Metaphysics

Metaphysics

A Guide and Anthology

**Tim Crane and
Katalin Farkas**

OXFORD
UNIVERSITY PRESS

OXFORD
UNIVERSITY PRESS

Great Clarendon Street, Oxford OX2 6DP

Oxford University Press is a department of the University of Oxford.
It furthers the University's objective of excellence in research, scholarship,
and education by publishing worldwide in

Oxford New York

Auckland Bangkok Buenos Aires Cape Town Chennai
Dar es Salaam Delhi Hong Kong Istanbul Karachi Kolkata
Kuala Lumpur Madrid Melbourne Mexico City Mumbai Nairobi
São Paulo Shanghai Taipei Tokyo Toronto

Oxford is a registered trade mark of Oxford University Press
in the UK and in certain other countries

Published in the United States
by Oxford University Press Inc., New York

First published 2004
Reprinted 2006

British Library Cataloguing in Publication Data

Data available

Library of Congress Cataloging in Publication Data

Data available

ISBN 978–0–19–926197–0

10 9 8 7 6 5

Typeset in Adobe Minion
by Newgen Imaging Systems (P) Ltd., Chennai, India
Printed in Great Britain by
Ashford Colour Press, Gosport, Hants

To the memory of David Lewis (1941–2001)

Preface

METAPHYSICS is that part of philosophy which asks the most general questions about the most general nature of reality. It is traditionally distinguished from epistemology, the theory of knowledge, which asks the most general questions about our knowledge of reality. Metaphysical enquiries deal with the nature of what there is, abstracting away from the particular details of goings on in our world, in an attempt to uncover the underlying structure, or fundamental classification, of reality. So, for example, while a theory in chemistry might describe the particular chemical changes undergone by certain chemical substances, metaphysics might ask about the nature of change itself. It is customary for books on metaphysics to mention the rather unusual origins of the word 'metaphysics'. Since some of our readers might be new to metaphysics, we will follow this custom. When Aristotle's works were collected and catalogued by Andronicus of Rhodes in the first century BC, the collection of writings dealing with substance, causation, and other topics was placed after the book now known as the *Physics* (from the Greek word for nature, *phusis*). For this reason, the work was described as 'what comes after the Physics', from which we derive our word 'metaphysics'. However, citing this etymology should not be taken to imply that metaphysics is something which comes after (or even before) physics in the contemporary sense of that word.

Metaphysics has always been controversial, and philosophers have often debated whether it is possible at all, and whether it has a distinctive method. These are philosophical questions in their own right, which have exercised the minds of some of the greatest thinkers of our tradition. However, in this book we set these questions aside and examine metaphysical enquiries on their own terms, without examining the philosophy or methodology of metaphysics itself. There are many different conceptions of what it is that is being done when philosophers investigate things metaphysically. For example: are metaphysicians analysing concepts, or are they investigating the preconditions of experience, or are they probing the necessary structure of reality? Although each of these conceptions has something to be said for it, none of them is plausible in general. The question of what metaphysics is is as hard to answer as the question of what science is, or of what art is; and we will not attempt to answer it here. If we were forced to provide an answer to the question 'what is metaphysics?', the best we could do is to paraphrase a famous remark of Wilfrid Sellars: it is the attempt to understand how things, in the most general sense of that word, hang together, in the most general sense of that word.

This Guide and Anthology attempts to introduce the main elements of metaphysics to students. One thing that distinguishes this book from some other recent anthologies on metaphysics is its inclusion of excerpts from the writings of some of the great philosophers of the past. We have done this not simply because the content of these contributions is still relevant to today's debate, but also because it is important in understanding a philosophical problem to understand something of its historical origins. This is one major way for us to understand why we have the problems that we have. Another distinctive feature of this book is the substantial introductory essays to each part of the book. These essays provide an entry into the subject for the newcomer, and a narrative binding together the articles selected in this part of the anthology. For the student, there are text boxes highlighting important concepts or arguments in an easily digestible form, and study questions and suggestions for reading to direct their further thinking on this subject. It should be noted that un-referenced quotations in our introductory essays are from the selections themselves.

We envisage that the book could be used by teachers in a number of different ways. The whole book could be used as a course text, for a year-long or semester-long course. Some of the more difficult readings could be put to one side for an introductory course. But it would also be possible to take a number of sections together as the basis for a more intensive course. For example: God, Idealism, and Freedom and Determinism might constitute the text for a somewhat introductory course. A more advanced course might weave together the related issues in Being, Universals, and Identity. Other possible combinations are: Universals, Time and Space, and Causation; Identity, Mind and Body, and Freedom and Determinism; Necessity, Identity, and Universals.

Acknowledgements

WE are very grateful to the anonymous readers for OUP for their extremely useful comments at different stages of the project; their comments were of great help in shaping the anthology section, and in revising the introductory material. We would also like to thank Helen Beebee, Gábor Betegh, István Bodnár, John Divers, Ferenc Huoranszki, Robin Le Poidevin, and Briggs Wright, for their oral and written comments on drafts of the material and for other forms of practical help. Thanks too to Ruth Anderson, our editor at OUP's Higher Education Department, for her constant encouragement, good advice, and support. We gratefully acknowledge the support of the Hungarian OTKA (grant number T032435). Finally, we give our sincere thanks to the following philosophers for their kind permission to allow the reproduction of their work in this anthology: Robert Adams, David Armstrong, Donald Davidson, Michael Dummett, Harry Frankfurt, Gilbert Harman, Paul Horwich, Barry Loewer, Hugh Mellor, Derek Parfit, Alvin Plantinga, Howard Robinson, Sydney Shoemaker, Jack Smart, Paul Snowdon, and Peter van Inwagen.

T.C.
K.F.
Budapest, December 2003

Contents

Part VIII **Identity**

Part IX **Mind and body**

List of boxes

Notes on contributors

Robert M. Adams (1937–   ). Professor of Philosophy, Yale University. He is the author of *Leibniz: Determinist, Theist, Idealist* and *Infinite Goods*, among other works.

St Anselm of Canterbury (1033–1109). Benedictine monk who became Archbishop of Canterbury in 1093. Influenced by St Augustine of Hippo, he was the author of many works of philosophical theology including *Proslogion*, *Monologion*, and *Cur Deus Homo?*

St Thomas Aquinas (1224/5–74). Born in Roccasecca in the Kingdom of Naples. Canonized in 1323. The most brilliant and influential of medieval philosophers, and the author of over 8 million words of philosophical writings, including the massive *Summa Theologiae*.

Aristotle (384–322). Born in Stagira in northern Greece, Aristotle studied with Plato in the latter's Academy in Athens. One of the greatest philosophers who ever lived, he can also be credited with inventing philosophy as an intellectual enquiry with its own distinct areas (logic, ethics, etc.).

D. M. Armstrong (1926–   ). Challis Professor of Philosophy Emeritus in the University of Sydney. Among his books are *Bodily Sensations, A Materialist Theory of the Mind, What is a Law of Nature?, A Combinatorial Theory of Possibility*, and *A World of States of Affairs*.

George Berkeley (1685–1753). Irish philosopher, born near Kilkenny, who eventually became Bishop of Cloyne in Ireland. He is known chiefly today for his defence of idealism in the *Three Dialogues* and the *Principles of Human Knowledge*, and for his *New Theory of Vision*.

Roderick M. Chisholm (1916–99). Was Professor of Philosophy at Brown University. Among his many books are *Theory of Knowledge, Person and Object, Perceiving*, and *The First Person*.

Samuel Clarke (1675–1729). English philosopher and theologian, and a follower of Sir Isaac Newton. Considered in his lifetime to be the equal of Locke.

Donald Davidson (1917–2003). Was Professor of Philosophy, University of California, Berkeley. Among his publications are *Inquiries into Truth and Interpretation, Essays on Actions and Events*, and *Subjective, Intersubjective, Objective*.

René Descartes (1596–1650). Often considered to be the founder of modern philosophy, Descartes's revolution was based on his rejection of the Aristotelian philosophy of the medieval scholastics or 'schoolmen'. His major works are the *Meditations*, the *Discourse on the Method*, and the *Principles of Philosophy*.

Michael Dummett (1925–   ). Wykeham Professor of Logic Emeritus in the University of Oxford. Among his books are *Frege: Philosophy of Language*, *Truth and Other Enigmas*, and *The Logical Basis of Metaphysics*.

Gareth Evans (1946–80). Was Wilde Reader in Mental Philosophy in the University of Oxford. He was the author of *The Varieties of Reference*.

Harry Frankfurt (1929–   ). Emeritus Professor of Philosophy, Princeton University. He is the author of *Demons, Dreamers and Madmen*, *The Importance of What We Care About*, and *Necessity, Volition and Love*, and many influential articles on ethics and metaphysics.

Gilbert Harman (1938–   ). Professor of Philosophy, Princeton University. Among his books are *Thought*, *Change in View*, and *The Nature of Morality*.

Paul Horwich (1947–   ). Professor of Philosophy, Graduate Center of the City University of New York. He is the author of *Probability and Evidence*, *Asymmetries in Time*, *Truth*, and *Meaning*.

David Hume (1711–76). Scottish philosopher, essayist, and historian, author of *A Treatise of Human Nature*, the *Enquiry Concerning Human Understanding*, and the *Enquiry Concerning the Principles of Morals*, and the leading figure of the Scottish Enlightenment. An empiricist and naturalist, with a strong sceptical streak, Hume's philosophy has been very influential in Anglo-American thinking in the twentieth century.

Immanuel Kant (1724–1804). Often considered the greatest of modern (as opposed to ancient or medieval) philosophers, Kant created a system of philosophy (the 'critical philosophy') which synthesized elements of earlier empiricism and rationalism. His *Critique of Pure Reason* was followed by the *Critique of Practical Reason* and the *Critique of Judgement*.

Saul Kripke (1940–   ). Professor of Philosophy, Graduate Center of the City University of New York. He is the author of *Naming and Necessity*, *Wittgenstein on Rules and Private Language*, and several influential articles in the philosophy of language and logic.

G. W. Leibniz (1646–1716). Along with Descartes and Spinoza, Leibniz was one of the greatest philosophers of the seventeenth century. He also made important contributions to mathematics.

David Lewis (1941–2001). Was Professor of Philosophy, Princeton University. He is the author of five volumes of philosophical papers, and also of *Convention, Counterfactuals, The Plurality of Worlds,* and *Parts of Classes*.

John Locke (1632–1704). English empiricist philosopher, whose *Essay Concerning Human Understanding* is one of the most influential works of English philosophy ever written.

Barry Loewer (1945–   ). Professor of Philosophy at Rutgers University, New Jersey. He is the editor (with Georges Rey) of *Meaning in Mind*, the editor (with Carl Gillett) of *Physicalism and its Discontents*, and the author of many articles on metaphysics, the philosophy of mind, and the philosophy of science.

J. L. Mackie (1917–81). Was Fellow of University College, Oxford. He was the author of *Problems from Locke, Truth, Probability and Paradox, The Miracle of Theism, Ethics*, and others.

J. M. E. McTaggart (1866–1925). One of the last of the nineteenth-century British idealists. *The Nature of Existence* is his major work.

D. H. Mellor (1938–   ). Professor of Philosophy Emeritus in the University of Cambridge. He is the author of *The Matter of Chance, Real Time, The Facts of Causation*, and *Matters of Metaphysics*, and articles on metaphysics and the philosophy of mind.

Thomas Nagel (1937–   ). Professor of Philosophy and Law, New York University. Among his books are *The Possibility of Altruism, Mortal Questions*, and *The View from Nowhere*.

William Paley (1743–1805). English philosopher, theologian, and moral philosopher. *The Principles of Moral and Political Philosophy* is his major work.

Derek Parfit (1942–   ). Fellow of All Souls College, Oxford. He is the author of *Reasons and Persons* and several articles on metaphysics and ethics.

Alvin Plantinga (1932–   ). Professor of Philosophy, University of Notre Dame. Among his books are *The Nature of Necessity, God, Freedom and Evil*, and *Warrant and Proper Function*.

Plato (*c*.428–347 BC). Follower of Socrates, who figures as a character in Plato's brilliant philosophical dialogues. Along with Aristotle, Plato was one of the great philosophers of antiquity, and his influence is comparable.

Arthur N. Prior (1914–69). Was Fellow of Balliol College, Oxford, and Professor of Philosophy at the University of Manchester. He was the author of *Past, Present and Future, Objects of Thought*, and *Papers on Time and Tense*.

W. V. Quine (1908–2000). Was Professor of Philosophy, Harvard University. Among his many books are *Word and Object, From a Logical Point of View, The Ways of Paradox, Philosophy of Logic*, and *Theories and Things*.

Howard Robinson (1945–   ). Professor of Philosophy at the Central European University, Budapest, and Honorary Research Fellow in the Department of Philosophy at the University of Liverpool. He is the author of *Matter and Sense* and *Perception*, and the editor (with John Foster) of *Essays on Berkeley*.

Sydney Shoemaker (1931–   ). Professor of Philosophy, Cornell University. Among his books are *Self-Knowledge and Self-Identity* and *Identity, Cause and Mind*.

J. J. C. Smart (1920–   ). Emeritus Professor of Philosophy, Australian National University. Among his books are *Philosophy and Scientific Realism, Our Place in the Universe*, and (with Bernard Williams) *Utilitarianism: For and Against*.

P. F. Snowdon (1946–   ). Grote Professor of the Philosophy of Mind and Logic at University College London. He is the author of articles on personal identity, and on the philosophy of perception, the mind–body problem, and conceptual analysis.

Peter van Inwagen (1942–   ). Professor of Philosophy, University of Notre Dame. He is the author of *An Essay on Free Will, Metaphysics, Material Beings, Ontology, Identity and Modality*, and many articles on metaphysics and the philosophy of religion.

Donald C. Williams (1899–1983). Was Professor of Philosophy at Harvard University. He was the author of a number of influential articles on metaphysics, and also of *The Ground of Induction* and *The Principles of Empirical Realism*.

Part I

God

Introduction

1. Introduction

ONE way to sum up the metaphysical projects of Western philosophy is in terms of the answers they give to two questions: what is the nature of the world, or reality? And why does it have that nature? In the Western philosophical tradition, these 'cosmological' questions have traditionally been answered by making reference to God as the creator of the world, and in terms of whom the nature of the world is given its fundamental explanation. Consequently, it is hard to understand a lot of Western metaphysics without grasping the role God played in the thinking of the great philosophers of the past. Of course, there are many questions about God which have been debated by theologians and philosophers—what kind of being God is, what are God's attributes, whether God acts in the world, whether religious experiences and miracles are evidence for God—but here we will focus only on how God can play a role in answering the question: why is there anything at all?

2. Why is there anything at all?

A metaphysical enquiry begins with asking *how* things are. Later in this book, for example, we ask questions about whether the world is in any way dependent on the human mind (Part II: Idealism and Realism); we will also examine questions about what the most fundamental things are (Part III: Being; Part IV: Universals and Particulars) and whether there are mental things as well as physical things (Part IX: Mind and Body). All these questions are part of the traditional task of metaphysics: what Aristotle called the enquiry into 'being as such'.

But in addition to asking how things are, philosophers have also asked *why* they are that way. Why is our world one way rather than another? Often the answers to this question are causal answers, giving the cause of the phenomenon we are trying to explain (see Part VI: Causation). We want to know why the First World War happened as it did; so we turn to historians, who attempt to tell us the causes of the war. And we can ask about the causes of these causes, and so on. Giving the cause of something is giving a causal explanation of it. But not all explanations, it seems, are causal explanations. If we ask why 2 is the only even prime number, then we should not expect a causal answer. The number 2 is not *caused* to be the even prime number. Or suppose we want to know why nothing can be red and green all over at the same time. A causal answer is not the right kind here either: something's being red does not *cause* it not to be green as well. Some truths seem to be necessary—for example, the truth that 2 is the even prime number, or that nothing can be red and green all over. Necessary truths are those which cannot have been otherwise. And necessary truths seem to need explanation too.

When asking why things are the way they are, we might be asking questions like the ones just mentioned: about specific truths and why they are true. But we might have in mind something even more general: why is anything *any* way at all? Indeed, why *is* there anything at all? Explanation is sometimes called 'contrastive', where what is meant is that we ask why *this* happened, rather than *that*. And so we seem to be able to ask, in the case of this very general question, why is there *anything* at all, rather than *nothing*?

As Derek Parfit argues (Chapter 1), a causal answer does not seem like the right kind of answer to this question. When considering the existence of the universe as a whole, there seem to be two options. Either the universe has always existed, and its age is infinite. Or the universe came into existence at some point. On the first option, a causal explanation of events would cite an infinite series of events, each one being caused by a preceding one. But in this case, what is being explained is just the events, one after each other; the existence of the whole series (i.e. the whole universe itself) is not causally explained. So there is no causal explanation of the universe. On the second option, there was a first event in the universe, before which there was nothing; and all events happening after that are explained by this. But in this case, the existence of the first event cannot be causally explained, and to that extent things as a whole have no explanation. Some have said that God caused the first event. We have not got to this idea yet; it will be discussed below in section 3. But the obvious immediate objection is that we are still lacking a causal explanation of God's existence.

Some philosophers might say that the existence of something rather than nothing is a necessary truth: it could not have failed to be true that there is something. So to the question, 'why is there something rather than nothing?', they give the answer that there simply could not have been nothing. So the question should not arise. But this is not very satisfactory, since we have seen that the fact that something is a necessary truth does not stop us looking for a rational explanation of it. We can still explain why 2 is the even prime number; even though it is a necessary truth, it could not have been otherwise. And we are still rationally entitled to look for an explanation of why nothing can be red and green all over.

A more popular response among contemporary philosophers is that the existence of the universe is a brute (i.e. inexplicable) fact. This what Parfit calls 'the Brute Fact View'. This view says that the universe just happens to exist. So we should try and eliminate our sense of puzzlement about the existence of the universe. Whatever we try and use as an explanation of why the universe exists, we can ask the same question about why *that* should exist. And the answer to that question could just as well be the answer to the question of why the universe itself exists: it just does. So we have to stop somewhere; why not stop with the assertion of the existence of something we more or less understand—the universe itself?

One reason for believing in the Brute Fact View is that there cannot be a causal explanation of why the universe exists, and the only explanations are causal explanations; so there cannot be any explanation of why the universe exists. But, as we have just seen, the second premiss of the argument is false: not all explanations are causal explanations. So this is not a good argument for the Brute Fact View.

According to the Brute Fact View, the existence of the universe is a coincidence. A coincidence is, by definition, something that has no explanation. Suppose that out of millions of entrants, you win the lottery, and on a day that happens to be your birthday. If you are slightly superstitious, you might wonder whether this fact—that you win the lottery on the day that is your birthday—is something that needs explaining. But if the lottery is fair, then it is just a coincidence. Why you won the lottery has an explanation— the ticket that you bought was selected by a random procedure. The fact that such-and-such a day is your birthday has an explanation—you were born on that day. But there is no explanation of the whole thing: the fact that you won on your birthday. The defenders of the Brute Fact View say that there are lots of explanations of particular events in the universe, but no explanation of the whole thing.

Parfit argues that there is something unsatisfactory about the unquestioned acceptance of the idea that the existence of the universe is a coincidence. For on the face of it, the existence of the universe in all its complexity looks like something rather improbable. And certain kinds of improbable events naturally call out for explanation. Consider a lottery which is regularly won by the lottery owner's mother. Our suspicions would be raised. The lottery owner might defend himself by saying: 'everyone who enters the lottery has an equal chance of winning. My mother's chance of winning is exactly the same as everyone else's. But each time the draw is made, someone had to win. I admit it is very good luck for her that she won each time. But this is the same kind of luck as if you gain a row of consecutive sixes in a game of dice. Each time the chance of individual die landing six is the same: one in six. You would have to accept that this is just good luck. And so, improbable as it is, my mother's winning is pure luck.' But we might think, with some justification, 'who believes in that kind of luck?' It seems perfectly reasonable to think that we should at least *look* for an explanation of this series of events; that is, that we should not be entitled to *assume* that it is a coincidence (even if, as things turn out, it is).

Do we know enough about the universe to know that its existence demands explanation? Physicists have drawn attention to the fact that if the initial conditions at the Big Bang had been very slightly different, then the universe would not have developed in such a way as to allow human life to evolve (see Leslie 1989 for details). This is called the evidence for 'fine-tuning'. Some have drawn the hasty conclusion from this that the reason why things were the way they were at the Big Bang was *so that* human life could evolve. This is called an 'anthropic' conclusion since it explains the physical facts of nature in terms of facts about human life: *anthropos* is the Greek word for 'human being'. But suppose that we do not draw the anthropic conclusion. Nonetheless, it can still seem a remarkable fact, rather like the fact that the lottery owner's mother tends to win the lottery, that out of all the millions of possible arrangements of the physical facts at the Big Bang, almost all of which would not have been such as to allow life, these ones prevailed.

A defender of the Brute Fact View will respond that we should not be misled by this remarkable fact into empty speculations about the explanation of the universe. They might say that the improbability of the universe is not really like the improbability of the lottery owner's mother winning the lottery. For in that case we have some idea of how something could possibly explain it; in the case of the universe, we do not. So to think that the physical set-up at the Big Bang needs explanation is to commit a fallacy somewhat akin to the fallacy of thinking your own winning the lottery needs explanation. It does not; it is a mere coincidence.

Parfit shows that even if the Brute Fact View is true, the question of why the universe exists is not a silly question. One reason he thinks this is that the truth of the Brute Fact View does not *itself* seem to be a brute fact. So the truth of the view itself might require explanation. But what is the possible range of views which one could adopt as answers to the question? Parfit discusses some: for example, the view that the world exists because it is good. But in traditional philosophy, the dominant answer to the question (why is there anything at all?), and the only real alternative to the Brute Fact View, is the *theistic* answer. A theist is someone who believes in God. The theist will say that the question has an answer and that God is the best answer to it. Let us look more closely at these answers.

3. God as an answer to the question

Philosophers who have seen God as an answer to our question have tended to argue in the following way. They first point out some very general, obvious, and widely accepted fact about the world. Then they argue that this fact needs explaining, and that the existence of God explains it. Here and in the selected readings we shall consider two important kinds of argument of this general form: Cosmological Arguments and Design Arguments.

Cosmological Arguments can take a number of forms. Gottfried Wilhelm Leibniz, for example, argued from a general principle that for every truth there is a sufficient reason why it is true rather than not (Chapter 5). He then argued that there must be a sufficient reason for the existence of the world, which is not itself the world. This reason must derive from a necessary being: that is, must be founded in the nature of God. In Chapter 2, St Thomas Aquinas proposes arguments of a similar general kind in the first three of his famous 'five ways' of proving that there is a God. The first way appeals to the fact of change. Changes are explained by other changes, but this cannot go on forever, 'since then there would be no first cause of the change, and as a result no subsequent causes'. So there must be a first cause of change, 'and this is what everyone understands by *God*'. The second way argues similarly from the fact that causes are always found to be in a series, and that this series must begin somewhere. The third way anticipates Leibniz's argument: there are some things which 'can be and need not be' (that is, do not exist necessarily); their existence is explained by what must be (that is, things which do exist necessarily). Things that must be may owe their necessity to other things, and these must ultimately owe their existence to something which exists in and of itself.

Cosmological Arguments, then, tend to claim that there is some general feature of the world which needs to be explained—changes depending on other changes, or the fact that every event has a cause—and then move to the conclusion that God is the only explanation for this feature. We can question both the claim and the conclusion. First, what is the reason for thinking that the fact that every event has a cause has to have an explanation? Why cannot it be a brute fact, in the sense described above in section 2, that every event has a cause? And second, even if we accept that this feature should have an explanation, why should the explanation be God? It might be objected that Aquinas makes things rather too easy for himself by concluding, 'this is what everyone under-stands by *God*'. Why isn't the right conclusion to draw simply the observation that there is *something*—something whose nature we do not yet know—which explains why the world is as it is? It seems a further step to move from this to the conclusion that this 'something' is God, understood as the thing whose existence is in serious dispute.

The fourth and fifth of Aquinas's 'five ways' are versions of what we are calling the Design Argument. (This argument is sometimes called the 'Argument *from* Design' but, as we shall see, it is question-begging to describe it in this way.) The Design Argument does not simply assume that the *existence* of the world requires explanation: rather, it assumes that the highly *specific* nature of the world is something which requires explanation. The world seems to exhibit a remarkable degree of order and coherence. Such a degree of order seems to point to the universe being the product of design. And there is no design without a designer; the designer is God. This argument received a famous formulation in the writings of the English theologian William Paley (Chapter 3). Paley begins his argument by asking what we should conclude if we were walking on a heath and were to find a watch. He claims that it is reasonable to conclude the 'watch must have had a maker: that there must have existed, at some time, and at some place or other, an artificer or artificers who formed it for the purpose which we find it actually to answer; who comprehended its construction, and designed its use'.

Certainly, we should accept that if something literally has been designed, then there must be someone who designed it. If not, it would not have been designed. This is why we should not call the argument 'the argument *from* design', since it is a trivial matter to argue from design to a designer. The question rather is: are there good reasons to think the universe literally has been designed? Charles Darwin said in his *Autobiography* that Paley's work gave him 'as much delight as did Euclid'. However, many people think that the appeal of the Design Argument is seriously weakened by the plausibility of Darwin's theory of evolution by natural selection. Darwin's view was that the complexity and variety of organisms was the result of random mutations coming to dominate other traits of organisms as successful responses to environmental pressure. Here there is no literal selection or design. The mechanisms of natural selection are 'blind' (hence the title of Richard Dawkins's (1986) well-known book *The Blind Watchmaker*, which is an allusion to Paley's argument). But the defender of the Design Argument can respond that evolutionary explanations do not explain the design of everything; they do not explain how large molecules got together in the first place to create life, nor can they explain the apparent design implicit in the fine-tuning of the universe.

However, there is a further difficulty. Suppose that we do accept that the universe was designed, and that therefore there is a designer. And suppose we have some other arguments for the designer being God. Why should we stop there? After all, we may well find as much order and complexity in God as we find in the world, so why are we not looking for an explanation of God's order or apparent design? This important question leads us to the heart of the traditional arguments for God's existence.

4. The Ontological Argument

We seem to have uncovered a similar problem with each of the Cosmological and Design Arguments. In each case, we start from an empirical premise—the universe exhibits design, or everything has a cause—and then we are supposed to get from there to the existence of God. But there is a gaping hole in the Design Argument: if the existence of a phenomenon with a certain kind of order or design is always something which demands explanation, then why doesn't *God's* order or design itself demand explanation? The assumption that any design demands explanation applies, it seems, to God just as much as the world. A similar point applies to the Cosmological Argument. If we think that everything in the universe must have a cause, what entitles us to stop at God? If all that we are assuming is just that everything needs a causal explanation, why doesn't God have to have a causal explanation too? Both the Design Argument and the Cosmological Argument, at least in the simple forms presented here, seem to beg the question.

The similarity between these two objections might not be an accident. For we might respond in each case that God is the *kind of thing* whose design does not need explaining, and it is in the *nature* of God not to need any causal explanation. If this is true, then we can see how a defender of these arguments might use this extra idea—essentially that God is a being whose existence and nature needs no explanation—to prop up the argument. For if we argue that the best explanation for the order in the universe is God, and that God's own order does not need explanation, then we have a good reason for believing in God. Likewise, if we argue that everything has a causal explanation, and that the first cause of the universe is God since God's existence needs no causal explanation, then we also have a good argument for God, construed as the first cause. As Aquinas says, 'we are forced to postulate something which *of itself must be*, owing this to nothing outside itself' (our emphasis).

But notice that what is now doing all the work is the additional premiss—that God's nature needs no explanation, or that God's existence does not require a cause. In other words, God is a being whose existence and nature is in some way self-explanatory. For if God were not self-explanatory in this way, then his existence and nature would be something that would be explained—or would need explaining—by something else. But if God's existence and nature need explanation by something else, then the Design and Cosmological Arguments seem to fail. (Note: since the philosophers we are talking about are discussing the Christian God and refer to him as 'he', we will follow them in this. Obviously there are many other ways in which a God or Gods could be conceived, which cannot be touched on in this Introduction.)

The idea that God's existence is in some sense self-explanatory is essentially the idea that lies behind the famous *Ontological Argument* for God's existence: the argument that says, roughly, that it is part of the very idea of God that he exists. ('Ontological' means: having to do with the theory of being or what there is; see Part III: Being.) If this is right, then it turns out that the Design and Cosmological Arguments, if they are to be presented in a plausible way, need to be supplemented with an idea that is at the heart of the Ontological Argument (see Mackie 1982). So the ontological argument appears to be the most fundamental argument for the existence of God.

The Ontological Argument was first put forward by St Anselm of Canterbury (1033–1109) in his *Proslogion* (Chapter 4). Anselm argued that our idea of God is the idea of something than which no greater can be thought. If someone has this idea, then it exists in the understanding or the mind; but something that exists only in the understanding is not as great as something which exists in reality. So if this something than which no greater can be thought only exists in the mind, then it cannot be that than which no greater can be thought. But this is a contradiction. So something than which no greater can be thought must exist in reality as well as in the mind. So God must exist.

Since it was invented by Anselm, this extraordinary argument has had a colourful history. Aquinas dismissed it, arguing that 'even if the word *God* were generally recognized to have that meaning, nothing would thereby be granted existence in the world of fact, but merely in thought' (1967: Ia. 2. 1). Descartes disagreed. In his *Meditations* he produced a form of the ontological argument: the idea of God is the idea of a 'supremely perfect being'; a supremely perfect being cannot lack existence (which is a 'supreme perfection') any more than a mountain can lack a valley. So God must exist (Descartes 1641: *Meditation* 5). Leibniz (Chapter 4) endorsed the general idea behind this argument—that the idea of God contains the idea of existence—but emphasized that the argument will not work unless it is first established that God is possible. For if the idea of God were the idea of something impossible, then even if the idea contained the idea of existence, he could not exist, since nothing impossible can exist. Hence 'only God has this privilege: that he must exist if he is possible'. So if you accept this line of reasoning, you must accept that if God does not exist, then he is impossible. (The relevant senses of 'possible' and 'necessary' are explained in Part V: Necessity.)

The most famous criticism of the ontological argument is Immanuel Kant's discussion in his *Critique of Pure Reason* (1787). Kant questioned the assumption behind the argument that existence is a property of things. He expresses this by saying that 'Being' is 'obviously not a real predicate; that is, it is not the concept of something which can be added to the concept of a thing' (1787: A598/B626). What Kant means by this is that we do not add anything to our *idea* of a thing, X, by saying that it is an *existing* X—as we might add something to our idea of X by saying that it is a red or square X. Hence we cannot divide up things into those which exist and those which do not; rather, the very idea of *being a thing* at all is the idea of being an *existing* thing. Descartes, however, assumes that existence is a property of things—since he says it is a perfection and perfections are properties. If Kant is right, then Descartes cannot use this assumption to move from the *idea* of a being with all possible perfections to the *existence* of such a being. As Kant says, 'whatever our concept of an object may contain, we must go outside it, if we are to ascribe existence to the object'. Some see this criticism as decisive; but others think Kant's view of existence should be challenged; still others believe that the heart of the ontological argument does not rely on the controversial view that existence is a property (see Plantinga 1975; see also Part II: Being).

5. Is the existence of God inconsistent with the facts?

Leibniz argued that if the ontological argument is to work, it must say that if God exists at all, he exists necessarily. So it would seem that to argue against God's existence, you have to argue that God is impossible. Many arguments against God's existence, however, do not argue that God is impossible, but only that the existence of God is incompatible with the contingent facts of our world. So it is with the argument for the existence of evil, sometimes called *the problem of evil*. The problem can be expressed as follows. Evil exists. So

---

Box I.1. Divine omnipotence and omniscience

According to a traditional, orthodox conception of God, God is all powerful (omnipotent) and all knowing (omniscient) and all good (omnibenevolent). The problem of evil discussed in the text challenges God's goodness—if God is all good, why did he create evil? But it also challenges God's omnipotence—is God unable to eliminate evil from the world? God's omnipotence raises other philosophical puzzles too. Can God make a stone too heavy for him to lift? If he can, then there is something he cannot do: lift the stone. But if he cannot, then there is equally something he cannot do: make the stone. Some philosophers try and avoid this problem by saying that it is no restriction on God's omnipotence to say that he cannot do something which is contradictory and therefore logically impossible. But others, including Descartes, say that if God really is omnipotent, then he can do this too, whether or not we can understand how it can be so; for 'it would be presumptuous to think that our imagination extends as far as his power' (Descartes, letter to Mersenne, 15 Apr. 1630; in Descartes 1984: vol. iii). And if God can do something impossible by making a stone he cannot lift, then why should he not do another impossible thing and lift it? (See Frankfurt 1964: 263.)

Also puzzling is God's omniscience. If God knows everything, then he presumably knows whether Francis Ford Coppola will make *The Godfather: Part IV* or not. But suppose Coppola has not yet decided whether he will make this movie. Then either there is a fact about whether he will make it, but he does not know it (though God does); or it has not yet been determined whether he will make it. In the first case, it looks as if Coppola is not free to decide whether to make *The Godfather: Part IV* (see Part X: Freedom and Determinism). But in the second case, there is something God does not know after all: whether Coppola will make the film, contradicting our assumption that God knows everything.

---

either God cannot abolish evil, or he will not. If he cannot, then he is not all powerful. If he will not, then he is not all good. But God is supposed to be all powerful and all good. So how is his existence compatible with the manifest existence of evil in the world?

As J. L. Mackie points out in his discussion of this problem (Chapter 6), one of the dominant responses to it is the 'free will defence'. God gave us free will, it is argued, and evil is a consequence of the free actions of human beings. To this it is natural to respond: but why couldn't God have made our wills so that we always choose the good? This response misses the point; for as Alvin Plantinga has argued, if we are to be genuinely free, then whether or not we choose the good cannot be determined by God. If God intends to 'produce moral good, then he must create significantly free creatures upon whose co-operation he depends' (Plantinga 1974: 190). It is worth asking whether this involves a restriction on God's omnipotence.

But whatever the answer to this question, it seems that the free will defence cannot solve the whole of the problem of evil. For as well as the evil which is brought about by human action, free or not, there is also the 'evil' which seems to occur naturally in the world. 'Evil' does not seem quite the right word for things like natural disasters and terrible diseases; the idea is that things like this are generally a bad thing for us which we would be better off without. Such 'natural evil' is often not the work of human beings, so the free will defence does not apply; so how can a benevolent God allow it to exist? Here the theist seems to be on less secure ground than with the free will defence. Should they say that such things have a hidden value, which is hard for us to detect? Or that any suffering improves those who survive it? Or should they end up saying that there are limitations to God after all? None of these responses seems adequate.

It is worth bearing in mind that whether or not one is a theist, the questions discussed in this section are of lasting philosophical interest and importance. If one is a theist, then one is obliged to defend rationally the consequences of one's views against the deep difficulties they encounter. But if one is not a theist, the question we have been addressing here—why is there something rather than nothing?—is one to which one is also obliged to have an answer. Even if the answer is the Brute Fact View, this is not a view to be adopted lightly, without full consideration of its presuppositions and consequences.

Chapter 1

Why anything? Why this?

Derek Parfit

WHY does the Universe exist? There are two questions here. First, why is there a Universe at all? It might have been true that nothing ever existed: no living beings, no stars, no atoms, not even space or time. When we think about this possibility, it can seem astonishing that anything exists. Second, why does *this* Universe exist? Things might have been, in countless ways, different. So why is the Universe as it is?

These questions, some believe, may have causal answers. Suppose first that the Universe has always existed. Some believe that, if all events were caused by earlier events, everything would be explained. That, however, is not so. Even an infinite series of events cannot explain itself. We could ask why this series occurred, rather than some other series, or no series. Of the supporters of the Steady State Theory, some welcomed what they took to be this theory's atheistic implications. They assumed that, if the Universe had no beginning, there would be nothing for a Creator to explain. But there would still be an eternal Universe to explain.

Suppose next that the Universe is not eternal, since nothing preceded the Big Bang. That first event, some physicists suggest, may have obeyed the laws of quantum mechanics, by being a random fluctuation in a vacuum. This would causally explain, they say, how the Universe came into existence out of nothing. But what physicists call a vacuum isn't really nothing. We can ask why it exists, and has the potentialities it does. In Hawking's phrase, 'What breathes fire into the equations?'

Similar remarks apply to all suggestions of these kinds. There could not be a causal explanation of why the Universe exists, why there are any laws of nature, or why these laws are as they are. Nor would it make a difference if there is a God, who caused the rest of the Universe to exist. There could not be a causal explanation of why God exists.

Many people have assumed that, since these questions cannot have causal answers, they cannot have any answers. Some therefore dismiss these questions, thinking them not worth considering. Others conclude that they do not make sense. They assume that, as Wittgenstein wrote, 'doubt can exist only where there is a question; and a question only where there is an answer'.

These assumptions are all, I believe, mistaken. Even if these questions could not have answers, they would still make sense, and they would still be worth considering. I am reminded here of the aesthetic category of the *sublime*, as applied to the highest mountains, raging oceans, the night sky, the interiors of some cathedrals, and other things that are superhuman, awesome, limitless. No question is more sublime than why there is a Universe: why there is anything rather than nothing. Nor should we assume that answers to this question must be causal. And, even if reality cannot be fully explained, we may still make progress, since what is inexplicable may become less baffling than it now seems.

1

One apparent fact about reality has recently been much discussed. Many physicists believe that, for life to be possible, various features of the Universe must be almost precisely as they are. As one example of such a feature, we can take the initial conditions in the Big Bang. If these conditions had been more than very slightly different, these physicists claim, the Universe would not have had the complexity that allows living beings to exist. Why were these conditions so precisely right?[1]

Some say: 'If they had not been right, we couldn't even ask this question.' But that is no answer. It could be baffling how we survived some crash even though, if we hadn't, we could not be baffled.

Others say: 'There had to be some initial conditions, and the conditions that make life possible were as likely as any others. So there is nothing to be explained.' To see what is wrong with this reply, we must distinguish two kinds of case. Suppose first that, when some radio telescope is aimed at most points in space, it records a random sequence of incoming waves. There might be nothing here that needed to be explained. Suppose next that, when the telescope is aimed in one direction, it records a sequence of waves whose pulses match the number π, in binary notation, to the first ten thousand digits. That particular number is, in one sense, just as likely as any other. But there *would* be something here that needed to be explained. Though each long number is unique, only a very few are, like π, mathematically special. What would need to be explained is why this sequence of waves exactly matched such a special number. Though this matching might be a coincidence, which had been randomly produced, that would be most unlikely. We could be almost certain that these waves had been produced by some kind of intelligence.

On the view that we are now considering, since any sequence of waves is as likely as any other, there would be nothing to be explained. If we accepted this view, intelligent beings elsewhere in space would not be able to communicate with us, since we would ignore their messages. Nor could God reveal himself. Suppose that, with some optical telescope, we saw a distant pattern of stars which spelled out in Hebrew script the first chapter of Genesis. This pattern of stars, according to this view, would not need to be explained. That is clearly false.

Here is another analogy. Suppose first that, of a thousand people facing death, only one can be rescued. If there is a lottery to pick this one survivor, and I win, I would

---

1. In my remarks about this question, I am merely summarizing, and oversimplifying, what others have claimed. See, for example, John Leslie, *Universes*, Routledge, 1989.

be very lucky. But there might be nothing here that needed to be explained. Someone had to win, and why not me? Consider next another lottery. Unless my gaoler picks the longest of a thousand straws, I shall be shot. If my gaoler picks that longest straw, there would be something to be explained. It would not be enough to say, 'This result was as likely as any other.' In the first lottery, nothing special happened: whatever the result, someone's life would be saved. In this second lottery, the result *was* special, since, of the thousand possible results, only one would save a life. Why was this special result *also* what happened? Though this might be a coincidence, the chance of that is only one in a thousand. I could be almost certain that, like Dostoyevsky's mock execution, this lottery was rigged.

The Big Bang, it seems, was like this second lottery. For life to be possible, the initial conditions had to be selected with great accuracy. This *appearance of fine-tuning*, as some call it, also needs to be explained.

It may be objected that, in regarding conditions as special if they allow for life, we unjustifiably assume our own importance. But life *is* special, if only because of its complexity. An earthworm's brain is more complicated than a lifeless galaxy. Nor is it only life that requires this fine-tuning. If the Big Bang's initial conditions had not been almost precisely as they were, the Universe would have either almost instantly recollapsed, or expanded so fast, and with particles so thinly spread, that not even stars or heavy elements could have formed. That is enough to make these conditions very special.

It may next be objected that these conditions cannot be claimed to be improbable, since such a claim requires a statistical basis, and there is only one Universe. If we were considering all conceivable Universes, it would indeed be implausible to make judgments of statistical probability. But our question is much narrower. We are asking what would have happened if, with the same laws of nature, the initial conditions had been different. That provides the basis for a statistical judgment. There is a range of values that these conditions might have had, and physicists can work out in what proportion of this range the resulting Universe could have contained stars, heavy elements, and life.

This proportion, it is claimed, is extremely small. Of the range of possible initial conditions, fewer than one in a billion billion would have produced a Universe with the complexity that allows for life. If this claim is true, as I shall here assume, there is something that cries out to be explained. Why was one of this tiny set *also* the one that actually obtained?

On one view, this was a mere coincidence. That is conceivable, since coincidences happen. But this view is hard to believe since, if it were true, the chance of this coincidence occurring would be below one in a billion billion.

Others say: 'The Big Bang *was* fine-tuned. In creating the Universe, God chose to make life possible.' Atheists may reject this answer, thinking it improbable that God exists. But this is not as improbable as the view that would require so great a coincidence. So even atheists should admit that, of these two answers to our question, the answer that invokes God is more likely to be true.

This reasoning revives one of the traditional arguments for belief in God. In its strongest form, this argument appeals to the many features of animals, such as eyes or wings, that look as if they have been designed. Paley's appeal to such features much impressed Darwin when he was young. Darwin later undermined this form of the argument, since evolution can explain this appearance of design. But evolution cannot explain the appearance of fine-tuning in the Big Bang.

This argument's appeal to probabilities can be challenged in a different way. In claiming it to be most improbable that this fine-tuning was a coincidence, the argument assumes that, of the possible initial conditions in the Big Bang, each was equally likely to obtain. That assumption may be mistaken. The conditions that allow for complexity and life may have been, compared with all the others, much more likely to obtain. Perhaps they were even certain to obtain.

To answer this objection, we must broaden this argument's conclusion. If these life-allowing conditions were either very likely or certain to obtain, then—as the argument claims—it would be no coincidence that the Universe allows for complexity and life. But this fine-tuning might have been the work, not of some existing being, but of some impersonal force, or fundamental law. That is what some theists believe God to be.

A stronger challenge to this argument comes from a different way to explain the appearance of fine-tuning. Consider first a similar question. For life to be possible on the Earth, many of the Earth's features have to be close to being as they are. The Earth's having such features, it might be claimed, is unlikely to be a coincidence, and should therefore be regarded as God's work. But such an argument would be weak. The Universe, we can reasonably believe, contains many planets, with varying conditions. We should expect that, on a few of these planets, conditions would be just right for life. Nor is it surprising that we live on one of these few.

Things are different, we may assume, with the appearance of fine-tuning in the Big Bang. While there are likely to be many other planets, there is only one Universe. But this difference may be less than it seems. Some physicists suggest that the observable Universe is only one out of many different worlds, which are all equally parts of reality. According to one such view, the other worlds are related to ours in a way that solves some of the mysteries of quantum physics. On the different and simpler view that is relevant here, the other worlds have the same laws of nature as our world, and they are produced by Big Bangs that are broadly similar, except in having different initial conditions.

On this *Many Worlds Hypothesis*, there is no need for fine-tuning. If there were enough Big Bangs, we should expect that, in a few of these, conditions would be just right to allow for complexity and life; and it would be no surprise that our Big Bang was one of these few. To illustrate this point, we can revise my second lottery. Suppose my gaoler picks a straw, not once, but very many times. That would explain his managing, once, to pick the longest straw, without that's being an extreme coincidence, or this lottery's being rigged.

On most versions of the Many Worlds Hypothesis, these many worlds are not, except through their origins, causally related. Some object that, since our world could not be causally affected by such other worlds, we can have no evidence for their existence, and can therefore have no reason to believe in them. But we do have such a reason, since their existence would explain an otherwise puzzling feature of our world: the appearance of fine-tuning.

Of these two ways to explain this appearance, which is better? Compared with belief in God, the Many Worlds Hypothesis is more cautious, since its claim is merely that there is more of the kind of reality that we can observe around us. But God's existence has been claimed to be intrinsically more probable. According to most theists, God is a being who is omnipotent, omniscient, and wholly good. The uncaused existence of such a being has been claimed to be simpler, and less arbitrary, than the uncaused existence of many highly complicated worlds. And simpler hypotheses, many scientists assume, are more likely to be true.

If such a God exists, however, other features of our world become hard to explain. It may not be surprising that God chose to make life possible. But the laws of nature could have been different, so there are many possible worlds that would have contained life. It is hard to understand why, out of all these possibilities, God chose to create our world. What is most baffling is the problem of evil. There appears to be suffering which any good person, knowing the truth, would have prevented if he could. If there is such suffering, there cannot be a God who is omnipotent, omniscient, and wholly good.

To this problem, theists have proposed several solutions. Some suggest that God is not omnipotent, or not wholly good. Others suggest that undeserved suffering is not, as it seems, bad, or that God could not prevent such suffering without making the Universe, as a whole, less good.

We must ignore these suggestions here, since we have larger questions to consider. I began by asking why things are as they are. Before returning to that question, we should ask *how* things are. There is much about our world that we have not discovered. And, just as there may be other worlds that are like ours, there may be worlds that are very different.

2

It will help to distinguish two kinds of possibilities. *Cosmic* possibilities cover everything that ever exists, and are the different ways that the whole of reality might be. Only one such possibility can be actual, or be the one that *obtains*. *Local* possibilities are the different ways that some part of reality, or *local world*, might be. If some local world exists, that leaves it open whether other worlds exist.

One cosmic possibility is, roughly, that *every* possible local world exists. This we can call the *All Worlds Hypothesis*. Another possibility, which might have obtained, is that nothing ever exists. This we can call the *Null Possibility*. In each of the remaining possibilities, the number of local worlds that exist is between none and all. There are countless numbers of these possibilities, since there are countless combinations of possible local worlds.

Of these different cosmic possibilities, one must obtain, and only one can obtain. So we have two questions: Which obtains, and Why?

These questions are connected. If some possibility would be easier to explain, we may have more reason to believe that this possibility obtains. This is how, rather than believing in only one Big Bang, we have more reason to believe in many. Whether we believe in one or many, we have the question why any Big Bang has occurred. Though this question is hard, the occurrence of many Big Bangs is not more puzzling than the occurrence of only one. Most kinds of thing, or event, have many instances. We also have the question why, in the Big Bang that produced our world, the initial conditions allowed for complexity and life. If there has been only one Big Bang, this fact is also hard to explain, since it is most unlikely that these conditions merely happened to be right. If instead there have been many Big Bangs, this fact is easy to explain, since it is like the fact that, among countless planets, there are some whose conditions allow for life. Since belief in many Big Bangs leaves less that is unexplained, it is the better view.

If some cosmic possibilities would be less puzzling than others, because their obtaining would leave less to be explained, is there some possibility whose obtaining would be in no way puzzling?

Consider first the Null Possibility, in which nothing ever exists. To imagine this possibility, it may help to suppose first that all that ever existed was a single atom. We then imagine that even this atom never existed.

Some have claimed that, if there had never been anything, there wouldn't have been anything to be explained. But that is not so. When we imagine how things would have been if nothing had ever existed, what we should imagine away are such things as living beings, stars, and atoms. There would still have been various truths, such as the truth that there were no stars or atoms, or that 9 is divisible by 3. We can ask why these things would have been true. And such questions may have answers. Thus we can explain why, even if nothing had ever existed, 9 would still have been divisible by 3. There is no conceivable alternative. And we can explain why there would have been no such things as immaterial matter, or spherical cubes. Such things are logically impossible. But why would *nothing* have existed? Why would there have been no stars or atoms, no philosophers or bluebell woods?

We should not claim that, if nothing had ever existed, there would have been nothing to be explained. But we can claim something less. Of all the cosmic possibilities, the Null Possibility would have needed the least explanation. As Leibniz pointed out, it is much the simplest, and the least arbitrary. And it is the easiest to understand. It can seem mysterious, for example, how things could exist without their existence having some cause, but there cannot be a causal explanation of why the whole Universe, or God, exists. The Null Possibility raises no such problem. If nothing had ever existed, that state of affairs would not have needed to be caused.

Reality, however, does not take its least puzzling form. In some way or other, a Universe has managed to exist. That is what can take one's breath away. As Wittgenstein wrote, 'not how the world is, is the mystical, but *that* it is.' Or, in the words of a thinker as unmystical as Jack Smart: 'That anything should exist at all does seem to me a matter for the deepest awe.'

Consider next the All Worlds Hypothesis, on which every possible local world exists. Unlike the Null Possibility, this may be how things are. And it may be the next least puzzling possibility. This hypothesis is not the same as—though it includes—the Many Worlds Hypothesis. On that more cautious view, the many other worlds have the same elements as our world, and the same fundamental laws, and differ only in such features as their constants and initial conditions. The All Worlds Hypothesis covers every conceivable kind of world, and most of these other worlds would have very different elements and laws.

If all these worlds exist, we can ask why they do. But, compared with most other cosmic possibilities, the All Worlds Hypothesis may leave less that is unexplained. For example, whatever the number of possible worlds that exist, we have the question, 'Why *that* number?' That question would have been least puzzling if the number that existed were *none*, and the next least arbitrary possibility seems to be that *all* these worlds exist. With every other cosmic possibility, we have a further question. If ours is the only world, we can ask: 'Out of all the possible local worlds, why is *this* the one that exists?' On any version of the Many Worlds Hypothesis, we have a similar question: 'Why do just *these* worlds exist, with *these* elements and laws?' But, if *all* these worlds exist, there is no such further question.

It may be objected that, even if all possible local worlds exist, that does not explain why our world is as it is. But that is a mistake. If all these worlds exist, each world is as it is in the way in which each number is as it is. We cannot sensibly ask why 9 is 9. Nor should we ask why our world is the one it is: why it is *this* world. That would be like asking, 'Why are *we* who we are?', or 'Why is it *now* the time that it is?' Those, on reflection, are not good questions.

Though the All Worlds Hypothesis avoids certain questions, it is not as simple, or unarbitrary, as the Null Possibility. There may be no sharp distinction between worlds that are and are not possible. It is unclear what counts as a kind of world. And, if there are infinitely many kinds, there is a choice between different kinds of infinity.

Whichever cosmic possibility obtains, we can ask why it obtains. All that I have claimed so far is that, with some possibilities, this question would be less puzzling. Let us now ask: Could this question have an answer? Might there be a theory that leaves nothing unexplained?

3

It is sometimes claimed that God, or the Universe, make themselves exist. But this cannot be true, since these entities cannot do anything unless they exist.

On a more intelligible view, it is logically necessary that God, or the Universe, exist, since the claim that they might not have existed leads to a contradiction. On such a view, though it may seem conceivable that there might never have been anything, that is not really logically possible. Some people even claim that there may be only one coherent cosmic possibility. Thus Einstein suggested that, if God created our world, he might have had no choice about which world to create. If such a view were true, everything might be explained. Reality might be the way it is because there was no conceivable alternative. But, for reasons that have been often given, we can reject such views.

Consider next a quite different view. According to Plato, Plotinus and others, the Universe exists because its existence is good. Even if we are confident that we should reject this view, it is worth asking whether it makes sense. If it does, that may suggest other possibilities.

This *Axiarchic View* can take a theistic form. It can claim that God exists because his existence is good, and that the rest of the Universe exists because God caused it to exist. But in that explanation God, *qua* Creator, is redundant. If God can exist because his existence is good, so can the whole Universe. This may be why some theists reject the Axiarchic View, and insist that God's existence is a brute fact, with no explanation.

In its simplest form, this view makes three claims:

(1) It would be best if reality were a certain way.
(2) Reality is that way.
(3) (1) explains (2).

(1) is an ordinary evaluative claim, like the claim that it would be better if there was less suffering. The Axiarchic View assumes, I believe rightly, that such claims can be in a strong sense true. (2) is an ordinary empirical or scientific claim, though of a sweeping kind. What is distinctive in this view is claim (3), according to which (1) explains (2).

Can we understand this third claim? To focus on this question, we should briefly ignore the world's evils, and suspend our other doubts about claims (1) and (2). We should suppose that, as Leibniz claimed, the best possible Universe exists. Would it then make sense to claim that this Universe exists *because* it is the best?

That use of 'because', Axiarchists should admit, cannot be easily explained. But even ordinary causation is mysterious. At the most fundamental level, we have no idea why some events cause others; and it is hard to explain what causation is. There are, moreover, non-causal senses of 'because' and 'why', as in the claim that God exists because his existence is logically necessary. We can understand that claim, even if we think it false. The Axiarchic View is harder to understand. But that is not surprising. If there is some explanation of the whole of reality, we should not expect this explanation to fit neatly into some familiar category. This extra-ordinary question may have an extra-ordinary answer. We should reject suggested answers which make no sense; but we should also try to see what might make sense.

Axiarchy might be expressed as follows. We are now supposing that, of all the countless ways that the whole of reality might be, one is both the very best, and is the way that reality is. On the Axiarchic View, *that is no coincidence*. This claim, I believe, makes sense. And, if it were no coincidence that the best way for reality to be is *also* the way that reality is, that might support the further claim that this was *why* reality was this way.

This view has one advantage over the more familiar theistic view. An appeal to God cannot explain why the Universe exists, since God would himself be part of the Universe, or one of the things that exist. Some theists argue that, since nothing can exist without some cause, God, who is the First Cause, must exist. As Schopenhauer objected, this argument's premise is not like some cab-driver whom theists are free to dismiss once they have reached their destination. The Axiarchic View appeals, not to an existing entity, but to an explanatory law. Since such a law would not itself be part of the Universe, it might explain why the Universe exists, and is as good as it could be. If such a law governed reality, we could still ask why it did, or why the Axiarchic View was true. But, in discovering this law, we would have made some progress.

It is hard, however, to believe the Axiarchic View. If, as it seems, there is much pointless suffering, our world cannot be part of the best possible Universe.

4

Some Axiarchists claim that, if we reject their view, we must regard our world's existence as a brute fact, since no other explanation could make sense. But that, I believe, is not so. If we abstract from the optimism of the Axiarchic View, its claims are these:

Of the countless cosmic possibilities, one both has some very special feature, and is the possibility that obtains. That is no coincidence. This possibility obtains because it has this feature.

Other views can make such claims. This special feature need not be that of being best. Thus, on the All Worlds Hypothesis, reality is *maximal*, or as full as it could be. Similarly, if nothing had ever existed, reality would have been *minimal*, or as empty as it could be. If the possibility that obtained were either maximal, or minimal, that fact, we might claim, would be most unlikely to be a coincidence. And that might support the further claim that this possibility's having this feature would be *why* it obtained.

Let us now look more closely at that last step. When it is no coincidence that two things are both true, there is something that explains why, given the truth of one, the other is also true. The truth of either might make the other true. Or both might be explained by some third truth, as when two facts are the joint effects of a common cause.

Suppose next that, of the cosmic possibilities, one is both very special and is the one that obtains. If that is no coincidence, what might explain why these things are both true? On the reasoning that we are now considering, the first truth explains the second, since this possibility obtains because it has this special feature. Given the kind of truths these are, such an explanation could not go the other way. This possibility could not have this feature because it obtains. If some possibility has some feature, it could not fail to have this feature, so it would have this feature whether or not it obtains. The All Worlds Hypothesis, for example, could not fail to describe the fullest way for reality to be.

While it is necessary that our imagined possibility has its special feature, it is not necessary that this possibility obtains. This difference, I believe, justifies the reasoning that we are now considering. Since this possibility must have this feature, but might not have obtained, it cannot have this feature because it obtains, nor could some third truth explain why it both has this feature and obtains. So, if these facts are no coincidence, this possibility must obtain *because* it has this feature.

When some possibility obtains because it has some feature, its having this feature may be why some agent, or some process of natural selection, made it obtain. These we can call the *intentional* and *evolutionary* ways in which some feature of some possibility may explain why it obtains.

Our world, theists claim, can be explained in the first of these ways. If reality were as good as it could be, it would indeed make sense to claim that this was partly God's work. But, since God's own existence could not be God's work, there could be no intentional explanation of why the whole of reality was as good as it could be. So we could reasonably conclude that this way's being the best explained *directly* why reality was this way. Even if God exists, the intentional explanation could not compete with the different and bolder explanation offered by the Axiarchic View.

Return now to other explanations of this kind. Consider first the Null Possibility. This, we know, does not obtain; but, since we are asking what makes sense, that does not matter. If there had never been anything, would that have had to be a brute fact, which had no explanation? The answer, I suggest, is No. It might have been no coincidence that, of all the countless cosmic possibilities, what obtained was the simplest, and least arbitrary, and the only possibility in which nothing ever exists. And, if these facts had been no coincidence, this possibility would have obtained because—or partly because—it had one or more of these special features. This explanation, moreover, could not have taken an intentional or evolutionary form. If nothing had ever existed, there could not have been some agent, or process of selection, who or which made this possibility obtain. Its being the simplest or least arbitrary possibility would have been, directly, why it obtained.

Consider next the All Worlds Hypothesis, which may obtain. If reality is as full as it could be, is that a coincidence? Does it merely happen to be true that, of all the cosmic possibilities, the one that obtains is at this extreme? As before, that is conceivable, but this coincidence would be too great to be credible. We can reasonably assume that, if this possibility obtains, that is because it is maximal, or at this extreme. On this *Maximalist View*, it is a fundamental truth that being possible, and part of the fullest way that reality could be, is sufficient for being actual. That is the highest law governing reality. As before, if such a law governed reality, we could still ask *why* it did. But, in discovering this law, we would have made some progress.

Here is another special feature. Perhaps reality is the way it is because its fundamental laws are, on some criterion, as mathematically beautiful as they could be. That is what some physicists are inclined to believe.

As these remarks suggest, there is no clear boundary here between philosophy and science. If there is such a highest law governing reality, this law is of the same kind as those that physicists are trying to discover. When we appeal to natural laws to explain some features of reality, such as the relations between light, gravity, space, and time, we are not giving causal explanations, since we are not claiming that one part of reality caused another part to be some way. What such laws explain, or partly explain, are the deeper facts about reality that causal explanations take for granted.

There would be a highest law, of the kind that I have sketched, if some cosmic possibility obtained because it had some special feature. This feature we can call the *Selector*. If there is more than one such feature, they are all partial Selectors. Just as there are various cosmic possibilities, there are various *explanatory* possibilities. For each of these special features, there is the explanatory possibility that this feature is the Selector, or is one of the Selectors. Reality would then be the way it is because, or partly because, this way had this feature.

There is one other explanatory possibility: that there is *no* Selector. If that is true, it is random that reality is as it is. Events may be in one sense random, even though they are causally inevitable. That is how it is random whether a meteorite strikes the land or the sea. Events are random in a stronger sense if they have no cause. That is what most physicists believe about some features of events involving sub-atomic particles. If it is random what reality is like, the Universe not only has no cause. It has no explanation of any kind. This claim we can call the *Brute Fact View*.

Few features can be plausibly regarded as possible Selectors. Though plausibility is a matter of degree, there is a natural threshold to which we can appeal. If we suppose that reality has some special feature, we can ask which of two beliefs would be more credible: that reality merely happens to have this feature, or that reality is the way it is because this way has this feature. If the second would be more credible, this feature can be called a *credible Selector*. Return for example to the question of how many possible local worlds exist. Of the different answers to this question, *all* and *none* give us, I have claimed, credible Selectors. If either all or no worlds existed, that would be unlikely to be a coincidence. But suppose that 58 worlds existed. This number has some special features, such as being the smallest number that is the sum of seven different primes. It may be just conceivable that this would be why 58 worlds existed; but it would be more reasonable to believe that the number that existed merely happened to be 58.

There are, I have claimed, some credible Selectors. Reality might be some way because that way is the best, or the simplest, or the least arbitrary, or because its obtaining makes reality as full and varied as it could be, or because its fundamental laws are, in some way, as elegant as they could be. Presumably there are other such features, which I have overlooked.

In claiming that there are credible Selectors, I am assuming that some cosmic and explanatory possibilities are more probable than others. That assumption may be questioned. Judgments of probability, it may again be claimed, must be grounded on facts about our world, so such judgments cannot be applied either to how the whole of reality might be, or to how reality might be explained.

This objection is, I believe, unsound. When we choose between scientific theories, our judgments of their probability cannot rest only on predictions based on established facts and laws. We need such judgments in trying to decide what these facts and laws are. And we can justifiably make such judgments when considering different ways in which the whole of reality may be, or might have have been. Compare two such cosmic possibilities. In the first, there is a lifeless Universe consisting only of some spherical iron stars, whose relative motion is as it would be in our world. In the second, things are the same, except that the stars move together in the patterns of a minuet, and they are shaped like either Queen Victoria or Cary Grant. We would be right to claim that, of these two possibilities, the first is more likely to obtain.

In making that claim, we would not mean that it is more likely *that* the first possibility obtains. Since this possibility is the existence of a lifeless Universe, we know that it does not obtain. We would be claiming that this possibility is intrinsically more likely, or that, to put it roughly, it had a greater chance of being how reality is. If some possibility is more likely to obtain, that will often make it more likely that it obtains; but though one kind of likelihood supports the other, they are quite different.

Another objection may again seem relevant here. Of the countless cosmic possibilities, a few have special features, which I have called credible Selectors. If such a possibility obtains, we have, I have claimed, a choice of two conclusions. Either reality, by an extreme coincidence, merely happens to have this feature, or—more plausibly—this feature is one of the Selectors. It may be objected that, when I talk of an extreme coincidence, I must be assuming that these cosmic possibilities are all equally likely to obtain. But I have now rejected that assumption. And, if these possibilities are *not* equally likely, my reasoning may seem to be undermined.

As before, that is not so. Suppose that, of the cosmic possibilities, those that have these special features are much more likely to obtain. As this objection rightly claims, it would not then be amazing if such a possibility merely happened to obtain. But that does not undermine my reasoning, since it is another way of stating my conclusion. It is another way of saying that these features are Selectors.

These remarks do show, however, that we should distinguish two ways in which some feature may be a Selector. *Probabilistic* Selectors make some cosmic possibility more likely to obtain, but leave it open whether it does obtain. On any plausible view, there are some Selectors of this kind, since some ways for reality to be are intrinsically more likely than some others. Thus of our two imagined Universes, the one consisting of spherical stars is intrinsically more likely than the one with stars that are shaped like Queen Victoria or Cary Grant. Besides Probabilistic Selectors, there may also be one or more *Effective* Selectors. If some possibility has a certain feature, this may make this possibility, not merely intrinsically more likely, but the one that obtains. Thus, if simplicity had been the Effective Selector, that would have made it true that nothing ever existed. And, if maximality is the Effective Selector, as it may be, that is what makes reality as full as it could be. When I talk of Selectors, these are the kind I mean.

5

There are, then, various cosmic and explanatory possibilities. In trying to decide which of these obtain, we can in part appeal to facts about our world. Thus, from the mere fact that our world exists, we can deduce that the Null Possibility does not obtain. And, since our world seems to contain pointless evils, we have reason to reject the Axiarchic View.

Consider next the Brute Fact View, on which reality merely happens to be as it is. No facts about our world could refute this view. But some facts would make it less likely that this view is true. If reality is randomly selected, what we should expect to exist are many varied worlds, none of which had features that, in the range of possibilities, were at one extreme. That is what we should expect because, in much the largest set of cosmic possibilities, that would be what exists. If our world has very special features, that would count against the Brute Fact View.

Return now to the question whether God exists. Compared with the uncaused existence of one or many complicated worlds, the hypothesis that God exists has been claimed to be simpler, and less arbitrary, and thus more likely to be true. But this hypothesis is not simpler than the Brute Fact View. And, if it is random which cosmic possibility obtains, we should not expect the one that obtains to be as simple, and unarbitrary, as God's existence is claimed to be. Rather, as I have just said, we should expect there to be many worlds, none of which had very special features. Ours may be the kind of world that, on the Brute Fact View, we should expect to observe.

Similar remarks apply to the All Worlds Hypothesis. Few facts about our world could refute this view; but, if all possible local worlds exist, the likely character of our world is much the same as on the Brute Fact View. That claim may seem surprising, given the difference between these two views. One view is about *which* cosmic possibility obtains, the other is about *why* the one that obtains obtains. And these views conflict, since, if we knew that either view was true, we would have strong reason not to believe the other. If all possible worlds exist, that is unlikely to be a brute fact. But, in their different ways, these views are both *non-selective*. On neither view do certain worlds exist *because* they have certain special features. So, if either view is true, we should not expect our world to have such features.

To that last claim, there is one exception. This is the feature with which we began: that our world allows for life. Though this feature is, in some ways, special, it is one that we cannot help observing. That restricts what we can infer from the fact that our world has this feature. Rather than claiming that being life-allowing is one of the Selectors, we can appeal to some version of the Many Worlds Hypothesis.

If there are very many worlds, we would expect a few worlds to be life-allowing, and our world is bound to be one of these few.

Consider next other kinds of special feature: ones that we are not bound to observe. Suppose we discover that our world has such a feature, and we ask whether that is no coincidence. It may again be said that, if there are many worlds, we would expect a few worlds to have this special feature. But that would not explain why that is true of *our* world. We could not claim—as with the feature of being life-allowing—that our world is bound to have this feature. So the appeal to many worlds could not explain away the coincidence. Suppose, for example, that our world were very good, or were wholly law-governed, or had very simple natural laws. Those facts would count against both of the unselective views: both the All Worlds Hypothesis and the Brute Fact View. It is true that, if all worlds exist, or there are very many randomly selected worlds, we should expect a few worlds to be very good, or wholly law-governed, or to have very simple laws. But that would not explain why our world had those features. So we would have some reason to believe that our world is the way it is because this way has those features.

Does our world have such features: ones that count against the unselective views? Our world's moral character seems not to count against these views, since it seems the mixture of good and bad that, on the unselective views, we should expect. But our world may have the other two features: being wholly law-governed, and having very simple laws. Neither feature seems to be required in order for life to be possible. And, among possible life-containing worlds, a far greater range would not have these features. Thus, for each law-governed world, there are countless variants that would fail in different ways to be wholly law-governed. And, compared with simple laws, there is a far greater range of complicated laws. So, on both the unselective views, we should not expect our world to have these features. If it has them, as physicists might discover, that would give us reasons to reject both the All Worlds Hypothesis and the Brute Fact View. We would have some reason to believe that there are at least two partial Selectors: being law-governed and having simple laws.

There may be other features of our world from which we can try to infer what reality is like, and why. But observation can take us only part of the way. If we can get further, that will have to be by pure reasoning.

6

Of those who accept the Brute Fact View, many assume that it must be true. According to these people, though reality merely happens to be some way, *that* it merely happens to be some way does not merely happen to be true. There could not be an explanation of why reality is the way it is, since there could not be a causal explanation, and no other explanation would make sense.

This assumption, I have argued, is mistaken. Reality might be the way it is because this way is the fullest, or the most varied, or obeys the simplest or most elegant laws, or has some other special feature. Since the Brute Fact View is not the only explanatory possibility, we should not assume that it must be true.

When supporters of this view recognize these other possibilities, they may switch to the other extreme, claiming that their view's truth is another brute fact. If that were so, not only would there be no explanation of reality's being as it is, there would also be no explanation of there being no such explanation. As before, though this might be true, we should not assume that it must be true. If some explanatory possibility merely happens to obtain, the one that obtains may not be the Brute Fact View. If it is randomly selected *whether* reality is randomly selected, and there are other possibilities, random selection may not be selected.

There is, moreover, another way in which some explanatory possibility may obtain. Rather than merely happening to obtain, this possibility may have some feature, or set of features, which explains why it obtains. Such a feature would be a Selector at a higher level, since it would apply not to factual but to explanatory possibilities. It would determine, not that reality be a certain way, but that it be determined in a certain way how reality is to be.

If the Brute Fact View is true, it may have been selected in this way. Of the explanatory possibilities, this view seems to describe the simplest, since its claim is only that reality has no explanation. This possibility's being the simplest might make it the one that obtains. Simplicity may be the higher Selector, determining that there is no Selector between the ways that reality might be.

Once again however, though this may be true, we cannot assume its truth. There may be some other higher Selector. Some explanatory possibility may obtain, for example, because it is the least arbitrary, or is the one that explains most. The Brute Fact View has neither of those features. Or there may be no higher Selector, since some explanatory possibility may merely happen to obtain.

These alternatives are the different possibilities at yet another, higher explanatory level. So we have the same two questions: Which obtains, and Why?

We may now become discouraged. Every answer, it may seem, raises a further question. But that may not be so. There may be some answer that is a necessary truth. With that necessity, our search would end.

Some truth is logically necessary when its denial leads to a contradiction. It cannot be in this sense necessary either that reality is a brute fact, or that there is some Selector. Both these claims can be denied without contradiction.

There are also non-logical necessities. The most familiar, causal necessity, cannot give us the truth we need. It could not be causally necessary that reality is, or isn't, a brute fact. Causal necessities come lower down. Similar remarks apply to the necessities involved in the essential properties of particular things, or natural kinds. Consider next the metaphysical necessity that some writers claim for God's existence. That claim means, they say, that God's existence does not depend on anything else, and that nothing else could cause God to cease to exist. But these claims do not imply that God must exist, and that makes such necessity too weak to end our questions.

There are, however, some kinds of necessity that would be strong enough. Consider the truths that undeserved suffering is bad, and that, if we believe the premises of a sound argument, we ought rationally to believe this argument's conclusion. These truths are not logically necessary, since their denials would not lead to contradictions. But they could not have failed to be true. Undeserved suffering does not merely happen to be bad.

When Leslie defends the Axiarchic View, he appeals to this kind of non-logical necessity. Not only does value rule reality, Leslie suggests, it could not have failed to rule. But this suggestion is hard to believe. While it is inconceivable that undeserved suffering might have failed to be in itself bad, it is clearly conceivable that value might have failed to rule, if only because it seems so clear that value does *not* rule.

Return now to the Brute Fact View, which is more likely to be true. If this view is true, could its truth be non-logically necessary? Is it inconceivable that there might have been some Selector, or highest law, making reality be some way? The answer, I have claimed, is No. Even if reality is a brute fact, it might not have been. Thus, if nothing had ever existed, that might have been no coincidence. Reality might have been that way because, of the cosmic possibilities, it is the simplest and least arbitrary. And, as I have also claimed, just as it is not necessary that the Brute Fact View is true, it is not necessary that this view's truth be another brute fact. This view might be true because it is the simplest of the explanatory possibilities.

We have not yet found the necessity we need. Reality may happen to be as it is, or there may be some Selector. Whichever of these is true, it may happen to be true, or there may be some higher Selector. These are the different possibilities at the next explanatory level, so we are back with our two questions: Which obtains, and Why?

Could these questions continue for ever? Might there be, at every level, another higher Selector? Consider another version of the Axiarchic View. Reality might be as good as it could be, and that might be true because its being true is best, and that in turn might be true because its being true is best, and so on for ever. In this way, it may seem, everything might be explained. But that is not so. Like an infinite series of events, such a series of explanatory truths could not explain itself. Even if each truth were made true by the next, we could still ask why the whole series was true, rather than some other series, or no series.

The point can be made more simply. Though there might be some highest Selector, this might not be goodness but some other feature, such as non-arbitrariness. What could select between these possibilities? Might goodness be the highest Selector because that is best, or non-arbitrariness be this Selector because that is the least arbitrary possibility? Neither suggestion, I believe, makes sense. Just as God could not make himself exist, no Selector could make itself the one that, at the highest level, rules. No Selector could settle *whether* it rules, since it cannot settle anything unless it does rule.

If there is some highest Selector, this cannot, I have claimed, be a necessary truth. Nor could this Selector make itself the highest. And, since this Selector would be the highest, nothing else could make that true. So we may have found the necessity we need. If there is some highest Selector, that, I suggest, must merely happen to be true.

Supporters of the Brute Fact View may now feel vindicated. Have we not, in the end, accepted their view?

We have not. According to the Brute Fact View, reality merely happens to be as it is. That, I have argued, may not be true, since there may be some Selector which explains, or partly explains, reality's being as it is. There may also be some higher Selector which explains there being this Selector. My suggestion is only that, at the end of any such explanatory chain, some highest Selector must merely happen to be the one that rules. That is a different view.

This difference may seem small. No Selector could *explain* reality, we may believe, if it merely happened to rule. But this thought, though natural, is a mistake. If some explanation appeals to a brute fact, it does not explain that fact; but it may explain others.

Suppose, for example, that reality is as full as it could be. On the Brute Fact View, this fact would have no explanation. On the Maximalist View, reality would be this way because the highest law is that what is possible is actual. If reality were as full as it could be, this Maximalist View would be better than the Brute Fact View, since it would explain reality's being this way. And this view would provide that explanation even if it merely happened to be true. It makes a difference where the brute fact comes.

Part of the difference here is that, while there are countless cosmic possibilities, there are few plausible explanatory possibilities. If reality is as full as it could be, that's being a brute fact would be very puzzling. Since there are countless cosmic possibilities, it would be amazing if the one that obtained merely happened to be at the maximal extreme. On the Maximalist View, this fact would be no coincidence. And, since there are few explanatory possibilities, it would not be amazing if the Maximalist highest law merely happened to be the one that rules.

We should not claim that, if some explanation rests on a brute fact, it is not an explanation. Most scientific explanations take this form. The most that might be true is that such an explanation is, in a way, merely a better a description.

If that were true, there would be a different defence of the kind of reasoning that we have been considering. Even to discover *how* things are, we need explanations. And we may need explanations on the grandest scale. Our world may seem to have some feature that would be unlikely to be a coincidence. We may reasonably suspect that this feature is the Selector, or one of the Selectors. That hypothesis might lead us to confirm that, as it seemed, our world does have this feature. And that might give us reason to conclude either that ours is the only world, or that there are other worlds, with the same or related features. We might thus reach truths about the whole Universe.

Even if all explanations must end with a brute fact, we should go on trying to explain why the Universe exists, and is as it is. The brute fact may not enter at the lowest level. If reality is the way it is because this way has some feature, to know *what* reality is like, we must ask *why*.

7

We may never be able to answer these questions, either because our world is only a small part of reality, or because, though our world is the whole of reality, we could never know that to be true, or because of our own limitations. But, as I have tried to show, we may come to see more clearly what the possible answers are. Some of the fog that shrouds these questions may then disappear.

It can seem astonishing, for example, how reality could be made to be as it is. If God made the rest of reality be as it is, what could have made God exist? And, if God does not exist, what else could have made reality be as it is? When we think about these questions, even the Brute Fact View may seem unintelligible. It may be baffling how reality could be even randomly selected. What kind of *process* could select whether, for example, time had no beginning, or whether anything ever exists? When, and how, could any selection be made?

This is not a real problem. Of all the possible ways that reality might be, there must be one that is the way reality actually is. Since it is logically necessary that reality be some way or other, it is necessary that one way be picked to be the way that reality is. Logic ensures that, without any kind of process, a selection is made. There is no need for hidden machinery.

Suppose next that, as many people assume, the Brute Fact View must be true. If our world has no very special features, there would then be nothing that was deeply puzzling. If it were necessary that some cosmic possibility be randomly selected, while there would be no explanation of why the selection went as it did, there would be no mystery in reality's being as it is. Reality's features would be inexplicable, but only in the way in which it is inexplicable how some particle randomly moves. If a particle can merely happen to move as it does, reality could merely happen to be as it is. Randomness may even be *less* puzzling at the level of the whole Universe, since we know that facts at this level could not have been caused.

The Brute Fact View, I have argued, is not necessary, and may not be true. There may be one or more Selectors between the ways that reality might be, and one or more Selectors between such Selectors. But, as I have also claimed, it may be a necessary truth that it be a brute fact whether there are such Selectors, and, if so, which the highest Selector is.

If that is a necessary truth, similar remarks apply. On these assumptions, there would again be nothing that was deeply puzzling. If it is necessary that, of these explanatory possibilities, one merely happens to obtain, there would be no explanation of why the one that obtains obtains. But, as before, that would be no more mysterious than the random movement of some particle.

The existence of the Universe can seem, in another way, astonishing. Even if it is not baffling that reality was made to be some way, since there is no conceivable alternative, it can seem baffling that the selection went as it did. Why is there a Universe at all? Why doesn't reality take its simplest and least arbitrary form: that in which nothing ever exists?

If we find this astonishing, we are assuming that these features should be the Selectors: that reality should be as simple and unarbitrary as it could be. That assumption has, I believe, great plausibility. But, just as the simplest cosmic possibility is that nothing ever exists, the simplest explanatory possibility is that there is no Selector. So we should not expect simplicity at both the factual and explanatory levels. If there is no Selector, we should not expect that there would also be no Universe. That would be an extreme coincidence.[2]

---

2. Of several discussions of these questions, I owe most to John Leslie's *Value and Existence*, (Blackwell, 1979) and to Robert Nozick's *Philosophical Explanations* (Oxford, 1981); then to Richard Swinburne's *The Existence of God*, (Oxford, 1979), John Mackie's *The Miracle of Theism*, (Oxford, 1982), Peter Unger's article in *Mid-West Studies in Philosophy*, Volume 9 (1989), and some unpublished work by Stephen Grover.

Chapter 2

The five ways

Thomas Aquinas

THE third question [**Does God exist?**] we approach as follows:

It seems there is no God:

For [1] if one of two mutually exclusive things were to exist unbounded, the other would be totally destroyed. But the word *God* implies some unbounded good. So if God existed, no evil would ever be encountered. Evil is, however, encountered in the world. So God does not exist.

Moreover, [2] when a few causes fully account for some effect it doesn't need more. But it seems that everything we observe in this world can be fully accounted for by other causes, without assuming a God: natural effects by natural causes, and contrived effects by human reasoning and will. There is therefore no need to assume that God exists.

But against that:

Exodus 3 represents God as saying: *I am who am.*

In reply:

There are five ways of proving there is a God:

The first and most obvious way is based on change. For certainly some things are changing: this we plainly see. Now anything changing is being changed by something else. (This is so because what makes things changeable is unrealized potentiality, but what makes them cause change is their already realized state: causing change brings into being what was previously only able to be, and can only be done by something which already is. For example, the actual heat of fire causes wood, able to be hot, to become actually hot, and so causes change in the wood; now what is actually hot can't at the same time be potentially hot but only potentially cold, can't at the same time be actual and potential in the same respect but only in different respects; so that what is changing can't be the very thing that is causing the same change, can't be changing itself, but must be being changed by something else.) Again this something else, if itself changing, must be being changed by yet another thing; and this last by another. But this can't go on for ever, since then there would be no first cause of the change, and as a result no subsequent causes. (Only when acted on by a first cause do

Thomas Aquinas, 'The five ways', from *Selected Philosophical Writings*, edited by Timothy McDermott (Oxford World's Classics, 1998), reprinted by permission of Oxford University Press.

intermediate causes produce a change; unless a hand moves the stick, the stick won't move anything else.) So we are forced eventually to come to a first cause of change not itself being changed by anything, and this is what everyone understands by *God*.

The second way is based on the very notion of agent cause. In the observable world causes are found ordered in series: we never observe, nor ever could, something causing itself, for this would mean it preceded itself, and this is not possible. But a series of causes can't go on for ever, for in any such series an earlier member causes an intermediate and the intermediate a last (whether the intermediate be one or many). Now eliminating a cause eliminates its effects, and unless there's a first cause there won't be a last or an intermediate. But if a series of causes goes on for ever it will have no first cause, and so no intermediate causes and no last effect, which is clearly false. So we are forced to postulate some first agent cause, to which everyone gives the name *God*.

The third way is based on what need not be and on what must be, and runs as follows. Some of the things we come across can be but need not be, for we find them being generated and destroyed, thus sometimes in being and sometimes not. Now everything cannot be like this, for a thing that need not be was once not; and if everything need not be, once upon a time there was nothing. But if that were true there would be nothing even now, because something that does not exist can only begin to exist through something that already exists. If nothing was in being nothing could begin to be, and nothing would be in being now, which is clearly false. Not everything then is the sort that need not be; some things must be, and these may or may not owe this necessity to something else. But just as we proved that a series of agent causes can't go on for ever, so also a series of things which must be and owe this to other things. So we are forced to postulate something which of itself must be, owing this to nothing outside itself, but being itself the cause that other things must be.

The fourth way is based on the levels found in things. Some things are found to be better, truer, more excellent than others. Such comparative terms describe varying degrees of approximation to a superlative; for example, things are hotter the nearer they approach what is hottest. So there is something which is the truest and best and most excellent of things, and hence the most fully in being; for Aristotle says that the truest things are the things most fully in being. Now *when many things possess a property in common, the one most fully possessing it causes it in the others: fire*, as Aristotle says, *the hottest of all things, causes all other things to be hot.* So there is something that causes in all other things their being, their goodness, and whatever other perfections they have. And this is what we call *God*.

The fifth way is based on the guidedness of nature. Goal-directed behaviour is observed in all bodies in nature, even those lacking awareness; for we see their behaviour hardly ever varying and practically always turning out well, which shows they truly tend to goals and do not merely hit them by accident. But nothing lacking awareness can tend to a goal except it be directed by someone with awareness and understanding: arrows by archers, for example. So everything in nature is directed to its goal by someone with understanding, and this we call *God*.

Hence:

to 1: As Augustine says: *Since God is supremely good, he would not allow any evil at all in his works if he wasn't sufficiently almighty and good to bring good even from evil.* It is therefore a mark of his unbounded goodness that God allows evils to exist and draws from them good.

to 2: Natural causes pursue fixed goals under the direction of some superior cause, and so their effects must also be traced back to God as the first of all causes. In the same manner contrived effects must also be traced back to a higher cause than human reasoning and will, for these are changeable and can cease to exist, and, as we have seen, everything that can change or cease to exist must be traced back to a first cause which cannot change and of itself must be.

Chapter 3
Selection from *Natural Theology*
William Paley

The design argument

State of the argument

IN crossing a heath, suppose I pitched my foot against a *stone*, and were asked how the stone came to be there, I might possibly answer, that, for anything I knew to the contrary, it had lain there for ever; nor would it, perhaps, be very easy to show the absurdity of this answer. But suppose I had found a *watch* upon the ground, and it should be inquired how the watch happened to be in that place, I should hardly think of the answer which I had before given—that, for anything I knew, the watch might have always been there. Yet why should not this answer serve for the watch as well as for the stone? Why is it not as admissible in the second case as in the first? For this reason, and for no other, viz., that, when we come to inspect the watch, we perceive (what we could not discover in the stone) that its several parts are framed and put together for a purpose, e.g. that they are so formed and adjusted as to produce motion, and that motion so regulated as to point out the hour of the day; that, if the different parts had been differently shaped from what they are, of a different size from what they are, or placed after any other manner, or in any other order than that in which they are placed, either no motion at all would have been carried on in the machine, or none which would have answered the use that is now served by it. To reckon up a few of the plainest of these parts, and of their offices, all tending to one result:—We see a cylindrical box containing a coiled elastic spring, which, by its endeavour to relax itself, turns round the box. We next observe a flexible chain (artificially wrought for the sake of flexure) communicating the action of the spring from the box to the fusee. We then find a series of wheels, the teeth of which catch in, and apply to, each other, conducting the motion from the fusee to the balance, and from the balance to the pointer, and, at the same time, by the size and shape of those wheels, so regulating that motion as to terminate in causing an index, by an equable and measured progression, to pass over a given space in a given time. We take notice that the wheels are made of brass, in order to keep them from rust; the springs of steel, no other metal being so elastic; that over the face

William Paley, selection from *Natural Theology* (C. Knight, 1836).

of the watch there is placed a glass, a material employed in no other part of the work, but in the room of which, if there had been any other than a transparent substance, the hour could not be seen without opening the case. This mechanism being observed, (it requires indeed an examination of the instrument, and perhaps some previous knowledge of the subject, to perceive and understand it; but being once, as we have said, observed and understood,) the inference, we think, is inevitable, that the watch must have had a maker: that there must have existed, at some time, and at some place or other, an artificer or artificers who formed it for the purpose which we find it actually to answer; who comprehended its construction, and designed its use.

I. Nor would it, I apprehend, weaken the conclusion, that we had never seen a watch made; that we had never known an artist capable of making one; that we were altogether incapable of executing such a piece of workmanship ourselves, or of understanding in what manner it was performed; all this being no more than what is true of some exquisite remains of ancient art, of some lost arts, and, to the generality of mankind, of the more curious productions of modern manufacture. Does one man in a million know how oval frames are turned? Ignorance of this kind exalts our opinion of the unseen and unknown artist's skill, if he be unseen and unknown, but raises no doubt in our minds of the existence and agency of such an artist, at some former time, and in some place or other. Nor can I perceive that it varies at all the inference, whether the question arise concerning a human agent, or concerning an agent of a different species, or an agent possessing, in some respect, a different nature.

II. Neither, secondly, would it invalidate our conclusion, that the watch sometimes went wrong, or that it seldom went exactly right. The purpose of the machinery, the design, and the designer, might be evident, and, in the case supposed, would be evident, in whatever way we accounted for the irregularity of the movement, or whether we could account for it or not. It is not necessary that a machine be perfect, in order to show with what design it was made: still less necessary, where the only question is, whether it were made with any design at all.

III. Nor, thirdly, would it bring any uncertainty into the argument, if there were a few parts of the watch, concerning which we could not discover, or had not yet discovered, in what manner they conduced to the general effect; or even some parts, concerning which we could not ascertain whether they conduced to that effect in any manner whatever. For, as to the first branch of the case, if by the loss, or disorder, or decay of the parts in question, the movement of the watch were found in fact to be stopped, or disturbed, or retarded, no doubt would remain in our minds as to the utility or intention of these parts, although we should be unable to investigate the manner according to which, or the connexion by which, the ultimate effect depended upon their action or assistance; and the more complex is the machine, the more likely is this obscurity to arise. Then, as to the second thing supposed, namely, that there were parts which might be spared without prejudice to the movement of the watch, and that he had proved this by experiment, these superfluous parts, even if we were completely assured that they were such, would not vacate the reasoning which we had instituted concerning other parts. The indication of contrivance remained, with respect to them, nearly as it was before.

IV. Nor, fourthly, would any man in his senses think the existence of the watch with its various machinery, accounted for, by being told that it was one out of possible combinations of material forms; that whatever he had found in the place where he found the watch, must have contained some internal configuration other; and that this configuration might be the structure now exhibited, viz., of the works of a watch, as well as a different structure.

V. Nor, fifthly, would it yield his inquiry more satisfaction, to be answered, that there existed in things a principle of order, which had disposed the parts of the watch into their present form and situation. He never knew a watch made by the principle of order; nor can he even form to himself an idea of what is meant by principle of order, distinct from the intelligence of the watchmaker.

VI. Sixthly, he would be surprised to hear that the mechanism of the watch was no proof of contrivance, only a motive to induce the mind to think so:

VII. And not less surprised to be informed, that the watch in his hand was nothing more than the result of the laws of *metallic* nature. It is a perversion language to assign any law as the efficient, operative cause of anything. A law presupposes an agent; for it is only the mode according to which an agent proceeds: it implies a power; for it is the order according to which that power acts. Without this agent, without this power, which are both distinct from itself, the *law* do nothing, is nothing. The expression, 'the law of metallic nature,' may sound stran and harsh to a philosophic ear; but it seems quite as justifiable as some others which are more familiar to him, such as 'the law of vegetable nature,' 'the law of animal nature,' or, indeed, as 'the law of nature' in general, when assigned as the cause of phenomena, in exclusion of agency and power, or when it is substituted into the place of these.

VIII. Neither, lastly, would our observer be driven out of his conclusion, or from his confidence in its truth, by being told that he knew nothing at all about the matter. He knows enough for his argument: he knows the utility of the end: he knows the subserviency and adaptation of the means to the end. These points being known, his ignorance of other points, his doubts concerning other points, affect not the certainty of his reasoning. The consciousness of knowing little need not beget a distrust of that which he does know.

State of the argument continued

Suppose in the next place, that the person who found the watch should, after some time, discover that, in addition to all the properties which he had hitherto observed in it, it possessed the unexpected property of producing, in the course of it movement, another watch like itself (the thing is conceivable); that it contained within it a mechanism, a system of parts, a mould, for instance, or a complete adjustment of lathes, files, and other tools, evidently and separately calculated for this purpose; let us inquire what effect ought such a discovery to have upon his former conclusion.

I. The first effect would be to increase his admiration of the contrivance, and his conviction of the consummate skill of the contriver. Whether he regarded the object of the contrivance, the distinct apparatus, the intricate, yet in many parts intelligible mechanism by which it was carried on, he would perceive, in this new observation, nothing but an additional reason for doing what he had already done—for referring the construction of the watch to design, and to supreme art. If that construction *without* this property, or which is the same thing, before this property had been noticed, proved intention and art to have been employed about it, still more strong would the proof appear, when he came to the knowledge of this further property, the crown and perfection of all the rest.

II. He would reflect, that though the watch before him were, in *some sense*, the maker of the watch which was fabricated in the course of its movements, yet it was in a very different sense from that in which a carpenter, for instance, is the maker of a chair—the author of its contrivance, the cause of the relation of its parts to their use. With respect to these; the first watch was no cause at all to the second; in no such sense as this was it the author of the constitution and order, either of the parts which the new watch contained, or of the parts by the aid and instrumentality of which it was produced. We might possibly say, but with great latitude of expression, that a stream of water ground corn; but no latitude of expression would allow us to say, no stretch of conjecture could lead us to think, that the stream of water built the mill, though it were too ancient for us to know who the builder was. What the stream of water does in the affair is neither more nor less than this; by the application of an unintelligent impulse to a mechanism previously arranged, arranged independently of it, and arranged by intelligence, an effect is produced, viz., the corn is ground. But the effect results from the arrangement. The force of the stream cannot be said to be the cause or the author of the effect, still less of the arrangement. Understanding and plan in the formation of the mill were not the less necessary for any share which the water has in grinding the corn; yet is this share the same as that which the watch would have contributed to the production of the new watch, upon the supposition assumed in the last section. Therefore,

III. Though it be now no longer probable that the individual watch which our observer had found was made immediately by the hand of an artificer, yet doth not this alteration in anywise affect the inference, that an artificer had been originally employed and concerned in the production. The argument from design remains as it was. Marks of design and contrivance are no more accounted for now than they were before. In the same thing, we may ask for the cause of different properties. We may ask for the cause of the colour of a body, of its hardness, of its heat; and these causes may be all different. We are now asking for the cause of that subserviency to a use; that relation to an end, which we have remarked in the watch before us. No answer is given to this question, by telling us that a preceding watch produced it. There cannot be design without a designer; contrivance, without a contriver; order, without choice; arrangement, without anything capable of arranging; subserviency and relation to a purpose, without that which could intend a purpose; means suitable to an end, and executing their office in accomplishing that end, without the end ever having been contemplated, or the means accommodated to it. Arrangement, disposition of parts, subserviency of means to an end, relation of instruments to a use, imply the presence of intelligence and mind. No one, therefore, can rationally believe, that the insensible, inanimate watch, from which the watch before us issued, was the proper cause of the mechanism we so much admire in it;—could be truly said to have constructed the instrument, disposed its parts, assigned their office, determined their order, action, and mutual dependency, combined their several motions into one result, and that also a result connected with the utilities of other beings. All these properties, therefore, are as much unaccounted for as they were before.

IV. Nor is anything gained by running the difficulty farther back, *i.e.*, by supposing the watch before us to have been produced from another watch, that from a former, and so on indefinitely. Our going back ever so far, brings us no nearer to the least degree of satisfaction upon the subject. Contrivance is still unaccounted for. We still want a contriver. A designing mind is neither supplied by this supposition, nor dispensed with. If the difficulty were diminished the farther we went back, by going back indefinitely we might exhaust it. And this is the only case to which this sort of reasoning applies. Where there is a tendency, or, as we increase the number of terms, a continual approach towards a limit, *there*, by supposing the number of terms to be what is called infinite, we may conceive the limit to be attained; but where there is no such tendency or approach, nothing is effected by lengthening the series. There is no difference as to the point in question, (whatever there may be as to many points,) between one series and another; between a series which is finite, and a series which is infinite. A chain, composed of an infinite number of links, can no more support itself than a chain composed of a finite number of links. And of this we are assured; (though we never *can* have tried the experiment,) because, by increasing the number of links, from ten for instance to a hundred, from a hundred to a thousand, &c., we make not the smallest approach, we observe not the smallest tendency towards self-support. There is no difference in this respect (yet there may be a great difference in several respects,) between a chain of a greater or less length, between one chain and another, between one that is finite and one that is infinite. This very much resembles the case before us. The machine which we are inspecting demonstrates, by its construction, contrivance and design. Contrivance must have had a contriver; design, a designer; whether the machine immediately proceeded from another machine or not. That circumstance alters not the case. That other machine may, in like manner, have proceeded from a former machine: nor does that alter the case; the contrivance must have had a contriver. That former one from one preceding it: no alteration still; a contriver is still necessary. No tendency is perceived, no approach towards a diminution of this necessity. It is the same with any and every succession of these machines; a succession of ten, of a hundred, of a thousand; with one series, as with another; a series which is finite, as with a series which is infinite. In whatever other respects they may differ, in this they do not. In all, equally, contrivance and design are unaccounted for.

The question is not simply, How came the first watch into existence? which question, it may be pretended, is done away by supposing the series of watches thus produced from one another to have been infinite, and consequently to have had no such *first*, for which it was necessary to provide a cause. This, perhaps, would have been nearly the state of the question, if nothing had been before us but an unorganized, unmechanized substance, without mark or indication of contrivance. It might be difficult to show that such substance could not have existed from eternity, either in succession (if it were possible, which I think it is not, for unorganized bodies to spring from one another,) or by individual perpetuity. But that is not the question now. To suppose it to be so, is to suppose that it made no difference whether he had found a watch or a stone. As it is, the metaphysics of that question have no place: for, in the watch which we are examining, are seen contrivance, design; an end, a purpose; means for the end, adaptation to the purpose. And the question which irresistibly presses upon our thoughts, is, Whence this contrivance and design? The thing required is the intending mind, the adapted hand, the intelligence by which that hand was directed. This question, this demand, is not shaken off, by increasing a number or succession of substances, destitute of these properties; nor the more, by increasing the number to infinity. If it be said, that, upon the supposition of one watch being produced from another in the course of that other's movements, and by means of the mechanism within it, we have a cause for the watch in my hand, viz., the watch from which it proceeded,—I deny, that for the design, the contrivance, the suitableness of means to an end, the adaptation of instruments to a use, (all of which we discover in the watch,) we have any cause whatever. It is in vain, therefore, to assign a series of such causes, or to allege that a series may be carried back to infinity; for I do not admit that we have yet any cause at all for the phenomena, still less any series of causes either finite or infinite. Here is contrivance, but no contriver; proofs of design, but no designer.

V. Our observer would further also reflect, that the maker of the watch before him was, in truth and reality, the maker of every watch produced from it: there being no difference (except that the latter manifests a more exquisite skill,) between the making of another watch with his own hands, by the mediation of files, lathes, chisels, &c., and the disposing, fixing, and inserting of these instruments, or of others equivalent to them, in the body of the watch already made in such a manner, as to form a new watch in the course of the movements which he had given to the old one. It is only working by one set of tools instead of another.

The conclusion which the *first* examination of the watch, of its works, construction, and movement, suggested, was, that it must have had, for cause and author of that construction, an artificer who understood its mechanism, and designed its use. This conclusion is invincible. A *second* examination presents us with a new discovery. The watch is found, in the course of its movement, to produce another watch, similar to itself; and not only so, but we perceive in it a system, or organization, separately calculated for that purpose. What effect would this discovery have, or ought it to have, upon our former inference? What, as hath already been said, but to increase, beyond measure, our admiration of the skill which had been employed in the formation of such a machine? Or shall it, instead of this, all at once turn us round to an opposite conclusion, viz., that no art or skill whatever has been concerned in the business, although all other evidences of art and skill remain as they were, and this last and supreme piece of art be now added to the rest? Can this be maintained without absurdity? Yet this is atheism.

Application of the argument

This is atheism: for every indication of contrivance, every manifestation of design, which existed in the watch, exists in the works of nature; with the difference, on the side of nature, of being greater and more, and that in a degree which exceeds all computation. I mean that the contrivances of nature surpass the contrivances of art, in the complexity, subtilty, and curiosity of the mechanism; and still more, if possible, do they go beyond them in number and variety; yet in a multitude of cases, are not less evidently mechanical, not less evidently contrivances, not less evidently accommodated to their end, or suited to their office, than are the most perfect productions of human ingenuity.

Chapter 4

Selection from *Proslogion*

Anselm of Canterbury

That God truly exists

WELL then, Lord, You who give understanding to faith, grant me that I may understand, as much as You see fit, that You exist as we believe You to exist, and that You are what we believe You to be. Now we believe that You are something than which nothing greater can be thought. Or can it be that a thing of such a nature does not exist, since 'the Fool has said in his heart, there is no God' [Psalm 4: 1]? But surely, when this same Fool hears what I am speaking about, namely, 'something-than-which-nothing-greater-can-be-thought', he understands what he hears, and what he understands is in his mind, even if he does not understand that it actually exists. For it is one thing for an object to exist in the mind, and another thing to understand that an object actually exists. Thus, when a painter plans beforehand what he is going to execute, he has [the picture] in his mind, but he does not yet think that it actually exists because he has not yet executed it. However, when he has actually painted it, then he both has it in his mind and understands that it exists because he has now made it. Even the Fool, then, is forced to agree that something-than-which-nothing-greater-can-be-thought exists in the mind, since he understands this when he hears it, and whatever is understood is in the mind. And surely that-than-which-a-greater-cannot-be-thought cannot exist in the mind alone. For if it exists solely in the mind, it can be thought to exist in reality also, which is greater. If then that-than-which-a-greater-cannot-be-thought exists in the mind alone, this same that-than-which-a-greater-*cannot*-be-thought is that-than-which-a-greater-*can*-be-thought. But this is obviously impossible. Therefore there is absolutely no doubt that something-than-which-a-greater-cannot-be-thought exists both in the mind and in reality.

That God cannot be thought not to exist

And certainly this being so truly exists that it cannot be even thought not to exist. For something can be thought to exist that cannot be thought not to exist, and this is greater

Anselm of Canterbury, selection from *Proslogion*, translated by M. Charlesworth, copyright © Oxford University Press 1965. From *Anselm of Canterbury, the Major Works*, edited by Brian Davies and G. R. Evans (Oxford World's Classics, 1998), reprinted by permission of Oxford University Press.

than that which can be thought not to exist. Hence, if that-than-which-a-greater-cannot-be-thought can be thought not to exist, then that-than-which-a-greater-cannot-be-thought is not the same as that-than-which-a-greater-cannot-be-thought, which is absurd. Something-than-which-a-greater-cannot-be-thought exists so truly then, that it cannot be even thought not to exist.

And You, Lord our God, are this being. You exist so truly, Lord my God, that You cannot even be thought not to exist. And this is as it should be, for if some intelligence could think of something better than You, the creature would be above its Creator and would judge its Creator—and that is completely absurd. In fact, everything else there is, except You alone, can be thought of as not existing. You alone, then, of all things most truly exist and therefore of all things possess existence to the highest degree; for anything else does not exist as truly, and so possesses existence to a lesser degree. Why then did 'the Fool say in his heart, there is no God' [Psalms 13: 1; 52: 1] when it is so evident to any rational mind that You of all things exist to the highest degree? Why indeed, unless because he was stupid and a fool?

Chapter 5
Selection from *Monadology*
G. W. Leibniz

. . .

36. But a *sufficient reason* must also be found for *contingent truths*, or *truths of fact*—for the series of things which fills the universe of created things, that is. Here the resolution into particular reasons could be continued endlessly, because of the immense variety of things in nature, and because of the infinite divisibility of bodies. There are an infinite number of shapes and of motions, present and past, which play a part in the efficient cause of my present writing; and there are an infinite number of tiny inclinations and dispositions of my soul, present and past, which play a part in its final cause.

37. But since all this detail only involves other prior and more detailed contingencies, each one of which also stands in need of a similar analysis in order to give an explanation of it, we are no further forward: the sufficient or final reason must lie outside the succession or *series* in this detailed specification of contingencies, however infinite it may be.

38. And that is why the final reason for things must be in a necessary substance, in which the detailed specification of changes is contained only eminently, as in their source; and that is what we call *God*.

39. Now, since this substance is a sufficient reason for all this detail, which is interconnected throughout, *there is only one God, and that God is enough.*

40. We can also see that this supreme substance, which is unique, universal, and necessary (because there is nothing outside it which is independent of it, and it is a straightforward consequence of possible being), must be incapable of limits, and must contain fully as much reality as is possible.

41. From which it follows that God is absolutely perfect, since *perfection* is nothing but the total amount of positive reality taken in the precise sense, leaving aside the limitations or boundaries of things that have them. And there, in something which has no boundaries—in God, that is—perfection is absolutely infinite.

42. It also follows that created things have their perfections from the influence of God, but that they have their imperfections from their own natures, which are necessarily bounded. For that is what distinguishes them from God. This original imperfection of created things is shown by the natural inertia of bodies.

43. And what is more, God is the source not only of existences, but also of essences, insofar as they are real; he is the source of what reality there is among possibilities. This is because God's understanding is the realm of eternal truths, or of the ideas on which they depend, and without God there would be no reality among possibilities: not only would nothing exist, but nothing would even be possible.

44. Because it is clear that if there is any reality among essences or possibilities, or among eternal truths, that reality must be grounded in something actually existent; therefore it must be grounded in the existence of the necessary being, in whom essence includes existence, that is, for whom being possible is sufficient for being actual.

45. Thus only God, or the necessary being, has this privilege: that he must exist if he is possible. And as nothing can prevent the possibility of something which contains no boundaries, no negation and therefore no contradiction, that in itself is enough for us to perceive the existence of God a priori. We have also proved his existence by means of the reality of eternal truths, and we have now also proved it a posteriori, because contingent things exist, and their final or sufficient reason could only be found in the necessary being, which has the reason for its existence within itself.

Chapter 6
Evil and omnipotence
J. L. Mackie

THE traditional arguments for the existence of God have been fairly thoroughly criticized by philosophers. But the theologian can, if he wishes, accept this criticism. He can admit that no rational proof of God's existence is possible. And he can still retain all that is essential to his position, by holding that God's existence is known in some other, non-rational way. I think, however, that a more telling criticism can be made by way of the traditional problem of evil. Here it can be shown, not that religious beliefs lack rational support, but that they are positively irrational, that the several parts of the essential theological doctrine are inconsistent with one another, so that the theologian can maintain his position as a whole only by a much more extreme rejection of reason than in the former case. He must now be prepared to believe, not merely what cannot be proved, but what can be *disproved* from other beliefs that he also holds.

The problem of evil, in the sense in which I shall be using the phrase, is a problem only for someone who believes that there is a God who is both omnipotent and wholly good. And it is a logical problem, the problem of clarifying and reconciling a number of beliefs: it is not a scientific problem that might be solved by further observations, or a practical problem that might be solved by a decision or an action. These points are obvious; I mention them only because they are sometimes ignored by theologians, who sometimes parry a statement of the problem with such remarks as 'Well, can you solve the problem yourself?' or 'This is a mystery which may be revealed to us later' or 'Evil is something to be faced and overcome, not to be merely discussed.'

In its simplest form the problem is this: God is omnipotent; God is wholly good; and yet evil exists. There seems to be some contradiction between these three propositions, so that if any two of them were true the third would be false. But at the same time all three are essential parts of most theological positions: the theologian, it seems, at once *must* adhere and *cannot consistently* adhere to all three. (The problem does not arise only for theists, but I shall discuss it in the form in which it presents itself for ordinary theism.)

However, the contradiction does not arise immediately; to show it we need some additional premises, or perhaps some quasi-logical rules connecting the terms 'good', 'evil', and 'omnipotent'. These additional principles are that good is opposed to evil, in such a way that a good thing always eliminates evil as far as it can, and that there are no limits to what an omnipotent thing can do. From these it follows that

J. L. Mackie, 'Evil and omnipotence', from *Mind*, 64 (1995), reprinted by permission of Oxford University Press.

a good omnipotent thing eliminates evil completely, and then the propositions that a good omnipotent thing exists, and that evil exists, are incompatible.

A. Adequate solutions

Now once the problem is fully stated it is clear that it can be solved, in the sense that the problem will not arise if one gives up at least one of the propositions that constitute it. If you are prepared to say that God is not wholly good, or not quite omnipotent, or that evil does not exist, or that good is not opposed to the kind of evil that exists, or that there are limits to what an omnipotent thing can do, then the problem of evil will not arise for you.

There are, then, quite a number of adequate solutions of the problem of evil, and some of these have been adopted, or almost adopted, by various thinkers. For example, a few have been prepared to deny God's omnipotence, and rather more have been prepared to keep the term 'omnipotence' but severely to restrict its meaning, recording quite a number of things that an omnipotent being cannot do. Some have said that evil is an illusion, perhaps because they held that the whole world of temporal, changing things is an illusion, and that what we call evil belongs only to this world, or perhaps because they held that although temporal things *are* much as we see them, those that we call evil are not really evil. Some have said that what we call evil is merely the privation of good, that evil in a positive sense, evil that would really be opposed to good, does not exist. Many have agreed with Pope that disorder is harmony not understood, and that partial evil is universal good. Whether any of these views is *true* is, of course, another question. But each of them gives an adequate solution of the problem of evil in the sense that if you accept it this problem does not arise for you, though you may, of course, have *other* problems to face.

But often enough these adequate solutions are only *almost* adopted. The thinkers who restrict God's power, but keep the term 'omnipotence', may reasonably be suspected of thinking, in other contexts, that his power is really unlimited. Those who say that evil is an illusion may also be thinking, inconsistently, that this illusion is itself an evil. Those who say that 'evil' is merely privation of good may also be thinking, inconsistently, that privation of good is an evil. (The fallacy here is akin to some forms of the 'naturalistic fallacy' in ethics, where some think, for example, that 'good' is just what contributes to evolutionary progress, and that evolutionary progress is itself good.) If Pope meant what he said in the first line of his couplet, that 'disorder' is only harmony not understood, the 'partial evil' of the second line must, for consistency, mean 'that which, taken in isolation, falsely appears to be evil', but it would more naturally mean 'that which, in isolation, really is evil'. The second line, in fact, hesitates between two views, that 'partial evil' isn't really evil, since only the universal quality is real, and that 'partial evil' is really an evil, but only a little one.

In addition, therefore, to adequate solutions, we must recognize unsatisfactory inconsistent solutions, in which there is only a half-hearted or temporary rejection of one of the propositions which together constitute the problem. In these, one of the constituent propositions is explicitly rejected, but it is covertly re-asserted or assumed elsewhere in the system.

B. Fallacious solutions

Besides these half-hearted solutions, which explicitly reject but implicitly assert one of the constituent propositions, there are definitely fallacious solutions which explicitly maintain all the constituent propositions, but implicitly reject at least one of them in the course of the argument that explains away the problem of evil.

There are, in fact, many so-called solutions which purport to remove the contradiction without abandoning any of its constituent propositions. These must be fallacious, as we can see from the very statement of the problem, but it is not so easy to see in each case precisely where the fallacy lies. I suggest that in all cases the fallacy has the general form suggested above: in order to solve the problem one (or perhaps more) of its constituent propositions is given up, but in such a way that it appears to have been retained, and can therefore be asserted without qualification in other contexts. Sometimes there is a further complication: the supposed solution moves to and fro between, say, two of the constituent propositions, at one point asserting the first of these but covertly abandoning the second, at another point asserting the second but covertly abandoning the first. These fallacious solutions often turn upon some equivocation with the words 'good' and 'evil', or upon some vagueness about the way in which good and evil are opposed to one another, or about how much is meant by 'omnipotence'. I propose to examine some of these so-called solutions, and to exhibit their fallacies in detail. Incidentally, I shall also be considering whether an adequate solution could be reached by a minor modification of one or more of the constituent propositions, which would, however, still satisfy all the essential requirements of ordinary theism.

1. 'Good cannot exist without evil' or 'Evil is necessary as a counterpart to good'

It is sometimes suggested that evil is necessary as a counterpart to good, that if there were no evil there could be no good either, and that this solves the problem of evil. It is true that it points to an answer to the question 'Why should there be evil?' But it does so only by qualifying some of the propositions that constitute the problem.

First, it sets a limit to what God can do, saying that God *cannot* create good without simultaneously creating evil, and this means either that God is not omnipotent or that there are *some* limits to what an omnipotent thing can do. It may be replied that these limits are always presupposed, that omnipotence has never meant the power to do what is logically impossible, and on the present view the existence of good without evil would be a logical impossibility. This interpretation of omnipotence may, indeed, be accepted as a modification of our original account which does not reject anything that is essential to theism, and I shall in general assume it in the subsequent discussion. It is, perhaps, the most common theistic view, but I think that some theists at least have maintained that God can do what is logically impossible. Many theists, at any rate, have held that logic itself is created or laid down by God, that logic is the way in which God arbitrarily chooses to think. (This is, of course, parallel to the ethical view that morally right actions are those which God arbitrarily chooses to command, and the two views encounter similar difficulties.) And *this* account of logic is clearly inconsistent with the view that God is bound by logical necessities—unless it is possible for an omnipotent being to bind himself, an issue which we shall consider later, when we come to the Paradox of Omnipotence. This solution of the problem of evil cannot, therefore, be consistently adopted along with the view that logic is itself created by God.

But, secondly, this solution denies that evil is opposed to good in our original sense. If good and evil are counterparts, a good thing will not 'eliminate evil as far as it can'. Indeed, this view suggests that good and evil are not strictly qualities of things at all. Perhaps the suggestion is that good and evil are related in much the same way as great and small. Certainly, when the term 'great' is used relatively as a condensation of 'greater than so-and-so', and 'small' is used correspondingly, greatness and smallness are counterparts and cannot exist without each other. But in this sense greatness is not a quality, not an intrinsic feature of anything; and it would be absurd to think of a movement in favour of greatness and against small-ness in this sense. Such a movement would be self-defeating, since relative greatness can be promoted only by a simultaneous promotion of relative smallness. I feel sure that no theists would be content to regard God's goodness as analogous to this—as if what he supports were not the *good* but the *better*, and as if he had the paradoxical aim that all things should be better than other things.

This point is obscured by the fact that 'great' and 'small' seem to have an absolute as well as a relative sense. I cannot discuss here whether there is absolute magnitude or not, but if there is, there could be an absolute sense for 'great'; it could mean of at least a certain size, and it would make sense to speak of all things getting bigger, of a universe that was expanding all over, and therefore it would make sense to speak of promoting greatness. But in *this* sense great and small are not logically necessary counterparts: either quality could exist without the other. There would be no logical impossibility in everything's being small or in everything's being great.

Neither in the absolute nor in the relative sense, then, of 'great' and 'small' do these terms provide an analogy of the sort that would be needed to support this solution of the problem of evil. In neither case are greatness and smallness *both* necessary counterparts *and* mutually opposed forces or possible objects for support or attack.

It may be replied that good and evil are necessary counterparts in the same way as any quality and its logical opposite: redness can occur, it is suggested, only if non-redness also occurs. But unless evil is merely the privation of good, they are not logical opposites, and some further argument would be needed to show that they are counterparts in the same way as genuine logical opposites. Let us assume that this could be given. There is still doubt of the correctness of the metaphysical principle that a quality must have a real opposite: I suggest that it is not really impossible that everything should be, say, red, that the truth is merely that if everything were red we should not notice redness, and so we should have no word 'red'; we observe and give names to qualities only if they have real opposites. If so, the principle that a term must have an opposite would belong only to our language or to our thought, and would not be an ontological principle, and, correspondingly, the rule that good cannot exist without evil would not state a logical necessity of a sort that God would just have to put up with. God might have made everything good, though *we* should not have noticed it if he had.

But, finally, even if we concede that this *is* an ontological principle, it will provide a solution for the problem of evil only if one is prepared to say, 'Evil exists, but only just enough evil to serve as the counterpart of good.' I doubt whether any theist will accept this. After all, the *ontological* requirement that non-redness should occur would be satisfied even if all the universe, except for a minute speck, were red, and, if there were a corresponding requirement for evil as a counterpart to good, a minute dose of evil would presumably do. But theists are not usually willing to say, in all contexts, that all the evil that occurs is a minute and necessary dose.

2. 'Evil is necessary as a means to good'

It is sometimes suggested that evil is necessary for good not as a counterpart but as a means. In its simple form this has little plausibility as a solution of the problem of evil, since it obviously implies a severe restriction of God's power. It would be a *causal* law that you cannot have a certain end without a certain means, so that if God has to introduce evil as a means to good, he must be subject to at least some causal laws. This certainly conflicts with what a theist normally means by omnipotence. This view of God as limited by causal laws also conflicts with the view that causal laws are themselves made by God, which is more widely held than the corresponding view about the laws of logic. This conflict would, indeed, be resolved if it were possible for an omnipotent being to bind himself, and this possibility has still to be considered. Unless a favourable answer can be given to this question, the suggestion that evil is necessary as a means to good solves the problem of evil only by denying one of its constituent propositions, either that God is omnipotent or that 'omnipotent' means what it says.

3. 'The universe is better with some evil in it than it could be if there were no evil'

Much more important is a solution which at first seems to be a mere variant of the previous one, that evil may contribute to the goodness of a whole in which it is found, so that the universe as a whole is better as it is, with some evil in it, than it would be if there were no evil. This solution may be developed in either of two ways. It may be supported by an aesthetic analogy, by the fact that contrasts heighten beauty, that in a musical work, for example, there may occur discords which somehow add to the beauty of the work as a whole. Alternatively, it may be worked out in connection with the notion of progress, that the best possible organization of the universe will not be static, but progressive, that the gradual overcoming of evil by good is really a finer thing than would be the eternal unchallenged supremacy of good.

In either case, this solution usually starts from the assumption that the evil whose existence gives rise to the problem of evil is primarily what is called physical evil, that is to say, pain. In Hume's rather halfhearted presentation of the problem of evil, the evils that he stresses are pain and disease, and those who reply to him argue that the existence of pain and disease makes possible the existence of sympathy, benevolence, heroism, and the gradually successful struggle of doctors and reformers to overcome these evils. In fact, theists often seize the opportunity to accuse those who stress the problem of evil of taking a low, materialistic view of good and evil, equating these with pleasure and pain, and of ignoring the more spiritual goods which can arise in the struggle against evils.

But let us see exactly what is being done here. Let us call pain and misery 'first order evil' or 'evil (1)'. What contrasts with this, namely, pleasure and happiness, will be called 'first order good' or 'good (1)'. Distinct from this is 'second order good' or 'good (2)' which somehow emerges in a complex situation in which evil (1) is a necessary component—logically, not merely causally, necessary. (Exactly *how* it emerges does not matter: in the crudest version of this solution good (2) is simply the heightening of happiness by the contrast with misery; in other versions it includes sympathy with suffering, heroism in facing danger, and the gradual decrease of first order evil and increase of first order good.) It is also being assumed that second order good is more important than first order good or evil, in particular that it more than outweighs the first order evil it involves.

Now this is a particularly subtle attempt to solve the problem of evil. It defends God's goodness and omnipotence on the ground that (on a sufficiently long view) this is the best of all logically possible worlds, because it includes the important second order goods, and yet it admits that real evils, namely first order evils, exist. But does it still hold that good and evil are opposed? Not, clearly, in the sense that we set out originally: good does not tend to eliminate evil in general. Instead, we have a modified, a more complex pattern. First order good (e.g. happiness) *contrasts with* first order evil (e.g. misery): these two are opposed in a fairly mechanical way; some second order goods (e.g. benevolence) try to maximize first order good and minimise first order evil; but God's goodness is not this, it is rather the will to maximize *second* order good. We might, therefore, call God's goodness an example of a third order goodness, or good (3). While this account is different from our original one, it might well be held to be an improvement on it, to give a more accurate description of the way in which good is opposed to evil, and to be consistent with the essential theist position.

There might, however, be several objections to this solution.

First, some might argue that such qualities as benevolence—and *a fortiori* the third order goodness which promotes benevolence—have a merely derivative value, that they are not higher sorts of good, but merely means to good (1), that is, to happiness, so that it would be absurd for God to keep misery in existence in order to make possible the virtues of benevolence, heroism, etc. The theist who adopts the present solution must, of course, deny this, but he can do so with some plausibility, so I should not press this objection.

Secondly, it follows from this solution that God is not in our sense benevolent or sympathetic: he is not concerned to minimize evil (1), but only to promote good (2), and this might be a disturbing conclusion for some theists.

But, thirdly, the fatal objection is this. Our analysis shows clearly the possibility of the existence of a *second* order evil, an evil (2) contrasting with good (2) as evil (1) contrasts with good (1). This would include malevolence, cruelty, callousness, cowardice, and states in which good (1) is decreasing and evil (1) increasing. And just as good (2) is held to be the important kind of good, the kind that God is concerned to promote, so evil (2) will, by analogy, be the important kind of evil, the kind which God, if he were wholly good and omnipotent, would eliminate. And yet evil (2) plainly exists, and indeed most theists (in other contexts) stress its existence more than that of evil (1). We should, therefore, state the problem of evil in terms of second order evil, and against this form of the problem the present solution is useless.

An attempt might be made to use this solution again, at a higher level, to explain the occurrence of evil (2): indeed the next main solution that we shall examine does just this, with the help of some new notions. Without any fresh notions, such a solution would have little plausibility: for example, we could hardly say that the really important good was a good (3), such as the increase of benevolence in proportion to cruelty, which logically required for its occurrence the occurrence of some second order evil. But even if evil (2) could be explained in this way, it is fairly clear that there would be third order evils contrasting with this third order good: and we should be well on the way to an infinite regress, where the solution of a problem of evil, stated in terms of evil (n), indicated the existence of an evil ($n + 1$), and a further problem to be solved.

4. 'Evil is due to human free will'

Perhaps the most important proposed solution of the problem of evil is that evil is not to be ascribed to God at all, but to the independent actions of human beings, supposed to have been endowed by God with freedom of the will. This solution may be combined with the preceding one: first order evil (e.g. pain) may be justified as a logically necessary component in second order good (e.g. sympathy) while second order evil (e.g. cruelty) is not *justified*, but is so ascribed to human beings that God cannot be held responsible for it. This combination evades my third criticism of the preceding solution.

The free will solution also involves the preceding solution at a higher level. To explain why a wholly good God gave men free will although it would lead to some important evils, it must be argued that it is better on the whole that men should act freely, and sometimes err, than that they should be innocent automata, acting rightly in a wholly determined way. Freedom, that is to say, is now treated as a third order good, and as being more valuable than second order goods (such as sympathy and heroism) would be if they were deterministically produced, and it is being assumed that second order evils, such as cruelty, are logically necessary accompaniments of freedom, just as pain is a logically necessary pre-condition of sympathy.

I think that this solution is unsatisfactory primarily because of the incoherence of the notion of freedom of the will: but I cannot discuss this topic adequately here, although some of my criticisms will touch upon it.

First I should query the assumption that second order evils are logically necessary accompaniments of freedom. I should ask this: if God has made men such that in their free choices they sometimes prefer what is good and sometimes what is evil, why could he not have made men such that they always freely choose the good? If there is no logical impossibility in a man's freely choosing the good on one, or on several occasions, there cannot be a logical impossibility in his freely choosing the good on every occasion. God was not, then, faced with a choice between making innocent automata and making beings who, in acting freely, would sometimes go wrong: there was open to him the obviously better possibility of making beings who would act freely but always go right. Clearly, his failure to avail himself of this possibility is inconsistent with his being both omnipotent and wholly good.

If it is replied that this objection is absurd, that the making of some wrong choices is logically necessary for freedom, it would seem that 'freedom' must here mean complete randomness or indeterminacy, including randomness with regard to the alternatives good and evil, in other words that men's choices and consequent actions can be 'free' only if they are not determined by their characters. Only on this assumption can God escape the responsibility for men's actions; for if he made them as they are, but did not determine their wrong choices, this can only be because the wrong choices are not determined by men as they are. But then if freedom is randomness, how can it be a characteristic of *will*? And, still more, how can it be the most important good? What value or merit would there be in free choices if these were random actions which were not determined by the nature of the agent?

I conclude that to make this solution plausible two different senses of 'freedom' must be confused; one sense which will justify the view that freedom is a third order good, more valuable than other goods would be without it, and another sense, sheer randomness, to prevent us from ascribing to God a decision to make men such that they sometimes go wrong when he might have made them such that they would always freely go right.

This criticism is sufficient to dispose of this solution. But besides this there is a fundamental difficulty in the notion of an omnipotent God creating men with free will, for if men's wills are really free this must mean that even God cannot control them, that is, that God is no longer omnipotent. It may be objected that God's gift of freedom to men does not mean that he *cannot* control their wills, but that he always *refrains* from controlling their wills. But why, we may ask, should God refrain from controlling evil wills? Why should he not leave men free to will rightly, but intervene when he sees them beginning to will wrongly? If God could do this, but does not, and if he is wholly good, the only explanation could be that even a wrong free act of will is not really evil, that its freedom is a value which outweighs its wrongness, so that there would be a loss of value if God took away the wrongness and the freedom together. But this is utterly opposed to what theists say about sin in other contexts. The present solution of the problem of evil, then, can be maintained only in the form that God has made men so free that he *cannot* control their wills.

This leads us to what I call the Paradox of Omnipotence: can an omnipotent being make things which he cannot subsequently control? Or, what is practically equivalent to this, can an omnipotent being make rules which then bind himself? (These are practically equivalent because any such rules could be regarded as setting certain things beyond his control and *vice versa*.) The second of these formulations is relevant to the suggestions that we have already met, that an omnipotent God creates the rules of logic or causal laws, and is then bound by them.

It is clear that this is a paradox: the questions cannot be answered satisfactorily either in the affirmative or in the negative. If we answer 'Yes', it follows that if God actually makes things which he cannot control, or makes rules which bind himself, he is not omnipotent once he has made them: there are *then* things which he cannot do. But if we answer 'No', we are immediately asserting that there are things which he cannot do, that is to say that he is already not omnipotent.

It cannot be replied that the question which sets this paradox is not a proper question. It would make perfectly good sense to say that a human mechanic has made a machine which he cannot control: if there is any difficulty about the question it lies in the notion of omnipotence itself.

This, incidentally, shows that although we have approached this paradox from the free will theory, it is equally a problem for a theological determinist. No one thinks that machines have free will, yet they may well be beyond the control of their makers. The determinist might reply that anyone who makes anything determines its ways of acting, and so determines its subsequent behaviour: even the human mechanic does this by his *choice* of materials and structure for his machine, though he does not know all about either of these: the mechanic thus determines, though he may not foresee, his machine's actions. And since God is omniscient, and since his creation of things is total, he both determines and foresees the ways in which his creatures will act. We may grant this, but it is beside the point. The question is not whether God *originally* determined the future actions of his creatures, but whether he can *subsequently* control their actions, or whether he was able in his original creation to put things beyond his subsequent control. Even on determinist principles the answers 'Yes' and 'No' are equally irreconcilable with God's omnipotence.

Before suggesting a solution of this paradox, I would point out that there is a parallel Paradox of Sovereignty. Can a legal sovereign make a law restricting its own future legislative power? For example, could the British parliament make a law forbidding any future parliament to socialize banking, and also forbidding the future repeal of this law itself? Or could the British parliament, which was legally sovereign in Australia in, say, 1899, pass a valid law, or series of laws, which made it no longer sovereign in 1933? Again, neither the affirmative nor the negative answer is really satisfactory. If we were to answer 'Yes', we should be admitting the validity of a law which, if it were actually made, would mean that parliament was no longer sovereign. If we were to answer

'No', we should be admitting that there is a law, not logically absurd, which parliament cannot validly make, that is, that parliament is not now a legal sovereign. This paradox can be solved in the following way. We should distinguish between first order laws, that is laws governing the actions of individuals and bodies other than the legislature, and second order laws, that is laws about laws, laws governing the actions of the legislature itself. Correspondingly, we should distinguish between two orders of sovereignty, first order sovereignty (sovereignty (1)) which is unlimited authority to make first order laws, and second order sovereignty (sovereignty (2)) which is unlimited authority to make second order laws. If we say that parliament is sovereign we might mean that any parliament at any time has sovereignty (1), or we might mean that parliament has both sovereignty (1) and sovereignty (2) at present, but we cannot without contradiction mean both that the present parliament has sovereignty (2) and that every parliament at every time has sovereignty (1), for if the present parliament has sovereignty (2) it may use it to take away the sovereignty (1) of later parliaments. What the paradox shows is that we cannot ascribe to any continuing institution legal sovereignty in an inclusive sense.

The analogy between omnipotence and sovereignty shows that the paradox of omnipotence can be solved in a similar way. We must distinguish between first order omnipotence (omnipotence (1)), that is unlimited power to act, and second order omnipotence (omnipotence (2)), that is unlimited power to determine what powers to act things shall have. Then we could consistently say that God all the time has omnipotence (1), but if so no beings at any time have powers to act independently of God. Or we could say that God at one time had omnipotence (2), and used it to assign independent powers to act to certain things, so that God thereafter did not have omnipotence (1). But what the paradox shows is that we cannot consistently ascribe to any continuing being omnipotence in an inclusive sense.

An alternative solution to this paradox would be simply to deny that God is a continuing being, that any times can be assigned to his actions at all. But on this assumption (which also has difficulties of its own) no meaning can be given to the assertion that God made men with wills so free that he could not control them. The paradox of omnipotence can be avoided by putting God outside time, but the free will solution of the problem of evil cannot be saved in this way, and equally it remains impossible to hold that an omnipotent God *binds himself* by causal or logical laws.

Conclusion

Of the proposed solutions of the problem of evil which we have examined, none has stood up to criticism. There may be other solutions which require examination, but this study strongly suggests that there is no valid solution of the problem which does not modify at least one of the constituent propositions in a way which would seriously affect the essential core of the theistic position.

Quite apart from the problem of evil, the paradox of omnipotence has shown that God's omnipotence must in any case be restricted in one way or another, that unqualified omnipotence cannot be ascribed to any being that continues through time. And if God and his actions are not in time, can omnipotence, or power of any sort, be meaningfully ascribed to him?

Study questions

1. Does Darwin's theory of evolution by natural selection refute the Design Argument?
2. Is there any way of reconciling the existence of natural evil with the existence of God?
3. The twelfth century monk Gaunilo complained that the form of argument used by Anselm could equally well be used to show that a perfect *island* must exist; since no such thing need exist, the form of argument must be invalid. How might you reconstruct Gaunilo's argument? Is his criticism of Anselm fair?
4. Is the notion of an all-perfect God a contradiction in terms?

Further reading

An excellent and readable collection of short readings is Helm (1999). A comprehensive anthology of readings of the philosophy of religion, with introductory material, is Davies (2000). Davies has also written a good short introduction to the philosophy of religion (1993). Two other useful recent anthologies are Stump and Muray (1999) and Quinn and Taliaferro (1997). A recent discussion of the question of why there is anything is Jacquette (2002: chapter 1). On the arguments for God's existence in general, see Swinburne (1986) for the case in favour, and J. L. Mackie (1982) for the case against. On the Cosmological Argument, see Davies (2000: part III, section 1) for some central readings; and Craig (1980) for a historical account of the different arguments. For a very clear discussion of Aquinas's cosmological arguments, see Anscombe and Geach (1961: 109–25), and Kenny (1969). On the Design Argument, see part III, section 2 of Davies (2000). Kenny (1969: chapter 6) contains a good discussion of Aquinas's argument for God as a final cause. Hume's *Dialogues Concerning Natural Religion* (1778) is one of the most important historical sources of sceptical arguments: Davies (2000) contains a good excerpt. Swinburne (1968) is a critical discussion of Hume. Chapter 4 of Geach (1977) is a good discussion of whether Darwin refuted the Design Argument. Dawkins (1986) argues that he did. On the Ontological Argument, see Davies (2000: part III, section 3) for some core readings; Alvin Plantinga's defence of the argument may be found here (chapter 35 of Davies 2000), and in Plantinga (1975). Oppy (1995) is a thorough, and in parts difficult, assessment of the argument in all its forms; Barnes (1972) is shorter and easier for the beginner. For further reading on the question of whether existence is a real property of things, see Part III: Being. On the problem of evil, see Davies (2000: Part V) and Adams and Adams (1990) for an excellent collection of readings. Geach (1977) and Hick (1975) are important discussions.

Part II

Realism and idealism

Introduction

1. Appearance and reality

IN George Berkeley's first dialogue between Hylas and Philonous (Chapter 8), we find Philonous describing a fine morning: the 'purple sky, the fragrant bloom upon the trees and flowers, the gentle influence of the rising sun'. Just like Philonous, we see colours, smell the fragrance of flowers, feel the warmth of the sun, and so on. All this adds up to how the world appears to us, sentient beings. For non-sentient beings such as cliffs or church towers, the world does not appear to be any way. These objects are just there, in the world; the rest of the world is nothing to them. In addition to our sensory capacities, we also classify things in the world by employing thoughts and concepts. It is because we can do these things that the question of truth and falsity arises for us. For the world sometimes appears different from the way it is: a straight stick might appear bent in water, a square tower might appear round from a distance. When the world appears different from the way it is, this can lead us into error. One traditional question in philosophy is whether we can ever get things right, and how we can have any assurance that we do. But this question—the question of how knowledge is possible—belongs to epistemology. Our concern in metaphysics is with how things are, rather than with how we know them. However, the possibility of effecting a strict separation between these two questions is not an easy matter. For our access to the world, to how things are, is through the way it appears to us. And therefore we can ask the question of whether there is anything *beyond* appearances; whether the world is in fact independent of the way it appears to us. This is a genuine metaphysical question.

Those who claim that the world exists and has properties independently from the experiencing and cognizing mind are called *realists*. When addressing the question of realism, one does not have to commit oneself to a uniform view about everything. It is possible to be a realist about certain things—like physical objects—and not be a realist about other things—like aesthetic values. In what follows, we shall be mainly concerned with realism about objects and properties in the world outside thinking, perceiving, sensing subjects; that is, about the world outside the mind, normally known as the *external world*.

What is the external world? There is a famous argument by Descartes (1641), which attempts to prove that each of us can be certain of his or her own existence. It goes as follows: is it possible to doubt my own existence? If I am trying to do this, I must at the same time be aware that I am considering the question of my own existence, that I am convinced of this or doubting that. But since it is *me* who is doing the considering or the doubting, I myself must exist. *Solipsism* is the philosophical position which says that by proving the existence of oneself, one completes the inventory of beings, since apart from oneself, nothing else exists. Since this book is jointly authored by two people, we cannot really accept solipsism. But in rejecting solipsism, what are we thereby accepting? Well, first of all, we are accepting that more things than oneself exist. Which things?

Certainly other people exist, and other things in the world around us, a world which is distinct from ourselves, and has existed for millions of years before we existed. This idea of the *world around us* is the idea of the 'external' world. It was about this world that we said that *it* appears to us in a certain way: for it is part of the very nature of appearances that when we see, hear, or taste something, it seems to us as if we perceived *the things in the world* having certain qualities. It is the sky which appears to be purple, and the flowers which appear to be fragrant. Reflecting on the way the world is presented to us in experience and thought, the assumption that what is presented—the flower, and its fragrance—is there, independently of its being presented, just seems undeniably true. It simply does not strike us as if the flower sprang out of the soil, or started to perfume the air just because we were there to perceive it. It seems, then, that the natural view of common sense is realist: the world exists and is the way it is independently from us.

But there is a further point that needs to be considered. We said that the very fact that the world appears to us is possible because we are equipped with certain faculties. So the question might arise: does the specific nature of these faculties somehow contribute to the way things appear to us? Or are appearances determined solely by the nature of the things that appear? One answer to this question is implied by the traditional distinction between primary and secondary qualities.

2. Primary and secondary qualities

In Chapter 7, from Locke's *Essay Concerning Human Understanding*, we find one of the most famous discussions of the distinction between primary and secondary qualities. The distinction is not actually Locke's invention: it is usual to credit Galileo with the first modern formulation of the idea. What is this distinction?

Locke first of all distinguishes *ideas of the mind*, and *qualities of bodies*: what the mind immediately perceives in itself is called an 'idea', and the power of a body or physical object to produce an idea in the mind is called a 'quality'. Let us consider a particular body: say a sharp knife. Locke's view is that the knife can produce various ideas in us: the idea of a certain longish triangular shape, an idea of movement as the knife is used to cut something; also the idea of a certain steely colour, the idea of cold when touching the blade; and also the idea of pain if we accidentally cut our finger. In some of these cases, we think the idea in us is produced by a quality in the knife which we call by the same name: the *quality* of having a longish triangular shape *in the knife*, produces the *idea* of a longish triangular shape *in us*. When this assumption is correct, as in the case of shape and in the case of movement, we have a *primary* quality. In some other cases, we think differently: we would never say that the idea of pain in us is produced by the *quality of pain* in the knife; in fact, there is nothing in the knife which would in any way resemble our idea of pain. Instead, the knife has a certain primary quality—a certain shape—in virtue of which it can produce the idea of pain in us. As Locke would put it, this quality is 'allowed as barely power': a power to produce a certain idea in us. Qualities like this are classified by Locke as belonging to the 'third group', and sometimes are called *tertiary* qualities. Finally, there are cases which we might be tempted to regard as more like the case of primary qualities, but which are *in fact* the same as the case of tertiary qualities. It might be natural to think that the idea of cold in us is produced by the quality of coldness in the knife, but this is a mistake. Coldness is not in the knife, just as pain is not; what is in the knife is a collection of some primary qualities which enable the knife to produce the idea of cold in us. The same is true for colours. Qualities like heat, cold, and colour are called *secondary* qualities.

Thus, primary qualities are those which are inseparable from bodies: this means that they are qualities of the bodies themselves, independently of anyone's experiences, and that all bodies have some or other determinate version of every primary quality. The list of primary qualities is given by Locke as follows: solidity, extension, figure, motion or rest, number. This list is not the same for all philosophers; for example, Descartes, although he recognizes the primary/secondary distinction, does not include solidity among the primary qualities. But extension, shape, motion or rest do figure on every list.

Secondary qualities can be defined only with reference to our sensory capacities: these are powers in bodies—powers they possess in virtue of having some primary qualities— to produce certain sensations in us. The list includes colours, sounds, smells, tastes—in fact, all those sensory modalities which belong to one sense only. In contrast, primary qualities are perceivable through more than one sense—for example, we can perceive shape through touch and sight.

Why should we think that colours or tastes are not really in bodies? One reason often mentioned is the world-view of modern physics which emerged in the seventeenth century, with Galileo and Descartes. On this view, the nature of the material world can be completely described by a physical theory which treats bodies as having only primary qualities. Colours, tastes, and the other secondary qualities drop out of the picture. But we could argue that colours are not in bodies even without appealing to science. To see this, we shall introduce what has become known as the 'inverted spectrum' hypothesis. Locke writes:

Neither would it carry any imputation of *falsehood* to our simple ideas, *if* by the different structure of our organs, it were so ordered, that *the same object should produce in several men's minds different ideas* at the same time; *v.g.* if the idea that a *violet* produced in one man's mind by his eyes, were the same that a *marigold* produced in another man's, and *vice versa*. (Locke 1690: book II, chapter xxxii, § 15)

Now consider the following hypothesis about the authors of this book. Violets regularly produce a colour idea in Farkas which she calls 'blue', and marigolds regularly produce a colour idea in her which she calls 'yellow'. Similarly, violets produce an idea in Crane he calls 'blue' and marigolds produce an idea he calls 'yellow'. But let us suppose that our visual organs have different structures, and the colour experience Farkas associates with 'blue' is the one Crane associates with 'yellow', and vice versa. We will probably not discover this difference, since we both say that violets are blue and marigolds are yellow, and also that violets have the same colour as the front cover of John McDowell's *Mind and World*, and marigolds have the same colour as David Papineau's *The Philosophy of Science*, and similarly with other judgements about colour. But even though disagreement never surfaces, it would still be true that Farkas sees the world in a completely different way from Crane. Is it the case that one of us is *right* about the colour of things and the other is *wrong*? Some philosophers, who accept a reduction of secondary qualities to primary qualities, will say yes (Jackson 1998). But this is a difficult line to take, since in the story as told, there seems to be no more reason to say that Farkas is right than there is reason to say that Crane is right. You might think that the question could be answered by referring to what the majority of perceivers experience: maybe yellowness should be described in terms of the typical experience which marigolds give rise to in normal perceivers. But this does not help, because we can also imagine that half of the population see things as Farkas does, and the other half see things as Crane does. As Locke says, such differences between us would not carry an imputation of falsehood. Yet each of us sees a violet as having a completely differ-ent colour. So the colour cannot really be in the violet; it essentially depends on the perceiver's mind.

Our initial assumption was that we experience things and their qualities: the purple-ness of the sky, the fragrance of the flowers. If some qualities are secondary qualities, then we should qualify this: for what we perceive in perceiving a secondary quality is not dependent on the nature of the perceived thing alone, but it also essentially depends on our perceiving faculties, on our minds. But it is important to clarify what sort of mind-dependence is being claimed here. If this mind-dependence thesis is to be plausible at all, it should not imply that what is experienced—flowers rather than trees, purpleness rather than blueness—is created by the specific *act* of perception. As we observed above, it is not as if the flower became fragrant *because* we smelled it on that specific occasion. If there is dependence here, it is not on the individual act of perception, but on the nature of perceptual capacities in general. This is an important point to remember: when philosophers say that the world is mind-dependent, they do not (or should not) mean that it is dependent on particular *acts* of mind, or particular mental *events*. Rather, the dependence of the world on the mind is normally understood as the dependence on general facts about what kind of creatures we are. Hence, mind-dependence is com-patible with *objectivity*, the view that there are true and false judgements, and inter-subjective standards of correctness.

3. Idealism

Even though Locke thinks that colours or tastes are not really in bodies independently of our experience, this is only a minor concession to mind-dependence. Otherwise, Locke was a firm believer in realism. He thought that matter, endowed with primary qualities, exists independently of our minds. The other authors in our selections disagree.

In Chapter 8, from his *Three Dialogues*, Berkeley starts with the following question: 'does the reality of sensible things consist in being perceived? or, is it something distinct from their being perceived, and that bears no relation to the mind?' Berkeley's spokesman, Philonous, proves first for secondary, then for primary qualities, that their reality consists in being perceived. One argument used throughout is the argument from the relativity of perception: if the same water feels cold to one hand, and warm to the other, surely what we thereby perceive is not in the water; for to think otherwise would allow things to have contradictory qualities. This applies also to primary qualities: for the same object can appear to have different sizes or shapes from different viewpoints or for different observers; if we think that we perceive something in the bodies, then again bodies should have contradictory qualities. As long as sensible things are understood as things immediately perceived, Philonous' conclusion is that these must exist in the mind, and not independently of it.

Philonous' opponent, Hylas, then suggests another view: that we do not perceive material things immediately; rather we perceive them through having some ideas—and only ideas are immediately perceived. Philonous remains unsatisfied with this position, for he cannot make sense of the relation between the thing allegedly represented by the idea and the idea itself. The conclusion is that only ideas and minds, which perceive ideas, exist. This view is known as *idealism*. Berkeley's famous dictum was that to exist is to be perceived (*esse est percipi*). In fact, this should be qualified: for he thought that to exist is *either* to be perceived *or* to be a perceiver. It is important to understand what Berkeley means here. His thesis is that the nature of the world is fundamentally mental, but he certainly does not deny that the 'external world'—that is, the world around us— exists. The purple sky, the fragrant flowers and so on are all real—it is just that they are not constituted by material substance, but by ideas. And neither is Berkeley committed to the implausible claim described above, that our individual acts of perception create the world around us. His argument does not require that what exists should exist in *his* mind or in *your* mind; but simply that it should exist in *some* mind. And in fact, ideas are constantly perceived by God, and exist in his mind. This accounts for the independence of objects of experience from particular human perceivers, as well as for the fact that we can share the same sensible world. (On this, see his *Second Dialogue* in Berkeley 1713.)

A contemporary defender of idealism, Howard Robinson develops the thought inherent in the primary/secondary distinction (Chapter 10). Traditionally, secondary qualities are powers or, in contemporary terminology, *dispositions*—which means that they are essentially identified in terms of what effects they would produce in certain circumstances (see Part IV: Universals, for more on the idea of a disposition). So colours, on Locke's view, are dispositions to produce experiences of a certain kind in perceivers. Non-dispositional properties are known these days as *categorical* properties: for example, the primary qualities of a surface, in virtue of which it absorbs certain wavelengths of light and reflects others, are categorical properties of the surface, and it is in virtue of having these properties that the surface has the colour it does. Now Locke certainly thought that bodies have dispositional properties in virtue of their categorical properties. But Robinson challenges the idea that we can attribute any non-dispositional property to matter which would be sufficient for a full conception of matter. Our conception of matter, he argues, is ultimately that of a collection of powers, rather than that of the categorical basis of these powers. For example, we might initially think that an object's *mass* is a paradigm of a categorical, i.e. non-dispositional, property. But when we examine what physics says about mass, we discover that mass is partly characterized (for example) in terms of how it affects accelerations under a given force; that is, it is characterized in dispositional terms. In the second part of the argument, Robinson argues against the view that the whole world could be a collection of powers. The nature of a power is given by what would constitute its actualization—that is, by the circumstances when the power actually acts in some way. Robinson thinks that when we characterize the actualization of a power, we cannot go on indefinitely to describe the effects in terms of the appearance of further powers; for in this case, objects would not have determinate natures. There must be a point where the actualization of a power is in fact constituted by something which is itself not a power. Searching for such properties, we find that 'the only categorical entities that can end the regress are mental states with sensible qualities as their objects'. Hence minds must exist, and matter can be understood only in terms of certain effects on the mind. The notion of mind-independent matter is incoherent.

Robinson's argument involves three important claims:

1. Objects have powers or dispositions in virtue of having categorical, non-dispositional properties.
2. Our conception of matter is a conception of powers.
3. The only categorical basis for material powers is the sensory qualities of mental states.

Each claim can be challenged. Against claim (1) it could be said that the distinction between the dispositional and the categorical is very hard to draw, and that the ultimate truth may be that all properties have some dispositional component or aspect (Martin in Crane 1995b; Blackburn 1990). Against claim (2) it could be said that the descriptions of powers and their manifestations which characterize matter in fact constitute a description only of our way of *finding out* about matter, and not necessarily a description of the entire nature of matter itself. We learn about material objects by seeing how they behave in certain circumstances; it is a significant step from this to say that all there is to matter is the totality of ways we have of finding out about it. And against claim (3) it could be said that until we have ruled out the other (non-mental) candidates for being the categorical basis for material powers, we should refrain from drawing the conclusion that the only categorical bases are mental. This stage of the argument appears to be an inference to the best explanation, and we should not make this inference until we have examined the alternatives.

A comment about physicalism and materialism is worth making at this point. In contemporary philosophy of mind, there is a debate between physicalists and anti-physicalists. Physicalism is the view that everything in the world is physical, that is, the subject matter of physical science. Though 'physicalism' is often used synonymously with 'materialism', there are some differences between the historical materialist position—which Berkeley was opposing—and the contemporary physicalist view (see Part IX: Mind and Body). Someone like Robinson is opposed to both physicalism (the view that everything is physical) and realism (the view that the world is mind independent). However, we should be careful about the relation between these views. Someone could believe that everything is the subject matter of physical science; and they could also say that physics is a science which is ultimately based on experiential evidence. So physics explains its evidence: that is, it explains the course of experience. Further, it is possible for the same philosopher to believe that the world consist of experiences (for Robinson's reasons or for some other) and hence that the world is mind dependent. But this is consistent with saying that the fundamental theory of the world is physics, since what this means is that physics is the fundamental theory which explains the course of experience. It turns out that physicalism and the denial of realism are compatible.

4. Knowledge and realism

Berkeley thought that his view was the only safeguard against scepticism, that is, against the view that sensible things have no reality. The view that realism leads to scepticism, and that the only escape from scepticism is the denial of realism, is something that has motivated a number of philosophers who argued against realism. The thought is that if the world is independent of our experiences, then there is never any assurance that the world is not completely different from what our experiences tell us about it. Indeed, some have *defined* realism as the view that even our best theory of the world might turn out to be false. On the other hand, if the world somehow constitutively depends on the experiencing mind, then it seems we can exclude the possibility of a radical mismatch between the way the world is, and the way it appears to us.

A specific form of the thought that the very possibility of knowledge requires the mind-dependence of the world lies behind Kant's *transcendental* idealism (Chapter 9). Kant's concern is the possibility of *a priori* knowledge of the world. Since he regards all a priori knowledge as necessary (see Part V: Necessity), this means that his concern is the possibility of knowing the necessary features of the world. As long as we believe that the mind is a passive recipient of inputs from the external world, there is no hope that we shall know anything about it a priori. Instead, we should assume that the mind itself *structures reality*, that we comprehend the world around us only as it conforms to 'forms of intuitions' provided by our sensibility, and categories provided by our understanding. Space and time are forms of intuition, and, for example, cause is a category; we experience things in space and time, and standing in causal relations, because our sensibility and understanding structures experience according to these. Space, time, and causation thus belong to the *phenomenal* world, the world as it appears to us. But Kant recognizes also something which is beyond the phenomenal world, the *thing in itself*. Our conception of this is entirely negative: we cannot say anything about it, for it lies outside the reach of any concepts by which we could comprehend it. Since the world around us is the phenomenal world, structured by the mind, reason discovers in the world what 'it has itself put into nature', and hence a priori knowledge of the world becomes possible. This is the thought encapsulated in Kant's 'Copernican revolution': that instead of assuming that our knowledge must conform to objects, we should suppose that objects conform to our knowledge.

5. Contemporary anti-realism

The debate about realism in modern philosophy was formulated simply in terms of the question of whether the world around us is mind dependent. To put it briefly, Locke's answer is *no*, Berkeley's *yes*, and Kant's is *yes* with respect to the phenomenal world, and *no* with respect to the thing in itself. Michael Dummett, however, whose ideas have shaped a significant part of the contemporary debate, understands the question of realism in a novel way. He considers realism as a possible position with respect to a number of areas—like the physical world, or mathematics—and calls statements about that area 'disputed statements'. Realism is characterized as 'the belief that statements of the disputed class possess an objective truth-value, independently of our means of knowing it: they are true in virtue of reality existing independently of us'. The opponent, called an 'anti-realist', holds that 'statements of the disputed class are to be understood only by reference to the sort of thing which we count as evidence for the statements of that class'. So, for example, a realist about statements about the past will say that the statement, 'The Hungarians bought their country from the Slovakians for a white horse in 896', has a truth-condition which transcends any ability we have to recognize that it is true. The anti-realist about the past, by contrast, will understand the statement in terms of the evidence which we would take to warrant its assertion or denial. The dispute between the realist and the anti-realist is therefore based on different conceptions of *meaning* and therefore *understanding*. The realist believes that to understand a statement is to know what it would be for that statement to be true—whether we can find out about this truth or not. The anti-realist thinks that understanding a statement amounts to knowing what would count as evidence for accepting or rejecting it. Armed with this conception of the debate between realism and anti-realism, Dummett argues that the realist's conception of meaning and understanding is deeply problematic.

Chapter 7

Selection from *Essay Concerning Human Understanding*

John Locke

Some further considerations concerning our simple ideas

Positive ideas from privative causes

§1. Concerning the simple ideas of sensation 'tis to be considered, that whatsoever is so constituted in nature, as to be able, by affecting our senses, to cause any perception in the mind, doth thereby produce in the understanding a simple idea; which, whatever be the external cause of it, when it comes to be taken notice of, by our discerning faculty, it is by the mind looked on and considered there, to be a real *positive* idea in the understanding, as much as any other whatsoever; though perhaps, the cause of it be but a privation in the subject.

§2. Thus the idea of heat and cold, light and darkness, white and black, motion and rest, are equally clear and *positive* ideas in the mind; though, perhaps, some of *the causes* which produce them, are barely *privations* in those subjects, from whence our senses derive those ideas. These the understanding, in its view of them, considers all as distinct positive ideas, without taking notice of the causes that produce them; which is an inquiry not belonging to the idea, as it is in the understanding; but to the nature of the things existing without us. These are two very different things, and carefully to be distinguished; it being one thing to perceive, and know the idea of white or black, and quite another to examine what kind of particles they must be, and how ranged in the superficies, to make any object appear white or black.

§3. A painter or dyer, who never inquired into their causes, hath the ideas of white and black, and other colours, as clearly, perfectly, and distinctly in his understanding, and perhaps more distinctly, than the philosopher, who hath busied himself in considering their natures, and thinks he knows how far either of them is in its cause positive or privative; and the *idea of black* is no less *positive* in his mind, than that of white, *however the cause* of that colour in the external object, may *be only a privation*.

John Locke, selection from *Essay Concerning Human Understanding*, book II, chapter viii. Edited by Roger Woolhouse (Penguin 1997), copyright © Roger Woolhouse 1997.

§4. If it were the design of my present undertaking, to inquire into the natural causes and manner of perception, I should offer this as a reason *why a privative cause might,* in some cases at least, *produce a positive idea, viz.* that all sensation being produced in us, only by different degrees and modes of motion in our animal spirits, variously agitated by external objects, the abatement of any former motion, must as necessarily produce a new sensation, as the variation or increase of it; and so introduce a new idea, which depends only on a different motion of the animal spirits in that organ.

§5. But whether this be so, or no, I will not here determine, but appeal to everyone's own experience, whether the shadow of a man, though it consists of nothing but the absence of light (and the more the absence of light is, the more discernible is the shadow) does not, when a man looks on it, cause as clear and positive an idea in his mind, as a man himself, though covered over with clear Sunshine? And the picture of a shadow, is a positive thing. Indeed, we have *negative names,* which stand not directly for positive ideas, but for their absence, such as *insipid, silence, nihil, etc.* which words denote positive ideas; *v.g. taste, sound, being,* with a signification of their absence.

§6. And thus one may truly be said to see darkness. For supposing a hole perfectly dark, from whence no light is reflected, 'tis certain one may see the figure of it, or it may be painted; or whether the ink, I write with, makes any other idea, is a question. The privative causes I have here assigned of positive ideas, are according to the common opinion; but in truth, it will be hard to determine, whether there be really any ideas from a privative cause, till it be determined, *whether rest be any more a privation than motion.*

Ideas in the mind, qualities in bodies

§7. To discover the nature of our ideas the better, and to discourse of them intelligibly, it will be convenient to distinguish them, as they are ideas or perceptions in our minds; and as they are modifications of matter in the bodies that cause such perceptions in us; that so we *may not* think (as perhaps usually is done) that they are exactly the images and *resemblances* of something inherent in the subject; most of those of sensation being in the mind no more the likeness of something existing without us, than the names, that stand for them are the likeness of our ideas, which yet upon hearing, they are apt to excite in us.

§8. Whatsoever the mind perceives in itself, or is the immediate object of perception, thought, or understanding, that I call *idea;* and the power to produce any idea in our mind, I call *quality* of the subject wherein that power is. Thus a snowball having the power to produce in us the ideas of *white, cold,* and *round,* the powers to produce those ideas in us, as they are in the snowball, I call *qualities;* and as they are sensations, or perceptions, in our understandings, I call them *ideas;* which ideas, if I speak of sometimes, as in the things themselves, I would be understood to mean those qualities in the objects which produce them in us.

Primary qualities

§9. Qualities thus considered in bodies are, first such as are utterly inseparable from the body, in what estate soever it be; such as in all the alterations and changes it suffers, all the force can be used upon it, it constantly keeps; and such as sense constantly finds in every particle of matter, which has bulk enough to be perceived, and the mind finds inseparable from every particle of matter, though less than to make itself singly be perceived by our senses. *v.g.* take a grain of wheat, divide it into two parts, each part has still *solidity, extension, figure,* and *mobility;* divide it again, and it retains still the same qualities: and so divide it on, till the parts become insensible, they must retain still each of them all those qualities. For division (which is all that a mill, or pestle, or any other body, does upon another, in reducing it to insensible parts) can never take away either solidity, extension, figure, or mobility from any body, but only makes two, or more distinct separate masses of matter, of that which was but one before; all which distinct masses, reckoned as so many distinct bodies, after division make a certain number. These I call *original* or *primary qualities* of body, which I think we may observe to produce simple ideas in us, *viz.* solidity, extension, figure, motion, or rest, and number.

§10. *Secondly,* such *qualities,* which in truth are nothing in the objects themselves, but powers to produce various sensations in us by their *primary qualities, i.e.* by the bulk, figure, texture, and motion of their insensible parts, as colours, sounds, tastes, *etc.* These I call *secondary qualities.* To these might be added a third sort which are allowed to be barely powers, though they are as much real qualities in the subject, as those which I, to comply with the common way of speaking, call *qualities,* but for distinction *secondary qualities.* For the power in fire to produce a new colour, or consistency in wax or clay by its primary qualities, is as much a quality in fire, as the power it has to produce in me a new idea or sensation of warmth or burning, which I felt not before, by the same primary qualities, *viz.* the bulk, texture and motion of its insensible parts.

How primary qualities produce their ideas

§11. The next thing to be considered, is how *bodies* produce ideas in us, and that is manifestly *by impulse,* the only way which we can conceive bodies operate in.

§12. If then external objects be not united to our minds, when they produce ideas in it; and yet we perceive *these original qualities* in such of them as singly fall under our senses, 'tis evident, that some motion must be thence continued by our nerves, or animal spirits, by some parts of our bodies, to the brains, or the seat of sensation, there to *produce in our minds the particular ideas we have of them.* And since the extension, figure, number, and motion of bodies of an observable bigness, may be perceived at a distance *by* the sight, 'tis evident some singly imperceptible bodies must come from them to the eyes, and thereby convey to the brain some *motion,* which produces these ideas, which we have of them in us.

How secondary

§13. After the same manner, that the ideas of these original qualities are produced in us, we may conceive, that the *ideas of secondary qualities* are also *produced*, viz. *by the operation of insensible particles on our senses*. For it being manifest, that there are bodies, and good store of bodies, each whereof are so small, that we cannot, by any of our senses, discover either their bulk, figure, or motion, as is evident in the particles of the air and water, and other extremely smaller than those, perhaps, as much smaller than the particles of air, or water, as the particles of air or water, are smaller than peas or hail-stones. Let us suppose at present, that the different motions and figures, bulk and number of such particles, affecting the several organs of our senses, produce in us those different sensations, which we have from the colours and smells of bodies, *v.g.* that a violet, by the impulse of such insensible particles of matter of peculiar figures, and bulks, and in different degrees and modifications of their motions, causes the ideas of the blue colour, and sweet scent of that flower to be produced in our minds. It being no more impossible, to conceive, that God should annex such ideas to such motions, with which they have no similitude; than that he should annex the idea of pain to the motion of a piece of steel dividing our flesh, with which that idea hath no resemblance.

§14. What I have said concerning *colours* and *smells*, may be understood also of *tastes*, and *sounds, and other the like sensible qualities*; which, whatever reality we by mistake, attribute to them, are in truth nothing in the objects themselves, but powers to produce various sensations in us, and *depend on those primary qualities, viz.* bulk, figure, texture, and motion of parts; as I have said.

Ideas of primary qualities are resemblances; of secondary, not

§15. From whence I think it is easy to draw this observation, That the *ideas of primary qualities* of bodies, *are resemblances* of them, and their patterns do really exist in the bodies themselves; but the ideas, *produced* in us *by* these *secondary qualities, have no resemblance* of them at all. There is nothing like our ideas, existing in the bodies themselves. They are in the bodies, we denominate from them, only a power to produce those sensations in us: and what is sweet, blue, or warm in idea, is but the certain bulk, figure, and motion of the insensible parts in the bodies themselves, which we call so.

§16. *Flame* is denominated *hot* and *light; snow, white* and *cold*; and *manna, white* and *sweet*, from the ideas they produce in us. Which qualities are commonly thought to be the same in those bodies, that those ideas are in us, the one the perfect resemblance of the other, as they are in a mirror; and it would by most men be judged very extravagant, if one should say otherwise. And yet he, that will consider, that *the same fire*, that at one distance *produces* in us the sensation of *warmth*, does at a nearer approach, produce in us the far different sensation of *pain*, ought to bethink himself, what reason he has to say, that his idea of *warmth*, which was produced in him by the fire, is actually *in the fire;* and his idea of *pain*, which the same fire produced in him the same way, is *not* in the *fire*. Why is whiteness and coldness in snow, and pain not, when it produces the one and the other idea in us; and can do neither, but by the bulk, figure, number, and motion of its solid parts?

§17. The particular *bulk, number, figure, and motion of the parts of fire, or snow, are really in them*, whether anyone's senses perceive them or no: and therefore they may be called *real qualities*, because they really exist in those bodies. But *light, heat, whiteness*, or *coldness, are no more really in them, than sickness or pain is in* manna. Take away the sensation of them; let not the eyes see light, or colours, nor the ears hear sounds; let the palate not taste, nor the nose smell, and all colours, tastes, odours, and sounds, as they are such particular ideas, vanish and cease, and are reduced to their causes, i.e. bulk, figure, and motion of parts.

§18. A piece of *manna* of a sensible bulk, is able to produce in us the idea of a round or square figure; and, by being removed from one place to another, the idea of motion. This idea of motion represents it, as it really is in the *manna* moving: a circle or square are the same, whether in idea or existence; in the mind, or in the *manna*: and this, both *motion and figure are really in the manna*, whether we take notice of them or no: this everybody is ready to agree to. Besides, *manna* by the bulk, figure, texture, and motion of its parts, has a power to produce the sensations of sickness, and sometimes of acute pains, or gripings in us. That these ideas of *sickness and pain are not in the* manna, but effects of its operations on us, and are nowhere when we feel them not: this also everyone readily agrees to. And yet men are hardly to be brought to think, that *sweetness and whiteness are not really in manna*; which are but the effects of the operations of *manna*, by the motion, size, and figure of its particles on the eyes and palate; as the pain and sickness caused by *manna*, are confessedly nothing, but the effects of its operations on the stomach and guts, by the size, motion, and figure of its insensible parts; (for by nothing else can a body operate, as has been proved:) as if it could not operate on the eyes and palate, and thereby produce in the mind particular distinct ideas, which in itself it has not, as well as we allow it can operate on the guts and stomach, and thereby produce distinct ideas, which in itself it has not. These ideas being all effects of the operations of *manna*, on several parts of our bodies, by the size, figure, number, and motion of its parts, why those produced by the eyes and palate, should rather be thought to be really in the *manna*, than those produced by the stomach and guts; or why the pain and sickness, ideas that are the effects of *manna*, should be thought to be nowhere, when they are not felt; and yet the sweetness and whiteness, effects of the same *manna* on other parts of the body, by ways equally as unknown, should be thought to exist in the *manna*, when they are not seen nor tasted, would need some reason to explain.

§19. Let us consider the red and white colours in *porphyry*: hinder light but from striking on it, and its colours vanish; it no longer produces any such ideas in us: upon the return of light, it produces these appearances on us again. Can anyone think any real alterations are made in the *porphyry*, by the presence or absence of light; and that those ideas of whiteness and redness, are really in *porphyry* in the light, when 'tis plain *it has no colour in the dark?* It has, indeed, such a configuration of particles, both night and day, as are apt by the rays of light rebounding from some parts of that hard stone, to produce in us the idea of redness, and from others the idea of whiteness: but whiteness or redness are not in it at any time, but such a texture, that hath the power to produce such a sensation in us.

§20. Pound an almond, and the clear white *colour* will be altered into a dirty one, and the sweet *taste* into an oily one. What real alteration can the beating of the pestle make in any body, but an alteration of the *texture* of it?

§21. Ideas being thus distinguished and understood, we may be able to give an account, how the same water, at the same time, may produce the idea of cold by one hand, and of heat by the other: whereas it is impossible, that the same water, if those ideas were really in it, should at the same time be both hot and cold. For if we imagine *warmth*, as it is *in our hands*, to be *nothing but a certain sort and degree of motion in the minute particles of our nerves, or animal spirits*, we may understand, how it is possible, that the same water may at the same time produce the sensation of heat in one hand, and cold in the other; which yet figure never does, that never producing the idea of a square by one hand, which has produced the idea of a globe by another. But if the sensation of heat and cold, be nothing but the increase or diminution of the motion of the minute parts of our bodies, caused by the corpuscles of any other body, it is easy to be understood, that if that motion be greater in one hand, than in the other; if a body be applied to the two hands, which has in its minute particles a greater motion, than in those of one of the hands, and a less, than in those of the other, it will increase the motion of the one hand, and lessen it in the other, and so cause the different sensations of heat and cold, that depend thereon.

§22. I have in what just goes before, been engaged in physical inquiries a little further than perhaps I intended. But it being necessary, to make the nature of sensation a little understood, and to make the *difference between the qualities in bodies, and the ideas produced by them in the mind*, to be distinctly conceived, without which it were impossible to discourse intelligibly of them; I hope, I shall be pardoned this little excursion into natural philosophy, it being necessary in our present inquiry, to distinguish the *primary*, and *real qualities* of bodies, which are always in them, (*viz.* solidity, extension, figure, number, and motion, or rest; and are sometimes perceived by us, *viz.* when the bodies they are in, are big enough singly to be discerned) from those *secondary* and *imputed qualities*, which are but the powers of several combinations of those primary ones, when they operate, without being distinctly discerned; whereby we also may come to know what ideas are, and what are not resemblances of something really existing in the bodies, we denominate from them.

Three sorts of qualities in bodies

§23. The *qualities* then that are in *bodies* rightly considered, are of *three sorts*.

First, the *bulk, figure, number, situation*, and *motion, or rest* of their solid parts; those are in them, whether we perceive them or no; and when they are of that size, that we can discover them, we have by these an idea of the thing, as it is in itself, as is plain in artificial things. These I call *primary qualities*.

Secondly, the *power* that is in any body, *by* reason of *its* insensible *primary qualities*, to operate after a peculiar manner on any of our senses, and thereby *produce in us* the *different ideas* of several colours, sounds, smells, tastes, *etc.* These are usually called sensible qualities.

Thirdly, the *power* that is in any body, *by* reason of the particular constitution of *its primary qualities, to* make such a *change* in the *bulk, figure, texture, and motion of another body*, as to make it operate on our senses, differently from what it did before. Thus the Sun has a power to make wax white, and fire to make lead fluid. These *are* usually called powers.

The first of these, as has been said, I think, may be properly called *real original*, or *primary qualities*, because they are in the things themselves, whether they are perceived or no; and upon their different modifications it is, that the secondary qualities depend.

The other two, are only powers to act differently upon other things, which powers result from the different modifications of those primary qualities.

The 1st. are resemblances. The 2nd. thought resemblances, but are not. The 3rd. neither are, nor are thought so

§24. But though *these two later sorts of qualities are powers barely*, and nothing but powers, relating to several other bodies, and resulting from the different modifications of the original qualities; yet they are generally otherwise thought of. For *the second sort, viz.* the powers to produce several ideas in us by our senses, *are looked upon as real qualities, in the things* thus affecting us: but *the third sort are called, and esteemed barely powers, v.g.* the idea of heat, or light, which we receive by our eyes, or touch from the Sun, are commonly thought *real qualities*, existing in the Sun, and something more than mere powers in it. But when we consider the Sun, in reference to wax, which it melts or blanches, we look upon the whiteness and softness produced in the wax, not as qualities in the Sun, but effects produced by *powers* in it: whereas, if rightly considered, these qualities of light and warmth, which are perceptions in me when I am warmed, or enlightened by the Sun, are no otherwise in the Sun, than the changes made in the wax, when it is blanched or melted, are in the Sun. They are all of them equally powers in the Sun, depending on its primary qualities; whereby it is able in the one case, so to alter the bulk, figure, texture, or motion of some of the insensible parts of my eyes, or hands, as thereby to produce in me the idea of light or heat; and in the other, it is able so to alter the bulk, figure, texture, or motion of the insensible parts of the wax, as to make them fit to produce in me the distinct ideas of white and fluid.

§25. The reason, *why the one are ordinarily taken for real qualities, and the other only for bare powers*, seems to be, because the ideas we have of distinct colours, sounds, *etc.* containing nothing at all in them, of bulk, figure, or motion, we are not apt to think them the effects of these primary qualities, which appear not to our senses, to operate in their production; and with which, they have not any apparent congruity, or conceivable connexion. Hence it is, that we are so forward to imagine, that those ideas are the resemblances of something really existing in the objects themselves: since sensation discovers nothing of bulk, figure, or motion of parts in their production; nor can reason show, how bodies by their bulk, figure, and motion, should produce in the mind the ideas of blue, or yellow, *etc.* But in the other case, in the operations of bodies, changing the qualities one of another, we plainly discover, that the quality produced, hath commonly no resemblance with anything in the thing producing it; wherefore we look on it as a bare effect of power. For though receiving the idea of heat, or light, from the Sun, we are apt to think, 'tis a perception and resemblance of such a quality in the Sun: yet when we see wax, or a fair face, receive change of colour from the Sun, we cannot imagine, that to be the reception or resemblance of anything in the Sun, because we find not those different colours in the Sun itself. For our senses, being able to observe a likeness, or unlikeness of sensible qualities in two different external objects, we forwardly enough conclude the production of any sensible quality in any subject, to be an effect of bare power, and not the communication of any quality, which was really in the efficient, when we find no such sensible quality in the thing that produced it. But our senses, not being able to discover any unlikeness between the idea produced in us, and the quality of the object producing it, we are apt to imagine, that our ideas are resemblances of something in the objects, and not the effects of certain powers, placed in the modification of their primary qualities, with which primary qualities the ideas produced in us have no resemblance.

Secondary qualities two-fold; first, immediately perceivable; secondly, mediately perceivable

§26. To conclude, beside those before-mentioned *primary qualities* in bodies, *viz.* bulk, figure, extension, number, and motion of their solid parts; all the rest whereby we take notice of bodies, and distinguish them one from another, are nothing else, but several powers in them, depending on those primary qualities; whereby they are fitted, either by immediately operating on our bodies, to produce several different ideas in us; or else by operating on other bodies, so to change their primary qualities, as to render them capable of producing ideas in us, different from what before they did. The former of these, I think, may be called *secondary qualities, immediately perceivable:* the latter, *secondary qualities, mediately perceivable.*

Chapter 8

Selection from *Three Dialogues between Hylas and Philonous*

George Berkeley

The first dialogue between Hylas and Philonous

PHILONOUS. Good morrow, Hylas: I did not expect to find you abroad so early.

HYLAS. It is indeed something unusual; but my thoughts were so taken up with a subject I was discoursing of last night, that finding I could not sleep, I resolved to rise and take a turn in the garden.

PHILONOUS. It happened well, to let you see what innocent and agreeable pleasures you lose every morning. Can there be a pleasanter time of the day, or a more delightful season of the year? That purple sky, these wild but sweet notes of birds, the fragrant bloom upon the trees and flowers, the gentle influence of the rising sun, these and a thousand nameless beauties of nature inspire the soul with secret transports; its faculties too being at this time fresh and lively, are fit for those meditations, which the solitude of a garden and tranquillity of the morning naturally dispose us to. But I am afraid I interrupt your thoughts: for you seemed very intent on something.

HYLAS. It is true, I was, and shall be obliged to you if you will permit me to go on in the same vein; not that I would by any means deprive myself of your company, for my thoughts always flow more easily in conversation with a friend, than when I am alone: but my request is, that you would suffer me to impart my reflexions to you.

PHILONOUS. With all my heart, it is what I should have requested myself, if you had not prevented me.

HYLAS. I was considering the odd fate of those men who have in all ages, through an affectation of being distinguished from the vulgar, or some unaccountable turn of thought, pretended either to believe nothing at all, or to believe the most extravagant things in the world. This however might be borne, if their paradoxes and scepticism did not draw after them some consequences of general disadvantage

This selection comprises most of the first of Berkeley's three dialogues. In the passage we have cut, Philonous applies his arguments to the qualities perceived by the senses, and he convinces Hylas that tastes, sounds, smells and colours exist in the perceiver's mind.

George Berkeley, selection from *Three Dialogues* (Oxford World's Classics, 1996), reprinted by permission of Oxford University Press.

to mankind. But the mischief lieth here; that when men of less leisure see them who are supposed to have spent their whole time in the pursuits of knowledge, professing an entire ignorance of all things, or advancing such notions as are repugnant to plain and commonly received principles, they will be tempted to entertain suspicions concerning the most important truths, which they had hitherto held sacred and unquestionable.

PHILONOUS. I entirely agree with you, as to the ill tendency of the affected doubts of some philosophers, and fantastical conceits of others. I am even so far gone of late in this way of thinking, that I have quitted several of the sublime notions I had got in their schools for vulgar opinions. And I give it you on my word, since this revolt from metaphysical notions to the plain dictates of Nature and common sense, I find my understanding strangely enlightened, so that I can now easily comprehend a great many things which before were all mystery and riddle.

HYLAS. I am glad to find there was nothing in the accounts I heard of you.

PHILONOUS. Pray, what were those?

HYLAS. You were represented in last night's conversation, as one who maintained the most extravagant opinion that ever entered into the mind of man, to wit, that there is no such thing as *material substance* in the world.

PHILONOUS. That there is no such thing as what philosophers call *material substance*, I am seriously persuaded: but if I were made to see anything absurd or sceptical in this, I should then have the same reason to renounce this, that I imagine I have now to reject the contrary opinion.

HYLAS. What! can anything be more fantastical, more repugnant to common sense, or a more manifest piece of scepticism, than to believe there is no such thing as *matter*?

PHILONOUS. Softly, good Hylas. What if it should prove, that you, who hold there is, are by virtue of that opinion a greater *sceptic*, and maintain more paradoxes and repugnancies to common sense, than I who believe no such thing?

HYLAS. You may as soon persuade me, the part is greater than the whole, as that, in order to avoid absurdity and scepticism, I should ever be obliged to give up my opinion in this point.

PHILONOUS. Well then, are you content to admit that opinion for true, which upon examination shall appear most agreeable to common sense, and remote from scepticism?

HYLAS. With all my heart. Since you are for raising disputes about the plainest things in Nature, I am content for once to hear what you have to say.

PHILONOUS. Pray, Hylas, what do you mean by a *sceptic*?

HYLAS. I mean what all men mean, one that doubts of everything.

PHILONOUS. He then who entertains no doubt concerning some particular point, with regard to that point cannot be thought a *sceptic*.

HYLAS. I agree with you.

PHILONOUS. Whether doth doubting consist in embracing the affirmative or negative side of a question?

HYLAS. In neither; for whoever understands English, cannot but know that *doubting* signifies a suspense between both.

PHILONOUS. He then that denieth any point, can no more be said to doubt of it, than he who affirmeth it with the same degree of assurance.

HYLAS. True.

PHILONOUS. And consequently, for such his denial is no more to be esteemed a *sceptic* than the other.

HYLAS. I acknowledge it.

PHILONOUS. How cometh it to pass then, Hylas, that you pronounce me a *sceptic*, because I deny what you affirm, to wit, the existence of matter? Since, for ought you can tell, I am as peremptory in my denial, as you in your affirmation.

HYLAS. Hold, Philonous, I have been a little out in my definition; but every false step a man makes in discourse is not to be insisted on. I said indeed, that a *sceptic* was one who doubted of everything; but I should have added, or who denies the reality and truth of things.

PHILONOUS. What things? Do you mean the principles and theorems of sciences? But these you know are universal intellectual notions, and consequently independent of matter; the denial therefore of this doth not imply the denying them.

HYLAS. I grant it. But are there no other things? What think you of distrusting the senses, of denying the real existence of sensible things, or pretending to know nothing of them. Is not this sufficient to denominate a man a *sceptic*?

PHILONOUS. Shall we therefore examine which of us it is that denies the reality of sensible things, or professes the greatest ignorance of them; since, if I take you rightly, he is to be esteemed the greatest *sceptic*?

HYLAS. That is what I desire.

PHILONOUS. What mean you by sensible things?

HYLAS. Those things which are perceived by the senses. Can you imagine that I mean anything else?

PHILONOUS. Pardon me, Hylas, if I am desirous clearly to apprehend your notions, since this may much shorten our inquiry. Suffer me then to ask you this farther question. Are those things only perceived by the senses which are perceived immediately? Or may those things properly be said to be *sensible*, which are perceived mediately, or not without the intervention of others?

HYLAS. I do not sufficiently understand you.

PHILONOUS. In reading a book, what I immediately perceive are the letters, but mediately, or by means of these, are suggested to my mind the notions of God, virtue, truth, &c. Now, that the letters are truly sensible things, or perceived by sense, there is no doubt: but I would know whether you take the things suggested by them to be so too.

HYLAS. No certainly, it were absurd to think *God* or *Virtue* sensible things, though they may be signified and suggested to the mind by sensible marks, with which they have an arbitrary connexion.

PHILONOUS. It seems then, that by *sensible things* you mean those only which can be perceived immediately by sense.

HYLAS. Right.

PHILONOUS. Doth it not follow from this, that though I see one part of the sky red, and another blue, and that my reason doth thence evidently conclude there must be some cause of that diversity of colours, yet that cause cannot be said to be a sensible thing, or perceived by the sense of seeing?

HYLAS. It doth.

PHILONOUS. In like manner, though I hear variety of sounds, yet I cannot be said to hear the cause of those sounds.

HYLAS. You cannot.

PHILONOUS. And when by my touch I perceive a thing to be hot and heavy, I cannot say with any truth or propriety, that I feel the cause of its heat or weight.

HYLAS. To prevent any more questions of this kind, I tell you once for all, that by *sensible things* I mean those only which are perceived by sense, and that in truth the senses perceive nothing which they do not perceive immediately: for they make no inferences. The deducing therefore of causes or occasions from effects and appearances, which alone are perceived by sense, entirely relates to reason.

PHILONOUS. This point then is agreed between us, that *sensible things are those only which are immediately perceived by sense.* You will farther inform me, whether we immediately perceive by sight anything beside light, and colours, and figures: or by hearing, anything but sounds: by the palate, anything beside tastes: by the smell, beside odours: or by the touch, more than tangible qualities.

HYLAS. We do not.

PHILONOUS. It seems therefore, that if you take away all sensible qualities, there remains nothing sensible.

HYLAS. I grant it.

PHILONOUS. Sensible things therefore are nothing else but so many sensible qualities, or combinations of sensible qualities.

HYLAS. Nothing else.

PHILONOUS. Heat then is a sensible thing.

HYLAS. Certainly.

PHILONOUS. Doth the reality of sensible things consist in being perceived? or, is it something distinct from their being perceived, and that bears no relation to the mind?

HYLAS. To *exist* is one thing, and to be *perceived* is another.

PHILONOUS. I speak with regard to sensible things only: and of these I ask, whether by their real existence you mean a subsistence exterior to the mind, and distinct from their being perceived?

HYLAS. I mean a real absolute being, distinct from, and without any relation to their being perceived.

PHILONOUS. Heat therefore, if it be allowed a real being, must exist without the mind.

HYLAS. It must.

PHILONOUS. Tell me, Hylas, is this real existence equally compatible to all degrees of heat, which we perceive: or is there any reason why we should attribute it to some, and deny it others? And if there be, pray let me know that reason.

HYLAS. Whatever degree of heat we perceive by sense, we may be sure the same exists in the object that occasions it.

PHILONOUS. What, the greatest as well as the least?

HYLAS. I tell you, the reason is plainly the same in respect of both: they are both perceived by sense; nay, the greater degree of heat is more sensibly perceived; and consequently, if there is any difference, we are more certain of its real existence than we can be of the reality of a lesser degree.

PHILONOUS. But is not the most vehement and intense degree of heat a very great pain?

HYLAS. No one can deny it.

PHILONOUS. And is any unperceiving thing capable of pain or pleasure?

HYLAS. No certainly.

PHILONOUS. Is your material substance a senseless being, or a being endowed with sense and perception?

HYLAS. It is senseless, without doubt.

PHILONOUS. It cannot therefore be the subject of pain.

HYLAS. By no means.

PHILONOUS. Nor consequently of the greatest heat perceived by sense, since you acknowledge this to be no small pain.

HYLAS. I grant it.

PHILONOUS. What shall we say then of your external object; is it a material substance, or no?

HYLAS. It is a material substance with the sensible qualities inhering in it.

PHILONOUS. How then can a great heat exist in it, since you own it cannot in a material substance? I desire you would clear this point.

HYLAS. Hold, Philonous, I fear I was out in yielding intense heat to be a pain. It should seem rather, that pain is something distinct from heat, and the consequence or effect of it.

PHILONOUS. Upon putting your hand near the fire, do you perceive one simple uniform sensation, or two distinct sensations?

HYLAS. But one simple sensation.

PHILONOUS. Is not the heat immediately perceived?

HYLAS. It is.

PHILONOUS. And the pain?

HYLAS. True.

PHILONOUS. Seeing therefore they are both immediately perceived at the same time, and the fire affects you only with one simple, or uncompounded idea, it follows that this same simple idea is both the intense heat immediately perceived, and the pain; and consequently, that the intense heat immediately perceived, is nothing distinct from a particular sort of pain.

HYLAS. It seems so.

PHILONOUS. Again, try in your thoughts, Hylas, if you can conceive a vehement sensation to be without pain, or pleasure.

HYLAS. I cannot.

PHILONOUS. Or can you frame to yourself an idea of sensible pain or pleasure in general, abstracted from every particular idea of heat, cold, tastes, smells? &c.

HYLAS. I do not find that I can.

PHILONOUS. Doth it not therefore follow, that sensible pain is nothing distinct from those sensations or ideas, in an intense degree?

HYLAS. It is undeniable; and to speak the truth, I begin to suspect a very great heat cannot exist but in a mind perceiving it.

PHILONOUS. What! are you then in that *sceptical* state of suspense, between affirming and denying?

HYLAS. I think I may be positive in the point. A very violent and painful heat cannot exist without the mind.

PHILONOUS. It hath not therefore, according to you, any real being.

HYLAS. I own it.

PHILONOUS. Is it therefore certain, that there is no body in nature really hot?

HYLAS. I have not denied there is any real heat in bodies. I only say, there is no such thing as an intense real heat.

PHILONOUS. But did you not say before, that all degrees of heat were equally real: or if there was any difference, that the greater were more undoubtedly real than the lesser?

HYLAS. True: but it was, because I did not then consider the ground there is for distinguishing between them, which I now plainly see. And it is this: because intense heat is nothing else but a particular kind of painful sensation; and pain cannot exist but in a perceiving being; it follows that no intense heat can really exist in an unperceiving corporeal substance. But this is no reason why we should deny heat in an inferior degree to exist in such a substance.

PHILONOUS. But how shall we be able to discern those degrees of heat which exist only in the mind, from those which exist without it?

HYLAS. That is no difficult matter. You know, the least pain cannot exist unperceived; whatever therefore degree of heat is a pain, exists only in the mind. But as for all other degrees of heat, nothing obliges us to think the same of them.

PHILONOUS. I think you granted before, that no unperceiving being was capable of pleasure, any more than of pain.

HYLAS. I did.

PHILONOUS. And is not warmth, or a more gentle degree of heat than what causes uneasiness, a pleasure?

HYLAS. What then?

PHILONOUS. Consequently it cannot exist without the mind in any unperceiving substance, or body.

HYLAS. So it seems.

PHILONOUS. Since therefore, as well those degrees of heat that are not painful, as those that are, can exist only in a thinking substance; may we not conclude that external bodies are absolutely incapable of any degree of heat whatsoever?

HYLAS. On second thoughts, I do not think it so evident that warmth is a pleasure, as that a great degree of heat is a pain.

PHILONOUS. I do not pretend that warmth is as great a pleasure as heat is a pain. But if you grant it to be even a small pleasure, it serves to make good my conclusion.

HYLAS. I could rather call it an *indolence*. It seems to be nothing more than a privation of both pain and pleasure. And that such a quality or state as this may agree to an unthinking substance, I hope you will not deny.

PHILONOUS. If you are resolved to maintain that warmth, or a gentle degree of heat, is no pleasure, I know not how to convince you otherwise, than by appealing to your own sense. But what think you of cold?

HYLAS. The same that I do of heat. An intense degree of cold is a pain; for to feel a very great cold, is to perceive a great uneasiness: it cannot therefore exist without the mind; but a lesser degree of cold may, as well as a lesser degree of heat.

PHILONOUS. Those bodies therefore, upon whose application to our own, we perceive a moderate degree of heat, must be concluded to have a moderate degree of heat or warmth in them: and those, upon whose application we feel a like degree of cold, must be thought to have cold in them.

HYLAS. They must.

PHILONOUS. Can any doctrine be true that necessarily leads a man into an absurdity?

HYLAS. Without doubt it cannot.

PHILONOUS. Is it not an absurdity to think that the same thing should be at the same time both cold and warm?

HYLAS. It is.

PHILONOUS. Suppose now one of your hands hot, and the other cold, and that they are both at once put into the same vessel of water, in an intermediate state; will not the water seem cold to one hand, and warm to the other?

HYLAS. It will.

PHILONOUS. Ought we not therefore by your principles to conclude, it is really both cold and warm at the same time, that is, according to your own concession, to believe an absurdity.

HYLAS. I confess it seems so.

PHILONOUS. Consequently, the principles themselves are false, since you have granted that no true principle leads to an absurdity.

HYLAS. But after all, can anything be more absurd than to say, *there is no heat in the fire?*

PHILONOUS. To make the point still clearer; tell me, whether in two cases exactly alike, we ought not to make the same judgment?

HYLAS. We ought.

PHILONOUS. When a pin pricks your finger, doth it not rend and divide the fibres of your flesh?

HYLAS. It doth.

PHILONOUS. And when a coal burns your finger, doth it any more?

HYLAS. It doth not.

PHILONOUS. Since therefore you neither judge the sensation itself occasioned by the pin, nor anything like it to be in the pin; you should not, conformably to what you have now granted, judge the sensation occasioned by the fire, or anything like it, to be in the fire.

HYLAS. Well, since it must be so, I am content to yield this point, and acknowledge, that heat and cold are only sensations existing in our minds: but there still remain qualities enough to secure the reality of external things.

PHILONOUS. But what will you say, Hylas, if it shall appear that the case is the same with regard to all other sensible qualities, and that they can no more be supposed to exist without the mind, than heat and cold?

HYLAS. Then indeed you will have done something to the purpose; but that is what I despair of seeing proved . . .

HYLAS. I frankly own, Philonous, that it is in vain to stand out any longer. Colours, sounds, tastes, in a word, all those termed *secondary qualities*, have certainly no existence without the mind. But by this acknowledgment I must not be supposed to derogate anything from the reality of matter or external objects, seeing it is no more than several philosophers maintain, who nevertheless are the farthest imaginable from denying matter. For the clearer understanding of this, you must know sensible qualities are by philosophers divided into *primary* and *secondary*.

The former are extension, figure, solidity, gravity, motion, and rest. And these they hold exist really in bodies. The latter are those above enumerated; or briefly, all sensible qualities beside the primary, which they assert are only so many sensations or ideas existing nowhere but in the mind. But all this, I doubt not, you are already apprised of. For my part, I have been a long time sensible there was such an opinion current among philosophers, but was never thoroughly convinced of its truth till now.

PHILONOUS. You are still then of opinion, that extension and figures are inherent in external unthinking substances.

HYLAS. I am.

PHILONOUS. But what if the same arguments which are brought against secondary qualities, will hold good against these also?

HYLAS. Why then I shall be obliged to think, they too exist only in the mind.

PHILONOUS. Is it your opinion, the very figure and extension which you perceive by sense, exist in the outward object or material substance?

HYLAS. It is.

PHILONOUS. Have all other animals as good grounds to think the same of the figure and extension which they see and feel?

HYLAS. Without doubt, if they have any thought at all.

PHILONOUS. Answer me, Hylas. Think you the senses were bestowed upon all animals for their preservation and well-being in life? or were they given to men alone for this end?

HYLAS. I make no question but they have the same use in all other animals.

PHILONOUS. If so, is it not necessary they should be enabled by them to perceive their own limbs, and those bodies which are capable of harming them?

HYLAS. Certainly.

PHILONOUS. A mite therefore must be supposed to see his own foot, and things equal or even less than it, as bodies of some considerable dimension; though at the same time they appear to you scarce discernible, or at best as so many visible points.

HYLAS. I cannot deny it.

PHILONOUS. And to creatures less than the mite they will seem yet larger.

HYLAS. They will.

PHILONOUS. Insomuch that what you can hardly discern, will to another extremely minute animal appear as some huge mountain.

HYLAS. All this I grant.

PHILONOUS. Can one and the same thing be at the same time in itself of different dimensions?

HYLAS. That were absurd to imagine.

PHILONOUS. But from what you have laid down it follows, that both the extension by you perceived, and that perceived by the mite itself, as likewise all those perceived by lesser animals, are each of them the true extension of the mite's foot, that is to say, by your own principles you are led into an absurdity.

HYLAS. There seems to be some difficulty in the point.

PHILONOUS. Again, have you not acknowledged that no real inherent property of any object can be changed, without some change in the thing itself?

HYLAS. I have.

PHILONOUS. But as we approach to or recede from an object, the visible extension varies, being at one distance ten or an hundred times greater than at another. Doth it not therefore follow from hence likewise, that it is not really inherent in the object?

HYLAS. I own I am at a loss what to think.

PHILONOUS. Your judgment will soon be determined, if you will venture to think as freely concerning this quality, as you have done concerning the rest. Was it not admitted as a good argument, that neither heat nor cold was in the water, because it seemed warm to one hand, and cold to the other?

HYLAS. It was.

PHILONOUS. Is it not the very same reasoning to conclude, there is no extension or figure in an object, because to one eye it shall seem little, smooth, and round, when at the same time it appears to the other, great, uneven, and angular?

HYLAS. The very same. But doth this latter fact ever happen?

PHILONOUS. You may at any time make the experiment, by looking with one eye bare, and with the other through a microscope.

HYLAS. I know not how to maintain it, and yet I am loth to give up *extension*, I see so many odd consequences following upon such a concession.

PHILONOUS. Odd, say you? After the concessions already made, I hope you will stick at nothing for its oddness. But on the other hand should it not seem very odd, if the general reasoning which includes all other sensible qualities did not also include extension? If it be allowed that no idea nor anything like an idea can exist in an unperceiving substance, then surely it follows, that no figure or mode of extension, which we can either perceive or imagine, or have any idea of, can be really inherent in matter; not to mention the peculiar difficulty there must be, in conceiving a material substance, prior to and distinct from extension, to be the *substratum* of extension. Be the sensible quality what it will, figure, or sound, or colour; it seems alike impossible it should subsist in that which doth not perceive it.

HYLAS. I give up the point for the present, reserving still a right to retract my opinion, in case I shall hereafter discover any false step in my progress to it.

PHILONOUS. That is a right you cannot be denied. Figures and extension being dispatched, we proceed next to *motion*. Can a real motion in any external body be at the same time both very swift and very slow?

HYLAS. It cannot.

PHILONOUS. Is not the motion of a body swift in a reciprocal proportion to the time it takes up in describing any given space? Thus a body that describes a mile in an hour, moves three times faster than it would in case it described only a mile in three hours.

HYLAS. I agree with you.

PHILONOUS. And is not time measured by the succession of ideas in our minds?

HYLAS. It is.

PHILONOUS. And is it not possible ideas should succeed one another twice as fast in your mind, as they do in mine, or in that of some spirit of another kind.

HYLAS. I own it.

PHILONOUS. Consequently the same body may to another seem to perform its motion over any space in half the time that it doth to you. And the same reasoning will hold as to any other proportion: that is to say, according to your principles (since the motions perceived are both really in the object) it is possible one and the same body shall be really moved the same way at once, both very swift and very slow. How is this consistent either with common sense, or with what you just now granted?

HYLAS. I have nothing to say to it.

PHILONOUS. Then as for *solidity*; either you do not mean any sensible quality by that word, and so it is beside our inquiry: or if you do, it must be either hardness or resistance. But both the one and the other are plainly relative to our sense: it being evident, that what seems hard to one animal, may appear soft to another, who hath greater force and firmness of limbs. Nor is it less plain, that the resistance I feel is not in the body.

HYLAS. I own the very sensation of resistance, which is all you immediately perceive, is not in the *body*, but the cause of that sensation is.

PHILONOUS. But the causes of our sensations are not things immediately perceived, and therefore not sensible. This point I thought had been already determined.

HYLAS. I own it was; but you will pardon me if I seem a little embarrassed: I know not how to quit my old notions.

PHILONOUS. To help you out, do but consider, that if extension be once acknowledged to have no existence without the mind, the same must necessarily be granted of motion, solidity, and gravity, since they all evidently suppose extension. It is therefore superfluous to inquire particularly concerning each of them. In denying extension, you have denied them all to have any real existence.

HYLAS. I wonder, Philonous, if what you say be true, why those philosophers who deny the secondary qualities any real existence, should yet attribute it to the primary. If there is no difference between them, how can this be accounted for?

PHILONOUS. It is not my business to account for every opinion of the philosophers. But among other reasons which may be assigned for this, it seems probable, that pleasure and pain being rather annexed to the former than the latter, may be one. Heat and cold, tastes and smells, have something more vividly pleasing or disagreeable than the ideas of extension, figure, and motion, affect us with. And it being too visibly absurd to hold, that pain or pleasure can be in an unperceiving substance, men are more easily weaned from believing the external existence of the secondary, than the primary qualities. You will be satisfied there is something in this, if you recollect the difference you made between an intense and more moderate degree of heat, allowing the one a real existence, while you denied it to the other. But after all, there is no rational ground for that distinction; for surely an indifferent sensation is as truly *a sensation*, as one more pleasing or painful; and consequently should not any more than they be supposed to exist in an unthinking subject.

HYLAS. It is just come into my head, Philonous, that I have somewhere heard of a distinction between absolute and sensible extension. Now though it be acknowledged that *great* and *small*, consisting merely in the relation which other extended beings have to the parts of our own bodies, do not really inhere in the substances themselves; yet nothing obliges us to hold the same with regard to *absolute extension*, which is something abstracted from *great* and *small*, from this or that particular magnitude or figure. So likewise as to motion, *swift* and *slow* are altogether relative to the succession of ideas in our own minds. But it doth not follow, because those modifications of motion exist not without the mind, that therefore absolute motion abstracted from them doth not.

PHILONOUS. Pray what is it that distinguishes one motion, or one part of extension from another? Is it not something sensible, as some degree of swiftness or slowness, some certain magnitude or figure peculiar to each?

HYLAS. I think so.

PHILONOUS. These qualities therefore stripped of all sensible properties, are without all specific and numerical differences, as the Schools call them.

HYLAS. They are.

PHILONOUS. That is to say, they are extension in general, and motion in general.

HYLAS. Let it be so.

PHILONOUS. But it is an universally received maxim, that *everything which exists, is particular*. How then can motion in general, or extension in general exist in any corporeal substance?

HYLAS. I will take time to solve your difficulty.

PHILONOUS. But I think the point may be speedily decided. Without doubt you can tell, whether you are able to frame this or that idea. Now I am content to put our dispute on this issue. If you can frame in your thoughts a distinct abstract idea of motion or extension, divested of all those sensible modes, as swift and slow, great and small, round and square, and the like, which are acknowledged to exist only in the mind, I will then yield the point you contend for. But if you cannot, it will be unreasonable on your side to insist any longer upon what you have no notion of.

HYLAS. To confess ingenuously, I cannot.

PHILONOUS. Can you even separate the ideas of extension and motion, from the ideas of all those qualities which they who make the distinction, term *secondary*.

HYLAS. What! is it not an easy matter, to consider extension and motion by themselves, abstracted from all other sensible qualities? Pray how do the mathematicians treat of them?

PHILONOUS. I acknowledge, Hylas, it is not difficult to form general propositions and reasonings about those qualities, without mentioning any other; and in this sense to consider or treat of them abstractedly. But how doth it follow that because I can pronounce the word *motion* by itself, I can form the idea of it in my mind exclusive of body? Or because theorems may be made of extension and figures, without any mention of *great* or *small*, or any other sensible mode or quality; that therefore it is possible such an abstract idea of extension, without any particular size or figure, or sensible quality, should be distinctly formed, and apprehended by the mind? Mathematicians treat of quantity, without regarding what other sensible qualities it is attended with, as being altogether indifferent to their demonstrations. But when laying aside the words, they contemplate the bare ideas, I believe you will find, they are not the pure abstracted ideas of extension.

HYLAS. But what say you to *pure intellect*? May not abstracted ideas be framed by that faculty?

PHILONOUS. Since I cannot frame abstract ideas at all, it is plain, I cannot frame them by the help of *pure intellect*, whatsoever faculty you understand by those words. Besides, not to inquire into the nature of pure intellect and its spiritual objects, as *virtue, reason, God,* or the like; thus much seems manifest, that sensible things are only to be perceived by sense, or represented by the imagination. Figures therefore and extension being originally perceived by sense, do not belong to pure intellect. But for your farther satisfaction, try if you can frame the idea of any figure, abstracted from all particularities of size, or even from other sensible qualities.

HYLAS. Let me think a little—I do not find that I can.

PHILONOUS. And can you think it possible, that should really exist in Nature, which implies a repugnancy in its conception?

HYLAS. By no means.

PHILONOUS. Since therefore it is impossible even for the mind to disunite the ideas of extension and motion from all other sensible qualities, doth it not follow, that where the one exist, there necessarily the other exist likewise?

HYLAS. It should seem so.

PHILONOUS. Consequently the very same arguments which you admitted, as conclusive against the secondary qualities, are without any farther application of force against the primary too. Besides, if you will trust your senses, is it not plain all sensible qualities coexist, or to them, appear as being in the same place?

Do they ever represent a motion, or figure, as being divested of all other visible and tangible qualities?

HYLAS. You need say no more on this head. I am free to own, if there be no secret error or oversight in our proceedings hitherto, that all sensible qualities are alike to be denied existence without the mind. But my fear is, that I have been too liberal in my former concessions, or overlooked some fallacy or other. In short, I did not take time to think.

PHILONOUS. For that matter, Hylas, you may take what time you please in reviewing the progress of our inquiry. You are at liberty to recover any slips you might have made, or offer whatever you have omitted, which makes for your first opinion.

HYLAS. One great oversight I take to be this: that I did not sufficiently distinguish the *object* from the *sensation*. Now though this latter may not exist without the mind, yet it will not thence follow that the former cannot.

PHILONOUS. What object do you mean? the object of the senses?

HYLAS. The same.

PHILONOUS. It is then immediately perceived.

HYLAS. Right.

PHILONOUS. Make me to understand the difference between what is immediately perceived, and a sensation.

HYLAS. The sensation I take to be an act of the mind perceiving; beside which, there is something perceived; and this I call the *object*. For example, there is red and yellow on that tulip. But then the act of perceiving those colours is in me only, and not in the tulip.

PHILONOUS. What tulip do you speak of? is it that which you see?

HYLAS. The same.

PHILONOUS. And what do you see beside colour, figure, and extension?

HYLAS. Nothing.

PHILONOUS. What you would say then is, that the red and yellow are coexistent with the extension; is it not?

HYLAS. That is not all; I would say, they have a real existence without the mind, in some unthinking substance.

PHILONOUS. That the colours are really in the tulip which I see, is manifest. Neither can it be denied, that this tulip may exist independent of your mind or mine; but that any immediate object of the senses, that is, any idea, or combination of ideas, should exist in an unthinking substance, or exterior to all minds, is in itself an evident contradiction. Nor can I imagine how this follows from what you said just now, to wit that the red and yellow were on the tulip *you saw*, since you do not pretend to *see* that unthinking substance.

HYLAS. You have an artful way, Philonous, of diverting our inquiry from the subject.

PHILONOUS. I see you have no mind to be pressed that way. To return then to your distinction between *sensation* and *object*; if I take you right, you distinguish in every perception two things, the one an action of the mind, the other not.

HYLAS. True.

PHILONOUS. And this action cannot exist in, or belong to any unthinking thing; but whatever beside is implied in a perception, may.

HYLAS. That is my meaning.

PHILONOUS. So that if there was a perception without any act of the mind, it were possible such a perception should exist in an unthinking substance.

HYLAS. I grant it. But it is impossible there should be such a perception.

PHILONOUS. When is the mind said to be active?

HYLAS. When it produces, puts an end to, or changes anything.

PHILONOUS. Can the mind produce, discontinue, or change anything but by an act of the will?

HYLAS. It cannot.

PHILONOUS. The mind therefore is to be accounted active in its perceptions, so far forth as volition is included in them.

HYLAS. It is.

PHILONOUS. In plucking this flower, I am active, because I do it by the motion of my hand, which was consequent upon my volition; so likewise in applying it to my nose. But is either of these smelling?

HYLAS. No.

PHILONOUS. I act too in drawing the air through my nose; because my breathing so rather than otherwise, is the effect of my volition. But neither can this be called *smelling*: for if it were, I should smell every time I breathed in that manner.

HYLAS. True.

PHILONOUS. Smelling then is somewhat consequent to all this.

HYLAS. It is.

PHILONOUS. But I do not find my will concerned any farther. Whatever more there is, as that I perceive such a particular smell or any smell at all, this is independent of my will, and therein I am altogether passive. Do you find it otherwise with you, Hylas?

HYLAS. No, the very same.

PHILONOUS. Then as to seeing, is it not in your power to open your eyes, or keep them shut; to turn them this or that way?

HYLAS. Without doubt.

PHILONOUS. But doth it in like manner depend on your will, that in looking on this flower, you perceive *white* rather than any other colour? Or directing your open eyes toward yonder part of the heaven, can you avoid seeing the sun? Or is light or darkness the effect of your volition?

HYLAS. No certainly.

PHILONOUS. You are then in these respects altogether passive.

HYLAS. I am.

PHILONOUS. Tell me now, whether *seeing* consists in perceiving light and colours, or in opening and turning the eyes?

HYLAS. Without doubt, in the former.

PHILONOUS. Since therefore you are in the very perception of light and colours altogether passive, what is become of that action you were speaking of, as an ingredient in every sensation? And doth it not follow from your own concessions, that the perception of light and colours, including no action in it, may exist in an unperceiving substance? And is not this a plain contradiction?

HYLAS. I know not what to think of it.

PHILONOUS. Besides, since you distinguish the *active* and *passive* in every perception, you must do it in that of pain. But how is it possible that pain, be it as little active as you please, should exist in an unperceiving substance? In short, do but consider the point, and then confess ingenuously, whether light and colours, tastes, sounds, &c. are not all equally passions or sensations in the soul. You may indeed call them *external objects*, and give them in words what subsistence you please. But examine your own thoughts, and then tell me whether it be not as I say?

HYLAS. I acknowledge, Philonous, that upon a fair observation of what passes in my mind, I can discover nothing else, but that I am a thinking being, affected with variety of sensations; neither is it possible to conceive how a sensation should exist in an unperceiving substance. But then on the other hand, when I look on sensible things in a different view, considering them as so many modes and qualities, I find it necessary to suppose a material *substratum*, without which they cannot be conceived to exist.

PHILONOUS. *Material substratum* call you it? Pray, by which of your senses came you acquainted with that being?

HYLAS. It is not itself sensible; its modes and qualities only being perceived by the senses.

PHILONOUS. I presume then, it was by reflexion and reason you obtained the idea of it.

HYLAS. I do not pretend to any proper positive idea of it. However I conclude it exists, because qualities cannot be conceived to exist without a support.

PHILONOUS. It seems then you have only a relative notion of it, or that you conceive it not otherwise than by conceiving the relation it bears to sensible qualities.

HYLAS. Right.

PHILONOUS. Be pleased therefore to let me know wherein that relation consists.

HYLAS. Is it not sufficiently expressed in the term *substratum*, or *substance*?

PHILONOUS. If so, the word *substratum* should import, that it is spread under the sensible qualities or accidents.

HYLAS. True.

PHILONOUS. And consequently under extension.

HYLAS. I own it.

PHILONOUS. It is therefore somewhat in its own nature entirely distinct from extension.

HYLAS. I tell you, extension is only a mode, and matter is something that supports modes. And is it not evident the thing supported is different from the thing supporting?

PHILONOUS. So that something distinct from, and exclusive of extension, is supposed to be the *substratum* of extension.

HYLAS. Just so.

PHILONOUS. Answer me, Hylas. Can a thing be spread without extension? or is not the idea of extension necessarily included in *spreading*?

HYLAS. It is.

PHILONOUS. Whatsoever therefore you suppose spread under anything, must have in itself an extension distinct from the extension of that thing under which it is spread.

HYLAS. It must.

PHILONOUS. Consequently every corporeal substance being the *substratum* of extension, must have in itself another extension by which it is qualified to be a *substratum*: and so on to infinity. And I ask whether this be not absurd in itself, and repugnant to what you granted just now, to wit, that the *substratum* was something distinct from, and exclusive of extension.

HYLAS. Ay but, Philonous, you take me wrong. I do not mean that matter is *spread* in a gross literal sense under extension. The word *substratum* is used only to express in general the same thing with *substance*.

PHILONOUS. Well then, let us examine the relation implied in the term *substance*. Is it not that it stands under accidents?

HYLAS. The very same.

PHILONOUS. But that one thing may stand under or support another, must it not be extended?

HYLAS. It must.

PHILONOUS. Is not therefore this supposition liable to the same absurdity with the former?

HYLAS. You still take things in a strict literal sense: that is not fair, Philonous.

PHILONOUS. I am not for imposing any sense on your words: you are at liberty to explain them as you please. Only I beseech you, make me understand something by them. You tell me, matter supports or stands under accidents. How! is it as your legs support your body?

HYLAS. No; that is the literal sense.

PHILONOUS. Pray let me know any sense, literal or not literal, that you understand it in.—How long must I wait for an answer, Hylas?

HYLAS. I declare I know not what to say. I once thought I understood well enough what was meant by matter's supporting accidents. But now the more I think on it, the less can I comprehend it; in short, I find that I know nothing of it.

PHILONOUS. It seems then you have no idea at all, neither relative nor positive of matter; you know neither what it is in itself, nor what relation it bears to accidents.

HYLAS. I acknowledge it.

PHILONOUS. And yet you asserted, that you could not conceive how qualities or accidents should really exist, without conceiving at the same time a material support of them.

HYLAS. I did.

PHILONOUS. That is to say, when you conceive the real existence of qualities, you do withal conceive something which you cannot conceive.

HYLAS. It was wrong I own. But still I fear there is some fallacy or other. Pray what think you of this? It is just come into my head, that the ground of all our mistakes lies in your treating of each quality by itself. Now, I grant that each quality cannot singly subsist without the mind. Colour cannot without extension, neither can figure without some other sensible quality. But as the several qualities united or blended together form entire sensible things, nothing hinders why such things may not be supposed to exist without the mind.

PHILONOUS. Either, Hylas, you are jesting, or have a very bad memory. Though indeed we went through all the qualities by name one after another; yet my arguments, or rather your concessions nowhere tended to prove, that the secondary qualities did not subsist each alone by itself; but that they were not *at all* without the mind. Indeed in treating of figure and motion, we concluded they could not exist without the mind, because it was impossible even in thought to separate them from all secondary qualities, so as to conceive them existing by themselves. But then this was not the only argument made use of upon that occasion. But (to pass by all that hath been hitherto said, and reckon it for nothing, if you will have it so) I am content to put the whole upon this issue. If you can conceive it possible for any mixture or combination of qualities, or any sensible object whatever, to exist without the mind, then I will grant it actually to be so.

HYLAS. If it comes to that, the point will soon be decided. What more easy than to conceive a tree or house existing by itself, independent of, and unperceived by any mind whatsoever? I do at this present time conceive them existing after that manner.

PHILONOUS. How say you, Hylas, can you see a thing which is at the same time unseen?

HYLAS. No, that were a contradiction.

PHILONOUS. Is it not as great a contradiction to talk of *conceiving* a thing which is *unconceived*?

HYLAS. It is.

PHILONOUS. The tree or house therefore which you think of, is conceived by you.

HYLAS. How should it be otherwise?

PHILONOUS. And what is conceived, is surely in the mind.

HYLAS. Without question, that which is conceived is in the mind.

PHILONOUS. How then came you to say, you conceived a house or tree existing independent and out of all minds whatsoever?

HYLAS. That was I own an oversight; but stay, let me consider what led me into it— It is a pleasant mistake enough. As I was thinking of a tree in a solitary place, where no one was present to see it, methought that was to conceive a tree as existing unperceived or unthought of, not considering that I myself conceived it all the while. But now I plainly see, that all I can do is to frame ideas in my own mind. I may indeed conceive in my own thoughts the idea of a tree, or a house, or a mountain, but that is all. And this is far from proving, that I can conceive them *existing out of the minds of all spirits*.

PHILONOUS. You acknowledge then that you cannot possibly conceive, how any one corporeal sensible thing should exist otherwise than in a mind.

HYLAS. I do.

PHILONOUS. And yet you will earnestly contend for the truth of that which you cannot so much as conceive.

HYLAS. I profess I know not what to think, but still there are some scruples remain with me. Is it not certain I see things at a distance? Do we not perceive the stars and moon, for example, to be a great way off? Is not this, I say, manifest to the senses?

PHILONOUS. Do you not in a dream too perceive those or the like objects?

HYLAS. I do.

PHILONOUS. And have they not then the same appearance of being distant?

HYLAS. They have.

PHILONOUS. But you do not thence conclude the apparitions in a dream to be without the mind?

HYLAS. By no means.

PHILONOUS. You ought not therefore to conclude that sensible objects are without the mind, from their appearance or manner wherein they are perceived.

HYLAS. I acknowledge it. But doth not my sense deceive me in those cases?

PHILONOUS. By no means. The idea or thing which you immediately perceive, neither sense nor reason inform you that it actually exists without the mind. By sense you only know that you are affected with such certain sensations of light and colours, &c. And these you will not say are without the mind.

HYLAS. True: but beside all that, do you not think the sight suggests something of *outness* or *distance?*

PHILONOUS. Upon approaching a distant object, do the visible size and figure change perpetually, or do they appear the same at all distances?

HYLAS. They are in a continual change.

PHILONOUS. Sight therefore doth not suggest or any way inform you, that the visible object you immediately perceive, exists at a distance, or will be perceived when you advance farther onward, there being a continued series of visible objects succeeding each other, during the whole time of your approach.

HYLAS. It doth not; but still I know, upon seeing an object, what object I shall perceive after having passed over a certain distance: no matter whether it be exactly the same or no: there is still something of distance suggested in the case.

PHILONOUS. Good Hylas, do but reflect a little on the point, and then tell me whether there be any more in it than this. From the ideas you actually perceive by sight, you have by experience learned to collect what other ideas you will (according to the standing order of Nature) be affected with, after such a certain succession of time and motion.

HYLAS. Upon the whole, I take it to be nothing else.

PHILONOUS. Now is it not plain, that if we suppose a man born blind was on a sudden made to see, he could at first have no experience of what may be suggested by sight.

HYLAS. It is.

PHILONOUS. He would not then according to you have any notion of distance annexed to the things he saw; but would take them for a new set of sensations existing only in his mind.

HYLAS. It is undeniable.

PHILONOUS. But to make it still more plain: Is not *distance* a line turned endwise to the eye?

HYLAS. It is.

PHILONOUS. And can a line so situated be perceived by sight?

HYLAS. It cannot.

PHILONOUS. Doth it not therefore follow that distance is not properly and immediately perceived by sight?

HYLAS. It should seem so.

PHILONOUS. Again, is it your opinion that colours are at a distance?

HYLAS. It must be acknowledged, they are only in the mind.

PHILONOUS. But do not colours appear to the eye as coexisting in the same place with extension and figures?

HYLAS. They do.

PHILONOUS. How can you then conclude from sight, that figures exist without, when you acknowledge colours do not; the sensible appearance being the very same with regard to both?

HYLAS. I know not what to answer.

PHILONOUS. But allowing that distance was truly and immediately perceived by the mind, yet it would not thence follow it existed out of the mind. For whatever is immediately perceived is an idea: and can any *idea* exist out of the mind?

HYLAS. To suppose that, were absurd: but inform me, Philonous, can we perceive or know nothing beside our ideas?

PHILONOUS. As for the rational deducing of causes from effects, that is beside our inquiry. And by the senses you can best tell, whether you perceive anything which is not immediately perceived. And I ask you, whether the things immediately perceived, are other than your own sensations or ideas? You have indeed more than once, in the course of this conversation, declared yourself on those points; but you seem by this last question to have departed from what you then thought.

HYLAS. To speak the truth, Philonous, I think there are two kinds of objects, the one perceived immediately, which are likewise called *ideas*; the other are real things or external objects perceived by the mediation of ideas, which are their images and representations. Now I own, ideas do not exist without the mind; but the latter sort of objects do. I am sorry I did not think of this distinction sooner; it would probably have cut short your discourse.

PHILONOUS. Are those external objects perceived by sense, or by some other faculty?

HYLAS. They are perceived by sense.

PHILONOUS. How! is there anything perceived by sense, which is not immediately perceived?

HYLAS. Yes, Philonous, in some sort there is. For example, when I look on a picture or statue of Julius Cæsar, I may be said after a manner to perceive him (though not immediately) by my senses.

PHILONOUS. It seems then, you will have our ideas, which alone are immediately perceived, to be pictures of external things: and that these also are perceived by sense, inasmuch as they have a conformity or resemblance to our ideas.

HYLAS. That is my meaning.

PHILONOUS. And in the same way that Julius Cæsar, in himself invisible, is nevertheless perceived by sight; real things in themselves imperceptible, are perceived by sense.

HYLAS. In the very same.

PHILONOUS. Tell me, Hylas, when you behold the picture of Julius Cæsar, do you see with your eyes any more than some colours and figures with a certain symmetry and composition of the whole?

HYLAS. Nothing else.

PHILONOUS. And would not a man, who had never known anything of Julius Cæsar, see as much?

HYLAS. He would.

PHILONOUS. Consequently he hath his sight, and the use of it, in as perfect a degree as you.

HYLAS. I agree with you.

PHILONOUS. Whence comes it then that your thoughts are directed to the Roman Emperor, and his are not? This cannot proceed from the sensations or ideas of sense by you then perceived; since you acknowledge you have no advantage over him in that respect. It should seem therefore to proceed from reason and memory: should it not?

HYLAS. It should.

PHILONOUS. Consequently it will not follow from that instance, that anything is perceived by sense which is not immediately perceived. Though I grant we may in one acceptation be said to perceive sensible things mediately by sense: that is, when from a frequently perceived connexion, the immediate perception of ideas by one sense suggests to the mind others perhaps belonging to another sense, which are wont to be connected with them. For instance, when I hear a coach drive along the streets, immediately I perceive only the sound; but from the experience I have had that such a sound is connected with a coach, I am said to hear the coach. It is nevertheless evident, that in truth and strictness, nothing can be *heard* but *sound*: and the coach is not then properly perceived by sense, but suggested from experience. So likewise when we are said to see a red-hot bar of iron; the solidity and heat of the iron are not the objects of sight, but suggested to the imagination by the colour and figure, which are properly perceived by that sense. In short, those things alone are actually and strictly perceived by any sense, which would have been perceived, in case that same sense had then been first conferred on us. As for other things, it is plain they are only suggested to the mind by experience grounded on former perceptions. But to return to your comparison of Cæsar's picture, it is plain, if you keep to that, you must hold the real things or archetypes of our ideas are not perceived by sense, but by some internal faculty of the soul, as reason or memory. I would therefore fain know, what arguments you can draw from reason for the existence of what you call *real things* or *material objects*. Or whether you remember to have seen them formerly as they are in themselves? or if you have heard or read of any one that did.

HYLAS. I see, Philonous, you are disposed to raillery; but that will never convince me.

PHILONOUS. My aim is only to learn from you, the way to come at the knowledge of *material beings*. Whatever we perceive, is perceived either immediately or mediately: by sense, or by reason and reflexion. But as you have excluded sense, pray shew me what reason you have to believe their existence; or what *medium* you can possibly make use of, to prove it either to mine or your own understanding.

HYLAS. To deal ingenuously, Philonous, now I consider the point, I do not find I can give you any good reason for it. But thus much seems pretty plain, that it is at least possible such things may really exist. And as long as there is no absurdity in supposing them, I am resolved to believe as I did, till you bring good reasons to the contrary.

PHILONOUS. What? is it come to this, that you only believe the existence of material objects, and that your belief is founded barely on the possibility of its being true? Then you will have me bring reasons against it: though another would think it reasonable, the proof should lie on him who holds the affirmative. And after all, this very point which you are now resolved to maintain without any reason, is in effect what you have more than once during this discourse seen good reason to give up. But to pass over all this: if I understand you rightly, you say our ideas do not exist without the mind; but that they are copies, images, or representations of certain originals that do.

HYLAS. You take me right.

PHILONOUS. They are then like external things.

HYLAS. They are.

PHILONOUS. Have those things a stable and permanent nature independent of our senses; or are they in a perpetual change, upon our producing any motions in our bodies, suspending, exerting, or altering our faculties or organs of sense.

HYLAS. Real things, it is plain, have a fixed and real nature, which remains the same, notwithstanding any change in our senses, or in the posture and motion of our bodies; which indeed may affect the ideas in our minds, but it were absurd to think they had the same effect on things existing without the mind.

PHILONOUS. How then is it possible, that things perpetually fleeting and variable as our ideas, should be copies or images of anything fixed and constant? Or in other words, since all sensible qualities, as size, figure, colour, &c. that is, our ideas are continually changing upon every alteration in the distance, medium, or instruments of sensation; how can any determinate material objects be properly represented or painted forth by several distinct things, each of which is so different from and unlike the rest? Or if you say it resembles some one only of our ideas, how shall we be able to distinguish the true copy from all the false ones?

HYLAS. I profess, Philonous, I am at a loss. I know not what to say to this.

PHILONOUS. But neither is this all. Which are material objects in themselves, perceptible or imperceptible?

HYLAS. Properly and immediately nothing can be perceived but ideas. All material things therefore are in themselves insensible, and to be perceived only by their ideas.

PHILONOUS. Ideas then are sensible, and their archetypes or originals insensible.

HYLAS. Right.

PHILONOUS. But how can that which is sensible be like that which is insensible? Can a real thing in itself *invisible* be like a *colour*, or a real thing which is not *audible*, be like a *sound*? In a word, can anything be like a sensation or idea, but another sensation or idea?

HYLAS. I must own, I think not.

PHILONOUS. Is it possible there should be any doubt in the point? Do you not perfectly know your own ideas?

HYLAS. I know them perfectly; since what I do not perceive or know, can be no part of my idea.

PHILONOUS. Consider therefore, and examine them, and then tell me if there be anything in them which can exist without the mind: or if you can conceive anything like them existing without the mind.

HYLAS. Upon inquiry, I find it is impossible for me to conceive or understand how anything but an idea can be like an idea. And it is most evident, that *no idea can exist without the mind*.

PHILONOUS. You are therefore by your principles forced to deny the reality of sensible things, since you made it to consist in an absolute existence exterior to the mind. That is to say, you are a downright *sceptic*. So I have gained my point, which was to shew your principles led to scepticism.

HYLAS. For the present I am, if not entirely convinced, at least silenced.

PHILONOUS. I would fain know what more you would require in order to a perfect conviction. Have you not had the liberty of explaining yourself all manner of ways? Were any little slips in discourse laid hold and insisted on? Or were you not allowed to retract or reinforce anything you had offered, as best served your purpose? Hath not everything you could say been heard and examined with all the fairness imaginable? In a word, have you not in every point been convinced out of your own mouth? And if you can at present discover any flaw in any of your former concessions, or think of any remaining subterfuge, any new distinction, colour, or comment whatsoever, why do you not produce it?

HYLAS. A little patience, Philonous. I am at present so amazed to see myself ensnared, and as it were imprisoned in the labyrinths you have drawn me into, that on the sudden it cannot be expected I should find my way out. You must give me time to look about me, and recollect myself.

PHILONOUS. Hark; is not this the college-bell?

HYLAS. It rings for prayers.

PHILONOUS. We will go in then if you please, and meet here again tomorrow morning. In the mean time you may employ your thoughts on this morning's discourse, and try if you can find any fallacy in it, or invent any new means to extricate yourself.

HYLAS. Agreed.

Chapter 9

Selection from *Critique of Pure Reason*

Immanuel Kant

Preface to second edition

WHETHER the treatment of such knowledge as lies within the province of reason does or does not follow the secure path of a science, is easily to be determined from the outcome. For if after elaborate preparations, frequently renewed, it is brought to a stop immediately it nears its goal; if often it is compelled to retrace its steps and strike into some new line of approach; or again, if the various participants are unable to agree in any common plan of procedure, then we may rest assured that it is very far from having entered upon the secure path of a science, and is indeed a merely random groping. In these circumstances, we shall be rendering a service to reason should we succeed in discovering the path upon which it can securely travel, even if, as a result of so doing, much that is comprised in our original aims, adopted without reflection, may have to be abandoned as fruitless.

That logic has already, from the earliest times, proceeded upon this sure path is evidenced by the fact that since Aristotle it has not required to retrace a single step, unless, indeed, we care to count as improvements the removal of certain needless subtleties or the clearer exposition of its recognised teaching, features which concern the elegance rather than the certainty of the science. It is remarkable also that to the present day this logic has not been able to advance a single step, and is thus to all appearance a closed and completed body of doctrine. If some of the moderns have thought to enlarge it by introducing *psychological* chapters on the different faculties of knowledge (imagination, wit, etc.), *metaphysical* chapters on the origin of knowledge or on the different kinds of certainty according to difference in the objects (idealism, scepticism, etc.), or *anthropological* chapters on prejudices, their causes and remedies, this could only arise from their ignorance of the peculiar nature of logical science. We do not enlarge but disfigure sciences, if we allow them to trespass upon one another's territory. The sphere of logic is quite precisely delimited; its sole concern is to give an exhaustive exposition and a strict proof of the formal rules of all thought, whether it be *a priori* or empirical, whatever be its origin or its object, and whatever hindrances, accidental or natural, it may encounter in our minds.

Immanuel Kant, selection from *Critique of Pure Reason*, translated by Norman Kemp-Smith (Macmillan, 1929), reproduced with permission of Palgrave Macmillan.

That logic should have been thus successful is an advantage which it owes entirely to its limitations, whereby it is justified in abstracting—indeed, it is under obligation to do so—from all objects of knowledge and their differences, leaving the understanding nothing to deal with save itself and its form. But for reason to enter on the sure path of science is, of course, much more difficult, since it has to deal not with itself alone but also with objects. Logic, therefore, as a propaedeutic, forms, as it were, only the vestibule of the sciences; and when we are concerned with specific modes of knowledge, while logic is indeed presupposed in any critical estimate of them, yet for the actual acquiring of them we have to look to the sciences properly and objectively so called.

Now if reason is to be a factor in these sciences, something in them must be known *a priori*, and this knowledge may be related to its object in one or other of two ways, either as merely *determining* it and its concept (which must be supplied from

B x.   elsewhere) or as also *making it actual.* The former is *theoretical,* the latter *practical* knowledge of reason. In both, that part in which reason determines its object completely *a priori*, namely, the *pure* part—however much or little this part may contain—must be first and separately dealt with, in case it be confounded with what comes from other sources. For it is bad management if we blindly pay out what comes in, and are not able, when the income falls into arrears, to distinguish which part of it can justify expenditure, and in which[1] line we must make reductions.

Mathematics and physics, the two sciences in which reason yields theoretical knowledge, have to determine their objects *a priori*, the former doing so quite purely, the latter having to reckon, at least partially, with sources of knowledge other than reason.

In the earliest times to which the history of human reason extends, *mathematics,* among that wonderful people, the Greeks, had already entered upon the sure path of science. But it must not be supposed that it was as easy for mathematics as it was for logic—in which reason has to deal with itself alone—to light upon, or rather to

B xi.   construct for itself, that royal road. On the contrary, I believe that it long remained, especially among the Egyptians, in the groping stage, and that the transformation must have been due to a *revolution* brought about by the happy thought of a single man, the experiment which he devised marking out the path upon which the science must enter, and by following which, secure progress throughout all time and in endless expansion is infallibly secured. The history of this intellectual revolution—far more important than the discovery of the passage round the celebrated Cape of Good Hope—and of its fortunate author, has not been preserved. But the fact that Diogenes Laertius, in handing down an account of these matters, names the reputed author of even the least important among the geometrical demonstrations, even of those which, for ordinary consciousness, stand in need of no such proof, does at least show that the memory of the revolution, brought about by the first glimpse of this new path, must have seemed to mathematicians of such outstanding importance as

---

1. [Reading, with Erdmann, *von welchem* for *von welcher.*]

to cause it to survive the tide of oblivion. A new light flashed upon the mind of the first man (be he Thales or some other) who demonstrated the properties of the isosceles triangle. The true method, so he found, was not to inspect what he B xii. discerned either in the figure, or in the bare concept of it, and from this, as it were, to read off its properties; but to bring out what[2] was necessarily implied in the concepts that he had himself formed *a priori*, and had put into the figure in the construction by which he presented it to himself. If he is to know anything with *a priori* certainty he must not ascribe to the figure anything save what necessarily follows from what he has himself set into it in accordance with his concept.

Natural science was very much longer in entering upon the highway of science. It is, indeed, only about a century and a half since Bacon, by his ingenious proposals, partly initiated this discovery, partly inspired fresh vigour in those who were already on the way to it. In this case also the discovery can be explained as being the sudden outcome of an intellectual revolution. In my present remarks I am referring to natural science only in so far as it is founded on *empirical* principles.

When Galileo caused balls, the weights of which he had himself previously determined, to roll down an inclined plane; when Torricelli made the air carry a weight which he had calculated beforehand to be equal to that of a definite volume of water; or in more recent times, when Stahl changed metals into oxides, and oxides B xiii. back into metal, by withdrawing something and then restoring it,[3] a light broke upon all students of nature. They learned that reason has insight only into that which it produces after a plan of its own, and that it must not allow itself to be kept, as it were, in nature's leading-strings, but must itself show the way with principles of judgment based upon fixed laws, constraining nature to give answer to questions of reason's own determining. Accidental observations, made in obedience to no previously thought-out plan, can never be made to yield a necessary law, which alone reason is concerned to discover. Reason, holding in one hand its principles, according to which alone concordant appearances can be admitted as equivalent to laws, and in the other hand the experiment which it has devised in conformity with these principles, must approach nature in order to be taught by it. It must not, however, do so in the character of a pupil who listens to everything that the teacher chooses to say, but of an appointed judge who compels the witnesses to answer questions which he has himself formulated. Even physics, therefore, owes the beneficent revolution in its point of view entirely to the happy thought, that while reason must B xiv. seek in nature, not fictitiously ascribe to it, whatever as not being knowable through reason's own resources has to be learnt, if learnt at all, only from nature, it must adopt as its guide, in so seeking, that which it has itself put into nature. It is thus that the study of nature has entered on the secure path of a science, after having for so many centuries been nothing but a process of merely random groping.

---

2. [Reading, with Adickes, *sondern das* for *sondern durch das.*]

3. I am not, in my choice of examples, tracing the exact course of the history of the experimental method; we have indeed no very precise knowledge of its first beginnings.

Metaphysics is a completely isolated speculative science of reason, which soars far above the teachings of experience, and in which reason is indeed meant to be its own pupil. Metaphysics rests on concepts alone—not, like mathematics, on their application to intuition. But though it is older than all other sciences, and would survive even if all the rest were swallowed up in the abyss of an all-destroying barbarism, it has not yet had the good fortune to enter upon the secure path of a science. For in it reason is perpetually being brought to a stand, even when the laws into which it is seeking to have, as it professes, an *a priori* insight are those that are confirmed by our most common experiences. Ever and again we have to retrace our steps, as not leading us in the direction in which we desire to go. So far, too, are the students of metaphysics from exhibiting any kind of unanimity in their contentions, that metaphysics has rather to be regarded as a battle-ground quite peculiarly suited for those who desire to exercise themselves in mock combats, and in which no participant has ever yet succeeded in gaining even so much as an inch of territory, not at least in such manner as to secure him in its permanent possession. This shows, beyond all questioning, that the procedure of metaphysics has hitherto been a merely random groping, and, what is worst of all, a groping among mere concepts.

B xv.

What, then, is the reason why, in this field, the sure road to science has not hitherto been found? Is it, perhaps, impossible of discovery? Why, in that case, should nature have visited our reason with the restless endeavour whereby it is ever searching for such a path, as if this were one of its most important concerns? Nay, more, how little cause have we to place trust in our reason, if, in one of the most important domains of which we would fain have knowledge, it does not merely fail us, but lures us on by deceitful promises, and in the end betrays us! Or if it be only that we have thus far failed to find the true path, are there any indications to justify the hope that by renewed efforts we may have better fortune than has fallen to our predecessors?

The examples of mathematics and natural science, which by a single and sudden revolution have become what they now are, seem to me sufficiently remarkable to suggest our considering what may have been the essential features in the changed point of view by which they have so greatly benefited. Their success should incline us, at least by way of experiment, to imitate their procedure, so far as the analogy which, as species of rational knowledge, they bear to metaphysics may permit. Hitherto it has been assumed that all our knowledge must conform to objects. But all attempts to extend our knowledge of objects by establishing something in regard to them *a priori*, by means of concepts, have, on this assumption, ended in failure. We must therefore make trial whether we may not have more success in the tasks of metaphysics, if we suppose that objects must conform to our knowledge. This would agree better with what is desired, namely, that it should be possible to have knowledge of objects *a priori*, determining something in regard to them prior to their being given. We should then be proceeding precisely on the lines of Copernicus' primary hypothesis.[4] Failing of satisfactory progress in explaining the

B xvi.

4. [*mit den ersten Gedanken des Kopernikus.*]

movements of the heavenly bodies on the supposition that they all revolved round the spectator, he tried whether he might not have better success if he made the spectator to revolve and the stars to remain at rest. A similar experiment can be tried in metaphysics, as regards the *intuition* of objects. If intuition must conform to the constitution of the objects, I do not see how we could know anything of the latter *a priori*; but if the object (as object of the senses) must conform to the constitution of our faculty of intuition, I have no difficulty in conceiving such a possibility. Since I cannot rest in these intuitions if they are to become known, but must relate them as representations to something as their object, and determine this latter through them, either I must assume that the *concepts*, by means of which I obtain this determination, conform to the object, or else I assume that the objects, or what is the same thing, that the *experience* in which alone, as given objects, they can be known, conform to the concepts. In the former case, I am again in the same perplexity as to how I can know anything *a priori* in regard to the objects. In the latter case the outlook is more hopeful. For experience is itself a species of knowledge which involves understanding; and understanding has rules which I must pre-suppose as being in me prior to objects being given to me, and therefore as being *a priori*. They find expression in *a priori* concepts to which all objects of experience necessarily conform, and with which they must agree. As regards objects which are thought solely through reason, and indeed as necessary, but which can never—at least not in the manner in which reason thinks them—be given in experience, the attempts at thinking them (for they must admit of being thought) will furnish an excellent touchstone of what we are adopting as our new method of thought, namely, that we can know *a priori* of things only what we ourselves put into them.[5]

This experiment succeeds as well as could be desired, and promises to metaphysics, in its first part—the part that is occupied with those concepts *a priori* to which the corresponding objects, commensurate with them, can be given in experience—the secure path of a science. For the new point of view enables us to explain how there can be knowledge *a priori*; and, in addition, to furnish satisfactory proofs of the laws which form the *a priori* basis of nature, regarded as the sum of the objects of experience—neither achievement being possible on the procedure hitherto followed. But this deduction of our power of knowing *a priori*, in the first part of metaphysics, has a consequence which is startling, and which has the appearance

B xvii.

B xviii.

B xix.

---

5. This method, modelled on that of the student of nature, consists in looking for the elements of pure reason in *what admits of confirmation or refutation by experiment*. Now the propositions of pure reason, especially if they venture out beyond all limits of possible experience, cannot be brought to the test through any experiment with their *objects*, as in natural science. In dealing with those *concepts* and *principles* which we adopt *a priori*, all that we can do is to contrive that they be used for viewing objects from two different points of view—on the one hand, in connection with experience, as objects of the senses and of the understanding, and on the other hand, for the isolated reason that strives to transcend all limits of experience, as objects which are thought merely. [Reading, with Adickes, *über alle* for *über*.] If, when things are viewed from this twofold standpoint, we find that there is agreement with the principle of pure reason, but that when we regard them only from a single point of view reason is involved in unavoidable self-conflict, the experiment decides in favour of the correctness of this distinction.

B xix.

of being highly prejudicial to the whole purpose of metaphysics, as dealt with in the second part. For we are brought to the conclusion that we can never transcend the limits of possible experience, though that is precisely what this science is concerned, above all else, to achieve. This situation yields, however, just the very experiment by which, indirectly, we are enabled to prove the truth of this first estimate of our *a priori* knowledge of reason, namely, that such knowledge has to do only with appearances, and must leave the thing in itself[6] as indeed real *per se*, but as not known by us. For what necessarily forces us to transcend the limits of experience and of all appearances is the *unconditioned*, which reason, by necessity and by right, demands in things in themselves, as required to complete the series of conditions. If, then, on the supposition that our empirical knowledge conforms to objects as things in themselves, we find that the unconditioned *cannot be thought without contradiction*, and that when, on the other hand, we suppose that our representation of things, as they are given to us, does not conform to these things as they are in themselves, but that these objects, as appearances, conform to our mode of representation, *the contradiction vanishes*; and if, therefore, we thus find that the unconditioned is not to be met with in things, so far as we know them, that is, so far as they are given to us, but only so far as we do not know them, that is, so far as they are things in themselves, we are justified in concluding that what we at first assumed for the purposes of experiment is now definitely confirmed.[7] But when all progress in the field of the supersensible has thus been denied to speculative reason, it is still open to us to enquire whether, in the practical knowledge of reason, data may not be found sufficient to determine reason's transcendent concept of the unconditioned, and so to enable us, in accordance with the wish of metaphysics, and by means of knowledge that is possible *a priori*, though only from a practical point of view, to pass beyond the limits of all possible experience. Speculative reason has thus at least made room for such an extension; and if it must at the same time leave it empty, yet none the less we are at liberty, indeed we are summoned, to take occupation of it, if we can, by practical data of reason.[8]

B xx.

B xxi.

B xxii.

6. [*die Sache an sich selbst.*]
7. This experiment of pure reason bears a great similarity to what in chemistry is sometimes entitled the experiment of *reduction*, or more usually the *synthetic* process. The *analysis of the metaphysician* separates pure *a priori* knowledge into two very heterogeneous elements, namely, the knowledge of things as appearances, and the knowledge of things in themselves; his *dialectic* combines these two again, in *harmony* with the necessary idea of the *unconditioned* demanded by reason, and finds that this harmony can never be obtained except through the above distinction, which must therefore be accepted.
8. Similarly, the fundamental laws of the motions of the heavenly bodies gave established certainty to what Copernicus had at first assumed only as an hypothesis, and at the same time yielded proof of the invisible force (the Newtonian attraction) which holds the universe together. The latter would have remained for ever undiscovered if Copernicus had not dared, in a manner contradictory of the senses, but yet true, to seek the observed movements, not in the heavenly bodies, but in the spectator. The change in point of view, analogous to this hypothesis, which is expounded in the *Critique*, I put forward in this preface as an hypothesis only, in order to draw attention to the character of these first attempts at such a change, which are always hypothetical. But in the *Critique* itself it will be proved, apodeictically not hypothetically, from the nature of our representations of space and time and from the elementary concepts of the understanding.

Chapter 10

Selection from *Matter and Sense*

Howard Robinson

1. Introduction

IT is generally agreed that material bodies are extended in space; they are three-dimensional objects. In the *Second Meditation* Descartes maintained that being extended was the essence of body, but most philosophers have been inclined to deny that extension alone is what constitutes body, for a body is something more than a bare geometrical figure. A bare geometrical figure is just a volume of empty space, but those spaces in which bodies are located are not empty but *occupied*. A body occupies a space in the sense that while it is located in that space no other material body can be located there: to occupy space is to exclude other bodies. It would seem that bodies must of necessity possess some property or properties over and above their geometrical properties; there must be something further which constitutes their materiality, their power to occupy the space in which they are located.

Locke recognised the need to characterise bodies more fully than they are characterised in Descartes's definition, and he saw that their materiality consisted in their ability to occupy space to the exclusion of other bodies. Consequently he introduced as his other essential and intrinsic characterisation of body the property of impenetrability, which just is the capacity of one body to prevent another body from occupying the space it occupies itself, whilst it occupies that space itself (*Essay*, II, 8, 23).

If we add impenetrability to shape and size, the modes of extension, our conception of body comes to be that of a volume of impenetrability. Most people have felt that this is still an inadequate characterisation of what it is to be a material body, and they point out that impenetrability is a dispositional property only. So, to say that something is impenetrable is to say what it will do or how it will act under certain circumstances, namely when another body of an appropriate sort attempts to occupy the space which it occupies itself. But to say how a thing will sometimes act is not to say what it is—it does not tell us the actual or intrinsic or internal nature of the object which supposedly will so act. It seems that the power, capacity, or disposition of an object to act in a certain way cannot be the whole nature of the object, for that power, capacity or disposition becomes actualised only in those movements when the object is acting in the appropriate way, but the object which possesses the disposition is thought to exist actually and really, and not merely potentially when it stands alone not exercising its disposition and interacting with other objects.

Yet there are those who think that it *is* both coherent and correct to conceive of bodies as volumes of impenetrability—that is, as conglomerations of spatially arranged powers or dispositions. This view has a striking similarity to that of modern science which sees the basic constituents of the material world as being purely dispositional entities which are characterised solely by reference to their ability to act upon and influence things in their vicinity. I shall discuss this view in section 4, but before doing so I shall examine attempts to avoid this purely dispositional conception of body by ascribing further non-dispositional properties to bodies over and above the properties of extension and impenetrability which we have already ascribed to them.

It is worth remarking, as a polemical aside, on Armstrong's attitude to this problem. He is fully aware of the difficulties involved in finding non-relational properties, other than geometrical ones, which it is plausible to impute to matter. He admits that he does not know the answer to this problem but excuses himself 'further consideration of the difficulty, on the grounds that it is a quite separate problem from the problems considered in this book' (1968: 283). In a sense it is a separate problem from that of giving a materialist account of mind; but it is a prior one, not a posterior one, for how can anyone reasonably ask people to accept a counterintuitive account of mind for the sake of furthering the materialist programme when it is uncertain whether there is a coherent concept of matter? We have in Armstrong's attitude to these problems a blatant example of the way in which the fashion for scientific realism obscures first the proper philosophical ordering of problems and consequently the actual situation concerning what is philosophically plausible.

2. Solidity: by impenetrability out of confusion

Those who search for something more categorical than a power or capacity with which to fill the volumes that bodies occupy have often lighted upon the quality of solidity as encountered in tactile experience. Harré, not himself a believer in such a quality, expresses clearly the view of those who do believe in it:

> Solidity is the alleged quality, the possession of which is responsible for the fact that two material things cannot occupy the same place at the same time and is logically connected with impenetrability . . . in that the former is supposed to account for the manifestation of the latter. Solidity is supposed to be the permanent state of a thing which ensures that a thing has the secondary power to resist any other body. (1970: 305)

I shall present three arguments against the view that solidity can figure in this way as the qualitative 'filler' of body.

(1) There are two *prima facie* coherent views concerning the relation between the quality solidity and the power impenetrability. First, it might be argued that in touch we experience a certain quality which we find to be possessed by all and only those bodies which resist penetration. This quality we call solidity because it is constantly conjoined with the power of impenetrability. According to this view one could not claim that the quality is identical with the power but only that it is the quality which give evidence of, or is causally associated with, the presence of the power. The second possible view is that in touch we experience the power called impenetrability: it can thus be called a quality in so far as that term simply signifies that it presents itself as a datum in experience. Neither of these two views will help the materialist out of his problems. In the first case, the quality of solidity does not explain or constitute the power to resist penetration; it is merely contingently connected with its presence and therefore it ought to make sense to imagine either without the other: there is no 'internal' connexion between the two features and, so conceived, solidity would be no better a candidate for what actually constitutes materiality than would, for example, colour, realistically interpreted. In the second case, the assertion is simply that at least one type of power can be directly experienced. This claim in no way alters the fact that impenetrability is just a power and that the world being revealed by touch is a world consisting of volumes of impenetrability. As the quotation from Harré suggests, what those who put their faith in solidity are after is both a quality and a power in a sense which means more than that the power is directly experienceable. What is desired is that the quality is a genuine quality, the power a power, and that the two are necessarily connected such that there could not be a quality like that if it were not also a power: the quality entails and therefore explains the power. It is difficult to *prove* that the importation of synthetic necessities into the phenomenal realm in this way is improper. It does, however, look as if this peculiar desired position seems legitimate only because it is a confusion of the other two: the contingently connected quality from the first becomes confused with the directly experienceable power from the second. Put at its weakest, such synthetic necessities should be objects of suspicion.

(2) For any sense, the same informational value could be embodied in a subjectively different type of sense experience. That this is so is attested by the fact that people with very few of our normal physical senses (e.g. a blind, deaf-mute) can come to understand the same theory about the world as we accept. Now consider the following proposition: what one's tactile experience is like—including what the quality of solidity seems to us to be like—is a function of the type of receptors by which we feel; that is, the receptor type is a causally necessary condition for the experience being as it is. If this proposition is accepted—as surely it must be—in company with the proposition that the quality of solidity as presented in touch is a real quality of objects, we must conclude that anyone whose receptors were fundamentally different, such that his experience was subjectively quite different from ours, would not get an accurate idea of solidity even if his idea possessed all the same formal properties (i.e. those relating to the causal properties of the object) as

ours. This is no better than the dogma which I shall consider in the next section, that it is reasonable to attribute absolute colour to objects. What is more, this felt solidity is meant not merely to be objective, but also to be the ground and explanation of the dispositional property of impenetrability; but if various receptors and, therefore, various experienced qualities could fill the bill of correlating with these causal powers, and each seem the natural experiential facet of solidity to the observer with the relevant type of sense, how can there be this logical or internal connexion with impenetrability? Are we to believe that the subject with our type of sense really apprehends the connexion directly, though others would merely learn it?

(3) Solidity as given in touch is a property of macroscopic objects and of microscopic ones if one takes a Newtonian corpuscularian view of the 'minute parts'. But it is not a property of the microscopic as that is conceived in modern physics: fields, energy and charges are not solid. The line of argument developed in (2) already suggests that it is unreasonable to treat sensible qualities as independent of our senses. We can add to this that science has no role for solidity beyond impenetrability. Therefore, if the ontology of modern science is correct, solidity is not an intrinsic feature of matter.

3. Secondary qualities as the ground of our being

We remain, therefore, in the position of conceiving of objects as nothing more than volumes of impenetrability. Perhaps we can escape from this 'powers' conception of body by ascribing one of the traditional secondary qualities, realistically conceived, to matter. Colour is the best candidate once tactile sensations have been disposed of, for sounds, tastes and smells are qualities emitted by objects, but colours seem to be qualities possessed intrinsically by them: the colour is where the object is and not something *from* the object. However, colours will not plausibly fill the bill either, for two reasons.

(1) We are searching for some property which will give categorical or substantial existence to material bodies; something which can save them from being mere collections of powers. How plausible is it to regard the substantiality of an object as consisting in and resting upon a volume of colour? If we adopt colour as the categorical element in material substance we will thereby be conceiving of bodies as volumes of colour possessing an overall shape and possessing dispositional properties at every point within that volume, such as to correspond to the forces exercised either by the whole volume or specifically at that point within the volume: these powers will be powers of the volume of colour, which will be the object itself. This theory is bizarre but it is not incoherent. The position is made neither better nor worse by including the other secondary qualities as well as colour.

(2) Second, one might deny that secondary qualities are intrinsic to objects except as powers. If this Lockean position is correct, then the qualities cannot play the role of replacing powers as the most substantial element in body, for they will themselves only be powers. There are at least three reasons for denying that

secondary qualities are intrinsic. First, if one rejects naive realism, it will follow that secondary qualities can be intrinsic in objects only at the price of allowing a dual instantiation; behind the read of my sense-datum is the red of a physical object. This dual instantiation is unreasonable in the case of secondary qualities in a way that it is not for primary qualities for a variety of reasons. One is that secondary qualities are never assigned a causal role (except, perhaps, as affecting minds), such roles always devolving upon the primary features of the world. The postulation of such qualities is, therefore, scientifically otiose. Our second reason for denying objective status to secondary qualities also functions as an additional argument under the first against dual instantiation. Smart has pointed out that secondary qualities do not bear any very essential relation to the primary qualities that underlie them (1963: 70–1). So the light waves that make something appear green or the particles the emission of which from an object make it smell a certain way will not be essentially similar groups, but collections of essentially heterogeneous waves or molecules which happen, because of the structure of our senses, to affect us in the same way. This suggests that the qualities as we sense them are the production of the idiosyncrasies of our senses and not objective features of the world. Finally, the second argument used against the perceivability of solidity works also as an argument against the objectivity of all sensed qualities. If it is the structural features of our experience that determine the usefulness of the senses, not their qualitative ones, and if, therefore, any structurally similar qualities would seem to be equally correct there can be no good ground for attributing the quality as sensed to the external world.

4. Potentiality and vacuity

We started with a purely geometrical conception of body; then we filled it with impenetrability. Then, feeling dissatisfaction with such a dispositional filling for the physical cake we tried solidity, hoping that that would act as the ground of the impenetrability. After the failure of this attempt we tried to fill body with colour but found this implausible. Consequently we are left with a conception of body which makes it spatial and dispositional only. This line of reduction of matter to something merely dispositional does not only apply to the Lockean or atomist picture of the physical world. More modern conceptions of matter are overtly and directly dispositional. Nowadays we are presented with an ontology which is avowedly devoid of quality, containing only quantitively discernible forces, fields and energies, all of which are entities existing only as forms of disposition, power and influence. Here we arrive at something of a paradox. On the one hand, those philosophers who, by arguments similar to our own, have reached this attenuated view of matter have tended to fall into idealism, regarding a world of powers as too insubstantial to command belief. On the other hand, this is the theory that physical science advocates. It is, therefore, not surprising that some realist philosophers of science have attempted to defend this etiolated conception of matter. If the arguments in the previous sections of this chapter are sound, the materialist and the non-idealist are obliged, the former to show that the view that there is nothing but such powers is not incoherent, and the latter to show that it is not incoherent to hold that everything material is so constituted. I hope to prove that they both fail to escape from this predicament.

Harré drawing on the theories of the eighteenth century Croatian priest and diplomat, Boscovitch, expresses the general form of the powers ontology as follows:

Every fundamental theory must, as expressed in the language of physics, be a field theory. (1970: 313)

The ultimate entities of the world, as we can understand it, must be point sources of mutual influence, that is centres of power distributed in space. They are perpetually redistributing themselves in space, that is, they are continuously changing their spatial relations, and, consequently, their mutual influences, since these are distance dependent. (ibid.: 308)

Unfortunately, little is said about the nature of powers and certain problems and limitations inherent in the notion thereby go neglected. Starting from the intuition that any real entity must possess a determinate nature we can generate an argument against the ontology of powers.[1]

(1) Every real object must possess a determinate nature.

(2) The nature of any power P is given by what would constitute its actualisation.

Therefore,

(3) If P is a real object it must be a power to a determinate actualisation.

(4) As P must have a determinate actualisation and the determinacy of a power rests upon the determinacy of its potential effect (that is, given (1), (2) and (3)) then if a power Q is the actualisation of P, the determinacy of P will depend upon the determinacy of Q; that is, of Q's actualisation.

It is plain that this principle leads by generalisation to a regress such that

(5) The list of effects constituting the determinate and complete nature of P will be finite only if the list contains (and thereby terminates at) an effect which is not a power.

However,

(6) An infinite list constitutes indeterminacy.

Therefore,

(7) A determinate power must issue at some point in its chain of consequences in an effect which is not itself a power.

---

1. The following is, I think, a fuller version of what is suggested in Holt, 1976–7. He argues that 'The idea that "bundles of causes" simply act on other bundles of causes is surely logically insupportable since the notion of any cause is incomplete without the specification of its effect' (p. 23).

It is necessary to clarify the notion of a determinate actualisation, as it relates to powers. What must be determinate is not the general potentiality of a power, but the state brought about by it on any given occasion of its actualisation. Thus it is conceivable that P is the power to make any white thing within six inches of it coloured. This may be a determinable power in that it randomly makes things different colours, and therefore the nature of the power can only be given generically as the power to make them coloured. But in the case of any given actualisation of this power the patient object must become a determinate colour. This is the sense in which a power must be determinate, namely that the state of affairs that constitutes its actualisation in any given case must be a determinate state of affairs.

As a further difficulty, it might be objected that the statement that the actualisation of something consists in a power is itself ambiguous. It might be said the 'The actualisation of P is to produce power Q' suggests that what P produces is some new power state, whereas what it would have to mean to cover the Boscovitchian scheme would be that P is the power to alter the location of Q and that the alteration could be precisely specified; thus it is not the power itself that is altered but only its location. But this answer will not suffice, for it must be possible in principle to specify the state brought about by the power, for the reason given above, and that state is the location at some place *of power* Q. To say that one alters a place is either nonsense or incomplete, for one only alters the place of something, and therefore a specification of what has been moved is essential for a determinate specification of what has been done.

However, it has still not been made clear what counts as an adequately non-potential specification of a state of affairs. Suppose a power to have as its actualisation the production of a change of shape in a certain object, shape being a paradigm of a quality and not a power, and that object possesses a certain power. Would the first power be determinate in virtue of the production of the quality change, or would the possession of the potentiality by the object entail that its determinacy require determinacy of the power of the object, that being part of the total state produced by the initial power? To set the stronger requirement would mean that a world in which all objects possessing qualities also possess powers would be as subject to the regress as a world which consisted solely of powers; and this is counter intuitive. The relevant factor is that feature of the resulting state of affairs which is nomically related to the power; that is, that feature which the power is designated as a power to produce. If this is qualitative then the regress is terminated, unless, as with location, the quality in question can only be completely expressed by reference to something further and that turns out to be a power.

Having explained the argument to (5) we must consider the most crucial controversial premise in the argument, (6). It might be denied that the regress is vicious on the grounds that, at any given step, one can say what the next power is, after a fashion—one merely can never finish the process. However, this cannot be virtuous. If a determinate conception of the power requires the specification of an infinite series of events, it is in principle an incompletable conception; but if a concept is in principle incompletable in this way it is indeterminate. (I said 'incompletable *in this way*' because the incompletability of, for example, *pi* is different, for in that case a definite point is being approached, whereas in the case of the powers it is precisely such a definiteness of end that is missing.) This can be seen intuitively if we consider a regressive specification of a power: P is the power to produce (alter) a power to produce (alter) a power to produce . . . Such a formula seems to tell us nothing about what is actually done.

I fear that at this point we shall be faced with objections from the philosophy of allusion and metaphor as practised by some philosophers of science. Using the magical net of holism they will try to fish sense out of a sea of nonsense. We will be told that the absolute interdependence of terms in empirical theory in no way impugns the intelligibility of the overall web of theory, which is self-sustaining, or is sustained by its place in scientific practice. Unfortunately, vagueness is of the essence of this viewpoint and it can, therefore, present no opposition to what I hope are the precise arguments given above. Indeed, the above argument shows that interdependence has its limits. PME showed (Robinson 1982: 6.2) that interdependence alone was not enough, requiring also empirical demonstration; the argument above shows that some concepts must not be essentially relative in their characterisation. These theses are not identical for some may hold that certain powers are demonstrable, *qua* powers, although one is likely to hold that the demonstrable and the non-relative are co-extensive. As argued in Robinson (1982: 5.5) none of this shows that there are concepts which we could have without a framework of grammar—that is another matter—but it does impose constraints on elements within that framework.

The argument, therefore, is sound. We have established that the world of powers is logically dependent on the world (real or potential) of categorical properties—although in nature, of course, the dependence may run the other way, as the actualities depend upon the powers for their generation. But what sort of thing are these actual or categorical entities? According to Harré they are sensible qualities; that is, such things at least as colours, sounds and smells (1970: 303). He is surely right in seeing the sensible qualities as the obvious candidates for actuality: the phenomenal realm is that area which cannot be reduced to potentialities. Bearing in mind the conclusion that we have reached regarding the mind-dependent nature of secondary qualities, we can say that the only categorical entities that can end the regress are mental states with sensible qualities as their objects.

In the context of the overall enterprise of this essay it is worth noticing that this entails that no one who believes that the physical world consists entirely of powers can be a materialist, upon pain of vacuity. For if mental states are only physical and therefore themselves only powers and lacking categorical experiential content the regress could never be terminated. It is indeed a happy coincidence that Armstrong adopts the view that all dispositions must have a categorical base (1968: 86). The arguments of sections 1–3 suggest that it is also fortunate for him that he did not try to say what that base could ultimately be. If we take the ontology of modern science, however, to be simply one of powers, it is interesting to note that this is incompatible with a materialist theory of mind.

It seems that determinacy in a power consists in its ability to contribute, directly or at a remove, to mentality. So if all physical entities or properties are ultimately powers it follows that they must all be able, in the appropriate context, so to contribute. This conclusion manages to be, on the one hand, interesting but, on the other, apparently very weak. It is interesting because it gives us a concept of matter analogous to phenomenalism, for it places the essence of matter in its ability to produce experience. It is apparently weak because there would appear to be no physical power which could not, in the appropriate context, causally contribute to mentality. This is so because there is no reason to limit the context to the actual world; that a given power could make the appropriate contribution in some world would be enough to establish its determinacy. But for any given power we could imagine some further powers in the company of which it would produce mentality. There might even, therefore, be a world which did not possess the capacity to produce mental states, but each element in which could so contribute in the context of different powers than those with which it actually shared that particular world. Thus any power, specified according to its physical potentialities after the manner of some scientific theory, will also trivially possess a mental potentiality realisable in some possible world. However, further examination will show that this weakness in our conclusion is apparent only, not real.

We have spoken so far of the requirement that each physical power should be able to make some contribution to the production of mentality. This suggests that the same power has two aspects, one concerned with its physical effects, the other with its mental. But because mentality is a 'dangler', not in any way deducible from physical theory, these two aspects cannot be regarded as functions of the same power, for two ranges of effects can be regarded as effects of the same power only when there is one law or formula which describes both. For example, suppose a field has the power to make an object weighing x lbs and situated a inches away move towards the centre of the field at 1 m.p.h.: and also the power to make an object weighing $2x$ lbs and $2a$ inches away move at 0.25 m.p.h. In such a case there is one clear formula at work relating distance from the centre, weight and acceleration. But if the laws governing the production of mental states cannot be integrated into those describing the other operations of matter then the mental power cannot be expressed as an aspect of the same power as the other physical powers.

It is important to remember that we are talking here about powers as such and not objects that possess powers. Naturally, one object might possess two different powers, but on the ontology we are considering the powers are the only objects and cannot, therefore, be treated as the owners of them: one power, that is, cannot be said to be the owner of two entirely discrete potentialities for two discrete potentialities simply are two powers, not one.

Using M for mental and P for physical we can say that the M power is emergent with respect to the P power. This, however, can be taken in two ways. Given that basic physical atoms contribute to the production of mind only by combining with many other such atoms in very complex structures it might be said that the M power is an emergent property of such complex physical structures; that is, that individual atomic P powers do not have a correlated M power. On the other hand, one might claim that, because each P power can make contributions in different combinations to producing different mental states, it has a correlated M power in its own right. (It would, of course, be a pre-condition for this latter view that the range of contributions to mentality of which the power was capable could be expressed in a systematic way. Otherwise there would be no determinate formula for the atomic M power and the same objection as we raised against consolidating the M and P powers would operate against unifying the atomic M power.) The first alternative is the natural one to choose, for ascribing some M power to each atomic P power as its companion, contingently associated with it, seems bizarre. However, we shall see that our opponent is in fact forced to adopt this remarkable view. For suppose that we choose the first alternative, so that M powers emerge into existence from P powers only when the latter are combined in complex structures. It will follow that the P powers should be able to exist without the M powers and this has already been shown to be incoherent. This follows in virtue of the following general principle: if some phenomenon A is emergent with respect to a realm B then the intelligibility or coherence of B (not merely the being-known of B) cannot rest upon the fact that it produces A. This is so because if A is emergent it is only contingently connected to B and B's internal laws, and being only so connected it can make no essential contribution to the sense or meaningfulness of talk about B.

Referring back to what was proved above, the point can be made in a slightly different form. Avoiding a vicious regress of powers required that any given power be part of a chain of powers which ends in the possible production (as the actualisation of the final power in the chain) of something categorical. But if there is a nomological chasm between the physical and mental no series of physical powers can end in this way, for the production of mentality can never be expressed as an aspect of a physical potentiality.

We can dismiss, therefore, the theory that mental potentiality is emergent with physical complexity; we must choose the other option, namely that mental potentiality exists together with physical at the atomic level. It has already been argued that one single power cannot be both an M and a P power, therefore it follows that there must be two types of basic atom. The question is whether we can characterise their relations and mutual influence in such a way that the ability of the M power to produce actual mental states can bring to an end the regress of P powers. We shall see that this cannot be done.

First, let us notice what a strange world we are postulating. *Prima facie* it is much more natural to think of M power as emerging with physical complexity, for the nature of atomic M powers is extremely opaque. They will not be observable or detectable among P powers for, having no P potential themselves, they could never influence any instrument of observation. We could only tell that they were present when a mental state was produced, and this would not be a means of detecting individual M powers, for more than one would be required to produce a mental state.

This follows because if one were sufficient and they existed independently of P power structures, it would follow that all M powers were always producing their appropriate mental state irrespective of whether an appropriate body was present. Assuming that minds exist only in conjunction with bodies of a certain sort it must be the case that the right combination of M powers comes about only as a result of particular combinations of P powers. However, this supposes interaction between M and P powers, in the form of the ability of P powers to determine the combination of M powers and such interaction is not possible. For it to be possible it would have to be the case that M powers could be influenced by P powers. But being influenced by a P power involves a form of P potentiality. This passive power cannot be regarded as an aspect of the mental potentiality and is therefore not a property of the M power. Nor can this passive power of the M power be dismissed on the grounds that it is merely passive and the real potentiality be attributed to the P power that influences it, for even if the effect that P powers had on M powers could be expressed in the same formula as that which described their influence on other P powers (e.g. as the power to change their location in a certain way) this would not of itself wholly explain the influence. There could not be a power which was a power to influence the location of something irrespective of the nature of that thing (though it might be able to influence everything that in fact existed), for natural influence is relative to the nature of the thing influenced. Fire, for example, will only burn what is combustible, and how something is determines whether it will burn just as much as the nature of fire determines whether that thing will burn. Passive potentiality cannot, therefore, be regarded as a mere privation.

On this ground we can say that interaction between pre-existing M and P powers is impossible; therefore neither the emergence of M potentiality nor the pre-existence of M powers infuses content into the notion a physical world consisting entirely of powers.

5. The last ditch: a nameless residue

One position remains to someone who believes in matter. He might abandon the ontology of bare powers and give those powers an owner of which we can know nothing. He might, that is, postulate as unknown and in principle unknowable residue which stands to the power rather as a magnet stands to its magnetic field—that is, as something categorical at its centre. This would be rather like Price's spatial occupants (1932: 275ff 14) or the Lockean (or supposedly Lockean) substratum.[2] Such a residue could not, of course, possess any knowable quality for the reasons given above for not allowing qualities to matter. But its nature could be regarded as analogous to an object with sensible qualities. This residue would be a very strange type of entity. Berkeley's scoff at substratum that it is nothing but the bare idea of being

---

2. *Essay*, II, 23, 2. For a persuasive statement of the view that Locke did not believe in the substratum see Ayers, 1975.

itself would be appropriate here: it would be nothing other than the idea of bare physical being. But though the idea might be disreputable it might do to save matter for those who are desperate in that cause. The introduction of a residue, which will be a categorical entity rather than a power, removes the need for the M potentiality, for the actual effect which terminates the regress of powers to affect powers could be the relocation of a categorical residue. The picture of interaction that follows this scheme would be that the P power moved the residual owner of the power (see diagram). As we finally have the owner of powers, the absence of which seemed so damaging in previous arguments, the P power can, by moving the residue, move the influences that belong to it.

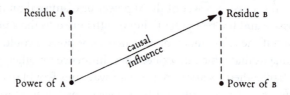

   Whether the postulation of a residue is helpful depends on the relationship that is taken to hold between powerfields and their owners. If an object A possesses a field F and A is moved, is the consequent movement of F a causal consequence of the movement of A, or something stronger? If the movement of F were only a causal consequence of the movement of A then A might have moved and F remained where it was. If we try to avoid this by saying that A has a power to move F, as F itself is a power of A, we are moving along the first steps of a regress. On the other hand, if A moves F, but not by some further power, then the causal connexion between the motions of A and F will be one of bare conjunction; it would be bizarre for someone operating with an ontology in which real potentiality was the only detectable feature to import Humean conjunction in this way. If the residue is to be of any help, therefore, we must be able to regard the connexion between it and the fields of power that it possesses as more than causal. I find this difficult to do, given that the field occupies a different area from that occupied by its owner. The field of a residue, that is, can never be regarded as constitutive of it in the way that, for example, the surface of something can be so regarded. The remaining of the residue or of any field owner in the same intrinsic state (whatever that may be) seems to be compatible with the presence or absence of a given field.

   In short, the situation is this. We introduced the residue to be the owner of the power in the belief that the movement of a power would be explained by the movement of the residue to which it belonged and of which it is, in some sense, a property. This seemed a reasonable thing to believe, because it was assumed to be necessarily the case that whenever something is moved so are its properties. However, whilst this applies in an intuitively obvious way to most qualities it is not obvious that it applies to powers. It is not, for example, true of relational properties.

An object moved which previously had the property of being two inches away from my hand will probably lose that property on being moved. Although real potentialities are not meant to be purely relational properties, like the spatial relation in our example, neither are they intrinsic to the object in the way that its shape or surfaces or mass are. That is, it makes no sense to suggest than an object might move and leave its shape, surfaces or mass behind it; but it does seem to make sense to think of a magnet being removed and its field of influence remaining, or its field moving away from it. What seems conceivable for the magnet should be conceivable for a residue if that is thought of in the only way it can be, namely on analogy with a quality-possessing centre to a field. It seems, then, that someone who accepts residues must either import bare Humean conjunction to explain their connexion with their powers, maintaining that this counts as more than a coincidental connexion, or think of the fields as essentially tied to their centres in a manner which defies intuition. Whether either of these options really makes sense I would not like to say. I am sure that they represent view-points which no one would happily settle for. But we are now dealing with extremely peculiar and etiolated concepts. For this reason absolute refutation is not possible. But the defence of obscurity and possible, but not demonstrable, vacuity is not a very impressive defence. Only a thin streak of verificationism is required in one's temperament to lead one to lose patience with such a concept of matter. The belief in mind-independent matter turns out to be too unclear to be clearly refuted. Dogmatism has its last ditch; it can be refuted only if it hedges by trying to work a compromise with the demands of intelligibility.

References

Armstrong, D. M. 1968. *A Materialist Theory of the Mind*, London: Routledge and Kegan Paul.

Ayers, M. R. 1975. Power and substance in Locke, *Philosophical Quarterly*, 25, 1–27, London: Routledge.

Harré R. 1970. *Principles of Scientific Thinking*, London: Macmillan.

Holt, P. J. 1976–7. Causality and our conception of matter, *Analysis*, 37, 20–9.

Locke, J. *Essay Concerning Human Understanding*, ed. A. C. Fraser, 1969, New York: Dover.

Price, H. H. 1932. *Perception*, London: Methuen.

Robinson, H. 1982. *Matter and Sense*, Cambridge.

Smart, J. J. C. 1963. *Philosophy and Scientific Realism*, London: Routledge and Kegan Paul.

Chapter 11
Realism

Michael Dummett

I was told at school that the scholastic doctrine known as realism, and opposed to nominalism, had nothing whatever to do with that opinion known as realism in later philosophy, and opposed to idealism. It was only much later that it struck me that the two disputes bore to one another an analogy which made the use of the same designation 'realism' for one side in each of them more than a pure equivocation: although the subject-matter of the two controversies differed, there was a resemblance in the form of the disputes. I wish to consider a number of such disputes over the propriety of realism concerning a certain subject-matter, and to describe in detail the analogies and differences between them: it is not my purpose here to achieve a resolution of these disputes.

I shall adopt the terminological expedient of treating 'realism' as a common noun, capable of a plural, so that I can speak of 'a realism' instead of having always to say 'realism concerning a given subject-matter'.

A dispute over a realism may be expressed by asking whether or not there really exist entities of a particular type—universals, or material objects: or, again, it may be asked, not whether they exist, but whether they are among the ultimate constitutents of reality. From this second formulation it is apparent that opposition to realism often takes the form of a species of reductionism: certain entities are not among the ultimate constituents of reality if they can be 'reduced' to entities of other types. For reasons which I shall set out later, however, I do not wish to adopt 'reductionism' as a generic term for the view opposed to realism, but shall use instead the colourless term 'anti-realism'.

A dispute over a realism can be described linguistically as being over the question whether certain expressions—general terms, or names of material objects— genuinely have a reference. This corresponds to the simpler of the two formulations in the material mode, namely that which describes the dispute as concerning the existence of entities of a certain type. It is, however, clear that neither of these two formulations is entirely happy: phenomenalism seems to be better described as the view that material objects are reducible to (constructions out of) sense-data, than as the view that there are no such things as material objects or that names of material objects do not really stand for anything. Moreover, in some cases I want to consider, such as realism about the past or about the future, the question does not turn on the referential character of any *terms* at all; and in at least one other, that of platonism in mathematics, the concentration on the reference of terms seems to me to deflect the dispute from what it is really concerned with; as Kreisel has remarked, the issue concerning platonism relates, not to the existence of mathematical objects, but to the objectivity of mathematical statements.

For these reasons, I shall take as my preferred characterisation of a dispute between realists and anti-realists one which represents it as relating, not to a class of entities or a class of terms, but to a class of *statements*, which may be, e.g., statements about the physical world, statements about mental events, processes or states, mathematical statements, statements in the past tense, statements in the future tense, etc. This class I shall, from now on, term 'the disputed class'. Realism I characterise as the belief that statements of the disputed class possess an objective truth-value, independently of our means of knowing it: they are true or false in virtue of a reality existing independently of us. The anti-realist opposes to this the view that statements of the disputed class are to be understood only by reference to the sort of thing which we count as evidence for a statement of that class. That is, the realist holds that the meanings of statements of the disputed class are not directly tied to the kind of evidence for them that we can have, but consist in the manner of their determination as true or false by states of affairs whose existence is not dependent on our possession of evidence for them. The anti-realist insists, on the contrary, that the meanings of these statements are tied directly to what we count as evidence for them, in such a way that a statement of the disputed class, if true at all, can be true only in virtue of something of which we could know and which we should count as evidence for its truth. The dispute thus concerns the notion of truth appropriate for statements of the disputed class; and this means that it is a dispute concerning the kind of *meaning* which these statements have.

I do not expect this characterisation to be fully explanatory, nor do I claim it as wholly accurate: my intention will become plainer when I turn, as I shall do in a moment, to the examples which I wish to consider. I wish before that to remark that the characterisation of a dispute over realism that I have just given does not fit every dispute which could be characterised in one of the ways with which I began. I pointed out that the present characterisation is in one respect more general than the earlier ones (in that it applies, as the earlier ones did not, to realism about the past). Now it might seem obvious that anything which, under any of the earlier characterisations, is a dispute over a realism, is one under the present characterisation: since, if we have a dispute over the existence of certain entities or over whether certain terms have a reference, we can represent it in my way simply by taking the disputed class to consist of statements about those entities or containing those terms: if, e.g. the entities are material objects, then the disputed class will consist of statements containing terms for material objects.

Nevertheless, the fact that the characterisation I have adopted is, in another respect, less general can be brought out in the case of realism about universals. It does not appear that the anti-realists in this case—the nominalists—who denied the existence of universals and the referential character of general terms, were anti-realists in the sense of the characterisation I have now adopted: that they were necessarily committed to a different view of the kind of truth possessed by statements containing general terms (that is by all statements) from that of the realists. It is not, of course, simply a matter of whether or not the truth of a statement of the disputed class is something objective. The realist and the anti-realist may agree that it is an objective matter whether, in the case of any given statement of the class, the criteria we use for judging such a statement to be true are satisfied: the difference between them lies in the fact that, for the anti-realist, the truth of the statement can only consist in the satisfaction of these criteria, whereas, for the realist, the statement can be true even though we have no means of recognising it as true. A nominalist does not seem to be committed to being an anti-realist in this sense: for this reason I shall not use realism about universals as an example. (Frege of course held that our statements cannot have an objective truth-value unless their constituents, including predicative and relational expressions, have an objective reference; but that the mistake in the realist view of universals consisted in taking predicates as standing for objects, i.e. entities capable of being referred to by means of singular terms. I think his solution to be correct, and this gives me another reason for regarding this case as very different from those I want to discuss.)

Among the cases I do want to consider are: realism about material objects, opposition to which has traditionally taken the form of phenomenalism; realism about the theoretical entities of science, which is opposed by scientific positivism; realism about mathematical statements, for which I shall use the standard name 'platonism', employed (not altogether happily) by Bernays and Quine, opposition to which is known as 'constructivism'; realism about mental states, events and processes, to which is opposed behaviourism; realism about the past and about the future. Before describing any of these in detail, however, I want to introduce one which is not a live dispute, one where very few people would seriously adopt a realist attitude, which can serve as an elementary example: the case of statements about a person's character. For the sake of this example, I assume that there is no vagueness in the characterisation of human actions—for instance, that no disagreement can arise over the application to a particular act of the predicate 'brave'. I shall also ignore the fact that the performance of a single act possessing a certain quality is not sufficient for the ascription of the corresponding character-trait to the agent—e.g. that the performance of a single brave act is not enough to guarantee that we can say without qualification that the agent is a brave man: I thus in effect assume that no one ever acts out of character, and that no one's character ever changes. Let us now suppose that we ask of a particular man whether he is brave or not. If he is still alive, his future behaviour is relevant, so let us suppose that he is now dead. If he ever performed a brave action, then he was brave; if he was ever in a situation of danger in which he did not act bravely, then he was not brave: but suppose that he led a very sheltered life, and throughout its whole course was never in a situation of danger. Then, we may say, the content of the statement, 'He was brave', reduces to that of the counterfactual conditional, 'If he had been in a situation of danger, he would have acted bravely', and that of the statement, 'He was not brave', to that of the opposite counterfactual, 'If he had been in a situation of danger, he would not have acted bravely'. (In general, for any counterfactual conditional, I shall call 'the opposite one' that which has the same antecedent and the contradictory consequent.)

Now it is beyond question that we might have adequate grounds for asserting one or other of these counterfactuals: bravery might invariably accompany other qualities which the man had displayed, or cowardice might run in families according to some definite pattern. But it is clear that it might be the case that, however much we knew about the behaviour of this man and of others, we might never know anything which we should regard as a ground for asserting either counterfactual. I shall make the assumption that a counterfactual conditional could not be simply true: if it is true, it must be true in virtue of the truth of some categorical statement. This principle is intuitively compelling, and I shall not here take time to argue for it: its status is, in fact, a slightly curious one.

It is tempting to generalise for arbitrary forms of statement the notion of being 'simply true': an attempt would be to say that a true statement is simply true if there is nothing in virtue of which we can say that it is true other than the fact which it itself states; this was the idea that lay behind the discussions whether there are disjunctive facts, negative facts, etc. However, it is clear that this definition would need refinement if we are to be capable of asserting any statements to be simply true, and it is not obvious how to provide this.

In the present context, it is no objection to the principle that a counterfactual, if true, must be true in virtue of the truth of some categorical (i.e. non-conditional) statement that there is disagreement as to which statements are genuinely categorical: for these disagreements reflect differences between a realist and an anti-realist view of the statements concerned, and therefore the application of the principle is not in doubt within the framework of a given realist or anti-realist position.

Our assumption is, then, that a counterfactual cannot be simply true, in the sense that, if true at all, it must be true in virtue of the truth of some statement not involving the non-material conditional. Now if we hold further that counterfactual statements about a man's behaviour in some supposititious circumstances can be true only in virtue of facts of the kind which we should count as grounds for asserting them, say facts about people's actual behaviour, then we shall have to admit that it might be the case that neither one of our pair of counterfactuals was true, since there was nothing in virtue of which either was true. Since we have agreed that, in the case in which this man never encountered danger, the statement, 'He was brave' reduces to the counterfactual, and its negation to the opposite counterfactual, we shall conclude that it may be the case that the statement, 'He was brave', is neither true nor false (taking its falsity to consist in the truth of its negation).

In arriving at this conclusion, we have rejected a realist view of statements about character: the only way of resisting the conclusion, otherwise than by allowing that a counterfactual could be simply true, would be to adopt such a realist view. On a realist view, the truth of the counterfactual must indeed rest on the truth of some categorical, but this categorical need not be a statement about anyone's behaviour. On the contrary, the statement, 'If he had encountered danger, he would have acted bravely', if true, would be true in virtue of the truth of the statement, 'He was brave': this latter statement would now be thought of, not as explained in part by reference to the use of the counterfactual, judged true or false by what we know of his and others' behaviour, but as relating directly to some psychic mechanism which determines the man's behaviour in the situations he encounters. On this realist view, statements about character relate to something which we mass, or that, say, two strips of carpet either are or are not of the same length, independently of whether we have applied the test for mass or equality of length. Of course, not every possible test is regarded as revealing information of this sort, i.e. as being capable of conferring sense on a form of statement whose instances will then have a truth-value independent of the execution of the test. We should not, for example, use the result of a single game of chess as a criterion for the truth of statements of the form, 'X is a better chess-player than Y', construed in the way described. What is lacking in this case is a certain kind of background, a background which we may vaguely describe as a theory with predictive power.

Discussion of measurable or dispositional *properties* obviously shades off into discussion of theoretical *objects* such as electrons. For scientific realism, a scientific theory (containing references to objects not directly observable) purports to reveal what the world is really like in itself, as opposed to how it presents itself to us, with our particular observational capacities, conceptual equipment and location in time and space. For a scientific positivist, however, a scientific theory is simply a convenient device allowing us to impose a pattern on the otherwise bewildering variety of laws connecting observables with observables, and its whole content consists in the laws of this kind which can be derived from it. The argument that the theory or model necessarily contains features not directly correlated with observation (since otherwise it would refer only to what is observable), and therefore, by setting up new correlations with these features, we may be led to discover new laws, the positivist may readily accept as not conflicting essentially with his position: he can allow that a theory has, besides its actual content, a certain suggestive power.

Where time is concerned, the appeal to pictorial images is especially compelling. Since Aristotle, philosophers have disagreed as to whether it is proper to ascribe present truth or falsity to statements about the future; and those who adopt the anti-realist position that it is not form to themselves a picture of the temporal process on which, although both past and present states of affairs are already in existence, future states of affairs are simply not yet *there* to render our statements about them true or false. A vivid description of such a picture is given in Broad's *Scientific Thought*. There are, however, two versions of this anti-realist view about the future. According to one, all future-tense statements must be interpreted as rendered true or false, if at all, only by present tendencies and present intentions. On this view, the only admissible use of the future tense which we have is that employed in announcements of the form, 'The marriage between X and Y will not now take place'—a use which permits one to say, 'It *was* going to occur, but it is no longer going to'. According to the other version of anti-realism about the future, we do have another use of future-tense statements, a use according to which they are not made definitively true or false by anything in the present, but will be rendered true or false at the time to which they refer: nevertheless, since they are not *yet* either true or false, the law of excluded middle does not hold for them.

Most philosophers would adopt a realist view of statements about the past; an exception is provided by Ayer in *Language, Truth and Logic*, where he argues that a statement about the past can be true only if there is something in the present (or future) which we count as (conclusive) evidence for it. Yet the justification of the realist view has occasioned much dispute. It seems natural to say that we can never have, now or in the future, direct evidence for the truth of a statement about what is now past, since all our evidence at any time must consist in what is the case at that time: it therefore appears to follow, as Russell concluded, that a Cartesian doubt about the past is unanswerable. Now the usual way of philosophers with a Cartesian doubt is to declare it senseless: but this would apparently involve us in holding an anti-realist view of statements about the past, the view, namely, that a statement about the past, if true, can be true only in virtue of what is or will be the case, and that therefore there may be statements about the past which are neither true nor false.

We recognise the truth of a mathematical statement by means of a proof or computation. We cannot in general recognise something as a proof of a statement unless we know the meaning of the statement; and, provided we know the meanings of all the statements in a proof, we can presumably recognise it as a proof. The second half of this assertion doubtless needs qualification: but we may roughly regard it as common ground that we know the meaning of a mathematical statement if and only if we know what to count as a proof of it. What distinguishes platonists from constructivists is that, for the latter, an explanation of the meaning of a mathematical statement essentially involves reference to, and in fact consists in, a stipulation of what is to count as a proof of it: understanding a statement amounts to being able to recognise, for any mathematical construction, whether or not it is a proof of it. For the platonist, on the other hand, the meaning of a mathematical statement is given in some way that does not invoke our methods of recognising the statement as true, i.e. our means of proof: our knowledge of what counts as a proof is indirectly derived from our understanding of the statement, instead of constituting that understanding. For the platonist, the meaning of a statement is given by a determination of its truth-conditions, false. *This* kind of rejection of the law of excluded middle does not reflect any divergence from realism.

In many of the cases I have mentioned, anti-realism takes the form of a species of reductionism. Thus phenomenalism holds that material-object statements are reducible to ones about sense-data, and scientific positivism that statements about electrons relate ultimately only to pointer-readings; statements about character are really about behaviour, we may say; and the behaviourist says the same about statements concerning desires, intentions, mental images, etc.; Ayer held that statements about the past relate only to present memories and records, while others have held that a meaningful statement about the future can relate only to present tendencies and intentions. In these cases there is a distinguishable class of statements expressing the existence of evidence for and against statements of the disputed class. Let us call this second class of statements 'the reductive class': if the disputed class is that of statements about material objects, the reductive class will be that of sense-datum statements; if the disputed class consists of statements about character, the reductive class will be that of statements about behaviour.

If there exists a reductive class, it is part of the anti-realist position that a statement of the disputed class can be true only if some suitable statement of the reductive class is also true. It is not always insisted that we must *know* the truth of some reductive statement giving the evidence for the truth of the statement of the disputed class: only that there must *be* some true statement of the reductive class whose truth, if we knew it, we should count as evidence. Nor is there necessarily claimed to be a *translation* of statements of the disputed class into statements of the reductive class: for it may be allowed that there is no finite disjunction of statements of the reductive class which expresses the existence of all conceivable evidence for a given statement of the disputed class. It is, as I said, a condition of the dispute's arising at all that it is agreed by both sides that, for any given statement of the disputed class, there need not exist any true statement of the reductive class which we should count as evidence either for or against the truth of the given statement.

The characterisation of a reductive class is not yet complete, however, as we see if we consider the case of mathematics. If we wanted to select a reductive class of statements serving to express the evidence for the truth of mathematical statements, a class disjoint from the class of mathematical statements themselves, we could only take it as consisting of statements such as that on a certain page is written a proof of such-and-such a statement. It is clear, however, that statements of this kind do not bear to mathematical statements the relation which phenomenalists suppose sense-datum statements to bear to material-object statements, or which statements about behaviour bear to statements about character. The difference lies in the fact that a statement about behaviour can be made and understood without using or understanding a statement about character which it supports, and likewise a statement about sense-data is supposed to be formulable without appeal to any material-object statement; but a statement asserting the existence of a proof cannot be understood without understanding the statement which the proof proves (unless we are prepared to adopt a thoroughgoing formalist position). We can judge that a description of an action is correct without so much as understanding the vocabulary of character-traits, and the same is supposed to hold for sense-datum and material-object statements; but we cannot recognise that something is correctly described as being a proof if we do not know what its conclusion is intended to be and understand that conclusion. We must therefore require of a reductive class of statements that members of this class, strong enough to constitute grounds for or against statements of the disputed class, should nevertheless be intelligible independently of them.

As soon as we make this further stipulation, we see that the claim that such a reductive class exists is an intrusive feature of the anti-realist position: anti-realism need not take the form of reductionism. We have seen that there is no reductive class for mathematical statements; and the same holds good for statements about the future or about the past: for neither a memory nor an intention can be characterised independently of what it is a memory *of* or an intention *to do*.

Now most of the argument about phenomenalism has centred on its insistence on the reductive class of statements about sense-data: attacks on phenomenalism have principally taken the form of charging that it has failed either to isolate the purported class of sense-datum statements or to explain how they acquire their meaning. I shall not here argue this well-known case, but simply assume that it is sound. I am going to argue that a realist view of the material world cannot be established simply by refuting phenomenalism; that the collapse of phenomenalism does not suffice to establish the correctness of a realist view of material-object statements, where this is taken to imply the validity of the law of excluded middle for such statements. To suppose that realism can be established in this negative way is to make the presumption that phenomenalism represents the only alternative to a realist view. But phenomenalism is a reductionist version of anti-realism, and the arguments against it all centre on this feature of it: the arguments against sense-data fail if it is not assumed that a sense-datum language is in principle intelligible prior to, and independently of, the material-object language. I them in different language. From what I have said it is evident that the error in this argument arose from neither the realists' nor the phenomenalists' noticing that some deductive inferences which would be valid on a realist view would fail on a phenomenalist view, and that this would necessarily result in a difference as to which material-object statements we have adequate indirect evidence for, and hence in which ones were believed.

The real difference between the dispute over platonism in mathematics and that over realisms of other kinds is not that in mathematics there is no independently intelligible reductive class of statements, but that there is not such a thing as indirect evidence for the truth of mathematical statements as well as direct evidence. In many cases, e.g. that of realism about character or about material objects, the anti-realist is bound to admit that the existence of actual direct evidence is not necessary for the truth of a statement of the disputed class. A statement about material objects can be true even though it is not a report of anyone's observation: it can be inferred from what is observed together with observationally based general laws. Likewise a statement attributing a character-trait to a man might be true even though he had never overtly manifested this trait. It is just in such cases that we say that the content of a statement of the disputed class can be expressed by means of a subjunctive conditional (beginning, say, 'If he had been in danger, . . . ' or 'If it had been measured, . . . '). This of course does not constitute an analysis of statements of the disputed class from the anti-realist point of view: for such an analysis we should need an accurate account of how such counterfactuals are supported, i.e. of just what constitutes acceptable indirect evidence.

The antecedent of such a conditional expresses the fulfilment of the condition for obtaining direct evidence. If statements of the disputed class can themselves be used to express direct judgments, e.g. as reports of observation, as with statements about observable properties of material objects, then the consequent of the conditional expresses an observation that the original statement is true, as in the 'table in the next room' example. Where statements of the disputed class cannot be used as reports of observation, as with statements about measurable properties of objects or about people's character, then there is a reductive class of statements whose truth constitutes direct evidence for statements of the disputed class (reports of pointer readings or of overt behaviour respectively), and the consequent of the conditional will belong to this reductive class.

This general description applies rather well to most of the disputes over realism I have mentioned: it is not intended to apply to the mathematical case, where, as I said, there is no indirect evidence. It does not, however, apply at all well either to the case of the past or that of the future. Philosophers have disagreed about whether memory-reports should be counted as giving direct evidence for the truth of past-tense statements (as opposed to indirect historical evidence). They indeed express direct judgments in the sense I explained: they are not asserted as the conclusion of any inference. Against this is the fact that someone who took a realist view of the past might not wish to accord to memory-reports that close connection with the meanings of statements in the past tense which would rule out the possibility of a Cartesian doubt about the past in the face of any number of sincere memory-reports. In any case, even if the realist accepted the equivalence of 'X happened in place P at time t' with 'If anyone had been in place P at time t, he would remember X as having happened', this translation would be of no help for the anti-realist's account of statements in the past tense, just because the antecedent is itself such a statement: so the anti-realist's explanation of what constitutes indirect evidence for the truth of a past-tense statement cannot use the reduction to counterfactual form even as a preliminary.

The situation in the case of statements about the future is different again, and yet more complicated. One who insisted that statements in the future tense can be interpreted only as referring to present tendencies and intentions might contrast expressions of intention as giving direct evidence with predictions arrived at inferentially as indirect: but he certainly would not interpret the predictions as being expressible by any kind of conditional. On the other hand, no one who agreed that only what happens at the time referred to can be conclusive evidence for or against a statement about the future, whether he rejected the law of excluded middle for statements about the future or not, would think of intentions as being that in virtue of which statements about the future were true: a doubt about the fulfilment of an intention cannot be a Cartesian doubt. From this point of view also, therefore, there is no question of the translation of statements about the future into subjunctive conditionals.

We have become so used to the cliché that inductive arguments establish their conclusions only with probability that we overlook the obvious fact that in practice we treat a great deal of inductive evidence as conclusive and a great many empirical statements which are not direct reports of observation as certain. For this reason it would be quite implausible for an anti-realist to claim that only those statements about observable properties of material objects were true which were actually reports of observation: instead, his claim is merely that those which are not are true (when they are true) in virtue *only* of the truth of the observational assertions on which they rest. There may indeed be some empirical statements whose truth can never be known with certainty, for which there cannot be any wholly conclusive evidence. For such statements there will, for the anti-realist, be no question of there being anything in virtue of which they are (definitively) true, but only of things in virtue of which they are probably true; the notion of absolute truth simply will not apply to such statements. But, though the realist must hold fast to the conception of an absolute truth-value as attaching to every statement, the anti-realist does not need to. For him the meaning of a statement is intrinsically connected with that which we count as evidence for or against the statement; and there is nothing to prevent a statement's being so used that we do not treat anything as conclusively verifying it. The use of inductive arguments as establishing, either conclusively or as subject to the possibility of revision, the truth of a statement thus becomes for the anti-realist an intrinsic feature of the meaning of that statement. (This is intended to apply only to two cases: that of statements that have not been and never will be verified or falsified by observation, though perhaps in principle capable of being; and that of statements which are incapable of being conclusively established. The traditional problem of the justification of induction has concerned the case of a statement for which it is left open in the formulation of the problem whether it will subsequently be verified or falsified by observation, and whose probability we have derived from an inductive argument: it is just this case which gives the question of realism applied to statements about the future its peculiar character. Thus I do not intend what I have said to suggest the possibility of any facile solution of the problem of 'justifying induction'.)

The problem of platonism is distinguished from all the other problems concerning realisms in that there is no such thing as indirect evidence for the truth of a mathematical statement. More properly, although indirect, inductive evidence indeed exists, as Polya has stressed, we should never count it as conclusive, and hence as being that in virtue of which a mathematical statement was true. Not only do we never treat probability arguments as decisive in mathematics, but there is no statement which can be supported *only* by probability arguments, since it can never be ruled out, for any statement not hitherto refuted, that we shall discover some intuitively acceptable proof of it. Furthermore, there is no such thing in mathematics, as there is in many of the cases we have discussed, as a set of conditions for verifying (obtaining direct evidence for) a statement. In all those cases in which, in the absence of direct evidence, the content of a statement reduces to that of a subjunctive conditional, the antecedent expresses the fulfilment of just such a condition: for a statement about observable properties, that the object should be in view; for one about measureable properties, that the procedure of measurement should be applied to it; for one about character, that the situation should occur which elicits the relevant behaviour. For most mathematical statements, we have no decision procedure, and hence there is no such thing as being in a position in which one can certainly obtain evidence for or against their truth; and when a decision procedure exists, one is always in a position to carry it out—there is no set of conditions which may not be fulfilled and whose fulfilment is a necessary condition for obtaining direct evidence.

For this reason, in mathematics an anti-realist (i.e. constructivist) position involves holding that a mathematical statement can be true only in virtue of *actual* evidence, that is, of our actually possessing a proof. In cases in which there is a reductive class, and in which indirect (inductive) evidence is admitted as conclusive, the reductive class forms the stock from which not only direct but also indirect evidence is drawn. (In some cases, such as that of measurable properties of material objects, the reductive class needs to be enlarged in order to be considered in this way.) For instance, we assumed that not only all direct evidence, but also all indirect evidence, for a statement about someone's character rested on his and other people's behaviour. If the anti-realist is prepared to take a realist view of statements of the reductive class, then he need not insist that a statement of the disputed class is true only if we actually know some true statement of the reductive class which conveys the existence of evidence for it: it may be true in virtue of the truth of some reductive statement whose truth we do not know, but which, if we did know of it, we should count as conclusive evidence in favour. For instance, the statement, 'He was brave', may be true in virtue of something which we do not know but which, if we did know, we should count as supporting the counterfactual, 'If he had been in danger, he would have acted bravely'. In a case in which we admit inductive evidence as conclusive, in which statements of the disputed class for which there is no direct evidence allow of translation into the conditional form, but in which there is no reductive class, both direct and indirect evidence is expressed by observationally based statements of the disputed class itself. Such a case is that of material-object statements in general (that is, if phenomenalism is rejected). In such a case there can be no question of an anti-realist's conceding that a statement of the disputed class could be true in virtue of something which we have not observed—that would be to abandon his whole position. (He could indeed allow the possibility of such a statement's being true in virtue of observations which we had made, but which we had not recognised as constituting indirect evidence for the truth of the statement.)

Since in mathematics there is neither a reductive class nor any conclusive indirect evidence, no sense can attach, for a constructivist, to the notion of a statement's being true if this is to mean any less than that we are actually in possession of a proof of it. The identification of mathematical truth with intuitive provability is thus not a possible constructivist standpoint, if 'intuitive provability' is understood as meaning the *existence* of an intuitively correct proof in a sense weaker than that of our being in possession of such a proof. A platonist who thought the concept of an intuitively correct proof was completely definite would indeed say that, for any given statement, either there exists a proof of it or there does not, independently of whether we know of the existence of such a proof or of a means of constructing one; and he would understand this in such a way that, if a proof was later discovered, he would then say that it had existed all along. In saying this, he would of course be taking a realist view of statements to the effect that there is an intuitively correct proof of a given mathematical proposition. But such a statement so closely resembles a mathematical statement that, if it is permissible to adopt a realist view of the one, it is permissible to adopt a realist view of the other. It is thus equally impossible for the platonist and for the constructivist to identify truth with intuitive provability: if the statement that there exists a proof of a given proposition possesses a determinate truth-value independently of our knowledge, then the statement that there exists a natural number having a certain definite property must also possess a determinate truth-value independently of whether we either know it or even could know it.

This need not mean, of course, that a platonist is committed to holding that *every* mathematical statement possesses a definite truth-value. His only claim is that, once we have definitely assigned the range of our variables and the application of our primitive predicates, all statements formed from these predicates by means of the sentential operators and of quantification over this range acquire a definite value, *true* or *false*. This presumably holds for number theory and for analysis; but it is still open to him to allow that for some theories—set theory, for instance—we have not yet assigned the range of our variables in a completely determinate manner, and hence that in such a theory there may be statements for which we have not yet determined a definite truth-value.

This completes what I wish to say on this topic here, though of course not all there is to say on it, nor even all that I have to say on it. It will be obvious anyone familiar with the elements of intuitionism that I have taken some of its basic features as a model for an anti-realist view. This involves acknowledging that all disputes over realism entail a disagreement about the criterion for the validity of deductive arguments containing statements of the disputed class. The reason why this has been so little stressed in some of these cases by philosophers may lie in their erroneously assuming that rejecting the law of excluded middle must take the form of introducing a middle truth-value. The use of intuitionism as a model involves acknowledgement also that anti-realism need not take the form of reductionism: and I have argued that, at least in one important case, realism scored too easy a victory because anti-realists chose to be reductionists when they need not, and should not, have been.

Study questions

1. The are many things in the world whose existence and properties are obviously dependent on human beings: all artefacts are like this. The fact that the Sydney Opera House exists and that it is 221 feet high is something that clearly depends on human beings. Do you think a realist could agree with this?
2. Do you think it is possible to create an argument like the 'inverted spectrum' about shapes?
3. Does Berkeley recognize a distinction between primary and secondary qualities? Does Robinson?
4. In the selection from the *Critique of Pure Reason*, Kant explains how physics was set on the secure path of science. What was the crucial moment in this?
5. What is Dummett's definition of realism and anti-realism?

Further reading

For an excellent discussion of primary and secondary qualities, which gives some insight into the history of the distinction, see Smith (1990). For Berkeley's views, see the essays in Foster and Robinson (1985), and Fogelin (2001) (on Berkeley's *Principles*) and Stoneham (2002) (on the *Three Dialogues*). Gardner (1999) is a rich yet accessible introduction to Kant's *Critique of Pure Reason*. For contemporary idealism, see Vesey (1980), which contains, among other things, influential papers by Bernard Williams, 'Wittgenstein on Idealism' (also in Williams 1981) and Myles Burnyeat (1982); Foster (1982) defends idealism in detail. For Dummett's anti-realism, see his papers 'The Philosophical Basis of Intuitionist Logic' and 'The Reality of the Past' in Dummett (1978). One of Dummett's most penetrating critics is John McDowell: see McDowell (1998). McDowell (1994) is an influential account of the relation between mind and reality. Hilary Putnam has pursued the question of realism in many different forms throughout his many writings; his (1999) is his latest thinking on the matter, influenced by McDowell. The question of objective truth, and what it is, is one only lightly touched on in this Guide and Anthology. See 'Objectivity' in van Inwagen (1993) for a clear introduction, and Wright (1992) for an important account of the matter. Also neglected here is the question of relativism; for which, see Bernard Williams's essay, 'The Truth in Relativism', in Williams (1981).

Part III

Being

Part III

Being

Introduction

1. Introduction

THE word 'being' has two senses. In the first sense, it means something that *is*, or exists: an entity, a thing. In the second sense, it refers to what all the things that are have in common. The most important questions concerning being can be thought of as corresponding to these two senses. The first question asks what is there; that is, what are the beings or entities in the world? The second question concerns what it is to be. The branch of metaphysics which deals with issues concerning being in general is called *ontology*. According to tradition, it was Aristotle who first engaged in a systematic science of being. Central to his ontology is the notion of substance; this notion, as we shall see, has involved many different interpretations throughout the history of philosophy, and most of these derive in some way or another from Aristotle's work. In what follows, we shall pursue some of these developments. The second question is what it is to be. It may seem at first that being or existence is simply a property of things, like being fat or being agreeable—what is special about it is that everything has it; for while not everything that there is is fat or agreeable, everything that there is, exists. This view, however, will turn out to be problematic, and many philosophers have denied that existence can be predicated of things in this way.

2. Aristotle on being

Our first question was about all the things that exist. Now the answer to this could be either very short or very long. Quine, for example, answers the question of what there is with one simple word: everything (see Chapter 15). Though we can hardly object to this, we might want something more informative. Another idea then is to look around and start to list things: this cup of coffee, these particles of dust moving in the air, the sound of a car from the street . . . and our list will be too long to fit in this book. Therefore, the sensible idea seems to be to establish some broad ontological categories; the fundamental types into which we classify beings.

This is what Aristotle attempts in his *Categories* (Chapter 12). He takes the reasonable starting point that when we talk, we talk about what there is, and presumably the simplest elements of speech will correspond to the basic elements of reality. Therefore, he starts to investigate words—rather than say sentences—or, as he puts it, 'what is said without combination'. First he distinguishes between what can be *said of* a subject and what cannot be said of a subject: this is best understood as a distinction between the general and the particular. A further distinction is between what is *in* a subject, and what is not. This notion has caused some difficult moments for Aristotle's interpreters, and probably the best way to understand it is to look at the examples. When something is white, whiteness is said to be in it; usually something's being in a subject indicates some feature or property of the subject in question; however, not all features of a subject are in it, as the example 'man' shows: 'man' is said of the individual man but is not *in* the individual man.

	said of a subject	not said of a subject
in a subject	(c) knowledge (it is in the soul, and it is said of knowledge-of-grammar)	(b) the individual knowledge-of-grammar, the individual white
not in a subject	(a) man (said of the individual man but is not in the individual man)	(d) individual man, individual horse

Aristotle defines primary substance as something that *is neither said of something nor is in something*. When something is said of a subject—like man of the individual man—the name can, of course, be *predicated* of the subject: 'Socrates is a man.' But Aristotle observes that sometimes the name of things that are *in* a subject—for example the individual paleness in a man—can *also be predicated* of the subject: 'the man is pale.' The subsequent tradition tended to ignore Aristotle's distinction between the two cases of something being predicated of a subject (i.e. 'said of' and 'being in'), and often defined substance simply as a *subject of predication that itself cannot be predicated of something else*. We shall come back to the important distinction between 'man' and 'pale' predicated of a primary substance, and Aristotle's notion of a secondary substance, in section 6, but first let us take a closer look at the simpler definition of substance. Until further notice, substance will be understood as primary substance.

When something is predicated of a subject, what is being said is that a certain thing has some property or stands in some relation to something, and accordingly, being the *ultimate bearer of properties* is part of the traditional understanding of substances. Aristotle claims that, since everything else is either said of or is in substances, without substances nothing would exist—they are thus somehow the primary beings. At first sight it might be plausible to claim that paleness or running or being grammatical could not exist without *something* or *someone* being pale or running or grammatical. But isn't there a dependence the other way around? Could a substance—a horse or a man—exist without *anything* being predicable about it; without having *some* colour or shape or being one kind of animal or another? This is hardly possible. But then it seems that, contrary to what Aristotle says, substances and whatever is predicated of them *mutually* need each other for their existence.

It is likely that Aristotle would have agreed that substances could not exist without properties. We shall understand his meaning better once we realize that he is engaged in a debate with Plato. Plato held that the sensible world that we see around ourselves has only a derived existence; ordinary objects of experience exemplify their properties by an imperfect resemblance to Forms, which are themselves the perfect exemplars of the same qualities. So on Plato's view, an individual man or horse has only a secondary existence compared to the existence of eternal and perfect Forms, and this is the view that Aristotle steadfastly opposes. (See further Part IV: Universals and Particulars.)

Aristotle indicates another distinctive feature of primary substances: that they can undergo change. 'It seems most distinctive of substance that what is numerically one and the same is able to receive contraries. In no other case could one bring forward anything, numerically one, which is able to receive contraries.' The same man might be pale at one time, and dark another time. In contrast, Aristotle claims that qualities like colours cannot change in this way: 'a colour which is numerically one and the same will not be black and white.' Is it true that colours cannot change? Consider the following example: white was fashionable last year, but it is not anymore. Is this not a case of the same thing receiving contraries?

We could infer Aristotle's answer to this question from what he says about beliefs and statements. The latter also appear at first sight counterexamples to the claim that only substances can change: truth and falsity are contraries, and a belief that someone is sitting might be true at one time, and false afterwards. However, this is not, according to Aristotle, a case of one thing receiving contraries. For when a belief changes its truth value, the belief *itself* is completely unchanged; what has changed is the *actual* thing— the state of affairs—and this results in a different truth value. We might express this point by saying that only substances can change their *intrinsic* properties; for everything else, changes are merely changes in their *relations* to other things. So just as the apparent change in the belief was not a change in the belief itself, but rather in its relation to facts, so the change in the fashionableness of white is not a change in white itself, but rather in its relation to other things. (See also Part VII: Time and Space, and Part VIII: Identity.)

3. Substance in the Rationalist and Empiricist traditions

The idea that substances are the primary beings and everything else depends for its existence on substances became a distinct and important aspect of the idea of substance in the rationalist tradition of modern (i.e. seventeenth- and eighteenth-century) philosophy. (Rationalists are those philosophers who believe that fundamental knowledge of the world can be gained through reason alone.) Descartes defined substance as the ultimate independent being: something whose existence is not dependent on anything else. In this strict sense, God is the only substance, since everything else depends for its existence on God. The created world includes substances only in a different, derived sense: created substances are different from each other in that they can exist without each other, though not, of course, without the concurrence of God. Thinking substance and extended substance are, in this sense, different substances according to Descartes (Descartes 1644: §§ 51 ff.; see also Part IX: Mind and Body).

Spinoza (1985) took the idea that substance is independent being even more seriously. He goes along with Descartes's idea that God is the only substance, and stops there. He rejects the Cartesian notion of substance in a derived sense, and states that things in the created world are nothing but modes of the one and only substance. Both Descartes and Spinoza believe that substances have attributes, that is, essential properties. For Descartes, each of the two distinct created substances has its own characteristic attribute: it is extension for body, and thought for mind. Spinoza thinks the only substance, God, possesses both attributes, and perhaps many others beside. All other features of a substance—like having a particular shape or colour—are modes.

The notion of substance plays a central role also in Leibniz's philosophy. He thought, like Aristotle, that the world consists of individual substances, and he put great emphasis on *individuality*. A heap of stones is not a substance, it is merely an aggregate of things; its unity, insofar as it exists, is accidental and not necessary. In contrast, substances should have essential unity or integrity; this Leibniz sometimes expresses by using the scholastic terminology of *unum per se* ('unity by itself') for substances (see Leibniz 1686). Although there is a considerable debate among interpreters about Leibniz's view of matter, it is clear, in any case, that on his view, the clearest (and possibly only) examples of such substances are immaterial minds (see Adams 1994).

Empiricists—those who think that all knowledge is based on experience—concentrate on another element in the notion of substance that we identified earlier: that substance is the ultimate bearer of properties. Empiricists hold that all our ideas originate from experience, and it is a particular picture of perception that leads to their characteristic view of substance. Speaking of the origins of ideas, Locke offers the following: 'our senses, conversant about particular sensible objects, do *convey into the mind*, several distinct *perceptions* of things, according to those various ways, wherein those objects do affect them: and thus we come by those ideas, we have of *yellow, white, heat, cold, soft, hard, bitter, sweet*, and all those which we call sensible qualities' (Locke 1690: I; 1 § 3). This is right at the beginning of Locke's *Essay Concerning Human Understanding* and for a good reason: the mind receiving the ideas of simple sensible qualities is the fundamental case of perception—more complicated cases should be based on this.

What happens, for example, when one perceives a *horse*, a complex thing, rather than a simple sensible quality? We can certainly identify some sensible qualities: the mind receives the ideas of *white, horse-shaped, neighing sound*, and so on. Is there anything *more* involved in our perception of a horse? Surely it is an important element of our experience that these ideas somehow go together; that we experience them as belonging to the *same thing*. But what more can be said of this 'same thing'? Locke suggests that since we are accustomed to some simple ideas going together, we assume that there is something in which they inhere, something that 'underlies' them, something that holds them together, and this is what we call pure substance or *substratum*. Notice that on this view, substratum *itself* cannot have any sensible properties: for it is precisely what would be *left* if we removed all sensible properties. Thus, we have only an obscure and confused idea of this pure substance: it is this 'we know not what' which, we suppose, holds together the qualities we experience. ('Substance' and 'substratum' are often used interchangeably in this context, though not in others. 'Substratum' is the specific understanding of substance as the bearer of properties which is itself without properties, or as a constituent of objects distinct from its properties.)

Although Locke maintains that our idea of substance is obscure, he does not seem to object to its existence; but other empiricists were more radical. Berkeley for instance offers a vigorous criticism of *material substratum* (see Chapter 8). Extension is a property of objects that we can perceive; and material substratum is supposed to be something that supports this property. The thing supported and the thing supporting are naturally understood to be distinct from each other: substratum is different from extension, and consequently, it itself cannot be extended. But Berkeley finds the idea of something non-extended *supporting* something extended unintelligible. Various attempts to understand the relation between the characterless substratum and the modes it supports lead to contradictions, and Berkeley concludes that the very idea of material substratum is incoherent. The ordinary objects of experience are thus no more than combinations of sensible qualities. Berkeley thought further that sensible qualities are nothing but ideas perceived by a mind, but this requires a separate argument. (For more on this, see Part II: Realism and Idealism.)

Interestingly, Berkeley did not think that similar considerations apply to *mental substance*: he thought that we are conscious of ourselves not as a mere collection of our ideas, but as a 'thinking, active principle that perceives, knows, wills and operates about ideas' (Berkeley 1710: 176). Hume, however, went even further. He famously claimed that 'for my part, when I enter most intimately into what I call *myself*, I always stumble on some particular perception or other, of heat or cold, light or shade, love or hatred, pain or pleasure' (Hume 1739–40: book I, part 4, § vi). We have thus no separate idea of the Self, something that could be understood as distinct from particular perceptions. 'When I see this table and that chimney, nothing is present to me but particular perceptions . . . When I turn my reflection on myself, I can never perceive this self without some or more perceptions; nor can I ever perceive any thing but the perceptions. 'Tis the composition of these, therefore, which forms the self' (Hume 1739–40: appendix). The resulting view is often called the 'Bundle Theory'; for material objects, on this view, are nothing but bundles of perceivable qualities, and the self is nothing but a bundle of particular perceptions—substance as the bearer of properties, and distinct from them, is thus excluded from the realm of existence.

4. The identity of indiscernibles

Suppose that, as the bundle theory claims, objects are constituted by their properties, and suppose we assume further the plausible principle that things that are different must differ in at least some of their constituents. The consequence is that different objects must differ in their properties; or, what is equivalent to this, indiscernible things, that is, things agreeing in all their properties, must be identical. This is the principle of the Identity of Indiscernibles, and a considerable part of the more recent debate on substratum is focused on this issue.

The principle was famously defended by Leibniz, and sometimes referred to as *Leibniz's Law*, although in the contemporary literature it is more customary to call another principle 'Leibniz's Law': the principle of the Indiscernibility of Identicals, which asserts that if *a* is identical to *b*, they must agree in all their properties (see Part VIII: Identity). But Leibniz's discussion of the principle of the Identity of Indiscernibles has very little to do with our present concerns; for Leibniz was not an empiricist, nor did he understand substance as substratum—in fact, he explicitly criticized Locke's treatment of substance as the 'I-know-not-what'—and certainly did not want to eliminate substances from his ontology. (For an important application of the principle by Leibniz, see Part VII: Time and Space.)

Since the bundle theory entails the principle of the Identity of Indiscernibles, if we found reasons to reject the principle, we should have an argument against the Bundle Theory. At first sight, we may wonder how the principle could fail to be true. As Robert

Adams says (Chapter 14), if Castor and Pollux are distinct individuals, Castor will necessarily have some properties that Pollux lacks: the property of being identical to Castor, and the property of not being identical to Pollux. A property of the first type—i.e. the property of being identical to a particular individual—is called 'thisness' or 'haecceity' ('haec' is Latin for 'this'). That there really are such properties is highly controversial, and those who choose to defend the Identity of Indiscernibles usually do not resort to this defence. When they claim that sameness of properties entails identity, they do not wish to include thisnesses or any property that presupposes thisness (see e.g. Ayer 1954: 29–30). We can mention two reasons for this restriction. First, one source of the Identity of Indiscernibles, as we saw, was an acceptance of the bundle theory, which, in turn, was motivated by thoroughgoing empiricism. Now suppose that Castor and Pollux are indeed completely indiscernible; then not even the most careful perception of either of them will reveal that something is Castor, or that something is Pollux. Experience will not provide us with the idea of 'being identical to Castor', and hence empiricists will be suspicious of such an idea.

However, a defence of the Identity of Indiscernibles is not necessarily motivated by empiricism, and the debate can be formulated in more general terms: is *particularity* or *individuality* an irreducible feature of the world, or is it reducible to something else— for example, to some properties—other than thisnesses—being present together? The second reason to defend the Identity of Indiscernibles restricted to properties which do not involve thisness is a suspicion about the ontological category of irreducible particulars, of which substrata are the paradigmatic examples. These suspicions will be spelled out presently, after we have considered a putative counterexample to the Identity of Indiscernibles.

A famous case discussed by Max Black (1952) and also by Robert Adams in our selection, is a universe which includes nothing but two exactly similar spheres at a certain distance from each other; each is made of pure iron, has a diameter of one mile, has the same temperature, colour, has the same history, etc. These spheres agree in all their properties, and yet, since they are apart, they seem clearly distinct. If this is logically possible, it appears to provide a straightforward counterexample to the principle of the Identity of Indiscernibles. A natural reply might be that the two spheres are, after all, distinguished by their spatial position, but this is no obvious help. If we think of space as relative, then both spheres have the same relative position with respect to an exactly similar sphere, and hence no distinguishing feature is forthcoming. Resorting to a position occupied in absolute space and time, on the other hand, arguably reintroduces the idea of irreducible particularity, since on this view, pure spatio-temporal locations would differ not in their properties, but in their simple individuality. (For more on relative and absolute space, see Part VII: Time and Space.)

Should we then deny the Identity of Indiscernibles? One reason for insisting on the bundle theory and the ensuing principle of the Identity of Indiscernibles is that the proposed alternatives were claimed to be unacceptable. Take Black's two spheres, and suppose that these agree in all their properties but nonetheless are distinct. If we still assume that things can differ only when their constituents do, this means that each sphere has to have an *additional* component besides their properties: our familiar substratum, the bearer of properties. Since each sphere has its own particular substratum, we apparently accounted for the distinctness of the two spheres. Now when we enquire about the essence of a particular substratum, about what makes this substratum what it is, this cannot be any of its properties. For if it were, then this property would be repeated in the other, indiscernible thing, and hence the two substrata, having the same essence, would become one, and could not account any more for the distinctness of the two spheres. Substratum thus must be a *bare particular*, an entity whose being the thing that it is does not involve any properties. But this is impossible, the argument continues, for everything has to have properties, for example every being must have trivial essential properties like 'having some shape if square', or 'existing or not existing at midnight, 31 December 2000' and so on. (See Part IV: Universals and Particulars, for a discussion of properties like this.) The notion of a bare particular is thus incoherent. The conclusion is that the hopelessness of the bare particular theory should, after all, make us look more kindly at the bundle theory.

We can, however, object to the claim that the bare particulars theory is the only alternative to the bundle theory. We should distinguish between the following two claims: (i) the being of a substratum *does not involve any* properties, and (ii) the being of a substratum *is not exhausted* by its properties. Only the second claim is needed to preserve the role of substrata as accounting for the distinctness of the indiscernible spheres. Suppose, accordingly, that both substrata have properties, including the property of being a substratum, and the trivially essential ones; and besides this, each has its own irreducible particularity. The bundle theorist might retort that we have just pushed the problem one level further, since when we look at the structure of a substratum, after separating all the properties it has, we are still left with a remainder which now we call its irreducible particularity, and this notion will lead to the same problems as above.

This reply reveals a deeper reason to suspect that something might have gone wrong in the set-up of the whole debate. Why should we, in the first place, think of properties as *constituents* of things? Tracing our steps back, we can find the source of this idea in the empiricist conception of experience. Locke, as well as Hume, offered us a picture of the mind receiving the ideas of sensible qualities, of white, of cold, of soft, and so on; and it was natural then to think of things as being constituted by these qualities—and perhaps something else beside. But this view can be questioned—as Roderick Chisholm (1969) maintains, our idea of say, a peach is not really the idea of a set of qualities like sweetness, roundness, fuzziness; it is much more natural to think of our perception of a peach as a perception *of something* that *is* sweet and round and fuzzy. So rather than thinking of experience as experience of qualities, we should think of it as experience of *things having certain qualities*, or even better, as experience of things being in a certain way. This opens the possibility of conceiving the *peach* rather than some component of it as a substance and bearer of properties. Substance understood in this way is not bare: for the thing that is the bearer for example of the property of roundness—the peach— is also the same thing that is sweet and fuzzy. This conception seems much closer to the original Aristotelian idea of substance.

We could now simply suspend the question of whether properties are constituents of objects, and frame the debate about the Identity of Indiscernibles in a more non-committal manner, rather in the way Robert Adams does in our selection. The question then remains simply whether thisness or haecceity is a feature of objects, and Adams's answer to this question is affirmative. (On questions relating to the final sections of Adams's paper, see Part V: Necessity.)

5. Constitution

Our discussion of substrata began with the observation that perceiving, say, a horse, we perceive qualities belonging to *one* and the same thing, or, if we accept Chisholm's way of putting it, we see *one thing* having certain qualities. Even if we put aside the question of whether properties are constituents of things, there are still undoubtedly some other things that really do constitute the horse: its bodily parts, its cells, the particles in its body. There are many particles constituting the horse, and yet it seems evident that the horse is one thing. Now why is that? What are the conditions for something being *one* thing? The question about constitution with respect to material objects has received increasing attention in the past couple of decades. (Recall that a similar question was in the centre of Leibniz's considerations on substance: he thought that a substance was a unity, an *unum per se*, rather than a simple aggregate, like a heap of stones.)

Peter van Inwagen, in the book from which our selection is taken (1990), offers a novel theory of material constitution. Van Inwagen seeks an answer to what he calls the Special Composition Question: 'in what circumstances do things compose or add up to something? When does unity arise out of plurality?' (van Inwagen 1990: 31). He criticizes some possible answers, like the theory that if things are in *contact*, or if there is some *physical bonding* between things, this is sufficient for them to compose something. Van Inwagen finds this implausible; if he shakes hands with someone, the contact between their hands does not make them one thing; not even if someone should bind or glue their hands together. His own answer is that things compose something when they form a *living organism*. This has the consequence that van Inwagen's inventory of beings is rather different from the usual one. Every physical thing is either a simple—a being that has no proper parts—or a living organism. Simples, which are, to the best of our knowledge, elementary particles, exist, because such things trivially compose themselves. But there are no such things as tables and chairs—philosophers' favourite objects—nor are there continents or stars. If there were such things, they would not be simples, and thus their proper parts should compose them; but things can compose only organisms, which rocks and continents are not. In our selection, van Inwagen tries to explain how this startling view can be reconciled with our ordinary way of thinking. (It should be noted here that some philosophers think that discoveries in quantum mechanics make van Inwagen's conception of simples highly problematic.)

6. Secondary substances

Let us now return to Aristotle, and the question we left hanging from section 2 about the difference between predicating 'man' and 'pale' of an individual man. The individual man is a primary substance, it is a *being* in the primary sense. Once we know that the individual man *is*, we might want to enquire further: *what is it?* It does not seem a full answer to this question to say that the man is pale, or that the man is knowledgeable about grammar; this is more of an answer to the question of what he is *like*, rather than what he *is*. According to the Aristotelian view—which also has a number of contemporary defenders—whenever we ask about a primary substance what it is, the answer is what Aristotle calls a *secondary substance*; in this case, the answer is that *he is a man*. Secondary substances are natural kinds; the prime examples are biological species, like human, horse, or hickory tree. The nature of a primary substance is set by the kind it belongs to; indeed, this shared nature is what makes something a member of a kind.

Secondary substances also provide an answer to the question of what makes an entity like an individual man *one*; for kinds are *individuative* categories. This means that each primary substance is distinct from other members of its kind, as well as from primary substances of other kinds, according to its own nature. Perhaps even more importantly, the nature of a primary substances is the source of all the possible changes that the substance can undergo without ceasing to be what it is. The nature of horses, for instance, determines the kind of changes that a horse can undergo without ceasing to exist. This will become important for questions of identity over time (see Part VIII: Identity).

7. What is it to be?

We have surveyed some debates about what there is in the world, and we saw that philosophers disagree on what ontological categories there are. The question of existence, of course, can be raised not only with respect to ontological categories, but also about specific members of a category; we may want to know whether the lost city of Atlantis exists. So now it is time to turn to our second question: what are we asking when we ask whether something exists? And what do we state when we state that something exists or that something does not exist? What is it to be?

There is an old puzzle about existence, which is discussed by Quine in Chapter 15. Actually, the puzzle is rather about non-existence: how is it possible ever to say truly that something does not exist—for example, to claim truly that the lost city of Atlantis does not exist, or that Pegasus does not exist? If these claims are true, then there are at least two things that do not exist; but what sense does it make to say that there *are* things that do not exist? As Quine puts it: 'Nonbeing must in some sense be, otherwise what is it that there is not?' There have been philosophers who accepted this claim at face value; Alexius Meinong (1853–1920) famously held that there are non-existent objects.

Meinong's fame these days is largely based on the fact that he was criticized for his view by Bertrand Russell (1905). The solution to the problem of non-existence advanced by Quine follows Russell. The main idea is that when we claim that Pegasus does not exist, we should not think of this as stating something *about Pegasus*. Take another example: the King of France does not exist. According to Russell's theory of descriptions, this statement should not be thought of as having a subject-predicate structure, with the King of France being the subject and non-existence predicated of him. The proper logical form of the statement can be rendered as follows: 'there is no unique thing which is King of France.' What we state here, in effect, is that a certain predicate is never satisfied—or that a certain property is never exemplified. Our statement is not about a thing, the King of France, but about the property of being King of France. If we stated that the King of France *does* exist, this statement would be, similarly, not about a thing, but about a property; we would say that the property of being King of France is exemplified. In Gottlob Frege's terminology, 'Exist' is not a first-level, but a second-level predicate, so existence is not a first-level, but a second-level property: a property of properties (Frege 1884: § 53; see McCulloch 1989: chapter 1 for an exposition of Frege's view). Quine also explains how this analysis applies to the case of Pegasus: we should replace 'Pegasus' by a description which aims to pick out Pegasus uniquely, and then proceed with the kind of paraphrase we saw above.

Quine takes this analysis further to develop a theory of existence. Whenever we state that something does exist, we state there is an *x* such that *x* satisfies some predicate. Quine's view is that the *ontological commitments* of a theory—that is, those things to whose existence the theory is committed—are those things which are the values of these variable *x*s. A theory requires the existence of those entities which have to be assigned as values to variables in order to make the statements of the theory true. Hence Quine's famous dictum: 'To be is to be the value of a variable.' This applies to kinds of beings as well as specific entities. For example, if our theory claims that there are prime numbers larger than a million, we commit ourselves to the existence of numbers; if our theory claims that Denmark has a queen, we commit ourselves to the existence of the Queen of Denmark.

The last step here may be objected to in the following way: Quine's analysis does not reveal what it is for something to be; it reveals only what it is for a theory to *say* that there is something. But of course, the theory might be wrong, in which case the entities assigned as values to its variables may not exist at all. What happens, if we have theories with rival ontological commitments, or as Quine puts it sometimes, rival conceptual schemes? How to decide, for example, between a theory which is committed only to the existence of physical objects, and another which is committed only to the existence of experiences? Quine thinks that we choose among rival conceptual schemes by judging the theories that include them largely on pragmatic grounds: by employing considerations of simplicity, economy, explanatory power, and that is the end of the matter. There is no more to ontology than pragmatic choices among different conceptual schemes.

8. Entity and identity

There is another idea in Quine's paper which may help us to say something about being in general. In a discussion with an imaginary philosopher, Wyman, Quine discusses the idea that there might be 'unactualized possibles': things which do not actually exist, but are merely possible. He objects to this idea as follows. Everything is identical to itself, and distinct from everything else. But when we consider unactualized possibles, it is not clear that the concept of identity can be applied to them in a meaningful way. Since there could be a fat man in that doorway, and also a bald man, this can be expressed by saying that there is a possible fat man and a possible bald man in that doorway. Now, are these two identical? Do we have two possible men in the doorway, or only one? What could decide this issue? asks Quine—obviously implying that nothing could.

Perhaps Quine is wrong in dismissing the prospects of finding something that could decide the identity of possible beings, but the point is rather that if he *were* right—that is, if nothing would determine the identity of a certain kind of putative entity—this would indeed be a good reason to deny the existence of such entities. Hence another famous Quinean slogan: 'No entity without identity.' We should, however, be careful to distinguish different interpretations of this claim. One is that for each entity, there should be a *fact of the matter* about what it is identical to; or in other words, that each entity should have determinate identity conditions. Now we may not always be able to *state* these conditions in an informative way, simply because (as we saw above) some entities may have primitive identity, which is not explainable by, or reducible to, other features of the world. Hence saying that an entity should have determinate identity conditions is not the same as saying that we should be able to *state criteria for its identity*. This latter is in fact another interpretation of the slogan, which seems to grasp Quine's meaning better. He says that each decision to include a type of entity in our conceptual scheme should be supported by providing criteria of identity for that type of entity. For example, for *physical objects*, it could be said that the criterion for identity is occupying the same area of space and time. Quine argues that in the case of universals we have no similar well-defined principle of individuation, so we should not posit their existence. (See Part IV: Universals and Particulars.)

Quine says elsewhere that the lack of a clear individuation principle has nothing to do with vagueness (Quine 1981: 100). What philosophers call vagueness is the phenomenon when the application of a certain predicate includes *borderline* cases. We cannot, for instance, say exactly when someone ceases to be young. A 20-year-old person is clearly young. A 70-year-old person is clearly not young. So the change from old to young has to happen between the two; but it seems that no amount of factual information will help us to settle the question of exactly when. Nor is this a case of being ignorant of the meaning of the word 'young'; we all understand it perfectly well, and yet there may be cases when we cannot really make a decision. Vague predicates like 'young', whose applicability turns on small changes, which do not make a difference in themselves, but gradually add up to a change that does, give rise to the *sorites* paradox (see Box III.1). There are many other examples of vagueness. Consider a colour spectrum: there are areas on it which are clearly red, and there are areas which are clearly orange; but between the two there will be borderline cases, where it is simply not clear whether an area belongs to one or the other.

Another case is the one Quine mentions: vague boundaries. If we want to establish exactly where the boundaries of, say, a desk lie, we get into trouble when we get down to its small-scale structure. The molecules at the surface would have less and less allegiance to the desk, and there will be cases where it is indeterminate whether a peripheral molecule belongs to the desk or the atmosphere. Another example is a mountain: as we descend from the mountain to the valley, it will be vague by which step we leave the mountain. Quine thinks that the desk is vague, because if we take very similar physical objects, which differ from each other only in the exclusion or inclusion of peripheral molecules, any of these could serve as *the* desk. Nevertheless, Quine contends, each of these physical objects is perfectly well individuated, for like any physical objects they are distinguished by their locations in space and time.

Quine does not pursue this line of enquiry, but it seems that his analysis has the consequence that the desk is *not a physical object*. For in his view, we cannot say that

---

Box III.1. The *sorites* (heap) paradox

Consider the following two statements:

1. If Sophie is now 15 years old, she is obviously young.
2. Someone who is young cannot cease to be young in a second.

These apparently uncontroversial statements have the consequence that Sophie will remain young forever, no matter what age she is. For if she is young now, then according to (2) she will be young a second later. Consider her again at this time: she is young, so she will not cease to be young yet another second later. And so on. Since no passing of a second will stop her being young, she will be young 2,365,200,000 seconds from now, when she is 90. And this is absurd. Yet our assumptions (1) and (2) seem innocent enough, as does our reasoning. Here we have a paradox: an unacceptable conclusion drawn from apparently true premisses by apparently valid reasoning.

This paradox is, of course, not restricted to claims about people's ages. One famous version of the paradox involves removing grains of sand from a heap of sand. Parallel reasoning as above will show that one grain of sand is a heap. Hence the paradox is known as the *sorites* paradox, from the Greek word 'sorites' which means *heap*. See Sainsbury (1995) for a good introduction.

---

the desk is *either* of the physical objects differing only by a few molecules; but it cannot be *all* of them, for they are clearly distinct, and so the desk would not be identical to itself. We could resolve the situation by accepting the argument presented by Gareth Evans and David Lewis in our selections. Evans argues that objects themselves cannot be vague. How should we explain then the vagueness of the desk? The answer is that whatever is in the world, the physical objects, is determinate. It is vague, however, *which of these determinate objects* is denoted by our words 'the desk'. So vagueness is not a feature of the world, but a feature of the relation between language and the world. If this argument is right, then contrary to what Quine says, we can establish a link between the requirement of determinate identity and the question of vagueness. For when we state that each entity has a determinate identity—like physical objects do, on Quine's account—this amounts to denying that objects themselves are vague.

Chapter 12
Selections from *Categories*
Aristotle

. . .

2

O<small>F</small> things that are said, some involve combination while others are said without combination. Examples of those involving combination are: man runs, man wins; and of those without combination: man, ox, runs, wins.

Of things there are: (*a*) some are *said of* a subject but are not *in* any subject. For example, man is said of a subject, the individual man, but is not in any subject. (*b*) Some are in a subject but are not said of any subject. (By 'in a subject' I mean what is in something, not as a part, and cannot exist separately from what it is in.) For example, the individual knowledge-of-grammar is in a subject, the soul, but is not said of any subject; and the individual white is in a subject, the body (for all colour is in a body), but is not said of any subject. (*c*) Some are both said of a subject and in a subject. For example, knowledge is in a subject, the soul, and is also said of a subject, knowledge-of-grammar. (*d*) Some are neither in a subject nor said of a subject, for example, the individual man or the individual horse—for nothing of this sort is either in a subject or said of a subject. Things that are individual and numerically one are, without exception, not said of any subject, but there is nothing to prevent some of them from being in a subject—the individual knowledge-of-grammar is one of the things in a subject.

3

Whenever one thing is predicated of another as of a subject, all things said of what is predicated will be said of the subject also. For example, man is predicated of the individual man, and animal of man; so animal will be predicated of the individual man also—for the individual man is both a man and an animal.

The differentiae of genera which are different[1] and not subordinate one to the other are themselves different in kind. For example, animal and knowledge: footed,

---

1. Read τῶν ἑτέρων γενῶν.

Aristotle, selection from *Categories*, chapters 4 and 5, translated by J. L. Ackrill. From *The Complete Works of Aristotle: The Revised Oxford Translation,* edited by Jonathan Barnes, copyright © 1984, Princeton University Press, reprinted by permission of Princeton University Press.

winged, aquatic, two-footed, are differentiae of animal, but none of these is a
20   differentia of knowledge; one sort of knowledge does not differ from another by
being two-footed. However, there is nothing to prevent genera subordinate one to
the other from having the same differentiae. For the higher are predicated of the genera below them, so that all differentiae of the predicated genus will be differentiae of
the subject also.

4

25   Of things said without any combination, each signifies either substance or quantity
or qualification or a relative or where or when or being-in-a-position or having or
doing or being-affected. To give a rough idea, examples of substance are man, horse;
of quantity: four-foot, five-foot; of qualification: white, grammatical; of a relative:
2^a1 double, half, larger; of where: in the Lyceum, in the market-place; of when: yesterday,
last-year; of being-in-a-position: is-lying, is-sitting; of having: has-shoes-on, has-
armour-on; of doing: cutting, burning; of being-affected: being-cut, being-burned.
5   None of the above is said just by itself in any affirmation, but by the combination
of these with one another an affirmation is produced. For every affirmation, it
10   seems, is either true or false; but of things said without any combination none is
either true or false (e.g. man, white, runs, wins).

5

A *substance*—that which is called a substance most strictly, primarily, and most of
all—is that which is neither said of a subject nor in a subject, e.g. the individual man
15   or the individual horse. The species in which the things primarily called substances
are, are called *secondary substances*, as also are the genera of these species. For example, the individual man belongs in a species, man, and animal is a genus of the
species; so these—both man and animal—are called secondary substances.
It is clear from what has been said that if something is said of a subject both its
20   name and its definition are necessarily predicated of the subject. For example, man
is said of a subject, the individual man, and the name is of course predicated (since
you will be predicating man of the individual man), and also the definition of man
25   will be predicated of the individual man (since the individual man is also a man).
Thus both the name and the definition will be predicated of the subject. But as for
things which are in a subject, in most cases neither the name nor the definition is
30   predicated of the subject. In some cases there is nothing to prevent the name from
being predicated of the subject, but it is impossible for the definition to be predicated. For example, white, which is in a subject (the body), is predicated of the subject; for a body is called white. But the definition of white will never be predicated
of the body.
35   All the other things are either said of the primary substances as subjects or in
them as subjects. This is clear from an examination of cases. For example, animal is

predicated of man and therefore also of the individual man; for were it predicated of none of the individual men it would not be predicated of man at all. Again, colour is in body and therefore also in an individual body; for were it not in some individual body it would not be in body at all. Thus all the other things are either said of the primary substances as subjects or in them as subjects. So if the primary substances did not exist it would be impossible for any of the other things to exist.[2]

Of the secondary substances the species is more a substance than the genus, since it is nearer to the primary substance. For if one is to say of the primary substance what it is, it will be more informative and apt to give the species than the genus. For example, it would be more informative to say of the individual man that he is a man than that he is an animal (since the one is more distinctive of the individual man while the other is more general); and more informative to say of the individual tree that it is a tree than that it is a plant. Further, it is because the primary substances are subjects for all the other things and all the other things are predicated of them or are in them, that they are called substances most of all. But as the primary substances stand to the other things, so the species stands to the genus: the species is a subject for the genus (for the genera are predicated of the species but the species are not predicated reciprocally of the genera). Hence for this reason too the species is more a substance than the genus.

But of the species themselves—those which are not genera—one is no more a substance than another: it is no more apt to say of the individual man that he is a man than to say of the individual horse that it is a horse. And similarly of the primary substances one is no more a substance than another: the individual man is no more a substance than the individual ox.

It is reasonable that, after the primary substances, their species and genera should be the only other things called secondary substances. For only they, of things predicated, reveal the primary substance. For if one is to say of the individual man what he is, it will be in place to give the species or the genus (though more informative to give man than animal); but to give any of the other things would be out of place— for example, to say white or runs or anything like that. So it is reasonable that these should be the only other things called substances. Further, it is because the primary substances are subjects for everything else that they are called substances most strictly. But as the primary substances stand to everything else, so the species and genera of the primary substances stand to all the rest: all the rest are predicated of these. For if you will call the individual man grammatical, then you will call both a man and an animal grammatical; and similarly in other cases.

It is a characteristic common to every substance not to be in a subject. For a primary substance is neither said of a subject nor in a subject. And as for secondary substances, it is obvious at once that they are not in a subject. For man is said of the

2. The Oxford text continues: 'For all the other things are either said of these as subjects or in them as subjects; so that if the primary substances did not exist, it would be impossible for any of the other things to exist.' Most scholars excise those sentences.

individual man as subject but is not in a subject: man is not *in* the individual man. Similarly, animal also is said of the individual man as subject, but animal is not *in*

15   the individual man. Further, while there is nothing to prevent the name of what is in a subject from being sometimes predicated of the subject, it is impossible for the definition to be predicated. But the definition of the secondary substances, as well as the name, is predicated of the subject: you will predicate the definition of man of

20   the individual man, and also that of animal. No substance, therefore, is in a subject.

This is not, however, peculiar to substance, since the differentia also is not in a subject. For footed and two-footed are said of man as subject but are not in a subject;

25   neither two-footed nor footed is *in* man. Moreover, the definition of the differentia is predicated of that of which the differentia is said. For example, if footed is said of man the definition of footed will also be predicated of man; for man is footed.

30   We need not be disturbed by any fear that we may be forced to say that the parts of a substance, being in a subject (the whole substance), are not substances. For when we spoke of things *in a subject* we did not mean things belonging in something as *parts*.

It is a characteristic of substances and differentiae that all things called from them are so called synonymously. For all the predicates from them are predicated either

35   of the individuals or of the species. (For from a primary substance there is no predicate, since it is said of no subject; and as for secondary substances, the species is predicated of the individual, the genus both of the species and of the individual.

3^{b}1 Similarly, differentiae too are predicated both of the species and of the individuals.) And the primary substances admit the definition of the species and of the genera, and the species admits that of the genus; for everything said of what is predicated

5   will be said of the subject also. Similarly, both the species and the individuals admit the definition of the differentiae. But synonymous things were precisely those with both the name in common and the same definition. Hence all the things called from substances and differentiae are so called synonymously.

10   Every substance seems to signify a certain 'this'. As regards the primary substances, it is indisputably true that each of them signifies a certain 'this'; for the thing revealed is individual and numerically one. But as regards the secondary substances, though it appears from the form of the name—when one speaks of man or

15   animal—that a secondary substance likewise signifies a certain 'this', this is not really true; rather, it signifies a certain qualification—for the subject is not, as the primary substance is, one, but man and animal are said of many things. However, it does not signify simply a certain qualification, as white does. White signifies noth-

20   ing but a qualification, whereas the species and the genus mark off the qualification of substance—they signify substance of a certain qualification. (One draws a wider boundary with the genus than with the species, for in speaking of animal one takes in more than in speaking of man.)

Another characteristic of substances is that there is nothing contrary to them. For

25   what would be contrary to a primary substance? For example, there is nothing contrary to an individual man, nor yet is there anything contrary to man or to animal.

This, however, is not peculiar to substance but holds of many other things also, for example, of quantity. For there is nothing contrary to four-foot or to ten or to anything of this kind—unless someone were to say that many is contrary to few or large to small; but still there is nothing contrary to any *definite* quantity.

Substance, it seems, does not admit of a more and a less. I do not mean that one substance is not more a substance than another (we have said that it is), but that any given substance is not called more, or less, that which it is. For example, if this substance is a man, it will not be more a man or less a man either than itself or than another man. For one man is not more a man than another, as one pale thing is more pale than another and one beautiful thing more beautiful than another. Again, a thing is called more, or less, such-and-such than itself; for example, the body that is pale is called more pale now than before, and the one that is hot is called more, or less, hot. Substance, however, is not spoken of thus. For a man is not called more a man now than before, nor is anything else that is a substance. Thus substance does not admit of a more and a less.

It seems most distinctive of substance that what is numerically one and the same is able to receive contraries. In no other case could one bring forward anything, numerically one, which is able to receive contraries. For example, a colour which is numerically one and the same will not be black and white, nor will numerically one and the same action be bad and good; and similarly with everything else that is not substance. A substance, however, numerically one and the same, is able to receive contraries. For example, an individual man—one and the same—becomes pale at one time and dark at another, and hot and cold, and bad and good.

Nothing like this is to be seen in any other case, unless perhaps someone might object and say that statements and beliefs are like this. For the same statement seems to be both true and false. Suppose, for example, that the statement that somebody is sitting is true; after he has got up this same statement will be false. Similarly with beliefs. Suppose you believe truly that somebody is sitting; after he has got up you will believe falsely if you hold the same belief about him. However, even if we were to grant this, there is still a difference in the *way* contraries are received. For in the case of substances it is by themselves changing that they are able to receive contraries. For what has become cold instead of hot, or dark instead of pale, or good instead of bad, has changed (has altered); similarly in other cases too it is by itself undergoing change that each thing is able to receive contraries. Statements and beliefs, on the other hand, themselves remain completely unchangeable in every way; it is because the *actual thing* changes that the contrary comes to belong to them. For the statement that somebody is sitting remains the same; it is because of a change in the actual thing that it comes to be true at one time and false at another. Similarly with beliefs. Hence at least the *way* in which it is able to receive contraries—through a change in itself—would be distinctive of substance, even if we were to grant that beliefs and statements are able to receive contraries. However, this is not true. For it is not because they themselves receive anything that statements and beliefs are said to be able to receive contraries, but because of what has

10 happened to something else. For it is because the actual thing exists or does not exist that the statement is said to be true or false, not because it is able itself to receive contraries. No statement, in fact, or belief is changed at all by anything. So, since nothing happens in them, they are not able to receive contraries. A substance, on

15 the other hand, is said to be able to receive contraries because it itself receives contraries. For it receives sickness and health, and paleness and darkness; and because it itself receives the various things of this kind it is said to be able to receive contraries. It is, therefore, distinctive of substance that what is numerically one and the same is able to receive contraries. This brings to an end our discussion of substance.

...

Chapter 13

Selection from *Essay Concerning Human Understanding*

John Locke

Of our complex ideas of substances

Ideas of substances, how made

§1. The mind being, as I have declared, furnished with a great number of the simple ideas, conveyed in by the *senses*, as they are found in exterior things, or by *reflection* on its own operations, takes notice also, that a certain number of these simple ideas go constantly together; which being presumed to belong to one thing, and words being suited to common apprehensions, and made use of for quick dispatch, are called, so united in one subject, by one name; which, by inadvertency, we are apt afterward to talk of, and consider as one simple idea, which indeed is a complication of many ideas together: because, as I have said, not imagining how these simple ideas can subsist by themselves, we accustom ourselves, to suppose some *substratum*, wherein they do subsist, and from which they do result; which therefore we call *substance*.

Our idea of substance in general

§2. So that if anyone will examine himself concerning his *notion of pure substance in general*, he will find he has no other idea of it at all, but only a supposition of he knows not what support of such qualities, which are capable of producing simple ideas in us; which qualities are commonly called accidents. If anyone should be asked, what is the subject wherein colour or weight inheres, he would have nothing to say, but the solid extended parts: and if he were demanded what is it, that the solidity and extension inhere in, he would not be in a much better case, than the Indian before-mentioned, who, saying that the world was supported by a great elephant, was asked, what the elephant rested on? to which his answer was, a great tortoise: but being again pressed to know what gave support to the broad-backed tortoise, replied, something, he knew not what. And thus here, as in all other cases, where we use words without having clear and distinct ideas, we talk like children;

John Locke, selection from *Essay Concerning Human Understanding*, book II, chapter xxiii, edited by Roger Woolhouse (Penguin, 1997), copyright © Roger Woolhouse 1997.

who, being questioned, what such a thing is, which they know not, readily give this satisfactory answer, that it is *something*, which in truth signifies no more, when so used, either by children or men, but that they know not what; and that the thing they pretend to know, and talk of, is what they have no distinct idea of at all, and so are perfectly ignorant of it, and in the dark. The idea then we have, to which we give the general name substance, being nothing, but the supposed, but unknown support of those qualities, we find existing, which we imagine cannot subsist, *sine re substante*, without something to support them, we call that support *substantia*; which, according to the true import of the word, is in plain English, *standing under*, or *upholding*.

Of the sorts of substances

§3. An obscure and relative idea of substance in general, being thus made, we come to have the *ideas of particular sorts of substances*, by collecting such combinations of simple ideas, as are by experience and observation of men's senses, taken notice of to exist together, and are therefore supposed to flow from the particular internal constitution, or unknown essence of that substance. Thus we come to have the ideas of a man, horse, gold, water, *etc.* of which substances, whether anyone has any other clear idea, further than of certain simple ideas co-existing together, I appeal to everyone's own experience. 'Tis the ordinary qualities, observable in iron, or a diamond, put together, that make the true complex idea of those substances, which a smith, or a jeweller, commonly knows better than a philosopher; who, whatever substantial forms he may talk of, has no other idea of those substances, than what is framed by a collection of those simple ideas which are to be found in them; only we must take notice, that our complex ideas of substances, besides all these simple ideas they are made up of, have always the confused idea of *something* to which they belong, and in which they subsist: and therefore when we speak of any sort of substance, we say it is a *thing* having such or such qualities, as body is a *thing* that is extended, figured, and capable of motion; a spirit, a *thing* capable of thinking; and so hardness, friability, and power to draw iron, we say, are qualities to be found in a loadstone. These, and the like fashions of speaking, intimate, that the substance is supposed always *something* besides the extension, figure, solidity, motion, thinking, or other observable ideas, though we know not what it is.

No clear idea of substance in general

§4. Hence when we talk or think of any particular sort of corporeal substances, as *horse, stone, etc.* though the idea we have of either of them, be but the complication, or collection of those several simple ideas of sensible qualities, which we use to find united in the thing called *horse* or *stone*, yet because we cannot conceive how they should subsist alone, nor one in another, we suppose them existing in, and supported by some common subject; *which support, we denote by the name substance*, though it be certain, we have no clear or distinct idea of that *thing* we suppose a support.

As clear an idea of spirit, as body

§5. The same happens concerning the operations of the mind, *viz.* thinking, reasoning, fearing, *etc.* which we concluding not to subsist of themselves, nor apprehending how they can belong to body, or be produced by it, we are apt to think these the actions of some other *substance*, which we call *spirit*; whereby yet it is evident, that having no other idea or notion of matter, but *something* wherein those many sensible qualities, which affect our senses, do subsist; by supposing a substance, wherein *thinking, knowing, doubting*, and a power of moving, *etc.* do subsist, *we have as clear a notion of the substance of spirit, as we have of body*; the one being supposed to be (without knowing what it is) the *substratum* to those simple ideas we have from without; and the other supposed (with a like ignorance of what it is) to be the *substratum* to those operations which we experiment in ourselves within. 'Tis plain then, that the idea of corporeal *substance* in matter, is as remote from our conceptions, and apprehensions, as that of spiritual *substance*, or *spirit*; and therefore from our not having any notion of the *substance* of spirit, we can no more conclude its non-existence, than we can, for the same reason, deny the existence of body: it being as rational to affirm, there is no body, because we have no clear and distinct idea of the *substance* of matter, as to say, there is no spirit, because we have no clear and distinct idea of the *substance* of a spirit.

Of the sorts of substances

§6. Whatever therefore be the secret and abstract nature of *substance* in general, all *the ideas we have of particular distinct sorts of substances*, are nothing but several combinations of simple ideas, co-existing in such, though unknown, cause of their union, as makes the whole subsist of itself. 'Tis by such combinations of simple *ideas*, and nothing else, that we represent particular sorts of *substances* to ourselves; such are the ideas we have of their several species in our minds; and such only do we, by their specific names, signify to others, *v.g. man, horse, sun, water, iron*; upon hearing which words, everyone, who understands the language, frames in his mind a combination of those several simple ideas, which he has usually observed, or fancied to exist together under that denomination; all which he supposes to rest in, and be, as it were, adherent to that unknown common subject, which inheres not in anything else. Though in the meantime it be manifest, and everyone upon inquiry into his own thoughts, will find that he has no other idea of any *substance, v.g.* let it be *gold, horse, iron, man, vitriol, bread*, but what he has barely of those sensible qualities, which he supposes to inhere, with a supposition of such a *substratum*, as gives as it were a support to those qualities, or simple ideas, which he has observed to exist united together. Thus the idea of the *Sun*, what is it, but an aggregate of those several simple ideas, bright, hot, roundish, having a constant regular motion, at a certain distance from us, and, perhaps, some other? as he who thinks and discourses of the *Sun*, has been more or less accurate, in observing those sensible qualities, ideas, or properties, which are in that thing, which he calls the *Sun*.

Power a great part of our complex ideas of substances

§7. For he has the perfectest idea of any of the particular sorts of *substance*, who has gathered, and put together, most of those simple ideas, which do exist in it, among which are to be reckoned its active powers, and passive capacities; which though not simple ideas, yet, in this respect, for brevity's sake, may conveniently enough be reckoned amongst them. Thus the power of drawing iron, is one of the ideas of the complex one of that substance we call a *loadstone*, and a power to be so drawn, is a part of the complex one we call *iron*; which powers pass for inherent qualities in those subjects. Because every *substance* being as apt, by the powers we observe in it, to change some sensible qualities in other subjects, as it is to produce in us those simple ideas, which we receive immediately from it, does, by those new sensible qualities introduced into other subjects, discover to us those powers, which do thereby mediately affect our senses, as regularly as its sensible qualities do it immediately, *v.g.* we immediately by our senses perceive in *fire* its heat and colour; which are, if rightly considered, nothing but powers in it, to produce those ideas in us: we also by our senses perceive the colour and brittleness of *charcoal*, whereby we come by the knowledge of another power in fire, which it has to change the colour and consistency of wood. By the former fire immediately, by the latter it mediately discovers to us these several powers, which therefore we look upon to be a part of the qualities of fire, and so make them a part of the complex ideas of it. For all those powers that we take cognizance of, terminating only in the alteration of some sensible qualities, in those subjects on which they operate, and so making them exhibit to us new sensible ideas; therefore it is that I have reckoned these powers amongst the simple ideas, which make the complex ones of the sorts of *substances*; though these powers considered in themselves, are truly complex ideas. And in this looser sense, I crave leave to be understood, when I name any of these *potentialities amongst the simple ideas*, which we recollect in our minds, when we think *of particular substances*. For the powers that are severally in them, are necessary to be considered, if we will have true distinct notions of the several sorts of substances.

And why

§8. Nor are we to wonder, that *powers make a great part of our complex ideas of substances*; since their secondary qualities are those, which in most of them serve principally to distinguish substances one from another, and commonly make a considerable part of the complex idea of the several sorts of them. For our senses failing us in the discovery of the bulk, texture, and figure of the minute parts of bodies, on which their real constitutions and differences depend, we are fain to make use of their secondary qualities, as the characteristical notes and marks, whereby to frame ideas of them in our minds, and distinguish them one from another. All which secondary qualities, as has been shown, are nothing but bare powers. For the colour and taste of *opium*, are, as well as its soporific or anodyne virtues, mere powers depending on its primary qualities, whereby it is fitted to produce different operations on different parts of our bodies.

Three sorts of ideas make our complex ones of substances

§9. *The ideas that make our complex ones of corporeal substances*, are of these three sorts. *First*, the ideas of the primary qualities of things, which are discovered by our senses, and are in them even when we perceive them not, such are the bulk, figure, number, situation, and motion of the parts of bodies, which are really in them, whether we take notice of them or no. *Secondly*, the sensible secondary qualities, which depending on these, are nothing but the powers those substances have to produce several ideas in us by our senses; which ideas are not in the things themselves otherwise than as anything is in its cause. *Thirdly*, the aptness we consider in any substance, to give or receive such alterations of primary qualities, as that the substance so altered should produce in us different ideas from what it did before; these are called active and passive powers: all which powers, as far as we have any notice or notion of them, terminate only in sensible simple ideas. For whatever alteration a *loadstone* has the power to make in the minute particles of iron, we should have no notion of any power it had at all to operate on iron, did not its sensible motion discover it; and I doubt not, but there are a thousand changes, that bodies we daily handle, have a power to cause in one another, which we never suspect, because they never appear in sensible effects.

Powers make a great part of our complex ideas of substances

§10. *Powers* therefore justly *make a great part of our complex ideas of substances*. He, that will examine his complex idea of gold, will find several of its ideas, that make it up, to be only powers, as the power of being melted, but of not spending itself in the fire; of being dissolved in *aqua regia*, are ideas, as necessary to make up our complex idea of gold, as its colour and weight: which, if duly considered, are also nothing but different powers. For to speak truly, yellowness is not actually in gold; but is a power in gold to produce that idea in us by our eyes, when placed in a due light: and the heat, which we cannot leave out of our idea of the Sun, is no more really in the Sun, than the white colour it introduces into wax. These are both equally powers in the Sun, operating, by the motion and figure of its insensible parts, so on a man, as to make him have the idea of heat; and so on wax, as to make it capable to produce in a man the idea of white.

The now secondary qualities of bodies would disappear, if we could discover the primary ones of their minute parts

§11. Had we senses acute enough to discern the minute particles of bodies, and the real constitution on which their sensible qualities depend, I doubt not but they would produce quite different ideas in us; and that which is now the yellow colour of gold, would then disappear, and instead of it, we should see an admirable texture of parts of a certain size and figure. This microscopes plainly discover to us: for what to our naked eyes produces a certain colour, is by thus augmenting the acuteness of our senses, discovered to be quite a different thing; and the thus altering, as it were, the proportion of the bulk of the minute parts of a coloured object to our usual sight, produces different ideas from what it did before. Thus sand, or pounded glass, which is opaque, and white to the naked eye, is pellucid in a microscope; and a hair seen this way, loses its former colour, and is in a great measure pellucid, with a mixture of some bright sparkling colours, such as appear from the refraction of diamonds, and other pellucid bodies. Blood to the naked eye, appears all red; but by a good microscope, wherein its lesser parts appear, shows only some few globules of red, swimming in a pellucid liquor; and how these red globules would appear, if glasses could be found that yet could magnify them 1000, or 10,000 times more, is uncertain.

Chapter 14

Primitive thisness and primitive identity

Robert M. Adams

Is the world—and are all possible worlds—constituted by purely qualitative facts, or does thisness hold a place beside suchness as a fundamental feature of reality? Some famous philosophers—Leibniz, Russell, and Ayer, for example—have believed in a purely qualitative constitution of things; others, such as Scotus, Kant, and Peirce, have held to primitive thisness. Recent discussions of direct, nondescriptive reference to individuals have brought renewed interest in the idea of primitive, non-qualitative thisness.

I am inclined to accept primitive thisness, but for reasons that do not depend very heavily on recent semantics. In the present essay I will try to justify my position—but even more to sort out some issues that are easily and often confused. I will begin (in section 1) by trying to elucidate some terms that will be important in the discussion. Leibniz will be discussed in section 2 as the archetypal believer in a purely qualitative universe. I will argue that his position is not inconsistent with the semantics of direct reference, and that proponents of primitive thisness must attack rather a certain doctrine of the Identity of Indiscernibles. Two types of argument against that doctrine will be analyzed and defended in sections 3 and 4.

Primitive thisness has been associated or even identified, in recent discussion, with primitive identity and non-identity of individuals in different possible worlds.[1] The association is appropriate, but the main issue about primitive transworld identity is quite different from that about primitive thisness, as will be argued in section 5, where I will also defend the primitiveness of transworld identity. The sixth and final section of the paper will be devoted to some problems about necessary connections between qualitative properties and primitive thisnesses.

Versions of this paper were read to colloquia at UCLA, UC Irvine, and Stanford. I am indebted to many, and particularly to Marilyn Adams, Kit Fine, Dagfinn Føllesdal, Ian Hacking, Robert Hambourger, David Kaplan, Kenneth Olson, John Perry, and Peter Woodruff, for discussion that helped in writing and rewriting the paper. My interest in the project grew out of discussions with Kaplan.

1. See David Kaplan, 'How to Russell a Frege-Church,' *Journal of Philosophy* 72 (1975, Nov. 6), pp. 716–29, at pp. 722–7.

Robert Merrihew Adams, 'Primitive Thisness and Primitive Identity', *Journal of Philosophy* 76/1. (Jan. 1979), copyright © *Journal of Philosophy*, 1979.

1. Thisness and suchness

Three notions that we will use call for some elucidation at the outset. They are the notions of an *individual*, of a *thisness*, and of a purely qualitative property or (as I shall call it) a *suchness*.

By 'individual' here I mean particulars such as persons, physical objects, and events. It is assumed that numbers and universals are not individuals in this sense, and that particular places and times are individuals if they have an absolute being and identity independent of their relation to particular physical objects and events.

A thisness[2] is the property of being identical with a certain particular individual—not the property that we all share, of being identical with some individual or other, but my property of being identical with me, your property of being identical with you, etc. These properties have recently been called 'essences,'[3] but that is historically unfortunate; for essences have normally been understood to be constituted by qualitative properties, and we are entertaining the possibility of nonqualitative thisnesses. In defining 'thisness' as I have, I do not mean to deny that universals have analogous properties—for example, the property of being identical with the quality red. But since we are concerned here principally with the question whether the identity and distinctness of individuals is purely qualitative or not, it is useful to reserve the term 'thisness' for the identities of individuals.

It may be controversial to speak of a 'property' of being identical with me. I want the word 'property' to carry as light a metaphysical load here as possible. 'Thisness' is intended to be a synonym or translation of the traditional term 'haecceity' (in Latin, *haecceitas*), which so far as I know was invented by Duns Scotus. Like many medieval philosophers, Scotus regarded properties as components of the things that have them. He introduced haecceities (thisness), accordingly, as a special sort of metaphysical component of individuals.[4] I am not proposing to revive this aspect of his conception of a haecceity, because I am not committed to regarding properties as components of individuals. To deny that thisnesses are purely qualitative is not necessarily to postulate 'bare particulars,' substrata without qualities of their own, which would be what was left of the individual when all its qualitative properties were subtracted. Conversely, to hold that thisnesses are purely qualitative is not to imply that individuals are nothing but bundles of qualities, for qualities may not be components of individuals at all.

---

2. 'Thisness' is the inevitable and historic word here. But we must not suppose that everything important that is expressed by a demonstrative is caught up in the relevant thisness. You might know many facts involving the thisness (in my sense) of Gerald Ford, for example, and yet be ignorant that *that* man (disappearing over the hill in a golf cart) is Ford. I believe this is a translation into my terminology of a point John Perry has made; see his 'Frege on demonstratives,' *Philosophical Review* 86/4 (Oct. 1977), pp. 474–97, and 'Indexicality and belief,' unpublished.
3. E.g., by Alvin Plantinga, *The Nature of Necessity* (Oxford; Clarendon Press, 1974), pp. 71f.
4. Johannes Duns Scotus, *Quaestiones in libros metaphysicorum*, VII. xii. schol. 3; cf. *Ordinatio*, II. 3. 1. 2, 57. I am indebted to Marilyn McCord Adams for acquainting me with these texts and views of Scotus, and for much discussion of the topics of this paragraph.

We could probably conduct our investigation, in somewhat different terms, without referring to thisnesses as properties; but the concept of a *suchness* is not so dispensable. Without the distinction between the qualitative and the nonqualitative, the subject of this paper does not exist. I believe the concept, and the distinction, can be made clear enough to work with, though not, I fear, clear enough to place them above suspicion.

We might try to capture the idea by saying that a property is purely qualitative— a suchness—if and only if it could be expressed, in a language sufficiently rich, without the aid of such referential devices as proper names, proper adjectives and verbs (such as 'Leibnizian' and 'pegasizes'), indexical expressions, and referential uses of definite descriptions. That seems substantially right, but may be suspected of circularity, on the ground that the distinction between qualitative and nonqualitative might be prior to the notions of some of those referential devices. I doubt that it really is circular, in view of the separation between semantical and metaphysical issues for which I shall argue in section 2; but it would take us too far afield to pursue the issue of circularity here.

There is another and possibly more illuminating approach to the definition of 'suchness'. All the properties that are, in certain senses, general (capable of being possessed by different individuals) and nonrelational are suchnesses. More precisely, let us say that a *basic suchness* is a property that satisfies the following three conditions. (1) It is not a thisness and is not equivalent to one. (2) It is not a property of being related in one way or another to one or more particular individuals (or to their thisnesses). This is not to deny that some basic suchnesses are in a sense relational (and thus do not fall in the Aristotelian category of Quality, though they count as 'purely qualitative' for present purposes). An example may help to clarify this. The property of owning the house at 1011 Rose Avenue, Ann Arbor, Michigan, is not a basic suchness, although several different individuals have had it, because it involves the thisness of that particular house. But the property of being a homeowner is a basic suchness, although relational, because having it does not depend on which particular home one owns. (3) A basic suchness is not a property of being identical with or related in one way or another to an extensionally defined set that has an individual among its members, or among its members' members, or among its members' members' members, etc. Thus, if being an American is to be analyzed as a relation to a set of actual people and places, it is not a basic suchness.

These three conditions may be taken as jointly sufficient for being a suchness, but it is not clear that they are also necessary for being a suchness. For it seems intuitively that any property that is constructed by certain operations out of purely qualitative properties must itself be purely qualitative. The operations I have in mind for the construction are of two sorts. (1) They may be logical, such as those expressed by 'not', 'or', and $\lceil (\exists x)\phi(\ , x) \rceil$, where the property ascribed to x by $\lceil (\exists y)\phi(y, x) \rceil$ is a basic suchness or constructed by allowed operations out of basic suchnesses. Or (2) they may be epistemic, such as those expressed by $\lceil$ believes that $p \rceil$ and $\lceil$ wishes that $p \rceil$, where p is a proposition constructed, by allowed operations, solely out of basic suchnesses. So if your thisness, or a property equivalent to the property of being (identical with) you, could be constructed in these ways as a complex of basic suchnesses, it would seem intuitively to be a suchness, although (by definition) it is not a *basic* suchness. Indeed, as we shall see, this is precisely the way in which Leibniz attempts to account for individuality in a purely qualitative universe.

So as not to beg the question against him, let us define a *suchness* as a property that is either a basic suchness or constructed out of basic suchnesses in such a way as I have indicated. This recursive definition of 'suchness' seems to me to capture the notion I want to discuss; but it depends on notions of property construction and of being a relation to a particular individual which may themselves be somewhat unclear or otherwise debatable. In any event, I am prepared to accept the notion of a suchness, and related notions of qualitativeness of facts, similarities, differences, etc., as primitive if they cannot be satisfactorily defined. Some philosophers may entirely reject this distinction between the qualitative and the nonqualitative, or may doubt that there are any properties that really ought to count as suchnesses under it. We shall not be concerned here with these doubts, but rather with what can be said, within the framework of the distinction, against those philosophers who think that all properties are suchnesses and all facts purely qualitative.

2. The Leibnizian position

Leibniz held, as I have suggested, that the thisness of each particular individual *is* a suchness. 'Singulars,' he said, 'are in fact *infimae species*,' the lowest or final species, the most specific members of the system of kinds. In this, as he sometimes remarked, he was extending to all individuals the doctrine of Thomas Aquinas about angels, that each one constitutes a separate species.[5]

The idea behind this claim is fairly simple, though the structure it postulates for thisnesses is infinitely complex. According to Leibniz, the terms of all propositions, at least as they are apprehended by the omniscience of God, are analyzable into simple, purely qualitative concepts. The construction of complex concepts out of simple ones is by logical operations; Leibniz thinks principally of conjunction and negation. The concept of an individual, which as we may put it expresses the property of being that individual, differs from more general concepts in being *complete*.[6] What makes a thing an individual, in other words, is that, in the logical construction of its concept, differentia is added to differentia until a concept is reached so specific that no new content can consistently be added to it.

---

5. Gottfried Wilhelm Leibniz, *Fragmente zur Logik*, ed. Franz Schmidt (Berlin: Akademie-Verlag, 1960), p. 476; cf. Leibniz, *Discourse on Metaphysics*, trans. P. G. Lucas and L. Griut (Manchester: Manchester University Press, 1953), sect. 9. This is not the place to debate points of interpretation, and I will sometimes speak of 'properties' where Leibniz usually restricts himself to 'concept' and 'predicate'; but I think I do not substantially misrepresent him on the points that concern us.
6. *Discourse on Metaphysics*, sect. 8.

Leibniz expresses this notion of completeness by saying that the concept of an individual implies every predicate of the individual. He inferred, notoriously, that alternative careers cannot be possible for the same individual. If a man never marries, for example, the concept of him must contain the predicate of never marrying, and so it would have been contradictory for *him* to have married.[7] I see no need to incorporate this implausible thesis in the theory of purely qualitative thisnesses. For if God can form complete concepts in the way that Leibniz supposes, he can also form the concept of a being that satisfies *either* one *or* another *or* another . . . of them.[8] If individuals are defined by disjunctive concepts of the latter sort, there are alternative careers, in different possible worlds, that they could have had. And if Leibnizian complete concepts are purely qualitative, so are disjunctions of them. The completeness of individual concepts, at least in the form actually maintained by Leibniz, is therefore not to be regarded as an integral part of the 'Leibnizian position' under discussion here.

If we want an up-to-date argument for primitive, *non*qualitative thisnesses, we may be tempted to seek it in the semantics of direct reference. Several philosophers have made a persuasive case for the view that we often succeed in referring to a particular individual without knowing any clearly qualitative property, or even any disjunction of such properties, that a thing must possess in order to be that individual. Such direct reference is commonly effected by the use of proper names and indexical expressions, and sometimes by what has been called the 'referential' use of descriptions.[9] If these claims are correct (as I believe they are), doesn't it follow that thisnesses are primitive and nonqualitative?

Yes and no. It follows that thisnesses are *semantically* primitive—that is, that we can express them (and know that we express them) without understanding each thisness (the property of being this or that individual) in terms of some other property or properties, better known to us, into which it can be analyzed or with which it is equivalent. But it does not follow that thisnesses *are* not analyzable into, equivalent with, or even identical with, purely qualitative properties or suchnesses, as claimed by Leibniz. Thus it does not follow that we are entitled to say that thisnesses are *metaphysically* primitive in the sense that interests us here, or (more precisely) that they are nonqualitative.

For Leibniz could certainly accept direct reference without giving up his conception of thisnesses as qualitative properties. All he must say is that we can refer to

---

7. See Leibniz's letter of 4/14 July, 1686 to Antoine Arnauld, in *The Leibniz–Arnaud Correspondence*, trans. H. T. Mason, (Manchester: Manchester University Press, 1967), pp. 53–66.

8. This point could also be put in terms of constructing complete concepts from predicates that are indexed to possible worlds. This possible amendment of Leibniz's position, and its analogy with Leibniz's commitment to the indexing of predicates to times, were noted by Benson Mates, 'Individuals and modality in the philosophy of Leibniz,' *Studia Leibnitiana* 4 (1972), p. 109.

9. Cf. Keith S. Donnellan, 'Reference and definite descriptions,' *Philosophical Review*, 75/3 (July 1966), pp. 281–304, and *idem*, 'Proper names and identifying descriptions,' in D. Davidson and G. Harman (eds), *The Semantics of Natural Languages*, 2nd edn. (Boston: Reidel, 1972), pp. 356–79; Saul Kripke, 'Naming and necessity,' in Davidson and Harman (eds), pp. 253–355.

individuals, and thus express their thisnesses, without understanding the analyses that show the thisnesses to be qualitative. And that he believed in any case. On his view the complete, definitive concept of an individual is infinitely complex and, therefore, cannot be distinctly apprehended by any finite mind, but only by God. Hence *we* must refer to the concept of the individual by reference to the individual (as 'the individual notion or haecceity of Alexander,'[10] for example), rather than referring to the individual as the one who satisfies the concept.

We may rely intuitively on direct reference in arguing for nonqualitative thisnesses, but the issue of direct reference is not the center of our metaphysical inquiry. The purely qualitative conception of individuality stands or falls, rather, with a certain doctrine of the Identity of Indiscernibles.

The Identity of Indiscernibles might be defined, in versions of increasing strength, as the doctrine that no two distinct individuals can share (1) all their properties, or (2) all their suchnesses, or (3) all their nonrelational suchnesses. Leibniz takes no pains to distinguish these three doctrines, because he holds all of them; but it is only the second that concerns us here. The first is utterly trivial. If thisnesses are properties, of course two distinct individuals, Castor and Pollux, cannot have all their properties in common. For Castor must have the properties of being identical with Castor and not being identical with Pollux, which Pollux cannot share.[11] The third doctrine, rejecting the possibility of individuals differing in relational suchnesses alone, is a most interesting thesis, but much more than needs to be claimed in holding that reality must be purely qualitative. Let us therefore here reserve the title 'Identity of Indiscernibles' for the doctrine that any two distinct individuals must differ in some suchness, *either* relational *or* nonrelational.

I say, the doctrine that they *must* so differ. Leibniz commonly states this principle, and the stronger principle about relations, in the language of necessity. And well he might; for he derives them from his theory of the nature of an individual substance, and ultimately from his conception of the nature of truth, which he surely regarded as absolutely necessary.[12] He was not perfectly consistent about this. He seemed to admit to Clarke that there could have been two perfectly indiscernible things. But, as Clarke remarked, some of Leibniz's arguments require the claim of necessity.[13] And it is only if necessity is claimed, that philosophically interesting objections can be raised to the Identity of Indiscernibles. For surely we have no reason to believe that

10. Leibniz, Discourse on Metaphysics, sect. 8.

11. This way of establishing a trivial version of the Identity of Indiscernibles was noticed by Whitehead and Russell, *Principia Mathematica*, vol. 1, 2nd edn. (Cambridge: Cambridge University Press, 1957), p. 57. It is the initial topic in Max Black's 'The identity of indiscernibles,' *Mind*, 61: (1952), pp. 153–64, and I think that Black does not quite distinguish it from any interesting version of the doctrine, because he does not explicitly distinguish relational properties that are suchnesses from those which are not.

12. See esp. his famous paper 'First truths,' and his *Discourse on Metaphysics*, sects. 8, 9.

13. *The Leibniz–Clarke Correspondence*, ed. H. G. Alexander (Manchester: Manchester University Press, 1956), Leibniz's fifth letter, sects. 25, 26, and Clarke's fifth reply, sects. 21–5 and 26–32. Clarke could not have seen the papers in which Leibniz most clearly implied the claim of necessity.

there actually are distinct individuals that share all their qualitative properties, relational as well as nonrelational.

Here we are concerned with the necessary connection between the Identity of Indiscernibles, in the sense I have picked out, and Leibniz's conception of thisnesses as suchnesses. If individuals are *infimae species*, then 'the principle of individuation is always some specific difference';[14] individuals must be distinguished by their suchnesses. Conversely, the clearest way of proving the distinctness of two properties is usually to find a possible case in which one would be exemplified without the other. In order to establish the distinctness of thisnesses from all suchnesses, therefore, one might try to exhibit possible cases in which two things would possess all the same suchnesses, but with different thisnesses. That is, one might seek counterexamples to refute the Identity of Indiscernibles.

Indeed a refutation of that doctrine is precisely what is required for the defense of nonqualitative thisnesses. For suppose the Identity of Indiscernibles is true. And suppose further, as Leibniz did and as believers in the doctrine may be expected to suppose, that it is true of possible worlds as well as of individuals, so that no two possible worlds are exactly alike in all qualitative respects. Then for each possible individual there will be a suchness of the disjunctive form:

having suchnesses $S_{\iota 1}$ in a world that has suchnesses $S_{\omega 1}$, *or*
having suchnesses $S_{\iota 2}$ in a world that has suchnesses $S_{\omega 2}$, *or* . . .

which that individual will possess in every world in which it occurs, and which no other individual will possess in any possible world.[15] This suchness will, therefore, be necessarily equivalent to the property of being that individual, and, since there will be such a suchness for every individual, it follows that every individual's thisness will be equivalent to a suchness.

Perhaps it does not follow immediately that every possible individual's thisness will *be* a suchness. If being an even prime and being the successor of 1 may be distinct though necessarily equivalent properties, some thisness and some suchness might also be distinct though necessarily equivalent. But if *every* thisness must be necessarily equivalent to a suchness, it will be hard to show that thisnesses distinct from suchnesses cannot be dispensed with, or that possible worlds cannot all be constituted purely qualitatively.

On the other hand, if it is possible for there to be distinct but qualitatively indiscernible individuals, it is possible for there to be individuals whose thisnesses are both distinct from all suchnesses and necessarily equivalent to no suchness. And in that case there is some point to distinguishing the thisnesses of individuals systematically from their suchnesses. For it is plausible to suppose that the structure of

---

14. Leibniz, *Fragmente zur Logik*, p. 476.
15. Of course the suchness will be constituted by a single disjunct if, as Leibniz held, each individual exists in only one possible world.

individuality is sufficiently similar in all cases that, if in some possible cases thisnesses would be distinct from all suchnesses, then thisnesses are universally distinct
from suchnesses—even if some thisnesses (including, for all we know, those of all
actual individuals) are necessarily equivalent to some suchnesses.

3. The dispersal arguments against the identity
of indiscernibles

The standard argument against the Identity of Indiscernibles, going back at least to
Kant,[16] is from spatial dispersal. Max Black's version[17] is fairly well known. We are
to imagine a universe consisting solely of two large, solid globes of iron. They always
have been, are, and always will be exactly similar in shape (perfectly spherical), size,
chemical composition, color—in short, in every qualitative respect. They even share
all their relational suchnesses; for example, each of them has the property of being
two diameters from another iron globe similar to itself. Such a universe seems to be
logically possible; hence it is concluded that there could be two qualitatively indiscernible things and that the Identity of Indiscernibles is false.

Similar arguments may be devised using much more complicated imaginary universes, which may have language-users in them. Such universes may be perfectly
symmetrical about a central point, line, or plane, throughout their history. Or they
may always repeat themselves to infinity in every direction, like a monstrous three-
dimensional wallpaper pattern.

The reason that is assumed to show that the indiscernibles in these imaginary
universes are not identical is not that they have different properties, but that they
are spatially dispersed, spatially distant from one another. The axiom about identity
that is used here is not that the same thing cannot both have and lack the same
property, but that the same thing cannot be in two places at once—that is, cannot
be spatially distant from itself.[18]

An argument for the possibility of non-identical indiscernibles, very similar
to the argument from spatial dispersal, and as good, can also be given from *temporal* dispersal. For it seems that there could be a perfectly cyclical universe in which
each event was preceded and followed by infinitely many other events qualitatively
indiscernible from itself. Thus there would be distinct but indiscernible *events*,
separated by temporal rather than spatial distances. And depending on our
criteria of transtemporal identity, it might also be argued that there would be
indiscernible persons and physical objects, similarly separated by temporal
distances.

---

16. Immanuel Kant, *Critique of Pure Reason*, A263f = B319f.
17. 'The identity of indiscernibles'.
18. This axiom might be doubted, but I simply assume it here. Occam denied that it is a necessary truth
    (*Reportatio*, IV, q. 4N and q. 5), in *Opera Plurima* (Lyon, 1494–6); I am indebted to Marilyn Adams
    for this information).

In a recent interesting article Ian Hacking argues that 'it is vain to contemplate possible spatiotemporal worlds to refute or establish the identity of indiscernibles.'[19] He holds that

Whatever God might create, we are clever enough to describe it in such a way that the identity of indiscernibles is preserved. This is a fact not about God but about description, space, time, and the laws that we ascribe to nature.[20]

The dichotomy between what God might create and our descriptions is important here. Hacking allows that there are consistent descriptions of non-identical indiscernibles and that there are possible states of affairs in which those descriptions would not exactly be false. On the other hand, he thinks that those same possible states of affairs could just as truly (not more truly, but just as truly) be described as containing only one thing in place of each of the sets of indiscernibles. The two descriptions are very different, but there is no difference at all in the possible reality that they represent. Thus, Hacking is not exactly asserting the Identity of Indiscernibles. But his rejection of primitive, nonqualitative thisness runs at least as deep as Leibniz's. He thinks that there cannot be any objective fact of the matter about how many individuals are present in the cases that seem to be counterexamples to the Identity of Indiscernibles. And on his view the constitution of reality, of what 'God might create,' as distinct from our descriptions of it, is purely qualitative.

Hacking's criticisms are directed against both the spatial- and the temporal-dispersal arguments for the possibility of non-identical indiscernibles. The most telling point he makes against them is that they overlook the possibility of alternative geometries and chronometries. If we have a space or time that is curved, then an individual can be spatially or temporally distant from itself, and distance does not prove distinctness. Hacking makes this point most explicitly about time,[21] but he could also use it to criticize the spatial argument, as follows: 'The most that God could create of the world imagined by Black is a globe of iron, having internal qualities Q which can be reached by traveling two diameters in a straight line from a globe of iron having qualities Q. This possible reality can be described as two globes in Euclidean space, or as a single globe in a non-Euclidean space so tightly curved that the globe can be reached by traveling two diameters in a straight line from itself. But the difference between these descriptions represents no difference in the way things could really be.'

There are at least two possible replies to Hacking. (1) He acknowledges that if 'absolute spacetime' is accepted, the spatial and temporal dispersal arguments are quite successful in refuting the Identity of Indiscernibles. But to hold, as he seems to,[22] that no weaker assumption would vindicate the arguments is to demand more

19. Ian Hacking, 'The identity of indiscernibles,' *Journal of Philosophy* 72, 9 (8 May 1975), pp. 249–56, at p. 249.
20. Ibid., pp. 255–6.
21. Ibid., p. 255. The point was also suggested, about space, by Black, this volume, ch. 6.
22. Hacking, 'Identity of indiscernibles,' pp. 251f, 254f.

than is needed. The dispersal arguments hold up very well even if places and times are defined in terms of relations of objects, provided that certain spatiotemporal relational properties of objects are accepted as primitive. For example, if it is a primitive feature of a possible reality that an iron globe such as Black describes can be reached by traveling some distance in one direction on a *Euclidean* straight line from an exactly similar globe, then non-identical indiscernibles are possible in reality and not just in description.

In order to reply to Hacking in this way, one must assume that a difference in geometries makes, in its own right, a difference in possible worlds, so the same paths in the same universe could not be described, without error, both as Euclidean straight paths and as non-Euclidean straight paths. One must assume that facts about what geometry the universe has are not reducible to facts about what laws of nature best explain other, more primitive facts about objects in space; in particular, one must assume that what geometry the universe has does not depend on a determination of the number of objects in space. Some philosophers may accept these assumptions, and I do not have any better than intuitive grounds for rejecting them. Like Hacking, nonetheless, I am inclined to reject them.

(2) The most obvious and fundamental difference between Black's imaginary Euclidean (or gently Riemannian) two-globe universe and its tightly curved one-globe counterpart seems to be that in one of them there are two iron globes, and in the other only one. Why can't that be a difference between possible realities in its own right? Indeed, I think it is extremely plausible to regard it so.[23]

To give this answer, of course, is to hold that the thisnesses of the two globes are metaphysically primitive. The function of the imaginary spatiotemporal world here is not to show how individual distinctness can be explained by spatiotemporal relations; no such explanation is needed if thisnesses are metaphysically primitive. The imaginary world simply provides an example in which it seems intuitively that two individuals would be distinct although it is clear that they would have all the same suchnesses.

The intuition involved here is akin to those which support belief in direct reference. This will be clearer if we imagine that we are on one of the two globes, with indiscernible twins on the other, so that the use of demonstratives will be possible. Then we can appeal to the intuition that it means something, which we understand quite well and which if true expresses a metaphysical reality, to say that this globe is not identical with that one, even in a situation in which we are not able to

---

23. Strictly speaking, I think it is highly plausible to regard it so *if* physical objects are accepted as primitive features of reality. Like Leibniz, I am inclined to take a phenomenalistic view of physical objects, and hence doubt the primitiveness of *their* thisnesses. Unlike Leibniz, I think there could be distinct but indiscernible sentient beings and mental events; cases that help to show the plausibility of this view may be provided by temporal dispersal arguments, or by another type of argument to be discussed in section 4 below.

distinguish them qualitatively. But the argument goes beyond direct reference in one important respect: it incorporates a judgment that the assertion of individual distinctness is not only intelligible independently of qualitative difference, but also consistent with the assumption that there is no qualitative difference.

4. Arguments from the possibility of almost indiscernible twins

We may just have an intuition that there could be distinct, though indiscernible, globes in these circumstances. But there may also be an argument for this view—which will depend in turn on other intuitions, like all arguments in these matters. The argument might rest on an intuition that the possibility of there being two objects in a given spatiotemporal relation to each other is not affected by any slight changes in such features as the color or chemical composition of one or both objects.[24] If we accept that intuition, we can infer the possibility of indiscernible twins from the uncontroversial possibility of *almost* indiscernible twins. No one doubts that there could be a universe like the universe of our example in other respects, if one of the two globes had a small chemical impurity that the other lacked. Surely, we may think, the absence of the impurity would not make such a universe impossible.

Spatiotemporal dispersal still plays a part in this argument. But one can argue against the Identity of Indiscernibles from the possibility of almost indiscernible twins in quite a different way, using an example that has to do primarily with minds rather than with bodies. Suppose I have an almost indiscernible twin. The only qualitative difference between him and me, and hence between his part of the universe and mine, is that on one night of our lives (when we are 27 years old) the fire-breathing dragon that pursues me in my nightmare has ten horns, whereas the monster in his dream has only seven. I assume that the number of horns is little noted nor long remembered, and that any other, causally associated differences between his and my lives and parts of the world are slight and quite local. No doubt there is a possible world (call it w) in which there are almost indiscernible twins of this sort; it is only an expository convenience to assume that I am one of them and that w is actual. But if such a world is even possible, it seems to follow that a world with perfectly indiscernible twins is also possible. For surely I could have existed, and so could my twin, if my monster had had only seven horns, like his. And that could have been even if there were no other difference from the lives we live in w, except in the details causally connected with the number of horns in my dream.

24. If we assume that differences in color or chemical composition necessarily involve microscopic differences in spatiotemporal configuration, the intuition would have to be that slight differences of that sort do not affect the logical or metaphysical possibility of a given macroscopic configuration of objects.

In that case we would have been distinct but qualitatively indiscernible—a relation which seems therefore to be logically possible.

Several points in this argument call for further mention or explanation. (1) The non-identity obtaining between me and my twin in *w* is proved by a qualitative difference between us there. (2) The argument depends on an intuition of transworld identity—that in a possible world (call it *w′*), otherwise like *w*, but in which my dragon has only seven horns, there could exist an individual identical with me and an individual identical with my twin, even though we would not be qualitatively different in that case. (3) The transitivity of identity is relied on in arguing that since my twin and I are not identical in *w* (as shown by the difference in our suchnesses there), it follows that we are not identical in any possible world, and therefore are distinct in *w′*, if we both exist in it.

(4) Because differences in modal properties can be purely qualitative, the conclusion that my twin and I would be qualitatively indiscernible in *w′* depends, additionally, on the assumption that in *w′* he as well as I would be a person who could have dreamed of a ten-horned monster in the circumstances in which I did in *w*. In other words, it is assumed that if *w* and *w′* are possible, so is a world *w″* just like *w* except that in *w″* it is my twin's beast that has ten horns and mine that has seven. (More precisely, it is assumed that *w* and *w″* would be equally possible if *w′* were actual.) The implications of the supposition that there are possible worlds that differ, as *w* and *w″* do, only by a transposition of individuals will be studied further in section 5 below.

(5) But we may notice here a consideration about time that seems to me to support assumptions (2) and (4). The mutual distinctness of two individual persons already existing cannot depend on something that has not yet happened. The identity and non-identity of most individuals, and surely of persons, are conceived of as determined, at any time of their existence, by their past and present. This is doubtless connected with the importance that origins seem to have in questions of transworld identity. Consider the state of *w* when my twin and I are 22, five years before the distinctive dreams. We are already distinct from each other, though nothing has yet happened to distinguish us qualitatively. I think it follows that our mutual distinctness is independent of the qualitative difference arising from our later dreams. We would be distinct, therefore, even if our dreams did not differ at age 27—that is, even if we were perfectly indiscernible qualitatively, as we would be in *w′*. Moreover, since my twin and I have our identities already established by age 22, which of us is which cannot depend on which has which dream five years later; it is possible that the seven-horned monster trouble my sleep, and the ten-horned his, when we are 27, as in *w″*. This argument depends, of course, on the assumption that in *w* my twin and I have histories that differ qualitatively during a certain period after we are 22, but not before then. It follows that *w* is not completely deterministic, but that does not keep *w* from being at least logically possible.[25]

25. I do not claim that Leibniz would accept this judgment of possibility.

5. Primitive trans-world identity

Issues of modality *de re* turn on identity questions. To say that a certain individual is only contingently a parent, but necessarily an animal, for example, is to say that there could have been a nonparent, but not a non-animal, that would have been the same individual as that one. It has become customary, and has been at least heuristically helpful, to represent such identities as identities of individuals in different possible worlds—'transworld identities' for short—although (as we have just seen) modal claims *de re* can be understood as identity claims even without the imagery of possible worlds. Whether modality *de re* really adds anything important to the stock of modal facts depends, I think, on whether there are transworld identities or non-identities, and if so, whether they are primitive or are rather to be analyzed in terms of some more fundamental relation(s) among possible worlds. I will try to show here that, if we are prepared to accept nonqualitative thisnesses, we have a very plausible argument for primitive transworld identities and non-identities.

It might be thought, indeed, that we would have a more than plausible argument—that if, by refuting the Identity of Indiscernibles, we can show that thisnesses are metaphysically primitive, it will follow trivially that transworld identity of individuals is also primitive. For the property of being identical with (for example) Aristotle is the same property in every possible world in which it occurs. Hence it cannot be distinct from all suchnesses when possessed by a famous philosopher in the actual world if it is identical with a suchness when possessed by one of Alexander the Great's tax collectors in some other possible world.

This argument is correct insofar as it makes the point that the thisness or identity of a particular individual is nonqualitative either at all places, times, and possible worlds at which it occurs, or at none of them. By the same token, however, there is nothing special about transworld identity in this connection. But the issue on which I wish to focus here is specifically about the primitiveness of *transworld* identities. It therefore cannot be the issue of whether they are purely qualitative.

When we ask about the primitiveness of a kind of identity, we typically want to know, about a certain range of cases, whether the belonging of two properties to a single subject can be explained as consisting in other, more basic relations obtaining between distinct subjects of the same or related properties.[26] Thus Aristotle is the subject of the diverse properties expressed by 'is a philosopher' and 'could have been a tax collector'. In asking whether the identity of the actual philosopher with the possible tax collector is primitive, we want to know whether it consists in some more fundamental relation between Aristotle's actual career and a career in which he would have been a tax collector. This issue is quite distinct from that of the qualitative or nonqualitative character of Aristotle's identity, in the same or in different worlds, as may be seen by reflecting on some other sorts of identity.

---

26. Cf. John Perry, 'Can the self divide?', *Journal of Philosophy* 59/6 (7 Sept. 1972), pp. 463–88, at pp. 466–8.

The claim that there are nonqualitative thisnesses does not clearly entail that *transtemporal* identity, for example, is primitive. For suppose there are two persisting individuals, Indi and Scerni, acknowledged to be qualitatively indiscernible, and therefore to possess nonqualitative thisnesses. It is not obvious that the identity of Indi at time t_1 with Indi at time t_2 (or the belonging of Indi's t_1 states and t_2 states to a single individual) cannot be explained as consisting in other, more basic relations among successive events or states or stages of Indi, without presupposing the transtemporal identity of any individual. Perhaps this can be done in terms of spatiotemporal continuity or memory links or causal connections or some other relation. The property of being Indi at any given time would still not be equivalent to any suchness. It could be analyzed in terms of the more basic relations among Indi's temporal stages. But the distinctness of those stages from the corresponding stages of Scerni would still be irreducibly nonqualitative, and this nonqualitative character would be passed on to the property of being Indi (at any time). The transtemporal aspect of Indi's identity, however, would not be indispensably primitive. In the present state of philosophical research it is probably unclear whether any transtemporal identity is indeed primitive; my point here is just that the thesis of the nonqualitativeness of thisnesses can be separated from that of the primitiveness of transtemporal identity.

If, to complete the separation of issues, we seek an example of a philosopher who is committed, with apparent consistency, both to the purely qualitative character of all thisnesses and to the primitiveness of some sort of individual identity, we can find it in Leibniz. He regards thisnesses as conjunctions of simpler, logically independent suchnesses. That the combination of properties is effected by the logical operation of conjunction is an essential part of his conceptual atomism. He assumes that there are some cases in which the instantiation of a conjunction of properties cannot be analyzed as consisting in any more fundamental fact. But if it is a primitive fact that the property *F and G* is instantiated, the identity of some possessor of *F* with a possessor of *G* must also be primitive, rather than analyzable as consisting in some more basic relation obtaining between distinct possessors of *F* and of *G* or related properties. The primitiveness of identity in such cases is in no way inconsistent with Leibniz's opinion that thisnesses are suchnesses; it is indeed required by the way in which he thinks thisnesses are constructed out of simpler suchnesses.

The primitive identities for Leibniz would probably not be transtemporal, and would certainly not be transworld. But no distance in space, time, or 'logical space' is needed for questions of identity. Suppose one of Aristotle's momentary perceptual states includes both tasting an olive and hearing a bird sing. In this supposition it is implied, and not yet explained by any more basic relation, that some individual that is tasting an olive is *identical* with one that is hearing a bird sing. And it seems that this sort of identity (identity of the individual subject of simultaneous qualities) could be primitive in a purely qualitative construction of reality.

So questions of the primitiveness of identity relations are in general distinct from the question of the qualitativeness or nonqualitativeness of thisnesses. But, in the case of transworld identity in particular, I think that primitive identities are much more plausible if nonqualitative thisnesses are accepted than if they are rejected. Suppose, on the one hand, that all thisnesses are purely qualitative. Then the thisness of any individual can be constructed as a disjunction of suchnesses, each suchness representing one possible career of the individual (as explained in section 2 above). It seems quite possible that in every case the grouping of disjuncts as alternative careers of a single individual could be explained by general principles about transworld identity of one or another kind of individuals, and the transworld identity of the particular individual could be analyzed as consisting in the satisfaction of the general principles by the relevant disjuncts. And if there should be borderline cases, in which the issue of transworld identity is not settled by general principles, one might well conclude that transworld identity or non-identity is undefined, rather than primitive, in those cases.

If, on the other hand, we reject the Identity of Indiscernibles in favor of nonqualitative thisnesses, it will not be hard to find examples that will provide support of great intuitive plausibility for primitive transworld identities and non-identities. Consider, again, a possible world w_1 in which there are two qualitatively indiscernible globes; call them Castor and Pollux.[27] Being indiscernible, they have of course the same duration; in w_1 both of them have always existed and always will exist. But it seems perfectly possible, logically and metaphysically, that either or both of them cease to exist. Let w_2 then, be a possible world just like w_1 up to a certain time t at which in w_2 Castor ceases to exist while Pollux goes on forever; and let w_3 be a possible world just like w_2 except that in w_3 it is Pollux that ceases to exist at t while Castor goes on forever. That the difference between w_2 and w_3 is real, and could be important, becomes vividly clear if we consider that, from the point of view of a person living on Castor before t in w_1 and having (of course) an indiscernible twin on Pollux, it can be seen as the difference between being annihilated and somebody else being annihilated instead. But there is no qualitative difference between w_2 and w_3. And there are no qualitative necessary and sufficient conditions for the transworld identity or non-identity of Castor and Pollux; for every qualitative condition satisfied by Castor in w_2 is satisfied by Pollux in w_1 and vice versa.[28]

27. The question may be raised whether giving names to the globes is consistent with their qualitative indiscernibility (cf. Black, 'The indiscernibility of identicals'). Two answers may be given. The imaginative answer is that we may suppose that the globes have (indiscernible) societies of language-users on them and we are speaking the language of the Castor-dwellers; in the language of the Pollux-dwellers, of course, 'Castor' names Pollux and 'Pollux' Castor, but that does not keep Castor from *being* Castor and Pollux Pollux. The sober answer is that 'Castor' and 'Pollux' are informal equivalents of variables bound by the existential quantifiers that would be used to introduce the example in a formal way.

28. We rely here on an intuition that the Castor-dweller can refer directly to the same individual (namely herself) in different possible worlds, despite the absence of qualitative necessary and sufficient conditions for the identity. This is related, in ways that should by now be familiar to us, to intuitions that have been used to support the semantics of direct reference—as, for example, that when we say, 'Nixon might have lost the 1968 election,' we refer to the actual individual, Nixon, in a non-actual situation even if we do not know any clearly qualitative property that the possible loser must have in order to be identical with the actual President. (The example is Kripke's; see his 'Naming and necessity,' pp. 264ff.)

A similar example can be constructed for transworld identity of *events*. Suppose all that happens in w_1 is that Castor and Pollux approach and recede from each other in an infinite series of indiscernible pulsations of the universe. In w_1 their pulsations go on forever, but they might not have. For every pair of them there is surely a possible world in which one member of the pair is the last pulsation, and a different possible world in which the other is the last pulsation. But there is no qualitative difference between these possible worlds; each contains the same number (N_0 the first infinite number) of exactly similar pulsations. There are therefore no qualitative necessary and sufficient conditions for the transworld identities and non-identities of the events in these possible worlds.

Any case of this sort, in which two possible worlds differ in the transworld identities of their individuals but not in their suchnesses, provides us at once with a clearer proof of a primitive transworld identity than has yet been found for a primitive transtemporal identity.[29] For the geometrical, topological, psychological, and causal relations out of which philosophers have hoped to construct transtemporal identity do not obtain among the alternative possible careers of an individual. 'Logical space' is not a space to which the concepts of physical space apply literally. There is no causal interaction between different possible worlds. One cannot remember events in another possible world in the same sense in which one's memory of events in the actual past might be important to personal identity. The most important transworld relations of individuals, which seem to be the foundation of all their other transworld relations, are qualitative similarity—which cannot explain different transworld identities in worlds that are qualitatively indiscernible—and identity itself. One might try to analyze the transworld identity of an individual in terms of qualitative similarities plus having the same parts, or the same parents; but then the transworld identity of some individuals (the parts or the parents) is presupposed. If the Identity of Indiscernibles is rejected, there seems to be no plausible way of analyzing transworld identity and non-identity in general in terms of other, more basic relations.

6. Thisness and necessity

I have argued that there are possible cases in which no purely qualitative conditions would be both necessary and sufficient for possessing a given thisness. It may be thought that this is too cautious a conclusion—that if thisnesses are nonqualitative, there cannot be any qualitative necessary conditions at all for possessing them. The following argument could be given for this view.

---

29. It is not essential to the argument to start from a world in which (as in w_1) there are non-identical indiscernibles. An essentially similar argument can be based on the case presented in section 4 above, in which I have an *almost* indiscernible twin. But, since the crux of the argument will be that every qualitative condition satisfied by me in w is satisfied by him in w'', and vice versa, we must still be prepared to accept nonqualitative thisnesses. And, as we saw in section 4, the case can also be used to argue for the possibility of a world containing perfectly indiscernible twins.

Let *T* be a thisness, and let *S* be a suchness. Many philosophers have believed that all necessary truths are *analytic*, in the sense that they are either truths of formal logic or derivable by valid logical rules from correct analyses of concepts or properties. This may be regarded as a broadly Leibnizian conception of necessity. Suppose it is right; and suppose that thisnesses are irreducibly nonqualitative. We may well wonder, then, how it could be a necessary truth that whatever has *T* has *S*. For it is surely not a truth of formal logic. And suchnesses are not analyzable in terms of thisnesses; so if thisnesses are not analyzable in terms of suchnesses, how can any connection between *T* and *S* fail to be synthetic?

The conclusion, that there cannot be any purely qualitative necessary condition for the possession of any given thisness, is absurd, however. It implies that you and I, for example, could have been individuals of any sort whatever—plutonium atoms, noises, football games, places, or times, if those are all individuals.[30] If we cannot trust our intuition that we could not have been any of those things, then it is probably a waste of time to study *de re* modalities at all. If there are any transworld identities and non-identities, there are necessary connections between thisnesses and some suchnesses.

But it is difficult to understand what makes these connections necessary; and that difficulty has doubtless motivated some philosophical doubts about *de re* modality.[31] Those who accept nonqualitative thisnesses but cling to the dogma that all necessary truths are analytic in the sense explained above may suppose that every nonqualitative thisness that is necessarily connected with suchnesses is analyzable as a conjunction of some or all of the suchnesses it implies, plus a relation to one or more particular individuals of some more fundamental sort. Either the latter individuals (or others still more basic to which one would come by recursive applications of the view) would have no qualitative necessary conditions of their identity at all, or there would be an infinite regress (perhaps virtuous) of thisnesses analyzable in terms of more fundamental thisnesses. Neither alternative seems particularly plausible.

It is better to abandon the identification of necessity with analyticity and suppose that necessities *de re* are commonly synthetic. Perhaps the best answer that can be given to the question, What makes it necessary that Jimmy Carter (for example) is not a musical performance? is this: It is a fact, which we understand very well to be true, though not analytic, that Jimmy Carter is a person. And there are necessary conditions of intra- and transworld identity which follow (analytically, indeed) from the concept or property of being a person and which entail that no individual that is in fact a person could under any circumstances be a musical performance.

30. In his *Examination of McTaggart's Philosophy*, vol. 1 (Cambridge: Cambridge University Press, 1933), p. 177, C. D. Broad pointed out that rejection of the Identity of Indiscernibles does not imply 'that it is logically possible that [a particular] *P*, which *in fact has* the nature *N*, should *instead* have had some other nature *N'*; e.g., that I might have been born in Rome in 55 BC, or that the Albert Memorial might have been a volcano in South America.'

31. Cf. W. V. Quine, *From a Logical Point of View*, 2nd edn. (New York: Harper Torchbooks, 1963), p. 155.

There are many notoriously perplexing questions about what suchnesses belong necessarily to which individuals. 'Could Cleopatra have been male?' 'Could I (who am blue-eyed) have been brown-eyed?' And so forth. It may be that some of these questions call for conceptual legislation rather than metaphysical discovery, for some of our concepts of kinds of individual may be somewhat vague with respect to necessary conditions of transworld identity. The acceptance of nonqualitative thisnesses does not oblige us to settle doubtful cases in favor of contingency. Indeed, I am inclined to decide a very large proportion of them in favor of necessity (or impossibility, as the case may be).

If a name is desired for the position I have defended here, according to which thisnesses and transworld identities are primitive but logically connected with suchnesses, we may call it *Moderate Haecceitism.*

Chapter 15

On what there is

W. V. Quine

A CURIOUS thing about the ontological problem is its simplicity. It can be put in three Anglo-Saxon monosyllables: 'What is there?' It can be answered, more-over, in a word—'Everything'—and everyone will accept this answer as true. However, this is merely to say that there is what there is. There remains room for disagreement over cases; and so the issue has stayed alive down the centuries.

Suppose now that two philosophers, McX and I, differ over ontology. Suppose McX maintains there is something which I maintain there is not. McX can, quite consistently with his own point of view, describe our difference of opinion by saying that I refuse to recognize certain entities. I should protest, of course, that he is wrong in his formulation of our disagreement, for I maintain that there are no entities, of the kind which he alleges, for me to recognize; but my finding him wrong in his formulation of our disagreement is unimportant, for I am committed to consid-ering him wrong in his ontology anyway.

When *I* try to formulate our difference of opinion, on the other hand, I seem to be in a predicament. I cannot admit that there are some things which McX countenances and I do not, for in admitting that there are such things I should be contradicting my own rejection of them.

It would appear, if this reasoning were sound, that in any ontological dispute the proponent of the negative side suffers the disadvantage of not being able to admit that his opponent disagrees with him.

This is the old Platonic riddle of nonbeing. Nonbeing must in some sense be, other-wise what is it that there is not? This tangled doctrine might be nicknamed *Plato's beard*; historically it has proved tough, frequently dulling the edge of Occam's razor.

It is some such line of thought that leads philosophers like McX to impute being where they might otherwise be quite content to recognize that there is nothing. Thus, take Pegasus. If Pegasus *were* not, McX argues, we should not be talking about anything when we use the word; therefore it would be nonsense to say even that Pegasus is not. Thinking to show thus that the denial of Pegasus cannot be coher-ently maintained, he concludes that Pegasus is.

McX cannot, indeed, quite persuade himself that any region of space–time, near or remote, contains a flying horse of flesh and blood. Pressed for further details on Pegasus, then, he says that Pegasus is an idea in men's minds. Here, however, a confusion begins to be apparent. We may for the sake of argument concede that there is an entity, and even a unique entity (though this is rather implausible), which is the mental Pegasus-idea; but this mental entity is not what people are talking about when they deny Pegasus.

McX never confuses the Parthenon with the Parthenon-idea. The Parthenon is physical; the Parthenon-idea is mental (according anyway to McX's version of ideas, and I have no better to offer). The Parthenon is visible; the Parthenon-idea is invisible. We cannot easily imagine two things more unlike, and less liable to confusion, than the Parthenon and the Parthenon-idea. But when we shift from the Parthenon to Pegasus, the confusion sets in—for no other reason than that McX would sooner be deceived by the crudest and most flagrant counterfeit than grant the nonbeing of Pegasus.

The notion that Pegasus must be, because it would otherwise be nonsense to say even that Pegasus is not, has been seen to lead McX into an elementary confusion. Subtler minds, taking the same precept as their starting point, come out with theories of Pegasus which are less patently misguided than McX's, and correspondingly more difficult to eradicate. One of these subtler minds is named, let us say, Wyman. Pegasus, Wyman maintains, has his being as an unactualized possible. When we say of Pegasus that there is no such thing, we are saying, more precisely, that Pegasus does not have the special attribute of actuality. Saying that Pegasus is not actual is on a par, logically, with saying that the Parthenon is not red; in either case we are saying something about an entity whose being is unquestioned.

Wyman, by the way, is one of those philosophers who have united in ruining the good old word 'exist'. Despite his espousal of unactualized possibles, he limits the word 'existence' to actuality—thus preserving an illusion of ontological agreement between himself and us who repudiate the rest of his bloated universe. We have all been prone to say, in our common-sense usage of 'exist', that Pegasus does not exist, meaning simply that there is no such entity at all. If Pegasus existed he would indeed be in space and time, but only because the word 'Pegasus' has spatio-temporal connotations, and not because 'exists' has spatio-temporal connotations. If spatio-temporal reference is lacking when we affirm the existence of the cube root of 27, this is simply because a cube root is not a spatio-temporal kind of thing, and not because we are being ambiguous in our use of 'exist'.[1] However, Wyman, in an ill-conceived effort to appear agreeable, genially grants us the nonexistence of Pegasus and then, contrary to what *we* meant by nonexistence of Pegasus, insists that Pegasus *is*. Existence is one thing, he says, and subsistence is another. The only way I know of coping with this obfuscation of issues is to *give* Wyman the word 'exist'.

1. The impulse to distinguish terminologically between existence as applied to objects actualized somewhere in space-time and existence (or subsistence or being) as applied to other entities arises in part, perhaps, from an idea that the observation of nature is relevant only to questions of existence of the first kind. But this idea is readily refuted by counterinstances such as 'the ratio of the number of centaurs to the number of unicorns'. If there were such a ratio, it would be an abstract entity, viz. a number. Yet it is only by studying nature that we conclude that the number of centaurs and the number of unicorns are both 'zero' and hence that there is no such ratio.

I'll try not to use it again; I still have 'is'. So much for lexicography; let's get back to Wyman's ontology.

Wyman's overpopulated universe is in many ways unlovely. It offends the aesthetic sense of us who have a taste for desert landscapes, but this is not the worst of it. Wyman's slum of possibles is a breeding ground for disorderly elements. Take, for instance, the possible fat man in that doorway; and, again, the possible bald man in that doorway. Are they the same possible man, or two possible men? How do we decide? How many possible men are there in that doorway? Are there more possible thin ones than fat ones? How many of them are alike? Or would their being alike make them one? Are no *two* possible things alike? Is this the same as saying that it is impossible for two things to be alike? Or, finally, is the concept of identity simply inapplicable to unactualized possibles? But what sense can be found in talking of entities which cannot meaningfully be said to be identical with themselves and distinct from one another? These elements are well-nigh incorrigible. By a Fregean therapy of individual concepts,[2] some effort might be made at rehabilitation; but I feel we'd do better simply to clear Wyman's slum and be done with it.

Possibility, along with the other modalities of necessity and impossibility and contingency, raises problems upon which I do not mean to imply that we should turn our backs. But we can at least limit modalities to whole statements. We may impose the adverb 'possibly' upon a statement as a whole, and we may well worry about the semantical analysis of such usage; but little real advance in such analysis is to be hoped for in expanding our universe to include so-called *possible entities*. I suspect that the main motive for this expansion is simply the old notion that Pegasus, for example, must be because otherwise it would be nonsense to say even that he is not.

Still, all the rank luxuriance of Wyman's universe of possibles would seem to come to naught when we make a slight change in the example and speak not of Pegasus but of the round square cupola on Berkeley College. If, unless Pegasus were, it would be nonsense to say that he is not, then by the same token, unless the round square cupola on Berkeley College were, it would be nonsense to say that it is not. But, unlike Pegasus, the round square cupola on Berkeley College cannot be admitted even as an unactualized *possible*. Can we drive Wyman now to admitting also a realm of unactualizable impossibles? If so, a good many embarrassing questions could be asked about them. We might hope even to trap Wyman in contradictions, by getting him to admit that certain of these entities are at once round and square. But the wily Wyman chooses the other horn of the dilemma and concedes that it is nonsense to say that the round square cupola on Berkeley College is not. He says that the phrase 'round square cupola' is meaningless.

Wyman was not the first to embrace this alternative. The doctrine of the meaninglessness of contradictions runs away back. The tradition survives, moreover, in writers who seem to share none of Wyman's motivations. Still, I wonder whether the

2. See Quine [1] p. 152.

first temptation to such a doctrine may not have been substantially the motivation which we have observed in Wyman. Certainly the doctrine has no intrinsic appeal; and it has led its devotees to such quixotic extremes as that of challenging the method of proof by *reductio ad absurdum*—a challenge in which I sense a *reductio ad absurdum* of the doctrine itself.

Moreover, the doctrine of meaninglessness of contradictions has the severe methodological drawback that it makes it impossible, in principle, ever to devise an effective test of what is meaningful and what is not. It would be forever impossible for us to devise systematic ways of deciding whether a string of signs made sense— even to us individually, let alone other people—or not. For it follows from a discovery in mathematical logic, due to Church, that there can be no generally applicable test of contradictoriness.

I have spoken disparagingly of Plato's beard, and hinted that it is tangled. I have dwelt at length on the inconveniences of putting up with it. It is time to think about taking steps.

Russell, in his theory of so-called singular descriptions, showed clearly how we might meaningfully use seeming names without supposing that there be the entities allegedly named. The names to which Russell's theory directly applies are complex descriptive names such as 'the author of *Waverley*', 'the present King of France', 'the round square cupola on Berkeley College'. Russell analyzes such phrases systematically as fragments of the whole sentences in which they occur. The sentence 'The author of *Waverley* was a poet', for example, is explained as a whole as meaning 'Someone (better: something) wrote *Waverley* and was a poet, and nothing else wrote *Waverley*'. (The point of this added clause is to affirm the uniqueness which is implicit in the word 'the', in '*the* author of *Waverley*'.) The sentence 'The round square cupola on Berkeley College is pink' is explained as 'Something is round and square and is a cupola on Berkeley College and is pink, and nothing else is round and square and a cupola on Berkeley College'.[3]

The virtue of this analysis is that the seeming name, a descriptive phrase, is paraphrased *in context* as a so-called incomplete symbol. No unified expression is offered as an analysis of the descriptive phrase, but the statement as a whole which was the context of that phrase still gets its full quota of meaning—whether true or false.

The unanalyzed statement 'The author of *Waverley* was a poet' contains a part, 'the author of *Waverley*', which is wrongly supposed by McX and Wyman to demand objective reference in order to be meaningful at all. But in Russell's translation, 'Something wrote *Waverley* and was a poet and nothing else wrote *Waverley*', the burden of objective reference which had been put upon the descriptive phrase is now taken over by words of the kind that logicians call bound variables, variables of quantification, namely, words like 'something', 'nothing', 'everything'. These words, far from purporting to be names specifically of the author of *Waverley*, do not

---

3. For more on the theory of descriptions see Quine [1], pp. 85f, 166f.

purport to be names at all; they refer to entities generally, with a kind of studied ambiguity peculiar to themselves.[4] These quantificational words or bound variables are, of course a basic part of language, and their meaningfulness, at least in context, is not to be challenged. But their meaningfulness in no way presupposes there being either the author of *Waverley* or the round square cupola on Berkeley College or any other specifically preassigned objects.

Where descriptions are concerned, there is no longer any difficulty in affirming or denying being. 'There *is* the author of *Waverley*' is explained by Russell as mean- ing 'Someone (or, more strictly, something) wrote *Waverley* and nothing else wrote *Waverley*'. 'The author of *Waverley* is not' is explained, correspondingly, as the alter- nation 'Either each thing failed to write *Waverley* or two or more things wrote *Waverley*'. This alternation is false, but meaningful; and it contains no expression purporting to name the author of *Waverley*. The statement 'The round square cupola on Berkeley College is not' is analyzed in similar fashion. So the old notion that statements of nonbeing defeat themselves goes by the board. When a statement of being or nonbeing is analyzed by Russell's theory of descriptions, it ceases to con- tain any expression which even purports to name the alleged entity whose being is in question, so that the meaningfulness of the statement no longer can be thought to presuppose that there be such an entity.

Now what of 'Pegasus'? This being a word rather than a descriptive phrase, Russell's argument does not immediately apply to it. However, it can easily be made to apply. We have only to rephrase 'Pegasus' as a description, in any way that seems adequately to single out our idea; say, 'the winged horse that was captured by Bellerophon'. Substituting such a phrase for 'Pegasus', we can then proceed to ana- lyze the statement 'Pegasus is', or 'Pegasus is not', precisely on the analogy of Russell's analysis of 'The author of *Waverley* is' and 'The author of *Waverley* is not'.

In order thus to subsume a one-word name or alleged name such as 'Pegasus' under Russell's theory of description, we must, of course, be able first to translate the word into a description. But this is no real restriction. If the notion of Pegasus had been so obscure or so basic a one that no pat translation into a descriptive phrase had offered itself along familiar lines, we could still have availed ourselves of the following artificial and trivial-seeming device: we could have appealed to the *ex hypothesi* unanalyzable, irreducible attribute of *being Pegasus*, adopting, for its expression, the verb 'is-Pegasus', or 'pegasizes'. The noun 'Pegasus' itself could then be treated as derivative, and identified after all with a description: 'the thing that is-Pegasus', 'the thing that pegasizes'.[5]

If the importing of such a predicate as 'pegasizes' seems to commit us to recog- nizing that there is a corresponding attribute, pegasizing, in Plato's heaven or in the minds of men, well and good. Neither we nor Wyman nor McX have been

---

4. For more explicit treatment of the bound variable see Quine [1], pp. 82, 102f.
5. For further remarks on such assimilation of all singular terms to descriptions see Quine [1] p. 167; also Quine [2], pp. 218–24.

contending, thus far, about the being or nonbeing of universals, but rather about that of Pegasus. If in terms of pegasizing we can interpret the noun 'Pegasus' as a description subject to Russell's theory of descriptions, then we have disposed of the old notion that Pegasus cannot be said not to be without presupposing that in some sense Pegasus is.

Our argument is now quite general. McX and Wyman supposed that we could not meaningfully affirm a statement of the form 'So-and-so is not', with a simple or descriptive singular noun in place of 'so-and-so', unless so-and-so is. This supposition is now seen to be quite generally groundless, since the singular noun in question can always be expanded into a singular description, trivially or otherwise, and then analyzed out *à la* Russell.

We commit ourselves to an ontology containing numbers when we say there are prime numbers larger than a million; we commit ourselves to an ontology containing centaurs when we say there are centaurs; and we commit ourselves to an ontology containing Pegasus when we say Pegasus is. But we do not commit ourselves to an ontology containing Pegasus or the author of *Waverley* or the round square cupola on Berkeley College when we say that Pegasus or the author of *Waverley* or the cupola in question is *not*. We need no longer labor under the delusion that the meaningfulness of a statement containing a singular term presupposes an entity named by the term. A singular term need not name to be significant.

An inkling of this might have dawned on Wyman and McX even without benefit of Russell if they had only noticed—as so few of us do—that there is a gulf between *meaning* and *naming* even in the case of a singular term which is genuinely a name of an object. The following example from Frege will serve. The phrase 'Evening Star' names a certain large physical object of spherical form, which is hurtling through space some scores of millions of miles from here. The phrase 'Morning Star' names the same thing, as was probably first established by some observant Babylonian. But the two phrases cannot be regarded as having the same meaning; otherwise that Babylonian could have dispensed with his observations and contented himself with reflecting on the meanings of his words. The meanings, then, being different from one another, must be other than the named object, which is one and the same in both cases.

Confusion of meaning with naming not only made McX think he could not meaningfully repudiate Pegasus; a continuing confusion of meaning with naming no doubt helped engender his absurd notion that Pegasus is an idea, a mental entity. The structure of his confusion is as follows. He confused the alleged *named object* Pegasus with the *meaning* of the word 'Pegasus', therefore concluding that Pegasus must be in order that the word have meaning. But what sorts of things are meanings? This is a moot point; however, one might quite plausibly explain meanings as ideas in the mind, supposing we can make clear sense in turn of the idea of ideas in the mind. Therefore Pegasus, initially confused with a meaning, ends up as an idea in the mind. It is the more remarkable that Wyman, subject to the same initial motivation as McX, should have avoided this particular blunder and wound up with unactualized possibles instead.

Now let us turn to the ontological problem of universals: the question whether there are such entities as attributes, relations, classes, numbers, functions. McX, characteristically enough, thinks there are. Speaking of attributes, he says: 'There are red houses, red roses, red sunsets; this much is prephilosophical common sense in which we must all agree. These houses, roses, and sunsets, then, have something in common; and this which they have in common is all I mean by the attribute of redness.' For McX, thus, there being attributes is even more obvious and trivial than the obvious and trivial fact of there being red houses, roses, and sunsets. This, I think, is characteristic of metaphysics, or at least of that part of metaphysics called ontology: one who regards a statement on this subject as true at all must regard it as trivially true. One's ontology is basic to the conceptual scheme by which he interprets all experiences, even the most commonplace ones. Judged within some particular conceptual scheme—and how else is judgment possible?—an ontological statement goes without saying, standing in need of no separate justification at all. Ontological statements follow immediately from all manner of casual statements of commonplace fact, just as—from the point of view, anyway, of McX's conceptual scheme—'There is an attribute' follows from 'There are red houses, red roses, red sunsets'.

Judged in another conceptual scheme, an ontological statement which is axiomatic to McX's mind may, with equal immediacy and triviality, be adjudged false. One may admit that there are red houses, roses, and sunsets, but deny, except as a popular and misleading manner of speaking, that they have anything in common. The words 'houses', 'roses', and 'sunsets' are true of sundry individual entities which are houses and roses and sunsets, and the word 'red' or 'red object' is true of each of sundry individual entities which are red houses, red roses, red sunsets; but there is not, in addition, any entity whatever, individual or otherwise, which is named by the word 'redness', nor, for that matter, by the word 'householdhood', 'rosehood', 'sunsethood'. That the houses and roses and sunsets are all of them red may be taken as ultimate and irreducible, and it may be held that McX is no better off, in point of real explanatory power, for all the occult entities which he posits under such names as 'redness'.

One means by which McX might naturally have tried to impose his ontology of universals on us was already removed before we turned to the problem of universals. McX cannot argue that predicates such as 'red' or 'is-red', which we all concur in using, must be regarded as names each of a single universal entity in order that they be meaningful at all. For we have seen that being a name of something is a much more special feature than being meaningful. He cannot even charge us—at least not by *that* argument—with having posited an attribute of pegasizing by our adoption of the predicate 'pegasizes'.

However, McX hits upon a different strategem. 'Let us grant,' he says, 'this distinction between meaning and naming of which you make so much. Let us even grant that "is red", "pegasizes", etc., are not names of attributes. Still, you admit they have meanings. But these *meanings*, whether they are *named* or not, are still universals, and

I venture to say that some of them might even be the very things that I call attributes, or something to much the same purpose in the end.'

For McX, this is an unusually penetrating speech; and the only way I know to
counter it is by refusing to admit meanings. However, I feel no reluctance toward
refusing to admit meanings, for I do not thereby deny that words and statements are
meaningful. McX and I may agree to the letter in our classification of linguistic
forms into the meaningful and the meaningless, even though McX construes meaningfulness as the *having* (in some sense of 'having') of some abstract entity which he
calls a meaning, whereas I do not. I remain free to maintain that the fact that a given
linguistic utterance is meaningful (or *significant*, as I prefer to say so as not to invite
hypostasis of meanings as entities) is an ultimate and irreducible matter of fact; or,
I may undertake to analyze it in terms directly of what people do in the presence of
the linguistic utterance in question and other utterances similar to it.

The useful ways in which people ordinarily talk or seem to talk about meanings
boil down to two: the *having* of meanings, which is significance, and *sameness* of
meaning, or synonymy. What is called *giving* the meaning of an utterance is simply
the uttering of a synonym, couched, ordinarily, in clearer language than the original.
If we are allergic to meanings as such, we can speak directly of utterances as significant or insignificant, and as synonymous or heteronymous one with another. The
problem of explaining these adjectives 'significant' and 'synonymous' with some
degree of clarity and rigor—preferably, as I see it, in terms of behavior—is as difficult
as it is important.[6] But the explanatory value of special and irreducible intermediary
entities called meanings is surely illusory.

Up to now I have argued that we can use singular terms significantly in sentences
without presupposing that there are the entities which those terms purport to
name. I have argued further that we can use general terms, for example, predicates,
without conceding them to be names of abstract entities. I have argued further that
we can view utterances as significant, and as synonymous or heteronymous with
one another, without countenancing a realm of entities called meanings. At this
point McX begins to wonder whether there is any limit at all to our ontological
immunity. Does *nothing* we may say commit us to the assumption of universals or
other entities which we may find unwelcome?

I have already suggested a negative answer to this question, in speaking of bound
variables, or variables of quantification, in connection with Russell's theory of
descriptions. We can very easily involve ourselves in ontological commitments by
saying, for example, that *there is something* (bound variable) which red houses and
sunsets have in common; or that *there is something* which is a prime number larger
than a million. But this is, essentially, the *only* way we can involve ourselves in ontological commitments: by our use of bound variables. The use of alleged names is no
criterion, for we can repudiate their namehood at the drop of a hat unless the
assumption of a corresponding entity can be spotted in the things we affirm in

---

6. See Essays II and III in Quine [1]

terms of bound variables. Names are, in fact, altogether immaterial to the ontological issue, for I have shown, in connection with 'Pegasus' and 'pegasize', that names can be converted to descriptions, and Russell has shown that descriptions can be eliminated. Whatever we say with the help of names can be said in a language which shuns names altogether. To be assumed as an entity is, purely and simply, to be reckoned as the value of a variable. In terms of the categories of traditional grammar, this amounts roughly to saying that to be is to be in the range of reference of a pronoun. Pronouns are the basic media of reference; nouns might better have been named propronouns. The variables of quantification, 'something', 'nothing', 'everything', range over our whole ontology, whatever it may be; and we are convicted of a particular ontological presupposition if, and only if, the alleged presuppositum has to be reckoned among the entities over which our variables range in order to render one of our affirmations true.

We may say, for example, that some dogs are white and not thereby commit ourselves to recognizing either doghood or whiteness as entities. 'Some dogs are white' says that some things that are dogs are white; and, in order that this statement be true, the things over which the bound variable 'something' ranges must include some white dogs, but need not include doghood or whiteness. On the other hand, when we say that some zoölogical species are cross-fertile we are committing ourselves to recognizing as entities the several species themselves, abstract though they are. We remain so committed at least until we devise some way of so paraphrasing the statement as to show that the seeming reference to species on the part of our bound variable was an avoidable manner of speaking.[7]

Classical mathematics, as the example of primes larger than a million clearly illustrates, is up to its neck in commitments to an ontology of abstract entities. Thus it is that the great mediaeval controversy over universals has flared up anew in the modern philosophy of mathematics. The issue is clearer now than of old, because we now have a more explicit standard whereby to decide what ontology a given theory or form of discourse is committed to: a theory is committed to those and only those entities to which the bound variables of the theory must be capable of referring in order that the affirmations made in the theory be true.

Because this standard of ontological presupposition did not emerge clearly in the philosophical tradition, the modern philosophical mathematicians have not on the whole recognized that they were debating the same old problem of universals in a newly clarified form. But the fundamental cleavages among modern points of view on foundations of mathematics do come down pretty explicitly to disagreements as to the range of entities to which the bound variables should be permitted to refer.

The three main mediaeval points of view regarding universals are designated by historians as *realism*, *conceptualism*, and *nominalism*. Essentially these same three doctrines reappear in twentieth-century surveys of the philosophy of mathematics under the new names *logicism*, *intuitionism*, and *formalism*.

7. For more on this topic, see Essay VI in Quine [1].

Realism, as the word is used in connection with the mediaeval controversy over universals, is the Platonic doctrine that universals or abstract entities have being independently of the mind; the mind may discover them but cannot create them. *Logicism,* represented by Frege, Russell, Whitehead, Church, and Carnap, condones the use of bound variables to refer to abstract entities known and unknown, specifiable and unspecifiable, indiscriminately.

Conceptualism holds that there are universals but they are mind-made. *Intuitionism,* espoused in modern times in one form or another by Poincaré, Brouwer, Weyl, and others, countenances the use of bound variables to refer to abstract entities only when those entities are capable of being cooked up individually from ingredients specified in advance. As Fraenkel has put it, logicism holds that classes are discovered while intuitionism holds that they are invented—a fair statement indeed of the old opposition between realism and conceptualism. This opposition is no mere quibble; it makes an essential difference in the amount of classical mathematics to which one is willing to subscribe. Logicists, or realists, are able on their assumptions to get Cantor's ascending orders of infinity; intuitionists are compelled to stop with the lowest order of infinity, and, as an indirect consequence, to abandon even some of the classical laws of real numbers.[8] The modern controversy between logicism and intuitionism arose, in fact, from disagreements over infinity.

Formalism, associated with the name of Hilbert, echoes intuitionism in deploring the logicist's unbridled recourse to universals. But formalism also finds intuitionism unsatisfactory. This could happen for either of two opposite reasons. The formalist might, like the logicist, object to the crippling of classical mathematics; or he might, like the *nominalists* of old, object to admitting abstract entities at all, even in the restrained sense of mind-made entities. The upshot is the same: the formalist keeps classical mathematics as a play of insignificant notations. This play of notations can still be of utility—whatever utility it has already shown itself to have as a crutch for physicists and technologists. But utility need not imply significance, in any literal linguistic sense. Nor need the marked success of mathematicians in spinning out theorems, and in finding objective bases for agreement with one another's results, imply significance. For an adequate basis for agreement among mathematicians can be found simply in the rules which govern the manipulation of the notations— these syntactical rules being, unlike the notations themselves, quite significant and intelligible.[9]

I have argued that the sort of ontology we adopt can be consequential—notably in connection with mathematics, although this is only an example. Now how are we to adjudicate among rival ontologies? Certainly the answer is not provided by the semantical formula 'To be is to be the value of a variable'; this formula serves rather, conversely, in testing the conformity of a given remark or doctrine to a prior onto-

---

8. See Quine [1], pp. 125ff.
9. See Goodman and Quine. For further discussion of the general matters touched on in the past two pages, see Bernays, Fraenkel, Black.

logical standard. We look to bound variables in connection with ontology not in order to know what there is, but in order to know what a given remark or doctrine, ours or someone else's, *says* there is; and this much is quite properly a problem involving language. But what there is is another question.

In debating over what there is, there are still reasons for operating on a semantical plane. One reason is to escape from the predicament noted at the beginning of this essay: the predicament of my not being able to admit that there are things which McX countenances and I do not. So long as I adhere to my ontology, as opposed to McX's, I cannot allow my bound variables to refer to entities which belong to McX's ontology and not to mine. I can, however, consistently describe our disagreement by characterizing the statements which McX affirms. Provided merely that my ontology countenances linguistic forms, or at least concrete inscriptions and utterances, I can talk about McX's sentences.

Another reason for withdrawing to a semantical plane is to find common ground on which to argue. Disagreement in ontology involves basic disagreement in conceptual schemes; yet McX and I, despite these basic disagreements, find that our conceptual schemes converge sufficiently in their intermediate and upper ramifications to enable us to communicate successfully on such topics as politics, weather, and, in particular, language. In so far as our basic controversy over ontology can be translated upward into a semantical controversy about words and what to do with them, the collapse of the controversy into question-begging may be delayed.

It is no wonder, then, that ontological controversy should tend into controversy over language. But we must not jump to the conclusion that what there is depends on words. Translatability of a question into semantical terms is no indication that the question is linguistic. To see Naples is to bear a name which, when prefixed to the words 'sees Naples', yields a true sentence; still there is nothing linguistic about seeing Naples.

Our acceptance of an ontology is, I think, similar in principle to our acceptance of a scientific theory, say a system of physics: we adopt, at least insofar as we are reasonable, the simplest conceptual scheme into which the disordered fragments of raw experience can be fitted and arranged. Our ontology is determined once we have fixed upon the over-all conceptual scheme which is to accommodate science in the broadest sense; and the considerations which determine a reasonable construction of any part of that conceptual scheme, for example, the biological or the physical part, are not different in kind from the considerations which determine a reasonable construction of the whole. To whatever extent the adoption of any system of scientific theory may be said to be a matter of language, the same—but no more—may be said of the adoption of an ontology.

But simplicity, as a guiding principle in constructing conceptual schemes, is not a clear and unambiguous idea; and it is quite capable of presenting a double or multiple standard. Imagine, for example, that we have devised the most economical set of concepts adequate to the play-by-play reporting of immediate experience. The entities under this scheme—the values of bound variables—are, let us suppose, individual subjective events of sensation or reflection. We should still find, no doubt, that a physicalistic conceptual scheme, purporting to talk about external objects, offers great advantages in simplifying our over-all reports. By bringing together scattered sense events and treating them as perceptions of one object, we reduce the complexity of our stream of experience to a manageable conceptual simplicity. The rule of simplicity is indeed our guiding maxim in assigning sense data to objects: we associate an earlier and a later round sensum with the same so-called penny, or with two different so-called pennies, in obedience to the demands of maximum simplicity in our total world-picture.

Here we have two competing conceptual schemes, a phenomenalistic one and a physicalistic one. Which should prevail? Each has its advantages; each has its special simplicity in its own way. Each, I suggest, deserves to be developed. Each may be said, indeed, to be the more fundamental, though in different senses: the one is epistemologically, the other physically, fundamental.

The physical conceptual scheme simplifies our account of experience because of the way myriad scattered sense events come to be associated with single so-called objects; still there is no likelihood that each sentence about physical objects can actually be translated, however deviously and complexly, into the phenomenalistic language. Physical objects are postulated entities which round out and simplify our account of the flux of experience, just as the introduction of irrational numbers simplifies laws of arithmetic. From the point of view of the conceptual scheme of the elementary arithmetic of rational numbers alone, the broader arithmetic of rational and irrational numbers would have the status of a convenient myth, simpler than the literal truth (namely, the arithmetic of rationals) and yet containing that literal truth as a scattered part. Similarly, from a phenomenalistic point of view, the conceptual scheme of physical objects is a convenient myth, simpler than the literal truth and yet containing that literal truth as a scattered part.[10]

Now what of classes or attributes of physical objects, in turn? A platonistic ontology of this sort is, from the point of view of a strictly physicalistic conceptual scheme, as much a myth as that physicalistic conceptual scheme itself is for phenomenalism. This higher myth is a good and useful one, in turn, in so far as it simplifies our account of physics. Since mathematics is an integral part of this higher myth, the utility of this myth for physical science is evident enough. In speaking of it nevertheless as a myth, I echo that philosophy of mathematics to which I alluded earlier under the name of formalism. But an attitude of formalism may with equal justice be adopted toward the physical conceptual scheme, in turn, by the pure aesthete or phenomenalist.

The analogy between the myth of mathematics and the myth of physics is, in some additional and perhaps fortuitous ways, strikingly close. Consider, for example, the crisis which was precipitated in the foundations of mathematics, at the turn of the century, by the discovery of Russell's paradox and other antinomies of set theory.

---

10. The arithmetical analogy is due to Frank, pp. 108f.

These contradictions had to be obviated by unintuitive, *ad hoc* devices;[11] our mathematical myth-making became deliberate and evident to all. But what of physics? An antinomy arose between the undular and the corpuscular accounts of light; and if this was not as out-and-out a contradiction as Russell's paradox, I suspect that the reason is that physics is not as out-and-out as mathematics. Again, the second great modern crisis in the foundations of mathematics—precipitated in 1931 by Gödel's proof that there are bound to be undecidable statements in arithmetic—has its companion piece in physics in Heisenberg's indeterminacy principle.

In earlier pages I undertook to show that some common arguments in favor of certain ontologies are fallacious. Further, I advanced an explicit standard whereby to decide what the ontological commitments of a theory are. But the question what ontology actually to adopt still stands open, and the obvious counsel is tolerance and an experimental spirit. Let us by all means see how much of the physicalistic conceptual scheme can be reduced to a phenomenalistic one; still, physics also naturally demands pursuing, irreducible *in toto* though it be. Let us see how, or to what degree, natural science may be rendered independent of platonistic mathematics; but let us also pursue mathematics and delve into its platonistic foundations.

From among the various conceptual schemes best suited to these various pursuits, one—the phenomenalistic—claims epistemological priority. Viewed from within the phenomenalistic conceptual scheme, the ontologies of physical objects and mathematical objects are myths. The quality of myth, however, is relative; relative, in this case, to the epistemological point of view. This point of view is one among various, corresponding to one among our various interests and purposes.

Bibliographical references

Bernays, Paul, 'Sur le platonisme dans les mathématiques,' *L'Enseignement mathématique* 34 (1935–36), 52–69.

Black, Max, *The Nature of Mathematics* (London: Kegan Paul, 1933; New York: Harcourt Brace, 1934).

Church, Alonzo, 'A note on the Entscheidungsproblem,' *Journal of Symbolic Logic 1* (1936), 40f, 101f. (For a possibly more convenient presentation of the argument, see Hilbert and Bernays, vol. 2, pp. 416–421.)

Fraenkel, A. A., 'Sur la notion d'existence dans les mathématiques,' *L'Enseignement mathématique 34* (1935–36), 18–32.

Frank, Philipp, *Modern Science and its Philosophy* (Cambridge, Mass: Harvard University Press, 1949).

Frege, Gottlob, 'On sense and nominatum,' in Feigl and Sellars, pp. 85–102. Translation of 'Ueber Sinn und Bedeutung,' *Zeitschrift für Philosophie und philosophische Kritik 100* (1892), 25–50.

Gödel, Kurt, 'Ueber formal unentscheidbare Sätze der Principia Mathematica und verwandter Systeme,' *ibid. 38* (1931), 173–198. (For an introductory account and further references see Quine [2], pp. 245ff.)

11. See Quine [1], pp. 90ff, 96ff, 122ff.

Goodman, Nelson, and W. V. Quine, 'Steps toward a constructive nominalism', *Journal of Symbolic Logic* 12 (1947), 105–122.

Hilbert, David, and Paul Bernays, *Grundlagen der Mathematik*. 2 vols. (Berlin: Springer, 1934, 1939; 2nd printing, Ann Arbor: Edwards, 1944).

Quine, W. V. [1], *From a Logical Point of View* (Cambridge, Mass: Harvard University Press, 1953).

Quine, W. V. [2], *Methods of Logic* (New York: Holt, 1950).

Chapter 16

Selection from *Material Beings*

Peter van Inwagen

Why the proposed answer to the special composition question, radical though it is, does not contradict our ordinary beliefs

THE thesis about composition and parthood that I am advocating has far-reaching ontological consequences: that every physical thing is either a living organism or a simple. (For suppose there is something that is neither a simple nor an organism. Since it is not a simple, it has proper parts. Since it is not an organism, then, if the thesis I am advocating is correct, it has no proper parts.) We might, in fact, think of simples as degenerate organisms, in the sense of 'degenerate' in which, for instance, a line segment is sometimes called a degenerate ellipse. An organism may be thought of as a thing whose intrinsic nature determines how it is to change its parts with the passage of time. Thus, a table could not be an organism since, if there were tables, they could change their parts purely as the result of the application of external forces. (An organ transplant is *not* a case of organism's changing its parts purely as the result of the application of external forces. See Section 15.) A simple fits this abstract characterization of what it is to be an organism: its intrinsic nature determines that it is always to be composed of the *same* parts. If we adopt this way of talking, we can say that all physical objects are organisms, either degenerate or living.[1]

The book from which this selection is taken, Peter van Inwagen's *Material Beings*, is an attempt to answer what van Inwagen calls the 'special composition question'. This is the question of what it is for some things to add up to a whole thing; or in what circumstances do a collection of things constitute a whole. Van Inwagen's answer to this question is that a thing is composed of some parts if their activity constitutes a life. It is a consequence of this that the only things which there really are organisms and their elementary parts. In the selections reprinted here, van Inwagen explains this idea further. Note that the references to 'section 17' (etc.) are to other sections of *Material Beings* and not to sections of this Guide and Anthology.

1. Or we might say that all physical objects are living organisms, some of them (the simples) having 'degenerate' *lives*. If we adopted both this convention and the convention mentioned in n. 34—that every organism is caught up in its own life—then the following three biconditionals will hold (according to the Proposed Answer) without the annoying 'special case' qualifications that are necessary in the absence of the two conventions:

    $\exists y$ (the xs compose y) iff the activity of the xs constitutes a life.
    The xs compose y iff the activity of the xs constitutes the life of y.
    x is a part of y iff x is caught up in the life of y.

The Proposed Answer, therefore, is consistent with the existence of simples. Does it *require* the existence of simples? That is, does it entail that organisms are composed of simples? There would seem to be two ways to avoid this conclusion. First, one might suppose—it can be argued that this is Aristotle's view of the matter—that organisms have no proper parts, that they are entirely composed of absolutely continuous stuffs. (Strictly speaking, this does not entail that there are no simples, but rather that living organisms are simples, albeit they are continuously assimilating and eliminating matter.) I take it, however, that we now know empirically that living organisms are not composed of absolutely continuous stuffs. Secondly, one might suppose that organisms have proper parts and that every proper part of an organism has proper parts. It is easy enough to propose models on which this thesis is true. Suppose, for example, that space is continuous and that every region of space that lies within the boundaries of an organism (or every such region topologically suitable for occupation by an object) is occupied by a part of that organism. I have argued elsewhere[2] that this supposition is false, but, true or false, it is not consistent with the proposed answer to the Special Composition Question. It is obvious that, while some regions of space inside an organism may be occupied by organisms, some of them are not. A second model, one that does not face that difficulty, is this: An organism like a man or a cat is composed of smaller organisms, cells; and cells in their turn are composed of 'subcells' (whose activity constitutes the life of the cell); 'and so ad infinitum.' Again, however, I take it that we know empirically that this is false. I know of no model for the mereological structure of organisms that is consistent both with the thesis that there are no simples and with the empirical facts. (And, anyway, current physics strongly suggests that quarks and leptons and gluons and photons have no proper parts and that all organisms are composed of quarks and leptons and gluons and photons.)[3] I shall, accordingly, assume that if the proposed answer to the Special Composition Question is correct, then all organisms are composed of simples. That is, I shall suppose that, for every organism, there are xs such that the xs are simples and the xs compose that organism. Note that this does not entail that, for every organism, and for any xs, if those xs compose that organism, then those xs are simples.

Most philosophers I have talked about these matters with think that my ontology contains too few objects. One philosopher (Peter Unger) thinks it contains too many. In the present section, I shall attempt to take some of the sting out of the charge that I believe in too few objects. (I shall put off till Section 17 the less pressing problem of answering the charge that it contains too many.) I shall show that my view, though radical, is not so far from being rational that it does not deserve a hearing.

Before I do this, however, I want to do what I can to disown a certain apparently almost irresistible characterization of my view, or of that part of my view that pertains

2. 'The Doctrine of Arbitrary Undetached Parts,' *Pacific Philosophical Quarterly* 62 (1981): 123–37.
3. See Haim Harani, 'The Structure of Quarks and Leptons,' *Scientific American*, April 1983, pp. 56–68.

to inanimate objects. Many philosophers, in conversation and correspondence, have insisted, despite repeated protests on my part, on describing my position in words like these: 'Van Inwagen says that tables are not real'; '. . . not true objects'; '. . . not actually *things*'; '. . . not substances'; '. . . not unified wholes'; '. . . nothing more than collections of particles.' These are words that darken counsel. They are, in fact, perfectly meaningless. My position vis-à-vis tables and other inanimate objects is simply that there *are* none. Tables are not defective objects or second-class citizens of the world; they are just not there at all. But perhaps this wretched material mode is a part of the difficulty. Let us abandon it. There are certain properties that a thing would have to have to be properly called a 'table' on anyone's understanding of the word, and nothing has all of these properties. If anything did have them, it would be real, a true object, actually a *thing*, a substance, a unified whole, and something more than a collection of particles. But nothing does. If there were tables, they would be composite material objects, and every composite material object is real, a true object, actually a *thing*, a substance, a unified whole, and something more than a collection of particles. But there are no tables. I hope I have made myself clear.

Is my thesis absurd? Why? The argument, I think would be something like this:

According to your proposal, there are no such things as tables or chairs or rocks or mountains or continents or stars. But there just obviously are such things as these. Therefore, your theory is wrong. In fact it's *so* obvious that there are such things as these that your theory is absurd.

Now these words can be interpreted in various ways. I believe that the strongest argument that can be found in them is the following, an argument that was invented, or at least made famous, by Moore:

Your position, if it rests on anything at all, rests on certain arguments. But the premises of these arguments, whatever they may be, could not possibly be so worthy of belief as what you are denying, *viz.* that there are such things as tables and stars.

Is this really true? What it *would* be true to say is this:

. . . the premises of these arguments, whatever they may be, could not possibly be so worthy of belief as the thesis that when English-speakers, immersed in the ordinary business of life, utter sentences like, 'There are two very valuable chairs in the next room' or 'There are stars larger than the sun', they very often say true things.

But I do not deny this. In fact, I affirm it. 'Now, *look*. "There are two very valuable chairs in the next room" entails "There are chairs", which is what you deny.' The objection is misconceived. 'There are two very valuable chairs in the next room' and 'There are chairs' are sentences, not propositions. Therefore, they neither entail nor are entailed and they are not the objects of affirmation and denial. Moreover, any of the propositions that an English speaker might express by uttering 'There are two very valuable chairs in the next room' on a particular occasion—there are, of course, many such propositions, owing to the indexical elements in the sentence—is,

I would argue, consistent with the propositions that I, as metaphysician, express by writing the words 'There are no chairs'.

This reply may strike some philosophers as a desperate, ad hoc evasion of a very cogent point. But, really, whatever the merits of the present case may be, this sort of maneuver is common enough. Here are three examples of similar cases. (1) I am a vociferous defender of the Principle of Noncontradiction. You ask me whether it's raining. I answer, 'Well, it is and it isn't.' You remind me of my allegiance to the Principle of Non-contradiction. I reply that the proposition I expressed by saying 'It is and it isn't' is consistent with the Principle of Noncontradiction. (2) I deny that there are sense data, after-images, pains, or other objects of immediate sensory awareness. One day you hear me complain of a nagging pain in my left shoulder. You say, 'There—you admit that there are pains!' I reply that the proposition I express when I say 'There's a nagging pain in my left shoulder' is consistent with my denial that there are objects of immediate sensory awareness. (3) I accept the Copernican Hypothesis. One day you hear me say, 'It was cooler in the garden after the sun had moved behind the elms.' You say, 'You see, you can't consistently maintain your Copernicanism outside the astronomer's study. You say that the sun moved behind the elms; yet, according to your official theory, the sun does not move.' I reply that the proposition I expressed by saying 'It was cooler in the garden after the sun had moved behind the elms' is consistent with the Copernican Hypothesis. This last example is particularly instructive. When I speak the words 'the sun moved behind the elms', I am reporting a fact. I am reporting a real alteration in the relations of external objects. Perhaps the words I use constitute what is in some sense a misleading description of this fact, but they do at least get one thing literally right: taken literally, they report an alteration in the spatial disposition of external objects and an alteration in the spatial disposition of external objects really does occur and is the basis for the report. Thus, 'The sun moved behind the elms' is not, even from the point of view of the most fanatical astronomical literalist, a report of a nonexistent, fabricated, or imaginary event; it is not like, say, 'The sun moved rapidly back and forth across the sky'. It may describe an actual event in a misleading or loose or even a wrong way, but the event it describes or misdescribes is there to be described or misdescribed. Something similar may be said about 'There are two very valuable chairs in the next room'. This sentence, when it is successfully used to report a fact, does report a fact about the existence of *something*. This much is shown by the fact that if the next room were wholly empty of matter, then what was expressed by this sentence would be false by anyone's standard. We may say that this sentence is 'essentially existential,' meaning that it can be used to report a fact, and that a correct paraphrase—correct by the most pedantic and literalistic standards—of this sentence into the language of formal logic must start with an existential quantifier. (In a similar spirit, we could say that 'The sun moved behind the elms' was 'essentially alterational.') In Section 11 we shall take up the question of what literally correct paraphrases of sentences like 'There are two chairs in the next room' should look like. I believe that the fact that such sentences can be used to say what is true and the fact that they are essentially existential together account for the *feeling* we have of making an assertion of existence, one that is objectively correct, when we utter them in appropriate circumstances. But from the three premises, (1) a certain man has said (using the words in their standard English senses) 'There are two chairs in the next room,' (2) what he said was true, and (3) what he said must be represented formally as an existential quantification, we cannot infer that there are chairs.

My position, therefore, is that when people say things in the ordinary business of life by uttering sentences that start 'There are chairs . . .' or 'There are stars . . .', they very often say things that are literally true. (' "Literally"? What does that mean?' Well, they can be *right*, in whatever sense someone can be right if he says that the sun traversed 59 minutes of arc during our conversation.) I can say this because I accept certain theses in the philosophy of language. Some people, I suppose, would reject these theses. These people would say that when I said 'It is and it isn't' and 'The sun moved behind the elms,' I said something false. If I agreed with them, I could not reply to the Moore-style objection to my ontology in the way that I have. Since I do not propose to defend my philosophy of language in the present work, I think it is worth pointing out that even if I did accept the austere philosophy of language that ascribes falsity to typical utterances of 'The sun moved behind the elms', I could nevertheless respond to 'Moore's gambit' in a way that is very much like the way I have responded to it. If someone maintains that 'The sun moved behind the elms' expresses a falsehood, he must still have some way to distinguish between this sentence and those sentences (like 'The sun exploded' and 'The sun turned green') that the vulgar would regard as the sentences that expressed falsehoods about the sun. He will require what we may call a 'term of alethic commendation' which he can correctly apply to 'The sun moved behind the elms' and withhold from 'The sun exploded'. Let us suppose that his term of alethic commendation is 'expresses a false-hood that for most practical purposes may be treated as a truth'. (It will make no real difference what term of alethic commendation we consider.) If, I say, I accepted this austere philosophy of language, then I should be more cautious about what I granted to a philosopher who attempted to refute my position by an argument in the style of Moore. I should not be willing to say that people who uttered things like 'There are two very valuable chairs in the next room' very often said what was true. I should be willing to say only that they very often said what might be treated as a truth for all practical purposes.

Mention of Moore brings to mind 'common sense.' Does my position not fly in the face of common sense? I do not think so. This is not because I think that my position is in accord with 'common sense,' but rather because I do not think that there is any such thing as the body of doctrine that philosophers call common sense. There is common sense: Common sense tells us to taste our food before we salt it and to cut the cards. It does not tell us that there are chairs. Now, in addition to common sense there is what we might call Universal Belief: that body of proposi-tions that has been accepted by every human being who has ever lived, bar a few imbeciles and madmen; which is accepted even by Spinoza and Bradley when the madness of philosophy is not upon them. Is the existence of chairs—or, at any rate, of things suitable for sitting on, like stones and stumps—a matter of Universal Belief? If it were, this would count strongly against my position, for any philosopher who denies what practically *everyone* believes is, so far as I can see, adopting a position according to which the human capacity for knowing the truth about things is radically defective. And why should he think that his own capacities are the exception to the rule? It is far from obvious, however, that it is a matter of Universal Belief that there are chairs. In fact, to say that any particular proposition that would be of interest to philosophers belongs to the body of Universal Belief is to put forward a philosophical thesis and no trivial one. It is difficult to settle such questions, in part because there are a lot of things that one might express by uttering 'philosophical' sentences like 'There are chairs', and some of them might be things that are irrelevant to the concerns of ordinary life. Moreover, the distinctions among various of these things may be subtle: It may be that the intellectual training provided by dealing with ordinary matters ill equips one to appreciate them.

In my view, my general thesis about what there is—that the only physical things are simples and living organisms—is not inconsistent with anything believed *ubique et ab omnibus*. In my view, my metaphysic does not shut me off from Universal Belief. I shall try to show why I think this is so by telling a fable, the story of the bligers.

When the first settlers arrived in the hitherto unpeopled land of Pluralia, they observed (always from a fair distance) what appeared to be black tigers, and they coined the name 'bliger' for them. 'Bligers' were even more shy of human beings than ordinary tigers, and they were never suspected of harming human beings or even of carrying off a chicken. The Pluralians were an intensely practical race of farmers who never hunted for sport, and, since nothing needed to be *done* about bligers, bligers were seldom in their thoughts. Occasionally, Pluralians would make idle remarks along the lines of 'There's a bliger crossing that field', and that was about the extent of their interaction with bligers. A few centuries after the settlement of Pluralia, however, a foreign zoological expedition discovered that, in a way, there were no bligers. 'A bliger (*Quasi-Tigris Multiplex Pluralianus*),' their report read, 'is really six animals. Its "legs" are four monkey-like creatures, its "trunk" a sort of sloth, and its "head" a species of owl. Any six animals of the proper species can combine temporarily to form a bliger. (Combinations lasting for several hours have been observed telescopically.) The illusion is amazing. Even a trained zoologist observing a bliger from a distance of ten meters would swear that he was seeing a single, unified animal. While the purpose of the combination is doubtless to protect its members from predators by producing the illusion of the presence of a large, dangerous carnivore, we can only guess at the evolutionary history of this marvelous symbiosis.'

Are there any bligers (in the story)? I think not. But I do not suppose that a Pluralian says anything false if he says 'There is a bliger crossing that field,' any more than I would suppose that he says something false when he says 'The sun is rising' or 'That cat is sharpening its claws.' But what do I mean when I say that there are no bligers? I am obviously not denying that there are occasions on which six animals arrange themselves in bliger fashion (as we might say). But it does not follow from this fact that there are bligers. That is, it does not follow that six animals arranged in bliger fashion compose anything, and that is what I mean to deny when I say that there are no bligers. Or put my thesis this way. Consider six animals arranged in bliger fashion; consider the region of space that they collectively occupy; there is no one thing that just exactly fills this region of space.

What I mean by saying that there are no chairs is precisely analogous to what I mean by saying that there are no bligers. To make things as simple as possible, let us suppose that chairs—if there are any—are made entirely of wood and let us suppose (though nothing remotely like this is true) that any object that is 'made entirely of wood' is composed of simples called 'wood-particles'. Now consider those regions of space that, according to those who believe in the existence of chairs, are occupied by chairs. Call them chair-receptacles. One of these chair-receptacles is beneath me as I write. Call it R. I concede the truth of this proposition:

(A) The chair-receptacle R is filled with rigidly interlocking wood-particles; the regions immediately contiguous with R contain no wood-particles; the wood-particles at the boundary of R (that is, the wood-particles within R that are not entirely surrounded by wood-particles) are bonded to nearby wood-particles much more strongly than they are bonded to the non-wood-particles immediately outside R; the strength of the mutual bondings of wood-particles within R is large in comparison with the forces produced by casual human muscular exertions.

What my answer to the Special Composition Question entails the denial of is not (A), but rather the two following theses (and, therefore, the proposition that either of them is entailed by (A)):

(B) There is something that fits exactly into R.
(C) There is something that the wood-particles within R compose.

Now if either (B) or (C) were true, there would be a chair. If either of them is false, then there are no chairs. (Or, at least, there is no chair in R.) Because it is (B) and (C) that I deny, and not (A), I am a metaphysician and not a madman. (I once actually met a madman who denied the existence of the moon. But *I* deny the existence of the moon, since it is neither an organism nor a simple. I deny that anything is a sphere of rock two thousand miles in diameter. What makes the man I met a madman and me a mere metaphysician? Part of the answer, no doubt, is that my denials are more systematic and coherent than his: he thinks that there's a *special* reason for denying the existence of the moon. But even in the particular case there are differences. He thinks that there is nothing in the 'lunar receptacle.' I say that the lunar receptacle contains untold myriads of things; I simply deny that these myriads compose a single thing. Moreover, I think that when people say 'Men have walked on the moon,' they say something true. He thinks they say something false; in fact, he will not even grant that what they say expresses a falsehood 'that for most practical purposes may be treated as a truth.')

What I differ from most philosophers about (though perhaps most philosophers have not thought about material objects in just these terms) is this: They believe that (A) entails (B) and (C) and I do not. But whether this entailment holds is a very subtle metaphysical question. I do not think it is absurd to suppose that (A) might be true and (B) and (C) false. The possibility is at least worth examining.

I have been arguing that my position is not absurd and is not at variance with Universal Belief. A good many philosophers may feel that it is absurd for all that, and at variance with Universal Belief as well. They may want to accuse me of a philosophical ploy that Saul Kripke has described in these words:

> The philosopher advocates a view apparently in patent contradiction to common sense. Rather than repudiating common sense, he asserts that the conflict comes from a philosophical misinterpretation of common language—sometimes he adds that the misinterpretation is encouraged by the 'superficial form' of ordinary speech. He offers his own analysis of the relevant common assertions, one that shows that they do not really say what they seem to say. . . .
>
> Personally, I think such philosophical claims are almost invariably suspect. What the claimant calls a 'misleading philosophical misconstrual' of the ordinary statement is probably the natural and correct understanding. The real misconstrual comes when the claimant continues, 'All the ordinary man really means is . . .' and gives a sophisticated analysis compatible with his own philosophy.[4]

I would make two points.

First, my view is not in patent contradiction with common sense, because, as I have said, there is no such body of extra-philosophical belief as 'common sense.' There are, of course, various philosophies like 'the Scottish philosophy of common sense' or 'Moore's philosophy of common sense' that my view contradicts, but then they contradict one another. (There may be some sort of problem of self-reference here. I can imagine a philosopher telling me that my assertion that there is no such thing as what philosophers call common sense is in patent contradiction with common sense.)

Second, I am not proposing an analysis of common language. I am offering a metaphysical theory. The only thing I have to say about what the ordinary man really means by 'There are two valuable chairs in the next room' is that he really means that there are two valuable chairs in the next room. And we all understand him perfectly, since we are native speakers of our common language. In my view, this sentence is sufficiently empty of metaphysical commitment that the proposition it typically

---

4. Saul A. Kripke, *Wittgenstein on Rules and Private Language: An Elementary Exposition* (Cambridge, Mass: Harvard University Press, 1982), p. 65.

expresses is consistent both with the thesis that (A) entails (B) and (C) and with the thesis that (A) does not entail (B) or (C), and that is all I have to say about the meaning of sentences of ordinary language. In a similar vein, I would say that what is ordinarily expressed by 'It was cooler in the garden when the sun had moved behind the elms' is consistent with both Ptolemaic and Copernican astronomy. (It may be that the word 'moved' occurs in the idiom this sentence exemplifies because the first people to use this idiom accepted some geocentric account of the apparent motion of the sun. But that would not entail that an astronomical theory was built into the *meaning* of this idiom.)

I will close this section with a remark about the ordinary man. If you were to tell the ordinary man that I thought that there were no chairs, he would probably think I was mad. But you would have misled him about my thesis. He would understand you to be saying—given his education and interests, what else could he understand you to be saying?—something that implied that whenever anyone uttered a sentence like 'There are two valuable chairs in the next room', that person was under an illusion of some sort. He would think that I regarded utterers of this sentence as he (perhaps) regards utterers of the sentence 'There are two horrible ghosts in the next house'. But my assertion (and yours and his) that there are no ghosts is not like my assertion that in Pluralia there are no bligers. My assertion that in Pluralia there are no bligers is not meant to deny that reports of bligers are reports of a real and unified set of phenomena. My assertion that there are no ghosts is meant to deny that reports of ghosts are reports of a real and unified set of phenomena. When people say they see ghosts, I believe (and I presume you do, too) that either there is nothing there, or, if there is something there, it's not the same sort of thing on each occasion. When Pluralians say they have seen a bliger, there generally is something there, and it's generally the same sort of thing. My assertion that there are no chairs is like my assertion that there are no bligers. But that is something that you will not convey to the ordinary man when you tell him that I think that there are no chairs, just as you would not have conveyed to the sixteenth-century ordinary man what Copernicus believed about the motion of the sun if you told him that, according to Copernicus, the sun does not move.

Unity and thinking

We have proposed the following 'Moderate' answer to the Special Composition Question:

(∃y the xs compose y) if and only if
the activity of the xs constitutes a life.

I have done my best to explain the content of this answer, and I have argued that this answer is not absurd. But to argue that an answer to a certain question is not absurd is not to argue that it is correct. Why should anyone suppose that this answer is correct?

I do not suppose that it is possible to prove a philosophical thesis, particularly a far-reaching and radical one. Moreover, the best reasons for accepting a philosophical thesis are generally of a sort that it is hard to capture in consecutive prose. The best reasons for accepting a philosophical thesis generally involve the ways in which a host of more or less unrelated problems, convictions, observations, and arguments interact with that thesis. I think that the best reasons for accepting my proposed answer to the Special Composition Question are available only to the philosopher who has examined the great philosophical puzzle cases about endurance in the light provided by this answer. We shall presently conduct an examination of some of these cases in that light. Nevertheless, it is possible to produce some arguments in the narrow sense—arguments having identifiable premises and a discernible logical structure—that support our answer. These arguments are perhaps rather weak, but I do not think they are entirely worthless and I shall devote the present section to them.

I begin with a point made in Section 8: Nihilism is false because (1) I exist, and (2) if I exist, I have parts. But what about (1)? Why should I suppose that I exist?

There are various arguments that, if I accepted them, would force me to concede that I did not exist. The only arguments that support this unattractive thesis that seem to me to be worth taking seriously (and I think they are worth taking more seriously than many philosophers do) are various arguments having to do with vagueness. We shall consider one of these arguments in Section 17.

The main arguments for the thesis that one exists are, of course, due to Descartes.

Why should I think that I exist? Why should *who* think that *who* exists? To raise the question whether one exists is to presuppose that one exists; even an omnipotent deceiver could not deceive one about one's own existence, owing to the fact that one would have to be *there* in order to be deceived. (Imagine an omnipotent deceiver who boasted, 'This morning I deceived Zeus. Although he doesn't exist, I made him think that he did.') In addition to the argument from the incoherency of denying one's own existence, Descartes employs a second argument: *Cogito, ergo sum*. Presumably this argument is not really (as Hobbes thought it was) of the same logical form as *ambulo, ergo sum*. Presumably Descartes meant by saying '*Cogito, ergo sum*' that he was in some sense directly aware of a thinking being, a being about whose existence he could not be mistaken, and that this being would have to be himself, since, for any being distinct from himself, he *could* be mistaken about that distinct being's existence.

These arguments have been challenged by various empiricists, such as Hume and Russell. A 'composite photograph' of the various empiricist counterarguments would look something like this. An occurrence of the question 'Do I indeed exist?' is a certain succession of ideas; suppose there are three of them, and call them *a*, *b*, and *c*. For this question to have an asker, however, is for the members of a certain very large set of ideas that contains *a*, *b*, and *c* to compose something. And the question whose occurrence is the succession *abc* can be correctly answered yes only if it has an asker: only if the members of that very large set of ideas compose something. But from the fact that *a*, *b*, and *c* occur in succession, it does not follow that there are *xs* such that *a*, *b*, *c*, and the *xs* compose something. An omnipotent deceiver could not, it is true, deceive any thinking being (any being composed of ideas in the right way) into thinking falsely that it existed. But it could cause an occurrence of the question 'Do I exist?' on an occasion when the answer to that question was no. And even if one does exist when one asks oneself whether one indeed exists, one has no right to be sure, without further argument, that this is not one of those occasions. A similar point applies to the second argument. Even if one does exist, the most one is aware of at any given moment is a succession of ideas; one is not aware of a thinking being, of a being composed of the members of some large collection of ideas of which the ideas one currently perceives are but a few.

Now, I find this all perfectly unintelligible. To mention just one difficulty among many, I do not understand what it means to say that I am composed of ideas. Whatever things compose me, they are all of them material—or, at any rate, are no further from being material than quarks and electrons are. But perhaps a materialist who doubts that I exist, or who rejects the Cartesian arguments for this conclusion, might offer an argument that is in some ways analogous to the argument of the empiricists.

He might say this: 'Consider those simples that we should normally say composed you. Suppose we're wrong about them. Suppose they don't compose you. Suppose they don't compose anything. Suppose, if you like, that Nihilism is true and that two or more simples never compose anything. Nevertheless, the simples that would compose you if there were such a thing as you—if there were any composite objects—stand to each other in just the causal relations they would stand in if they composed you: The same electrical currents flow, the same chemical reactions take place, and so on. Now, as a good token-token materialist, you believe that each of your particular, occurrent thoughts is identical with some particular physical process in your head. But even if these particles we're talking about compose nothing, that doesn't stop all these processes from going on, and thus it doesn't prevent the occurrence of thoughts. Perhaps, then, the thought that, according to vulgar opinion, is your wondering whether you exist can't be so described; perhaps it's no one's thought. Still, it occurs. Therefore, perhaps, there are occurrences of the question "Do I exist?" on occasions on which the answer to that question is no.'

A less dramatic way to put this point would be the following. 'You have offered paraphrases of sentences about artifacts into sentences that refer only to simples. Why do you suppose that the same thing can't be done in respect of sentences about you and other thinkers? Why couldn't we introduce a variable polyadic predicate— say, "the *xs* are arranged intellectually"—and paraphrase talk apparently about thinkers into talk that refers only to simples?'

I have no knock-down response to this challenge. What I am going to say will perhaps be thought to beg the question, but it is the best I can do.

Consider the sentences 'The sun shines' and 'The shelf supports the books'. According to the view I am advocating, there are no stars to do any shining and no shelves to do any supporting. Still, as one might put it, the shining and the supporting somehow get done. How, in my view, do they get done? Well, they get done in virtue of the cooperation of simples. The simples that are arranged shelf-wise cooperate to support weight; the simples that are arranged siderially cooperate to produce light. Our initial impression is that there is a certain huge object, the sun, that does a thing called shining. Later, under the influence of our theory, we decide that what we took to be the product of the activity of a single object was the product of the joint activity of many. Our initial impression is that there is a certain middle-sized object, the shelf, that does a thing called supporting weight. Later, under the influence of our theory, we decide that what we took to be an accomplishment of a single object was an accomplishment of many.

Could *this* be true: Our initial impression is that there is a certain object, I, that does a thing called thinking; later, under the influence of our theory, we decide that what we took to be the activity of a single object was the activity of many? Peirce says somewhere that one's thinking is really no more than a persistent habit of cooperation among one's brain cells. Couldn't he be right? In fact, couldn't we go him one better and say that one's thinking is really no more than a persistent habit of cooperation among certain simples? And if we have the cooperating simples, what need have we for *one*?

In my view, we do have a need for 'one,' that is, for the individual thing that thinks. I do not see how we can regard thinking as a mere cooperative activity. Things can work together to produce light. They may do this by composing a single object—a firefly, say—that emits light. But things that work together to produce light are not forced, by the very nature of the task set them, to produce light *by* composing a single object that emits light. And things that work together to support weight are not forced, by the very nature of the task set them, to support weight *by* composing a single object that holds things aloft. (As regards the second case, it seems obvious enough that it is no argument for the thesis that Tom and Tim have a mereological sum to point out that they are carrying a beam: Tom's activity and Tim's activity are jointly sufficient to account for the fact that the beam remains aloft and moves along.) But things cannot work together to think—or, at least, things can work together to think only in the sense that they can compose, in the strict and mereological understanding of the word, an object that thinks. (I am, incidentally, using 'think' in a very liberal sense, sufficiently liberal that I will count such items as *feeling pain* as instances of thinking.) Now, surely, planning for tomorrow or feeling pain cannot be activities that a lot of simples can perform collectively, as simples can collectively shine or collectively support a weight? One is reminded, when one considers this question, of the so-called Chinese Room examples that figure in debates about artificial intelligence.[5] One popular reply to the arguments in which these examples figure is that it is the *system* (the system consisting of the man, the rule books, and the scraps of paper) that does the thinking. This may or may not

---

5. See John R. Searle et al., 'Minds, Brains, and Programs,' commentaries by various hands, and reply by Searle, *Behavioral and Brain Sciences* 3 (1980): 417–56.

be a good reply, but it does seem to presuppose the following thesis: There is a certain object, a real and not a virtual object, a 'system,' which is such that the man and the books and the scraps of paper compose it. Thus the proponents of the 'systems' reply do not suppose that thinking can be a cooperative activity: They suppose that there is one object that does the thinking and differ from their opponents in believing that such an object, a system consisting of a man, some books, and some paper, is the sort of thing that *can* think. It is, of course, a consequence of our answer to the Special Composition Question that there are no systems (except, possibly, individual living organisms), although there are no doubt objects that cooperate systematically. I believe that those philosophers who deny that the Chinese Room can think are actually motivated by an inarticulate realization that the 'system' supposedly composed of the human rule-follower, the rule books, and the scraps of paper does not exist; an inarticulate realization that these individual objects (supposing *them* to exist) are the only things *there*; a realization that they do not add up to anything. But, I would judge, these philosophers, having failed to raise the Special Composition Question, misdescribe the source of their intuitions by conceding (not explicitly; they concede by failing to dispute) that there is such a thing as the man-book-paper system and proceeding to argue that it is not the sort of thing that thinks. But once the existence of the 'system' is conceded, the battle is lost; worse, the whole dispute degenerates into cloudy exchanges about whether a 'system' can have the same causal powers as a human brain. (It should be evident from the preceding, by the way, that if my answer to the Special Composition Question is correct, computers—computers of the sort IBM sells—cannot think. They cannot think because they do not exist.)

I therefore exist. And yet I have parts. (Someone might argue that the Cartesian arguments we have employed are valid only on the assumption that the subject is an immaterial being, and hence a being without proper parts. I don't see this. It seems to me that Descartes's arguments for his own existence can be evaluated independently of what the evaluator knows or believes about his own nature; they are simply neutral in relation to questions about the metaphysics of thinkers. I concede that Descartes believed that he could deduce his immateriality from the fact that he was the sort of being whose existence could be proved by 'Cartesian' methods. But you, I hope, will concede that his attempted deduction of this conclusion was irremediably invalid.) Therefore, there is at least one case in which a material being has parts. When, in general, does this happen? What allows a material being to have parts? What makes this possible?

We have argued that this state of affairs is possible because it is actual. And our argument for the conclusion that it was actual depended on the notion of thinking: We argued that a thinking being existed and was composite. But we did *not* argue that the fact that this being was a thinking being in any way explained or accounted for the fact that it was a composite being. A proof of actuality is a proof of possibility, but such a proof does not invariably explain the possibility whose existence it demonstrates, for we may very well know that a certain thing is actual (and hence possible) and nevertheless have no explanation of how such a thing could be possible. For example, the absence of money from a bank vault may prove that someone entered the vault during the night, and, if it does prove this, will a fortiori prove that it was *possible* for someone to enter the vault during the night. But the absence of money will in no way explain how it was possible for someone to enter the vault. We can easily imagine officials of the bank and the police saying both that it is undeniable that someone was in the vault and that they have no idea how anyone could possibly have got into the vault. We may also note that, in a case like this, no one will suppose that the absence of money from the vault is even a part of the explanation of how someone could enter the vault: Everyone will suppose that if someone could get into the vault and take money from it, a person could also get into the vault by the same method, whatever it may be, and, if he chose, take no money.

In my view, the fact that I am a thinking being shows that there is at least one composite material object. But it does not explain how it is possible for there to be a composite material object. The fact that I think presupposes but does not explain the fact that certain simples compose something. And I do not suppose that the fact that I think is even a part of the explanation of the fact that certain simples are capable of composing me. I see no initial reason to deny that the factor that accounts for the unity of those simples might exist in the absence of thinking. It is possible (for all I know) that I might cease to think—that I might lose the very capacity for thought—and continue to exist. It is possible (for all I know) that there are composite objects that are essentially incapable of thought. And if there are such objects, the mereological unity of the simples that compose them may be due to precisely the same factor to which the mereological unity of the simples that compose me is due.

When I reflect on the matter, it does not seem to me that thinking has anything to do with my existence. The capacity for thought (even the capacity for sensation) seems to be, metaphysically speaking, a rather superficial property of myself. It may be the most valuable or important of my possessions, the sine qua non of an existence that is of any value whatever to me. There is no reason to suppose—whatever Saint Anselm and Descartes may have thought—that mere existence is a valuable thing. But the fact that a certain feature of a being is of preeminent, even transcendent, value to that being does not even seem to show that that feature is metaphysically essential to it. Descartes, of course, believed that his essence not only contained but *was* thinking. His arguments for this conclusion, however, are fallacious. His real reason for thinking this, whatever arguments he may have devised, seems to me to have been this: If one arranged in thought the objects of one's awareness according to their perceived distance from oneself (compare Moore: 'I am closer to my hands than I am to my feet'),[6] one would place one's thoughts at the very center. One's thoughts seem to be as close to one as anything could be. The

---

6. Reported by Morton White in 'Memories of G. E. Moore,' *Journal of Philosophy* 57 (1960): 805–10. The attribution is on p. 806. I am grateful to José Benardete for this reference.

other things—the hands and feet and eyes—are 'out there' and hence not a part of one. The thoughts are 'right here' and hence a part of one. I do not say that these words, or anything like them, have been offered as an *argument* by Descartes or by anyone else. I do say that their content is responsible for the plausibility of Descartes's conclusions and (since the more plausible the conclusion of an argument, the less critical the audience to whom the argument is addressed) explain the perennial popularity of Descartes's arguments.

If thinking is not my essence, what is? What is the ground of my unity? That is, what binds the simples that compose me into a single being? It seems to me to be plausible to say that what binds them together is that their activities constitute a life, a homeodynamic storm of simples, a self-maintaining, well-individuated, jealous event. But if I exist because the activity of certain simples constitutes a life, then it would be wholly implausible to suppose that I exist and that no other organisms do. If I exist, then you do too, and so all other human beings. That is to say, if in one case in which simples are arranged 'anthroponomically' they compose an object, then in all cases in which simples are arranged anthroponomically they compose an object.

Might it not be that simples (or any other objects) compose an object just in the case that their activity constitutes a *human* life? Might it not be that the xs compose something if and only if the xs are arranged anthroponomically? This would be an arbitrary position indeed. If objects whose activity constitutes a human life compose something, then so do objects whose activities constitute a feline or a murine life. ('But the notion of life is a vague notion. Not all lives are like the lives of human beings and cats and mice. What about bacterial and viral lives? Don't the lives of the lower links of the Great Chain of Being trail off into vague, temporary episodes of molecular interaction? Where will you draw the line?' I shall discuss these questions in connection with the general topic of vagueness in Sections 17, 18, and 19.[7])

It would, I have suggested, be arbitrary to say of any simples whose activity constitutes a life that they fail to compose an object. If this suggestion is correct, then the 'if' half of our answer to the Special Composition Question is correct. But what about the 'only if' half of the answer? That, after all, is the really radical part of the answer. Why should one suppose that there are no artifacts and stones and heavenly bodies? If it is arbitrary to suppose (given that simples arranged anthroponomically compose a human being) that simples arranged pigwise do not compose pigs, then, surely, it is arbitrary to suppose that simples arranged penwise do not compose pens? Surely a pen (or a stone or a star) would normally be taken to be as much a central or perfectly clear or paradigmatic case of an existent object as people and pigs are? Why stop with organisms?

7. But consider the following quotation from a book by the chemist Robert Shapiro, *Origins: A Skeptic's Guide to the Creation of Life on Earth* (New York: Bantam Books, 1986): 'The smallest free-living organisms are probably the mycoplasmas, tiny bacteria. . . . As we shall see, viruses are generally smaller than mycoplasmas, but they are not separate living beings. They function as parts of organisms, not as complete ones' (pp. 117–18).

The answer (insofar as I have an answer) is threefold. (1) Cartesian arguments show that we are forced to grant existence to *some* organisms (to the ones that think, at least), owing to the fact that thinking cannot be understood as a disguised cooperative activity. But *all* the activities apparently carried out by shelves and stars and other artifacts and natural bodies can be understood as disguised cooperative activities. And, therefore, we are not forced to grant existence to *any* artifacts or natural bodies. (I have not, of course, proved this general statement. I have done no more than give examples. Perhaps the example of paraphrase given in the preceding section and the discussion of cooperative activity in the present section have gone some way toward making this general statement plausible.) (2) What answer to the Special Composition Question would generate artifacts and natural bodies?[8] *Contact, Fastening, Cohesion, Fusion,* and Universalism would generate various of these things, though they might generate more or fewer of them than the friends of artifacts would be comfortable with. *Contact,* for example, does not obviously provide us with cups, since it is not obvious that one should say that the simples within a certain cup-receptacle are in contact. And if *Contact* does provide us with cups, then it also provides us with an object that is the sum of the dinner table and the complete service for eight that is laid out on it. (As a further bonus, it generously provides us with a host of metaphysical problems about this complicated domestic object; does it, for example, cease to exist when the saltcellar falls to the floor, or does it simply cease to have the saltcellar as a part?) In any case, all these answers are demonstrably wrong. Perhaps some answer of the *Series* type will generate all the comfortable furniture of earth (and will generate no discomfiting spare furniture, like tables-cum-services-for-eight). But we in fact know of no plausible answer of the *Series* type. If we supposed that there were no material objects but organisms and simples, we should be relieved of the task of trying to devise an answer to the Special Composition Question that would accommodate them. (3) It is not only discomfiting spare furniture that generates embarrassing metaphysical problems. The comfortable furniture of earth can be very embarrassing indeed. If we supposed that there were no material objects but organisms and simples, we should be spared these embarrassments.

---

8. *Editor's note:* Van Inwagen's answer to this question refers to earlier discussion in *Material Beings.*

Chapter 17

Can there be vague objects?

Gareth Evans

IT is sometimes said that the world might itself *be* vague. Rather than vagueness being a deficiency in our mode of describing the world, it would then be a necessary feature of any true description of it. It is also said that amongst the statements which may not have a determinate truth value as a result of their vagueness are identity statements. Combining these two views we would arrive at the idea that the world might contain certain objects about which it is a *fact* that they have fuzzy boundaries. But is this idea coherent?

Let 'a' and 'b' be singular terms such that the sentence '$a = b$' is of indeterminate truth value, and let us allow for the expression of the idea of indeterminacy by the sentential operator '∇'.

Then we have:

(1) $\nabla(a = b)$.

(1) reports a fact about b which we may express by ascribing to it the property '$\hat{x}[\nabla(x = a)]$':

(2) $\hat{x}[\nabla(x = a)]b$.

But we have:

(3) $\sim\nabla(a = a)$

and hence:

(4) $\sim\hat{x}[\nabla(x = a)]a$.

But by Leibniz's Law, we may derive from (2) and (4):

(5) $\sim(a = b)$

contradicting the assumption, with which we began, that the identity statement '$a = b$' is of indeterminate truth value.

If 'Indefinitely' and its dual, 'Definitely' ('Δ') generate a modal logic as strong as S5, (1)–(4) and, presumably, Leibniz's Law, may each be strengthened with a 'Definitely' prefix, enabling us to derive

(5') $\Delta\sim(a = b)$

which is straightforwardly inconsistent with (1).

Chapter 18

Vague identity: Evans misunderstood

David Lewis

GARETH Evans's article 'Can there be vague objects?' is over-brief, cryptic, and often misunderstood.[1] As misunderstood, Evans is a pitiful figure: a 'technical philosopher' out of control of his technicalities, taken in by a fallacious proof of an absurd conclusion. Rightly understood, Evans endorses neither the bad proof nor the bad conclusion. Instead he is making a good argument in favour of a very different conclusion. To honour his memory, and to make his point more clearly available, it is worth setting the record straight.

Evans discusses a purported proof that there can be no such thing as a vague identity statement. There are two problems about this proof. One problem is that its conclusion is plainly false. There are vague identity statements. Example: 'Princeton = Princeton Borough'. (It is unsettled whether the name 'Princeton' denotes just the Borough, the Borough plus the surrounding Township, or one of countless some-what larger regions.) The other problem is that if we understand vagueness as semantic indeterminacy, a deficiency in our language, we can diagnose a fallacy. The proof twice invokes an alleged equivalence between statements of the forms (1) and (2):

(1) it is vague whether . . . a . . . ,
       symbolized as $\nabla(. . . a . . .)$,
(2) a is such that it is vague whether . . . it . . . ,
       symbolized as $\hat{x}\nabla(. . . x . . .)a$.

If vagueness is semantic indeterminacy, then wherever we have vague statements, we have several alternative precisifications of the vague language involved, all with equal claim to being 'intended'. These alternative precisifications play a role analogous to alternative worlds in modal logic. The operator 'it is vague whether . . . ' is analogous to an operator of contingency, and means 'it is true on some but not all of the precisifications that . . . '. A term like 'Princeton' that denotes different things on different precisifications is, analogically speaking, non-rigid. When a is non-

---

1. The misunderstanding I have in mind can be found in about half of the published discussions of 'Can there be vague objects?' known to me; though never, I think, in the pages of *Analysis*.

rigid, the alleged equivalence between (1) and (2) is fallacious. It is analogous to the fallacious modal equivalence between 'It is contingent whether the number of planets is nine' (true) and 'The number of planets is such that it is contingent whether it is nine' (false), or between 'It is contingent whether the number of planets is the number of planets' (false) and 'The number of planets is such that it is contingent whether it is the number of planets' (true). For a fuller discussion see Thomason 1982.[2]

The misunderstanding is that Evans overlooks the fallacy, endorses the proof, and embraces the absurd conclusion that there can be no vague identity statements. Besides ascribing folly to a man who was no fool, this interpretation makes nonsense of the title and first paragraph of Evans's article:

> *Can there be vague objects?* It is sometimes said that the world might itself *be* vague. Rather than vagueness being a deficiency in our mode of describing the world, it would then be a necessary feature of any true description of it. It is also said that amongst the statements which may not have a determinate truth value as a result of their vagueness are identity statements. Combining these two views we would arrive at the idea that the world might contain certain objects about which it is a *fact* that they have fuzzy boundaries. But is this idea coherent?

How could Evans think that the purported proof—which occupies the rest of the article—addresses his question whether vagueness is due to vague objects, as opposed to vagueness in our mode of describing? A proof that there cannot be vague identity statements would be trouble for the vagueness-in-describing view, no less than for vague objects.

The correct interpretation is that Evans trusts the reader—unwisely!—to join him in taking for granted that there are vague identity statements, that a proof to the contrary cannot be right, and that the vagueness-in-describing view affords a diagnosis of the fallacy. His point is that the vague-objects view cannot accept this diagnosis, because it says that a name like 'Princeton' rigidly denotes a certain vague object. In fact, the vague-objects view does not afford *any* diagnosis of the fallacy, so it is stuck with the unwelcome proof of an absurd conclusion, so it is in bad trouble. (Or better, what is in trouble is the vague-objects view combined with the view that vague identity yields identity statements with indeterminate truth value.) On this interpretation, every bit of what Evans says fits into place. However, he has left some important things unsaid.

You might think that charity can be overdone and the textual evidence is inconclusive. One way, Evans comes out saying too much; the other way, too little. What's to choose?

Therefore I end by reporting an exchange of letters in 1978 that ought to settle the matter. A friend sent me a draft taking Evans to task for overlooking the fallacy, endorsing the proof, and embracing the conclusion. I wrote back, hesitantly

2. Thomason, Richmond [1982] 'Identity and Vagueness', Philosophical Studies 43, pp. 329–32.

proposing the interpretation that I have here called correct; and I sent a copy (with my friend's name blanked out) to Evans. Evans replied: 'Exactly! Just so! Yes, Yes, Yes! I am covered with relief that you see so clearly what I was doing . . . and that you were able to ward off the misunderstanding of Anonymous so effectively.'[3]

3. I thank Antonia Phillips for her kind permission to quote this passage.

Study questions

1. List all the different notions of substance.
2. On the one hand, when we describe an object, we describe its properties. This suggests that an object might *just* be a bundle of properties. On the other hand, this would imply that there cannot be two objects with exactly the same properties. But this seems like a possibility. So perhaps objects cannot be bundles of properties after all. What should we say instead?
3. 'Substance is the thing that undergoes change. Change is when one and the same thing receives contrary properties. So substance, what undergoes change, must be the same throughout this change. This means that the substance itself is not changing. But then there is a contradiction in the notion of substance: for it is the thing which undergoes change, but itself does not change.'

    This argument is rather similar to the argument which aims to prove that substance, understood as bearer of properties, cannot have any properties itself. We saw that this view can be questioned. Is it possible, with an analogous reasoning, to show that the argument about change is not correct?
4. Does van Inwagen think that marigolds exist?
5. What are we saying , according to Quine, when we say 'Atlantis does not exist'?
6. How could you prove with a *sorites* argument that it is impossible for anyone to grow tall?

Further reading

On Aristotle's view of substance, see Barnes (1995). For Locke, see Ayers (1991), a significant scholarly work on Locke, but also a thorough philosophical defence of some Lockean doctrines. An excellent introductory book on substance in the rationalist tradition is Woolhouse (1993).

For contemporary defences of substance, see Lowe (1998), Wiggins (1980 and 2001), and Anscombe (1981). For an attack on substance, see Simons (1998a). On the 'bundle theory', see van Cleve (1985) and Armstrong (1997). For more on Quine's massively influential views of existence, see his (1958c) and (1960: chapter 7). For an interesting discussion of Quine's views, see Strawson (1976). A fascinating though demanding discussion of existence, arguing against the Russell–Quine view, is Evans (1982: chapter 10). Despite the intuitive appeal of the problem of vagueness (see Box III.1), much of the literature on this subject is forbiddingly difficult. The essay by Cargile in Keefe and Smith (1997), and the introduction to that volume, are both fairly accessible. A full account of the problem, with an ingenious though controversial solution, is Williamson (1994). See also Part VIII: Identity, for constitution.

Part IV

Universals and particulars

Introduction

1. Introduction

IN addition to particular objects, the world also appears to contain the *properties* or *qualities* of these things, and *relations* between them. In addition to Brutus and Julius Caesar, there are also such things as Caesar's *ambition*, and Brutus' *love* for Caesar—things which do not seem to be objects in quite the way that Brutus and Caesar are. But the existence and nature of such properties or qualities has been a matter of philosophical controversy since the ancient Greeks. In this section, we discuss three important questions about properties and their relation to the objects which have them: (i) what kind of entities are properties? Are they a fundamentally different kind of entity from particular objects, or should talk of properties be explained in terms of talk of objects? (ii) What is the relationship between properties and the language we use to talk about them? Does each distinct predicate or general term in our language pick out a distinct property? Are there determinable properties (like *redness*) as well as determinate ones (like very specific *shades* of red)? (iii) What is the relationship between properties and causation? Do a cause's effects depend on the properties of the cause? Can properties be distinguished by their contribution to producing characteristic effects?

Some terminological preliminaries. The words 'property', 'quality', and 'relation' will be used as neutral terms: anyone who thinks that some things are red, say, believes in the property or quality of *redness*, and anyone who believes that some rabbits are bigger than others believes in the relation of *being bigger than something*. Likewise, on this usage, anyone who believes that two or more things can be red (or bigger than something etc.) believes in *sameness of type* or *qualitative identity*. It will not be assumed, therefore, that qualitative identity *is* numerical identity, the logical relation which properly deserves the name 'identity' (see Part VIII: Identity). The philosophical problem we will be discussing here is how to give a philosophical account of properties and relations, and of sameness of type/qualitative identity, given that these things exist.

2. Plato: one over many

The question discussed in our selections from Plato is known as the question of 'one over many': how can many things be one, or the same? Among individual things in the world, we find things which are the same colour, the same shape, and so on. Yet no two individual things can literally be numerically identical (see Part VIII: Identity). So what can it mean to say that two things are the same in any sense? In the excerpt from his dialogue *Parmenides* reproduced here (Chapter 19), we find Socrates discussing this question with Parmenides, the ancient Greek philosopher famous for thinking that reality must ultimately be one, and that there is no real diversity in the world. Socrates defends the view that when two things have something F in common, there is literally something in which they 'partake'. This is called the *Form of F* or the *Form of F-ness*. So, for example, when two things are beautiful, they partake in the Form of beauty. It is partaking in the Form of beauty which makes something beautiful.

The question of what Forms are, and how we can know them, was one of the pre-occupations of Plato's philosophy. The discussion with Parmenides focuses mostly on whether Forms are divided among the things which partake in them. Parmenides asks whether 'the Form as a whole—one thing—is in each of the many'. This question gives rise to a dilemma. If the Form as a whole is in each of the things which partake of it, then it will be 'as a whole in things which are many and separate; and thus it would be separate from itself'—and this seems absurd. But if the Form is divided among the things which partake in it, then things which partake in the Form will only partake in a part of the Form. Parmenides illustrates this idea with the vivid image of a sail covering many people; we might say that one whole sail covers many people, but what we really mean by this is that the whole sail covers all the people by a part of the sail covering each person. But the problem with this is how the parts of the Form relate to the Form itself. Do they relate to the Form by partaking of it? If so, a regress threatens: for do the parts of the Form relate to the whole Form by partaking in *another* part of it? This obscure idea really does not answer the question. So we have the dilemma which Socrates is trying to resolve in the excerpt from *Parmenides* reprinted here.

The need to choose between the two horns of this dilemma can arise independently of the specific details of Plato's theory of Forms. It is a quite general predicament for anyone who believes that properties, like beauty or colour, are entities of a different kind from the particular objects which have them. Some philosophers in effect adopt the first horn of the dilemma and insist that properties are what are called *universals*, entities which are 'wholly present' whenever a particular instantiates them (see Armstrong 1978: vol. ii). On this view, the property of (e.g.) courage exists in Brutus; it also exists in Mark Anthony. And it exists in its entirety in each of them. It is not that a *part* of courage is destroyed when Brutus dies. Courage itself does not change at all, it is not diminished, by the death of Brutus. Hence it must be, in its entirety, in Brutus and Anthony and anyone else who is courageous. These philosophers accept the apparently absurd consequence that courage and other properties can be in more than one place at one time.

Other philosophers take the second horn of the dilemma and hold that properties are never wholly present in an individual; an individual can only ever instantiate a part of the property (the trope theory described in section 3 below, and defended by D. C. Williams in Chapter 22, takes this line). They then must accept the consequence that when Brutus dies, courage itself is diminished.

In our second excerpt from Plato, this time from his later work, the *Republic*, the question discussed by Socrates and his interlocutor Glaucon is how we can know about the Forms. The context of this discussion is one of the main themes of the *Republic*: who should rule in an ideal state. Plato is well known for the argument that philosophers should rule, since they have a knowledge of the ultimate reality of things. In this section of the *Republic*, Socrates draws the famous analogy between our everyday knowledge and the experience of prisoners living in a cave, unable to move and watching shadows cast by activity happening in front of a distant fire. If the prisoners had no other experience, Socrates argues, they would conclude that the shadows on the wall of the cave were real objects. These prisoners, he says, 'are like us': their position is analogous to people who think that the ordinary objects of experience are real things. However, the philosopher who comes to know the Forms—'things that are grasped by reasoning' as they are called in the *Parmenides*—is analogous to someone who can leave the cave and see real things illuminated by the sun. Hence it is only philosophers who have genuine knowledge of reality itself, which lies outside the world of experience.

Plato's theory of Forms, then, seems to involve two main ideas: first, that Forms are themselves—in some way—one; and second, that Forms do not exist in the world of experience: they are 'transcendent'. As we have seen in an earlier chapter, however, Aristotle had a different view (see Part III: Being). Aristotle thought that Forms reside in the substances whose matter is organized by the Form: Forms are not transcendent but 'immanent'. The Form of a horse, for example, resides in each individual horse. The difference between Plato and Aristotle here is over the question of what is most fundamentally real. Does the ultimate reality of the world lie within the ordinary things of experience? Or does it transcend those things? To say that a Form of the horse is in the horse is to say that the horse is fully real in itself; the reality of an individual horse does not have to be underwritten by the horse's relationship to something outside the world of experience.

3. Theories of properties

Aristotle and Plato therefore provide us with two very different solutions to the problem of one over many, solutions which in certain respects are still being discussed today. A contemporary defender of an Aristotelian view is D. M. Armstrong. In Chapter 20, Armstrong argues against the Platonistic view that properties and relations are transcendent universals. As a *Naturalist* (see Part IX: Mind and Body), Armstrong thinks that universals must inhabit the space-time world, the world of experience. His general metaphysical picture is that the world consists of what he calls *states of affairs*: objects having or instantiating properties, considered as Aristotelian universals.

A chief motivation for this theory derives from what Armstrong calls the 'truth-maker principle': that for every contingent truth there 'must be something in the world which makes it true'. Consider two truths about the same object, such as 'Brutus is honourable' and 'Brutus is courageous'. It is natural to think that what makes these truths true is not the mere existence of Brutus, but rather something different in each case: in the first case, the property of being honourable is involved in making it true, in the second the property of being courageous (see Martin 1980). Armstrong argues further (Chapter 20, section iv) that it is still not enough that Brutus and these properties must exist; rather Brutus must *have* the properties in question. It would not be true that Brutus is courageous simply if Brutus and courageousness were to exist; Brutus must *instantiate* courageousness. And an object instantiating a property is a state of affairs. (As Armstrong notes, states of affairs are what others call 'facts': see Part VI: Causation.)

To understand this picture of the world as constituted of states of affairs—particulars instantiating universals—we need to understand further the ideas of universal and instantiation. What is instantiation? It is what Armstrong calls the 'fundamental tie' which binds particulars to universals. It should not be thought of as a *relation* which stands in need of further explanation: rather, the notion of instantiation is a primitive notion in Armstrong's Realist theory. If it were a relation, then an infinite regress would threaten: if object *a* and property *F* are bound together by the instantiation relation *I*, then this binding together is itself an instantiation of the instantiation relation *I*; if it is an instantiation of this relation, then it too must bear the instantiation relation to the universal instantiation; and so on.

In an earlier work, Armstrong (1978) had used such regress arguments against his opponents: any attempt to do without universals in one's ontology is undermined by what he calls the 'relation regress'. So, for example, the attempt to do without universals by appealing to the resemblance relations between particulars was challenged by Armstrong to characterize the resemblance relation without launching on a regress: *a* and *b* are *F* because they *resemble* some paradigm *F*, say *c*; but '*x* resembles *y*' is a predicate which is true of many situations, so these situations too must *resemble* some paradigm of the resemblance situation; and so on. In Chapter 21 David Lewis shows that Armstrong's own theory is vulnerable to this kind of objection; the lesson he draws is that no theory can be expected to reduce the fundamental idea of predication—something's being true of something—to any more fundamental idea. So just as Armstrong appeals to a primitive relation of instantiation, so his opponents can appeal to their own primitives: see below for examples of alternative primitive notions.

Suppose we accept the idea that there is a primitive relation of instantiation which binds universals to objects. What about universals themselves? The traditional realist view is that unlike particulars, which can only exist in their entirety in one region of space and time, universals can exist in their entirety (can be 'wholly present') in more than one place at one time. What does this mean? Something's being 'wholly' *F* is naturally contrasted with its being partly *F*; and something being partly present is naturally understood in terms of some of its *parts* being present. So for something to be wholly present would be for *all* of its parts to be present. But it is absurd to say that all of the parts of courage are present in Brutus; for we have no idea what it means to say that courage has parts at all. And certainly on a view like Armstrong's, courage has no parts; so what sense can be made of a universal's being 'wholly' present?

Some will react to this with scepticism about the very idea of a universal, and be tempted into a position which denies that there are any such things. This position has become known as *nominalism* (see Armstrong 1978; Lewis, Chapter 21). Some care is needed for readers new to this area, since 'nominalism' is also used for the view which denies the existence of *abstract* entities (like numbers, for example). When Quine (in Chapter 15) rejects nominalism, he is rejecting the view that there are no abstract objects. But Quine is nonetheless a nominalist in Armstrong's and Lewis's sense, since he rejects universals. Rejecting universals and rejecting abstract objects are different positions, so it is confusing that the same word is used for both rejections.

Here, however, we will follow Lewis and Armstrong and use 'nominalism' for the view that only particulars exist, whether abstract or concrete. How does nominalism explain sameness of type or qualitative identity? Clearly, qualitative 'identity' cannot be genuine (numerical) identity, on this view, since two men could be qualitatively identical—in both being courageous, for example—but there be no numerically identical entity which they both share in or 'partake'. So the nominalist must instead give an explanation of qualitative identity in some other terms. One nominalist proposal, for example, is that qualitative identity/sameness of type should be explained in terms of *resemblance*. To say that objects A and B are both F, on this view, is to say that they resemble each other in respect of F-ness; or (better) that they resemble a paradigm F thing. Criticisms of this kind of idea can be found in Russell (1912); notice that the theory has recently received a new defence by Rodriguez-Pereyra (2002).

A more popular nominalist proposal was initiated by Quine (Chapter 15) and developed by Lewis (Chapter 21). This is the view which Armstrong christened *class nominalism*: it says that for two objects to be F is for them to belong to the class of Fs. In other words, the property of being F is understood as the *extension* of the predicate 'x is F': for an object to be F is for it to be a member of the class which is the extension of that predicate. Classes (or sets) are here understood as they are in set theory, a branch of mathematics (see Burgess 2001 for an introduction to set theory). A class is simply a collection of objects, and set theory is the theory of the mathematical properties of such collections.

At first sight, it might seem a bit unclear how this theory answers our question about sameness of type. The theory says that for something to be red is for it to be a member of the class of red things. It is natural to respond: how can this *explain* what it is for something to be red? A class nominalist might reply that this misses the point. Class nominalism can certainly explain what it is for something to be red in scientific terms, in terms of the light which is absorbed and reflected by red objects. But, they can say, it is a mistake to think there is any more fundamental philosophical explanation in terms of notions like 'instantiation' or 'partaking in a Form'. The philosophically basic explanation just says that all red things belong to the class of red things, and that the class of red things can be called the 'property of being red'. No more is needed.

But there is a problem with this view. Class nominalism says that properties differ when classes do; so if classes are identical then properties are. Classes are identical when they have the same members (in set theory this is called the *axiom of extensionality*: for an introduction, see Burgess 2001: 55). So if two predicates are *co-extensive*—that is, they have the same extensions or are true of all the same things—then the predicates pick out the same property. Quine points out that all creatures with hearts ('cordates') are also creatures with kidneys ('renates'). Hence the class of cordates is identical with the class of renates, since they have the same members. On the class nominalist view, this means that the property *being a renate* is the same property as *being a cordate*. Quine is happy to accept this conclusion. But there is surely something unsatisfactory here. Being a renate has something to do with kidneys, and being a cordate has something to do with hearts, so surely they are different properties of the animals?

Lewis's version of class nominalism is able to answer this question. His theory appeals to his well-known *modal realism*: the view that other possible worlds and their inhabitants (called *possibilia*) are as real as the actual world (see Part V: Necessity). For Lewis, properties are sets of such possibilia. If it is possible—as it surely is—that there could be something which has a heart but does not have a kidney, or vice versa, then the set of all possible renates is different from the set of all possible cordates, and hence the properties are different.

Lewis has more difficulty with predicates which seem to be *necessarily* co-extensive, like 'triangular' and 'trilateral', for in this case, there can be no member of the class of all possible trilaterals which is not a member of the class of all possible triangles (see Lewis 1986*b*: § 1.5 for some discussion). Putting this worry to one side, it is plain that Lewis's theory solves the initial problem we posed for Quine's nominalism. But it does so at a price: to accept Lewis's solution, you have to accept his modal realism. For you cannot believe that properties are sets of possibilia unless you believe in possibilia; for the simple reason that you cannot believe in the set of *X*s unless you believe *X*s exist. And for reasons discussed elsewhere, Lewis's modal realism is very hard to believe (see Part V: Necessity).

Does this mean, then, that the only viable form of nominalism is one which accepts possibilia? If so, and we cannot accept them, then it would seem that we must return to the theory of universals. But in fact, there is an alternative: the *trope theory* defended by D. C. Williams in Chapter 22. Trope theory starts in a completely different place from the other forms of nominalism and from the theory of universals. Rather than assuming particular objects and/or universals as the basic entities in the universe, trope theory assumes that the basic entities in the world are neither of these. Courage is a property (whether class or universal) which may be had by many people, but *Brutus' courage* is a particular instance of that property which is unique to Brutus. No one else can have Brutus' courage. But Brutus' courage is not Brutus himself, since Brutus, has many other qualities: his height, his weight, his hair colour, and so on. All these qualities which make up Brutus and are unique to him are his particularized properties or 'tropes'. According to trope theory, tropes are the basic elements of reality. What we call particular objects—things like Brutus—are bundles of tropes. What we call properties—things like courage—are classes of exactly resembling tropes. Objects and properties are constructions out of tropes. This elegant approach to the problem is nominalist in the sense that it denies the existence of universals—tropes are particulars—but it does not encounter Quine's renate/cordate problem, since the sets of all exactly resembling *having a kidney* tropes and all exactly resembling *having a heart* tropes will be distinct, even in the actual world.

We have distinguished three types of theory of properties and relations: Armstrong's theory of universals, Lewis's nominalism, and Williams's trope theory. It is helpful to distinguish these theories by how they answer two questions: (i) is qualitative identity numerical identity? And (ii) are particulars reducible? Understanding the theories in this way (as demonstrated in Box IV.1) also allows us to locate a position discussed in Part II: Being: the theory that particulars are 'bundles of universals'.

4. Properties and predicates

What is the relationship between properties (however conceived: as universals, classes, or tropes) and the predicates we use to talk about them? A predicate is sometimes defined as what you get when you remove the names or singular terms from sentences containing them. Thus, 'Caesar was ambitious' with the name 'Caesar' removed leaves us with 'is ambitious', and philosophers and logicians often mark the place left by 'Caesar'

Box IV.1. Theories of properties and particulars

The differences between the different theories of particulars and properties can be represented by the way they answer two questions: (i) *is qualitative identity numerical identity?* and (ii) *are particulars reducible to some other category of entity?* Armstrong's *theory of universals and particulars* says yes to (i) and no to (ii); the *bundle theory* says yes to (i) and yes to (ii); *nominalism* says no to (i) and no to (ii); and *trope theory* says no to (i) and yes to (ii). These options may be illustrated by the following matrix:

Is qualitative identity numerical identity?

Are particulars reducible?	YES	NO
YES	Bundle theory	Trope theory
NO	The theory of universals and particulars	Class and resemblance nominalisms

---

with what is known as a free variable '*x*': '*x* is ambitious.' Now it is certainly true that our grasp on the notion of a property comes partly through our understanding of the general terms or predicates which we apply to objects. We understand the idea of Brutus being courageous partly in terms of the predicate '*x* is courageous' being true of Brutus, the subject of the sentence. One approach to the whole question of properties is to push ontological questions no further than the linguistic distinction just made: 'property' and 'predicate' are on this view interchangeable terms.

But this approach cannot be satisfactory. For one thing, the linguistic distinction between subject and predicate will not capture what is meant by a distinction between object and property. As F. P. Ramsey argued (1925), one could express the same idea expressed by 'Caesar is ambitious' by saying that 'Ambition is a characteristic of Caesar'—but in the first, *Caesar* is the subject, and in the second, *ambition* is. But whatever ambition is, it is surely not an object in the same sense that Caesar is; so the subject-predicate distinction cannot be the same as the object-property distinction.

But there is another important reason why something's having a property cannot be the same as a predicate's being true of it. There are many cases where there are many distinct predicates true of an object, but where it is implausible to think that the object in question has the same number of properties. For example, suppose Brutus weighs 95 kilos. It is also true that he weighs less than 100 kilos; and that he weighs more than 50 kilos; and so on. There is no limit in principle to the different ways in which Brutus' weight could be specified. All these predications say that *distinct* weight-predicates are true of Brutus. But surely it is very implausible to think that Brutus has as many *weights* as he has true weight-descriptions. Isn't it more plausible to think that any one time in his life, Brutus has just one weight, and it is his having this one weight which makes true all the true predications of his weight? If this is right, it would mean that true predications do not correspond one to one with the predications for which they are the truth-makers.

Some philosophers, notably Lewis (in Chapter 21), respond by distinguishing between two kinds of property: sparse and abundant. For every distinct predicate there is a distinct abundant property; but this is not true for sparse properties, sometimes also called 'natural properties'. 'Natural properties would be the ones whose sharing makes for resemblance, and the ones relevant to causal powers,' Lewis says. Notice, of course, that since Lewis is a class nominalist, he thinks that the distinction between sparse and abundant properties is a distinction between kinds of classes—since properties *are* classes. Lewis's view is that we need both sparse and abundant properties, since they play different roles in our theories of the world: abundant properties provide the extensions of all of our natural language predicates; while sparse properties are what are discovered by science. Some philosophers, however, think that there are only sparse properties; there are no abundant properties (see Armstrong 1997; Mellor 1993).

Are everyday properties like weights and colours sparse properties? For those who believe that sparse properties are discovered by science, this will depend on whether there are scientific theories of weights and colours (which of course there are). But this in itself does not necessarily mean that there is such a property as (for example) *being red* or *being heavy*. To explain why, it is useful to introduce another important distinction in the theory of properties. Properties like weight are known as *determinable* properties, and the specific weights things have (like weighing exactly 95 kilos) are known as *determinates* of these determinables (the distinction derives from Johnston 1921; for a contemporary exposition, see Yablo 1992). In fact, the distinction between determinables and determinates is not absolute, but a relative one. For example: Red is a determinate of the determinable Colour; but Red is a determinable of which Crimson is a determinate; and Crimson is a determinable of which the most specific shade of Crimson is a determinate. It is natural to think that for any determinable kind of property, there is always a *most determinate* property: that is, a property which is not a determinable with any further determinates. The most determinate properties are the most specific weights, lengths, colours, etc.

What is the relationship between the determinate/determinable distinction and the sparse/abundant distinction? One reason for thinking properties are sparse was put forward in our discussion of weight above: properties are the *truth-makers* for the many distinct predications which are true of an object. If we have this reason for believing in sparse properties, then we are led to the conclusion that there are no determinable sparse properties. All sparse properties are the most determinate properties. There are no determinable sparse properties because whenever a determinable predicate is true of something, it is always made true by the instantiation of a more determinate property. For example: consider a red apple. It is true that this apple is red; but this is made true by the apple's being a specific determinate shade of red.

This means that if you believe only in sparse properties, and you believe that they are the truth-makers for determinable predications (for example, of redness), then, you should believe that, strictly speaking, there is no such property as redness itself. There are only very specific determinate colour properties, which we group together as shades of red, green, and so on. Although this might seem like a rather surprising conclusion to draw, it is actually a natural consequence of thinking of properties in the sparse way. (However, it is worth noting that there are powerful arguments to show that determinable predications often have more explanatory power than determinate ones: see Yablo 1992.)

5. Properties and causation

Suppose that we have settled on a view about in what general ontological category (universal, particular, etc.) properties belong, and that we have some idea about how properties differ from other kinds of entity. The natural question then arises: how are properties distinguished from each other? We have a pretty good idea when, for example, material objects are distinguished from one another: at the very least, when they occupy different spatio-temporal positions at the same time (but see Part VIII: Identity, for other views). But what should we say about properties? If we had accepted the linguistic view of properties discussed in the previous section, then we would have an easy answer to this: for each semantically distinct predicate (i.e. predicates which are distinct in meaning) of a language, there is a distinct property (with synonymous predicates picking out the same property). But we found reasons to deny this view; so what should we say instead?

The main alternative to the linguistic view is the view that properties are distinguished by their causal powers; or (more precisely) by the causal powers they confer upon the objects which have them. This view—the causal theory of properties—is represented here by Sydney Shoemaker (Chapter 23). The idea of a causal power may be introduced with reference to the familiar concept of a *disposition*. Having a disposition—like being soluble, fragile, or flexible, for example—is having a property, which is characterized *causally*, in terms of the typical effects that are produced in typical circumstances. For example: for a sugar cube to be (water-) soluble is for it to be caused to dissolve when put in water. Being soluble is one of the sugar cube's causal powers.

However, although the notion of a disposition is a useful way of getting an initial grasp on the notion of a causal power, Shoemaker does not say that all properties are dispositions. This is because he thinks that 'dispositional' is a way of classifying *predicates* rather than properties themselves, and not all properties are classifiable by dispositional predicates. A predicate is dispositional when it is part of the meaning of the predicate that things of which it is true will behave in certain ways in certain circumstances. This is certainly true for '*x* is flexible' and '*x* is soluble'. But it is not true for '*x* is round' or '*x* is made of copper'. As Shoemaker says, 'there are causal powers associated with being made of copper—for example, being an electrical conductor. But presumably this association is not incorporated into the meaning of the term "copper".' Shoemaker intends his causal theory of properties not simply to apply to those properties which are describable by dispositional predicates, but to all properties. So the notion of a disposition will not suffice for his purposes. Moreover, he does not want to say that properties *are* or *have* causal powers. It is objects which have powers, and they have them in virtue of the properties they have. His thesis is that 'what makes a property the property it is . . . is its potential for contributing to the causal powers of the things that have it'. It follows from this that properties cannot differ if their total contribution in all possible circumstances to the causal powers of objects is the same.

Chapter 19

Selections from *Parmenides* and *Republic*

Plato

From Parmenides

'But tell me this: is it your view that, as you say, there are certain forms from which these other things, by getting a share of them, derive their names—as, for instance, they come to be like by getting a share of likeness, large by getting a share of largeness, and just and beautiful by getting a share of justice and beauty?'

'It certainly is,' Socrates replied.

'So does each thing that gets a share get as its share the form as a whole or a part of it? Or could there be some other means of getting a share apart from these two?'

'How could there be?' he said.

'Do you think, then, that the form as a whole—one thing—is in each of the many? Or what do you think?'

'What's to prevent its being one,[1] Parmenides?' said Socrates.

'So, being one and the same, it will be at the same time, as a whole, in things that are many and separate; and thus it would be separate from itself.'

'No it wouldn't,' Socrates said. 'Not if it's like one and the same day. That is in many places at the same time and is none the less not separate from itself. If it's like that, each of the forms might be, at the same time, one and the same in all.'

Plato's *Parmenides*, from which our first excerpt is taken, is a dialogue which describes an imagined meeting between Socrates and the two great philosophers from Elea, Parmenides and Zeno. The dialogue concerns the question of 'one over many', and the text prior to our excerpt has described Socrates questioning Zeno about his views on this matter. We join the action when Parmenides starts asking Socrates about his own 'theory of forms'. The main theme of Plato's *Republic*, from which our second excerpt is taken, is the nature of the state and how it should be governed. The story of the cave is introduced as part of a discussion of the knowledge of what is real, in the context of Plato's view that philosophers should be the rulers of the ideal state.

1. Removing the brackets in a10–11.

'Socrates,' he said, 'how neatly you make one and the same thing be in many places at the same time! It's as if you were to cover many people with a sail, and then say that one thing as a whole is over many. Or isn't that the sort of thing you mean to say?'

c   'Perhaps,' he replied.

'In that case would the sail be, as a whole, over each person, or would a part of it be over one person and another part over another?'

'A part.'

'So the forms themselves are divisible, Socrates,' he said, 'and things that partake of them would partake of a part; no longer would a whole form, but only a part of it, be in each thing.'

'It does appear that way.'

'Then are you willing to say, Socrates, that our one form is really divided? Will it still be one?'

'Not at all,' he replied.

d   'No,' said Parmenides. 'For suppose you are going to divide largeness itself. If each of the many large things is to be large by a part of largeness smaller than largeness itself, won't that appear unreasonable?'

'It certainly will,' he replied.

'What about this? Will each thing that has received a small part of the equal have something by which to be equal to anything, when its portion is less than the equal itself?'

'That's impossible.'

'Well, suppose one of us is going to have a part of the small. The small will be larger than that part of it, since the part is a part of it: so the small itself will

e   be larger! And that to which the part subtracted is added will be smaller, not larger, than it was before.'

'That surely couldn't happen,' he said.

'Socrates, in what way, then, will the other things get a share of your forms, if they can do so neither by getting parts nor by getting wholes?'

'By Zeus!' Socrates exclaimed. 'It strikes me that's not at all easy to determine!'

'And what do you think about the following?'

'What's that?'

132   'I suppose you think each form is one on the following ground: whenever some number of things seem to you to be large, perhaps there seems to be some one character, the same as you look at them all, and from that you conclude that the large is one.'

'That's true,' he said.

'What about the large itself and the other large things? If you look at them all in the same way with the mind's eye, again won't some one thing appear large, by which all these appear large?'[2]

'It seems so.'

---

2. Alternatively: 'If you look at them all in the same way with the mind's eye, won't some one large again appear, by which all these appear large?'

'So another form of largeness will make its appearance, which has emerged alongside largeness itself and the things that partake of it, and in turn another over all these, by which all of them will be large. Each of your forms will no longer be one, but unlimited in multitude.' b

'But, Parmenides, maybe each of these forms is a thought,'[3] Socrates said, 'and properly occurs only in minds. In this way each of them might be one and no longer face the difficulties mentioned just now.'

'What do you mean?' he asked. 'Is each of the thoughts one, but a thought of nothing?'

'No, that's impossible,' he said.

'Of something, rather?'

'Yes.'

'Of something that is, or of something that is not?' c

'Of something that is.'

'Isn't it of some one thing, which that thought thinks is over all the instances, being some one character?'

'Yes.'

'Then won't this thing that is thought to be one, being always the same over all the instances, be a form?'

'That, too, appears necessary.'

'And what about this?' said Parmenides. 'Given your claim that other things partake of forms, won't you necessarily think either that each thing is composed of thoughts and all things think, or that, although they are thoughts, they are unthinking?'[4]

'That isn't reasonable either, Parmenides,' he said. 'No, what appears most likely d to me is this: these forms are like patterns set in nature, and other things resemble them and are likenesses; and this partaking of the forms is, for the other things, simply being modeled on them.'

'If something resembles the form,' he said, 'can that form not be like what has been modeled on it, to the extent that the thing has been made like it? Or is there any way for something like to be like what is not like it?'

'There is not.'

'And isn't there a compelling necessity for that which is like to partake of the same one form as what is like it?'[5]

'There is.'

'But if like things are like by partaking of something, won't that be the form itself?'

'Undoubtedly.'

'Therefore nothing can be like the form, nor can the form be like anything else. Otherwise, alongside the form another form will always make its appearance, and if

---

3. Alternatively: 'But, Parmenides, maybe each of the forms is a thought of these things.'6. Reading *parionta autous nomizein onomazein* in b5.

4. Alternatively: 'or that, although they are thoughts, they are not thought?'

5. Removing the bracket in e1.

133 that form is like anything, yet another; and if the form proves to be like what partakes of it, a fresh form will never cease emerging.'

'That's very true.'

'So other things don't get a share of the forms by likeness; we must seek some other means by which they get a share.'

'So it seems.'

'Then do you see, Socrates,' he said, 'how great the difficulty is if one marks things off as forms, themselves by themselves?'

From Republic

514 Next, I said, compare the effect of education and of the lack of it on our nature to an experience like this: Imagine human beings living in an underground, cavelike dwelling, with an entrance a long way up, which is both open to the light and as wide as the cave itself. They've been there since childhood, fixed in the same place, with their necks and legs fettered, able to see only in front of them, because their bonds prevent them from turning their heads around. Light is provided by a fire burning far

b above and behind them. Also behind them, but on higher ground, there is a path stretching between them and the fire. Imagine that along this path a low wall has been built, like the screen in front of puppeteers above which they show their puppets.

I'm imagining it.

Then also imagine that there are people along the wall, carrying all kinds of

c artifacts that project above it—statues of people and other animals, made out of stone, wood, and every material. And, as you'd expect, some of the carriers are talk-

515 ing, and some are silent.

It's a strange image you're describing, and strange prisoners.

They're like us. Do you suppose, first of all, that these prisoners see anything of themselves and one another besides the shadows that the fire casts on the wall in front of them?

b How could they, if they have to keep their heads motionless throughout life?

What about the things being carried along the wall? Isn't the same true of them?

Of course.

And if they could talk to one another, don't you think they'd suppose that the names they used applied to the things they see passing before them?[6]

They'd have to.

And what if their prison also had an echo from the wall facing them? Don't you think they'd believe that the shadows passing in front of them were talking whenever one of the carriers passing along the wall was doing so?

I certainly do.

c Then the prisoners would in every way believe that the truth is nothing other than the shadows of those artifacts.

They must surely believe that.

6. Reading *parionta autous nomizein onomazein* in b5.

Consider, then, what being released from their bonds and cured of their ignorance would naturally be like, if something like this came to pass.[7] When one of them
was freed and suddenly compelled to stand up, turn his head, walk, and look up
toward the light, he'd be pained and dazzled and unable to see the things whose   d
shadows he'd seen before. What do you think he'd say, if we told him that what he'd
seen before was inconsequential, but that now—because he is a bit closer to the
things that are and is turned towards things that are more—he sees more correctly?
Or, to put it another way, if we pointed to each of the things passing by, asked him
what each of them is, and compelled him to answer, don't you think he'd be at a loss
and that he'd believe that the things he saw earlier were truer than the ones he was
now being shown?

Much truer.

And if someone compelled him to look at the light itself, wouldn't his eyes hurt,
and wouldn't he turn around and flee towards the things he's able to see, believing   e
that they're really clearer than the ones he's being shown?

He would.

And if someone dragged him away from there by force, up the rough, steep path,
and didn't let him go until he had dragged him into the sunlight, wouldn't he be
pained and irritated at being treated that way? And when he came into the light,
with the sun filling his eyes, wouldn't he be unable to see a single one of the things   516
now said to be true?

He would be unable to see them, at least at first.

I suppose, then, that he'd need time to get adjusted before he could see things in
the world above. At first, he'd see shadows most easily, then images of men and
other things in water, then the things themselves. Of these, he'd be able to study the
things in the sky and the sky itself more easily at night, looking at the light of the
stars and the moon, than during the day, looking at the sun and the light of the sun.   b

Of course.

Finally, I suppose, he'd be able to see the sun, not images of it in water or some
alien place, but the sun itself, in its own place, and be able to study it.

Necessarily so.

And at this point he would infer and conclude that the sun provides the seasons
and the years, governs everything in the visible world, and is in some way the cause   c
of all the things that he used to see.

It's clear that would be his next step.

What about when he reminds himself of his first dwelling place, his fellow
prisoners, and what passed for wisdom there? Don't you think that he'd count himself happy for the change and pity the others?

Certainly.

And if there had been any honors, praises, or prizes among them for the one who
was sharpest at identifying the shadows as they passed by and who best remembered

---

7. Reading *hoia tis an eiē phusei, ei* in c5.

d   which usually came earlier, which later, and which simultaneously, and who could thus best divine the future, do you think that our man would desire these rewards or envy those among the prisoners who were honored and held power? Instead, wouldn't he feel, with Homer, that he'd much prefer to 'work the earth as a serf to another, one without possessions,'[8] and go through any sufferings, rather than share their opinions and live as they do?

e   I suppose he would rather suffer anything than live like that.

Consider this too. If this man went down into the cave again and sat down in his same seat, wouldn't his eyes—coming suddenly out of the sun like that—be filled with darkness?

They certainly would.

And before his eyes had recovered—and the adjustment would not be quick—while his vision was still dim, if he had to compete again with the perpetual pris-
517 oners in recognizing the shadows, wouldn't he invite ridicule? Wouldn't it be said of him that he'd returned from his upward journey with his eyesight ruined and that it isn't worthwhile even to try to travel upward? And, as for anyone who tried to free them and lead them upward, if they could somehow get their hands on him, wouldn't they kill him?

They certainly would.

b   This whole image, Glaucon, must be fitted together with what we said before. The visible realm should be likened to the prison dwelling, and the light of the fire inside it to the power of the sun. And if you interpret the upward journey and the study of things above as the upward journey of the soul to the intelligible realm, you'll grasp what I hope to convey, since that is what you wanted to hear about. Whether it's true or not, only the god knows. But this is how I see it: In the knowable realm, the form of the good is the last thing to be seen, and it is reached only with difficulty. Once one has seen it, however, one must conclude that it is the cause of all that is correct and beautiful in anything, that it produces both light and its source in the visible
c   realm, and that in the intelligible realm it controls and provides truth and under-standing, so that anyone who is to act sensibly in private or public must see it.

I have the same thought, at least as far as I'm able.

Come, then, share with me this thought also: It isn't surprising that the ones who get to this point are unwilling to occupy themselves with human affairs and that their souls are always pressing upwards, eager to spend their time above, for, after all,
d   this is surely what we'd expect, if indeed things fit the image I described before.

It is.

What about what happens when someone turns from divine study to the evils of human life? Do you think it's surprising, since his sight is still dim, and he hasn't yet become accustomed to the darkness around him, that he behaves awkwardly and appears completely ridiculous if he's compelled, either in the courts or elsewhere, to contend about the shadows of justice or the statues of which they are the shadows

---

8. *Odyssey* xi.489–90.

and to dispute about the way these things are understood by people who have never seen justice itself?

e

That's not surprising at all.

No, it isn't. But anyone with any understanding would remember that the eyes may be confused in two ways and from two causes, namely, when they've come from the light into the darkness *and* when they've come from the darkness into the light. Realizing that the same applies to the soul, when someone sees a soul disturbed and unable to see something, he won't laugh mindlessly, but he'll take into consideration whether it has come from a brighter life and is dimmed through not having yet become accustomed to the dark or whether it has come from greater ignorance into greater light and is dazzled by the increased brilliance. Then he'll declare the first soul happy in its experience and life, and he'll pity the latter—but even if he chose to make fun of it, at least he'd be less ridiculous than if he laughed at a soul that has come from the light above.

518

b

What you say is very reasonable.

If that's true, then here's what we must think about these matters: Education isn't what some people declare it to be, namely, putting knowledge into souls that lack it, like putting sight into blind eyes.

c

They do say that.

But our present discussion, on the other hand, shows that the power to learn is present in everyone's soul and that the instrument with which each learns is like an eye that cannot be turned around from darkness to light without turning the whole body. This instrument cannot be turned around from that which is coming into being without turning the whole soul until it is able to study that which is and the brightest thing that is, namely, the one we call the good. Isn't that right?

d

Yes.

Then education is the craft concerned with doing this very thing, this turning around, and with how the soul can most easily and effectively be made to do it. It isn't the craft of putting sight into the soul. Education takes for granted that sight is there but that it isn't turned the right way or looking where it ought to look, and it tries to redirect it appropriately.

So it seems.

Now, it looks as though the other so-called virtues of the soul are akin to those of the body, for they really aren't there beforehand but are added later by habit and practice. However, the virtue of reason seems to belong above all to something more divine, which never loses its power but is either useful and beneficial or useless and harmful, depending on the way it is turned. Or have you never noticed this about people who are said to be vicious but clever, how keen the vision of their little souls is and how sharply it distinguishes the things it is turned towards? This shows that

e

519

its sight isn't inferior but rather is forced to serve evil ends, so that the sharper it sees, the more evil it accomplishes.

Absolutely.

However, if a nature of this sort had been hammered at from childhood and freed from the bonds of kinship with becoming, which have been fastened to it by feasting, greed, and other such pleasures and which, like leaden weights, pull its vision downwards—if, being rid of these, it turned to look at true things, then I say that the same soul of the same person would see these most sharply, just as it now does the things it is presently turned towards.

Probably so.

And what about the uneducated who have no experience of truth? Isn't it likely— indeed, doesn't it follow necessarily from what was said before—that they will never adequately govern a city? But neither would those who've been allowed to spend their whole lives being educated. The former would fail because they don't have a single goal at which all their actions, public and private, inevitably aim; the latter would fail because they'd refuse to act, thinking that they had settled while still alive in the faraway Isles of the Blessed.

That's true.

It is our task as founders, then, to compel the best natures to reach the study we said before is the most important, namely, to make the ascent and see the good. But when they've made it and looked sufficiently, we mustn't allow them to do what they're allowed to do today.

What's that?

To stay there and refuse to go down again to the prisoners in the cave and share their labors and honors, whether they are of less worth or of greater.

Then are we to do them an injustice by making them live a worse life when they could live a better one?

You are forgetting again that it isn't the law's concern to make any one class in the city outstandingly happy but to contrive to spread happiness throughout the city by bringing the citizens into harmony with each other through persuasion or compulsion and by making them share with each other the benefits that each class can confer on the community.[9] The law produces such people in the city, not in order to allow them to turn in whatever direction they want, but to make use of them to bind the city together.

9. See 420b–421c, 462a–466c.

Chapter 20

Selection from *Universals: An Opinionated Introduction*

D. M. Armstrong

Universals as attributes

I. Uninstantiated universals?

Iᶠ we abandon the idea that particulars are nothing but bundles of universals but still want to recognize universals, then we must return to the traditional view that particulars, tokens, *instantiate* universals: having properties and standing to each other in relations. If we do this, then there are a number of controversial questions that have to be settled. One key question is this. Should we, or should we not, accept a **Principle of Instantiation** for universals? That is, should we, or should we not, demand that every universal be instantiated? That is, for each property universal must it be the case that it is a property of some particular? For each relation universal must it be the case that there are particulars between which the relation holds?

We certainly should not demand that every universal should be instantiated *now*. It would be enough if a particular universal was not instantiated now, but was instantiated in the past, or would be instantiated in the future. The Principle of Instantiation should be interpreted as ranging over all time: past, present, and future. But should we uphold the principle even in this relatively liberal form?

This is a big parting of the ways. We can call the view that there are uninstantiated universals the Platonist view. It appears to have been the view held by Plato, who was also, apparently, the first philosopher to introduce universals. (He spoke of Forms or Ideas—but there was nothing psychological about the Ideas.)

Once you have uninstantiated universals you need somewhere special to put them, a 'Platonic heaven,' as philosophers often say. They are not to be found in the ordinary world of space and time. And since it seems that any instantiated universal might have been uninstantiated—for example, there might have been nothing past, present, or future that had that property—then if uninstantiated universals are in a Platonic heaven, it will be natural to place all universals in that heaven. The result is that we get two realms: the realm of universals and the realm of particulars,

It is suggested that Chapter 11 of D. M. Armstrong's *Nominalism and Realism* and Chapters 13–17 of his *A Theory of Universals* be used as companion readings to this chapter.

the latter being ordinary things in space and time. Such universals are often spoken of as *transcendent*. (A view of this sort was explicitly held by Russell in his earlier days before he adopted a bundle-of-universals view. See his introductory book *The Problems of Philosophy*, 1912, Chs. 9 and 10.) **Instantiation** then becomes a very big deal: a relation between universals and particulars that crosses realms. The Latin tag used by the Scholastics for a theory of this sort is *universalia ante res*, 'universals before things.' Such a view is unacceptable to Naturalists, that is, to those who think that the space-time world is all the world that there is. This helps to explain why Empiricists, who tend to be sympathetic to Naturalism, often reject universals.

It is interesting to notice that a separate-realm theory of universals permits of a blob[1] as opposed to a layer-cake view of particulars. For on this view, what is it for a thing to have a property? It is not the thing's having some internal feature, but rather its having a relationship, the instantiation relationship, to certain universals or Forms in another realm. The thing itself could be bloblike. It is true that the thing could also be given a property structure. But then the properties that make up this structure cannot be universals but must be particulars. They would have to be tropes. Perhaps this second possibility is the natural candidate for the sixth box in the diagram in Chapter 1 (Section III). The particular involves property tropes, but these property tropes are put into natural classes by their instantiating a certain universal in the realm of the universals. At any rate, without bringing in tropes in addition it seems that Platonic theories of universals have to treat particulars as bloblike rather than layer-caked. I think that this is an argument against Platonic theories.

If, however, we reject uninstantiated universals, then we are at least in a position, if we want to do it, to bring the universals down to earth. We can adopt the view whose Latin tag is *universalia in rebus*, 'universals in things.' We can think of a thing's properties as constituents of the thing and think of the properties as universals. This may have been the position of Aristotle. (The scholars differ. Some make him a Nominalist. Some think he believed in this-worldly universals. Certainly, he criticized Plato's otherworldly universals.) *Universalia in rebus* is, of course, a layer-cake view, with properties as universals as part of the internal structure of things. (Relations will be *universalia inter res*, 'universals between things' [Abbott 1886].)

There are difficulties in this position, of course, objections that can be brought, as with every other solution to the Problem of Universals. One thing that has worried many philosophers, including perhaps Plato, is that on this view we appear to have multiple location of the same thing. Suppose *a* is F and *b* is also F, with F a property universal. The very same entity has to be part of the structure of two things at two places. How can the universal be in two places at once? I will come back to this question later in this chapter.

Just to round things off I will mention the third Scholastic tag: *universalia post res*, 'universals after things.' This was applied to Nominalist theories. It fits best with

---

1. *Editors' note*: Armstrong's term 'blob' refers to theories that deny objective properties as constituents of particulars; 'layer-cake' theories are those that admit such objective properties.

Predicate or **Concept Nominalism**, where properties, et cetera, are as it were created by the classifying mind: shadows cast on things by our predicates or concepts.

But our present task is to decide whether or not we ought to countenance uninstantiated universals. The first point to be made is that the onus of proof seems to be firmly on the side of the Platonists. It can hardly be doubted that there is a world of space and time. But a separate realm of universals is a mere hypothesis, or postulation. If a postulation has great explanatory value, then it may be a good postulation. But it has to prove itself. Why should we postulate uninstantiated universals?

One thing that has moved many philosophers is what we may call the argument from the meaning of general terms. Plato, in his *Republic*, had Socrates say, 'shall we proceed as usual and begin by assuming the existence of a single essential nature or Form for every set of things which we call by the same name?' (595, trans. F. M. Cornford). Socrates may have been thinking along the following lines. Ordinary names, that is, proper names, have a bearer of the name. If we turn to general terms—words like 'horse' and 'triangular' that apply to many different things—then we need something that stands to the word in the same general sort of relation that the bearer of the proper name stands to the proper name. There has to be an object that constitutes or corresponds to the meaning of the general word. So there has to be something called horseness, and triangularity. But now consider a general word that applies to nothing particular at all, a word like 'unicorn' for instance. It is perfectly meaningful. And if it is meaningful, must there not be something in the world that constitutes or corresponds to the word? So there must be uninstantiated universals.

This 'argument from meaning' is a very bad argument. (In fairness to Socrates, it is not clear whether he was using it. Other philosophers have, though, often at a rather unself-conscious level.) The argument depends on the assumption that in every case where a general word has meaning, there is something in the world that constitutes or corresponds to that meaning. Gilbert Ryle spoke of this as the 'Fido'-Fido fallacy. Fido corresponds to the word 'Fido', but there does not have to be some single thing corresponding to a general word.

To go along with the argument from meaning is to be led into a very promiscuous theory of universals. If it is correct, then we know a priori that for each general word with a certain meaning, there exists a universal. This lines up predicates and properties in a nice neat way, but it is a way that we ought to be very suspicious of. Is it that easy to discover what universals there are?

Plato had another line of thought that led him toward uninstantiated universals. This is the apparent failure of things in the ordinary world to come up to exact standards. It seems that nothing in the world is perfectly straight or circular, yet in geometry we discuss the properties of perfectly straight lines or perfect circles. Again, no thing is perfectly changeless. Yet again, it may well be that no act is perfectly just. Certainly no person is perfectly virtuous and no state is perfectly just. Yet in ethical and political discussion (e.g., in the *Republic*) we can discuss the nature of virtue and justice. In general, we perceive the world as falling short of certain standards. This can be explained if, whether we know it or not, we are comparing ordinary things to Forms, which the ordinary things can never fully instantiate. (This can lead one, and perhaps led Plato, to the difficult notion of degrees of instantiation, with the highest degree never realized.)

It is interesting to notice that this argument did not quite lead Plato where he wanted to go in every case. Consider geometry. In geometry one might wish to consider the properties of, say, two intersecting circles. These circles will be perfectly circular. But also, of course, there is only *one* Form of the circle. So what are these two perfect circles? Plato, apparently, had to introduce what he called the Mathematicals. Like the mathematical Forms they were perfect and thus were unlike ordinary things. But unlike the Forms, there could be many tokens of the same type, and in this they were like ordinary things. They were particulars, although perfect particulars. But if this is so, though perhaps the falling away from standards gave Plato an argument for the Mathematicals, it is not clear that it is any argument for the Forms.

But in any case, cannot ideal standards simply be things that we merely think of? We can quite knowingly form thoughts of that which does not exist. In the case of ideal standards nothing comes up to the standard, but by extrapolating from ordinary things that approximate to the standard in different degrees, we can form the thought of something that does come up to the standard. It turns out to be useful to do so. Why attribute metaphysical reality to such standards? They could be useful fictions. As a matter of fact, in the geometrical case it appears that such notions as that of a perfectly straight line or a perfectly circular object may be acquired directly in experience. For cannot something look perfectly straight or perfectly circular, even if it is not in fact so?

One should note that one thing that seems to keep a theory of uninstantiated universals going is the widespread idea that it is sufficient for a universal to exist if it is merely possible that it should be instantiated. I have found in discussion that this idea has particular appeal if it is empirically possible (that is, compatible with the laws of nature) that the alleged universal should have actual instances. Suppose, for instance, that somebody describes a very complex pattern of wallpaper but does not ever sketch the pattern or manufacture the wallpaper. Suppose nobody else does either in the whole history of the universe. It is clear that there was nothing in the laws of nature that prevented the pattern's ever having an instance, from ever having a token of the type. But is not that pattern a monadic universal, a complex and structural universal to be sure, but a universal nonetheless?

In this way, apparently, it is natural for philosophers to argue. But for myself I do not see the force of the argument. Philosophers do not reason that way about particulars. They do not argue that it is empirically possible that present-day France should be a monarchy and therefore that the present king of France exists, although, unfortunately for French royalists, he is not instantiated. Why argue in the same way about universals? Is it that philosophers think that universals are so special that they can exist whether or not particular things, which are contingent only, exist? If so, I think that this is no better than a prejudice, perhaps inherited from Plato.

There is one subtle variation of the argument to uninstantiated universals from their empirical possibility that I think has more weight. It has been developed by Michael Tooley (1987, 3.1.4 and 3.2). However, it depends upon deep considerations about the nature of the laws of nature, which cannot be discussed here. And in any case, the argument depends upon the laws' being found to have a very special structure, which it is unlikely that they actually have. As a result, it seems that the best that the argument shows is that uninstantiated universals are possible rather than actual. And even this conclusion may be avoidable (see Armstrong 1983, Ch. 8).

It may also be thought that considerations from mathematics, and the properties and relations postulated by mathematicians, push toward the recognition of uninstantiated universals. However, the whole project of bringing together the theory of universals with the disciplines of mathematics, although very important, cannot be undertaken here. I have sketched out, rather broadly, the way that I think it ought to go in a book on the nature of possibility (1989, Chapter 10).

From this point on, therefore, I am going to assume the truth of the Principle of Instantiation. As already noted, this does not compel one to abandon a two-realm doctrine. It does not compel one to bring the universals down among ordinary things. But it does *permit* one to do this, and to do so seems the natural way to develop the theory once one rejects uninstantiated universals.

II. Disjunctive, negative, and conjunctive universals

For simplicity, in this section I will consider property universals only. But the points to be made appear to apply to relations also. We have already rejected uninstantiated universals. But it seems that the potential class of universals needs to be cut down a great deal further if we are to get a plausible theory. I will begin by giving reasons for rejecting disjunctive property universals. By a **disjunctive property** I mean a disjunction of (property) universals. Let us assume that particular electric charges and particular masses are universals. Then having charge C or having mass M (with C and M dummies for determinate, that is, definite values) would be an example of a disjunctive property. Why is it not a universal? Consider two objects. One has charge C but lacks mass M. The other lacks charge C but has mass M. So they have the disjunctive property having charge C or having mass M. But surely that does not show that, in any serious sense, they thereby have something identical? The whole point of a universal, however, is that it should be identical in its different instances.

There is another reason to deny that a disjunction of universals is a universal. There is some very close link between universals and causality. The link is of this nature. If a thing instantiates a certain universal, then, in virtue of that, it has the power to act in a certain way. For instance, if a thing has a certain mass, then it has the power to act upon the scalepan of a balance, or upon scales, in a certain way.

Furthermore, different universals bestow different powers. Charge and mass, for instance, manifest themselves in different ways. I doubt if the link between universals and powers is a necessary one, but it seems real. Moreover, if, as seems abstractly possible, two different universals bestowed the very same powers, how could one ever know that they were two different universals? If they affect all apparatus, including our brains, in exactly the same way, will we not judge that we are dealing with one universal only?

Now suppose that a thing has charge C but lacks mass M. In virtue of charge C, it has certain powers to act. For instance, it repels things with like charge. Possession of the disjunctive property C or M adds nothing to its power. This suggests that while C may be a genuine universal, C or M is not.

So I think that we should reject disjunctive universals. A similar case seems to hold against negative universals: the lack or absence of a property is not a property. If having charge C is the instantiation of a universal, then not having C is not the instantiating of a universal.

First, we may appeal to identity again. Is there really something in common, something identical, in everything that lacks charge C? Of course, there might be some universal property that just happened to be coextensive with lacking charge C. But the lack itself does not seem to be a factor found in each thing that lacks charge C.

Second, causal considerations seem to point in the same direction. It is a strange idea that lacks or absences do any causing. It is natural to say that a thing acts in virtue of positive factors alone. This also suggests that absences of universals are not universals.

It is true that there is some linguistic evidence that might be thought to point the other way. We do say things like 'lack of water caused his death'. At the surface, the statement says that a lack of water caused an absence of life. But how seriously should we take such ways of expressing ourselves? Michael Tooley has pointed out that we are unhappy to say 'lack of poison causes us to remain alive'. Yet if the surface way of understanding the first statement is correct, then the second statement should be understood in the same way and thought to be true. Certain counterfactual statements are true in both cases: If he had had water, then he would (could) have still been alive; if we had taken poison, we would have been dead now. These are causal truths. But they tell us very little about the actual causal factors operative in the two cases. We believe, I think, that these actual causal factors could be spelled out in purely positive terms.

It is interesting to notice that conjunctions of universals (having both charge C and mass M) escape the two criticisms leveled against disjunctive and negative universals. With conjunctions we do have identity. The very same conjunction of factors is present in each instance. There is no problem about causality. If a thing instantiates the conjunction, then it will have certain powers as a consequence. These powers will be different from those that the thing would have had if it had had just one of the conjuncts. It may even be that the conjunction can do more than the sum of what each property would do if each was instantiated alone. (As scientists say: There could be synergism. The effect could be more than the sum of each cause acting by itself.)

But there is one condition that ought to be put on conjunctive universals. Some thing (past, present, future) must actually have both properties and at the same time. This, of course, is simply the Principle of Instantiation applied to conjunctive universals.

III. Predicates and universals

What has been said about uninstantiated universals, and also about disjunctions and negations of universals, has brought out a most important point. It is that there is no automatic passage from predicates (linguistic entities) to universals. For instance, the expression 'either having charge C or having mass M' is a perfectly good predicate. It could apply to, or be true of, innumerable objects. But as we have seen, this does not mean that there is a universal corresponding to this predicate.

Wittgenstein made a famous contribution to the Problem of Universals with his discussion of **family resemblances**. Wittgenstein was an antimetaphysician, and his object was to dissolve rather than to solve the Problem of Universals. He seems to have thought that what he said about family resemblances was (among other things) a step toward getting rid of the problem. But I think that the real moral of what he said is only that predicates and universals do not line up in any simple way.

In his *Philosophical Investigations* (1953, Secs. 66 and 67) he considered the notion of a *game*. He had this to say about it:

66. Consider for example the proceedings that we call "games". I mean board-games, card-games, ball-games, Olympic games, and so on. What is common to them all?—Don't say: "There *must* be something common, or they would not be called 'games' "—but *look and see* whether there is anything common to all.—For if you look at them you will not see something that is common to *all*, but similarities, relationships, and a whole series of them at that. To repeat: don't think, but look!—Look for example at board-games, with their multifarious relationships. Now pass to card-games; here you find many correspondences with the first group, but many common features drop out, and others appear. When we pass next to ball-games, much that is common is retained, but much is lost.—Are they all 'amusing'? Compare chess with noughts and crosses. Or is there always winning and losing, or competition between players? Think of patience. In ball games there is winning and losing; but when a child throws his ball at the wall and catches it again, this feature has disappeared. Look at the parts played by skill and luck; and at the games like ring-a-ring-a-roses; here is the element of amusement, but how many other characteristic features have disappeared! And we can go through the many, many other groups of games in the same way; we can see how similarities crop up and disappear.

And the result of this examination is: we see a complicated network of similarities overlapping and criss-crossing: sometimes overall similarities, sometimes similarities of detail.

67. I can think of no better expression to characterize these similarities than "family resemblances"; for the various resemblances between members of a family: build, features, colour of eyes, gait, temperament, etc. etc. overlap and criss-cross in the same way.—And I shall say: 'games' form a family.

This has been a very influential passage. Wittgenstein and his followers applied the point to all sorts of notions besides those of a game, including many of the central notions discussed by philosophers. But what should a believer in universals think that Wittgenstein has shown about universals?

Let us agree, as we probably should, that there is no universal of gamehood. But now what of this 'complicated network of similarities overlapping and criss-crossing' of which Wittgenstein speaks? All the Realist has to do is to analyze each of these similarities in terms of common properties. That analysis of similarity is not a difficult or unfamiliar idea, though it is an analysis that would be contested by a Nominalist. But there will not be any property that runs through the whole class and makes them all games. To give a crude and oversimplified sketch, the situation might be like this:

Particulars:	*a*	*b*	*c*	*d*	*e*
Their properties:	FGHJ	GHJK	HJKL	JKLM	KLMN

Here F to N are supposed to be genuine property universals, and it is supposed that the predicate 'game' applies in virtue of these properties. But the class of particulars {*a* . . . *e*}, which is the class of all tokens of games, is a family in Wittgenstein's sense. Here, though, I have sketched an account of such families that is completely compatible with Realism about universals.

However, Wittgenstein's remarks do raise a big question. How does one decide whether one is or is not in the presence of a genuine property or relation? Wittgenstein says of games, 'don't think, but look.' As a general recipe, at least, that seems far too simple.

I do not think that there is any infallible way of deciding what are the true universals. It seems clear that we must not look to semantic considerations. As I said in Section I of this chapter, those who argue to particular universals from semantic data, from predicates to a universal corresponding to that predicate, argue in a very optimistic and unempirical manner. I call them **a priori realists**. Better, I think, is **a posteriori realism**. The best guide that we have to just what universals there are is total science.

For myself, I believe that this puts physics in a special position. There seem to be reasons, (scientific, empirical, a posteriori reasons) to think that physics is *the* fundamental science. If that is correct, then such properties as mass, charge, extension, duration, space–time interval, and other properties envisaged by physics may be the true monadic universals. (They are mostly ranges of quantities. Quantities raise problems that will need some later discussion.) Spatio-temporal and causal relations will perhaps be the true polyadic universals.

If this is correct, then the ordinary types—the type red, the type horse, in general, the types of the manifest image of the world—will emerge as preliminary, rough-and-ready, classifications of reality. For the most part they are not false, but they are rough-and-ready. Many of them will be family affairs, as games appear to be. To the one type will correspond a whole family of universals and not always a very close family. And even where the ordinary types do carve the beast of reality along its true joints, they may still not expose those joints for the things that they are. But let it be emphasized that any identification of universals remains rather speculative. In what I have just been saying I have been trying to combine a philosophy of universals with Physicalism. Others may have other ideas.

IV. States of affairs

In the Universals theory that we are examining, particulars instantiate properties, pairs of particulars instantiate (dyadic) relations, triples of particulars instantiate (triadic) relations, and so on as far as is needed. Suppose that a is F, with F a universal, or that a has R to b, with R a universal. It appears that we are required to recognize a's being F and a's having R to b as items in our ontology. I will speak of these items as **states of affairs**. Others have called them facts (e.g., Wittgenstein 1961, Skyrms 1981).

Why do we need to recognize states of affairs? Why not recognize simply particulars, universals (divided into properties and relations), and, perhaps, instantiation? The answer appears by considering the following point. If a is F, then it is entailed that a exists and that the universal F exists. However, a could exist, and F could exist, and yet it fail to be the case that a is F (F is instantiated, but instantiated elsewhere only). a's being F involves something more than a and F. It is no good simply adding the fundamental tie or nexus of instantiation to the sum of a and F. The existence of a, of instantiation, and of F does not amount to a's being F. The something more must be a's being F—and this is a state of affairs.

This argument rests upon a general principle, which, following C. B. Martin, I call the truth-maker principle. According to this principle, for every contingent truth at least (and perhaps for all truths contingent or necessary) there must be something in the world that makes it true. 'Something' here may be taken as widely as may be wished. The 'making' is not causality, of course: Rather, it is that in the world in virtue of which the truth is true. Gustav Bergmann and his followers have spoken of the 'ontological ground' of truths, and I think that this is my 'something in the world' that makes truths true. An important point to notice is that different truths may all have the same truth-maker, or ontological ground. For instance, that this thing is colored, is red, and is scarlet are all made true by the thing's having a particular shade of color.

The truth-maker principle seems to me to be fairly obvious once attention is drawn to it, but I do not know how to argue for it further. It is to be noted however that some of those who take perfectly seriously the sort of metaphysical investigation that we are here engaged upon nevertheless reject the principle (see in particular Lewis 1986c).

Accepting the truth-maker principle will lead one to reject Quine's view (1961) that *predicates* do not have to be taken seriously in considering the ontological implications of statements one takes to be true. Consider the difference between asserting that a certain surface is red and asserting that it is green. An upholder of the truth-maker principle will think that there has to be an ontological ground, a difference in the world, to account for the difference between the predicate 'red' applying to the surface and the predicate 'green' so applying. Of course, what that ontological ground is, is a further matter. There is no high road from the principle to universals and states of affairs.

Returning now to states of affairs, it may be pointed out that there are some reasons for accepting states of affairs even if the truth-maker principle is rejected. First, we can apparently refer to states of affairs, preparatory to saying something further about them. But it is generally, if not universally, conceded by philosophers that what can be referred to exists. Second, states of affairs are plausible candidates for the terms of causal relations. The state of affairs of a's being F may be the cause of b's being G. Third, as we shall see in Section VIII of this chapter, states of affairs can help to solve a fairly pressing problem in the theory of universals: how to understand the multiple location of property universals and the nonlocation of relation universals.

It is interesting to see that states of affairs seem not to be required by a Class Nominalist or a Resemblance Nominalist, and of course that is an important economy for their respective theories. The Class Nominalist analyzes a's being F as a's being a member of a class (or natural class) containing $\{a, b, c, \ldots\}$. But here we have simply a and the class. The class-membership relation is internal, dictated by the nature of the terms. So we need not recognize it as something additional to the terms. The terms by themselves are sufficient truth-makers. Hence we do not need states of affairs.

The Resemblance Nominalist analyzes a's being F as a matter of resemblance relations holding between a and, say, suitable paradigm Fs. But that relation is also internal, dictated by what I called the particularized nature of a and the paradigm objects. Once again, states of affairs are not needed.

(But it seems that a Predicate Nominalist *will* require states of affairs. a's being F is analyzed as a's falling under the predicate F. But how can the falling under be dictated simply by a and the linguistic object F? Falling under is an external relation.)

Now for something very important. States of affairs have some rather surprising characteristics. Let us call a, b, F, R, et cetera, the constituents of states of affairs. It turns out that it is possible for there to be two different states of affairs that nevertheless have *exactly the same constituents*.

Here is a simple example. Let R be a nonsymmetrical relation (for instance, loves). Let it be the case, contingently, that a has R to b and b has R to a. Two distinct states of affairs exist: a's having R to b, and b's having R to a (a's loving b and b's loving a). Indeed, these states of affairs are *wholly* distinct, in the sense that it is possible for either state of affairs to fail to obtain while the other exists. Yet the two states of affairs have exactly the same constituents.

You can get the same phenomenon with properties as well as relations (as pointed out by Lewis 1986c). Assume, as I think it is correct to assume, that a conjunction of states of affairs is itself a state of affairs. Then consider (1) a's being F and b's being

G; and (2) a's being G and b's being F. Two wholly distinct states of affairs, it may be, but the very same constituents.

At this point, it is worth realizing that states of affairs may be required not simply by those who recognize universals but also by any philosophy that recognizes properties and relations, whether as universals or as particulars. This is very important, because we saw in examining Natural Class and Resemblance theories what difficulties there are in denying properties and relations (in espousing a blob view).

Suppose that a has R_1 to b, with R_1 a particular, but a nonsymmetrical, relation. If b has 'the same' relation to a, then, on a philosophy of tropes, we have b's having R_2 to a: two states of affairs with different (though overlapping) constituents. For the loving that holds between a and b is a different object from the loving that holds between b and a. Nevertheless a's having R_1 to b entails the existence of constituents a, R_1, and b, but the existence of these constituents does not entail that a has R_1 to b. So states of affairs still seem to be something more than their constituents.

With tropes, you never get different states of affairs constructed out of exactly the same constituents. But given just one set of constituents, more than one state of affairs having just these constituents is *possible*. From a, trope R_1, and b, for instance, we could get a's having R_1 to b or b's having R_1 to a. There is a way for a philosophy of tropes to avoid having to postulate states of affairs. But let us leave that aside until the next chapter.

I have spoken of the constituents of states of affairs. Could we also think and speak of them as *parts* of states of affairs? I think that it would be very unwise to think and speak of them in this way. Logicians have paid some attention to the notions of whole and part. They have worked out a formal calculus for manipulating these notions, which is sometimes called the calculus of individuals or, better, **mereology** (in Greek *meros* means a part). One philosopher who helped to work this out was Nelson Goodman, and in his book *The Structure of Appearance* (1966), an account of mereology is given. There is one mereological principle that is very important for us here: If there are a number of things, and if they have a sum, that is, a whole of which they are parts, then they have just one sum.

I say *if* they have a sum, because it is controversial whether a number of things *always* have a sum. Do the square root of 2 and the Sydney Opera House have a sum? Philosophers differ on how permissive a mereology should be, that is, on whether there are limits to what you can sum, and if there are limits, where the limits fall. I myself would accept total permissiveness in summing. But all that is needed here is something that is agreed by all: where things can be summed, for each collection of things there is just one sum. We have just seen, however, that the complete constituents of a state of affairs are capable of being, and may actually even be, the complete constituents of a different state of affairs. Hence constituents do not stand to states of affairs as parts to whole.

It is worth noticing that complex universals have constituents rather than parts. At any rate this is so if we accept the Principle of Instantiation. Consider, for instance, conjunctive universals. If being P and Q is a conjunctive universal, then there must exist some particular, x, such that x is both P and Q. But to say that is to say that there exists at least one state of affairs of the form x is P and x is Q. For the conjunctive universal to exist is for there to be a state of affairs of a certain sort. As a result, it is misleading to say that P and Q are *parts* of the conjunctive universal, a thing that I myself did say in the past (1978b, Ch. 15, Sec. II).

A very important type of complex universal is a *structural* property. A structural property involves a thing instantiating a certain pattern, such as a flag. Different parts (mereological parts) of the thing that instantiates the structural property will have certain properties. If the structural property involves relations, as a flag does, some or all of these parts will be related in various ways. It is easy to see that states of affairs must be appealed to. If a has P, and b has Q, and a has R to b, then and only then the object $[a + b]$ has the structural property that may be presented in a shorthand way as P-R-Q.

A final point before leaving this particularly important section. The fact that states of affairs, if they exist, have a nonmereological mode of composition may have consequences for the theory examined in the previous chapter: the view that particulars are no more than bundles of universals. (I understand that this point comes from Mark Johnston.) We have seen that different states of affairs can have exactly the same constituents (a's loving b, and b's loving a). We have previously argued against the Bundle theory that two bundles containing exactly the same universals are impossible. They would be the very same bundle. Yet, considering the matter independently of the Bundle theory, why should not two different particulars be exactly alike? But now suppose that, as is plausible, we treat a bundling of universals as a state of affairs. Why should not exactly the same universals be bundled up in different ways?

In reply, I think it must be admitted that this is conceivable. But it would depend upon the Bundle theorist's working out a scheme that allowed for different bundling of the very same things. This is not provided for in the actual Bundle theories that have been developed. So if they want to take this path, then the onus is on Bundle theorists to try to develop their theory in a new way.

V. A world of states of affairs?

In the previous section it was argued that a philosophy that admits both particulars and universals ought to admit states of affairs (facts), which have particulars and universals as constituents (not as parts). As a matter of fact we saw that to introduce properties and relations at all, even as particulars, would apparently involve states of affairs. But our present concern is with universals.

The suggestion to be put forward now is that we should think of the world as a world of states of affairs, with particulars and universals only having existence within states of affairs. We have already argued for a Principle of Instantiation for universals. If this is a true principle, then the way is open to regard a universal as an identical element present in certain states of affairs. A particular that existed outside states of affairs would not be clothed in any properties or relations. It may be called a *bare* particular. If the world is to be a world of states of affairs we must add to the Principle of Instantiation a Principle of the Rejection of Bare Particulars.

This second principle looks plausible enough. In a Universals theory, it is universals that give a thing its nature, kind, or sort. A bare particular would not instantiate any universals, and thus would have no nature, be of no kind or sort. What could we make of such an entity? Perhaps a particular need not have any relations to any other particular—perhaps it could be quite isolated. But it must instantiate at least one property.

References

Abbott, F. E. (1886) *Scientific Theism*, Macmillan.

Adams, R. (1979) 'Primitive Thisness and Primitive Identity', *Journal of Philosophy* 76.

Aristotle. *Basic Works*, ed. R. McKeon, Random House, 1941.

Armstrong, D. M. (1978a) *Nominalism and Realism*, vol. 1 of *Universals and Scientific Realism*, Cambridge University Press.

——. (1978b) *A Theory of Universals*, vol. 2 of *Universals and Scientific Realism*, Cambridge University Press.

——. (1980) 'Against "Ostrich Nominalism": A Reply to Michael Devitt', *Pacific Philosophical Quarterly* 61.

——. (1983) *What Is a Law of Nature?* Cambridge University Press.

——. (1988a) 'Can a Naturalist Believe in Universals?', in *Science in Reflection*, ed. E. Ullmann-Margalit, Kluwer Academic Publishers.

——. (1988b) 'Are Quantities Relations?' *Philosophical Studies* 54.

——. (1989) *A Combinatorial Theory of Possibility*, Cambridge University Press.

Bar-Elli, G. (1988) 'Can a Naturalist Believe in Universals? A Comment', in *Science in Reflection*, ed. E. Ullmann-Margalit, Kluwer Academic Publishers.

Bergmann, G. (1967) *Realism*, University of Wisconsin Press.

Blanshard, B. (1939) *The Nature of Thought*, Allen and Unwin.

——. (1962) *Reason and Analysis*, Open Court.

Butler, J. *The Analogy of Religion*, Everyman, 1906.

Campbell, K. K. (1981) 'The Metaphysic of Abstract Particulars', *Midwest Studies in Philosophy*, vol. 6, ed. P. A. French, T. E. Uehling, and H. K. Wettstein, University of Minnesota Press.

——. (forthcoming) *Abstract Particulars*, Blackwell.

Denkel, A. (1989) 'Real Resemblances', *Philosophical Quarterly* 39.

Devitt, M. (1980) ' "Ostrich Nominalism" or "Mirage Realism"?' *Pacific Philosophical Quarterly* 61.

Foster, J. (1983) 'Induction, Explanation and Natural Necessity', *Proceedings of the Aristotelian Society*, vol. 83.

Goodman, N. (1966) *The Structure of Appearance*, 2nd edn., Bobbs-Merrill.

Hume, D. *A Treatise of Human Nature*, 2 vols., Everyman, 1911.

Jackson, F. (1977) 'Statements about Universals', *Mind* 76.

Küng, G. (1967) *Ontology and the Logistic Analysis of Language*, rev. edn., Reidel.

Leibniz, G. W. *The Leibniz-Clarke Correspondence*, ed. H. G. Alexander, Manchester University Press, 1956.

Lewis, D. (1983) 'New Work for a Theory of Universals', *Australasian Journal of Philosophy* 61.

——. (1986a) *On the Plurality of Worlds*, Blackwell.

——. (1986b) 'Against Structural Universals', *Australasian Journal of Philosophy* 64.

——. (1986c) 'Comment on Forrest and Armstrong', *Australasian Journal of Philosophy* 64.

——. (1986d) *Philosophical Papers*, vol. 2, Oxford University Press.

Martin, C. B. (1980) 'Substance Substantiated', *Australasian Journal of Philosophy* 58.

Matthews, G. B., and S. M. Cohen (1968) 'The One and the Many', *Review of Metaphysics* 21.

McTaggart, J. McT. E. (1921) *The Nature of Existence*, 2 vols., Cambridge University Press.

Pap, A. (1959) 'Nominalism, Empiricism and Universals: 1', *Philosophical Quarterly* 9.

Plato. Philebus, trans. A. E. Taylor, in *Plato: Philebus and Epinomis*, ed. R. Klibansky, Nelson, 1956.

——. *Republic*, trans. F. Cornford, Oxford University Press, 1941.

Price, H. H. (1953) *Thinking and Experience*, Hutchinson.

Quilter, J. (1985) 'What Has Properties?', *Proceedings of the Russellian Society*, Philosophy Dept., Sydney University, 10.

Quine, W. V. (1961) 'On What There Is', in *From a Logical Point of View*, by W. V. Quine, Harper & Row.

——. (1980) 'Soft Impeachment Disowned', *Pacific Philosophical Quarterly* 61.

Quinton, A. (1957) 'Properties and Classes', *Proceedings of the Aristotelian Society*, vol. 58.

——. (1973) *The Nature of Things*, Routledge and Kegan Paul.

Russell, B. (1912) *The Problems of Philosophy*, Home University Library.

——. (1940) *An Inquiry into Meaning and Truth*, Allen and Unwin.

——. (1948) *Human Knowledge, Its Scope and Limits*, Allen and Unwin.

——. (1959) *My Philosophical Development*, Allen and Unwin.

Seargent, D. A. J. (1985) *Plurality and Continuity, an Essay in G. F. Stout's Theory of Universals*, Martinus Nijhoff.

Sellars, W. (1963) 'Philosophy and the Scientific Image of Man', in *Science, Perception and Reality*, by W. F. Sellars, Routledge and Kegan Paul.

Skyrms, B. (1981) 'Tractarian Nominalism', *Philosophical Studies* 40.

Sober, Elliott. (1982) 'Why Logically Equivalent Predicates May Pick Out Different Properties', *American Philosophical Quarterly* 19.

Stout, G. F. (1921) *The Nature of Universals and Propositions*, Oxford University Press (British Academy Lecture), reprinted in G. F. Stout, *Studies in Philosophy and Psychology*, Macmillan, 1930.

——. (1936) Universals Again, *Proceedings of the Aristotelian Society*, supp. vol. 15.

Tooley, M. (1987) *Causation*, Clarendon Press.

Williams, D. C. (1966) 'The Elements of Being', in *The Principles of Empirical Realism*, by D. C. Williams, Charles Thomas.

Wittgenstein, L. (1953) *Philosophical Investigations*, Blackwell.

——. (1961) *Tractatus Logico-Philosophicus*, trans. D. F. Pears and B. F. McGuinness, Routledge and Kegan Paul.

Wolterstorff, N. (1970) *On Universals*, University of Chicago Press.

Chapter 21

Selection from *New Work for a Theory of Universals*

David Lewis

Introduction

D. M. ARMSTRONG offers a theory of universals as the only adequate answer to a 'compulsory question' for systematic philosophy: the problem of One over Many.[1] I find this line of argument unpersuasive. But I think there is more to be said for Armstrong's theory than he himself has said. For as I bear it in mind considering various topics in philosophy, I notice time and again that it offers solutions to my problems. Whatever we may think of the problem of One over Many, universals can earn their living doing other much-needed work.

I do not say that they are indispensable. The services they render could be matched using resources that are Nominalistic in letter, if perhaps not in spirit.[2] But neither do I hold any presumption against universals, to the effect that they are to be accepted only if we have no alternative. I therefore suspend judgement about universals themselves. I only insist that, one way or another, their work must be done.

I shall investigate the benefits of adding universals to my own usual ontology. That ontology, though Nominalistic, is in other respects generous. It consists of *possibilia*—particular, individual things, some of which comprise our actual world

I am indebted to comments by Gilbert Harman, Lloyd Humberstone, Frank Jackson, Mark Johnston, Donald Morrison, Kim Sterelny, and others; and especially to discussion and correspondence with D. M. Armstrong over several years, without which I might well have believed to this day that set theory applied to *possibilia* is all the theory of properties that anyone could ever need.

1. D. M. Armstrong, *Universals and Scientific Realism* (Cambridge: Cambridge University Press, 1978), henceforth cited as *Universals*; see also his 'Against "Ostrich" Nominalism: A Reply to Michael Devitt', *Pacific Philosophical Quarterly*, 61 (1980), 440–49.
2. In this paper, I follow Armstrong's traditional terminology: 'universals' are repeatable entities, wholly present wherever a particular instantiates them; 'Nominalism' is the rejection of such entities. In the conflicting modern terminology of Harvard, classes count as 'universals' and 'Nominalism' is predominantly the rejection of classes. Confusion of the terminologies can result in grave misunderstanding; see W. V. Quine, 'Soft Impeachment Disowned', *Pacific Philosophical Quarterly*, 61 (1980), 450–51.

David Lewis, selection from 'New Work for a Theory of Universals', from the *Australasian Journal of Philosophy*, 64 (1983), reprinted by permission of Oxford University Press.

and others of which are unactualized[3]—together with the iterative hierarchy of classes built up from them. Thus I already have at my disposal a theory of properties as classes of *possibilia*. Properties, so understood, are not much like universals. Nor can they, unaided, take over the work of universals. Nevertheless, they will figure importantly in what follows, since for me they are part of the environment in which universals might operate.

The friend of universals may wonder whether they would be better employed not as an addition to my ontology of *possibilia* and classes, but rather as a replacement for parts of it. A fair question, and an urgent one; nevertheless not a question considered in this paper.

In the next section, I shall sketch Armstrong's theory of universals, contrasting universals with properties understood as classes of *possibilia*. Then I shall say why I am unconvinced by the One over Many argument. Then I shall turn to my principal topic: how universals could help me in connection with such topics as duplication, supervenience, and divergent worlds; a minimal form of materialism; laws and causation; and the content of language and thought. Perhaps the list could be extended.

Universals and properties

Language offers us several more or less interchangeable words: 'universal'; 'property', 'quality', 'attribute', 'feature', and 'characteristic'; 'type', 'kind', and 'sort'; and perhaps others. And philosophy offers us several conceptions of the entities that such words refer to. My purpose is not to fix on one of these conceptions; but rather to distinguish two (at opposite extremes) and contemplate helping myself to both. Therefore some regimentation of language is called for; I apologise for any inconvenience caused. Let me reserve the word 'universal' for those entities, if such there be, that mostly conform to Armstrong's account. And let me reserve the word 'property' for classes—any classes, but I have foremost in mind classes of things. To have a property is to be a member of the class.[4]

Why call them 'properties' as well as 'classes'?—Just to underline the fact that they need not be classes of *actual* things. The property of being a donkey, for instance, is the class of *all* the donkeys. This property belongs to—this class contains—not only the actual donkeys of this world we live in, but also all the unactualised, otherworldly donkeys.

3. Among 'things' I mean to include all the gerrymandered wholes and parts admitted by the most permissive sort of mereology. Further, I include such physical objects as spatiotemporal regions and force fields, unless an eliminative reduction of them should prove desirable. Further, I include such nonphysical objects as gods and spooks, though not—I hope—as parts of the same world as us. Worlds themselves need no special treatment. They are things—big ones, for the most part.

4. My conception of properties resembles the doctrine of Class Nominalism considered in *Universals*, I, pp. 28–43. But, strictly speaking, a Class Nominalist would be someone who claims to solve the One over Many problem simply by means of properties taken as classes, and that is far from my intention.

Likewise I reserve the word 'relation' for arbitrary classes of ordered pairs, triples, ... Thus a relation among things is a property of 'tuples of things. Again, there is no restriction to actual things. Corresponding roughly to the division between properties and relations of things, we have the division between 'monadic' and 'polyadic' universals.

Universals and properties differ in two principal ways. The first difference concerns their instantiation. A universal is supposed to be wholly present wherever it is instantiated. It is a constituent part (though not a spatiotemporal part) of each particular that has it. A property, by contrast, is spread around. The property of being a donkey is partly present wherever there is a donkey, in this or any other world. Far from the property being part of the donkey, it is closer to the truth to say that the donkey is part of the property. But the precise truth, rather, is that the donkey is a member of the property.

Thus universals would unify reality (*Cf. Universals*, I, p. 109) in a way that properties do not. Things that share a universal have not just joined a single class. They literally have something in common. They are not entirely distinct. They overlap.

By occurring repeatedly, universals defy intuitive principles. But that is no damaging objection, since plainly the intuitions were made for particulars. For instance, call two entities *copresent* if both are wholly present at one position in space and time. We might intuit offhand that copresence is transitive. But it is not so, obviously, for universals. Suppose for the sake of argument that there are universals: round, silver, golden. Silver and round are copresent, for here is a silver coin; golden and round are copresent, for there is a gold coin; but silver and golden are not copresent. Likewise, if we add universals to an ontology of *possibilia*, for the relation of being part of the same possible world.[5] I and some otherworldly dragon are not worldmates; but I am a worldmate of the universal golden, and so is the dragon. Presumably I need a mixed case involving both universals and particulars. For why should any two universals ever fail to be worldmates? Lacking such failures, the worldmate relation among universals alone is trivially transitive.

The second difference between universals and properties concerns their abundance. This is the difference that qualifies them for different work, and thereby gives rise to my interest in having universals and properties both.

A distinctive feature of Armstrong's theory is that universals are sparse. There are the universals that there must be to ground the objective resemblances and the

---

5. If universals are to do the new work I have in store for them, they must be capable of repeated occurrence not only within a world but also across worlds. They would then be an exception to my usual principle—meant for particulars, of course—that nothing is wholly present as part of two different worlds. But I see no harm in that. If two worlds are said to overlap by having a coin in common, and this coin is supposed to be wholly round in one world and wholly octagonal in the other, I stubbornly ask what shape it is, and insist that shape is not a relation to worlds. (See my 'Individuation by Acquaintance and by Stipulation', *Philosophical Review*, 92 (1983), 3–32.) I do not see any parallel objections if worlds are said to overlap by sharing a universal. What contingent, nonrelational property of the universal could we put in place of shape of the coin in raising the problem? I cannot think of any.

causal powers of things, and there is no reason to believe in any more. All of the following alleged universals would be rejected:

not golden,	first examined before 2000 A.D.
golden or wooden,	being identical,
metallic,	being alike in some respect,
self-identical,	being exactly alike,
owned by Fred,	being part of,
belonging to class C,	owning,
grue,	being paired with by some pair in R

(where C and R are utterly miscellaneous classes). The guiding idea, roughly, is that the world's universals should comprise a minimal basis for characterising the world completely. Universals that do not contribute at all to this end are unwelcome, and so are universals that contribute only redundantly. A satisfactory inventory of universals is a non-linguistic counterpart of a primitive vocabulary for a language capable of describing the world exhaustively.

(That is rough: Armstrong does not dismiss redundant universals out of hand, as the spirit of his theory might seem to demand. Conjunctive universals—as it might be, golden-and-round—are accepted, though redundant; so are analysable structural universals. The reason is that if the world were infinitely complex, there might be no way to cut down to a minimal basis. The only alternative to redundancy might be inadequacy, and if so we had better tolerate redundancy. But the redundancy is mitigated by the fact that complex universals consist of their simpler—if perhaps not absolutely simple—constituents. They are not distinct entities. See *Universals*, II, pp. 30–42 and 67–71.)

It is quite otherwise with properties. Any class of things, be it ever so gerrymandered and miscellaneous and indescribable in thought and language, and be it ever so superfluous in characterizing the world, is nevertheless a property. So there are properties in immense abundance. (If the number of things, actual and otherwise, is beth-2, an estimate I regard as more likely low than high, then the number of properties of things is beth-3. And that is a big infinity indeed, except to students of the outer reaches of set theory.) There are so many properties that those specifiable in English, or in the brain's language of synaptic interconnections and neural spikes, could be only an infinitesimal minority.

Because properties are so abundant, they are undiscriminating. Any two things share infinitely many properties, and fail to share infinitely many others. That is so whether the two things are perfect duplicates or utterly dissimilar. Thus properties do nothing to capture facts of resemblance. That is work more suited to the sparse universals. Likewise, properties do nothing to capture the causal powers of things. Almost all properties are causally irrelevant, and there is nothing to make the relevant ones stand out from the crowd. Properties carve reality at the joints—and everywhere else as well. If it's distinctions we want, too much structure is no better than none.

It would be otherwise if we had not only the countless throng of all properties, but also an élite minority of special properties. Call these the *natural* properties.[6] If we had properties and universals both, the universals could serve to pick out the natural properties. Afterwards the universals could retire if they liked, and leave their jobs to the natural properties. Natural properties would be the ones whose sharing makes for resemblance, and the ones relevant to causal powers. Most simply, we could call a property *perfectly* natural if its members are all and only those things that share some one universal. But also we would have other lessthan-perfectly natural properties, made so by families of suitable related universals.[7] Thus we might have an imperfectly natural property of being metallic, even if we had no such single universal as metallic, in virtue of a close-knit family of genuine universals one or another of which is instantiated by any metallic thing. These imperfectly natural properties would be natural to varying degrees.

Let us say that an *adequate* theory of properties is one that recognises an objective difference between natural and unnatural properties; preferably, a difference that admits of degree. A combined theory of properties and universals is one sort of adequate theory of properties.

But not the only sort. A Nominalistic theory of properties could achieve adequacy by other means. Instead of employing universals it could draw primitive distinctions among particulars. Most simply, a Nominalist could take it as a primitive fact that some classes of things are perfectly natural properties; others are less-than-perfectly natural to various degrees; and most are not at all natural. Such a Nominalist takes 'natural' as a primitive predicate, and offers no analysis of what he means in predicating it of classes. His intention is to select the very same classes as natural properties that the user of universals would select. But he regards the universals as idle machinery, fictitiously superimposed on the primitive objective difference between the natural properties and the others.[8]

Alternatively, a Nominalist in pursuit of adequacy might prefer to rest with primitive objective resemblance among things. (He might not think that 'natural' was a very natural primitive, perhaps because it is to be predicated of classes.) Then he

---

6. See *Universals*, I, pp. 38–41; Anthony Quinton, 'Properties and Classes', *Proceedings of the Aristotelian Society*, 48 (1957), 33–58; and W. V. Quine, 'Natural Kinds', in his *Ontological Relativity* (New York: Columbia University Press, 1969). See also George Bealer, *Quality and Concept* (Oxford: Oxford University Press, 1982), especially pp. 9–10 and 177–87. Like me, Bealer favours an inegalitarian twofold conception of properties: there are abundant 'concepts' and sparse 'qualities', and the latter are the ones that 'determine the logical, causal, and phenomenal order of reality' (p. 10). Despite this point of agreement, however, Bealer's views and mine differ in many ways.

7. Here I assume that some solution to the problem of resemblance of universals is possible, perhaps along the lines suggested by Armstrong in *Universals*, II, pp. 48–52 and 101–31; and that such a solution could be carried over into a theory of resemblance of perfectly natural properties, even if we take naturalness of properties as primitive.

8. This is the Moderate Class Nominalism considered in *Universals*, I, pp. 38–41. It is akin to the views of Quinton, 'Properties and Classes'; but plus the unactualised members of the natural classes, and minus any hint that 'natural' could receive a psychologistic analysis.

could undertake to define natural properties in terms of the mutual resemblance of their members and the failure of resemblance between their members and their non-members. Unfortunately, the project meets with well-known technical difficulties. These can be solved, but at a daunting price in complexity and artificiality of our primitive. We cannot get by with the familiar dyadic 'resembles'. Instead we need a predicate of resemblance that is both contrastive and variably polyadic. Something like

$x_1, x_2, \ldots$ resemble one another and do not likewise resemble any of $y_1, y_2, \ldots$

(where the strings of variables may be infinite, even uncountable) must be taken as understood without further analysis.[9] If adequate Nominalism requires us to choose between this and a primitive predicate of classes, we might well wonder whether the game is worth the candle. I only say we might wonder; I know of no consideration that seems to me decisive.

At this point, you may see very well why it could be a good idea to believe in universals as well as properties; but you may see no point in having properties as well as universals. But properties have work of their own, and universals are ill-suited to do the work of properties.

It is properties that we need, sometimes natural and sometimes not, to provide an adequate supply of semantic values for linguistic expressions. Consider such

9. Such a theory is a form of Resemblance Nominalism, in Armstrong's classification, but it is unlike the form that he principally considers. See *Universals*, I, pp. 44–63. For discussions of the problem of defining natural classes in terms of resemblance, and of the trickery that proves useful in solving this problem, see Nelson Goodman, *The Structure of Appearance* (Cambridge, Mass.: Harvard University Press, 1951), chapters 4–6; W. V. Quine, 'Natural Kinds'; and Adam Morton, 'Complex Individuals and Multigrade Relations', *Noûs*, 9 (1975), 309–18.

To get from primitive resemblance to perfectly natural properties, I have in mind a definition as follows. We begin with R as our contrastive and variably polyadic primitive. We want it to turn out that $x_1, x_2, \ldots Ry_1, y_2, \ldots$ iff some perfectly natural property is shared by all of $x_1, x_2, \ldots$ but by none of $y_1, y_2, \ldots$ We want to define N, another variably polyadic predicate, so that it will turn out that $Nx_1, x_2, \ldots$ iff $x_1, x_2, \ldots$ are all and only the members of some perfectly natural property. Again we must allow for, and expect, the case where there are infinitely many x's. We define $Nx_1, x_2, \ldots$ as:

$\exists y_1, y_2, \ldots \forall z(z, x_1, x_2, \ldots Ry_1, y_2, \ldots \equiv z = x_1 \lor z = x_2 \lor \ldots).$

Then we finish the job by defining a perfectly natural property as a class such that, if $x_1, x_2, \ldots$ are all and only its members, then $Nx_1, x_2, \ldots$.

We might have taken N as primitive instead of R. But would that have been significantly different, given the interdefinability of the two? On the other hand, taking N as primitive also seems not significantly different from taking perfect naturalness of classes as primitive. It is only a difference between speaking in the plural of individuals and speaking in the singular of their classes, and that seems no real difference. Is plural talk a disguised form of class talk? Or *vice versa*? (See the discussion in *Universals*, I, pp. 32–4; also Max Black, 'The Elusiveness of Sets', *Review of Metaphysics*, 24 (1971), 614–36; Eric Stenius, 'Sets', *Synthese*, 27 (1974), 161–88; and Kurt Gödel, 'Russell's Mathematical Logic', *The Philosophy of Bertrand Russell*, edited by P. A. Schilpp (Cambridge: Cambridge University Press, 1944.) At any rate, it is not at all clear to me that Moderate Class Nominalism and Resemblance Nominalism in its present form are two different theories, as opposed to a single theory presented in different styles.

sentences as these:

(1) Red resembles orange more than it resembles blue.
(2) Red is a colour.
(3) Humility is a virtue.
(4) Redness is a sign of ripeness.

Prima facie, these sentences contain names that cannot be taken to denote particular, individual things. What is the semantic role of these words? If we are to do compositional semantics in the way that is best developed, we need entities to assign as semantic values to these words, entities that will encode their semantic roles. Perhaps sometimes we might find paraphrases that will absolve us from the need to subject the original sentence to semantic analysis. That is the case with (1), for instance.[10] But even if such paraphrases sometimes exist—even if they *always* exist, which seems unlikely—they work piecemeal and frustrate any systematic approach to semantics.

Armstrong takes it that such sentences provide a subsidiary argument for universals, independent of his main argument from the One over Many problem. (*Universals*, I, pp. 58–63; also 'Against "Ostrich" Nominalism'.[11]) I quite agree that we have here an argument for something. But not for universals as opposed to properties. Properties can serve as the requisite semantic values. Indeed, properties are much better suited to the job than universals are. That is plain even from the examples considered. It is unlikely that there are any such genuine universals as the colours (especially determinable colours, like red, rather than determinate shades), or ripeness, or humility. Armstrong agrees (*Universals*, I, p. 61) that he cannot take (1)–(4) as straightforwardly making reference to universals. He must first subject them to paraphrase. Even if there always is a paraphrase that does refer to, or quantify over, genuine universals, still the need for paraphrase is a threat to systematic semantics. The problem arises exactly because universals are sparse. There is no corresponding objection if we take the requisite semantic values as properties.

10. In virtue of the close resemblance of red and orange, it is possible for a red thing to resemble an orange one very closely; it is not possible for a red thing to resemble a blue one quite so closely. Given our ontology of *possibilia*, all possibilities are realised. So we could paraphrase (1) by

(1') Some red thing resembles some orange thing more than any red thing resembles any blue thing

so long as it is understood that the things in question needn't be part of our world, or of any one world. Or if we did not wish to speak of unactualised things, but we were willing to take ordinary-language modal idioms as primitive, we could instead give the paraphrase:

(1″) A red thing can resemble an orange thing more closely than a red thing can resemble a blue thing.

It is necessary to use the ordinary-language idioms, or some adequate formalisation of them, rather than standard modal logic. You cannot express (1″) in modal logic (excluding an enriched modal logic that would defeat the point of the paraphrase by quantifying over degrees of resemblance or whatnot) because you cannot express cross-world relations, and in particular cannot express the needed cross-world comparison of similarity.

11. He derives the argument, and a second semantic argument to be considered shortly, from Arthur Pap, 'Nominalism, Empiricism and Universals: I', *Philosophical Quarterly*, 9 (1959), 330–40, and Frank Jackson, 'Statements about Universals', *Mind*, 86 (1997), 427–29.

Other sentences make my point more dramatically.

(5) Grueness does not make for resemblance among all its instances.
(6) What is common to all who suffer pain is being in some or another state that occupies the pain role, presumably not the same state in all cases.

The point is not that these sentences are true—though they are—but that they require semantic analysis. (It is irrelevant that they are not ordinary language.) A universal of grueness would be anathema; as would a universal such that, necessarily, one has it if he is in some state or other that occupies the pain role in his case.[12] But the corresponding properties are no problem.

Indeed, we have a comprehension schema applying to any predicate phrase whatever, however complicated. (Let it even be infinitely long; let it even include imaginary names for entities we haven't really named.) Let x range over things, P over properties (classes) of things. Then:

$$\exists_1 P \,\square\, \forall x \,(x \text{ has } P \equiv \phi x).$$

We could appropriately call this 'the property of ϕ-ing' in those cases where the predicate phrase is short enough to form a gerund, and take this property to be the semantic value of the gerund. Contrast this with the very different relationship of universals and predicates set forth in *Universals*, II, pp. 7–59.

Consider also those sentences which *prima facie* involve second-order quantification. From *Universals*, I, p. 62, and 'Against "Ostrich" Nominalism' we have these.

(7) He has the same virtues as his father.
(8) The dresses were of the same colour.
(9) There are undiscovered fundamental physical properties.
(10) Acquired characteristics are never inherited.
(11) Some zoological species are cross-fertile.

Prima facie, we are quantifying either over properties or over universals. Again, paraphrases might defeat the presumption, but in a piecemeal way that threatens systematic semantics. In each case, properties could serve as the values of the variables of quantification. Only in case (9) could universals serve equally well. To treat the other cases, not to mention

(12) Some characteristics, such as the colours, are more disjunctive than they seem.

as quantifications over universals, we would again have to resort to some preliminary paraphrase. (Armstrong again agrees: *Universals*, I, p. 63.) This second semantic argument, like the first, adduces work for which properties are better qualified than universals.

---

12. Or better, in the case of creatures of his kind. See my 'Mad Pain and Martian Pain', in *Readings in Philosophy of Psychology*, I, edited by Ned Block (Cambridge, Mass.: Harvard University Press, 1980), 216–22.

Which is not to deny that a partnership might do better still. Let it be granted that we are dealing with quantifications over properties. Still, these quantifications—like most of our quantifications—may be tacitly or explicitly restricted. In particular, they usually are restricted to natural properties. Not to perfectly natural properties that correspond to single universals, except in special cases like (9), but to properties that are at least somewhat more natural than the great majority of the utterly miscellaneous. That is so for all our examples, even (12). Then even though we quantify over properties, we still need either universals or the resources of an adequate Nominalism in order to say which of the properties we mostly quantify over.

I also think that it is properties that we need in characterising the content of our intentional attitudes. I believe, or I desire, that I live in one of the worlds in a certain class, rather than any world outside that class. This class of worlds is a property had by worlds. I believe, or I desire, that my world has that property. (The class of worlds also may be called a *proposition*, in one of the legitimate senses of that word, and my 'propositional attitude' of belief or desire has this proposition as its 'object'.) More generally, subsuming the previous case, I believe or I desire that I myself belong to a certain class of *possibilia*. I ascribe a certain property to myself, or I want to have it. Or I might ascribe a property to something else, or even to myself, under a relation of acquaintance I bear to that thing.[13] Surely the properties that give the content of attitudes in these ways cannot be relied on to be perfectly natural, hence cannot be replaced by universals. It is interesting to ask whether there is any lower limit to their naturalness (see the final section of this paper), but surely no very exacting standard is possible. Here again properties are right for the job, universals are not.

One over many

Armstrong's main argument for universals is the 'One over Many'. It is because I find this argument unconvincing that I am investigating alternative reasons to accept a theory of universals.

Here is a concise statement of the argument, taken by condensation from 'Against "Ostrich" Nominalism' (p. 102). A very similar statement could have been drawn from the opening pages of *Universals*:

I would wish to start by saying that many different particulars can all have what appears to be the same nature and draw the conclusion that, as a result, there is a *prima facie* case for postulating universals. We are continually talking about different things having the same property or quality, being of the same sort or kind, having the same nature, and so on. Philosophers draw the distinction between sameness of token and sameness of type. But they are only making explicit a distinction which ordinary language (and so, ordinary thought) perfectly recognises. I suggest that the fact of sameness of type is a Moorean fact: one of the

13. See my 'Attitudes *De Dicto* and *De Se*', *Philosophical Review*, 88 (1979), 513–43; and 'Individuation by Acquaintance and by Stipulation'.

many facts which even philosophers should not deny, whatever philosophical account or analysis they give of such facts. Any comprehensive philosophy must try to give some account of Moorean facts. They constitute the compulsory questions in the philosophical examination paper.

From this point of departure, Armstrong makes his case by criticising rival attempts to answer the compulsory question, and by rejecting views that decline to answer it at all.

Still more concisely, the One over Many problem is presented as the problem of giving some account of Moorean facts of apparent sameness of type. Thus understood, I agree that the question is compulsory; I agree that Armstrong's postulation of shared universals answers it; but I think that an adequate Nominalism also answers it.

An effort at systematic philosophy must indeed give an account of any purported fact. There are three ways to give an account. (1) 'I deny it'—this earns a failing mark if the fact is really Moorean. (2) 'I analyse it thus'—this is Armstrong's response to the facts of apparent sameness of type. Or (3) 'I accept it as primitive'. Not every *account* is an *analysis*! A system that takes certain Moorean facts as primitive, as unanalysed, cannot be accused of failing to make a place for them. It neither shirks the compulsory question nor answers it by denial. It does give an account.

An adequate Nominalism, of course, is a theory that takes Moorean facts of apparent sameness of type as primitive. It predicates mutual resemblance of the things which are apparently of the same type; or it predicates naturalness of some property that they all share, *i.e.* that has them all as members; and it declines to analyse these predications any further. That is why the problem of One over Many, rightly understood, does not provide more than a *prima facie* reason to postulate universals. Universals afford one solution, but there are others.

I fear that the problem does not remain rightly understood. Early in *Universals* it undergoes an unfortunate double transformation. In the course of a few pages (*Universals*, I, pp. 11–16) the legitimate demand for an account of Moorean facts of apparent sameness of type turns into a demand for an analysis of predication in general. The *analysandum* becomes the schema '*a* has the property *F*'. The turning point takes only two sentences (p. 12):

How is [the Nominalist] to account for the apparent (if usually partial) identity of numerically different particulars? How can two different things both be white or both be on a table?

And very soon (pp. 16–17) those who 'refuse to countenance universals but who at the same time see no need for any reductive analyses [of the schema of predication]', those according to whom 'there are no universals but the proposition that *a* is *F* is perfectly all right as it is', stand accused of dodging the compulsory question.

When the demand for an account—for a place in one's system—turned into a demand for an analysis, then I say that the question ceased to be compulsory. And when the *analysandum* switched, from Moorean facts of apparent sameness of type to predication generally, then I say that the question ceased to be answerable at all.

The transformed problem of One over Many deserves our neglect. The ostrich that will not look at it is a wise bird indeed.

Despite his words, I do not think that Armstrong really means to demand, either from Nominalists or from himself, a *fully* general analysis of predication. For none is so ready as he to insist that not just any shared predicate makes for even apparent sameness of type. (That is what gives his theory its distinctive interest and merit.) It would be better to put the transformed problem thus: one way or another, all predication is to be analysed. Some predications are to be analysed away in terms of others. Here we have one-off analyses for specific predicates—as it might be, for 'grue'. But all those predications that remain, after the one-off analyses are finished, are to be analysed wholesale by means of a general analysis of the schema '*a* has property *F*'.

There is to be no unanalysed predication. Time and again, Armstrong wields this requirement against rival theories. One theory after another falls victim to the 'relation regress': in the course of analysing other predications, the theory has resort to a new predicate that cannot, on pain of circularity, be analysed along with the rest. So falls Class Nominalism (including the version with primitive naturalness that I deem adequate): it employs predications of class membership, which predications it cannot without circularity analyse in terms of class membership. So falls Resemblance Nominalism: it fails to analyse predications of resemblance. So fall various other, less deserving Nominalisms. And so fall rival forms of Realism, for instance Transcendent, Platonic Realism: this time, predications of participation evade analysis. Specific theories meet other, specific objections; suffice it to say that I think these inconclusive against the two Nominalisms that I call adequate. But the clincher, the one argument that recurs throughout the many refutations, is the relation regress. And this amounts to the objection that the theory under attack does not achieve its presumed aim of doing away with all unanalysed predication and therefore fails to solve the transformed problem of One over Many.

Doing away with all unanalysed predication is an unattainable aim, and so an unreasonable aim. No theory is to be faulted for failing to achieve it. For how could there be a theory that names entities, or quantifies over them, in the course of its sentences, and yet altogether avoids primitive predication? Artificial tricks aside,[14] the thing cannot be done.

What's true is that a theory may be faulted for its overabundant primitive predications, or for unduly mysterious ones, or for unduly complicated ones. These are not fatal faults, however. They are to be counted against a theory, along with its

---

14. Let S be the syntactic category of sentences, let N be the category of names, and for any categories x and y, let x/y be the category of expressions that attach to y-expressions to make x-expressions. Predicates, then, are category S/N. (Or $(S/N)/N$ for two-place predicates, and so on.) To embed names (or variables in the category of names) into sentences without primitive predication, take any category Q which is neither S nor N, nor S/N, and let there be primitives of categories Q/N and S/Q. Or take Q_1 and Q_2, different from S and N and S/N and each other, and let the primitives be of categories Q_1/N, Q_2/Q_1, and S/Q_2. Or . . . I cannot see how this trickery could be a genuine alternative to, rather than a disguise for, primitive predication.

faults of overly generous ontology or of disagreement with less-than-Moorean commonsensical opinions. Rival philosophical theories have their prices, which we seek to measure. But it's all too clear that for philosophers, at least, there ain't no such thing as a free lunch.

How does Armstrong himself do without primitive predication?—He doesn't. Consider the predicate 'instantiates' (or 'has'), as in 'particular *a* instantiates universal *F*' or 'this electron has unit charge'. No one-off analysis applies to this specific predicate. 'Such identity in nature [as results from the having of one universal in many particulars] is literally inexplicable, in the sense that it cannot be further explained.' (*Universals*, I, p. 109.) Neither do predications of 'instantiates' fall under Armstrong's general analysis of (otherwise unanalysed) predication. His is a non-*relational* Realism: he declines, with good reason, to postulate a dyadic universal of instantiation to bind particulars to their universals. (And if he did, it would only postpone the need for primitive predication.) So let all who have felt the bite of Armstrong's relation regress rise up and cry '*Tu quoque!*' and let us mark well that Armstrong is prepared to give *one* predicate 'what has been said to be the privilege of the harlot: power without responsibility. The predicate is informative, it makes a vital contribution to telling us what is the case, the world is different if it is different, yet ontologically it is supposed not to commit us. Nice work: if you can get it.' (Compare Armstrong on Quine's treatment of predication, 'Against "Ostrich" Nominalism', pp. 104–5.)

Let us dump the project of getting rid of primitive predication, and return to the sensible—though not compulsory—project of analysing Moorean facts of apparent sameness of type. Now does the relation regress serve Armstrong better? I think not. It does make better sense within the more sensible project, but it still bites Armstrong and his rivals with equal force. Let the Nominalist say 'These donkeys resemble each other, so likewise do those stars, and there analysis ends.' Let the Platonist say 'This statue participates in the Form of beauty, likewise that lecture participates in the Form of truth, and there analysis ends.' Let Armstrong say 'This electron instantiates unit charge, likewise that proton instantiates tripartiteness, and there analysis ends.' It is possible to complain in each case that a fact of sameness of type has gone unanalysed, the types being respectively resemblance, participation, and instantiation. But it is far from evident that the alleged facts are Moorean, and still less evident that the first two are more Moorean than the third. None of them are remotely the equals of the genuine Moorean fact that, in some sense, different lumps of gold are the same in kind.

Michael Devitt has denounced the One over Many problem as a mirage better left unseen.[15] I have found Devitt's discussion instructive and I agree with much of what

---

15. ' "Ostrich Nominalism" or "Mirage Realism"?', *Pacific Philosophical Quarterly*, 61 (1980), 433–39. Devitt speaks on behalf of Quine as well as himself; Quine indicates agreement with Devitt in 'Soft Impeachment Disowned'.

he says. But Devitt has joined Armstrong in transforming the One over Many problem. He takes it to be the problem of analysing the schema

> *a* and *b* have the same property (are of the same type), *F*-ness

otherwise than by means of a one-off analysis for some specific *F*. To that problem it is fair to answer as he does that

> *a* is *F*; *b* is *F*

is analysis enough, once we give over the aim of doing without primitive predication. But Devitt has set himself too easy a problem. If we attend to the modest, untransformed One over Many problem, which is no mirage, we will ask about a different *analysandum*:

> *a* and *b* have some common property (are somehow of the same type)

in which it is not said what *a* and *b* have in common. This less definite *analysandum* is not covered by what Devitt has said. If we take a clearly Moorean case, he owes us an account: either an analysis or an overt resort to primitive predication of resemblance.

...

Chapter 22

On the elements of being: I

Donald C. Williams

Fᴵʀsᴛ philosophy, according to the traditional schedule, is analytic ontology, examining the traits necessary to whatever is, in this or any other possible world. Its cardinal problem is that of substance and attribute, or at any rate something cognate with this in that family of ideas which contains also subsistence and inherence, subject and predicate, particular and universal, singular and general, individual and class, and matter and form. It is the question how a thing can be an instance of many properties while a property may inhere in many instances, the question how everything is a *case* of a *kind*, a this-such, an essence endowed with existence, an existent differentiated by essence, and so forth. Concerned with what it means to be a thing or a kind at all, it is in some wise prior to and independent of the other great branch of metaphysics, speculative cosmology: what kinds of things are there, what stuff are they made of, how are they strung together? Although 'analytic ontology' is not much practised as a unit under that name today, its problems, and especially the problem of subsistence and inherence, are as much alive in the latest manifestos of the logical analysts, who pretend to believe neither in substances nor in universals, as they were in the counsels of Athens and of Paris. Nothing is clear until that topic is clear, and in this essay I hope to clarify it in terms of a theory or schema which over a good many years I have found so serviceable that it may well be true.

Metaphysics is the thoroughly empirical science. Every item of experience must be evidence for or against any hypothesis of speculative cosmology, and every experienced object must be an exemplar and test case for the categories of analytic ontology. Technically, therefore, one example ought for our present theme to be as good as another. The more dignified examples, however, are darkened with a patina of tradition and partisanship, while some frivolous ones are peculiarly perspicuous. Let us therefore imagine three lollipops, made by a candy man who buys sticks from a big supplier and molds candy knobs on them. Lollipop No. 1 has a red round peppermint head, No. 2 a brown round chocolate head, No. 3 a red square peppermint head. The circumstance here which mainly provokes theories of subsistence and inherence is similarity with difference: each lollipop is partially similar to each other and partially different from it. If we can give a good account of this circumstance in this affair we shall have the instrument to expose the anatomy of everything, from an electron or an apple to archangels and the World All.

Donald C. Williams, 'On the Elements of Being: I', from *Review of Metaphysics*, 2/7(1953), copyright © 1953 by *Review of Metaphysics*, reprinted with permission.

My chief proposal to that end may be put, to begin with, as nothing more tremendous than that we admit literally and seriously that to say that *a* is partially similar to *b* is to say that a part of *a* is wholly or completely similar to a part of *b*. This is a truism when we construe it with respect to ordinary concrete parts, for example, the sticks in the lollipops. On physical grounds, to be sure, it is not likely that any three solid objects, not even three sticks turned out by mass industry, are exactly similar, but they often look as if they were, and we can intelligibly stipulate for our argument that our exemplary sticks do exactly resemble each other through and through. To say then that each of the lollipops is partially similar to each other, that is, with respect to stick, is to say that there is a stick in each which is perfectly similar to the stick in every other, even though each stick remains as particular and distinct an individual as the whole lollipop. We would seldom give a proper name to a lollipop, and still more seldom to the stick in one, but we might easily do so—'Heraplem' for lollipop No. 1, for example, 'Paraplete' for its stick, 'Boanerp' for No. 2 and 'Merrinel' for its stick. Heraplem and Boanerp are partially similar because Paraplete and Merrinel are perfectly similar.

But what now of the rest of each lollipop and what of their more subtle similarities, of color, shape, and flavor? My proposal is that we treat them in exactly the same way. Since we can not find more parts of the usual gross sort, like the stick, to be wholly similar from lollipop to lollipop, let us discriminate subtler and thinner or more diffuse parts till we find some of these which *are* wholly similar. This odd-sounding assignment, of course, is no more than we are accustomed to do, easily and without noticing. Just as we can distinguish in the lollipops Heraplem and Boanerp the gross parts called 'sticks', namely, Paraplete and Merrinel, so we can distinguish in each lollipop a finer part which we are used to call its 'color' and another called its 'shape'—not its kind of color or shape, mind you, but these particular cases, this reddening, this occurrence or occasion of roundness, each as uniquely itself as a man, an earthquake, or a yell. With only a little more hardihood than christened the lollipops and sticks we can christen our finer components: 'Harlac' and 'Bantic' for the respective color components, let us say, and 'Hamis' and 'Borcas' for the respective shape components. In these four new names the first and last letters are initials of 'Heraplem' and 'Boanerp', and of 'color' and 'shape', respectively, but this is a mnemonic device for us, irrelevant to their force as names. 'Harlac', for example, is not to be taken as an abbreviation for the description, 'the color component of Heraplem'. In a real situation like the one we are imagining, 'Harlac' is defined ostensively, as one baptizes a child or introduces a man, present in the flesh; the descriptive phrase is only a scaffolding, a temporary device to bring attention to bear on the particular entity being denoted, as a mother of twins might admonish the vicar, 'Boadicea is the cross-looking one'. Heraplem and Boanerp are partially similar, then, not merely because the respective gross parts Paraplete and Merrinel (their sticks) are wholly similar, but also because the respective fine parts, Hamis and Borcas (their 'shapes'), are wholly similar—all this without prejudice to the fact that Hamis is numerically as distinct from Borcas, to which it is wholly similar, and from Harlac, with which it is conjoined in Heraplem, as Harlac is from Bantic to which it is neither similar nor conjoined, and as the stick Paraplete is from the stick Merrinel, and as the whole lollipop, Heraplem, is from the whole Boanerp. The sense in which Heraplem and Boanerp 'have the same shape', and in which 'the shape of one is identical with the shape of the other', is the sense in which two soldiers 'wear the same uniform', or in which a son 'has his father's nose', or our candy man might say 'I use the same identical stick, Ledbetter's Triple-X, in all my lollipops'. They do not 'have the same shape' in the sense in which two children 'have the same father', or two streets have the same manhole in the middle of their inter-section, or two college boys 'wear the same tuxedo' (and so can't go to dances together). But while similar in the indicated respects, Heraplem and Boanerp are partially dissimilar in as much as their knobs or heads are partially dissimilar, and these are partially dissimilar because some of their finer parts, for example, Harlac and Bantic, their colors, are dissimilar.

In like manner, to proceed, we note that Harlac, the color component of No. 1 (Heraplem), though numerically distinct from, is wholly similar to the color com-ponent of No. 3. But No. 1 has not only a color component which is perfectly sim-ilar to the color component of No. 3; it has also a flavor component perfectly similar to the flavor component of No. 3. (It does not matter whether we think of the flavor as a phenomenal quality or as a molecular structure in the stuff of the candy.) The flavor-plus-color of No. 1 (and likewise of No. 3) is a complex whose own con-stituents are the flavor and the color, and so on for innumerable selections and combinations of parts, both gross and fine, which are embedded in any one such object or any collection thereof.

Crucial here, of course, is the admission of a 'fine' or 'subtle' part, a 'diffuse' or 'permeant' one, such as a resident color or occurrent shape, to at least as good stand-ing among the actual and individual items of the world's furniture as a 'gross' part, such as a stick. The fact that one part is thus finer and more diffuse than another, and that it is more susceptible of similarity, no more militates against its individual actuality than the fact that mice are smaller and more numerous than elephants makes them any the less real. To borrow now an old but pretty appropriate term, a gross part, like the stick, is 'concrete', as the whole lollipop is, while a fine or diffuse part, like the color component or shape component, is 'abstract'. The color-cum-shape is less abstract or more concrete or more nearly concrete than the color alone but it is more abstract or less concrete than color-plus-shape-plus-flavor, and so on till we get to the total complex which is wholly concrete.

I propose now that entities like our fine parts or abstract components are the prim-ary constituents of this or any possible world, the very alphabet of being. They not only are actual but are the only actualities, in just this sense, that whereas entities of all other categories are literally composed of them, they are not in general composed of any other sort of entity. That such a crucial category has no regular name is quite characteristic of first principles and is part of what makes the latter worth pursuing. A description of it in good old phraseology has a paradoxical ring: our thin parts are 'abstract particulars'.[1] We shall have occasion to use 'parts' for concreta and 'components' for our abstracta (and 'constituent' for both), as some British philosophers use 'component' for property and 'constituent' for concrete part. Santayana, however, used 'trope' to stand for the *essence* of an *occurrence*;[2] and I shall divert the word, which is almost useless in either his or its dictionary sense, to stand for the abstract particular which is, so to speak, the *occurrence* of an *essence*. A trope then is a particular entity either abstract or consisting of one or more concreta in combination with an abstractum. Thus a cat and the cat's tail are not tropes, but a cat's smile is a trope, and so is the whole whose constituents are the cat's smile plus her ears and the aridity of the moon.

Turning now briefly from the alphabet of being to a glimpse of its syllabary, we observe two fundamental ways in which tropes may be connected with one another: the way of location and the way of similarity. These are categorially different, and indeed systematic counterparts of one another—mirror images, as it were. Location is external in the sense that a trope *per se* does not entail or necessitate or determine its location with respect to any other trope, while similarity is internal in the sense that, given any two tropes, there are entailed or necessitated or determined whether and how they are similar. (What further this *prima facie* difference amounts to we cannot pursue here.) Location is easiest thought of as position in physical space-time, but I intend the notion to include also all the analogous spreads and arrangements which we find in different conscious fields and indeed in any realm of existence which we can conceive—the whole interior stretch and structure of a Leibnizian monad, for example. Both modes of connection are describable in terms of 'distance' and 'direction'. We are very familiar in a general way with the numberless distances and directions which compose locations in space and time, somewhat less familiar with the idea of what I suggest is the limiting value of such location (though very familiar with the phenomenon itself): the collocation, or peculiar interpretation, the unique congress in the same volume, which we call 'belonging to (or inhering in, or characterizing) the same thing'. With various interests and intentions, this nexus has been mentioned by Russell as 'compresence', by Mill as 'co-inherence', by G. F. Stout as 'concrescence', by Professor Goodman as 'togetherness', and by Whitehead, Keynes, and Mill again as 'concurrence'.[3] With respect to similarity, on the other hand, we are comparatively familiar with the notion of its limiting value, the precise, or almost precise, similarity such as obtained between the

1. I argued the general legitimacy of such a category in 'The Nature of Universals and of Abstractions', *The Monist*, (1931), 583–93.
2. *The Realm of Matter* (London: Constable & Co., 1930), chapter VI.
3. See Russell, *Human Knowledge* (London: George Allen & Unwin), pp. 294, 297, 304, etc.; Stout, 'The Nature of Universals and Propositions' (note 7 below); Nelson Goodman, *The Structure of Appearance* (Cambridge, Mass.: Harvard University Press, 1951), p. 178; Whitehead, *Concept of Nature* (Cambridge: Cambridge University Press, 1920), pp. 157–8; J. M. Keynes, *Treatise on Probability* (London: Macmillan, 1921), p. 385; J. S. Mill, *A System of Logic* (London: Longmans, 1930), p. 67. Mills is quoting Bain.

colors of our first and third lollipops, less familiar with the idea of the lesser similarity which obtains between a red and a purple, and rather uncertain, unless we are psychologists or phenomenologists, about such elaborate similarity distances and directions as are mapped on the color cone.

Any possible world, and hence, of course, this one, is completely constituted by its tropes and their connections of location and similarity, and any others there may be. (I think there are no others, but that is not necessary to the theory of tropes.) Location and similarity (or whatever else there is) provide all the relations, as the tropes provide the terms, but the total of the relations is not something over and above the total of the terms, for a relation R between tropes a and b is a constitutive trope of the complex $r'(a, b)$, while conversely the terms a and b will be in general composed of constituents in relation—though perhaps no more than the spread of a smooth or 'homoeomerous' quale such as a color.

Any trope belongs to as many sets or sums of tropes as there are ways of combining it with other tropes in the world. Of special interest however are (1) the set or sum of tropes which have to it the relation of *concurrence* (the limiting value of location), and (2) the set or sum of those which have to it the relation of *precise similarity* (the limiting value of similarity, sometimes mischievously called 'identity'). For a given trope, of course, one or both of these sets or sums might contain nothing except the trope itself, but it is hard to imagine a world in which there would not be many tropes that belong to well populated sets or sums of both sorts, and in our world such sets or sums are very conspicuous. Speaking roughly, now, the set or sum of tropes concurrent with a trope, such as our color component Harlac, is the concrete particular or 'thing' which it may be said to 'characterize', in our example the lollipop Heraplem, or, to simplify the affair, the knob of the lollipop at a moment. Speaking roughly, again, the set or sum of tropes precisely similar to a given trope, say Harlac again, is the abstract universal or 'essence' which it may be said to exemplify, in our illustration a definite shade of Redness. (The tropes approximately similar to the given one compose a less definite universal.)

The phrase 'set or sum' above is a deliberate hedge. A set is a *class* of which the terms are members; a sum is a whole of which the terms are parts, in the very primitive sense of 'part' dealt with by recent calculi of individuals.[4] In the accompanying figure, for instance, the class of six squares, the class of three rows, and the class of

4. Nelson Goodman and Henry Leonard, 'The Calculus of Individuals and Its Uses', *Journal of Symbolic Logic*, 5 (1940), 45–55; Goodman, *The Structure of Appearance*, pp. 42 ff; Appendix E, by Alfred Tarski, in J. H. Woodger, *The Axiomatic Method in Biology* (Cambridge: Cambridge University Press, 1937), 161–72.

two columns are different from each other and from the one figure; but the sum of squares, the sum of rows, and the sum of columns are identical with one another and with the whole. What a difference of logical 'type' amounts to, particularly in the philosophy of tropes, is far from clear, but everybody agrees that a sum is of the same type with its terms, as a whole is of the same type with its parts, a man of the same type with his arms and legs. The concept of a class or set, on the other hand, is notably more complex and questionable. A class is surely not, in any clear sense, what it is too often called,[5] 'an abstract entity', but there is some excuse for considering it of a different 'type' from its members. Convinced that tropes compose a concretum in a manner logically no different from that in which any other exhaustive batch of parts compose it, we have every incentive to say that the concretum is not the set but the sum of the tropes; and let us so describe it. Whether the counterpart concept of the universal can be defined as the sum of similars—all merely grammatical difficulties aside—is not so clear. There is little doubt that the set or class will do the job. For all the paradoxes which attend the fashionable effort to equate the universal Humanity, for example, with the class of concrete men (including such absurdities as that being a featherless biped is the same as having a sense of humor) disappear when we equate it rather with our new set, the class of abstract humanities—the class whose members are not Socrates, Napoleon, and so forth, but the human trope in Socrates, the one in Napoleon, and so forth. Still wilder paradoxes resulted from the more radical nominalistic device of substituting the *sum* of concrete men for their class,[6] and most even of these are obviated by taking our sum of similar tropes instead. I suspect, however, that some remain, and because concurrence and similarity are such symmetrical counterparts, I shall not be surprised if it turns out that while the concurrence complex must be a sum, the similarity complex must be a set.

In suggesting how both concrete particulars and abstract universals are composed of tropes, I aver that those two categories do not divide the world between them. It does not consist of concrete particulars in addition to abstract universals, as the old scheme had it, nor need we admit that it must be 'constructible' *either* from concrete particulars *or* from abstract universals as recent innovators argue (Carnap and Goodman, respectively, for example). The notions of the abstract and the universal (and hence of the concrete and the particular) are so far independent that their combinations box the logical compass. Socrates is a concrete particular; the component of him which is his wisdom is an abstract particular or 'trope'; the total Wisdom of which all such wisdoms are components or members is an abstract universal; and the total Socratesity of which all creatures exactly like him are parts or members is a 'concrete universal', not in the idealistic but in a strictly accurate

5. Goodman, *The Structure of Appearance*, p. 150; W. V. Quine, *Methods of Logic* (New York: Holt, 1950), p. 204.
6. Witness the doughty struggle of Quine and Goodman in 'Steps Toward a Constructive Nominalism', *Journal of Symbolic Logic*, 12 (1947), 105–22.

sense. It was because of the unfortunate limitation of ordinary philosophic discourse to the two combinations, concrete particular and abstract universal, that in order to call attention to our tropes we had to divert such phrases as 'the humanity of Socrates' or 'the redness of the lollipop', which normally would stand for kinds of degrees of humanity and redness, to stand for their particular cases of Humanity and Redness, respectively, and so we have been driven in turn to using the capital letters in 'Humanity' and 'Redness' to restore the 'abstract nouns' to their normal duty of naming the respective universals. A similar explanation, but a longer one, would have to be given of our less definite phrases like 'the shape of Boanerp' or 'the color of it'.

Having thus sorted out the rubrics, we can almost automatically do much to dispel the ancient mystery of predication, so influential in the idea of logical types. The prevalent theory has been that if y can be 'predicated' of x, or 'inheres in' or 'characterizes' x, or if x is an 'instance' of y, then x and y must be sundered by a unique logical and ontological abyss. Most of the horror of this, however, which has recently impelled some logicians to graceless verbalistic contortions, is due to taking predication as one indissoluble and inscrutable operation, and vanishes when our principles reveal predication to be composed of two distinct but intelligible phases. 'Socrates is wise', or generically 'a is φ', means that the concurrence sum (Socrates) includes a trope which is a member of the similarity set (Wisdom). When we contrast a thing with a property or 'characteristic' of it, a 'substantive' with an 'adjective', we may intend either or both of these connections. The particular wisdom in Socrates is in one sense 'characteristic', i.e., it is a component, of him—this is the sense in which Stout held, quite properly to my way of thinking, that 'characters are abstract particulars which are predicable of concrete particulars'.[7] The universal Wisdom is in the second sense the 'characteristic' of each such wisdom—this is the sense in which Moore could hold plausibly that even an event, such as a sneeze, *has* characteristics and is not one.[8] In the third or ordinary sense, however, the universal Wisdom 'characterizes' the whole Socrates. From this imbroglio emerge at least two senses of 'instance', the sense in which Socrates is a (concrete) 'instance' of Wisdom and that in which his wisdom component is an (abstract) 'instance' of it, and the two notions of class, the ordinary concreta class consisting of Socrates, Plato, and all other whole wise creatures, and the abstracta class of their wisdoms, our similarity set.

Raying out around the problem of predication is many another half-magical notion about essence and existence which we now can prosily clarify. Thus, Mr Broad and Mr Dawes Hicks, while believing in 'Abstracta', have described them

7. 'Are the Characteristics of Particular Things Universal or Particular?', a symposium by G. E. Moore, G. F. Stout, and G. Dawes Hicks, *Aristotelian Society Supplementary Volume*, 3 (1923), 95–128, p. 114. His theory of abstract particulars, here and in 'The Nature of Universals and Propositions', *Proceedings of the British Academy*, 10 (192–23), is almost identical with the one I am defending; if there is a difference it is in his obscure idea of the class as a unique form of unity not reducible to similarity.

8. *Loc. cit.*, p. 98. Mr Moore, I cannot help thinking, already a very uncommonplace minion of the commonplace, almost fiercely resists understanding the Stout theory.

in the same fantastic terms in which Santayana described his essences, as placeless and timeless, and hence 'real but non-existent'.[9] This remarkable but not unusual proposition might for a Platonist be grounded in a whole theory of universals *ante rem*, but mostly it results from not distinguishing between its two principal sources: the specious eternity a *universal* has because, as Stout put it, it 'spreads undivided, operates unspent',[10] which for us is just the fact that similarity is a 'saltatory' relation, overleaping spatial and temporal distances undiminished and without cost in stuff or energy; and the specious eternity an *abstractum* has because in attending to it we normally 'abstract from' its spatiotemporal location (which nevertheless it has and keeps). As the obscurity of Essence is thus mostly resolved by looking at it stereoscopically, to distinguish the dimensions of the universal and of the abstract, so too that dark mingling of glory and degradation which haunts Existence and the individual is mostly resolved by the ideas of concreteness and particularity. The Individual is hallowed both by the utter self-identity and self-existence of the particular occurrent and by the inexhaustible richness and the inimitability of the concrete. At the same time, however, it is debased by the very same factors. It seems ignobly arbitrary and accidental, *qua* particular, with respect to its mere self in its external relations, because it thus lacks the similarity, classification, and generalization which could interpret it; and it has the confusion and unfathomability of the concrete, wherein every form struggles in a melee of forms so stupendous that the Aristotelians mistook it for formless matter.

A philosophy of tropes calls for completion in a dozen directions at once. Some of these I must ignore for the present because the questions would take us too far, some because I do not know the answers. Of the first sort would be a refinement and completion of our account of substance and of the similarity manifold. Of the second sort would be an assimilation of the very categories of our theory—concurrence, similarity, abstractness, and so forth—to the theory itself, as tropes like the rest, instead of relegating them to the anomalous immunities of 'transcendentals' (as the old Scholastics said) and 'metalanguage' (as the new scholastics say). What in fact I shall do here is to defend the fundamental notion that there are entities at once abstract, particular, and actual, and this in two ways: the affirmative way of showing how experience and nature evince them over and over, and the negative way of settling accounts with old dialectical objections to them.

I deliberately did not use the word 'abstract' to describe our tropes till we had done our best to identify them in other ways, lest the generally derogatory connotation of the word blind us to the reality of objects as plain as the sunlight (for indeed the sunlight *is* an abstract existent). The many meanings of 'abstract' which make it repulsive to the empirical temper of our age suggest that an abstractum is the product of some magical feat of mind, or the denizen of some remote immaterial eternity.

---

9. Broad, *Mind and Its Place in Nature* (London: Routledge & Kegan Paul, 1925), p. 19; Dawes Hicks, *Critical Realism* (London: Macmillan, 1938), pp. 76–8. Broad can justly marvel that we can cognize what is mental or physical only by 'cognizing objects which are neither' (p. 5).

10. 'Are the Characteristics, etc.,' p. 116.

Dictionaries, journalists, and philosophical writers are almost equally vague and various about it. Santayana has it that 'abstract' means imprecise, but also 'verbal, unrealizable, or cognitively secondary'.[11] The abstract is equated with the abstruse, the ethereal, the mental, the rational, the incorporeal, the ideally perfect, the non-temporal, the primordial or ultimate, the purely theoretical, the precariously speculative and visionary; or again with the empty, the deficient, the non-actual or merely potential, the downright imaginary, and the unreal. In some quarters 'abstract' means symbolical, figurative, or merely representative, in contrast with what is real in its own right. On the same page the word may connote alternately the two extremes of precious precision and the vague, confused, or indefinite. Mathematics or logic is called 'abstract' partly because it is about formal structures, partly because it treats them only hypothetically;[12] but a symbolic calculus is called 'abstract' because it isn't about anything. Semanticists and professors of composition shudder away from statements on such 'high levels of abstraction' as 'Herbivority is conducive to bovine complacency' in contrast with the 'concrete' virility of 'Cows like grass', though the two sentences describe exactly the same state of affairs. Logical philosophers proclaim their 'renunciation of abstract entities' without making clear either what makes an entity 'abstract' or how one goes about 'renouncing' an entity.

One wonders, in view of this catalog, if there is anything which would not on occasion be called 'abstract'. Most people would deny that a cat is abstract, but an idealist would say she is. Yet it would be a mistake to infer that 'abstract' has been a wholly indiscriminate epithet. All the uses we have observed, and doubtless others, have stemmed from two roots which in turn are related in a very intimate way. They represent what various persons believed, often mistakenly, is implied by those root ideas. One of them is the use of 'abstract' to mean *transcending individual existence*, as a universal, essence, or Platonic idea is supposed to transcend it. But even though this use of 'abstract' is probably as old as the word itself, I think it was in fact derived, by the natural mistake which we earlier noted, from the other aboriginal use, more literally in accord with the word's Latin construction, which is virtually identical with our own. At its broadest the 'true' meaning of 'abstract' is *partial, incomplete*, or *fragmentary*, the trait of what is less than its including whole. Since there must be, for everything but the World All, at least something, and indeed many things, of which it is a proper part, everything but the World All is 'abstract' in this broad sense. It is thus that the idealist can denounce the cat as 'abstract'. The more usual practice of philosophers, however, has been to require for 'abstractness' the more special sort of incompleteness which pertains to what we have called the 'thin' or 'fine' or 'diffuse' sort of constituent, like the color or shape of our lollipop, in contrast with the 'thick', 'gross', or chunky sort of constituent, like the stick in it.[13]

11. *Realms of Being*, p. 32.
12. C. I. Lewis, *Mind and the World-Order* (London: Charles Scribner's Sons, 1929), pp. 242, 249.
13. Although this has been for centuries the root meaning of 'abstract', the nearest to a straightforward statement of it which I have found is by Professor Ledger Wood in the *Dictionary of Philosophy*, edited by D. D. Runes (London: Routledge, 1944), p. 2: 'a designation applied to a partial aspect or

If now one looks at things without traditional prepossessions, the existence of abstracta seems as plain as any fact could be. There is something ironically archaic in the piety with which the new nominalists abhor abstract entities in favor of that 'common-sense prejudice pedantically expressed',[14] the dogma of Aristotle that there can be no real beings except 'primary substances', concrete individuals, as absolute and 'essential' units, and thus turn their backs on one of the greatest insights of the Renaissance, that the apparent primacy of such chunky middle-sized objects is only a function of our own middle size and practical motivation. The great modern philosophies have rather sought the real in putative 'simple natures' at one end of the scale and the one great ocean of action at the other end. I have no doubt that whole things like lollipops, trees, and the moon, do exist in full-blooded concreteness, but it is not they which are 'present to the senses',[15] and it is not awareness of abstracta which is 'difficult, . . . not to be attained without pains and study'.[16] To claim primacy for our knowledge of concreta is 'mysticism' in the strict sense, that is, a claim to such acquaintance with a plethoric being as no conceivable stroke of psychophysics could account for. What we primarily *see* of the moon, for example, is its shape and color and not at all its whole concrete bulk—generations lived and died without suspecting it had a concrete bulk; and if now we impute to it a solidity and an aridity, we do it item by item quite as we impute wheels to a clock or a stomach to a worm. Evaluation is similarly focussed on abstracta. What most men value the moon for is its brightness; what a child wants of a lollipop is a certain flavor and endurance. He would much rather have these abstracta without the rest of the bulk than the bulk without the qualities. Integral to the debate between the metaphysical champions of the concrete particular and of the abstract universal has been a discussion whether the baby's first experiences are of whole concrete particulars (his ball, his mother, and so forth) or of abstract universals (redness, roundness, and so forth). For what it may be worth, perhaps not much, a little observation of a baby, or oneself in a babyish mood, will convince the candid and qualified that the object of such absorption is not the abstract universal (the infant does not 'fall from the clouds upon the top-most twig of the tree of Porphyry')[17] and certainly not the concrete particular (that 'foreign thing and a marvel to the spirit'[18] which a lifetime of

quality considered in isolation from a total object, which is, in contrast, designated concrete.' Even here the word 'isolation', as we shall see, is delusive.

14. Russell, *History of Western Philosophy* (London: George Allen & Unwin, 1946), p. 163.
15. I have in mind Willard Quine's epistemological ballad about Homo javanensis, whose simple faculties 'could only treat of things concrete and present to the senses'. 'Identity, Ostension, and Hypostasis', *Journal of Philosophy*, 47 (1950), 621–33, p. 631 n.
16. This is Berkeley on abstract ideas, *The Principles of Human Knowledge* (London: 1710), Introduction, §10. It is cited at length by William James, *The Principles of Psychology* (London: Macmillan, 1901), volume 1, p. 469, who argues, correctly I think, that what is difficult is not the recognition of abstracta but the recognition that they are abstract, and the conception of the universal, and that these are at worst no more laborious than the counterpart conception of the concretum.
17. Brand Blanshard, *The Nature of Thought* (New York: Humanities Press, 1964), volume I, p. 569.
18. Santayana, *The Unknowable* (Oxford: Clarendon Press, 1923), p. 29.

observation and twenty centuries of research hardly begin to penetrate), but is in sooth the abstract particular or trope, *this* redness, *this* roundness, and so forth.

Though the uses of the trope to account for substances and universals are of special technical interest, the impact of the idea is perhaps greater in those many regions not so staled and obscured by long wont and old opinion and not so well supplied with alternative devices. While substances and universals can be 'constructed' out of tropes, or apostrophized *in toto* for sundry purposes, the trope cannot well be 'constructed' out of them and provides the one rubric which is hospitable to a hundred sorts of entity which neither philosophy, science, nor common sense can forego. This is most obvious in any attempt to treat of the mind, just because the mind's forte is the tuning, focussing, or spotlighting which brings abstracta into relief against a void or nondescript background. A pain is a trope *par excellence*, a mysterious bright pain in the night, for example, without conscious context or classification, yet as absolutely and implacably its particular self as the Great Pyramid. But all other distinguishable contents are of essentially the same order: a love, or a sorrow, or 'a single individual pleasure'.[19]

The notion, however, gets its best use in the theory of knowledge. The 'sensible species' of the Scholastics, the 'ideas' of Locke and Berkeley, the ideas and impressions of Hume, the sense data of recent epistemology—once they are understood as tropes, and as neither things nor essences, a hundred riddles about them dissolve, and philistine attacks on theory of knowledge itself lose most of their point. We need not propose that a red sensum, for example, is perfectly abstract (whatever that might be). But even though it have such distinguishable components as a shape and a size as well as a color, and though the color itself involve the 'attributes' of hue, brightness, and saturation, still it is abstract in comparison with a whole colored solid. According to reputable psychologists, furthermore, there can be data much more abstract, professed 'empiricists' to the contrary notwithstanding: data which have color and no other character, or even hue and no other 'attribute'. The person who uses the theory of tropes to sharpen his sight of what really is present and what is not may not credit such still more delicate components, attributed to the mind, as the imageless thought of the old German schools, or the non-imaginal ideas of Descartes, or the pure concepts of the Scholastics, or the ethereal Gestalten of more recent German evangels; but if any of these do exist, they exist as tropes. The same is to be said, I suppose, of the still darker categories of pure mental act, intentionalities, dispositions, and powers. Such actual but relatively complex mental processes as trains of thought, moral decisions, beliefs, and so forth, taken as particular occurrents, whether comparatively brief or lifelong, and not (as nearly all phrases in this department at least equally suggest) as recurrent kinds, are tropes and compounded of tropes—and the kinds too, of course, are compounds of tropes in their own way. A whole soul or mind, if it is not a unique immaterial substance on its own, is a trope.

19. C. S. Peirce, without the notion of trope, denounces this perfectly intelligible phrase as 'words without meaning', *Collected Papers*, edited by C. Hartshorne and P. Weiss (Cambridge, Mass.: Harvard University Press, 1931), volume I, p. 172.

Chapter 23

Causality and properties

Sydney Shoemaker

1

IT is events, rather than objects or properties, that are usually taken by philo-sophers to be the terms of the causal relationship. But an event typically consists of a change in the properties or relationships of one or more objects, the latter being what Jaegwon Kim has called the 'constituent objects' of the event.[1] And when one event causes another, this will be in part because of the properties possessed by their constituent objects. Suppose, for example, that a man takes a pill and, as a result, breaks out into a rash. Here the cause and effect are, respectively, the taking of the pill and the breaking out into a rash. Why did the first event cause the second? Well, the pill was penicillin, and the man was allergic to penicillin. No doubt one could want to know more—for example, about the biochemistry of allergies in general and this one in particular. But there is a good sense in which what has been said already explains why the one event caused the other. Here the pill and the man are the constituent objects of the cause event, and the man is the constituent object of the effect event. Following Kim we can also speak of events as having 'constituent properties' and 'consitutent times'. In this case the constituent property of the cause event is the relation expressed by the verb 'takes', while the constituent property of the effect event is expressed by the predicate 'breaks out into a rash'. The constituent times of the events are their times of occurrence. Specifying the constituent objects and properties of the cause and effect will tell us what these events consisted in, and together with a specification of their constituent times will serve to identify them; but it will not, typically, explain why the one brought about the other. We explain this by mentioning certain properties of their constituent objects. Given that the pill was penicillin, and that the man was allergic to penicillin, the taking of the pill by the man was certain, or at any rate very likely, to result in an allergic response like a rash. To take another example, suppose a branch is blown against a window and breaks it. Here the constituent objects include the branch and the window, and the causal relationship holds because of, among other things, the massiveness of the one and the fragility of the other.

1. See Jaegwon Kim, 'Causation, Nomic Subsumption, and the Concept of Event', *The Journal of Philosophy*, 70 (1973), 27–36. I should mention that it was reflection on this excellent paper that first led me to the views developed in the present one.

It would appear from this that any account of causality as a relation between events should involve, in a central way, reference to the properties of the constituent objects of the events. But this should not encourage us to suppose that the notion of causality is to be analyzed away, in Humean fashion, in terms of some relationship between properties—for example, in terms of regularities in their instantiation. For as I shall try to show, the relevant notion of a property is itself to be explained in terms of the notion of causality in a way that has some strikingly non-Humean consequences.

2

Philosophers sometimes use the term 'property' in such a way that for every predicate *F* true of a thing there is a property of the thing which is designated by the corresponding expression of the form 'being *F*'. If 'property' is used in this broad way, every object will have innumerable properties that are unlikely to be mentioned in any causal explanation involving an event of which the object is a constituent. For example, my typewriter has the property of being over one hundred miles from the current heavyweight boxing champion of the world. It is not easy to think of a way in which its having this property could help to explain why an event involving it has a certain effect, and it seems artificial, at best, to speak of my typewriter's acquisition of this property as one of the causal effects of the movements of the heavyweight champion.

It is natural, however, to feel that such properties are not 'real' or 'genuine' properties. Our intuitions as to what are, and what are not, genuine properties are closely related to our intuitions as to what are, and what are not, genuine changes. A property is genuine if and only if its acquisition or loss by a thing constitutes a genuine change in that thing. One criterion for a thing's having changed is what Peter Geach calls the 'Cambridge criterion'. He formulates this as follows: 'The thing called "*x*" has changed if we have "*F(x)* at time *t*" true and "*F(x)* at time *t'*" false, for some interpretations of "*F*", "*t*", and "*t'*".'[2] But as Geach points out, this gives the result that Socrates undergoes a change when he comes to be shorter than Theaetetus in virtue of the latter's growth, and even that he undergoes a change every time a fresh schoolboy comes to admire him. Such 'changes', those that intuitively are not genuine changes, Geach calls 'mere "Cambridge" changes'. For Geach, real changes are Cambridge changes, since they satisfy the Cambridge criterion, but some Cambridge changes, namely those that are *mere* Cambridge changes, fail to be real changes. Since it is mere Cambridge changes, rather than Cambridge changes in general, that are to be contrasted with real or genuine changes, I shall introduce the hyphenated expression 'mere-Cambridge' to characterize these. And I shall apply

2. Peter Geach, *God and the Soul* (London: Routledge & Kegan Paul, 1969), p. 71. See also Jaegwon Kim, 'Non-Causal Relations', *Noûs*, 8 (1974), 41–52, and 'Events as Property Exemplifications', in *Action and Theory* edited by M. Brand and D. Walton (Dordrecht; Reidel, 1976), 159–77.

the terms 'Cambridge' and 'mere-Cambridge' to properties as well as to changes. Mere-Cambridge properties will include such properties as being 'grue' (in Nelson Goodman's sense), historical properties like being over twenty years old and having been slept in by George Washington, relational properties like being fifty miles south of a burning barn,[3] and such properties as being such that Jimmy Carter is President of the United States.

It is worth mentioning that in addition to distinguishing between real and mere-Cambridge properties and changes, we must also distinguish between real and mere-Cambridge resemblance or similarity, and between real and mere-Cambridge differences. Cambridge similarities hold in virtue of the sharing of Cambridge properties. And mere-Cambridge similarities hold in virtue of the sharing of mere-Cambridge properties: there is such a similarity between all grue things; there is one between all things fifty miles south of a burning barn; there is one between all beds slept in by George Washington; and there is one between all things such that Jimmy Carter is President of the United States. It will be recalled that the notion of similarity, or resemblance, plays a prominent role in Hume's account of causality. His first definition of *cause* in the *Treatise* is 'an object precedent and contiguous to another, and where all the objects resembling the former are plac'd in a like relation of priority and contiguity to those objects, that resemble the latter.'[4] Hume clearly regarded the notion of resemblance as quite unproblematical and in no need of elucidation.[5] Yet it is plain that he needs a narrower notion of resemblance than that of Cambridge resemblance if his definition of causality is to have the desired content. Cambridge resemblances are too easily come by; any two objects share infinitely many Cambridge properties, and so 'resemble' one another in infinitely many ways. There are also infinitely many Cambridge differences between any two objects. What Hume needs is a notion of resemblance and difference which is such that some things resemble a given thing more than others do, and such that some things may resemble a thing exactly (without being numerically identical to it) while others resemble it hardly at all. Only 'real' or 'genuine' resemblance will serve his purposes. If it turns out, as I think it does, that in order to give a satisfactory account of the distinction between real and mere-Cambridge properties, changes, similarities, and differences we must make use of the notion of causality, the Humean project of defining causality in terms of regularity or 'constant conjunction', notions that plainly involve the notion of resemblance, is seriously undermined.

I have no wish to legislate concerning the correct use of the terms 'property', 'change', 'similar', and so forth. It would be rash to claim that the accepted use of the term 'property' is such that what I have classified as mere-Cambridge properties are

---

3. I take this example from Kim, 'Causation, Nomic Subsumption, and the Concept of Event'.
4. David Hume, *A Treatise of Human Nature*, edited by L. A. Selby-Bigge (Oxford: Oxford University Press, 1888), book I, part III, section XIV, p. 170.
5. 'When any objects *resemble* each other, the resemblance will at first strike the eye, or rather the mind, and seldom requires a second examination', *Treatise*, book I, part III, section I, p. 70.

not properties. But I do think that we have *a* notion of what it is to be a property which is such that this is so—in other words, which is such that not every phrase of the form 'being so and so' stands for a property which something has just in case the corresponding predicate of the form 'is so and so' is true of it, and is such that sometimes a predicate is true of a thing, not because (or only because) of any properties *it* has, but because something else, perhaps something related to it in certain ways, has certain properties. It is this narrow conception of what it is to be a property, and the correlative notions of change and similarity, that I am concerned to elucidate in this essay. (I should mention that I am concerned here only with the sorts of properties with respect to which change is possible; my account is not intended to apply to such properties of numbers as being even and being prime.)

3

John Locke held that '*Powers make a great part of our complex* Ideas *of substances*.'[6] And there is one passage in which Locke seems to suggest that all qualities of substances are powers: he says, in explanation of his usage of the term 'quality', that 'the Power to produce any *Idea* in our mind, I call *quality* of the Subject wherein that power is'.[7] This suggests a theory of properties, namely that properties are causal powers, which is akin to the theory I shall be defending. As it happens, this is not Locke's view. If one ascribed it to him on the basis of the passage just quoted, one would have to ascribe to him the view that all qualities are what he called 'secondary qualities'—powers to produce certain mental effects ('ideas') in us. But Locke recognized the existence of powers that are not secondary qualities, namely powers (for example, the power in the sun to melt wax) to produce effects in material objects. These have been called 'tertiary qualities'. And he distinguished both of these sorts of powers from the 'primary qualities' on which they 'depend'. Nevertheless, the view which Locke's words unintentionally suggest is worth considering.

What would seem to be the same view is sometimes put by saying that all properties are dispositional properties. But as thus formulated, this view seems plainly mistaken. Surely we make a distinction between dispositional and nondispositional properties, and can mention paradigms of both sorts. Moreover, it seems plain that what dispositional properties something has, what powers it has, depends on what nondispositional properties it has—just as Locke thought that the powers of things depend on their primary qualities and those of their parts.

In fact, I believe, there are two different distinctions to be made here, and these are often conflated. One is not a distinction between kinds of *propeties* at all, but rather a distinction between kinds of *predicates*. Sometimes it belongs to the meaning, or

6. John Locke, *Essay Concerning Human Understanding*, edited by Peter H. Nidditch (Oxford: Oxford University Press, 1975), book II, chapter 23, section VIII, p. 300.
7. *Essay*, book II, chapter 8, section VIII, p. 134.

sense, of a predicate that if it is true of a thing then under certain circumstances the thing will undergo certain changes or will produce certain changes in other things. This is true of what are standardly counted as dispositional predicates, for example, 'flexible', 'soluble', 'malleable', 'magnetized', and 'poisonous'. Plainly not all predicates are of this sort. Whether color predicates are is a matter of controversy. But whatever we say about this, it seems plain that predicates like 'square', 'round' and 'made of copper' are not dispositional in this sense. There are causal powers associated with being made of copper—for example, being an electrical conductor. But presumably this association is not incorporated into the meaning of the term 'copper'.

The first distinction, then, is between different sorts of predicates and I think that the term 'dispositional' is best employed as a predicate of predicates, not of properties. A different distinction is between powers, in a sense I am about to explain, and the properties in virtue of which things have the powers they have.[8] For something to have a power, in this sense, is for it to be such that its presence in circumstances of a particular sort will have certain effects.[9] One can think of such a power as a function from circumstances to effects. Thus if something is poisonous its presence in someone's body will produce death or illness; in virtue of this, being poisonous is a power. Here it is possible for things to have the same power in virtue of having very different properties. Suppose that one poisonous substance kills by affecting the heart, while another kills by directly affecting the nervous system and brain. They produce these different effects in virtue of having very different chemical compositions. They will of course differ in their powers as well as in their properties, for one will have the power to produce certain physiological effects in the nervous system, while the other will have the power to produce quite different physiological effects in the heart. But there is one power they will share, in virtue of having these different powers, namely that of producing death if ingested by a human being. Properties here play the role, vis-à-vis powers, that primary qualities play in Locke; it is in virtue of a thing's properties that the thing has the powers (Locke's secondary and tertiary qualities) that it has.

There is a rough correspondence between this distinction between powers and properties and the earlier distinction between dispositional and nondispositional predicates. By and large, dispositional predicates ascribe powers while nondispositional monadic predicates ascribe properties that are not powers in the same sense.

8. What does 'in virtue of' mean here? For the moment we can say that a thing has a power in virtue of having certain properties if it is a lawlike truth that whatever has those properties has that power. On the theory I shall be defending it turns out that this is a matter of the possession of the properties entailing the possession of the power (that is, its being true in all possible worlds that whatever has the properties has the power).
9. In speaking of 'circumstances', I have in mind the relations of the objects to other objects; instead of speaking of 'presence in circumstances of a particular sort', I could instead speak of 'possession of particular relational properties'. Being in such and such circumstances is a mere-Cambridge property of an object, not a genuine (intrinsic) property of it.

4

On the view of properties I want to propose, while properties are typically not powers of the sort ascribed by dispositional predicates, they are related to such powers in much the way that such powers are related to the causal effects which they are powers to produce. Just as powers can be thought of as functions from circumstances to causal effects, so the properties on which powers depend can be thought of as functions from properties to powers (or, better, as functions from sets of properties to sets of powers). One might even say that properties are second-order powers; they are powers to produce first-order powers (powers to produce certain sorts of events) if combined with certain other properties. But the formulation I shall mainly employ is this: what makes a property the property it is, what determines its identity, is its potential for contributing to the causal powers of the things that have it. This means, among other things, that if under all possible circumstances properties X and Y make the same contribution to the causal powers of the things that have them, X and Y are the same property.

To illustrate this, let us take as our example of a property the property of being 'knife-shaped'—I shall take this to be a highly determinate property which belongs to a certain knife in my kitchen and to anything else of exactly the same shape. Now if all that I know about a thing is that it has this property, I know nothing about what will result from its presence in any circumstances. What has the property of being knife-shaped could be a knife, made of steel, but it could instead be a piece of balsa wood, a piece of butter, or even an oddly shaped cloud of some invisible gas. There is no power which necessarily belongs to all and only the things having this property. But if this property is combined with the property of being knife-sized and the property of being made of steel, the object having these properties will necessarily have a number of powers. It will have the power of cutting butter, cheese, and wood, if applied to these substances with suitable pressure, and also the power of producing various sorts of sense-impressions in human beings under appropriate observational conditions and also the power of leaving an impression of a certain shape if applied to soft wax and then withdrawn, and so on. The combination of the property of being knife-shaped with the property of being made of glass will result in a somewhat different set of powers, which will overlap with the set which results from its combination with the property of being made of steel. Likewise with its combination with the property of being made of wood, the property of being made of butter, and so on.

Let us say that an object has power P conditionally upon the possession of the properties in set Q if it has some property r such that having the properties in Q together with r is causally sufficient for having P, while having the properties in Q is not by itself causally sufficient for having P. Thus, for example, a knife-shaped object has the power of cutting wood conditionally upon being knife-sized and made of steel; for it is true of knife-shaped things, but not of things in general, that if they are knife-sized and made of steel they will have the power to cut wood. When a thing has a power conditionally upon the possession of certain properties, let us say that this amounts to its having a *conditional power*. Our knife-shaped object has the conditional power of being able to cut wood if knife-sized and made of steel. The identity condition for conditional powers is as follows: if A is the conditional power of having power P conditionally upon having the properties in set Q, and B is the conditional power of having P' conditionally upon having the properties in set Q', then A is identical to B just in case P is identical to P' and Q is identical to Q'. Having introduced this notion of a conditional power, we can express my view by saying that properties are clusters of conditional powers. (I shall count powers *simpliciter* as a special case of conditional powers.) I have said that the identity of a property is determined by its causal potentialities, the contributions it is capable of making to the causal powers of things that have it. And the causal potentialities that are essential to a property correspond to the conditional powers that make up the cluster with which the property can be identified; for a property to have a causal potentiality is for it to be such that whatever has it has a certain conditional power.

This account is intended to capture what is correct in the view that properties just are powers, or that all properties are dispositional, while acknowledging the truth of a standard objection to that view, namely that a thing's powers or dispositions are distinct from, because 'grounded in', its intrinsic properties.[10]

Before I give my reasons for holding this view, I should mention one *prima facie* objection to it. Presumably the property of being triangular and the property of being trilateral do not differ in the contributions they make to the causal powers of the things that have them, yet it is natural to say that these, although necessarily coextensive, are different properties. It seems to me, however, that what we have good reason for regarding as distinct are not these properties, as such, but rather the concepts of triangularity and trilaterality, and the meanings of the expressions 'triangular' and 'trilateral'. If we abandon, as I think we should, the idea that properties are the meanings of predicate expressions, and if we are careful to distinguish concepts from what they are concepts of, I see no insuperable obstacle to regarding the properties themselves as identical.

5

My reasons for holding this theory of properties are, broadly speaking, epistemological. Only if some causal theory of properties is true, I believe, can it be explained how properties are capable of engaging our knowledge, and our language, in the way they do.

10. After this was written I found that Peter Achinstein has advanced a causal account of property identity which, despite a different approach, is in some ways similar to the account proposed here. See his 'The Identity of Properties', *American Philosophical Quarterly*, 11 (1974), 257–76. There are also similarities, along with important differences, between my views and those presented by D. H. Mellor in 'In Defense of Dispositions', *The Philosophical Review*, 83 (1974), 157–81, and those presented by R. Harré and E. H. Madden in *Causal Powers: A Theory of Natural Necessity* (Oxford: Blackwell, 1975).

We know and recognize properties by their effects, or, more precisely, by the effects of the events which are the activations of the causal powers which things have in virtue of having the properties. This happens in a variety of ways. Observing something is being causally influenced by it in certain ways. If the causal potentialities involved in the possession of a property are such that there is a fairly direct causal connection between the possession of it by an object and the sensory states of an observer related to that object in certain ways, e.g., looking at it in good light, we say that the property itself is observable. If the relationship is less direct, e.g., if the property can affect the sensory states of the observer only by affecting the properties of something else which the observer observes, a scientific instrument, say, we speak of inferring that the thing has the property from what we take to be the effects of its possession. In other cases we conclude that something has a property because we know that it has other properties which we know from other cases to be correlated with the one in question. But the latter way of knowing about the properties of things is parasitic on the earlier ways; for unless the instantiation of the property had, under some circumstances, effects from which its existence could be concluded, we could never discover laws or correlations that would enable us to infer its existence from things other than its effects.

Suppose that the identity of properties consisted of something logically independent of their causal potentialities. Then it ought to be possible for there to be properties that have no potential whatever for contributing to causal powers, i.e., are such that under no conceivable circumstances will their possession by a thing make any difference to the way the presence of that thing affects other things or to the way other things affect it. Further, it ought to be possible that there be two or more different properties that make, under all possible circumstances, exactly the same contribution to the causal powers of the things that have them. Further, it ought to be possible that the potential of a property for contributing to the production of causal powers might change over time, so that, for example, the potential possessed by property A at one time is the same as that possessed by property B at a later time, and that possessed by property B at the earlier time is the same as that possessed by property A at the latter time. Thus, a thing might undergo radical change with respect to its properties without undergoing any change in its causal powers, and a thing might undergo radical change in its causal powers without undergoing any change in the properties that underlie these powers.

The supposition that these possibilities are genuine implies, not merely (what might seem harmless) that various things might be the case without its being in any way possible for us to know that they are, but also that it is impossible for us to know various things which we take ourselves to know. If there can be properties that have no potential for contributing to the causal powers of the things that have them, then nothing could be good evidence that the overall resemblance between two things is greater than the overall resemblance between two other things; for even if A and B have closely resembling effects on our senses and our instruments while C and D do not, it might be (for all we know) that C and D share vastly more properties of the causally impotent kind than do *A* and *B*. Worse, if two properties can have exactly the same potential for contributing to causal powers, then it is impossible for us even to know (or have any reason for believing) that two things resemble one another by sharing a single property. Moreover, if the properties and causal potentialities of a thing can vary independently of one another, then it is impossible for us to know (or have any good reason for believing) that something has retained a property over time, or that something has undergone a change with respect to the properties that underlie its causal powers. On these suppositions, there would be no way in which a particular property could be picked out so as to have a name attached to it; and even if, *per impossibile*, a name did get attached to a property, it would be impossible for anyone to have any justification for applying the name on particular occasions.

It may be doubted whether the view under attack has these disastrous epistemo-logical consequences. Surely, it may be said, one can hold that it is a contingent matter that particular properties have the causal potentialities they have, and nevertheless hold, compatibly with this, that there are good theoretical reasons for thinking that as a matter of fact different properties differ in their causal potentialities, and that any given property retains the same potentialities over time. For while it is logically possible that the latter should not be so, according to the contingency view, the sim-plest hypothesis is that it is so; and it is reasonable to accept the simplest hypothesis compatible with the data.

Whatever may be true in general of appeals to theoretical simplicity, this one seems to me extremely questionable. For here we are not really dealing with an explanatory hypothesis at all. If the identity of properties is made independent of their causal potentialities, then in what sense do we explain sameness or difference of causal potentialities by positing sameness or difference of properties? There are of course cases in which we explain a constancy in something by positing certain underlying constancies in its properties. It is genuinely explanatory to say that something retained the same causal power over time because certain of its proper-ties remained the same. And this provides, *ceteris paribus*, a simpler, or at any rate more plausible, explanation of the constancy than one that says that the thing first had one set of underlying properties and then a different set, and that both sets were sufficient to give it that particular power. For example, if the water supply was pois-onous all day long, it is more plausible to suppose that this was due to the presence in it of one poisonous substance all day rather than due to its containing cyanide from morning till noon and strychnine from noon till night. But in such cases we presuppose that the underlying property constancies carry with them constancies in causal potentialities, and it is only on this presupposition that positing the underly-ing constancies provides the simplest explanation of the constancy to be explained. Plainly this presupposition cannot be operative if what the 'inference to the best explanation' purports to explain is, precisely, that sameness of property goes with sameness of causal potentialities. It is not as if a property had the causal potential-ities in question as a result of having yet *other* causal potentialities, the constancy of the latter explaining the constancy of the former. This disassociation of property identity from identity of causal potentiality is really an invitation to eliminate reference to properties from our explanatory hypotheses altogether; if it were correct then we could, to use Wittgenstein's metaphor, 'divide through' by the properties and leave the explanatory power of what we say about things untouched.

It might be objected that even if my arguments establish that the causal potentialities of a genuine property cannot change over time, they do not establish that these causal potentialities are essential to that property, in the sense of belonging to it in all possible worlds. The immutability of properties with respect to their causal potentialities, it might be said, is simply a consequence of the immutability of laws—of the fact that it makes no sense to speak of a genuine law holding at one time and not at another. And from the fact that the laws governing a property cannot change over time it does not follow, it may be said, that the property cannot be governed by different laws in different possible worlds.

Let me observe first of all that in conceding that the immutability of the causal potentialities of genuine properties is a consequence of the immutability of laws, the objection concedes a large part of what I want to maintain. It is not true in general of mere-Cambridge properties that their causal potentialities cannot change over time; for example, this is not true of *grueness* on the Barker–Achinstein definition of *grue*, where something is grue just in case it is green and the time is before T (say A.D. 2000) or it is blue and the time is T or afterwards.[11] That genuine properties are marked off from mere-Cambridge properties by their relation to causal laws (and that it is nonsense to speak of a world in which it is the mere-Cambridge properties rather than the genuine ones that are law-governed in a way that makes their causal potentialities immutable) is a central part of my view.

There is, moreover, a *prima facie* case for saying that the immutability of the causal potentialities of a property does imply their essentiality; or in other words, that if they cannot vary across time, they also cannot vary across possible worlds. Most of us do suppose that *particulars* can (or do) have different properties in different possible worlds. We suppose, for example, that in some possible worlds I am a plumber rather than a philosopher, and that in some possible worlds my house is painted yellow rather than white. But it goes with this that particulars can change their properties over time. It is possible that I, the very person who is writing this essay, might have been a plumber, because there is a possible history in which I start with the properties (in this case relational as well as intrinsic) which I had at some time in my actual history, and undergo a series of changes which result in my eventually being a plumber. If I and the world were never such that it was then possible for me to *become* a plumber, it would not be true that I might have been a plumber, or (in other words) that there is a possible world in which I am one. There is, in short, a close linkage between identity across time and identity across possible

11. See S. F. Barker and P. Achinstein, 'On the New Riddle of Induction', *The Philosophical Review*, 69 (1960), 511–22. The definition given there is not equivalent to that originally given by Goodman, in *Fact, Fiction and Forecast*, 3rd edition (Indianapolis: Bobbs-Merrill, 1975), p. 74, and it is the latter which is employed elsewhere in the present essay.

worlds; the ways in which a given thing can be different in different possible worlds depend on the ways in which such a thing can be different at different times in the actual world. But now let us move from the case of particulars to that of properties. There is no such thing as tracing a property through a series of changes in its causal potentialities—not if it is a genuine property, i.e., one of the sort that figures in causal laws. And so there is no such thing as a possible history in which a property starts with the set of causal potentialities it has in the actual world and ends with a different set. To say the least, this calls into question the intelligibility of the suggestion that the very properties we designate with words like 'green', 'square', 'hard', and so on, might have had different causal potentialities than they in fact have.

However, this last argument is not conclusive. My earlier arguments, however, if sound, establish that there is an intimate connection between the identity of a property and its causal potentialities. But it has not yet been decisively established that *all* of the causal potentialities of a property are essential to it. The disastrous epistemological consequences of the contingency view would be avoided if for each property we could identify a proper subset of its causal potentialities that are essential to it and constitutive of it, and this would permit some of a property's causal potentialities, those outside the essential cluster, to belong to it contingently, and so not belong to it in some other possible worlds. There would, in this case, be an important difference between the trans-world identity of properties and that of particulars— and it is a difference which there is in my own view as well. If, as I believe, the assertion that a certain particular might have had different properties than it does in the actual world (that in some other possible world it does have those properties) implies that there is a possible history 'branching off' from the history of the actual world in which it acquires those properties, this is because there is, putting aside historical properties and 'identity properties' (like being identical to Jimmy Carter), no subset of the properties of such a thing which constitutes an individual essence of it, i.e., is such that, in any possible world, having the properties in that subset is necessary *and sufficient* for being that particular thing. To put this otherwise, the reason why the possible history in which the thing has different properties must be a branching-off from the history of the actual world is that the individual essence of a particular thing must include historical properties. Now I am not in a position to object to the suggestion that properties differ from particulars in having individual essences which do not include historical properties and which are sufficient for their identification across possible worlds; for I hold that the totality of a property's causal potentialities constitutes such an individual essence. So a possible alternative to my view is one which holds that for each property there is a proper subset of its causal potentialities that constitutes its individual essence. Such a view has its attractions, and is compatible with much of what I say in this essay; in particular, it is compatible with the claim that within any possible world properties are identical just in case they have the same causal potentialities. But I shall argue in section 9 that this view is unworkable, and that there is no acceptable alternative to the view that all of the causal potentialities of a property are essential to it.

6

As was intended, my account of properties does not apply to what I have called mere-Cambridge properties. When my table acquired the property of being such that Gerald Ford is President of the United States, which it did at the time Nixon resigned from the presidency, this presumably had no effect on its causal powers. Beds that were slept in by George Washington may command a higher price than those that lack this historical property, but presumably this is a result, not of any causal potentialities in the beds themselves, but of the historical beliefs and interests of those who buy and sell them. And grueness, as defined by Goodman, is not associated in the way greenness and blueness are with causal potentialities. (In this sense, which differs from that invoked in section 5, something is grue at a time just in case it is green at that time and is first examined before T, say, A.D. 2000, or is blue at that time and is not first examined before T.) It can happen that the only difference between something that is grue and something that is not is that one of them has and the other lacks the historical property of being (or having been) first examined before the time T mentioned in Goodman's definition of *grue*; and presumably this does not in itself make for any difference in causal potentialities. It can also happen that two things share the property of being grue in virtue of having properties that have different potentialities—that is, in virtue of one of them being green (and examined before T) and the other being blue (and not so examined).

There is an epistemological way of distinguishing genuine and mere-Cambridge properties that is *prima facie* plausible. If I wish to determine whether an emerald is green at t, the thing to do, if I can manage it, is to examine the emerald at t. But examination of a table will not tell me it is such that Gerald Ford is President of the United States, or whether it is fifty miles south of a burning barn. And if I am ignorant of the date, or if t is after T (the date in Goodman's definition), examination of an emerald will not tell me whether it is grue. Likewise, while scrutiny of a bed may reveal a plaque claiming that it was slept in by George Washington, it will not tell me whether this claim is true. Roughly, if a question about whether a thing has a property at a place and time concerns a genuine nonrelational property, the question is most directly settled by observations and tests in the vicinity of that place and time, while if it concerns a mere-Cambridge property it may be most directly settled by observations and tests remote from that place and time, and observations and tests made at that place and time will either be irrelevant (as in the case of the property of being such that Jimmy Carter is President) or insufficient to settle the question (as in the case of grue).

It would be difficult to make this into a precise and adequate criterion of genuineness of property, and I do not know whether this could be done. But I think that to the extent that it is adequate, its adequacy is explained by my account of properties in terms of causal powers. Properties reveal their presence in actualizations of their causal potentialities, a special case of this being the perception of a property. And the most immediate and revealing effects of an object's having a property at a particular place and time are effects that occur in the immediate vicinity of that place and time. To be sure, we cannot rule out on purely philosophical grounds the possibility of action at a spatial and/or temporal distance. And the more prevalent such action is, the less adequate the proposed epistemological criterion will be. But there do seem to be conceptual limitations on the extent to which causal action can be at a spatial or temporal distance. It is doubtful, to say the least, whether there could be something whose causal powers are *all* such that whenever any of them is activated the effects of its activation are spatially remote from the location of the thing at that time, or occur at times remote from the time of activation.

Causation and causal powers are as much involved in the verification of ascriptions of mere-Cambridge properties as in the verification of ascriptions of genuine ones. But in the case of mere-Cambridge properties some of the operative causal powers will either belong to something other than the object to which the property is ascribed, or will belong to that object at a time other than that at which it has that property. Thus if I verify that a man has the property of being fifty miles south of a burning barn, it will be primarily the causal powers of the barn, and of the intervening stretch of land (which, we will suppose, I measure), rather than the causal powers of the man, that will be responsible for my verifying observations.

7

It will not have escaped notice that the account of properties and property identity I have offered makes free use of the notion of a property and the notion of property identity. It says, in brief, that properties are identical, whether in the same possible world or in different ones, just in case their coinstantiation with the same properties gives rise to the same powers. This is, if anything, even more circular than it looks. For it crucially involves the notion of sameness of powers, and this will have to be explained in terms of sameness of circumstances and sameness of effects, the notions of which both involve the notion of sameness of property. And of course there was essential use of the notion of a property in my explanation of the notion of a conditional power.

It is worth observing that there is a distinction between kinds of powers that corresponds to the distinction, mentioned earlier, between genuine and mere-Cambridge properties.[12] Robert Boyle's famous example of the key can be used to illustrate this.[13] A particular key on my key chain has the power of opening locks of a certain design. It also has the power of opening my front door. It could lose the former power only by undergoing what we would regard as real change, for example, a change in its shape. But it could lose the latter without undergoing such a change; it could do so in virtue of the lock on my door being replaced by one of a different

---

12. This was called to my attention by Nicholas Sturgeon.
13. See Boyle, 'The Origins and Forms of Qualities', in *The Works of the Honourable Robert Boyle*, 5 volumes (London: A. Millar, 1744), volume II, pp. 461 ff.

design. Let us say that the former is an intrinsic power and the latter a mere-Cambridge power. It is clear that in my account of properties the word 'power' must refer only to intrinsic powers. For if it refers to mere-Cambridge powers as well, then what seems clearly to be a mere-Cambridge property of my key, namely being such that my door has a lock of a certain design, will make a determinate contribution to its having the powers it has, and so will count as a genuine property of it. But it seems unlikely that we could explain the distinction between intrinsic and mere-Cambridge powers without making use of the notion of a genuine change and that of a genuine property. And so again my account of the notion of a property in terms of the notion of a power can be seen to be circular.

How much do these circularities matter? Since they are, I think, unavoidable, they preclude a reductive analysis of the notion of a property in terms of the notion of causality. But they by no means render my account empty. The claim that the causal potentialities of a property are essential to it, and that properties having the same causal potentialities are identical, is certainly not made vacuous by the fact that the explanation of the notion of a causal potentiality, or a conditional power, must invoke the notion of a property. As I see it, the notion of a property and the notion of a causal power belong to a system of internally related concepts, no one of which can be explicated without the use of the others. Other members of the system are the concept of an event, the concept of similarity, and the concept of a persisting substance. It can be worthwhile, as a philosophical exercise, to see how far we can go in an attempt to reduce one of these concepts to others—for both the extent of our success and the nature of our failures can be revealing about the nature of the connections between the concepts. But ultimately such attempts must fail. The goal of philosophical analysis, in dealing with such concepts, should not be reductive analysis but rather the charting of internal relationships. And it is perfectly possible for a 'circular' analysis to illuminate a net-work of internal relationships and have philosophically interesting consequences.

8

According to the theory of properties I am proposing, all of the causal potentialities possessed by a property at any time in the actual world are essential to it and so belong to it at all times and in all possible worlds. This has a very strong consequence, namely that causal necessity is just a species of logical necessity. If the introduction into certain circumstances of a thing having certain properties causally necessitates the occurrence of certain effects, then it is impossible, logically impossible, that such an introduction could fail to have such an effect, and so logically necessary that it has it. To the extent that causal laws can be viewed as propositions describing the causal potentialities of properties, it is impossible that the same properties should be governed by different causal laws in different possible worlds, for such propositions will be necessarily true when true at all.

It is not part of this theory, however, that causal laws are analytic or knowable *a priori*. I suppose that it is analytic that flexible things bend under suitable pressure, that poisonous things cause injury to those for whom they are poisonous, and so on. But I do not think that it is analytic that copper is an electrical conductor, or that knife-shaped things, if knife-sized and made of steel, are capable of cutting butter. Nor does it follow from the claim that such truths are necessary that they are analytic. Kripke has made a compelling case for the view that there are propositions that are necessary *a posteriori*, that is, true in all possible worlds but such that they can only be known empirically.[14] And such, according to my theory, is the status of most propositions describing the causal potentialities of properties. The theory can allow that our knowledge of these potentialities is empirical, and that it is bound to be only partial. But in order to show how, in the theory, such empirical knowledge is possible, I must now bring out an additional way in which the notion of causality is involved in the notion of a property.

One of the formulations of my theory says that every property is a cluster of conditional powers. But the converse does not seem to me to hold; not every cluster of conditional powers is a property. If something is both knife-shaped and made of wax, then it will have, among others, the following conditional powers: the power of being able to cut wood conditionally upon being knife-sized and made of steel (this it has in virtue of being knife-shaped), and the power of being malleable conditionally upon being at a temperature of 100°F (this it has in virtue of being made of wax). Intuitively, these are not common components of any single property. By contrast, the various conditional powers a thing has in virtue of being knife-shaped—for example, the power of being able to cut wood conditionally upon being knife-sized and made of steel, the power of being able to cut butter conditionally upon being knife-sized and made of wood, the power of having a certain visual appearance conditionally upon being green, the power of having a certain other visual appearance conditionally upon being red, and so on—are all constituents of a single property, namely the property of being knife-shaped. The difference, I think, is that in the one case the set of conditional powers has, while in the other it lacks, a certain kind of causal unity. I shall now try to spell out the nature of this unity.

Some subsets of the conditional powers which make up a genuine property will be such that it is a consequence of causal laws that whatever has any member of the subset necessarily has all of its members. Thus, for example, something has the power of leaving a six-inch-long knife-shaped impression in soft wax conditionally upon being six inches long if and only if it has the power of leaving an eight-inch-long knife-shaped impression in soft wax conditionally upon being eight inches long. Now some conditional powers will belong to more than one property cluster; thus, for example, there are many different shape properties that give something the power of being able to cut wood conditionally upon being made of steel. But where a conditional power can be shared by different properties in this way, it will belong to a particular property cluster only if there is another member of that cluster which

14. See Saul Kripke, 'Naming and Necessity', in *Semantics of Natural Language*, edited by D. Davidson and G. Harman (Dordrecht: Reidel, 1972), 253–355.

is such that it is a consequence of causal laws that whatever has that other member has the conditional power in question. And at the core of each cluster there will be one or more conditional powers which are such that as a consequence of causal laws whatever has any of them has all of the conditional powers in the cluster. For example, if something has, conditionally upon being made of steel, the power of leaving a knife-shaped impression in soft wax, then it cannot fail to be knife-shaped, and so cannot fail to have all of the other conditional powers involved in being knife-shaped. I suggest, then, that conditional powers X and Y belong to the same property if and only if it is a consequence of causal laws that either (1) whatever has either of them has the other, or (2) there is some third conditional power such that whatever has it has both X and Y.

Returning now to the conditional power of being able to cut wood conditionally upon being made of steel and the conditional power of being malleable conditionally upon being at a temperature of 100°F, it seems to me that these do not qualify under the proposed criterion as belonging to a common property. It is obviously not true that whatever has one of them must have the other. And it does not appear that there is any third conditional power which is such that whatever has it must have the two conditional powers in question.

If I am right in thinking that the conditional powers constituting a property must be causally unified in the way indicated, it is not difficult to see how knowledge of the causal potentialities of properties can develop empirically. The behavior of objects, that is, the displays of their powers, will reveal that they have certain conditional powers. Once it is discovered that certain conditional powers are connected in a lawlike way, we can use these to 'fix the reference' of a property term to the cluster containing those conditional powers and whatever other conditional powers are related to them in the appropriate lawlike relationships.[15] And we can then set about to determine empirically what the other conditional powers in the cluster are.

9

As I observed earlier, my theory appears to have the consequence that causal laws are logically necessary, and that causal necessity is just a species of logical necessity. While to some this may be an attractive consequence, to many it will seem counterintuitive. It does seem to most of us that we can conceive of possible worlds which resemble the actual world in the kinds of properties that are instantiated in them, but differ from it in the causal laws that obtain. My theory must maintain either that we cannot really conceive of this or that conceivability is not proof of logical possibility.

Anyone who finds both of these alternatives unacceptable, but is persuaded by the arguments in section 5 that the identity of properties is determined by their causal potentialities, will look for ways of reconciling that conclusion with the view that there can be worlds in which some of the causal laws are different from, and

15. For the notion of 'reference fixing', see Kripke, 'Naming and Necessity', pp. 269–75.

incompatible with, those that obtain in the actual world. I want now to consider two ways in which one might attempt to achieve such a reconciliation. First, it might be held that while propositions describing the causal potentialities of properties are necessarily true if true at all, there are other lawlike propositions, namely those asserting lawlike connections between conditional powers, which are contingent and so true in some possible worlds and false in others. According to this view, when we seem to be conceiving of worlds in which the same properties are governed by different laws, what we are really conceiving of are worlds in which the same conditional powers stand one to another in different lawlike connections than they do in the actual world, and so are differently clustered into properties. Second, it might be held that my condition for the identity of properties across possible worlds is too strict. The theory I have advanced might be called the 'total cluster theory'; it identifies a property with a cluster containing all of the conditional powers which anything has in virtue of having that property, and maintains that in any possible world anything that has that property must have all of the members of that cluster. One might attempt to replace this with a 'core cluster theory', which identifies the property with some proper subset of the conditional powers something has in virtue of having that property. On this theory, it is only some of the causal potentialities possessed by a property in the actual world, namely those constituted by the conditional powers in its core cluster, that are essential to it—so it is possible for the same property to have somewhat different causal potentialities in different possible worlds, because of different laws relating the conditional powers in its core cluster with other conditional powers.

   I do not believe, however, that either of these attempted reconciliations is successful. The first involves the suggestion that it is at least sometimes a contingent matter whether two conditional powers belong to the same property, and hence that there could be a world in which some of the same conditional powers are instantiated as in this world, but in which, owing to the holding of different laws, these are differently clustered into properties. The difficulty with this is that the specification of a conditional power always involves, in two different ways, reference to properties that are instantiated in our world and which, *ex hypothesi*, would not be instantiated in the alternative world in question. It involves reference to the properties on which the power is conditional, and also to the properties in the instantiation of which the exercise of the power would result. For example, one of the conditional powers in the property of being knife-shaped is the power, conditionally upon being made of steel, of leaving a knife-shaped impression if pressed into soft wax and then withdrawn. This conditional power, although not by itself identical to the property of being knife-shaped, could not be exercised without that property being instantiated. Neither could it be exercised without the property of being made of steel being instantiated. And a conditional power could not be instantiated in a world in which the causal laws would not allow an exercise of it. So in general, a conditional power could not be instantiated in a world in which the causal laws did not permit the instantiation of the properties whose instantiation would be involved in its instantiation or in its exercise.

Nothing I have said precludes the possibility of there being worlds in which the causal laws are different from those that prevail in this world. But it seems to follow from my account of property identity that if the laws are different then the properties will have to be different as well. And it does not appear that we have the resources for describing a world in which the properties that can be instantiated differ from what I shall call the 'actual world properties', that is, those that can be instantiated in the actual world. We have just seen that we cannot do this by imagining the conditional powers that exist in this world to be governed by different laws, and so to be differently grouped into properties.

It might seem that we can at least imagine a world in which *some* of the properties that can be instantiated are actual world properties while others are not. But a specification of the causal potentialities of one property will involve mention of other properties, a specification of the causal potentialities of those other properties will involve mention of still other properties, and so on. If there could be a world in which some but not all of the actual world properties can be instantiated, this could only be because those properties were causally insulated, as it were, from the rest— that is, were such that their causal potentialities could be fully specified without reference to the rest and vice versa. It seems unlikely that any proper subset of the actual world properties is causally insulated in this way—and any that are insulated from all properties we know about are thereby insulated from our knowledge and our language. But could there be a world in which the properties that can be instantiated include all of the actual world properties plus some others? This would be possible only if the two sets of properties, the actual world properties and the properties that cannot be instantiated in the actual world, were causally insulated from one another. And because of this, it would be impossible for us to say anything about the properties that cannot be instantiated in the actual world; for what we can describe is limited to what can be specified in terms of properties that can be so instantiated. What we could describe of such a world would have to be compatible with the laws that specify the causal potentialities of the actual world properties and, what we have found to be inseparable from these, the laws describing the lawlike connections between the conditional powers that constitute these properties.

Now let us consider the second attempt to reconcile the claim that the identity of a property is determined by its causal potentialities with the apparent conceivability of worlds in which the causal laws that obtain are different from, and incompatible with, those that obtain in the actual world. This involves the proposal that we adopt a 'core cluster theory' in place of the 'total cluster theory', and make the identity of a property dependent on a proper subset, rather than on the totality, of the causal potentialities it has in the actual world. Like the first attempted reconciliation, this involves the idea that at least some of the lawlike connections between conditional powers hold only contingently; it is this that is supposed to make it possible for the composition of the total cluster associated with a property to differ from one possible world to another, owing to different conditional powers being causally linked with the conditional powers in the property's essential core cluster. But it would seem that the lawlike connections between those conditional powers included in the essential core cluster will have to hold of logical necessity, i.e., in all possible worlds. For if they held only contingently, then in some possible worlds they would not hold. In such a world, the individual conditional powers which in the actual world constitute the essential core of the property could be instantiated, but the property itself could not be instantiated. Even if these conditional powers could be instantiated together in such a world, their coinstantiation would not count as the instantiation of a property, and so of that property, since the requisite causal unity would be lacking. But I have already argued, in discussing the first attempted reconciliation, that it is not possible that there should be a world in which conditional powers that are instantiated in the actual world can be instantiated while actual world properties cannot be instantiated.

But if, as I have just argued, the lawlike connections between conditional powers within the essential core cluster will have to hold of logical necessity, then we are faced with a problem. Some lawlike connections between conditional powers will hold contingently (according to the core cluster theory), while others will hold as a matter of logical necessity. How are we to tell which are which? It does not appear that we can distinguish these lawlike connections epistemologically, i.e., by the way in which they are known. For if, as I am assuming, there are truths that are necessary *a posteriori*, the fact that a connection is discovered empirically is no guarantee that it does not hold necessarily. Nor can it be said that we identify the necessary connections by the fact that they hold between conditional powers belonging to some property's essential core cluster; for this presupposes that we have some way of identifying essential core clusters, and how are we to do this if we do not already know which connections between conditional powers are necessary and which are contingent?

It might be suggested that what constitutes a set of conditional powers as constituting an essential core cluster is just its being a lawlike truth that whatever has any of its members has all of them, and that it is by discovering such lawlike truths that we identify essential core clusters. Given that the lawlike connections between members of essential core clusters hold of logical necessity, this would amount to the claim that if two conditional powers are so related that the possession of either of them is both causally necessary and causally sufficient for the possession of the other, then the lawlike connection between them holds as a matter of logical necessity, while if the possession of one is causally sufficient but not causally necessary for the possession of the other then the lawlike connection may be contingent. I have no knockdown argument against this view, but it seems to me implausible. If it is possible for it to be a contingent fact that the possession of one conditional power is causally sufficient for the possession of another, then it seems to me that it ought to be possible for it to be a contingent fact that the possession of one conditional power is both causally necessary and causally sufficient for the possession of another; that is, it ought to be possible for it to be contingently true of two conditional powers that the possession of either of them is causally sufficient for the possession of the other. So if we deny that the latter is a possibility, we should also deny that the former is.

It may be suggested that it is our linguistic conventions that make certain causal potentialities essential to a property, and so determine the makeup of a property's essential core cluster. But this cannot be so. It may in some cases belong to the conventionally determined sense of a property word that the property it designates has certain causal potentialities; while I think there is no need for property words to have such Fregean senses, and think that such words often function much as Kripke thinks natural kind terms do, I have no wish to deny that a property word can have a conventionally determined sense. But there is only so much that linguistic conventions can do; and one thing they cannot do is to dictate to reality, creating lawlike connections and *de re* necessities. Having discovered that certain conditional powers necessarily go together, and so are appropriately related for being part of an essential core cluster, we can lay down the convention that a certain word applies, in any possible world, to those and only those things having those conditional powers. But this leaves open the question of how we know that the conditional powers in question are appropriately related—that they must go together in any world in which either can be instantiated. And here appeal to convention cannot help us.

It begins to appear that if we hold that some lawlike connections are contingent, there is no way in which we could discover which of the lawlike connections between conditional powers are logically necessary and which are logically contingent, and so no way in which we could identify the essential core clusters of properties. This means that when we conceive, or seem to be conceiving, of a possible world in which the actual world properties are governed by somewhat different laws, there is no way in which we can discover whether we are conceiving of a genuine possibility. All that any of our empirical investigations can tell us is what lawlike connections obtain in the actual world; and without some way of telling which of these connections are contingent and which necessary, this gives us no information about what can be the case in other possible worlds. This makes all talk about what logically might be and might have been completely idle, except where questions of logical possibility can be settled *a priori*. If the core cluster theory makes the modal status of causal connections, their being necessary or contingent, epistemologically indeterminate in this way, it does not really save the intuitions which lead us to resist the total cluster theory, according to which all such connections are necessary. Unless we are prepared to abandon altogether the idea that there is a 'fact of the matter' as to whether there are logically possible circumstances in which a given property would make a certain contribution to the causal powers of its subject, I think we must accept the total cluster theory and its initially startling consequence that all of the causal potentialities of a property are essential to it.

10

If, as my theory implies, there are no situations that are logically but not causally possible, how is it that we are apparently able to conceive or imagine such situations?

Saul Kripke has suggested one answer to a very similar question.[16] He holds that it is a necessary truth that heat is molecular motion, but recognizes that it seems as if we can imagine heat turning out to be something other than this. According to Kripke, this appearance of conceivability is something to be explained away, and he explains it away by claiming that the seeming conceivability of heat turning out not to be molecular motion consists in the actual conceivability of something else, namely of sensations of a certain sort, those that we in fact get from heat, turning out to be caused by something other than molecular motion. The latter really is conceivable, he holds, and for understandable reasons we mistake its conceivability for the conceivability of something that is in fact not conceivable.

But if conceivability is taken to imply possibility, this account commits one to the possibility that the sensations we get from heat might standardly be caused by something other than molecular motion (and so something other than heat); more than that, it commits one to the possibility that this might be so and that these sensations might be related to other sensations and sense-experiences in all the ways they are (or have been to date) in the actual world. And since the property of having such sensations is one that is actualized in this world, this would commit one, in my view, to the claim that it is compatible with the laws of nature that prevail in the actual world that these sensations should be so caused and so related to other experiences. Now this claim may be true—if 'may be' is used epistemically. But it is hard to see how we are entitled to be confident that it is. For might there not be laws, unknown to us, that make it impossible that the standard cause of these sensations should be anything other than it is, given the way they are related to the rest of our experience? If the seeming conceivability of heat turning out to be something other than molecular motion does not prove the actual possibility of this, why should the seeming conceivability of certain sensations being caused by something other than molecular motion prove the actual, and so causal, possibility of that? And if seeming conceivability no more proves possibility in the latter case than in the former, there seems little point in distinguishing between conceivability and seeming conceivability; we may as well allow that it is conceivable (and not just seemingly conceivable) that heat should turn out to be molecular motion, and then acknowledge that conceivability is not conclusive proof of possibility. We could use the term 'conceivable' in such a way that it is conceivable that P just in case not-P is not provable a priori. Or we could use it in such a way that it is conceivable that P just in case it is epistemically possible that it is possible that P should be the case—that is, just in case P's being possible is compatible, for all we know, with what we know. These uses of 'conceivable' are not equivalent, but on both of them it is possible to conceive of what is not possible.

11

Although many of the implications of the account I have advanced are radically at odds with Humean views about causality, it does enable us to salvage one of the

16. 'Naming and Necessity', pp. 331–42.

central tenets of the Humean view, namely the claim that singular causal statements are 'implicitly general'. As I see it, the generality of causal propositions stems from the generality of properties, that is, from the fact that properties are universals, together with the fact which I began this essay by pointing out, namely that causal relations hold between particular events in virtue of the properties possessed by the constituent objects of those events, and the fact, which I have tried to establish in the essay, that the identity of a property is completely determined by its potential for contributing to the causal powers of the things that have it. If I assert that one event caused another, I imply that the constituent objects of the cause event had properties which always contribute in certain ways to the causal powers of the things that have them, and that the particular episode of causation at hand was an actualization of some of these potentialities. I may of course not know what the relevant properties of the cause event were; and if I do know this, I may know little about their causal potentialities. This is closely related to the now familiar point that in claiming to know the truth of a singular causal statement one is not committed to knowing the laws in virtue of which it holds.[17] Moreover, a single causal statement does not commit one to the claim that the instantiation of the relevant properties in relevant similar circumstances always produces the effect that it did in the case at hand; for the laws governing these properties may be statistical, the powers to which the properties contribute may, accordingly, be statistical tendencies or propensities, and the causation may be nonnecessitating. Also, the claim that singular causal statements are implicitly general does not, as here interpreted, imply anything about how such statements are know—in particular, it does not imply the Humean view that causal relationships can only be discovered *via* the discovery of regularities or 'constant conjunctions'. But where the present theory differs most radically from theories in the Humean tradition is in what it claims about the modality of the general propositions, the laws, that explain the truth of singular causal propositions; for whereas on the Humean view the truth of these propositions is contingent, on my view it is logically necessary. I thus find myself, in what I once would have regarded as reactionary company, defending the very sort of 'necessary connection' account of causality which Hume is widely applauded for having refuted.

Postscript

(The following was appended to the original publication of this essay as a 'Note Added in Proof'.)

Richard Boyd has offered the following as a counter example to the account of properties proposed in this essay. Imagine a world in which the basic physical elements include substances A, B, C, and D. Suppose that X is a compound of A and B, and Y is a compound of C and D. We can suppose that it follows from the laws of

---

17. See, for example, Donald Davidson, 'Causal Relations', *The Journal of Philosophy*, 64 (1967), 691–703.

nature governing the elements that these two compounds, although composed of different elements, behave exactly alike under all possible circumstances—so that the property of being made of X and the property of being made of Y share all of their causal potentialities. (This means, among other things, that it follows from the laws that once a portion of X or Y is formed, it cannot be decomposed into its constituent elements.) It would follow from my account of properties that being made of X and being made of Y are the same property. And this seems counterintuitive. If, as appears, X and Y would be different substances, the property of being composed of the one should be different from the property of being composed of the other.

I think that this example does show that my account needs to be revised. I propose the following as a revised account which is still clearly a causal account of properties: for properties F and G to be identical, it is necessary *both* that F and G have the same causal potentialities *and* (this is the new requirement) that whatever set of circumstances is sufficient to cause the instantiation of F is sufficient to cause the instantiation of G, and vice versa. This amounts to saying that properties are individuated by their possible causes as well as by their possible effects. No doubt Boyd's example shows that other things I say in the essay need to be amended.

Study questions

1. Explain, with examples, the distinction between determinable and determinate properties or predicates.
2. When challenged by Parmenides to say how one Form can be wholly in many places at the same time, Socrates responds by saying that one day can be in many places at the same time, and the Forms might be like that. What do you think of this response?
3. How can a class nominalist give an account of what it is that all red things have in common?
4. Does the causal theory of properties have the consequence that the laws of nature are metaphysically necessary? Is this a good thing or a bad thing for the theory?

Further reading

For the interpretation of Plato's theory of Forms, see Irwin (1999). For Aristotle on form and matter, see Barnes (1995). Armstrong (1989a), from which our selection is taken, is an excellent introduction to the whole issue of universals by one of the leading contributors to the contemporary debate; Armstrong's latest substantial contribution to this debate is his (1997). Ramsey (1925) criticized the very idea of a particular/universal distinction; his ideas have recently been pursued by MacBride (1998). Ramsey's paper is reprinted in the excellent anthology edited by Mellor and Oliver (1997). In this anthology, see also the essays by Mellor (on a proposal for distinguishing between properties in terms of their place in the laws of nature), Jackson (on an argument for universals), and the debate between Armstrong and Devitt (on nominalism). For discussions of the notion of a disposition, see Blackburn (1990), Martin (1994), Crane (1995b), Mumford (1998), and Molnar (2003). A form of nominalism which is based on the notion of resemblance is defended by Rodriguez-Pereyra (2002). Trope theory is defended by Campbell (1990). A number of philosophers in recent years have begun to defend the causal theory of properties: Heil (2003) is a clear exponent of the view.

Part V

Necessity

Introduction

1. Introduction

A GATHA Christie writes in her autobiography that she had always been fascinated with mathematics, and she thought that at some point in her life, if she had continued her education, she would have become a mathematician, and would never have written any detective stories. As it happened, her somewhat whimsical mother transferred her to another school and her ambitions were never fulfilled. If we do not believe that everything that happens to us is inevitable or dictated by fate, we will believe that it was *possible* that Agatha Christie should have become a mathematician. Now, we could express this by saying that there is a possible world where Agatha Christie is a mathematician, perhaps the same world where *Murder on the Orient Express* was never written. If it was possible for Agatha Christie to become a mathematician, the fact that she did not is a *contingent* fact: something which is the case but did not have to be the case. But while Agatha Christie's failure to contribute to mathematics seems a contingent matter, mathematics itself does not. If we agree that $1 + 1 = 2$ is necessary—that is, true no matter what—we could express this by saying that $1 + 1 = 2$ is true in all possible worlds. A statement is therefore necessary if it is true in all possible worlds, possible if it is true in some possible world, and contingent if it is true in some possible world but false in some other.

'Modality' refers to, in its broadest sense, the way or 'mode' in which a certain truth is true. Necessity and possibility, the modalities we are concerned with in this section, are called 'alethic' or 'logical' modalities. ('Alethic' comes from the Greek word for *truth*.) A necessary truth is a truth that could not fail to be true; truths of logic and mathematics are the obvious examples of necessary truths. There is a straightforward connection between necessity and possibility: a possible truth is one which is not necessarily false. Contingent truths are those which are true, but not necessarily true. The difference between contingency and possibility should not be overlooked: according to the usual understanding, necessary truths are also possible (since of course they are not necessarily false), but they are obviously not contingent.

2. Modality and epistemology

Philosophers have classified truths in various ways. One such classification is *epistemic*: that is, concerns the way we get to know things. Thus, Leibniz made a distinction between truths of *reason* and truths of *fact*; for those of the former, he says, the explanation of their truth can be found by analysis alone: 'by resolving them into simpler ideas and truths, until we arrive at the basic ones' whose denial involves an explicit contradiction. For those of the latter, this cannot be done (1714: § 33). Hume distinguished among the objects of enquiry between *relations of ideas* and *matters of fact*; propositions of the first kind 'are discoverable by the mere operation of thought, without dependence on what is anywhere existent in the universe' and are 'intuitively or demonstratively certain';

propositions of the second kind are justified by the present testimony of the senses, memory, and reasoning involving cause and effect (Hume 1748: § IV, part i). Kant gave us the terminology most commonly used today for distinguishing truths epistemically: *a priori* truths can be known (or justified) independently of experience, *a posteriori* truths are known (or justified) on the basis of experience.

There was considerable disagreement among these philosophers about the details and significance of this classification, but on one issue they seemed to agree: that the *epistemic* status of truths is intrinsically linked with their *modal* status; so much so that the two kinds of categorizations are often run together. For example, according to Leibniz, 'truths of reasoning are necessary, and their opposite is impossible, those of fact are contingent and their opposite is possible'. Similarly, Hume writes: 'the contrary of every matter of fact is still possible; because it can never imply a contradiction' (Hume 1748: § IV, part i). The reverse is also argued for: necessary truths, insofar as they are known, must be known by thought alone. Hence Leibniz claims that 'necessary truths, such as we find in pure mathematics and particularly in arithmetic and geometry, must have principles whose proof does not depend on instances nor, consequently, on the testimony of the senses' (Leibniz 1765: 50). Kant concurs when he writes that 'experience teaches us that a thing is so and so, but not that it cannot be otherwise . . . [thus] if we have a proposition which in being thought is thought as *necessary*, it is an *a priori* judgement' (Kant 1787: 43). (See also Part VI: Causation, for Hume's argument that we cannot gain the idea of necessary connection through experience.)

We saw that the existence of necessary truths which are known by thinking alone has been acknowledged by philosophers in both the empiricist and rationalist traditions. Some empiricists, however, felt uneasy about this—after all, the basic tenet of empiricism is that all ideas and knowledge derive from experience. This was the case with representatives of logical positivism, a stringent empiricist school of thought active in the first part of the twentieth century. (For an extreme expression of this unease, see Ayer 1936: chapter 4.) The logical positivists held that we should be able to establish the truth of every factual statement through sense-experience; but everyone seemed to agree that sense-experience can never reveal anything to be necessary or certain. This caused a problem since the logical positivists also wanted to hold that truths of logic and mathematics were necessary. The solution they advanced located the source of these truths in our determination to use words in a particular way.

We can illustrate this idea by considering definitions. We introduce the expression 'π' to stand for the ratio of the circumference and the diameter of a circle. In other words, we commit ourselves to use the expression 'π' in such a way that the statement 'π is the ratio of the circumference and the diameter of a circle' is always true. Due to this commitment, the statement is true no matter what; at the same time, we need no sense-experience to tell us that it is, for once we know what 'π' means or stands for, the truth of the statement is clear. Of course, not every statement in logic or mathematics is a definition, but the logical positivists thought that the basic idea extends to all cases. For example, 'for all x, x is identical to x' is universally true because we *decide* to use the words 'identical', 'all', etc., in such a way that the statement would always be true.

Logical and mathematical statements were thus held to be *analytic*: that is, known through, and true in virtue of, the meaning of the words which constitute them. These statements were a priori, since what was needed to know them was simply knowledge of the meaning of words. The statements were also, in a fashion, necessary. But according to the logical positivists, this necessity is not a fact about the world; rather, it is simply a consequence of the rules we introduce for using certain words. (It is easy to discover in this theory the replay of the Humean distinction between relations of ideas and matters of fact.) This view is known as the linguistic (or analytic) theory of necessity.

On this theory, the question of necessity and possibility ceases to have a metaphysical dimension, that is, anything to do with the fundamental nature of the *world*. What questions remained about modalities were purely logical questions; by this we do not mean questions about the *status* of logical statements (that was supposed to be handled by the theory that they are analytic), but rather questions about the correct rules of modal inference; we may ask, for example, whether the following forms of inference are valid (the '$\Box$' or 'box' sign stands for 'Necessarily . . .'; the '$\Diamond$' or 'diamond' sign stands for 'Possibly . . .'):

(1) $\Box p$ entails p
(2) $\Diamond \Box p$ entails $\Box p$

An important advance in the logic of modalities was made in the first part of the twentieth century by C. I. Lewis and others, by providing various axiomatic systems to handle modal inferences. Incidentally, (1) above is recognized as valid in all these systems, whereas (2) is recognized as valid only in some axiomatic systems. As for the question of what makes the statement 'Necessarily p' true, Lewis sides with the logical positivists: what makes it true is simply that 'p' is analytic. (C. I. Lewis should not be confused with David Lewis, whose contributions to the philosophy of modality we shall discuss below.)

3. Scepticism about modality: Quine

Even the somewhat meagre sense of necessity afforded by the linguistic theory of necessity became threatened by several criticisms advanced by Quine. One general attack concerned the intelligibility of the notion of analyticity (Quine 1951); and since analyticity was meant to be the sole source of necessity, this was bad news for modality.

Furthermore, Quine argued that even if we grant the legitimacy of the notion of analyticity, modal logic would face problems if we tried to introduce quantification—expressions which talk about quantities of things, like 'some' and 'all', standardly symbolized by $\exists$ and $\forall$—into this logic (Quine 1953 and 1960: § 41). The linguistic theory of necessity says that

(3) Necessarily, nine is greater than seven

is true because 'nine is greater than seven' is analytic, whereas

(4) Necessarily, the number of planets is greater than seven

is false, because 'the number of planets is greater than seven' is not analytic—even though of course the number of planets *is* nine. This shows that the attempt to explain necessity by analyticity has the consequence that we can distinguish between necessary and non-necessary features of an object *only relative to the way the object is specified*. If we specify the number as 'nine', we can say that it is necessarily greater than seven; if we specify it as 'the number of planets', we cannot.

Quine argued that if we introduce quantification into modal logic, we will get into trouble on this score. For example, we will be asked to infer from (3) the following:

(5) There is an *x* such that necessarily, *x* is greater than seven

and here we cannot say that '*x* is greater than seven' is analytic. The analyticity or otherwise of this sentence will depend on what means we use to refer to *x*. The obvious way to avoid this problem would be to say that the value of the variable '*x*' (for example, the number nine) *itself* has the necessary feature of being greater than seven, independently of how we choose to talk about it—but as we saw, this is at variance with the idea that necessity is explained by analyticity. Saying that the number nine itself is necessarily such-and-such would introduce the kind of necessity that empiricists were trying to get rid of: necessity as a feature of the world itself, rather than as a consequence of the way we use words.

We can express Quine's point by using the distinction between so-called *de dicto* and *de re* modalities. We talk about *de dicto* necessity (or possibility) when a whole sentence or proposition is modified by the 'necessarily' (or 'possibly') operator, as in (3) and (4): we take the whole content of the proposition, and we state that *it* is necessary ('dictum' is Latin for *saying*: hence the necessity attaches to the proposition, what is said). In contrast, we use modal terms *de re* when we attribute a modal feature to some *particular thing* ('res' is Latin for *thing*). For example:

(6) Nine is such that it is necessarily greater than seven.

This sentence is supposed to say something about the number nine itself, independently of how we choose to pick it out. Saying that nine is necessarily greater than seven amounts to saying that 'being greater than seven' is an *essential* property of the number nine. Essential—as opposed to *accidental*—properties of a thing are those properties without which the thing could not exist. If we want to express truths about essential properties, it is important that modalities should be understood *de re*; if we had only *de dicto* necessities, we could not say that nine is necessarily or essentially greater than seven—for this would be true if we refer to nine as 'nine', and false when we refer to it as 'the number of planets'. Quine, as it should be expected, is thoroughly sceptical about this notion of essential properties which he labels 'Aristotelian essentialism'. So the gist of Quine's argument can be put by saying that the analytic theory of necessity allows only *de dicto* modalities, but quantified modal logic would require *de re* modalities and essentialism. So much the worse then for quantified modal logic; indeed, so much the worse for modal logic, since if we do not introduce quantification, there is no reason to call a sentence 'necessary' instead of simply calling it 'analytic'—if there is any point calling anything analytic at all (Quine 1953: 156).

4. The return of metaphysical modality: Kripke

The metaphysics of modality took a radical new turn in the late 1960s and 1970s with the emergence of Saul Kripke's *Naming and Necessity* (see Chapter 24). Kripke's revolutionary contribution involved rethinking the relation between epistemic and modal categories. The categories of a priori and a posteriori concern the way *we can get to know* things. Necessity and possibility, on the other hand, concern the way things *are*, so these are metaphysical categories. It may be the case, Kripke says, that some of these categories will turn out to coincide; but this would be a substantial thesis, and it certainly does not follow directly from their initial characterization. Of course, the point could be really appreciated if we found some statements which did not fit into the traditional classification which connected the necessary with the a priori, and the contingent with the a posteriori. And this was indeed what Kripke did: he argued that certain identity statements were *necessary and a posteriori*.

When talking about the modal status of identity, we should separate two questions: one concerns the nature of *identity*, the other the nature of *identity statements*. Let's start with the second. Almost everyone who believes in some sort of necessity will agree that some identity statements are necessary and some are contingent.

(7) Cicero is Cicero

is necessary; for how could it fail to be true? But consider Kripke's example:

(8) The inventor of bifocals was the first Postmaster General of the United States.

As it happens, both of these descriptions pick out Benjamin Franklin, so the statement is true. But it would be absurd to hold that the statement is *necessarily true*: surely things could have happened in such a way that Franklin did not invent bifocals, or did not become Postmaster General, or even that he did neither of these but two other people did. In the case of definite descriptions like 'the inventor of bifocals' we can easily imagine possible circumstances where they denote something other than they actually denote. To use Kripke's terminology, they are *non-rigid designators*: they may denote different things in different possible worlds. In general, when we have identity statements containing such non-rigid designators, we should expect the statement to be contingent.

Kripke claimed—and many followed him—that unlike definite descriptions, *proper names are rigid designators*, meaning that they denote the same thing in every possible world where that thing exists. Things could have happened to Nixon in many different ways: he might not have been a president, or a Republican; he might not have been called 'Richard' or indeed 'Nixon'; but when we describe all these possible ways of how things could have happened, we are still talking about the same person—Nixon—and we use our word 'Nixon' to talk about this person. We use descriptions to pick out objects in terms of their properties; we use names to talk about the *objects* as such, not as specified as the bearer of certain properties. Consider then a true identity statement including two proper names. The names denote the same thing in this world, and since they are rigid designators, they denote the same one thing in all other possible worlds. This means that the statement is true in every possible world, so it is necessarily true.

The striking fact is that many of these statements are a posteriori. No amount of a priori reasoning will tell us that George Eliot is identical to Mary Ann Evans; this is something that we learn in an empirical way. But if Kripke is right, then the statement is also necessary, since both names are rigid designators. We have thus an a posteriori necessary statement. The traditional assumption that only a priori statements can be necessary is thus refuted. Thinking back to what we said in section 2, we can see where Kant's reasoning went wrong. It may be true that you can never learn from experience *that* a statement is necessary; but when you learn that George Eliot is Mary Ann Evans, you learn a statement which *is* necessary. You do not thereby learn *that it is necessary*. Kant perhaps assumed that when grasping a necessary statement, we also grasp the fact that it is necessary, but there is really no reason to assume that this is the case. (Kripke has also argued that, contrary to the traditional view, there are a priori contingent statements as well. However, the status of these is much more controversial than that of the necessary a posteriori statements.)

The second question to be addressed here concerns the nature of identity. There is a general argument which purports to show that identity is necessary (see Box V.1). The basic idea is simple: if everything is identical to itself and nothing is ever identical to anything else, then *all* identity is self-identity, and most philosophers agree that self-identity is necessary. But how is this consistent with the view, mentioned earlier, that some identity statements are contingent? Consider again:

(8) The inventor of bifocals was the first Postmaster General of the United States.

Box V.1. The argument for the necessity of identity

There is a famous and simple argument which apparently shows that identity must be a necessary relation: that if *A* is identical to *B*, then *A* is necessarily identical to *B*. The argument was first presented by Barcan Marcus (1947), and endorsed by Kripke (1971). It can be given informally as follows:

(1.) Suppose that *A* is identical to *B*.
(2.) If *A* is identical to *B*, then whatever is true of *A* is true of *B*.
(3.) It is necessary that *A* is identical to *A*.
(4.) Therefore it is true of *A* that it is necessarily identical to *A*.
(5.) Therefore it is true of *B* that it is necessarily identical to *A*.
(6.) If *A* is identical to *B*, then *A* is necessarily identical to *B*.

The argument seems flawless. Premiss (2) is Leibniz's Law (see Part VIII: Identity). Premiss (3) is just the necessity of self-identity: it is necessary that everything is itself. (4) follows from (3) straightforwardly; and (5) is just a result of applying Leibniz's Law to (4). But despite the simplicity of the argument, the conclusion seems to be of great metaphysical significance. (Notice, incidentally, the similarity between the structure of this argument and the argument against vague identity in Chapter 17.)

Box V.2. The varieties of necessity

Philosophers talk about different kinds of necessity, and it can sometimes be a little confusing what they mean when they say something is necessary. Here is our way of understanding the main varieties of necessity employed in contemporary philosophy.

1. Metaphysical necessities: the most general kind of necessary truth. A truth is metaphysically necessary when it is true at all possible worlds.
2. Logical necessities: these are those metaphysical necessities which are truths of logic. For example, 'for all x, $x = x$' or 'p or not-p'. Although all logical necessities are metaphysical necessities, not all metaphysical necessities are logical necessities. 'Cicero $=$ Tully' expresses a metaphysical necessity, as does 'nothing can be red and green all over at the same time'. But these are not truths of logic, or consequences of logical truths.
3. Conceptual necessities: these are those metaphysical necessities which are a consequence of truths about our concepts. (They could also be called 'analytic necessities'.) Although some philosophers have tried to explain logical necessity in terms of conceptual necessity, it is nonetheless clear that not all conceptual necessities are logical necessities. For example, 'all bachelors are unmarried' is necessarily true, but it is not a logical necessity.
4. Nomological (or physical) necessity: truths which are consequences of the laws of nature (or physics). If the laws of nature are metaphysically necessary, then nomological necessities are true in all worlds; but if they are contingent, then nomological necessities are true only in those worlds which have our laws.

Thinking of things in this way, we can see that classifying a necessity as logical or conceptual is partly a matter of how it is *known*: whether it can be known through the study of logic or conceptual analysis for example. Whereas calling a necessity metaphysical is simply saying that it is true in all worlds, regardless of how we come to know it. (It should be borne in mind that many contemporary philosophers are suspicious of the category of conceptual necessity. For a defence of the category, and of conceptual analysis, see Jackson 1998.)

Now what is actually denoted by each of the descriptions turns out to be the very same thing, which is indeed necessarily identical to itself. Notice, however, that speaking in this way assumes that we can think of modality in *de re* terms—that is, we can do precisely what Quine thought was unacceptable: talk about things having necessary features independently of the way we refer to them (cf. Quine 1953: 156).

To sum up: Kripke's view about identity, widely accepted today, has two components. First, he accepts that there are both necessary and contingent statements apparently expressing identity. But contrary to the traditional view, he thinks that the modal status of such statements depends not on their being a priori or a posteriori, but on whether they involve rigid or non-rigid designators. The second component of the view is that we can *also* address the question of identity independently of the first issue, that is, independently of how we refer to objects; and viewed in this way, identity turns out to be necessary. (However, not everyone agrees with this: for an argument for the contingency of identity see Gibbard 1975.)

5. Possible worlds

We have come a long way from the idea that necessity is not a feature of the world, but simply a consequence of certain statements being analytic. With modality back in the world, the question arises: what are the conditions for a modal statement to be true? Which feature of the world is responsible for some modal statements being true, and some others false? Various answers to this question focus on the notion of possible worlds. Possible-world-talk has undoubtedly helped to clarify a number of issues about modalities, but some have hoped, in addition, that possible worlds can do more than simply provide a helpful way of expressing ourselves. Their hope was that by designing a theory of what possible worlds are, we could provide truth-conditions for modal statements. We shall look at three suggestions of how this could be done.

One of the most important views of possible worlds has been developed by David Lewis. As Lewis says in Chapter 25, he is a *modal realist*: he thinks that all possible worlds are of the same kind, and they all exist. We have an idea of what our world is: it consists of concrete particulars with properties—people, planets, or plutonium atoms—which stand in spatio-temporal and causal relations to one another. Our world is the comprehensive object made of all these. On Lewis's view, other possible worlds also consist of particulars existing in their own space and time, though people or plutonium atoms may not be among them—for it is possible that there should be no people or plutonium atoms. Causal and spatio-temporal relations obtain only *within* a world; each world is isolated from all others in space and time, and there is no causal interaction between worlds. The difference between what we call the actual world on the one hand, and what we call merely possible worlds on the other, is not metaphysical, but rather personal: the actual world simply happens to be *our* world. 'Actual', on this view, is an indexical expression like 'here': its reference is determined by the context of its use. The claim that there is a possible world where *Murder on the Orient Express* was never written, if true, is literally true: there must be a comprehensive, spatio-temporally and causally closed entity which contains no such book among the concrete particulars that make it up.

As Lewis himself is ready to admit, modal realism is not exactly common sense: 'When modal realism tells you—as it does—that there are uncountable infinities of donkeys and protons and puddles and stars, and of planets very like Earth, and of cities very like Melbourne, and of people very like yourself . . . small wonder if you are reluctant to believe it' (Lewis 1986a: 133). Though the departure from common sense may be smaller than it might seem at first, it is still a departure. But Lewis also thinks that there are theoretical benefits to the view which make it worth paying this price. The major benefit is that it provides a *reductive explanation* of modality. Possible worlds are defined as spatio-temporally and causally isolated entities. There are no modal notions on the defining side of this definition. Therefore, if we say that 'Necessarily A' is true if and only if 'A' is true in all possible worlds, we have provided truth-conditions for this modal claim in non-modal terms. And this is not all; reducing modality is no mean feat in itself, but we can appreciate the significance of the theory even more if we reflect upon the fact that many other notions in philosophy have modal components. Such is the case with properties: as we saw in Part IV, Lewis offers a theory of properties which makes use of the existence of possible objects or *possibilia*. Also, Lewis's theory of causation analyses it in terms of counterfactuals; and modal realism provides a powerful tool to analyse the truth-conditions of counterfactual statements (see Part VI: Causation). Yet another example of a modal notion is the notion of the *content* of a thought or a *proposition*; Lewis was one of the pioneers of the idea that a proposition should be understood as the set of all those worlds in which a sentence expressing that proposition is true. (For more details, see Lewis 1986*b*: chapters 1.2–1.6; and Stalnaker 1984: 2 ff.)

Impressive as it is, Lewis's theory has not attracted many followers. Some philosophers suggest an alternative which could reap the advantages of the theory of possible worlds—provide truth-conditions for modal statements, clarify the relation between various modal properties—without committing us to a plurality of concrete Lewisian worlds. For obvious reasons, Lewis calls this view 'ersatz modal realism' or 'ersatzism'. The basic idea is that there is only *one* world of concrete individuals, and this world contains entities which represent, or correspond to, the way the world might have been. On one version, the entities in question are abstract *propositions*. Propositions are the contents of our sentences and of our beliefs, and they can be true or false. Take the proposition that Agatha Christie was a novelist and the proposition that Agatha Christie was a mathematician; both are abstract entities, both exist, but the first is true and the second is false. Rather than following Lewis, and identifying a proposition with the set of worlds in which a sentence expressing the proposition is true, the view in question instead identifies a possible world with a set of *propositions*: the propositions which would be true if the world in question were actual. Then we could say that a possible world where Agatha Christie is a mathematician is a set of propositions which contains the proposition that Agatha Christie is a mathematician.

This thought needs elaboration, for not every set of propositions forms a possible world. One thing is that the set must be comprehensive: it should specify not only how things are with Agatha Christie, but also how things are with everything else. So to form a possible world, a set of propositions is required to be maximal: for every proposition *p*, either *p* or its negation should be included in the set. Furthermore, a set including both the proposition that Agatha Christie was born in New York and that Agatha Christie was born in Madrid does not represent a possible world. So we should make sure that the propositions in the set are consistent. Consistency, however, is a modal notion: propositions are consistent when it is *possible* that they are true at the same time. Unlike in Lewis's theory, modal notions cannot be analysed in non-modal terms. Ersatz theories do have a lot to offer: they can explain what possible-world-talk is about, and then use possible worlds with a clear conscience to clarify modal claims and to display the logical form of modal arguments. What they cannot offer is a reductive account of modality; they have to take modality as primitive.

According to this ersatzist view, once we acknowledge that propositions exist, then sets of them—possible worlds—exist. But they are clearly different from our familiar world of concrete particulars—they are ersatz worlds. Alvin Plantinga's theory (see Chapter 26) is a version of ersatzism. Plantinga constructs his worlds from states of affairs, rather than propositions (though this may in the end be just a terminological variation from the proposition view, since he leaves open the question of whether states of affairs are the same as propositions or not). On Lewis's view, all worlds—including the non-actual ones—are concrete entities. By contrast, on Plantinga's view, all worlds—including the actual one—are abstract entities. This may sound a bit puzzling at first, for if abstract entities exist outside of space and time, how could the actual world be an abstract entity? We need to clarify the terminology. Call the world where we live *Our World*. This world, as we said, includes concrete particulars—us, atoms, etc.—and, according to those who believe in abstract entities, it includes also entities like states of affairs and propositions. Philosophers often call Our World the actual world, but Plantinga uses the term 'actual' in a different way. What he calls the 'actual world' is only a part of Our World; it is an abstract entity, a set of states of affairs. States of affairs are of two kinds: some obtain, and some do not. Plantinga calls states of affairs which obtain 'actual', and those which do not 'possible'. He insists, however, that both actual and possible states of affairs—being abstract entities—exist in the same way; they are part of Our World. (As we shall see, David Armstrong in Chapter 27 uses the term 'state of affairs' in a different way.) David Lewis, following the more usual terminology, puts this point by saying that although ersatz worlds are all *actual*—that is, as we might say, part of Our World—there is only one which is *actualized*.

Plantinga's conception of actuality is different from Lewis's in at least two ways. For Lewis, actuality is a relative property; each world is actual from its own point of view, and there is no more to actuality than this. Plantinga, in contrast, thinks that actuality is an absolute property, which is held only by one possible world. Furthermore, Plantinga would agree that only Our World exists; whereas Lewis denies this. Since, as we said, Our World is sometimes called the actual world, Plantinga is often characterized as an actualist: someone who thinks that actuality is an absolute property and that everything that exists is actual—that is, part of Our World. Plantinga himself describes the actualist view he is committed to as the claim that there are no non-existent objects (Chapter 26, § II). Again, we should be careful here, since in this sense, Lewis, at least on his own account, would also turn out to be an actualist—since he believes that all possible worlds exist—whereas on the usual understanding just mentioned, Lewis is opposed to actualism (see Lewis 1986b: 2.1).

The third theory, represented here by David Armstrong (Chapter 27), is *combinatorialism*. Armstrong defends Naturalism, which he understands as 'the doctrine that nothing at all exists except the single world of space and time' (Armstrong 1989a: 3) Armstrong's ontology is the most parsimonious so far: it excludes Lewis's plurality of concrete worlds, and also the abstract entities favoured by the proposition theory and by Plantinga. On Armstrong's view, possible worlds are combinations of the elements of the actual world. The world contains simple individuals and simple properties. Just when a simple object, a, has the simple property F, a's being F is an atomic state of affairs. States of affairs on this view are not abstract entities; and when *a* is not *G*, then the state of affairs *a*'s being *G* does not exist. (Hence the difference from Plantinga's terminology). However, the statement '*a* is *G*', though false, expresses a possibility: *a*'s being *G*. Any conjunction of such combinations, which makes use of all the simple individuals and simple properties is a possible world. Armstrong insists that by introducing possible states of affairs, no addition to the ontology of the space-time world is needed.

By offering a combinatorial analysis of possibility, Armstrong succeeds in doing what Lewis has done and the other ersatzers have not: he has given a reduction of modality in non-modal terms. In addition, the theory is much less ontologically costly than Lewis's. However, the success of the theory turns on whether it can answer two serious objections. First, the theory assumes that the simple properties are independent from each other; for suppose, contrary to this, that 'N' = 'having negative charge' and 'P' = 'having positive charge' are both simple properties; if we have unlimited recombination, then we cannot exclude the possible world which has both '*a* is P' and '*a* is N'. But this is not possible. If we tried to limit the acceptable recombinations to those which are *possible*, then we would be back where the other ersatzers were: short of a reductive theory of modality. Thus we must assume that having one simple property is not incompatible with having any other simple property; and the question is whether this assumption is plausible. The second problem, often raised in connection with the combinatorial theory, is that combinations do not allow possible worlds which include alien individuals or properties—that is, entities which do not exist in this world. (See Armstrong 1989*a*: chapter 4 for a discussion of these problems.)

Finally, let us say a few words about the problem of so called 'transworld identity', which emerges in connection with *de re* modal statements. Suppose we want to say *of* Agatha Christie that she could have been a mathematician. According to possible worlds theory, this is true if there is a possible world where *she*, Agatha Christie is a mathematician. This might raise the following question: *which* individual in that world is Agatha Christie—so that *her* being a mathematician makes the modal claim true? Kripke argues that this question is partly based on a confusion: for the point of *de re* claims is precisely that we can describe possible worlds in a way which assumes that the answer to this question is settled. This, however, is only part of a theory about *de re* modality: for various theories about possible worlds can agree that we can describe worlds in *de re* terms, yet they would give different answers to the question of what makes *de re* modal statements true.

It is plausible to assume that the actual Agatha Christie is an individual bound in our space and time. If this assumption is accepted, then the label 'transworld *identity*' turns out to be somewhat misleading: for on most theories of possible worlds, this space-time bound actual individual cannot be literally identical to a merely possible individual. On Lewis's theory, merely possible individuals exist in other space and time; none of those is identical to the actual Agatha Christie. Lewis thinks that Agatha Christie has *counterparts* in other possible worlds: individuals who resemble her in various respects. If one of Agatha Christie's counterparts is a mathematician, the claim that Agatha Christie could have been a mathematician is true. On abstract ersatz theories like Plantinga's, Agatha Christie exists in another possible world if the proposition or state of affairs that

Agatha Christie exists is a member of the set of propositions or states of affairs which make that world up. If it makes sense to talk about the possible Agatha Christie as an individual at all, it must be an abstract entity; and the actual concrete Agatha Christie can hardly be literally identical to it. Finally, on Armstrong's view, possible worlds are recombinations of simple objects and simple properties into possible states of affairs; but possible states of affairs do not exist, hence there is not anything existing to which the actual Agatha Christie could be identical.

Chapter 24

Selection from *Naming and Necessity*

Saul Kripke

. . . Philosophers have talked (and, of course, there has been considerable controversy in recent years over the meaningfulness of these notions) [about] various categories of truth, which are called '*a priori*', 'analytic', 'necessary'—and sometimes even 'certain' is thrown into this batch. The terms are often used as if *whether* there are things answering to these concepts is an interesting question, but we might as well regard them all as meaning the same thing. Now, everyone remembers Kant (a bit) as making the distinction between '*a priori*' and 'analytic'. So maybe this distinction is still made. In contemporary discussion very few people, if any, distinguish between the concepts of statements being *a priori* and their being necessary. At any rate I shall *not* use the terms '*a priori*' and 'necessary' interchangeably here.

Consider what the traditional characterizations of such terms as '*a priori*' and 'necessary' are. First the notion of a prioricity is a concept of epistemology. I guess the traditional characterization from Kant goes something like: *a priori* truths are those which can be known independently of any experience. This introduces another problem before we get off the ground, because there's another modality in the characterization of '*a priori*', namely, it is supposed to be something which *can* be known independently of any experience. That means that in some sense it's *possible* (whether we do or do not in fact know it independently of any experience) to know this independently of any experience. And possible for whom? For God? For the Martians? Or just for people with minds like ours? To make this all clear might [involve] a host of problems all of its own about what sort of possibility is in question here. It might be best therefore, instead of using the phrase '*a priori* truth', to the extent that one uses it at all, to stick to the question of whether a particular person or knower knows something *a priori* or believes it true on the basis of *a priori* evidence.

I won't go further too much into the problems that might arise with the notion of a prioricity here. I will say that some philosophers somehow change the modality in this characterization from *can* to *must*. They think that if something belongs to the realm of *a priori* knowledge, it couldn't possibly be known empirically. This is just a mistake. Something may belong in the realm of such statements that *can* be known *a priori* but still may be known by particular people on the basis experience. To give a really common sense example: anyone who has worked with a computing

Saul Kripke, selection from *Naming and Necessity* (Blackwell, 1981), reprinted with permission of Blackwell Publishing Ltd.

machine knows that the computing machine may give an answer to whether such and such a number is prime. No one has calculated or proved that the number is prime; but the machine has given the answer: this number is prime. We, then, if we believe that the number is prime, believe it on the basis of our knowledge of the laws of physics, the construction of the machine, and so on. We therefore do not believe this on the basis of purely *a priori* evidence. We believe it (if anything is *a posteriori* at all) on the basis of *a posteriori* evidence. Nevertheless, maybe this could be known *a priori* by someone who made the requisite calculations. So 'can be known *a priori*' doesn't mean '*must* be known *a priori*'.

The second concept which is in question is that of necessity. Sometimes this is used in an epistemological way and might then just mean *a priori*. And of course, sometimes it is used in a physical way when people distinguish between physical and logical necessity. But what I am concerned with here is a notion which is not a notion of epistemology but of metaphysics, in some (I hope) nonpejorative sense. We ask whether something might have been true, or might have been false. Well, if something is false, it's obviously not necessarily true. If it is true, might it have been otherwise? Is it possible that, in this respect, the world should have been different from the way it is? If the answer is 'no', then this fact about the world is a necessary one. If the answer is 'yes', then this fact about the world is a contingent one. This in and of itself has nothing to do with anyone's knowledge of anything. It's certainly a philosophical thesis, and not a matter of obvious definitional equivalence, either that everything *a priori* is necessary or that everything necessary is *a priori*. Both concepts may be vague. That may be another problem. But at any rate they are dealing with two different domains, two different areas, the epistemological and the metaphysical. Consider, say, Fermat's last theorem—or the Goldbach conjecture. The Goldbach conjecture says that an even number greater than 2 must be the sum of two prime numbers. If this is true, it is presumably necessary, and, if it is false, presumably necessarily false. We are taking the classical view of mathematics here and assume that in mathematical reality it is either true or false.

If the Goldbach conjecture is false, then there is an even number, n, greater than 2, such that for no primes p_1 and p_2, both $< n$, does $n = p_1 + p_2$. This fact about n, if true, is verifiable by direct computation, and thus is necessary if the results of arithmetical computations are necessary. On the other hand, if the conjecture is true, then every even number exceeding 2 is the sum of two primes. Could it then be the case that, although in fact every such even number is the sum of two primes, there might have been such an even number which was not the sum of two primes? What would that mean? Such a number would have to be one of, 4, 6, 8, 10, . . .; and, by hypothesis, since we are assuming Goldbach's conjecture to be true, each of these can be shown, again by direct computation, to be the sum of two primes. Goldbach's conjecture, then, cannot be contingently true or false; whatever truth-value it has belongs to it by necessity.

But what we can say, of course, is that right now, as far as we know, the question can come out either way. So, in the absence of mathematical proof deciding this question, none of us has any *a priori* knowledge about this question in either direction. We don't know whether Goldbach's conjecture is true or false. So right now we certainly don't know anything *a priori* about it.

Perhaps it will be alleged that we *can* in principle know *a priori* whether it is true. Well, maybe we can. Of course an infinite mind which can search through all the numbers can or could. But I don't know whether a finite mind can or could. Maybe there just is no mathematical proof whatsoever which decides the conjecture. At any rate this might or might not be the case. Maybe there is a mathematical proof deciding this question; maybe every mathematical question is decidable by an intuitive proof or disproof. Hilbert thought so; others have thought not; still others have thought the question unintelligible unless the notion of intuitive proof is replaced by that of formal proof in a single system. Certainly no one formal system decides all mathematical question, as we know from Gödel. At any rate, and this is the important thing, the question is not trivial; even though someone said that it's necessary, if true at all, that every number is the sum of two primes, it doesn't follow that anyone knows anything *a priori* about it. It doesn't even seem to me to follow without some further philosophical argument (it is an interesting philosophical question) that anyone *could* know anything a *a priori* about it. The 'could', as I said, involves some other modality. We mean that even if no one, perhaps even in the future, knows or will know *a priori* whether Goldbach's conjecture is right, in principle there is a way, which *could* have been used, of answering the question *a priori*. This assertion is not trivial.

The terms 'necessary' and '*a priori*', then, as applied to statements, are *not* obvious synonyms. There may be a philosophical argument connecting them, perhaps even identifying them; but an argument is required, not simply the observation that the two terms are clearly interchangeable. (I will argue below that in fact they are not even coextensive—that necessary *a posteriori* truths, and probably contingent *a priori* truths, both exist.)

I think people have thought that these two things must mean the same for these reasons:

First, if something not only happens to be true in the actual world but is also true in all possible worlds, then, of course, just by running through all the possible worlds in our heads, we ought to be able with enough effort to see, if a statement is necessary, that it is necessary, and thus know it *a priori*. But really this is not so obviously feasible at all.

Second, I guess it's thought that, conversely, if something is known *a priori* it must be necessary, because it was known without looking at the world. If it depended on some contingent feature of the actual world, how could you know it without looking? Maybe the actual world is one of the possible worlds in which it would have been false. This depends on the thesis that there can't be a way of knowing about the actual world without looking that wouldn't be a way of knowing the same thing about every possible world. This involves problems of epistemology and the nature of knowledge; and of course it is very vague as stated. But it is not really *trivial* either. More important than any particular example of something which is alleged to be necessary and not *a priori* or *a priori* and not necessary, is to see that the notions are different, that it's not trivial to argue on the basis of something's being something which maybe we can only know *a posteriori*, that it's not a necessary truth. It's not trivial, just because something is known in some sense *a priori*, that what is known is a necessary truth.

Another term used in philosophy is 'analytic', Here it won't be too important to get any clearer about this in this talk. The common examples of analytic statements, nowadays, are like 'bachelors are unmarried'. Kant (someone just pointed out to me) gives as an example 'gold is a yellow metal', which seems to me an extraordinary one, because it's something I think that can turn out to be false. At any rate, let's just make it a matter of stipulation that an analytic statement is, in some sense, true by virtue of its meaning and true in all possible worlds by virtue of its meaning. Then something which is analytically true will be both necessary and *a priori*. (That's sort of stipulative.)

Another category I mentioned was that of certainty. Whatever certainty is, it's clearly not obviously the case that everything which is necessary is certain. Certainty is another epistemological notion. Something can be known, or at least rationally believed, *a priori*, without being quite certain. You've read a proof in the math book; and, though you think it's correct, maybe you've made a mistake. You often do make mistakes of this kind. You've made a computation, perhaps with an error.

There is one more question I want to go into in a preliminary way. Some philosophers have distinguished between essentialism, the belief in modality *de re*, and a mere advocacy of necessity, the belief in modality *de dicto*. Now, some people say: Let's *give* you the concept of necessity.[1] A much worse thing, something creating great additional problems, is whether we can say of any particular that it has necessary or contingent properties, even make the distinction between necessary and contingent properties. Look, it's only a *statement* or a *state of affairs* that can be either necessary or contingent! Whether a *particular* necessarily or contingently has a certain property depends on the way it's described. This is perhaps closely related to the view that the way we refer to particular things is by a description. What is Quine's famous example? If we consider the number 9, does it have the property of necessary oddness? Has that number got to be odd in all possible worlds? Certainly it's true in all possible worlds, let's say, it couldn't have been otherwise, that *nine* is odd. Of course, 9 could also be equally well picked out as *the number of planets*. It is

---

1. By the way, it's a common attitude in philosophy to think that one shouldn't introduce a notion until it's been rigorously defined (according to some popular notion of rigor). Here I am just dealing with an intuitive notion and will keep on the level of an intuitive notion. That is, we think that some things, though they are in fact the case, might have been otherwise. I might not have given these lectures today. If that's right, then it is *possible* that I wouldn't have given these lectures today. Quite a different question is the epistemological question, how any particular person knows that I gave these lectures today. I suppose in that case he does know this is *a posteriori*. But, if someone were born with an innate belief that I was going to give these lectures today, who knows? Right now, anyway, let's suppose that people know this *a posteriori*. At any rate, the two questions being asked are different.

not necessary, not true in all possible worlds, that the number of planets is odd. For example if there had been eight planets, the number of planets would not have been odd. And so it's thought: Was it necessary or contingent that Nixon won the election? (It might seem contingent, unless one has some view of some inexorable processes. . . .) But this is a contingent property of Nixon only relative to our referring to him as 'Nixon' (assuming 'Nixon' doesn't mean 'the man who won the election at such and such a time'). But if we designate Nixon as 'the man who won the election in 1968', then it will be a necessary truth, of course, that the man who won the election in 1968, won the election in 1968. Similarly, whether an object has the same property in all possible worlds depends not just on the object itself, but on how it is described. So it's argued.

It is even suggested in the literature, that though a notion of necessity may have some sort of intuition behind it (we do think some things could have been otherwise; other things we don't think could have been otherwise), this notion [of a distinction between necessary and contingent properties] is just a doctrine made up by some bad philosopher, who (I guess) didn't realize that there are several ways of referring to the same thing. I don't know if some philosophers have not realized this; but at any rate it is very far from being true that this idea [that a property can meaningfully be held to be essential or accidental to an object independently of its description] is a notion which has no intuitive content, which means nothing to the ordinary man. Suppose that someone said, pointing to Nixon, 'That's the guy who might have lost'. Someone else says 'Oh no, if you describe him as "Nixon", then he might have lost; but, of course, describing him as the winner, then it is not true that he might have lost'. Now which one is being the philosopher, here, the unintuitive man? It seems to me obviously to be the second. The second man has a philosophical theory. The first man would say, and with great conviction, 'Well, of course, the winner of the election *might have been someone else.* The actual winner, had the course of the campaign been different, might have been the loser, and someone else the winner; or there might have been no election at all. So, such terms as "the winner" and "the loser" don't designate the same objects in all possible worlds. On the other hand, the term "Nixon" is just a *name* of *this man'.* When you ask whether it is necessary or contingent that *Nixon* won the election, you are asking the intuitive question whether in some counterfactual situation, *this man* would in fact have lost the election. If someone thinks that the notion of a necessary or contingent property (forget whether there *are* any nontrivial necessary properties [and consider] just the *meaningfulness* of the notion[2]) is a philosopher's notion with no intuitive content, he is wrong.

2. The example I gave asserts a certain property—electoral victory—to be *accidental* to Nixon, independently of how he is described. Of course, if the notion of accidental property is meaningful, the notion of essential property must be meaningful also. This is not to say that there *are* any essential properties—though, in fact, I think there are. The usual argument questions the *meaningfulness* of essentialism, and says that whether a property is accidental or essential to an object depends on how it is described. It is thus *not* the view that all properties are accidental. Of course, it is also not the view, held by some idealists, that all properties are essential, all relations internal.

Of course, some philosophers think that something's having intuitive content is very inconclusive evidence in favor of it. I think it is very heavy evidence in favor of any-thing, myself. I really don't know, in a way, what more conclusive evidence one can have about anything, ultimately speaking. But, in any event, people who think the notion of accidental property unintuitive have intuition reversed, I think.

Why have they thought this? While there are many motivations for people thinking this, one is this: The question of essential properties so-called is supposed to be equiva-lent (and it is equivalent) to the question of 'identity across possible worlds'. Suppose we have someone, Nixon, and there's another possible world where there is no one with all the properties Nixon has in the actual world. Which one of these other people, if any, is Nixon? Surely you must give some criterion of identity here! If you have a criterion of identity, then you just look in the other possible worlds at the man who is Nixon; and the question whether, in that other possible world, Nixon has certain prop-erties, is well defined. It is also supposed to be well defined, in terms of such notions, whether it's true in all possible worlds, or there are some possible worlds in which Nixon didn't win the election. But, it's said, the problems of giving such criteria of identity are very difficult. Sometimes in the case of numbers it might seem easier (but even here it's argued that it's quite arbitrary). For example, one might say, and this is surely the truth, that if position in the series of numbers is what makes the number 9 what it is, then if (in another world) the number of planets had been 8, the number of planets would be a different number from the one it actually is. You wouldn't say that that number then is to be identified with our number 9 in this world. In the case of other types of objects, say people, material objects, things like that, has anyone given a set of necessary and sufficient conditions for identity across possible worlds?

Really, adequate, necessary and sufficient conditions for identity which do not beg the question are very rare in any case. Mathematics is the only case I really know of where they are given even *within* a possible world, to tell the truth. I don't know of such conditions for identity of material objects over time, or for people. Everyone knows what a problem this is. But, let's forget about that. What seems to be more objectionable is that this depends on the wrong way of looking at what a possible world is. One thinks, in this picture, of a possible world as if it were like a foreign country. One looks upon it as an observer. Maybe Nixon has moved to the other country and maybe he hasn't, but one is given only qualities. One can observe all his qualities, but, of course, one doesn't observe that someone is Nixon. One observes that something has red hair (or green or yellow) but not whether something is Nixon. So we had better have a way of telling in terms of properties when we run into the same thing as we saw before; we had better have a way of telling, when we come across one of these other possible worlds, who was Nixon.

Some logicians in their formal treatment of modal logic may encourage this picture. A prominent example, perhaps, is myself. Nevertheless, intuitively speaking, it seems to me not to be the right way of thinking about the possible worlds. A pos-sible world isn't a distant country that we are coming across, or viewing through a telescope. Generally speaking, another possible world is too far away. Even if we travel faster than light, we won't get to it. A possible world is *given by the descriptive conditions we associate with it.* What do we mean when we say 'In some other possible world I would not have given this lecture today?' We just imagine the situation where I didn't decide to give this lecture or decided to give it on some other day. Of course, we don't imagine everything that is true or false, but only those things relevant to my giving the lecture; but, in theory, everything needs to be decided to make a total description of the world. We can't really imagine that except in part; that, then, is a 'possible world'. Why can't it be part of the *description* of a possible world that it contains *Nixon* and that in that world *Nixon* didn't win the election? It might be a question, of course, whether such a world *is* possible. (Here it would seem, *prima facie*, to be clearly possible.) But, once we see that such a situation is possible, then we are given that the man who might have lost the election or did lose the election in this possible world is Nixon, because that's part of the description of the world. 'Possible worlds' are *stipulated*, not *discovered* by powerful telescopes. There is no reason why we cannot *stipulate* that, in talking about what would have happened to Nixon in a certain counterfactual situation, we are talking about what would have happened to *him*.

Of course, if someone makes the demand that every possible world has to be described in a purely qualitative way, we can't say, 'Suppose Nixon had lost the election', we must say, instead, something like, 'Suppose a man with a dog named Checkers, who looks like a certain David Frye impersonation, is in a certain possible world and loses the election.' Well, does he resemble Nixon enough to be identified with Nixon? A very explicit and blatant example of this way of looking at things is David Lewis's counterpart theory,[3] but the literature on quantified modality is

---

3. David K. Lewis, 'Counterpart Theory and Quantified Modal Logic', *Journal of Philosophy* 65 (1968), 113–126. Lewis's elegant paper also suffers from a purely formal difficulty: on his interpretation of quantified modality, the familiar law $(y)((x)A(x) \supset A(y))$ fails, if $A(x)$ is allowed to contain modal operators. (For example, $(\exists y)((x) \Diamond (x \neq y))$ is satisfiable but $(\exists y) \Diamond (y \neq y)$ is not.) Since Lewis's formal model follows rather naturally from his philosophical views on counterparts, and since the failure of universal instantiation for modal properties is intuitively bizarre, it seems to me that this failure constitutes an additional argument against the plausibility of his philosophical views. There are other, lesser, formal difficulties as well. I cannot elaborate here.

   Strictly speaking, Lewis's view is not a view of 'transworld identification'. Rather, he thinks that similarities across possible worlds determine a counterpart relation which need be neither symmetric nor transitive. The counterpart of something in another possible world is *never* identical with the thing itself. Thus, if we say 'Humphrey might have won the election (if only he had done such-and-such), we are not talking about something that might have happened to *Humphrey* but to someone else, a "counterpart".' Probably, however, Humphrey could not care less whether someone *else*, no matter how much resembling him, would have been victorious in another possible world. Thus, Lewis's view seems to me even more bizarre than the usual notions of transworld identification that it replaces. The important issues, however, are common to the two views: the supposition that other possible worlds are like other dimensions of a more inclusive universe, that they can be given only by purely qualitative descriptions, and that therefore either the identity relation or the counterpart relation must be established in terms of qualitative resemblance.

   Many have pointed out to me that the father of counterpart theory is probably Leibnitz. I will not go into such a historical question here. It would also be interesting to compare Lewis's views with the Wheeler-Everett interpretation of quantum mechanics. I suspect that this view of physics may suffer from philosophical problems analogous to Lewis's counterpart theory; it is certainly very similar in spirit.

replete with it.[4] Why need we make this demand? That is not the way we ordinarily think of counterfactual situations. We just say 'suppose this man had lost'. It is *given* that the possible world contains *this man*, and that in that world, he had lost. There may be a problem about what intuitions about possibility come to. But, if we have such an intuition about the possibility of *that* (*this man's* electoral loss), then it is about the possibility of *that*. It need not be identified with the possibility of a man looking like such and such, or holding such and such political views, or otherwise qualitatively described, having lost. We can point to the *man*, and ask what might have happened to *him*, had events been different.

It might be said 'Let's suppose that this is true. It comes down to the same thing, because whether Nixon could have had certain properties, different from the ones he actually has, is equivalent to the question whether the criteria of identity across possible worlds include that Nixon does not have these properties'. But it doesn't really come to the same thing, because the usual notion of a criterion of transworld identity demands that we give purely qualitative necessary and sufficient conditions for someone being Nixon. If we can't imagine a possible world in which Nixon doesn't have a certain property, then it's a necessary condition of someone being Nixon. Or a necessary property of Nixon that he [has] that property. For example, supposing Nixon is in fact a human being, it would seem that we cannot think of a possible counterfactual situation in which he was, say, an inanimate object; perhaps it is not even possible for him not to have been a human being. Then it will be a necessary fact about Nixon that in all possible worlds where he exists at all, he is human or anyway he is not an inanimate object. This has nothing to do with any requirement that there be purely qualitative *sufficient* conditions for Nixonhood which we can spell out. And should there be? Maybe there is some argument that there should be, but we can consider these questions about *necessary* conditions without going into any question about *sufficient* conditions. Further, even if there were a purely qualitative set of necessary and sufficient conditions for being Nixon, the view I advocate would not demand that we find these conditions *before* we can ask whether Nixon might have won the election, nor does it demand that we restate the question in terms of such conditions. We can simply consider *Nixon* and ask what might have happened to *him* had various circumstances been different. So the two views, the two ways of looking at things, do seem to me to make a difference.

Notice this question, whether Nixon could not have been a human being, is a clear case where the question asked is not epistemological. Suppose Nixon actually turned out to be an automaton. That might happen. We might need evidence whether Nixon is a human being or an automaton. But that is a question about our knowledge. The question of whether Nixon might have not been a human being, given that he is one, is not a question about knowledge, *a posteriori* or *a priori*. It's

---

4. Another *locus classicus* of the views I am criticizing, with more philosophical exposition than Lewis's paper, is a paper by David Kaplan on transworld identification. Unfortunately, this paper has never been published. It does not represent Kaplan's present position.

a question about, even though such and such things are the case, what might have been the case otherwise.

This table is composed of molecules. Might it not have been composed of molecules? Certainly it was a scientific discovery of great moment that it was composed of molecules (or atoms). But could anything be this very object and not be composed of molecules? Certainly there is some feeling that the answer to that must be 'no'. At any rate, it's hard to imagine under what circumstances you would have this very object and find that it is not composed of molecules. A quite different question is whether it is in fact composed of molecules in the actual world and how we know this. (I will go into more detail about these questions about essence later on.)

I wish at this point to introduce something which I need in the methodology of discussing the theory of names that I'm talking about. We need the notion of 'identity across possible worlds' as it's usually and, as I think, somewhat misleadingly called,[5] to explicate one distinction that I want to make now. What's the difference between asking whether it's necessary that 9 is greater than 7 or whether it's necessary that the number of planets is greater than 7? Why does one show anything more abut essence than the other? The answer to this might be intuitively 'Well, look, the number of planets might have been different from what it in fact is. It doesn't make any sense, though, to say that nine might have been different from what it in fact is'. Let's use some terms quasi-technically. Let's call something a *rigid designator* if in every possible world it designates the same object, a *nonrigid* or *accidental designator* if that is not the case. Of course we don't require that the objects exist in all possible worlds. Certainly, Nixon might not have existed if his parents had not gotten married, in the normal course of things. When we think of a property as essential to an object we usually mean that it is true of that object in any case where it would have existed. A rigid designator of a necessary existent can be called *strongly rigid*.

One of the intuitive theses I will maintain in these talks is that *names* are rigid designators. Certainly they seem to satisfy the intuitive test mentioned above: although someone other than the U.S. President in 1970 might have been the U.S. President in 1970 (e.g., Humphrey might have), no one other than Nixon might have been Nixon. In the same way, a designator rigidly designates a certain object if it designates that object wherever the object exists; if, in addition, the object is a necessary existent, the designator can be called *strongly rigid*. For example, 'the President of the U.S. in 1970' designates a certain man, Nixon; but someone else

5. Misleadingly, because the phrase suggests that there is a special problem of 'transworld identifica- tion', that we cannot trivially stipulate whom or what we are talking about when we imagine another possible world. The term 'possible world' may also mislead; perhaps it suggests the 'foreign country' picture. I have sometimes used 'counterfactual situation' in the text; Michael Slote has suggested that 'possible state (or history) of the world' might be less misleading than 'possible world'. It is better still, to avoid confusion, not to say, 'In some possible world, Humphrey would have won' but rather, simply, 'Humphrey might have won'. The apparatus of possible words has (I hope) been very useful as far as the set-theoretic model-theory of quantified modal logic is concerned, but has encouraged philosophical pseudo-problems and misleading pictures.

(e.g., Humphrey) might have been the President in 1970, and Nixon might not have; so this designator is not rigid.

In these lectures, I will argue, intuitively, that proper names are rigid designators, for although the man (Nixon) might not have been the President, it is not the case that he might not have been Nixon (though he might not have been *called* 'Nixon'). Those who have argued that to make sense of the notion of rigid designator, we must antecedently make sense of 'criteria of transworld identity' have precisely reversed the cart and the horse; it is *because* we can refer (rigidly) to Nixon, and stipulate that we are speaking of what might have happened to *him* (under certain circumstances), that 'transworld identifications' are unproblematic in such cases.[6]

The tendency to demand purely qualitative descriptions of counterfactual situations has many sources. One, perhaps, is the confusion of the epistemological and the metaphysical, between a prioricity and necessity. If someone identifies necessity with a prioricity, and thinks that objects are named by means of uniquely identifying properties, he may think that it is the properties used to identify the object which, being known about it *a priori*, must be used to identify it in all possible worlds, to find out which object is Nixon. As against this, I repeat: (1) Generally, things aren't 'found out' about a counterfactual situation, they are stipulated; (2) possible worlds need not be given purely qualitatively, as if we were looking at them through a telescope. And we will see shortly that the properties an object has in every counterfactual world have nothing to do with properties used to identify it in the actual world.[7]

Does the 'problem' of 'transworld identification' make any sense? Is it *simply* a pseudo-problem? The following, it seems to me, can be said for it. Although the statement that England fought Germany in 1943 perhaps cannot be *reduced* to any statement about individuals, nevertheless in some sense it is not a fact 'over and above' the collection of all facts about persons, and their behavior over history. The sense in which facts about nations are not facts 'over and above' those about persons can be expressed in the observation that a description of the world mentioning all facts about persons but omitting those about nations can be a *complete* description of the world, from which the facts about nations follow. Similarly, perhaps, facts about material objects are not facts 'over and above' facts about their constituent molecules. We may then ask, given a description of a non-actualized possible situation in terms of people, whether England still exists in that situation, or whether a certain nation (described, say, as the one where Jones lives) which would exist in that situation, is England. Similarly, given certain counterfactual vicissitudes in the history of the molecules of a table, *T*, one may ask whether *T* would exist, in that

6. Of course I don't imply that language contains a name for every object. Demonstratives can be used as rigid designators, and free variables can be used as rigid designators of unspecified objects. Of course when we specify a counterfactual situation, we do not describe the whole possible world, but only the portion which interests us.

7. See *Naming and Necessity* Lecture I, p. 53 (on Nixon), and Lecture II, pp. 74–7.

situation, or whether a certain bunch of molecules, which in that situation would constitute a table, constitute the very same table *T*. In each case, we seek criteria of identity across possible worlds for certain particulars in terms of those for other, more 'basic', particulars. If statements about nations (or tribes) are not *reducible* to those about other more 'basic' constituents, if there is some 'open texture' in the relationship between them, we can hardly expect to give hard and fast identity criteria; nevertheless, in concrete cases we may be able to answer whether a certain bunch of molecules would still constitute *T*, though in some cases the answer may be indeterminate. I think similar remarks apply to the problem of identity over time; here too we are usually concerned with determinacy, the identity of a 'complex' particular in terms of more 'basic' ones. (For example, if various parts of a table are replaced, is it the same object?[8])

Such a conception of 'transworld identification', however, differs considerably from the usual one. First, although we can try to describe the world in terms of molecules, there is no impropriety in describing it in terms of grosser entities: the statement that *this table* might have been placed in another room is perfectly proper, in and of itself. We *need* not use the description in terms of molecules, or even grosser parts of the table, though we *may*. Unless we assume that some particulars are 'ultimate', 'basic' particulars, no type of description need be regarded as privileged. We can ask whether *Nixon* might have lost the election without further subtlety, and usually no further subtlety is required. Second, it is not assumed that necessary and sufficient conditions for what kinds of collections of molecules make up this table are possible; this fact I just mentioned. Third, the attempted notion deals with criteria of identity of particulars in terms of other *particulars*, not qualities. I can refer to the table before me, and ask what might have happened to it under certain circumstances; I can also refer to its molecules. If, one the other hand, it is demanded that I describe each counterfactual situation purely qualitatively, then I can only ask whether *a table*, of such and such color, and so on, would have certain properties; whether the table in question would be *this table*, table *T*, is indeed moot, since all reference to objects, as opposed to qualities, has disappeared. It is often said that, if a counterfactual situation is described as one which would have happened to *Nixon*, and if it is not assumed that such a description is reducible to

---

8. There is some vagueness here. If a chip, or molecule, of a given table had been replaced by another one, we would be content to say that we have the same table. But if too many chips were different, we would seem to have a different one. The same problem can, of course, arise for identity over time.

   Where the identity relation is vague, it may seem intransitive; a chain of apparent identities may yield an apparent non-identity. Some sort of 'counter-part' notion (though not with Lewis's philosophical underpinnings of resemblance, foreign country worlds, etc.), may have some utility here. One could say that strict identity applies only to the particulars (the molecules), and the counterpart relation to the particulars 'composed' of them, the tables. The counterpart relation can then be declared to be vague and intransitive. It seems, however, utopian to suppose that we will ever reach a level of ultimate, basic particulars for which identity relations are never vague and the danger of intransitivity is eliminated. The danger usually does not arise in practice, so we ordinarily can speak simply of identity without worry. Logicians have not developed a logic of vagueness.

a purely qualitative one, then mysterious 'bare particulars' are assumed, property-less substrata underlying the qualities. This is not so: I think that Nixon is a Republican, not merely that he lies in back of Republicanism, whatever that means; I also think he might have been a Democrat. The same holds for any other properties Nixon may possess, except that some of these properties may be essential. What I do deny is that a particular is nothing but a 'bundle of qualities', whatever that may mean. If a quality is an abstract object, a bundle of qualities is an object of an even higher degree of abstraction, not a particular. Philosophers have come to the opposite view through a false dilemma: they have asked, are these objects *behind* the bundle of qualities, or is the object *nothing but* the bundle? Neither is the case; this table is wooden, brown, in the room, etc. It has all these properties and is not a thing without properties, behind them; but it should not therefore be identified with the set, or 'bundle', of its properties, nor with the subset of its essential properties. Don't ask: how can I identify this table in another possible world, except by its properties? I have the table in my hands, I can point to it, and when I ask whether *it* might have been in another room, I am talking, by definition, about *it*. I don't have to identify it after seeing it through a telescope. If I am talking about it, I am talking about *it*, in the same way as when I say that our hands might have been painted green, I have stipulated that I am talking about greenness. Some properties of an object may be essential to it, in that it could not have failed to have them. But these properties are not used to identify the object in another possible world, for such an identification is not needed. Nor need the essential properties of an object be the properties used to identify it in the actual world, if indeed it is identified in the actual world by means of properties (I have up to now left the question open).

So: the question of transworld identification makes *some* sense, in terms of asking about the identity of an object *via* questions about its component parts. But these parts are not qualities, and it is not an object resembling the given one which is in question. Theorists have often said that we identify objects across possible worlds as objects resembling the given one in the most important respects. On the contrary, Nixon, had he decided to act otherwise, might have avoided politics like the plague, though privately harboring radical opinions. Most important, even when we *can* replace questions about an object by questions about its parts, we *need* not do so. We can refer to the object and ask what might have happened to *it*. So, we do not begin with worlds (which are supposed somehow to be real, and whose qualities, but not whose objects, are perceptible to us), and then ask about criteria of transworld identification; on the contrary, we begin with the objects, which we *have*, and can identify, in the actual world. We can then ask whether certain things might have been true of the objects.

. . .

I think the next topic I shall want to talk about is that of statements of identity. Are these necessary or contingent? The matter has been in some dispute in recent philosophy. First, everyone agrees that descriptions can be used to make contingent identity statements. If it is true that the man who invented bifocals was the first

Postmaster General of the United States—that these were one and the same—it's contingently true. That is, it might have been the case that one man invented bifocals and another was the first Postmaster General of the United States. So certainly when you make identity statements using descriptions—when you say 'the x such that φx and the x such that ψx are one and the same'—that can be a contingent fact. But philosophers have been interested also in the question of identity statements between names. When we say 'Hesperus is Phosphorus' or 'Cicero is Tully', is what we are saying necessary or contingent? Further, they've been interested in another type of identity statement, which comes from scientific theory. We identify, for example, light with electromagnetic radiation between certain limits of wavelengths, or with a stream of photons. We identify heat with the motion of molecules; sound with a certain sort of wave disturbance in the air; and so on. Concerning such statements the following thesis is commonly held. First, that these are obviously contingent identities: we've found out that light is a stream of photons, but of course it might not have been a stream of photons. Heat is in fact the motion of molecules; we found that out, but heat might not have been the motion of molecules. Secondly, many philosophers feel damned lucky that these examples are around. Now, why? These philosophers, whose views are expounded in a vast literature, hold to a thesis called 'the identity thesis' with respect to some psychological concepts. They think, say, that pain is just a certain material state of the brain or of the body, or what have you—say the stimulation of C-fibers. (It doesn't matter what.) Some people have then objected, 'Well, look, there's perhaps a *correlation* between pain and these states of the body; but this must just be a contingent correlation between two different things, because it was an empirical discovery that this correlation ever held. Therefore, by "pain" we must mean something different from this state of the body or brain; and, therefore, they must be two different things.'

Then it's said, 'Ah, but you see, this is wrong! Everyone knows that there can be contingent identities.' First, as in the bifocals and Postmaster General case, which I have mentioned before. Second, in the case, believed closer to the present paradigm, of theoretical identifications, such as light and a stream of photons, or water and a certain compound of hydrogen and oxygen. These are all contingent identities. They might have been false. It's no surprise, therefore, that it can be true as a matter of contingent fact and not of any necessity that feeling pain, or seeing red, is just a certain state of the human body. Such psychophysical identifications can be contingent facts just as the other identities are contingent facts. And of course there are widespread motivations—ideological, or just not wanting to have the 'nomological dangler' of mysterious connections not accounted for by the laws of physics, one to one correlations between two different kinds of thing, material states, and things of an entirely different kind, which lead people to want to believe this thesis.

I guess the main thing I'll talk about first is identity statements between names. But I hold the following about the general case. First, that characteristic theoretical identifications like 'Heat is the motion of molecules', are not contingent truths but necessary truths, and here of course I don't mean just physically necessary, but necessary in the highest degree—whatever that means. (Physical necessity *might* turn out to be necessity in the highest degree. But that's a question which I don't wish to prejudge. At least for this sort of example, it might be that when something's physically necessary, it always is necessary *tout court*.) Second, that the way in which these have turned out to be necessary truths does not seem to me to be a way in which the mind-brain identities could turn out to be either necessary or contingently true. So this analogy has to go. It's hard to see what to put in its place. It's hard to see therefore how to avoid concluding that the two are actually different.

Let me go back to the more mundane case about proper names. This is already mysterious enough. There's a dispute about this between Quine and Ruth Barcan Marcus.[9] Marcus says that identities between names are necessary. If someone thinks that Cicero is Tully, and really uses 'Cicero' and 'Tully' as names, he is thereby committed to holding that his belief is a necessary truth. She uses the term 'mere tag'. Quine replies as follows, 'We may tag the planet Venus, some fine evening, with the proper name "Hesperus". We may tag the same planet again, some day before sunrise, with the proper name "Phosphorus". When we discover that we have tagged the same planet twice our discovery is empirical. And not because the proper names were descriptions.'[10] First, as Quine says when we discovered that we tagged the same planet twice, our discovery was empirical. Another example I think Quine gives in another book is that the same mountain seen from Nepal and from Tibet, or something like that, is from one angle called 'Mt. Everest' (you've heard of that); from another it's supposed to be called 'Gaurisanker'. It can actually be an empirical discovery that Gaurisanker is Everest. (Quine says that the example is actually false. He got the example from Erwin Schrödinger. You wouldn't think the inventor of wave mechanics got things that wrong. I don't know where the mistake is supposed to come from. One could certainly imagine this situation as having been the case; and it's another good illustration of the sort of thing that Quine has in mind.)

What about it? I wanted to find a good quote on the other side from Marcus in this book but I am having trouble locating one. Being present at that discussion, I remember[11] that she advocated the view that if you really have names, a good dictionary should be able to tell you whether they have the same reference. So someone should be able, by looking in the dictionary, to say that Hesperus and Phosphorus are the same. Now this does not seem to be true. It does seem, to many people, to be a consequence of the view that identities between names are necessary. Therefore the view that identity statements between names are necessary has usually been rejected. Russell's conclusion was somewhat different. He did think there should never be any empirical question whether two names have the same reference. This isn't satisfied for ordinary names, but it is satisfied when you're naming your own sense datum, or

9. Ruth Barcan Marcus, 'Modalities and Intensional Languages' (comments by W. V. Quine, plus discussion), *Boston Studies in the Philosophy of Science*, volume I, Reidel, Dordrecht, Holland, 1963, pp. 77–116.

10. p. 101.

11. p. 115.

something like that. You say, 'Here, this, and that (designating the same sense datum by both demonstratives).' So you can tell without empirical investigation that you're naming the same thing twice; the conditions are satisfied. Since this won't apply to ordinary cases of naming, ordinary 'names' cannot be genuine names.

What should we think about this? First, it's true that someone can use the name 'Cicero' to refer to Cicero and the name 'Tully' to refer to Cicero also, and not know that Cicero is Tully. So it seems that we do not necessarily know *a priori* that an identity statement between names is true. It doesn't follow from this that the statement so expressed is a contingent one if true. This is what I've emphasized in my first lecture. There is a very strong feeling that leads one to think that, if you can't know something by *a priori* ratiocination, then it's got to be contingent: it might have turned out otherwise; but nevertheless I think this feeling is wrong.

Let's suppose we refer to the same heavenly body twice, as 'Hesperus' and 'Phosphorus'. We say: Hesperus is that star over there in the evening; Phosphorus is that star over there in the morning. Actually, Hesperus is Phosphorus. Are there really circumstances under which Hesperus wouldn't have been Phosphorus? Supposing that Hesperus is Phosphorus, let's try to describe a possible situation in which it would not have been. Well, it's easy. Someone goes by and he calls two *different* stars 'Hesperus' and 'Phosphorus'. It may even be under the same conditions as prevailed when we introduced the names 'Hesperus' and 'Phosphorus'. But are those circumstances in which Hesperus is not Phosphorus or would not have been Phosphorus? It seems to me that they are not.

Now, of course I'm committed to saying that they're not, by saying that such terms as 'Hesperus' and 'Phosphorus', when used as names, are rigid designators. They refer in every possible world to the planet Venus. Therefore, in that possible world too, the planet Venus is the planet Venus and it doesn't matter what any other person has said in this other possible world. How should *we* describe this situation? He can't have pointed to Venus twice, and in the one case called it 'Hesperus' and in the other 'Phosphorus', as we did. If he did so, then 'Hesperus is Phosphorus' would have been true in that situation too. He pointed maybe neither time to the planet Venus—at least one time he didn't point to the planet Venus, let's say when he pointed to the body he called 'Phosphorus'. Then in that case we can certainly say that the name 'Phosphorus' might not have referred to Phosphorus. We can even say that in the very position when viewed in the morning that we found Phosphorus, it might have been the case that Phosphorus was not there—that something else was there, and that even, under certain circumstances it would have been *called* 'Phosphorus'. But that still is not a case in which Phosphorus was not Hesperus. There might be a possible world in which, a possible counterfactual situation in which, 'Hesperus' and 'Phosphorus' weren't names of the things they in fact are names of. Someone, if he did determine their reference by identifying descriptions, might even have used the very identifying descriptions we used. But still that's not a case in which Hesperus wasn't Phosphorus. For there couldn't have been such a case, given that Hesperus is Phosphorus.

Now this seems very strange because in advance, we are inclined to say, the answer to the question whether Hesperus is Phosphorus might have turned out either way. So aren't there really two possible worlds—one in which Hesperus was Phosphorus, the other in which Hesperus wasn't Phosphorus—in advance of our discovering that these were the same? First, there's one sense in which things might turn out either way, in which it's clear that that doesn't imply that the way it finally turns out isn't necessary. For example, the four color theorem might turn out to be true and might turn out to be false. It might turn out either way. It still doesn't mean that the way it turns out is not necessary. Obviously, the 'might' here is purely 'epistemic'—it merely expresses our present state of ignorance, or uncertainty.

But it seems that in the Hesperus–Phosphorus case, something even stronger is true. The evidence I have before I know that Hesperus is Phosphorus is that I see a certain star or a certain heavenly body in the evening and call it 'Hesperus', and in the morning and call it 'Phosphorus'. I know these things. There certainly is a possible world in which a man should have seen a certain star at a certain position in the evening and called it 'Hesperus' and a certain star in the morning and called it 'Phosphorus'; and should have concluded—should have found out by empirical investigation—that he names two different stars, or two different heavenly bodies. At lease one of these stars or heavenly bodies was not Phosphorus; otherwise it couldn't have come out that way. But that's true. And so it's true that given the evidence that someone has antecedent to his empirical investigation, he can be placed in a sense in exactly the same situation, that is a qualitatively identical epistemic situation, and call two heavenly bodies 'Hesperus' and 'Phosphorus', without their being identical. So in that sense we can say that it might have turned out either way. Not that it might have turned out either way as to Hesperus's being Phosphorus. Though for all we knew in advance, Hesperus wasn't Phosphorus, that couldn't have turned out any other way, in a sense. But being put in a situation where we have exactly the same evidence, qualitatively speaking, it could have turned out that Hesperus was not Phosphorus; that is, in a counterfactual world in which 'Hesperus' and 'Phosphorus' were not used in the way that we use them, as names of this planet, but as names of some other objects, one could have had qualitatively identical evidence and concluded that 'Hesperus' and 'Phosphorus' named two different objects.[12] But we, using the names as we do right now, can say in advance, that if Hesperus and Phosphorus are one and the same, then in no other possible world can they be different. We use 'Hesperus' as the name of a certain body and 'Phosphorus' as the name of a certain body. We use them as names of those bodies in all possible worlds. If, in fact, they are the *same* body, then in any other possible world we have to use them as a name of that object. And so in any other possible world it will be true that Hesperus is Phosphorus. So two things are true: first, that we do not know *a priori* that Hesperus is Phosphorus, and are in no

12. There is a more elaborate discussion of this point in the third lecture, where its relation to a certain sort of counterpart theory is also mentioned.

position to find out the answer except empirically. Second, this is so because we could have evidence qualitatively indistinguishable from the evidence we have and determine the reference of the two names by the positions of two planets in the sky, without the planets being the same.

Of course, it is only a contingent truth (not true in every other possible world) that the star seen over there in the evening is the star seen over there in the morning, because there are possible worlds in which Phosphorus was not visible in the morning. But that contingent truth shouldn't be identified with the statement that Hesperus is Phosphorus. It could only be so identified if you thought that it was a necessary truth that Hesperus is visible over there in the evening or that Phosphorus is visible over there in the morning. But neither of those are necessary truths even if that's the way we pick out the planet. These are the contingent marks by which we identify a certain planet and give it a name.

Chapter 25

Selection from *On the Plurality of Worlds*

David Lewis

A philosophers' paradise

1.1. The thesis of plurality of worlds

THE world we live in is a very inclusive thing. Every stick and every stone you have ever seen is part of it. And so are you and I. And so are the planet Earth, the solar system, the entire Milky Way, the remote galaxies we see through telescopes, and (if there are such things) all the bits of empty space between the stars and galaxies. There is nothing so far away from us as not to be part of our world. Anything at any distance at all is to be included. Likewise, the world is inclusive in time. No long-gone ancient Romans, no long-gone pterodactyls, no long-gone primordial clouds of plasma are too far in the past, nor are the dead dark stars too far in the future, to be part of this same world. Maybe, as I myself think, the world is a big physical object; or maybe some parts of it are entelechies or spirits or auras or deities or other things unknown to physics. But nothing is so alien in kind as not to be part of our world, provided only that it does exist at some distance and direction from here, or at some time before or after or simultaneous with now.

The way things are, at its most inclusive, means the way this entire world is. But things might have been different, in ever so many ways. This book of mine might have been finished on schedule. Or, had I not been such a commonsensical chap, I might be defending not only a plurality of possible worlds, but also a plurality of impossible worlds, whereof you speak truly by contradicting yourself. Or I might not have existed at all—neither I myself, nor any counterpart of me. Or there might never have been any people. Or the physical constants might have had somewhat different values, incompatible with the emergence of life. Or there might have been altogether different laws of nature; and instead of electrons and quarks, there might have been alien particles, without charge or mass or spin but with alien physical properties that nothing in this world shares. There are ever so many ways that a world might be; and one of these many ways is the way that this world is.

David Lewis, selection from *On the Plurality of Worlds* (Blackwell, 1986), reprinted with permission of Blackwell Publishing Ltd.

Are there other worlds that are other ways? I say there are. I advocate a thesis of plurality of worlds, or *modal realism*,[1] which holds that our world is but one world among many. There are countless other worlds, other very inclusive things. Our world consists of us and all our surroundings, however remote in time and space; just as it is one big thing having lesser things as parts, so likewise do other worlds have lesser other-worldly things as parts. The worlds are something like remote planets; except that most of them are much bigger than mere planets, and they are not remote. Neither are they nearby. They are not at any spatial distance whatever from here. They are not far in the past or future, nor for that matter near; they are not at any temporal distance whatever from now. They are isolated: there are no spatiotemporal relations at all between things that belong to different worlds. Nor does anything that happens at one world cause anything to happen at another. Nor do they overlap; they have no parts in common, with the exception, perhaps, of immanent universals exercising their characteristic privilege of repeated occurrence.

The worlds are many and varied. There are enough of them to afford worlds where (roughly speaking) I finish on schedule, or I write on behalf of *impossibilia*, or I do not exist, or there are no people at all, or the physical constants do not permit life, or totally different laws govern the doings of alien particles with alien properties. There are so many other worlds, in fact, that absolutely *every* way that a world could possibly be is a way that some world *is*. And as with worlds, so it is with parts of worlds. There are ever so many ways that a part of a world could be; and so many and so varied are the other worlds that absolutely every way that a part of a world could possibly be is a way that some part of some world is.

The other worlds are of a kind with this world of ours. To be sure, there are differences of kind between things that are parts of different worlds—one world has electrons and another has none, one has spirits and another has none—but these differences of kind are no more than sometimes arise between things that are parts of one single world, for instance in a world where electrons coexist with spirits. The difference between this and the other worlds is not a categorial difference.

Nor does this world differ from the others in its manner of existing. I do not have the slightest idea what a difference in manner of existing is supposed to be. Some things exist here on earth, other things exist extraterrestrially, perhaps some exist no place in particular; but that is no difference in manner of existing, merely a difference in location or lack of it between things that exist. Likewise, some things exist here at our world, others exist at other worlds; again, I take this to be a difference between things that exist, not a difference in their existing. You might say that strictly speaking, only this-worldly things *really* exist; and I am ready enough to agree; but on my view this 'strict' speaking is *restricted* speaking, on a par with saying that all the beer is in the fridge and ignoring most of all the beer there is. When we quantify over less than all there is, we leave out things that (unrestrictedly speaking) exist

1. Or 'extreme' modal realism, as Stalnaker calls it—but in what dimension does its extremity lie?

simpliciter. If I am right, other-worldly things exist *simpliciter*, though often it is very sensible to ignore them and quantify restrictedly over our worldmates. And if I am wrong, other-worldly things fail *simpliciter* to exist. They exist, as the Russell set does, only according to a false theory. That is not to exist in some inferior manner—what exists only according to some false theory just does not exist at all.

The worlds are not of our own making. It may happen that one part of a world makes other parts, as we do; and as other-worldly gods and demiurges do on a grander scale. But if worlds are causally isolated, nothing outside a world ever makes a world; and nothing inside makes the whole of a world, for that would be an impossible kind of self-causation. We make languages and concepts and descriptions and imaginary representations that apply to worlds. We make stipulations that select some worlds rather than others for our attention. Some of us even make assertions to the effect that other worlds exist. But none of these things we make are the worlds themselves.

Why believe in a plurality of worlds?—Because the hypothesis is serviceable, and that is a reason to think that it is true. The familiar analysis of necessity as truth at all possible worlds was only the beginning. In the last two decades, philosophers have offered a great many more analyses that make reference to possible worlds, or to possible individuals that inhabit possible worlds. I find that record most impressive. I think it is clear that talk of *possibilia* has clarified questions in many parts of the philosophy of logic, of mind, of language, and of science—not to mention metaphysics itself. Even those who officially scoff often cannot resist the temptation to help themselves abashedly to this useful way of speaking.

Hilbert called the set-theoretical universe a paradise for mathematicians. And he was right (though perhaps it was not he who should have said it). We have only to believe in the vast hierarchy of sets, and there we find entities suited to meet the needs of all the branches of mathematics;[2] and we find that the very meagre primitive vocabulary of set theory, definitionally extended, suffices to meet our needs for mathematical predicates; and we find that the meagre axioms of set theory are first principles enough to yield the theorems that are the content of the subject. Set theory offers the mathematician great economy of primitives and premises, in return for accepting rather a lot of entities unknown to *Homo javanensis*. It offers an improvement in what Quine calls ideology, paid for in the coin of ontology. It's an offer you can't refuse. The price is right; the benefits in theoretical unity and economy are well worth the entities. Philosophers might like to see the subject reconstructed or reconstrued; but working mathematicians insist on pursuing their subject in paradise, and will not be driven out. Their thesis of plurality of sets is fruitful; that gives them good reason to believe that it is true.

Good reason; I do not say it is conclusive. Maybe the price is higher than it seems because set theory has unacceptable hidden implications—maybe the next round of

---

2. With the alleged exception of category theory—but here I wonder if the unmet needs have more to do with the motivational talk than with the real mathematics.

set-theoretical paradoxes will soon be upon us. Maybe the very idea of accepting controversial ontology for the sake of theoretical benefits is misguided—so a sceptical epistemologist might say, to which I reply that mathematics is better known than any premise of sceptical epistemology. Or perhaps some better paradise might be found. Some say that mathematics might be pursued in a paradise of *possibilia*, full of unactualised idealisations of things around us, or of things we do—if so, the parallel with mathematics serves my purpose better than ever! Conceivably we might find some way to accept set theory, just as is and just as nice a home for mathematics, without any ontological commitment to sets. But even if such hopes come true, my point remains. It has been the judgement of mathematicians, which modest philosophers ought to respect, that *if* that is indeed the choice before us, then it is worth believing in vast realms of controversial entities for the sake of enough benefit in unity and economy of theory.

As the realm of sets is for mathematicians, so logical space is a paradise for philosophers. We have only to believe in the vast realm of *possibilia*, and there we find what we need to advance our endeavours. We find the wherewithal to reduce the diversity of notions we must accept as primitive, and thereby to improve the unity and economy of the theory that is our professional concern—total theory, the whole of what we take to be true. What price paradise? If we want the theoretical benefits that talk of *possibilia* brings, the most straightforward way to gain honest title to them is to accept such talk as the literal truth. It is my view that the price is right, if less spectacularly so than in the mathematical parallel. The benefits are worth their ontological cost. Modal realism is fruitful; that gives us good reason to believe that it is true.

Good reason; I do not say it is conclusive. Maybe the theoretical benefits to be gained are illusory, because the analyses that use *possibilia* do not succeed on their own terms. Maybe the price is higher than it seems, because modal realism has unacceptable hidden implications. Maybe the price is *not* right; even if I am right about what theoretical benefits can be had for what ontological cost, maybe those benefits just are not worth those costs. Maybe the very idea of accepting controversial ontology for the sake of theoretical benefits is misguided. Maybe—and this is the doubt that most interests me—the benefits are not worth the cost, because they can be had more cheaply elsewhere. Some of these doubts are too complicated to address here, or too simple to address at all; others will come in for discussion in the course of this book.

Chapter 26

Actualism and possible worlds

Alvin Plantinga

T H E idea of possible worlds has both promised and, I believe, delivered understanding and insight in a wide range of topics. Pre-eminent here, I think, is the topic of broadly logical possibility, both *de dicto* and *de re*. But there are others: the nature of propositions, properties, and sets; the function of proper names and definite descriptions; the nature of counter-factuals; time and temporal relations; causal determinism; in philosophical theology, the ontological argument, theological determinism, and the problem of evil (see [7], chapters IV–X). In one respect, however, the idea of possible worlds may seem to have contributed less to clarity than to confusion; for if we take this idea seriously, we may find ourselves committed to the dubious notion that there are or could have been things that do not exist. Let me explain.

I. The canonical conception of possible worlds

The last quarter century has seen a series of increasingly impressive and successful attempts to provide a semantic understanding for modal logic and for interesting modal fragments of natural language (see, for example [4]; [5], p. 169; and [6]). These efforts suggest the following conception of possible worlds: call it 'the Canonical Conception'. Possible worlds themselves are typically 'taken as primitive', as the saying goes: but by way of informal explanation it may be said that a possible world is a *way things could have been*—a *total* way. Among these ways things could have been there is one—call it 'α'—that has the distinction of being actual; this is the way things actually are. α is the one possible world that obtains or is actual; the rest are merely possible. Associated with each possible world W, furthermore, is a set of individuals or objects: the *domain* of W, which we may call '$\psi(W)$'. The members of $\psi(W)$ are the objects that *exist in W*; and of course different objects may exist in different worlds. As Saul Kripke put it in [4], p. 65,

Intuitively, $\psi(W)$ is the set of all individuals existing in W. Notice, of course, that $\psi(W)$ need not be the same set for different arguments W, just as, intuitively, in worlds other than the real one, some actually existing individuals may be absent, while new individuals . . . may appear.[1]

---

1. For the sake of definiteness I substantially follow the semantics developed in this piece. The essentials of the canonical conception, however, are to be found not just here but in very many recent efforts to provide a semantics for modal logic or modal portions of natural language.

Each possible world W, then, has its domain $\psi(W)$; but there is also the union—call it U—of the domains of all the worlds. This set contains the objects that exist in α, the actual world, together with those, if any, that do not exist in α but do exist in other possible worlds.

On the Canonical Conception, furthermore, *propositions* are thought of as set-theoretical entities—sets of possible worlds, perhaps, or functions from sets of worlds to truth and falsehood. If we think of propositions as sets of worlds, then a proposition is true in a given world W if W is a member of it. *Necessary* propositions are then the propositions true in every world; possible propositions are true in at least one world; impossible propositions are not true in any. Still further, the members of U are thought of as *having properties* and *standing in relations* in possible worlds. Properties and relations, like propositions, are set-theoretic entities: functions, perhaps, from possible worlds to sets of n-tuples of members of U. If, for simplicity, we ignore relations and stick with properties, we may ignore the n-tuples and say that a property is a function from worlds to sets of members of U. A property P, then, has an *extension* at a given world W: the set of objects that is the value of P for that world W. An object has a property P in a world W if it is in the extension of P for W; and of course an object may have different properties in different worlds. In the actual world, W. V. O. Quine is a distinguished philosopher; but in some other world he lacks that property and is instead, let us say, a distinguished politician. Modal properties of objects may now be explained as much like modal properties of propositions: an object x has a property P *accidentally* or *contingently* if it has P, but does not have P in every possible world; thus, the property of being a philosopher is accidental to Quine. X has P *essentially* or *necessarily*, on the other hand, if x has P in every possible world. While *being a philosopher* is accidental to Quine, *being a person*, perhaps, is essential to him; perhaps there is no possible world in which he does not have that property.

Quantification with respect to a given possible world, furthermore, is over the domain of that world; such a proposition as

(1) $(\exists x)$ x is a purple cow

is true in a given world W only if $\psi(W)$, the domain of W, contains an object that has, in W, the property of being a purple cow. To put it a bit differently, (1) is true, in a world W, only if there is a member of U that is contained in the extension of *being a purple cow* for W and is also contained in $\psi(W)$; the fact, if it is a fact, that some member of U not contained in $\psi(W)$ has the property of being a purple cow in W is irrelevant. And now we can see how such propositions as

(2) $\Diamond(\exists x)$ x is a purple cow

and

(3) $(\exists x)$ $\Diamond$ x is a purple cow

are to be understood. (2) is true if there is a possible world in which (1) is true; it is therefore true if there is a member of U that is also a member of $\psi(W)$ for some world W in which it has the property of being a purple cow. (3), on the other hand, is true if and only if $\psi(\alpha)$, the domain of α, the actual world, contains an object that in some world W has the property of being a purple cow. (2), therefore, would be true and (3) false if no member of $\psi(\alpha)$ is a purple cow in any world, but some member of U exists in a world in which it is a purple cow; (3) would be true and (2) false if some member of $\psi(\alpha)$ is a purple cow in some world, but no member of U is a purple cow in any world in which it exists.

Now here we should pause to celebrate the sheer ingenuity of this scheme. Life is short, however; let us note simply that the Canonical Conception is indeed ingenious and that it has certainly contributed to our understanding of matters modal. In one regard, however, I think it yields confusion rather than clarity; for it suggests that there are things that do not exist. How, exactly, does the question of nonexistent objects rear its ugly head? Of course the Canonical Scheme does not as such tell us that there are some objects that do not exist; for perhaps $\psi(\alpha)$, the domain of the actual world coincides with U. That is, the Canonical Conception does not rule out the idea that among the possible worlds there are some in which exists everything that exists in any world; and for all the scheme tells us, α may be just such a world. There is, however, a very plausible proposition whose conjunction with the Canonical Conception entails that $\psi(\alpha) \neq U$. It is certainly plausible to suppose that there could have been an object distinct from each object that does in fact exist; i.e.,

(4) Possibly, there is an object distinct from each object that exists in α.

If (4) is true, then (on the Canonical Scheme) there is a possible world W in which there exists an object distinct from each of the things that exists in α. $\psi(W)$, therefore, contains an object that is not a member of $\psi(\alpha)$; hence the same can be said for U. Accordingly, U contains an object that does not exist in α; this object, then, does not exist in the actual world and hence does not exist. We are committed to the view that there are some things that don't exist, therefore, if we accept the Canonical Conception and consider that there could have been a thing distinct from each thing that does in fact exist.

And even if we reject (4), we shall still be committed, on the canonical scheme, to the idea that there *could have been* some nonexistent objects. For surely there are possible worlds in which you and I do not exist. These worlds are impoverished, no doubt, but not on that account impossible. There is, therefore, a possible world W in which you and I do not exist; but then $\psi(W) \neq U$. So if W had been actual, U, the set of possible objects, would have had some members that do not exist; there would have been some nonexistent objects. You and I, in fact, would have been just such objects. The canonical conception of possible worlds, therefore, is committed to the idea that there are or could have been nonexistent objects.

II. The actualist conception of possible worlds

I said that the canonical conception of possible worlds produces confusion with respect to the notion of nonexistent objects. I said this because I believe there neither are nor could have been things that do not exist; the very idea of a non- existent object is a confusion, or at best a notion, like that of a square circle, whose exemplification is impossible. In the present context, however, this remark may beg some interesting questions. Let us say instead that the canonical conception of possible worlds exacts a substantial ontological toll. If the insight and understanding it undeniably provides can be achieved only at this price, then we have a reason for swallowing hard, and paying it—or perhaps a reason for rejecting the whole idea of possible worlds. What I shall argue, however, is that we can have the insight without paying the price. (Perhaps you will think that this procedure has, in the famous phrase, all the advantages of theft over honest toil; if so, I hope you are mistaken.) Suppose we follow Robert Adams ([1], p. 211) in using the name 'Actualism' to designate the view that there neither are nor could be any nonexistent objects. Possible worlds have sometimes been stigmatized as 'illegitimate totalities of undefined objects'; from an actualist point of view this stigmatisation has real point. But suppose we try to remove the stigmata; our project is to remain actualists while appropriating what the possible worlds scheme has to offer. I shall try to develop an actualist conception of possible worlds under the following five headings:

(1) worlds and books;
(2) properties;
(3) essences and the α-transform;
(4) domains and propositions; and
(5) essences and truth conditions.

1. *Worlds and books.*   We begin with the notion of *states of affairs*. It is obvious, I think, that there are such things as states of affairs: for example, *Quine's being a distinguished philosopher*. Other examples are *Quine's being a distinguished politician*, *9's being a prime number*, and the state of affairs consisting in all men's being mortal. Some states of affairs—*Quine's being a philosopher* and *7 + 5's being 12* for example—obtain or are actual. *Quine's being a politician*, however, is a state of affairs that is not actual and does not obtain. Of course it isn't my claim that this state of affairs *does not exist*, or that there simply is no such state of affairs; indeed there is such a state of affairs and it exists just as serenely as your most solidly actual state of affairs. But it does not obtain; it isn't actual. It *could have been* actual, however, and had things been appropriately different, it *would* have been actual; it is a *possible* state of affairs. *9's being prime*, on the other hand, is an impossible state of affairs that neither does nor could have obtained.

Now a possible world is a possible state of affairs. But not just any possible state of affairs is a possible world; to achieve this distinction, a state of affairs must be *complete* or *maximal*. We may explain this as follows. Let us say that a state of affairs S *includes* a state of affairs S^* if it is not possible that S obtain and S^* fail to obtain; and let us say that S *precludes* S^* if it is not possible that both obtain. A maximal state of affairs, then, is one that for every state of affairs S, either includes or precludes S. And a possible world is a state of affairs that is both possible and maximal.

As on the Canonical Conception, just one of these possible worlds—α—has the distinction of being such that every state of affairs it includes is actual; so α is the actual world. Each of the others *could have been* actual but in fact is not. A possible world, therefore, is a state of affairs, and is hence an abstract object. So α, the actual world, is an abstract object. It has no center of mass; it is neither a concrete object nor a mereological sum of concrete objects; indeed α, like *Ford's being ingenious*, has no spatial parts at all. Note also that we begin with the notions of possibility and actuality for states of affairs. Given this explanation of possible worlds, we couldn't sensibly go on to explain possibility as inclusion in some possible world, or actuality as inclusion in the actual world; the explanation must go the other way around.

It is also obvious, I believe, that there are such things as *propositions*—the things that are true or false, believed, asserted, denied, entertained, and the like. That there are such things is, I believe, undeniable; but questions may arise as to their nature. We might ask, for example, whether propositions are sentences, or utterances of sentences, or equivalence classes of sentences, or things of quite another sort. We might also ask whether they are *states of affairs:* are there really *two* sorts of things, propositions and states of affairs, or only one? I am inclined to the former view on the ground that propositions have a property—truth or falsehood—not had by states of affairs. But in any event there are propositions and there are states of affairs; and what I say will be true, I hope, even if propositions just are states of affairs.

We may concur with the Canonical Conception in holding that propositions are true or false *in* possible worlds. A proposition p is true in a state of affairs S if it is not possible that S be actual and p be false; thus,

(5) Quine is a philosopher

is true in the state of affairs *Quine's being a distinguished philosopher.* A proposition p is true in a world W, then, if it is impossible that W obtain and p be false; and the propositions true-in-α, evidently, are just the true propositions. Here, of course, it is *truth* that is the basic notion. Truth is not to be explained in terms of truth-in-the-actual-world or truth-in-α; the explanation goes the other way around. Truth-in-α, for example, is to be defined in terms of truth plus modal notions. The set of propositions true in a given world W is the *book* on W. Books, like worlds, have a maximality property: for any proposition p and book B, either B contains p or B contains $\bar{p}$, the denial of p. The book on α, the actual world, is the set of true propositions. It is clear that some propositions are true in exactly one world;

(6) α is actual,

for example, is true in α and α alone. If we wish, therefore, we can take a book to be, not a set of propositions, but a proposition true in just one world.

2. *Properties.*   On the canonical conception, objects have properties in worlds. As actualists we may endorse this sentiment: an object x has a property P in a world W

if and only if x is such that W includes its having P. We *are* obliged, however, to reject the Canonical Conception of properties. On that conception, a property is a set-theoretical entity of some sort; perhaps a function from worlds to sets of individuals. This conception suffers from two deficiencies. In the first place, it entails that there are no distinct but necessarily coextensive properties—i.e., no distinct properties P and P^* such that there is no world W in which some object has P but not P^*. But surely there are. The property of being the square of 3 is necessarily coextensive with the property of being $\int_0^3 x^2 dx$; but surely these are not the very same properties. If the ontological argument is correct, the property of knowing that God does not exist is necessarily coextensive with that of being a square circle; but surely these are not the *same* property, even if that argument is correct.

The second deficiency is more important from the actualist point of view. Clearly enough the property of being a philosopher, for example, would have existed even if one of the things that *is* a philosopher—Quine, let's say—had not. But now consider the Canonical Conception: on this view, *being a philosopher* is a function from possible worlds to sets of individuals; it is a set of ordered pairs whose first members are worlds and whose second members are sets of individuals. And this is in conflict with the truth just mentioned. For if Quine had not existed, neither would any set that contains him. Quine's singleton, for example, could not have existed if Quine had not. For from the actualist point of view, if Quine had not existed, there would have been no such thing as Quine at all, in which case there would have been nothing for Quine's singleton to contain; so if Quine had not existed, Quine's singleton, had it existed, would have been empty. But surely the set whose only member is Quine could not have existed but been empty; in those worlds where Quine does not exist, neither does his singleton. And of course the same holds for sets that contain Quine together with other objects. The set S of philosophers, for example— the set whose members are all the philosophers there are—would not have existed if Quine had not. Of course, if Quine had not existed, there would have been a set containing all the philosophers and nothing else; but S, the set that does in *fact* contain just the philosophers, would not have existed.

And here we come upon a crucial difference between sets and properties. No distinct sets have the same members; and no set could have lacked any member it has or had any it lacks. But a pair of distinct properties—*being cordate* and *being renate*, for example, or *being Plato's teacher* and *being the shortest Greek philosopher*—can have the same extension; and a property such as *being snubnosed* could have been exemplified by something that does not in fact exemplify it. We might put the difference this way: all sets but not all properties have their extensions essentially. If this is so, however, the actualist must not follow the canonical scheme in taking properties to be functions from worlds to sets of individuals. If no set containing Quine exists in any world where Quine does not, the same must be said for any set whose transitive closure contains him. So properties cannot be functions from worlds to sets of individuals; for if they were, then if Quine had not existed, neither would any of his properties; which is absurd.

As actualists, then, we must reject the canonical conception of properties; a property is not a function or indeed any set whose transitive closure contains contingent objects. We must agree with the canonical conception, however, in holding that properties are the sorts of things exemplified by objects, and exemplified by objects in possible worlds. An object x has a property P in a world W if x is such that W includes x's *having P*. Quine, for example, has the property of being a distinguished philosopher; since that is so he has that property in α, the actual world. No doubt he has it in many other worlds as well. Abstract objects as well as concrete objects have properties in worlds. The number 9 has the property of numbering the planets in α; but in some other worlds 9 lacks that property, having its complement instead. The proposition

(7) Quine is a distinguished philosopher

has the property *truth* in the actual world; in some other worlds it is false. A property P is *essential* to an object x if x has P in every world in which x exists; x has P *accidentally*, on the other hand, if it has P, but does not have it essentially. Thus Quine has the property of being a philosopher accidentally; but no doubt the property of being a person is essential to him. (7) has *truth* accidentally; but

(8) All distinguished philosophers are philosophers

has truth essentially. Indeed, a necessary proposition is just a proposition that has truth essentially; we may therefore see modality *de dicto* as a special case of modality *de re*. Some properties—truth, for example—are essential to some of the things that have them, but accidental to others. Some, like *self-identity*, are essential to all objects, and indeed *necessarily* essential to all objects; that is, the proposition

(9) Everything has self-identity essentially

is necessarily true. Others are essential to those objects that have them, but are had by only some objects; *being a member*, for example, or *being a person.*

Among the properties essential to all objects is *existence*. Some philosophers have argued that existence is not a property; these arguments, however, even when they are coherent, seem to show at most that existence is a special kind of property. And indeed it is special; like self-identity, existence is essential to each object, and necessarily so. For clearly enough, every object has existence in each world in which it exists. That is not to say, however, that every object is a *necessary being*. A necessary being is one that exists in every possible world; and only some objects—numbers, properties, pure sets, propositions, states of affairs, God—have this distinction. Many philosophers have thought there couldn't be a necessary being, that in no possible world is there a being that exists in every possible world. But from the present point of view this is a whopping error; surely there are as many necessary as contingent beings.

Among the necessary beings, furthermore, are states of affairs and hence possible worlds themselves. Now an object x exists in a world W if and only if it is not possible that W be actual and x fail to exist. It follows that every possible world exists in every possible world and hence in itself; α, for example, exists in α. This notion has engendered a certain amount of resistance, but not, so far as I can see, for anything like cogent reasons. A possible world W is a state of affairs; since it is not possible that W fail to exist, it is not possible that W be actual and W fail to exist. But that is just what it means to say that W exists in W. That α exists in α is thus, so far as I can see, totally unproblematic.

3. *Essences and the α-transform.*   Among the properties essential to an object, there is one (or some) of particular significance; these are its *essences*, or individual natures, or, to use Scotus' word, its *haecceities*. I'll use 'essence'; it's easier. Scotus did not discover essences; they were recognized by Boethius, who put the matter thus:

> For were it permitted to fabricate a name, I would call that certain quality, singular and incommunicable to any other subsistent, by its fabricated name, so that the form of what is proposed would become clearer. For let the incommunicable property of Plato be called 'Platonity'. For we can call this quality 'Platonity' by a fabricated word, in the way in which we call the quality of man 'humanity'. Therefore, this Platonity is one man's alone, and this not just anyone's, but Plato's. For 'Plato' points out a one and definite substance, and property, that cannot come together in another.[2]

So far as I know, this is the earliest explicit recognition of individual essences; accordingly we might let 'Boethianism' name the view that there are such things. On the Boethian conception, an essence of Plato is a property he has essentially; it is, furthermore, 'incommunicable to any other' in that there is no possible world in which there exists something distinct from him that has it. It is, we might say, essential to him and essentially unique to him. One such property, says Boethius, is the property of being Plato, or the property of being identical with Plato. Some people have displayed a certain reluctance to recognise such properties as this, but for reasons that are at best obscure. In any event it is trivially easy to state the conditions under which an object has Platonity; an object has it, clearly enough, if and only if that object is Plato.

But this is not the only essence of Plato. To see the others we must note that Plato has *world-indexed* properties. For any property P and world W, there is the world-indexed property P-*in*-W; and an object x exemplifies P-in-W if x is such that W includes x's having P. We have already encountered one world-indexed property: truth-in-α. Truth-in-α characterizes all the propositions that are in fact true. Furthermore it characterizes them in every possible world; there are worlds in which

(7) Quine is a distinguished philosopher

lacks truth, but none in which it lacks truth-in-α. (7) could have been false; but even if it *had* been, α would have included the truth of (7), so that (7) would have been true-in-α. Truth-in-α is *noncontingent*; every object has it, or its complement, essentially.

2. In *Librium de interpretatione editio secunda*, PL 64, 462d–464c. Quoted in [2], pp. 135–136.

But the same goes for every world-indexed property; if P is a world-indexed property, then no object has P, or its complement, accidentally.

Where P is a property, let's say that the world-indexed property P-in-α (call it 'P_α') is the α-transform of P; and if $\mathcal{P}$ is a predicate expressing property P, its α-transform $\mathcal{P}_\alpha$ expresses P_α. And now consider any property Q that Quine alone has: *being the author of* Word and object, for example, or *being born at P, T*, where P is the place and T the time at which he was born. Q is accidental to Quine; but its α-transform Q_α is essential to him. Indeed, Q_α is one of Quine's essences. To be an essence of Quine, we recall, a property E must be essential to him and such that there is no possible world in which there exists an object distinct from him that has E. Since Q_α is world-indexed, it satisfies the first condition. But it also satisfies the second. To see this, we must observe first that the property of being identical with Quine is essential to anything that has it: i.e.,

(10) Necessarily, anything identical with Quine has *being identical with Quine* essentially.

But then it follows that anything that has the complement of *identity-with-Quine*— that is, *diversity from Quine*—has that property essentially:

(11) Necessarily, anything diverse from Quine has diversity from Quine essentially.

We must also observe that

(12) Necessarily, an essence of an object x entails each property essential to x,

where a property P entails a property Q if it is not possible that P be exemplified by an object that lacks Q. And now suppose there is a world W in which there exists an object x that is distinct from Quine but has Q_α Then there must be an essence E that is exemplified in W and entails (11) and (12), both *being distinct from Quine and* Q_α. Since E entails Q_α, E is exemplified in α—and exemplified by some object that is distinct from Quine and has Q. But by hypothesis there is nothing in α that is distinct from Quine and has Q; accordingly, Q_α is an essence of Quine.

For any property P unique to Quine, therefore, P_α, its α-transform, is one of his essences. So for any definite description (ιx) Fx that denotes Quine, there is a description (ιx) $F_\alpha x$ that *essentially* denotes him—singles him out by expressing one of his essences. Here we see an explanation of a phenomenon noted by Keith Donnellan [3]. A sentence containing a description, he says, can sometimes be used to express a proposition equivalent to that expressed by the result of supplanting the description by a proper name of what it denotes. Thus the sentence

(13) the author of *Word and Object* is ingenious

can be used to express a proposition equivalent to

(14) Quine is ingenious.

The proposition expressed by (13) is true in a world *W* where not Quine but someone else—Gerald R. Ford, let's say—writes *Word and Object* if and only if it is *Quine* who is ingenious in *W*; Ford's ingenuity or lack thereof in *W* is irrelevant. We may see this phenomenon as an implicit application of the α-transform to 'the author of *Word and Object*', what (13) thus expresses can be put more explicitly as

(15) the (author of *Word and Object*)$_\alpha$ is ingenious,

a proposition true in the very same worlds as (14).

Now what Donnellan noted is that sentences containing *descriptions* display this phenomenon. For any predicate $\mathcal{P}$, however, there is its α-transform $\mathcal{P}_\alpha$. We should therefore expect to find Donnellan's phenomenon displayed in other contexts as well—by universal sentences for example. These expectations are not disappointed. Rising to address the Alpine Club, I say

(16) every member of the Alpine Club is a splendid climber!

Here, but for an untoward bit of prolixity, I might as well have gone through the membership roll, uttering a long conjunctive sentence of the form

(17) N_1 is a splendid climber & N_2 is a splendid climber & . . . & N_n is a splendid climber

where for each member of the Club there is a conjunct attaching 'is a splendid climber' to his name. If M_1 . . . M_n are the members of the Club, the proposition expressed by (16) is true, in a given world *W*, only if each of M_1 . . . M_n is a splendid climber in *W*; the fact, if it is a fact, that in *W* the Club contains some nonclimbers, or some unsplendid ones, is irrelevant. But then (16) can be put more explicitly as

(18) every (member of the Alpine Club)$_\alpha$ is a splendid climber.

We may state the point a bit differently. Suppose '*S*' is a name of the set of members of the Alpine Club; then (16), (17), and (18) express a proposition equivalent to

(19) every member of *S* is a splendid climber.

If we use (16) without implicitly applying the α-transform, of course, what we assert is not equivalent to (19); for what we then assert is true in a world *W* only if *in W* the Alpine Club contains none but splendid climbers.[3]

4. *Domains and propositions.*   But now back to our main concern. As actualists we reject the canonical conception of properties while agreeing that objects have properties in worlds and that some of their properties are essential to them; and among the properties essential to an object we have noted, in particular, its essences. But what about domains? On the Canonical Conception, each possible world has its

---

3. The α-transform can also help us fathom the behavior of proper names; in particular it can help us bridge the gap between a broadly Fregean view and the anti-Fregean claims of Donnellan, Kaplan, Kripke, and others. See [8].

domain: the set of objects that exist in it. Here I have two *caveats*. First, what are domains *for*? For quantifiers to range over, naturally enough. But now we must be careful. On the usual domain-and-variables account, quantification is understood as follows. Consider a universally quantified sentence such as

(20) All spotted dogs are friendly

or

(20) (x) (if x is a spotted dog, then x is friendly).

Here, the quantifier is said to range over a set D of objects; and what (20) says is true if and only if every spotted dog in D is also friendly. But this seems fair enough; why must we be careful? Because it suggests that (20) expresses a proposition equivalent if not identical to

(21) every member of D is friendly, if a spotted dog

where D is the domain of the quantifier in (20). And this suggestion is clearly false. For consider a possible world where D and its members exist, the latter being, if spotted dogs, then friendly, but where there are other spotted dogs—dogs not in D—of a nasty and churlish disposition. What (21) expresses is true in that world; what (20) expresses, however, is flatly false therein. (20) and (21) are materially but not logically equivalent—both true or both false, but not true in the same worlds. We may say, if we wish, that in a sentence of the form '$(x)Fx$' the quantifier has a domain D; but propositions expressed by such a sentence will not in general be equivalent to the claim that every member of D has F.

   And now for the second and, in the present context, more relevant caveat. On the canonical scheme, each world W has a domain: the set of objects that exist in W. And though it is seldom stated, it is always taken for granted that a possible world W with domain $\psi(W)$ has *essentially* the property of having $\psi(W)$ as its domain. Having $\psi(\alpha)$ as domain is essential to α; had another world β been actual, other individuals might have existed, but $\psi(\alpha)$ would have been the domain of α. From an actualist point of view, however, this pair of claims, i.e.,

(22) for any world W there is a set $\psi(W)$ that contains just those objects that exist in W,

and

(23) if D is the domain of W, then W has essentially the property of having D as its domain

leads to trouble. For a set, as we have already seen, can exist only in those worlds where all of its members exist. Hence $\psi(\alpha)$ would not have existed if any of its members had not. $\psi(\alpha)$, therefore, would not have existed had Socrates, let's say, failed to exist. But if, as (23) affirms, α has essentially the property of being such that $\psi(\alpha)$ is its domain, then α can exist only if $\psi(\alpha)$ does. Hence if Socrates had not existed, the same would have held for $\psi(\alpha)$ and α itself. If we accept both (22) and (23), we are burdened with the alarming consequence that possible worlds are not necessary beings; even the most insignificant pebble on the beach has the distinction of being such that if it had failed to exist, there would have been no such thing as α (or any other world whose domain includes that pebble) at all.

This difficulty induces another with respect to the Canonical Conception of propositions as set theoretical entities—sets of possible worlds, let's say. That conception must be rejected in any event; for it entails that there are no distinct but logically equivalent propositions. But clearly this is false.

(24) All bachelors are unmarried

and

(25) $\int_0^3 x^2 dx > 7$

are equivalent. There are those, however, who believe the first without believing or even grasping the second. The first, therefore, has a property not had by the second and is, accordingly, distinct from it. But the principal difficulty with the Canonical Conception is due to the deplorable fragility of sets and domains—their deplorable liability to nonexistence in the worlds where some of their members do not exist. For consider any true proposition p; on the Canonical Conception p will be a set of worlds containing α. But now suppose some object—the Taj Mahal, let's say—had not existed; then neither would $\psi(\alpha)$, α, or p. So if the Taj Mahal had not existed, the same would have held for the truths that $7 + 5 = 12$ and that Socrates was wise; and this is absurd. On the Canonical Conception, only necessarily false propositions together with such items as

(26) there are no contingent beings

turn out to be necessary beings. This is a distinction, surely, that they do not deserve.

How, then, shall we as actualists think of the domains of possible worlds? We may, if we wish, concur with the Canonical Conception that for each world W there is indeed the set $\psi(W)$ that contains just those objects that exist in W. On the actualist view, however, domains lose much of their significance; and they also display some anomalous properties. First of all, domains, as we have seen, are typically contingent beings. If Socrates had not existed, no set that includes him would have, so that $\psi(\alpha)$ would not have existed. Possible worlds, however, are necessary beings; hence worlds do not in general have their domains essentially. If Socrates had not existed, there would have been a set distinct from $\psi(\alpha)$ that would have been the domain of α; and if *no* contingent beings had existed, the domain of α would have contained only necessary beings. Second, the domain of any possible world W, from the actualist perspective, is a subset of $\psi(\alpha)$. Since there are no objects distinct from those that exist in α, $\psi(W)$ cannot contain an object distinct from each that exists in α. Of course, the actualist will happily concede that there *could have been* an object distinct from any that exists in α. Hence there is a possible world W in which there exists an object distinct from any that actually exists. The actualist must hold, therefore, that $\psi(W)$ is a subset of $\psi(\alpha)$—despite the fact that W includes the existence of an object that does not exist in α. How can this be managed? How can the actualist understand

(27) There could have been an object distinct from each object that actually exists

if he holds that $\psi(W)$, for any W, is a subset of $\psi(\alpha)$?

5. *Essences and truth conditions.* Easily enough; he must appeal to essences. Socrates is a contingent being; his essence, however, is not. Properties, like propositions and possible worlds, are necessary beings. If Socrates had not existed, his essence would have been unexemplified, but not nonexistent. In worlds where Socrates exists, Socrateity is his essence; *exemplifying Socrateity* is essential to him. Socrateity, however, does not have essentially the property of being exemplified by Socrates; it is not exemplified by him in worlds where he does not exist. In those worlds, of course, it is not exemplified at all; so *being exemplified by Socrates if at all* is essential to Socrateity, while *being exemplified by Socrates* is accidental to it.

Associated with each possible world W, furthermore, is the set $\psi_E(W)$, the set of essences exemplified in W. $\psi_E(W)$ is the *essential* domain of W; and U_E, the union of $\psi_E(W)$ for all worlds W is the set of essences. Essential domains have virtues where domains have vices. Properties exist in every world; so, therefore, do sets of them; and hence essential domains are necessary beings. Furthermore, if $\psi_E(W)$ is the essential domain of a world W, then W has essentially the property of having $\psi_E(W)$ as its essential domain. And just as properties of other sorts are sometimes unexemplified, so there may be unexemplified essences. If Socrates had not existed, then Socrateity would have been an unexemplified essence. Very likely there are in fact some unexemplified essences; probably there is a world W whose essential domain $\psi_E(W)$ contains an essence that is not in fact exemplified. U_E, therefore, no doubt contains some unexemplified essences.

We are now prepared to deal with (27). Before we do so, however, let us see how some simpler types of propositions are to be understood from the actualist perspective. Consider first

(1) $(\exists x)$ x is a purple cow.

(1) is true if and only if some member of U_E is coexemplified with the property of being a purple cow; and (1) is true in a world W if $\psi_E(W)$ contains an essence that is coexemplified with that property in W.

(2) Possibly $(\exists x)$ x is a purple cow

is true if there is a world in which (1) is true—if, that is, there is an essence that in some world is coexemplified with *being a purple cow*. (2) is therefore noncontingent—either necessarily true or necessarily false.

(3) (∃x) possibly x is a purple cow,

on the other hand, is true if some member of U_E is coexemplified with the property of possibly being a purple cow. So (3) is true if some exemplified essence is coexemplified in some possible world with the property *being a purple cow*. More generally, (3) is true in a possible world W if some member of $\psi_E(W)$ is coexemplified in some world W^* with *being a purple cow*. (3) entails (2); but if, as seems likely, it is possible that there be purple cows but also possible that there be no things that could have been purple cows, then (2) does not entail (3).

When we turn to singular propositions, it is evident that one like

(28) Ford is ingenuous G

is true in a world W if and only if an essence of Ford is coexemplified with ingenuousness in W.

But what about

(29) Ford is not ingenuous?

The sentence (29) is in fact ambiguous, expressing two quite different propositions. On the one hand it expresses a proposition predicating a lack of ingenuousness of Ford, a proposition true in just those worlds where an essence of Ford is coexemplified with lack of ingenuousness. This proposition could be put more explicitly as

(29*) Ford is disingenuous;

i.e., Ford has the complement of ingenuousness. But (29) also expresses the denial of (28):

(29**) it is not the case that Ford is ingenuous.

(28) is clearly false in worlds where Ford does not exist; (29**), therefore, is true in those worlds. Indeed, a crucial difference between (29*) and (29**) is that the former but not the latter entails that Ford exists; (29**), unlike (29*), is true in worlds where Ford does not exist.

We may see the distinction between (29*) and (29**) as a *de re–de dicto* difference. (29*) predicates a property of Ford: disingenuousness. (29**), on the other hand, predicates falsehood of (28) but nothing of Ford. (29*) is true in those worlds where an essence of Ford is coexemplified with disingenuousness. Since there neither are nor could have been nonexistent objects, there neither are nor could have been nonexistent exemplifications of disingenuousness. (29*), therefore, entails that Ford exists. (29**), however, does not. It is true where (28) is false, and true in those worlds in which Ford neither exists nor has any properties.

We may see the ambivalence of the sentence (29) as due to scope ambiguity. In (29**) the sign for negation applies to a sentence and contains the name 'Ford' within its scope. In (29*), however, the sign for negation applies, not to a sentence, but to a predicate, yielding another predicate; and 'Ford' is not within its scope. Where 'Ford' has widest scope, as in (29*), the resulting sentence expresses a proposition that predicates a property of Ford and entails his existence; where the name has less than widest scope the proposition expressed may fail to predicate a property of Ford and may be true in worlds where he does not exist. This interplay between *de re–de dicto* distinctions and scope ambiguity is to be seen elsewhere. A sentence like

(30) If Socrates is wise, someone is wise

is ambiguous in the same way as (29). It can be read as predicating a property of Socrates: the property of being such that if he is wise, then someone is. What it expresses, so read, is put more explicitly as

(30*) Socrates is such that if he is wise, then someone is wise,

a proposition true in just those worlds where Socrates exists. But (30) can also express a proposition that predicates a relation of the propositions *Socrates is wise* and *someone is wise*. Since these propositions stand in that relation in every possible world, this proposition is necessarily true. Unlike (30*), therefore, it is true in worlds where Socrates does not exist. Similarly for

(31) If anything is identical with Socrates, then something is a person.

If we give 'Socrates' widest scope in (31), then what it expresses is a contingent proposition that predicates a property of Socrates and is true only in those worlds where he exists. If we give it narrow scope, however, (31) expresses a necessary proposition—provided, of course, that *being a person* is essential to Socrates.

What about singular existential propositions?

(32) Ford exists

is true in just those worlds where an essence of Ford is coexemplified with existence—the worlds where Ford exists.

(33) Ford does not exist,

however, is ambiguous in the very same way as (29); it may express either

(33*) Ford has nonexistence (the complement of existence)

or

(33**) it is not the case that Ford exists.

(33**) is the negation of (32) and is true in just those worlds where (32) is false. (33*), however, is true in just those worlds where an essence of Ford is coexemplified with nonexistence. As actualists we insist that there neither are nor could have been things that don't exist; accordingly there is no world in which an essence is coexemplified with nonexistence; so (33*) is a necessary falsehood.

We may now return to

(27) there could have been an object distinct from each object that actually exists.

On the Canonical Conception, (27) is true only if there is a member x of U such that x does not exist in fact but does exist in some possible world distinct from α; (27), therefore, is true, on that conception, if and only if there are some things that don't exist but could have. On the actualist conception, however, there are no things that don't exist. How then shall we understand (27)? Easily enough; (27) is true if and only if there is a world where

(34) there is an object that does not exist in α

is true. But (34) is true in a world W if and only if there is an essence that is exemplified in W but not in α. (27) is true, therefore, if and only if there is at least one essence that is exemplified in some world but not exemplified in fact—if and only if, that is, there is an unexemplified essence. Hence (27) is very likely true. As actualists, therefore, we may state the matter thus:

(35) although there could have been some things that don't *in fact* exist, there are no things that don't exist but could have.

These, then, are the essentials of the actualist conception of possible worlds. It has the virtues but not the vices of the Canonical Conception; we may thus achieve the insights provided by the idea of possible worlds without supposing that there are or could have been things that don't exist.[4]

References

[1] ROBERT ADAMS, 'Theories of Actuality,' Noûs, 8 (1974), 211–231.

[2] HECTOR-NERI CASTAÑEDA, 'Individuation and Non-Identity: A New Look,' American Philosophical Quarterly, 12 (1975), 131–140.

[3] KEITH DONNELLAN, 'Speaking of Nothing,' Philosophical Review, 83 (1974), 3–31.

[4] SAUL KRIPKE, 'Semantical Considerations on Modal Logic,' Acta Philosophica Fennica, 16 (1963), 83–94.

[5] DAVID LEWIS, 'General Semantics', in Semantics of Natural Language, ed. by Gilbert Harman and Donald Davidson (Dordrecht: Reidel, 1972), pp. 169–218.

[6] RICHARD MONTAGUE, Formal Philosophy, ed. by Richmond Thomason (New Haven: Yale University Press, 1974).

[7] ALVIN PLANTINGA, The Nature of Necessity (Oxford: Clarendon Press, 1974).

[8] ALVIN PLANTINGA, 'The Boethian Compromise,' American Philosophical Quarterly, 15 (1978), 129–138.

4. In 'An Actualist Semantics for Modal Logic', Thomas Jager has developed and axiomatized a semantics for quantified modal logic that presupposes neither that things have properties in worlds in which they don't exist, nor that there are or could have been objects that do not exist. In the intended applied semantics, the domain of a model is taken to be a set of essences; and a proposition expressed by a sentence of the form $(\exists x)Fx$ is true in a world if and only if some essence is coexemplified, in that world, with the property expressed by F. Copies may be obtained from Professor Thomas Jager, Department of Mathematics, Calvin College, Grand Rapids, MI 49506, U.S.A.

Chapter 27

Selection from *A Combinatorial Theory of Possibility*

D. M. Armstrong

Possibility in a simple world

I. Preliminary remarks

THE Naturalist theory of possibility now to be advanced will be called a Combinatorial theory. It traces the very idea of possibility to the idea of the combinations—*all* the combinations—of given, actual elements. Combination is to be understood widely. It includes the notions of expansion (perhaps 'repetition' is a less misleading term) and also contraction.

It is to be emphasized that the central idea is not original, although naturally I hope I will be making some contribution to the details. The central idea is in the *Tractatus*, and it is one of the central ideas of the *Tractatus*. Perhaps its charter is 3.4:

A proposition determines a place in logical space. The existence of this logical place is guaranteed by *the mere existence of the constituents*. [My italics.]

I myself encountered the Combinatorial idea, and was converted, in Brian Skyrms's article 'Tractarian Nominalism' (1981), which is reprinted in Armstrong (1989*a*) as an appendix. But a Combinatorial conception of possibility was put forward earlier by Max Cresswell (1972) and before that at least toyed with, quite a vigorous toying, by Quine (1969, pp. 147–52). The Combinatorial theory of Cresswell and Quine does not involve the fictionalist element that mine will have.

I shall develop the theory in a particular way, a way determined by my own metaphysical views, in particular by my acceptance of (*in re*) universals (see Armstrong 1978a, b). It seems a peculiarly apt way to develop a Combinatorial theory. But I expect that a version of this theory of possibility could be developed by those who articulate their Naturalism in a different way than I do (in particular, those who are Nominalists) or, perhaps who are not Naturalists at all.

The theory will be developed in stages, and not all that is said at the beginning will represent the final view to be presented. I will start with a view of the world which is, with the exception of its explicit recourse to universals, close to the *Tractatus* account.

A Combinatorial theory of possibility for such a world will be developed. A conception of possible worlds will also be developed: Such worlds will be called the Wittgenstein worlds. After that, some ladders will have to be kicked away. The scheme must be added to, and in a degree modified, to yield a deeper view.

II. Sketch of an ontology

The world I begin with contains a number of individuals (first-order particulars), $a, b, c. . . .$ The number is not specified. It might be a finite number, it might be infinite (one of the infinite cardinals). I think that it is an empirical question, to be decided on *a posteriori*, scientific, grounds, if it can be decided at all, how many individuals the world contains.

We make the preliminary assumption, however, to be abstracted from subsequently, that these individuals are *simple*. The force of the word 'simple' must not be overestimated here. It does not mean that these individuals may not have indefinitely many properties, or stand in indefinitely many relations to indefinitely many other individuals. The simplicity of the individuals is constituted by the fact that they have no individuals as proper parts.

Candidates for such individuals would be point-instants, but point-instants which are conceived of not as 'bare' point-instants but as things having properties and standing in relations to other point-instants. If we so conceive of the individuals, then ordinary particulars will be complexes of such individuals, complexes having both spatial and *temporal* parts. But I stress that such point-instants are mere candidates for the simple individuals. Like Wittgenstein, my argument abstracts from the concrete nature of the individuals postulated.

The world also contains, in finite or infinite number, simple properties, F, G, ... The simplicity of simple properties is constituted by their lacking proper constituents, where a constituent of a property is itself a property, or, in the case of structural properties, a property or relation. The term 'constituent' replaces the term 'part' which I would once have used. This is because these constituents have a non-mereological relation to the properties and relations of which they are constituents. The word 'part' is best kept for the part-whole relation studied in mereology. More of this anon.

For the present, we are not endowing these properties with further properties or giving them relations to other properties. For the present, that is, we are not contemplating *higher-order* properties and relations.

These simple properties are conceived of as *universals*. By this is meant no more than that any property can be possessed by more than one, indeed by indefinitely many, individuals. If a is F, and if the distinct individual b is also F, then a and b are identical in this respect.

If F and G are properties, then there is no property of *being F or G*. Similarly there are no properties of *not being F* and *not being G*. There are no disjunctive or negative properties. The corresponding *predicates* exist, of course, and are likely to be applicable to various individuals. But properties are not to be conceived of as the meanings of predicates, and no simple relationship between predicates and properties can be assumed. Properties are universals, identical in different individuals.[1] But what properties there are is in no case to be determined *a priori*. It is to be determined empirically, *a posteriori*, on the basis of total science.

Finally, the world contains a finite or infinite number of relations, R, S, ... Like properties, they are universals. They are simple because they lack proper constituents, whether these constituents be relations or properties. They may be dyadic, tetradic, ... Indeed, I can think of no convincing *a priori* reason why the number of places in a simple relation should not be infinite, although I cannot imagine what an example would be like.

It seems, however, that a Principle of *Instantial Invariance* should be enforced on relations. For all numbers, *n*, if a relation is *n*-adic in one instantiation, then it is *n*-adic in all its instantiations. The rationale for this is straightforward enough. If one has, say, R*ab* and R*cde*, then it is hard to see how R could be *identical* in its different instantiations.[2] This does have the consequence that so-called anadic or multigrade relations, that is, relations which can take a different number of terms in different instantiations, are not genuine universals. Perhaps they are a more or less closely knit *family* of universals, with the predicate applying in virtue of just one or more members of the family.

Like the properties, although the relations are simple this does not rule out their having properties, and there being relations between relations. But for the present we do not consider the possibility of their having such higher-order properties and relations.

As in the case of properties, relations are not to be promiscuously postulated. For instance, there is no automatic inference from polyadic predicates to relations of that -adicity. What relations there are is, again, to be established *a posteriori* on the basis of scientific theory.

Properties and relations have been distinguished. But more or less under the inspiration of Russell, we can see properties as a mere limiting case among the universals.

---

1. The argument to universals is perhaps best presented as an inference to the best explanation from the facts of resemblance, talk of sameness of sort and kind, the application of one predicate to an indefinite and unforeseen multitude of individuals, etc. See Swoyer (1983). Of course, it will have to be shown that it is the *best* explanation of these phenomena. That involves a critique of various forms of Nominalism. See my 1978a. Arguments against disjunctive and negative properties are developed in my 1978b, Chapter 14. It should be noted also that as the argument of this essay develops, a new and more relaxed sense of the word 'property' will be introduced, a sense in which a disjunction of universals or the negation of a universal can be said to be a property. But these relaxed properties are still not universals.

2. Perhaps the force of the Principle of Instantial Invariance can be brought out in the following way. Suppose that R*ab*, R*cde* and R*fg*, with R supposed to be the same relation in each case. Does not R in the second case lack *complete* resemblance, complete resemblance in its own intrinsic nature, to R in the first and third cases? But without complete resemblance, there is not identity.

   Another argument is: Properties appear to be no more than the monadic case of universals. But if that is so, and if Instantial Invariance is denied, why not both R*ab* and R*c*, with R the same universal? This conclusion, however, seems very unintuitive.

Properties are the monadic case. Relations are the dyadic, triadic, . . . n-adic cases, that is, the polyadic cases.

We have already suggested that point-instants are a candidate for individuals. As candidates for the relations, we have causal and spatio-temporal relations. Candidates for properties might be such things as charge and mass, non-relationally conceived. But, to re-emphasize, these examples should be thought of more as aids to the understanding than an attempt to advance a doctrine.

Individuals, properties and relations are brought together in what Wittgenstein called *facts* and what I shall call *states of affairs*. Once properties and relations have been introduced, the necessity for recognizing states of affairs should be clear. The existence of the individual a and the property F by no means ensures that a is F. If we are ontologically serious, we shall require a truth-maker to correspond to this truth: the state of affairs of a's being F.[3]

If a and F are simples, then we can call a's being F an *atomic* state of affairs. As emphasized in the *Tractatus*, each atomic state of affairs is logically independent of all the others. States of affairs that are independent of each other in this way may be called 'Hume independent'.

We shall speak of a and F as *constituents* of the state of affairs. It is clear that they are not *parts* of the state of affairs, in the sense of 'part' studied in mereology, the so-called calculus of individuals. If a exists and F exists, then their mereological sum, $a + F$, automatically exists. But as we have noted, the state of affairs of a's being F does not automatically exist. If a has R to b, and b has R to a, with R non-symmetrical, then we have two independent states of affairs. But the two states of affairs have exactly the same constituents. By contrast, there is just one sum of a, R and b. It is because non-simple properties and relations involve states of affairs (as we will see) that I speak of their constituents rather than their parts.

It is indeed vital to understand that states of affairs are non-mereological 'wholes'. Consider the relationship between a state of affairs, such as a's being F, and the two constituents of the state of affairs, a and F. The obtaining of the state of affairs entails the existence of the constituents, but the constituents could exist in the absence of that state of affairs. This might suggest a whole-part relation as studied by mereology. But if that suggestion were true, then the state of affairs would contain a surplus that would be a distinct existence from the constituents, and detachable from them. But there is no such extra 'factor' in the state of affairs.

It is well known to metaphysicians, at least since the time of F. H. Bradley, that there is no escape from a non-mereological mode of composition here by postulating a relation, R, that holds together a and F in the state of affairs. Now, a's having

---

3. We could put Quine's famous test for ontological commitment by saying that he requires a truth-maker for the referential component of true statements but not for any other component. I hold that predicates also require truth-makers, although the semantic relations between predicates and universals differ from case to case. I have called Quine's stance on the predicate 'Ostrich nominalism' (see my 1978a, p. 16, and 1980; for dissent, see Devitt 1980 and Quine 1980). The deniers of states of affairs may also be described as ontological ostriches, although, of course, they need not be *Nominalists*.

R to F again entails, but is not entailed by, the existence of the putative constituents, a, R and F.

It may be worth noting that this contrast between parts of individuals and constituents of states of affairs holds even if, contrary to the position taken in this essay, properties and relations are taken to be particulars rather than universals.[4] Suppose that a exists, the *particularized* asymmetrical relation R exists, and b exists. The sum $a + R + b$ automatically exists. No state of affairs involving these three constituents need exist. Suppose, however, that a state of affairs involving just these three constituents exists. It might be either a's having R to b, or b's having R to a. It appears that the recognition of properties and relations in an ontology, whether universals or particulars, leads to the recognition of states of affairs and so to the recognition of constituents of the states of affairs, constituents that are not in the mereological sense parts of the states of affairs.

Going back to a point of mere terminology, the choice between the phrases 'states of affairs' and 'facts' is a little delicate. 'Facts' may seem to have the advantage that there cannot be false facts, whereas language does seem to permit talk of non-existent states of affairs. But we shall see shortly that this apparent advantage is not really an advantage. It is in fact useful to have a relaxed sense of 'state of affairs' in which it is possible to talk of non-existent states of affairs.

A positive reason for not using the term 'fact' is our very strong tendency to speak of any true proposition as a fact, and of true propositions that are not logically equivalent as different facts. My (existent) states of affairs are truth-makers for propositions, where the one truth-maker may be the ontological ground for more than one true proposition. For instance, the state of affairs that a certain particular has a certain determinate shade of colour might make it true that the particular is scarlet, is red and is coloured.

We have now introduced states of affairs and have pointed out, without fully investigating, the special relation in which they stand to their constituents. This may suggest a tinker-toy picture in which states of affairs are built up from the constituents. But now I want to argue for a greatly enhanced position for that which the constituents constitute. The constituents are essentially aspects of, abstractions from, the states of affairs.

Consider the totality of atomic states of affairs. (The following formulation is indebted to Skyrms's 1981 article.) We may think of an individual, such as a, as no more than an *abstraction* from all those states of affairs in which a figures, F as an abstraction from all those states of affairs in which F figures, and similarly for relation R. By 'abstraction' is not meant that a, F and R are in any way other-worldly, still less 'mental' or unreal. What is meant is that, whereas by an act of selective attention they may be *considered* apart from the states of affairs in which they figure, they have no existence outside states of affairs.

---

4. See, for instance, the views of G. F. Stout and D. C. Williams. I discuss such views in my 1978a, Ch. 8, and, more sympathetically, in *Universals* (1989b).

Here is a way of conceiving of properties and relations which, if correct, makes clear the dependence of these 'entities' upon states of affairs (see Seargent 1985, Chapter 4). Properties are to be thought of as *ways that individuals are*. (If properties of properties are admitted, they will be further ways that ways are.) Relations are to be thought of as ways in which a certain number of individuals stand to each other. This conception of properties and relations makes it clear that there can be no uninstantiated properties and relations. A *possible* property or relation, even an empirically (nomically) possible property or relation, is not *ipso facto* a property or a relation.

Properties and relations thus depend on individuals, and are found only in states of affairs. What of individuals? Are they equally dependent on properties and relations? Not on relations. An individual which does not stand in any relations to other individuals (or, at any rate, external relations, which, it will subsequently be argued, are the prime candidates for our polyadic universals) seems to be a possibility. But could an individual be propertyless? Can it exist, but not in any particular way?

I do not think it can. An individual, to be an individual, must surely be *one* thing. But to be one must it not 'fall under a concept', as Frege would put it, that is to say, have some unit-making property? Without that, it is not even *an* individual. So I think we can reject bare individuals as well as uninstantiated properties and relations. States of affairs rule!

Before leaving this ontological sketch I will call attention to what may be called Ramsey's problem (1925).

The problem is this. What in this scheme marks off particulars from universals? It is customary to say that universals are ones which run through many. We have Fa and Fb, and again Rcd and Ref, where F and R are such ones. All very well. But equally do we not have Fa, Ga, Rab. . . where now a is a one which runs through many? Ramsey concludes that there is no major distinction here. His opinion has recently been endorsed by Hugh Mellor (1980, pp. 123–4). It may have been Wittgenstein's view.

I have three answers to the Ramsey problem.

First, there is the answer of Aristotle. Primary substance is that of which things are predicated, but is not itself predicated of anything. Properties are properties *of* individuals. Relations are relations *holding between* individuals. But individuals are not individuals *of* their properties. Nor do individuals hold between the relations which relate them. So, at any rate, ordinary discourse assures us. It seems reasonable to take this asymmetry recognized by discourse as marking a rather fundamental ontological asymmetry.

Second, the theory of states of affairs developed in this section treats individuals and universals in a quite different fashion. Universals have a definite -adicity. They are monadic, dyadic. . ., an -adicity which, I argued, does not change from instantiation to instantiation. Given a universal, then the number of individuals it links in a token state of affairs is fixed. But given an individual, the -adicity of the universals that it instantiates is by no means fixed. The individual must, I think, instantiate at least one monadic universal. But after that it is on its own. What relations it has to other individuals, and what the -adicity of these relations is, is a contingent matter. So individuals and universals belong to different categories.

Third, I argue in Armstrong (1989*a*) Chapter 4 that there is (a) sense in which individuals are all the same. In abstraction from their properties and relations they are barely numerically different. (This is the rejection of the doctrine of *haecceity*.) By contrast, properties and relations do each have their own haecceity, or, better, their own quiddity or nature.

I conclude, then, against Ramsey, that the one that runs through the many where many individuals have the one property is not to be assimilated to the one that runs through the many where the one individual has many properties.

III. The Wittgenstein worlds

Once we have the notion of an atomic state of affairs, we can introduce the notion of a *molecular* state of affairs. Notice that here they are confined to *conjunctions* of states of affairs. (And, we may note in advance, they are supervenient on the existence of their conjuncts.) Molecular states of affairs do not involve negative or disjunctive states of affairs. There is, however, no bar to molecular states of affairs being infinite. If the world is in fact infinite (in time, say), then it will be a certain infinite conjunction of states of affairs.

We may now introduce the notion of a *possible* atomic state of affairs, and, in particular, a *merely possible* atomic state of affairs. The word 'possible' here modifies the sense of the phrase 'state of affairs'. For, as the phrase was introduced in Section II of this chapter, all states of affairs are actual.

The notion of a possible state of affairs is introduced semantically, by means of the notion of an atomic *statement*. Let *a* be a simple individual, and F and G two simple properties. Let *a* be F, but not G. Now consider the statements '*a* is F' and '*a* is G'. The former is true, and may be called an atomic statement. But the latter may *also* be called an atomic statement. While failing to correspond to an atomic state of affairs, it corresponds to the *form* of an atomic state of affairs: '*a*' picks out an actual atomic individual, 'G' falsely predicates a genuine simple property of this individual.

I pause here to note that no particular knowledge of what in fact these individuals and properties are is assumed. What we have here is a though-experiment in which we imagine ourselves formulating a false atomic statement. In my view, Wittgenstein's avowal of ignorance here was a stroke of genius, and not, as is often thought, a cowardly evasion. It pays tribute to the fact that we have no *a priori* insight into, and even now only a little *a posteriori* insight into, the building-blocks of the world: the true individuals and the true universals. What does somewhat muddy Wittgenstein's insight is the thought that it should still be possible, by logical analysis alone, to get from *ordinary* true or false statements down to the atomic bedrock. This in turn is connected with the idea that necessities must one and all be analytic or tautological. Kripke has shown us the way ahead here. Some of his ideas about *a posteriori* (i.e., synthetic) necessities of identity will be incorporated into my argument as it advances.

Returning to the main line of the argument, 'a is G' is a false atomic statement. What it states, that a is G, is false. But we can also say that a's being G is a possible (merely possible) atomic state of affairs. I repeat what I have already said in Part I. A merely possible state of affairs does not exist, subsist or have any sort of being. It is no addition to our ontology. It is 'what is not'. It would not even be right to say that we can *refer* to it, at any rate if reference is taken to be a relation. Perhaps it is best to speak of *ostensible* reference. The parallel is with the ostensible (but very useful) reference that we make to ideal gasses, frictionless planes and so forth, in scientific investigations.

Instead of treating mere possibilities as non-existents, one could instead identify them with sets. For instance, the possibility that a is G could be identified with the set whose sole members are a and G. Whatever sets are, it is hard to deny that, given the existence of a and G, then this set exists. As a result, an Actualist can identify possibilities with something actual. As a matter of fact, Lycan (1979), who appears to have introduced the term 'Combinatorialism', takes it for granted that the Combinatorialist will adopt this approach (p. 305). The same assumption seems to be made by Lewis. In particular, Lewis interprets Skyrms's Combinatorial theory in this way, basing himself on the following text:

We may 'in the vulgar way', think of an atomic fact [in some world–DMA] as associated with a representation consisting of... an n-ary relation followed by n objects. (Skyrms 1981, p. 200)

Lewis interprets this passage as *identifying* possibilities with the 'representation', and so takes Skyrms's theory to be an *Ersatz* one.

However, Skyrms's phrase 'in the vulgar way' leaves his intentions ambiguous. And in correspondence he has told me that he is a Fictionalist rather than an *Ersatzer*. He takes mere possibilities to be non-existents. I think this is the right way to go. My reason is the simple one already advanced (Armstrong 1989a, Chapter 2, Section X). When we talk about possibilities we are talking about something represent*ed*, not a representation. (An ideal gas is not a representation.) Perhaps this argument will be dismissed as 'ordinary language'. But I think my view has a technical advantage as well. It seems that sets are supervenient on their members, that is, ultimately, things which are not sets. Supervenience, however, is a notion to be defined in terms of possible worlds, and hence in terms of possibility. It seems undesirable, therefore, to make use of sets in defining possibility.

So we take mere possibilities to be non-existents. Having introduced the notion of a possible atomic state of affairs, we can go on to introduce the notion of a possible molecular state of affairs. These are just conjunctions of possible atomic states of affairs, perhaps infinite conjunctions.

We have postulated here a stock, perhaps an infinite stock, of simple individuals, properties and relations, inextricably linked in states of affairs. It is at the heart of the matter that *any* statement involving these elements, and which respects the form of states of affairs (has the form 'Fa', 'Rab', 'Sabc', etc.), states a possibility. So the possible atomic states of affairs are *all the combinations*. (The *merely* possible atomic states of affairs are the *re*combinations, the ones that do not exist.) In this way, the notion of possibility is given an analysis, an analysis which uses the universal quantifier. What remains to be seen is whether a plausible theory of properties and relations can be developed which permits this promiscuous recombination.

Now for possible worlds. The simplest way to specify a possible world would be to say that *any conjunction* of possible atomic states of affairs, including the unit conjunction, constitutes such a world. This is essentially correct, but three qualifications should be noted.

First, this suggestion would permit 'contracted' worlds, worlds which lack some of the simple individuals and/or simple properties and/or simple relations with which we started. As a matter of fact, we shall shortly admit such contracted worlds into our scheme. But certain complications are involved in doing so which it is desirable to postpone. So let us for the present restrict our conjunctions of possible atomic facts to those which at some point in the conjunction make use of *every* simple individual, property and relation involved in the *actual* world, involved, that is, in all the actual states of affairs.

Second, we need to eschew propertyless individuals. So an individual, a, say, must figure in at least one possible state of affairs of the form 'Fa'. The states of affairs it figures in cannot *all* be of the form 'Rab . . .'.

Third, even if these two constraints on molecular possible states of affairs are satisfied, what we have is not strictly a possible world. We have to make explicit a further condition: that this *is* the (supposed) totality of atomic states of affairs. But having taken notice of this potential problem, let us bracket it for the time being. Here, however, it may be noted that this totality condition will be used to provide truth-makers for negative statements. This is important because, as we will note in a moment, our scheme cannot admit negative states of affairs or negative universals.

Given these qualifications, then, any conjunction of possible atomic states of affairs constitutes a possible world. I will call these possible worlds the Wittgenstein worlds.

The possible atomic states of affairs are all the combinations of the simple individuals, properties and relations which respect the form of atomic states of affairs. The possible worlds are all the conjunctions of possible atomic states of affairs which respect the constraints discussed earlier. This, I take it, was Wittgenstein's inspiration (allowing that the details differ a little, in particular because Wittgenstein makes no use of universals, explicitly at least). The notion of possibility is analysed, reduced I think it can be said, to the combination of elements. Most of these combinations do not exist. They are the *mere* logical possibilities.

It remains to be seen whether the power and simplicity of this notion can carry it, or some suitable modification of it, through the difficulties which can be proposed.

One consequence of the view as so far developed is that we cannot admit negative states of affairs, or negative universals. Negative states of affairs were not stipulated in our construction. It is clear that they must be rejected. Suppose we try to admit both a's being F and $\sim$(a's being F) as possible states of affairs. Our Combinatorial scheme would then allow us to select *both* these states of affairs for the one possible world, when in fact a 'world' containing both these possibilities is an impossible world.

If, however, we try to deal with the problem by introducing an extra constraint forbidding contradictory conjunctions in the one world, then we are using in our statement of constraints that very notion of modality which it was our hope to analyse. For contradictory states of affairs would be ones for which one state of affairs *must* obtain, and the other fail to obtain.

This, of course, faces us with a further task: that of providing a semantics for '~(a is F)'. How does this contingent statement hook onto the world? It is rather easy to see how '(a is F) v (a is G)' hooks on. The truth-conditions are perspicuous. Not so with negation. The matter must be left aside for the present, but it will be dealt with in Armstrong (1989a) Chapter 7.

The situation is the same with negative properties and relations. If F is a property, then *not being* F is not a property, although there might be a genuine property with just that extension. If R is a relation, then *not being R* is not a relation. To admit both F and *not being F*, say, would be to ruin the Combinatorial scheme in just the way that negative states of affairs ruin it. In our Combinatorial scheme, *all simple properties and relations are compossible.*

IV. Fictionalism[5]

I have indicated my preference for a *Fictionalist* form of Combinatorialism as opposed to a more orthodox *Ersatz* version of the theory, a preference shared by Skyrms. I say that the (merely) possible worlds and possible states of affairs do not exist, although we can make ostensible or fictional reference to them. The *Ersatzer* identifies these entities with actually existing entities: suitable sets containing individuals and universals, if his building-blocks are the same as mine.

My quarrel with the *Ersatzer* is perhaps not very deep, and I should not be too distressed if I were forced back to his position. But the quarrel is real. Mere representations of possibilities, which is what the *Ersatzer* uses, are not to be identified with the possibilities that we seek to represent.

What account of fictional statements, then, should we accept? Not, clearly, an account in terms of possible worlds! But not only would such an account lead to circularity, it also ignores the fact that the notion of the fictional is linked to what is false, or non-existent, but has no special link with possibilities. *Alice in Wonderland* and *Through the Looking Glass* are works of fiction. But some of the fictional situations that are described there are impossible. So are some of the situations portrayed in Escher drawings. Again, we might have the fiction that heat is not the motion of molecules. Yet if we accept Kripke's view of this proposition, as I think we should, it is an impossible fiction.

What is wanted, then, is an Actualist, one-world, account of fiction, and one that will accept both the merely possible and the impossible as fictions. I do not know in

5. *Author's note* (2003): I now think it was a mistake to make Fictionalism a part of the combinatorial theory. For incisive criticism see Nolan (1997). The truth-makers for the truths of possibility, I say now, are just the 'atoms' involved, much as Wittgenstein suggested in the *Tractatus* (Wittgenstein 1921).

detail what account to give, but it would be truly surprising if no such satisfying account were available.

I used to think that, with modifications that are minor in this context, Lewis's multiverse taken as a fiction would serve. The trouble with this idea is that the fiction would be a fiction of a monstroulsy swollen actuality. But the merely possible worlds are *alternatives* to the actual world and to each other.

Picking up a suggestion that I have heard from Lewis (!), perhaps the matter can be handled this way. Each possible world is a different fiction about the way the world is. Logical space is the great fiction of a book of all these fictions: the book of worlds. We, of course, can only spell out a very small number of the individual fictions (ones that are very short). But we can indicate the general principles that determine just what there is in the book.

But, the Modal Realist may protest, must there not be some ontological gulf between the possible, even the merely possible, and the impossible? My answer to this is that making ostensible reference to the (merely) possible and, in particular, to the notion of (merely) possible worlds is, for certain philosophical and other purposes, a particularly useful thing to do. The usefulness springs from the fact that certain definite *constraints* have been put on such fictions. The constraints are somewhat less than the constraints that are put on useful scientific fictions such as ideal gasses, frictionless planes and economic men (constraints that would take some work to spell out). But there are definite constraints none the less. For instance, the general form of states of affairs must be respected, and possible worlds must answer to certain further restrictions which we will be spelling out. In speaking about the merely possible in ordinary discourse we have some informal or implicit sense of these restrictions. A Combinatorialist theory is meant to tell us just precisely what these restrictions are.

And it may well be an aid to the intellectual imagination, a creature which constantly needs the crutches of metaphor and make-believe, to treat mere possibilities as something real.

Of course, we want to say that (some) statements of mere possibility are *true*. I do not think this creates any difficulty. Some statements about ideal gasses, frictionless planes and economic men are true, while others are false. What is more, when statements about ideal gasses, frictionless planes and economic men are true, then they have truth-makers in the one and only real world. It may be tricky to spell out the exact way that such true statements correspond to the world, but surely it can be done.

If we compare 'p' and 'it is possible that p', what we can say in general is that we demand much less of the second statement than we do of the second in order to account it true. Nevertheless, we do make demands, demands which a theory of possibility, such as this essay, tries to spell out. These demands may be most simply and vividly formulated by a fictional device. We set up non-existent 'merely possible worlds' alongside the actual world, using certain principles, Combinatorial principles as I maintain. 'It is possible that p' is then said to be true if and only if a world can be found in which p is true. Like a true statement about ideal gasses, however, the truth-maker for 'it is possible that *p*' is to be found in *our* world.

V. Rejection of essentialism

One issue we should face immediately. It may be held that this particular Combinatorial account of possibility is too latitudinarian because it would permit anything to be of almost any nature. It would permit Bertrand Russell to be a poached egg, to adapt an example of Pavel Tichy's. Yet is this really a possibility?

Russell, of course, is not a simple individual. But we are at present assuming that he is made up of simple individuals. Could these individuals have had certain properties, certain relations to each other, and perhaps to other individuals having certain properties, such that the original individuals so propertied and related constitute a poached egg?

The difficulty really is to see why not. Perhaps Russell could not have been a poached egg if he has certain essential properties, properties which he has in all those possible worlds in which he exists. But it is notoriously difficult to give any principled reason for picking out a subset of his properties as essential. His humanity is the orthodox candidate. But once such a candidate is proposed, doubts can be raised. What is the difference between Russell's being some very stupid human being and being a dog, a jellyfish . . . or a poached egg? It seems to be a matter of the way it strikes one's imagination.

I do not think such doubts are in any way conclusive. But the point is that it is so hard to give reasons on one side or the other of the debate whether Russell has any essential properties, that it seems reasonable to let the matter be decided elsewhere: by what seems to be on other grounds the best theory of possibility. It is a case of spoils to the victor.

Meanwhile, I think some explanation can be given, from the standpoint of an unrestricted Combinatorial theory, why certain possibilities seem so far-fetched. I shall begin by drawing the distinction between the *thin* and the *thick* particular.

The thin particular is what we have to this point spoken of as the individual. It is the particular in abstraction from all its properties and relations, the particular *qua* particular only. I have not spoken of it as the *bare* particular because that might suggest that it could exist in independence of any properties and relations. But although always clothed it is *thin*.

But we also think of the properties of particulars, and especially their non-relational properties, as *in some sense* part of the particular. As we will now see, states of affairs can accommodate the point.

The first point to notice is that states of affairs are particulars rather than universals. For *a*'s being F is no more susceptible of repetition than *a* is. The constituents of a state of affairs are particulars and universals, but what they make up is a particular. In my 1978a (Chapter 11, Section III) I called this 'the victory of particularity'. (It does something to help explain, without justifying, the appeal of Nominalism.)

Consider now the states of affairs involving a certain particular, but confine ourselves to the non-relational properties of that particular. Roll up all these properties into a conjunctive property. (Unlike disjunctive and negative properties, there seems to be no objection to conjunctive properties.) We can identify the state of affairs of that particular having that property as the *thick* particular. That property, and its conjuncts, are not parts of the particular in the orthodox mereological sense. But they are constituents of the state of affairs, and so in a sense they are parts of the particular.

Now, that the *thick* particular has a certain non-relational property is a necessary truth, for it is true in every possible world that contains that thick particular. (In general, however, it will not be an analytic truth, or one that is known a *priori*.)

Having introduced the notion of the thick as well as the thin particular (the individual), we can see that it is possible to work with particulars of intermediate thickness. In a rather vague and imprecise way, it seems that this is what ordinary thought and discourse do. When considering possibilities for Russell we are unlikely to take him merely as a thin particular, nor yet as a thick particular. What we do is to presuppose certain truths, or what we take to be truths, about Russell. The truth-makers for these will be certain states of affairs—a certain simple individual having certain properties and relations, including perhaps relations to further individuals. The possibilities which interest us concerning Russell keep these states of affairs constant. If they are not kept constant, then we will not be so inclined to say that the possibility is a possibility *about Russell.*

So it seems that it can be maintained with reasonable plausibility that the individuals (as opposed to their properties and relations) that constitute Russell could, collectively, have properties that would make them a poached egg, although it might well be that we would not count this collection of particulars as *Russell's* being a poached egg. The essentialist alternative has its own implausible arbitrariness. As a result, we do not have here a particular reproach to (although equally no advantage for) a Combinatorialist scheme.

Perhaps, then, Combinatorialism can meet this first of the many challenges it must face.

Works cited

Armstrong, D. M. 1978a. *Nominalism and Realism.* Vol. 1 of *Universals and Scientific Realism.* Cambridge, Cambridge University Press.

Armstrong, D. M. 1978b. *A Theory of Universals.* Vol. 2 of *Universals and Scientific Realism.* Cambridge, Cambridge University Press.

Armstrong, D. M. 1980. 'Against "Ostrich" Nominalism: A Reply to Michael Devitt', *Pacific Philosophical Quarterly,* 61: 440–9.

Armstrong, D. M. 1989a. *A Combinatorial Theory of Possibility.* Cambridge, Cambridge University Press.

Armstrong, D. M. 1989. *Universals.* Boulder, Colo., Westview Press.

Cresswell, M. 1972. 'The World Is Everything That Is the Case', *Australasian Journal of Philosophy,* 50. Reprinted in *The Possible and the Actual.* Ed. M. J. Loux. Ithaca, N. Y., Cornell University Press, 1979.

Devitt, M. 1980. ' "Ostrich Nominalism" or "Mirage Realism" ', *Pacific Philosophical Quarterly*, 61: 433–9.

Lycan, W. G. 1979. 'The Trouble with Possible Worlds', in *The Possible and the Actual*. Ed. M. J. Loux. Ithaca, N. Y., Cornell University Press.

Mellor, D. H. 1980. 'Necessities and Universals in Natural Laws', in *Science, Belief and Behaviour*. Ed. D. H. Mellor. Cambridge, Cambridge University Press.

Quine, W. V. 1969. 'Propositional Objects', in Quine, *Ontological Relativity and Other Essays*. New York, Columbia University Press.

Quine, W. V. 1980. 'Soft Impeachment Disowned', *Pacific Philosophical Quarterly*, 61: 450–1.

Ramsey, F. P. 1925. 'Universals'. Reprinted in *Foundations*. Ed. D. H. Mellor. London, Routledge & Kegan Paul, 1978.

Seargent, D. 1985. *Plurality and Continuity*. The Hague, Martinus Nijhoff.

Skyrms, B. 1981. 'Tractarian Nominalism', *Philosophical Studies*, 40: 199–206.

Swoyer, C. 1983. 'Realism and Explanation', *Philosophical Inquiry*, 5: 14–28.

Wittgenstein, L. 1921. *Tractatus Logico-Philosophicus*. Trans. D. F. Pears and B. F. McGuiness. London: Routledge & Kegan Paul, 1961.

Study questions

1. Traditionally, philosophers argued that if we know a statement from experience, it must be contingent, for necessity cannot be experienced through the senses. How could you argue against this position?

2. Consider the following:

   'If we ask whether it is necessary that the author of *Murder on the Orient Express* was the author of *Murder on the Orient Express*, it seems that there are two possible answers, depending on two different readings of the necessity claim:

   (a) Necessarily, the author of *Murder on the Orient Express* is the author of *Murder on the Orient Express*.

   (b) The author of *Murder on the Orient Express* is necessarily the author of *Murder on the Orient Express*.

   On the first reading, the statement is true, on the second, it is false.'

   What would be Quine's view of this argument? What would be Kripke's view of it?

3. We said Plantinga thinks that actuality is an absolute property, something that only one possible world has; and he also thinks that everything that exists is part of Our World. As Plantinga describes the 'Canonical Conception' in his paper, would a representative of the Canonical Conception agree with either or both of these two claims?

4. What are the merely terminological, and what are the substantial, differences between Plantinga's view and Armstrong's view?

Further reading

On the history of some questions related to modality, see Coffa (1991). For the history of modal logic from antiquity (not from a metaphysical, but rather from a logical point of view), see Kneale and Kneale (1962); see index on 'modal logic'. Ayer (1936: chapter 4) is a good short introduction to the linguistic theory of necessity; for a longer treatment, mainly for enthusiasts, see Carnap (1947). Quine criticized analyticity and the linguistic theory of necessity in (1958e) and (1958f); these are both hard-going. Boghossian (1996) is a very illuminating criticism of some aspects of the traditional view about analyticity. The 'Introduction' to Loux (1979) contains an accessible overview of the development of modal logic in the first part of the twentieth century. Kripke (1971) and (1972) are both deep but easily readable, and contain an elaboration of Kripke's views. For an argument for the contingency of identity, see the somewhat challenging Gibbard (1975). For more on the relation between apriority and necessity, see Casullo (1977) and Kitcher (1980), both reprinted in Moser (1987). On possible worlds, a very good collection is Loux (1979); see also Divers (2002) for a thorough and detailed up-to-date account of the nature of, and the debate about, possible worlds. Lewis's view on modality, with excellent and clear presentation of problems and other views, is given in Lewis (1986b). For modal fictionalism, see Rosen (1990).

Part VI

Causation

Part VI

Causation

Introduction

1. Introduction

DAVID Hume called causation 'the cement of the universe'. The image is a powerful one because our world is, it seems, bound together by causes and effects. But philosophers have struggled to understand the underlying nature of causation: what, in the most general terms, is it for one thing to cause something? Our starting point here, as for so many areas of metaphysics, is Aristotle. Aristotle distinguished what he called 'four causes' (four uses of the word 'cause'): these are known as the efficient cause, the formal cause, the material cause, and the final cause. These distinctions will be explained in section 2 below.

Over the centuries since Aristotle wrote, one particular notion of cause—Aristotle's 'efficient cause'—has become the dominant one in metaphysical discussion. This discussion may be summarized in terms of two questions. First, what kinds of entities are causes and effects? Are they objects, events, facts, or some other kind of entity? Second, what is the nature of the causal relation which holds between these entities, whatever their nature may be? Can this relation be explained in terms of the idea of a law of nature? Is it in any sense a necessary relation? And how is it related to determinism, the thesis that everything which happens is determined or fixed by what happens at an earlier time?

2. The senses of 'cause'

Aristotle distinguished between four ways in which something can be said to be a cause. Take a particular statue of Hercules, for example. According to Aristotle, we might say that its cause is the bronze from which it is made; or that its cause is the form or structure it has; or that its cause is the sculptor who made it; or that its cause is the purpose for which it was made (say to adorn a temple). It might sound odd, in a contemporary context, to talk of all these things as causes; in what sense, for example, is the 'form' of something a *cause*? However, if we understand the idea of 'giving a cause' broadly, in terms of giving an account of *why something is the way it is*, then things become clearer. For each of the four answers above is, in a different sense, an answer to the question, 'why is the statue the way it is?' Since it is standard these days to describe explanations as 'answers to why-questions' (Hempel 1965) it might be more in keeping with contemporary philosophical practice to talk of four kinds of *explanation* here, rather than four *causes*. (Indeed, some commentators have talked in terms of Aristotle's 'four becauses' rather than 'four causes'.)

Aristotle's four causes (or becauses) are classified as follows. In answer to the question 'why is this statue the way it is?' we might give:

  (i) The *material cause*: because it is made out of bronze
  (ii) The *formal cause*: because it has the form of a statue
  (iii) The *efficient cause*: because Polyclitus made it
  (iv) The *final cause*: because it is needed to adorn the temple

While we certainly can understand all these kinds of explanation, contemporary philosophy has tended to focus on the third of Aristotle's four causes—the efficient cause—as 'the' notion of cause. Efficient causation is a matter of one thing making something else happen. One reason for this is that, since the seventeenth century, 'final' causes have been viewed with suspicion: nature does not contain such intrinsic goals or purposes. Also, although the distinction between the matter of which something is made and its structure is clearly a significant one, few philosophers now think in terms of Aristotelian notions of 'form' and 'matter'. Aristotle's important discussion is useful as a way of distinguishing different explanatory concerns; here, however, we shall follow the later tradition and concentrate on 'efficient' causation.

3. Efficient causation and events

So to our first question: what kind of thing is a cause? The efficient cause of something explains why it happens. Things that happen are events. So it is natural to say that all effects of efficient causes are events. But are all causes events? Donald Davidson (Chapter 31) argues that they are.

Davidson distinguishes between the question of giving an analysis of the causal relation—of the kind we will discuss below—and giving what he calls the 'logical form' of causal statements. The logical form of a statement is the underlying structure which explains its inferential powers. We can understand the inferential powers of the statement that all pigs like acorns by treating it as a universally quantified generalization of the form, 'for all x, if x is a pig, x likes acorns', since we then can see how the statement 'D likes acorns' follows straightforwardly from 'D is a pig'. Davidson's declared aim in this selection is to uncover the logical form of causal statements. Their logical form involves an implicit quantification over events. The claim that 'the flood caused the famine' has an underlying logical structure of the form: There is an event x and an event y such that: x is a flood and y is a famine and x caused y. From this we can infer straightforwardly that something caused the famine, for example. Causal statements, according to Davidson, are *extensional* in the sense that substitution of one correct description of an event for another will not change the truth value of the whole statement: if the famine is also truly described as 'the worst disaster to have struck this century' then the statement 'the flood caused the worst disaster to have struck this century' is equally true.

What are events? According to Davidson, they are concrete particulars, in the same sense that physical objects like tables and human beings are concrete particulars. Concrete particulars, unlike properties, are 'unrepeatable' in the sense that they are only ever in one place at one time (see Part IV: Universals). A particular animal, say, is unrepeatable in at least the sense that that very same animal can only occupy one place at a time. Events are particulars in this sense; but this does not mean that events are concrete physical objects. There is an intuitive difference between an animal and the animal's life: the animal's life takes a certain amount of time, the animal does not; there are earlier and later parts of an animal's life, but there are not earlier and later parts of the animal. We might sum this up—although this is controversial—by saying that events, unlike concrete physical objects, have temporal parts. Davidson himself does not describe the difference between concrete objects and events this way, but it is certainly consistent with what he says about events. (However, it should be pointed out here that many philosophers, influenced by W. V. Quine and David Lewis, will say that objects have temporal parts too: for the details of this debate see Part VIII: Identity, section 3.)

Because events are things that happen, and it is natural to think that causes and effects are things that happen, it is very natural to assume that causes and effects are events. But is there any alternative to this thesis of Davidson's? On reflection it is plain that our everyday ways of describing causation allow many kinds of things to be causes, other than events. It was Brutus who killed Caesar; Brutus did this because of Caesar's ambition; and the fact that Caesar was assassinated caused the people to revolt. But neither Brutus, nor the fact that Caesar was assassinated, nor Caesar's ambition is an event. One is an object, another a fact, and the other a property or feature. None of these entities is an event. So if we think all descriptions of causation are descriptions of a relation between events, then we will have to construct paraphrases of the sentences above which explicitly mention events. So, for example, we might say that Brutus killed Caesar by stabbing him, and this stabbing—an event—is the kind of thing which can count as the real cause of Caesar's death.

Some philosophers dispute this. Some say that we should take seriously the idea that objects or substances *themselves* are causes, and not just the events in which they partake (Lowe 2002: chapter 11). Others say that it is properties, like fragility or mass, which are the real causes. (Perhaps following Hume's words in his *Treatise* (1739–40): 'where several different objects produce the same effect, it must be by means of some quality, which we discover to be common among them.') There are a number of ways of filling out this proposal. Some agree with Davidson that causes are events, but say in addition that events have their effects 'in virtue of their properties': thus the dropping caused the bottle to break, but only because it was a dropping of a bottle which was fragile, from a certain height, and so on. Others (e.g. Ehring 1997) say that we should think of causes as individual property instances or 'tropes': the cause of the bottle breaking was its particular fragility, for example. (For some discussion of tropes, see Part IV: Universals and Particulars.) Finally, some philosophers (e.g. Mellor 1995; Bennett 1998) treat causes as facts, conceived of as what is expressed by a complete indicative sentence, a sentence which may be substituted for '*p*' in constructions like 'It is a fact that *p*.' Hence the true sentence 'Brutus killed Caesar' expresses a fact, since it may be embedded in the construction 'It is a fact that . . . ' This does not mean that the killing of Caesar is not an event. The relation between events and facts is rather this: where the term e refers to an occurring event, there will always be a fact expressible in a sentence of the form 'e occurs'. (Analogously, the relation between facts and objects is this: where the term o refers to an existing object, there will always be a fact expressible in a sentence of the form 'o exists'. See Ramsey 1927.) On most views of facts, facts have objects and properties as *constituents*: thus the fact of the form a *is* F has the particular a and the property F as its constituents. Not all philosophers accept that there are facts; but if they do they normally accept that facts should be characterized in this way.

These last three proposals—that causes have their effects in virtue of their properties, that they are tropes, and that they are facts—have something in common. They all see *properties* as having a major role in causation. When Brutus stabs Caesar, it is because of certain properties of Brutus, his dagger, Caesar, and the stabbing that the stabbing has the effect of killing Caesar. Some properties of the stabbing—that it took place on the Ides of March, for example—or of the objects involved—the colour of the dagger, for example—make no difference to whether Caesar dies. Therefore, the defenders of property or fact causation will say that Davidson's extensional approach to causal statements does not pick out causes specifically enough. For if properties are causes, then not all descriptions of events will be descriptions of causes strictly speaking; for some true descriptions of events will describe them in terms of properties (like the colour of Brutus' dagger) which have no role in the causal process.

Davidson responds to this in 'Causal Relations' (§ 4) by distinguishing between statements of *causation* and statements of *causal explanation*. He therefore has to explain how causation and causal explanations are related: since he cannot simply say that all causal explanations are statements of a causal connection between events: they are not. But in addition, Davidson has a number of arguments against the view that causation relates facts or instances of properties or anything expressed by sentences. One of the most famous of these—introduced in the paragraph beginning 'It is obvious that the connective . . . ' in § 1 of Chapter 31—has acquired the name 'the slingshot' (for reasons that need not concern us). We lack the space to discuss this here. For a commentary on this argument as used in this context, see Lowe (2002: 169–73); for a discussion of this style of argument in general, see Neale (1995).

4. Causal necessity and law

Suppose, for the sake of argument, we have settled the question of what causation relates (the 'relata' of causation). We now need to consider our second question of the nature of the causal relation itself. When two entities are related as cause and effect, what makes them so related?

Physicalists or materialists will tend to answer this question in purely physical terms, in terms of a force or energy passing between bodies (see Dowe 2000 for an extended defence of this idea; see Part IX: Mind and Body, for physicalism). But physicalist proposals like this are not put forward as analyses of the very idea of causation; rather they are supposed to be accounts of the natural or scientific basis of our claims about causation. We can certainly make sense of causal claims such as 'her reluctance caused him to postpone the wedding' or 'the Chancellor's stringent economic constraints caused the economic recovery'. But we have little or no idea how to understand claims like these in terms of the physical transfer of energy. The idea of causation seems to be one which has a much wider application than simply its application in cases of physical interaction. So our task here will be to try and understand this idea; we will leave its supposed physical basis for further investigation.

Let's consider an example of the search for causes. Suppose a fire has destroyed a house and the fire brigade are looking for the cause. What kind of thing are they looking for? Something which happened before the fire did, to be sure. But the mere fact that an event *B* follows event *A* is not *enough* to make *A* the cause of *B*. Suppose that a man was smoking a cigarette inside the house before the fire; the mere fact that this occurred before the fire is not enough to establish it as the cause. The cause must be the thing which *produced* or *brought about* the effect. But 'producing' and 'bringing about' seem to be synonyms for 'cause' here, so they can hardly help us with an analysis. What kind of relation is this 'bringing about'?

Philosophers have traditionally thought about causation in terms of the idea of *necessitation*: what *must* happen, given other things. The basic idea is that if the cause happened, then (in some sense) the effect must happen. But in what sense? Suppose it was the case that the sinister intruder tossed his cigarette onto a pile of newspapers. Then we can conclude that, given the laws of nature, the newspapers *must* burn. But this causal necessity does not seem to be the necessity of logic: there is no logical con-tradiction in asserting both 'The intruder threw his cigarette onto the newspapers' and 'The newspapers did not burn.' So if there is a necessity here, it seems to lie in the way the natural world is, and not in logic. But such 'natural necessity' seems a very strange thing. To explain causation in terms of natural necessity might look like explaining one obscure idea in terms of another.

This was certainly Hume's view (Chapter 29). In one of the most famous discussions of causation in Western philosophy, Hume argued that all reasoning about matters of fact is based on reasoning about cause and effect, and that this reasoning is never a priori. We think of this reasoning as discovering necessary connections between causes and effects. But, Hume argues, when we look for the source of this necessary connection in our experience of the world, we come up with nothing. 'All events seem entirely loose and separate,' he writes, 'one event follows another; but we can never observe any tie between them. They seem *conjoined*, but never *connected*.' According to Hume's empiricism, all our ideas must be based on prior impressions or experiences. So on what impressions is our idea of necessary connection based? Hume denied that this idea was derived from any impression or experience of necessary links between events. Rather, the idea of necessary connection has its source in our repeated experience of one thing following another, and our consequent expectation of like things following like. It is this feature of the world which therefore constitutes causation: the constant conjunction of like events following like. Hence, Hume's famous definition of cause: 'an object, followed by another, and where all the objects similar to the first are followed by objects similar to the second. Or in other words where, if the first object had not been, the second never had existed.'

Hume's 'constant conjunction' theory of causation has been subject to much scrutiny, most of it focusing on whether the constant conjunction between events of similar kinds is sufficient for a causal link between events of those kinds. It may be that every time you visit the countryside it rains; there is no contradiction in supposing so. But it would be absurd to suppose that there is a causal link between your visiting the countryside and it raining. In response, defenders of Hume say that we must distinguish between accidental regularities like the one just mentioned, and lawlike (or 'nomological') regu-larities, like 'unsupported bodies fall to the ground at a constant rate of acceleration'. Hence the successor of Hume's theory of causation is known as the *regularity* account of causation.

According to David Lewis (Chapter 30), a regularity account of causation says that a cause is a 'member of a minimal set of actual conditions that are jointly sufficient, given the laws, for the existence of the event'. Thus, the man dropping the cigarette onto the newspapers is a member of a set of actual conditions which, given the laws, entail that the fire started (see Mackie 1965). The other conditions in this set are, for example, the fact that the newspaper is dry, that the room was full of oxygen, and so on. Notice then that the dryness of the newspaper, the presence of oxygen, are also causes of the fire according to the regularity theory, since they are members of the smallest set of conditions which is sufficient, given the laws, for the existence of the effect.

Some philosophers resist the idea that these other entities are causes, and say that they are only the 'circumstances' or 'background conditions'. They then attempt to produce a theory of causation which will distinguish causes from circumstances. But it is very hard to apply these definitions to actual cases without stretching the facts to fit the theory, or making *ad hoc* stipulations. When we talk about things like '*the* cause of Caesar's death', this is best regarded as loose talk. Caesar died because his heart stopped; but he also died because he was stabbed; if he had been as strong as an ox maybe he would have been able to escape his assassins; and maybe he also died because he was ambitious. What general reason is there to think that every event has only one immediate cause? We are perfectly happy with the idea that an effect may have had many causes stretching back in time (many 'mediate' causes). So surely it makes just as much sense to say that there many causes of an effect immediately before it happened. The truth is surely that every effect has many causes; so it cannot be an objection to the regularity theory that it cannot distinguish causes from 'circumstances' or 'background conditions'.

But the regularity theory of causation has other problems. For one thing, the fundamental assertion that all causation is explained by underlying regularities needs justification (see Anscombe 1971). Hume himself had a justification for his version of the regularity theory: his theory of ideas and impressions. Since, he argued, we have no impression of real connection between causes and effects, we cannot claim that causation consists in such a real connection. Our only impressions are of one event following another, so that is all our idea of necessary connection could amount to. But if we do not have Hume's motivation for this thesis, what motivation can we offer? So-called *singularist* theories of question deny that there is any adequate motivation; causation needs to be explained primarily for the single case. Two questions need to be distinguished here. First, whether there can be a causal relationship between a particular cause and effect which implies *no* regularity at all. And second, even when causation does imply a regularity, whether the presence of the regularity *explains* the causal link. Singularists typically say no to the second question; sometimes, however, they say yes to the first as well (see Foster 1985). (See Lewis's discussion in 'Causation' for other problems with the regularity theory.)

5. Causation and 'the thing that made the difference'

Is there an alternative to the regularity theory of causation for those who are, like Hume, sceptical of natural necessities? David Lewis proposed an answer to this question (Chapter 30) with his influential 'counterfactual analysis' of causation. Lewis's starting point is the second part of Hume's famous definition of 'cause' in the first *Enquiry*: one object is a cause of another 'where, if the first object had not been, the second never had existed'. That is, a cause c of an effect e is something such that if c had not existed, e would not have existed. This is called the 'counterfactual' analysis because it analyses causation in terms of what *would* have been the case if certain other things *had* been the case; that is, in terms of matters which are *contrary to fact* or 'counterfactual'.

Lewis sees his counterfactual analysis as filling out the intuitive idea that the cause is the thing that makes the difference to whether the effect happened or not. We can express the idea that it was your peeling the apple which caused it to turn brown, by saying that if you had not peeled it, then it would not have turned brown. Your peeling it was the thing that made the difference to its turning brown. But couldn't it have turned brown if someone else had peeled it or because it had spontaneously lost its skin? Surely yes; but when we are asking whether c was the thing that actually made the difference, we are asking whether things *would* have been the same if c had been absent, not whether things *could* have been the same. To say that things *could* have been different is just to say that the occurrence of c and e are contingent (see Part V: Necessity). But to say that things *would* have been different is arguably to say something about the *dependence* of e on c.

In other words, if c really is the cause of e, then we expect the following 'counterfactual conditional' to be true: 'if c had not existed, then e would not have existed.' But we can expect this without needing to have any opinion on the truth of the conditional: 'if c had not existed, e could not have existed.' An event e could have been the case for all sorts of other reasons; but what we are interested in when talking of causes is what *would* have been the case if c had been absent.

Lewis can make progress by analysing causation in terms of counterfactual conditionals because he has an independently motivated theory of counterfactual conditionals (see Lewis 1973). His theory appeals to unactualized possible worlds (see Part V: Necessity) and a relation between worlds of *comparative overall similarity*. Possible worlds can be more or less similar to one another, either in the laws of nature which obtain in them, or in the arrangement of particular matters of fact in the worlds. Taking all these factors into consideration, we can form judgements about which worlds are overall similar to others. The actual world truth-conditions of a counterfactual of the form 'If it had not been the case that C, it would not have been the case that E' (where C and E are sentences) is given as follows: In the closest possible worlds to the actual world where 'C' is false, 'E' is false. This is to say that the proposition expressed by 'E' is *counterfactually dependent* on the proposition expressed by 'C'.

Lewis confines his attention to relationships between events. When one event, e, counterfactually depends on another, c, he says that e is *causally dependent* on c. Causal dependence is a relationship between events, while counterfactual dependence is a relationship between propositions. Following Lewis, we use upper case letters for sentences expressing propositions (C, E, etc.) and lower case for the corresponding events (c, e, etc.). When there is a chain of causally dependent events, $d_1, d_2, d_3 \ldots d_n$, linking an event c to event e, then (Lewis says) c is a cause of e. Causation is thereby defined in terms of a chain of causal dependence. Why does Lewis define causation in this indirect way? Why not simply identify causation with causal dependence—that is, with counterfactual dependence among events? His reason is that causation is transitive and causal dependence is not. (A relation R is transitive iff aRb and bRc implies aRc.) Lewis thinks that there can be cases where a causally depends on b, b causally depends on c, but a does not causally depend on c. Nonetheless, Lewis says, it will still be true that, in this case, c is a cause of a. Thus suppose you shoot the president, and this brings about a revolution, which in turn brings about the president's rival ascending to power. Let's suppose that each later stage in this process causally depends on the previous stage. Lewis would say that even though it is true that your act caused the president's rival to ascend to power, it need not thereby be true that the president's rival's ascent is causally dependent on your shooting, since it need not be true that in the closest world in which you did not shoot, he did not ascend to power (maybe the whole situation is so politically unstable that someone else would have shot if you had not). So we have causation between my action and the eventual outcome without causal dependence.

It is for this reason that Lewis calls causation the *ancestral* of the relation of causal dependence. The ancestral of a relation R is that relation which stands to R as the relation *x is an ancestor of y* stands to the relation *x is a parent of y*. The relation 'ancestor' might be loosely defined as follows: x is an ancestor of y iff x is a parent of y, or x is a parent of a parent of y, or x is a parent of a parent of a parent of y . . . and so on. So while 'x is a parent of y' is not transitive, 'x is an ancestor of y' is. The same structure holds, according to Lewis, for the relations 'x causally depends on y' and 'x is a cause of y'. (It is worth pointing out here that not all theorists accept that causation is transitive. See Mellor 1995 for a denial of the transitivity of causation.)

The counterfactual theory gives substance to the idea that a cause is something that made a difference, since something that made a difference is precisely the thing such that if it had been absent, the difference in question would not have been made. But despite its evident intuitive appeal, the theory has had persistent difficulty dealing with the powerful form of counterexamples which Lewis ('Postscripts' in Lewis 1986a) later came to call 'redundant causation'. These are cases where there evidently is a causal relation between c and e, but it is not true that if c were not the case e would not have been the case (see Box VI.1 for some illustrations). Lewis ultimately responded to these kinds of case by amending his theory of causation in various ways (1986a, 2000). When pursuing this topic further it is worth asking whether Lewis (2000) has effectively abandoned the counterfactual analysis of causation.

6. Causation and determinism

So far we have been assuming that causation must be deterministic, that causes determine their effects. Both the regularity theory (Hume) and the counterfactual theory (Lewis) are framed in terms of determinism. The thesis of determinism has been formulated in various ways. For the purposes of this discussion, we can adopt Lewis's formulation of it: 'the prevailing laws of nature are such that there do not exist any two possible worlds which are exactly alike up to some time, which differ thereafter, and in which those laws are never violated.' Indeterminism is the denial of determinism: given the laws of nature, there are two possible worlds which are exactly alike up to some time, but differ thereafter without any violation of law.

Box VI.1. The varieties of redundant causation

Redundant causation comes in a number of forms. The first form is normally called 'causal overdetermination':

(a) *Actual (or symmetrical) overdetermination.* Two assassins, working independently, fire and simultaneously kill the tyrant. There is no reason to suppose that one assassin's firing has more of a right to be called a cause than the other's: so they are both causes. But if so, then it is not true that if the first assassin had not fired, then the tyrant would not have died. And likewise with the second assassin.

This seems to be a counterexample to the claim that if *A* caused *B*, then if *A* had not been the case *B* would not have been the case (the counterfactual theory of causation). But it is not a very intuitive kind of scenario; how do we know if such simultaneous overdetermination is really possible? However, this worry does not apply to the second variety of redundant causation, 'pre-emption':

(b) *Pre-emption (or assymetrical/potential overdetermination).* Suppose now that the assassins are working together. The first one fires, and the second one fires shortly after, to ensure that the job gets done. But the first assassin's bullet hits the tyrant and kills him, the second assassin's bullet missing because, let us suppose, the tyrant fell to the ground. Here it is clear that the first assassin's shot killed the tyrant; but it is not true that if he had not shot, then the tyrant would not have died.

Lewis responded to examples like this by appealing to his distinction between causal dependence and causation (see main text). It is true that the death is not causally dependent on either the first assassin or the second firing. But it is dependent on some intermediate cause, c_i, which (we may suppose) is dependent on the first assassin shooting. Hence there is a chain of causal dependence (and hence causation) between the first assassin's shot and the death, even though it is not true that the death would not have happened if he had not shot. This response works so long as we can be assured that there is an intermediate event, c_i, lying between the cause and the effect. But we cannot just stipulate that there *must* be such an event. Why can't there be cases of 'late' pre-emption, where the pre-empting cause steps in, right 'at the last minute', and pre-empts the other cause? Lewis acknowledges that such late pre-emption cannot be dealt with in the above way. (For discussion, see Lewis 1986a; Menzies 1995.)

It is obvious that part of the reason the pre-empting cause *is* a cause, and the pre-empted cause is not, is that there is an actual, real process linking the pre-empting cause to the effect, but no such real process in the case of the pre-empted cause. The pre-empted process is somehow 'cut off'. Can this idea somehow help the counterfactual theory? One might think so, were it not for an ingenious variant on the pre-empting case invented by Jonathan Schaffer (2000):

(c) *Trumping pre-emption.* Two officers, a junior and a senior, shout an order at their troops: 'charge!' The troops advance. The orders are shouted in exactly the same manner, we may suppose, but the troops advance because of the order of the senior officer and not because of the order of the junior. But, again, it is not true that if the senior officer had not shouted, the troops would not have advanced.

This counterexample, fanciful as it may seem, cannot be answered in the way the others were. For there is pre-emption here; and two actual processes (no 'cutting' of causal chains); but there are not two causes. The counterfactual analysis appears doomed.

Many physicists and philosophers believe that modern physics shows that the world is indeterministic; that is, that some of its fundamental laws are probabilistic. A probabilistic law is one which fixes a certain outcome only with a certain probability or chance. A real case of this is the laws of radioactivity, described by D. H. Mellor (Chapter 32). These laws say that each atom of a radioactive isotope of an element like uranium has a certain chance of decaying within a certain time interval. The laws do not say that every atom will decay; only that it has a certain chance of decaying. So, for example, two worlds could have identical histories up until a certain time t, then after t they differ in that in one a certain atom a decays, and in the other a does not decay. And this involves no violation of the laws of nature.

Some philosophers and scientists will say that such indeterminism is really an *epistemological* phenomenon; that is, it is not a genuine feature of reality, but a consequence of our ignorance of some factors which are responsible in a deterministic way for the decay. These factors are sometimes called 'hidden variables'. In our selection from his book *The Facts of Causation* (1995), Mellor discusses the arguments for and against the existence of such hidden variables. He argues that there are no good reasons for believing in them, but it is possible for determinists to dig their heels in and insist that there always must be deterministic causes of every event. His own view, however, and the view of many physicists and philosophers, is that the world is irreducibly indeterministic.

If the world is irreducibly indeterministic in this way, where does this leave causation? There are two possibilities: some events are not caused; or some events have indeterministic causes. The idea that some events have no causes does not seem to be a contradiction in terms; but if we are talking about the kinds of events which laws like the laws of radioactivity cover, then it is very implausible. For as Mellor shows, it would seem to imply (among other things) that we do not cause atomic explosions when we bombard radioactive material in an atomic bomb. The alternative must be true: there is indeterministic causation. Mellor shows how this conclusion is not in conflict with any of the 'connotations' of causation: i.e. with those ideas which we use to understand causation. In the selected passage, he mentions four such connotations: (i) causes generally precede their effects in time; (ii) causes are contiguous to their immediate effects; (iii) causes and effects are evidence for each other; and (iv) causes explain their effects. (In a later chapter of his book, he discusses a fifth connotation: that causes are *means* to the *ends* which are their effects.) Mellor argues that none of these connotations require determinism to be true; so indeterministic causation is not ruled out by causation's connotations.

What does it mean for causation to be indeterministic? Mellor's answer is: a cause must raise the chance of its effect. That is, it must make the chance of the effect higher than it would have been if the cause had not been there (note the similarity with Lewis's counterfactual theory here: and note that in this selection Mellor uses the symbol '$\Rightarrow$' instead of Lewis's '$\Box\!\!\rightarrow$' for the counterfactual conditional). So to say that Fred's smoking is an indeterministic cause of Fred's getting cancer is to say that the chance of Fred's getting cancer would be higher if he were to smoke than if he were not. The chance of an effect E is understood as an 'objective probability': that is, the probability of E happening, independently of what anyone believes, or however many events like E there have been or will be. (For more on chance, see chapter 4 of Mellor (1995).)

As the beginning of Chapter 32 makes clear, Mellor also thinks that causation can be deterministic. But by saying that causation can be deterministic and indeterministic, Mellor does not mean that there are *two* kinds of causation, deterministic and indeterministic. Rather, there is just causation; all causes raise the chances of their effects; but deterministic causation is just a special case where the chances in question are 0 or 1 (i.e. 0 per cent or 100 per cent chance). This can be illustrated in Mellor's notation. He writes '$ch_C(E) = p$' as an abbreviation for 'the chance that a cause C gives an effect E $= p$', where 'p' is some number between 0 and 1, measuring the chance of p's occurrence. But these numbers can also *be* 0 or 1 themselves. So to say that C is a deterministic cause of E is to say, among other things, that $ch_{\sim C}(E) = 0$, and $ch_E(C) = 1$. Deterministic causes give their effects a probability of 1; and the effect has a zero chance in the absence of its deterministic cause.

Chapter 28

Selection from *Metaphysics*

Aristotle

WE call a cause (1) that from which (as immanent material) a thing comes into being, e.g. the bronze of the statue and the silver of the saucer, and the classes which include these. (2) The form or pattern, i.e. the formula of the essence, and the classes which include this (e.g. the ratio 2 : 1 and number in general are causes of the octave) and the parts of the formula. (3) That from which the change or the freedom from change first begins, e.g. the man who has deliberated is a cause, and the father a cause of the child, and in general the maker a cause of the thing made and the change-producing of the changing. (4) The end, i.e. that for the sake of which a thing is, e.g. health is the cause of walking. For why does one walk? We say 'in order that one may be healthy', and in speaking thus we think we have given the cause. The same is true of all the means that intervene before the end, when something else has put the process in motion (as e.g. thinning or purging or drugs or instruments intervene before health is reached); for all these are for the sake of the end, though they differ from one another in that some are instruments and others are actions.

These, then, are practically all the senses in which causes are spoken of, and as they are spoken of in several senses it follows that there are several causes of the same thing, and in no accidental sense, e.g. both the art of sculpture and the bronze are causes of the statue not in virtue of anything else but *qua* statue; not, however, in the same way, but the one as matter and the other as source of the movement. And things can be causes of one another, e.g. exercise of good condition, and the latter of exercise; not, however, in the same way, but the one as end and the other as source of movement.—Again, the same thing is sometimes cause of contraries; for that which when present causes a particular thing, we sometimes charge, when absent, with the contrary, e.g. we impute the shipwreck to the absence of the steersman, whose presence was the cause of safety; and both—the presence and the privation—are causes as sources of movement.

All the causes now mentioned fall under four senses which are the most obvious. For the letters are the causes of syllables, and the material is the cause of manufactured things, and fire and earth and all such things are the causes of bodies, and the parts are causes of the whole, and the hypotheses are causes of the conclusion, in the sense that they are that out of which these respectively are made; but of these some are cause as *substratum* (e.g. the parts), others as *essence* (the whole, the synthesis,

Aristotle, selection from *Metaphysics*, book 5, translated by W. D. Ross. From *The Complete Works of Aristotle: The Revised Oxford Translation*, edited by Jonathan Barnes, copyright © 1984, Princeton University Press, reprinted by permisssion of Princeton University Press.

and the form). The semen, the physician, the man who has deliberated, and in general the agent, are all *sources of change* or of rest. The remainder are causes as the *end* and the good of the other things; for that, for the sake of which other things are, is naturally the best and the end of the other things; let us take it as making no difference whether we call it good or apparent good.

These, then, are the causes, and this is the number of their kinds, but the *varieties* of causes are many in number, though when summarized these also are comparatively few. Causes are spoken of in many senses, and even of those which are of the same kind some are causes in a prior and others in a posterior sense, e.g. both the physician and the professional man are causes of health, and the ratio 2 : 1 and number are causes of the octave, and the classes that include any particular cause are always causes of the particular effect. Again, there are accidental causes and the classes which include these, e.g. while in one sense the sculptor causes the statue, in another sense Polyclitus causes it, because the sculptor happens to be Polyclitus; and the classes that include the accidental cause are also causes, e.g. a man—or in general an animal—is the cause of the statue, because Polyclitus is a man, and a man is an animal. Of accidental causes also some are more remote or nearer than others, as, for instance, if the white and the musical were called causes of the statue, and not only Polyclitus or a man. But besides all these varieties of causes, whether proper or accidental, some are called causes as being able to act, others as acting, e.g. the cause of the house's being built is the builder, or the builder when building.—The same variety of language will be found with regard to the effects of causes, e.g. a thing may be called the cause of this statue or of a statue or in general of an image, and of this bronze or of bronze or of matter in general; and similarly in the case of accidental effects. Again, both accidental and proper causes may be spoken of in combination, e.g. we may say not 'Polyclitus' nor 'the sculptor', but 'Polyclitus the sculptor'.

Yet all these are but six in number, while each is spoken of in two ways; for (1) they are causes either as the individual, or as the class that includes the individual, or as the accidental, or as the class that includes the accidental, and these either as combined, or as taken simply; and (2) all may be taken as acting or as having a capacity. But they differ inasmuch as the acting causes and the individuals exist, or do not exist, simultaneously with the things of which they are causes, e.g. this particular man who is curing, with this particular man who is recovering health, and this particular builder with this particular thing that is being built; but this is not always so with potential causes; for the house does not perish at the same time as the builder.

Chapter 29

Selection from *Enquiry Concerning Human Understanding*

David Hume

Sceptical doubts concerning the operations of the understanding

Part I

20   ALL the objects of human reason or enquiry may naturally be divided into two kinds, to wit, *Relations of Ideas*, and *Matters of Fact*. Of the first kind are the sciences of Geometry, Algebra, and Arithmetic; and in short, every affirmation which is either intuitively or demonstratively certain. *That the square of the hypothenuse is equal to the square of the two sides*, is a proposition which expresses a relation between these figures. *That three times five is equal to the half of thirty*, expresses a relation between these numbers. Propositions of this kind are discoverable by the mere operation of thought, without dependence on what is anywhere existent in the universe. Though there never were a circle or triangle in nature, the truths demonstrated by Euclid would for ever retain their certainty and evidence.

21   Matters of fact, which are the second objects of human reason, are not ascertained in the same manner; nor is our evidence of their truth, however great, of a like nature with the foregoing. The contrary of every matter of fact is still possible; because it can never imply a contradiction, and is conceived by the mind with the same facility and distinctness, as if ever so conformable to reality. *That the sun will not rise to-morrow* is no less intelligible a proposition, and implies no more contradiction, than the affirmation, *that it will rise*. We should in vain, therefore, attempt to demonstrate its falsehood. Were it demonstratively false, it would imply a contradiction, and could never be distinctly conceived by the mind.

It may, therefore, be a subject worthy of curiosity, to enquire what is the nature of that evidence which assures us of any real existence and matter of fact, beyond

David Hume, selection from *Enquiry Concerning Human Understanding*, § IV, part i and § VII, part ii, 3rd edition, edited by P. H. Nidditch (Oxford University Press, 1975), reprinted by permission of Oxford University Press.

the present testimony of our senses, or the records of our memory. This part of philosophy, it is observable, has been little cultivated, either by the ancients or moderns; and therefore our doubts and errors, in the prosecution of so important an enquiry, may be the more excusable; while we march through such difficult paths without any guide or direction. They may even prove useful, by exciting curiosity, and destroying that implicit faith and security, which is the bane of all reasoning and free enquiry. The discovery of defects in the common philosophy, if any such there be, will not, I presume, be a discouragement, but rather an incitement, as is usual, to attempt something more full and satisfactory than has yet been proposed to the public.

22 All reasonings concerning matter of fact seem to be founded on the relation of *Cause and Effect.* By means of that relation alone we can go beyond the evidence of our memory and senses. If you were to ask a man, why he believes any matter of fact, which is absent; for instance, that his friend is in the country, or in France; he would give you a reason; and this reason would be some other fact; as a letter received from him, or the knowledge of his former resolutions and promises. A man finding a watch or any other machine in a desert island, would conclude that there had once been men in that island. All our reasonings concerning fact are of the same nature. And here it is constantly supposed that there is a connexion between the present fact and that which is inferred from it. Were there nothing to bind them together, the inference would be entirely precarious. The hearing of an articulate voice and rational discourse in the dark assures us of the presence of some person: Why? because these are the effects of the human make and fabric, and closely connected with it. If we anatomize all the other reasonings of this nature, we shall find that they are founded on the relation of cause and effect, and that this relation is either near or remote, direct or collateral. Heat and light are collateral effects of fire, and the one effect may justly be inferred from the other.

23 If we would satisfy ourselves, therefore, concerning the nature of that evidence, which assures us of matters of fact, we must enquire how we arrive at the knowledge of cause and effect.

I shall venture to affirm, as a general proposition, which admits of no exception, that the knowledge of this relation is not, in any instance, attained by reasonings *a priori*; but arises entirely from experience, when we find that any particular objects are constantly conjoined with each other. Let an object be presented to a man of ever so strong natural reason and abilities; if that object be entirely new to him, he will not be able, by the most accurate examination of its sensible qualities, to discover any of its causes or effects. Adam, though his rational faculties be supposed, at the very first, entirely perfect, could not have inferred from the fluidity and transparency of water that it would suffocate him, or from the light and warmth of fire that it would consume him. No object ever discovers, by the qualities which appear to the senses, either the causes which produced it, or the effects which will arise from it; nor can our reason, unassisted by experience, ever draw any inference concerning real existence and matter of fact.

24   This proposition, *that causes and effects are discoverable, not by reason but by experience*, will readily be admitted with regard to such objects, as we remember to have once been altogether unknown to us; since we must be conscious of the utter inability, which we then lay under, of foretelling what would arise from them. Present two smooth pieces of marble to a man who has no tincture of natural philosophy; he will never discover that they will adhere together in such a manner as to require great force to separate them in a direct line, while they make so small a resistance to a lateral pressure. Such events, as bear little analogy to the common course of nature, are also readily confessed to be known only by experience; nor does any man imagine that the explosion of gunpowder, or the attraction of a loadstone, could ever be discovered by arguments *a priori*. In like manner, when an effect is supposed to depend upon an intricate machinery or secret structure of parts, we make no difficulty in attributing all our knowledge of it to experience. Who will assert that he can give the ultimate reason, why milk or bread is proper nourishment for a man, not for a lion or a tiger?

    But the same truth may not appear, at first sight, to have the same evidence with regard to events, which have become familiar to us from our first appearance in the world, which bear a close analogy to the whole course of nature, and which are supposed to depend on the simple qualities of objects, without any secret structure of parts. We are apt to imagine that we could discover these effects by the mere operation of our reason, without experience. We fancy, that were we brought on a sudden into this world, we could at first have inferred that one Billiard-ball would communicate motion to another upon impulse; and that we needed not to have waited for the event, in order to pronounce with certainty concerning it. Such is the influence of custom, that, where it is strongest, it not only covers our natural ignorance, but even conceals itself, and seems not to take place, merely because it is found in the highest degree.

25   But to convince us that all the laws of nature, and all the operations of bodies without exception, are known only by experience, the following reflections may, perhaps, suffice. Were any object presented to us, and were we required to pronounce concerning the effect, which will result from it, without consulting past observation; after what manner, I beseech you, must the mind proceed in this operation? It must invent or imagine some event, which it ascribes to the object as its effect; and it is plain that this invention must be entirely arbitrary. The mind can never possibly find the effect in the supposed cause, by the most accurate scrutiny and examination. For the effect is totally different from the cause, and consequently can never be discovered in it. Motion in the second Billiard-ball is a quite distinct event from motion in the first; nor is there anything in the one to suggest the smallest hint of the other. A stone or piece of metal raised into the air, and left without any support, immediately falls: but to consider the matter *a priori*, is there anything we discover in this situation which can beget the idea of a downward, rather than an upward, or any other motion, in the stone or metal?

    And as the first imagination or invention of a particular effect, in all natural operations, is arbitrary, where we consult not experience; so must we also esteem the supposed tie or connexion between the cause and effect, which binds them together, and renders it impossible that any other effect could result from the operation of that cause. When I see, for instance, a Billiard-ball moving in a straight line towards another; even suppose motion in the second ball should by accident be suggested to me, as the result of their contact or impulse; may I not conceive, that a hundred different events might as well follow from that cause? May not both these balls remain at absolute rest? May not the first ball return in a straight line, or leap off from the second in any line or direction? All these suppositions are consistent and conceivable. Why then should we give the preference to one, which is no more consistent or conceivable than the rest? All our reasonings *a priori* will never be able to show us any foundation for this preference.

In a word, then, every effect is a distinct event from its cause. It could not, therefore, be discovered in the cause, and the first invention or conception of it, *a priori*, must be entirely arbitrary. And even after it is suggested, the conjunction of it with the cause must appear equally arbitrary; since there are always many other effects, which, to reason, must seem fully as consistent and natural. In vain, therefore, should we pretend to determine any single event, or infer any cause or effect, without the assistance of observation and experience.

Hence we may discover the reason why no philosopher, who is rational and modest, has ever pretended to assign the ultimate cause of any natural operation, or to show distinctly the action of that power, which produces any single effect in the universe. It is confessed, that the utmost effort of human reason is to reduce the principles, productive of natural phenomena, to a greater simplicity, and to resolve the many particular effects into a few general causes, by means of reasonings from analogy, experience, and observation. But as to the causes of these general causes, we should in vain attempt their discovery; nor shall we ever be able to satisfy ourselves, by any particular explication of them. These ultimate springs and principles are totally shut up from human curiosity and enquiry. Elasticity, gravity, cohesion of parts, communication of motion by impulse; these are probably the ultimate causes and principles which we shall ever discover in nature; and we may esteem ourselves sufficiently happy, if, by accurate enquiry and reasoning, we can trace up the particular phenomena to, or near to, these general principles. The most perfect philosophy of the natural kind only staves off our ignorance a little longer: as perhaps the most perfect philosophy of the moral or metaphysical kind serves only to discover larger portions of it. Thus the observation of human blindness and weakness is the result of all philosophy, and meets us at every turn, in spite of our endeavours to elude or avoid it. 26

Nor is geometry, when taken into the assistance of natural philosophy, ever able to remedy this defect, or lead us into the knowledge of ultimate causes, by all that accuracy of reasoning for which it is so justly celebrated. Every part of mixed mathematics proceeds upon the supposition that certain laws are established by nature in her operations; and abstract reasonings are employed, either to assist experience in the discovery of these laws, or to determine their influence in particular instances, where it depends upon any precise degree of distance and quantity. Thus, 27 it is a law of motion, discovered by experience, that the moment or force of any body in motion is in the compound ratio or proportion of its solid contents and its velocity; and consequently, that a small force may remove the greatest obstacle or raise the greatest weight, if, by any contrivance or machinery, we can increase the velocity of that force, so as to make it an overmatch for its antagonist. Geometry assists us in the application of this law, by giving us the just dimensions of all the parts and figures which can enter into any species of machine; but still the discovery of the law itself is owing merely to experience, and all the abstract reasonings in the world could never lead us one step towards the knowledge of it. When we reason *a priori*, and consider merely any object or cause, as it appears to the mind, independent of all observation, it never could suggest to us the notion of any distinct object, such as its effect; much less, show us the inseparable and inviolable connexion between them. A man must be very sagacious who could discover by reasoning that crystal is the effect of heat, and ice of cold, without being previously acquainted with the operation of these qualities.

. . .

On the idea of necessary connexion

Part II

58   But to hasten to a conclusion of this argument, which is already drawn out to too great a length: We have sought in vain for an idea of power or necessary connexion in all the sources from which we could suppose it to be derived. It appears that, in single instances of the operation of bodies, we never can, by our utmost scrutiny, discover any thing but one event following another; without being able to comprehend any force or power by which the cause operates, or any connexion between it and its supposed effect. The same difficulty occurs in contemplating the operations of mind on body—where we observe the motion of the latter to follow upon the volition of the former, but are not able to observe or conceive the tie which binds together the motion and volition, or the energy by which the mind produces this effect. The authority of the will over its own faculties and ideas is not a whit more comprehensible: So that, upon the whole, there appears not, throughout all nature, any one instance of connexion which is conceivable by us. All events seem entirely loose and separate. One event follows another; but we never can observe any tie between them. They seem *conjoined*, but never *connected*. And as we can have no idea of any thing which never appeared to our outward sense or inward sentiment, the necessary conclusion *seems* to be that we have no idea of connexion or power at all, and that these words are absolutely without any meaning, when employed either
59   in philosophical reasonings or common life.

But there still remains one method of avoiding this conclusion, and one source which we have not yet examined. When any natural object or event is presented, it is impossible for us, by any sagacity or penetration, to discover, or even conjecture, without experience, what event will result from it, or to carry our foresight beyond that object which is immediately present to the memory and senses. Even after one instance or experiment, where we have observed a particular event to follow upon another, we are not entitled to form a general rule, or foretell what will happen in like cases; it being justly esteemed an unpardonable temerity to judge of the whole course of nature from one single experiment, however accurate or certain. But when one particular species of event has always, in all instances, been conjoined with another, we make no longer any scruple of foretelling one upon the appearance of the other, and of employing that reasoning, which can alone assure us of any matter of fact or existence. We then call the one object, *Cause*; the other, *Effect*. We suppose that there is some connexion between them; some power in the one, by which it infallibly produces the other, and operates with the greatest certainty and strongest necessity.

It appears, then, that this idea of a necessary connexion among events arises from a number of similar instances which occur of the constant conjunction of these events; nor can that idea ever be suggested by any one of these instances, surveyed in all possible lights and positions. But there is nothing in a number of instances, different from every single instance, which is supposed to be exactly similar; except only, that after a repetition of similar instances, the mind is carried by habit, upon the appearance of one event, to expect its usual attendant, and to believe that it will exist. This connexion, therefore, which we *feel* in the mind, this customary transition of the imagination from one object to its usual attendant, is the sentiment or impression from which we form the idea of power or necessary connexion. Nothing farther is in the case. Contemplate the subject on all sides; you will never find any other origin of that idea. This is the sole difference between one instance, from which we can never receive the idea of connexion, and a number of similar instances, by which it is suggested. The first time a man saw the communication of motion by impulse, as by the shock of two billiard balls, he could not pronounce that the one event was *connected*: but only that it was *conjoined* with the other. After he has observed several instances of this nature, he then pronounces them to be *connected*. What alteration has happened to give rise to this new idea of *connexion*? Nothing but that he now *feels* these events to be *connected* in his imagination, and can readily foretell the existence of one from the appearance of the other. When we say, therefore, that one object is connected with another, we mean only that they have acquired a connexion in our thought, and give rise to this inference, by which they become proofs of each other's existence: A conclusion which is somewhat extraordinary, but which seems founded on sufficient evidence. Nor will its evidence be weakened by any general diffidence of the understanding, or sceptical suspicion concerning every conclusion which is new and extraordinary. No conclusions can be more agreeable to scepticism than such as make discoveries concerning the weakness and narrow limits of human reason and capacity.

And what stronger instance can be produced of the surprising ignorance and weakness of the understanding than the present? For surely, if there be any relation

60

among objects which it imports to us to know perfectly, it is that of cause and effect. On this are founded all our reasonings concerning matter of fact or existence. By means of it alone we attain any assurance concerning objects which are removed from the present testimony of our memory and senses. The only immediate utility of all sciences, is to teach us, how to control and regulate future events by their causes. Our thoughts and enquiries are, therefore, every moment, employed about this relation: Yet so imperfect are the ideas which we form concerning it, that it is impossible to give any just definition of cause, except what is drawn from something extraneous and foreign to it. Similar objects are always conjoined with similar. Of this we have experience. Suitably to this experience, therefore, we may define a cause to be *an object, followed by another, and where all the objects similar to the first are followed by objects similar to the second.* Or in other words *where, if the first object had not been, the second never had existed.* The appearance of a cause always conveys the mind, by a customary transition, to the idea of the effect. Of this also we have experience. We may, therefore, suitably to this experience, form another definition of cause, and call it, *an object followed by another, and whose appearance always conveys the thought to that other.* But though both these definitions be drawn from circumstances foreign to the cause, we cannot remedy this inconvenience, or attain any more perfect definition, which may point out that circumstance in the cause, which gives it a connexion with its effect. We have no idea of this connexion, nor even any distinct notion what it is we desire to know, when we endeavour at a conception of it. We say, for instance, that the vibration of this string is the cause of this particular sound. But what do we mean by that affirmation? We either mean *that this vibration is followed by this sound, and that all similar vibrations have been followed by similar sounds:* Or, *that this vibration is followed by this sound, and that upon the appearance of one the mind anticipates the senses, and forms immediately an idea of the other.* We may consider the relation of cause and effect in either of these two lights; but beyond these, we have no idea of it.[1]

---

1. According to these explications and definitions, the idea of *power* is relative as much as that of *cause*; and both have a reference to an effect, or some other event constantly conjoined with the former. When we consider the *unknown* circumstance of an object, by which the degree or quantity of its effect is fixed and determined, we call that its power: And accordingly, it is allowed by all philosophers, that the effect is the measure of the power. But if they had any idea of power, as it is in itself, why could not they measure it in itself? The dispute whether the force of a body in motion be as its velocity, or the square of its velocity; this dispute, I say, needed not be decided by comparing its effects in equal or unequal times; but by a direct mensuration and comparison.

   As to the frequent use of the words, Force, Power, Energy, &c., which every where occur in common conversation, as well as in philosophy; that is no proof, that we are acquainted, in any instance, with the connecting principle between cause and effect, or can account ultimately for the production of one thing by another. These words, as commonly used, have very loose meanings annexed to them; and their ideas are very uncertain and confused. No animal can put external bodies in motion without the sentiment of a *nisus* or endeavour; and every animal has a sentiment or feeling from the stroke or blow of an external object, that is in motion. These sensations, which are merely animal, and from which we can *à priori* draw no inference, we are apt to transfer to inanimate objects, and

To recapitulate, therefore, the reasonings of this section: Every idea is copied from 61 some preceding impression or sentiment; and where we cannot find any impression, we may be certain that there is no idea. In all single instances of the operation of bodies or minds, there is nothing that produces any impression, nor consequently can suggest any idea, of power or necessary connexion. But when many uniform instances appear, and the same object is always followed by the same event; we then begin to entertain the notion of cause and connexion. We then *feel* a new sentiment or impression, to wit, a customary connexion in the thought or imagination between one object and its usual attendant; and this sentiment is the original of that idea which we seek for. For as this idea arises from a number of similar instances, and not from any single instance, it must arise from that circumstance, in which the number of instances differ from every individual instance. But this customary connexion or transition of the imagination is the only circumstance in which they differ. In every other particular they are alike. The first instance which we saw of motion communicated by the shock of two billiard balls (to return to this obvious illustration) is exactly similar to any instance that may, at present, occur to us; except only, that we could not, at first, *infer* one event from the other; which we are enabled to do at present, after so long a course of uniform experience. I know not whether the reader will readily apprehend this reasoning. I am afraid that, should I multiply words about it, or throw it into a greater variety of lights, it would only become more obscure and intricate. In all abstract reasonings there is one point of view which, if we can happily hit, we shall go farther towards illustrating the subject than by all the eloquence and copious expression in the world. This point of view we should endeavour to reach, and reserve the flowers of rhetoric for subjects which are more adapted to them.

---

to suppose, that they have some such feelings, whenever they transfer or receive motion. With regard to energies, which are exerted, without our annexing to them any idea of communicated motion, we consider only the constant experienced conjunction of the events; and as we *feel* a customary connexion between the ideas, we transfer that feeling to the objects; as nothing is more usual than to apply to external bodies every internal sensation, which they occasion.

Chapter 30

Causation*

David Lewis

H UME defined causation twice over. He wrote 'we may define a cause to be *an object followed by another, and where all the objects, similar to the first, are followed by objects similar to the second*. Or, in other words *where, if the first object had not been, the second never had existed*.'[1]

Descendants of Hume's first definition still dominate the philosophy of causation: a causal succession is supposed to be a succession that instantiates a regularity. To be sure, there have been improvements. Nowadays we try to distinguish the regularities that count—the 'causal laws'—from mere accidental regularities of succession. We subsume causes and effects under regularities by means of descriptions they satisfy, not by overall similarity. And we allow a cause to be only one indispensable part, not the whole, of the total situation that is followed by the effect in accordance with a law. In present-day regularity analyses, a cause is defined (roughly) as any member of any minimal set of actual conditions that are jointly sufficient, given the laws, for the existence of the effect.

More precisely, let C be the proposition that c exists (or occurs) and let E be the proposition that e exists. Then c causes e, according to a typical regularity analysis,[2] iff (1) C and E are true; and (2) for some non-empty set $\mathcal{L}$ of true law-propositions and some set $\mathcal{F}$ of true propositions of particular fact, $\mathcal{L}$ and $\mathcal{F}$ jointly imply $C \supset E$, although $\mathcal{L}$ and $\mathcal{F}$ jointly do not imply E and $\mathcal{F}$ alone does not imply $C \supset E$.[3]

Much needs doing, and much has been done, to turn definitions like this one into defensible analyses. Many problems have been overcome. Others remain: in particular, regularity analyses tend to confuse causation itself with various other causal relations. If c belongs to a minimal set of conditions jointly sufficient for e, given the laws, then c may well be a genuine cause of e. But c might rather be an effect of e: one which could

* I thank the American Council of Learned Societies, Princeton University, and the National Science Foundation for research support.

1. *An Enquiry Concerning Human Understanding*, sect. 7.
2. Not one that has been proposed by any actual author in just this form, so far as I know.
3. I identify a *proposition*, as is becoming usual, with the set of possible worlds where it is true. It is not a linguistic entity. Truth-functional operations on propositions are the appropriate Boolean operations on sets of worlds; logical relations among propositions are relations of inclusion, overlap, etc. among sets. A sentence of a language *expresses* a proposition iff the sentence and the proposition are true at exactly the same worlds. No ordinary language will provide sentences to express all propositions; there will not be enough sentences to go around.

not, given the laws and some of the actual circumstances, have occurred otherwise than by being caused by *e*. Or *c* might be an epiphenomenon of the causal history of *e*: a more or less inefficacious effect of some genuine cause of *e*. Or *c* might be a pre-empted potential cause of *e*: something that did not cause *e*, but that would have done so in the absence of whatever really did cause *e*.

It remains to be seen whether any regularity analysis can succeed in distinguishing genuine causes from effects, epiphenomena, and pre-empted potential causes—and whether it can succeed without falling victim to worse problems, without piling on the epicycles, and without departing from the fundamental idea that causation is instantiation of regularities. I have no proof that regularity analyses are beyond repair, nor any space to review the repairs that have been tried. Suffice it to say that the prospects look dark. I think it is time to give up and try something else.

A promising alternative is not far to seek. Hume's 'other words'—that if the cause had not been, the effect never had existed—are no mere restatement of his first definition. They propose something altogether different: a counterfactual analysis of causation.

The proposal has not been well received. True, we do know that causation has something or other to do with counterfactuals. We think of a cause as something that makes a difference, and the difference it makes must be a difference from what would have happened without it. Had it been absent, its effects—some of them, at least, and usually all—would have been absent as well. Yet it is one thing to mention these platitudes now and again, and another thing to rest an analysis on them. That has not seemed worth while.[4] We have learned all too well that counterfactuals are ill understood, wherefore it did not seem that much understanding could be gained by using them to analyse causation or anything else. Pending a better understanding of counterfactuals, moreover, we had no way to fight seeming counter-examples to a counterfactual analysis.

But counterfactuals need not remain ill understood, I claim, unless we cling to false preconceptions about what it would be like to understand them. Must an adequate understanding make no reference to unactualized possibilities? Must it assign sharply determinate truth conditions? Must it connect counterfactuals rigidly to covering laws? Then none will be forthcoming. So much the worse for those standards of adequacy. Why not take counterfactuals at face value: as statements about possible alternatives to the actual situation, somewhat vaguely specified, in which the actual laws may or may not remain intact? There are now several such treatments of counterfactuals, differing only in details.[5] If they are right, then sound foundations have been laid for analyses that use counterfactuals.

In this paper, I shall state a counterfactual analysis, not very different from Hume's second definition, of some sorts of causation. Then I shall try to show how

---

4. One exception: Ardon Lyon, 'Causality', *British Journal for Philosophy of Science*, 18.1 (May 1967), 1–20.
5. See e.g. Robert Stalnaker. 'A Theory of Conditionals', in Nicholas Rescher (ed.), *Studies in Logical Theory* (Oxford, Blackwell, 1968), repr. in F. Jackson (ed.), *Conditionals* (Oxford, Oxford University Press, 1991), 28–45; and my *Counterfactuals* (Oxford, Blackwell, 1973).

this analysis works to distinguish genuine causes from effects, epiphenomena, and pre-empted potential causes.

My discussion will be incomplete in at least four ways. Explicit preliminary settings-aside may prevent confusion.

1. I shall confine myself to causation among *events*, in the everyday sense of the word: flashes, battles, conversations, impacts, strolls, deaths, touchdowns, falls, kisses, and the like. Not that events are the only things that can cause or be caused; but I have no full list of the others, and no good umbrella-term to cover them all.

2. My analysis is meant to apply to causation in particular cases. It is not an analysis of causal generalizations. Presumably those are quantified statements involving causation among particular events (or non-events), but it turns out not to be easy to match up the causal generalizations of natural language with the available quantified forms. A sentence of the form 'c-events cause e-events,' for instance, can mean any of

    (a) For some c in c and some e in e, c causes e,

    (b) For every e in e, there is some c in c such that c causes e,

    (c) For every c in c, there is some e in e such that c causes e,

    not to mention further ambiguities. Worse still, 'Only c-events cause e-events' ought to mean

    (d) For every c, if there is some e in e such that c causes e, then c is in c

    if 'only' has its usual meaning. But no; it unambiguously means (b) instead! These problems are not about causation, but about our idioms of quantification.

3. We sometimes single out one among all the causes of some event and call it 'the' cause, as if there were no others. Or we single out a few as the 'causes', calling the rest mere 'causal factors' or 'causal conditions'. Or we speak of the 'decisive' or 'real' or 'principal' cause. We may select the abnormal or extraordinary causes, or those under human control, or those we deem good or bad, or just those we want to talk about. I have nothing to say about these principles of invidious discrimination.[6] I am concerned with the prior question of what it is to be one of the causes (unselectively speaking). My analysis is meant to capture a broad and non-discriminatory concept of causation.

4. I shall be content, for now, if I can give an analysis of causation that works properly under determinism. By determinism I do not mean any thesis of universal causation, or universal predictability-in-principle, but rather this: the prevailing laws of nature are such that there do not exist any two possible worlds which are exactly alike up to some time, which differ thereafter, and in which those laws are never violated. Perhaps by ignoring indeterminism I squander the most striking advantage of a counterfactual analysis over

---

6. Except that Morton G. White's discussion of causal selection, in *Foundations of Historical Knowledge* (New York, Harper & Row, 1965), 105–81, would meet my needs, despite the fact that it is based on a regularity analysis.

a regularity analysis: that it allows undetermined events to be caused.[7] I fear, however, that my present analysis cannot yet cope with all varieties of causation under indeterminism. The needed repair would take us too far into disputed questions about the foundations of probability.

Comparative similarity

To begin, I take as primitive a relation of *comparative overall* similarity among possible worlds. We may say that one world is *closer to actuality* than another if the first resembles our actual world more than the second does, taking account of all the respects of similarity and difference and balancing them off one against another.

(More generally, an arbitrary world *w* can play the role of our actual world. In speaking of our actual world without knowing just which world is ours, I am in effect generalizing over all worlds. We really need a three-place relation: world w_1 is closer to world *w* than world w_2 is. I shall henceforth leave this generality tacit.)

I have not said just how to balance the respects of comparison against each other, so I have not said just what our relation of comparative similarity is to be. Not for nothing did I call it primitive. But I have said what *sort* of relation it is, and we are familiar with relations of that sort. We do make judgements of comparative overall similarity—of people, for instance—by balancing off many respects of similarity and difference. Often our mutual expectations about the weighting factors are definite and accurate enough to permit communication. I shall have more to say later about the way the balance must go in particular cases to make my analysis work. But the vagueness of overall similarity will not be entirely resolved. Nor should it be. The vagueness of similarity does infect causation; and no correct analysis can deny it.

The respects of similarity and difference that enter into the overall similarity of worlds are many and varied. In particular, similarities in matters of particular fact trade off against similarities of law. The prevailing laws of nature are important to the character of a world; so similarities of law are weighty. Weighty, but not sacred. We should not take it for granted that a world that conforms perfectly to our actual laws is *ipso facto* closer to actuality than any world where those laws are violated in any way at all. It depends on the nature and extent of the violation, on the place of the violated laws in the total system of laws of nature, and on the countervailing similarities and differences in other respects. Likewise, similarities or differences of particular fact may be more or less weighty, depending on their nature and extent. Comprehensive and exact similarities of particular fact throughout large spatio-temporal regions seem to have special weight. It may be worth a small miracle to prolong or expand a region of perfect match.

Our relation of comparative similarity should meet two formal constraints. (1) It should be a weak ordering of the worlds: an ordering in which ties are permitted,

7. That this ought to be allowed is argued in G. E. M. Anscombe, *Causality and Determination: An Inaugural Lecture* (Cambridge, CUP, 1971), repr. as Ch. V above; and in Fred Dretske and Aaron Snyder, 'Causal Irregularity', *Philosophy of Science*, 39.1 (Mar. 1972), 69–71.

but any two worlds are comparable. (2) Our actual world should be closest to actuality, resembling itself more than any other world resembles it. We do *not* impose the further constraint that for any set *A* of worlds there is a unique closest *A*-world, or even a set of *A*-worlds tied for closest. Why not an infinite sequence of closer and closer *A*-worlds, but no closest?

Counterfactuals and counterfactual dependence

Given any two propositions *A* and *C*, we have their *counterfactual* $A \,\square\!\rightarrow C$: the proposition that if *A* were true, then *C* would also be true. The operation $\square\!\rightarrow$ is defined by a rule of truth, as follows. $A \,\square\!\rightarrow C$ is true (at a world *w*) iff either (1) there are no possible *A*-worlds (in which case $A \,\square\!\rightarrow C$ is *vacuous*), or (2) some *A*-world where *C* holds is closer (to *w*) than is any *A*-world where *C* does not hold. In other words, a counterfactual is non-vacuously true iff it takes less of a departure from actuality to make the consequent true along with the antecedent than it does to make the antecedent true without the consequent.

We did not assume that there must always be one or more closest *A*-worlds. But if there are, we can simplify: $A \,\square\!\rightarrow C$ is non-vacuously true iff *C* holds at all the closest *A*-worlds.

We have not presupposed that *A* is false. If *A* is true, then our actual world is the closest *A*-world, so $\square\!\rightarrow C$ is true iff *C* is. Hence $A \,\square\!\rightarrow C$ implies the material conditional $A \supset C$; and *A* and *C* jointly imply $A \,\square\!\rightarrow C$.

Let $A_1, A_2, \ldots$ be a family of possible propositions, no two of which are compossible; let $C_1, C_2, \ldots$ be another such family (of equal size). Then if all the counterfactuals $A_1 \,\square\!\rightarrow C_1, A_2 \,\square\!\rightarrow C_2, \ldots$ between corresponding propositions in the two families are true, we shall say that the *C*'s *depend counterfactually* on the *A*'s. We can say it like this in ordinary language: whether C_1 or C_2 or . . . depends (counterfactually) on whether A_1 or A_2 or . . . .

Counterfactual dependence between large families of alternatives is characteristic of processes of measurement, perception, or control. Let $R_1, R_2, \ldots$ be propositions specifying the alternative readings of a certain barometer at a certain time. Let $P_1, P_2, \ldots$ specify the corresponding pressures of the surrounding air. Then, if the barometer is working properly to measure the pressure, the *R*'s must depend counterfactually on the *P*'s. As we say it: the reading depends on the pressure. Likewise, if I am seeing at a certain time, then my visual impressions must depend counterfactually, over a wide range of alternative possibilities, on the scene before my eyes. And if I am in control over what happens in some respect, then there must be a double counterfactual dependence, again over some fairly wide range of alternatives. The outcome depends on what I do, and that in turn depends on which outcome I want.[8]

---

8. Analyses in terms of counterfactual dependence are found in two papers of Alvin I. Goldman: 'Toward a Theory of Social Power', *Philosophical Studies*, 23 (1972), 221–68; and 'Discrimination and Perceptual Knowledge', presented at the 1972 Chapel Hill Colloquium.

Causal dependence among events

If a family $C_1, C_2, \ldots$ depends counterfactually on a family $A_1, A_2, \ldots$ in the sense just explained, we will ordinarily be willing to speak also of causal dependence. We say, for instance, that the barometer reading depends causally on the pressure, that my visual impressions depend causally on the scene before my eyes, or that the outcome of something under my control depends causally on what I do. But there are exceptions. Let $G_1, G_2, \ldots$ be alternative possible laws of gravitation, differing in the value of some numerical constant. Let $M_1, M_2, \ldots$ be suitable alternative laws of planetary motion. Then the M's may depend counterfactually on the G's, but we would not call this dependence causal. Such exceptions as this, however, do not involve any sort of dependence among distinct particular events. The hope remains that causal dependence among events, at least, may be analysed simply as counterfactual dependence.

We have spoken thus far of counterfactual dependence among propositions, not among events. Whatever particular events may be, presumably they are not propositions. But that is no problem, since they can at least be paired with propositions. To any possible event e, there corresponds the proposition $O(e)$ that holds at all and only those worlds where e occurs. Thus $O(e)$ is the proposition that e occurs.[9] (If no two events occur at exactly the same worlds—if, that is, there are no absolutely necessary connections between distinct events—we may add that this correspondence of events and propositions is one to one.) Counterfactual dependence among events is simply counterfactual dependence among the corresponding propositions.

Let $c_1, c_2, \ldots$ and $e_1, e_2, \ldots$ be distinct possible events such that no two of the c's and no two of the e's are compossible. Then I say that the family $e_1, e_2, \ldots$ of events *depends causally* on the family $c_1, c_2, \ldots$ iff the family $O(e_1), O(e_2), \ldots$ of propositions depends counterfactually on the family $O(c_1), O(c_2), \ldots$ As we say it: whether e_1 or e_2 or $\ldots$ occurs depends on whether c_1 or c_2 or $\ldots$ occurs.

---

9. Beware: if we refer to a particular event e by means of some description that e satisfies, then we must take care not to confuse $O(e)$, the proposition that e itself occurs, with the different proposition that some event or other occurs which satisfies the description. It is a contingent matter, in general, what events satisfy what descriptions. Let e be the death of Socrates—the death he actually died, to be distinguished from all the different deaths he might have died instead. Suppose that Socrates had fled, only to be eaten by a lion. Then e would not have occurred, and $O(e)$ would have been false; but a different event would have satisfied the description 'the death of Socrates' that I used to refer to e. Or suppose that Socrates had lived and died just as he actually did, and afterwards was resurrected and killed again and resurrected again, and finally became immortal. Then no event would have satisfied the description. (Even if the temporary deaths are real deaths, neither of the two can be *the* death.) But e would have occurred, and $O(e)$ would have been true. Call a description of an event e *rigid* iff (1) nothing but e could possibly satisfy it, and (2) e could not possibly occur without satisfying it. I have claimed that even such commonplace descriptions as 'the death of Socrates' are non-rigid, and in fact I think that rigid descriptions of events are hard to find. That would be a problem for anyone who needed to associate with every possible every e a sentence $\varphi(e)$ true at all and only those worlds where e occurs. But we need no such sentences—only propositions, which may or may not have expressions in our language.

We can also define a relation of dependence among single events rather than families. Let c and e be two distinct possible particular events. Then e *depends causally* on c iff the family $O(e)$, $\sim O(e)$ depends counterfactually on the family $O(c)$, $\sim O(c)$. As we say it: whether e occurs or not depends on whether c occurs or not. The dependence consists in the truth of two counterfactuals: $O(c \,\square\!\rightarrow O(e)$ and $\sim O(c) \,\square\!\rightarrow \sim O(e)$. There are two cases. If c and e do not actually occur, then the second counterfactual is automatically true because its antecedent and consequent are true: so e depends causally on c iff the first counterfactual holds. That is, if e would have occurred if c had occurred. But if c and e are actual events, then it is the first counterfactual that is automatically true. Then e depends causally on c iff, if c had not been, e never had existed. I take Hume's second definition as my definition not of causation itself, but of causal dependence among actual events.

Causation

Causal dependence among actual events implies causation. If c and e are two actual events such that e would not have occurred without c, then c is a cause of e. But I reject the converse. Causation must always be transitive; causal dependence may not be; so there can be causation without causal dependence. Let c, d, and e be three actual events such that d would not have occurred without c and e would not have occurred without d. Then c is a cause of e even if e would still have occurred (otherwise caused) without c.

We extend causal dependence to a transitive relation in the usual way. Let c, d, e, . . . be a finite sequence of actual particular events such that d depends causally on c, e on d, and so on throughout. Then this sequence is a *causal chain*. Finally, one event is a *cause* of another iff there exists a causal chain leading from the first to the second. This completes my counterfactual analysis of causation.

Counterfactual versus nomic dependence

It is essential to distinguish counterfactual and causal dependence from what I shall call *nomic dependence*. The family C_1, C_2, . . . of propositions depends nomically on the family A_1, A_2, . . . iff there are a non-empty set $\mathcal{L}$ of true law-propositions and a set $\mathcal{F}$ of true law-propositions of particular fact such that $\mathcal{L}$ and $\mathcal{F}$ jointly imply (but $\mathcal{F}$ alone does not imply) all the material conditionals $A_1 \supset C_1$, $A_2 \supset C_2$, . . . between the corresponding propositions in the two families. (Recall that these same material conditionals are implied by the counterfactuals that would comprise a counterfactual dependence.) We shall say also that the nomic dependence holds *in virtue of* the premise sets $\mathcal{L}$ and $\mathcal{F}$.

Nomic and counterfactual dependence are related as follows. Say that a proposition B is *counterfactually independent* of the family A_1, A_2, . . . of alternatives iff

B would hold no matter which of the As were true—that is, iff the counterfactuals $A_1 \,\square\!\!\rightarrow B, A_2 \,\square\!\!\rightarrow B \ldots$ all hold. If the C's depend nomically on the A's in virtue of the premise sets $\mathcal{L}$ and $\mathcal{F}$, and if in addition (all members of) $\mathcal{L}$ and $\mathcal{F}$ are counterfactually independent of the A's, then it follows that the C's depend counterfactually on the A's. In that case, we may regard the nomic dependence in virtue of $\mathcal{L}$ and $\mathcal{F}$ as explaining the counterfactual dependence. Often, perhaps always, counterfactual dependences may be thus explained. But the requirement of counterfactual independence is indispensable. Unless $\mathcal{L}$ and $\mathcal{F}$ meet that requirement, nomic dependence in virtue of $\mathcal{L}$ and $\mathcal{F}$ does not imply counterfactual dependence, and, if there is counterfactual dependence anyway, does not explain it.

Nomic dependence is reversible, in the following sense. If the family $C_1, C_2, \ldots$ depends nomically on the family $A_1, A_2, \ldots$, in virtue of $\mathcal{L}$ and $\mathcal{F}$, then also $A_1, A_2, \ldots$ depends nomically on the family $AC_1, AC_2, \ldots$, in virtue of $\mathcal{L}$ and $\mathcal{F}$, where A is the disjunction $A_1 \vee A_2 \vee \ldots$. Is counterfactual dependence likewise reversible? That does not follow. For, even if $\mathcal{L}$ and $\mathcal{F}$ are independent of $A_1, A_2, \ldots$ and hence establish the counterfactual dependence of the C's on the A's, still they may fail to be independent of $AC_1, AC_2, \ldots$, and hence may fail to establish the reverse counterfactual dependence of the A's on the AC's. Irreversible counterfactual dependence is shown below: @ is our actual world, the dots are the other worlds, and distance on the page represents similarity 'distance'.

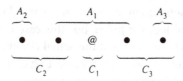

The counterfactuals $A_1 \,\square\!\!\rightarrow C_1, A_2 \,\square\!\!\rightarrow C_2$, and $A_3 \,\square\!\!\rightarrow C_3$ hold at the actual world; wherefore the C's depend on the A's. But we do not have the reverse dependence of the A's on the AC's, since instead of the needed $AC_2 \,\square\!\!\rightarrow A_2$ and $AC_3 \,\square\!\!\rightarrow A_3$ we have $AC_2 \,\square\!\!\rightarrow A_1$ and $AC_3 \,\square\!\!\rightarrow A_1$.

Just such irreversibility is commonplace. The barometer reading depends counterfactually on the pressure—that is as clear-cut as counterfactuals ever get—but does the pressure depend counterfactually on the reading? If the reading had been higher, would the pressure have been higher? Or would the barometer have been malfunctioning? The second sounds better: a higher reading would have been an incorrect reading. To be sure, there are actual laws and circumstances that imply and explain the actual accuracy of the barometer, but these are no more sacred than the actual laws and circumstances that imply and explain the actual pressure. Less sacred, in fact. When something must give way to permit a higher reading, we find it less of a departure from actuality to hold the pressure fixed and sacrifice the accuracy, rather than vice versa. It is not hard to see why. The barometer, being more localized and more delicate than the weather, is more vulnerable to slight departures from actuality.[10]

We can now explain why regularity analyses of causation (among events, under determinism) work as well as they do. Suppose that event c causes event e according to the sample regularity analysis that I gave at the beginning of this paper, in virtue of premise sets $\mathcal{L}$ and $\mathcal{F}$. It follows that $\mathcal{L}$, and $\mathcal{F} \sim O(c)$ jointly do not imply $O(e)$. Strengthen this: suppose further that they do imply $\sim O(e)$. If so, the family $O(e)$, $\sim O(e)$, depends nomically on the family $O(c)$, $\sim O(c)$ in virtue of $\mathcal{L}$ and $\mathcal{F}$. Add one more supposition: that $\mathcal{L}$ and $\mathcal{F}$ are counterfactually independent of $O(c)$, $\sim O(c)$. Then it follows according to my counterfactual analysis that e depends counterfactually and casually on c, and hence that c causes e. If I am right, the regularity analysis gives conditions that are almost but not quite sufficient for explicable causal dependence. That is not quite the same thing as causation; but causation without causal dependence is scarce, and if there is inexplicable causal dependence we are (understandably!) unaware of it.[11]

Effects and epiphenomena

I return now to the problems I raised against regularity analyses, hoping to show that my counterfactual analysis can overcome them.

The *problem of effects*, as it confronts a counterfactual analysis, is as follows. Suppose that c causes a subsequent event e, and that e does not also cause c. (I do not rule out closed causal loops *a priori*, but this case is not to be one.) Suppose further that, given the laws and some of the actual circumstances, c could not have failed to cause e. It seems to follow that if the effect e had not occurred, then its cause c would not have occurred. We have a spurious reverse causal dependence of c on e, contradicting our supposition that e did not cause c.

The *problem of epiphenomena*, for a counterfactual analysis, is similar. Suppose that e is an epiphenomenal effect of a genuine cause c of an effect f. That is, c causes first e and then f, but e does not cause f. Suppose further that, given the laws and some of the actual circumstances, c could not have failed to cause e; and that, given the laws and others of the circumstances, f could not have been caused otherwise than by c. It seems to follow that if the epiphenomenon e had not occurred, then its

10. Granted, there are contexts or changes of wording that would incline us the other way. For some reason, 'If the reading had been higher, that would have been because the pressure was higher' invites my assent more than 'If the reading had been higher, the pressure would have been higher.' The counterfactuals from readings to pressures are much less clear-cut than those from pressures to readings. But it is enough that some legitimate resolutions of vagueness give an irreversible dependence of readings on pressures. Those are the resolutions we want at present, even if they are not favored in all contexts.

11. I am not here proposing a repaired regularity analysis. The repaired analysis would gratuitously rule out inexplicable causal dependence, which seems bad. Nor would it be squarely in the tradition of regularity analyses any more. Too much else would have been added.

cause c would not have occurred and the further effect f of that same cause would not have occurred either. We have a spurious causal dependence of f on e, contradicting our supposition that e did not cause f.

One might be tempted to solve the problem of effects by brute force: insert into the analysis a stipulation that a cause must always precede its effect (and perhaps a parallel stipulation for causal dependence). I reject this solution. (1) It is worthless against the closely related problem of epiphenomena, since the epiphenomenon e does precede its spurious effect f. (2) It rejects *a priori* certain legitimate physical hypotheses that posit backward or simultaneous causation. (3) It trivializes any theory that seeks to define the forward direction of time as the predominant direction of causation.

The proper solution to both problems, I think, is flatly to deny the counterfactuals that cause the trouble. If e had been absent, it is not that c would have been absent (and with it f, in the second case). Rather, c would have occurred just as it did but would have failed to cause e. It is less of a departure from actuality to get rid of e by holding c fixed and giving up some or other of the laws and circumstances in virtue of which c could not have failed to cause e, rather than to hold those laws and circumstances fixed and get rid of e by going back and abolishing its cause c. (In the second case, it would of course be pointless not to hold f fixed along with c.) The causal dependence of e on c is the same sort of irreversible counterfactual dependence that we have considered already.

To get rid of an actual event e with the least overall departure from actuality, it will normally be best not to diverge at all from the actual course of events until just before the time of e. The longer we wait, the more we prolong the spatio-temporal region of perfect match between our actual world and the selected alternative. Why diverge sooner rather than later? Not to avoid violations of laws of nature. Under determinism *any* divergence, soon or late, requires some violation of the actual laws. If the laws were held sacred, there would be no way to get rid of e without changing all of the past; and nothing guarantees that the change could be kept negligible except in the recent past. That would mean that if the present were ever so slightly different, then all of the past would have been different—which is absurd. So the laws are not sacred. Violation of laws is a matter of degree. Until we get up to the time immediately before e is to occur, there is no general reason why a later divergence to avert e should need a more severe violation than an earlier one. Perhaps there are special reasons in special cases—but then these may be cases of backward causal dependence.

Pre-emption

Suppose that c_1 occurs and causes e; and that c_2 also occurs and does not cause e, but would have caused e if c_1 had been absent. Thus c_2 is a potential alternative cause of e, but is pre-empted by the actual cause c_1. We may say that c_1 and c_2

overdetermine e, but they do so asymmetrically.[12] In virtue of what difference does c_1 but not c_2 cause e?

As far as causal dependence goes, there is no difference: e depends neither on c_1 nor on c_2. If either one had not occurred, the other would have sufficed to cause e. So the difference must be that, thanks to c_1, there is no causal chain from c_2 to e; whereas there is a causal chain of two or more steps from c_1 to e. Assume for simplicity that two steps are enough. Then e depends causally on some intermediate event d, and d in turn depends on c_1. Causal dependence is here intransitive: c_1 causes e via d even though e would still have occurred without c_1.

So far, so good. It remains only to deal with the objection that e does *not* depend causally on d, because if d had been absent then c_1 would have been absent and c_2, no longer pre-empted, would have caused e. We may reply by denying the claim that if d had been absent then c_1 would have been absent. That is the very same sort of spurious reverse dependence of cause on effect that we have just rejected in simpler cases. I rather claim that if d had been absent, c_1 would somehow have failed to cause d. But c_1 would still have been there to interfere with c_2, so e would not have occurred.

---

12. I shall not discuss symmetrical cases of overdetermination, in which two overdetermining factors have equal claim to count as causes. For me these are useless as test cases because I lack firm naïve opinions about them.

Chapter 31

Causal relations*

Donald Davidson

WHAT is the logical form of singular causal statements like: 'The flood caused the famine,' 'The stabbing caused Caesar's death,' 'The burning of the house caused the roasting of the pig'? This question is more modest than the question how we know such statements are true, and the question whether they can be analysed in terms of, say, constant conjunction. The request for the logical form is modest because it is answered when we have identified the logical or grammatical roles of the words (or other significant stretches) in the sentences under scrutiny. It goes beyond this to define, analyse, or set down axioms governing, particular words or expressions.

1

According to Hume, 'we may define a cause to be an object, followed by another, and where all the objects similar to the first are followed by objects similar to the second.' This definition pretty clearly suggests that causes and effects are entities that can be named or described by singular terms; probably events, since one can follow another. But in the *Treatise*, under 'rules by which to judge of causes and effects', Hume says that 'where several different objects produce the same effect, it must be by means of some quality, which we discover to be common among them. For as like effects imply like causes, we must always ascribe the causation to the circumstances wherein we discover the resemblance.' Here it seems to be the 'quality' or 'circumstances' of an event that is the cause rather than the event itself, for the event itself is the same as others in some respects and different in other respects. The suspicion that it is not events, but something more closely tied to the descriptions of events, that Hume holds to be causes is fortified by Hume's claim that causal statements are never necessary. For if events were causes, then a true description of some event would be 'the cause of *b*', and, given that such an event exists, it follows logically that the cause of *b* caused *b*.

* I am indebted to Harry Lewis and David Nivison, as well as to other members of seminars at Stanford University to whom I presented the ideas in this paper during 1966–7, for many helpful comments. I have profited greatly from discussion with John Wallace of the questions raised here; he may or may not agree with my answers. My research was supported in part by the National Science Foundation.

Mill said that the cause 'is the sum total of the conditions positive and negative taken together . . . which being realized, the consequent invariably follows'. Many discussions of causality have concentrated on the question whether Mill was right in insisting that the 'real Cause' must include all the antecedent conditions that jointly were sufficient for the effect, and much ingenuity has been spent on discovering factors, pragmatic or otherwise, that guide and justify our choice of some 'part' of the conditions as the cause. There has been general agreement that the notion of cause may be at least partly characterized in terms of sufficient and (or) necessary conditions.[1] Yet it seems to me we do not understand how such characterizations are to be applied to particular causes.

Take one of Mill's examples: some man, say Smith, dies, and the cause of his death is said to be that his foot slipped in climbing a ladder. Mill would say we have not given the whole cause, since having a foot slip in climbing a ladder is not always followed by death. What we were after, however, was not the cause of death in general but the cause of Smith's death: does it make sense to ask under what conditions Smith's death invariably follows? Mill suggests that part of the cause of Smith's death is 'the circumstance of his weight', perhaps because if Smith had been light as a feather his slip might not have injured him. Mill's explanation of why we don't bother to mention this circumstance is that it is too obvious to bear mention, but it seems to me that if it was Smith's fall that killed him, and Smith weighed 12 stone, then Smith's fall was the fall of a man who weighed 12 stone, whether or not we know it or mention it. How could Smith's actual fall, with Smith weighing, as he did, 12 stone, be any more efficacious in killing him than Smith's actual fall?

The difficulty has nothing to do with Mill's sweeping view of the cause, but attends any attempt of this kind to treat particular causes as necessary or sufficient conditions. Thus Mackie asks, 'What is the exact force of [the statement of some experts] that this short-circuit caused this fire?' And he answers, 'Clearly the experts are not saying that the short-circuit was a necessary condition for this house's catching fire at this time; they know perfectly well that a short-circuit somewhere else, or the overturning of a lighted oil stove . . . might, if it had occurred, have set the house on fire' (ibid. 245). Suppose the experts know what they are said to; how does this bear on the question whether the short circuit was a necessary condition of this particular fire? For a short-circuit elsewhere could not have caused *this* fire, nor could the overturning of a lighted oil stove.

To talk of particular events as conditions is bewildering, but perhaps causes aren't events (like the short-circuit, or Smith's fall from the ladder), but correspond rather to sentences (perhaps like the fact that this short-circuit occurred, or the fact that Smith fell from the ladder). Sentences can express conditions of truth for others— hence the word 'conditional'.

---

1. For a recent example, with reference to many others, see J. L. Mackie, 'Causes and Conditions', *American Philosophical Quarterly*, 2/4 (Oct. 1965), 245–64.

If causes correspond to sentences rather than singular terms, the logical form of a sentence like:

(1) The short-circuit caused the fire.

would be given more accurately by:

(2) *The fact that* there was a short-circuit *caused it to be the case that* there was a fire.

In (2) the italicized words constitute a sentential connective like 'and' or 'if . . then . . .' This approach no doubt receives support from the idea that causal laws are universal conditionals, and singular causal statements ought to be instances of them. Yet the idea is not easily implemented. Suppose, first that a causal law is (as it is usually said Hume taught) nothing but a universally quantified material conditional. If (2) is an instance of such, the italicized words have just the meaning of the material conditional, 'If there was a short-circuit, then there was a fire.' No doubt (2) entails this, but not conversely, since (2) entails something stronger, namely the conjuction 'There was a short-circuit *and* there was a fire.' We might try treating (2) as the conjunction of the appropriate law and 'There was a short-circuit and there was a fire—indeed this seems a possible interpretation of Hume's definition of cause quoted above—but then (2) would no longer be an instance of the law. And aside from the inherent implausibility of this suggestion as giving the logical form of (2) (in contrast, say, to giving the grounds on which it might be asserted) there is also the oddity that an inference from the fact that there was a short-circuit and there was a fire, and the law, to (2) would turn out to be no more than a conjoining of the premises.

Suppose, then, that there is a non-truth-functional causal connective, as has been proposed by many.[2] In line with the concept of a cause as a condition, the causal connective is conceived as a conditional, though stronger than the truth-functional conditional. Thus Arthur Pap writes, 'The distinctive property of causal implication as compared with material implication is just that the falsity of the antecedent is no ground for inferring the truth of the causal implication' (p. 212). If the connective Pap had in mind were that of (2), this remark would be strange, for it is a property of the connective in (2) that the falsity of either the 'antecedent' or the 'consequent' is a ground for inferring the falsity of (2). That treating the causal connective as a kind of conditional unsuits it for the work of (1) or (2) is perhaps even more evident from Burks's remark that 'p is causally sufficient for q is logically equivalent to $\sim q$ is causally sufficient for $\sim p$' (p. 369). Indeed, this shows not only that Burks's connective is not that of (2), but also that it is not the subjunctive causal connective

---

2. e.g. by: Mackie, 'Causes and Conditions', 254; Arthur W. Burks, 'The Logic of Causal Propositions', *Mind*, 60/239 (July 1951), 363–82; and Arthur Pap, 'Disposition Concepts and Extensional Logic', in *Minnesota Studies in the Philosophy of Science*, 2, eds. H. Feigl, M. Scriven, and G. Maxwell (Minneapolis, 1958), 196–224.

'would cause'. My tickling Jones would cause him to laugh, but his not laughing would not cause it to be the case that I didn't tickle him.

These considerations show that the connective of (2), and hence by hypothesis of (1), cannot, as is often assumed, be a conditional of any sort, but they do not show that (2) does not give the logical form of singular causal statements. To show this needs a stronger argument, and I think there is one, as follows.

It is obvious that the connective in (2) is not truth-functional, since (2) may change from true to false if the contained sentences are switched. Nevertheless, substitution of singular terms for others with the same extension in sentences like (1) and (2) does not touch their truth value. If Smith's death was caused by the fall from the ladder and Smith was the first man to land on the moon, then the fall from the ladder was the cause of the death of the first man to land on the moon. And if the fact that there was a fire in Jones's house caused it to be the case that the pig was roasted, and Jones's house is the oldest building on Elm Street, then the fact that there was a fire in the oldest building on Elm Street caused it to be the case that the pig was roasted. We must accept the principle of extensional substitution, then. Surely also we cannot change the truth value of the likes of (2) by substituting logically equivalent sentences for sentences in it. Thus (2) retains its truth if for 'there was a fire' we substitute the logically equivalent '$\hat{x}(x = x \ \& \text{ there was a fire}) = \hat{x}(x = x)$'; retains it still if for the left side of this identity we write the coextensive singular term '$\hat{x}(x = x \ \& \text{ Nero fiddled})$'; and still retains it if we replace '$\hat{x}(x = x \ \& \text{ Nero fiddled}) = \hat{x}(x = x)$' by the logically equivalent 'Nero fiddled'. Since the only aspect of 'there was a fire' and 'Nero fiddled' that matters to this chain of reasoning is the fact of their material equivalence, it appears that our assumed principles have led to the conclusion that the main connective of (2) is, contrary to what we supposed, truth-functional.[3]

Having already seen that the connective of (2) cannot be truth-functional, it is tempting to try to escape the dilemma by tampering with the principles of substitution that led to it. But there is another, and, I think, wholly preferable way out: we may reject the hypothesis that (2) gives the logical form of (1), and with it the ideas that the 'caused' of (1) is a more or less concealed sentential connective, and that causes are fully expressed only by sentences.

2

Consider these six sentences:

(3) *It is a fact that* Jack fell down.
(4) Jack fell down *and* Jack broke his crown.

3. This argument is closely related to one spelled out by Dagfinn Føllesdal, 'Quantification into Causal Contexts', in *Boston Studies in the Philosophy of Science*, 2, ed. R. S. Cohen and M. W. Wartofsky (New York, 1966), 263–74, to show that unrestricted quantification into causal contexts leads to difficulties. His argument is in turn a direct adaptation of Quine's (*Word and Object* (Cambridge, Mass., 1960), 197–8) to show that (logical) modal distinctions collapse under certain natural assumptions. My argument derives directly from Frege.

(5) Jack fell down *before* Jack broke his crown.

(6) Jack fell down, *which caused it to be the case that* Jack broke his crown.

(7) *Jones forgot the fact that* Jack fell down.

(8) *That* Jack fell down *explains the fact that* Jack broke his crown.

Substitution of equivalent sentences for, or substitution of coextensive singular terms or predicates in, the contained sentences, will not alter the truth value of (3) or (4): here extensionality reigns. In (7) and (8), intensionality reigns, in that similar substitution in or for the contained sentences is not guaranteed to save truth. (5) and (6) seem to fall in between; for in them substitution of coextensive singular terms preserves truth, whereas substitution of equivalent sentences does not. However this last is, as we just saw with respect to (2), and hence also (6), untenable middle ground.

Our recent argument would apply equally against taking the 'before' of (5) as the sentential connective it appears to be. And of course we don't interpret 'before' as a sentential connective, but rather as an ordinary two-place relation true of ordered pairs of times; this is made to work by introducing an extra place into the predicates ('*x* fell down' becoming '*x* fell down at *t*') and an ontology of times to suit. The logical form of (5) is made perspicuous, then, by:

(5) There exist times *t* and *t'* such that Jack fell down at *t*, Jack broke his crown at *t'*, and *t* preceded *t'*.

This standard way of dealing with (5) seems to me essentially correct, and I propose to apply the same strategy to (6), which then comes out:

(6) There exists events *e* and *e'* such that *e* is a falling down of Jack, *e'* is a breaking of his crown by Jack, and *e* caused *e'*.

Once events are on hand, an obvious economy suggests itself: (5) may as well be construed as about events rather than times. With this, the canonical version of (5) becomes just (6'), with 'preceded' replacing 'caused'. Indeed, it would be difficult to make sense of the claim that causes precede, or at least do not follow, their effects if (5) and (6) did not thus have parallel structures. We will still want to be able to say when an event occurred, but with events this requires an ontology of pure numbers only. So 'Jack fell down at 3 p.m.' says that there is an event *e* that is a falling down of Jack, and the time of *e*, measured in hours after noon, is 3; more briefly, $(\exists e \, (F \, (\text{Jack},e) \, \& \, t(e) = 3)$.

On the present plan, (6) means some fall of Jack's caused some breaking of Jack's crown; so (6) is not false if Jack fell more than once, broke his crown more than once, or had a crown-breaking fall more than once. Nor, if such repetitions turned out to be the case, would we have grounds for saying that (6) referred to one rather than another of the fracturings. The same does not go for 'The short-circuit caused the fire' or 'The flood caused the famine' or 'Jack's fall caused the breaking of Jack's crown'; here singularity is imputed. ('Jack's fall', like 'the day after tomorrow', is no less a singular term because it may refer to different entities on different occasions.) To do justice to 'Jack's fall caused the breaking of Jack's crown' what we need is something like 'The one and only falling down of Jack caused the one and only breaking of his crown by Jack'; in some symbols of the trade, '($\imath e$) F (Jack, e) caused ($\imath e$) B (Jack's crown, e).'

Evidently (1) and (2) do not have the same logical form. If we think in terms of standard notations for first-order languages, it is (1) that more or less wears its form on its face; (2), like many existentially quantified sentences, does not (witness 'Somebody loves somebody'). The relation between (1) and (2) remains obvious and close: (1) entails (2), but not conversely.[4]

3

The salient point that emerges so far is that we must distinguish firmly between causes and the features we hit on for describing them, and hence between the question whether a statement says truly that one event caused another and the further question whether the events are characterized in such a way that we can deduce, or otherwise infer, from laws or other causal lore, that the relation was causal. 'The cause of this match's lighting is that it was struck.—Yes, but that was only *part* of the cause; it had to be a dry match, there had to be adequate oxygen in the atmosphere, it had to be struck hard enough, etc.' We ought now to appreciate that the 'Yes, but' comment does not have the force we thought. It cannot be that the striking of this match was only part of the cause, for this match was in fact dry, in adequate oxygen, and the striking was hard enough. What is partial in the sentence 'The cause of this match's lighting is that it was struck' is the *description* of the cause; as we add to the description of the cause, we may approach the point where we can deduce, from this description and laws, that an effect of the kind described would follow.

If Flora dried herself with a coarse towel, she dried herself with a towel. This is an inference we know how to articulate, and the articulation depends in an obvious way on reflecting in language an ontology that includes such things as towels: if there is a towel that is coarse and was used by Flora in her drying, there is a towel that was used by Flora in her drying. The usual way of doing things does not, however, give similar expression to the similar inference from 'Flora dried herself with a towel on the beach at noon' to 'Flora dried herself with a towel', or for that matter, from the last to 'Flora dried herself.' But if, as I suggest, we render 'Flora

---

4. A familiar device I use for testing hypotheses about logical grammar is translation into standard quantificational form; since the semantics of such languages is transparent, translation into them is a way of providing a semantic theory (a theory of the logical form) for what is translated. In this employment, canonical notation is not to be conceived as an improvement on the vernacular, but as a comment on it.

    For elaboration and defence of the view of events sketched in this section, see my 'The Logical Form of Action Sentences', in Nicholas Rescher (ed.), *The Logic of Action and Preference* (Pittsburgh, 1967).

dried herself' as about an event, as well as about Flora, these inferences turn out
to be quite parallel to the more familiar ones. Thus if there was an event that was a
drying by Flora of herself and that was done with a towel, on the beach, at noon,
then clearly there was an event that was a drying by Flora of herself—and so on.

The mode of inference carries over directly to causal statements. If it was a drying
she gave herself with a coarse towel on the beach at noon that caused those awful
splotches to appear on Flora's skin, then it was a drying she gave herself that did it;
we may also conclude that it was something that happened on the beach, something
that took place at noon, and something that was done with a towel, that caused the
tragedy. These little pieces of reasoning seem all to be endorsed by intuition, and it
speaks well for the analysis of causal statements in terms of events that on that
analysis the arguments are transparently valid.

Mill, we are now in a better position to see, was wrong in thinking we have not
specified the whole cause of an event when we have not wholly specified it. And
there is not, as Mill and others have maintained, anything elliptical in the claim that
a certain man's death was caused by his eating a particular dish, even though death
resulted only because the man had a particular bodily constitution, a particular
state of present health, and so on. On the other hand Mill was, I think, quite right
in saying that 'there certainly is, among the circumstances that took place, some
combination or other on which death is invariably consequent . . . the whole of
which circumstances perhaps constituted in this particular case the conditions of
the phenomenon . . .' (*A System of Logic*, 1.5.3.) Mill's critics are no doubt justified
in contending that we may correctly give the cause without saying enough about it
to demonstrate that it was sufficient; but they share Mill's confusion if they think
every deletion from the description of an event represents something deleted from
the event described.

The relation between a singular causal statement like 'The short-circuit caused
the fire' and necessary and sufficient conditions seems, in brief, to be this. The fuller
we make the description of the cause, the better our chances of demonstrating that
it was sufficient (as described) to produce the effect, and the worse our chances of
demonstrating that it was necessary; the fuller we make the description of the effect,
the better our chances of demonstrating that the cause (as described) was necessary,
and the worse our chances of demonstrating that it was sufficient. The symmetry
of these remarks strongly suggests that in whatever sense causes are correctly said to
be (described as) sufficient, they are as correctly said to be necessary. Here is an
example. We may suppose there is some predicate '$P(x,y,e)$' true of Brutus, Caesar,
and Brutus's stabbing of Caesar and such that any stab (by anyone of anyone) that
is P is followed by the death of the stabbed. And let us suppose further that this law
meets Mill's requirements of being *unconditional*—it supports counterfactuals of
the form 'If Cleopatra had received a stab that was P, she would have died.' Now we
can prove (assuming a man dies only once) that Brutus's stab was sufficient for
Caesar's death. Yet it was not the cause of Caesar's death, for Caesar's death was the
death of a man with more wounds than Brutus inflicted, and such a death could not

have been caused by an event that was P ('P' was chosen to apply only to stabbings administered by a single hand). The trouble here is not that the description of the cause is partial, but that the event described was literally (spatio-temporally) only part of the cause.

Can we then analyse 'a caused b' as meaning that a and b may be described in such a way that the existence of each could be demonstrated, in the light of causal laws, to be a necessary and sufficient condition of the existence of the other? One objection, foreshadowed in previous discussion, is that the analysandum does, but the analysans does not, entail the existence of a and b. Suppose we add, in remedy, the condition that either a or b as described, exists. Then on the proposed analysis one can show that the causal relation holds between any two events. To apply the point in the direction of sufficiency, imagine some description '$(\iota x)Fx$' under which the existence of an event a may be shown sufficient for the existence of b. Then the existence of an arbitrary event c may equally be shown sufficient for the existence of b: just take as the description of c the following: '$(\iota y)(y = c\ \&\ (\exists!x)Fx)$'.[5] It seems unlikely that any simple and natural restrictions on the form of allowable descriptions would meet this difficulty, but since I have abjured the analysis of the causal relation, I shall not pursue the matter here.

There remains a legitimate question concerning the relation between causal laws and singular causal statements that maybe raised independently. Setting aside the abbreviations successful analysis might authorize, what form are causal laws apt to have if from them, and a premiss to the effect that an event of a certain (acceptable) description exists, we are to infer a singular causal statement saying that the event caused, or was caused by, another? A possibility I find attractive is that a full-fledged causal law has the form of a conjunction:

(L) $\begin{cases} \text{(S)} & (e)(n)((Fe\ \&\ t(e) = n)\rightarrow(\exists!f)(Gf\ \&\ t(f) = n + \epsilon\ \&\ C(e,f)))\ \text{and} \\[2ex] \text{(N)} & (e)(n)((Ge\ \&\ t(e) = n + \epsilon)\rightarrow(\exists!f)(Ff\ \&\ t(f) = n\ \&\ C(f,e))). \end{cases}$

Here the variables 'e' and 'f' range over events, 'n' ranges over numbers, F and G are properties of events, '$C(e,f)$' is read 'e causes f', and 't' is a function that assigns a number to an event to mark the time the event occurs. Now, given the premiss:

(P) $(\exists!e)(Fe\ \&\ t(e) = 3)$

(C) $(\iota e)(Fe\ \&\ t(e) = 3)$ caused $(\iota e)(Ge\ \&\ t(e) = 3 + \epsilon)$.

It is worth remarking that part (N) of (L) is as necessary to the proof of (C) from (P) as it is to the proof of (C) from the premiss '$(\exists!e)(Ge\ \&\ t(e) = 3\ \epsilon))$'. This is perhaps more reason for holding that causes are, in the sense discussed above, necessary as well as sufficient conditions.

Explaining 'why an event occurred', on this account of laws, may take an instructively large number of forms, even if we limit explanation to the resources of deduction.

---

5. Here I am indebted to Professor Carl Hempel, and in the next sentence to John Wallace.

Suppose, for example, we want to explain the fact that there was a fire in the house at 3.01 p.m. Armed with appropriate premisses in the form of (P) and (L), we may deduce: that there was a fire in the house at 3.01 p.m.; that it was caused by a short-circuit at 3.00 p.m.; that there was only one fire in the house at 3.01 p.m.; that this fire was caused by the one and only short-circuit that occurred at 3.00 p.m. Some of these explanations fall short of using all that is given by the premisses; and this is lucky, since we often know less. Given only (S) and (P), for example, we cannot prove there was only one fire in the house at 3.01 p.m., though we can prove there was exactly one fire in the house at 3.01 p.m. that was caused by the short-circuit. An interesting case is where we know a law in the form of (N), but not the corresponding (S). Then we may show that, given that an event of a particular sort occurred, there must have been a cause answering to a certain description, but, given the same description of the cause, we could not have predicted the effect. An example might be where the effect is getting pregnant.

If we explain why it is that a particular event occurred by deducing a statement that there is such an event (under a particular description) from a premiss known to be true, then a simple way of explaining an event, for example the fire in the house at 3.01 p.m., consists in producing a statement of the form of (C); and this explanation makes no use of laws. The explanation will be greatly enhanced by whatever we can say in favour of the truth of (C); needless to say, producing the likes of (L) and (P), if they are known true, clinches the matter. In most cases, however, the request for explanation will describe the event in terms that fall under no full-fledged law. The device to which we will then resort, if we can, is apt to be redescription of the event. For we can explain the occurrence of any event a if we know (L), (P), and the further fact that $a = (\iota e)(Ge \;\&\; t(e) = 3 + \epsilon)$. Analogous remarks apply to the redescription of the cause, and to cases where all we want to, or can, explain is the fact that there was *an* event of a certain sort.

The great majority of singular causal statements are not backed, we may be sure, by laws in the way (C) is backed by (L). The relation in general is rather this: if 'a caused b' is true, then there are descriptions of a and b such that the result of substituting them for 'a' and 'b' in 'a caused b' is entailed by true premisses of the form of (L) and (P); and the converse holds if suitable restrictions are put on the descriptions.[6] If this is correct, it does not follow that we must be able to dredge up a law if we know a singular causal statement to be true; all that follows is that we know there must be a covering law. And very often, I think, our justification for accepting a singular causal statement is that we have reason to believe an appropriate causal law exists, though we do not know what it is. Generalizations like 'If you strike a well-made match hard enough against a properly prepared surface, then, other conditions being favourable, it will light' owe their importance not to the fact that

6. Clearly this account cannot be taken as a definition of the causal relation. Not only is there the inherently vague quantification over expressions (of what language?), but there is also the problem of spelling out the 'suitable restrictions'.

we can hope eventually to render them untendentious and exceptionless, but rather to the fact that they summarize much of our evidence for believing that full-fledged causal laws exist covering events we wish to explain.[7]

If the story I have told is true, it is possible to reconcile, within limits, two accounts thought by their champions to be opposed. One account agrees with Hume and Mill to this extent: it says that a singular causal statement 'a caused b' entails that there is a law to the effect that 'all the objects similar to a are followed by objects similar to b' and that we have reason to believe the singular statement only in so far as we have reason to believe there is such a law. The second account (persuasively argued by C. J. Ducasse)[8] maintains that singular causal statements entail no law and that we can know them to be true without knowing any relevant law. Both of these accounts are entailed, I think, by the account I have given, and they are consistent (I therefore hope) with each other. The reconciliation depends, of course, on the distinction between knowing there is a law 'covering' two events and knowing what the law is: in my view, Ducasse is right that singular causal statements entail no law; Hume is right that they entail there is a law.

4

Much of what philosophers have said of causes and causal relations is intelligible only on the assumption (often enough explicit) that causes are individual events, and causal relations hold between events. Yet, through failure to connect this basic aperçu with the grammar of singular causal judgements, these same philosophers have found themselves pressed, especially when trying to put causal statements into quantificational form, into trying to express the relation of cause to effect by a sentential connective. Hence the popularity of the utterly misleading question: can causal relations be expressed by the purely extensional material conditional, or is some stronger (non-Humean) connection involved? The question is misleading because it confuses two separate matters: the logical form of causal statements and the analysis of causality. So far as form is concerned, the issue of non-extensionality does not arise, since the relation of causality between events can be expressed (no matter how 'strong' or 'weak' it is) by an ordinary two-place predicate in an ordinary, extensional first-order language. These plain resources will perhaps be outrun by an adequate account of the

7. The thought in these paragraphs, like much more that appears here, was first adumbrated in my 'Actions, Reasons, and Causes', Journal of Philosophy, 60 (1963), 685–700, esp. 696–9; repr. in Bernard Berofsky (ed.), Free will and Determinism (New York, 1966). This conception of causality was subsequently discussed and, with various modifications, employed by Samuel Gorovitz, 'Causal Judgments and Causal Explanations', Journal of Philosophy, 62 (1965), 695–711, and by Bernard Berofsky, 'Causality and General Laws', ibid. 63 (1966), 148–57.
8. See his 'Critique of Hume's Conception of Causality', Journal of Philosophy, 63 (1966), 141–8; Causation and the Types of Necessity (Seattle, 1924); Nature, Mind, and Death (La Salle, Ill., 1951), pt. 2. I have omitted from my 'second account' much that Ducasse says that is not consistent with Hume.

form of causal laws, subjunctives, and counterfactual conditionals, to which most attempts to analyse the causal relation turn. But this is, I have urged, another question.

This is not to say there are no causal idioms that directly raise the issue of apparently non-truth-functional connectives. On the contrary, a host of statement forms, many of them strikingly similar, at least at first view, to those we have considered, challenge the account just given. Here are samples: 'The failure of the sprinkling system caused the fire,' 'The slowness with which controls were applied caused the rapidity with which the inflation developed,' 'The collapse was caused, not by the fact that the bolt gave way, but by the fact that it gave way so suddenly and unexpectedly,' 'The fact that the dam did not hold caused the flood.' Some of these sentences may yield to the methods I have prescribed, especially if failures are counted among events, but others remain recalcitrant. What we must say in such cases is that in addition to, or in place of, giving what Mill calls the 'producing cause', such sentences tell, or suggest, a causal story. They are, in other words, rudimentary causal explanations. Explanations typically relate statements, not events. I suggest therefore that the 'caused' of the sample sentences in this paragraph is not the 'caused' of straightforward singular causal statements, but is best expressed by the words 'causally explains'.[9]

A final remark. It is often said that events can be explained and predicted only in so far as they have repeatable characteristics, but not in so far as they are particulars. No doubt there is a clear and trivial sense in which this is true, but we ought not to lose sight of the less obvious point that there is an important difference between explaining the fact that there was *an* explosion in the broom closet and explaining the occurrence of *the* explosion in the broom closet. Explanation of the second sort touches the particular event as closely as language can ever touch any particular. Of course this claim is persuasive only if there are such things as events to which singular terms, especially definite descriptions, may refer. But the assumption, ontological and metaphysical, that there are events, is one without which we cannot make sense of much of our most common talk; or so, at any rate, I have been arguing. I do not know any better, or further, way of showing what there is.

---

9. Zeno Vendler has ingeniously marshalled the linguistic evidence for a deep distinction, in our use of 'cause', 'effect', and related words, between occurrences of verb-nominalizations that are fact-like or propositional, and occurrences that are event-like. See Zeno Vendler, 'Effects, Results and Consequences', in R. J. Butler (ed.), *Analytic Philosophy* (New York, 1962), pp. 1–15. Vendler concludes that the 'caused' of 'John's action caused the disturbance' is always flanked by expressions used in the propositional or fact-like sense, whereas 'was an effect of' or 'was due to' in 'The shaking of the earth was an effect of (was due to) the explosion' is flanked by expressions in the event-like sense. My distinction between essentially sentential expressions and the expressions that refer to events is much the same as Vendler's and owes much to him, though I have used more traditional semantic tools and have interpreted the evidence differently. My suggestion that 'caused' is sometimes a relation, sometimes a connective, with corresponding changes in the interpretation of the expressions flanking it, has much in common with the thesis of J. M. Shorter's 'Causality, and a Method of Analysis', in *Analytic Philosophy*, 2 (1965), 145–57.

Chapter 32

Selections from *The Facts of Causation*

D. H. Mellor

Deterministic and indeterministic causation

Singular and general causation

To understand causation we need to answer three distinct questions. First, what kinds of entities can be causes and effects? Second, when entities of those kinds are causes and effects, what makes them so? And third, what follows from their being so: what are the consequences of causation? But although these questions are distinct, their answers will obviously affect each other. What causation is, and what it entails, will depend on what causes and effects are, and *vice versa*.

We therefore cannot expect to treat these questions entirely separately. But we must start somewhere, and I will start by saying something about what causes and effects are. First, whatever they are, they must be entities of the same kinds, since most if not all causes are also effects. Suppose for example that a climber, Don, is killed by falling while climbing. The cause here, Don's falling, is also an effect, of whatever made him fall; and his dying, the effect, is also a cause, for example of grief in others. Thus finding out what causes are will also tell us what effects are.

Second and more important, causes and effects appear at first sight to include two very different sorts of entity. One sort are general properties. Suppose smoking causes cancer. The causation here seems to link two properties, being a smoker and having cancer, regardless of who has these properties or when. Causation

This selection comprises excerpts from chapters 1 and 5 of D. H. Mellor's *The Facts of Causation*. We have cut sections 5–7 of Mellor's chapter 1, which discuss which kind of conditional ('if . . . then . . .') statement should be used for expressing claims about causation; and also section 2 of chapter 5, which discusses the view that apparently indeterministic phenomena like radioactivity can be explained by a determinist by postulating 'hidden variables'. Note that Mellor uses the symbols 'C $\Rightarrow$ E' to express the counterfactual conditional (if it were the case that C, it would be the case that E); and he writes '$ch_C(E) = p$' as an abbreviation for 'the chance that a cause C gives an effect E $= p$', where p is a number between 0 and 1.

which links such properties, unlocalised in space or time, we may call *general* causation.

Don's falling causing him to die, by contrast, is a piece of what I shall call *singular* causation. Here the cause and effect are both local. Neither is everywhere in space and time, only where and when Don falls and dies. This is the kind of causation that concerns me in this book. However, much of what I shall say will apply also to general causation, since the two sorts of causation, although different, must be linked: it cannot be a coincidence that smoking causes cancer and that Don's son Bill's smoking causes him to get cancer. The link is indeed disputed, but as the dispute only concerns the nature of general causation, which is not my business, I shall simply state my view of it: namely, that general causation is a generalisation of singular causation. Smoking causes cancer iff (if and only if) smokers' cancers are generally caused by their smoking.

If this is so, the real mark of general causation is generalisation, not lack of location. General causal facts can be as local as singular ones. I might for example claim not that smoking causes cancer everywhere and always but only that it causes cancer in Britain this century. My claim is local, but is still a general claim about the British this century. Localising the scope of a general claim does not make it singular.

This distinction between general and singular causation does not imply a distinction between general and singular causes and effects. For if general causation is just singular causation generalised, then it links the same kinds of entities: not general properties like being a smoker or having cancer, or types of events like falling or dying, but one or more instances of such properties or event-types, like Britons smoking and getting cancer, or Don's falling and dying.

I shall therefore take it for granted in what follows that all causes and effects are singular. This does not however mean that the causal links between them must be singular. The causation that links Bill's smoking to his getting cancer might be general. It might for example be the statistical fact that everywhere and always (or at least in Britain this century), among people relevantly like Bill, the fraction who get cancer is higher among those who smoke than among those who do not. Or it might be a law of nature that people like Bill have a greater chance of getting cancer if they smoke than if they do not: a law of which the statistical fact would then be a highly probable consequence. In neither case would there be a singular causal link between Bill's smoking and his getting cancer. The two might still be linked by a chain of intermediate causes and effects, such as a build-up of tar in his lungs and chemical changes in his cells. But this intermediate causation would also reduce to statistical correlations, or probabilistic laws, linking inhaled smoke with tar absorption, absorbed tar with cell changes, and so on.

There might therefore be no more to singular causation than individual instances of general laws or correlations. In fact, as we shall see, there is more to it: singular causation really is as singular as the causes and effects it links. But that question is not begged by taking causes and effects to be singular.

Two sorts of cause

Taking causes and effects to be singular is innocuous largely because it says almost nothing about what causes and effects are. They are at first sight very varied, as the following examples show. People and other animals affect each other, are caused by their parents and cause their offspring. Medicines cause our illnesses to go away. There are inanimate things like icebergs, which are caused by cooling water and cause ships to sink. There are instances of properties, like a tyre's high pressure, caused by inflating it, and which causes it to be rigid. My lighting a fire, thus causing a temperature difference between it and me, is an action causing an instance of a relation (hotter than). A spark causing the fuel and air in a car engine cylinder to ignite, thus causing the engine to run and the car to move, is one inanimate event causing another, which in turn causes a change.

Fortunately all these seemingly diverse causes and effects can be reduced to two basic sorts. The first of these is a species of what I shall call *states of affairs*, by which I mean what are stated by sentences, statements or propositions like 'Don falls', whether they are true or false: Don's falling is a state of affairs whether he falls or not. How sentences, statements and propositions relate to each other and to states of affairs is a complex and contentious question, whose answer fortunately does not matter here. (In particular, as the differences between sentences, statements and propositions will rarely matter in what follows, I shall mostly use one of these terms to stand for all of them.) What does matter here is the difference between *true* statements (etc.) and *false* ones, i.e. between those states of affairs that are *actual* and those that are not. Actual states of affairs, corresponding to true statements, I shall call *facts*, like the fact that Don falls, which exists iff 'Don falls' is true. Facts, so understood, are one of my two basic sorts of causes and effects.

Many objections have been raised to the idea of causes and effects as facts. The answers to most of them will have to wait until we learn more about what causation entails, but two of them can be answered now. The premise of the first objection is that statements of cause and effect, if true at all, are true everywhere and at all times. This makes it look as if facts, which correspond to truths, cannot have the restricted locations in space and time with which I have credited singular causes and effects.

Although the premise of this objection is contentious, I accept it. This does not of course mean that we can only use sentences which are true at all times to state causes and effects. We can perfectly well use tensed sentences like 'Don died', a sentence which, because it implies that Don's death is past, was not always true. But as I (1998 chs 2–3) and others have shown, we can always say in tenseless terms what makes tensed sentences true. We can do this in English by using the present tenses of verbs *atemporally*, by which I mean using them as a speaker does who, as the 1979 *Collins English Dictionary* puts it, 'does not wish to make any explicit temporal reference'. Thus we may say atemporally that any utterance of 'Don died' is true iff it is made after Don dies, and similarly in all other cases.

In short, replacing 'Don died because he fell' and 'Don's fall caused his death' with the atemporal 'Don dies because he falls' and 'Don's fall causes his death', loses nothing but the implication that this piece of causation occurs before I write or you read this sentence. But as we are concerned with all causation whenever it occurs, that implication is irrelevant. This is why, at the cost of some occasional inelegance, I shall from now on report all causation atemporally.

But then 'Don falls' and 'Don dies', if true at all, are true everywhere and always. How then can the facts that correspond to these truths have a restricted location in space and time? To see how, note first that we can and often do identify facts by their location. Thus 'it rains in Paris on 1 March 1998' and 'it rains in London on 9 July 2001', if atemporally true, state different facts, located at those places and times. And whether we say so or not, the fact is that Don dies somewhere and at some time: say in the Lake District in June 1988—not in London and not in May. Similarly for any other located fact P. Even if its location is not stated in 'P', 'P at s at t' will still be true, everywhere and always, for some but not all places s and times t, with a smallest such s and t (e.g. the foot of Castle Rock, 2.23 pm on 4 June), included in all the others, which is P's location.

(This has the obvious and obviously true consequence that non-actual states of affairs have no location: for if 'P' is false then 'P at s at t' will also be false for all s and t. Thus while the fact that Shakespeare wrote *Hamlet* is located in London in about 1600, the state of affairs of Marlowe writing *Hamlet*, since it is not a fact, is not located anywhere.)

The other objection to facts is to the so-called *correspondence* theory of truth, i.e. to the thesis that statements are made true by corresponding facts. The objection is that only by definition can facts correspond to all true statements, thus making the theory either vacuous or false. With this objection I agree: facts, as I use the term 'fact', cannot be used to define truth. But I am not using facts to define truth: I am using truths to define facts. In so doing I am taking for granted some other account of what in the world, if anything, makes sentences like 'Don dies' and 'Don dies because he falls' true. We shall see later what the answers to those questions are: here all that matters is that they will not be 'the fact that Don dies' and 'the fact that Don dies because he falls'. This being so, the vacuity or falsity of correspondence theories of truth is no reason to deny that causes and effects can be facts, i.e. entities that correspond by definition to truths.

So much, for the time being, for facts. But we need more than facts, plentiful though they are. Some causes and effects cannot be facts because they cannot even be states of affairs: they do not correspond to anything which can be true or false. Hence the other sort of causes and effects, which correspond to names and other referring terms, like 'Don' and 'Don's fall', that cannot be used on their own to make any statement, true or false. These non-factual causes and effects are *particulars*, and they come in two sorts. There are what I shall call *things*, including people, animals, plants and inanimate objects ranging in size from quarks to galaxies; and there are *events*, like Don's fall and his death. Although the nature and even the existence of events is disputed, they are in fact the commonest kind of causal particulars, which is why

I shall make them my exemplars. How they are related to things that are also causes and effects is a complex question, for whose answer we shall again have to wait [10].*

This division of causes and effects into facts and particulars is not only exclusive, it is also exhaustive. All singular causes and effects are either facts or particulars. If this is not at once obvious, it will I hope become so as we tackle more and more cases. Meanwhile I shall recommend the idea by showing how to represent some of the causes and effects listed at the start of this section in one or other of these two ways. Thus parents (things) cause an offspring (thing) by an action of theirs (an event) causing its conception (an event). We affect others when our actions (events) cause some change in them (event or fact). We can also affect ourselves in the same way. Thus Bill's wife Kim causes herself to recover from an illness (fact) by taking her medicine (event or fact). And so on: as the reader may easily verify, all my other examples can be put in terms of causation linking facts or particulars or both.

How these two basic sorts of cause and effect are related, and which if either is the more basic, are questions whose answers must again await more information about causation [11]. Fortunately we can avoid the issue for the present, because most causation can be represented equally well either way. Thus we may say 'Don dies because he falls', which represents the cause and the effect as facts. Or we may say 'Don's fall causes his death', which represents them as particular events. For the moment it does not matter which way we put it.

However, to discuss causation generally without begging the answers to these questions, I need a single way of representing causation of both sorts. To get it I propose for the time being to represent causal particulars as facts, namely as the facts that those particulars exist (if they are things) or occur (if they are events) somewhere in the past, present or future of the actual world. And since the difference between things and events, and thus between existing and occurring, is not relevant here, I shall for brevity say of both kinds of particulars that they 'exist'. (Those who think that possible but non-actual particulars exist, in other possible worlds, should read my 'exists' as 'is actual'.)

Putting all this more generally and formally, we may use the following form of sentence to report all causation between facts:

(1) 'E because C'.

Instances of (1), like 'Don dies because he falls' are *molecular* sentences, so-called because they contain other sentences 'C' ('Don falls') and 'E' ('Don dies') linked by the sentential connective 'because'.

(I realise of course that 'because' is not an exclusively causal connective, being used also to give proofs—'There is no greatest prime number, because if there were . . .'—and explanations of non-causal kinds. There are thus many non-causal instances of (1), which I must exclude. I could exclude them by using an exclusively causal connective, like 'the fact that . . . causes it to be the case that . . .'. But I would rather

---

* NOTE: Numbers in square brackets refer to numbered sections of Mellor's book.

avoid such turgid locutions if I can, and fortunately I can. For since these locutions exist, we can make (1) causal by fiat, i.e. by restricting its instances to those that do have exclusively causal equivalents. This for brevity I hereby do.)

The form of sentence I shall use to report causation between any two particulars *c* and *e* is

(2) '*c* causes *e*'.

This form, unlike (1), needs no restriction to make it causal, being clearly causal to start with. On the contrary, (2) is itself only a restricted form of the more general but equally causal

(2′) '*c* causes or affects *e*'

to be discussed later [12]. Since however, as we shall see, the difference between causing and affecting something is not a causal one, we shall beg no question here by using the simpler (2).

(2) differs radically in form from (1) in that its instances, like 'Don's fall causes his death', since they contain no other sentences, are not molecular. They are *atomic* sentences, containing only the referring terms '*c*' ('Don's fall') and '*e*' ('Don's death'), linked by the relational predicate 'causes'. Nevertheless, despite this difference, we can always turn them into equivalent sentences of form (1) by letting 'C' and 'E' be '*c* exists' and '*e* exists', to give

(2″) '*e* exists because *c* exists',

a form which is, by definition, to mean whatever (2) means.

Thus 'Don's death exists because Don's fall exists' means 'Don's fall causes his death'. Whether this means the same as 'Don dies because he falls' remains to be seen. Meanwhile (2″) lets us waive that question without begging it by making (1) the form of all causal statements.

Causation's incomplete truth table

When is 'E because C' true? Part of the answer we know already. For to say that causation links facts is really just to say that 'E because C' entails 'C' and 'E'. No one will deny this: no one will deny that 'Don dies because he falls' entails both that Don falls and that he dies. To die because he falls he must fall and he must die; and similarly for all other cases of causation. Only actual states of affairs have actual causes and effects.

Put formally, this means that 'E because C' is at least a partial truth function of 'C' and 'E'. That is, the truth values (true or false) of 'C' and 'E' determine the truth value of 'E because C' in three of the four possible cases: 'E because C' is false whenever (i) 'C' and 'E' are both false, (ii) 'C' is true and 'E' is false and (iii) 'C' is false and 'E' is true.

'C'	'E'	'E because C'
True	True	?
True	False	False
False	True	False
False	False	False

Figure 1. Truth table for 'E because C'.

But when 'C' and 'E' are both true 'E because C' does not always have the same truth value. If 'E because C' were always false then too, causation would link no facts at all: there would be no causation. While if it were always true, causation would link every pair of facts both ways round, making it universal and hence symmetrical, since 'E because C', *via* 'C' and 'E', would entail 'C because E'. But that is absurd: Don's dying because he falls does not entail that he falls because he dies! So 'E because C' is neither always true nor always false when 'C' and 'E' are true. The truth table of the causal connective 'because' must therefore be incomplete, as shown in Fig. 1: 'E because C' is not a complete truth function of 'C' and 'E'.

The basic question about causation therefore is this: what more, besides the truth of 'C' and 'E', is needed to make 'E because C' true? Many conditions have been proposed, for example that causes must precede their effects, or be next to them in space and time. These we shall look at later. But the most important, obscure and contentious condition is that causes must somehow *necessitate* or *determine* their effects. We shall see in the end that this condition is too strong; but first we must see what it is. That is the main business of this chapter.

Deterministic causation

By causes that determine their effects I shall mean ones that are in the circumstances both *sufficient* and *necessary* for them. 'Sufficient' here means that the existence of the cause ensures, in a sense yet to be made clear, that its effects also exist. 'Necessary' here means that its non-existence ensures in the same sense that its effects do not exist.

These two conditions are clearly independent, and not all philosophers require deterministic causes to satisfy both of them. It is indeed more usual to read 'determinism' as requiring only that causes be sufficient for their effects. So before going on I should say why I also require deterministic causes to be necessary for their effects. It is really only a matter of convenience. For it will eventually turn out that causes need not, in my sense, determine their effects [5], and my account of indeterministic causation will then cover causes that are sufficient but not necessary, or necessary but not sufficient. This being so, it is simpler to tackle sufficient and necessary causes together, since they raise the same key question: in what sense does a sufficient cause's existence ensure that its effects exist and a necessary one's non-existence ensure that they do not?

Before tackling this question, however, I should say again what I mean, when causes and effects are facts, by saying that they 'exist'. All I mean is this: the cause C and effect E reported by 'E because C' exist iff 'C' and 'E' are true, i.e. if the states of affairs C and E are actual [2]. Thus the facts that Don falls and that he dies exist iff 'Don falls' and 'Don dies' are true, i.e. iff Don falls and dies. If Don neither falls nor dies, i.e. if 'Don falls' and 'Don dies' are false, then the states of affairs those sentences report are not facts: the facts that Don falls and that he dies do not then exist.

This is all my talk of facts existing means. In particular, it implies nothing about the nature of facts, e.g. whether we can identify them with true propositions, and thus states of affairs with propositions generally [2]. All I mean by 'the fact C exists' is that 'C' is true. And one advantage of this weak sense of 'fact' is that, without begging any questions about what facts are, I can use 'C' both as a sentence and also, as above, to abbreviate 'the fact that C' or 'the state of affairs that C'—and similarly for 'E'—provided of course I make it clear which of these things I mean.

This double use of 'C' and 'E' lets me turn (1) into

(1′) 'C causes E',

which is an abbreviation of 'the fact that C causes it to be a fact that E'. (1′) has the form of (2), 'c causes e', while by definition meaning 'E because C', a device that will greatly simplify later discussion of factual causes and effects [9]. Meanwhile, to reduce the risk of ambiguity between instances of (1′) and of (2), I shall use phrases like 'Don's falling' to refer to the fact that he falls, as opposed to the event, his fall. Thus where it matters I shall use 'Don's falling causes his dying' to mean 'Don dies because he falls' as opposed to 'Don's fall causes his death'.

Given this terminology, we can now turn to deterministic causation, i.e. to true causal instances of 'E because C' where C is in the circumstances both sufficient and necessary for E. Suppose then that Don's falling is in the circumstances—he is brittle-boned and fifteen metres above rocks but otherwise alive and well—sufficient and necessary for his dying. (That is, for his dying roughly then, there and as he does. How much the time, place and manner of his dying could vary without it being a different fact is a question we can waive for now.) In other words, in the circumstances, Don's falling ensures that he does die, and his not falling would ensure that he did not die. What does 'ensure' mean here?

Whatever it means, it must not be entailed by the truth table for 'E because C' shown above in Fig. 1. This says that 'E because C' entails 'E': the fact that C causes E is logically sufficient for E. But as we have seen, all this means is that only actual effects have actual causes: Don's falling cannot cause Don's dying unless he actually dies. But this truism applies to all causation, whether deterministic or not. It cannot be what makes C itself, as opposed to the fact that C causes E, sufficient for E. So what does make C sufficient for E?

. . .

Radioactivity

We have seen* how, and in what sense, the existence of sufficient causes and the non-existence of necessary ones necessitate the existence and non-existence respectively of their effects, by giving them chances of 1 and 0. Now we know what this causal kind of necessitation is, we can see whether causation really needs it. Must causes be in this sense sufficient and necessary for their effects: is what I shall call *causal determinism* true?

Modern physics suggests that it is not. Take the decay of atoms of radioelements [2.1]. These are radioactive isotopes of chemical elements like radium and uranium whose atoms decay when subatomic particles, such as α or β particles, 'tunnel' out of their nuclei, thereby turning them into atoms of other elements. This process of decay is not deterministic [2.1]: its laws do not make any atom of a radioelement E certain to decay (D) in any given interval of time. Instead they give each such atom x in its normal state a certain chance of decaying within any subsequent time interval of length t units (seconds, hours, etc.). This chance, $ch(D(x, t))$, is given by

(15) $ch(D(x,t)) = 1 - e^{-\lambda t}$,

where e^y is the sum to infinity of $1 + y/1 + y^2/1 \times 2 + \cdots y^n/n! + \cdots$ for any real number y, and '$D(x,t)$' means that x decays within t units of time. λ is a constant, E's so-called *decay constant*, often re-expressed as its half life, the value of t for which $ch(D(x,t)) = 1/2$ [2.1]. And since $e^y \approx 1 + y$ when y is very small, $ch(D(x,t)) \approx 1 \lambda t$ when t is very small, so that λ is itself a chance, namely the chance, which I shall write '$ch(Dx)$', of any normal E atom x decaying in any sufficiently small unit time.

(15) entails that any normal E atom has a finite chance of decaying, and also of not decaying, within any finite time interval. Take a sufficiently small unit interval, from t_0 to $t_0 + 1$. Then it is a fact about the nuclear structure of every E atom x at t_0 that $ch(Dx) = \lambda$, where $0 < \lambda < 1$ [2.1]. So one E atom h may decay, Dh, in the interval from t_0 to $t_0 + 1$ while another, i, does not, $\sim Di$. Since (15) gives neither Dh nor $\sim Di$ a chance of 1, this seem to entail that the causes of these facts are insufficient and thus indeterministic.

In fact this does not follow: we could simply deny that Dh and $\sim Di$ have causes. For since to say that all causation is deterministic is not to say that all contingent facts have causes, we can easily reconcile causal determinism with natural radioactive decay by denying that it has any causes at all. But determinism is not so easily reconciled with what I shall call *forced* decay. Suppose that at t_0 we bombard the nucleus of our E atom h (Bh) with a subatomic particle. If h were in its normal state its chance of decaying by $t_0 + 1$, $ch(Dh)$, would be λ, which we may take to be minute: say 10^{-10}. But bombarding h makes it almost certain to decay by $t_0 + 1$, i.e. raises $ch(Dh)$ to a value, λ', very close to 1: say to $1 - 10^{-10}$. Suppose now that h does decay by $t_0 + 1$. In these circumstances did it not do so *because* it was bombarded: is not 'Dh because Bh' true?

If so, we have a cause that is neither sufficient nor necessary for its effect. For Bh to be sufficient for Dh, $ch_{Bh}(Dh)$, h's chance of decaying if bombarded, must be 1,

---

* In Chapters 1.5–1.7, and 3, 4 and 5 of Mellor's book. See Introduction, §6, for more details.

which it is not: it is $1 - 10^{-10}$. For Bh to be necessary for Dh, $ch_{\sim Bh}(Dh)$, h's chance of decaying if not bombarded must be 0, which it is not: it is 10^{-10}. The effect has a finite chance of existing without this apparent cause and a finite chance of not existing with it.

Causal determinists must therefore deny that bombarding h causes it to decay. But then they must also deny that we cause atomic bombs to explode by forcing together two masses of fissile material, such as uranium–235 (^{235}U). For this apparent causation also relies on indeterministic facts like those I have just cited. Take a particular thing d made of ^{235}U. When d's atoms split, releasing energy, they usually emit between one and three neutrons, and we can simplify matters without begging any questions by supposing that they always emit two. These neutrons may then hit the nuclei of other ^{235}U atoms before leaving d, the mean chance of their doing so increasing of course as d's mass gets larger. If they do hit other nuclei, they raise the chance that those nuclei will split, emitting more energy and two more neutrons, almost to 1. So once d's mass is large enough for an emitted neutron's mean chance of hitting another nucleus to exceed 1/2, d becomes *supercritical*: the chance of a rapidly accelerating chain reaction, splitting ^{235}U atoms and releasing energy so fast that d explodes, rises almost to 1.

This then is how atomic explosions are produced: high explosive is used to force two *subcritical* masses of fissile material together into a supercritical mass, which then explodes. But this process is not deterministic. As with the forced decay of single E atoms, the chance that a supercritical mass will explode is still less than 1, and the chance that a subcritical mass will explode is greater than 0. So if causes must be sufficient and necessary for their effects, an atomic explosion cannot be caused by turning a subcritical mass of fissile material into a supercritical one. Yet that *is* how atomic explosions are caused.

Hidden variables

Determinists could however take atomic explosions, and the forced decay of E atoms, to be caused by *hidden variables*: unknown differences between E atoms like h and i that provide deterministic causes of Dh and $\sim Di$.

. . .

A hidden variable could consistently with (15), provide deterministic causes of radioactive decay. However, unfortunately for causal determinists, no such variable has been shown to exist and many physicists think none does exist.

Determinists might then conclude that even the forced decays of radioactive atoms, and hence atomic explosions, have no causes at all. This conclusion is incredible enough to make a strong case for letting causation be indeterministic. But an even stronger case can be made, namely that many effects which do have deterministic causes also have indeterministic ones. For no deterministic cause of an effect E can explain E's apparent causation by a C which does *not* determine it. Thus, a hidden cause Ch of a bombarded atom h's decay will not make *bombarding h* cause it to decay. Yet this is what it needs to do. For what our examples suggest is not just that a fact E has *some* cause, but that E's causes include the fact C that we bring about in order to make E a fact. But if C does not already determine E, no other deterministic causes of E can make C determine it.

The existence of hidden variables is, in short, irrelevant: apparent cases of indeterministic causation are as persuasive with them as without them. Take Bill's smoking causing him to get cancer. So far, for the sake of argument, I have taken this cause to determine this effect, which of course it does not. Bill's chance of getting cancer is greater if he smokes than if he does not, but it is still less than 1; and it would still be greater than 0 if he did not smoke. Must we then deny that Bill gets cancer because he smokes? Surely not. Yet with or without hidden variables his smoking can only cause him to get cancer if causes need not determine their effects.

To see this, suppose there *are* hidden variables here: suppose there are always relevant metabolic differences between smokers who get cancer and smokers who do not; and similarly for non-smokers. Let us grant then that, unlike an atomic explosion, Bill's getting cancer in an interval $(t_0, t_1]$ has a deterministic cause: namely, his having during $[t_0, t_1)$ a metabolic property C such that, if he smokes during $[t_0, t_1)$, his chance of getting cancer in $(t_0, t_1]$ is 1 if he is C during $[t_0, t_1)$ and 0 if he is not.

But some indeterministic causation is still needed here, as we can see by asking what causes Bill to be C. First, if causation must be deterministic, it cannot be the fact that he smokes. For as with radioactivity, if Bill's being C is a deterministic cause of his getting cancer, then his chances of being C during $[t_0, t_1)$ and of getting cancer in $(t_0, t_1]$ must be the same. So if the latter is less than 1 if he smokes and greater than 0 if he does not, so also must the former be. Indeterminism in the causation of his cancer by his smoking reappears as indeterminism in the causation of its deterministic cause, or of the deterministic cause of that cause, or . . . and so on.

However, although Bill's smoking may cause him indeterministically to get cancer by causing the deterministic causes of his getting it, it need not. For smoking *could* correlate with cancer not by causing it *via* causing C but by being a side effect of C. But this hypothesis, while attractive to tobacco firms, is useless to a causal determinist, since it too demands some indeterministic causation. For if Bill's being C caused him to smoke and to get cancer deterministically, then his chances of getting cancer would have to be 1 if he smoked and 0 if he did not, which by hypothesis they are not.

In short, causal determinists can no more explain the appearance of causal indeterminism here than they can in the case of atomic explosions. Causation can only link Bill's smoking directly or indirectly to his getting cancer if some of the causation involved is indeterministic. So if causation must be deterministic, much apparent causation, with or without hidden variables, must be illusory. Is it?

The connotations of causation

It takes more than plausible cases to show that causation can be indeterministic. For as intuitions about cases can be as contentious as the theses they are used to support, determined determinists may simply deny that these really are cases of indeterministic causation. They may insist in the nuclear case that there *must* be hidden variables because, like Einstein, they cannot believe that God plays dice. Or they may insist that without such variables there can be no causation, since it is part of our concept of causation that causes determine their effects.

Neither side can rest here. Determinists must say what they think we mean by our talk of causing atomic explosions, or of smoking causing cancer, when we think these causes do not determine their effects. Their opponents must say why, if causation does not entail determinism, it seems to—and what it does entail instead. One way or the other these apparent cases of indeterministic causation must be explained or explained away. But which is it to be? To answer that question we need to ask why we apply our concept of causation as we do. To reverse an old and over-rated adage, we must ask not just for the use of terms like 'cause' and 'effect' but for the point of their use, i.e. for what we mean by them. What, in other words, do we take to follow from saying or denying that one fact or particular causes another: what are the connotations of causation?

Putting the question like this does not commit me to what Strawson (1959) has called *descriptive* metaphysics. I am not, as he puts it (p. 9), 'content to describe the actual structure of our thought about the world'. It is not safe to constrain our meta-physics by the structure of 'our thought', as enshrined in everyday speech, since much of that is demonstrably false. The metaphysics of time yields several examples of this, one of which I gave in the Introduction. Another is the assumption that whether a celestial event is happening *now* is always a matter of fact, an assumption which the special theory of relativity shows to be false (Reichenbach 1928 §§19–20). It may matter to semantics that much of our thought still presupposes a spatially unrestricted concept of simultaneity. It does not matter to metaphysics. What matters there is that this is a mistake which can be and has been corrected. And the question whose answer does not matter at all is whether the concept with which the special theory of relativity has replaced classical simultaneity is similar enough to deserve the same name.

So it is with causation. Much of our thought may well presuppose that causes determine their effects. Yet, given the evidence, we also think that smoking causes cancer and that we cause atomic explosions. But as we have seen, given what we now know about the relevant metabolic and subatomic processes, these thoughts cannot all be true. Something must give: no metaphysics of causation can rescue all our thought about it.

What then should we say? If our indeterministic cases lacked most of causation's other connotations (as we shall see shortly that 'C causes C' does) we should of course say that these are not cases of causation. But in fact we should say no such thing, since nearly all causation's connotations survive in these cases [5.5.–7; 7]. Only determinism goes, and even then it remains as an ideal special case [8]. The concept we need to replace deterministic causation with is thus obviously similar enough to it to deserve the name 'causation', which is why I shall call it that. But even if it were not, that would not matter. All that matters is seeing how, and how far, the other connotations of causation can survive the loss of determinism.

To see this we need not examine all causation's connotations, since many of them stay too close to home to tell us much. Anscombe (1971), for example, says that 'causality consists in the derivativeness of an effect from its causes' (p. 67), which she says does not entail determinism. Maybe not: but to show how and when effects can 'derive' from causes that do not determine them we need an independent account of 'derivativeness', which we lack. Salmon (1984) similarly defines causation in terms of 'the two basic concepts of *propagation* and *production*' (p. 139). But in his examples (e.g. 'the electrical discharge produces a fire') 'produces' is just a synonym for 'causes', to which 'propagates' merely adds the truism that effects can be caused by causing their causes, i.e. that causation is not intransitive. This tells us nothing, because no constraint on indeterministic causation needs to make it intransitive in the first place.

It has been said (e.g. by Taylor 1966, p. 39) that causation's connotations are all too close to home for it to be analysed in non-causal terms. Fortunately this is not true. Causation has several obvious connotations that will serve our turn. Here are four.

Temporal: causes generally *precede* their effects.

Contiguity: causes are *contiguous* to their immediate effects.

Evidential: causes and effects are *evidence* for each other.

Explanatory: causes *explain* their effects.

All these connotations link causation to very different concepts, and they all need accounting for. The first two require our theories of causation, time and space to say between them why causes precede and are contiguous to their immediate effects. (An immediate effect of a cause C is an E such that C causes E but not by causing any D that causes E.) Similarly for causation's other connotations. Our theory of causation must combine with our theories of evidence and explanation to say what makes causes and effects evidence for each other and how causes explain their effects.

These connotations do therefore constrain causation: for example, by ruling out self-causation [1.6]. The reason nothing can cause itself is that nothing can precede, be evidence for or explain itself. Nor can anything be the means to itself that, as we shall see later, causes must be to their effects [7]. What makes 'C causes C' false for all C is the fact that 'C causes E' loses almost all its connotations when E = C.

Causation's connotations also constrain time, evidence and explanation. But those constraints I shall not discuss, apart from those on time [17]. Causation is my business here, not evidence or explanation. About them I need only assume enough to show why their links with causation do not require causes to determine their effects. That is the task of this chapter. In the next, we shall see what causation's connotations do require the chances of effects to be.

It is obvious that none of causation's connotations entails determinism. No one will deny that a cause can precede and be contiguous to effects for which it is neither sufficient nor necessary; nor will anyone deny that it can be evidence for them and they for it. None of the many conflicting theories of evidence requires it to be either conclusive (sufficient) or exclusive (necessary), let alone both. No one for example thinks that statistical evidence must be the only evidence that a drug is safe, nor that such evidence must leave no chance of error. Similarly, statistical explanations of the roughly equal numbers of male and female births can obviously fail to be either sufficient or necessary for what they explain.

If it is easy to see *that* our connotations let causation be indeterministic, it is less easy to say *why* they do so. But we must see why if we are to see how causation's connotations do constrain the chances of effects. For this is not at all obvious. It is not for example obvious that causation's temporal and contiguity connotations depend on effects having chances. Yet they do, as we shall see [17.4–5], which is why I have listed them here. But I cannot invoke them here, since they too are contentious. Just as the cases above persuade me that a cause need not determine its effects, so other cases persuade others that it need not always precede nor—when they are immediate effects—be contiguous to them.

In fact every cause must do both these things, but only because its effects must have chances with and without it. So to derive our constraint on causation from the assumption that causes precede or are contiguous to their immediate effects would beg the question. We must go the other way round, deriving causation's temporal and contiguity connotations from constraints derived from other, less contentious, connotations. But first we must see why these do not entail determinism. Let us take them in turn.

Evidence

That causes and effects are evidence for each other is a long-standing and uncontentious connotation of causation. Hume (1748) thought that:

all reasonings concerning matter of fact seem to be founded on the relation of *Cause and Effect*. By means of that relation alone we can go beyond the evidence of our memory and sense (§22).

This may be too strong: some evidence for matters of fact may not be founded on causation. But obviously most of it is. And certainly causes generally do provide at least some evidence for their effects. For example, if Don dies because he falls, his falling as he does must give some reason to fear that he will die. Effects likewise generally provide evidence for their causes: Bill's getting cancer is some evidence that he is a smoker. And effects of common causes provide evidence for each other: thus 'heat and light are collateral effects of fire, and the one effect may justly be inferred from the other' (Hume 1748 §22).

That causation generates evidence in these three ways is obvious enough. It is also fairly obvious that the strength of this evidence could be measured by the probabilities which causes and effects give each other. These are the evidential probabilities $P(P,Q)$ that are measured by the credence $cr(P)$ which I ought to have in P if Q is my evidence about P [3.3]. They raise many questions [2], but again we only need two innocuous assumptions about them.

The first is the Evidence condition [3.3], that for all P and p,

(10) $ch(P) = p$ entails $P(P, ch(P) = p) = p$.

Take the chances of radioactive decay. The half life of radium's most stable form, ^{226}Ra, is 1622 years: i.e. the chance of any normal ^{226}Ra atom x decaying in that time is 1/2. So on this evidence the evidential probability that x *will* decay in the next 1622 years is also 1/2.

This if anything is what makes a cause C evidence for an effect E: the chance $ch_C(E) = p$ which C gives E entails that $P(E, C \& ch_C(E) = p) = p$. Of course more needs saying about how this entailment can make C itself evidence for E [3.3]. But the Evidence condition at least makes $P(E,C)$'s dependence on $ch_C(E)$ fairly obvious and straightforward.

It is however far less obvious how chances can make E evidence for C, or two effects E and E′ of a common cause C evidence for each other. The problem here is that E and E′ do not give C, or each other, whatever chances they may have. Don's dying is not what gave his falling whatever chance it has, and the light of a fire is not what gives the fire its chance of giving off heat. Yet it is as obvious that the evidential probabilities $P(C,E)$, $P(E,E′)$ and $P(E′,E)$ exist as it is that $P(E,C)$ does, and indeed the evidence of our senses depends on them [6.3].

But this is no excuse for postulating chances to correspond *via* (10) to all these evidential probabilities. The distinction between chance and evidential probability is fundamental, and failure to draw it only generates nonsense, such as the so-called *anthropic principle* (Leslie 1989). This principle exploits our knowledge that the laws and initial conditions of our world have led to us, i.e. that, given us, the evidential probability of their not doing so is 0. But from this tautology anthropicists infer that our world's laws and initial conditions had a zero *chance* of not leading to us, thus making our existence probable in a sense that calls for teleological explanation. This is absurd: it is like inferring, from seeing clearly that a coin lands on edge (evidential probability 1), that it had no chance of doing otherwise (chance 1)!

In short, even if $P(C,E)$ and $P(E,E′)$ always depend on chances, as I believe they do, they must do so in a far less obvious and straightforward way than $P(E,C)$ does. Just how they do so is however a question we can leave until later [6.3], since the connection which (10) entails between the chance and the evidential probability that C gives E is enough to show how causation can be indeterministic, as follows.

First we must note that the truth of 'E because C' cannot make C and E evidence for each other just by entailing 'C&E'. When I see Don fall and infer that he will die, I am not making the trivial inference from 'Don dies because he falls' to 'Don dies': I am inferring 'Don dies' from 'Don falls'. How can the fact that Don dies because he falls make this what Hume would have called a 'just' inference?

The short answer is that it cannot, since the inference would be equally just if Don did not die. His falling is evidence that he will die even if he lives: we often have evidence for the truth of predictions that turn out to be false. But if Don does not die, he cannot die because he falls: so that cannot be what makes his falling evidence for his dying. What makes it evidence must be something which does not entail that he dies. What can it be?

It cannot be the fact that *if* Don falls he dies, since the material conditional 'Don falls ⊃ Don dies', the strict 'Don falls ⊣ Don dies' and the closest-world 'Don falls ⇒Don dies' all satisfy *modus ponens* [1.7]: they all conjoin with 'Don falls' to entail 'Don dies'. So if Don falls but does not die, all these conditionals are false. And if 'Don falls ⇒ Don dies' is false then so, by the Necessity condition, is 'Don falls ⇒ ch(Don dies) = 1': since $ch(E) = 1$ must entail E if 'C ⇒ $ch(E) = 1$' is to express C's sufficiency for E [3.1]. In short, Don's falling cannot be sufficient for his dying if he falls and lives. But it can still be evidence for it. So a cause need not be sufficient for its effects to be evidence for them.

Causation's evidential connotation thus cannot entail causal determinism. But the chance that C gives E may still be what makes C evidence for E, since conditionals like 'Don falls ⇒ ch(Don dies) = p' can be true even if Don falls and lives, provided $p < 1$. Yet it may still be that not any $p < 1$ will do: that causation's evidential connotation limits the chances that causes can give their effects. And so it does, as we shall see. But first we must see why causation's explanatory connotation also fails to entail determinism.

Explanation

It is an obvious connotation of causation that causes explain their effects—but not *vice versa*. To see what this implies, we must choose between two ways of putting it. Hempel's classic (1965) account treats an explanation as a statement giving 'an answer to a why-question' (p. 334). Put this way, it is not causes that explain their effects but rather statements of causes that explain statements of their effects. A true 'E because C' gives a causal explanation not of E but of what Hempel calls the *explanandum* statement 'E', the explanation being not C but the *explanans* statement 'C'.

I put the matter in terms not of statements but of facts, which comes to the same thing provided *explananda* and *explanantia* must be true. And so they must, since the relevant why-question is 'why did Don die?', not 'why "Don dies"?' It is the fact that Don dies, not the statement 'Don dies', that needs explaining. No one who thinks that 'Don dies' is false will think that what this statement says, as opposed to the fact that someone says it, either requires or admits of explanation.

As for *explananda*, so for *explanantia*. No one who thinks that the statement 'Don falls' is false, i.e. that Don does not fall, will take this statement to explain anything. It is not 'Don falls' but the fact that Don falls which explains the fact that he dies. The mere content of a statement, as opposed to the fact that it is true, explains nothing.

Thus to satisfy its explanatory connotation, 'E because C' must entail 'C' and 'E', as it does [1.3]: no one denies this. Nor does anyone really deny that, put in terms of facts, causes do explain their effects. The explanatory connotation only seems to be denied by those who, like Davidson (1980 Essay 7), take causes and effects to be particulars, i.e., entities that correspond not to truths like 'Don falls' and 'Don dies' but to referring terms like 'Don's fall' and 'Don's death'. And here I agree. It takes more than a referring term to be an *explanans* or an *explanandum*: it takes a true sentence. This indeed implies that particular events like Don's fall and Don's death, while they may be causes and effects, can neither be nor have explanations. But facts about them can, including the facts that these particulars exist [1.2]. We can still say therefore that Don's fall explains Don's death, meaning by this that his death exists because his fall does.

Read like this, no one denies causation's explanatory connotation. Even Davidson takes the causal 'because' to be 'best expressed by the words "causally explains"' (1980 Essay 7, p. 162). We can all agree that the causing of one fact by another satisfies the explanatory connotation.

We can also all agree that indeterministic causation can satisfy this connotation. No account of explanation and its link with causation requires causal explanations to be deterministic. Only one, the so-called 'deductive-nomological' or 'DN' account of Hempel (1965 §2), even comes close to doing so. Since it is also the best known and best articulated account, this is the one I will discuss. Showing how even Hempel can admit indeterministic causal explanations should suffice to make my case.

Hempel takes singular causes and effects to be particulars, not facts. On the other hand, he does constrain causal links between facts by requiring causally linked particulars to instantiate deterministic laws, as follows:

The law tacitly implied by the assertion that *b* [Don's death], as an event of kind *B* [a death], was caused by *a* [Don's fall] as an event of kind *A* [a fall] is a general statement of causal connection to the effect that, under suitable circumstances, an instance of *A* is invariably accompanied by an instance of *B* (p. 349).

Thus, for Don's fall to cause Don's death, the circumstances S—his being brittle-boned, fifteen metres above rocks, etc.—must be 'suitable', i.e. be of a kind S* such that it is a law that falls in S* circumstances are invariably accompanied by deaths.

The trouble here lies in the phrase 'invariably accompanied'. For only a chance 1 of *B* events accompanying *A* events will make them accompany *A* events invariably. The phrase thus implies that for *a* to cause *b*, the law N which they instantiate must be deterministic. That is, N must make the existence of an *A* event in any S* circumstances sufficient for there to be a *B* event, i.e. it must make 'there is an *A* event $\Rightarrow$ *ch*(there is a *B* event) = 1' true.

And as for the existence of particular events, so for causes and effects generally. Hempel's account of causal explanation makes 'E because C' require causes to be sufficient for their effects. But not necessary in the without-which-not sense: his account says nothing about E's chances *without* C. However, if Hempel's idea of causation is weaker in this respect than our deterministic one [2.4], his idea of explanation is stronger. For a DN explanation is, as its full name implies, deductive: it entails what it explains. But causes rarely if ever entail their effects [1.6]. In particular, if the relevant law N is contingent, the effect, Don's dying, will not be entailed even by its total cause—Don's falling fifteen metres onto rocks with brittle bones, etc.—let alone by his simply falling. So his falling cannot by itself provide a DN explanation of his dying: what does that is the combination of the total cause of his dying with the law N that makes it the total cause.

Hempel's deductive condition seems then to stop most if not all causes satisfying causation's explanatory connotation. But this is not so. For by making 'Don dies because he falls' entail the existence of a deterministic law linking this cause and effect, Hempel makes it entail that some such explanation, including Don's falling, exists. And this provides a clear and far more credible derivative sense of 'explain' in which Don's falling does explain his dying: by making 'Don dies because he falls' entail that there is a law which makes his falling sufficient for his dying.

Hempel's account can thus accommodate a non-deductive sense in which sufficient causes do explain their effects. And so it should, since no one thinks that all explanations are deductive. Even Hempel (1965 §3) admits what he calls 'inductive—statistical' explanations, with indeterministic laws, which explain facts they do not entail by giving them chances less than 1. And even if Hempel himself will not let *causes* give their effects chances less than 1, we can do so; and if we do, we can then let those causes explain their effects in some such probabilistic way.

To say all this is not to endorse Hempel's own account of probabilistic explanation, which is highly contentious. What is not now contentious is that explanation can be probabilistic, i.e., that it can give what it explains a probability less than 1. So no one now thinks that causation's explanatory connotation requires causes even to be sufficient for their effects, let alone necessary.

Conclusion

We have seen that four at least of causation's major connotations can survive causal indeterminism. A cause which does not determine its effects can still be evidence for them, and they for it and for each other. It can also precede, be contiguous to and explain them. Nothing about time, space, evidence or explanation need deprive indeterministic causation of any of its temporal, contiguity, evidential and explanatory connotations. Our apparent cases of indeterministic causation may indeed be as causal as they seem to be.

Bibliography

Anscombe, G. E. M. (1971) 'Causality and determination', in *Causation*, ed. E. Sosa and M. Tooley (1993), Oxford: Oxford University Press, 88–104.

Davidson, D. (1980) *Essays on Actions and Events*, Oxford: Clarendon Press.

Hempel, C. G. (1965) 'Aspects of scientific explanation', in *Aspects of Scientific Explanation and Other Essays in the Philosophy of Science*, New York: The Free Press, 331–496.

Hume, D. (1748) *An Enquiry concernign Human Understanding, Enquiries concerning the Human Understanding and concerning the Principles of Morals*, ed. L. A. Selby-Bigge (1902), Oxford: Clarendon Press, 5–165.

Leslie, J. (1989) *Universes*, London: Routledge.

Mellor, D. H. (1998) *Real Time II*, London: Routledge.

Reichenbach, H. (1928) *The Philosophy of Space and Time*, English transl. (1958), New York: Dover.

Salmon, W. C. (1984) *Scientific Explanation and the Causal Structure of the World*, Princeton, New Jersey: Princeton University Press.

Strawson, P. F. (1959) *Individuals*, London: Methuen.

Taylor, R. (1966) *Action and Purpose*, Englewood Cliffs, New Jersey: Prentice-Hall.

Study questions

1. What is the relationship between causation and the laws of nature?
2. Must causation be a physical relation?
3. What does it mean to say that causation is transitive? Is it true?
4. We frequently talk as if absences can be causes: 'he died because of lack of food', 'the absence of a smoke alarm hastened the fire', etc. But an absence is the non-existence of something. How, then, can causation be a relation at all, since a relation between two things entails the existence of those things?

Further reading

Causation is a very difficult subject for which, unlike some other areas of metaphysics, there is not a large amount of introductory material. However, Lowe (2002: chapters 8–10) is a good place to start. Aristotle's views on causation are discussed by Hankinson (1995). For a discussion of Hume's views on causation, see Stroud (1981); Strawson (1989) challenges the traditional understanding of Hume on causation, and contains some interesting discussions of causation in general. An in-depth criticism of Strawson is Broackes (1993). The anthology edited by Sosa and Tooley (1993) contains many classic papers: apart from the ones reproduced here, see the essays by Anscombe (1971) for a critique of the idea that causation must involve necessity or regularity, Ducasse and Tooley for similar views, and Kim and Horwich for some clear criticisms of Lewis. On laws of nature, see Dretske (1977). Lewis's 'Causation' is reprinted in his (1986a) with several illuminating postscripts; his final view on causation is contained in his (2000). Peter Menzies has proposed a development of the counterfactual analysis, which manages to avoid the problems of pre-emption: see his (1989) and (1996). Collins, Hall, and Paul (eds.) (forthcoming) is an up-to-date collection of essays on the counterfactual theory of causation, also containing Lewis's account of how absences can be causes, 'Void and Object'. The idea that absences can be causes threatens the idea that causation is a relation; for a defence of this idea, see Menzies (2003). Mellor (1995) defends the idea that causation relates facts, within the context of a theory of probabilistic causation, combined with a defence of the view that the *truth-makers* (for this notion, see Part IV: Universals and Particulars) for causal truths or facts need not be relational at all.

Part VII

Time and space

Introduction

1. Introduction

Aт the beginning of his famous discussion of time in his *Physics*, Aristotle posed two questions about time: does time exist? And if it does exist, what is its nature? These two questions, asked here of time and also of space, will be the focus of our discussion in this section.

Our first question is whether space and time have any kind of real existence: is the existence of space and time something distinct from that of the objects and events which occupy them? Or is their existence entirely dependent on the existence of these things, or even on the human mind? The second question, to some extent independent of the first, is what the specific nature of space and time is, and what the differences between them amount to. Should time be thought of as the fourth dimension of a four-dimensional space–time, and if so, what distinguishes this temporal dimension from the three spatial dimensions? One apparently obvious difference between time and space is that time seems to have an essential 'direction': in some sense, movement through time is possible only in one direction—from the past to the future—whereas movement through space is possible in any direction. Is this difference real, and if so what explains it? Should it be explained in terms of the existence of a 'moving now' which marks off the present from the future?

2. Space and time and their occupants

The question of whether space and time are real may be understood in a number of ways. One way of understanding it is as asking about whether space and time are ultimately illusory. We shall examine below one notorious argument for the view that time is a kind of illusion (section 4). But another way of understanding the question is as asking whether space and time have an existence which is independent of the things and events which inhabit or occupy them. If all the objects and events were removed from space and time, would there be anything left?

Sir Isaac Newton (1642–1727) gave an unequivocal answer to this question: 'absolute, true and mathematical time, of itself, and from its own nature, flows equably without relation to anything external' (1729: Scholium to Definition VIII). And he thought the same about space, which he called God's *sensorium*: that is, the arena in which inhabit the things of which God was aware. These are Newton's doctrines of absolute time and absolute space. We will not go far wrong if we think of absolute space and absolute time as the 'containers' in which objects exist and events occur. On this view, space and time are capable of existing independently of objects and events. Since something which is capable of independent existence is one of the things philosophers have called a *substance,* Newton's view is sometimes called *substantivalism*: the view that space and time are substances.

Gottfried Wilhelm Leibniz objected to this view of Newton's, and debated it in a correspondence with Newton's follower Samuel Clarke (Chapter 37). In our selection from this correspondence, we join Leibniz and Clarke as they enter into a discussion of Newton's views of space and time. Leibniz had previously claimed 'space to be something merely relative, as time is; I hold it to be an order of co-existences, as time is an order of succession' (1956: 26). In other words, space and time have no existence over and above the objects and events which inhabit them; our talk about space and time is really talk about spatial and temporal *relations* between events and objects. For this reason, Leibniz's view is known as *relationism*.

That is Leibniz's conclusion; but what is his argument? He considers Clarke's view that, given Newton's view of space, God could cause the entire contents of the universe to move forward in a straight line; and that, given Newton's view of time, God could have created the universe a million years earlier than he actually did. Leibniz finds these possibilities absurd, and gives two reasons for this, each based on one of his fundamental philosophical principles: the principle of the identity of indiscernibles, and the principle of sufficient reason.

The identity of indiscernibles says that 'there is no such thing as two individuals indiscernible from each other'. Or in other words, if objects X and Y share all their properties then they are identical (see Part III: Being). So a universe which is being shifted forward in a straight line would share all its properties with our universe ('all the parts of the universe should have had the same situation among themselves as that which they actually had,' Leibniz says). Therefore there would be no reason to say it is different in any way from the actual universe. Therefore the supposition that the universe might be moved in space is incoherent; and parallel reasoning applies to time.

A natural response to this argument, given by Clarke, is that it begs the question. For if Newton *is* right, then there is a difference between these two universes: their different positions in absolute space. Whether or not we could *tell* that they have these different positions is a separate question; defending Newton's argument for the distinction between absolute and relative rest and motion, Clarke argues by analogy that a ship could be moving whether or not a sailor locked in a cabin could detect its motion. His conclusion is that 'two places, though exactly alike, are not the same place. Nor is the motion or rest of the universe, the same state.'

Leibniz's second argument is based on his principle of sufficient reason, which says that for everything that happens, there must be a reason why it happens rather than not; or for every truth, there must be a reason why it, and not its negation, is true. So if God had decided to create the universe a million years earlier than he actually did, there would have had to have been a reason why he decided to do this rather than not. But, Leibniz argues, there can be no reason for God to prefer the earlier date of creation to the later one: since that would necessarily involve discerning some other difference between the two created universes which would provide the basis for God's choice. But there is no such difference; so there is no reason. And since 'God does nothing without reason' the apparent possibility of the universe being created a million years earlier is a 'mere chimera'.

The theological basis of this argument may seem to have little connection with contemporary philosophy of time, which is largely secular in character. But it is possible to reconstrue Leibniz's argument in terms of the idea of scientific explanation. When we are considering why something occurs, it might be argued, a sound scientific method should be able to give some account, in principle, of why it happened *then* and *there* rather than at some other time or place. If this is inexplicable under one hypothesis but not under another, then this gives us reason (other things being equal) to prefer the latter hypothesis. It is arguable that this is the situation we are in here: Newton's hypothesis of absolute space and time makes it inexplicable why certain events (e.g. the beginning of the universe) occur when and where they do. On Leibniz's account these questions do not arise. This might give us a reason to prefer Leibniz's account, if we were to accept the key principle about explanation.

Does Leibniz deny that space and time are real? This depends on whether you think that in order to be real, space and time have to be substances. If you think this, then you will say that Leibniz denies the reality of time and space. But there are ways in which things can be real without their being substances (see Part II: Being). Things can have *dependent* existence or reality. It is plausible that relations between objects have such a dependent existence: they depend on the things being related. In this case, if Leibniz's relationalist view of space and time is true, it would not be a denial of the reality of space and time, but instead an account of what they consist in.

3. Time and change

Suppose we have settled the question of whether, and in what way, space and time are real. The question still remains as to what distinguishes them. One traditional answer is to say with Aristotle (in Chapter 33) that time is intrinsically connected to change. Aristotle says, not entirely perspicuously, that time is 'the number of change in respect of before and after'. One natural way of understanding this is that time is the *measure* of change: that is, how long things take. Aristotle argued that time should not be identified with change, since change can be fast or slow, but it makes no sense to say that time is fast or slow. (Notice that Aristotle talks of 'change or movement' as if these were the same thing; when he talks of 'movement' in the selection below, we shall take him to mean 'change'.) But, nonetheless, time would not exist without change, he argues, since if nothing were perceived to have changed then we would not notice that time had passed. Someone (like one of Aristotle's 'heroes of Sardinia') who falls asleep for some time, and wakes up without noticing a change, may not have any reason to think that any time has passed.

It is certainly true that we recognize differences in time by recognizing that things have changed: the sun changes its position in the sky, the hands of the clock move around the clock face, and so on. But surely these changes are just the evidence we have for time passing; why should they be what the passage of time consists in? For in general we think that the evidence we have for something is normally independent of that thing, and that therefore the thing could exist without the evidence for it existing. Therefore if change is simply the evidence for time, it seems that time could exist without change, contrary to what Aristotle says (for more discussion of this issue, see Horwich, Chapter 36, and Shoemaker 1969).

Is there any other reason for thinking that change is essential to time? The Cambridge philosopher J. M. E. McTaggart (1866–1925) said that there is a sense in which an event, like the assassination of Caesar, is constantly changing its position in time: it is constantly moving back into the past. But is this what we really mean by change? Well, if we think of change purely in terms of some (monadic or relational) predicate being true of something at one time and not being true of it at a later time, then what McTaggart is talking about is certainly change. At one time, the predicate 'x occurred exactly 1000 years ago' was true of the assassination of Caesar; a year later, this was not true. So in this sense, every event changes with the passing of time. P. T. Geach called this very liberal conception of change 'Cambridge change' in honour of McTaggart (Geach 1969). It is certainly true that all real changes are Cambridge changes, but it is questionable whether all Cambridge changes are real changes (see Part VIII: Identity).

Do events really change their position in time? This partly depends on how we think of positions in time. McTaggart distinguished two ways we have of thinking of time and events in time: in terms of something's being past, present, or future; and in terms of something being earlier than, later than, or simultaneous with something else. Each of these ways of thinking is called a 'time series' since they are ways of ordering events in time. So the first way of thinking orders events in time by characterizing them as present, some past, and some future. McTaggart called this (famously, but unmemorably) the 'A series'. The second way of thinking orders events in time by placing some before some fixed point, some after that point, and some simultaneous with it. This he called the 'B series'.

So, for example, your reading this book is an event in the present; the writing of it is in the past, and the moment when you finish reading it is in the future. This is the A-series way of ordering events. But also your reading this book is earlier than your finishing it, and it is later than the writing of the book, and simultaneous with many other events: for example, with your drinking coffee. This is the B-series way of ordering events. The difference between the A and the B series is that the A-series positions of events are temporary, while their B-series positions are permanent. Your reading this book is present, but it will cease to be so. But your reading this book will always be later than the writing of it, even when it ceases to be present.

The upshot seems to be that events change their positions in the A series constantly, but permanently retain their positions in the B series. Against this it could be objected that it is *things* or *substances* that change, not events (see Part III: Being, for the idea of substance). Suppose a man gradually changes from being hairy to being bald. Then surely it is the *man* who has changed, not the *event* of him being hairy. To say that this event is perpetually changing by 'receding into the past', as McTaggart does, is simply to adopt a rather artificial way of describing a perfectly familiar phenomenon. Surely it is more natural to say that the only thing that is receding is the man's hairline, not any event.

We might defend this point by observing that events themselves are changes, and so if events change, then we are really saying that changes change—and what can that mean? But as A. N. Prior points out (Chapter 35), reflection shows that there is nothing wrong with the idea of a change changing: for example, acceleration, as opposed to a simple motion, is understood in terms of rate of change of velocity, itself a change. So this would not be a good reason for thinking that events do not change.

The idea that all events undergo change is nonetheless puzzling. But if there really *is* an A series, then it is irresistible to think of the present moment as 'moving' through it, and therefore changing its position. To progress further with these issues, then, we have to consider whether any sense can be made of things 'moving in time' at all.

4. Direction and the 'flow of time'

So in what sense, if any, do things 'move' in time? It is frequently pointed out that time can be distinguished from space by the fact that time has an intrinsic *direction*, whereas space does not. What this means is not just that things change *in time* but that they can only change from the way they *were* in the past, to the way they *are* in the present, and to the way they *will* be in the future. Things cannot change from being present to being future. That is what we mean by saying that what is done cannot be undone. Change— or anything that happens—can only happen in one direction; there is no parallel to this in the case of mere spatial variation in properties.

The direction of time is sometimes associated with the idea that time *flows*. Our everyday ways of thinking and talking about time are full of images of time as involving a kind of movement (time's arrow) or even as a kind of agency: time the destroyer, time's winged chariot, old father time, a bearded ancient with a scythe, and so on. In his most famous speech, Macbeth talks of each day creeping 'in this petty pace from day to day, to the last syllable of recorded time'. It is undeniable that it is, in a certain way, very natural to think of time *itself* as moving, or flying, or even creeping. But what literal sense can we make out of these images and metaphors? It cannot be literally true that time moves or flows. Flowing or moving are things which take place in time: if something has moved, it was at one place *at one time*, then at another place *at another time*. So if time were to move, *time itself* would have to be at one place at one time and another at another. But what can this mean? Similar puzzles arise with the idea of flow: at what rate does time flow? The easy answer—'at the rate of one hour per hour'—sounds like a joke (see Prior, Chapter 35, for more on this).

As we shall see, it is possible to make sense of the idea that time has a direction while denying that time flows. So flow and direction are two different ideas. But first we must examine the serious attempts to make sense of the flow of time. Those who believe in the flow of time normally try and explain it in terms of McTaggart's A series. For time to flow, on this conception, is for there to be a distinction in reality between past, present, and future. Some events are really past, some really present, and some really future. But, as we saw, these are not permanent features of events: each event is changing its position in the A series constantly. We can think of this, in the phrase used by Paul Horwich (Chapter 36), as the 'moving now' constantly making its way 'gradually along the array in the direction from past to future'. This real difference between past, present, and future—understood in terms of a 'moving now'—is what explains both the possibility of change and the direction of time.

It is this picture of time which McTaggart (Chapter 34) argued was incoherent. He argued that the picture of time as 'flowing' does express the essence of time, but that this picture is incoherent: time is unreal. It is worth pausing for a moment to consider what someone might possibly mean by saying something like this. McTaggart does not say this to be frivolous or paradoxical for the sake of it. Rather, he is trying to make a point about the fundamental nature of reality, about what is most real. The overall style of argument is that the world appears to contain a certain phenomenon, but such a phenomenon is contradictory; so the underlying reality of the world must be something else, which gives rise to the illusion of this phenomenon being part of reality. This is what McTaggart is trying to do with his argument against the reality of time: time is unreal, a kind of illusion; the ultimate reality which gives rise to this illusion cannot be a temporal reality.

McTaggart's argument has the following structure: (1) change is essential to time; (2) change requires the A series to be real; (3) the A series is contradictory and therefore unreal; (4) therefore there is no change; (5) therefore there is no time. It is clear that this argument is valid: that is, the conclusion follows from the premisses. But are the premisses true?

McTaggart agrees with Aristotle that change is of the essence of time. But he thinks that only with the A series can there be real change. Aristotle seems to agree: 'if there were no time, there would be no "now" and vice versa'. (Note the 'vice versa'.) McTaggart expresses this by saying that 'there can be no change unless facts change': that is, unless facts change their position in the A series. This part of McTaggart's argument is discussed critically and in detail by Horwich (Chapter 36). The most controversial part of the argument is the part which is supposed to show that the A series is contradictory. It will be useful to outline the main elements of the argument here (but for more details see the selections from Horwich and McTaggart, and the Further Reading).

McTaggart's argument for the premiss that the A series is contradictory is initially very simple. As time passes, every event has each A-series position: every event passes from being future, to being present, to being past. But these positions are incompatible: for if something is future, it cannot be past or present; and if something is present, it cannot be past or future; and if something is past, it cannot be present or future. But nothing can have incompatible properties. Reality can contain no contradictions. Therefore past, present, and future cannot exist.

The obvious response to this argument is that the A-series positions—past, present, and future—do not all belong to each event at the same time. Your reading this book is present *now* but it is not *now* in the past or *now* in the future. It *will be* in the past; and it *was* in the future. Events do not have all A-series positions *simultaneously*, but successively. Once this is made explicit, then it seems that the contradiction is only apparent. It would be rather like saying that *person* is a contradictory notion because every person is both a child and an adult, and nothing can be both child and adult. To which the correct response is: nothing can be both child and adult at the *same time*. There is no contradiction, as soon as things are spelled out fully.

McTaggart rejects this response. He describes it as saying that a present event, for example, is 'present at a moment of present time, past at some moment of future time, and future at some moment of past time'. But he then points out that these *moments* themselves are located in the A series too, so each moment too will have all A-series positions. And so these moments will have incompatible properties; and so cannot exist. To respond in the same way that these moments will not have all these incompatible A-series positions at the *same time* raises again the question when they have them. If it is answered that the moments have these positions only in relation to other moments, then (McTaggart argues) an infinite regress arises. These moments 'again, to avoid a like contradiction, must in turn be specified as past, present, and future. And since this continues indefinitely, the first set of terms never escapes from contradiction at all' (p. 33).

Although it is clear what McTaggart is attempting to do here—to argue that the A series gives rise to an infinite regress—commentators have been divided on whether he succeeds. Let us try and defend McTaggart in the following way, concentrating for simplicity on the contrast between past and present. Take some event e, which is happening at present (say, your reading this book). So it is true that e is present; at some later time it is true that e is past. e cannot be simultaneously past and present. What we should say is that e can be present at one time and past at another. But the question is, what makes it *true* that e is present at one time and past at another? If what makes it true is simply that e occurs at some position in the B series, then it appears that we have conceded that the only reality in question is the B-series reality: the ordering of events as earlier and later. Call the point in the B series at which e occurs t. Then the 'B way' of describing the situation is:

(i) 'e is present' is true at t
(ii) 'e is past' is true later than t

This reconciles the contradiction between 'e is present' and 'e is past', but only by expressing it in B-series terms. For 'e is present' to be true at t is just for e to occur at t. And if it is true that e occurs at t, it will always be true. The changing, 'dynamic' A series has been eliminated.

To maintain the reality of the A series, McTaggart's opponent has to say something about what makes it true that e is present at one time and not at another in irreducibly A-series terms:

(i)* 'e is present' is true now
(ii)* 'e is past' is true at some future time

McTaggart can then respond by saying that (i)* is incompatible with

(iii)* 'e is present' is true in the past

—since if 'e is present' is true in the past, it cannot be true now. And (iii)* expresses a truth about what will be the case after you have finished reading this. To express the sense in which (i)* and (iii)* are not really incompatible, we then have to move to another level of A-series properties: we should say that (i)* is true now, while (iii)* will be true at some future time. But then at this level too McTaggart will easily find incompatibilities between truths about e; and to resolve these in A-series terms we have to move to a higher level; and so on.

So does McTaggart's argument work? One critical response is that McTaggart has not shown that there really is any contradiction expressed by saying that every event is past, present, and future. For the defender of the reality of the A series can say that any statement is always made from some temporal perspective or point of view. From any such point of view, we can say that some events are past, some are present, and some are future. We can of course *describe* a temporal point of view in non-A-series terms (e.g. as '1 January 2002')—but in *expressing* how things are from a point of view we need to use 'indexical' expressions like 'now', 'I', 'my point of view', 'here', 'in the present', etc.—expressions which change their reference depending on when, where, and by whom they are being uttered. (Indexical expressions are also called 'token-reflexives'.) This is why we are inclined to say, in reaction to McTaggart's initial claim, 'but what is past is not present *now*!' For we can describe how something can be past and not present only in indexical terms. But we cannot, so to speak, 'step outside' any temporal point of view and say whether things are past, present, and future 'in themselves', from *no point of view*. This is because, according to the defender of the A series, from no point of view there is no past, present, or future. But it seems that McTaggart is trying to force the defender of the A series to say, in effect, that there *is* a perspective from which every event *really is* past, present, and future. And in trying to find such a perspective, we are forced to move up McTaggart's hierarchy, at each stage unable to resolve the apparent contradictions. But perhaps what the defender of the A series should say is that if the A series is real, there is *no* temporal perspective from which everything is past, present, and future. So there is no way of even stating a genuine contradiction in the first place (see Lowe 2002, Broad 1938).

The idea that from no point of view nothing is past, present, and future could be taken in one of two ways. The first is to say that since there must be such a thing as temporal reality as it is from no point of view, McTaggart's first claim—that time requires a real A series—must be false. There can be a complete description of time in B-series terms. This is the approach taken by the 'B theory' of time, defended by Mellor (1981, 1998), Smart (Chapter 38), and Horwich (Chapter 36), and will be discussed below. The second is to say that since McTaggart's first claim is correct, then there cannot be such a thing as temporal reality as it is from no point of view. For if there were, then a description of this reality would have to include a description of the A-series positions of events. But this, as McTaggart has shown, is impossible. Therefore there can be no complete description of temporal reality independently of temporal perspective. This is the conclusion of a well-known argument of Dummett's (1960).

But if a theory of time is to defend the A series, and therefore reject McTaggart's argument, then how should it understand the differences between past, present, and future? As we have seen, it should not say that there *are* (laid out in some 'tenseless' B realm) all the events, and pastness, presentness, and futurity are properties of these events. For this would leave it open to McTaggart's objection: the properties are incompatible. Rather, the A theory might understand the attribution of pastness and futurity in terms of expressions (known as 'operators') applied to whole present-tense sentences. An operator in this logical sense is an expression which, when added to a whole sentence, turns that sentence into a new sentence. (So, for example, adding 'It is not the case' to the sentence 'It is raining' creates the new sentence 'It is not the case that it is raining'.) The idea behind this 'tense logic' is to take the present tense as the starting point, and to add the operators 'It was the case that' and 'It will be the case that' to express pastness and futurity. This way of understanding the idea of the flow of time is developed in A. N. Prior's paper (Chapter 35). Prior's views on time are one source of the contemporary doctrine of *presentism*: that only the present is real.

5. Space, time, and space–time

As we have just seen, another way to respond to McTaggart's argument is to say that it shows that only the B series is real: the order of events in time is just given in terms of the idea of events being earlier than, later than, or simultaneous with others. This view is sometimes called the 'tenseless' view of time (since it takes all facts about time to be expressible without reference to a tensed language: i.e. a language with terms like 'will be', 'was', and so on). It is also called the 'B theory of time'.

It is important to recognize that although one could arrive at this theory by employing McTaggart's argument against the A series (as Mellor 1981, 1998 does), this is not the only route to the B theory of time. Indeed, one could think that McTaggart's argument is fallacious, and nonetheless assert that past, present, and future are unreal. McTaggart's argument is not the only argument for this conclusion; there may be other reasons for believing it even if McTaggart fails. One such reason for believing in the B theory of time is that it is the account of time which fits into modern physics' picture of the world as a so-called 'block universe'. Thus the reasons we have for believing in this picture are also reasons for believing in the B theory of time. This is the view defended by J. J. C. Smart (in Chapter 38). The block universe view treats the universe as a four-dimensional entity, with the three dimensions of space and the fourth dimension of time. (This is what physicists call 'space–time'.) A dimension, roughly speaking, is a way in which things can fail to coincide. Two objects—say, two rabbits—may fail to coincide in space–time by being in different regions of space at the same time, or being in the same region of space at different times. Just as there is nothing special about any particular place that makes it *here*, so there is nothing special about any particular time that makes it *now*. Utterances of 'now' and 'here' simply refers to whenever or wherever they are uttered. All events, whether past, present, or future, occupy some real position in the block universe.

This approach to the nature of time is sometimes called 'spatializing time'. It is not surprising, then, that the question arises again of how we should distinguish between space and time. If we do not employ a real A series, then how can we explain change and the direction of time, which we used the A series to explain, in our exposition above? The B (or block universe) theorist will respond by defending Russell's conception of change, which McTaggart attacks in his article: change is when something is true of an object at one time and not true of it at another. This conception of change is still 'Cambridge change': but note that it is described in purely B-series terms. If the B theory wants to rule out spurious 'changes' which are covered by this definition (as our house, for example, 'changes' in its distance from us as we walk away from it) then they have to impose further conditions on change. But they will insist that they can do this without departing from the concepts of the B series.

The other aspect of time of which the B theory has to give an account is the direction of time. For although it has dispensed with the idea of the 'flow' of time, the phenomenon of direction—which A-series 'flow' was arguably intended to explain—still remains. We described the direction of time above in terms of the idea that one can only travel in one direction in time, whereas one can travel in any direction in space. The significance of the question of the possibility of time travel (specifically, time travel into the past) is to challenge this assumption and argue that direction is not an essential feature of time (see Box VII.1). But for those B theorists who accept that direction is an essential or necessary feature of time, they have to find some explanation for it. A dominant tradition here (including the work of Reichenbach 1956 and Mellor 1998) has been to explain the direction of time in terms of the direction of causation (see Part VI: Causation).

Box VII.1. Time travel

Philosophers often explain the difference between space and time by saying that time has an intrinsic direction, whereas space does not. Events in time seem to be ordered by *asymmetric* relations like *earlier than* and *later than*, in a way that has no parallel in spatial order. (A relation R is asymmetric when *aRb* implies not-*bRa*.) This direction seems to be revealed by the fact that it is only possible to travel in one direction in time—from the present into the future—whereas we can travel in any direction in the three spatial dimensions: up or down, left or right, backwards or forwards.

But is this really true? Science fiction stories are full of time travellers and their journeys into the past and the future. If what the science fiction stories describe is metaphysically coherent, and therefore possible, then it would seem that our initial supposition is wrong: so it is *possible* for someone to travel in both directions in time, just as in space. And if this is possible, then the apparent 'direction' of time would seem to be a superficial feature of time, and not an essential feature. Another consequence, it seems, is that backwards causation would be possible: an effect could precede its cause.

Science fiction stories represent time travel into the future as well as travel into the past. But on reflection, it is clear that, however glamorous it might be, time travel into the future is not especially metaphysically puzzling. For if what is worrying about time travel is that it shows that time does not have an essential direction, then time travel into the future is not relevant to this worry: *towards the future* is just the normal direction in which we travel in time. Indeed, the conditions which would permit forward time travel seem to be already intelligible for us. It is often pointed out that modern physics entails that if someone were to travel, at something close to the speed of light, to a close star, they might find that their journey takes some twenty or so years; on their return home, however, they would discover that the Earth had aged millions of years. This is due to the effects of very fast speeds on other physical processes. Amazing as this story otherwise seems, it is no more baffling from a metaphysical point of view than the stories of Sleeping Beauty and Rip van Winkle. For this reason, D. H. Mellor has observed that calling such cases *forward time travel* is 'a misleadingly portentous description of situations in which our mental and bodily processes take longer than they normally do' (Mellor 1998: 124).

The really puzzling phenomenon is backwards time travel. Could someone travel into the past? And if they got there, what could they do? It has been argued that backwards time travel too is consistent with modern physics (see Horwich 1990: chapter 7). But the apparently obvious objection to the very idea of time travel into the past is that the time traveller could do something which undermined the conditions for his own existence and therefore his own actions. For example, the time traveller might kill his grandfather. And this would mean he would never have come into existence. But then he would never have returned to the past to kill his grandfather . . . However, if we take the idea of backwards time travel seriously, we must press the question: is it *really* possible for the time traveller to kill his grandfather? In H. G. Wells's story, *The Time Machine*, the hero uses his time machine to return to the moment before his fiancée was murdered, to attempt to prevent the murder. Each time he returns, something stops him from preventing the murder: he cannot change the past. So although everything is in place to allow him to prevent the terrible deed (and so in *that* sense he 'can' prevent it: he has the resources), it never comes about. Some will say that if time travel into the past is really possible, and there are reasons for thinking that it is, then this is how things should be (see Lowe 2002, and Lewis's discussion in Chapter 39). But others turn this point on its head and argue that the fact that time travel would allow you to kill your grandfather is just one of the many absurdities at the heart of backwards time travel, and one of the things that shows it to be impossible (see Mellor 2002).

Finally, there is the very important question of how our *experience* of time is, how time seems to us. For even if the B theory of time is right, and the past, present, and future are unreal, we certainly *think* in these terms; so any theory which denies them has to explain this. Moreover, we attach great significance to whether something is past, present, or future. We are relieved when something is in the past, and we feel more distress at our future non-existence than we do at our past non-existence. Why is this? If past, present, and future do not really exist, but if there is some basis to our attitudes here, then the B theory of time is not complete until it has explained what this basis is.

Chapter 33

Selection from *Physics*

Aristotle

10

30   Next for discussion after the subjects mentioned is time. The best plan will be
to begin by working out the difficulties connected with it, making use of the
current arguments. First, does it belong to the class of things that exist or to that of
things that do not exist? Then secondly, what is its nature? To start, then: the fol-
218ª1   lowing considerations would make one suspect that it either does not exist at all or
barely, and in the obscure way. One part of it has been and is not, while the other is
going to be and is not yet. Yet time—both infinite time and any time you like to
take—is made up of these. One would naturally suppose that what is made up of
things which do not exist could have no share in reality.

   Further, if a divisible thing is to exist, it is necessary that, when it exists, all or
5   some of its parts must exist. But of time some parts have been, while others are
going to be, and no part of it *is*, though it is divisible. For the 'now' is not a part: a
part is a measure of the whole, which must be made up of parts. Time, on the other
hand, is not held to be made up of 'nows'.

   Again, the 'now' which seems to bound the past and the future—does it always
10   remain one and the same or is it always other and other? It is hard to say.

   If it is always different and different, and if none of the *parts* in time which are
other and other are simultaneous (unless the one contains and the other is
contained, as the shorter time is by the longer), and if the 'now' which is not, but
15   formerly was, must have ceased to be at some time, the '*nows*' too cannot be simultaneous with one another, but the prior 'now' must always have ceased to be. But the
prior 'now' cannot have ceased to be in itself (since it then existed); yet it cannot
have ceased to be in another 'now'. For we may lay it down that one 'now' cannot be
20   next to another, any more than a point to a point. If then it did not cease to be in
the next 'now' but in another, it would exist simultaneously with the innumerable
'nows' between the two—which is impossible.

   Yes, but neither is it possible for the 'now' to remain always the same. No determinate divisible thing has a single termination, whether it is continuously extended
25   in one or in more than one dimension; but the 'now' is a termination, and it is possible to cut off a determinate time. Further, if coincidence in time (i.e. being neither

Aristotle, selection from *Physics*, book 4, translated by R. P. Hardie and R. K. Gaye. From *The Complete Works of Aristotle: The Revised Oxford Translation*, edited by Jonathan Barnes, copyright © 1984, Princeton University Press, reprinted by permission of Princeton University Press.

prior nor posterior) means to be in one and the same 'now', then, if both what is before and what is after are in this same 'now', things which happened ten thousand years ago would be simultaneous with what has happened to-day, and nothing would be before or after anything else.

This may serve as a statement of the difficulties about the attributes of time.　　30

As to what time is or what is its nature, the traditional accounts give us as little light as the preliminary problems which we have worked through.

Some assert that it is the movement of the whole, others that it is the sphere itself.　　218ᵇ1

Yet part, too, of the revolution is a time, but it certainly is not a revolution; for what is taken is part of a revolution, not a revolution. Besides, if there were more heavens than one, the movement of any of them equally would be time, so that there would be many times at the same time.　　5

Those who said that time is the sphere of the whole thought so, no doubt, on the ground that all things are in time and all things are in the sphere of the whole. The view is too naive for it to be worth while to consider the impossibilities implied in it.

But as time is most usually supposed to be motion and a kind of change, we must　　10 consider this view.

Now the change or movement of each thing is only *in* the thing which changes or *where* the thing itself which moves or change may chance to be. But time is present equally everywhere and with all things.

Again, change is always faster or slower, whereas time is not; for fast and slow are　　15 defined by time—fast is what moves much in a short time, slow what moves little in a long time; but time is not defined by time, by being either a certain amount or a certain kind of it.

Clearly then it is not movement. (We need not distinguish at present between movement and change.)　　20

11

But neither does time exist without change; for when the state of our minds does not change at all, or we have not noticed its changing, we do not think that time has elapsed, any more than those who are fabled to sleep among the heroes in Sardinia do when they are awakened; for they connect the earlier 'now' with the later and　　25 make them one, cutting out the interval because of their failure to notice it. So, just as, if the 'now' were not different but one and the same, there would not have been time, so too when its difference escapes our notice the interval does not seem to be time. If, then, the non-realization of the existence of time happens to us when we do not distinguish any change, but the mind seems to stay in one indivisible state,　　30 and when we perceive and distinguish we say time has elapsed, evidently time is not independent of movement and change. It is evident, then, that time is neither move-　　219ᵃ1 ment nor independent of movement.

We must take this as our starting-point and try to discover—since we wish to know what time is—what exactly it has to do with movement.

Now we perceive movement and time together; for even when it is dark and we are not being affected through the body, if any movement takes place in the mind we at once suppose that some time has indeed elapsed; and not only that but also, when some time is thought to have passed, some movement also along with it seems to have taken place. Hence time is either movement or something that belongs to movement. Since then it is not movement, it must be the other.

But what is moved is moved from something to something, and all magnitude is continuous. Therefore the movement goes with the magnitude. Because the magnitude is continuous, the movement too is continuous, and if the movement, then the time; for the time that has passed is always thought to be as great as the movement.

The distinction of before and after holds primarily, then, in place; and there in virtue of relative position. Since then before and after hold in magnitude, they must hold also in movement, these corresponding to those. But also in time the distinction of before and after must hold; for time and movement always correspond with each other. The before and after in motion identical in substratum with motion yet differs from it in being, and is not identical with motion.

But we apprehend time only when we have marked motion, marking it by before and after; and it is only when we have perceived before and after in motion that we say that time has elapsed. Now we mark them by judging that one thing is different from another, and that some third thing is intermediate to them. When we think of the extremes as different from the middle and the mind pronounces that the 'nows' are two, one before and one after, it is then that we say that there is time, and this that we say is time. For what is bounded by the 'now' is thought to be time—we may assume this.

When, therefore, we perceive the 'now' as one, and neither as before and after in a motion nor as the same element but in relation to a 'before' and an 'after', no time is thought to have elapsed, because there has been no motion either. On the other hand, when we do perceive a 'before' and an 'after', then we say that there is time. For time is just this—number of motion in respect of 'before' and 'after'.

Hence time is not movement, but only movement in so far as it admits of enumeration. An indication of this: we discriminate the more or the less by number, but more or less movement by time. Time then is a kind of number. (Number, we must note, is used in two ways—both of what is counted or countable and also of that with which we count. Time, then, is what is counted, not that with which we count: these are different kinds of thing.)

Just as motion is a perpetual succession, so also is time. But every simultaneous time is the same; for the 'now' is the same in substratum—though its being is different—and the 'now' determines time, in so far as time involves the before and after.

The 'now' in one sense is the same, in another it is not the same. In so far as it is in succession, it is different (which is just what its being now was supposed to mean), but its substratum is the same; for motion, as was said, goes with magnitude, and time, as we maintain, with motion. Similarly, then, there corresponds to the point the body which is carried along, and by which we are aware of the motion and of the before and after involved in it. This is an identical *substratum* (whether a point or a stone or something else of the kind), but it is different in definition— as the sophists assume that Coriscus' being in the Lyceum is a different 20 thing from Coriscus' being in the market-place. And the body which is carried along is different, in so far as it is at one time here and at another there. But the 'now' corresponds to the body that is carried along, as time corresponds to the motion. For it is by means of the body that is carried along that we become aware of the before and after in the motion, and if we regard these as countable we get 25 the 'now'. Hence in these also the 'now' as substratum remains the same (for it is what is before and after in movement), but its being is different; for it is in so far as the before and after is that we get the 'now'. This is what is most knowable; for motion is known because of that which is moved, locomotion because of that which 30 is carried. For what is carried is a 'this', the movement is not. Thus the 'now' in one sense is always the same, in another it is not the same; for this is true also of what is carried.

Clearly, too, if there were no time, there would be no 'now', and vice versa. Just as 220ª1 the moving body and its locomotion involve each other mutually, so too do the number of the moving body and the number of its locomotion. For the number of the locomotion is time, while the 'now' corresponds to the moving body, and is like the unit of number.

Time, then, also is both made continuous by the 'now' and divided at it. For here 5 too there is a correspondence with the locomotion and the moving body. For the motion or locomotion is made one by the thing which is moved, because *it* is one— not because it is one in substratum (for there might be pauses in the movement of such a thing)—but because it is one in definition; for this determines the movement as 'before' and 'after'. Here, too, there is a correspondence with the point; for the point also both connects and terminates the length—it is the beginning of one and 10 the end of another. But when you take it in this way, using the one point as two, a pause is necessary, if the same point is to be the beginning and the end. The 'now' on the other hand, since the body carried is moving, is always different.

Hence time is not number in the sense in which there is number of the same 15 point because it is beginning and end, but rather as the extremities of a line form a number, and not as the parts of the line do so, both for the reason given (for we can use the middle point as two, so that on that analogy time might stand still), and further because obviously the 'now' is no *part* of time nor the section any part of the movement, any more than the points are parts of the line—for it is two *lines* that are 20 *parts* of one line.

In so far then as the 'now' is a boundary, it is not time, but an attribute of it; in so far as it numbers, it is number; for boundaries being only to that which they bound, but number (e.g. ten) is the number of these horses, and belongs also elsewhere.

It is clear, then, that time is number of movement in respect of the before and 25 after, and is continuous since it is an attribute of what is continuous.

The smallest number, in the strict sense, is two. But of number as concrete, sometimes there is a minimum, sometimes not: e.g. of a line, the smallest in respect of *multiplicity* is two (or, if you like, one), but in respect of *size* there is no minimum; for every line is divided *ad infinitum*. Hence it is so with time. In respect of number the minimum is one (or two); in point of extent there is no minimum.

It is clear, too, that time is not described as fast or slow, but as many or few and as long or short. For as continuous it is long or short and as a number many or few; but it is not fast or slow—any more than any number with which we count is fast or slow.

Further, there is the same time everywhere at once, but not the same time before and after; for while the present change is one, the change which has happened and that which will happen are different. Time is not number with which we count, but the number of things which are counted; and this according as it occurs before or after is always different, for the 'nows' are different. And the number of a hundred horses and a hundred men is the same, but the things numbered are different—the horses for the men. Further, as a movement can be one and the same again and again, so too can time, e.g. a year or a spring or an autumn.

Not only do we measure the movement by the time, but also the time by the movement, because they define each other. The time marks the movement, since it is its number, and the movement the time. We describe the time as much or little, measuring it by the movement, just as we know the number by what is numbered, e.g. the number of the horses by one horse as the unit. For we know how many horses there are by the use of the number; and again by using the one horse as unit we know the number of the horses itself. So it is with the time and the movement; for we measure the movement by the time and vice versa. It is reasonable that this should happen; for the movement goes with the distance and the time with the movement, because they are quanta and continuous and divisible. The movement has these attributes because the distance is of this nature, and the time has them because of the movement. And we measure both the distance by the movement and the movement by the distance; for we say that the road is long, if the journey is long and that this is long, if the road is long—the time, too, if the movement, and the movement, if the time.

Time is a measure of motion and of being moved, and it measures the motion by determining a motion which will measure the whole motion, as the cubit does the length by determining an amount which will measure out the whole. Further to be in time means, for movement, that both it and its essence are measured by time (for simultaneously it measures both the movement and its essence, and this is what being in time means for it, that its essence should be measured).

Clearly, then, to be in time has the same meaning for other things also, namely, that their being should be measured by time. To be in time is one of two things: to exist when time exists, and as we say of some things that they are 'in number'. The latter means either what is a part or mode of number—in general, something which belongs to number—or that things have a number.

Now, since time is number, the 'now' and the before and the like are in time, just as unit and odd and even are in number, i.e. in the sense that the one set belongs to number, the other to time. But things are in time as they are in number. If this is so, they are contained by time as things in number are contained by number and things in place by place.

Plainly, too, to be in time does not mean to coexist with time, any more than to be in motion or in place means to coexist with motion or place. For if 'to be in something' is to mean this, then all things will be in anything, and the world will be in a grain; for when the grain is, then also is the world. But this is accidental, whereas the other is necessarily involved: that which is in time necessarily involves that there is time when *it* is, and that which is in motion that there is motion when *it* is.

Since what is in time is so in the same sense as what is in number is so, a time greater than everything in time can be found. So it is necessary that all the things in time should be contained by time, just like other things also which are in anything, e.g. the things in place by place.

A thing, then, will be affected by time, just as we are accustomed to say that time wastes things away, and that all things grow old through time, and that people forget owing to the lapse of time, but we do not say the same of getting to know or of becoming young or fair. For time is by its nature the cause rather of decay, since it is the number of change, and change removes what is.

Hence, plainly, things which are always are not, as such, in time; for they are not contained by time, nor is their being measured by time. An indication of this is that none of them is *affected* by time, which shows that they are not in time.

Since time is the measure of motion, it will be the measure of rest too. For all rest is in time. For it does not follow that what is in time is moved, though what is in motion is necessarily moved. For time is not motion, but number of motion; and what is at rest can be in the number of motion. Not everything that is not in motion can be said to be at rest—but only that which can be moved, though it actually is not moved, as was said above.

To be in number means that there is a number of the thing, and that its being is measured by the number in which it is. Hence if a thing is in time it will be measured by time. But time will measure what is moved and what is at rest, the one *qua* moved, the other *qua* at rest; for it will measure their motion and rest respectively.

Hence what is moved will not be measured by the time simply in so far as it has quantity, but in so far as its *motion* has quantity. Thus none of the things which are neither moved nor at rest are in time; for to be in time is to be measured by time, while time is the measure of motion and rest.

Plainly, then, neither will everything that does not exist be in time, i.e. those non-existent things that cannot exist, as the diagonal's being commensurate with the side.

Generally, if time is the measure of motion in itself and of other things accidentally, it is clear that a thing whose being is measured by it will have its being in rest or motion. Those things therefore which are subject to perishing and becoming—generally, those which at one time exist, at another do not—are necessarily in time;

30   for there is a greater time which will extend both beyond their being and beyond the time which measures their being. Of things which do not exist but are contained by time some were, e.g. Homer once was, some will be, e.g. a future event; this depends

222ª1   on the direction in which time contains them; if on both, they have both modes of existence. As to such things as it does not contain in any way, they neither were nor are nor will be. These are those non-existents whose opposites always are, as the

5   incommensurability of the diagonal always is—and this will not be in time. Nor will the commensurability, therefore; hence this eternally is not, because it is contrary to what eternally is. A thing whose contrary is not eternal can be and not be, and it is of such things that there is coming to be and passing away.

13

10   The 'now' is the link of time, as has been said (for it connects past and future time), and it is a limit of time (for it is the beginning of the one and the end of the other). But this is not obvious as it is with the point, which is fixed. It divides potentially, and in so far as it is dividing the 'now' is always different, but in so far as it connects

15   it is always the same, as it is with mathematical lines. For the intellect it is not always one and the same point, since it is other and other when one divides the line; but in so far as it is one, it is the same in every respect.

So the 'now' also is in one way a potential dividing of time, in another the termination of both parts, and their unity. And the dividing and the uniting are the

20   same thing and in the same reference, but in essence they are not the same.

So one kind of 'now' is described in this way: another is when the time of something is *near*. He will come now, because he will come to-day; he has come now, because he came to-day. But the things in the *Iliad* have not happened now, nor is the flood now—not that the time from now to them is not continuous, but because they are not near.

25   'At some time' means a time determined in relation to the first of the two types of 'now', e.g. at some time Troy was taken, and at some time there will be a flood; for it must be determined with reference to the 'now'. There *will* thus be a determinate time from this 'now' to that, and there *was* such in reference to the past event. But if there be no time which is not 'sometime', every time will be determined.

30   Will time then fail? Surely not, if motion always exists. Is time then always different or does the same time recur? Clearly, it is the same with time as with motion. For if one and the same motion sometimes recurs, it will be one and the same time, and if not, not.

Since the 'now' is an end and a beginning of time, not of the same time however,

222ᵇ1   but the end of that which is past and the beginning of that which is to come, it follows that, as the circle has its convexity and its concavity, in a sense, in the same

5   thing, so time is always at a beginning and at an end. And for this reason it seems to be always different; for the 'now' is not the beginning and the end of the same

thing; if it were, it would be at the same time and in the same respect two opposites. And time will not fail; for it is always at a beginning.

'Just now' refers to the part of future time which is near the indivisible present 'now' (When are you walking?—Just now; because the time in which he is going to do so is near), and to the part of past time which is not far from the 'now' (When are you walking?—I have been walking just now). But to say that Troy has just now been taken—we do not say that, because it is too far from the 'now'. 'Lately', too, refers to the part of past time which is near the present 'now'. 'When did you go?' 'Lately', if the time is near the existing now. 'Long ago' refers to the distant past.

'Suddenly' refers to what has departed from its former condition in a time imperceptible because of its smallness; but it is the nature of *all* change to alter things from their former condition. In time all things come into being and pass away; for which reason some called it the wisest of all things, but the Pythagorean Paron called it the most stupid, because in it we also forget; and his was the truer view. It is clear then that it must be in itself, as we said before, a cause of destruction rather than of coming into being (for change, in itself, makes things depart from their former condition), and only accidentally of coming into being, and of being. A sufficient evidence of this is that nothing comes into being without itself moving somehow and acting, but a thing can be destroyed even if it does not move at all. And this is what, as a rule, we chiefly mean by a thing's being destroyed by time. Still, time does not work even this change; but this sort of change too happens to occur in time.

We have stated, then, that time exists and what it is, and in how many ways we speak of the 'now', and what 'at some time', 'lately', 'just now', 'long ago', and 'suddenly' mean.

Chapter 34

Selection from *The Nature of Existence*

J. M. E. McTaggart

Time

Iᴛ will be convenient to begin our enquiry by asking whether anything existent can possess the characteristic of being in time. I shall endeavour to prove that it cannot.

It seems highly paradoxical to assert that time is unreal, and that all statements which involve its reality are erroneous. Such an assertion involves a departure from the natural position of mankind which is far greater than that involved in the assertion of the unreality of space or the unreality of matter. For in each man's experience there is a part—his own states as known to him by introspection—which does not even appear to be spatial or material. But we have no experience which does not appear to be temporal. Even our judgements that time is unreal appear to be themselves in time.

Yet in all ages and in all parts of the world the belief in the unreality of time has shown itself to be singularly persistent. In the philosophy and religion of the West—and still more, I suppose, in the philosophy and religion of the East—we find that the doctrine of the unreality of time continually recurs. Neither philosophy nor religion ever hold themselves apart from mysticism for any long period, and almost all mysticism denies the reality of time. In philosophy, time is treated as unreal by Spinoza, by Kant, and by Hegel. Among more modern thinkers, the same view is taken by Mr Bradley. Such a concurrence of opinion is highly significant, and is not the less significant because the doctrine takes such different forms, and is supported by such different arguments.

I believe that nothing that exists can be temporal, and that therefore time is unreal. But I believe it for reasons which are not put forward by any of the philosophers I have just mentioned.

Positions in time, as time appears to us prima facie, are distinguished in two ways. Each position is Earlier than some and Later than some of the other positions. To constitute such a series there is required a transitive asymmetrical relation, and

J. M. E. McTaggart, selection from chapter 33 of *The Nature of Existence* (Cambridge University Press, 1927).

a collection of terms such that, of any two of them, either the first is in this relation to the second, or the second is in this relation to the first. We may take here either the relation of 'earlier than' or the relation of 'later than', both of which, of course, are transitive and asymmetrical. If we take the first, then the terms have to be such that, of any two of them, either the first is earlier than the second, or the second is earlier than the first.

In the second place, each position is either Past, Present, or Future. The distinctions of the former class are permanent, while those of the latter are not. If M is ever earlier than N, it is always earlier. But an event, which is now present, was future, and will be past.

Since distinctions of the first class are permanent, it might be thought that they were more objective, and more essential to the nature of time, than those of the second class. I believe, however, that this would be a mistake, and that the distinction of past, present, and future is as *essential* to time as the distinction of earlier and later, while in a certain sense it may ... be regarded as more *fundamental* than the distinction of earlier and later. And it is because the distinctions of past, present, and future seem to me to be essential for time that I regard time as unreal.

For the sake of brevity I shall give the name of the A series to that series of positions which runs from the far past through the near past to the present, and then from the present through the near future to the far future, or conversely. The series of positions which runs from earlier to later, or conversely, I shall call the B series. The contents of any position in time form an event. The varied simultaneous contents of a single position are, of course, a plurality of events. But, like any other substance, they form a group, and this group is a compound substance. And a compound substance consisting of simultaneous events may properly be spoken of as itself an event.[1]

The first question which we must consider is whether it is essential to the reality of time that its events should form an A series as well as a B series. It is clear, to begin with, that, in present experience, we never *observe* events in time except as forming

---

1. It is very usual to contemplate time by the help of a metaphor of spatial movement. But spatial movement in which direction? The movement of time consists in the fact that later and later terms pass into the present, or—which is the same fact expressed in another way—that presentness passes to later and later terms. If we take it the first way, we are taking the B series as sliding along a fixed A series. If we take it the second way, we are taking the A series as sliding along a fixed B series. In the first case time presents itself as a movement from future to past. In the second case it presents itself as a movement from earlier to later. And this explains why we say that events come out of the future, while we say that we ourselves move towards the future. For each man identifies himself especially with his present state, as against his future or his past, since it is the only one which he is directly perceiving. And this leads him to say that he is moving with the present towards later events. And as those events are now future, he says that he is moving towards the future.

Thus the question as to the movement of time is ambiguous. But if we ask what is the movement of either series, the question is not ambiguous. The movement of the A series along the B series is from earlier to later. The movement of the B series along the A series is from future to past.

both these series. We perceive events in time as being present, and those are the only events which we actually perceive. And all other events which, by memory or by inference, we believe to be real, we regard as present, past, or future. Thus the events of time as observed by us form an *A* series.

It might be said, however, that this is merely subjective. It might be the case that the distinction of positions in time into past, present, and future is only a constant illusion of our minds, and that the real nature of time contains only the distinctions of the *B* series—the distinctions of earlier and later. In that case we should not perceive time as it really is, though we might be able to *think* of it as it really is.

This is not a very common view, but it requires careful consideration. I believe it to be untenable, because, as I said above, it seems to me that the *A* series is essential to the nature of time, and that any difficulty in the way of regarding the *A* series as real is equally a difficulty in the way of regarding time as real.

It would, I suppose, be universally admitted that time involves change. In ordinary language, indeed, we say that something can remain unchanged through time. But there could be no time if nothing changed. And if anything changes, then all other things change with it. For its change must change some of their relations to it, and so their relational qualities. The fall of a sand-castle on the English coast changes the nature of the Great Pyramid.

If, then, a *B* series without an *A* series can constitute time, change must be possible without an *A* series. Let us suppose that the distinctions of past, present, and future do not apply to reality. In that case, can change apply to reality?

What, on this supposition, could it be that changes? Can we say that, in a time which formed a *B* series but not an *A* series, the change consisted in the fact that the event ceased to be an event, while another event began to be an event? If this were the case, we should certainly have got a change.

But this is impossible. If *N* is ever earlier than *O* and later than *M*, it will always be, and has always been, earlier than *O* and later than *M*, since the relations of earlier and later are permanent. *N* will thus always be in a *B* series. And as, by our present hypothesis, a *B* series by itself constitutes time, *N* will always have a position in a time-series, and always has had one. That is, it always has been an event, and always will be one, and cannot begin or cease to be an event.

Or shall we say that one event *M* merges itself into another event *N*, while still preserving a certain identity by means of an unchanged element, so that it can be said, not merely that *M* has ceased and *N* begun, but that it is *M* which has become *N*? Still the same difficulty recurs. *M* and *N* may have a common element, but they are not the same event, or there would be no change. If, therefore, *M* changed into *N* at a certain moment, then, at that moment, *M* would have ceased to be *M*, and *N* would have begun to be *N*. This involves that, at that moment, *M* would have ceased to be an event, and *N* would have begun to be an event. And we saw, in the last paragraph, that, on our present hypothesis, this is impossible.

Nor can such change be looked for in the different moments of absolute time, even if such moments should exist. For the same argument will apply here. Each such moment will have its own place in the *B* series, since each would be earlier or later than each of the others. And, as the *B* series depends on permanent relations, no moment could ever cease to be, nor could it become another moment.

Change, then, cannot arise from an event ceasing to be an event, nor from one event changing into another. In what other way can it arise? If the characteristics of an event change, then there is certainly change. But what characteristics of an event can change? It seems to me that there is only one class of such characteristics. And that class consists of the determinations of the event in question by the terms of the *A* series.

Take any event—the death of Queen Anne, for example—and consider what changes can take place in its characteristics. That it is a death, that it is the death of Anne Stuart, that it has such causes, that it has such effects—every characteristic of this sort never changes. 'Before the stars saw one another plain', the event in question was the death of a queen. At the last moment of time—if time has a last moment—it will still be the death of a queen. And in every respect but one, it is equally devoid of change. But in one respect it does change. It was once an event in the far future. It became every moment an event in the nearer future. At last it was present. Then it became past, and will always remain past, though every moment it becomes further and further past.[2]

Such characteristics as these are the only characteristics which can change. And, therefore, if there is any change, it must be looked for in the *A* series, and in the *A* series alone. If there is no real *A* series, there is no real change. The *B* series, therefore, is not by itself sufficient to constitute time, since time involves change.

The *B* series, however, cannot exist except as temporal, since earlier and later, which are the relations which connect its terms, are clearly time-relations. So it follows that there can be no *B* series when there is no *A* series, since without an *A* series there is no time.

We must now consider three objections which have been made to this position. The first is involved in the view of time which has been taken by Mr Russell, according to which past, present, and future do not belong to time *per se*, but only in relation to a knowing subject. An assertion that *N* is present means that it is simultaneous with that assertion, an assertion that it is past or future means that it is earlier or later than that assertion. Thus it is only past, present, or future in relation to some assertion. If there were no consciousness, there would be events which were earlier and later than others, but nothing would be in any sense past, present, or future. And if there were events earlier than any consciousness, those events would never be future or present, though they could be past.

---

2. The past, therefore, is always changing, if the *A* series is real at all, since at each moment a past event is further in the past than it was before. This result follows from the reality of the *A* series, and is independent of the truth of our view that all change depends exclusively on the *A* series. It is worth while to notice this, since most people combine the view that the *A* series is real with the view that the past cannot change—a combination which is inconsistent.

If *N* were ever present, past, or future in relation to some assertion *V*, it would always be so, since whatever is ever simultaneous to, earlier than, or later than *V* will always be so. What, then, is change? We find Mr Russell's views on this subject in his *Principles of Mathematics*, section 442. 'Change is the difference, in respect of truth or falsehood, between a proposition concerning an entity and the time *T*, and a proposition concerning the same entity and the time *T'*, provided that these propositions differ only by the fact that *T* occurs in the one where *T'* occurs in the other.' That is to say, there is change, on Mr Russell's view, if the proposition 'At the time *T* my poker is hot' is true, and the proposition 'At the time *T'* my poker is hot' is false.

I am unable to agree with Mr Russell. I should, indeed, admit that, when two such propositions were respectively true and false, there would be change. But then I maintain that there can be no time without an *A* series. If, with Mr Russell, we reject the *A* series, it seems to me that change goes with it, and that therefore time, for which change is essential, goes too. In other words, if the *A* series is rejected, no proposition of the type 'At the time *T* my poker is hot' can ever be true, because there would be no time.

It will be noticed that Mr Russell looks for change, not in the events in the time-series, but in the entity to which those events happen, or of which they are states. If my poker, for example, is hot on a particular Monday, and never before or since, the event of the poker being hot does not change. But the poker changes, because there is a time when this event is happening to it, and a time when it is not happening to it.

But this makes no change in the qualities of the poker. It is always a quality of that poker that it is one which is hot on that particular Monday. And it is always a quality of that poker that it is one which is not hot at any other time. Both these qualities are true of it at any time—the time when it is hot and the time when it is cold. And therefore it seems to be erroneous to say that there is any change in the poker. The fact that it is hot at one point in a series and cold at other points cannot give change, if neither of these facts change—and neither of them does. Nor does any other fact about the poker change, unless its presentness, pastness, or futurity change.

Let us consider the case of another sort of series. The meridian of Greenwich passes through a series of degrees of latitude. And we can find two points in this series, *S* and *S'*, such that the proposition 'At *S* the meridian of Greenwich is within the United Kingdom' is true, while the proposition 'At *S'* the meridian of Greenwich is within the United Kingdom' is false. But no one would say that this gave us change. Why should we say so in the case of the other series?

Of course there is a satisfactory answer to this question if we are correct in speaking of the other series as a time-series. For where there is time, there is change. But then the whole question is whether it is a time-series. My contention is that if we remove the *A* series from the prima facie nature of time, we are left with a series which is not temporal, and which allows change no more than the series of latitudes does.

If, as I have maintained, there can be no change unless facts change, then there can be no change without an *A* series. For, as we saw with the death of Queen Anne, and also in the case of the poker, no fact about anything can change, unless it is a fact about its place in the A series. Whatever other qualities it has, it has always. But that which is future will not always be future, and that which was past was not always past.

It follows from what we have said that there can be no change unless some propositions are sometimes true and sometimes false. This is the case of propositions which deal with the place of anything in the A series— 'The Battle of Waterloo is in the past', 'It is now raining'. But it is not the case with any other propositions.

Mr Russell holds that such propositions are ambiguous, and that to make them definite we must substitute propositions which are always true or always false— 'The Battle of Waterloo is earlier than this judgement', 'The fall of rain is simultaneous with this judgement'. If he is right, all judgements are either always true, or always false. Then, I maintain, no facts change. And then, I maintain, there is no change at all.

I hold, as Mr Russell does, that there is no A series. (My reasons for this will be given below.) And ... I regard the reality lying behind the appearance of the A series in a manner not completely unlike that which Mr Russell has adopted. The difference between us is that he thinks that, when the A series is rejected, change, time, and the B series can still be kept, while I maintain that its rejection involves the rejection of change, and, consequently, of time, and of the B series.

The second objection rests on the possibility of non-existent time-series—such, for example, as the adventures of Don Quixote. This series, it is said, does not form part of the A series. I cannot at this moment judge it to be either past, present, or future. Indeed, I know that it is none of the three. Yet, it is said, it is certainly a B series. The adventure of the galley-slaves, for example, is later than the adventure of the windmills. And a B series involves time. The conclusion drawn is that an A series is not essential to time.

I should reply to this objection as follows. Time only belongs to the existent. If any reality is in time, that involves that the reality in question exists. This, I think, would be universally admitted. It may be questioned whether all of what exists is in time, or even whether anything really existent is in time, but it would not be denied that, if anything is in time, it must exist.

Now what is existent in the adventures of Don Quixote? Nothing. For the story is imaginary. The states of Cervantes' mind when he invented the story, the states of my mind when I think of the story—these exist. But then these form part of an A series. Cervantes' invention of the story is in the past. My thought of the story is in the past, the present, and—I trust—the future.

But the adventures of Don Quixote may be believed by a child to be historical. And in reading them I may, by an effort of my imagination, contemplate them as if they really happened. In this case, the adventures are believed to be existent, or are contemplated as existent. But then they are believed to be in the A series, or are contemplated as being in the A series. The child who believes them to be historical will believe that they happened in the past. If I contemplate them as existent, I shall contemplate them as happening in the past. In the same way, if I believed the events described in Jefferies' *After London* to exist, or contemplated them as existent, I should believe them to exist in the future, or contemplate them as existing in the future. Whether we place the object of our belief or of our contemplation in the present, the past, or the future will depend upon the characteristics of that object. But somewhere in the *A* series it will be placed.

Thus the answer to the objection is that, just as far as a thing is in time, it is in the *A* series. If it is really in time, it is really in the *A* series. If it is believed to be in time, it is believed to be in the *A* series. If it is contemplated as being in time, it is contemplated as being in the *A* series.

The third objection is based on the possibility that, if time were real at all, there might be in reality several real and independent time-series. The objection, if I understand it rightly, is that every time-series would be real, while the distinctions of past, present, and future would only have a meaning within each series, and would not, therefore, be taken as absolutely real. There would be, for example, many presents. Now, of course, many points of time can be present. In each time-series many points are present, but they must be present successively. And the presents of the different time-series would not be successive, since they are not in the same time.[3] And different presents, it would be said, cannot be real unless they are successive. So the different time-series, which are real, must be able to exist independently of the distinction between past, present, and future.

I cannot, however, regard this objection as valid. No doubt in such a case, no present would be *the* present—it would only be the present of a certain aspect of the universe. But then no time would be *the* time—it would only be the time of a certain aspect of the universe. It would be a real time-series, but I do not see that the present would be less real than the time.

I am not, of course, maintaining that there is no difficulty in the existence of several distinct *A* series. In the second part of this chapter I shall endeavour to show that the existence of *any A* series is impossible. What I assert here is that, if there could be an *A* series at all, and if there were any reason to suppose that there were several distinct *B* series, there would be no additional difficulty in supposing that there should be a distinct *A* series for each *B* series.

We conclude, then, that the distinctions of past, present, and future are essential to time, and that, if the distinctions are never true of reality, then no reality is in time. This view, whether true or false, has nothing surprising in it. It was pointed out above that we always perceive time as having these distinctions. And it has generally been held that their connection with time is a real characteristic of time, and not an illusion due to the way in which we perceive it. Most philosophers, whether they did or did not believe time to be true of reality, have regarded the distinctions of the *A* series as essential to time.

3. Neither would they be simultaneous, since that equally involves being in the same time. They would stand in no time-relation to one another.

When the opposite view has been maintained it has generally been, I believe, because it was held (rightly, as I shall try to show) that the distinctions of past, present, and future cannot be true of reality, and that consequently, if the reality of time is to be saved, the distinction in question must be shown to be unessential to time. The presumption, it was held, was for the reality of time, and this would give us a reason for rejecting the *A* series as unessential to time. But, of course, this could only give a presumption. If the analysis of the nature of time has shown that, by removing the *A* series, time is destroyed, this line of argument is no longer open.

I now pass to the second part of my task. Having, as it seems to me, succeeded in proving that there can be no time without an *A* series, it remains to prove that an *A* series cannot exist, and that therefore time cannot exist. This would involve that time is not real at all, since it is admitted that the only way in which time can be real is by existing.

Past, present, and future are characteristics which we ascribe to events, and also to moments of time, if these are taken as separate realities. What do we mean by past, present, and future? In the first place, are they relations or qualities? It seems quite clear to me that they are not qualities but relations, though, of course, like other relations, they will generate relational qualities in each of their terms.[4] But even if this view should be wrong, and they should in reality be qualities and not relations, it will not affect the result which we shall reach. For the reasons for rejecting the reality of past, present, and future, which we are about to consider, would apply to qualities as much as to relations.

If, then, anything is to be rightly called past, present, or future, it must be because it is in relation to something else. And this something else to which it is in relation must be something outside the time-series. For the relations of the *A* series are changing relations, and no relations which are exclusively between members of the time-series can ever change. Two events are exactly in the same places in the time-series, relatively to one another, a million years before they take place, while each of them is taking place, and when they are a million years in the past. The same is true of the relation of moments to one another, if moments are taken as separate realities. And the same would be true of the relations of events to moments. The changing relation must be to something which is not in the time-series.

Past, present, and future, then, are relations in which events stand to something outside the time-series. Are these relations simple, or can they be defined? I think that they are clearly simple and indefinable. But, on the other hand, I do not think that they are isolated and independent. It does not seem that we can know, for example, the meaning of pastness, if we do not know the meaning of presentness or of futurity.

---

4. It is true, no doubt, that my anticipation of an experience *M*, the experience itself, and the memory of the experience are three states which have different original qualities. But it is not the future *M*, the present *M*, and the past *M* which have these three different qualities. The qualities are possessed by three different events—the anticipation of *M*, *M* itself, and the memory of *M*—each of which in its turn is future, present, and past. Thus this gives no support to the view that the changes of the *A* series are changes of original qualities.

We must begin with the *A* series, rather than with past, present, and future, as separate terms. And we must say that a series is an *A* series when each of its terms has, to an entity *X* outside the series, one, and only one, of three indefinable relations, pastness, presentness, and futurity, which are such that all the terms which have the relation of presentness to *X* fall between all the terms which have the relation of pastness to *X*, on the one hand, and all the terms which have the relation of futurity to *X*, on the other hand.

We have come to the conclusion that an *A* series depends on relations to a term outside the *A* series. This term, then, could not itself be in time, and yet must be such that different relations to it determine the other terms of those relations, as being past, present, or future. To find such a term would not be easy, and yet such a term must be found, if the *A* series is to be real. But there is a more positive difficulty in the way of the reality of the *A* series.

Past, present, and future are incompatible determinations. Every event must be one or the other, but no event can be more than one. If I say that any event is past, that implies that it is neither present nor future, and so with the others. And this exclusiveness is essential to change, and therefore to time. For the only change we can get is from future to present, and from present to past.

The characteristics, therefore, are incompatible. But every event has them all.[5] If *M* is past, it has been present and future. If it is future, it will be present and past. If it is present, it has been future and will be past. Thus all the three characteristics belong to each event. How is this consistent with their being incompatible?

It may seem that this can easily be explained. Indeed, it has been impossible to state the difficulty without almost giving the explanation, since our language has verb-forms for the past, present, and future, but no form that is common to all three. It is never true, the answer will run, that *M* is present, past, and future. It *is* present, *will be* past, and *has been* future. Or it *is* past, and *has been* future and present, or again *is* future, and *will be* present and past. The characteristics are only incompatible when they are simultaneous, and there is no contradiction to this in the fact that each term has all of them successively.

But what is meant by 'has been' and 'will be'? And what is meant by 'is', when, as here, it is used with a temporal meaning, and not simply for predication? When we say that *X* has been *Y*, we are asserting *X* to be *Y* at a moment of past time. When we say that *X* will be *Y*, we are asserting *X* to be *Y* at a moment of future time. When we say that *X* is *Y* (in the temporal sense of 'is'), we are asserting *X* to be *Y* at a moment of present time.

Thus, our first statement about *M*—that it is present, will be past, and has been future—means that *M* is present at a moment of present time, past at some moment of future time, and future at some moment of past time. But every moment, like

---

5. If the time-series has a first term, that term will never be future, and if it has a last term, that term will never be past. But the first term, in that case, will be present and past, and the last term will be future and present. And the possession of two incompatible characteristics raises the same difficulty as the possession of three.

every event, is both past, present, and future. And so a similar difficulty arises. If *M* is present, there is no moment of past time at which it is past. But the moments of future time, in which it is past, are equally moments of past time, in which it cannot be past. Again, that *M* is future and will be present and past means that *M* is future at a moment of present time, and present and past at different moments of future time. In that case it cannot be present or past at any moments of past time. But all the moments of future time, in which *M* will be present or past, are equally moments of past time.

And thus again we get a contradiction, since the moments at which *M* has any one of the three determinations of the *A* series are also moments at which it cannot have that determination. If we try to avoid this by saying of these moments what had been previously said of *M* itself—that some moment, for example, is future, and will be present and past—then 'is' and 'will be' have the same meaning as before. Our statement, then, means that the moment in question is future at a present moment, and will be present and past at different moments of future time. This, of course, is the same difficulty over again. And so on infinitely.

Such an infinity is vicious. The attribution of the characteristics past, present, and future to the terms of any series leads to a contradiction, unless it is specified that they have them successively. This means, as we have seen, that they have them in relation to terms specified as past, present, and future. These again, to avoid a like contradiction, must in turn be specified as past, present, and future. And, since this continues infinitely, the first set of terms never escapes from contradiction at all.[6]

The contradiction, it will be seen, would arise in the same way supposing that pastness, presentness, and futurity were original qualities, and not, as we have decided that they are, relations. For it would still be the case that they were characteristics which were incompatible with one another, and that whichever had one of them would also have the other. And it is from this that the contradiction arises.

The reality of the *A* series, then, leads to a contradiction, and must be rejected. And, since we have seen that change and time require the *A* series, the reality of change and time must be rejected. And so must the reality of the *B* series, since that requires time. Nothing is really present, past, or future. Nothing is really earlier or later than anything else or temporally simultaneous with it. Nothing really changes. And nothing is really in time. Whenever we perceive anything in time—which is the only way in which, in our present experience, we do perceive things—we are perceiving it more or less as it really is not.[7]

6. It may be worth while to point out that the vicious infinite has not arisen from the impossibility of *defining* past, present, and future, without using the terms in their own definitions. On the contrary, we have admitted these terms to be indefinable. It arises from the fact that the nature of the terms involves a contradiction, and that the attempt to remove the contradiction involves the employment of the terms, and the generation of a similar contradiction.

7. Even on the hypothesis that judgements are real it would be necessary to regard ourselves as perceiving things in time, and so perceiving them erroneously.

Chapter 35

Changes in events and changes in things

Arthur N. Prior

THE basic question to which I wish to address myself in this lecture is simply the old one, does time really flow or pass? The problem, of course, is that genuine flowing or passage is something which occurs *in* time, and *takes* time to occur. If time itself flows or passes, must there not be some 'super-time' in which it does so? Again, whatever flows or passes does so at some *rate*, but a rate of flow is just the amount of movement in a given *time*, so how could there be a rate of flow of time itself? And if time does not flow at any rate, how can it flow at all?

A natural first move towards extricating ourselves from these perplexities is to admit that talk of the flow or passage of time is just a metaphor. Time may be, as Isaac Watts says, *like* an ever-rolling stream, but it isn't really and literally an ever-rolling stream. But *how* is it like an ever-rolling stream? What is the literal truth behind this metaphor? The answer to this is not, at first sight, difficult. Generally when we make such remarks as 'Time does fly, doesn't it?—why, it's already the 16th', we mean that some date or moment which we have been looking forward to as future has ceased to be future and is now present and on its way into the past. Or more fundamentally, perhaps, some future *event* to which we have been looking forward with hope or dread is now at last occurring, and soon will have occurred, and will have occurred a longer and longer time *ago*. We might say, for example, 'Time does fly— I'm already 47'—that is, my birth is already that much past, 'and soon I shall be 48', i.e. it will be more past still. Suppose we speak about something 'becoming more past' not only when it moves from the comparatively near past to the comparatively distant past, but also when it moves from the present to the past, from the future to the present, and from the comparatively distant future to the comparatively near future. Then whatever is happening, has happened, or will happen is all the time 'becoming more past' in this extended sense; and just this is what we mean by the flow or passage of time. And if we want to give the *rate* of this flow or passage, it is surely very simple—it takes one exactly a year to get a year older, i.e. events become more past at the rate of a year per year, an hour per hour, a second per second.

Does this remove the difficulty? It is far from obvious that it does. It's not just that an hour per hour is a queer sort of rate—*this* queerness, I think, has been exaggerated, and I shall say more about it in a minute—but the whole idea of events changing is

Arthur N. Prior, 'Changes in Events and Changes in Things', from *Papers on Time and Tense* (Clarendon Press, 1968), reprinted by permission of Oxford University Press.

at first sight a little strange, even if we abandon the admittedly figurative description of this change as a *movement*. By and large, to judge by the way that we ordinarily talk, it's *things* that change, and events don't change but *happen*. Chairs, tables, horses, people change—chairs get worn out and then mended, tables get dirty and then clean again, horses get tired and then refreshed, people learn things and forget them, or are happy and then miserable, active and then sleepy, and so on, and all these are changes, and chairs, tables, horses, and people are all what I mean by things as opposed to events. An accident, a coronation, a death, a prize-giving, are examples of what we'd call events, and it does seem unnatural to describe these as changing— what these do, one is inclined to say, is not to change but to happen or occur.

One of the things that make us inclined to deny that events undergo changes is that events *are* changes—to say that such and such an event has occurred is generally to say that some thing has, or some things have, changed in some way. To say, for instance, that the retirement of Sir Anthony Eden occurred in such and such a year is just to say that Sir Anthony then retired and so suffered the change or changes that retirement consists in—he had been Prime Minister, and then was not Prime Minister. Sir Anthony's retirement is or was a change concerning Sir Anthony; to say that it itself changes or has changed sounds queer because it sounds queer to talk of a change changing.

This queerness, however, is superficial. When we reflect further we realize that changes do change, especially if they go on for any length of time. (In this case we generally, though not always, call the change a *process* rather than an event, and there are other important differences between events and processes besides the length of time they take, but these differences are not relevant to the present discussion, so I shall ignore them and discuss changes generally, events and processes alike.) Changes do change—a movement, for example, may be slow at first and then rapid, a prize-giving or a lecture may be at first dull and afterwards interesting, or vice versa, and so on. It would hardly be too much to say that modern science began when people became accustomed to the idea of changes changing, e.g. to the idea of acceleration as opposed to simple motion. I've no doubt the ordinary measure of acceleration, so many feet per second per second, sounded queer when it was first used, and I think it still sounds queer to most students when they first encounter it. Ordinary speech is still resistant to it, and indeed to the expression of anything in the nature of a comparison of a comparison. We are taught at school that 'more older', for example, is bad English, but why shouldn't I say that I am more older than my son than he is than my daughter? And if we have learned to talk of an acceleration of a foot per second per second without imagining that the second 'second' must somehow be a different kind of 'second' from the first one—without imagining that if motion takes place in ordinary time, acceleration must take place in some super-time—can we not accustom ourselves equally to a change of 'a second per second' without any such imagining?

Changes do change, then, but this does not leave everything quite simple and solved. For there's still something odd about the change that we describe figuratively as the flow or passage of time—the change from an event's being future to its being present, and from its being more and more past. For the other changes in events which I have mentioned are ones which go on in the event *while it is occurring*; for example, if a lecture gets duller or a movement faster then this is something it does *as it goes on*; but the change from past to still further past isn't one that occurs while the event is occurring, for all the time that an event is occurring it isn't past but present, in fact the presentness of an event just *is* its happening, its occurring, as opposed to its merely having happened or being merely about to happen. We might put it this way: the things that change are *existing* things, and it's while they exist that they change, e.g. it's existing men, not non-existent men, that get tired and then pick up again; Julius Caesar, for example, isn't now getting tired and picking up again, unless the doctrine of immortality is true and he exists now as much as he ever did. And such changes as the change in the rate of movement are similarly changes that go on in events or processes while they exist, that is, while they exist in the only sense in which events and processes do exist, namely while they are occurring. But getting more and more past seems to be something an event does when it *doesn't* exist, and this seems very queer indeed.

We may retrace our steps to this point by looking at some of the literature of our subject. Professor C. D. Broad, in the second volume of his *Examination of McTaggart's Philosophy*, says that the ordinary view that an event, say the death of Queen Anne, is in the indefinitely distant future and then less and less future and then present and then goes into the more and more distant past—this ordinary story, Broad says, cannot possibly be true because it takes the death of Queen Anne to be at once a mere momentary thing and something with an indefinitely long history. We can make a first answer to this by distinguishing between the history that an event *has*, and the bit of history that it *is*. The bit of history that Queen Anne's death is, or was, is a very very short bit, but that doesn't prevent the history that it has from being indefinitely long. Queen Anne's death is part of the history of Queen Anne, and a very short part of it; what is long is not this part of the history of Queen Anne, but rather the history of this part of her history—the history of this part of her history is that first it was future, then it was present, and so on, and this can be a long history even if the bit of history that it is the history *of* is very short. There is not, therefore, the flat contradiction that Broad suggests here. There is, however, the difficulty that we generally think of the history of a thing as the sum of what it does and what happens to it *while it is there*—when it ceases to be, its history has ended—and this does make it seem odd that there should be an indefinitely long history of something which itself occupies a time which is indefinitely short.

But if there is a genuine puzzle here, it concerns what is actually going on also. For whatever goes on for any length of time—and that means: whatever goes on— will have future and past phases as well as the immediately present one; its going on is in fact a continual passage of one phase after another from being future through being present to being past. Augustine's reflections, in the eleventh chapter of his

Confessions, on the notion of a 'long time', are relevant here. Just when, he asks, is a long time long? Is it long when it is present, or when it is past or future? We need not, I think, attach much importance to the fact that Augustine concentrates on so abstract a thing as a 'time' or an interval; his problems can be quite easily restated in terms of *what goes on* over the interval; in fact he himself slips into this, and talks about his childhood, a future sunrise, and so on. When, we may ask, does a process go on for a long time—while it is going on, or when it lies ahead of us, or is all over?

Augustine is at first driven to the view that it is when it is present that a time is long, for only what *is* can be long or short (paragraph 18). We can give the same answer with processes—it is when they are going on that they go on for a long time. But then, as Augustine points out, there are these phases. A hundred years is a long time, but it's not really present all at once, and even if we try to boil down the present to an hour, 'that one hour passes away in flying particles'. 'The present hath no space' (20). Augustine had apparently not heard of the 'specious present', but even if he had it would not have helped him much—most of the happenings we are interested in take longer than that. He tries out the hypotheses that the past and the future, and past and future events, in some sense after all 'are'—that there is some 'secret place' where they exist all the time, and from which they come and to which they go. If there is no such place, then where do those who foresee the future and recall the past discern these things? 'For that which is not, cannot be seen' (22).

Well, Augustine says, he doesn't know anything about that, but one thing that he does know is that wherever 'time past and to come' may 'be', 'they are not there as future, or past, but present. For if there also they be future, they are not yet there; if there also they be past, they are no longer there. Wheresoever then is whatsoever is, it is only as present' (23). Of course there are present 'traces' or images of past things in our memories, and present signs and intentions on the basis of which we make our future forecasts (23, 24), and sometimes Augustine seems satisfied with this— past, present, and future, he says, 'do exist in some sort, in the soul, but otherwhere do I not see them' (26). But sometimes he seems far from content with this—*that which* we remember and anticipate, he says, is different from these signs, and is *not* present (23, 24)—and, one must surely add, is *not* 'in the soul'.

It is time now to be constructive, and as a preparation for this I shall indulge in what may seem a digression, on the subject of Grammar. English philosophers who visit the United States are always asked sooner or later, whether they are 'analysts'. I'm not at all sure what the answer is in my own case, but there's another word that Professor Passmore once invented to describe some English philosophers who are often called 'analysts', namely the word 'grammaticist', and that's something I wouldn't at all mind calling myself. I don't deny that there are genuine metaphysical problems, but I think you have to talk about grammar at least a little bit in order to solve most of them. And in particular, I would want to maintain that most of the present group of problems about time and change, though not quite all of them, arise from the fact that many expressions which look like nouns, i.e., names of objects, are not really nouns at all but concealed verbs, and many expressions which look like verbs are not really verbs but concealed conjunctions and adverbs. That is a slight over-simplification, but before we can get it stated more accurately we must look more closely at verbs, conjunctions, and adverbs.

I shall assume that we are sufficiently clear for our present purposes as to what a noun or name is, and what a sentence is; and given these notions, we can define a verb or verb-phrase as an expression that constructs a sentence out of a name or names. For instance, if you tack the verb 'died' on the name 'Queen Anne' you get the sentence 'Queen Anne died', and if you tack the phrase 'is an undertaker' on the name 'James Bowels' you get the sentence 'James Bowels is an undertaker', so that this is a verb-phrase. I say 'out of a name *or names*' because some verbs have to have an object as well as a subject. Thus if you put the verb 'loves' between the names 'Richard' and 'Joan' you get the sentence 'Richard loves Joan'; this verb constructs this sentence out of these two names; and the phrase 'is taller than' would function similarly. Logicians call verbs and verb-phrases 'predicates'; 'died' and 'is an under-taker' would be 'one-place' predicates, and 'loves' and 'is taller than' are 'two-place' predicates. There are also expressions which construct sentences, not out of names, but out of other sentences. If an expression constructs a sentence out of two or more other sentences it is a conjunction, or a phrase equivalent to a conjunction. For example 'Either—or—' functions in this way in 'Either it will rain or it will snow'. If the expression constructs a sentence out of one other sentence it is an adverb or adverbial phrase, like 'not' or 'It is not the case that', or 'allegedly' or 'It is alleged that', or 'possibly' or 'It is possible that'. Thus by attaching these expressions to 'It is raining' we obtain the sentences

> It is not raining;
> It is not the case that it is raining;
> It is allegedly raining;
> It is alleged that it is raining;
> It is possibly raining;
> It is possible that it is raining.

One very important difference between conjunctions and adverbs, on the one hand, and verbs, on the other, is that because the former construct sentences out of sentences, i.e. the same sort of thing as they end up with, they can be applied again and again to build up more and more complicated sentences, like 'It is allegedly possible that he will not come', which could be spread out as

> It is said that (it is possible that (it is not the case that (he will come))).

You can also use the same adverb twice and obtain such things as double negation, alleged allegations, and so on. Verbs, because they do not end up with the same sort of expression as what they start with, cannot be piled up in this way. Having constructed 'Queen Anne died' by the verb 'died' out of the name 'Queen Anne', you cannot do it again—'Queen Anne died died' is not a sentence.

Turning now to our main subject, I want to suggest that putting a verb into the past or future tense is exactly the same sort of thing as adding an adverb to the sentence. 'I *was* having my breakfast' is related to 'I am having my breakfast' in exactly the same way as 'I am *allegedly* having my breakfast' is related to it, and it is only an historical accident that we generally form the past tense by modifying the present tense, e.g. by changing 'am' to 'was', rather than by tacking on an adverb. In a rationalized language with uniform constructions for similar functions we could form the past tense by prefixing to a given sentence the phrase 'It was the case that', or 'It has been the case that' (depending on what sort of past we meant), and the future tense by prefixing 'It will be the case that'. For example, instead of 'I will be eating my breakfast' we could say

It will be the case that I am eating my breakfast,

and instead of 'I was eating my breakfast' we could say

It was the case that I am eating my breakfast.

The nearest we get to the latter in ordinary English is 'It was the case that I *was* eating my breakfast', but this is one of those anomalies like emphatic double negation. The construction I am sketching embodies the truth behind Augustine's suggestion of the 'secret place' where past and future times 'are', and his insistence that wherever they are, they are not there as past or future but as present. The past is not the present but it *is* the past present, and the future is not the present but it *is* the future present.

There is also, of course, the past future and the future past. For these adverbial phrases, like other adverbial phrases, can be applied repeatedly—the sentences to which they are attached do not have to be simple ones; it is enough that they be sentences, and they can be sentences which already have tense-adverbs, as we might call them, within them. Hence we can have such a construction as

It will be the case that (it has been the case that (I am taking off my coat)).

or in plain English, 'I will have taken off my coat'. We can similarly apply repeatedly such *specific* tense-adverbs as 'It was the case forty-eight years ago that'. For example, we could have

It will be the case seven months hence that (it was the case forty-eight years ago that (I am being born)),

that is, it will be my forty-eighth birthday in seven months' time.

To say that a change has occurred is to say at least this much: that something which was the case formerly is not the case now. That is, it is at least to say that for some sentence p we have

It was the case that p, and it is not the case that p.

This sentence p can be as complicated as you like, and can itself contain tense-adverbs, so that one example of our formula would be

> It was the case five months ago that (it was the case only forty-seven years ago that (I am being born)), and it is not now the case that (it was the case only forty-seven years ago that (I am being born)),

that is, I am not as young as I used to be. This last change, of course, is a case of precisely that recession of events into the past that we are really talking about when we say that time flows or passes, and the piling of time-references on top of one another, with no suggestion that the time-words must be used in a different sense at each level, simply reflects the fact that tense-adverbs *are* adverbs, not verbs.

An important point to notice now is that while *I* have been talking about words—for example, about verbs and adverbs—for quite a long time, the sentences that I have been using as examples have *not* been about words but about real things. When a sentence is formed out of another sentence or other sentences by means of an adverb or conjunction, it is not *about* those other sentences, but about whatever they are themselves about. For example, the compound sentence 'Either I will wear my cap or I will wear my beret' is not about the sentences 'I will wear my cap' and 'I will wear my beret'; like them, it is about me and my headgear, though the information it conveys about these is a little less definite than what either of them would convey separately. Similarly, the sentence 'It will be the case that I am having my tooth out' is not about the sentence 'I am having my tooth out'; it is about me. A genuine sentence about the sentence 'I am having my tooth out' would be one stating that it contained six words and nineteen letters, but 'It will be the case that I am having my tooth out', i.e. 'I will be having my tooth out', is quite obviously not a sentence of this sort at all.

Nor is it about some abstract entity named by the clause 'that I am having my tooth out'. It is about me and my tooth, and about nothing else whatever. The fact is that it is difficult for the human mind to get beyond the simple subject–predicate or noun–verb structure, and when a sentence or thought hasn't that structure but a more complex one we try in various ways to force it into the subject–predicate pattern. We thus invent new modes of speech in which the subordinate sentences are replaced by noun–phrases and the conjunctions or adverbs by verbs or verb-phrases. For example, instead of saying

> (1) *If* you have oranges in your larder you have been to the greengrocer's,

we may say

> (2) Your having oranges in your larder *implies* your having been to the greengrocer's,

which looks as if it has the same form as 'Richard loves Joan' except that 'Your having oranges in your larder' and 'Your having been to the grocer' seem to name more abstract objects than Richard and Joan, and implying seems a more abstract activity than loving. We can rid ourselves of this suggestion if we reflect that (2) is nothing more than a paraphrase of (1). Similarly,

(3) It is now six years since it was the case that I am falling out of a punt,

could be rewritten as

(4) My falling out of a punt has receded six years into the past.

This suggests that something called an event, my falling out of a punt, has gone through a performance called receding into the past, and moreover has been going through this performance even after it has ceased to exist, i.e. after it has stopped happening. But of course (4) is just a paraphrase of (3), and like (3) is not about any objects except me and that punt—there is no real reason to believe in the existence either now or six years ago of a further object called 'my falling out of a punt'.

What I am suggesting is that what looks like talk about events is really at bottom talk about things, and that what looks like talk about changes in events is really just slightly more complicated talk about changes in things. This applies *both* to the changes that we say occur in events when they are going on, like the change in speed of a movement ('movement' is a *façon de parler*; there is just the moving car, which moves more quickly than it did), *and* the changes that we say occur in events when they are not going on any longer, or not yet, e.g. my birth's receding into the past ('birth' is a *façon de parler*—there's just me being born, and then getting older).

It's not all quite as simple as this, however. This story works very well for me and my birth and my fall out of the punt, but what about Queen Anne? Does Queen Anne's death getting more past mean that *Queen Anne* has changed from having died 250 years ago to having died 251 years ago, or whatever the period is?—that *she* is still 'getting older', though in a slightly extended sense? The trouble with this, of course, is just that Queen Anne doesn't exist now any more than her death does. There are at least two different ways in which we might deal with this one. We might, in the first place, say that our statement really is about Queen Anne (despite the fact that she 'is no more'), and really is, or at least entails, a statement of the form

It was the case that *p*, and is not now the case that *p*,

namely

It was the case that it was the case only 250 years ago that Queen Anne is dying, and is not now the case that it was the case only 250 years ago that Queen Anne is dying,

but we may add that this statement does not record a 'change' in any natural sense of that word, and certainly not a change in Queen Anne. A genuine record of change, we could say, must not only be of the form above indicated but must meet certain further conditions which we might specify in various ways. And we could say that although what is here recorded *isn't* a change in the proper sense, it is *like* a change in fitting the above formula. The flow of time, we would then say, is merely metaphorical, not only because what is meant by it isn't a genuine movement, but further because what is meant by it isn't a genuine change; but the force of the metaphor can still be explained—we use the metaphor because what we call the flow of time does fit the above formula. On this view it might be that not only the recession of Queen Anne's death but my own growing older will not count as a change in the strict sense, though growing older is normally *accompanied* by genuine changes, and the phrase is commonly extended to cover these—increasing wisdom, bald patches, and so on.

But can a statement really be *about* Queen Anne after she has ceased to be? I do not wish to dogmatize about this, but an alternative solution is worth mentioning. We might paraphrase 'Queen Anne has died' as 'Once there was a person named "Anne", who reigned over England, etc., but there is not now any such person'. This solution exploits a distinction which we may describe as one between *general facts* and *individual facts*. That someone has stolen my pencil is a general fact; that John Jones has stolen my pencil, if it is a fact at all, is an individual fact. It has often been said—for example, it was said by the Stoic logicians—that there are no general facts without there being the corresponding individual facts. It cannot, for example, be the case that 'someone' has stolen my pencil, unless it is the case that some specific individual—if not John Jones, then somebody else—has stolen it. And in cases of this sort the principle is very plausible, indeed it is obviously true. I have read that some of the schoolmen described the subject of sentences like 'someone has stolen my pencil' as an *individuum vagum*, but of course this is a makeshift—forcing things into a pattern again. There are no 'vague individuals', and if a pencil has been stolen at all it has been stolen not by a vague individual but by some quite definite one, or else by a number of such. There are vague statements, however, and vague thoughts, and the existence of such statements and thoughts is as much a fact about the real world as any other; and when we describe the making of such statements and the entertaining of such thoughts, we do encounter at least partly general facts to which no wholly individual facts correspond. If I allege or believe that someone has stolen my pencil, there may be *no* specific individual with respect to whom I allege or believe that *he* stole my pencil. There is *alleged or believed to be* an individual who stole it, but there is *no individual who is alleged or believed* to have stolen it (not even a vague one). So while it is a fact that I allege or believe that someone stole it, there is no fact of the form 'I allege (or believe) that *X* stole it'. The one fact that there is is no doubt an individual fact in so far as it concerns me, but is irreducibly general as far as the thief is concerned. (There may indeed be *no* thief—I am perhaps mistaken about the whole thing—but this is another question; our present point is that there may be no one who is even said or thought to be a thief, though it is said or thought *that there is* a thief.)

Returning now to Queen Anne, what I am suggesting is that the sort of thing that we unquestionably do have with 'It is said that' and 'It is thought that', we also have with 'It will be the case that' and 'It was the case that'. It *was the case that someone* was called 'Anne', reigned over England, etc., even though *there is not now anyone* of whom it was the case that *she* was called 'Anne', reigned over England, etc. What we must be careful about here is simply getting our prefixes in the right order. Just as

(1) I think that (for some specific X (X stole my pencil))

does not imply

(2) For some specific X (I think that (X stole my pencil)),

so

(3) It was the case that (for some specific X (X is called 'Anne', reigns over England, etc.))

does not imply

(4) For some specific X (it was the case that (X is called 'Anne', reigns over England, etc.)).

On this view, the fact that Queen Anne has been dead for some years is not, in the strict sense of 'about', a fact about Queen Anne; it is not a fact about anyone or anything—it is a *general* fact. Or if it is about anything, what it is about is not Queen Anne—it is about the earth, maybe, which has rolled around the sun so many times since there was a person who was called 'Anne', reigned over England, etc. (It would then be a *partly* general fact—individual in so far as it concerns the earth, but irreducibly general as far as the dead queen is concerned. But if there are—as there undoubtedly are—irreducibly partly general facts, could there not be irreducibly wholly general ones?) Note, too, that the fact that this fact is not about Queen Anne cannot itself be a fact about Queen Anne—its statement needs rephrasing in some such way as 'There is no person who was called "Anne", etc., and about whom it is a fact that, etc.'

On this view, the recession of Queen Anne's death into the further past is quite decidedly not a change in Queen Anne, not because we are using 'change' in so tight a sense that it is not a change at all, but because Queen Anne doesn't herself enter into this recession, or indeed, now, into any fact whatever. But the recession *is* still a change or quasi-change in the sense that it fits the formula 'It was the case that p, but is not now the case that p'—this formula continues to express what is common to the flow of a literal river on the one hand (where it was the case that such and such drops were at a certain place, and this is the case no longer) and the flow of time on the other.

Chapter 36
Selection from *Asymmetries in Time*
Paul Horwich

Direction

1. The 'moving now' conception of time

THE quintessential property of time, it may seem, is the difference between the past and the future. And here I don't just mean that the past and the future are separate regions, or that the past and future directions along the continuum of instants are opposite to one another, but rather that these two directions are somehow fundamentally unlike. This idea is fostered by the desire to explain pervasive temporally asymmetric phenomena, such as causation, knowledge, decay, and the phenomenological feeling of 'moving into the future'. And it is reflected in the use of such phrases as 'time's arrow' and in our inclination to say that time 'goes' in one direction and not the other. Despite the fact that these expressions have an air of metaphor about them, they clearly imply *anisotropy*—that is, a significant lack of symmetry between the two directions of the temporal continuum. We tend to believe, in short, that time *itself* is temporally asymmetric.

This view of time contrasts with our attitude towards space. We can pick any straight line and define two opposite directions along it. Although the directions are numerically distinct from one another, we would regard them as essentially similar. We wouldn't expect the result of an experiment to depend on the direction in which our apparatus is pointing. Thus we suppose that space is isotropic. Not that this supposition is taken to be *necessarily* true. Aristotelian space, for example, is anisotropic in that directions toward and away from the center of the universe are ascribed quite different causal properties: fire naturally goes one way, and earth another. Similarly it should not be surprising if the question of time's anisotropy proves to be an empirical, contingent matter.

Often, however, those who proclaim the anisotropy of time are not motivated by scientific considerations but are gripped by a certain metaphysical picture. They have in mind that time is more than just a fixed sequence of events ordered by such relations as *later than* and *simultaneous with*, but that it also contains a peculiar property—being *now*—which moves gradually along the array in the direction from past to future. This idea is sometimes combined with a further metaphysical doctrine: namely, that there

Paul Horwich, selection from *Asymmetries in Time* (MIT Press, 1990).

is an ontological distinction between the past and the future—a distinction that can be represented in a tree model of reality, in which the past consists of a fixed, definite course of events and the future contains nothing but a manifold of branching possibilities. These alleged aspects of time—which I shall describe in more detail as we proceed—are thought to especially distinguish it from space, which possesses no such features. Recent advocates of this sort of view include Broad (1938), Gale (1969), Geach (1972), and Schliesinger (1980). On the other hand, there are many philosophers—for example, Russell (1903), Williams (1951), Smart (1955), and Grünbaum (1963)—who reject the 'moving *now*' conception and think that the past and future have exactly the same ontological status. They maintain that the word 'now' is an indexical expression (on a par with 'here' and 'I') whose special function is to designate whatever time happens to be the time at which the word-token is uttered. On this account, the thought that an event *E* is first in the future, will become present, and then fade into the past does not presuppose a 'moving *now*', but it implies merely that *E* is later than the time at which that thought is entertained, simultaneous with some subsequent time, and earlier than times after that.

Our job in this chapter will be to try to settle these issues—that is, to decide whether there really is any objective feature of the world that corresponds to the idea of a 'moving *now*' and to assess the merits of the tree model. To this end I shall begin by describing and defending McTaggart's notorious proof that there is no such thing as the 'moving *now*'. But I won't endorse his entire line of thought. McTaggart argues that the 'moving property' theory of *now* is self-contradictory, but he thinks that this conception is nevertheless essential to time. He concludes therefore that time does not exist and that, though 'now' indeed functions as an indexical, it refers not to times but rather to other entities that are somewhat like instants of time but only pale substitutes for them. I shall support McTaggart's rejection of the 'moving *now*' but not his further claim that genuine time could not exist without it. We shall see that the best defense against McTaggart's attack on the 'moving *now*' involves a commitment to the tree model of reality. Therefore, in exposing and undermining the antifatalistic and the verificationist motivations for that ontological picture, I hope to reinforce McTaggart's criticism of the 'moving *now*'.

After reaching these conclusions, I shall try to explain why we are nevertheless so captivated by the 'moving *now*' conception. And in the next chapter we shall see that the metaphysical asymmetries suggested by the 'moving *now*' and the tree model are not needed for time to be anisotropic. Even if those ideas are wholly incorrect, there remains the possibility that time is intrinsically asymmetric in virtue of some purely physical, empirical phenomenon.

To begin with, it is worth a moment's digression to note that although McTaggart follows Leibniz (the Leibniz/Clarke correspondance; see Alexander 1956) in trying to prove *a priori* that time does not exist, their two arguments are totally unrelated. This is because Leibniz and McTaggart disagree radically about the sort of thing time would have to be, in order to be real. For Leibniz, real time would be a substance—a Newtonian continuum of thinglike instants at which events are

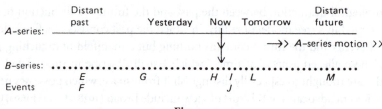

Figure 1

located, ordered by the relation *later than*. But according to McTaggart, something quite different would have to be involved for time to exist: namely, a property, *being now*, which glides along the continuum of instants in the future direction. Moreover there is no need, in his view, for substantial instants. It would suffice if there were merely states of the world ordered by the relation, *later than*, just so long as the property, *now*, moves through these states, singling out progressively later and later ones, as shown in Fig. 1.

In McTaggart's terminology temporal locations may be specified in terms of two alternative systems of coordinates: the *A*-series, which locates an event relative to *now* (as being in the distant past, the recent past, the present, tomorrow, etc.), and the *B*-series, which locates an event relative to other events (as earlier than *F*, or simultaneous with *G*, etc.). His view is that time requires that there be a *B*-series, which in turn requires an *A*-series; but that the *A*-series is self-contradictory. Thus Leibniz and McTaggart are arguing against the instantiation of different conceptions of time. Leibniz tries to show that a continuum of instants cannot exist because it would violate the principles of Sufficient Reason and Identity of Indiscernibles. McTaggart contends that the 'moving *now*' model of time is indispensible yet incoherent.

2. McTaggart's argument for the unreality of time

The outline of McTaggart's proof is as follows:

1. Events are located in a *B*-series (ordered with respect to *later than*), only if time exists.
2. Time exists, only if there is genuine change.
3. There is genuine change in the world, only if events are located in a real *A*-series.

THEREFORE:

i. Events are ordered with respect to *later than*, only if they are located in a real *A*-series.

4. If events are located in a real *A*-series, then each event acquires the absolute properties *past*, *now*, and *future*.
5. There is a contradiction in supposing that any event has any two of these absolute properties.

THEREFORE:

ii. A real *A*-series cannot exist.

THEREFORE:

(M) Events are not ordered with respect to *later than.*

Evidently this is a perfectly valid argument: there is nothing wrong with the deductive reasoning by which the preliminary conclusions, i and ii, are derived from their respective premises, and by which McTaggart's final conclusion, (M), is then drawn. It remains, however, to justify these premises. Let us consider what may be said on their behalf.

1. *Events are located in a B-series, only if time exists.* In order to see that McTaggart's first premise is correct, one must remember that it is not time in the Newtonian sense—an array of thinglike instants—whose reality is in question. Rather, the consequent of (1)—time exists—is supposed to be construed in a very broad way, as something like 'the world exhibits temporality'. And in that case, premise 1 becomes a trivial truth.

2. *Time exists, only if there is genuine change.* It might seem as though there could be time without change. For consider the scenarios schematized in Fig. 2. Cases like these are good candidates for time without change, and many philosophers who believe there could be time without change (e.g., Shoemaker 1969) have thought that it would suffice to show that worlds like those can occur. Such possibilities, however, are not what McTaggart is intent to deny. His view is that even in those cases there is still, contrary to first appearances, change of a certain kind taking place: namely, states *A* and *B* are receding further and further into the past, and *D* is approaching the present. The *now* is in motion.

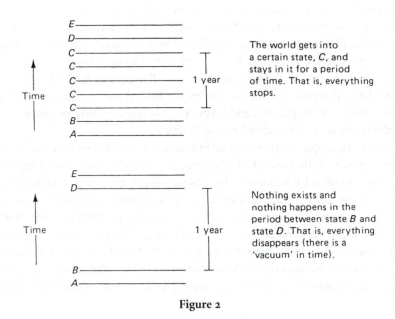

Figure 2

According to McTaggart, this sort of change is not only necessarily present if time passes, but also it is the only sort of *genuine* change that there could be. Consider, for example, a hot poker, which gradually cools in the period from t_1 to t_2. McTaggart denies that its being hot at t_1 and cold at t_2 constitutes a genuine change. For, he says, it was and will be true throughout the history of the universe that this poker is hot at t_1 and cold at t_2. Those facts are eternal; they always were, and always will obtain. That kind of variation with respect to time no more qualifies as genuine change than a variation of the temperature along the poker's length. What is required for genuine change, on the other hand, is that the sum total of facts at one time be not the same as the sum total of facts at another time.

Here, by the way, is the place at which I would quarrel with McTaggart's proof, although the rationale for digging in at exactly this point will become clear only in retrospect. When we see what he has in mind by 'genuine change', this will undermine whatever initial inclination we may have had to agree that the reality of time requires such a thing. In other words, McTaggart's demonstration, in the second part of his argument, that 'genuine change' is self-contradictory should not persuade us that time is unreal but, rather, should force us to acknowledge that time does not require 'genuine change' after all.

3. *There is genuine change in the world, only if events are located in a real* A-*series.* A variation in the facts would not occur if time consisted in the B-series alone. For the B-series is a fixed ordering of events with respect to one another (and with respect to instants of time, if there are such entities). Therefore the B-series provides only for temporal facts like 'the poker is hot at t_1', which, if it obtains at all, obtains forever. Genuine change can come about only in virtue of the relative motion of the A- and the B-series, in which the *now* moves gradually in the direction from earlier to later. This generates genuine changes of the follwoing kind: E is in the distant future, E is in the near future, E is now, E is in the past, and so on.

Note that there are certain metaphysically innocuous construals of the terms 'past', 'now', and 'future' that must be rejected by McTaggart, since they would not imply a real A-series. Consider, for example, the use of 'now' in sentences such as 'E is now (present) at t'. This usually means 'E occurs at t', which is a B-series fact. Similarly 'E is past at t' means 'E is earlier than t', and 'E is future at t' means 'E is later than t'. Past, present, and future have become *relative* properties, whose exemplification is accommodated by the B-series.

Alternatively, suppose that 'now' is an indexical expression, like 'here' and 'I', whose referent depends on the context of utterance. In particular, 'now' would rigidly pick out the time, whatever it happens to be, at which the word is used. And suppose that at t_1 I truthfully say 'E is now', and at t_2 I say 'E is not now'. Each of these utterances expresses facts, and each of the facts obtains throughout all time. One might be tempted to dispute this claim. One might doubt that 'E is now', said at t_1, expresses a fact that obtains at t_2, since that sentence uttered at t_2 would be false. But this would be a non sequitur because the sentence does not say the same thing at the two different times. The word 'now', used at t_1, simply provides a way of referring to the time

t_1. And the fact expressed by the first remark—though perhaps not the same as the fact expressed by 'E is at t_1'—is just as permanent. Consequently McTaggart holds that for there to be genuine change and a real A-series, 'past', 'present', and 'future' can be neither relational predicates nor indexicals.

So far McTaggart has tried to show that time requires the existence of a genuinely moving *now*. And, as I have already said, this preliminary conclusion may be resisted. The remainder of his argument is a demonstration that the 'moving *now*' conception is self-contradictory. This is part of his reasoning that I believe is correct and important.

4. *If events are located in a real A-series, then each event acquires the absolute properties past, now, and future.* A real A-series entails that for every event such as E, there is a fact, included in the totality of facts that constitutes the universe, consisting of E's having the quality of *presentness*, that is,

E is   (or, E is now)

but also the universe must contain the facts

E will be   (or, E is future)

and

E was   (or, E is past)

Given what is meant by 'a real A-series,' such facts are not relations between events and times. They are not, in other words, the exemplification of merely *relative* properties, which can both apply and fail to apply to the same event relative to different frames of reference. Rather, such facts consist in the exemplification by events of absolute properties.

5. *There is a contradiction in supposing that any event possesses any two of these absolute properties.* Past, present, and future (which are equivalent to 'earlier than now', 'now', and 'later than now') are incompatible attributes. Therefore the supposition that one event has them all involves a contradiction. That is to say, it is impossible that the history of the universe contain the three facts: E is past, E is now, E is future.

One will be tempted to object, as follows. There is a contradiction only if the A-series qualities are attributed *simultaneously* to E; but such simultaneous attribution is not required by the existence of the A-series; rather, its existence entails only that each of the A-series qualities apply to E at some time or other. That is to say, McTaggart's premise 4 will be satisfied even if the A-series determinations are acquired *successively*, and in that case no contradiction arises. In other words, the requirement described in premise 4 may be met by the existence of the facts:

E is future at t_1
E is present at t_2
E is past at t_3

which are quite compatible. There is no need to take premise 4 to imply that all the A-series determinations would have to apply at the same time.

However, one must beware of resolving the contradiction in ways that involve eliminating any real A-series. And this is exactly what has just happened. For the meanings of 'future', 'present', and 'past' in the preceding sentences are 'later than', 'simultaneous with', and 'earlier than'. The facts described are generated by the B-series. Genuine change has been lost in the reformulation. To preserve genuine change—to have a real A-series—it is not enough that there be a variation in *relative* presentness from one time to another (like the variation in the velocity of an object relative to different reference frames). Rather, there must be variation of facts. Thus it is necessary to construe premise 4 in such a way that the transitions from '*E* will be' to '*E* is' to '*E* was' are transitions between mutually exclusive, absolute states.

At this point McTaggart's opponent might well complain that revealing such a variation of facts was precisely the intention behind his reformulation of premise 4. The idea, he says, was *not* to transform *past, present,* and *future* into mere relations (which admittedly only succeeds in eliminating the A-series) but rather to suggest that the facts '*E* is past', and so on, might themselves obtain only relative to a temporal perspective. In other words, the premise 4 should have been formulated more perspicuously with the following sentences:

The fact that *E is future* obtains at t_1
The fact that *E is present* obtains at t_2
The fact that *E is past* obtains at t_3

Thus, there *is*, after all, a variation, from one time to another, as to which facts obtain.

In response to this suggestion, however, we are justified in resisting the crucial assumption that the italicized internal sentences express facts. For a strong case can be made that this latest formulation of premise 4 trades on an idiosyncratic and unmotivated conception of *fact*. After all, we do not regard

X is to the left of *Y*

and

X is not to the left of *Y*

as explicit descriptions of facts. Rather, we suppose that whenever such claims are true, they are partial accounts of facts whose explicit descriptions take the form

X is to the left of *Y* relative to *Z*

and

X is not to the left of *Y* relative to *W*

Similarly one does not say that the facts, fully articulated, include

It is raining

and

It is not raining

But rather, for example,

It is raining in Manchester

and

It is not raining in Florida

The general point is that we reserve the term 'fact' for those aspects of reality whose explicit descriptions are sentences that are true *simpliciter*—and not merely true relative to some context or point of view, and false relative to others. Consequently, if we are going to say that 'E is past' is sometimes true and sometimes false, then unless some good reason is given to depart from our usual conception of fact, we should not countenance this sentence as an explicit characterization of a fact. The real facts, as we said initially, are described by sentences of the form 'E is past at t', in which pastness has been transformed into a relation.

These remarks do not absolutely preclude the idea that facts may be relative: that is, dependent on a frame of reference. The point is, rather, that such a perspectival view of reality would require a radical change in our conception of fact, and that any such revision would call for some independent motivation. So far, in our discussion of this problem, no reason to abandon the usual notion of fact has been offered. And this is why the response to McTaggart that we are now considering is inadequate as it stands. However, that is not to say that no such argument for perspectivalism *could* be given. Indeed, a strategy to that end, based on verificationist considerations, is suggested by Dummett (1960). I shall take it up in the next section, in connection with Aristotle's tree model of reality.

I have been arguing that McTaggart's contradiction is not avoided by the supposition that the futurity, presentness, and pastness of E obtain relative to three times, t_1, t_2, and t_3. Notice that it is equally futile to try to escape his conclusion by rendering the facts as follows:

E is future, in the past
E is now, in the present
E is past, in the future

In the first place, this strategy is subject to the same criticism as before: the initial occurrences of 'future', 'present', and 'past' have been transformed into relative properties. So these sentences can be reformulated as

E is later than past times
E is simultaneous with the present time
E is earlier than future times

which do not entail the existence of the facts required by a real *A*-series. And in the second place, such second-order temporal attributions are just as problematic, from McTaggart's point of view, as the first-order ones. For they are compatible with one another only if we assume that the *past, present,* and *future* are disjoint regions of time (or of events). And that assumption is contrary to his requirement: that every event and time has the qualities of *past, present,* and *future.* This being so, we can derive from the first statement (supposing that 'past' and 'present' are coextensive)

E is future, in the present

which conflicts with the second statement. Therefore the contradiction is not avoided by introducing second-order temporal attributions. This is because, from the fact that each of the first-order attributions must hold, it follows that each of the second-order attributions must hold. And they conflict just as blatantly as the first-order attributions.

The most common criticism of McTaggart's argument (e.g., Broad 1938; Prior 1967) is exactly the point just dealt with: to claim that consistency may be achieved by a reformulation in terms of higher-order temporal attributions. It is not appreciated that McTaggart himself considers and refutes this strategy. To repeat, he denies that his requirement that the world contain the facts:

E is past
E is present
E is future

is misstated when construed literally, in which case the facts are mutually inconsistent with one another; and therefore he denies that the required facts are accurately represented by, for example,

E is past, in the future
E is now, in the present
E is future, in the past

For the operative occurrences of 'past', 'present', and 'future' have been turned into relations. Therefore McTaggart denies that the initial contradiction is treated by introducing second-order attributions. Nevertheless he is quite happy to conduct the argument at the second level. For, from his first-order requirement, it follows that *every* second-order attribution must hold—and this is also a contradiction.

Thus, McTaggart shows that a certain very tempting, 'moving *now*' conception of time is not actualized. But he does not succeed in proving that time is unreal, because the first part of his argument is not persuasive (Mellor 1981). In other words, we need not agree with him (premise 2) that it is essential to the reality of time that there be 'genuine change', in his sense. This claim is implausible and never really substantiated. If we are persuaded, as I think we should be, by the second part of his argument, we will conclude that there can be no 'real *A*-series' or 'genuine change'. Rather, change is always variation in one thing with respect to another, the totality of absolute facts about those functional relations remaining forever constant.

3. The tree model of reality

Affiliated with the 'moving *now*' conception of time is another unorthodox metaphysical theory—roughly speaking, that only past and present events exist, and future ones do not. Reality, in this view, is thought to resemble an unlimited tree: from any point, there is a single definite path downward (history is fixed) but above each point we encounter a proliferation of many possible branches (the future is open). Thus, statements about the past and present are, right now, determinately true or false, unlike current claims about the future, which do not attain a truth value until the predicted events either occur or fail to occur. Only the advance of the *now* settles which path through the tree is taken and which predictions are true.

In Fig. 3, *N* represents the present state of the world. The chain of stars represents the fixed past. (Note that there is just one way down the tree from N.) And the branches growing up from *N* represent the many things that might happen later; thus the future is open. The only statements about the future that hold at *N* are those that are obtain in all of the branches that stem from N. If something—for example, a sea battle tomorrow—occurs in some branches but not in others, then from the perspective of *N*, there is no fact of the matter as to whether there will be a sea battle tomorrow.

Aristotle, with whom this sort of view is often credited, was not the first philosopher to deal with time; but he was the first to offer more than provocative aphorisms and to try, in a scientific spirit, to clarify and demystify our conception of temporality. And he reached the conclusion that time is *doubly* asymmetrical. In the *Physics* (Book IV) he endorses the 'moving *now*' and in *De Interpretatione*—according to one

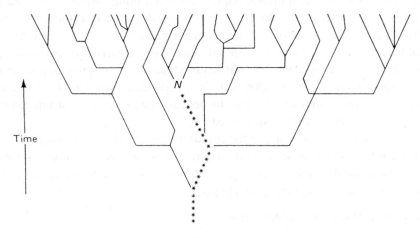

Figure 3

natural construal of it—he advocates a truth-value asymmetry as the only way to avoid fatalism.

I am going to argue, on the contrary, that there is no ontological asymmetry between past and future and that the threat of fatalism can be averted without radical measures of this sort. To begin with, however, I want to explore the relationship between the tree model of reality and the 'moving *now*' conception of time. We shall see that although advocates of the 'moving *now*' can base a defense against McTaggart on the tree model, there is, on the other hand, no incentive for advocates of the tree model to endorse the 'moving *now*' conception of time.

On the latter point, notice that the tree model does not preclude an indexical construal of 'now'; and so there is no compulsion to hold that reality contains not merely the tree but also a quality—*now*—that moves up the tree, selecting which branches are to be actual. To see more vividly why this addition to the tree model is not needed, suppose that the past, as well as the future, were not determined by the present. Suppose, in other words, that more than one possible course of history were compatible with the current state of the world. Then a network of possibilities would branch out into the past. And in that case both the past and the future would be open. One would think that if the openness of the future called for a future-directed *now*, then the openness of the past would similarly entail a past-directed *now*. Yet there surely would be no philosopher who would go quite so far as to postulate a *pair* of oppositely moving *nows*. (When would they meet?) This suggests that a fondness for the tree model does not produce a taste for the 'moving *now*' conception of time.

On the other hand, one can quite understand why advocates of a 'moving *now*' would be inclined to sympathize with the tree model. McTaggart's argument that the 'moving *now*' does not exist depends on exposing a contradiction between facts '*E* is past', '*E* is present', and '*E* is future', all of which must, given a genuinely moving *now*, belong to the totality of absolute facts in the world. However, as Dummett (1960) has observed, this argument requires the assumption (which, as we shall see in a minute, is questionable) that there *is* such a totality of facts. If there is no such thing—if the facts change from one temporal perspective to another—then the only trouble-some contradictions are contradictions from a particular temporal perspective. But a 'moving *now*' does not require that *E* be past, present, and future from a single temporal perspective. So if there is no time-neutral body of absolute facts, there is no contradiction. Thus, by denying the assumption of this totality, McTaggart's objection can be sidestepped.

But only at substantial cost. For the crucial move—denying the assumption that there is a totality of facts—seems quite bizarre, unless it is independently motivated. As we saw in our discussion of McTaggart's proof, it looks simply ad hoc, and contrary to our usual conception of fact, to say

The fact that *E is future* obtains at *t₁*

rather than

E is the future at t_1

or, in other words

E is later than t_1

Thus, there might seem to be no reason to countenance facts that obtain at some times and not at others. The attraction of the tree model of reality is precisely its ability to supply this rationale. For the tree model purports to show, independently of anything to do with *now*, that there is no complete, time-neutral body of facts. At any point the facts consist of a certain course of history, plus the present state and whatever is in every future branch. But this body of facts changes. And there is no summing up, from a temporally neutral point of view, to obtain an overall picture of reality. Thus defenders of the 'moving *now*' will be happy to embrace the tree model. For, in the context of that model, their best reply to McTaggart is not ad hoc: genuine change can be achieved without contradiction. By the same token a thorough criticism of the 'moving *now*' conception must eventually deal with the tree model of reality.

Bibliography

Alexander, H. G. (ed.). 1956. *The Leibniz-Clarke Correspondence*. Manchester: Manchester University Press.

Broad, C. D. 1938. *Examination of McTaggart's Philosophy*. Cambridge: Cambridge University Press.

Dummett, M. 1960. 'A Defense of McTaggart's Proof of the Unreality of Time', *Philosophical Review* 69: 497–504.

Gale, R. (ed.). 1967. *The Philosophy of Time*. New York: Anchor Books.

Gale, R. 1969. *The Language of Time*. London: Routledge and Kegan Paul.

Geach, P. T. 1972. *Logic Matters*. Berkeley: University of California Press.

Grünbaum, A. 1963. *Philosophical Problems of Space and Time*. New York: Knopf: 2nd edn., Dordrecht: Reidel, 1973.

Mellor, D. H. 1981. *Real Time*. Cambridge: Cambridge University Press.

Prior, A. 1967. *Past, Present and Future*. Oxford: Oxford University Press.

Russell, B. 1903. *The Principles of Mathematics*. New York: Norton.

Schliesinger, G. 1980. *Aspects of Time*. Indianapolis: Hackett Publishing Company.

Shoemaker, S. S. 1969. 'Time without Change', *Journal of Philosophy* 66: 363–381.

Smart, J. J. C. 1955. 'Spatializing Time' reprinted in *The Philosophy of Time*. Edited by R. Gale. New York: Anchor Books, 1967.

Williams, D. C. 1951. 'The Myth of Passage', *Journal of Philosophy* 48: 457–472.

Chapter 37

Selection from *The Leibniz–Clarke Correspondence*

Mr Leibnitz's fourth paper[1] being an answer to Dr Clarke's third reply

1. In things absolutely indifferent, there is no [foundation for][2] choice; and consequently no election, nor will; since choice must be founded on some reason, or principle.

2. A mere will without any motive, is a fiction, not only contrary to God's perfection, but also chimerical and contradictory; inconsistent with the definition of the will, and sufficiently confuted in my Theodicy.

3. 'Tis a thing indifferent, to place three bodies, equal and perfectly alike, in any order whatsoever; and consequently they will never be placed in any order, by him who does nothing without wisdom. But then he being the author of things, no such things will be produced by him at all; and consequently there are no such things in nature.

4. There is no such thing as two individuals indiscernible from each other. An ingenious gentleman of my acquaintance, discoursing with me, in the presence of Her Electoral Highness the Princess Sophia,[3] in the garden of Herrenhausen; thought he could find two leaves perfectly alike. The Princess defied him to do it, and he ran all over the garden a long time to look for some; but it was to no purpose. Two drops of water, or milk, viewed with a microscope, will appear distinguishable from each other. This is an argument against atoms; which are confuted, as well as a vacuum, by the principles of true metaphysics.

5. Those great principles of a *sufficient reason*, and of the *identity of indiscernibles*, change the state of metaphysics. That science becomes real and demonstrative by means of these principles; whereas before, it did generally consist in empty words.

6. To suppose two things indiscernible, is to suppose the same thing under two names. And therefore to suppose that the universe could have had at first another position of time and place, than that which it actually had; and yet that all the parts

---

1. Despatched with letter dated 2 June 1716 (p. 195).
2. Clarke's addition.
3. Sophia, Electress of Hanover, mother of George I of England. Herrenhausen was the residence of the Electors of Hanover.

Selection from *The Leibniz–Clarke Correspondence*, edited by H. G. Alexander (Manchester University Press, 1956). References in the text and in the footnotes to other papers and replies, and to the introduction and appendix, are to Leibniz (1956).

of the universe should have had the same situation among themselves, as that which they actually had; such a supposition, I say, is an impossible fiction.

7. The same reason, which shows that extramundane space is imaginary, proves that all empty space is an imaginary thing; for they differ only as greater and less.

8. If space is a property or attribute, it must be the property of some substance. But what substance will that bounded empty space be an affection or property of, which the persons I am arguing with, suppose to be between two bodies?

9. If infinite space is immensity, finite space will be the opposite to immensity, that is, 'twill be mensurability, or limited extension. Now extension must be the affection of some thing extended. But if that space be empty, it will be an attribute without a subject, an extension without any thing extended. Wherefore by making space a property, the author falls in with my opinion, which makes it an order of things, and not any thing absolute.

10. If space is an absolute reality; far from being a property or an accident opposed to substance, it will have a greater reality than substances themselves.[4] God cannot destroy it, nor even change it in any respect. It will be not only immense in the whole, but also immutable and eternal in every part. There will be an infinite number of eternal things besides God.

11. To say that infinite space has no parts, is to say that it does not consist of finite spaces; and that infinite space might subsist, though all finite spaces should be reduced to nothing. It would be, as if one should say, in the Cartesian supposition of a material extended unlimited world, that such a world might subsist, though all the bodies of which it consists, should be reduced to nothing.

12. The author ascribes parts to space, p. 19. of the 3rd edition of his *Defense of the Argument against Mr. Dodwell*;[5] and makes them inseparable one from another. But, p. 30 of his *Second Defense*,[5a] he says they are parts *improperly so called*: which may be understood in a good sense.

13. To say that God can cause the whole universe to move forward in a right line, or in any other line, without making otherwise any alteration in it; is another chimerical supposition. For, two states indiscernible from each other, are the same state; and consequently, 'tis a change without any change. Besides, there is neither rhyme nor reason in it. But God does nothing without reason; and 'tis impossible there should be any here. Besides, it would be *agendo nihil agere*, as I have just now said, because of the indiscernibility.

14. These are *idola tribus*, mere chimeras, and superficial imaginations. All this is only grounded upon the supposition, that imaginary space is real.

15. It is a like fiction, (that is) an impossible one, to suppose that God might have created the world some millions of years sooner. They who run into such kind of fictions, can give no answer to one that should argue for the eternity of the world. For since God does nothing without reason, and no reason can be given why he did not create the

---

4. 'il sera plus subsistant que les substance'.
5. Clarke, *Works*, vol. III, p. 763 and p. 794.
5a. *Clarke, Works*, vol. III, p. 763 and p. 794.

488 THE LEIBNIZ–CLARKE CORRESPONDENCE

world sooner; it will follow, either that he has created nothing at all, or that he created the world before any assignable time, that is, that the world is eternal. But when once it has been shown, that the beginning, whenever it was, is always the same thing; the question, why it was not otherwise ordered, becomes needless and insignificant.

16. If space and time were any thing absolute, that is, if they were any thing else, besides certain orders of things; then indeed my assertion would be a contradiction. But since it is not so, the hypothesis [that space and time are any thing absolute][6] is contradictory, that is, 'tis an impossible fiction.

17. And the case is the same as in geometry; where by the very supposition that a figure is greater than it really is, we sometimes prove that it is not greater. This indeed is a contradiction; but it lies in the hypothesis, which appears to be false for that very reason.

18. Space being uniform, there can be neither any external nor internal reason, by which to distinguish its parts, and to make any choice among them. For, any external reason to discern between them, can only be grounded upon some internal one. Otherwise we should discern what is indiscernible, or choose without discerning. A will without reason, would be the chance of the Epicureans.[7] A God, who should act by such a will, would be a God only in name. The cause of these errors proceeds from want of care to avoid what derogates from the divine perfections.

19. When two things which cannot both be together, are equally good; and neither in themselves, nor by their combination with other things, has the one any advantage over the other; God will produce neither of them.

20. God is never determined by external things, but always by what is in himself; that is, by his knowledge of things, before any thing exists without himself.

21. There is no possible reason, that can limit the quantity of matter; and therefore such limitation can have no place.

22. And supposing an arbitrary limitation of the quantity of matter, something might always be added to it without derogating from the perfection of those things which do already exist; and consequently something must always be added, in order to act according to the principle of the perfection of the divine operations.

23. And therefore it cannot be said, that the present quantity of matter is the fittest for the present constitution of things. And supposing it were, it would follow that this present constitution of things would not be the fittest absolutely, if it hinders God from using more matter. It were therefore better to choose another constitution of things, capable of something more.

24. I should be glad to see a passage of any philosopher, who takes *sensorium* in any other sense than Goclenius does.

25. If Scapula says that *sensorium* is the place in which the understanding resides, he means by it the organ of internal sensation. And therefore he does not differ from Goclenius.

---

6. Clarke's addition.
7. Epicurus held that while most atoms moved in regular courses, some occasionally made entirely uncaused swerves. Such a swerve occurring in the atoms of a man's brain gives rise to what the man regards as an act of free will.

26. *Sensorium* has always signified the organ of sensation. The *glandula pinealis* would be, according to Cartesius, the sensorium, in the above-mentioned sense of Scapula.

27. There is hardly any expression less proper upon this subject, than that which makes God to have a sensorium. It seems to make God the soul of the world. And it will be a hard matter to put a justifiable sense upon this word, according to the use Sir Isaac Newton makes of it.

28. Though the question be about the sense put upon that word by Sir Isaac Newton, and not by Goclenius; yet I am not to blame for quoting the philosophical dictionary of that author, because the design of dictionaries is to show the use of words.

29. God perceives things in himself. Space is the place of things, and not the place of God's ideas: unless we look upon space as something that makes an union between God and things, in imitation of the imagined union between the soul and the body; which would still make God the soul of the world.

30. And indeed the author is much in the wrong, when he compares God's knowledge and operation, with the knowledge and operation of souls. The soul knows things, because God has put into it a principle representative of things without. But God knows things, because he produces them continually.

31. The soul does not act upon things, according to my opinion, any otherwise than because the body adapts itself to the desires of the soul, by virtue of the harmony, which God has pre-established between them.

32. But they who fancy that the soul can give a new force to the body; and that God does the same in the world, in order to mend the imperfections of his machine; make God too much like the soul, by ascribing too much to the soul, and too little to God.

33. For, none but God can give a new force to nature; and he does it only supernaturally. If there was need for him to do it in the natural course of things; he would have made a very imperfect work. At that rate, he would be with respect to the world, what the soul, in the vulgar notion, is with respect to the body.

34. Those who undertake to defend the vulgar opinion concerning the soul's influence over the body, by instancing in God's operating on things external; make God still too much like a soul of the world. To which I add, that the author's affecting to find fault with the words, *intelligentia supramundana*, seems also to incline that way.

35. The images, with which the soul is immediately affected,[8] are within itself; but they correspond to those of the body. The presence of the soul is imperfect, and can only be explained by that correspondence. But the presence of God is perfect, and manifested by his operation.

36. The author wrongly supposes against me, that the presence of the soul is connected with its influence over the body; for he knows, I reject that influence.

37. The soul's being diffused through the brain, is no less inexplicable, than its being diffused through the whole body. The difference is only in more and less.

38. They who fancy that active force lessens of itself in the world, do not well understand the principal laws of nature, and the beauty of the works of God.

---

8. 'affected' is used here not in the sense of 'caused' or 'influenced', but rather in the sense in which a quality is an affect of an object.

39. How will they be able to prove, that this defect is a consequence of the dependence of things?

40. The imperfection of our machines, which is the reason why they want to be mended, proceeds from this very thing, that they do not sufficiently depend upon the workman. And therefore the dependence of nature upon God, far from being the cause of such an imperfection, is rather the reason why there is no such imperfection in nature, because it depends so much upon an artist, who is too perfect to make a work that wants to be mended. 'Tis true that every particular machine of nature, is, in some measure, liable to be disordered; but not the whole universe, which cannot diminish in perfection.

41. The author contends, that space does not depend upon the situation of bodies. I answer: 'tis true, it does not depend upon such or such a situation of bodies; but it is that order, which renders bodies capable of being situated, and by which they have a situation among themselves when they exist together; as time is that order, with respect to their successive position. But if there were no creatures, space and time would be only in the ideas of God.

42. The author seems to acknowledge here, that his notion of a miracle is not the same with that which divines and philosophers usually have. It is therefore sufficient for my purpose, that my adversaries are obliged to have recourse to what is commonly called a miracle.

43. I am afraid the author, by altering the sense commonly put upon the word *miracle*, will fall into an inconvenient opinion. The nature of a miracle does not at all consist in usualness or unusualness; for then monsters would be miracles.

44. There are miracles of an inferior sort, which an angel can work. He can, for instance, make a man walk upon the water without sinking. But there are miracles, which none but God can work; they exceeding all natural powers. Of which kind, are creating and annihilating.

45. 'Tis also a supernatural thing, that bodies should attract one another at a distance, without any intermediate means; and that a body should move round, without receding in the tangent, though nothing hinder it from so receding. For these effects cannot be explained by the nature of things.

46. Why should it be impossible to explain the motion of animals by natural forces? Tho' indeed, the beginning of animals is no less inexplicable by natural forces, than the beginning of the world.

P.S.[9]

All those who maintain a vacuum, are more influenced by imagination than by reason. When I was a young man, I also gave into the notion of a vacuum and atoms;

---

9. This 'postscript' was actually written and despatched by Leibniz as a postscript to a private letter to Caroline, dated 12 May 1716. It was occasioned by Caroline's mention of experiments on the vacuum in her letter of 15 May 1716. See Appendix B, p. 194.

but reason brought me into the right way. It was a pleasing imagination. Men carry their inquiries no farther than those two things: they (as it were) nail down their thoughts to them: they fancy, they have found out the first elements of things, a *non plus ultra*. We would have nature to go no farther; and to be finite, as our minds are: but this is being ignorant of the greatness and majesty of the author of things. The least corpuscle is actually subdivided *in infinitum*, and contains a world of other creatures, which would be wanting in the universe, if that corpuscle was an atom, that is, a body of one entire piece without subdivision. In like manner, to admit a vacuum in nature, is ascribing to God a very imperfect work: 'tis violating the grand principle of the necessity of a sufficient reason; which many have talked of, without understanding its true meaning; as I have lately shown, in proving, by that principle, that space is only an order of things, as time also is, and not at all an absolute being. To omit many other arguments against a vacuum and atoms, I shall here mention those which I ground upon God's perfection, and upon the necessity of a sufficient reason. I lay it down as a principle, that every perfection, which God could impart to things without derogating from their other perfections, has actually been imparted to them. Now let us fancy a space wholly empty. God could have placed some matter in it, without derogating in any respect from all other things: therefore he has actually placed some matter in that space: therefore, there is no space wholly empty: therefore all is full. The same argument proves that there is no corpuscle, but what is subdivided. I shall add another argument, grounded upon the necessity of a sufficient reason. 'Tis impossible there should be any principle to determine what proportion of matter there ought to be, out of all the possible degrees from a plenum to a vacuum, or from a vacuum to a plenum.[10] Perhaps it will be said, that the one should be equal to the other: but, because matter is more perfect than a vacuum, reason requires that a geometrical proportion should be observed, and that there should be as much more matter than vacuum, as the former deserves to have the preference before the latter. But then there must be no vacuum at all; for the perfection of matter is to that of a vacuum, as something to nothing. And the case is the same with atoms: what reason can any one assign for confining nature in the progression of subdivision? These are fictions merely arbitrary, and unworthy of true philosophy. The reasons alleged for a vacuum, are mere sophisms.

Dr Clarke's fourth reply[11]

1 and 2. This notion leads to universal necessity and fate, by supposing that motives have the same relation to the will of an intelligent agent, as weights have to a balance;[12] so that of two things absolutely indifferent, an intelligent agent can no

10. 'de determiner la proportion de la matière, ou du rempli au vuide, ou du vuide au plein'.
11. Transmitted 26 June 1716 (p. 196).
12. See above, Mr. Leibnitz's Second Paper, § 1.

more choose either, than a balance can move itself when the weights on both sides are equal. But the difference lies here. A balance is no agent, but is merely passive and acted upon by the weights; so that, when the weights are equal, there is nothing to move it. But intelligent beings are agents; not passive, in being moved by the motives, as a balance is by weights; but they have active powers and do move themselves, sometimes upon the view of strong motives, sometimes upon weak ones, and sometimes where things are absolutely indifferent. In which latter case, there may be very good reason to act, though two or more ways of acting may be absolutely indifferent. This learned writer always supposes the contrary, as a principle; but gives no proof of it, either from the nature of things, or the perfections of God.

3 and 4. This argument, if it was true, would prove that God neither has created, nor can possibly create any matter at all. For the perfectly solid parts of all matter, if you take them of equal figure and dimensions (which is always possible in supposition,) are exactly alike; and therefore it would be perfectly indifferent if they were transposed in place; and consequently it was impossible (according to this learned author's argument,) for God to place them in those places wherein he did actually place them at the creation, because he might as easily have transposed their situation. 'Tis very true, that no two leaves, and perhaps no two drops of water are exactly alike; because they are bodies very much compounded. But the case is very different in the parts of simple solid matter. And even in compounds, there is no impossibility for God to make two drops of water exactly alike. And if he should make them exactly alike, yet they would never the more become one and the same drop of water, because they were alike. Nor would the place of the one, be the place of the other; though it was absolutely indifferent, which was placed in which place. The same reasoning holds likewise concerning the original determination of motion, this way or the contrary way.

5 and 6. Two things, by being exactly alike, do not cease to be two. The parts of time, are as exactly like to each other, as those of space: yet two points of time, are not the same point of time, nor are they two names of only the same point of time. Had God created the world but this moment, it would not have been created at the time it was created. And if God has made (or can make) matter finite in dimensions, the material universe must consequently be in its nature moveable; for nothing that is finite, is immoveable. To say therefore that God could not have altered the time or place of the existence of matter, is making matter to be necessarily infinite and eternal, and reducing all things to necessity and fate.

7. Extra-mundane space, (if the material world be finite in its dimensions,) is not imaginary, but real. Nor are void spaces in the world, merely imaginary. In an exhausted receiver,[13] though rays of light, and perhaps some other matter, be there in an exceeding small quantity; yet the want of resistance plainly shows, that the greatest part of that space is void of matter. For subtleness or fineness of matter,

---

13. This was occasioned by a passage in the private letter wherein Mr. Leibniz's paper came inclosed. [This was Leibniz's letter of 2 June 1716, the relevant parts of which are given in Appendix B, p. 195.]

cannot be the cause of want of resistance. Quicksilver is as subtle, and consists of as fine parts and as fluid, as water; and yet makes more than ten times the resistance: which resistance arises therefore from the quantity, and not from the grossness of the matter.

8. Space void of body, is the property of an incorporeal substance. Space is not bounded by bodies, but exists equally within and without bodies. Space is not inclosed between bodies; but bodies, existing in unbounded space, are, themselves only, terminated by their own dimensions.

9. Void space, is not an attribute without a subject; because, by void space, we never mean space void of every thing, but void of body only. In all void space, God is certainly present, and possibly many other substances which are not matter; being neither tangible, nor objects of any of our senses.

10. Space is not a substance, but a property;[14] and if it be a property of that which is necessary, it will consequently (as all other properties of that which is necessary must do,) exist more necessarily, (though it be not itself a substance,) than those substances themselves which are not necessary. Space is immense, and immutable, and eternal; and so also is duration. Yet it does not at all from hence follow, that any thing is eternal *hors de Dieu*. For space and duration are not *hors de Dieu*, but are caused by, and are immediate and necessary consequences of his existence.[15] And without them, his eternity and ubiquity (or omnipresence) would be taken away.

11 and 12. Infinites are composed of finites, in no other sense, than as finites are composed of infinitesimals. In what sense space has or has not parts, has been explained before, Reply III, § 3. Parts, in the corporeal sense of the word, are separable, compounded, ununited, independent on, and moveable from, each other: but infinite space, though it may by us be partially apprehended, that is, may in our imagination be conceived as composed of parts; yet those parts (improperly so called) being essentially indiscernible and immoveable from each other, and not partable without an express contradiction in terms, (see above, Reply II, § 4 and Reply III, § 3;) space consequently is in itself essentially one, and absolutely indivisible.

13. If the world be finite in dimensions, it is moveable by the power of God and therefore my argument drawn from that moveableness is conclusive. Two places, though exactly alike, are not the same place. Nor is the motion or rest of the universe, the same state; any more than the motion or rest of a ship, is the same state, because a man shut up in the cabin cannot perceive whether the ship sails or not, so long as it moves uniformly. The motion of the ship, though the man perceives it not, is a real different state, and has real different effects; and, upon a sudden stop, it would have other real effects; and so likewise would an indiscernible motion of the universe. To this argument, no answer has ever been given. It is largely insisted on

14. Clarke qualifies this use of the term *property* in a note contained in the preface to Des Maiseaux's editions of the Correspondence. Cf. Introduction, p. xxix.
15. [Clarke quotes here from the General Scholium in the *Principia*, the passage, 'He is eternal and infinite, . . . cannot be never and nowhere. He is omnipresent not virtually only but also substantially; for virtue cannot subsist without substance', Appendix, pp. 167–8.]

by Sir Isaac Newton in his *Mathematical Principles*, (Definit. 8.) where, from the consideration of the properties, causes, and effects of motion, he shows the difference between real motion, or a body's being carried from one part of space to another; and relative motion, which is merely a change of the order or situation of bodies with respect to each other. This argument is a mathematical one; showing, from real effects, that there may be real motion where there is none relative; and relative motion, where there is none real: and is not to be answered, by barely asserting the contrary.

14. The reality of space is not a supposition, but is proved by the foregoing arguments, to which no answer has been given. Nor is any answer given to that other argument, that space and time are quantities, which situation and order are not.

15. It was no impossibility for God to make the world sooner or later than he did: nor is it at all impossible for him to destroy it sooner or later than it shall actually be destroyed. As to the notion of the world's eternity; they who suppose matter and space to be the same, must indeed suppose the world to be not only infinite and eternal, but necessarily so; even as necessarily as space and duration, which depend not on the will, but on the existence of God. But they who believe that God created matter in what quantity, and at what particular time, and in what particular spaces he pleased, are here under no difficulty. For the wisdom of God may have very good reasons for creating this world, at that particular time he did; and may have made other kinds of things before this material world began, and may make other kinds of things after this world is destroyed.

16 and 17. That space and time are not the mere order of things, but real quantities (which order and situation are not;) has been proved above, (See Third Reply, § 4; and in this paper, § 13,) and no answer yet given to those proofs. And till an answer be given to those proofs, this learned author's assertion is (by his own confession in this place) a contradiction.

18. The uniformity of all the parts of space, is no argument against God's acting in any part, after what manner he pleases. God may have good reasons to create finite beings, and finite beings can be but in particular places. And, all places being originally alike, (even though place were nothing else but the situation of bodies;) God's placing one cube of matter behind another equal cube of matter, rather than the other behind that; is a choice no way unworthy of the perfections of God, though both these situations be perfectly equal: because there may be very good reasons why both the cubes should exist and they cannot exist but in one or other of equally reasonable situations. The Epicurean chance, is not a choice of will, but a blind necessity of fate.

19. This argument, (as I now observed, § 3,) if it proves anything, proves that God neither did nor can create any matter at all; because the situation of equal and similar parts of matter, could not but be originally indifferent: as was also the original determination of their motions, this way, or the contrary way.

20. What this tends to prove, with regard to the argument before us; I understand not.

21. That God cannot limit the quantity of matter, is an assertion of too great consequence, to be admitted without proof. If he cannot limit the duration of it neither, then the material world is both infinite and eternal necessarily and independently upon God.

22 and 23. This argument, if it were good, would prove that whatever God can do, he cannot but do; and consequently that he cannot but make every thing infinite and every thing eternal. Which is making him no governor at all, but a mere necessary agent, that is, indeed no agent at all, but mere fate and nature and necessity.

24–28. Concerning the use of the word, *sensory*; (though Sir Isaac Newton says only, *as it were the sensory*,) enough has been said in my Third Reply, § 10; and Second Reply, § 3; and First Reply, § 3.

29. Space is the place of all things, and of all ideas: just as duration is the duration of all things, and of all ideas. That this has no tendency to make God the soul of the world, see above, Reply II, § 12. There is no union between God and the world. The mind of man might with greater propriety be styled the soul of the images of things which it perceives, than God can be styled the soul of the world, to which he is present throughout, and acts upon it as he pleases, without being acted upon by it. Though this answer was given before, (Reply II, § 12.) yet the same objection is repeated again and again, without taking any notice of the answer . . .

Chapter 38

The space–time world

J. J. C. Smart

Anthropocentric cosmologies

In the Middle Ages, the Aristotelian view that man stood at the centre of the cosmos prevailed. There was a spherical earth around which the various sub-lunary and superlunary spheres rotated. This cosmology was clearly very congenial to Christian theology. Even though the theologian admitted the existence of superior created intelligences, those of the angels, he still gave to man a unique place in the cosmos. According to him, the great theme of cosmic history was the fall and redemption of man, and it was God himself who took on human form. No wonder that there was resistance against the non-anthropocentric cosmologies of Copernicus and later scientists. Modern cosmology is even less anthropocentric. According to some modern cosmological hypotheses, there may be hundreds of thousands, or even millions, of inhabited planetary systems in our galaxy alone. It is likely that some of the inhabitants of some of these systems will be incomparably superior in intelligence to human beings. It would be an unlikely coincidence if we were the top dogs: indeed, it is quite improbable when we think of the millions of years of evolution before us, provided that we avoid blowing up our planet in the meantime. (Almost certainly life on some planets of remote stars will have got going long before life on ours did.) The view of man which was canvassed in the last chapter is corrective of an anthropocentric outlook: in regarding man as a physical mechanism we regard him as part of nature. It is so common in literary and popular thought to think of man not as part of nature but somehow as set over against it that a conscious effort to think of man as part of nature is very valuable. After a bit it becomes second nature to do so, and one gets a new and highly satisfying view of the world. Flying in the dark over the empty countryside, our aeroplane eventually comes down over the lights of a great city: how unnatural all this is, we feel, after so many miles of primeval bush and mountain. And then, we may reflect, it is not unnatural at all: birds make nests, but men make street lights and neon signs.

Anthropocentricity of some temporal concepts

There is one feature of common ways of thinking which projects another sort of anthropocentric idea on to the universe at large. One can easily get the idea that the notions of past, present, and future apply objectively to the universe. In contrast,

J. J. C. Smart, 'The Space–Time World', from *Philosophy and Scientific Realism* (Routledge & Kegan Paul, 1963).

I shall argue that the concepts of past, present, and future have significance relative only to human thought and utterance and do not apply to the universe as such. They contain a hidden anthropocentricity. So also do tenses. On the other hand, the concepts of 'earlier', 'simultaneous', and 'later' are impeccably non-anthropocentric. I shall argue for a view of the world as a four-dimensional continuum of space–time entities, such that out of relation to particular human beings or other language users there is no distinction of 'past', 'present', and 'future'. Moreover, the notion of the flow of time is the result of similar confusions. Our notion of time as flowing, the transitory aspect of time as Broad has called it, is an illusion which prevents us seeing the world as it really is.

The space–time world

A man or stone or star is commonly regarded as a three-dimensional object which nevertheless *endures* through time. This enduring through time clearly brings a fourth dimension into the matter, but this fact is obscured by our ordinary language. In our ordinary way of talking we stress the three-dimensionality of bodies, and by our notion of the permanent in change we conceal the fact that bodies extend through time. For philosophical reasons, therefore, it is of interest to discuss a way of talking which does not make use of the notion of the permanent in change. This explicitly four-dimensional way of talking has had important applications in physics. It needs, however, a bit of philosophical tidying up.

   In what follows I shall want to make use of tenseless verbs. I shall indicate tenselessness by putting these verbs in italics. Tenseless verbs are familiar in logic and mathematics. When we say that two plus two *equals* four we do not mean that two plus two equals four at the present moment. Nor do we mean that two plus two always equalled four in the past, equals four now, and will always equal four in the future. This would imply that two plus two will equal four at midnight tonight, which has no clear sense. It could perhaps be taken to mean that if someone says 'two plus two *equals* four' at midnight tonight, then he will speak truly, but then 'at midnight tonight' does not occur in the proposition that is mentioned.

   It is perfectly possible to think of things and processes as four-dimensional space–time entities. The instantaneous state of such a four-dimensional space–time solid will be a three-dimensional 'time slice'[1] of the four-dimensional solid. Then instead of talking of things or processes changing or not changing we can now talk of one time slice of a four-dimensional entity *being* different or not different from some other time slice. (Note the tenseless participle of the verb 'to be' in the last sentence.)

   When we think four-dimensionally, therefore, we replace the notions of change and staying the same by the notions of the similarity or dissimilarity of time slices of four-dimensional solids. It may be objected that there is one sort of change which

---

1. This vivid expression is used by J. H. Woodger. See his 'Technique of Theory Construction', *International Encyclopedia of Unified Science*, Vol. 2, No. 5 (University of Chicago Press, 1939).

cannot be thus accommodated. For of any event, or of any time slice, it may be said on a certain occasion that it is in the future, and that later on it becomes present, and that later still it becomes past. It seems essential to say such things as that, for example, event E was future, is present, and will become past. The notion of change seems to be reintroduced into our four-dimensional scheme of things.

The objector is going too fast. If we are going to eliminate the notion of change we had better, to preserve consistency, eliminate also words such as 'past', 'present', 'future', and 'now'. Let us replace the words 'is past' by the words '*is* earlier than this utterance'. (Note the transition to the tenseless 'is'.) Similarly, let us replace 'is present' and 'now' by '*is* simultaneous with this utterance', and 'is future' by '*is* later than this utterance'. By 'utterance' here, I mean, in the case of spoken utterances the actual sounds that are uttered. In the case of written sentences (which extend through time) I mean the earliest time slices of such sentences (ink marks on paper). Notice that I am here talking of self-referential *utterances*, not self-referential *sentences*. (The same sentence can be uttered on many occasions.) We can, following Reichenbach, call the utterance itself a 'token', and this sort of reflexivity 'token-reflexivity'. Tenses can also be eliminated, since such a sentence as 'he will run' can be replaced by 'he *runs* at some future time' (with tenseless 'runs') and hence by 'he *runs* later than this utterance'. Similarly, 'he runs' means 'he *runs* (tenseless) simultaneous with this utterance', and 'he ran' means 'he *runs* (tenseless) earlier than this utterance'.[2] All the jobs which can be done by tenses can be done by means of the tenseless way of talking and the self-referential utterance 'this utterance'. Of course, every time you use the words 'this utterance' you refer to a different utterance. So though I have just said that 'all the jobs' we can do with tenses and with words such as 'past', 'present', 'future', and 'now' can be done in our tenseless language together with the self-referential utterance 'this utterance', there is nevertheless one sort of thing that we cannot say in our tenseless language. We cannot translate a sentence of the form 'This event was future, is present and will be past'.

So far from this last fact being a criticism of the tenseless way of talking, it is, I think, pure gain. The inability to translate talk of events changing in respect of pastness, presentness, and futurity into our tenseless language can be taken simply as a proof of the concealed token reflexivity of tenses and of words such as 'past', 'present', 'future', and 'now'. If 'past' means 'earlier than this utterance' it is going to have a different reference every time it is used. If uttered in 1950 it refers to events earlier than 1950 and if uttered in 1965 it refers to events earlier than 1965. The notion of events 'changing from future to past' is simply a confused acknowledgment of this quite simple sort of fact. Once we see this we banish from the universe much unnecessary mystery.

If past, present, and future were real properties of events, then it would require explanation that an event which becomes present in 1965 becomes present at that

2. H. Reichenbach has given an excellent discussion of tenses and similar notions in terms of 'token-reflexivity' in §§ 50–1 of his *Elements of Symbolic Logic* (Macmillan, New York, 1947).

date and not at some other (and this would have to be an explanation over and above the explanation of why an event of this sort *occurred* in 1965). Indeed, every event is 'now' at some time or another, and so the notion of 'now' cannot be that of an objective property in nature which singles out some events from others. When we talk in our four-dimensional language of space–time we must clearly talk neither of events nor of things changing, since we have replaced the notion of a thing as the permanent in change by that of a four-dimensional entity, some of whose time slices *are* or *are* not different from others. But even in our language of the permanent in change we must still not think of *events* changing. Things (and processes) come into existence, change, or stay the same, whereas to say that an event (such as the beginning of a football match) 'came into existence' or 'changed' would be absurd. The only exception to this rule is that we *can* say that events 'become present', or 'become past', or even 'become probable' or 'become unlikely'. (On the other hand, it is somewhat strained to say that a *thing* becomes past or probable.) These phenomena of language can be neatly explained once we recognise the fact that utterances of words such as 'past', 'present', and 'future' refer to themselves. So also with 'probable' and 'unlikely', since here 'probable' and 'unlikely' mean 'probable, or unlikely, in terms of *present* evidence'.

Some philosophers have talked as though events 'become' or 'come into existence'. 'Become' is a transitive verb, and so to say that an event 'becomes' must presumably mean that it 'becomes present', and this, we have seen, misleads by concealing the token-reflexivity of 'present' and suggesting that the becoming present of an event is a real change like, for example, the becoming brown of a grassy hillside in summer. Similarly, an event cannot come into existence—a new building can come into existence, but the building of it cannot meaningfully be said to come into existence. (In the four-dimensional way of talking, of course, we must not say even that *things* come into existence—we replace talk of a building coming into existence at *t* by talk of the earliest time slice of the building *being* at *t*.) Some philosophers have erected these misconceptions about the grammar of the verbs 'to become' and 'to come into existence' into a metaphysics, as when, for example, Whitehead said that 'actual occasions become'.

We can also see how misleading it is to talk of the flow of time, or of our advance through time. To say that by next year a year of time will have gone by is simply to say that our conscious experiences of a year later than this utterance *are* (tenseless) a year later than this utterance. Our consciousness does not literally advance into the future, because if it did we could intelligibly ask 'How fast does it advance?' We should need to postulate a hyper-time with reference to which our advance in time could be measured (seconds per hyper-seconds), but there seems to be no reason to postulate such an entity as a hyper-time. (There is still something odd about movement in time even if it is said, as it might be, that the hyper-time has an *order* but no metric. This would rule out talk of 'seconds per hyper-seconds', but it would not affect the fact that change in time would still be a change with respect to hyper-time. Moreover, anyone who thought that time-flow was necessary for time would presumably want to say that hyper-time-flow was necessary for hyper-time. He would therefore be driven to postulate a hyper-hyper-time, and so on without end.)

It is true that sometimes in relativity theory it is said that time 'runs more slowly' in a moving system than it does in a system at rest relative to us. This, however, is not to imply any movement or 'running' of time. What is meant, by this misleading locution, is that according to the conventions of simultaneity of our system of axes the space–time interval between events on our clock is greater than that between simultaneous events on a clock in the moving system. Equally, since we are moving relative to the other system, clocks in our system 'run slow' relative to the moving system. Indeed, so far from relativity leading to difficulties for us, the reverse is the case. The four-dimensional way of talking which we have advocated could still have been possible in pre-relativity days, but it has derived additional theoretical advantages from Minkowski's discovery that the Lorentz transformations of special relativity can be regarded simply as a rotation of axes in space–time. This is not the place to go into an exposition of relativity, but I wish to record the conviction that many of the puzzles and paradoxes of relativity (or rather those things which are sometimes wrongly thought to be puzzles and paradoxes) can most easily be resolved by drawing diagrams of Minkowski space–time, in which most of these at first sight counter-intuitive facts will at once look quite obvious. (We must, of course, bear in mind that the geometry of space–time is not Euclidean.)

If I am right in supposing that 'now' is equivalent to 'simultaneous with this utterance', then I am able, as we have seen, to reject the notion of an objective 'now', the notion that even in past ages when there were perhaps no sentient beings there was nevertheless a moment which was distinguishable as 'the present' or 'now'.[3] An utterance of the word 'now' refers to itself, since it refers to the set of events simultaneous with itself. Now the special theory of relativity shows that there is no unique set of events which is 'now' or 'simultaneous with this utterance'. Which time slice of the four-dimensional manifold constitutes a 'now' depends on the frame of reference in which we are at rest. Our four-dimensional cake can be sliced at different angles. It is worth mentioning this consideration, since I have known one very eminent disciple of Whitehead (and therefore of an objective 'becoming') to have been genuinely worried by it. For our purposes we can easily modify the notions of 'now' or 'present' to mean 'simultaneous, relative to the utterer's frame of reference, of this utterance'. Similar modifications must be made for 'past' and 'future'.

The notions of 'past', 'present', and 'future' are more complex than those of 'earlier' and 'later', since the former notions do, and the latter notions do not, involve reference to the utterer's position in space–time. 'Earlier' and 'later' fit into the tenseless locution that I have advocated, whereas 'past', 'present', and 'future' do not.

---

3. See the passage from H. Bergmann, *Der Kampf um das Kausalgesetz in der jüngsten Physik* (Braunschweig, 1929), pp. 27–8, which is quoted in A. Grünbaum's paper 'Carnap's Views on the Foundations of Geometry', in P. A. Schilpp (ed.), *The Philosophy of Rudolf Carnap* (Open Court, La Salle, Illinois, 1963). Grünbaum's paper contains an excellent critique of the idea of an objective 'now'.

It may now be objected: 'So much the worse for the tenseless way of talking.' For it may be said that so far from the tensed language being definable in terms of the tenseless one (together with the notion of self-referential utterances), the tenseless '*is*' has to be defined in terms of the tensed one. As Wilfrid Sellars has objected,[4] a tenseless sentence '*x is φ at t*' is equivalent to the tensed one 'Either *x* was *φ* at *t* or is *φ* at *t* or will be *φ* at *t*'. So '*x is φ at t*' is not like '7 *is* a prime number', which does *not* mean '7 was, is, or will be a prime number'.

Now there is, I agree, a difference between '*x is φ at t*' and '7 *is* a prime number'. But it does not appear to be happily expressed by saying that the former sentence is not really tenseless. It is better expressed by saying that '*is* a prime number at such and such a time' is not a meaningful predicate. The difference can be brought out within the *predicates* of '*x is φ at t*' and '7 *is* a prime number' and has nothing to do with the copula. It is true that in extending the tenseless way of talking from pure mathematics to discourse about the space–time world it is natural to introduce '*x is φ at t*' via the locution '*x* was, is, or will be *φ* at *t*'. This is because it is tacitly agreed that *x* is a space–time entity and so earlier, simultaneous with or later than our present utterance, though in the present context which it is does not matter. But though it is natural to wean users of tensed language from their tenses in this way, it is by no means logically necessary that a tenseless language should be introduced in this manner.

A fable may be of use here. Consider a tribe whose religious and social life depended on the exact numerical age in years of the king, and that for this reason their very language made a difference between three sorts of numbers: those numbers which were less than the number of years which was the king's age, the number which was equal to this number, and the numbers which were greater than this number. Indeed, our tribe do not think of the three sorts of numbers as numbers, but believe that there are three sort of entities, alphas, betas, and gammas. They are, of course, slightly puzzled that every year (until the king dies) a gamma becomes a beta and a beta becomes an alpha. Someone might get the bright idea of introducing the notion of number as 'number = alpha or beta or gamma'. Would this show that the notion of 'number' had anything to do with the age of the king? It has indeed been introduced by reference to notions that have to do with the age of the king, but in such a way that this kingly reference 'cancels out'. Sellars argues that Tom, in 1955, Dick, in 1956, and Harry, in 1957, could agree that Eisenhower should be (tenselessly) President in 1956, but that their reasons would be different. Tom's reason would be 'Eisenhower will be President in 1956', Dick's reason would be 'Eisenhower is President in 1956', and Harry's reason would be 'Eisenhower was President in 1956'. These considerations, says Sellars, make it quite clear that the tenseless present, introduced via 'was, is, or will be', is quite other than the tenseless present of mathematics. As against this, I would say this: the fact that, since they

4. In his essay, 'Time and the World Order', in H. Feigl and G. Maxwell (eds.), *Minnesota Studies in the Philosophy of Science*, Vol. III (University of Minnesota Press, 1962), pp. 527–616, see p. 533.

speak from different temporal perspectives, Tom, Dick, and Harry give different reasons for saying 'Eisenhower *is* (tenseless) President in 1956' does not show that they mean anything non-tenseless. For a reason '*q*' offered for '*p*' in the explanation '*p* because *q*', may well contain extraneous and irrelevant elements. It does not therefore seem to me that Sellars has given any convincing reason for saying that there is any important difference between the tenseless '*is*' of 'Eisenhower *is* President in 1956' and '7 + 5 *is* equal to 12'. Of course Eisenhower is a temporal entity, and so 'in 1956' has sense in relation to him, and numbers are non-temporal entities, and so there is no question of 'in 1956' in the case of the second proposition. This distinction can perfectly well be made explicit in the *predicates* of the two sentences and need not be done in the *copulae*. This also explains why it is natural (though there is no need to suppose that it is logically *necessary*) to introduce the tenseless *is* in the case of 'Eisenhower *is* President in 1956' *via* the idiom 'was, is, or will be', whereas it would, as Sellars notes, not be natural to do so in cases like '7 + 5 *is* equal to 12'.

A sentence of the form '*x* is ϕ at *t*' is, of course, not timeless, any more than '*x* is ϕ at such and such a place at *t*' is *spaceless*. Timelessness is not the same as tense-lessness. '7 *is* a prime number' is both tenseless and timeless. (There is no sense in saying '7 *is* a prime number at *t*'.) The tenseless way of talking does not therefore imply that physical things or events are eternal in the way in which the number 7 is.

As we have already noted, it is sometimes said that 'this utterance' is to be analysed as 'the utterance which is- now'. If so, of course, tenses or the notions of past, present, and future *are* fundamental. My reply to this move is to say that this is simply a dogmatic rejection of the analysis in terms of token-reflexiveness. On this analysis 'now' is elucidated in terms of 'this utterance', and not vice-versa. This seems to me to be a perfectly legitimate procedure. How does one settle the argument with someone who says that 'this utterance' has to be analysed in terms of 'utterance now'? Any analysis is a way of looking at language, and there is no one way. I advocate my way, because it fits our ordinary way of talking much more closely to our scientific way of looking at the world and it avoids unnecessary mystification. If someone is adamant that his analysis is the correct analysis of ordinary language I am prepared to concede him this rather empty point. Ordinary language is, then, on his account, more at variance with science than is my version of ordinary language. Nevertheless, the two analyses are in practice pretty well equivalent: in ordinary life a linguist will detect no difference between 'ordinary language', as in accordance with my analysis, and 'ordinary language', as in accordance with my opponent's analysis. Our ordinary language is just not quite so 'ordinary' as is our opponent's, but it is just as good even for ordinary purposes. It is perhaps more 'ordinary' to say that sugar 'melts' than that it 'dissolves', but the greater scientific correctness of the latter locution does not in any way unfit it for even the most practical purposes. Similarly, the additional theoretical advantages of looking at temporal language in the present way suggest that we should prefer this analysis to the other. Perhaps the objector is saying that the present analysis is impossible for any language, whether 'ordinary' or scientific. But it is not at all evident why the objector should think that an utterance like 'this utterance' cannot be *directly* self-referential. We hear a token of the form 'this utterance' and simply understand that this token utterance is the one referred to. We can at a later date *say* what the utterance referred to was: we can enumerate sufficient of its characteristics to identify it. It is always logically possible, of course, that some *other* utterance should possess this list of characteristics—we can misidentify an utterance just as we can misidentify a stone, a tree, or a person. But in fact we need not and do not. Moreover, if we *did* misidentify it, how would the proposal to elucidate 'this' in terms of 'now' have prevented us?

The self-reference of specific utterances of words such as 'here' and 'now' is sufficient to deal with the following puzzle: it is logically possible that in remote regions of space–time the universe might repeat itself exactly.[5] We cannot therefore uniquely single out an entity (say this table) by referring to it by means of some set of properties—elsewhere in the universe there might be another table with exactly the same qualities and relations to other objects. A token-reflexive expression can, however, uniquely pick out this table—this table is near the utterance of *this token'*. Of course there may well be other Smarts in other regions of space–time uttering precisely similar tokens, but they can all refer uniquely to their environments by token-reflexive means. There is, however, no need for words such as 'now' or tenses—this utterance' or 'this token' is always enough to do the trick. Sellars makes a similar point when he argues that token-reflexives are needed to distinguish the real world from fictional worlds. (The real world is a system of entities which includes *this.*) There are obvious difficulties here, which perhaps can be got round only if one accepts Sellars' own interesting but debatable views on the concept of existence. I should wish to say too, however, that tenses and words such as 'present' or 'now' are unimportant here, and that a simple token-reflexive device (corresponding to 'this utterance') is enough to do the trick. For cosmological *theory*, moreover, token-reflexivity is *not* needed. Here one can simply assert, as part of the theory, either that the universe repeats itself in remote parts of space–time or that it does not. It is only in *applying* the theory to observations that unique references have actually to be made.

It should be hardly necessary, at this stage, I should hope, to emphasise that when in the tenseless way of talking we banish tenses, we really must banish them. Thus, when we say that future events exist we do *not* mean that they exist now (present tense). The view of the world as a four-dimensional manifold does not therefore imply that, as some people seem to have thought, the future is already 'laid up'. To say that the future is already laid up is to say that future events exist *now*, whereas when I say of future events that they *exist* (tenselessly) I am doing so simply because, in this case, they *will* exist. The tensed and tenseless locutions are like oil and water—they

---

5. See A. W. Burks, 'A Theory of Proper Names', *Philosophical Studies*, Vol. 2, 1951, pp. 36–45, and N. L. Wilson, 'The Identity of Indiscernibles and the Symmetrical Universe', *Mind*, Vol. 62, 1953, pp. 506–11.

do not mix, and if you try to mix them you get into needless trouble. We can now see also that the view of the world as a space–time manifold no more implies determinism than it does the fatalistic view that the future 'is already laid up'. It is compatible both with determinism and with indeterminism, *i.e.* both with the view that earlier time slices of the universe are determinately related by laws of nature to later time slices and with the view that they are not so related.

When we use tenses and token-reflexive words such as 'past', 'present', and 'future' we are using a language which causes us to see the universe very much from the perspective of our position in space–time. Our view of the world thus acquires a certain anthropocentricity, which can best be eliminated by passing to a tenseless language. By the use of such expressions as 'earlier than this utterance' and 'later than this utterance' we make quite explicit the reference to our particular position in space–time. Once we recognise this anthropocentric reference and bring it out into the open we are less likely to project it on to the universe. The tenseless and minimally token-reflexive language enables us to see the world, in Spinoza's phrase, *sub specie aeternitatis*.

The temporal asymmetry of the world

We have rejected the notions of 'time flow' and of 'absolute becoming'. We conceive of the universe as a space–time manifold. We may now be struck by a puzzling fact. Why is it that the universe seems to be asymmetrical in the time direction, whereas, on a large scale, it seems to be quite symmetrical in the various space directions?[6] For example, there are photographs, fossil records, footprints in sand, and innumerable other such species of traces of the past, and yet nothing at all comparable in the case of the future. We know a great deal about past history and yet the future is obscure to us. In some cases, of course, we can predict the future, just as we can retrodict the past, but this does not affect the present issue, since our knowledge through traces greatly exceeds that which we should get through retrodiction alone. Human memories themselves provide a special case of the concept of a trace, since they presumably arise from traces in the neurophysiological structure of the brain.

The question of why the universe is asymmetrical in this way, of why there seems to be nothing analogous to traces of future events, is one which the adherent of time flow or of 'objective becoming' may fail to find puzzling. For he may relate it to the alleged fact that 'time flows one way' or may say that 'there can be traces of the past because past events exist, whereas there cannot be traces of future events because they have not come into existence yet'. We have seen reason to reject this sort of talk. Happily, however, our puzzle is soluble, and soluble in an illuminating

---

6. Though the world may be asymmetrical as regards *rotations*. This is suggested by the recent discovery in physics that parity is not conserved. In an article 'The Temporal Asymmetry of the World', *Analysis*, Vol. 14, 1953–54, pp. 79–83, I asserted the asymmetry of the world with regard to rotations, but this was due to elementary confusion of thought on my part, and not to prescience of the discovery about parity!

scientific manner rather than by means of the facile devices of the *a priori* meta-physician. The solution of this problem is one of the most fascinating chapters in recent scientific philosophy, and the most up-to-date discussion of it will be found in some of the recent writings of A. Grünbaum.[7] Important contributions are those by H. Reichenbach,[8] E. Schrödinger,[9] and others. An important suggestion on different lines is by K. R. Popper.[10]

The directionality which puzzles us does not show up in the laws of classical mechanics, electromagnetism, or in quantum mechanics. Any solution of these laws of the form $f(t)$ has a corresponding solution $f(-t)$. However, as K. R. Popper has shown,[11] even in classical mechanics and electromagnetism a directionality becomes apparent if besides the *laws* we consider *boundary conditions*. Consider a spherical light wave emitted from a point in space, for example from an electric bulb. The equations of propagation of the spherical wave are certainly unchanged by a transformation from t to $-t$. In other words, a train of spherical waves *converging* to a point is equally compatible with the laws of nature. Nevertheless, as Popper points out, the initial conditions for the second interpretation are quite improbable. Rays of light would have to be sent out from all points on a sphere of a radius of cosmic dimensions, the rays of light travelling along radii of the sphere towards its centre. Though such a combination of occurrences would be compatible with the laws of nature, it would constitute an infinitely improbable coincidence. There would have to be a most unlikely harmonising of emissions from the points of the sphere so as to simulate in reverse a spherical wave emitted from a point. Some extraordinary hypothesis would be needed to account for such a queer thing. When, on the other hand, we consider the spherical wave emitted from a lamp we do not have to postulate any improbable initial conditions. Moreover, the rays converging from a distant sphere would still not come from infinity.

In some cases, therefore, we can give an account of temporal asymmetry without going beyond the differential equations of classical physics, together with a consideration of boundary conditions. The consideration of boundary conditions involves us in probability considerations. For a widely applicable explanation of temporal asymmetry, however, we must pass to thermodynamics and statistical mechanics. Notice that here again probability plays a central role. For example, consider a chamber divided into two compartments A and B. In A is a gas at temperature θ_1, and in B is a gas at temperature θ_2. When the partition between the chambers is removed the gases mix and settle down to a temperature intermediate between

---

7. *Op. cit.* See also his 'The Nature of Time', in R. Colodny (ed.), *Frontiers of Science and Philosophy* (University of Pittsburgh Press, 1962).

8. *The Direction of Time* (Cambridge University Press, 1957).

9. 'Irreversibility', *Proceedings of the Royal Irish Academy*, Vol. 52, 1950, pp. 189–95.

10. *Nature*, Vol. 177, 1956, p. 538. See also the letters by E. L. Hill and A. Grünbaum, and reply by Popper, *Nature*, Vol. 179, 1957, pp. 1296–7, and Grünbaum's paper 'Popper on Irreversibility', in *The Critical Approach, Essays in Honor of Karl Popper*, edited by M. Bunge (The Free Press, Glencoe, Illinois, 1963).

11. See previous footnote.

θ_1 and θ_2. It is, of course, conceivable that on the average the faster-moving molecules stayed in A and the slower-moving ones stayed in B, but statistics show that this would be almost infinitely improbable. For this reason also we never observe that a gas at temperature θ_3 separates spontaneously into two spatially distinct gases at different temperatures θ_1 and θ_2 respectively. An important objection has, however, been raised against this reasoning, and it will be helpful to consider it. This is the 'reversibility objection'. It goes as follows. According to gas theory, the probability of a molecule's having a velocity v in a certain direction is equal to the probability of its having a velocity $-v$ in that direction (*i.e.* a velocity v in the *opposite* direction). Now if all the velocities of the molecules of the gas at temperature θ_3 were reversed we should get the opposite process to our mixing process above, and the gases would separate out into the two parts A and B at temperature θ_1 and θ_2. That is, contrary to what was asserted above, separation processes must be as common as mixing processes.

Kinetic theory, of the sort we are considering in connection with the reversibility objection, presupposes that we are dealing with a closed and finite system of particles. In order therefore to apply these considerations to the universe as a whole let us make the assumption that the universe contains a finite number of particles, that there is no creation or annihilation of matter, and that the universe is not expanding or contracting. These assumptions are contrary to what is probably the case, but it is nevertheless instructive here to suppose that they hold good. With these assumptions it is possible to talk of the entropy (roughly the amount of disorganisation) of the universe as a whole. The entropy of the universe is increasing much as the disorder of a pack of cards increases as they are shuffled. When the shuffling reaches completion the universe is in its 'heat death': there is no order anywhere, such as is exemplified by hot sun and cold earth, but everywhere there is a flat uniformity. A pack of cards, if it is shuffled for long enough, will emerge from a state of randomness back into a state in which the cards are arranged in suits. Similarly, if the universe were finite and non-expanding its entropy curve would ultimately begin to descend again. Instead of increasing, entropy would begin to decrease. This illustrates the theorem that reversed states are as probable as non-reversed ones.

Let us consider the part of the entropy curve of the universe in which we ourselves are. (Remember that we are assuming for the sake of argument that it is legitimate to speak in this way of the entropy of the universe as a whole.) Now, as Reichenbach points out, we are not in practice concerned with the entropy of the whole universe: it is something of which we can have no knowledge. There are, however, vast numbers of what Reichenbach calls 'branch systems': such a system is one whose state of disorder 'branches' off from that of a wider system, and which remains relatively isolated until it merges with the wider system again. For example, consider a footprint on a beach. The state of order of the grains of sand that make up the footprint is greater than it was before the footprint was imprinted. This is compatible with the law that entropy, or disorder, always increases, because of the more than compensating increase of the entropy of the man who makes the footprints and is metabolically depleted as he walks. Ultimately as a result of wind and weather the footprint will merge into the flatness of the beach again, and its entropy level will return to that of the wider system. Another example of a branch system is exemplified by blocks of ice in a beaker of water which gradually melt and return to the temperature of the surroundings. Written and fossil records, magnetic tapes and photographic plates, all provide further examples of branch systems. In these cases it is useful, following Reichenbach, to talk of macroentropy, for we are primarily concerned with the states of order or disorder of entities much larger than molecules, such as grains of sand and pieces of print. Macroentropy is analogous to, and of course ultimately reducible to, microentropy, the state of disorder of assemblages or molecules, such as is considered in statistical mechanics.

Branch systems, we have noted, return ultimately to the entropy curve of the universe (on the assumption, as before, that we can meaningfully talk of the entropy of the whole universe). Now all branch systems with which we are acquainted run in the same direction. These provide a background against which we can test the direction of any particular process. A process is in the direction of positive time if it is in the direction of increase of entropy of branch systems, for example if it begins when ice *is* put into a beaker and finishes when the ice *is* melted. (It would, of course, have been more idiomatic if I had said 'when the ice has melted', but I have stuck to the tenseless 'is' in order to dodge unwarranted accusations of circularity.)

Now consider a finite non-expanding universe which ultimately attains its heat death, after which its entropy curve will run on a downgrade. In the era of the universe which is on the far side of the heat death branch systems will point the opposite way to branch systems in our era. Intelligent beings who lived in this era would get an illusion of time flow which is the opposite of ours.

Some philosophers have thought that a universe in which the direction of positive time went the other way would be a 'crazy' or 'irrational' world. As F. H. Bradley put it: 'Death would come before birth, the blow would follow the wound, and all must seem irrational.'[12] Similarly, J. N. Findlay has characterised such a world as one 'where a ripple would first form on the edge of a pond, and then swell steadily towards the centre, to be followed by a set of even larger, converging ripples, until on the arrival of the last, largest ripple at the centre, a stone would emerge with sudden noise, leaving the water behind it miraculously still. Or where a set of foot-prints would become more and more clear-cut with the lapse of time, until they were ultimately walked upon (and blotted out) by some suitable creature moving in reverse.'[13] Findlay says that such a world 'wouldn't strike us as queer but definitely crazy'. I contend, on the contrary, that the 'backwards' universe would both be and seem just like our 'forwards' universe. For one thing, our intuitive sense of time direction presumably is causally explicable by reference to the accumulation of memory traces in our brains. As A. Grünbaum has said, 'The flux of time consists

12. *Appearance and Reality*, 2nd Ed. (Oxford University Press, 1930), p. 190.
13. J. N. Findlay, review of C. Ehrenfels' *Cosmogony*, in *Philosophy*, Vol. 25, 1950, pp. 346–7.

in the *instantaneous awareness* of both the temporal order *and* the set-theoretical increase of the membership of the set of remembered (recorded) events, an awareness in which the instant of its own occurrence contributes a *distinguished element*.'[14] Grünbaum's statement needs a little tidying up, for if he were literally correct we should expect an old man who was losing memory traces faster than he was acquiring them to get the feeling of time flowing backwards. And this does not seem to be so. Nevertheless, it is difficult to believe that our intuitive sense of the direction of time does not arise from the formation of memory traces in our brain, which constitute 'branch systems'. Ignoring for the moment the possibility of the obliteration of memory traces, it is the case that in our world if time t_1 is earlier than time t_2 we have more memories at t_2 than at t_1. It is not surprising that we get the feeling of the advance of time as like the mercury running up a thermometer tube, though in fact what is changing is not time but the stock of our memory traces. Now in the reversed universe if t_1 is earlier than t_2 (according to our reckoning) there will be more memory traces in a person of that universe at t_1 than at t_2. Such a person will feel as though time is flowing in the direction from t_2 to t_1. So far from his world seeming crazy or irrational it will seem to him exactly as our world does to us. If an era of the universe in which its entropy curve is on the upgrade is followed by one in which the entropy curve is on a downgrade there is complete symmetry between the two eras. Indeed, from the point of view of someone in the other era he is on the upgrade and our era follows his and is on a downgrade.

We have, of course, made the artificial assumption of a non-expanding universe with a fixed and finite number of particles in it. On other assumptions there would not be symmetrically opposed eras. However, we have seen enough to understand that the temporal asymmetry of the universe (or at the least of our own cosmic era) comes not from the nature of time itself, but from very general facts, largely of a statistical sort, about the things in the universe. These facts can perfectly well be expressed within the theory of the universe as a space–time manifold.[15]

Conclusion

In this chapter I have been defending the view of the world as a four-dimensional system of entities in space–time. Concepts such as 'past' and 'future' have been shown to be anthropocentric in that they relate to particular human utterances. My advocacy of the four-dimensional picture of the world is therefore, among other things, part of the same campaign against anthropocentricity and romanticism in metaphysics that I have been waging elsewhere, as in the chapters on secondary qualities, consciousness, and man as a mechanism. It is surely no accident that

---

14. 'Carnap's Views on the Foundations of Geometry', *op. cit.*
15. For a critique of theories of time flow and of 'absolute becoming', together with a defence of the view of the universe as a space–time manifold, the reader may be further referred to Donald Williams' excellent article, 'The Myth of Passage', *Journal of Philosophy*, Vol. 48, 1951, pp. 457–72.

romantic, vitalistic, and anti-mechanistic philosophies such as those of Bergson and Whitehead are also those which lay great emphasis on the alleged transitory aspect of time, process or absolute becoming. While I concede that our present notions of space and time may perhaps have to be revised, the idea of the world as a space–time manifold is nearer the truth than these romantic and obscure philosophical theories.

Chapter 39

The paradoxes of time travel

David Lewis

Tᴵᴹᴱ travel, I maintain, is possible. The paradoxes of time travel are oddities, not impossibilities. They prove only this much, which few would have doubted: that a possible world where time travel took place would be a most strange world, different in fundamental ways from the world we think is ours.

I shall be concerned here with the sort of time travel that is recounted in science fiction. Not all science fiction writers are clearheaded, to be sure, and inconsistent time travel stories have often been written. But some writers have thought the problems through with great care, and their stories are perfectly consistent.[1]

If I can defend the consistency of some science fiction stories of time travel, then I suppose parallel defenses might be given of some controversial physical hypotheses, such as the hypothesis that time is circular or the hypothesis that there are particles that travel faster than light. But I shall not explore these parallels here.

What is time travel? Inevitably, it involves a discrepancy between time and time. Any traveler departs and then arrives at his destination; the time elapsed from departure to arrival (positive, or perhaps zero) is the duration of the journey. But if he is a time traveler, the separation in time between departure and arrival does not equal the duration of his journey. He departs; he travels for an hour, let us say; then he arrives. The time he reaches is not the time one hour after his departure. It is later, if he has traveled toward the future; earlier, if he has traveled toward the past. If he has traveled far toward the past, it is earlier even than his departure. How can it be that the same two events, his departure and his arrival, are separated by two unequal amounts of time?

It is tempting to reply that there must be two independent time dimensions; that for time travel to be possible, time must be not a line but a plane.[2] Then a pair of events may have two unequal separations if they are separated more in one of the time dimensions than in the other. The lives of common people occupy straight

---

1. I have particularly in mind two of the time travel stories of Robert A. Heinlein: 'By His Bootstraps', in R. A. Heinlein, *The Menace from Earth* (Hicksville, NY, 1959), and '—All You Zombies—', in R. A. Heinlein, *The Unpleasant Profession of Jonathan Hoag* (Hicksville, NY, 1959).

2. Accounts of time travel in two-dimensional time are found in Jack W. Meiland, 'A Two-Dimensional Passage Model of Time for Time Travel', *Philosophical Studies*, vol. 26 (1974), pp. 153–73; and in the initial chapters of Isaac Asimov, *The End of Eternity* (Garden City, NY, 1955). Asimov's denouement, however, seems to require some different conception of time travel.

David Lewis, 'The Paradoxes of Time Travel', from *American Philosophical Quarterly*, 13, (1976).

diagonal lines across the plane of time, sloping at a rate of exactly one hour of time$_1$ per hour of time$_2$. The life of the time traveler occupies a bent path, of varying slope.

On closer inspection, however, this account seems not to give us time travel as we know it from the stories. When the traveler revisits the days of his childhood, will his playmates be there to meet him? No; he has not reached the part of the plane of time where they are. He is no longer separated from them along one of the two dimensions of time, but he is still separated from them along the other. I do not say that two-dimensional time is impossible, or that there is no way to square it with the usual conception of what time travel would be like. Nevertheless I shall say no more about two-dimensional time. Let us set it aside, and see how time travel is possible even in one-dimensional time.

The world—the time traveler's world, or ours—is a four-dimensional manifold of events. Time is one dimension of the four, like the spatial dimensions except that the prevailing laws of nature discriminate between time and the others—or rather, perhaps, between various timelike dimensions and various spacelike dimensions. (Time remains one-dimensional, since no two timelike dimensions are orthogonal.) Enduring things are timelike streaks: wholes composed of temporal parts, or *stages*, located at various times and places. Change is qualitative difference between different stages—different temporal parts—of some enduring thing, just as a 'change' in scenery from east to west is a qualitative difference between the eastern and western spatial parts of the landscape. If this paper should change your mind about the possibility of time travel, there will be a difference of opinion between two different temporal parts of you, the stage that started reading and the subsequent stage that finishes.

If change is qualitative difference between temporal parts of something, then what doesn't have temporal parts can't change. For instance, numbers can't change; nor can the events of any moment of time, since they cannot be subdivided into dissimilar temporal parts. (We have set aside the case of two-dimensional time, and hence the possibility that an event might be momentary along one time dimension but divisible along the other.) It is essential to distinguish change from 'Cambridge change,' which can befall anything. Even a number can 'change' from being to not being the rate of exchange between pounds and dollars. Even a momentary event can 'change' from being a year ago to being a year and a day ago, or from being forgotten to being remembered. But these are not genuine changes. Not just any old reversal in truth value of a time-sensitive sentence about something makes a change in the thing itself.

A time traveler, like anyone else, is a streak through the manifold of space-time, a whole composed of stages located at various times and places. But he is not a streak like other streaks. If he travels toward the past he is a zig-zag streak, doubling back on himself. If he travels toward the future, he is a stretched-out streak. And if he travels either way instantaneously, so that there are no intermediate stages between the stage that departs and the stage that arrives and his journey has zero duration, then he is a broken streak.

I asked how it could be that the same two events were separated by two unequal amounts of time, and I set aside the reply that time might have two independent dimensions. Instead I reply by distinguishing time itself, *external time* as I shall also call it, from the *personal time* of a particular time traveler: roughly, that which is measured by his wristwatch. His journey takes an hour of his personal time, let us say; his wristwatch reads an hour later at arrival than at departure. But the arrival is more than an hour after the departure in external time, if he travels toward the future; or the arrival is before the departure in external time (or less than an hour after), if he travels toward the past.

That is only rough. I do not wish to define personal time operationally, making wristwatches infallible by definition. That which is measured by my own wristwatch often disagrees with external time, yet I am no time traveler; what my misregulated wristwatch measures is neither time itself nor my personal time. Instead of an operational definition, we need a functional definition of personal time: it is that which occupies a certain role in the pattern of events that comprise the time traveler's life. If you take the stages of a common person, they manifest certain regularities with respect to external time. Properties change continuously as you go along, for the most part, and in familiar ways. First come infantile stages. Last come senile ones. Memories accumulate. Food digests. Hair grows. Wristwatch hands move. If you take the stages of a time traveler instead, they do not manifest the common regularities with respect to external time. But there is one way to assign coordinates to the time traveler's stages, and one way only (apart from the arbitrary choice of a zero point), so that the regularities that hold with respect to this assignment match those that commonly hold with respect to external time. With respect to the correct assignment properties change continuously as you go along, for the most part, and in familiar ways. First come infantile stages. Last come senile ones. Memories accumulate. Food digests. Hair grows. Wristwatch hands move. The assignment of coordinates that yields this match is the time traveler's personal time. It isn't really time, but it plays the role in his life that time plays in the life of a common person. It's enough like time so that we can—with due caution—transplant our temporal vocabulary to it in discussing his affairs. We can say without contradiction, as the time traveler prepares to set out, 'Soon he will be in the past.' We mean that a stage of him is slightly later in his personal time, but much earlier in external time, than the stage of him that is present as we say the sentence.

We may assign locations in the time traveler's personal time not only to his stages themselves but also to the events that go on around him. Soon Caesar will die, long ago; that is, a stage slightly later in the time traveler's personal time than his present stage, but long ago in external time, is simultaneous with Caesar's death. We could even extend the assignment of personal time to events that are not part of the time traveler's life, and not simultaneous with any of his stages. If his funeral in ancient Egypt is separated from his death by three days of external time and his death is separated from his birth by three score years and ten of his personal time, then we may add the two intervals and say that his funeral follows his birth by three score years and ten and three days of *external personal time*. Likewise a bystander might truly say, three years after the last departure of another famous time traveler, that 'he may even now—if I may use the phrase—be wandering on some plesiosaurus-haunted oolitic coral reef, or beside the lonely saline seas of the Triassic Age.'[3] If the time traveler does wander on an oolitic coral reef three years after his departure in his personal time, then it is no mistake to say with respect to his extended personal time that the wandering is taking place 'even now'.

We may liken intervals of external time to distances as the crow flies, and intervals of personal time to distances along a winding path. The time traveler's life is like a mountain railway. The place two miles due east of here may also be nine miles down the line, in the west-bound direction. Clearly we are not dealing here with two independent dimensions. Just as distance along the railway is not a fourth spatial dimension, so a time traveler's personal time is not a second dimension of time. How far down the line some place is depends on its location in three-dimensional space, and likewise the location of events in personal time depend on their locations in one-dimensional external time.

Five miles down the line from here is a place where the line goes under a trestle; two miles further is a place where the line goes over a trestle; these places are one and the same. The trestle by which the line crosses over itself has two different locations along the line, five miles down from here and also seven. In the same way, an event in a time traveler's life may have more than one location in his personal time. If he doubles back toward the past, but not too far, he may be able to talk to himself. The conversation involves two of his stages, separated in his personal time but simultaneous in external time. The location of the conversation in personal time should be the location of the stage involved in it. But there are two such stages; to share the locations of both, the conversation must be assigned two different locations in personal time.

The more we extend the assignment of personal time outwards from the time traveler's stages to the surrounding events, the more will such events acquire multiple locations. It may happen also, as we have already seen, that events that are not simultaneous in external time will be assigned the same location in personal time— or rather, that at least one of the locations of one will be the same as at least one of the locations of the other. So extension must not be carried too far, lest the location of events in extended personal time lose its utility as a means of keeping track of their roles in the time traveler's history.

A time traveler who talks to himself, on the telephone perhaps, looks for all the world like two different people talking to each other. It isn't quite right to say that the whole of him is in two places at once, since neither of the two stages involved in the conversation is the whole of him, or even the whole of the part of him that is

---

3. H. G. Wells, *The Time Machine, An Invention* (London 1895), epilogue. The passage is criticized as contradictory in Donald C. Williams, "The Myth of Passage," *The Journal of Philosophy*, vol. 48 (1951), p. 463.

located at the (external) time of the conversation. What's true is that he, unlike the rest of us, has two different complete stages located at the same time at different places. What reason have I, then, to regard him as one person and not two? What unites his stages, including the simultaneous ones, into a single person? The problem of personal identity is expecially acute if he is the sort of time traveler whose journeys are instantaneous, a broken streak consisting of several unconnected segments. Then the natural way to regard him as more than one person is to take each segment as a different person. No one of them is a time traveler, and the peculiarity of the situation comes to this: all but one of these several people vanish into thin air, all but another one appear out of thin air, and there are remarkable resemblances between one at his appearance and another at his vanishing. Why isn't that at least as good a description as the one I gave, on which the several segments are all parts of one time traveler?

I answer that what unites the stages (or segments) of a time traveler is the same sort of mental, or mostly mental, continuity and connectedness that unites anyone else. The only difference is that whereas a common person is connected and continuous with respect to external time, the time traveler is connected and continuous only with respect to his own personal time. Taking the stages in order, mental (and bodily) change is mostly gradual rather than sudden, and at no point is there sudden change in too many different respects all at once. (We can include position in external time among the respects we keep track of, if we like. It may change discontinuously with respect to personal time if not too much else changes discontinuously along with it.) Moreover, there is not too much change altogether. Plenty of traits and traces last a lifetime. Finally, the connectedness and the continuity are not accidental. They are explicable; and further, they are explained by the fact that the properties of each stage depend causally on those of the stages just before in personal time, the dependence being such as tends to keep things the same.[4]

To see the purpose of my final requirement of causal continuity, let us see how it excludes a case of counterfeit time travel. Fred was created out of thin air, as if in the midst of life; he lived a while, then died. He was created by a demon, and the demon had chosen at random what Fred was to be like at the moment of his creation. Much later someone else, Sam, came to resemble Fred as he was when first created. At the very moment when the resemblance became perfect, the demon destroyed Sam. Fred and Sam together are very much like a single person: a time traveler whose personal time starts at Sam's birth, goes on to Sam's destruction and Fred's creation, and goes on from there to Fred's death. Taken in this order, the stages of Fred-*cum*-Sam have the proper connectedness and continuity. But they lack causal continuity, so Fred-*cum*-Sam is not one person and not a time traveler. Perhaps it was pure coincidence that Fred at his creation and Sam at his destruction were exactly alike;

---

4. I discuss the relation between personal identity and mental connectedness and continuity at greater length in 'Survival and Identity', in *The Identities of Persons*, ed. by Amélie Rorty (Berkeley and Los Angeles, 1976).

then the connectedness and continuity of Fred-*cum*-Sam across the crucial point are accidental. Perhaps instead the demon remembered what Fred was like, guided Sam toward perfect resemblance, watched his progress, and destroyed him at the right moment. Then the connectedness and continuity of Fred-*cum*-Sam has a causal explanation, but of the wrong sort. Either way, Fred's first stages do not depend causally for their properties on Sam's last stages. So the case of Fred and Sam is rightly disqualified as a case of personal identity and as a case of time travel.

We might expect that when a time traveler visits the past there will be reversals of causation. You may punch his face before he leaves, causing his eye to blacken centuries ago. Indeed, travel into the past necessarily involves reversed causation. For time travel requires personal identity—he who arrives must be the same person who departed. That requires causal continuity, in which causation runs from earlier to later stages in the order of personal time. But the orders of personal and external time disagree at some point, and there we have causation that runs from later to earlier stages in the order of external time. Elsewhere I have given an analysis of causation in terms of chains of counterfactual dependence, and I took care that my analysis would not rule out causal reversal *a priori*.[5] I think I can argue (but not here) that under my analysis the direction of counterfactual dependence and causation is governed by the direction of other *de facto* asymmetries of time. If so, then reversed causation and time travel are not excluded altogether, but can occur only where there are local exceptions to these asymmetries. As I said at the outset, the time traveler's world would be a most strange one.

Stranger still, if there are local—but only local—causal reversals, then there may also be causal loops: closed causal chains in which some of the causal links are normal in direction and others are reversed. (Perhaps there must be loops if there is reversal; I am not sure.) Each event on the loop has a causal explanation, being caused by events elsewhere on the loop. That is not to say that the loop as a whole is caused or explicable. It may not be. Its inexplicability is especially remarkable if it is made up of the sort of causal processes that transmit information. Recall the time traveler who talked to himself. He talked to himself about time travel, and in the course of the conversation his older self told his younger self how to build a time machine. That information was available in no other way. His older self knew how because his younger self had been told and the information had been preserved by the causal processes that constitute recording, storage, and retrieval of memory traces. His younger self knew, after the conversation, because his older self had known and the information had been preserved by the causal processes that constitute telling. But where did the information come from in the first place? Why did the whole affair happen? There is simply no answer. The parts of the loop are explicable, the whole of it is not. Strange! But not impossible, and not too different from

---

5. 'Causation', *The Journal of Philosophy*, vol. 70 (1973), pp. 556–67; the analysis relies on the analysis of counterfactuals given in my *Counterfactuals* (Oxford, 1973).

inexplicabilities we are already inured to. Almost everyone agrees that God, or the Big Bang, or the entire infinite past of the universe or the decay of a tritium atom, is uncaused and inexplicable. Then if these are possible, why not also the inexplicable causal loops that arise in time travel?

I have committed a circularity in order not to talk about too much at once, and this is a good place to set it right. In explaining personal time, I presupposed that we were entitled to regard certain stages as comprising a single person. Then in explaining what united the stages into a single person, I presupposed that we were given a personal time order for them. The proper way to proceed is to define personhood and personal time simultaneously, as follows. Suppose given a pair of an aggregate of person-stages, regarded as a candidate for personhood, and an assignment of coordinates to those stages, regarded as a candidate for his personal time. Iff the stages satisfy the conditions given in my circular explanation with respect to the assignment of coordinates, then both candidates succeed: the stages do comprise a person and the assignment is his personal time.

I have argued so far that what goes on in a time travel story may be a possible pattern of events in four-dimensional space-time with no extra time dimension; that it may be correct to regard the scattered stages of the alleged time traveler as comprising a single person; and that we may legitimately assign to those stages and their surroundings a personal time order that disagrees sometimes with their order in external time. Some might concede all this, but protest that the impossibility of time travel is revealed after all when we ask not what the time traveler *does*, but what he *could do*. Could a time traveler change the past? It seems not: the events of a past moment could no more change than numbers could. Yet it seems that he would be as able as anyone to do things that would change the past if he did them. If a time traveler visiting the past both could and couldn't do something that would change it, then there cannot possibly be such a time traveler.

Consider Tim. He detests his grandfather, whose success in the munitions trade built the family fortune that paid for Tim's time machine. Tim would like nothing so much as to kill Grandfather, but alas he is too late. Grandfather died in his bed in 1957, while Tim was a young boy. But when Tim has built his time machine and traveled to 1920, suddenly he realizes that he is not too late after all. He buys a rifle; he spends long hours in target practice; he shadows Grandfather to learn the route of his daily walk to the munitions works; he rents a room along the route; and there he lurks, one winter day in 1921, rifle loaded, hate in his heart, as Grandfather walks closer, closer, ...

Tim can kill Grandfather. He has what it takes. Conditions are perfect in every way: the best rifle money could buy, Grandfather an easy target only twenty yards away, not a breeze, door securely locked against intruders, Tim a good shot to begin with and now at the peak of training, and so on. What's to stop him? The forces of logic will not stay his hand! No powerful chaperone stands by to defend the past from interference. (To imagine such a chaperone, as some authors do, is a boring evasion, not needed to make Tim's story consistent.) In short, Tim is as much able to kill Grandfather as anyone ever is to kill anyone. Suppose that down the street another sniper, Tom, lurks waiting for another victim, Grandfather's partner. Tom is not a time traveler, but otherwise he is just like Tim: same make of rifle, same murderous intent, same everything. We can even suppose that Tom, like Tim, believes himself to be a time traveler. Someone has gone to a lot of trouble to deceive Tom into thinking so. There's no doubt that Tom can kill his victim; and Tim has everything going for him that Tom does. By any ordinary standards of ability, Tim can kill Grandfather.

Tim cannot kill grandfather. Grandfather lived, so to kill him would be to change the past. But the events of a past moment are not subdivisible into temporal parts and therefore cannot change. Either the events of 1921 timelessly do include Tim's killing of Grandfather, or else they timelessly don't. We may be tempted to speak of the 'original' 1921 that lies in Tim's personal past, many years before his birth, in which Grandfather lived; and of the 'new' 1921 in which Tim now finds himself waiting in ambush to kill Grandfather. But if we do speak so, we merely confer two names on one thing. The events of 1921 are doubly located in Tim's (extended) personal time, like the trestle on the railway, but the 'original' 1921 and the 'new' 1921 are one and the same. If Tim did not kill Grandfather in the 'original' 1921, then if he does kill Grandfather in the 'new' 1921, he must both kill and not kill Grandfather in 1921—in the one and only 1921, which is both the 'new' and the 'original' 1921. It is logically impossible that Tim should change the past by killing Grandfather in 1921. So Tim cannot kill Grandfather.

Not that past moments are special; no more can anyone change the present or the future. Present and future momentary events no more have temporal parts than past ones do. You cannot change a present or future event from what it was originally to what it is after you change it. What you *can* do is to change the present or the future from the unactualized way they would have been without some action of yours to the way they actually are. But that is not an actual change: not a difference between two successive actualities. And Tim can certainly do as much; he changes the past from the unactualized way it would have been without him to the one and only way it actually is. To "change" the past in this way, Tim need not do anything momentous; it is enough just to be there, however unobtrusively.

You know, of course, roughly how the story of Tim must go on if it is to be consistent: he somehow fails. Since Tim didn't kill Grandfather in the 'original' 1921, consistency demands that neither does he kill Grandfather in the 'new' 1921. Why not? For some commonplace reason. Perhaps some noise distracts him at the last moment, perhaps he misses despite all his target practice, perhaps his nerve fails, perhaps he even feels a pang of unaccustomed mercy. His failure by no means proves that he was not really able to kill Grandfather. We often try and fail to do what we are able to do. Success at some tasks requires not only ability but also luck, and lack of luck is not a temporary lack of ability. Suppose our other sniper, Tom, fails to kill Grandfather's partner for the same reason, whatever it is, that Tim fails to kill Grandfather. It does not follow that Tom was unable to do so.

No more does it follow in Tim's case that he was unable to do what he did not succeed in doing.

We have this seeming contradiction: '*Tim doesn't, but can, because he has what it takes*' versus '*Tim doesn't, and can't, because it's logically impossible to change the past.*' I reply that there is no contradiction. Both conclusions are true, and for the reasons given. They are compatible because 'can' is equivocal.

To say that something can happen means that its happening is compossible with certain facts. *Which* facts? That is determined, but sometimes not determined well enough, by context. An ape can't speak a human language—say, Finnish—but I can. Facts about the anatomy and operation of the ape's larynx and nervous system are not compossible with his speaking Finnish. The corresponding facts about my larynx and nervous system are compossible with my speaking Finnish. But don't take me along to Helsinki as your interpreter: I can't speak Finnish. My speaking Finnish is compossible with the facts considered so far, but not with further facts about my lack of training. What I can do, relative to one set of facts, I cannot do, relative to another, more inclusive, set. Whenever the context leaves it open which facts are to count as relevant, it is possible to equivocate about whether I can speak Finnish. It is likewise possible to equivocate about whether it is possible for me to speak Finnish, or whether I am able to, or whether I have the ability or capacity or power or potentiality to. Our many words for much the same thing are little help since they do not seem to correspond to different fixed delineations of the relevant facts.

Tim's killing Grandfather that day in 1921 is compossible with a fairly rich set of facts: the facts about his rifle, his skill and training, the unobstructed line of fire, the locked door and the absence of any chaperone to defend the past, and so on. Indeed it is compossible with all the facts of the sorts we would ordinarily count as relevant in saying what someone can do. It is compossible with all the facts corresponding to those we deem relevant in Tom's case. Relative to these facts, Tim can kill Grandfather. But his killing Grandfather is not compossible with another, more inclusive set of facts. There is the simple fact that Grandfather was not killed. Also there are various other facts about Grandfather's doings after 1921 and their effects: Grandfather begat Father in 1922 and Father begat Tim in 1949. Relative to these facts, Tim cannot kill Grandfather. He can and he can't, but under different delineations of the relevant facts. You can reasonably choose the narrower delineation, and say that he can; or the wider delineation, and say that he can't. But choose. What you mustn't do is waver, say in the same breath that he both can and can't, and then claim that this contradiction proves that time travel is impossible.

Exactly the same goes for Tom's parallel failure. For Tom to kill Grandfather's partner also is compossible with all facts of the sorts we ordinarily count as relevant, but not compossible with a larger set including, for instance, the fact that the intended victim lived until 1934. In Tom's case we are not puzzled. We say without hesitation that he can do it, because we see at once that the facts that are not compossible with his success are facts about the future of the time in question and therefore not the sort of facts we count as relevant in saying what Tom can do.

In Tim's case it is harder to keep track of which facts are relevant. We are accustomed to exclude facts about the future of the time in question, but to include some facts about its past. Our standards do not apply unequivocally to the crucial facts in this special case: Tim's failure, Grandfather's survival, and his subsequent doings. If we have foremost in mind that they lie in the external future of that moment in 1921 when Tim is almost ready to shoot, then we exclude them just as we exclude the parallel facts in Tom's case. But if we have foremost in mind that they precede that moment in Tim's extended personal time, then we tend to include them. To make the latter be foremost in your mind, I chose to tell Tim's story in the order of his personal time, rather than in the order of external time. The fact of Grandfather's survival until 1957 had already been told before I got to the part of the story about Tim lurking in ambush to kill him in 1921. We must decide, if we can, whether to treat these personally past and externally future facts as if they were straightforwardly past or as if they were straightforwardly future.

Fatalists—the best of them—are philosophers who take facts we count as irrelevant in saying what someone can do, disguise them somehow as facts of a different sort that we count as relevant, and thereby argue that we can do less than we think—indeed, that there is nothing at all that we don't do but can. I am not going to vote Republican next fall. The fatalist argues that, strange to say, I not only won't but can't; for my voting Republican is not compossible with the fact that it was true already in the year 1548 that I was not going to vote Republican 428 years later. My rejoinder is that this is a fact, sure enough; however, it is an irrelevant fact about the future masquerading as a relevant fact about the past, and so should be left out of account in saying what, in any ordinary sense, I can do. We are unlikely to be fooled by the fatalist's methods of disguise in this case, or other ordinary cases. But in cases of time travel, precognition, or the like, we're on less familiar ground, so it may take less of a disguise to fool us. Also, new methods of disguise are available, thanks to the device of personal time.

Here's another bit of fatalist trickery. Tim, as he lurks, already knows that he will fail. At least he has the wherewithal to know it if he thinks, he knows it implicitly. For he remembers that Grandfather was alive when he was a boy, he knows that those who are killed are thereafter not alive, he knows (let us suppose) that he is a time traveler who has reached the same 1921 that lies in his personal past, and he ought to understand—as we do—why a time traveler cannot change the past. What is known cannot be false. So his success is not only not compossible with facts that belong to the external future and his personal past, but also is not compossible with the present fact of his knowledge that he will fail. I reply that the fact of his foreknowledge, at the moment while he waits to shoot, is not a fact entirely about that moment. It may be divided into two parts. There is the fact that he then believes (perhaps only implicitly) that he will fail; and there is the further fact that his belief is correct, and correct not at all by accident, and hence qualifies as an item of knowledge. It is only the latter fact that is not compossible with his success, but it is only the former that is entirely about the moment in question. In calling Tim's state at that moment knowledge, not just belief, facts about personally earlier but externally later moments were smuggled into consideration.

I have argued that Tim's case and Tom's are alike, except that in Tim's case we are more tempted than usual—and with reason—to opt for a semi-fatalist mode of speech. But perhaps they differ in another way. In Tom's case, we can expect a perfectly consistent answer to the counterfactual question: what if Tom had killed Grandfather's partner? Tim's case is more difficult. If Tim had killed Grandfather, it seems offhand that contradictions would have been true. The killing both would and wouldn't have occurred. No Grandfather, no Father; no Father, no Tim; no Tim, no killing. And for good measure: no Grandfather, no family fortune; no fortune, no time machine; no time machine, no killing. So the supposition that Tim killed Grandfather seems impossible in more than the semi-fatalistic sense already granted.

If you suppose Tim to kill Grandfather and hold all the rest of his story fixed, of course you get a contradiction. But likewise if you suppose Tom to kill Grandfather's partner and hold the rest of his story fixed—including the part that told of his failure—you get a contradiction. If you make *any* counterfactual supposition and hold all else fixed you get a contradiction. The thing to do is rather to make the counterfactual supposition and hold all else as close to fixed as you consistently can. That procedure will yield perfectly consistent answers to the question: what if Tim had not killed Grandfather? In that case, some of the story I told would not have been true. Perhaps Tim might have been the time-traveling grandson of someone else. Perhaps he might have been the grandson of a man killed in 1921 and miraculously resurrected. Perhaps he might have been not a time traveler at all, but rather someone created out of nothing in 1920 equipped with false memories of a personal past that never was. It is hard to say what is the least revision of Tim's story to make it true that Tim kills Grandfather, but certainly the contradictory story in which the killing both does and doesn't occur is not the least revision. Hence it is false (according to the unrevised story) that if Tim had killed Grandfather then contradictions would have been true.

What difference would it make if Tim travels in branching time? Suppose that at the possible world of Tim's story the space-time manifold branches; the branches are separated not in time, and not in space, but in some other way. Tim travels not only in time but also from one branch to another. In one branch Tim is absent from the events of 1921; Grandfather lives; Tim is born, grows up, and vanishes in his time machine. The other branch diverges from the first when Tim turns up in 1921; there Tim kills Grandfather and Grandfather leaves no descendants and no fortune; the events of the two branches differ more and more from that time on. Certainly this is a consistent story; it is a story in which Grandfather both is and isn't killed in 1921 (in the different branches); and it is a story in which Tim, by killing Grandfather, succeeds in preventing his own birth (in one of the branches). But it is not a story in which Tim's killing of Grandfather both does occur and doesn't: it simply does, though it is located in one branch and not in the other. And it is not a story in which Tim changes the past. 1921 and later years contain the events of both branches, coexisting somehow without interaction. It remains true at all the personal times of Tim's life, even after the killing, that Grandfather lives in one branch and dies in the other.[6]

6. The present paper summarizes a series of lectures of the same title, given as the Gavin David Young Lectures in Philosophy at the University of Adelaide in July 1971. I thank the Australian–American Educational Foundation and the American Council of Learned Societies for research support. I am grateful to many friends for comments on earlier versions of this paper; especially Philip Kitcher, William Newton-Smith, J. J. C. Smart, and Donald Williams.

Study questions

1. If there were no events (that is, if nothing ever happened), would there still be time? If there were no objects, would there still be space?
2. According to the 'block universe' view, the future is as real as the past. How can such a view explain why the future is not 'fixed' in the way the past seems to be? Is this lack of 'fixity' an illusion?
3. In Chapter 39, David Lewis argues that backwards time travel is possible, and that there is a *sense* in which a backwards time traveller could kill his grandfather. How does he avoid the paradoxical consequences which seem to follow from these two claims?
4. Can there be time without change? Why does this question matter?

Further reading

Two good books to take you further in these issues about space and time are Le Poidevin (2003) and Dainton (2001), which have good introductions to some ideas in the physics of space and time too. Dainton's book also contains an excellent glossary and a list of internet resources. Le Poidevin and MacBeath (1993) is a good collection of readings, some of which are also reprinted in this Guide and Anthology. An older collection which is still useful is Gale (1968). For Aristotle's views on time, see Owen (1979), Sorabji (1988), and Bostock (1988). For the Newton/Leibniz debate, see Dainton (2001: chapters 10 and 11). The debate between the 'A' and 'B' theories of time discussed above is still very much alive. D. H. Mellor (1981, 1998) has been one of the leading defenders of the so-called 'new' theory of time: that is, the B theory that does not require that A (or 'tensed') statements be *translated* into B (or 'tenseless') terms; for a collection of papers on this issue, see Oaklander and Smith (1994). Price (1996) is a sophisticated attempt to explain the apparent 'arrow' of time from the point of view of someone who believes in the 'block universe'. One view not discussed in any detail in this Guide and Anthology is *presentism*: the view that only the present is real. For some discussions of presentism, see Lowe (2002: 42–3) and Percival (2002).

Part VIII

Identity

Introduction

1. Introduction

THE philosophical problems of identity have deep links with a number of the other areas of this book: universals, through the idea of sameness and difference of kind; being, through the idea of what are the most fundamental things which remain through change; mind and body, through the idea of the identity theory of mind and body; and time, through the idea of sameness and difference over time. Our concern in this chapter will largely be with the last of these; and with the problem of personal identity as a special case of the problem of change. We will also look at the question of the relationship between a thing and its parts at a time.

These traditional problems only have a distant connection with questions about one's own 'identity' as these might arise in everyday life: that is, one's racial, social, or sexual identity. Questions of identity in this sense are really questions about one's most important properties or relations, those properties (determining sexual orientation, for example) or relations (to a social group, for example) which are most important in determining who one is. Whatever philosophical problems arise with the notion of one's identity in this sense do not fall within the scope of traditional metaphysics.

2. The features of identity

In his *Tractatus*, Wittgenstein said, 'to say of *two* things that they are identical is nonsense, and to say of *one* thing that it is identical with itself is to say nothing at all' (Wittgenstein 1921: 5.5303). Some philososphers have seen this fact as indicating why there is no real problem of identity. David Lewis, for example, writes:

Identity is utterly simple and unproblematic. Everything is identical to itself; nothing is ever identical to anything else except itself. There is never any problem about what makes something identical to itself; nothing can ever fail to be. And there is never any problem about what makes two things identical; two things can never be identical. (Lewis 1986*b*: 192–3)

It is true that identity is, in a certain way, a very simple concept. Identity statements—claims about the identity of things—are often very easy to understand. Let's take a simple example. The original name of the English novelist George Eliot was 'Mary Ann Evans'. Now since the English word 'is' is used to express other ideas than identity (as in 'The Pope is Catholic', where it is the 'is' of predication), we shall use the '=' sign to indicate that what is being expressed is identity. We can then express the true identity claim thus: 'Mary Ann Evans = George Eliot'. The relation expressed by the '=' sign can be characterized in terms of certain distinguishing logical features: symmetry, reflexivity, transitivity, and being governed by what is known as *Leibniz's Law of the Indiscernibility of Identicals*. Box VIII.2 describes the first three of these logical features of the relation of identity. What is of interest to us here is Leibniz's Law. This says that if any objects *A* and *B* are identical, then whatever is true of *A* is true of *B* (that is, they are indiscernible).

Box VIII.1. The ship of Theseus

Theseus was a warrior of ancient Greek legend. Thomas Hobbes (1655) tells the story that after Theseus died, his ship was placed in the harbour in Athens to honour his memory. As time went on, parts of the ship started to decay and had to be replaced by new parts. Eventually, all the original parts of the ship were replaced. No problem, we might say: Theseus' ship still exists, and is lying in the harbour. After all, we think that an object can survive gradual change in its parts. But suppose now that the old parts of the ship were collected together in a warehouse, and assembled (in their admittedly fragile state) in exactly the same arrangement as they had in the original ship. Now there are two ships. We seemed to have already agreed that Theseus' ship is in the harbour, on the grounds that an object can survive a gradual replacement of its parts. But we should also agree that an artefact can be dismantled and reassembled in another place. Applying this idea to the case of the ship, it seems we should conclude that the ship in the warehouse is Theseus' ship. So we seem to have a reason to think that each ship is Theseus' ship. But this cannot be right; how can two ships be the same as one ship? So which one is the real ship of Theseus? (See Lowe 2002: 25–40 for further discussion.)

This law must be distinguished from the thesis of the Identity of Indiscernibles, also defended by Leibniz and also sometimes called 'Leibniz's Law'. The Identity of Indiscernibles says that if objects A and B have all the same properties, then A and B are identical. Although this might seem like an obvious truth at first sight, it is actually quite controversial for reasons which we discuss elsewhere (see the discussion in Part III: Being, section 6).

What we—following most contemporary philosophers—are calling 'Leibniz's Law' is something which should be quite uncontroversial. For if George Eliot really is the very same person as Mary Ann Evans, then how could something be true of Eliot which is not true of Evans? If George Eliot wrote *Middlemarch* then it follows from Leibniz's Law and the fact that Mary Ann Evans = George Eliot that Mary Ann Evans wrote *Middlemarch*. Of course it does: for 'they' are the same person.

It is helpful to distinguish Leibniz's Law, formulated in this way—'if A = B then whatever is true of A is true of B'—from a related but distinct principle which says that if two names refer to the same object, then they can always be substituted for one another without altering the truth or falsehood of sentences in which they occur. This principle (sometimes called 'the substitutivity of co-referring singular terms') does not seem to be generally true. Consider, for example, the fact that some people have read George Eliot's books under the false impression that she is a man. Such people, ignorant of the identity of George Eliot with Mary Ann Evans, would surely not thereby believe that

Mary Ann Evans is a man. So the sentence,

  'Some people believe that George Eliot is a man.'

can be true, while the sentence,

  'Some people believe that Mary Ann Evans is a man.'

is false. Yet the sentences differ only in containing the co-referring names 'George Eliot' and 'Mary Ann Evans'. So how can one be true and the other false? There seems to be a problem, then, with substituting co-referring names within sentences containing (for example) words like 'believes that . . . '. (This is sometimes called 'Frege's puzzle of identity': see Wiggins 1976; also Salmon 1986.)

But this problem does not touch Leibniz's Law, properly understood. For since Mary Ann Evans = George Eliot, it is true *of* Eliot that some people believed she was a man, and it is equally true *of* Evans. Leibniz's Law is not a controversial thesis, but surely one of the essential characteristics of the concept of identity. (As Frege said, 'this explanation of Leibniz's could be called an axiom that brings out the nature of the relation of identity; as such it is fundamentally important'. Quoted in Wiggins 2001: 27.) Identity, so characterized in terms of symmetry, reflexivity, transitivity, and Leibniz's Law, seems to be the paradigm of a fundamental logical concept. So what can anyone mean when they say that there are philosophical problems of identity?

3. Leibniz's Law and the problem of change

The problem arises when we begin to reflect on the obvious fact that things change. Consider a simple case: a metal bar, call it *B*, is hot yesterday, and cools down so that it is cold today. Intuitively, it is the very same (i.e. *identical*) thing, *B*, which is hot yesterday and cold today. But being hot and being cold are incompatible properties: nothing can be both hot and cold. Yet Leibniz's Law implies that if *B* today = *B* yesterday, then if *B* is cold today then *B* is cold yesterday; and if *B* is hot yesterday so is *B* today. Genuine identicals must be indiscernible. So how then can anything change and remain the same thing? (See Box VIII.1: The Ship of Theseus.)

Before considering the possible solutions to this ancient problem, let's just clarify what we mean here by *change*. When an object changes, a predicate (like 'is cold') is true of it which was not previously true of it. But the mere idea of a predicate's coming to be true of something does not capture our idea of change, since a predicate can come to be true of something when it has not changed in any way. When you first discovered that the number *pi* was irrational, for example, the predicate '*x* is thought by you to be irrational' comes to be true of *pi*. But surely the number *pi* has not changed at all; indeed, if numbers exist at all, they cannot change. At best what we have here is what has been called 'mere Cambridge change' (see Part VII: Time and Space, section 3) of which real change is a species. What real change involves is the gaining or losing of an object's *intrinsic* properties, those properties it has in and of itself, as opposed to its *relational* properties, those properties it has because of its relationships to other things. An object's mass is an intrinsic property, for instance, and a change in an object's mass is a paradigm case of real change. An object's position in time, by contrast, seems to be a paradigmatic example of a relation or a relational property, and a change in an object's position in time does not seem to be a real change in the object (for more on the notion of intrinsic properties, see Part IV: Universals and Particulars). Relations and relational properties raise interesting questions of their own, and some changes in relations can be real changes, but we have enough trouble dealing with change in intrinsic properties, so we will concentrate on this. Our problem here is about how an object can remain the same while changing its *intrinsic* properties, and for this reason David Lewis calls it 'the problem of temporary intrinsics' (Chapter 41). But we shall continue to call it 'the problem of change'.

The problem of change involves three assumptions, which it will be convenient to name:

1. *Change*: an object can have an intrinsic property *F* at one time and not have *F* at another time.
2. *Identity across time*: the same identical object can exist in its entirety at different times.
3. *Leibniz's Law*: if *A* = *B*, whatever *A* and *B* are, then whatever is true of *A* is true of *B* and vice versa.

Our metal bar has the intrinsic property of being hot, at one time, and the intrinsic property of being not hot, at another time (*Change*); it is the same entire bar which exists at both times (*Identity across time*); given these two assumptions, the conflict with Leibniz's Law is obvious. If the bar at the earlier time is hot, and is identical with the bar at the later time, then according to Leibniz's Law the bar at the later time should be hot. But it is not, so how can it be identical with the bar at the earlier time? It looks as if one of (1)–(3) should be given up. But which?

Can *Change* be denied? Recent philosophy provides us with two radical ways of denying it. In Chapter 40, Roderick Chisholm argues that, strictly speaking, material objects cannot survive change in their properties. The important phrase here is 'strictly speaking'. Chisholm follows the eighteenth century philosopher Bishop Butler in distinguishing identity in the 'loose and popular' sense from identity in the 'strict and philosophical' sense. In the strict and philosophical sense expressed by Leibniz's Law, no object can be *F* and not-*F*. Here Chisholm grasps the nettle and accepts that in this sense objects do not change; when an object loses a property, it ceases to exist. (Similarly, when an object loses a part, it ceases to exist. The theory of parts and wholes is called *mereology*. Hence Chisholm's view about an object and its parts is known as *mereological essentialism*: the view that an object's parts are essential to it.)

But although he denies that one object can really undergo change, Chisholm maintains that one can carry on *talking* as if there is one object existing over time, since it is convenient to do so; and he gives an account of how 'successive entities' (*entia successiva*) may be related in a way that mimics genuine identity over time. Using a phrase of Hume's, Chisholm says that we 'may feign identity when what we are dealing with is in fact only a succession of related objects'.

The second radical solution is to give up *Change* by giving up its implicit assumption that objects *exist* at more than one time, whether they change or not. This is the *presentist* view that only the present is real, or exists (see Part VII: Time and Space, section 4). Since, according to presentism, the past and the future do not exist, neither do any objects exist in the past and the future. All objects exist only in the present, and since no object has incompatible properties in the present, no object has incompatible properties when it exists. If presentism is true, then the problem disappears.

But presentism is a very radical view. It says the past and future have no reality at all. Yet there are clearly truths about the past—for example, that we were born—and about the future—for example, that we will die. What makes these truths true, if not facts about the past and the present? Another question which the presentist has to answer is when exactly the present is: how long does it last? It seems that as soon as we try and refer to the present, it ends up disappearing 'into' the past.

Lewis's approach, in Chapter 41, is to deny *Identity across time* (as defined above). Instead of thinking of the whole metal bar as being the thing to which the properties of hotness and coldness belong, Lewis instead argues that these properties actually belong to *parts* of the bar. The bar *yesterday* is what is hot, and the bar *today* is what is cold; and on Lewis's view the bar yesterday and the bar today are parts of the whole bar, which is extended across its whole life in space *and* time. The bar yesterday and the bar today are *temporal parts* of the bar. And just as there is no problem with the bar being cold at one of its spatial parts (say, at one end) and hot at another, there is no problem with the idea that it might be cold at one of its temporal parts and hot at another. Since it is not being claimed that one thing is both hot and cold at the same time and place, the problem disappears.

Lewis describes his approach in terminology which has now become standard (the terminology comes from Johnston (1987*b*)). Say that things *persist* when they exist at more than one time. Then there are two ways for something to persist: either by existing in their entirety at each moment, which Lewis calls 'enduring'; or by being extended across space–time, and at each moment a spatio-temporal part of the object existing. This he calls 'perduring'. The endurance approach to the problem of persistence treats objects as three-dimensional entities, extended across the three spatial dimensions. The perdurance approach treats objects as four-dimensional entities, extended across space and time. Hence the perdurance approach is sometimes called 'four-dimensionalism' (see Sider 2001; the idea derives from Quine 1961*b*; see Part VII: Time and Space, for the idea of a dimension). Four-dimensionalism about objects is distinct from four-dimensionalism about space and time. One could believe in the four-dimensionalist view of space–time without believing that objects are four-dimensional entities (see Mellor 1981: chapter 8). The distinctive feature of four-dimensionalism about objects (or perdurance) is that objects have temporal parts.

These are the proposed solutions to the problem of change which involve giving up *Change* and *Identity across time*. But if we cannot be persuaded to give up these assumptions, what should we say? Can we give up Leibniz's Law? Surely not. To think that something could be true of *A* but not true of *B* when *A just is B* is mind-boggling. If we gave up Leibniz's Law, essential as it is to the notion of identity, then it would cease to be clear what it is that we are holding on to when we say that *Identity across time* is true. But perhaps there are other options.

Perhaps we should take more seriously into account the time at which properties are had. One way to do this is to say that the kinds of properties we are talking about— properties that an object can have or lack throughout its life—are 'time-indexed': that is, they are only ever had *at a time*, so specifying what properties a thing has should involve specifying when it has them. Another way of saying the same kind of thing is to say that all (temporary) properties are really *relations* to times: to say that the bar is hot today is not really to ascribe to it an intrinsic property *hotness*, but to say that it stands in the relation *being hot at* to a time, namely yesterday. (This is discussed by Lewis in Chapter 41 and also by Merricks 1994.) The essence of this solution is that the bar's being *hot-at-time t* and *cold-at-time t + 1* are not really conflicting properties, so it is not the case that something is true of the bar yesterday which is not true of it today.

The difficulty with this approach is that it while attempting to *account* for real change, it actually seems to *eliminate* it. For we previously said that real change was something having a property at one time and not having it at another. However, if properties are essentially 'time-indexed' in this kind of way, then it is not true that objects which change come to lack the very same properties which they previously had. For if the heat of the bar is really *being-hot-at-t*, then the bar does not come to lack this property: for today (*t + 1*) it is equally true that the bar has the property of *being-hot-at-t*. And it will always have *this* property. So it looks as if this approach to the problem ends up denying *Change* after all. (For an alternative way of relating identity to time, see Gallois 2003.)

4. The problem develops: parts and wholes

In any case, whatever moves we make to defend this approach, it seems that bringing in a reference to the time at which a property is had will not solve all the problems of identity. In particular, it does not help with the problem of how an object is related to its parts, and how it can survive the loss of its parts. This problem has been vividly presented in an argument of Peter van Inwagen's (1981). (A similar kind of argument was originally raised by Geach 1962, in defence of his thesis of 'relative identity', and discussed *inter alia* by Wiggins 1980 and Lowe 1989.) We will briefly expound this argument here; it has connections with the discussion of substance in Part III: Being.

Consider a particular human body—which we shall simply call 'Body'—on a particular day, say Monday. Body has as one of its parts its left hand. Now consider the rest of Body on Monday, considered apart from its left hand. We can call this 'Body-minus-its-left-hand' or 'Body-minus' for short. Body-minus is that piece of matter consisting of Body minus its left hand. It is plain that

(1) Body on Monday ≠ Body-minus

since Body has a hand and Body-minus does not. Now suppose that on Tuesday, Body's left hand is amputated. Body still exists, we want to say; it has only lost its left hand. It is natural to insist that Body is still the numerically same object after the amputation; that is,

(2) Body on Monday = Body on Tuesday

But it seems that Body on Tuesday is the same thing as Body-minus, since that was defined as Body minus its left hand, and that is what Body on Tuesday seems to be,

Box VIII.2. The logical properties of identity

Identity is normally considered to be a relation (see Part IV: Universals and Particulars). If it is a relation, then it is different from many other relations. For many relations (e.g. *being taller*) hold between at least two things, whereas we know that identity only holds between a thing and itself. If A and B are two objects, then 'A = B' is false. But there are other relations which *can* hold between a thing and itself: a vain man can admire himself, for example.

Symmetry, reflexivity, and transitivity are among the most important logical properties of relations. Suppose R is a relation, a, b, and c are related objects, and a sentence of the form 'aRb' says that a bears relation R to b. Then we can describe these three important properties as follows:

Reflexivity: aRa

Symmetry: if aRb then bRa

Transitivity: if aRb and bRc then aRc

Some relations have some of these properties, some have them all, some have none. The relation of *loving*, for example, is neither symmetrical, reflexive, nor transitive. If Anthony loves Cleopatra, then it does not *follow* that Cleopatra loves Anthony, even if it is true (loving is not symmetrical); if Anthony loves Cleopatra, then it does not follow that Anthony loves Anthony or that Cleopatra loves Cleopatra (loving is not reflexive); and if Anthony loves Cleopatra and Cleopatra loves Caesar, then it does not follow that Anthony loves Caesar (loving is not transitive). Other relations have some but not all of these properties: *being taller*, for example, is transitive, but not reflexive or symmetrical.

Identity is reflexive, transitive, and symmetrical. Any relation with all these three properties is called an *equivalence relation*. There are other equivalence relations apart from identity: *having the same biological father* as someone else is an equivalence relation, for example.

too. So:

(3) Body on Tuesday = Body-minus.

But (2), (3), and the transitivity of identity (see Box VIII.2) imply

(4) Body on Monday = Body-minus,

which contradicts our assumption (1).

This argument is very worrying for someone who believes in endurance, since it is based on what seem to be (at first sight) very innocuous assumptions. And notice that it would not help to say that properties are 'time-indexed'—even if we originally found a solution of that kind plausible. There is no room for this solution here. Some other solution is needed.

Van Inwagen's own solution is that Body-minus does not exist. But Body-minus is just the 'complement' of Body's left hand; so if Body's left hand exists, then isn't it arbitrary to say that Body-minus does not exist? Van Inwagen agrees, and concludes that Body's left hand does not exist either! Van Inwagen later developed the radical view that the only material beings which exist are organisms and fundamental particles (see Van Inwagen 1990 and see Part III: Being). In the context of this view, it is easy to understand why he can say that Body exists, because Body is an organism (for a somewhat similar view to Van Inwagen's see Merricks 2001).

Another solution is to deny (2): Body on Monday is not identical to Body on Tuesday. One could deny (2) because one thought, for Chisholm's reasons, that no material entities can maintain their identity (in the 'strict and philosophical sense') if they change. Or one could deny it for Lewis's 'perdurantist' reasons: Body on Monday is not identical to Body on Tuesday because they are distinct temporal parts of the four-dimensional entity which Body actually is. (For critical discussion of temporal parts, see Thomson 1983 and Lowe 2002: chapter 4.)

The assumption (2) which is challenged here embodies our commonsensical assumptions *Change* or *Identity across time*. Is there a response to the puzzle which can retain (2) and therefore these common-sense beliefs? Since the unacceptable conclusion, (4), follows from the transitivity of identity and (2) and (3), then it looks as if the only option is to give up (3). (Denying transitivity should really be a last resort.) In other words, Body on Tuesday is not identical with Body-minus. At first sight, this seems crazy. After all, Body on Tuesday occupies exactly the same region of space as Body-minus, it is made of the same matter, and it has all the same parts. So what can it mean to say they are distinct?

The defender of this view will respond that part of what it means is that Body and Body-minus have different *persistence conditions*: that is, what it takes for Body to continue to exist is different from what it takes for Body-minus to continue to exist. Suppose we cut off Body-minus's right hand. Then, on this view, Body continues to exist, but Body-minus ceases to exist, since Body-minus was defined as that piece of matter consisting of Body minus its left hand (and this includes the right hand). So something is true of Body—it can survive the loss of its right hand—which is not true of Body-minus, so by Leibniz's Law they are distinct. The idea behind this approach is that entities of certain kinds have persistence conditions appropriate to things of those kinds (see Lowe 1989, Wiggins 1980). It is in the nature of organisms, like Body, to persist throughout the loss of their parts; whereas made-up (or 'gerrymandered') entities like Body-minus do not have such conditions. This view involves a return to an Aristotelian view of secondary substances, natural kinds which contain within themselves the principles of their own persistence (see Part III: Being, section 5). However, the inescapable consequence of the view is that two distinct objects (albeit objects of different kinds) can be in the same place at the same time. And some find this hard to accept (see Burke 1994, Gibbard 1975).

5. Personal identity

Chisholm's solution to the problem of change, as we saw, was to deny that in the 'strict and philosophical sense' any material object can change its properties. We might be happy with this solution—'OK, nothing *really* is the same from day to day, but the *entia successiva* are similar enough to be grouped together as the same thing for all practical purposes'—except when we come to consider our own identity. The problem of identity over time applies equally to us: how can *we* persist through change? Yet it seems unacceptable to treat persons as conglomerations of *entia successiva*. Surely there is a real unity which underlies our continued existence?

Chisholm agrees. He argues elsewhere that persons or people persist through change by retaining their identity (Chisholm 1976). A consequence of this, for Chisholm, is that persons are not material beings. But our ordinary conception of persons treats them as material beings. That is, we normally think of ourselves as embodied creatures with physical and biological properties (call them bodily properties) as well as thoughts, feelings, and emotions. Which of these kinds of properties—the bodily or the psychological—are most important in determining the identity of persons over time?

The problem of personal identity has revolved around this question. For it seems that there can be cases—real or imaginary—where one's bodily properties can change radically and one's psychological properties can stay the same, or where one's psychological properties can change radically and one's bodily properties stay the same (see below for some examples). Which criteria—bodily or psychological—are the criteria which determine a person's identity? Notice that the issue here is not about materialism *versus* dualism (see Part IX: Mind and Body). Of course, one could have a dualist conception of the person (see Swinburne 1984) which would imply the priority of the psychological criterion; but this does not mean that a materialist view of persons would have to choose the bodily criterion. For the materialist has to decide whether what determines a person's identity over time is the sameness of their body or the psychological characteristics embodied in their brain. Hence the choice between bodily and psychological criteria is not settled by choosing materialism; and this is illustrated by the fact that most discussions of personal identity in the late twentieth century assumed materialism, but did not assume that materialism by itself solves the problem.

One materialist theory which takes the bodily criterion of personal identity very seriously is the *animalist* theory defended by David Wiggins (1980, 2001) and Paul Snowdon (Chapter 43). The heart of the animalist theory is the apparently obvious claim that we can call express by saying 'I am an animal, of the species *homo sapiens*'. If this is true, then the conditions for our continued existence (our persistence conditions) are the conditions for the continued existence of these particular animals. Snowdon recognizes that the biggest challenge to this view come from a famous style of thought-experiment involving imaginary brain transfers. A simple version goes as follows: suppose that your brain is put into the living body of another person, *X*, and *X*'s brain goes into your body. Where would you be then? Many philosophers have argued that in a case like this, you and *X* would have 'swapped bodies': you would now be where *X*'s body is, and *X* would be where your body is. The reason behind this judgement is that your identity resides in your psychological characteristics, and your psychological characteristics are based in your brain. Hence, where your brain goes, there you go, too.

Snowdon responds by arguing that despite the intuitive pull of this conclusion, there are also strong arguments in favour of the alternative that I am an animal. Therefore, at the very least what we have here are two conflicting opinions, creating an antinomy or paradox, and not a knock-down argument in favour of the psychological view of personal identity.

Snowdon then goes on to defend the animalist line, and draws some general conclusions about the nature of this debate; though he recognizes that there is no simple dismissal of the psychological response to the brain-transplant thought-experiment (see Olson 1997 for a different defence of animalism).

Like many philosophers (e.g. Johnston 1987a), Snowdon is attempting to redefine the terms of what has become an intractable debate. A similar attempt was made in a very influential paper by Derek Parfit (Chapter 42). Parfit argued that the problems of personal identity can be resolved by shifting our attention away from the question, 'will I be identical with A or B?', and onto another question, 'what is it that *matters* most to us in our continued existence?' Parfit uses a version of the brain-transplant thought-experiment where a person apparently *divides*, rather than just having its brain moved into another body. (This version is called a 'fission' case, and is in many ways analogous to the case of the Ship of Theseus: see Box VIII.1.)

Suppose a person A divides into two others, B and C (see Parfit's paper for a description of how such division might come about). B and C are, at the time of the division, indistinguishable. The question then is: is A identical with either of the resulting people, B and C? Because identity is a one–one relation (one thing cannot be identical with two) A cannot be identical with both. But since B and C are indistinguishable in their qualities, there is no basis on which to say that A is identical with one rather than the other. So it looks as if A is identical with neither. Or at the very least, it looks as if we cannot *determine* whether A is identical with B or C. Maybe there is some fact of the matter about A's continued identity which we can never know. But it seems as if we have already taken into account any facts which could determine A's identity when we told the story; so A's identity on this conception would be a very mysterious 'further fact'. To say that A is identical with B or C, but we do not know which, sounds rather implausible (though it does have its defenders: see Chisholm 1976).

So suppose we do agree with Parfit that A is identical with neither B nor C. Does this mean that A fails to survive the fission in any sense? Only if, Parfit argues, survival presupposes identity. He then makes a case that it does not: A can survive as B *and* as C. Survival, unlike identity, can be a one–many relation (one thing can survive as many others), and Parfit says that what should matter to us in a case like this is the continuity of our psychological traits, our thoughts and intentions and so on. The continuity of these does not presuppose identity. So identity should not matter to us.

One way to see the plausibility of Parfit's case is to ask yourself whether fission would be as bad as death for you. Suppose you had the choice between painless fission and painless obliteration. Would you be indifferent between these two options? If you would prefer fission, then it seems that you think fission is not as bad for you as death. And if it is not as bad as death, then maybe this is because it *is not* death: something of you is surviving. However, it should be noted that it is controversial to draw substantial metaphysical conclusions from these imaginary cases; we should also consider the ways in which the conclusions we draw depend on how the stories are told (Williams 1973: chapter 4). And the defender of personal identity over time will resist the suggestion that the only reason that fission might be preferable to death is that one person can survive as two; for on their view, fission, unlike death, at least gives you a 50 per cent *chance* of surviving as the same identical person.

Chapter 40

Identity through time

Roderick M. Chisholm

> *The identity of a person is a perfect identity; wherever it is real, it admits of no degrees; and it is impossible that a person should be in part the same, and in part different . . . For this cause, I have first considered personal identity, as that which is perfect in its kind, and the natural measure of that which is imperfect.*
>
> Thomas Reid[1]

1. The Ship of Theseus

To understand the philosophical problems involved in persistence, in the fact that one and the same thing may endure through a period of time, we will begin with what Reid would have called the 'imperfect' cases and remind ourselves of some ancient philosophical puzzles. One such puzzle is suggested by the familiar dictum of Heraclitus: 'You could not step twice in the same river; for other and yet other waters are ever flowing on.'[2] Another is the problem of the Ship of Theseus.[3]

Updating the latter problem somewhat, let us imagine a ship—the Ship of Theseus—that was made entirely of wood when it came into being. One day a wooden plank is cast off and replaced by an aluminum one. Since the change is only slight, there is no question as to the survival of the Ship of Theseus. We still have the ship we had before; that is to say, the ship that we have now is identical with the ship we had before. On another day, another wooden plank is cast off and also replaced by an aluminum one. Still the same ship, since, as before, the change is only slight. The changes continue, in a similar way, and finally the Ship of Theseus is made entirely of aluminum. The aluminum ship, one may well argue, *is* the wooden ship

1. Thomas Reid, *Essays on the Intellectual Powers of Man*, essay III, ch. 14 in Sir William Hamilton (ed.), *The Works of Thomas Reid, D. D.* (Edinburgh: Maclachlan & Stewart, 1854), p. 345.
2. Fragment 41–2, as translated in Milton C. Nahm, *Selections from Early Greek Philosophy* (New York: F. S. Crofts, 1934), p. 91.
3. See Plato, *Phaedo*, 58A, and Xenophon, *Memorabilia*, 4. 8. 2. Leibniz speaks of the Ship of Theseus in *New Essays Concerning Human Understanding*, II, ch. 27, sect. 4, noting that any ordinary physical body may be said to be 'like a river which always changes its water, or like the ship of Theseus which the Athenians were always repairing' (Open Court edn), p. 240.

538 RODERICK M. CHISHOLM

we started with, for the ship we started with survived each particular change, and identity, after all, is transitive.

But what happened to the discarded wooden planks? Consider this possibility, suggested by Thomas Hobbes: 'If some man had kept the old planks as they were taken out, and by putting them afterwards together in the same order, had again made a ship of them, this, without doubt, had also been the same numerical ship with that which was at the beginning; and so there would have been two ships numerically the same, which is absurd.'[4] Assuming, as perhaps one has no right to do, that each of the wooden planks survived intact throughout these changes, one might well argue that the reassembled wooden ship *is* the ship we started with. 'After all, it is made up of the very same parts, standing in the very same relations, whereas that ugly aluminum object doesn't have a single part in common with our original ship.'

To compound the problem still further, let us suppose that the captain of the original ship had solemnly taken the vow that, if his ship were ever to go down, he would go down with it. What, now, if the two ships collide at sea and he sees them start to sink together? Where does his duty lie—with the aluminum ship or with the reassembled wooden ship?

'The carriage' is another ancient version of the problem. Socrates and Plato change the parts of their carriages piece by piece until, finally, Socrates' original carriage is made up of all the parts of Plato's carriage and Plato's carriage is made up of all the parts of Socrates' original carriage. Have they exchanged their carriages or not, and if so, at what point?

Perhaps the essence of the problem is suggested by an even simpler situation. Consider a child playing with his blocks. He builds a house with ten blocks, uses it as a garrison for his toy soldiers, disassembles it, builds many other things, then builds a house again, with each of the ten blocks occupying the position it had occupied before, and he uses it again as a garrison for his soldiers. Was the house that was destroyed the same as the one that subsequently came into being?

These puzzles about the persistence of objects through periods of time have their analogues for the extension of objects through places in space. Consider the river that is known in New Orleans as 'the Mississippi'. Most of us would say that the source of the river is in northern Minnesota. But what if one were to argue instead that the source is in Montana, where it is known as 'the Missouri'? Or that its source is in Pittsburgh, where it is known as 'the Ohio', or that its source is farther back where it is called 'the Allegheny', or in still another place where it is called 'the Monongahela'?[5]

The accompanying diagram (Fig. 1) provides us with a schematic illustration.

Of the river that has its central point at (d), one might wonder whether it flows south-easterly from (a), or due south from (b), or south-westerly from (c). (For

4. Thomas Hobbes, *Concerning Body*, ch. 11 ('Of identity and difference'), sect. 7.
5. Cf. W. V. Quine: 'Thus take the question of the biggest fresh lake. Is Michigan–Huron admissible, or is it a pair of lakes? . . . Then take the question of the longest river. Is the Mississippi–Missouri admissible, or is it a river and a half?' (*Word and Object* (New York: John Wiley, 1960), p. 128).

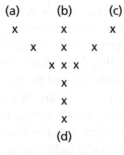

Figure 1

simplicity, we ignore the Allegheny and the Monongahela.) If we are puzzled about the beginning of the Mississippi, we should be equally puzzled about the end of the Rhine. Reading our diagram from bottom to top (and again oversimplifying), we could say that if the Rhine begins at (d), then it ends either with the Maas at (a), or with the Waal at (b), or with the Lek at (c).[6]

Perhaps we can imagine three philosophers looking down at the river(s) that end(s) at (*d*). One insists that the river flows between (*a*) and (*d*), another that it flows between (*b*) and (*d*) and the third that it flows between (*c*) and (*d*); and each insists that, since the arms (or tributaries) to which the other two philosophers refer are distinct not only from each other but from the river itself, neither of the other two can be right. Their dispute, clearly, would be analogous in significant respects to the problem of the Ship of Theseus.

What are we to say of such puzzles? We might follow the extreme course that Carneades took and simply deny the principle of the transitivity of identity.[7] In other words, we might say that things identical with the same thing need not be identical with each other. But if we thus abandon reason and logic at the very outset, we will have no way of deciding at the end what is the most reasonable thing to say about ourselves and *our* persistence through time.

We might be tempted to deny the possibility of alteration. Thus one could say: 'Strictly speaking, nothing alters—nothing is such that at one time it has one set of properties and at another time it has another set of properties. What happens is, rather, that at one time there is a thing having the one set of properties and at the other time there is another thing having the other set of properties.' But this supposition, if

6. Using terms not commonly applied to rivers, we may note for future reference that when our diagram is read from top to bottom it illustrates *fusion* and when it is read from bottom to top it illustrates *fission*.

7. See note c of the article 'Carneades' in Pierre Bayle's *A General Dictionary: Historical and Critical*, trans. Rev. J. P. Bernard, Rev. Thomas Birch, John Lockeman et al. (10 vols, London: James Bettenham, 1734–41): 'He found uncertainty in the most evident notions. All logicians know that the foundation of the syllogism, and consequently the faculty of reasoning, is built on this maxim: Those things which are identical with a third are the same with each other (*Quae sunt idem uno tertio sunt idem inter se*). It is certain that Carneades opposed it strongly and displayed all his subtleties against it.'

we apply it to ourselves, is inconsistent with the data with which we have begun. Each of us knows with respect to himself that he now has properties he didn't have in the past and that formerly he had properties he doesn't have now. ('But a thing x isn't identical with a thing y unless they have all their properties in common. And if the present you has one set of properties and the past you another, how can they be the same thing?') The answer is, of course, that there aren't two you's, a present one having one set of properties and a past one having another. It is rather that you *are* now such that you have these properties and lack those, whereas formerly you *were* such that you had those properties and lacked these. The 'former you' *has* the same properties that the 'present you' now has, and the 'present you' *had* the same properties that the 'former you' then had.[8]

Bishop Butler suggested that it is only in 'a loose and popular sense' that we may speak of the persistence of such familiar things as ships, plants and houses. And he contrasted this 'loose and popular sense' with 'the strict and philosophical sense' in which we may speak of the persistence of *persons*.[9] Let us consider these suggestions.

2. Playing loose with the 'Is' of identity

We will not pause to ask what Butler meant in fact. Let us ask what he could have meant. He suggested that there is a kind of looseness involved when we say that such things as the Ship of Theseus persist through time. What kind of looseness is this?

It could hardly be that the Ship of Theseus, in contrast with other things, is only loosely identical with itself. Surely one cannot say that, while some things are only loosely identical with themselves, other things are tightly identical with themselves.[10] The statement 'This thing is more loosely identical with itself than that thing', if it says anything at all, tells us only that the first thing is more susceptible than the second to loss of identity, and this means only that the first is more readily perishable than the second.

---

8. Further aspects of this kind of problem are discussed in Roderick M. Chisholm, *Person and Object* (La Salle, Ill.: Open Court, 1976), Appendix A ('The Doctrine of Temporal Parts').

9. Dissertation 1, in *The Whole Works of Joseph Butler, LL.D.* (London: Thomas Tegg, 1839), pp. 263–70. But compare Locke's third letter to the Bishop of Worcester: 'For it being his body both before and after the resurrection, everyone ordinarily speaks of his body as the same, though, in a strict and philosophical sense, as your lordship speaks, it be not the very same.'

10. I have heard it suggested, however, that (a) whereas the evening star is strictly identical with the evening star, nevertheless (b) the evening star is identical but not strictly identical with the morning star. The facts of the matter would seem to be only these: the evening star (i.e., the morning star) is necessarily self-identical; it is not necessarily such that it is visible in the evening or in the morning; it would be contradictory to say that the evening star exists and is not identical with the evening star, or that the morning star exists and is not identical with the morning star; but it would not be contradictory to say that the morning star exists and the evening star exists and the morning star is not identical with the evening star; and whatever is identical with the evening star (i.e., with the morning star) has all the properties that it does.

We should construe Butler's remark as saying, not that there is a loose kind of identity, but rather that there is a loose sense of 'identity'—a loose (and popular) use of the 'is' of identity.

What would be a *loose* sense of 'A is B', or 'A is identical with B'—a sense of 'A is B' which is consistent with a denial of the *strict* sense of 'A is B'? I suggest this: we use the locution 'A is B', or 'A is identical with B', in a *loose* sense, if we use it in such a way that it is consistent with saying 'A has a certain property that B does not have' or 'Some things are true of A that aren't true of B'.

Do we ever use the locution 'A is B' in this loose way? It would seem, unfortunately, that we do.

I will single out five different types of such misuse.

(1) One may say: 'Route 6 is Point Street in Providence and is Fall River Avenue in Seekonk.' Here we would seem to have the 'is' of identity, since it is followed in each occurrence by a term ('Point Street' and 'Fall River Avenue') and not by a predicate expression. But since Point Street and Fall River Avenue have different properties (one is in Providence and not in Seekonk, and the other is in Seekonk and not in Providence), the statement may be said to play loose with 'is'.

As our brief discussion of the rivers may make clear, this use of 'is' is readily avoided. We have only to replace 'is' by 'is part of' and then switch around the terms, as in: 'Point Street in Providence is part of Route 6 and Fall River Avenue in Seekonk is part of Route 6.' Or we could also say, of course: 'Point Street is part of Route 6 in Providence and Fall River Avenue is part of Route 6 in Seekonk.'[11]

(2) One may say 'This train will be two trains after Minneapolis', or, traveling in the other direction, 'Those two trains will be one train after Minneapolis'. In the first case ('fission'), we are not saying that there is one thing which will subsequently be identical with two things. We are saying, rather, that there is one thing which will be divided into two things, neither of them being identical with the original thing, but each of them being a part of the original thing. And in the second case ('fusion'), we are not saying that there are two things which are subsequently to become identical with each other, or with a third thing. We are saying rather that there are two things which will both become parts of a third thing. (Why not cite an amoeba as an instance of 'fission'? There is the offchance that amoebas are persons, or at least may be thought to be persons, and in such a case, as we shall see, our treatment would have to be somewhat different.)

11. This example of the roads, like that of the rivers above ('the Mississippi–Missouri'), may suggest that the key to our puzzles about identity through time may be found in the doctrine of 'temporal parts'. According to this doctrine, every individual thing x is such that, for every period of time through which x exists, there is a set of parts which are such that x is made up of them at that time and they do not exist at any other time. (Compare: every individual thing x is such that, for every portion of space that x occupies at any time, there is at that time a set of parts of x which then occupy that place and no other place.) I consider this doctrine in detail in *Person and Object*, Appendix A. I there conclude that it will not help us with our problems about identity through time and that there is no sufficient reason for accepting it.

(3) One may say: 'The President of the United States was Eisenhower in 1955, Johnson in 1965, and Ford in 1975.'[12] Here one may seem to be saying that there is, or was, something—namely, the President of the United States—which was identical with Eisenhower in 1955, with Johnson in 1965, and with Ford in 1975. And so, given that Eisenhower, Johnson and Ford were three different people, one may seem to be saying that there is one thing which has been identical with three different things. But this talk, too, is readily avoided. We have only to reformulate the original sentence in such a way that the temporal expression ('in 1955', 'in 1965' and 'in 1975') may be seen to modify, not the verb 'was', but the term 'the President of the United States'. Thus we could say: 'The President of the United States in 1955 (the person who officially presided over the United States in 1955) was Eisenhower; the President of the United States in 1965 was Johnson; and the President of the United States in 1975 was Ford.'[13]

(4) Pointing to a musical instrument, one man may say to another: 'What you have there is the same instrument that I play, but the one that I play isn't as old as that one.' The first 'is' might be taken to be the 'is' of identity, for it would seem to be followed by a term ('the same instrument that I play'), but the man is saying, of the thing designated by the first term ('what you have there'), that it is older than the thing designated by the second. But of course he didn't need to talk that way. He could have said: 'What you have there is an instrument of the same sort as the one that I play.'

We note a second example of this way of playing loose with 'is'—not because the example introduces any new considerations (for it doesn't), but because it has attracted the attention of philosophers.

Consider the following list:

Socrates is mortal.
Socrates is mortal.

12. Contrast P. T. Geach, *Reference and Generality* (Ithaca, NY: Cornell University Press, 1962), p. 157:'. . . different official personages may be one and the same man.' Possibly an illustration would be: 'The fire-chief isn't the same personage as the Sunday-school superintendent (for one is charged with putting out fires and the other with religious instruction); yet Jones is both.' But here one seems to be playing loose with 'isn't', for what one has in mind, presumably, is something of this sort: 'Being the fire-chief commits one to different things than does being the Sunday-school superintendent, and Jones is both.'
13. There may be temptations in thus playing loose with 'is'. Suppose there were a monarchy wherein the subjects found it distasteful ever to affirm that the monarch vacated his throne. Instead of saying that there have been so many dozen kings and queens in the history of their country, they will say that the monarch has now existed for many hundreds of years and has had so many dozen different names. At certain times it has been appropriate that these names be masculine, like 'George' and 'Henry', and at other times it has been appropriate that they be feminine, like 'Victoria' and 'Elizabeth'. What, then, if we knew about these people and were to hear such talk as this: 'There has existed for many hundreds of years an x such that x is our monarch; x is now feminine, though fifty years ago x was masculine, and fifty years before that x was feminine'? We should not conclude that there was in that land a monarch who is vastly different from any of the people in ours. We should conclude rather that the speakers were either deluded or pretending.

How many sentences have been listed? We could say either 'exactly one' or 'exactly two'. That these incompatible answers are both possible indicates that the question is ambiguous. And so it has been suggested that, to avoid the ambiguity, we introduce the terms 'sentence-token' and 'sentence-type' and then say 'There are two sentence-tokens on the list and one sentence-type'. But if we say this, then we can say: 'The first item on the list is the same sentence-type as the second (for they are syntactically just alike and say the same thing), but the two are different sentence-tokens (for they are two, one being in one place and the other in another).' Here, once again, we are playing loose with 'is'.[14] We *needn't* speak this way in order to deal with the ambiguity of 'How many sentences are there?' We could say there *are* two sentence-tokens and they are tokens *of* the same (sentence-)type. The example does not differ in principle, then, from 'The instrument Jones plays is the same as the one Smith plays but is somewhat older'.

It is sometimes said that we should distinguish the two locutions 'A is identical with B and A is a so-and-so' and 'A is the same so-and-so as B'. It has even been suggested that, for purposes of philosophy, the first of these two locutions should be abandoned in favour of the second.[15] According to this suggestion, we should never say, simply and absolutely, 'A is identical with B'; we should 'relativize the ascription of identity to a sortal', and say something of the form 'A is the same so-and-so as B', where the expression replacing 'so-and-so' is a count-term, or sortal, such as 'man', 'dog', 'horse'. But this suggestion has point only if we can find instances of the following:

A is the same so-and-so as B, and A is a such-and-such but is not the same such-and-such as B.

Are there really any such A's and B's?

What would be an instance of the above formula? In other words, what would be an instance of an A which is 'the same so-and-so' as something B, but which is not 'the same such-and-such' as B? The only instances which have ever been cited, in defending this doctrine of 'relativized identity', would seem to be instances of one or the other of the four ways of playing loose with 'is' that we have just distinguished. For example: 'Different official personages may be one and the same man' or 'This is the same word as that'. What the suggestion comes to, then, is that we abandon the strict use of 'is' and replace it by one or more of the loose uses just

---

14. Other examples are suggested by: 'He has a copy of *The Republic* on his desk and another on the table, and he doesn't have any other books. How many books does he have?' 'He played the *Appassionata* once in the afternoon and once again in the evening, but nothing further. How many sonatas did he play?'

15. Compare P. T. Geach in *Logic Matters* (Berkeley and Los Angeles: University of California Press, 1972), pp. 238–49; and *Reference and Generality*, pp. 149ff. The suggestion is criticized in detail by David Wiggins, in *Identity and Spatio-Temporal Continuity* (Oxford: Blackwell, 1967), pp. 1–26. Compare W. V. Quine in a review of *Reference and Generality* in *Philosophical Review*, 73 (1964), pp. 100–4, and Fred Feldman, 'Geach and relativized identity', *Review of Metaphysics* 22 (1968), pp. 547–55.

discussed. There may be advantages to this type of permissiveness, but it will not help us with our philosophical problems.[16]

Do these ways of playing loose with 'is' suggest a true interpretation of the thesis we have attributed to Bishop Butler—the thesis according to which it is only in 'a loose and popular sense' that we may speak of the persistence through time of such familiar physical things as ships, plants and houses? Is it only by playing loose with 'is' that we may say, of the Ship of Theseus, that it is one and the same thing from one period of time to another?

We *can*, of course, play loose with 'is' in one or another of these ways when we talk about the Ship of Theseus. Knowing that it is going to be broken up into two ships, we might say: 'It's going to be two ships.' Or knowing that it was made by joining two other ships, we might say: 'Once it had been two ships.' Or knowing that it makes the same ferry run as does the Ship of Callicles, we might say: 'The Ship of Theseus and the Ship of Callicles are the same ferry.' But the Ship of Theseus doesn't have to be talked about in these loose and popular ways any more than anything else does.

(5) It may be that the Ship of Theseus and the carriage and other familiar things involve still another way of playing loose with 'is'. Thus Hume said that it is convenient to 'feign identity' when we speak about things which, though they 'are supposed to continue the same, are such only as consist of succession of parts, connected together by resemblance, contiguity, or causation'.[17] What Hume here has in mind by 'feigning' may have been put more clearly by Thomas Reid. (Though Reid and Hume were far apart with respect to most of the matters that concern us here, they seem to be together with respect to this one.) Reid wrote:

All bodies, as they consist of innumerable parts that may be disjoined from them by a great variety of causes, are subject to continual changes of their substance, increasing, diminishing, changing insensibly. When such alterations are gradual, because language could not afford a different name for every different state of such a changeable being, it retains the same name, and is considered as the same thing. Thus we say of an old regiment that it did such a thing a century ago, though there now is not a man alive who then belonged to it. We say a tree is the same in the seed-bed and in the forest. A ship of war, which has successively changed her anchors, her tackle, her sails, her masts, her planks, and her timbers, while she keeps the same name is the same.[18]

I believe that Reid is here saying two things. The first is that, whenever there is a change of parts, however insignificant the parts may be, then some old thing ceases to be, and some new thing comes into being. This presupposes that, strictly speaking,

---

16. Compare P. T. Geach: 'Even if the man Peter Geach is the same person as the man Julius Caesar, they are certainly different men; they were for example born at different times to a different pair of parents' (*God and the Soul* (London: Routledge & Kegan Paul, 1969), p. 6). John Locke says very similar things; see the Fraser edn of the *Essay Concerning Human Understanding*, pp. 445, 450ff.

17. David Hume, *A Treatise of Human Nature*, bk I, sect. 6; L. A. Selby-Bigge edn., (Oxford: Clarendon Press, 1896), p. 255.

18. Reid, *Essays on the Intellectual Powers of Man*, p. 346.

the parts of a thing are essential to it, and therefore when, as we commonly say, something loses a part, then that thing strictly and philosophically ceases to be.[19]

The second thing I take Reid to be saying is this. If, from the point of view of our practical concerns, the new thing that comes into being upon the addition of parts is sufficiently similar to the old one, then it is much more convenient for us to treat them as if they were one than it is for us to take account of the fact that they are diverse. This point could also be put by saying that such things as the Ship of Theseus and indeed most familiar physical things are really 'fictions', or as we would say today, 'logical constructions'. They are logical constructions upon things which *cannot* survive the loss of their parts.

If Reid is right, then, 'The Ship of Theseus was in Athens last week and will be in Kerkyra Melaina next week' need not be construed as telling us that there *is* in fact a certain ship that was in Athens last week and will be in Kerkyra Melaina next week. It does not imply that any ship that was in the one place is identical with any ship that will be in the other place. And so if this is true, and if all the same we say 'A ship that was in Athens last week is identical with a ship that will be in Kerkyra Melaina next week', then, once again, we are playing loose with the 'is' of identity.

3. An interpretation of Bishop Butler's theses

We have found a way, then, of interpreting Bishop Butler's two theses.

According to the first, familiar physical things such as trees, ships, bodies and houses persist 'only in a loose and popular sense'. This thesis may be construed as presupposing that these things are 'fictions', logical constructions or *entia per alio*. And it tells us that, from the fact that any such physical thing may be said to exist at a certain place P at a certain time *t* and also at a certain place Q at a certain other time *t*, we may *not* infer that what exists at P at *t* is identical with what exists at Q at *t'*.

According to the second thesis, persons persist 'in a strict and philosophical sense'. This may be construed as telling us that persons are not thus 'fictions', logical constructions or *entia per alio*. And so it implies that, if a person may be said to exist at a certain place P at a certain time *t* and also at a certain place Q at a certain other time *t'*, then we *may* infer that something existing at P at *t* is identical with something existing at Q at *t'*.

We now consider the two theses in turn.

4. Feigning identity

Could we think of familiar physical things, such as ships and trees and houses, as being logical constructions? Let us consider just one type of physical thing, for what we say about it may be applied, *mutatis mutandis*, to the others (see Fig. 2).

19. This thesis is discussed and defended in my *Person and Object*, Appendix B ('Mereological essentialism').

Mon	AB
Tue	BC
Wed	CD

Figure 2

Consider the history of a very simple table. On Monday it came into being when a certain thing A was joined with a certain other thing B. On Tuesday A was detached from B and C was joined to B, these things occurring in such a way that a table was to be found during every moment of the process. And on Wednesday B was detached from C and D was joined with C, these things, too, occurring in such a way that a table was to be found during every moment of the process. Let us suppose that no other separating or joining occurred.

I suggest that in this situation there are the following three wholes among others: AB, that is, the thing made up of A and B; BC, the thing made up of B and C; and CD, the thing made up of C and D. I will say that AB 'constituted' our table on Monday, that BC 'constituted' our table on Tuesday, and that CD 'constituted' our table on Wednesday. Although AB, BC and CD are three different things, they all constitute the same table. We thus have an illustration of what Hume called 'a succession of objects'.[20]

One might also say, of each of the three wholes, AB, BC and CD, that it 'stands in for' or 'does duty for' our table on one of the three successive days. Thus if we consider the spatial location of the three wholes, we see that the place of the table was occupied by AB on Monday, by BC on Tuesday, and by CD on Wednesday. Again, the table was red on Monday if and only if AB was red on Monday, and it weighed 10 pounds on Monday if and only if AB weighed 10 pounds on Monday. And analogously for BC on Tuesday and for CD on Wednesday.

The situation may seem to involve two somewhat different types of individual thing. On the one hand, there is what might be called the *ens successivum*—the 'successive table' that is made up of different things at different times.[21] And on the other hand, there are the things that do duty on the different days for the successive table: namely,

20. See Hume, *Treatise of Human Nature*, bk I, pt iv, sect. 6 (Selby-Bigge edn., p. 255): 'all objects, to which we ascribe identity, without observing their invariableness and uninterruptedness, are such as consist of a succession of related objects.' In this same section. Hume affirms a version of the principle of mereological essentialism.

21. We could define an *ens successivum* by saying, with St Augustine, that it is 'a single thing . . . composed of many, all of which exist not together'; see *Confessions*, bk IV, ch. 11. St Thomas says in effect that a *successivum* is a thing such that some of its parts do not coexist with others of its parts ('una pars non est cum alia parte'); see the *Commentary on the Sentences*, bk I, dist. VIII, Q. 2, Art. 1, ad 4. The term *ens successivum* has traditionally been applied to such things as periods of time (e.g., days, weeks, months) and events; compare Aristotle's *Physics*, bk III, ch. 6, 206a.

AB, BC and CD. But any *ens successivum* may be viewed as a logical construction upon the various things that may be said to do duty for it.

Considering, then, just the simple situation I have described, can we express the information we have about the *ens successivum* in statements that refer only to the particular things that stand in or do duty for it? It should be clear that we can, but let us consider the situation in some detail.

Looking back to our diagram, we can see that Monday's table evolved into Tuesday's table, and that Tuesday's table evolved into Wednesday's table. We began with AB; then A was separated from B and replaced by C, but in such a way that there was a table to be found at every moment during the process; then, in a similar way, B was separated from C and replaced by D. We could say, then, that BC was a 'direct table successor' of AB and that CD was a 'direct table successor' of AB.

Making use of the undefined concept of *part*, or *proper part*, we may define the concept of 'table successor' in the following way:

> D. III. 1 x is at t a direct table successor of y at $t' = D_f$ (i) t does not begin before t'; (ii) x is a table at t and y is a table at t'; and (iii) there is a z, such that z is a part of x at t and a part of y at t', and at every moment between t' and t, inclusive, z is itself a table.

Thus z is a table which is a proper part of a table. (If we cut off a small part of a table, we may still have a table left. But if the thing that is left is a table, then, since it was there before, it was then a table that was a proper part of a table.) The concept *part*, as it is understood here, is discussed in detail in Appendix B ('Mereological essentialism').[22]

We may also say, more generally, that the CD of Wednesday is a 'table successor' of the AB of Monday, even though CD is not a *direct* table successor of AB. The more general concept is this:

> D. III. 2 x is at t a table successor of y at $t' = D_f$ (i) t does not begin before t'; (ii) x is a table at t, and y is a table at t'; and (iii) x has at t every property P such that (a) y has P at t' and (b) all direct table successors of anything having P have P.

The definition assures us that a direct table successor of a direct table successor is a table successor; so, too, for a direct table successor of a direct table successor . . . of a direct table successor.[23]

We may now say that things that are thus related by table succession 'constitute the same successive table'.

22. See Chisholm, *Person and Object*.
23. Definition D. III. 2 thus makes use of the general device by means of which Frege defined the ancestral relation; see G. Frege, *The Foundations of Arithmetic* (Oxford: Blackwell, 1950), sect. 79. A more intuitive reading of clause (iii) might be: '(iii) x belongs at t to every class c which is such that (a) y belongs to c at t' and (b) all direct table successors of anything belonging to c belong to c.'

D. III. 3 x constitutes at t the same successive table that y constitutes at $t' = $ $_{Df}$
either (a) x and only x is at t a table successor of y at t', or (b) y and only
y is at t' a table successor of x at t.

Each such thing may be said to 'constitute a successive table'.

D. III. 4 x constitutes at t a successive table $= $ $_{Df}$ There are a y and a t' such that
y is other than x, and x constitutes at t the same table that y constitutes
at t'.

We are on the way, then, to reducing our successive table to those things that are
said to constitute it.

Certain propositions, ostensibly about the successive table, may be reduced in
a straightforward way to propositions about the things that are said to constitute it.
For example:

D. III. 5 There is exactly one successive table at place P at time $t = $ $_{Df}$ There is
exactly one thing at place P at time t that constitutes a successive table
at t.

Our definition of 'constituting the same successive table' (D. III. 3) assures us that
nothing will constitute more than one successive table at any given time.

Some of the properties that the table has at any given time are thus such that the
table borrows them from the thing that constitutes it at that time; but others are
not. An example of a property of the first sort may be that of *being red*; an example
of a property of the second sort may be that of *having once been blue*. How are we
to mark off the former set of properties?

Some properties may be said to be 'rooted outside the times at which they are had'.
Examples are the property of *being a widow* and the property of *being a future
President*. If we know of anything that it has the former property at any given time, then
we can deduce that the thing existed prior to that time. And if we know of anything
that it has the latter property at any given time, then we can deduce that the thing
continues to exist after that time. Let us say:

D. III. 6 G is rooted outside times at which it is had $= $ $_{Df}$ Necessarily, for any x
and for any period of time t, x has the property G throughout t only if
x exists at some time before or after t.

Some properties may—but need not—be rooted outside the times at which they
are had. An example is the property of *being such that it is or was red*. Our successive table may derive this from its present constituent—if its present constituent is
red. But it may derive it from a former constituent—if its present constituent is not
red. The definition of this type of property is straightforward:

D. III. 7 G may be rooted outside times at which it is had $= $ $_{Df}$ G is equivalent to
a disjunction of two properties one of which is, and the other of which is
not, rooted outside times at which it is had.

Some properties, finally, are *not* such that they may be rooted outside the times at which they are had.[24] An example is *being red*.

Of the properties that our successive table has at any given time, which are the ones that it borrows from the thing that happens to constitute it at that time? The answer is: those of its properties which are *not* essential to it, and those of its properties which are *not* such that they may be rooted outside the times at which they are had. But the essential properties of the successive table—e.g., that it *is* a successive table—and those of its properties which may be rooted outside the times at which they are had—e.g., that it was blue or that it was or will be blue—are not such that, for any time, they are borrowed from the thing that constitutes the successive table at that time.

We may say, more generally, of the *ens successivum* and the thing that constitutes it at any given time, that they are exactly alike at that time with respect to all those properties which are such that they are not essential to either and they may not be rooted outside the times at which they are had.

Consider now the following definitional schema:

D. III. 8 The successive table that is at place P at time *t* is F at *t* = D*f* There is exactly one thing at place P at *t* that constitutes a successive table at *t*, and that thing is F at *t*.

This definition is applicable only if the predicates that replace the schematic letter 'F' are properly restricted. For the properties designated by such predicates should be those which are not essential to either and are not such that they may be rooted outside the times at which they are had. Hence acceptable replacements for 'F' would be: 'red', '10 feet square', and 'such that it weighs 10 pounds'.

But not all the properties of the successive table are derivable in this straightforward way from the properties of things that constitute it. For example, if AB ceased to be after Monday, we could say of the successive table on Monday, but not of AB, that it was going to persist through Wednesday. Or if CD came into being on Wednesday, we could say of the successive table on Wednesday, but not of CD, that it is at least two days old. Moreover, on Monday, the successive table, but not AB, was such that it would be constituted by CD on Wednesday; while on Wednesday, the successive table, but not CD, was such that it was constituted by AB on Monday.

Nevertheless all such truths about the successive table may be reduced to truths about AB, BC and CD. That this is so should be apparent from these definitions.

D. III. 9 The successive table that is at place P at time *t* has existed for at least three days = D*f* There is exactly one *x* such that *x* is at place P at time *t* and *x* constitutes a successive table at *t*; there are a *y* and a time *t'* such that *x* is

---

24. The distinction among these several types of property are used in my *Person and Object*, ch. 4, to mark off those states of affairs that are *events*. (We had noted in the previous chapter that, although 'John is walking' refers to an event, 'John will walk' and 'John is such that either he is walking or he will walk' do not refer to events.)

at *t* a table-successor of *y* at *t'*; and *t* and *t'* are separated by a period of three days.

This definition tells us, then, what it is for a successive table to persist through time. And the following definition suggests the way in which, at any time, the successive table may borrow its properties from things that constitute it at *other* times:

D. III. 10   The successive table that is at place P at time *t* is constituted by *x* at *t'* = D_f There is a *y* such that *y* is at place P at time *t*; *y* constitutes a successive table at *t*; and either *x* is identical with *y*, and *t* is identical with *t'*, or *y* constitutes at *t* the same successive table that *x* constitutes at *t'*.

It should now be obvious how to say such things as 'the successive table is red on Monday and green on Wednesday'.

One may object, 'You are committed to saying that AB, BC, CD, and our table are four different things. It may well be, however, that each of the three things AB, BC, CD satisfies the conditions of any acceptable definition of the term "table". Indeed your definitions presuppose that each of them *is* a table. Hence you are committed to saying that, in the situation described, there are *four* tables. But this is absurd; for actually you have described only *one* table.'

We will find a reply to this objection, if we distinguish the strict and philosophical sense of such expressions as 'There are four tables' from their ordinary, or loose and popular, sense. To say that there are four tables, in the strict and philosophical sense, is to say that there are four different things, each of them a table. But from the fact that there are four tables, in this strict and philosophical sense, it will not follow that there are four tables in the ordinary, or loose and popular, sense. If there are to be four tables in the ordinary, or loose and popular, sense, it must be the case that there are four things, not only such that each constitutes a table, but also such that no two of them constitute the same table. In other words, there must be four *entia successiva*, each of them a table.

We may, therefore, explicate the ordinary, or loose and popular, sense of 'There are *n* so-and-so's at *t*' (or 'The number of so-and-so's at *t* is *n*') in the following way:

D. III. 11   There are, in the loose and popular sense, *n* so-and-so's at *t* = D_f There are *n* things each of which constitutes a so-and-so at *t*, and no two of which constitute the same so-and-so at *t*.

The term 'so-and-so' in this schematic definition may be replaced by any more specific count-term, e.g., 'table' or 'ship'. And the *definiendum* could be replaced by 'The number of successive so-and-so's at *t* is *n*'.

Hence the answer to the above objection is this: in saying that there are exactly *three* tables in the situation described, one is speaking in the strict and philosophical sense and not in the loose and popular sense. In saying that there is exactly *one* table, one is speaking in the loose and popular sense and not in the strict and philosophical sense.

But the statement that there are *four* tables—AB, BC, CD and the successive table—is simply the result of confusion. One is trying to speak both ways at once.[25] The sense in which we may say that there *is* the successive table is not the sense in which we may say that there *is* the individual thing AB, or BC, or CD.[26]

The foregoing sketch, then, makes clear one way in which we may feign identity when what we are dealing with is in fact only a 'succession of related objects'. The ways in which we do thus feign identity are considerably more subtle and complex. Playing loose with 'is' and 'same', we may even speak of the sameness of a table when we are dealing with successions of objects which are related, not by what I have called table succession, but in much more tenuous ways. Nevertheless, it should be clear that if we are saying something we really know, when we thus speak of the sameness of a table, what we are saying could be re-expressed in such a way that we refer only to the related objects and not to the ostensible entities we think of them as making up. And so, too, for other familiar things—ships and trees and houses—that involve successions of related objects that stand in or do duty for them at different times.

We could say, then, that such things are *entia per alio*. They are ontological parasites that derive all their properties from other things—from the various things that do duty for them. An *ens per alio* never is or has anything on its own. It is what it is in virtue of the nature of something other than itself. At every moment of its history an *ens per alio* has something other than itself as its stand-in.

But if there are *entia per alio*, then there are also *entia per se*.

---

25. Compare Hume: 'Tho' we commonly be able to distinguish pretty exactly betwixt numerical and specific identity, yet it sometimes happens that we confound them, and in our thinking and reasoning employ the one for the other'. (*Treatise of Human Nature*, bk I, pt iv, sect. 6 ('Of Personal Identity'), Selby-Bigge edn., pp. 257–8.

26. It may be noted that we have defined the loose and popular sense of the expression 'There are *n* so-and-so's at *t*' and not the more general 'The number of so-and-so's that there ever will have been is *n*'. For the loose and popular sense of this latter expression is not sufficiently fixed to be explicated in any strict and philosophical sense. The following example may make this clear. In the infantry of the United States Army during World War II each private carried materials for half a tent—something like one piece of canvas, a pole and ropes. Two privates could then assemble their materials and create a tent which would be disassembled in the morning. On another night the two privates might find different tent companions. Occasionally, when the company was in camp, the various tent parts were collected, stored away, and then reissued, but with no attempt to assign particular parts to their former holders. Supposing, to simplify the matter considerably, that all the tents that there ever will have been were those that were created by the members of a certain infantry company, how, making use of our ordinary criteria, would we go about answering the question 'Just how many tents *have* there been?' Would an accounting of the history of the joinings of the various tent parts be sufficient to give us the answer?

Chapter 41
Selection from *On the Plurality of Worlds*
David Lewis

O U R question of overlap of worlds parallels the this-worldly problem of identity through time; and our problem of accidental intrinsics parallels a problem of temporary intrinsics, which is the traditional problem of change.[1] Let us say that something *persists* iff, somehow or other, it exists at various times; this is the neutral word. Something *perdures* iff it persists by having different temporal parts, or stages, at different times, though no one part of it is wholly present at more than one time; whereas it *endures* iff it persists by being wholly present at more than one time. Perdurance corresponds to the way a road persists through space; part of it is here and part of it is there, and no part is wholly present at two different places. Endurance corresponds to the way a universal, if there are such things, would be wholly present wherever and whenever it is instantiated. Endurance involves overlap: the content of two different times has the enduring thing as a common part. Perdurance does not.

(There might be mixed cases: entities that persist by having an enduring part and a perduring part. An example might be a person who consisted of an enduring entelechy ruling a perduring body; or an electron that had a universal of unit negative charge as a permanent part, but did not consist entirely of universals. But here I ignore the mixed cases. And when I speak of ordinary things as perduring, I shall ignore their enduring universals, if such there be.)

Discussions of endurance versus perdurance tend to be endarkened by people who say such things as this: 'Of course you are wholly present at every moment of your life, except in case of amputation. For at every moment all your parts are there: your legs, your lips, your liver . . . .' These endarkeners may think themselves partisans of endurance, but they are not. They are perforce neutral, because they lack the conceptual resources to understand what is at issue. Their speech betrays—and they may acknowledge it willingly—that they have no concept of a temporal part. (Or at any rate none that applies to a person, say, as opposed to a process or a stretch of time.) Therefore they are on neither side of a dispute about whether or not persisting things

---

1. My discussion of this parallel problem is much indebted to Armstrong, 'Identity Through Time', and to Johnston. I follow Johnston in terminology.

David Lewis, selection from *On the Plurality of Worlds* (Blackwell, 1986), reprinted with permission of Blackwell Publishing Ltd.

are divisible into temporal parts. They understand neither the affirmation nor the denial. They are like the people—fictional, I hope—who say that the whole of the long road is in their little village, for not one single lane of it is missing. Meaning less than others do by 'part', since they omit parts cut crosswise, they also mean less than others do by 'whole'. They say the 'whole' road is in the village; by which they mean that every 'part' is; but by that, they only mean that every part cut lengthwise is. Divide the road into its least lengthwise parts; they cannot even raise the question whether those are in the village wholly or only partly. For that is a question about crosswise parts, and the concept of a crosswise part is what they lack. Perhaps 'cross-wise part' really does sound to them like a blatant contradiction. Or perhaps it seems to them that they understand it, but the village philosophers have persuaded them that really they couldn't, so their impression to the contrary must be an illusion. At any rate, I have the concept of a temporal part; and for some while I shall be addressing only those of you who share it.[2]

Endurance through time is analogous to the alleged trans-world identity of common parts of overlapping worlds; perdurance through time is analogous to the 'trans-world identity', if we may call it that, of a trans-world individual composed of distinct parts in non-overlapping worlds. Perdurance, which I favour for the temporal case, is closer to the counterpart theory which I favour for the modal case; the difference is that counterpart theory concentrates on the parts and ignores the trans-world individual composed of them.

The principal and decisive objection against endurance, as an account of the persistence of ordinary things such as people or puddles, is the problem of temporary intrinsics. Persisting things change their intrinsic properties. For instance shape: when I sit, I have a bent shape; when I stand, I have a straightened shape. Both shapes are temporary intrinsic properties; I have them only some of the time. How is such change possible? I know of only three solutions.

(It is *not* a solution just to say how very commonplace and indubitable it is that we have different shapes at different times. To say that is only to insist—rightly—that it must be possible somehow. Still less is it a solution to say it in jargon—as it might be, that bent-on-Monday and straight-on-Tuesday are compatible because they are 'time-indexed properties'— if that just means that, somehow, you can be bent on Monday and straight on Tuesday.)

First solution: contrary to what we might think, shapes are not genuine intrinsic properties. They are disguised relations, which an enduring thing may bear to times. One and the same enduring thing may bear the bent-shape relation to some times, and the straight-shape relation to others. In itself, considered apart from its relations to other things, it has no shape at all. And likewise for all other seeming temporary intrinsics; all of them must be reinterpreted as relations that something with an

---

2. I attempt to explain it to others in *Philosophical Papers*, volume I, pages 76–7. But I have no great hopes, since any competent philosopher who does not understand something will take care not to understand anything else whereby it might be explained.

absolutely unchanging intrinsic nature bears to different times. The solution to the problem of temporary intrinsics is that there aren't any temporary intrinsics. This is simply incredible, if we are speaking of the persistence of ordinary things. (It might do for the endurance of entelechies or universals.) If we know what shape is, we know that it is a property, not a relation.

Second solution: the only intrinsic properties of a thing are those it has at the present moment. Other times are like false stories; they are abstract representations, composed out of the materials of the present, which represent or misrepresent the way things are. When something has different intrinsic properties according to one of these ersatz other times, that does not mean that it, or any part of it, or anything else, just *has* them—no more so than when a man is crooked according to the *Times*, or honest according to the *News*. This is a solution that rejects endurance; because it rejects persistence altogether. And it is even less credible than the first solution. In saying that there are no other times, as opposed to false representations thereof, it goes against what we all believe. No man, unless it be at the moment of his execution, believes that he has no future; still less does anyone believe that he has no past.

Third solution: the different shapes, and the different temporary intrinsics generally, belong to different things. Endurance is to be rejected in favour of perdurance. We perdure; we are made up of temporal parts, and our temporary intrinsics are properties of these parts, wherein they differ one from another. There is no problem at all about how different things can differ in their intrinsic properties.

Some special cases of overlap of worlds face no problem of accidental intrinsics. One arises on the hypothesis that there are universals, wholly present recurrently as non-spatiotemporal parts of all their particular instances. If so, these universals must recur as freely between the worlds as they do within a world. For there is qualitative duplication between the worlds, by the principle of recombination; and universals are supposed to recur whenever there is duplication. Doubtless there are electrons in other worlds than ours. If a universal of unit negative charge is part of each and every this-worldly electron, then equally it is part of the other-worldly electrons; in which case, since parthood is transitive, it is a common part of all the worlds where there are electrons; and that is overlap. We expect trouble with the accidental intrinsic properties of the common part. But what are those properties in this case? I cannot think of any. There isn't much to the intrinsic nature of a universal. Maybe it's intrinsically simple, or maybe it's intrinsically composed, somehow, of other universals; but if so, that seems to be an essential matter, so we still have no intrinsic accidents to trouble us. (Likewise these seem to be no temporary intrinsics to trouble us, so there is no problem about universals enduring through time.) If indeed there are no accidental intrinsics to raise a problem, then overlap confined to the sharing of universals seems entirely innocent. And also it seems inevitable, if there are universals at all. So my rejection of overlap must be qualified: whatever the universals may do, at any rate no two worlds have any particular as a common part.

If there are universals, identical between worlds as they are between instances within a world, then for them we may as well help ourselves to the simplest method of representation *de re*: what is true of a universal according to a world is what is true of *it*, when we restrict quantifiers to that world. What is true of it at a world will then be, first, that it has its constant essential intrinsic nature; and, second, that it has various relationships—notably, patterns of instantiation—to other things of that world. For instance it will be true of unit negative charge, at one world, that it is instantiated by exactly seventeen things, which are close together; and at another world, that it is instantiated by infinitely many widely scattered things. Thus its extrinsic 'properties', taken as disguised relations, vary. Its extrinsic properties, properly speaking, do not. But the way we name them does, so that for instance we can say that at one world but not the other, the universal has the property of being instantiated by seventeen close-together things.[3]

Another special case of overlap would be, if not altogether innocent, at least safe from the problem of accidental intrinsics. This is simply the case in which something does have accidental intrinsic properties, but they are constant within a limited range of worlds, and the proposed overlap is confined to the worlds in that limited range. Such limited overlap could not give us all we need by way of representation *de re*. For the thing does have some accidental intrinsic properties; so there must be some world which represents it as lacking some of these properties; that must be a world outside the limited range of overlap; so when that world represents the thing as lacking the properties, that representation *de re* must work not by trans-world identity but in some other way. Limited overlap would have to be combined with some other treatment of representation *de re*, presumably some form of counterpart theory.

Even so, limited overlap might be wanted. The most likely case would be limited overlap when branching worlds share a common inital segment. I distinguish *branching* of worlds from *divergence*. In branching, worlds are like Siamese twins.

---

3. A universal can safely be part of many worlds because it hasn't any accidental intrinsics. But mightn't the same be said of some simple particulars—tropes, if such there be, or fundamental particles, or momentary slices thereof? Maybe these things have no accidental intrinsic properties—it certainly seems hard to think of plausible candidates. If they haven't, then they too could safely be shared between overlapping worlds. We would not face a problem of accidental intrinsics. But I suggest that we would face a parallel problem of accidental external relations. Suppose we have a pair of two of these simple particulars A and B, both of which are common parts of various worlds. A and B are a certain distance apart. Their distance, it seems, is a relation of A and B and nothing else—it is not really a three-place relation of A, B, and this or that world. That means that A and B are precisely the same distance apart in all the worlds they are both part of. That means (assuming that we explain representation *de re* in terms of trans-world identity when we can) that it is impossible that A and B should both have existed and been a different distance apart. That seems wrong: it is hard to suppose that the distance is essential to the pair, equally hard to suppose that distance is not the plain two-place relation that it seems to be. So trans-world identity, even for simple particulars without accidental intrinsic properties, is *prima facie* trouble. An advocate of it will have some explaining to do, both as to how he gets around the problem of accidental external relations, and also as to what motivates it when it cannot provide a fully general account of representation *de re*. Such explaining may be found in Johnston, *Particulars and Persistence*, chapter 4.

There is one initial spatiotemporal segment; it is continued by two different futures—different both numerically and qualitatively—and so there are two over-lapping worlds. One world consists of the initial segment plus one of its futures; the other world consists of the identical initial segment plus the other future.

In divergence, on the other hand, there is no overlap. Two worlds have two duplicate initial segments, not one that they share in common. I, and the world I am part of, have only one future. There are other worlds that diverge from ours. These worlds have initial segments exactly like that of our world up to the present, but the later parts of these worlds differ from the later parts of ours. (Or we could make it relativistic: what is duplicated is the past cone from some spacetime point, as it might be from here and now.) Not I, but only some very good counterparts of me, inhabit these other worlds.

I reject genuine branching in favour of divergence. However there might be some reason to go the other way. Consider the philosophers who say that the future is unreal. It is hard to believe they mean it. If ever anyone is right that there is no future, then that very moment is his last, and what's more is the end of everything. Yet when these philosophers teach that there is no more time to come, they show no trace of terror or despair! When we see them planning and anticipating, we might suspect that they believe in the future as much as anyone else does. Maybe they only insist on restricting their quantifiers, and all they mean is that nothing future is present?—No, for they seem to think that what they are saying is controversial. What is going on?

Perhaps their meaning is clearer when they turn linguistic, and say that there is no determinate truth about the future. A modal realist who believed in genuine branching, in which his world overlaps with others by having initial segments in common, could agree with that. To have determinate truth about the future, it helps to have a future; but also, it helps to have only one future. If there are two futures, and both are equally mine with nothing to choose between them, and one holds a sea fight and the other doesn't, what could it mean for me to say that *the* future holds a sea fight? Not a rhetorical question: we have three options. (1) It is false that the future holds a sea fight; because 'the future' is a denotationless improper description. (2) It is true that the future holds a sea fight; because 'the future' denotes neither of the two partial futures but rather their disunited sum, which does hold a sea fight. (3) It is neither true nor false that the future holds a sea fight; because 'the future' has inde-terminate denotation, and we get different truth values on different resolutions of the indeterminacy. Offhand, the third option—indeterminacy—seems best. (At least it lets us talk in the ordinary way about matters on which the futures do not differ; what has the same truth value on all resolutions is determinately true or false.) But whichever way we go, our customary thought about 'the' future is in bad trouble. Against the common sense idea that we have one single future, advocates of many may join forces with advocates of none; but the advocates of many have the better of it, for they have no cause to despair. I do not suggest that philosophers of the unreal or indeterminate future are, in fact, modal realists who accept branching. But modal realists can make good sense of much that they say. So whatever motivates these philosophers to deny that we have a single future might equally motivate a modal realist to accept branching.

Why not, given that the overlap is limited enough not to raise the problem of accidental intrinsics? Well, one man's reason is another man's *reductio*. The trouble with branching exactly is that it conflicts with our ordinary presupposition that we have a single future. If two futures are equally mine, one with a sea fight tomorrow and one without, it is nonsense to wonder which way it will be—it will be both ways—and yet I do wonder. The theory of branching suits those who think this wondering *is* nonsense. Or those who think the wondering makes sense only if reconstrued: you have leave to wonder about the sea fight, provided that really you wonder not about what tomorrow will bring but about what today predetermines. But a modal realist who thinks in the ordinary way that it makes sense to wonder what *the* future will bring, and who distinguishes this from wondering what is already predetermined, will reject branching in favour of divergence. In divergence also there are many futures; that is, there are many later segments of worlds that begin by duplicating initial segments of our world. But in divergence, only one of these futures is truly ours. The rest belong not to us but to our other-worldly counterparts. Our future is the one that is part of the same world as ourselves. It alone is connected to us by the relations—the (strictly or analogically) spatiotemporal relations, or perhaps natural external relations generally—that unify a world. It alone is influenced causally by what we do and how we are in the present. We wonder which one is the future that has the special relation to ourselves. We care about it in a way that we do not care about all the other-worldly futures. Branching, and the limited overlap it requires, are to be rejected as making nonsense of the way we take ourselves to be related to our futures; and divergence without overlap is to be preferred.[4]

There is a less weighty argument against branching, and indeed against overlap generally. What unifies a world, I suggested, is that its parts stand in suitable external relations, preferably spatiotemporal. But if we have overlap, we have spatiotemporal relations between the parts of different worlds. For instance, let P be the common part—say, a shared initial segment—of two different worlds W_1 and W_2, let R_1 be the remainder of W_1, and let R_2 be the remainder of W_2. Then the appropriate unifying relations obtain between P and R_1, and also between P and R_2. But now the relations obtain between parts of two different worlds: between P, which is *inter alia* a part of the world W_1, and R_2, which is part of the different world W_2.

Of course it is also true that P and R_2 are parts of a single world W_2. So at least we can still say that whenever two things are appropriately related, there is some world they are both parts of, even if they may be parts of other worlds besides. Or can we say even that? In a sense, even R_1 and R_2 are related, in a stepwise back-and-forward way, via P. For instance, R_1 and R_2 might stand to one another in the complex temporal relation: successor-of-a-predecessor-of. Yet R_1 and R_2 are not both parts of

---

4. In his 'Theories of Actuality', Adams makes the same point; but while I use it in favour of modal realism without overlap, Adams uses it in favour of ersatzism.

any one world. Thus overlap complicates what we must say in explaining how worlds are unified by spatiotemporal interrelation, and thereby differ from trans-world individuals composed of parts of several worlds. The complication is unwelcome, but I think it's nothing worse. Overlap spoils the easiest account of how worlds are unified by interrelation: namely, the mereological analogue of the definition of equivalence classes. But alternative accounts are available (as in the parallel problem about time discussed in my 'Survival and Identity'), so I presume that a modal realist who wished to accept overlap would not be in serious difficulty on this score. Still less is there any problem if the only overlap we accept is the sharing of universals; we need only say that a world is unified by the spatiotemporal (or whatever) interrelation of its *particular* parts.

   If we stay with the simple account of how worlds are unified, we will conclude that where there is branching, there is one single world composed of all the branches. That would not be branching *of* worlds, but branching *within* worlds; and so the overlap of branches would not be overlap of worlds. Branching within worlds, I think, is to be accepted: it is possible that the spacetime of a world might have such a shape, and if that is a possible way for a world to be then it is a way that some world is. Some world; but there is no reason to think that such a world is ours. Respect for common sense gives us reason to reject any theory that says that we ourselves are involved in branching, or that if we are not, that can only be because (contrary to accepted theory) our world is governed by deterministic laws. But we needn't reject the very possibility that a world branches. The unfortunate inhabitants of such a world, if they think of 'the future' as we do, are of course sorely deceived, and their peculiar circumstances do make nonsense of how they ordinarily think. But that is their problem; not ours, as it would be if the worlds generally branched rather than diverging.

   I noted that our special cases of trans-world identity, sharing of universals and sharing of initial segments in branching, avoid the problem of accidental intrinsics. They avoid another well-known problem as well. A friend of overlap might wish to say that trans-world identity follows lines of qualitative similarity. Or he might not; whether to say this is part of the topic of haecceitism, considered in §4.4 of *On the Plurality of Worlds*. But if he does, his problem is that identity is transitive, similarity in general is not. But it is *approximate* similarity that fails to be transitive; whereas the supposed sharing of universals, and likewise the supposed sharing of initial segments in branching, would follow lines of *exact* similarity. When we have the exact similarity in a respect between two instances of unit negative charge, or the perfect match when two worlds start out exactly alike in their history, there is no discrepancy of formal character to stop us from taking these as cases of trans-world identity.

Works cited

Adams, Robert M. 'Theories of Actuality', *Noûs*, 8 (1974), pp. 211–31; reprinted in Loux, *The Possible and the Actual*.

Armstrong, D. M. 'Identity Through Time', in *Time and Cause: Essays Presented to Richard Taylor*, ed. by Peter van Inwagen, Reidel, 1980.

Johnston, Mark. *Particulars and Persistence*. Ph.D. dissertation, Princeton University, 1983.

Lewis, David. 'Survival and Identity', in *The Identities of Persons*, ed. by Amélie O. Rorty, University of California Press, 1976; reprinted, with added postscripts, in Lewis, *Philosophical Papers*, volume I.

—— *Philosophical Papers*, (two volumes). Oxford University Press, 1983 and 1986.

Loux, Michael. *The Possible and the Actual: Readings in the Metaphysics of Modality*. Cornell University Press, 1979.

Chapter 42
Personal identity
Derek Parfit[1]

WE can, I think, describe cases in which, though we know the answer to every other question, we have no idea how to answer a question about personal identity. These cases are not covered by the criteria of personal identity that we actually use.

Do they present a problem?

It might be thought that they do not, because they could never occur. I suspect that some of them could. (Some, for instance, might become scientifically possible.) But I shall claim that even if they did they would present no problem.

My targets are two beliefs: one about the nature of personal identity, the other about its importance.

The first is that in these cases the question about identity must have an answer.

No one thinks this about, say, nations or machines. Our criteria for the identity of these do not cover certain cases. No one thinks that in these cases the questions 'Is it the same nation?' or 'Is it the same machine?' must have answers.

Some people believe that in this respect they are different. They agree that our criteria of personal identity do not cover certain cases, but they believe that the nature of their own identity through time is, somehow, such as to guarantee that in these cases questions about their identity must have answers. This belief might be expressed as follows: 'Whatever happens between now and any future time, either I shall still exist, or I shall not. Any future experience will either be *my* experience, or it will not.'

This first belief—in the special nature of personal identity—has, I think, certain effects. It makes people assume that the principle of self-interest is more rationally compelling than any moral principle. And it makes them more depressed by the thought of aging and of death.

I cannot see how to disprove this first belief. I shall describe a problem case. But this can only make it seem implausible.

Another approach might be this. We might suggest that one cause of the belief is the projection of our emotions. When we imagine ourselves in a problem case, we do feel that the question 'Would it be me?' must have an answer. But what we take to be a bafflement about a further fact may be only the bafflement of our concern.

---

1. I have been helped in writing this by D. Wiggins, D. F. Pears, P. F. Strawson, A. J. Ayer, M. Woods, N. Newman, and (through his publications) S. Shoemaker.

Derek Parfit, 'Personal Identity', from *Philosophical Review*, 80 (1971).

I shall not pursue this suggestion here. But one cause of our concern is the belief which is my second target. This is that unless the question about identity has an answer, we cannot answer certain important questions (questions about such matters as survival, memory, and responsibility).

Against this second belief my claim will be this. Certain important questions do presuppose a question about personal identity. But they can be freed of this presupposition. And when they are, the question about identity has no importance.

I

We can start by considering the much discussed case of the man who, like an amoeba, divides.[2]

Wiggins has recently dramatized this case.[3] He first referred to the operation imagined by Shoemaker.[4] We suppose that my brain is transplanted into someone else's (brainless) body, and that the resulting person has my character and apparent memories of my life. Most of us would agree, after thought, that the resulting person is me. I shall here assume such agreement.[5]

Wiggins then imagined his own operation. My brain is divided, and each half is housed in a new body. Both resulting people have my character and apparent memories of my life.

What happens to me? There seem only three possibilities: (1) I do not survive; (2) I survive as one of the two people; (3) I survive as both.

The trouble with (1) is this. We agreed that I could survive if my brain were successfully transplanted. And people have in fact survived with half their brains destroyed. It seems to follow that I could survive if half my brain were successfully transplanted and the other half were destroyed. But if this is so, how could I *not* survive if the other half were also successfully transplanted? How could a double success be a failure?

We can move to the second description. Perhaps one success is the maximum score. Perhaps I shall be one of the resulting people.

---

2. Implicit in John Locke, *Essay Concerning Human Understanding*, ed. by John W. Yolton, vol. 2, chap. 27, sec. 18 (London, 1961) and discussed by (among others) A. N. Prior in 'Opposite Number', *Review of Metaphysics*, 11 (1957–1958), and 'Time, Existence and Identity', *Proceedings of the Aristotelian Society*, vol. 57 (1965–1966); J. Bennett in 'The Simplicity of the Soul', *Journal of Philosophy*, vol. 64 (1967); and R. Chisholm and S. Shoemaker in 'The Loose and Popular and the Strict and the Philosophical Senses of Identity', in *Perception and Personal Identity: Proceeding of the 1967 Oberlin Colloquium in Philosophy*, ed. Norman Care and Robert H. Grimm (Cleveland, 1967).

3. David Wiggins, *Identity and Spatio-Temporal Continuity* (Oxford, 1967), p. 50.

4. Sydney S. Shoemaker, *Self-Knowledge and Self-Identity* (Ithaca, NY, 1963), p. 22.

5. Those who would disagree are not making a mistake. For them my argument would need a different case. There must be some multiple transplant, faced with which these people would both find it hard to believe that there must be an answer to the question about personal identity, and be able to be shown that nothing of importance turns upon this question.

The trouble here is that in Wiggins' case each half of my brain is exactly similar, and so, to start with, is each resulting person. So how can I survive as only one of the two people? What can make me one of them rather than the other?

It seems clear that both of these descriptions—that I do not survive, and that I survive as one of the people—are highly implausible. Those who have accepted them must have assumed that they were the only possible descriptions.

What about our third description: that I survive as both people?

It might be said, 'If "survive" implies identity, this description makes no sense— you cannot be two people. If it does not, the description is irrelevant to a problem about identity.'

I shall later deny the second of these remarks. But there are ways of denying the first. We might say, 'What we have called "the two resulting people" are not two people. They are one person. I do survive Wiggins' operation. Its effect is to give me two bodies and a divided mind.'

It would shorten my argument if this were absurd. But I do not think it is. It is worth showing why.

We can, I suggest, imagine a divided mind. We can imagine a man having two simultaneous experiences, in having each of which he is unaware of having the other.

We may not even need to imagine this. Certain actual cases, to which Wiggins referred, seem to be best described in these terms. These involve the cutting of the bridge between the hemispheres of the brain. The aim was to cure epilepsy. But the result appears to be, in the surgeon's words, the creation of 'two separate spheres of consciousness,'[6] each of which controls one half of the patient's body. What is experienced in each is, presumably, experienced by the patient.

There are certain complications in these actual cases. So let us imagine a simpler case.

Suppose that the bridge between my hemispheres is brought under my voluntary control. This would enable me to disconnect my hemispheres as easily as if I were blinking. By doing this I would divide my mind. And we can suppose that when my mind is divided I can, in each half, bring about reunion.

This ability would have obvious uses. To give an example: I am near the end of a maths exam, and see two ways of tackling the last problem. I decide to divide my mind, to work, with each half, at one of two calculations, and then to reunite my mind and write a fair copy of the best result.

What shall I experience?

When I disconnect my hemispheres, my consciousness divides into two streams. But this division is not something that I experience. Each of my two streams of consciousness seems to have been straightforwardly continuous with my one stream of consciousness up to the moment of division. The only changes in each stream are the disappearance of half my visual field and the loss of sensation in, and control over, half my body.

6. R. W. Sperry, in *Brain and Conscious Experience*, ed. J. C. Eccles (New York, 1966), p. 299.

Consider my experiences in what we can call my 'right-handed' stream. I remember that I assigned my right hand to the longer calculation. This I now begin. In working at this calculation I can see, from the movements of my left hand, that I am also working at the other. But I am not aware of working at the other. So I might, in my right-handed stream, wonder how, in my left-handed stream, I am getting on.

My work is now over. I am about to reunite my mind. What should I, in each stream, expect? Simply that I shall suddenly seem to remember just having thought out two calculations, in thinking out each of which I was not aware of thinking out the other. This, I submit, we can imagine. And if my mind was divided, these memories are correct.

In describing this episode, I assumed that there were two series of thoughts, and that they were both mine. If my two hands visibly wrote out two calculations, and if I claimed to remember two corresponding series of thoughts, this is surely what we should want to say.

If it is, then a person's mental history need not be like a canal, with only one channel. It could be like a river, with islands, and with separate streams.

To apply this to Wiggins' operation: we mentioned the view that it gives me two bodies and a divided mind. We cannot now call this absurd. But it is, I think, unsatisfactory.

There were two features of the case of the exam that made us want to say that only one person was involved. The mind was soon reunited, and there was only one body. If a mind was permanently divided and its halves developed in different ways, the point of speaking of one person would start to disappear. Wiggins' case, where there are also two bodies, seems to be over the borderline. After I have had his operation, the two 'products' each have all the attributes of a person. They could live at opposite ends of the earth. (If they later met, they might even fail to recognize each other.) It would become intolerable to deny that they were different people.

Suppose we admit that they are different people. Could we still claim that I survived as both, using 'survive' to imply identity?

We could. For we might suggest that two people could compose a third. We might say, 'I do survive Wiggins' operation as two people. They can be different people, and yet be me, in just the way in which the Pope's three crowns are one crown.'[7]

This is a possible way of giving sense to the claim that I survive as two different people, using "survive" to imply identity. But it keeps the language of identity only by changing the concept of a person. And there are obvious objections to this change.[8]

---

7. Cf. David Wiggins, *op. cit*, p. 40.
8. Suppose the resulting people fight a duel. Are there three people fighting, one on each side, and one on both? And suppose one of the bullets kills. Are there two acts, one murder and one suicide? How many people are left alive? One? Two? (We could hardly say, 'One and a half.') We could talk in this way. But instead of saying that the resulting people are the original person—so that the pair is a trio—it would be far simpler to treat them as a pair, and describe their relation to the original person in some new way. (I owe this suggested way of talking, and the objections to it, to Michael Woods.)

The alternative, for which I shall argue, is to give up the language of identity. We can suggest that I survive as two different people without implying that I am these people.

When I first mentioned this alternative, I mentioned this objection: 'If your new way of talking does not imply identity, it cannot solve our problem. For that is about identity. The problem is that all the possible answers to the question about identity are highly implausible.'

We can now answer this objection.

We can start by reminding ourselves that this is an objection only if we have one or both of the beliefs which I mentioned at the start of this paper.

The first was the belief that to any question about personal identity, in any describable case, there must be a true answer. For those with this belief, Wiggins' case is doubly perplexing. If all the possible answers are implausible, it is hard to decide which of them is true, and hard even to keep the belief that one of them must be true. If we give up this belief, as I think we should, these problems disappear. We shall then regard the case as like many others in which, for quite unpuzzling reasons, there *is* no answer to a question about identity. (Consider 'Was England the same nation after 1066?')

Wiggins' case makes the first belief implausible. It also makes it trivial. For it undermines the second belief. This was the belief that important questions turn upon the question about identity. (It is worth pointing out that those who have only this second belief do not think that there must *be* an answer to this question, but rather that we must decide upon an answer.)

Against this second belief my claim is this. Certain questions do presuppose a question about personal identity. And because these questions *are* important, Wiggins' case does present a problem. But we cannot solve this problem by answering the question about identity. We can solve this problem only by taking these important questions and prizing them apart from the question about identity. After we have done this, the question about identity (though we might for the sake of neatness decide it) has no further interest.

Because there are several questions which presuppose identity, this claim will take some time to fill out.

We can first return to the question of survival. This is a special case, for survival does not so much presuppose the retaining of identity as seem equivalent to it. It is thus the general relation which we need to prize apart from identity. We can then consider particular relations, such as those involved in memory and intention.

'Will I survive?' seems, I said, equivalent to 'Will there be some person alive who is the same person as me?'

If we treat these questions as equivalent, then the least unsatisfactory description of Wiggins' case is, I think, that I survive with two bodies and a divided mind.

Several writers have chosen to say that I am neither of the resulting people. Given our equivalence, this implies that I do not survive, and hence, presumably, that even if Wiggins' operation is not literally death, I ought, since I will not survive it, to regard it *as* death. But this seemed absurd.

It is worth repeating why. An emotion or attitude can be criticized for resting on a false belief, or for being inconsistent. A man who regarded Wiggins' operation as death must, I suggest, be open to one of these criticisms.

He might believe that his relation to each of the resulting people fails to contain some element which is contained in survival. But how can this be true? We agreed that he *would* survive if he stood in this very same relation to only *one* of the resulting people. So it cannot be the nature of this relation which makes it fail, in Wiggins' case, to be survival. It can only be its duplication.

Suppose that our man accepts this, but still regards division as death. His reaction would now seem wildly inconsistent. He would be like a man who, when told of a drug that could double his years of life, regarded the taking of this drug as death. The only difference in the case of division is that the extra years are to run concurrently. This is an interesting difference. But it cannot mean that there are *no* years to run.

I have argued this for those who think that there must, in Wiggins' case, be a true answer to the question about identity. For them, we might add, 'Perhaps the original person does lose his identity. But there may be other ways to do this than to die. One other way might be to multiply. To regard these as the same is to confuse nought with two.'

For those who think that the question of identity is up for decision, it would be clearly absurd to regard Wiggins' operation as death. These people would have to think, 'We could have chosen to say that I should be one of the resulting people. If we had, I should not have regarded it as death. But since we have chosen to say that I am neither person, I *do*.' This is hard even to understand.[9]

My first conclusion, then, is this. The relation of the original person to each of the resulting people contains all that interests us—all that matters—in any ordinary case of survival. This is why we need a sense in which one person can survive as two.[10]

One of my aims in the rest of this paper will be to suggest such a sense. But we can first make some general remarks.

II

Identity is a one–one relation. Wiggins' case serves to show that what matters in survival need not be one–one.

Wiggins' case is of course unlikely to occur. The relations which matter are, in fact, one–one. It is because they are that we can imply the holding of these relations by using the language of identity.

This use of language is convenient. But it can lead us astray. We may assume that what matters *is* identity and, hence, has the properties of identity.

In the case of the property of being one–one, this mistake is not serious. For what matters is in fact one–one. But in the case of another property, the mistake *is* serious.

9. Cf. Sydney Shoemaker, in *Perception and Personal Identity*, p. 54.
10. Cf. David Wiggins, *op. cit.*

Identity is all-or-nothing. Most of the relations which matter in survival are, in fact, relations of degree. If we ignore this, we shall be led into quite ill-grounded attitudes and beliefs.

The claim that I have just made—that most of what matters are relations of degree—I have yet to support. Wiggins' case shows only that these relations need not be one–one. The merit of the case is not that it shows this in particular, but that it makes the first break between what matters and identity. The belief that identity *is* what matters is hard to overcome. This is shown in most discussions of the problem cases which actually occur: cases, say, of amnesia or of brain damage. Once Wiggins' case has made one breach in this belief, the rest should be easier to remove.[11]

To turn to a recent debate: most of the relations which matter can be provisionally referred to under the heading 'psychological continuity' (which includes causal continuity). My claim is thus that we use the language of personal identity in order to imply such continuity. This is close to the view that psychological continuity provides a criterion of identity.

Williams has attacked this view with the following argument. Identity is a one–one relation. So any criterion of identity must appeal to a relation which is logically one–one. Psychological continuity is not logically one–one. So it cannot provide a criterion.[12]

Some writers have replied that it is enough if the relation appealed to is always in fact one–one.[13]

I suggest a slightly different reply. Psychological continuity is a ground for speaking of identity when it is one–one.

If psychological continuity took a one-many or branching form, we should need, I have argued, to abandon the language of identity. So this possibility would not count against this view.

We can make a stronger claim. This possibility would count in its favor.

The view might be defended as follows. Judgments of personal identity have great importance. What gives them their importance is the fact that they imply

11. Bernard Williams' 'The Self and the Future', *Philosophical Review*, 79 (1970), 161–80, is relevant here. He asks the question 'Shall I survive?' in a range of problem cases, and he shows how natural it is to believe (1) that this question must have an answer, (2) that the answer must be all-or-nothing, and (3) that there is a 'risk' of our reaching the wrong answer. Because these beliefs are so natural, we should need in undermining them to discuss their causes. These, I think, can be found in the ways in which we misinterpret what it is to remember (cf. Sec. III below) and to anticipate (cf. Williams' 'Imagination and the Self', *Proceedings of the British Academy*, 52 [1966], 105–24); and also in the way in which certain features of our egoistic concern—e.g., that it is simple, and applies to all imaginable cases—are 'projected' onto its object. (For another relevant discussion, see Terence Penelhum's *Survival and Disembodied Existence* [London, 1970], final chapters.)

12. 'Personal Identity and Individuation', *Proceedings of the Aristotelian Society*, 57 (1956–1957), 229–53; also *Analysis*, 21 (1960–1961), 43–48.

13. J. M. Shorter, 'More about Bodily Continuity and Personal Identity', *Analysis*, 22 (1961–1962), 79–85; and Mrs. J. M. R. Jack (unpublished), who requires that this truth be embedded in a causal theory.

psychological continuity. This is why, whenever there is such continuity, we ought, if we can, to imply it by making a judgment of identity.

If psychological continuity took a branching form, no coherent set of judgments of identity could correspond to, and thus be used to imply, the branching form of this relation. But what we ought to do, in such a case, is take the importance which would attach to a judgment of identity and attach this importance directly to each limb of the branching relation. So this case helps to show that judgments of personal identity do derive their importance from the fact that they imply psychological continuity. It helps to show that when we can, usefully, speak of identity, this relation is our ground.

This argument appeals to a principle which Williams put forward.[14] The principle is that an important judgment should be asserted and denied only on importantly different grounds.

Williams applied this principle to a case in which one man is psychologically continuous with the dead Guy Fawkes, and a case in which two men are. His argument was this. If we treat psychological continuity as a sufficient ground for speaking of identity, we shall say that the one man is Guy Fawkes. But we could not say that the two men are, although we should have the same ground. This disobeys the principle. The remedy is to deny that the one man is Guy Fawkes, to insist that sameness of the body is necessary for identity.

Williams' principle can yield a different answer. Suppose we regard psychological continuity as more important than sameness of the body.[15] And suppose that the one man really is psychologically (and causally) continuous with Guy Fawkes. If he is, it would disobey the principle to deny that he is Guy Fawkes, for we have the same important ground as in a normal case of identity. In the case of the two men, we again have the same important ground. So we ought to take the importance from the judgment of identity and attach it directly to this ground. We ought to say, as in Wiggins' case, that each limb of the branching relation is as good as survival. This obeys the principle.

To sum up these remarks: even if psychological continuity is neither logically, nor always in fact, one–one, it can provide a criterion of identity. For this can appeal to the relation of *non-branching* psychological continuity, which is logically one–one.[16]

The criterion might be sketched as follows. '*X* and *Y* are the same person if they are psychologically continuous and there is no person who is contemporary with either and psychologically continuous with the other.' We should need to explain what we mean by 'psychologically continuous' and say how much continuity the criterion requires. We should then, I think, have described a sufficient condition for speaking of identity.[17]

---

14. *Analysis*, 21 (1960–1961), 44.
15. For the reasons given by A. M. Quinton in 'The Soul,' *Journal of Philosophy*, 59 (1962), 393–409.
16. Cf. S. Shoemaker, 'Persons and Their Pasts,' *American Philosophical Quarterly*, 7 (1970), 269; and 'Wiggins on Identity,' *Philosophical Review*, 79 (1970), 542.
17. But not a necessary condition, for in the absence of psychological continuity bodily identity might be sufficient.

We need to say something more. If we admit that psychological continuity might not be one–one, we need to say what we ought to do if it were not one–one. Otherwise our account would be open to the objections that it is incomplete and arbitrary.[18]

I have suggested that if psychological continuity took a branching form, we ought to speak in a new way, regarding what we describe as having the same significance as identity. This answers these objections.[19]

We can now return to our discussion. We have three remaining aims. One is to suggest a sense of 'survive' which does not imply identity. Another is to show that most of what matters in survival are relations of degree. A third is to show that none of these relations needs to be described in a way that presupposes identity.

We can take these aims in the reverse order.

III

The most important particular relation is that involved in memory. This is because it is so easy to believe that its description must refer to identity.[20] This belief about memory is an important cause of the view that personal identity has a special nature. But it has been well discussed by Shoemaker[21] and by Wiggins.[22] So we can be brief.

It may be a logical truth that we can only remember our own experiences. But we can frame a new concept for which this is not a logical truth. Let us call this 'q-memory.'

To sketch a definition[23] I am q-remembering an experience if (1) I have a belief about a past experience which seems in itself like a memory belief, (2) someone did have such an experience, and (3) my belief is dependent upon this experience in the same way (whatever that is) in which a memory of an experience is dependent upon it.

According to (1) q-memories seem like memories. So I q-remember *having* experiences.

This may seem to make q-memory presuppose identity. One might say, 'My apparent memory of *having* an experience is an apparent memory of *my* having an experience. So how could I q-remember my having other people's experiences?'

This objection rests on a mistake. When I seem to remember an experience, I do indeed seem to remember *having* it.[24] But it cannot be a part of what I seem to

18. Cf. Bernard Williams, 'Personal Identity and Individuation,' *Proceedings of the Aristotelian Society*, 57 (1956–1957), 240–41, and *Analysis*, 21 (1960–1961), 44; and also Wiggins, *op. cit.*, p. 38: 'If coincidence under [the concept] *f* is to be *genuinely* sufficient we must not withhold identity. . . simply because transitivity is threatened.'

19. Williams produced another objection to the 'psychological criterion,' that it makes it hard to explain the difference between the concepts of identity and exact similarity (*Analysis*, 21 [1960–1961], 48). But if we include the requirement of causal continuity we avoid this objection (and one of those produced by Wiggins in his note 47).

20. Those philosophers who have held this belief, from Butler onward, are too numerous to cite.

21. *Op. cit.*

22. In a paper on Butler's objection to Locke (not yet published).

23. I here follow Shoemaker's 'quasi-memory.' Cf. also Penelhum's 'retrocognition,' in his article on 'Personal Identity,' in the *Encyclopedia of Philosophy*, ed. Paul Edwards.

24. As Shoemaker put it, I seem to remember the experience 'from the inside' (*op. cit.*).

remember about this experience that I, the person who now seems to remember it, am the person who had this experience.[25] That I am is something that I automatically assume. (My apparent memories sometimes come to me simply as the belief that *I* had a certain experience.) But it is something that I am justified in assuming only because I do not in fact have *q*-memories of other people's experiences.

Suppose that I did start to have such *q*-memories. If I did, I should cease to assume that my apparent memories must be about my own experiences. I should come to assess an apparent memory by asking two questions: (1) Does it tell me about a past experience? (2) If so, whose?

Moreover (and this is a crucial point) my apparent memories would now come to me *as q*-memories. Consider those of my apparent memories which do come to me simply as beliefs about my past: for example, 'I did that.' If I knew that I could *q*-remember other people's experiences, these beliefs would come to me in a more guarded form: for example, 'Someone—probably I—did that.' I might have to work out who it was.

I have suggested that the concept of *q*-memory is coherent. Wiggins' case provides an illustration. The resulting people, in his case, both have apparent memories of living the life of the original person. If they agree that they are not this person, they will have to regard these as only *q*-memories. And when they are asked a question like 'Have you heard this music before?' they might have to answer 'I am sure that I *q*-remember hearing it. But I am not sure whether I remember hearing it. I am not sure whether it was I who heard it, or the original person.'

We can next point out that on our definition every memory is also a *q*-memory. Memories are, simply, *q*-memories of one's own experiences. Since this is so, we could afford now to drop the concept of memory and use in its place the wider concept *q*-memory. If we did, we should describe the relation between an experience and what we now call a 'memory' of this experience in a way which does not presuppose that they are had by the same person.[26]

This way of describing this relation has certain merits. It vindicates the 'memory criterion' of personal identity against the charge of circularity.[27] And it might, I think, help with the problem of other minds.

25. This is what so many writers have overlooked. Cf. Thomas Reid: 'My memory testifies not only that this was done, but that it was done by me who now remember it' ('Of Identity,' in *Essays on the Intellectual Powers of Man*, ed. A. D. Woozley [London, 1941], p. 203). This mistake is discussed by A. B. Palma in 'Memory and Personal Identity,' *Australasian Journal of Philosophy*, 42 (1964), 57.

26. It is not logically necessary that we only *q*-remember our own experiences. But it might be necessary on other grounds. This possibility is intriguingly explored by Shoemaker in his 'Persons and Their Pasts' (*op. cit.*). He shows that *q*-memories can provide a knowledge of the world only if the observations which are *q*-remembered trace out fairly continuous spatiotemporal paths. If the observations which are *q*-remembered traced out a network of frequently interlocking paths, they could not, I think, be usefully ascribed to persisting observers, but would have to be referred to in some more complex way. But in fact the observations which are *q*-remembered trace out single and separate paths; so we can ascribe them to ourselves. In other words, it is epistemologically necessary that the observations which are *q*-remembered should satisfy a certain general condition, one particular form of which allows them to be usefully self-ascribed.

27. Cf. Wiggins' paper on Butler's objection to Locke.

But we must move on. We can next take the relation between an intention and a later action. It may be a logical truth that we can intend to perform only our own actions. But intentions can be redescribed as q-intentions. And one person could q-intend to perform another person's actions.

Wiggins' case again provides the illustration. We are supposing that neither of the resulting people is the original person. If so, we shall have to agree that the original person can, before the operation, q-intend to perform their actions. He might, for example, q-intend, as one of them, to continue his present career, and, as the other, to try something new.[28] (I say 'q-intend *as* one of them' because the phrase 'q-intend that one of them' would not convey the directness of the relation which is involved. If I intend that someone else should do something, I cannot get him to do it simply by forming this intention. But if I am the original person, and he is one of the resulting people, I can.)

The phrase 'q-intend *as* one of them' reminds us that we need a sense in which one person can survive as two. But we can first point out that the concepts of q-memory and q-intention give us our model for the others that we need: thus, a man who can q-remember could q-recognize, and be a q-witness of, what he has never seen; and a man who can q-intend could have q-ambitions, make q-promises, and be q-responsible for.

To put this claim in general terms: many different relations are included within, or are a consequence of, psychological continuity. We describe these relations in ways which presuppose the continued existence of one person. But we could describe them in new ways which do not.

This suggests a bolder claim. It might be possible to think of experiences in a wholly 'impersonal' way. I shall not develop this claim here. What I shall try to describe is a way of thinking of our own identity through time which is more flexible, and less misleading, than the way in which we now think.

This way of thinking will allow for a sense in which one person can survive as two. A more important feature is that it treats survival as a matter of degree.

IV

We must first show the need for this second feature. I shall use two imaginary examples.

The first is the converse of Wiggins' case: fusion. Just as division serves to show that what matters in survival need not be one–one, so fusion serves to show that it can be a question of degree.

---

28. There are complications here. He could form *divergent* q-intentions only if he could distinguish, in advance, between the resulting people (e.g. as 'the left-hander' and 'the right-hander'). And he could be confident that such divergent q-intentions would be carried out only if he had reason to believe that neither of the resulting people would change their (inherited) mind. Suppose he was torn between duty and desire. He could not solve this dilemma by q-intending, as one of the resulting people, to do his duty, and, as the other, to do what he desires. For the one he q-intended to do his duty would face the same dilemma.

Physically, fusion is easy to describe. Two people come together. While they are unconscious, their two bodies grow into one. One person then wakes up.

The psychology of fusion is more complex. One detail we have already dealt with in the case of the exam. When my mind was reunited, I remembered just having thought out two calculations. The one person who results from a fusion can, similarly, *q*-remember living the lives of the two original people. None of their *q*-memories need be lost.

But some things must be lost. For any two people who fuse together will have different characteristics, different desires, and different intentions. How can these be combined?

We might suggest the following. Some of these will be compatible. These can coexist in the one resulting person. Some will be incompatible. These, if of equal strength, can cancel out, and if of different strengths, the stronger can be made weaker. And all these effects might be predictable.

To give examples—first, of compatibility: I like Palladio and intend to visit Venice. I am about to fuse with a person who likes Giotto and intends to visit Padua. I can know that the one person we shall become will have both tastes and both intentions. Second, of incompatibility: I hate red hair, and always vote Labour. The other person loves red hair, and always votes Conservative. I can know that the one person we shall become will be indifferent to red hair, and a floating voter.

If we were about to undergo a fusion of this kind, would we regard it as death?

Some of us might. This is less absurd than regarding division as death. For after my division the two resulting people will be in every way like me, while after my fusion the one resulting person will not be wholly similar. This makes it easier to say, when faced with fusion, 'I shall not survive,' thus continuing to regard survival as a matter of all-or-nothing.

This reaction is less absurd. But here are two analogies which tell against it.

First, fusion would involve the changing of some of our characteristics and some of our desires. But only the very self-satisfied would think of this as death. Many people welcome treatments with these effects.

Second, someone who is about to fuse can have, before-hand, just as much 'intentional control' over the actions of the resulting individual as someone who is about to marry can have, beforehand, over the actions of the resulting couple. And the choice of a partner for fusion can be just as well considered as the choice of a marriage partner. The two original people can make sure (perhaps by 'trial fusion') that they do have compatible characters, desires, and intentions.

I have suggested that fusion, while not clearly survival, is not clearly failure to survive, and hence that what matters in survival can have degrees.

To reinforce this claim we can now turn to a second example. This is provided by certain imaginary beings. These beings are just like ourselves except that they reproduce by a process of natural division.

We can illustrate the histories of these imagined beings with the aid of a diagram. The lines on the diagram represent the spatiotemporal paths which would be traced out by the bodies of these beings. We can call each single line (like the double line) a 'branch'; and we can call the whole structure a 'tree.' And let us suppose that each 'branch' corresponds to what is thought of as the life of one individual. These individuals are referred to as 'A,' 'B + 1,' and so forth.

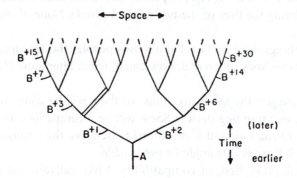

Now, each single division is an instance of Wiggins' case. So A's relation to both B + 1 and B + 2 is just as good as survival. But what of A's relation to B + 30?

I said earlier that what matters in survival could be provisionally referred to as 'psychological continuity.' I must now distinguish this relation from another, which I shall call 'psychochological connectedness.'

Let us say that the relation between a q-memory and the experience q-remembered is a 'direct' relation. Another 'direct' relation is that which holds between a q-intention and the q-intended action. A third is that which holds between different expressions of some lasting q-characteristic.

'Psychological connectedness,' as I define it, requires the holding of these direct psychological relations. 'Connectedness' is not transitive, since these relations are not transitive. Thus, if X q-remembers most of Y's life, and Y q-remembers most of Z's life, it does not follow that X q-remembers most of Z's life. And if X carries out the q-intentions of Y, and Y carries out the q-intentions of Z, it does not follow that X carries out the q-intentions of Z.

'Psychological continuity,' in contrast, only requires overlapping chains of direct psychological relations. So 'continuity' is transitive.

To return to our diagram. A is psychologically continuous with B + 30. There are between the two continuous chains of overlapping relations. Thus, A has q-intentional control over B + 2, B + 2 has q-intentional control over B + 6, and so on up to B + 30. Or B + 30 can q-remember the life of B + 14, B + 14 can q-remember the life of B + 6, and so on back to A.[29]

A, however, need *not* be psychologically connected to B + 30. Connectedness requires direct relations. And if these beings are like us, A cannot stand in such

29. The chain of continuity must run in one direction of time. B + 2 is not, in the sense I intend, psychologically continuous with B + 1.

relations to every individual in his indefinitely long 'tree.' Q-memories will weaken with the passage of time, and then fade away. Q-ambitions, once fulfilled, will be replaced by others. Q-characteristics will gradually change. In general, A stands in fewer and fewer direct psychological relations to an individual in his 'tree' the more remote that individual is. And if the individual is (like B + 30) sufficiently remote, there may be between the two *no* direct psychological relations.

Now that we have distinguished the general relations of psychological continuity and psychological connectedness, I suggest that connectedness is a more important element in survival. As a claim about our own survival, this would need more arguments than I have space to give. But it seems clearly true for my imagined beings. A is as close psychologically to B + 1 as I today am to myself tomorrow. A is as distant from B + 30 as I am from my great-great-grandson.

Even if connectedness is not more important than continuity, the fact that one of these is a relation of degree is enough to show that what matters in survival can have degrees. And in any case the two relations are quite different. So our imagined beings would need a way of thinking in which this difference is recognized.

V

What I propose is this.

First, A can think of any individual, anywhere in his 'tree,' as 'a descendant self.' This phrase implies psychological continuity. Similarly, any later individual can think of any earlier individual on the single path[30] which connects him to A as 'an ancestral self.'

Since psychological continuity is transitive, 'being an ancestral self of' and 'being a descendant self of' are also transitive.

To imply psychological connectedness I suggest the phrases 'one of my future selves' and 'one of my past selves.'

These are the phrases with which we can describe Wiggins' case. For having past and future selves is, what we needed, a way of continuing to exist which does not imply identity through time. The original person does, in this sense, survive Wiggins' operation: the two resulting people are his later selves. And they can each refer to him as 'my past self.' (They can share a past self without being the same self as each other.)

Since psychological connectedness is not transitive, and is a matter of degree, the relations 'being a past self of' and 'being a future self of' should themselves be treated as relations of degree. We allow for this series of descriptions: 'my most recent self', 'one of my earlier selves', 'one of my distant selves', 'hardly one of *my* past selves (I can only *q*-remember a few of his experiences)', and, finally, 'not in any way one of *my* past selves—just an ancestral self.'

---

30. Cf. David Wiggins, *op. cit.*

This way of thinking would clearly suit our first imagined beings. But let us now turn to a second kind of being. These reproduce by fusion as well as by division.[31] And let us suppose that they fuse every autumn and divide every spring. This yields the following diagram:

If A is the individual whose life is represented by the three-lined 'branch,' the two-lined 'tree' represents those lives which are psychologically continuous with A's life. (It can be seen that each individual has his own 'tree,' which overlaps with many others.)

For the imagined beings in this second world, the phrases 'an ancestral self' and 'a descendant self' would cover too much to be of much use. (There may well be pairs of dates such that every individual who ever lived before the first date was an ancestral self of every individual who ever will live after the second date.) Conversely, since the lives of each individual last for only half a year, the word 'I' would cover too little to do all of the work which it does for us. So part of this work would have to be done, for these second beings, by talk about past and future selves.

We can now point out a theoretical flaw in our proposed way of thinking. The phrase 'a past self of' implies psychological connectedness. Being a past self of is treated as a relation of degree, so that this phrase can be used to imply the varying degrees of psychological connectedness. But this phrase can imply only the degrees of connectedness between different lives. It cannot be used within a single life. And our way of delimiting successive lives does not refer to the degrees of psychological connectedness. Hence there is no guarantee that this phrase, 'a past self of,' could be used whenever it was needed. There is no guarantee that psychological connectedness will not vary in degree within a single life.

This flaw would not concern our imagined beings. For they divide and unite so frequently, and their lives are in consequence so short, that within a single life psychological connectedness would always stand at a maximum.

But let us look, finally, at a third kind of being.

In this world there is neither division nor union. There are a number of everlasting bodies, which gradually change in appearance. And direct psychological relations, as before, hold only over limited periods of time. This can be illustrated with a third

31. Cf. Sydney Shoemaker in 'Persons and Their Pasts,' *op. cit.*

diagram (which is found below). In this diagram the two shadings represent the degrees of psychological connectedness to their two central points.

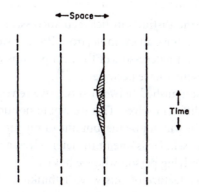

These beings could not use the way of thinking that we have proposed. Since there is no branching of psychological continuity, they would have to regard themselves as immortal. It might be said that this is what they are. But there is, I suggest, a better description.

Our beings would have one reason for thinking of themselves as immortal. The parts of each 'line' are all psychologically continuous. But the parts of each 'line' are not all psychologically connected. Direct psychological relations hold only between those parts which are close to each other in time. This gives our beings a reason for *not* thinking of each 'line' as corresponding to one single life. For if they did, they would have no way of implying these direct relations. When a speaker says, for example, 'I spent a period doing such and such,' his hearers would not be entitled to assume that the speaker has any memories of this period, that his character then and now are in any way similar, that he is now carrying out any of the plans or intentions which he then had, and so forth. Because the word 'I' would carry none of these implications, it would not have for these 'immortal' beings the usefulness which it has for us.[32]

To gain a better way of thinking, we must revise the way of thinking that we proposed above. The revision is this. The distinction between successive selves can be made by reference, not to the branching of psychological continuity, but to the degrees of psychological connectedness. Since this connectedness is a matter of degree, the drawing of these distinctions can be left to the choice of the speaker and be allowed to vary from context to context.

On this way of thinking, the word 'I' can be used to imply the greatest degree of psychological connectedness. When the connections are reduced, when there has been any marked change of character or style of life, or any marked loss of memory, our imagined beings would say, 'It was not I who did that, but an earlier self.' They could then describe in what ways, and to what degree, they are related to this earlier self.

32. Cf. Austin Duncan Jones, 'Man's Mortality,' *Analysis*, 28 (1967–1968), 65–70.

This revised way of thinking would suit not only our 'immortal' beings. It is also the way in which we ourselves could think about our lives. And it is, I suggest, surprisingly natural.

One of its features, the distinction between successive selves, has already been used by several writers. To give an example, from Proust: 'we are incapable, while we are in love, of acting as fit predecessors of the next persons who, when we are in love no longer, we shall presently have become. . . .'[33]

Although Proust distinguished between successive selves, he still thought of one person as being these different selves. This we would not do on the way of thinking that I propose. If I say, 'It will not be me, but one of my future selves,' I do not imply that I will be that future self. He is one of my later selves, and I am one of his earlier selves. There is no underlying person who we both are.

To point out another feature of this way of thinking. When I say, 'There is no person who we both are,' I am only giving my decision. Another person could say, 'It will be you,' thus deciding differently. There is no question of either of these decisions being a mistake. Whether to say 'I,' or 'one of my future selves,' or 'a descendant self' is entirely a matter of choice. The matter of fact, which must be agreed, is only whether the disjunction applies. (The question 'Are X and Y the same person?' thus becomes 'Is X *at least* an ancestral [or descendant] self of Y?')

VI

I have tried to show that what matters in the continued existence of a person are, for the most part, relations of degree. And I have proposed a way of thinking in which this would be recognized.

I shall end by suggesting two consequences and asking one question.

It is sometimes thought to be especially rational to act in our own best interests. But I suggest that the principle of self-interest has no force. There are only two genuine competitors in this particular field. One is the principle of biased rationality: do what will best achieve what you actually want. The other is the principle of impartiality: do what is in the best interests of everyone concerned.

The apparent force of the principle of self-interest derives, I think, from these two other principles.

The principle of self-interest is normally supported by the principle of biased rationality. This is because most people care about their own future interests.

Suppose that this prop is lacking. Suppose that a man does not care what happens to him in, say, the more distant future. To such a man, the principle of self-interest can only be propped up by an appeal to the principle of impartiality. We must say, 'Even if you don't care, you ought to take what happens to you then equally into account.' But for this, as a special claim, there seem to me no good arguments. It can

33. *Within a Budding Grove* (London, 1949), I, 226 (my own translation).

only be supported as part of the general claim, 'You ought to take what happens to everyone equally into account.'[34]

The special claim tells a man to grant an *equal* weight to all the parts of his future. The argument for this can only be that all the parts of his future are *equally* parts of *his* future. This is true. But it is a truth too superficial to bear the weight of the argument. (To give an analogy: The unity of a nation is, in its nature, a matter of degree. It is therefore only a superficial truth that all of a man's compatriots are *equally* his compatriots. This truth cannot support a good argument for nationalism.)[35]

I have suggested that the principle of self-interest has no strength of its own. If this is so, there is no special problem in the fact that what we ought to do can be against our interests. There is only the general problem that it may not be what we want to do.

The second consequence which I shall mention is implied in the first. Egoism, the fear not of near but of distant death, the regret that so much of one's *only* life should have gone by—these are not, I think, wholly natural or instinctive. They are all strengthened by the beliefs about personal identity which I have been attacking. If we give up these beliefs, they should be weakened.

My final question is this. These emotions are bad, and if we weaken them we gain. But can we achieve this gain without, say, also weakening loyalty to, or love of, other particular selves? As Hume warned, the 'refined reflections which philosophy suggests . . . cannot diminish . . . our vicious passions . . . without diminishing . . . such as are virtuous. They are . . . applicable to all our affections. In vain do we hope to direct their influence only to one side.'[36]

That hope *is* vain. But Hume had another: that more of what is bad depends upon false belief. This is also my hope.

34. Cf. Thomas Nagel's *The Possibility of Altruism* (Oxford, 1970), in which the special claim is in effect defended as part of the general claim.

35. The unity of a nation we seldom take for more than what it is. This is partly because we often think of nations, not as units, but in a more complex way. If we thought of ourselves in the way that I proposed, we might be less likely to take our own identity for more than what it is. We are, for example, sometimes told, 'It is irrational to act against your own interests. After all, it will be you who will regret it.' To this we could reply, 'No, not me. Not even one of my future selves. Just a descendant self.'

36. 'The Sceptic,' in 'Essays Moral, Political and Literary,' *Humes's Moral and Political Philosophy* (New York, 1959), p. 349.

Chapter 43

Persons, animals, and ourselves

P. F. Snowdon

List of discussed theses

Iɴ this chapter certain propositions are regularly referred to by numbers or abbreviated names. For ease of reference, a list of the most important ones is set out straight away.

   (1) I am a person.
  (1E) I am essentially a person.
   (2) The notion of a person involves distinctive criteria of identity.
   (3) I am an animal (of the species Homo sapiens).
  (3E) I am essentially such an animal.
   (4) The notion of such an animal involves distinctive criteria of identity.
   (5) If an object is an animal then it is not possible for that object to carry on existing without remaining an animal.
   (6) There are possible circumstances in which I carry on existing without being an animal.
  AAT (short for Animal Attribute Theory of Personhood): X is a person if and only if X is an animal . . . of a kind whose typical members perceive, feel, remember, etc. . . . , conceive of themselves as perceiving, feeling, etc. . . .
   PA (short for Psychological Animalism): any psychologically endowed thing must be an animal.

I

It is regrettable that, for a long time, the notions of 'human being' and 'animal' were neglected in discussions of, what is called, 'personal identity'.[1] The neglect is regrettable

I wish to thank Drs Martha Klein, Grant Gillett, Galen Strawson, and Christopher Gill for helpful comments on an earlier version.

1. It is quite possible to study the discussion of personal identity from the 1950s and 1960s in the works of e.g. Williams and Shoemaker, and hardly encounter the concepts of animal and human being. Fashions have, of course, changed. However, one purpose of this paper is to indicate that the right to think of ourselves as animals has to be earned.

P. F. Snowdon, 'Persons, Animals, and Ourselves', from *The Person and the Human Mind*, edited by C. Gill (Clarendon Press, 1990), reprinted by permission of Oxford University Press.

for two reasons. First, it meant that certain *problems* were not recognized. Second, it meant that certain *truths* were not recognized. At least, that is what I shall claim. As a piece of rather rough and ready history we can say this neglect has been ended, as far as recent discussion goes, by the writings of David Wiggins, some of whose arguments I shall discuss.[2] However, I want to begin by specifying some propositions with which the discussion will be concerned.

When philosophers ask what the criteria of personal identity are, it is clear that they do not distinguish the question they are considering from the question as to what the criteria of identity are for *themselves*. This is manifest from the practice of testing a suggested criterion by asking; must I fulfil that condition to remain in existence? If they recognize no distinction between these questions it is, I think, because they are making two assumptions. The first is about themselves, and would be expressed by each of them thus:

(1E) I am essentially a person.

(Obviously, if they accept (1E) they will also accept:

(1) I am a person.

I introduce (1) because I shall refer to it later.) The second assumption I shall express, perhaps infelicitously, as follows;

(2) The notion of a person involves certain distinctive criteria of identity.

I am going to assume that it is clear without much amplification, what the attitude is which the words in (2) are intended to express. It should be made explicit that when it is said (as in (2)) that a certain kind has distinctive criteria, it is meant, not that they are unique to that kind, but that they are the ones to which the kind is tied.

Let me introduce three other claims, related as the above are, but containing a different concept from that of person. They are:

(3) I am an animal (of the species Homo sapiens).
(3E) I am essentially such an animal.
(4) The notion of such an animal involves distinctive criteria of identity.

Assuming that the identified claims are sufficiently clear to consider, the question arises as to which of them are true. There are, I believe, two approaches which have been elaborated in the literature. The first accepts (1E), (2), and (4), but denies (3E) and (3). This I shall call the Lockean theory, for this combination corresponds to a natural way of stating (some of) Locke's conclusions in his chapter on identity.[3] Amongst current

2. See 'Locke, Butler and the Stream of Consciousness: And Men as a Natural Kind', in A. O. Rorty (ed.), *The Identities of Persons* (Berkeley, 1976), pp. 139–73, and also, and principally, *Sameness and Substance* (Oxford, 1980), esp. ch. 6. Although I discuss (in sects. IX and X) some claims made by Wiggins, I do not regard what is written here as anything like a complete assessment of his complex arguments or of the motivations which underly the development of his theory.
3. Locke expresses his views in *An Essay Concerning Human Understanding*, ed. P. H. Nidditch (Oxford, 1975), II. xxvii. In other parts of the *Essay*, of course, Locke made claims that would count against

writers we can cite Shoemaker as someone who accepts the Lockean view.[4] The second approach accepts, in effect, all the claims (1)–(4). I take Wiggins, in chapter 6 of *Sameness and Substance*, to be propounding this. In this account the crucial thought is that to be a person just is to be an animal of a certain kind.

It would be incorrect to assume that we are limited to choosing between these two approaches, but the disagreement between them highlights a crucial question; is (3) true? I want, in this paper, to consider (some of) the arguments for and against it. In Section II, I shall give what I consider to be the main argument against (3). In Section III, a group of what seem to be very strong considerations in favour of (3) will be propounded. We shall then have something like an antinomy, with (3) and its negation strongly supported. Subsequent sections will mainly be concerned to pursue (but certainly not to suggest how to conclude) the debate about resolving this antinomy, a debate which will touch on some of the other numbered propositions.

In the discussion I shall take some things for granted. Given the first-person content of (3), I shall state these assumptions as assumptions about myself, but it should be obvious that these are merely applications to myself of quite general assumptions. First, there certainly is an animal where I am now. This animal is as natural a member of the Order of Primates as are, for example, particular monkeys and apes. This particular animal, which I shall call H, is, clearly, the animal I am if I am an animal. Second, if I am not H, it is not because I am an entity currently existing separately from H or from what is going on in H. That is, the discussion will be conducted in a materialist framework. Third, despite the difficulties that arise, I shall not consider the option of relativizing identity as a possible escape route.[5]

II

The argument against (3) draws on familiar resources so I shall expound it in a brief way. Expressed in a very general form, it infers that (3) is false from two premises. They are:

(5) If an object is an animal then it is not possible for that object to carry on existing without remaining an animal.

(6) There are possible circumstances in which I carry on existing without being an animal.

supposing that he would acceept (1E). In calling this first combination the 'Lockean theory' I am, therefore, thinking only of his ch. on identity. Also, in calling it Lockean I am not giving expression to a conviction that acceptance of this combination commits one to acceptance of the actual analysis of personal identity which Locke himself advocated.

4. See S. Shoemaker, 'Personal Identity: A Materialist's Account', in S. Shoemaker and R. Swinburne, *Personal Identity* (Oxford, 1984), 67–132.

5. For an explanation and criticism of the thesis that identity statements are relative see Wiggins, *Sameness and Substance*, ch. 2. This thesis is not the only one which might be suggested in response to the difficulties raised by our questions and which I ignore. Another such response is that the difficulties show that our concepts of person and self are inadequate and should be regarded as lacking application. In ignoring them here, I am not implying that these suggestions are not worth discussing.

The inference (to the falsity of (3)) from (5) and (6) is, I hope, beyond criticism on logical grounds. How plausible, though, are the premisses?[6]

About (5) I shall, at this stage, say little. It is standard to distinguish between two sorts of sorts. The first sort are those to which a thing can belong at a given time and then cease to belong, despite remaining in existence. A clear example is that of being pretty. The second sort are those which have the following property: if an entity belongs to one of them at a given time, then that entity must belong to it as long as that entity remains in being. Call these *abiding sorts*. Different kinds of properties, of course, possess this property, but it would be widely agreed, and it is surely plausible to say, that 'being an animal' is an abiding sort.

What of (6), the second premiss? This is supported by describing circumstances which it is taken are possible (in the relevant sense of possible) and about which it is claimed to be true (*a*) that I survive, but (*b*) that there is no animal that I am. If we grant both (*a*) and (*b*) of the imagined possible circumstances then it seems that (6) is correct. The examples which, it might be supposed, reveal this have been used in recent discussion, not in arguments explicitly directed against (3), but rather in ones against the claim that (fairly full) bodily continuity is a necessary condition for survival of the person. So (*b*) has not normally been emphasized in the presentation of such cases.

Viewed in an abstract way, one source of the plausibility of agreeing that there are possible circumstances where (*a*) and (*b*) hold are the fundamental and apparently plausible intuitions Locke had about personal identity. These intuitions are, first, that the survival of a person is crucially linked to the persistence of, in some sense, his

6. It is, to some degree, a matter of choice how to formulate the sort of argument against (3) which I am interested in setting down. It would have been possible to use the following, slightly different, premisses. (5') If an object is a certain animal then it is not possible for that object to carry on existing without remaining that animal. (6') There are possible circumstances in which I carry on existing without being this animal H. This is as valid a ground for the denial of (4) as the argument in the main text, and has the advantage that to sustain (6') we need not envisage the supposed possibility of vat-sustained consciousness; we need only envisage brain transplants into other human bodies. There are, therefore, possible grounds for objection to (6), which are not grounds for objecting to (6'), and which, if relied on to block the argument involving (6), would not amount to full solutions of the problems raised by this sort of case. However, in the present discussion, there is, I hope, no reliance on objections with that character. The reason for using (5) and (6), rather than (5') and (6'), is that a defence of (5) is slightly more straightforward than one for (5'). (A remark by Colin McGinn prompted this clarification.) A far more important contrast is between the sort of grounds developed in the text for (6), (and which could have been developed for (6')), which are grounds to do with brain transplants, and another sort of ground which has sometimes been influential. When (6) is supported in this second way, something along the following lines is said: 'Surely it is just possible for you to switch from this body to another one; surely you can envisage simply waking up, after a night's sleep, in a new body, and, perhaps, looking across the room and seeing your old body.' Crucially, when argued this way, the basic description is simply in terms of the person or self transferring from his initial body to something else. In contrast, the account on which the argument in the text relies is in terms of a switch of a real substantial item (namely the brain) which is assumed (and not simply fantastically) to have certain functions. This latter basis evidently has a link to reality which is missing in the other one, which can, therefore, be dismissed as a fantasy which our account of the actual nature and identity of the things involved need not countenance as any sort of real possibility.

consciousness or capacity for consciousness; and second, that, in principle (although maybe not in fact) the persistence of a stream of consciousness (the direction in which it might go) is not clearly linked to any particular substance.[7] Locke developed his theory of personal identity to make these ideas coherent and explicit, a task in which, it is generally agreed, he failed. What is important for us though, is not the theory he developed, but the appeal of the ideas behind it.

Locke expresses one of his intuitions this way:

Thus everyone finds, that whilst comprehended under that consciousness, the little finger is as much part of itself, as what is most so. Upon separation of this little finger, should this consciousness go along with the little finger and leave the rest of the body, 'tis evident the little finger would be the Person, the same Person . . . (*Essay*, II. xxvii. 17).

Locke's talk of the finger is fanciful, but Locke's story updated is, of course, the brain-removal story, the development of which is due to Shoemaker.[8] Imagine a surgeon removing from your head the whole of your brain. He needs to preserve during the operation its long-run capacity to function. He then relocates it in a stable environment so that it can resume its normal function. The brain is, we think, the seat or organ of consciousness and of attendant psychological functions—such as memory; calculation, and thought. So, given that the organ for these is refunctioning, those operations are resumed. Sequences of events of this sort have seemed possible, in the relevant sense, to many people, and have also seemed to be the circumstances about which we should hold (*a*) that I survive the operation but (*b*) there is no animal I am after it. Now, we can vary the precise details of the story to reinforce our sense that these judgements are appropriate. In particular we can tell different stories about what happens during the operation and what happens after it. Such stories have been told repeatedly and well in recent discussions. I do not, therefore, want to elaborate the familiar transplant stories in order to elicit agreement to (*a*) but I do take it that (*a*) can be made to seem very plausible; and that (*b*) can be rendered plausible by envisaging the new stable environment as consisting in a totally artificial support system which both meets the brain's energy requirements and gives it suitable input and output channels, a piece of equipment commonly known as a Vat. Prima facie, this support system could resemble ones which are quite familiar in the study of other important organs—for example, hearts or kidneys. The crucial point is that no one has the slightest inclination to think these systems sustain an animal—rather they provide temporary support for an organ from an animal. That, I suggest, is the natural way to think of such an experiment even if it involves the brain.

---

7. It would be wrong to think that a belief in the possibility of circumstances where (*a*) and (*b*) obtain has to reflect a commitment to the plausibility of both these fundamental Lockean intuitions. The belief can be generated by a combination of what I have called Locke's first intuition (which is an almost universal one) and the rather less extreme intuition that the particular substance, if any, to which a particular stream of consciousness is essentially linked need not be on the scale of the whole animal.

8. See *Self-Knowledge and Self-Identity* (New York, 1963), 22–5.

Since both (5) and (6) are plausible, we have a strong case against (3). I shall call someone who accepts that (3) is false a 'non-animalist'.

III

At this point some will accept that (3) is false. But the denial of (3) itself faces serious problems. I want to advance three reasons which seem to strongly favour (3).

The first reason basically consists in pointing out that any denier of (3) must meet the challenge of providing a better explanation of how (3) can be false than was managed by Locke. Locke's explanation would be this; just as we need to distinguish the lump of matter here and the animal here, to recognize, that is, that they are two different sorts of thing, so we must also recognize a third sort—the person here. (3) can be false because I am something of that third sort—a person. But Locke also, and not surprisingly, says what sort of thing a person is: 'a person is a thinking intelligent being that has reason and reflection and can consider itself as itself, the same thinking thing in different times and places'.[9] That is to say: Locke thinks that that captures the kind of thing *I* am, so that, being that kind of thing, I can be contrasted with the animal here (another kind of thing) and the lump of stuff here (still another kind of thing).

Now, it is not at all hard to sympathize with this definition of the concept of a person; in effect, it makes 'person' a functional predicate, applicable to entities capable of a certain sort of higher cognition. Crucially, it allows 'person' to apply across animal species and, for all that it says, to non-animals. However, there are two comments I want to make. (i) It is hard to believe that 'person' as explained by Locke is an abiding sort; if it is not, then it does not mark out a basic sort of thing, the distinctive persistence conditions of which we can trace. One reason this is hard to believe is that, as defined, it appears very similar to lots of across-species functional classifications which do not mark out abiding sorts, e.g. 'is a teacher', 'can play chess at a grandmaster level', 'is a prodigious calculator'. The point can be put this way: if you concentrate on the functions alluded to in the definition, then there seems no difficulty in supposing that a creature at one time capable of carrying them out should itself lose that capacity. (ii) Surely if we ask to what entities the functional predicate (person), as elucidated by Locke, does apply, the answer we all want to give is—a certain kind of animal, namely human beings. They are animals which reason, reflect, and talk of themselves! So, rather amusingly, Locke defines a notion which he thinks picks out a sort of thing to be contrasted with the animal sort, but which actually applies to certain animals. In this sense of 'person', some animals are persons: they are fundamentally animals, which function so as to be persons. So Locke does not provide a coherent framework underpinning the person and animal contrast. I have not at this point been concerned with difficulties in what Locke says about personal identity; rather the objection has been that Locke's account of

9. *Essay*, II. xxvii. 9.

the conditions for falling under the person-concept does not leave room for contrasting the person I am with this animal which I am calling H.

What is the force of this difficulty in Locke's theory for us? My aim at the moment is to set up a powerful case *for* (3), so that, given the intuitively plausible argument of the previous section, we generate an antinomy (in a loose sense). The question, therefore, is how far does the Lockean difficulty support (3)? It is not, I think, a very direct argument for (3). It gives support, however, on certain assumptions. If we are inclined to agree that, if I am not an animal, then there is some other sort of thing I must be; that that sort of thing is a person; and that Locke characterizes more or less adequately what it is to be a person, then there seems to be no room for the denial of (3). In fact, these assumptions are not uncommon, so we have an argument with some bite.

The second argument for (3) points out a related problem in denying (3), but this time not to do with the concept of a person. If someone says (3) is false he is saying that when *I* say on this occasion (call it O) 'I am an animal' that remark is false. But we have to ask such a person this question: cannot animals ever think about themselves? cannot animals use the first-person pronoun? The answer has surely to be that they can; surely some animals could and have evolved with that capacity. Now, if it is agreed that animals can, then, surely, H (this animal) is one such. But if H can talk of itself using 'I', then it seems that the remarks made at O through the mouth of H are such remarks. Clearly there could not be any better candidate for such a case. (What must the animal H do to speak about itself which it did not do then?) If, however, that remark was a case where an animal spoke of itself, and what it said was 'I am an animal', then that must rank as a truth. That seems to settle the question we begin with. (I call that the reductio argument).

I have, so far, presented two lines of thought, pointing out these problems with the conclusion of our first argument: (i) that Locke's elucidation of 'person' quite fails to sustain it, (ii) that it is an animal talking here, so when it says 'I am an animal' that must be true. I want to mention a third point (or type of point)— namely, that to think of yourself as a animal (to acknowledge that) coheres with, and acts as, a potential explanation of the way we do think of ourselves. Here are three examples. It has always been a serious embarrassment to Lockean, or Lockean inspired, accounts of our identity, that we think of those accidents and illnesses which disturb the normal flow of our mental life as things we live through and hence undergo. If we are the animals, then this would be, of course, the correct way to think. More controversially, it seems to me that many of us are inclined to side with Bernard Williams's (tentative) judgement as to what the mental-characteristic switching machine of 'The Self and the Future' achieves; he prefers to think that he stays with his body.[10] Again, this opinion is validated if we think of the subjects involved as animals. Finally, in all actual circumstances that we are acquainted with, the principle 'some person, some human being' holds. To deny (3) is, then, to deny

10. See 'The Self and the Future' in *Problems of the Self* (Cambridge 1973), p. 63.

the most obvious ground for all our convictions about actual cases, and many of our convictions about supposedly possible cases.

IV

I have now set up an antimony concerning the proposition 'I am an animal'. In the face of it, there are two things we might do. We might provide a full resolution of, that is, a full adjudication of, all the arguments involved. There are three options available: first, accept the argument against (3) and defuse the arguments for it; second, accept the arguments (or some of them) for (3) and defuse the argument against it; third, defuse both sets of arguments. Alternatively, we might be less ambitious; we might aim to strengthen one conclusion, giving us confidence that the alternative side is wrong, without, however, pin-pointing any error in the considerations apparently supporting it. I want to do the less ambitious sort of thing: I want, first of all, to strengthen the case for (3), by considering replies that non-animalists might make to the arguments for (3).

Before I do that, I wish to set aside a suggestion of Shoemaker's which, it might be thought, could solve our problem.[11] In discussing personal identity, Shoemaker becomes worried about the status of (3). He points out, though, that even if we wish to assert a non-identity between myself and H, we can interpret (3) in a way which makes it come out true. It will be true if we interpret 'am' as meaning 'am composed of the same stuff as . . .'. Even if I am not identical with H, I am now composed of the same stuff as H. Does this suggestion contribute anything to a solution of our antinomy? Shoemaker's suggestion arises from his belief that the argument I presented in Section 11 (or, at least, something like it) is correct, and that the fundamental problem over (3) is that we have a strong intuition that, despite the correctness of the argument, (3) expresses a truth. Viewing the problem this way, his response is, naturally enough, to search for an interpretation of the words in (3) which, despite the soundness of the argument, allows it to be true. The problem which I have tried to establish is that (3), when interpreted in a way which makes the earlier argument count against it, that is, when it is interpreted as involving an identity, also has powerful arguments in favour of it. This problem is not, therefore, alleviated in the slightest by making (3) come out true *on some interpretation or other*. Shoemaker's suggestion is irrelevant to the achievement of a resolution of our problem.

V

The third sort of argument for (3) attempted to display it as something acceptance of which can explain and ground the basic ways we think when considering ourselves in normal, abnormal, and unrealistic circumstances. The rejoinder to this will be that there may be ways of accounting for our attitudes which equally fit the cases

11. Shoemaker, in Shoemaker and Swinburne, *Personal Identity*, sec. XI.

and which do not involve (3). It seems to me that the most likely possible alternative position here is that supported, in different ways, by Mackie and Nagel which treats a person as tied to that object which crucially sustains the mental operations the occurrence of which are required for a person, namely, his brain.[12] It can be argued that this view accounts for everything cited in support of (3) in the third argument. Indeed, this approach is overall in a very good position because it also accepts the intuitions about brain transplants we are inclined to have. That is, it accepts something like (6). One of its strengths is that it can accommodate the first argument. Now such a view need not deny (3), but it might do so. Therefore, unless something is said to block this suggestion, the third argument must be acknowledged to be inconclusive.

The first argument attempted to show that Locke's definition of what a person is provides no coherent ground for sustaining the assertion of (1) along with a denial of (3). In fact, what was argued is that, according to Locke's definition of 'person' and in light of the facts, this animal here (H) is a person. This confronts a nonanimalist with a choice. Since he, evidently, does not wish to abandon (1), he has either to say: (A) let's stick with Locke's definition (or something like it) and say: 'I am a person, H is a person, and so there are two persons here'; or (B) modify our account of person so that H is not counted a person; there may, therefore, be only one person here.

But both of these options are very unappealing. The reason that (B) is unacceptable is that there is nothing about H which can ground the denial to him of the status of a person. After all, H can think, is self-conscious, can deliberate, hold moral opinions, etc. No one should withhold from such a creature the title of 'person'. (A) is equally unappealing. In the first place, the suggestion that there are two persons in this chair is not one that anyone would accept.[13] In the second place, if H is a person, then persons cannot be things which, in their natures, are distinct from animals. The confidence of the non-animalist must be shaken by this.

I am suggesting, therefore, that the difficulties which were developed for Locke's approach, turn out on investigation to be (or, perhaps better, turn into) general

---

12. See J. L. Mackie, *Problems From Locke* (Oxford, 1976), ch. 6, esp. p. 200, and Thomas Nagel, *The View From Nowhere* (New York, 1986), ch. 3, esp. p. 40. This view was earlier endorsed by Wiggins; see *Identity and Spatio-Temporal Continuity* (Oxford, 1967), p. 51.

13. It will occur to some that my claim that no one would agree that there are two persons here is false. David Lewis and John Perry, in contributions to the personal identity debate (stimulated by Parfit's discussion of the split-brain transplant case), suggested views which would not rule this out in principle. That is true, and my remark is a little too strong. However, their approach will not allow the quite general consequence that there are, come what may, two persons here. They hold that, just as we can say with roads, where e.g. the road from Oxford to London and the road from Oxford to Aylesbury take the same route out of Oxford and, thereafter, diverge, that there are two roads which overlap at certain places, so we can say about a body whose brain was about to be split, that the pre-splitting stage involved two, at that point, overlapping persons. However, even theorists taking this view would not suppose that if there is no split then there are still two completely overlapping persons. Hence, neither they nor anyone else would be prepared to accept the consequence which grounds the objection to (A).

ones; any non-animalist seems to have problems about counting persons, which I have not found any way of resolving satisfactorily.

What is also troublesome, it seems to me, is the reductio argument. There is, as far as I can see, though, one desperate option available to the non-animalist.[14] If they grant the asumptions, they must agree that 'I am an animal', (3), as uttered by me now, is true. However, that does not exclude regarding it as false, so long as an ambiguity is postulated. Now, the ambiguity to be postulated must concern the reference of 'I': that is, it must be supposed to have a dual reference. They will have to say, there is not just one thing talking of itself, there are two. One is an animal; interpreted as referring to it, (3) is true. Another, however, is an entity of the person variety, an entity with that distinctive sort of life history; interpreted as referring to it, (3) as false.

In this way they can absorb the argument and maintain their own view. That is to say, the reductio argument is not a reductio strictly speaking; it does not reduce to absurdity the supposition that (3) expresses a falsehood. Rather, it reduces to absurdity the supposition that (3) does not express a truth. However, there is, surely, a strong inclination to regard what is involved in thus avoiding the objection as absurd. In the first place it concedes that the animal H can talk and think of itself, and is presumably therefore a person. So this reply is committed to the thesis that there are two persons. In the second place, the effort, while thinking first-person thoughts, of trying to keep the present suggestion alive induces extreme intellectual vertigo. Thus, how would one handle such a practical question as 'what ought I to do now?' while allowing that there is both the animal-person and the non-animal-person simultaneously thinking? Should we allow, and how should we cope with, the possibility of the animal-I concluding that he ought to do F and the non-animal-I concluding that he ought to do G? It is, surely, very hard not to think that 'I', unlike 'you' and 'there', is an indexical expression for which in normal conversational circumstances no supplement to its mere use can be needed in order to determine its reference. I think, therefore, that the present reply to the reductio argument is very hard to defend.

VI

Having set up a dilemma over (3), I have considered what might be said in reply to the arguments for (3). The conclusion has been that, with two of the arguments at least, the replies only sink the opponent of (3) into further problems. At the moment, therefore, I do not see any room to manœuvre for the opponent of (3),

---

14. Another reply that can be made is that from (i) the animal is speaking and it says 'I am an animal', we should no more infer that what was said is true, than we should infer from (ii) the mouth is speaking and it says 'I am a mouth', that what is said is true. This comparison, however, is very difficult to sustain. Thus, to the mouth we ascribe no intentions, plans, action-capacities, beliefs, awareness and so on. If those are ascribed to the animal, then how can it be denied that it can speak? If it can speak, then it can refer to itself. So, to hold out against the 'reductio-argument' on the basis of this reply, it must be claimed that the animal lacks these psychological characteristics. That, however, is not a serious option.

the non-animalist. It is reasonable therefore to conclude that (3) is true.[15] This means that I need to answer the Lockean argument which attacked (3). What options are there?

I want to distinguish three options. First, we can question (5); given the trouble the argument causes, maybe the thought that an object can be an animal and then cease to be should be revalued; maybe it is true.[16] Second, we can deny premiss (6), by saying this: we agree that the envisaged circumstances are, in the relevant sense, possible, but we deny that I and this animal ever, as it were, come apart in them. This requires us to identify which of the possible outcomes in the original case would be the outcome, given that we are not prepared to assent to both (a) and (b). The available alternatives are, roughly, that, after the operation, there is still an animal, or there is no longer me, or it is a borderline case to the same degree for both myself and the animal. There is, though, a third option: premiss (6) can be denied by claiming that the circumstances envisaged as possible, and about which we are invited to make judgements, are not actually possible at all in the relevant sense. This is a response available to someone who accepts recent ideas about genuine (metaphysical) possibility being determined empirically.

Now, it is not my intention to say what is wrong with the argument against (3). I do not know what, if anything, is to be rejected about it. I want, however, to consider the options, beginning with the suggestion that (5) ought to be abandoned.

VII

Should we reject (5)? To discuss this I shall take (5) to say: if something is an animal, then it (that thing) cannot cease to be animal. There is, it must be agreed, some attraction to resolving things by abandoning (5). People are often strongly wedded to the intuitions about brain transplants, and so, if the arguments for animalism are as strong as I claimed, premiss (5) has the least strong attachment, and can go.

---

15. I think that my acceptance of (3) on the grounds that have been presented might be challenged in at least two separate ways. First, it might be said that there is something spurious about the difficulties now alleged to be involved in denying (3). It is impossible to dismiss this suggestion outright, but unless something more specific is said, consideration of it cannot be taken any further. Second, it might be suggested that it is methodologically improper to regard (3) as more strongly supported than its denial simply because difficulties have been found in direct replies to the arguments for (3). After all, maybe the same will happen to direct replies to the argument against (3), and which arguments were discussed first should not affect the view we take. I do not have the space or enough understanding of the issues raised by this objection to discuss it properly. However, my inclination is to say (i) that given a prior expectation that an acceptable view about the truth-value of (3) can be found without commitment to grossly counterintuitive claims, it is reasonable at this point to regard (3) as true, given the difficulties of denying (3), but also (ii) that we should be prepared to revise our attitude to (3) if the difficulties pile up for an acceptance of it.

16. I had this option in mind when, in sec. v, I remarked that someone who believes that a person is tied, essentially, to his brain, need not deny (3).

I think, however, that we should be reluctant to abandon (5). In part, the attractions of making (5) the casualty in the conflict derive from its having received least attention so far; what can be said in its favour has not yet been said. I want, therefore, to sketch such a case. What we are trying to show is that if, at t, there is an animal, and at $t + n$ there is something which at that time is not an animal, then the thing which, at $t + n$, is not an animal is not the same thing as the thing which, at t, was an animal. We have, fundamentally, two notions in play. The first is that of an animal, the idea of what is to count as an animal. The second is that of a single persisting thing, the idea of an individual which exists over time. To make a case for (5) we need to bring these notions together—to show that being an animal is being a persisting thing, hence to lose an animal is to lose a thing (an individual).

The claim which I want to endorse (or, given how unambitious these remarks are, perhaps, better, *remind* you of) about persisting material things, that is to say, about what we recognize as such, is that we regard the persistence in a certain materially continuous form of a fundamental explanatory unity as the persistence of a thing. The details of what amounts to the persistence of such an explanatory unity I shall not attempt to fill in. However, I shall assume that the idea is a sound one. On the other side, it is plausible, surely, to think that an animal is, precisely, a materially continuous locus of fundamental explanation.[17] So, in our example, the move from the pre-operational animal to the post-operational functioning brain, marks a significant explanatory change; the powers and explanations are fundamentally different. If both these claims are correct, then premiss (5) is vindicated. Animals are kinds of things.

Thinking of identity in this way provides the major ground for retaining (5), but it is, perhaps, worthwhile to add three things. The first two are that thesis (5) is, surely, intuitively plausible, and has received assent by most people who seriously study identity. The third is that (6) (or something like it) receives a sort of confirmation in reactions to a famous Monty Python sketch, in which it is said that something is an 'ex-parrot'. Why is that so funny? The explanation, which involves (5), is that the predicate-modifier 'ex-', forms a new predicate, when concatenated to a predicate F (. . .), which counts as true of an item i, at a time just in case i was F but is no longer F at that time. Abiding predicates cannot sensibly be modified in this way; nothing ever is an ex-F, where F is an abiding predicate. According to (5), plus certain assumptions, '—is a parrot' is an abiding predicate. The humour of the remark, I want to suggest, lies in this logical incongruity.

I have not, in these remarks, properly argued for (5), the rejection of which may be the correct way to destroy the case against (3). I have tried to show, however, that (5) is anchored in a popular and persuasive way of thinking about identity, and is not easily rejectable.

17. The viewpoint I have expressed in these simple, not to say over-simple, claims has received further, more cautious and, I think, convincing expression in recent writings. See Wiggins, *Sameness and Substance*, esp ch. 3 sec. III, and R. G. Millikan, *Language, Thought and Other Biological Categories* (Cambridge, Mass., 1984), ch. 17.

VIII

If (5) is accepted, premiss (6) is all that is left to reject. I want to consider the first way of rejecting it, that of accepting that we are dealing with possibilities, but disputing the inclination to affirm both (*a*) and (*b*). One line here is to deny (*b*). But this suggestion I have, in effect, rejected in the previous discussion (that concerned with (5)). It seems that the kind of object an animal is, the kinds of explanations definitive of it, are simply not preserved in the thing remaining after the operation. It is, surely, a mistake to see the animal as preserved and much more plausible to regard the functioning brain as a preserved *organ*.

This leaves it open to argue directly for the rejection of (*a*). I shall consider one remark made by Bernard Williams in support of this. The argument invokes (or expresses) a supposed tie between a person and his body. Since the brain transplant leaves the body behind, grounds for linking a person to his body undermine the idea that he is transplanted with the brain. Here is how Williams tries to ground this idea, considering the possibility of a switch of persons between an emperor's and a peasant's body.

> The requirement is . . . that the emperor's body, with the peasant's personality, should be on the throne, and the peasant's body, with the emperor's personality in the corner. What does this mean? In particular, what has happened to the voices? The voice ought to count as a bodily function, yet how would the peasant's gruff blasphemies be uttered in the emperor's cultivated tones, or the emperor's witticisms in the peasant's growls?[18]

In fairness to Williams it should be said that he was not dealing with brain transplants, nor did he generalize strongly from the quoted remarks. However, it is, I think, hard to be impressed by this illustration of a link between a person and his body. It seems superficial to view those reponses to situations which are constitutive of personality as not expressible in different ways. Even if inexpressible, could they not still be his reactions? Further, even if part of the personality must be acknowledged to have been lost, it seems a relatively insignificant loss.[19]

The general claim which will need to be supported if it is to provide a criticism of (6) is that, in brain transplants too much is lost of what the particular person was (lost, because it requires the body which was left behind) to make it acceptable to think that the person (or the same self) remains. Now, it would be wrong, I think, to dismiss out of hand this way of resisting (6). My criticism is, rather, that Williams's illustration of it does not make it seem very strong. On one view, what is at issue is the very close identification of philosophers with their mental life, so that the artificial preservation of the organ for that makes them suppose *they* survive. The present

---

18. 'Personal Identity and Individuation', in *Problems of the Self*, p. 12.
19. A vivid way of revealing what this suggestion is up against is to imagine us urging it (by some communicating channel) on the conscious subject housed in the brain in the vat (something about which this objection to (6) is not being sceptical) as a basis for that subject's concluding he (or it?) is not identical with the person who donated the brain. The remarks do not seem particularly powerful for that role. (A remark of Professor Dummett produced this way of putting the problem.)

counter-suggestion is that this is simply a part of what there is in us, and we would lose, in brain transplants, too much of the body-linked elements to survive. I have not tried to refute such a bold conjecture, but no one has satisfactorily supported it.

IX

That is as far as I want (or am able) to take the question as to where exactly the argument based on (5) and (6) goes wrong. I find myself thinking that the resolution must lie in such a criticism since attempts to deny (3) seemed futile. However, before considering a rather different sort of argument which might be thought to help us, I want to note and try to counteract a certain rigidity in my discussion so far of the argument based on (5) and (6). My approach (in section VII and VIII, may have given the impression that there might be such a thing as *the* reply to that argument (that is, to the argument identified as containing (5) and (6)). In fact, if (5) is accepted, then the appropriate reply may, indeed surely will, (see note 6 above) depend upon what the supposed circumstances are which are being taken by a proponent of the argument to support (6). The present (unsuccessful) discussion should therefore be thought of as directed against (6) *as supported by full brain transplant cases*. (6) might be supported by, amongst other things, less than full brain transplants (e.g. split-brain or hemisphere transplants), or by transplant of more than the brain (e.g. complete head transplants). Bearing this in mind, it seems that a reply of the sort I claimed to find in Williams's paper, and which was considered in section VIII, has a better chance of working against (6), as supported by cases where less is transplanted, than it has of working against (6), as supported by cases where more substantial animal-parts are involved. My general point, though, is simply that a defender of (3) need not expect there to be a *single* criticism which will counter all the different sorts of transplant cases which have been taken to support (5).

The conviction that (3) is true would be strengthened if there were other arguments for it. I want to enquire whether there is another way to support (3), namely on the basis of the account of being a person advanced by Wiggins in chapter 6 of *Sameness and Substance*. If this account, which he calls the animal attribute theory and which asserts that necessarily persons are sorts of animals, is accepted, then, given the undoubted truth of (1) we can infer (3).

What then, is the animal attribute theory (which I shall call AAT)? Here is (an abbreviated form of) what is proposed:

'(Perhaps) X is a person if and only if X is an animal . . . of a kind whose typical members perceive, feel, remember, etc. . . . . conceive of themselves as perceiving, feeling, etc. . . .'[20]

We can best explain the significance of the account by contrasting it with Locke's account. There are three features of Locke's elucidation which are abandoned. First, Locke did not restrict in any way the sort of thing that can be a person, except as

---

20. *Sameness and Substance*, p. 171.

a thing possessing the specified set of mental capacities. The AAT restricts persons to animals. Second, the AAT has an open-ended list of psychological capacities required for personhood. Third, the AAT allows that an actual creature can count as a person without it having the relevant psychological capacities, namely if it is a member of an animal kind whose typical members have those capacities. We should also note that these three dimensions of modification (or difference) are independent. For example, we could adopt the limitations to animals, but retain Locke's list of psychological characteristics (with or without linking the psychological characteristics to the kind). Other combinations are obvious. A full discussion of the proposal would, therefore, be a matter of real complexity.

How should we react to this theory? I want to express a difficulty with one of its aspects. The short Lockean list of cognitive features supposedly required for personhood is replaced by a more complex list which is, as it stands, open-ended. We are told to 'note carefully these . . . dots'.[21] By what route, by gaining what knowledge, shall we be able to complete the definition and eliminate the dots? It is clear that the psychological attributes are supposed to be those of a typical human being; the dots will get eliminated, therefore, when psychology and biology tell us what the characteristic mental capacities of human beings are. There is, that is, a (surely, unobjectionable) commitment in the approach to something which may be called human psychological nature. Understood this way, the proposal invites the question: why is it necessary to have the typical psychological capacities of a human in order to be a person? I do not myself see what the answer to this question is.

This line of thought queried the list of cognitive capacities offered in the animal-attribute theory. We can also question, with some justification, the idea that for an object S to be a person, it need not itself possess the characteristic capacities, but must be a member of kind which typically does. In one respect this is an illiberal proposal. The second element in it rules out the possibility of being a person for a freakishly gifted member of a kind the typical members of which do not attain personhood. If an experiment in foetal development produced a highly intelligent and self-conscious orang-utan, I think we could count it as an (unfortunate) person. In another respect the proposal is liberal, for according to it human beings who are incapable of any advanced cognition are, by virtue of being human, to count as persons. There are uses of 'persons' which fit this suggestion. Thus in assessing the claim that a person dies in a certain hospital each day we would count it as true so long as a human being, however cognitively endowed at the time of death or, at any stage in their life, died each day. Such a use of 'person' is not sensibly defined in Locke's way. It is not clear, however, that it is sensibly defined in the animal-attribute way, since it seems to mean little more than 'individual human being'. There are however other uses for which this liberal suggestion fails to account. We say (or some do) that the very young are not yet persons, have not reached personhood, and that people suffering irreversible and severe loss of mental capacity are no longer persons.

---

21. *Sameness and Substance*, p. 171.

It is, in part, the existence of such claims (or at least the tendency for such claims to be made) that grounds the conviction that there is a distinctive and interesting person-concept.

I want to leave this problem unresolved and ask the crucial question: is it correct to require that all persons are of necessity animals? We can bring against this suggestion the willingness of many to think there can be persons who are not animals: for example, God, Satan, and angels. It may be said that these are impossibilities. That is, I agree, not ruled out simply because people believe in them. The existence of a willingness to think this way suggests, however, what—as I want to claim—is the correct conception of the issue. However precisely the contrast is to be drawn, there is agreement that persons are, at most, a sub-class of mentally endowed subjects. Cats are mentally endowed (with perception and sensation, etc.) but are not persons. So we can represent the concept of a person as involving at least both the notion of a mentally endowed subject and possession of some further mental qualities. Call these further mental properties the P-factor. The necessary animality of persons might be viewed as required either by the general notion of mental endowment or by the P-factor, or by its being a further restriction on the person-notion that a mentally endowed and P-factor possessing entity counts as a person only if it is also an animal. This third idea is the one which looks implausible given the widespread belief in non-animal persons. We cannot treat such believers as making the same sort of mistake as would be made by someone who failed to see the connection between kennels and dogs (or between pigs and sties). It would, also, surely, be implausible to allow that things other than animals can be mentally endowed (in the basic ways) but that only animals can possess the extra P-factor. If non-animals can perceive and feel, why cannot they also think, reflect, have self-consciousness, and so on?[22] This means that a defender of the animal-attribute view of persons is committed to defending the claim that necessarily only animals are mentally endowed. (I shall call this psychological animalism PA, in contrast to the animal-attribute theory of persons).

If this identification of the issue to be fought over is correct, then some comments are appropriate. (i) The difference between Locke's and the animal-attribute theorists's account of persons is, on the animal-attribute view when considered in its full commitment, not large. For Locke's definition, couched as it is in psychological terms, defines a notion which, given PA, could only apply to animals. (ii) PA will need to be supported by its proponents. However, they have, I think, a prior task—that of explaining how the claim *could* be true. In what way might the essential tie between mental state and animal nature arise? This will not be easy since it runs counter to well-entrenched psychological and philosophical dogmas. (iii) I think it becomes sensible, if I am right, to hold that the animal-attribute theory of persons is not a theoretically

---

22. There are some who think that this question is not unanswerable. They think that it is possible to find grounds for restricting the P-factor to animals which are not grounds for restricting sentience to animals. A proper consideration of this approach would need to be much more thorough than the very brief one I have provided.

interesting claim. It is not a thesis which it is appropriate or valuable to argue for. Rather, the debate should be, in part, about psychological animalism.

We can confirm this by considering one passage from Wiggins's (extremely rich) argument. He is, in this passage as I interpret it, trying to support the animal-attribute view of persons. He says:

To these claims I think that the animal attribute theorist who embraces their conservative implications will want to add that here at last we begin to see the proper grounds for what has sometimes appeared to be only fear or prejudice, but now starts to seem the plainest good sense. This is our defensible or indefensible conviction that, however we may conceive of higher animals such as dolphins or horses or apes, such artifacts as robots and automata have no title to any kind of civil right—or even to the consideration that we ought to accord to the lowlier sentient creatures . . . No weaker claim than that entered by the animal attribute view could do justice to the depth and passion of most people's resistance to the idea that automata can approximate to life or sentience, and it is certain that we still believe that, to have genuine feeling or purposes or concerns, a thing must *at least* be an animal of some sort.[23]

The suggestion made here is that there is some confirmation of the animal-attribute view of persons in its being a ground for certain fundamental convictions we have. The idea is that the combination of some firm opinions, together with its being the case that a certain theory would, if true, be an explanation or ground for them, is a sort of support for that theory. What opinions, however, are to be grounded? They are:

  (i)   artefacts have no rights;
  (ii) automata cannot approximate to life and sentience;
  (iii) only animals have genuine feelings and concerns.

The suggested ground for them, it seems, is AAT, a theory about what it is to be a person. Now (i) might be grounded in AAT only if the auxiliary assumption is made that persons alone have rights. The natural question would then be: why assume that only persons have rights? The answer must be that only persons possess those morally important attributes which support rights. This means that (i) is properly grounded by convictions of sort (ii) and (iii). But convictions of sort (ii) and (iii) are not consequences of a necessary link between personhood and animality; rather any assertion of such a link must be grounded on independent defences of (ii) and (iii).

I hope that consideration of this passage reveals that PA is the crucial claim (and not AAT). Of course, PA itself, if true, will ground (3), which is what we were looking to AAT for. However, a defence of PA would be an enormous task.

X

The strategy explored in the last section was that of attempting to show we must think of ourselves as possessing a certain feature (being animals) by showing that the feature must belong to persons. But it is obvious that there may be crucial features

---

23. *Sameness and Substance*, pp. 174–5.

we must acknowledge ourselves as possessing, which have nothing to do with our being *persons.* There are, then, two questions which should be distinguished:

(7) how should we elucidate the notion of a person?
(8) how should we think of ourselves?

I shall make some remarks on (and in response to) these questions, and conclude the discussion of our antinomy.

In his discussion Wiggins claims that unless we think of persons as animals (having a determinate, biological nature which can be discovered only by empirical investigation) there are very serious consequences. For example, he says:

one is bound to wonder what changes it would bring to the theory and practice of politics, if all inquiry and all description came to be organised by a conception of human personality that was focussed only by a systematic specification, rather than the idea of something that we can try to discover about, and may even be surprised by.[24]

By a 'systematic specification' he means one setting out the conditions for being a person by specifying, in a relatively a priori manner, a finite list of functional requirements (as in the Lockean definition). What is puzzling in this passage is the assumption that adopting a 'systematic' account of what is necessary for person-hood will have any implications at all for our conception of human nature, or for the idea that we are essentially human. What is dangerous here is rather ways of thinking of *ourselves*, ways which are nothing to do with what we think of as condi-tions for personhood. Wiggins's remark neglects the important distinction between issue (7) and issue (8). We can have a relatively 'systematic' concept of personhood because we can allow that the things which qualify (ourselves for one) have a real nature not implied by or involved in that concept.

It may be replied: if this 'systematic' account is combined with the view that persons, as a sort, have distinctive criteria of identity, we cannot dismiss the problems raised by a 'systematic' account so easily. Leaving aside the question whether that reply is cogent, it merely acts as an incentive to suggest that, in so far as personhood is a more general notion than that of simply being human, the notion is not one tied to, or implying, criteria of identity. That is to say, I think we should seriously consider abandoning proposition (2) of section 1. Here, I shall do no more than put the idea forward. Locke, and many people who discuss criteria of personal identity, assume that a person is a type of continuant, a different type from animals, and the aim is to articulate the requirements for persistence of such things. Wiggins rejects the contrast between person and animal, but still holds that (2) is true, because being a person is being a sort of animal. If we are suspicious both of the tie between person and animal, suggested by Wiggins, and the contrast between them suggested by Lockeans, we can resolve the problem by allowing that different kinds of things (animals and maybe non-animals) can equally be persons, and for them to be so is not for them to share persistence

24. Ibid. p. 179.

requirements. One reason for thinking that this is not totally unacceptable is the chaotic mess, and the evident arbitrarinesses, exhibited by the debate about criteria of personal identity. Maybe this is not so much a result of the great difficulty of the search, but rather of there being nothing to find.[25]

It may also be fair to see this proposal linked with another; namely, that the extant notion of being a person is not susceptible of a clear and tight analysis. We have a use of the term which applies it to a range of creatures (and not necessarily to all human beings at all times) which is guided by two things. The first is the aim of marking a class important from the moral point of view; and the second is that this importance derives from their sharing certain higher cognitive and psychological capacities. It is being claimed that it is simply untrue to say that our attributions are guided by much in the way of agreed conditions. If this is roughly correct, then it supports the rejection of (2) in two ways. First, if to be a person is to be capable of certain morally important, psychological functions, it will apply to things, of whatever sort of continuants, which are capable in the right way. Second, in being an imprecise notion, it can hardly mark out a distinctive and theoretically important sort of continuant.

Having queried (2) we can query (1E). If I had been brain-damaged at birth, I would not have become a person (taking the notion along the lines of the previous paragraph). Since I might never have become a person, I am not essentially a person.

Returning to our original six propositions, the combination I am proposing, although in no sense properly arguing for, is that (1), (3), (3E), and (4) are true; (1E) and (2) are dubious. However, this combination includes (3) against which there is a powerful objection which has not been properly answered. That important task is one for another occasion.

25. It should not be assumed that dropping (2) dissolves all these issues called 'problems of personal identity'. On the contrary, there will, of course, remain problems about our human, animal identity. The suggestion is rather that the mistaken conviction that as well as these problems there are also problems about the identity of another fundamental kind of thing, persons, has led to an unrestrained field day for groundless and subjective fantasies. It should not be assumed, either, that adoption of the view being recommended is necessarily inconsistent with some of the revisionary conclusions about what is of value in human life which, as normally argued for, seem to depend on (2).

Study questions

1. In which different ways do we employ the idea of things being 'the same' as another? Do all these ways involve the logical notion of identity? (You may want to consult the introduction to Part IV: Universals and Particulars, when addressing this question.)
2. What does it mean to say that an object has temporal parts? What can be said for or against this idea?
3. Can you make sense of the idea of surviving without being identical to the thing which survives? How?
4. Consider this view: 'The logical concept of identity is an abstraction which has no real application to the messy empirical world. The source of the puzzles of identity is the result of trying to apply this strict logical concept where it cannot really be applied.' Is this true?

Further reading

A very clear introduction to the issues in this section, which argues for a distinctive solution to the problems of change, is Lowe (2002: chapters 2–4). See also, the Further Reading for Part III: Being, for readings on substance. The four-dimensionalist (or 'perdurance') view derives from Quine (1961b). Armstrong (1980) gives a very clear discussion of the problem and a defence of the perdurance view; Heller (1990) and Sider (2001) provide further defences of the view. The three-dimentionalist (endurance) view is defended by Thomson (1983) and Merricks (1994). See Haslanger (forthcoming) for an excellent recent survey of the issues. Van Inwagen (1981) is an attack on the idea that objects have 'arbitrary undetached parts' like Body-minus, described above. Wiggins (1968) defends the view that more than one thing can be in the same place at the same time; see also Lowe (1989) and Hughes (1997). This is criticized by Burke (1994). These issues are now frequently discussed under the heading of 'material constitution': a very useful collection of essays with that name is Rea (1997). This collection also contains Gibbard (1975) a defence of the claim that objects can be identical with the portion of matter that makes them up and hence that identity can be contingent; this should be read in conjunction with Kripke (1971) (see also Part V: Necessity). An sophisticated yet very lucid introduction to the problem of personal identity is Garrett (1998). Olson (1997) defends an uncompromising animalist position. The essays of Bernard Williams (1973) remain among the classic readings on this problem (especially, 'The Self and the Future', 'Imagination and the Self' and 'Personal Identity and Individuation').

Mind and body

Part IX

Mind and body

Introduction

1. Introduction

THE metaphysical problems surrounding the nature of mind and body fall into two broad groups. In the first group belong questions about the fundamental metaphysical classification of mental phenomena. How do the metaphysical categories of substance, attribute (or property), event, and process apply to the mind? Is the mind a substance, or should we rather think of the mind in terms of mental states and processes? Or should we employ some other fundamental category—for example, the category of the *person*? The second group of questions is concerned with the relationship between the mental and the physical/material world. Dualists hold that mental and physical things are of two radically different natures; monists hold that their natures are of one kind. Materialist monists hold that this nature is wholly material; idealist monists hold that this nature is wholly mental. What is the fundamental nature of this debate between materialists and dualists?

There is also a debate about what it means to classify the phenomena of mind as *mental*. Is there a 'mark' of the mental, something all mental things have in common? Are all mental things, for example, distinguished by their intentionality (or representational character) or by their relation to consciousness? Or is the mental a hybrid category which has no principle of unity at all? We shall touch on this question briefly in this section, but not deal with it systematically. We shall take it for granted that mental phenomena include intentional phenomena like thoughts, beliefs, intentions, and emotions, which may or may not involve consciousness, as well as essentially conscious phenomena like sensations, perceptual experiences, and imaginings.

2. The interaction between mind and body

Descartes's theory of mind provides the paradigmatic starting point for any investigation into the philosophy of mind. Although his philosophy of mind has sometimes been criticized as being the source of many misconceptions (the so-called 'Cartesian legacy': see McCulloch 2003) it nonetheless provides an impressive vision of the integrity and the autonomy of the mental which still needs to be considered today in any full account of the metaphysics of mind. Descartes's project is also much misunderstood and therefore often criticized without good reason (see Patterson 2000 for an attempt to rectify some of these misunderstandings). Here we should note, first of all, that Descartes addresses both the kinds of questions above. His overall metaphysical position is, famously, dualist: he thought that each individual mind or soul is an immaterial substance, and the whole material world is a distinct substance. 'Substance' here is intended in the traditional metaphysical sense of a *being capable of independent existence* (see Part III: Being). So minds are capable of existing independently of the material world; and the material world is capable of existing independently of minds. (So notice that Descartes does not say that an individual human body (say) is a substance; nor does he say that minds are 'made of mental stuff' as some contemporary philosophers say he did.)

Substances are distinguished by their characteristic attributes. The characteristic attribute of mental substance is *thought*. In Chapter 44, Descartes explains what he means by 'thought' in this sense. Kinds of mental phenomena—like individual judgements or decisions, for example—are called *modes* of thought. In the selection from the Sixth Meditation reprinted here, we see that Descartes also argues that souls are 'joined' to their bodies in a kind of union. An interesting question is how Descartes can combine this view with the narrower definition of 'thought' described earlier in the selection.

Leibniz was one of Descartes's most formidable critics. Like many critics of Descartes, Leibniz argued that Descartes could not explain how minds and bodies could causally interact. Leibniz argued that in fact they do not interact, but rather they exist in a kind of pre-established harmony. It is important to realize that for Leibniz, this was not a harmony between two *substances*, since Leibniz did not think that bodies are substances at all (see Part III: Being). In fact, Leibniz was an *idealist*; he thought that the ultimate reality of the world is mental. This ultimate reality consists of simple substances, which he called 'monads', which are causally isolated from one another but which 'perceive' the entire universe. The harmony therefore holds between the mechanical unfolding of the physical world according to the laws of physics, and the pattern of perceptions in the monads.

3. The physical world

The debate between Descartes and Leibniz is partly about the existence of mental causation. They differ in that Descartes thinks that mind and body causally interact, whereas Leibniz thinks that the mental life of a substance is in a state of pre-established harmony with the phenomena of the physical world: there is no mind–body causation. However, they both agree that minds cannot be material beings at all. This is one the biggest differences between the classic discussions of mind in modern philosophy (i.e. the seventeenth/eighteenth centuries) and discussions today. While almost all great philosophers of the modern era denied that the mind is material, these days many (if not most) philosophers accept some sort of materialism or physicalism. What explains this change?

'Materialism' and 'physicalism' are terms which are used in many ways, some of them vague and imprecise, and some inconsistent with each other. When philosophers of the seventeenth and eighteenth centuries opposed materialism, what they took themselves to be opposing was the view that everything is matter, or that the fundamental reality of the world is material substance. The contemporary descendants of seventeenth-century materialists, the *physicalists*, do not tend to express their doctrine in terms of matter. The reasons for this are complex, but can be summarized as follows. 'Physicalism' was a term coined by the early twentieth-century logical positivist philosopher Otto Neurath (see Carnap 1955: 312) for the view that gives priority to physics, among all branches of knowledge, in telling us what there is and how we know about it. Let's call this proposed feature of physics its 'ontological authority'. Now physics, as it developed in the nineteenth and twentieth centuries, allows many more entities to exist in addition to matter. Forces, waves, and fields are not matter in any obvious or everyday sense;

but they are certainly physical, in the sense of being part of the subject matter of physics. Now if being physical is being the subject matter of physics, then physicalism (understood as the claim that physics has ontological authority) can differ from traditional materialism because it says that there is more in the world than matter. (It should be borne in mind, however, that some contemporary philosophers use the terms 'physicalism' and 'materialism' as synonyms.)

The view that physics has ontological authority has become a dominant one in English-speaking philosophy in recent years (see Papineau 2001 for an account of how this came about). But, so far, the view is a bit vague; how can we make it more precise? One way would be to say that the only entities there really are the ones dealt with by a true physical theory. But this would mean that we would be wrong about many things which exist. We think that there are cities, football matches, wars, and restaurants; but none of these things is strictly speaking the subject matter of physics. No physics textbook, for example, will mention these entities.

However, we might respond that although these entities are not themselves part of the subject matter of physics, they are built up or constituted out of entities which are: that is, all the entities mentioned are made up of things which are made of up things like atoms and molecules, which are clearly physical by the above definition. So a less extreme physicalist view would be that everything which exists is either a physical thing or entirely made up out of physical things. This view would deny the existence of Cartesian souls, for example, since they are neither physical, nor made up out of anything physical.

Suppose that this is what physicalism says. Why should we believe it? One very influential reason is that it makes best sense of the causal structure of our world (Loewer 2001). The basic idea here is that every uncontroversially physical thing which happens is the product of purely physical causal processes. There is nothing physical which needs an entirely non-physical cause to bring it about. This principle is sometimes called the 'causal closure' of the physical (Kim 1998) or the 'completeness of physics' (Papineau 2001) and it is sometimes said to be a working hypothesis of physics itself (Lewis 1966). If this principle is true, then there seems to be no room for something non-physical in the world which itself has physical effects. So everything which has physical effects must itself be physical, or be completely determined by the purely physical. If there are non-physical things, then they can have no physical effects: they are 'epiphenomena'. Some doubt whether there can be such epiphenomena; but the issue is deeply controversial (see Further Reading for details).

Sometimes physicalism is described as the view that there is only one kind of substance in the world. Or it is said that physicalism is the view that everything is made out of physical 'stuff'. This can be confusing if 'substance' is taken in some of its traditional philosophical senses (see Part III: Being). For physicalism need not necessarily be committed to the view that there are substances in the Aristotelian or Cartesian senses; and as we saw above, Cartesians do not think that minds are made out of 'stuff' at all (hence 'substance' cannot mean 'stuff'). If by 'substance' we mean *particular object*, then the physicalism outlined above can be described as the view that all substances (i.e. objects) are physical or made up of things that are physical. But what does a physicalist say about items in the other ontological categories—e.g. properties and states of affairs

(Armstrong 1997)? Here the standard view is to say that all instances of properties or states of affairs are completely determined by, or 'supervene upon', the instances of physical properties or states of affairs, in the sense that if you fix the physical facts of the world, then all the other facts come for free. Imagine God faced with the task of creating a world just like this one in every respect. Physicalism says that all God would have to do to perform this task would be to create its physical nature. Everything else would be determined by this (see Lewis 1994).

4. Causal theories of mind

Given this picture of the physical world, where does the mental fit in? One extreme answer to this question is: nowhere. This is the point of view of *eliminative materialism*: the philosophy which says that a correct account of reality has no place for mental categories (see Quine 1958b; Churchland 1981). Eliminative materialists say that for an entity to be real, it has to be scientifically tractable: that is, part of the subject matter of a bona fide science. They then argue that our common-sense mental classifications—in particular the scheme of interpretation involving belief, desire, and the other propositional attitudes—cannot be turned into a science. But this extreme view lacks serious argumentative support, and we can put it to one side here (for more on eliminative materialism, see Crane 2003: chapter 2).

Eliminative materialism says more than that everything real is physical; it also says that nothing real is mental. But it is possible to argue that everything is physical *and* that some things which are physical are mental too. This would be a *reduction* of the mental to the physical, rather than an *elimination* of the mental. Sometimes it can be hard to see the distinction between a reduction and an elimination. For it is natural to ask: if you are 'reducing' the mind, isn't this in some sense a way of getting rid of it? Tempting as this question is, it is mistaken. A reduction of the mind does not eliminate it; rather it just tells us something more about it. An analogy: as science developed, light was discovered to be (and hence 'reduced to') electromagnetic radiation. This was not the discovery that light does not exist. But consider a different kind of case: some scientists used to think that the difference between living and non-living things is explained in terms of the presence of a vital force in living things. But with the development of biochemistry, this theory was eventually abandoned. No one describes this in the following terms: 'we have now discovered that vital force is a biochemical process.' Light was reduced; vital force was eliminated. (We will return to the nature of reduction in section 5 below.)

A classic reductionist claim is the *identity theory* of mind and brain (see Smart 1953, Feigl 1958, Armstrong 1968). This says that mental states like beliefs, and mental events like pains, are identical with certain brain states and events. An argument for this conclusion is presented by David Lewis (Chapter 47). Where earlier defenders of the identity theory like Smart (1953) had argued for it on the grounds of general parsimony (i.e. why postulate an extra category of entities if science does not require it?) Lewis presents a deductive argument with two premises. The first is that our concepts of mental states are causal concepts. Our ordinary concepts of thought, desire, intention, and so on are concepts of states which play a certain 'causal role': the role of mediating between the 'input' received from perceptions and other mental states, and the 'output' produced in behaviour. In the words of D. M. Armstrong, who independently proposed a similar argument in 1968, the concept of a mental state is the concept of a state apt for bringing about a certain kind of behaviour. Why believe this? Both Armstrong and Lewis think that some support for these views comes from the behaviourist account of mental states—see e.g. Ryle (1948). Behaviourists had argued that mental concepts could be defined or described purely in terms of the behaviour with which they are associated. Armstrong and Lewis reject this idea; but nonetheless they believe that there are important links between mental states and behaviour, as well as to other mental states. These links constitute the *causal role* of a mental state. For example, a belief might be what plays the causal role of being caused by perceptions and other beliefs, and giving rise to actions in conjunction with desires. These causal roles, Lewis believes, are captured in the network of assumptions and principles which summarize our ordinary understanding of mental states. Like many philosophers, Lewis views this network as a theory, rather like a scientific theory. It is sometimes called 'folk psychology' or 'common-sense psychology'.

Lewis then argues that we have reason to believe that science will discover the occupant of causal role R to be an independently identifiable physical state. Why does he think this? Essentially because he believes in the causal closure of the physical world. Given that all physical effects are produced by physical causes, then since mental states by definition have physical effects (this is part of their causal role), they must themselves be physical. It is left to empirical science to find out exactly what these physical occupants of these causal roles are.

Note that the definitions which Lewis indicates common sense can provide are definitions of mental *properties*, like pain or hope, considered as such; they are not definitions of individual states like *Macbeth's hope that he will be king*, or individual events like *Hamlet's seeing the ghost of his father*. In other words, the mental states and events in question are *types* or *kinds* of mental states and events, not what are sometimes called *token* states or events. This is why Lewis's theory (and those like it, e.g. Armstrong's) is sometimes called a 'type identity theory'. It is also called the 'property identity theory'. We can easily switch between talk of states and talk of properties as follows: a thing is in a state of type F (or state-type F) when it has property F. (For example: a creature is in the state-type *pain* when it has the property of *being in pain*.)

Gilbert Harman (Chapter 46) also presents a causal theory of mind, and describes some further reasons for believing in such a theory. But where Lewis had argued that the causal theory of mind is a premiss in the argument for the identity theory, Harman argues that the causal theory (or functionalism) is an *alternative* to the identity theory. While for Lewis, the truth of the causal analysis of mental concepts is part of the reason for believing in the identity theory, for Harman, the falsity of the identity theory is part of the reason for believing in the causal theory of mental states! This rather confusing state of affairs can be explained by the fact that Lewis and Harman are thinking of the causal theory or functionalism in rather different ways. It is worth spelling this out in a little detail since it is easy to become confused about this aspect of functionalism.

Functionalists see mental properties as defined by their causal roles: the pattern of causes and effects typical of that property. For any such causally defined property, we can distinguish between the causal role definitive of the property and what it is that *occupies* the causal role. Fragility is such a property: something is fragile, roughly speaking, when it breaks or is otherwise damaged when it is dropped, struck, or treated with insufficient care. We can distinguish then between this causal role and what it is that occupies the causal role. Although glass and porcelain are both fragile, because they both have the property just described, the causal role is occupied (or 'realized') by one kind of material structure in porcelain, and by another kind in glass. Suppose we ask: what *is* fragility, itself? We then have a choice: we could say that it is what glass and porcelain share (the 'role property') or we could say that it is what occupies or realizes the role (the 'realizer' property). Each answer makes good sense. An analogous choice arises with other terms defined by their role: 'who is the prime minister, exactly?' 'He is the man who heads the cabinet, etc. . . . ' or 'he is Tony Blair' are both good answers, depending on what is meant by the question.

This enables us to see the difference between the two types of functionalist about mental properties. Some functionalists (like Harman or Hilary Putnam 1975) identify a mental property with the role property common to all those people who satisfy the causal role; others (like Lewis or Armstrong) identify a mental property with the realizer property (remember Lewis talks about pain as the *occupant* of the causal role). This is why 'realizer functionalists' like Lewis and Armstrong can combine their identity theory with their functionalism: for what realizes the functional role can also be a physical state. The 'role functionalist', by contrast, emphasizes the multiple or variable realiza- tion of mental states: the physical basis of a mental state may vary from creature to crea- ture, while their mental state can stay the same. Pain may be realized by one kind of physical structure in humans, and another in dolphins, for example. Hence they argue that the mental state, pain, is the state which is common across realizations. And hence pain cannot be identical with any of the realizations, since identity is transitive: if pain = state *X* in humans, and pain = state *Y* in dolphins, then it follows that state *X* in humans = state *Y* in dolphins, which by hypothesis is false.

This variable/multiple realization objection is often taken to be a knock-down objection to Lewis/Armstrong type identity theory. But it is not. They respond by allow- ing that pain may be one thing in dolphins and another in humans. But this does not mean that the identification of pain with a physical state is false; it just means that they need to spell out exactly what is being identified with what. When we are identifying pain with a brain state in humans, what we are doing is saying that *pain-in-humans* = state *X* in humans. And this is quite consistent with saying that *pain-in-dolphins* = state *Y* in dolphins. This is just like saying that *fragility-in-glass* = physical-chemical state *X* and *fragility-in-porcelain* = physical-chemical state *Y*. The identity theory does not say that state *X* = state *Y*, any more than it says that 15 = 27 just because the winning number in this week's lottery is 15 and in last week's lottery was 27 (Lewis 1968). Identity claims need to be relativized to the kind of phenomenon talked about.

How should we decide between these two views, 'role functionalism' and 'realizer functionalism-plus-the-identity-theory'? The variable/multiple realization hypothesis will not decide the issue. At stake here are some large issues about mental causation, the nature of 'functional' properties, and the causal priority of the physical (see Kim 1998: chapter 4 for further discussion).

5. Non-reductive physicalist theories of mind

The identity theory of mind gives a reductionist or reductive physicalist account of mental properties: it says they are brain properties. But not all physicalists are reductionists. Some physicalists propose a non-reductive version of physicalism. Davidson (1970) is one. But in what sense is a non-reductive physicalist really a *physicalist*? To answer this question, we need to return to the topic of reduction and reductionism.

Reduction has meant many things in recent philosophy; here it is useful to distinguish two. The first we can call *ontological reduction*, or (so to speak) reduction of entities. This does not mean, of course, that we take an entity of one kind—say mental—and 'reduce it' to one of another kind—say, physical. We do not reduce anything: either it is physical or it is not. We are not downplaying its importance or demeaning it in any other way by claiming it is physical: we are just telling you more about it. What an ontological reduction does, in outline, is to take a certain class X of entities, and assert that they are a subclass of another class Y. Thus all members of X are also members of Y; all Xs are Ys. With the class X understood as the class of mental properties and the class Y understood as the class of physical properties, this is what the property identity theory says.

The second idea of reduction is not ontological, but *explanatory*. This is what we mean when we say that one theory 'reduces to' another (as some philosophers have claimed that thermodynamics reduces to statistical mechanics). Plainly, when we say that one theory reduces to another, we do not mean that the theories are identical; no one thinks that thermodynamics = statistical mechanics. They are different theories. Rather, what we mean here is that one theory *explains* why the other theory is true; explains why its generalizations and laws are the way they are, and so on. Explanatory reduction is a much more complex and messy idea than ontological reduction, partly because the idea of explanation is a much less simple idea than the idea of identity. But it is fairly easy to see how it can be applied to the metaphysics of mind: an explanatory reduction of the mental is where the truth of a theory of the mind—either folk/common-sense theory, or a scientific psychology—is explained in terms of some other kind of theory—normally, neuroscience. (By an 'explanatory reduction of a theory' we will mean 'an explanatory reduction of the truth of a theory'.)

These two forms of reduction are independent. One could deny ontological reductionism for certain kinds of entities, but hold that there can still be an explanatory reduction of the theories of these entities. Consider, for example, the view (rather like Harman's) that says that mental properties cannot be identified with physical properties, but also insists that we should be able to explain how a physical object like the brain can come to have mental properties. This explanation would have to be a way of linking the theories of the mental and the physical: for example, by showing how one might derive a psychological theory from neuroscience. This view is an example of explanatory reduction combined with a denial of ontological reduction.

But the opposite is possible too: one could be an ontological reductionist about entities of a certain kind, while denying that there can be any explanatory reduction of the different theories of these entities. Davidson's *anomalous monism* is an example of this kind of view. Davidson believes that all particular mental events are physical events, (hence monism), but that there can be no explanation of the theory of the mind in terms of physics. As he puts it, there can be no 'psychophysical laws', laws linking mental and physical types or kinds (hence 'anomalous'). Davidson therefore combines an ontological reduction of mental events, by identifying them with physical events, with a denial of explanatory reduction.

Davidson's argument for this conclusion is based on three premises: (1) mental events causally interact with physical events; (2) where there is a causal relation between two events, there is a law of nature under which they fall; (3) there are no psychophysical laws. These premises are all in certain ways plausible, but they appear to be incompatible. (See Part VI: Causation, for Davidson's views on events and causation, see Davidson 1970 for the argument for (3).) This appearance of incompatibility is resolved as follows. Since the same event can be described in many ways, we must distinguish between events themselves and descriptions of them. From (1) and (2) it follows that in any mental–physical causal interaction, the interacting events fall under some law. That is, they have some descriptions under which they fall under some law. But by (3) we know this cannot be a psychophysical law, so it must be a physical law. But if events fall under a physical law, then they must have true physical descriptions. And if an event has a true physical description, then it must be a physical event. Therefore all mental events which interact causally with physical events are themselves physical events. If all mental events do interact with physical events in one way or another, then all mental events are physical events.

In Chapter 48, Davidson defends this argument, and also defends himself against the objection that although the argument for anomalous monism is based on the existence of mental causation, it does not properly account for such causation. The objection (voiced by Kim and others) is that even if particular mental events cause physical events by being themselves physical, this does not allow the *properties* of mental events to play any causal role. It is plausible to say that when an event has an effect, it does so in virtue of some of its properties rather than others (see Part VI: Causation, for a defence of this claim). If this is so, then we need to distinguish between causation by events and causation by the properties of events. So it is one thing to say that the event of your perceiving the ball caused you to try and catch it, but another to say that the event had this effect *because it was a perception* (that is, because it had a certain mental property). Mental causation seems to require the second claim as well as the first claim to be true; but Davidson's theory, it seems, can only allow the first and not the second. This is because mental properties neither identical with physical properties nor are they the sorts of things that can be causes. In Chapter 48, Davidson responds to this criticism by further clarifying his conception of events and causation. It emerges that what is at issue between Davidson and his critics is the nature of causation itself, and not anything specific to the mind.

6. The problem of consciousness: the mind–body problem

Physicalism meets its biggest challenge when it comes to consider consciousness. As Thomas Nagel puts it in Chapter 49, 'consciousness is what makes the mind–body problem

---

Box IX.1. The zombie argument

Descartes argued that he could clearly and distinctly conceive of his mind as existing without his body, and that since what can be conceived to be separate is actually distinct, then his mind and body are distinct entities. Some contemporary philosophers use a similar argument for the conclusion that physicalism is false: that not all facts are determined by the physical facts. This has become known as the 'zombie argument' (Kirk 1974, Chalmers 1996, Sturgeon 2000: chapter 5). A 'zombie' in this sense is a (supposedly) possible creature physically identical to a conscious person, but lacking consciousness. Of course, no one believes that there actually are such creatures; the point is whether they are metaphysically possible. Physicalism is the view that everything either is something physical or is completely and necessarily determined by the physical: this is also known as the *supervenience* of everything on the physical. So if it were possible for the physical aspect of the world to be as it is, and yet the world contain no consciousness, then it would not be true that everything is necessarily determined by the physical. Therefore physicalism cannot allow that zombies are possible.

How could we know whether zombies are possible? Defenders of the argument give Hume's reason: that nothing we can clearly conceive or imagine is absolutely impossible. The idea is that we can conceive or imagine zombies, and this is a good reason for thinking they are possible (see Chalmers 1996: chapter 6). We may then represent the whole argument like this:

(1) If zombies are possible, then physicalism is false, since physicalism holds that everything is determined by the physical.
(2) Zombies are conceivable.
(3) Zombies are possible, since what is conceivable is (or is very good evidence for what is) possible.
(4) Therefore physicalism is false.

The controversial step in the argument is the move from (2) to (3). For more on this, see the introduction to Gendler and Hawthorne (2001).

---

really intractable'. Physicalist theories of mind, like those of Armstrong and Lewis, attempt to give causal role analyses of all mental states and processes, including conscious ones (like being in pain, or consciously perceiving). But sceptics about these theories have argued that it is conceivable that these causal role analyses of mental phenomena could be true of a creature and yet that creature not be conscious. If this is true, then it seems to follow that the causal–physical facts supposedly definitive of a conscious mental state cannot themselves suffice for that conscious state to exist, since (in Nagel's words) they are 'logically compatible with its absence'.

Nagel's point can be taken in a metaphysical or an epistemological way. Taken in the metaphysical way, the point is that physicalism is false, since no physical facts can suffice for the existence of consciousness (see Chalmers 1996; and Box IX.1 for a summary of the argument). Taken in the epistemological way, Nagel's point is that, although physicalism may be true, we have a difficulty in understanding how it can be true (Levine 2000 has developed the argument in this way). Nagel's remarks about the analogy between our attitude to the physicalist reduction of mind and an ancient Greek's attitude to the idea that matter is energy suggest that his attitude is the epistemological one.

The issues raised by Nagel's discussion of consciousness have dominated recent discussion of the traditional mind–body problem. As matters stand at present, the mind–body problem can be seen as a dilemma, posed by two questions. First: if the mind is not physical, then how can it have effects in the physical world? But, second: if the mind is physical, then how can we understand consciousness? The first question drives us towards physicalism, while the second drives us towards dualism.

Chapter 44

Selection from *Meditations on First Philosophy*

René Descartes

Second meditation

The nature of the human mind, and how it is better known than the body

So serious are the doubts into which I have been thrown as a result of yesterday's meditation that I can neither put them out of my mind nor see any way of resolving them. It feels as if I have fallen unexpectedly into a deep whirlpool which tumbles me around so that I can neither stand on the bottom nor swim up to the top. Nevertheless I will make an effort and once more attempt the same path which I started on yesterday. Anything which admits of the slightest doubt I will set aside just as if I had found it to be wholly false; and I will proceed in this way until I recognize something certain, or, if nothing else, until I at least recognize for certain that there is no certainty. Archimedes used to demand just one firm and immovable point in order to shift the entire earth; so I too can hope for great things if I manage to find just one thing, however slight, that is certain and unshakeable.

I will suppose then, that everything I see is spurious. I will believe that my memory tells me lies, and that none of the things that it reports ever happened. I have no senses. Body, shape, extension, movement and place are chimeras. So what remains true? Perhaps just the one fact that nothing is certain.

Yet apart from everything I have just listed, how do I know that there is not something else which does not allow even the slightest occasion for doubt? Is there not a God, or whatever I may call him, who puts into me[1] the thoughts I am now having? But why do I think this, since I myself may perhaps be the author of these thoughts? In that case am not I, at least, something? But I have just said that I have no senses and no body. This is the sticking point: what follows from this? Am I not so bound up with a body and with senses that I cannot exist without them? But I have convinced myself that there is absolutely nothing in the world, no sky, no earth, no minds, no bodies. Does it now follow that I too do not exist? No: if I convinced

1. '. . . puts into my mind' (French version).

René Descartes, selection from *Meditations on First Philosophy* from *The Philosophical Writings of Descartes,* trans. John Cottingham, Robert Stoothoff and Donald Murdoch, Vol. II (Cambridge University Press, 1984).

myself of something[2] then I certainly existed. But there is a deceiver of supreme power and cunning who is deliberately and constantly deceiving me. In that case I too undoubtedly exist, if he is deceiving me; and let him deceive me as much as he can, he will never bring it about that I am nothing so long as I think that I am something. So after considering everything very thoroughly, I must finally conclude that this proposition, *I am, I exist*, is necessarily true whenever it is put forward by me or conceived in my mind.

But I do not yet have a sufficient understanding of what this 'I' is, that now necessarily exists. So I must be on my guard against carelessly taking something else to be this 'I', and so making a mistake in the very item of knowledge that I maintain is the most certain and evident of all. I will therefore go back and meditate on what I originally believed myself to be, before I embarked on this present train of thought. I will then subtract anything capable of being weakened, even minimally, by the arguments now introduced, so that what is left at the end may be exactly and only what is certain and unshakeable.

What then did I formerly think I was? A man. But what is a man? Shall I say 'a rational animal'? No; for then I should have to inquire what an animal is, what rationality is, and in this way one question would lead me down the slope to other harder ones, and I do not now have the time to waste on subtleties of this kind. Instead I propose to concentrate on what came into my thoughts spontaneously and quite naturally whenever I used to consider what I was. Well, the first thought to come to mind was that I had a face, hands, arms and the whole mechanical structure of limbs which can be seen in a corpse, and which I called the body. The next thought was that I was nourished, that I moved about, and that I engaged in sense-perception and thinking; and these actions I attributed to the soul. But as to the nature of this soul, either I did not think about this or else I imagined it to be something tenuous, like a wind or fire or ether, which permeated my more solid parts. As to the body, however, I had no doubts about it, but thought I knew its nature distinctly. If I had tried to describe the mental conception I had of it, I would have expressed it as follows: by a body I understand whatever has a determinable shape and a definable location and can occupy a space in such a way as to exclude any other body; it can be perceived by touch, sight, hearing, taste or smell, and can be moved in various ways, not by itself but by whatever else comes into contact with it. For, according to my judgement, the power of self-movement, like the power of sensation or of thought, was quite foreign to the nature of a body; indeed, it was a source of wonder to me that certain bodies were found to contain faculties of this kind.

But what shall I now say that I am, when I am supposing that there is some supremely powerful and, if it is permissible to say so, malicious deceiver, who is deliberately trying to trick me in every way he can? Can I now assert that I possess even the most insignificant of all the attributes which I have just said belong to the nature of a body? I scrutinize them, think about them, go over them again, but

26

27

2. '. . . or thought anything at all' (French version).

nothing suggests itself; it is tiresome and pointless to go through the list once more. But what about the attributes I assigned to the soul? Nutrition or movement? Since now I do not have a body, these are mere fabrications. Sense-perception? This surely does not occur without a body, and besides, when asleep I have appeared to perceive through the senses many things which I afterwards realized I did not perceive through the senses at all. Thinking? At last I have discovered it—thought; this alone is inseparable from me. I am, I exist—that is certain. But for how long? For as long as I am thinking. For it could be that were I totally to cease from thinking, I should totally cease to exist. At present I am not admitting anything except what is necessarily true. I am, then, in the strict sense only a thing that thinks;[3] that is, I am a mind, or intelligence, or intellect, or reason—words whose meaning I have been ignorant of until now. But for all that I am a thing which is real and which truly exists. But what kind of a thing? As I have just said—a thinking thing.

What else am I? I will use my imagination.[4] I am not that structure of limbs which is called a human body. I am not even some thin vapour which permeates the limbs—a wind, fire, air, breath, or whatever I depict in my imagination; for these are things which I have supposed to be nothing. Let this supposition stand;[5] for all that I am still something. And yet may it not perhaps be the case that these very things which I am supposing to be nothing, because they are unknown to me, are in real- ity identical with the 'I' of which I am aware? I do not know, and for the moment I shall not argue the point, since I can make judgements only about things which are known to me. I know that I exist; the question is, what is this 'I' that I know? If the 'I' is understood strictly as we have been taking it, then it is quite certain that knowl- edge of it does not depend on things of whose existence I am as yet unaware; so it cannot depend on any of the things which I invent in my imagination. And this very word 'invent' shows me my mistake. It would indeed be a case of fictitious invention if I used my imagination to establish that I was something or other; for imagining is simply contemplating the shape or image of a corporeal thing. Yet now I know for certain both that I exist and at the same time that all such images and, in general, everything relating to the nature of body, could be mere dreams <and chimeras>. Once this point has been grasped, to say 'I will use my imagination to get to know more distinctly what I am' would seem to be as silly as saying 'I am now awake, and see some truth; but since my vision is not yet clear enough, I will deliberately fall asleep so that my dreams may provide a truer and clearer representation.' I thus realize that none of the things that the imagination enables me to grasp is at all rel- evant to this knowledge of myself which I possess, and that the mind must therefore

28

3. The word 'only' is most naturally taken as going with 'a thing that thinks', and this interpretation is followed in the French version. When discussing this passage with Gassendi, however, Descartes suggests that he meant the 'only' to govern 'in the strict sense'; see below p. 276.
4. '. . . to see if I am not something more' (added in French version).
5. Lat. *maneat* ('let it stand'), first edition. The second edition has the indicative *manet*: 'The proposi- tion still stands, *viz.* that I am nonetheless something.' The French version reads: 'without changing this supposition, I find that I am still certain that I am something'.

be most carefully diverted from such things[6] if it is to perceive its own nature as distinctly as possible.

But what then am I? A thing that thinks. What is that? A thing that doubts, understands, affirms, denies, is willing, is unwilling, and also imagines and has sensory perceptions.

This is a considerable list, if everything on it belongs to me. But does it? Is it not one and the same 'I' who is now doubting almost everything, who nonetheless understands some things, who affirms that this one thing is true, denies everything else, desires to know more, is unwilling to be deceived, imagines many things even involuntarily, and is aware of many things which apparently come from the senses? Are not all these things just as true as the fact that I exist, even if I am asleep all the time, and even if he who created me is doing all he can to deceive me? Which of all these activities is distinct from my thinking? Which of them can be said to be separate from myself? The fact that it is I who am doubting and understanding and willing is so evident that I see no way of making it any clearer. But it is also the case that the 'I' who imagines is the same 'I'. For even if, as I have supposed, none of the objects of imagination are real, the power of imagination is something which really exists and is part of my thinking. Lastly, it is also the same 'I' who has sensory perceptions, or is aware of bodily things as it were through the senses. For example, I am now seeing light, hearing a noise, feeling heat. But I am asleep, so all this is false. Yet I certainly *seem* to see, to hear, and to be warmed. This cannot be false; what is called 'having a sensory perception' is strictly just this, and in this restricted sense of the term it is simply thinking.

. . .

Sixth meditation

The existence of material things, and the real distinction between mind and body[7]

It remains for me to examine whether material things exist. And at least I now know they are capable of existing, in so far as they are the subject-matter of pure mathematics, since I perceive them clearly and distinctly. For there is no doubt that God is capable of creating everything that I am capable of perceiving in this manner; and I have never judged that something could not be made by him except on the grounds that there would be a contradiction in my perceiving it distinctly. The conclusion that material things exist is also suggested by the faculty of imagination, which I am aware of using when I turn my mind to material things. For when I give more attentive consideration to what imagination is, it seems to be nothing else but

6. '. . . from this manner of conceiving things' (French version).
7. '. . . between the soul and body of man' (French version).

an application of the cognitive faculty to a body which is intimately present to it, and which therefore exists.

To make this clear, I will first examine the difference between imagination and pure understanding. When I imagine a triangle, for example, I do not merely understand that it is a figure bounded by three lines, but at the same time I also see the three lines with my mind's eye as if they were present before me; and this is what I call imagining. But if I want to think of a chiliagon, although I understand that it is a figure consisting of a thousand sides just as well as I understand the triangle to be a three-sided figure, I do not in the same way imagine the thousand sides or see them as if they were present before me. It is true that since I am in the habit of imagining something whenever I think of a corporeal thing, I may construct in my mind a confused representation of some figure; but it is clear that this is not a chiliagon. For it differs in no way from the representation I should form if I were thinking of a myriagon, or any figure with very many sides. Moreover, such a representation is useless for recognizing the properties which distinguish a chiliagon from other polygons. But suppose I am dealing with a pentagon: I can of course understand the figure of a pentagon, just as I can the figure of a chiliagon, without the help of the imagination; but I can also imagine a pentagon, by applying my mind's eye to its five sides and the area contained within them. And in doing this I notice quite clearly that imagination requires a peculiar effort of mind which is not required for understanding; this additional effort of mind   73
clearly shows the difference between imagination and pure understanding.

Besides this, I consider that this power of imagining which is in me, differing as it does from the power of understanding, is not a necessary constituent of my own essence, that is, of the essence of my mind. For if I lacked it, I should undoubtedly remain the same individual as I now am; from which it seems to follow that it depends on something distinct from myself. And I can easily understand that, if there does exist some body to which the mind is so joined that it can apply itself to contemplate it, as it were, whenever it pleases, then it may possibly be this very body that enables me to imagine corporeal things. So the difference between this mode of thinking and pure understanding may simply be this: when the mind understands, it in some way turns towards itself and inspects one of the ideas which are within it; but when it imagines, it turns towards the body and looks at something in the body which conforms to an idea understood by the mind or perceived by the senses. I can, as I say, easily understand that this is how imagination comes about, if the body exists; and since there is no other equally suitable way of explaining imagination that comes to mind, I can make a probable conjecture that the body exists. But this is only a probability; and despite a careful and comprehensive investigation, I do not yet see how the distinct idea of corporeal nature which I find in my imagination can provide any basis for a necessary inference that some body exists.

But besides that corporeal nature which is the subject-matter of pure mathemat-   74
ics, there is much else that I habitually imagine, such as colours, sounds, tastes, pain and so on—though not so distinctly. Now I perceive these things much better by means of the senses, which is how, with the assistance of memory, they appear to

have reached the imagination. So in order to deal with them more fully, I must pay equal attention to the senses, and see whether the things which are perceived by means of that mode of thinking which I call 'sensory perception' provide me with any sure argument for the existence of corporeal things.

To begin with, I will go back over all the things which I previously took to be perceived by the senses, and reckoned to be true; and I will go over my reasons for thinking this. Next, I will set out my reasons for subsequently calling these things into doubt. And finally I will consider what I should now believe about them.

First of all then, I perceived by my senses that I had a head, hands, feet and other limbs making up the body which I regarded as part of myself, or perhaps even as my whole self. I also perceived by my senses that this body was situated among many other bodies which could affect it in various favourable or unfavourable ways; and I gauged the favourable effects by a sensation of pleasure, and the unfavourable ones by a sensation of pain. In addition to pain and pleasure, I also had sensations within me of hunger, thirst, and other such appetites, and also of physical propensities towards cheerfulness, sadness, anger and similar emotions. And outside me, besides 75 the extension, shapes and movements of bodies, I also had sensations of their hardness and heat, and of the other tactile qualities. In addition, I had sensations of light, colours, smells, tastes and sounds, the variety of which enabled me to distinguish the sky, the earth, the seas, and all other bodies, one from another. Considering the ideas of all these qualities which presented themselves to my thought, although the ideas were, strictly speaking, the only immediate objects of my sensory awareness, it was not unreasonable for me to think that the items which I was perceiving through the senses were things quite distinct from my thought, namely bodies which produced the ideas. For my experience was that these ideas came to me quite without my consent, so that I could not have sensory awareness of any object, even if I wanted to, unless it was present to my sense organs; and I could not avoid having sensory awareness of it when it was present. And since the ideas perceived by the senses were much more lively and vivid and even, in their own way, more distinct than any of those which I deliberately formed through meditating or which I found impressed on my memory, it seemed impossible that they should have come from within me; so the only alternative was that they came from other things. Since the sole source of my knowledge of these things was the ideas themselves, the supposition that the things resembled the ideas was bound to occur to me. In addition, I remembered that the use of my senses had come first, while the use of my reason came only later; and I saw that the ideas which I formed myself were less vivid than those which I perceived with the senses and were, for the most part, made up of elements of sensory ideas. In this way I easily convinced myself that I had nothing at all in the intellect which I had 76 not previously had in sensation. As for the body which by some special right I called 'mine', my belief that this body, more than any other, belonged to me had some justification. For I could never be separated from it, as I could from other bodies; and I felt all my appetites and emotions in, and on account of, this body; and finally, I was aware of pain and pleasurable ticklings in parts of this body, but not in other bodies external to it. But why should that curious sensation of pain give rise to a particular distress of mind; or why should a certain kind of delight follow on a tickling sensation? Again, why should that curious tugging in the stomach which I call hunger tell me that I should eat, or a dryness of the throat tell me to drink, and so on? I was not able to give any explanation of all this, except that nature taught me so. For there is absolutely no connection (at least that I can understand) between the tugging sensation and the decision to take food, or between the sensation of something causing pain and the mental apprehension of distress that arises from that sensation. These and other judgements that I made concerning sensory objects, I was apparently taught to make by nature; for I had already made up my mind that this was how things were, before working out any arguments to prove it.

Later on, however, I had many experiences which gradually undermined all the faith I had had in the senses. Sometimes towers which had looked round from a distance appeared square from close up; and enormous statues standing on their pediments did not seem large when observed from the ground. In these and countless other such cases, I found that the judgements of the external senses were mistaken. And this applied not just to the external senses but to the internal senses as well. For what can be more internal than pain? And yet I had heard that those who had had a 77 leg or an arm amputated sometimes still seemed to feel pain intermittently in the missing part of the body. So even in my own case it was apparently not quite certain that a particular limb was hurting, even if I felt pain in it. To these reasons for doubting, I recently added two very general ones. The first was that every sensory experience I have ever thought I was having while awake I can also think of myself as sometimes having while asleep; and since I do not believe that what I seem to perceive in sleep comes from things located outside me, I did not see why I should be any more inclined to believe this of what I think I perceive while awake. The second reason for doubt was that since I did not know the author of my being (or at least was pretending not to), I saw nothing to rule out the possibility that my natural constitution made me prone to error even in matters which seemed to me most true. As for the reasons for my previous confident belief in the truth of the things perceived by the senses, I had no trouble in refuting them. For since I apparently had natural impulses towards many things which reason told me to avoid, I reckoned that a great deal of confidence should not be placed in what I was taught by nature. And despite the fact that the perceptions of the senses were not dependent on my will, I did not think that I should on that account infer that they proceeded from things distinct from myself, since I might perhaps have a faculty not yet known to me which produced them.

But now, when I am beginning to achieve a better knowledge of myself and the author of my being, although I do not think I should heedlessly accept everything 78 I seem to have acquired from the senses, neither do I think that everything should be called into doubt.

First, I know that everything which I clearly and distinctly understand is capable of being created by God so as to correspond exactly with my understanding of it. Hence the fact that I can clearly and distinctly understand one thing apart from another is enough to make me certain that the two things are distinct, since they are capable of being separated, at least by God. The question of what kind of power is required to bring about such a separation does not affect the judgement that the two things are distinct. Thus, simply by knowing that I exist and seeing at the same time that absolutely nothing else belongs to my nature or essence except that I am a thinking thing, I can infer correctly that my essence consists solely in the fact that I am a thinking thing. It is true that I may have (or, to anticipate, that I certainly have) a body that is very closely joined to me. But nevertheless, on the one hand I have a clear and distinct idea of myself, in so far as I am simply a thinking, non-extended thing; and on the other hand I have a distinct idea of body,[8] in so far as this is simply an extended, non-thinking thing. And accordingly, it is certain that I[9] am really distinct from my body, and can exist without it . . .

8. The Latin term *corpus* as used here by Descartes is ambiguous as between 'body' (i.e. corporeal matter in general) and 'the body' (i.e. this particular body of mine). The French version preserves the ambiguity.

9. '. . . that is, my soul, by which I am what I am' (added in French version).

Chapter 45

Selection from *New System of the Nature of Substances*

G. W. Leibniz

...

[10] I am as ready as anyone to do justice to the moderns; nevertheless I think they have carried reform too far, among other things in conflating natural things with artificial ones, through not having sufficiently grand ideas of the majesty of nature. They take the difference between nature's machines and ours to be only that between great and small. This recently led a very able man, the author of *Conversations on the Plurality of Worlds*, to say that on close inspection nature appears less wonderful than we had thought, it being only something like a crafts-man's window display. I think that this gives an inappropriate and unworthy idea of nature, and that it is only my system which shows the true and immense distance there is between the least productions and mechanisms of divine wisdom and the greatest masterpieces produced by the skill of a limited mind—a difference which is not merely one of degree, but one of kind. It needs to be recognized, then, that nature's machines have a truly infinite number of organic parts, and are so well provided for and proof against all accidents that it is not possible to destroy them. A natural machine is still a machine even in its smallest parts; and, what is more, it always remains the same machine it was, being merely transformed by being packed up in different ways; sometimes extended, sometimes contracted and as it were concentrated, when we think that it is destroyed.

[11] Furthermore, by means of the soul or form, there is in us a true unity which corresponds to what we call 'I'; this can have no place in artificial machines or in a simple mass of matter, however organized it may be. Such masses can only be thought of as like an army or a flock, or like a pond full of fish, or like a watch composed of springs and wheels. Yet if there were no true substantial unities there would be nothing substantial or real in such a collection. It was this that forced M. Cordemoy to abandon Descartes and adopt Democritus' doctrine of atoms in order to find a true unity. But *atoms of matter* are contrary to reason, quite apart from being still composed of parts, since the invincible attachment of one part to another (even if it could rationally be understood or imagined) would certainly not

G. W. Leibniz, selection from *New System of the Nature of Substances*, translated by Richard Francks and R. S. Woolhouse from *G. W. Leibniz: Philosophical Texts* (Oxford University Press, 1998), reprinted by permission of Oxford University Press.

take away the difference between them. It is only *atoms of substance*, that is to say real unities absolutely devoid of parts, that can be the sources of actions, and the absolute first principles of the composition of things, and as it were the ultimate elements in the analysis of substances (substantial things). They might be called *metaphysical points*; they have *something of the nature of life* and a kind of *perception*, and *mathematical points* are their *point of view* for expressing the universe. But when a corporeal substance is contracted, all its organs together make what to us is only a *physical point*. Thus the indivisibility of physical points is only apparent. Mathematical points really are indivisible, but they are only modalities. It is only metaphysical or substantial points (constituted by forms or souls) which are both indivisible and real, and without them there would be nothing real, since without true unities there would be no multiplicity.

[12] Having decided these things, I thought I had reached port, but when I set myself to think about the union of the soul with the body I was as it were carried back into the open sea. For I could find no way of explaining how the body can make something pass over into the soul or vice versa, or how one created substance can communicate with another. As far as we can see from his writings, M. Descartes gave up the game at this point, but his disciples, seeing that the popular opinion is incomprehensible, said that we are aware of the properties of bodies because God produces thoughts in the soul on the occasion of the motions of matter; and when in its turn our soul wishes to move the body, they said that it is God who moves the body for it. And as the communication of motion also seemed incomprehensible to them, they held that God gives motion to one body on the occasion of the motion of another. This is what they call the *System of Occasional Causes*, which has been made very fashionable by the excellent reflections of the author of the *The Search after Truth*.

[13] It must be admitted that they have gone a long way with this problem in telling us what cannot happen; but their account of what actually does happen does not appear to have solved it. It is quite true that in the strict metaphysical sense, one created substance has no real influence upon another, and that all things, with all their reality, are continually produced by the power of God. But to solve problems it is not enough to make use of a general cause and to introduce what is called a *deus ex machina*. For to do this, without giving any other explanation in terms of the order of secondary causes, is really to have recourse to a miracle. In philosophy we must try to show the way in which things are carried out by the divine wisdom by explaining them in accordance with the notion of the subject we are dealing with.

[14] Being thus obliged to admit that it is impossible that the soul or any other true substance should receive anything from outside, except through divine omnipotence, I was led gradually to an idea which surprised me, but which seems inevitable, and which in fact has very great advantages and very considerable attractions. This is that we should say that God first created the soul, or any other real unity, in such a way that everything in it arises from its own nature, with a perfect *spontaneity* as regards itself, and yet with a perfect *conformity* to things outside it. And thus, since our inner sensations (that is, those which are in the soul itself and not in the brain or in the

subtle parts of the body) are only a sequence of phenomena relating to external things, or are really appearances or systematic dreams, as it were, these internal perceptions in the soul itself must arise from its own original constitution, that is to say from its representational nature (its ability to express external things which are in relation with its organs), which it has had since its creation, and which constitutes its individual character. And this means that since each of these substances accurately represents the whole universe in its own way and from a particular point of view, and since its perceptions or expressions of external things occur in the soul at just the right time in virtue of its own laws, as in a world apart, as if there existed nothing but God and that soul (to use the expression of a certain lofty-minded person [Teresa], famous for her sanctity), there will be a perfect agreement between all these substances, which produces the same effect as would be observed if they communicated with one another by means of a transmission of species or qualities, such as most ordinary philosophers [Scholastics] suppose. Furthermore, the organized mass in which the point of view of the soul lies is more immediately expressed by it, and is in turn ready, just when the soul desires it, to act of itself according to the laws of the bodily mechanism, without either one interfering with the laws of the other, the animal spirits and the blood having exactly at the right moment the motions which correspond to the passions and perceptions of the soul. It is this mutual relationship, arranged in advance in each substance in the universe, which produces what we call their communication, and which alone constitutes *the union of soul and body*. And in this way we can understand how the soul has its seat in the body by an immediate presence, which is as close as could be, since the soul is in the body in the way in which unity is in that resultant of unities which is multiplicity.

[15] This hypothesis is certainly possible. For why could not God give to a substance at the outset a nature or internal force which could produce in it in an orderly way (as in a *spiritual or formal automaton; but a free one*, in the case of a substance which is endowed with a share of reason) everything that is going to happen to it, that is to say, all the appearances or expressions it is going to have, and all without the help of any created thing? This is the more likely since the nature of a substance necessarily requires and essentially involves some progress or change, without which it would have no force to act. And as the nature of the soul is to represent the universe in a very exact way (though with more or less distinctness), the succession of representations which the soul produces for itself will naturally correspond to the succession of changes in the universe itself: just as on the other hand the body has also been adapted to the soul for the occasions when we think of the soul as acting externally. What is all the more reasonable about this is that bodies are made only for minds which are capable of entering into association with God, and of celebrating his glory. Thus as soon as we see that this *Theory of Agreements* is possible, we see also that it is the most reasonable, and that it gives a wonderful sense of the harmony of the universe and the perfection of the works of God.

[16] It also has the great advantage that instead of saying that we are free only in appearance and in a way which is sufficient for practical purposes, as several clever

people have held, we must rather say that we are determined only in appearance, and that, in strict metaphysical language, we are perfectly independent of the influence of all other created things. This again puts into a marvellous light the immortality of our soul and the perfectly unbroken conservation of our individuality, which is perfectly well-regulated by its own nature and sheltered from all external accidents, however it may appear to the contrary. Never has any system made our elevated position more clear. Every mind is like a world apart, sufficient to itself, independent of every other created thing, involves the infinite, and expresses the universe, and so it is as lasting, as continuous in its existence, and as absolute as the universe of created things itself. Thus we should conclude that each mind should always play its part in the way most fitted to contribute to the perfection of the society of all minds which constitutes their moral union in the City of God. There is also here a new and surprisingly clear proof of the existence of God. For this perfect agreement of so many substances which have no communication with one another could come only from their common cause.

[17] Besides all these advantages which this theory has in its favour, we may say that it is something more than a theory, since it hardly seems possible to explain things in any other intelligible way, and because several serious difficulties which have perplexed men's minds up until now seem to disappear of themselves when we fully understand it. Our ordinary ways of speaking may also be easily preserved. For we may say that the substance whose state explains a change in an intelligible way (so that we may conclude that it is this substance to which the others have in this respect been adapted from the beginning, in accordance with the order of the decrees of God) is the one which, so far as this change goes, we should therefore think of as *acting* upon the others. So the action of one substance upon another is not an emission or a transplantation of an entity as is commonly thought, and it can be reasonably understood only in the way I have just described. It is true that we can easily understand in connection with matter both the emission and the receiving of parts, by means of which we quite properly explain all the phenomena of physics mechanically. But a material mass is not a substance, and so it is clear that action as regards an actual substance can only be as I have described.

[18] These considerations, however metaphysical they may seem, are nevertheless marvellously useful in physics for grounding the laws of motion, as my dynamics will be able to show. For we can say that when bodies collide, each one is affected only by its own elasticity, caused by the motion which is already in it. And as for absolute motion, nothing can determine it mathematically, since everything ends in relations: the result being that there is always a perfect equivalence of theories, as in astronomy; so that, whatever number of bodies we take, we may arbitrarily assign either rest or some degree of velocity to whichever we like, without it being possible for us to be refuted by the phenomena of motion, whether in a straight line, a circle, or composite. It is still reasonable, however, in conformity with the notion of activity which we have established here, to attribute genuine motions to bodies in accordance with what explains the phenomena in the most intelligible way.

Chapter 46
Selections from *Thought*
Gilbert Harman

Mental processes

1. Dualism

W<small>E</small> are tempted to take conscious experience to be paradigmatically mental. Moreover, a headache, an itch, a sudden thought, a feeling of joy, a pang of longing, or the awareness of a beautiful blue may seem very different from any physical process such as the excitation of nerve ends in the brain. We have a direct acquaintance with experiences and mental processes in general that, it seems, we can never have with physical processes. Some such line of thought may persuade us to accept a form of dualism—the idea that mental and physical processes are basically and irreducibly different. We may even decide that there must be two basic kinds of *substances*, minds and bodies.

Such dualism tends naturally to a form of dualistic interactionism—the theory that there is a causal interaction between the mental and the physical. For in visual perception, physical processes involving reflected light cause visual experiences and thoughts about what is seen. And mental processes culminating in decisions to undertake a particular course of action affect the movement of one's body.

But dualistic interactionism conflicts with the plausible and widely held view that in some sense there are no facts over and above the purely physical facts. Scientists believe that the totality of physical facts completely determines all other facts and that, in particular, all mental processes are completely determined by whatever physical processes there are. (This is not to say that physical processes themselves are causally determined by prior physical processes. According to quantum theory, that sort of determinism is false. But it is compatible with quantum theory to suppose that physical processes completely determine all nonphysical processes.) This rules out a mental realm distinct from a physical realm with which it occasionally interacts.

True, the idea that physical facts determine everything else is more trivial than may at first appear. If scientists discover a phenomenon that has physical effects but is not reducible to phenomena currently accepted as physical, they classify the new phenomenon as a new *physical* phenomenon. Some years ago, physical phenomena were thought to be entirely a matter of the movements of particles. When electromagnetic phenomena had to be accommodated, scientists did not suggest that there were two interacting but distinct realms, the physical and the electromagnetic. Instead they modified their conception of the physical to include electromagnetic phenomena.

But should we then suppose, e.g., that the mind is something like a *mental field*, different from and not reducible to other physical phenomena but interacting with them? Although the suggestion might be defended by appeal to alleged instances of mental telepathy, ESP, and psychokinesis, along with speculation that free choice operates in the area of quantum indeterminacy, that would really be to indulge in a kind of crackpot science. We should be able to understand mental processes without such hypotheses.

Furthermore, the idea that free will requires an underlying neurophysiological indeterminism, perhaps at the quantum level, is a philosophical mistake. It is true that explanation by reasons, whether of beliefs or decisions, is *non*deterministic. But, as I will argue in detail below, that does not mean that such explanation involves any commitment to an underlying *in*determinism. Explanation by reasons is compatible with an underlying indeterminism and with an underlying determinism. It involves no commitment either way.

Aside from worries about free will, the main support of dualism is the idea that one has a direct acquaintance with experiences and mental processes which one cannot have with respect to merely physical processes. It is true that when one has a headache there is an important sense in which one can be aware of an experience without being aware of a physical process. For one can be aware *that* a headache is occurring without being aware that a physical process is occurring. But that shows nothing. That one is unaware that a headache is a physical process by no means establishes that a headache is not a physical process. When one is aware of a headache there are many facts about the headache of which one is unaware. Facts about awareness provide no real evidence for dualism.

2. An identity theory

On the other hand, there are difficulties in the suggestion that a headache might just *be* a particular neurophysiological process, e.g., a certain pattern of electrical discharges in the brain; and similarly for other experiences and mental processes. For, if the suggestion is that in general for there to be a headache *is* for there to be such and such a pattern of electrical discharges—so that wherever there is the appropriate pattern of electrical discharges there is *ipso facto* a headache—then we must ask about relevant patterns of electrical discharge that do not happen to occur in a living brain but occur, e.g., in a cloud during an electrical storm or in something struck by lightning. Are such occurrences also experiences of headaches, occurring apart from the other sorts of experiences that go to make up the life of a person or animal? If we think *yes*, we will be led perhaps to suppose that experiences are all around, occurring occasionally in trees, etc. And that is to be led again into a kind of mystical crazy science not appropriate to the present investigation. But if we agree that it is only in the context of a living brain that such occurrences *are* experiences of headaches, then we must say why that is so. How can exactly the same sort of physical process *be* a conscious experience when it occurs in one context but not when it occurs in another?

Further reflection along these lines shows that an identity theory is wrong if it always identifies a mental process or experience with the same sort of physical process. For suppose that neurophysiologists were to decide that a certain area of the brain serves as a 'pain center.' On the identity theory, different patterns of electrical activity in this area would *be* different sorts of pains. But now suppose that a brain surgeon removes the pain center in someone's brain and replaces it with a plastic transitorized construction that is functionally equivalent, although its inner workings are different from those in the natural brain center. The artificial replacement accepts the same input electrical pulses and emits the same output pulses that the natural brain center would. But patterns of electrical activity characteristic of various sorts of pains in the natural pain center do not occur at all in the artificial pain center. Quite different patterns occur instead. Could a person with an artificial pain center feel pain? Given the functional equivalence of the artificial to the natural pain center, he will occasionally act as if he is in pain and, indeed, say that he is in pain—(so that it would be difficult to convince *him* that he is not in pain). But if such a person could have a headache, then the occurrence of a headache cannot be simply identified with the occurrence of the specified pattern of electrical activity in the pain center. It follows that variously different physical processes, involving variously different physical substances, may be the underlying physical bases for the same experiences and mental processes. A general identity theory, according to which a particular sort of mental process is always the same as a particular sort of physical process, is mistaken.

Of course, the idea that scientists might construct an artificial pain center is, so far, just a myth. But the point of the myth is a valid one. One person's brain differs in many ways from another's. There is no reason to suppose that similar neurophysiological processes in different people underlie similar mental processes.

3. Behaviorism

A behaviorist theory would provide a way out of the preceding difficulty. Behaviorism analyzes mental life in terms of dispositions to behave in various ways in various circumstances. In chapter one (of *Thought*), I discussed a form of the theory according to which behavioristic analyses hold by virtue of meaning. But behaviorism can also be taken simply to offer an account of the nature of mental processes that makes no claims about the meaning of words used to describe these processes.

A behaviorist says that a mental state is a relatively long-term disposition to behave in certain ways. A belief that it will rain is a disposition to do such things as carry an umbrella; a desire for money is the disposition to perform acts that tend, other things equal, to get one money; intelligence is a general disposition to do the appropriate thing to obtain that which one is tending toward; good humor is the disposition to respond well to circumstances and the actions of others, etc. Similarly, an experience is a short-term behavioral disposition. A pain is, e.g., a disposition to soothe the painful spot (coupled with a disposition to complain). Finally, a mental process is a change in the dispositions characterizing mental states and experiences. For example, theoretical reasoning is a change (or a series of changes) in belief, i.e., a change in certain relatively long-term dispositions to act in various ways.

Different underlying physical mechanisms can be responsible for exactly the same dispositions. According to behaviorism, replacing a person's pain center with an artificial model cannot affect his capacity to feel pain unless it interferes with his dispositions to respond in various ways in certain situations. So behaviorism easily accounts for the facts that undermine a crude identity theory.

Nevertheless, the objection to behaviorism I mentioned in chapter one still applies. There is no noncircular way to specify the relevant dispositions. For they are dispositions to act in certain ways given certain situations; and the relevant situations essentially include beliefs about the situation and desires concerning it. What a man will do if he hits his thumb with a hammer depends on who he believes is watching and what desires he has concerning his relationship to the watchers. But beliefs are dispositions to act in certain ways only given certain desires, whereas desires are dispositions to act in certain ways only given certain beliefs. A belief that it will rain will be manifested in the carrying of an umbrella only in the presence of a desire not to get wet; and the desire for money will manifest itself in acts that tend to get one money only if one believes that those acts will get one money. Since even in theory there is no noncircular way to specify relevant dispositions in pure behavioral terms, behaviorism cannot provide an adequate account of mental processes and experience.

4. A modified Ramsey method

I mentioned in chapter one (of *Thought*) that the connection between a man's behavior and the inner psychological states and processes responsible for it is like the connection between evidence and a theory that explains the evidence. The failure of behaviorism is a special case of the failure of theoretical reductionism. Theoretical facts cannot be identified with purely evidential facts.

It is useful to think of commonsense psychological views as forming a more or less complete theory. Crudely put, the theory says that desires and beliefs together influence what we do, that perception modifies belief in certain ways, that desires can result from deprivation of food and water, that reasoning can bring about changes in belief and desire, and so forth. Various desires and beliefs are here taken to be theoretical states postulated to explain behavior.

Ramsey suggested that references to theoretical states and processes be replaced with existentially quantified variables in the overall theory. Ramsey's method applied to commonsense psychology yields the theory that *there are states and processes* related in certain specified ways to each other and to perception, deprivation, and action, etc.

If there are states and processes appropriately interrelated, they can be identified with beliefs, desires, reasoning, and so forth. But our reflections so far cast doubt on the existence of such states and processes. We have just seen that dispositional states and modifications of these states will not do the trick. And earlier we saw that particular sorts of mental states or processes cannot be identified with always the same physical states and processes. Yet if we were to decide that mental states and processes were *sui generis* and not constituted by neurophysiological states and processes, we would be flying in the face of scientific good sense. For then we would have returned to a form of dualism.

The solution to this problem is to modify Ramsey's method for handling theoretical terms. Ramsey has us quantify over the theoretical states first: *There are states and processes such that for any person. . . .* But we have learned that the physical states and processes underlying particular mental states and processes in one person can be different from those underlying the mental states and processes of a different person or even of the same person at a different time. The solution is to change the order of the quantifiers: *For any person (at a particular time) there are states and processes. . . .* Any person has states and processes in him related in certain specified ways to themselves and to perception, deprivation, action, etc. Those are his mental states and processes. On the other hand, it need not be true (and almost certainly is not true) that there are particular states and processes which in every person are related in the relevant ways, since the relevant states and processes almost certainly vary from person to person and in any one person over time.

So a kind of identity theory can be accepted. Instances of mental states and processes are instances of physical states and processes, although different instances of the same mental states and processes need not be instances of the same physical states and processes. But more must be said to clarify this account.

5. Functionalism

A psychological theory, commonsense or otherwise, may usefully be interpreted as a psychological model. To have a theory of another person's psychological makeup is to have a model of the workings of his mind. We have somewhat different models for different people, although all psychological models share certain structural features.

A psychological model represents a more or less rigorously specified device that is intended to be able to duplicate the relevant behavior of a person. If the device is sufficiently described, it should be realizable as a robot or, as I shall say, an automaton.

An abstract automaton is specified by its program. The program indicates possible reactions to input, how internal states plus input can yield other internal states, and how internal states and input can lead to various sorts of output. In a psychological model, input can represent the effect of perception and output can represent intentional action.

An abstract automaton may be nondeterministic or deterministic, depending on its program. If the program implies that any combination of internal states and input always has a unique result, the program specifies a deterministic automaton. If some combinations might be followed by any of a number of different results, the program specifies a nondeterministic automaton. We shall see in section 7 (of Chapter 3 of *Thought*) that automata serving as psychological models should be nondeterministic.

The same abstract automaton can be instantiated in quite different mechanisms, e.g., in an old-fashioned computer using tubes and wires and in a more recent model using semiconductors and printed circuits. An object can instantiate an abstract automaton as long as it is capable of internal states and processes related as required by the program. It does not matter how it is constructed.

A detailed psychological model could be identified with an individual psychology. Anything that instantiates the associated automaton would have that individual psychology; and vice versa. Thus a person instantiates the automaton that serves as the model of his individual psychology. Given sufficient technology, a robot could be constructed that would also instantiate that individual psychology. From this point of view, the fact that the same psychological states and processes can be physically realized in different ways is an instance of the point that abstract automaton states and processes can be physically realized in different ways.

As Aristotle pointed out, mental states and processes are to be functionally defined. They are constituted by their function or role in the relevant program. To understand desire, belief, and reasoning is to understand how desires, beliefs, and instances of reasoning function in a human psychology.

A person's beliefs form his representation of the world, his desires represent his ends, goals, plans, and intentions. Perception yields new information about the world; natural needs for food, water, sleep, etc., put constraints on goals and intentions. Theoretical reasoning is a process that functions to improve his representation of the way things are. Practical reasoning is a way of modifying plans and intentions, in the light of the way things are represented to be, so as to increase the chances of success at reaching goals and ends. Pain functions to indicate danger or damage to parts of a person's body so as to get him out of a harmful situation or to care for the injury or to avoid such situations in the future. Certain emotions, such as fear, serve to concentrate his attention in a particular situation or some threat in the environment and enable him to avoid distractions.

These remarks are crude, but they bring out the way in which attention to the functional role of mental states and processes helps in explaining what they are.

. . .

Chapter 47

Psychophysical and theoretical identifications

David Lewis

PSYCHOPHYSICAL identity theorists often say that the identifications they anticipate between mental and neural states are essentially like various uncontroversial theoretical identifications: the identification of water with H_2O, of light with electromagnetic radiation, and so on. Such theoretical identifications are usually described as pieces of voluntary theorizing, as follows. Theoretical advances make it possible to simplify total science by positing bridge laws identifying some of the entities discussed in one theory with entities discussed in another theory. In the name of parsimony, we posit those bridge laws forthwith. Identifications are made, not found.

In 'An Argument for the Identity Theory',[1] I claimed that this was a bad picture of psychophysical identification, since a suitable physiological theory could *imply* psychophysical identities—not merely make it reasonable to posit them for the sake of parsimony. The implication was as follows:

Mental state M = the occupant of causal role R (by definition of M).
Neural state N = the occupant of causal role R (by the physiological theory).
∴ Mental state M = neural state N (by transitivity of =).

If the meanings of the names of mental states were really such as to provide the first premise, and if the advance of physiology were such as to provide the second premise, then the conclusion would follow. Physiology and the meanings of words would leave us no choice but to make the psychophysical identification.

In this sequel, I shall uphold the view that psychophysical identifications thus described would be like theoretical identifications, though they would not fit the usual account thereof. For the usual account, I claim, is wrong; theoretical identifications *in general* are implied by the theories that make them possible—not posited independently. This follows from a general hypothesis about the meanings of

Previous versions of this paper were presented at a conference on Philosophical Problems of Psychology held at Honolulu in March, 1968; at the annual meeting of the Australasian Association of Philosophy held at Brisbane in August, 1971; and at various university colloquia.

1. *Journal of Philosophy*, **63** (1966): 17–25.

David Lewis, 'Psychophysical and Theoretical Identifications', from the *Australasian Journal of Philosophy*, 50 (1972), reprinted by permission of Oxford University Press.

theoretical terms: that they are definable functionally, by reference to causal roles.[2] Applied to common-sense psychology—folk science rather than professional science, but a theory nonetheless—we get the hypothesis of my previous paper[3] that a mental state M (say, an experience) is definable as the occupant of a certain causal role R—that is, as the state, of whatever sort, that is causally connected in specified ways to sensory stimuli, motor responses, and other mental states.

First, I consider an example of theoretical identification chosen to be remote from past philosophizing; then I give my general account of the meanings of theoretical terms and the nature of theoretical identifications; finally I return to the case of psychophysical identity.

I

We are assembled in the drawing room of the country house; the detective reconstructs the crime. That is, he proposes a *theory* designed to be the best explanation of phenomena we have observed: the death of Mr. Body, the blood on the wallpaper, the silence of the dog in the night, the clock seventeen minutes fast, and so on. He launches into his story:

X, Y and Z conspired to murder Mr. Body. Seventeen years ago, in the gold fields of Uganda, X was Body's partner...Last week, Y and Z conferred in a bar in Reading...Tuesday night at 11:17, Y went to the attic and set a time bomb...Seventeen minutes later, X met Z in the billiard room and gave him the lead pipe...Just when the bomb went off in the attic, X fired three shots into the study through the French windows...

And so it goes: a long story. Let us pretend that it is a single long conjunctive sentence.

The story contains the three names 'X', 'Y' and 'Z'. The detective uses these new terms without explanation, as though we knew what they meant. But we do not. We never used them before, at least not in the senses they bear in the present context. All we know about their meanings is what we gradually gather from the story itself. Call these *theoretical terms* (*T-terms* for short) because they are introduced by a theory. Call the rest of the terms in the story *O-terms*. These are all the *other* terms except the T-terms; they are all the *old, original* terms we understood before the theory was proposed. We could call them our 'pre-theoretical' terms. But 'O' does *not* stand for 'observational'. Not all the O-terms are observational terms, whatever those may be. They are just any old terms. If part of the story was mathematical— if it included a calculation of the trajectory that took the second bullet to the chandelier without breaking the vase—then some of the O-terms will be mathematical. If the story says that something happened because of something else, then the

2. See my 'How to Define Theoretical Terms', *Journal of Philosophy*, **67** (1970): 427–46.
3. Since advocated also by D. M. Armstrong, in *A Materialist Theory of the Mind* (New York: Humanities Press, 1968). He expresses it thus: 'The concept of a mental state is primarily the concept of a state of the person apt for bringing about a certain sort of behaviour [and secondarily also, in some cases] apt for being brought about by a certain sort of stimulus', p. 82.

O-terms will include the intensional connective 'because', or the operator 'it is a law that', or something of the sort.

Nor do the theoretical terms name some sort of peculiar theoretical, unobservable, semi-fictitious entities. The story makes plain that they name *people*. Not theoretical people, different somehow from ordinary, observational people—just people!

On my account, the detective plunged right into his story, using 'X', 'Y' and 'Z' as if they were names with understood denotation. It would have made little difference if he had started, instead, with initial existential quantifiers: 'There exist X, Y and Z such that. . .' and then told the story. In that case, the terms 'X', 'Y' and 'Z' would have been bound variables rather than T-terms. But the story would have had the same explanatory power. The second version of the story, with the T-terms turned into variables bound by existential quantifiers, is the Ramsey sentence of the first. Bear in mind, as evidence for what is to come, how little difference the initial quantifiers seem to make to the detective's assertion.

Suppose that after we have heard the detective's story, we learn that it is true of a certain three people: Plum, Peacock and Mustard. If we put the name 'Plum' in place of 'X', 'Peacock' in place of 'Y', and 'Mustard' in place of 'Z' throughout, we get a true story about the doings of those three people. We will say that Plum, Peacock and Mustard together *realize* (or are a *realization* of) the detective's theory.

We may also find out that the story is not true of any other triple.[4] Put in any three names that do not name Plum, Peacock and Mustard (in that order) and the story we get is false. We will say that Plum, Peacock and Mustard *uniquely realize* (are the *unique realization* of) the theory.

We might learn both of these facts. (The detective might have known them all along, but held them back to spring his trap; or he, like us, might learn them only after his story had been told.) And if we did, we would surely conclude that X, Y and Z in the story were Plum, Peacock and Mustard. I maintain that we would be compelled so to conclude, given the senses borne by the terms 'X', 'Y' and 'Z' in virtue of the way the detective introduced them in his theorizing, and given our information about Plum, Peacock and Mustard.

In telling his story, the detective set forth three roles and said that they were occupied by X, Y and Z. He must have specified the meanings of the three T-terms 'X', 'Y' and 'Z' thereby; for they had meanings afterwards, they had none before, and nothing else was done to give them meanings. They were introduced by an implicit functional definition, being reserved to name the occupants of the three roles. When we find out who are the occupants of the three roles, we find out who are X, Y, and Z. Here is our theoretical identification.

In saying that the roles were occupied by X, Y and Z, the detective implied that they were occupied. That is, his theory implied its Ramsey sentence. That seems right; if we learnt that no triple realized the story, or even came close, we would have

---

4. The story itself might imply this. If, for instance, the story said 'X saw Y give Z the candlestick while the three of them were alone in the billiard room at 9:17'. then the story could not possibly be true of more than one triple.

to conclude that the story was false. We would also have to deny that the names 'X', 'Y' and 'Z' named anything; for they were introduced as names for the occupants of roles that turned out to be unoccupied.

I also claim that the detective implied that the roles were uniquely occupied, when he reserved names for their occupants and proceeded as if those names had been given definite referents. Suppose we learnt that two different triples realized the theory: Plum, Peacock, Mustard; and Green, White, Scarlet. (Or the two different triples might overlap: Plum, Peacock, Mustard; and Green, Peacock, Scarlet.) I think we would be most inclined to say that the story was false, and that the names 'X', 'Y' and 'Z' did not name anything. They were introduced as names for the occupants of certain roles; but there is no such thing as *the* occupant of a doubly occupied role, so there is nothing suitable for them to name.

If, as I claim, the T-terms are definable as naming the first, second, and third components of the unique triple that realizes the story, then the T-terms can be treated like definite descriptions. If the story is uniquely realized, they name what they ought to name; if the story is unrealized or multiply realized, they are like improper descriptions. If too many triples realize the story, 'X' is like 'the moon of Mars'; if too few triples—none—realize the story, 'X' is like 'the moon of Venus'. Improper descriptions are not meaningless. Hilary Putnam has objected that on this sort of account of theoretical terms, the theoretical terms of a falsified theory come out meaningless.[5] But they do not, if theoretical terms of unrealized theories are like improper descriptions. 'The moon of Mars' and 'The moon of Venus' do not (in any normal way) name anything here in our actual world; but they are not meaningless, because we know very well what they name in certain alternative possible worlds. Similarly, we know what 'X' names in any world where the detective's theory is true, whether or not our actual world is such a world.

A complication: what if the theorizing detective has made one little mistake? He should have said that Y went to the attic at 11:37, not 11:17. The story as told is unrealized, true of no one. But another story is realized, indeed uniquely realized: the story we get by deleting or correcting the little mistake. We can say that the story as told is *nearly realized*, has a unique *near-realization*. (The notion of a near-realization is hard to analyze, but easy to understand.) In this case the T-terms ought to name the components of the near-realization. More generally: they should name the components of the nearest realization of the theory, provided there is a unique nearest realization and it is near enough. Only if the story comes nowhere near to being realized, or if there are two equally near nearest realizations, should we resort to treating the T-terms like improper descriptions. But let us set aside this complication for the sake of simplicity, though we know well that scientific theories are often nearly realized but rarely realized, and that theoretical reduction is usually blended with revision of the reduced theory.

5. 'What Theories Are Not', in Nagel, Suppes and Tarski eds., *Logic, Methodology and Philosophy of Science* (Stanford University Press, 1962): 247.

This completes our example. It may seem atypical: the T-terms are names, not predicates or functors. But that is of no importance. It is a popular exercise to recast a language so that its nonlogical vocabulary consists entirely of predicates; but it is just as easy to recast a language so that its nonlogical vocabulary consists entirely of names (provided that the logical vocabulary includes a copula). These names, of course, may purport to name individuals, sets, attributes, species, states, functions, relations, magnitudes, phenomena or what have you; but they are still names. Assume this done, so that we may replace all T-terms by variables of the same sort.

II

We now proceed to a general account of the functional definability of T-terms and the nature of theoretical identification. Suppose we have a new theory, T, introducing the new terms $t_1 \ldots t_n$. These are our T-terms. (Let them be names.) Every other term in our vocabulary, therefore, is an O-term. The theory T is presented in a sentence called the *postulate* of T. Assume this is a single sentence, perhaps a long conjunction. It says of the entities—states, magnitudes, species, or whatever—named by the T-terms that they occupy certain *causal roles*; that they stand in specified causal (and other) relations to entities named by O-terms, and to one another. We write the postulate thus:[6]

$$T[\mathbf{t}].$$

Replacing the T-terms uniformly by free variables $x_1 \ldots x_n$, we get a formula in which only O-terms appear:

$$T[\mathbf{x}].$$

Any n-tuple of entities which satisfies this formula is a realization of the theory T. Prefixing existential quantifiers, we get the *Ramsey sentence* of T, which says that T has at least one realization:

$$\exists \mathbf{x}\, T[\mathbf{x}].$$

We can also write a *modified Ramsey sentence* which says that T has a unique realization:[7]

$$\exists_1 \mathbf{x}\, T[\mathbf{x}].$$

The Ramsey sentence has exactly the same O-content as the postulate of T; any sentence free of T-terms follows logically from one if and only if it follows from the

6. Notation: boldface names and variables denote n-tuples; the corresponding subscripted names and variables denote components of n-tuples. For instance, $\mathbf{t}$ is $<t_1 \ldots t_n>$. This notation is easily dispensable, and hence carries no ontic commitment to n-tuples.
7. That is, $\exists y \forall \mathbf{x}(T[\mathbf{x}] \equiv \mathbf{y} = \mathbf{x})$. Note that $\exists_1 x_1 \ldots \exists_1 x_n\, T[\mathbf{x}]$ does not imply $\exists_1 \mathbf{x}\, T[\mathbf{x}]$, and does not say that T is uniquely realized.

other.[8] The modified Ramsey sentence has slightly more O-content. I claim that this surplus O-content does belong to the theory T—there are more theorems of T than follow logically from the postulate alone. For in presenting the postulate as if the T-terms have been well-defined thereby, the theorist has implicitly asserted that T is uniquely realized.

We can write the *Carnap sentence* of T: the conditional of the Ramsey sentence and the postulate, which says that if T is realized, then the T-terms name the components of some realization of T:

$$\exists x\ T[x] \supset T[t].$$

Carnap has suggested this sentence as a meaning postulate for T[9] but if we want T-terms of unrealized or multiply realized theories to have the status of improper descriptions, our meaning postulates should instead be a *modified Carnap sentence*, this conditional with our modified Ramsey sentence as antecedent:

$$\exists_1 x\ T[x] \supset T[t],$$

together with another conditional to cover the remaining cases:[10]

$$\sim\exists_1 x\ T[x] \supset t = *.$$

This pair of meaning postulates is logically equivalent[11] to a sentence which explicitly defines the T-terms by means of O-terms:

$$t = \imath\, x\ T[x].$$

This is what I have called functional definition. The T-terms have been defined as the occupants of the causal roles specified by the theory T; as *the* entities, whatever those may be, that bear certain causal relations to one another and to the referents of the O-terms.

If I am right, T-terms are eliminable—we can always replace them by their definientia. Of course, this is not to say that theories are fictions, or that theories are uninterpreted formal abacuses, or that theoretical entities are unreal. Quite the opposite! Because we understand the O-terms, and we can define the T-terms from them, theories are fully meaningful; we have reason to think a good theory true; and if a theory is true, then whatever exists according to the theory really *does* exist.

---

8. On the assumptions—reasonable for the postulate of a scientific theory—that the T-terms occur purely referentially in the postulate, and in such a way that the postulate is false if any of them are denotationless. We shall make these assumptions henceforth.

9. Most recently in *Philosophical Foundations of Physics* (New York: Basic Books, 1966): 265–74. Carnap, of course, has in mind the case in which the O-terms belong to an observation language.

10. $t = *$ means that each t_i is denotationless. Let $*$ be some chosen necessarily denotationless name; then $*$ is $<*\ldots*>$ and $t = *$ is equivalent to the conjunction of all the identities $t_i = *$.

11. Given a theory of descriptions which makes an identity true whenever both its terms have the status of improper descriptions, false whenever one term has that status and the other does not. This might best be the theory of descriptions in Dana Scott, 'Existence and Description in Formal Logic', in R. Schoenman, ed., *Bertrand Russell: Philosopher of the Century* (London: Allen & Unwin, 1967).

I said that there are more theorems of T than follow logically from the postulate alone. More precisely: the theorems of T are just those sentences which follow from the postulate together with the corresponding functional definition of the T-terms. For that definition, I claim, is given implicitly when the postulate is presented as bestowing meanings on the T-terms introduced in it.

It may happen, after the introduction of the T-terms, that we come to believe of a certain n-tuple of entities, specified otherwise than as the entities that realize T, that they do realize T. That is, we may come to accept a sentence

$$T[\mathbf{r}]$$

where $r_1 \ldots r_n$ are either O-terms or theoretical terms of some other theory, introduced into our language independently of $t_1 \ldots t_n$. This sentence, which we may call a *weak reduction premise* for T, is free of T-terms. Our acceptance of it might have nothing to do with our previous acceptance of T. We might accept it as part of some new theory; or we might believe it as part of our miscellaneous, unsystematized general knowledge. Yet having accepted it, for whatever reason, we are logically compelled to make theoretical identifications. The reduction premise, together with the functional definition of the T-terms and the postulate of T, logically implies the identity:

$$\mathbf{t} = \mathbf{r}.$$

In other words, the postulate and the weak reduction premise definitionally imply the identities $t_i = r_i$.

Or we might somehow come to believe of a certain n-tuple of entities that they *uniquely* realize T; that is, to accept a sentence

$$\forall \mathbf{x}(T[\mathbf{x}] \equiv \mathbf{x} = \mathbf{r})$$

where $r_1 \ldots r_n$ are as above. We may call this a *strong reduction premise* for T, since it definitionally implies the theoretical identifications by itself, without the aid of the postulate of T. The strong reduction premise logically implies the identity

$$\mathbf{r} = \imath \mathbf{x} T[\mathbf{x}]$$

which, together with the functional definition of the T-terms, implies the identities $t_i = r_i$ by transitivity of identity.

These theoretical identifications are not voluntary posits, made in the name of parsimony; they are deductive inferences. According to their definitions, the T-terms name the occupants of the causal roles specified by the theory T. According to the weak reduction premise and T, or the strong reduction premise by itself, the occupants of those causal roles turn out to be the referents of $r_1 \ldots r_n$. Therefore, those are the entities named by the T-terms. That is how we inferred that X, Y and Z were Plum, Peacock and Mustard; and that, I suggest, is how we make theoretical identifications in general.

III

And that is how, someday, we will infer that[12] the mental states $M_1, M_2, \ldots$ are the neural states $N_1, N_2, \ldots$.

Think of common-sense psychology as a term-introducing scientific theory, though one invented long before there was any such institution as professional science. Collect all the platitudes you can think of regarding the causal relations of mental states, sensory stimuli, and motor responses. Perhaps we can think of them as having the form:

When someone is in so-and-so combination of mental states and receives sensory stimuli of so-and-so kind, he tends with so-and-so probability to be caused thereby to go into so-and-so mental states and produce so-and-so motor responses.

Add also all the platitudes to the effect that one mental state falls under another—'toothache is a kind of pain', and the like. Perhaps there are platitudes of other forms as well. Include only platitudes which are common knowledge among us—everyone knows them, everyone knows that everyone else knows them, and so on. For the meanings of our words are common knowledge, and I am going to claim that names of mental states derive their meaning from these platitudes.

Form the conjunction of these platitudes; or better, form a cluster of them—a disjunction of all conjunctions of *most* of them. (That way it will not matter if a few are wrong.) This is the postulate of our term-introducing theory. The names of mental states are the T-terms.[13] The O-terms used to introduce them must be sufficient for speaking of stimuli and responses, and for speaking of causal relations among these and states of unspecified nature.

From the postulate, form the definition of the T-terms; it defines the mental states by reference to their causal relations to stimuli, responses, and each other. When we learn what sort of states occupy those causal roles definitive of the mental states, we will learn what states the mental states are—exactly as we found out who X was when we found out that Plum was the man who occupied a certain role, and exactly as we found out what light was when we found that electromagnetic radiation was the phenomenon that occupied a certain role.

Imagine our ancestors first speaking only of external things, stimuli, and responses—and perhaps producing what we, but not they, may call *Aüsserungen* of

---

12. In general, or in the case of a given species, or in the case of a given person. It might turn out that the causal roles definitive of mental states are occupied by different neural (or other) states in different organisms. See my discussion of Hilary Putnam 'Psychological Predicates' in *Journal of Philosophy*, **66** (1969): 23–5.

13. It may be objected that the number of mental states is infinite, or at least enormous; for instance, there are as many states of belief as there are propositions to be believed. But it would be better to say that there is one state of belief, and it is a relational state, relating people to propositions. (Similarly, centigrade temperature is a relational state, relating objects to numbers.) The platitudes involving belief would, of course, contain universally quantified proposition-variables; likewise, for other mental states with intentional objects.

mental states—until some genius invented the theory of mental states, with its newly introduced T-terms, to explain the regularities among stimuli and responses. But that did not happen. Our common-sense psychology was never a newly invented term-introducing scientific theory—not even of prehistoric folk-science. The story that mental terms were introduced as theoretical terms is a myth.

It is, in fact, Sellars' myth of our Rylean ancestors.[14] And though it is a myth, it may be a good myth or a bad one. It is a good myth if our names of mental states do in fact mean just what they would mean if the myth were true.[15] I adopt the working hypothesis that it is a good myth. This hypothesis can be tested, in principle, in whatever way any hypothesis about the conventional meanings of our words can be tested. I have not tested it; but I offer one item of evidence. Many philosophers have found Rylean behaviorism at least plausible; more have found watered down, 'criteriological' behaviorism plausible. There is a strong odor of analyticity about the platitudes of common-sense psychology. The myth explains the odor of analyticity and the plausibility of behaviorism. If the names of mental states are like theoretical terms, they name nothing unless the theory (the cluster of platitudes) is more or less true. Hence it is analytic that *either* pain, etc., do not exist *or* most of our platitudes about them are true. If this *seems* analytic to you, you should accept the myth, and be prepared for psychophysical identifications.

The hypothesis that names of mental states are like functionally defined theoretical terms solves a familiar problem about mental explanations. How can my behavior be explained by an explanans consisting of nothing but particular-fact premises about my present state of mind? Where are the covering laws? The solution is that the requisite covering laws are implied by the particular-fact premises. Ascriptions to me of various particular beliefs and desires, say, cannot be true if there are no such states as belief and desire; cannot be true, that is, unless the causal roles definitive of belief and desire are occupied. But these roles can only be occupied by states causally related in the proper lawful way to behavior.

Formally, suppose we have a mental explanation of behavior as follows.

$$\frac{C_1[t], C_2[t], \ldots}{E}$$

14. Wilfrid Sellars, 'Empiricism and the Philosophy of Mind', in Feigl and Scriven, eds., *Minnesota Studies in the Philosophy of Science*, I (University of Minnesota Press, 1956): 309–20.

15. Two myths which cannot both be true together can nevertheless both be good together. Part of my myth says that names of color-sensations were T-terms, introduced using names of colors as O-terms. If this is a good myth, we should be able to define 'sensation of red' roughly as 'that state apt for being brought about by the presence of something red (before one's open eyes, in good light, etc.)'. A second myth says that names of colors were T-terms introduced using names of color-sensations as O-terms. If this second myth is good, we should be able to define 'red' roughly as 'that property of things apt for bringing about the sensation of red'. The two myths could not both be true, for which came first: names of color-sensations or of colors? But they could both be good. We could have a circle in which colors are correctly defined in terms of sensations and sensations are correctly defined in terms of colors. We could not discover the meanings *both* of names of colors and of names of color-sensations just by looking at the circle of correct definitions, but so what?

Here E describes the behavior to be explained; $C_1[t]$, $C_2[t]$, . . . are particular-fact premises describing the agent's state of mind at the time. Various of the mental terms t_1 . . . t_n appear in these premises, in such a way that the premises would be false if the terms named nothing. Now let $L_1[t]$, $L_2[t]$, . . . be the platitudinous purported causal laws whereby—according to the myth—the mental terms were introduced. Ignoring clustering for simplicity, we may take the term-introducing postulate to be the conjunction of these. Then our explanation may be rewritten:

$$\frac{\exists_1 x \left(\begin{array}{l} L_1[x] \ \& \ L_2[x] \& \dots \& \\ C_1[x] \ \& \ C_2[x] \& \dots \end{array} \right)}{E}$$

The new explanans is a definitional consequence of the original one. In the expanded version, however, laws appear explicitly alongside the particular-fact premises. We have, so to speak, an existential generalization of an ordinary covering-law explanation.[16]

The causal definability of mental terms has been thought to contradict the necessary infallibility of introspection.[17] Pain is one state; belief that one is in pain is another. (Confusingly, either of the two may be called 'awareness of pain'.) Why cannot I believe that I am in pain without being in pain—that is, without being in whatever state it is that occupies so-and-so causal role? Doubtless I am so built that this normally does not happen; but what makes it impossible?

I do not know whether introspection is (in some or all cases) infallible. But if it is, that is no difficulty for me. Here it is important that, on my version of causal definability, the mental terms stand or fall together. If common-sense psychology fails, all of them are alike denotationless.

Suppose that among the platitudes are some to the effect that introspection is reliable: 'belief that one is in pain never occurs unless pain occurs' or the like. Suppose further that these platitudes enter the term-introducing postulate as conjuncts, not as cluster members; and suppose that they are so important that an n-tuple that fails to satisfy them perfectly is not even a near-realization of common-sense psychology. (I neither endorse nor repudiate these suppositions.) Then the necessary infallibility of introspection is assured. Two states cannot be pain and belief that one is in pain, respectively (in the case of a given individual or species) if the second *ever* occurs without the first. The state that *usually* occupies the role of belief that one is in pain may, of course, occur without the state that *usually* occupies the role of pain; but in that case (under the suppositions above) the former no longer is the state of belief that one is in pain, and the latter no longer is pain. Indeed, the victim no longer is in any mental state whatever, since his states no longer realize (or nearly realize) common-sense psychology. Therefore, it is impossible to believe that one is in pain and not be in pain.

---

16. See 'How to Define Theoretical Terms': 440–1.
17. By Armstrong, in *A Materialist Theory of the Mind*, pp. 100–13. He finds independent grounds for denying the infallibility of introspection.

Chapter 48

Selection from *Thinking Causes*

Donald Davidson

Iₙ 1970 I proposed a theory about the relation between the mental and the physical that I called Anomalous Monism (*AM*).[1] *AM* holds that mental entities (particular time- and space-bound objects and events) are physical entities, but that mental concepts are not reducible by definition or natural law to physical concepts. The position is, in a general way, familiar: it endorses ontological reduction, but eschews conceptual reduction. What was new was the argument, which purported to derive *AM* from three premises, namely, (1) that mental events are causally related to physical events, (2) that singular causal relations are backed by strict laws, and (3) that there are no strict psycho-physical laws.[2] The first premiss seemed to me obvious, the second true though contested (I did not present arguments for it), and the third true and worth arguing for. Many readers have found my arguments against the existence of strict psycho-physical laws obscure; others have decided the three premises are mutually inconsistent. But the complaints have most often been summed up by saying that *AM* makes the mental causally inert. The criticisms are connected: if *AM* makes the mental causally inert, then *AM* apparently implies the falsity of the first premiss and hence the inconsistency of the three premises. The third premiss seems to many critics the relevant offender, so they urge that it should be dropped.

In this paper I attempt three things: first, to defend *AM* against misunderstandings and misrepresentations. This will involve some clarification, and perhaps modification, of the original thesis. Second, I want to maintain that the three premises from which I argue to *AM* are consistent when taken together, and so *AM* is a tenable thesis (it is weaker than the premises). Third, I shall say why I do not think *AM* makes the mental causally powerless. I do not plan here to argue for the truth of *AM* or the premises on which it rests.

In 'Mental Events' (Davidson 1970) I endorsed the idea that mental concepts[3] are supervenient, in a sense I explained, on physical concepts. I thought this would make it clear that, contrary to first impressions, *AM* and its entailing premises were after all consistent. So what I am defending in this paper is in effect not only *AM* itself, but

---

1. Davidson 1970.
2. This summary simplifies the original thesis and argument. Those not familiar with 'Mental Events' should consult it for caveats and additional assumptions.
3. In the present paper I do not distinguish concepts from properties or predicates, except to the extent that I allow that physics may well come to require predicates not now available.

AM in conjunction with the three premisses and the doctrine of supervenience. (In what follows, I shall abbreviate the expression 'anomalous monism conjoined with premisses (1) − (2)' by '*AM* + *P*'; '*AM* + *P* + *S*' will mean supervenience in addition to *AM* + *P*.)

When I wrote 'Mental Events' I thought I knew that G. E. Moore had used the word 'supervenience' to describe the relation between evaluative terms like 'good' and descriptive terms like 'sharp' or 'inexpensive' or 'pleasure-producing'. Moore's idea seemed clear enough: something is good only because it has properties that can be specified in descriptive terms, but goodness can't be reduced to a descriptive property. In fact, Moore apparently never used the word 'supervenient'. I had probably found the word in R. M. Hare's *The Language of Morals* (1952), and applied it, as he had, to Moore. (Hare has since complained that I got the concept wrong: for him supervenience implies a form of what I call nomological reduction.[4]) In any case, the idea I had in mind is, I think, most economically expressed as follows: a predicate *p* is supervenient on a set of predicates *S* if and only if *p* does not distinguish any entities that cannot be distinguished by *S*.[5] Supervenience so understood obviously applies in an uninteresting sense to cases where *p* belongs to *S*, to cases where *p* is explicitly definable by means of the predicates in *S*, and to cases where there is a law to the effect that the extension of *p* is identical with the extension of a predicate definable in terms of the predicates in *S*. The interesting cases are those where *p* resists any of these forms of reduction. I gave as a non-controversial example of an interesting case the supervenience of semantic predicates on syntactical predicates: a truth predicate for a language cannot distinguish any sentences not distinguishable in purely syntactical terms, but for most languages truth is not definable in such terms. The example gives one possible meaning to the idea that truths expressible by the subvenient predicates 'determine' the extension of the supervenient predicate, or that the extension of the supervenient predicate 'depends' on the extensions of the subvenient predicates.

---

4. Hare (1984, p. 3) says, '. . . supervenience brings with it the claim that there is some "law" which binds what supervenes to what it supervenes upon . . . what supervenience requires is that what supervenes is seen as an instance of some universal proposition linking it with what it supervenes upon.' But so far as I can see, Hare's characterization of supervenience, on the page before the one from which the above quotation is taken, does not imply the existence of laws or law-like generalizations linking what supervenes to what it supervenes on. Hare compares his version of supervenience with Kim's 'weak' supervenience, but Kim himself (correctly, I think) finds my version of supervenience very close to his 'weak' supervenience, and as not entailing connecting laws.

5. In 'Mental Events', I said the supervenience of the mental on the physical 'might be taken to mean that there cannot be two events alike in all physical respects but differing in some mental respect'. I intended this to be equivalent to the present formulation, but apparently it is easily misunderstood. In answer to a question about 'Mental Events', I gave an unambiguous definition of supervenience which is clearly equivalent to the present one: a predicate *p* is supervenient on a set of predicates *S* if for every pair of objects such that *p* is true of one and not of the other there is a predicate in *S* that is true of one and not of the other. I suggested that it is a common fallacy in philosophy (of which the naturalistic fallacy is an example) to switch the order of the quantifiers in this formula. See Davidson 1985, p. 242.

How can the possibility of a supervenient relation between the mental and the physical help to show that AM (or $AM + P$) is consistent, since supervenience says nothing about causality? The answer is simple: supervenience in any form implies monism; but it does not imply either definitional or nomological reduction. So if (non-reductive) supervenience is consistent (as the syntax-semantics example proves it is), so is AM. But supervenience is also consistent with premises (1) and (2), which are not implied by AM, since (1) and (2) concern causality, and supervenience says nothing about causality.

It is difficult, then, to see how $AM + P$ together with supervenience can imply a contradiction. So it surprised me to read in a recent article by Jaegwon Kim that not only are the premises of AM inconsistent with one another, but 'the notion of supervenience Davidson favours' is also inconsistent with the first premiss of AM (Kim 1989b, p. 6).

Let us look at these supposed inconsistencies. According to Kim,

The fact is that under Davidson's anomalous monism, mentality does no causal work. Remember: on anomalous monism, events are causes only as they instantiate physical laws, and this means that an event's mental properties make no causal difference. And to suppose that altering an event's mental properties would also alter its physical properties and thereby affect its causal relations is to suppose that psycho-physical anomalism, a cardinal tenet of anomalous monism, is false.

Of course, if 'mentality does no causal work' means that mental events do not enter into causal relations, the first premiss of AM is false, for it says mental events cause, and are caused by, physical events. This is not enough to prove AM itself inconsistent, but it certainly would show the three premises of AM inconsistent with one another. And if Kim's last sentence quoted above is correct, then AM is inconsistent with any form of supervenience.

Why does Kim think $AM + P + S$ is inconsistent? At least part of the answer is contained in the sentence in which Kim asks us to 'remember' what he thinks is a feature of $AM + P$; and here I believe Kim speaks for many of the critics of my position. What Kim asks us to 'remember' is that 'on anomalous monism, events are causes only as they instantiate laws'. This is not anything I have claimed. I could not have claimed it, since given my concept of events and of causality, it makes no sense to speak of an event being a cause 'as' anything at all. $AM + P + S$ is formulated on the assumption that events are non-abstract particulars, and that causal relations are extensional relations between such events. In his article, Kim does not dispute these two theses. But there is then no room for a concept of 'cause as' which would make causality a relation among three or four entities rather than between two. On the view of events and causality assumed here,[6] it makes no more sense to say event c caused event e as instantiating law l than it makes to say a weighs less than b as belonging to sort s. If causality is a relation between events, it holds between them no matter how they are described. So there can be descriptions of two events (physical

6. This view is spelled out in detail in the articles in the second part of Davidson 1980.

descriptions) which allow us to deduce from a law that if the first event occurred the second would occur, and other descriptions (mental descriptions) of the same events which invite no such inference. We can say, if we please (though I do not think this is a happy way of putting the point), that events instantiate a law only as described in one way rather than another, but we cannot say that an event caused another only as described. Redescribing an event cannot change what it causes, or change the event's causal efficacy. Events, unlike agents, do not care how what they cause is described: an agent may kill a bird because she wanted to perform an action that could be described as 'my killing of that bird'. But her killing of the bird might have been identical with her killing of the goose that laid the golden egg though 'My killing of the goose that laid the golden egg' may have been the last description she wanted to have describe an action of hers.

Kim thinks that $AM + P$ cannot remain consistently anomalous if it holds that altering an event's mental properties would also alter its physical properties. This seems to be a mistake. $AM + P + S$ (which includes supervenience) does hold that altering an event's mental properties would also alter its physical properties. But supervenience does not imply the existence of psycho-physical laws. To see this, it is only necessary to recognize that although supervenience entails that any change in a mental property p of a particular event e will be accompanied by a change in the physical properties of e, it does not entail that a change in p in other events will be accompanied by an identical change in the physical properties of those other events. Only the latter entailment would conflict with $AM + P$.

The definition of supervenience implies that a change in mental properties is always accompanied by a change in physical properties, but it does not imply that the same physical properties change with the same mental properties. Supervenience implies the first, because if a change in a mental property were not accompanied by a change in physical properties, there would be two events distinguished by their mental properties that were not distinguished by their physical properties, and supervenience, as I defined it, rules this out. Kim says supervenience 'is best regarded as independent' of the thesis of $AM + P$. This is true in the sense that neither supervenience nor $AM + P$ entails the other. But it is not true that the consistency of supervenience is irrelevant to the consistency of $AM + P$ since, as I just argued, supervenience helps in showing not only that $AM + P$ is consistent, but also that there is a version of $AM + P$ that gives a plausible picture of the relation between the mental and the physical. Kim may have made this remark because he mistakenly thinks that my 'weak' version of supervenience entails that 'the removal of all mental properties from events of this world would have no consequence whatever on how physical properties are distributed over them' (Kim 1989b, p. 35, n. 8). In fact supervenience entails the reverse. For consider two events with the same physical properties, but one with some mental property and the other with that property removed. These cannot be the same event, since one has a property the other lacks. But then contrary to the definition of supervenience, mental properties would distinguish two events not distinguished by their physical properties.

But the point seems clear enough whatever one wants to say about supervenience: if causal relations and causal powers inhere in particular events and objects, then the way those events and objects are described, and the properties we happen to employ to pick them out or characterize them, cannot affect what they cause. Naming the American invasion of Panama 'Operation Just Cause' does not alter the consequences of the event.

So far I have said little about laws because laws are not mentioned in the definition of supervenience, and the logical possibility of supervenience is important in establishing the consistency of $AM + P$. But of course the thesis that there are no strict psycho-physical laws is one of the premises on the basis of which I argued for AM. So even if AM is consistent, there is a question whether the denial of such laws somehow undermines the claim that mental events are causally efficacious. I say 'somehow' since it would seem that the efficacy of an event cannot depend on how the event is described, while whether an event can be called mental, or can be said to fall under a law, depends entirely on how the event can be described.

Let me digress briefly. The second assumption from which I argued to AM was that if two events are related as cause and effect, there must be a law that covers the case. In 'Mental Events' I explained in some detail what I meant by a law in this context, and what I meant by 'covering'. A law (formulated in some language) covers a case if the law, conjoined with a sentence that says the event (described appropriately) occurred, entails a sentence that asserts the existence of the effect (appropriately described). I made clear that what I was calling a law in this context was something that one could at best hope to find in a developed physics: a generalization that was not only 'law-like' and true, but was as deterministic as nature can be found to be, was free from caveats and *ceteris paribus* clauses; that could, therefore, be viewed as treating the universe as a closed system. I stressed that it was only laws of this kind (which I called 'strict' laws) that I was arguing could not cover events when those events were described in the mental vocabulary. I allowed that there are not, and perhaps could not be expected to be, laws of this sort in the special sciences. Most, if not all, of the practical knowledge that we (or engineers, chemists, geneticists, geologists) have that allows us to explain and predict ordinary happenings does not involve strict laws. The best descriptions we are able to give of most events are not descriptions that fall under, or will ever fall under, strict laws.[7]

There are two reasons for reminding those interested in AM (or $AM + P$ or $AM + P + S$) of these facts. The first is simply that much of the criticism of $AM + P$ has ignored the distinction I painfully spelled out in 'Mental Events' between the 'strict' laws I think exist covering singular causal relations and the less than strict laws that can be couched in mental terms. Thus, Kim, in the article I mentioned,

7. Davidson 1970/1980, pp. 216–23. There I said, 'I suppose most of our practical lore (and science) is heteronomic [i.e. not in the form of strict laws, and not reducible to such]. This is because a law can hope to be precise, explicit, and as exceptionless as possible only if it draws its concepts from a comprehensive closed theory', p. 219. Also see Vermazen and Hintikka 1985, pp. 242–52, and Pettit, Sylvan, and Norman 1987, pp. 41–8.

begins by saying correctly that $AM + P$ denies that there are precise or strict laws about mental events, but goes on to criticize $AM + P$ for maintaining that 'the mental is anomalous not only in that there are no laws relating mental events to other mental events but none relating them to physical events either' (Kim 1989b, p. 33). In fact I have repeatedly said that if you want to call certain undeniably important regularities laws—the familiar regularities that link the mental with the mental (as formulated, for example in decision theory) or the mental with the physical—I have no objection; I merely say these are not, and cannot be reduced to, *strict* laws.

Because he ignores the distinction between strict laws and other sorts of regularities, it is by no means clear that Kim really holds views at odds with $AM + P$. Kim maintains, plausibly it seems to me, that any satisfactory account of the relation between the mental and the physical must permit appeal to 'local correlations and dependencies between specific mental and physical properties'. But then he adds, 'The trouble is that once we begin talking about correlations and dependencies between specific psychological and physical properties, we are in effect talking about psycho-physical laws, and these laws raise the specter of unwanted physical reductionism. Where there are psycho-physical laws, there is always the threat, or promise, of psycho-physical reduction.' (Kim 1989b, p. 42.) But if the laws are not strict, the threat is averted, and the promise false. Kim offers no reason to think the laws can be strict; I have given arguments (which he does not mention or discuss in this article; see Kim 1989b, p. 42) why I think they cannot. It is not clear that Kim has come to grips with $AM+P$.

Kim is by no means the only critic of $AM + P$ to fail to notice the crucial importance of the distinction between strict and non-strict laws. Thus J. A. Fodor writes that he is going to defend the view that intentional (mental) properties are 'causally responsible' and that there are 'intentional causal laws . . . contrary to the doctrine called "anomalous monism" '. His defence is that in common sense and in many (all?) of the 'special' sciences, there are plenty of laws that are far from strict. He cites as an example of a law in geology that mountains are apt to have snow on them; it is *because* Mt. Everest is a mountain that it has snow on it.[8] But as I have just pointed out, this defence of the causal efficacy of the mental is consistent with $AM + P$.

It is a question whether others who have attacked $AM + P$ have taken the distinction between types of regularity fully into account. Fred Dretske, who has also maintained that $AM + P$ makes the mental causally inert, has never claimed

---

8. See Fodor 1989. The argument Fodor gives there is, though he does not realize it, a *defence* of AM, since he argues that although there may be no strict laws in geology, this does not show that such properties as being a mountain are not causally efficacious. As he says, to suppose that the lack of such strict laws makes geological properties epiphenomenal is absurd: 'there are likely to be parallel arguments that *all properties are inert excepting only those expressed by the vocabulary of physics.*' I think this is exactly right if one adds, 'expressible in the vocabulary of physics or in a vocabulary definitionally or nomologically reducible to the vocabulary of physics'. The same point is made in Fodor 1987, pp. 5–6. There, the example is 'A meandering river erodes its outer banks unless, for example, the weather changes and the river dries up'.

that there are strict psycho-physical laws (see Dretske 1989). There is thus no clear reason to believe that the sort of account he wants to offer of how the mental causes the physical is itself inconsistent with $AM + P$. I don't think his account succeeds; but that is another matter. Dagfinn Føllesdal has also thought there must be psycho-physical laws; but he gives as an example of such a 'law', 'Any severely dehydrated person who drinks water will improve' (Føllesdal 1985, p. 321). $AM + P$ does not rule out such laws, for such a law is obviously far from strict, and it is not likely that it can be made truly exceptionless.

The second reason for paying attention to the distinction between the laws of an ideal physics and other generalizations (whether or not we call them laws) has to do with the logic of the argument that leads from the premises to AM. The argument does not depend on the claim that there are no psycho-physical laws: the argument demands only that there are no laws that (i) contain psychological terms that cannot be eliminated from the laws nor reduced to the vocabulary of physics and (ii) that have the features of lacking *ceteris paribus* clauses and of belonging to a closed system like the laws of a finished physics. In other words, I argued from the assumptions that mental events are causally related to physical events, and that all causally related events instantiate the laws of physics, to the conclusion that mental events are identical with physical events: thus monism. The extent to which mental concepts fall short of being reducible to physical concepts measures the degree of anomaly. As far as I can see, the positions of both Kim and Fodor on the relation between the physical and the mental are consistent with AM and $AM + P$, and it seems to me possible that the same is true of Dretske and Føllesdal.

There remains an issue, however, that separates my views from Kim's and perhaps also from Fodor's. Fodor holds that mental (or intentional) concepts can't be reduced to the concepts of a finished physics, so in this respect his position is that of $AM + P$. Kim, on the other hand, believes in reduction. But he may simply have different standards for reduction than I do; if this is so, our difference on this point may be mainly verbal. But behind what may be merely a verbal point there lies a substantive issue: both Fodor and Kim seem to think that unless there are psycho-physical laws of *some* sort, the mental would have been shown to be powerless. I think the reasoning that leads them (and others) to this conclusion is confused.

Let's be clear about what is at stake. At this point I am not concerned with the question whether or not there are psycho-physical laws. In the sense in which Kim and Fodor think there are laws linking mental and physical concepts, I also think there are laws; what I have claimed is that such laws are not strict, and that mental concepts are not reducible by definition or by strict 'bridging' laws to physical concepts. But unlike my critics, I do not think it would prove that the mental is causally inert even if there were no psycho-physical laws of any kind.

Suppose I create a table in which all the entries are definite descriptions of one sort or another of events. I refer to the events by giving the column and the row where the description is to be found: column 179 row 1044 for example is the event of my writing this sentence. Let us call the events listed in the table 'table-events'.

The vocabulary needed to describe (needed to provide a definite description of) each event is just the vocabulary needed to pick out the column and row. These events have their causes and effects: for example event 179-1044 caused a certain rearrangement of electric flows in the random access memory of my computer. There are, I imagine, no interesting tablo-physical laws whatever, that is, laws linking events described in the table language and events described in the vocabulary of physics. Yet this fact does not show that table-events are not causally efficacious.

It will be retorted that it is simply irrelevant to the causal efficacy of table-events that they are table-events—that they are described in the table vocabulary. This is true. But it is also irrelevant to the causal efficacy of physical events that they can be described in the physical vocabulary. It is *events* that have the power to change things, not our various ways of describing them. Since the fact that an event is a mental event, i.e. that it can be described in a psychological vocabulary, can make no difference to the causes and effects of that event, it makes no sense to suppose that describing it in the psychological vocabulary might deprive the event of its potency. An event, mental or physical, by any other name smells just as strong.

The point seems so simple and so clear that it is hard to see how it can be doubted. Suppose Magellan notices that there are rocks ahead, an event that, through the intervening events such as his uttering orders to the helmsman, causes the ship to alter course. Magellan's noticing is a mental event, and it is causally efficacious. That event is also a physical event, a change in Magellan's body, and describable in the vocabulary of physics. As long as the predicates used to describe the mental event are not strictly reducible to the predicates of physics, all this is in accord with $AM + P$.

Yet according to Kim and others, $AM + P$ implies that the mental is causally inert: Kim asks 'What role does mentality play on Davidson's anomalous monism?', and he answers, 'None whatever'. Why does he think this? We get a hint when he says 'on anomalous monism, events are causes or effects only as they instantiate physical laws.' The same idea is expressed by the phrase 'in virtue of': mentality is causally effective only if events are causes *in virtue of their mental properties* (see Kim 1989b, p. 43). 'Because of' has been recruited to express the same idea. Kim has even implied that it is my explicit view that 'it is only under its physical description that a mental event can be seen to enter into a causal relation with a physical event (or any other event) by being subsumed under a causal law' (Kim 1984b, p. 267). Those who are familiar with the literature will recognize other ways of putting the point: on $AM + P$ (so one reads) the mental does not cause anything *qua* mental; the mental is not efficacious *as such*. This is the vein in which Ernest Sosa writes that 'The key to [Davidson's] proposed solution . . . is the idea that mental events enter into causal relations *not* as mental but only as physical' (Sosa 1984, p. 277). Sosa does at least recognize that this is not my way of putting things, but he does not realize that I couldn't put things this way. For me, it is events that have causes and effects. Given this extensionalist view of causal relations, it makes no literal sense, as I remarked above, to speak of an event causing something as mental, or by virtue of its mental properties, or as described in one way or another.

    . . .

References

Davidson, D. (1970), 'Mental Events', in Foster and Swanson (1970): 79–101; reprinted in Davidson (1980).

—— (1980), *Essays on Actions and Events*, Oxford: Clarendon Press.

—— (1985), 'Replies to Essays X–XII', in Vermazen and Hintikka (1985): 242–52.

Dretske, F. (1989), 'Reasons and Causes', *Philosophical Perspectives*, 3: 1–15.

Fodor, J. (1987), *Psychosemantics*, Cambridge, Mass.: MIT Press.

—— (1989), 'Making Mind Matter More', *Philosophical Topics*, 17: 59–80.

Føllesdal, D. (1985), 'Causation and Explanation: A Problem in Davidson's View on Action and Mind', in Le Pore and McLaughlin (1985): 311–23.

Foster, L., and Swanson, J. (1970) (eds.), *Experience* and *Theory*, Amherst, Mass.: University of Massachusetts Press.

Hare, R. (1952), *The Language of Morals*, Oxford: Clarendon Press.

—— (1984), 'Supervenience', *Aristotelian Society Supplementary Volume*, 58: 1–16.

Kim, J. (1984*b*), 'Epiphenomenal and Supervenient Causation', *Midwest Studies in Philosophy*, 9: 257–70.

—— (1989*b*), 'The Myth of Nonreductive Materialism', *Proceedings of the American Philosophical Association*, 63: 31–47.

Pettit, P., Sylvan, R., and Norman, J. (1987) (eds.), *Metaphysics and Morality*, Oxford: Basil Blackwell.

Sosa, E. (1984), 'Mind–Body Interaction and Supervenient Causation', *Midwest Studies in Philosophy*, 9: 271–81.

Vermazen, B., and Hintikka, M. (1985) (eds.), *Essays on Davidson: Actions and Events*, Oxford: Clarendon Press.

Chapter 49

What is it like to be a bat?

Thomas Nagel

CONSCIOUSNESS is what makes the mind–body problem really intractable. Perhaps that is why current discussions of the problem give it little attention or get it obviously wrong. The recent wave of reductionist euphoria has produced several analyses of mental phenomena and mental concepts designed to explain the possibility of some variety of materialism, psychophysical identification, or reduction.[1] But the problems dealt with are those common to this type of reduction and other types, and what makes the mind–body problem unique, and unlike the water–H_2O problem or the Turing machine–IBM machine problem or the lightning–electrical discharge problem or the gene–DNA problem or the oak tree–hydrocarbon problem, is ignored.

Every reductionist has his favorite analogy from modern science. It is most unlikely that any of these unrelated examples of successful reduction will shed light on the relation of mind to brain. But philosophers share the general human weakness for explanations of what is incomprehensible in terms suited for what is familiar and well understood, though entirely different. This has led to the acceptance of implausible accounts of the mental largely because they would permit familiar kinds of reduction. I shall try to explain why the usual examples do not help us to understand the relation between mind and body—why, indeed, we have at present no conception of what an explanation of the physical nature of a mental phenomenon would be. Without consciousness the mind–body problem would be much less interesting. With consciousness it seems hopeless. The most important and characteristic feature of conscious mental phenomena is very poorly understood. Most reductionist theories do not even try to explain it. And careful examination

---

1. Examples are J. J. C. Smart, *Philosophy and Scientific Realism* (London: Routledge & Kegan Paul, 1963); David K. Lewis, 'An Argument for the Identity Theory', *Journal of Philosophy*, LXIII (1966), reprinted with addenda in David M. Rosenthal, *Materialism & the Mind–Body Problem*, (Engelwood Cliffs, NJ: Prentice-Hall, 1971); Hilary Putnam, 'Psychological Predicates', in *Art, Mind, & Religion*, ed. W. H. Capitan and D. D. Merrill (Pittsburgh: University of Pittsburgh Press, 1967), reprinted in *Materialism*, ed. Rosenthal, as 'The Nature of Mental States'; D. M. Armstrong, *A Materialist Theory of the Mind* (London: Routledge & Kegan Paul, 1968); D. C. Dennett, *Content and Consciousness* (London: Routledge & Kegan Paul, 1969). I have expressed earlier doubts in 'Armstrong on the Mind', *Philosophical Review*, LXXIX (1970), 394–403; a review of Dennett, *Journal of Philosophy*, LXIX (1972); and chapter 11 above. See also Saul Kripke, 'Naming and Necessity', in *Semantics of Natural Language*, ed. D. Davidson and G. Harman (Dordrecht: Reidel, 1972), esp. pp. 334–42; and M. T. Thornton, 'Ostensive Terms and Materialism', *The Monist*, LVI (1972), 193–214.

Thomas Nagel, 'What is it Like to be a Bat?', from *Philosophical Review*, 83 (1974).

will show that no currently available concept of reduction is applicable to it. Perhaps a new theoretical form can be devised for the purpose, but such a solution, if it exists, lies in the distant intellectual future.

Conscious experience is a widespread phenomenon. It occurs at many levels of animal life, though we cannot be sure of its presence in the simpler organisms, and it is very difficult to say in general what provides evidence of it. (Some extremists have been prepared to deny it even of mammals other than man.) No doubt it occurs in countless forms totally unimaginable to us, on other planets in other solar systems throughout the universe. But no matter how the form may vary, the fact that an organism has conscious experience *at all* means, basically, that there is something it is like to *be* that organism. There may be further implications about the form of the experience; there may even (though I doubt it) the implications about the behavior of the organism. But fundamentally an organism has conscious mental states if and only if there is something that it is like to *be* that organism— something it is like *for* the organism.

We may call this the subjective character of experience. It is not captured by any of the familiar, recently devised reductive analyses of the mental, for all of them are logically compatible with its absence. It is not analyzable in terms of any explanatory system of functional states, or intentional states, since these could be ascribed to robots or automata that behaved like people though they experienced nothing.[2] It is not analyzable in terms of the causal role of experiences in relation to typical human behavior—for similar reasons.[3] I do not deny that conscious mental states and events cause behavior, nor that they may be given functional characterizations. I deny only that this kind of thing exhausts their analysis. Any reductionist program has to be based on an analysis of what is to be reduced. If the analysis leaves something out, the problem will be falsely posed. It is useless to base the defense of materialism on any analysis of mental phenomena that fails to deal explicitly with their subjective character. For there is no reason to suppose that a reduction which seems plausible when no attempt is made to account for consciousness can be extended to include consciousness. Without some idea, therefore, of what the subjective character of experience is, we cannot know what is required of physicalist theory.

While an account of the physical basis of mind must explain many things, this appears to be the most difficult. It is impossible to exclude the phenomenological features of experience from a reduction in the same way that one excludes the phenomenal features of an ordinary substance from a physical or chemical reduction of it—namely, by explaining them as effects on the minds of human observers.[4]

2. Perhaps there could not actually be such robots. Perhaps anything complex enough to behave like a person would have experiences. But that, if true, is a fact which cannot be discovered merely by analyzing the concept of experience.

3. It is not equivalent to that about which we are incorrigible, both because we are not incorrigible about experience and because experience is present in animals lacking language and thought, who have no beliefs at all about their experiences.

4. Cf. Richard Rorty, 'Mind–Body Identity, Privacy, and Categories', *Review of Metaphysics*, XIX (1965), esp. 37–8.

If physicalism is to be defended, the phenomenological features must themselves be given a physical account. But when we examine their subjective character it seems that such a result is impossible. The reason is that every subjective phenomenon is essentially connected with a single point of view, and it seems inevitable that an objective, physical theory will abandon that point of view.

Let me first try to state the issue somewhat more fully than by referring to the relation between the subjective and the objective, or between the *pour soi* and the *en soi*. This is far from easy. Facts about what it is like to be an X are very peculiar, so peculiar that some may be inclined to doubt their reality, or the significance of claims about them. To illustrate the connexion between subjectivity and a point of view, and to make evident the importance of subjective features, it will help to explore the matter in relation to an example that brings out clearly the divergence between the two types of conception, subjective and objective.

I assume we all believe that bats have experience. After all, they are mammals, and there is no more doubt that they have experience than that mice or pigeons or whales have experience. I have chosen bats instead of wasps or flounders because if one travels too far down the phylogenetic tree, people gradually shed their faith that there is experience there at all. Bats, although more closely related to us than those other species, nevertheless present a range of activity and a sensory apparatus so different from ours that the problem I want to pose is exceptionally vivid (though it certainly could be raised with other species). Even without the benefit of philo- sophical reflection, anyone who has spent some time in an enclosed space with an excited bat knows what it is to encounter a fundamentally *alien* form of life.

I have said that the essence of the belief that bats have experience is that there is something that it is like to be a bat. Now we know that most bats (the microchiroptera, to be precise) perceive the external world primarily by sonar, or echolocation, detecting the reflections, from objects within range, of their own rapid, subtly mod- ulated, high-frequency shrieks. Their brains are designed to correlate the outgoing impulses with the subsequent echoes, and the information thus acquired enables bats to make precise discriminations of distance, size, shape, motion, and texture comparable to those we make by vision. But bat sonar, though clearly a form of per- ception, is not similar in its operation to any sense that we possess, and there is no reason to suppose that it is subjectively like anything we can experience or imagine. This appears to create difficulties for the notion of what it is like to be a bat. We must consider whether any method will permit us to extrapolate to the inner life of the bat from our own case,[5] and if not, what alternative methods there may be for understanding the notion.

Our own experience provides the basic material for our imagination, whose range is therefore limited. It will not help to try to imagine that one has webbing on one's arms, which enables one to fly around at dusk and dawn catching insects in

---

5. By 'our own case' I do not mean just 'my own case', but rather the mentalistic ideas that we apply unproblematically to ourselves and other human beings.

one's mouth; that one has very poor vision, and perceives the surrounding world by a system of reflected high-frequency sound signals; and that one spends the day hanging upside down by one's feet in an attic. Insofar as I can imagine this (which is not very far), it tells me only what it would be like for *me* to behave as a bat behaves. But that is not the question. I want to know what it is like for a *bat* to be a bat. Yet if I try to imagine this, I am restricted to the resources of my own mind, and those resources are inadequate to the task. I cannot perform it either by imagining additions to my present experience, or by imagining segments gradually subtracted from it, or by imagining some combination of additions, subtractions, and modifications.

To the extent that I could look and behave like a wasp or a bat without changing my fundamental structure, my experiences would not be anything like the experiences of those animals. On the other hand, it is doubtful that any meaning can be attached to the supposition that I should possess the internal neurophysiological constitution of a bat. Even if I could by gradual degrees be transformed into a bat, nothing in my present constitution enables me to imagine what the experiences of such a future stage of myself thus metamorphosed would be like. The best evidence would come from the experiences of bats, if we only knew what they were like.

So if extrapolation from our own case is involved in the idea of what it is like to be a bat, the extrapolation must be incompletable. We cannot form more than a schematic conception of what it *is* like. For example, we may ascribe general *types* of experience on the basis of the animal's structure and behavior. Thus we describe bat sonar as a form of three-dimensional forward perception; we believe that bats feel some versions of pain, fear, hunger, and lust, and that they have other, more familiar types of perception besides sonar. But we believe that these experiences also have in each case a specific subjective character, which it is beyond our ability to conceive. And if there is conscious life elsewhere in the universe, it is likely that some of it will not be describable even in the most general experiential terms available to us.[6] (The problem is not confined to exotic cases, however, for it exists between one person and another. The subjective character of the experience of a person deaf and blind from birth is not accessible to me, for example, nor presumably is mine to him. This does not prevent us each from believing that the other's experience has such a subjective character.)

If anyone is inclined to deny that we can believe in the existence of facts like this whose exact nature we cannot possibly conceive, he should reflect that in contemplating the bats we are in much the same position that intelligent bats or Martians[7] would occupy if they tried to form a conception of what it was like to be us. The structure of their own minds might make it impossible for them to succeed, but we know they would be wrong to conclude that there is not anything precise that it is like to be us: that only certain general types of mental state could be ascribed to us

6. Therefore the analogical form of the English expression 'what it is *like*' is misleading. It does not mean 'what (in our experience) it *resembles*', but rather 'how it is for the subject himself'.

7. Any intelligent extraterrestrial beings totally different from us.

(perhaps perception and appetite would be concepts common to us both; perhaps not). We know they would be wrong to draw such a skeptical conclusion because we know what it is like to be us. And we know that while it includes an enormous amount of variation and complexity, and while we do not possess the vocabulary to describe it adequately, its subjective character is highly specific, and in some respects describable in terms that can be understood only by creatures like us. The fact that we cannot expect ever to accommodate in our language a detailed description of Martian or bat phenomenology should not lead us to dismiss as meaningless the claim that bats and Martians have experiences fully comparable in richness of detail to our own. It would be fine if someone were to develop concepts and a theory that enabled us to think about those things; but such an understanding may be permanently denied to us by the limits of our nature. And to deny the reality or logical significance of what we can never describe or understand is the crudest form of cognitive dissonance.

This brings us to the edge of a topic that requires much more discussion than I can give it here: namely, the relation between facts on the one hand and conceptual schemes or systems of representation on the other. My realism about the subjective domain in all its forms implies a belief in the existence of facts beyond the reach of human concepts. Certainly it is possible for a human being to believe that there are facts which humans never *will* possess the requisite concepts to represent or comprehend. Indeed, it would be foolish to doubt this, given the finiteness of humanity's expectations. After all, there would have been transfinite numbers even if everyone had been wiped out by the Black Death before Cantor discovered them. But one might also believe that there are facts which *could* not ever be represented or comprehended by human beings, even if the species lasted for ever—simply because our structure does not permit us to operate with concepts of the requisite type. This impossibility might even be observed by other beings, but it is not clear that the existence of such beings, or the possibility of their existence, is a precondition of the significance of the hypothesis that there are humanly inaccessible facts. (After all, the nature of beings with access to humanly inaccessible facts is presumably itself a humanly inaccessible fact.) Reflection on what it is like to be a bat seems to lead us, therefore, to the conclusion that there are facts that do not consist in the truth of propositions expressible in a human language. We can be compelled to recognize the existence of such facts without being able to state or comprehend them.

I shall not pursue this subject, however. Its bearing on the topic before us (namely, the mind–body problem) is that it enables us to make a general observation about the subjective character of experience. Whatever may be the status of facts about what it is like to be a human being, or a bat, or a Martian, these appear to be facts that embody a particular point of view.

I am not adverting here to the alleged privacy of experience to its possessor. The point of view in question is not one accessible only to a single individual. Rather it is a *type*. It is often possible to take up a point of view other than one's own, so the comprehension of such facts is not limited to one's own case. There is a sense in which phenomenological facts are perfectly objective: one person can know or say of another what the quality of the other's experience is. They are subjective, however, in the sense that even this objective ascription of experience is possible only for someone sufficiently similar to the object of ascription to be able to adopt his point of view—to understand the ascription in the first person as well as in the third, so to speak. The more different from oneself the other experiencer is, the less success one can expect with this enterprise. In our own case we occupy the relevant point of view, but we will have as much difficulty understanding our own experience properly if we approach it from another point of view as we would if we tried to understand the experience of another species without taking up *its* point of view.[8]

This bears directly on the mind–body problem. For if the facts of experience—facts about what it is like *for* the experiencing organism—are accessible only from one point of view, then it is a mystery how the true character of experiences could be revealed in the physical operation of that organism. The latter is a domain of objective facts *par excellence*—the kind that can be observed and understood from many points of view and by individuals with differing perceptual systems. There are no comparable imaginative obstacles to the acquisition of knowledge about bat neurophysiology by human scientists, and intelligent bats or Martians might learn more about the human brain than we ever will.

This is not by itself an argument against reduction. A Martian scientist with no understanding of visual perception could understand the rainbow, or lightning, or clouds as physical phenomena, though he would never be able to understand the human concepts of rainbow, lightning, or cloud, or the place these things occupy in our phenomenal world. The objective nature of the things picked out by these concepts could be apprehended by him because, although the concepts themselves are connected with a particular point of view and a particular visual phenomenology, the things apprehended from that point of view are not: they are observable from the point of view but external to it; hence they can be comprehended from other points of view also, either by the same organisms or by others. Lightning has an objective character that is not exhausted by its visual appearance, and this can be investigated by a Martian without vision. To be precise, it has a *more* objective character than is revealed in its visual appearance. In speaking of the move from

---

8. It may be easier than I suppose to transcend inter-species barriers with the aid of the imagination. For example, blind people are able to detect objects near them by a form of sonar, using vocal clicks or taps of a cane. Perhaps if one knew what that was like, one could by extension imagine roughly what it was like to possess the much more refined sonar of a bat. The distance between oneself and other persons and other species can fall anywhere on a continuum. Even for other persons the understanding of what it is like to be them is only partial, and when one moves to species very different from oneself, a lesser degree of partial understanding may still be available. The imagination is remarkably flexible. My point, however, is not that we cannot *know* what it is like to be a bat. I am not raising that epistemological problem. My point is rather that even to form a *conception* of what it is like to be a bat (and *a fortiori* to know what it is like to be a bat) one must take up the bat's point of view. If one can take it up roughly, or partially, then one's conception will also be rough or partial. Or so it seems in our present state of understanding.

subjective to objective characterization, I wish to remain noncommittal about the existence of an end point, the completely objective intrinsic nature of the thing, which one might or might not be able to reach. It may be more accurate to think of objectivity as a direction in which the understanding can travel. And in understanding a phenomenon like lightning, it is legitimate to go as far away as one can from a strictly human viewpoint.[9]

In the case of experience, on the other hand, the connexion with a particular point of view seems much closer. It is difficult to understand what could be meant by the *objective* character of an experience, apart from the particular point of view from which its subject apprehends it. After all, what would be left of what it was like to be a bat if one removed the viewpoint of the bat? But if experience does not have, in addition to its subjective character, an objective nature that can be apprehended from many different points of view, then how can it be supposed that a Martian investigating my brain might be observing physical processes which were my mental processes (as he might observe physical processes which were bolts of lightning), only from a different point of view? How, for that matter, could a human physiologist observe them from another point of view?[10]

We appear to be faced with a general difficulty about psychophysical reduction. In other areas the process of reduction is a move in the direction of greater objectivity, toward a more accurate view of the real nature of things. This is accomplished by reducing our dependence on individual or species-specific points of view toward the object of investigation. We describe it not in terms of the impressions it makes on our senses, but in terms of its more general effects and of properties detectable by means other than the human senses. The less it depends on a specifically human viewpoint, the more objective is our description. It is possible to follow this path because although the concepts and ideas we employ in thinking about the external world are initially applied from a point of view that involves our perceptual apparatus, they are used by us to refer to things beyond themselves—toward which we *have* the phenomenal point of view. Therefore we can abandon it in favor of another, and still be thinking about the same things.

Experience itself, however, does not seem to fit the pattern. The idea of moving from appearance to reality seems to make no sense here. What is the analogue in this case to pursuing a more objective understanding of the same phenomena by abandoning the initial subjective viewpoint toward them in favour of another that is more objective but concerns the same thing? Certainly it *appears* unlikely

9. The problem I am going to raise can therefore be posed even if the distinction between more subjective and more objective descriptions or viewpoints can itself be made only within a larger human point of view. I do not accept this kind of conceptual relativism, but it need not be refuted to make the point that psychophysical reduction cannot be accommodated by the subjective-to-objective model familiar from other cases.

10. The problem is not just that when I look at the *Mona Lisa*, my visual experience has a certain quality, no trace of which is to be found by someone looking into my brain. For even if he did observe there a tiny image of the *Mona Lisa*, he would have no reason to identify it with the experience.

that we will get closer to the real nature of human experience by leaving behind the particularity of our human point of view and striving for a description in terms accessible to beings that could not imagine what it was like to be us. If the subjective character of experience is fully comprehensible only from one point of view, then any shift to greater objectivity—that is, less attachment to a specific viewpoint—does not take us nearer to the real nature of the phenomenon: it takes us farther away from it.

In a sense, the seeds of this objection to the reducibility of experience are already detectable in successful cases of reduction; for in discovering sound to be, in reality, a wave phenomenon in air or other media, we leave behind one viewpoint to take up another, and the auditory, human or animal viewpoint that we leave behind remains unreduced. Members of radically different species may both understand the same physical events in objective terms, and this does not require that they understand the phenomenal forms in which those events appear to the senses of members of the other species. Thus it is a condition of their referring to a common reality that their more particular viewpoints are not part of the common reality that they both apprehend. The reduction can succeed only if the species-specific viewpoint is omitted from what is to be reduced.

But while we are right to leave this point of view aside in seeking a fuller understanding of the external world, we cannot ignore it permanently, since it is the essence of the internal world, and not merely a point of view on it. Most of the neobehaviorism of recent philosophical psychology results from the effort to substitute an objective concept of mind for the real thing, in order to have nothing left over which cannot be reduced. If we acknowledge that a physical theory of mind must account for the subjective character of experience, we must admit that no presently available conception gives us a clue how this could be done. The problem is unique. If mental processes are indeed physical processes, then there is something it is like, intrinsically,[11] to undergo certain physical processes. What it is for such a thing to be the case remains a mystery.

11. The relation would therefore not be a contingent one, like that of a cause and its distinct effect. It would be necessarily true that a certain physical state felt a certain way. Saul Kripke in *Semantics of Natural Language*, (ed. Davidson and Harman) argues that causal behaviorist and related analyses of the mental fail because they construe, e.g., 'pain' as a merely contingent name of pains. The subjective character of an experience ('its immediate phenomenological quality' Kripke calls it (p. 340)) is the essential property left out by such analyses, and the one in virtue of which it is, necessarily, the experience it is. My view is closely related to his. Like Kripke, I find the hypothesis that a certain brain state should *necessarily* have a certain subjective character incomprehensible without further explanation. No such explanation emerges from theories which view the mind–brain relation as contingent, but perhaps there are other alternatives, not yet discovered.

A theory that explained how the mind–brain relation was necessary would still leave us with Kripke's problem of explaining why it nevertheless appears contingent. That difficulty seems to me surmountable, in the following way. We may imagine something by representing it to ourselves either perceptually, sympathetically, or symbolically. I shall not try to say how symbolic imagination works, but part of what happens in the other two cases is this. To imagine something perceptually, we put ourselves in a conscious state resembling the state we would be in if we perceived it. To imagine

What moral should be drawn from these reflections, and what should be done next? It would be a mistake to conclude that physicalism must be false. Nothing is proved by the inadequacy of physicalist hypotheses that assume a faulty objective analysis of mind. It would be truer to say that physicalism is a position we cannot understand because we do not at present have any conception of how it might be true. Perhaps it will be thought unreasonable to require such a conception as a condition of understanding. After all, it might be said, the meaning of physicalism is clear enough: mental states are states of the body; mental events are physical events. We do not know *which* physical states and events they are, but that should not prevent us from understanding the hypothesis. What could be clearer than the words 'is' and 'are'?

But I believe it is precisely this apparent clarity of the word 'is' that is deceptive. Usually, when we are told that X is Y we know *how* it is supposed to be true, but that depends on a conceptual or theoretical background and is not conveyed by the 'is' alone. We know how both 'X' and 'Y' refer, and the kinds of things to which they refer, and we have a rough idea how the two referential paths might converge on a single thing, be it an object, a person, a process, an event or whatever. But when the two terms of the identification are very disparate it may not be so clear how it could be true. We may not have even a rough idea of how the two referential paths could converge, or what kind of things they might converge on, and a theoretical framework may have to be supplied to enable us to understand this. Without the framework, an air of mysticism surrounds the identification.

This explains the magical flavor of popular presentations of fundamental scientific discoveries, given out as propositions to which one must subscribe without really understanding them. For example, people are now told at an early age that all matter is really energy. But despite the fact that they know what 'is' means, most of them never form a conception of what makes this claim true, because they lack the theoretical background.

At the present time the status of physicalism is similar to that which the hypothesis that matter is energy would have had if uttered by a pre-Socratic philosopher. We do not have the beginnings of a conception of how it might be true. In order to

---

something sympathetically, we put ourselves in a conscious state resembling the thing itself. (This method can be used only to imagine mental events and states—our own or another's.) When we try to imagine a mental state occurring without its associated brain state, we first sympathetically imagine the occurrence of the mental state: that is, we put ourselves into a state that resembles it mentally. At the same time, we attempt perceptually to imagine the nonoccurrence of the associated physical state, by putting ourselves into another state unconnected with the first: one resembling that which we would be in if we perceived the nonoccurrence of the physical state. Where the imagination of physical features is perceptual and the imagination of mental features is sympathetic, it appears to us that we can imagine any experience occurring without its associated brain state, and vice versa. The relation between them will appear contingent even if it is necessary, because of the independence of the disparate types of imagination.

(Solipsism, incidentally, results if one misinterprets sympathetic imagination as if it worked like perceptual imagination: it then seems impossible to imagine any experience that is not one's own.)

understand the hypothesis that a mental event is a physical event, we require more than an understanding of the word 'is'. The idea of how a mental and a physical term might refer to the same thing is lacking, and the usual analogies with theoretical identification in other fields fail to supply it. They fail because if we construe the reference of mental terms to physical events on the usual model, we either get a reappearance of separate subjective events as the effects through which mental reference to physical events is secured, or else we get a false account of how mental terms refer (for example, a causal behaviorist one).

Strangely enough, we may have evidence for the truth of something we cannot really understand. Suppose a caterpillar is locked in a sterile safe by someone unfamiliar with insect metamorphosis, and weeks later the safe is reopened, revealing a butterfly. If the person knows that the safe has been shut the whole time, he has reason to believe that the butterfly is or was once the caterpillar, without having any idea in what sense this might be so. (One possibility is that the caterpillar contained a tiny winged parasite that devoured it and grew into the butterfly.)

It is conceivable that we are in such a position with regard to physicalism. Donald Davidson has argued that if mental events have physical causes and effects, they must have physical descriptions. He holds that we have reason to believe this even though we do not—and in fact *could* not—have a general psychophysical theory.[12] His argument applies to intentional mental events, but I think we also have some reason to believe that sensations are physical processes, without being in a position to understand how. Davidson's position is that certain physical events have irreducibly mental properties, and perhaps some view describable in this way is correct. But nothing of which we can now form a conception corresponds to it; nor have we any idea what a theory would be like that enabled us to conceive of it.[13]

Very little work has been done on the basic question (from which mention of the brain can be entirely omitted) whether any sense can be made of experiences' having an objective character at all. Does it make sense, in other words, to ask what my experiences are *really* like, as opposed to how they appear to me? We cannot genuinely understand the hypothesis that their nature is captured in a physical description unless we understand the more fundamental idea that they *have* an objective nature (or that objective processes can have a subjective nature).[14]

I should like to close with a speculative proposal. It may be possible to approach the gap between subjective and objective from another direction. Setting aside

12. See 'Mental Events' in *Experience and Theory*, ed. Lawrence Foster and J. W. Swanson (Amherst: University of Massachusetts Press, 1970); though I do not understand the argument against psychophysical laws.

13. Similar remarks apply to my paper 'Physicalism', *Philosophical Review*, LXXIV (1965), 339–56, reprinted with postscript in *Modern Materialism*, ed. John O'Connor (New York: Harcourt Brace Jovanovich, 1969).

14. This question also lies at the heart of the problem of other minds, whose close connection with the mind–body problem is often overlooked. If one understood how subjective experience could have an objective nature, one would understand the existence of subjects other than oneself.

temporarily the relation between the mind and the brain, we can pursue a more objective understanding of the mental in its own right. At present we are completely unequipped to think about the subjective character of experience without relying on the imagination—without taking up the point of view of the experiential subject. This should be regarded as a challenge to form new concepts and devise a new method—an objective phenomenology not dependent on empathy or the imagination. Though presumably it would not capture everything, its goal would be to describe, at least in part, the subjective character of experiences in a form comprehensible to beings incapable of having those experiences.

We would have to develop such a phenomenology to describe the sonar experiences of bats; but it would also be possible to begin with humans. One might try, for example, to develop concepts that could be used to explain to a person blind from birth what it was like to see. One would reach a blank wall eventually, but it should be possible to devise a method of expressing in objective terms much more than we can at present, and with much greater precision. The loose intermodal analogies—for example, 'Red is like the sound of a trumpet'—which crop up in discussions of this subject are of little use. That should be clear to anyone who has both heard a trumpet and seen red. But structural features of perception might be more accessible to objective description, even though something would be left out. And concepts alternative to those we learn in the first person may enable us to arrive at a kind of understanding even of our own experience which is denied us by the very ease of description and lack of distance that subjective concepts afford.

Apart from its own interest, a phenomenology that is in this sense objective may permit questions about the physical[15] basis of experience to assume a more intelligible form. Aspects of subjective experience that admitted this kind of objective description might be better candidates for objective explanations of a more familiar sort. But whether or not this guess is correct, it seems unlikely that any physical theory of mind can be contemplated until more thought has been given to the general problem of subjective and objective. Otherwise we cannot even pose the mind–body problem without sidestepping it.

15. I have not defined the term 'physical'. Obviously it does not apply just to what can be described by the concepts of contemporary physics, since we expect further developments. Some may think there is nothing to prevent mental phenomena from eventually being recognized as physical in their own right. But whatever else may be said of the physical, it has to be objective. So if our idea of the physical ever expands to include mental phenomena, it will have to assign them an objective character— whether or not this is done by analyzing them in terms of other phenomena already regarded as physical. It seems to me more likely, however, that mental–physical relations will eventually be expressed in a theory whose fundamental terms cannot be placed clearly in either category.

Study questions

1. Should the mind be thought of as a kind of substance, in the sense described in Part III: Being? If so, what kind of substance is it?
2. What is the problem of mental causation for dualists? What is the problem of mental causation for physicalists?
3. How would you go about arguing that the mind is separable from the body? Can any good argument be given for this conclusion?
4. How would you characterize the functionalist view of mind? What is the reason for being a functionalist?

Further reading

A good general introduction to the metaphysical problems of the philosophy of mind is Kim (1996). An excellent anthology of readings, covering all aspects of the philosophy of mind, is Rosenthal (ed.) (1991). For a good introduction to Descartes's theory of mind, see James (2000); for Leibniz, see Macdonald Ross (1984). An excellent introduction to the mind–body problem is Campbell (1970). On the argument for physicalism, see Lewis (1966) and Armstrong (1968). Lewis (1994) is his later statement of his position. More recent defences of physicalism, and the central premiss of the 'causal closure of the physical', are found in Papineau (2001) and Loewer (2001). On the variable/multiple realization argument, see Putnam (1975) and Lewis (1968). Davidson's anomalous monism was first presented in his classic (1970); a good introduction to Davidson's views is Evnine (1991). On the problem of consciousness, see Chalmers (1996) and Levine (2000). On the problem of mental causation for non-reductive physicalists, see Crane (1995*a*) and Kim (1989). More difficult, but worth persevering with, is Yablo (1992).

Part X

Freedom and determinism

Introduction

1. Introduction

WE are all familiar with the feeling that we are free. This feeling can be characterized by saying that in many cases, when we face several possible alternatives, it is *up to us* what we do; and once we act in some way rather than another, it is still true that we could have done otherwise. No one should expect these alternatives to be unlimited: our circumstances—including the laws of physics—will obviously constrain what we can do. Perhaps our circumstances are more limited than we would like; perhaps we are less free than we desire to be. Yet undoubtedly we have a clear idea of what it would be to act freely, to have things under our own control, to take our fate into our own hands. It is almost impossible to imagine what our life would be like without this. Harry Frankfurt in Chapter 51 in fact argues that free will is essentially related to what makes a person a person.

Freedom is pertinent to our life not only as we perceive it in our choices, but also through the fact that we attribute it to others. Many of our attitudes that are constitutive of our relations to other people, like resentment or gratitude, go with the tacit assumption that the receivers of these attitudes are free (see Strawson 1974). One especially important phenomenon is the attribution of moral responsibility. Blaming or praising someone for what she has done presupposes that she acted freely; the main reason to exempt someone from the responsibility for her actions is learning that she was forced to act as she did, that she could not help doing what she did.

2. Action, choice, will

The problem of freedom is often referred to as the problem of *free will*, but this can be a little misleading: for not everyone thinks that the question of freedom is the same as the freedom of the *will*.

On one obvious understanding, freedom has to do with *actions*: we are free when we are free to do or not to do something. A prisoner is not free because he cannot act freely; he cannot leave the prison if he wants to. Locke says that 'liberty is a power to act or not act, according as the mind directs' (1690: book II, chapter xxi, § 71). The will, on Locke's account, is the faculty of the mind responsible for these 'directions'. The question of whether the will itself is free does not make sense, according to him (see also Hobbes 1651: 44–5, 146). For the question would amount to asking whether we are free to will this or that, which in turn would be asking whether we are free to will as we will. 'A question, which, I think needs no answer: and they, who can make a question of it, must suppose one will to determine the acts of another, and another to determine that, and so on *in infinitum*' (1690: book II, chapter xxi, § 25).

It is clear that freedom in Locke's sense matters a great deal. We value the freedom to act as we choose; losing it is a frightening thought. But there is another sense we might find important. Anxiety about this further sense is forcefully expressed in George Orwell's anti-utopian novel *1984*. The protagonist of the novel, Winston Smith, lives in an absolute dictatorship ruled by 'the Party'; every aspect of his life is bound by the strictest rules, and the punishment for his breaking the rules is terrible. But what the Party wants from people is not simply that they should do what they are told to do; as one of the Inner Party members explains to Winston, 'we are different from the perse-cutors of the past. We are not content with negative obedience, nor even with the most abject submission. When finally you surrender to us, it must be of your own free will' (Orwell 1949: 210). Even during indescribable pain and torture, Winston tries to hold out. The thought he clings to is that though they can make him do or say anything, they cannot get inside him: 'to die hating them, that was freedom.' But the hope that he can do this proves to be futile. When Winston is finally released from prison, no one has to force him to comply with orders; thoroughly defeated, he has interiorized his captors' wishes. He has learned to love them.

There is a thought contained within this story which is applicable to more familiar circumstances of our lives. Manipulation—or hypnosis, or brainwashing—may be just as effective in controlling people as employing external force. Once the manipulated person has the beliefs and desires planted in her by the manipulators, she may be free—in Locke's sense—to act as she chooses. But would not real freedom require something more—that our beliefs and desires and choices should be *our own*? If we agree with this, then freedom will require more than the ability to act as we choose: it will also require that choices should genuinely originate in us, and not in something that is not within our power. Robert Kane's notion of 'ultimate responsibility', as described by Barry Loewer in Chapter 53, is one version of this idea.

Locke—who perhaps was not so worried about psychological manipulation or ideologi-cal brainwashing—would have found this requirement unintelligible, for the reason given above. Before getting deeper into this question, to which we will return in section 8 below, we first must introduce the idea of determinism.

3. Determinism

We generally consider only human beings to be free. We do not consider other members of the animal kingdom to possess freedom (see Pink 2004). But the striking contrast, in this respect, is between ourselves and the physical world around us: freedom is not applicable to atoms, tidal waves, or planets. At the same time, our freedom should some-how fit into this world: for whether we are entirely part of the physical world or not, our free actions certainly bring about changes in the physical world. An important aspect of the debate about free will is the effort to understand how this is possible.

Traditionally, one reason to think that there is a problem about how freedom is possible was the assumption that the world is *deterministic*. A rough definition of deter-minism is: the view that *everything that happens is such that given whatever happened before, nothing else could happen*. Determinism should be distinguished from *fatalism*: the view that everything that happens must happen, no matter what. Determinism allows that things could have been different from the way they actually are—if things in the past had been different. We could express the difference in terms of possible worlds as follows: fatalism says that there is only one possible world; determinism allows that there are many possible worlds, but these different possible worlds have to have different initial conditions. What determinism does not allow is this: that two possible worlds should have identical history up until a certain time, and diverge in their history from then on. If determinism is incompatible with free will, so is fatalism. But the other direction may not be true: as we shall see below, some philosophers think that determinism can accommodate freedom, even though fatalism cannot.

Why believe that determinism is true? Here is one line of reasoning. Many philosophers since the ancient times have held that the principle that *every event has a cause* is one of the fundamental principles of metaphysics. It is difficult to justify this *principle of universal causation* (or causality) with independent arguments, and so it has often been regarded as some sort of axiom. The main idea behind it is that it is impossible for something just to 'pop into existence', or change in some way, without something making it do so. Furthermore, it was believed for a long time that causation is deterministic; that is, it is part of the very idea of causation that causes are invariably followed by their effects (see Part VI: Causation). If every event has a cause, and causes are invariably followed by their effects, then every state of the universe is an inevitable consequence of the previous one. (This kind of determinism is often called 'causal determinism'; for another variety, see Box X.1.)

Box X.1. Logical determinism and the sea battle

The Principle of Bivalence states that every statement is either true or false. Aristotle's *De Interpretatione* 9 is the source of a famous argument which states that if the Principle of Bivalence applies to statements about the future, then the future is determined. For if the statement that there will be a sea battle tomorrow is either true or false *now*, then either it is true already that there will be a sea battle tomorrow, or it is true already that there will not be a sea battle tomorrow. We do not *know* which is true, but since one of them *is* true, whatever happens in the future is already settled. (This argument is similar to the one about God's omniscience, in Box I.1. God's omniscience could be used to argue for bivalence: for only what is true can be known. If God knows everything, including statements about the future, then these statements must be true eternally.)

The argument entails determinism but not fatalism in the sense we defined it: for the truth of 'there will be a sea battle tomorrow' is compatible with 'it is possible that there will not be a sea battle tomorrow', if we take possibility as metaphysical possibility—just as Franz Jozef's being emperor is compatible with his possibly not being emperor. (For the different senses of necessity and possibility, see Box V.2.) The argument thus allows that there should be different possible worlds, each with their own set of truths about everything that ever happens in that world. Since it is a matter of controversy whether determinism is compatible with free will, it is not obvious that logical determinism entails the impossibility of free will.

However, if we wanted to uphold that the future is not determined, how could we find fault with the argument? One obvious reply is to restrict the Principle of

Bivalence to statements about the past and the present, though this suggestion seems rather *ad hoc*. What other ways are there to resist the conclusion of this argument?

(Note that the Principle of Bivalence is distinguished from the Law of Excluded Middle: the latter says that every statement of the form ' either *p* or not *p*' is true.)

The view that the principle of universal causation leads to determinism was already present (though perhaps not unanimously accepted) in the ancient debate on the question of free will, for example between the Epicureans and the Stoics. These philosophers often discuss another idea: that causes are followed by their effects according to some principles which relate causes and effects. For example: on atomist theories, that the motion of atoms is influenced by their weight and collision with other atoms. This can be seen as an early precursor of the view which emerged in the seventeenth century, which stated that events progress according to the immutable laws of physics, the science which is most fundamental in describing and explaining what happens in the world.

The thesis of determinism can then be reformulated in terms of laws of these kinds: that the description of the world at any given time, together with the laws of nature, entails the description of the world at any subsequent time. In this formulation, the question of whether the world is deterministic turns on the *character of its laws*. This requires a slight change to our original explanation of determinism. There we said that determinism does not allow that the history of two possible worlds should diverge only from a certain time onward. We should now add that on the more specific understanding of determinism, this is true only insofar as the worlds have the same laws. Whether these two definitions are equivalent turns on the (non-trivial) question of whether the laws of nature are necessary. If we think that laws are not necessary, that is, that there are possible worlds with different laws, then we should adopt David Lewis's formulation of determinism: 'the prevailing laws of nature are such that there do not exist any two possible worlds which are exactly alike up to some time, which differ thereafter, and in which those laws are never violated' (Chapter 30).

These two conceptions of determinism—in terms of causation and in terms of laws—are of course connected. Classically, the laws were regarded as causal laws—that is, relating causes and effects—so saying that every event has a cause amounts to saying that every event falls under causal laws. (Davidson 1970 uses the connection between causes and laws in his argument for materialism: see Part IX: Mind and Body.) Thus the notion of cause keeps appearing in discussions of determinism to this day, including much of what follows. Still, the new formulation makes it possible to separate the question of causation from the question of determinism. The fact is, as some commentators (e.g. Russell 1918) have pointed out, that the laws of modern physics (whether Newtonian or Einsteinian) typically do not mention causes or causation at all. Think of such well-known examples as $F = ma$ or $E = mc^2$. Some have thought that this separation is a good thing: for the notion of cause, being too obscure and of not much use in science anyway, should not hinder the discussion of the more important question of whether the laws of physics are deterministic or not.

4. The consequence argument

The claim that determinism is incompatible with free will is as old as the debate about free will. Cicero reports, without endorsing, the view of some ancient thinkers (presumably the Epicureans or the Academics) who argued as follows. Our actions are consequences of 'impulses'. These are, roughly, mental states which bring about actions—something like intentions in the contemporary way of thinking. If everything comes about because of an antecedent cause, then presumably impulses will have antecedent causes too. Cicero's ancient thinkers then consider the case when the cause of an impulse is something outside us:

But if the cause of impulse is not located in us, neither is impulse itself in our power. If that is so, not even the results of impulse are in our power. Therefore neither acts of assent, nor actions are in our power. (Cicero in Long and Sedley 1987: 387)

If every event has a cause, then if we follow the causal origin of our actions back to impulses, then further to the causes of impulses, and so on, sooner or later we arrive at a cause which is located outside of us, something entirely outside our power. And it seems that if the causal origin of our actions is something not in our power, neither are the actions themselves.

Peter van Inwagen (Chapter 52) offers a strict version of this incompatibility argument, which he calls the 'consequence argument'. One advantage of his way of formulating the argument is that it locates clearly all the assumptions—and hence the possible weaknesses—of the argument. Van Inwagen adopts a version of the second, more specific formulation of determinism: he understands it as the view that a complete description of the world at any given time, in conjunction with the laws of physics, entails the complete description of the world at another time, and he argues that determinism so understood is incompatible with free will.

Let us consider something that someone did—for example Franz Jozef, Emperor and King of Austria–Hungary, signing the declaration of war on Serbia, on 28 July 1914, thereby beginning the First World War. No doubt many people contributed to the decision to declare war; there must have been all sorts of pressures on Franz Jozef to make this decision; however, what he finally did was his own choice and his own responsibility. He must have seen it in this way, if we are to believe what he said in a manifesto to the people of the Monarchy: 'In this grave hour I am fully aware of the significance of my decision and of my responsibility before Almighty God. I have examined and considered everything.' Now consider a state of the world a long time ago, before any people existed, even before life had made its appearance on Earth. Call this state the 'primeval state'. If determinism is true, then the description of the primeval state, together with the laws of nature, entails the description of the world on 28 July 1914, including Franz Jozef's signing the declaration of war. Clearly, it was not up to Franz Jozef how the world was in the primeval state. Equally clearly, it has never been up to Franz Jozef (or any other human being) whether the world is deterministic. These two facts together have the inevitable consequence that Franz Jozef signed the declaration of war on 28 July 1914—so this was not up to him, either.

If determinism is true, it seems, nothing we ever do is up to us. And if free will is a necessary condition of moral responsibility, this means that determinism implies that no one is morally responsible for what they do. This was the view of Cicero's ancient thinkers: 'if actions are not in our power, the result is that neither commendations nor reproofs nor honours nor punishments are just' (Cicero in Long and Sedley 1987: 387).

5. The incompatibility of free will and determinism

If we accept that free will is incompatible with determinism, one of them has to be given up. Those who choose to stick to determinism and to give up free will are sometimes called 'pessimists' or 'hard determinists'. It is very difficult to design an argument which would be effective against a resolute pessimist. Nonetheless, most philosophers would try to avoid this position. As we said earlier, freedom just seems to be too important to be given up. Therefore we shall turn our attention to the other variety of incompatibilism.

Those incompatibilists who choose to deny determinism in order to salvage freedom are called 'libertarians'. We saw that the thesis of determinism is a complex one, and it involves somewhat different ideas. First we should be clear about what we might be denying when we deny determinism.

Focusing on van Inwagen's argument, a first natural thought might be this: when we deny determinism, we could be denying that everything is physical, that is, that everything is under the sway of physical laws. According to this line of thought, volitions, choices, decisions belong to the psychological realm, and in this realm the laws of physics do not obtain. If this is to be an answer to the incompatibility argument, we should also add that the psychological realm is not deterministic. For if it were, we could apply the consequence argument again, this time treating determinism as a thesis about the character of physical *and* psychological laws. Moreover, though non-physical indeterminism may be part of a libertarian conception of free will, it is not sufficient in itself for the libertarian's purposes. Perhaps free choices originate in the psychological realm; but for freedom to be real, choices should have consequences in the physical world too. Franz Jozef's signing the declaration of war involved several physical events, like the moving of the particles of ink, pressure on the surface of the paper, etc. Now consider again the primeval state: that state is entirely physical. If the physical world is determined (that is, deterministic laws apply to everything physical), the physical events involved in Franz Jozef's signing are inevitable consequences of how things were in the primeval state. Here questions about the intervening psychological events simply drop out, so the consequence argument applies in the same way. The upshot is that whatever the libertarian believes about physicalism, she is committed to the claim that the physical realm—as well as whatever other non-physical realms there may be—is indeterministic.

From the seventeenth till the beginning of the twentieth century, the dominant view was that the physical world is describable by deterministic Newtonian laws, and hence is deterministic. In that intellectual climate, the position of the libertarian, who offers a philosophical argument against our best scientific theory, must have seemed unattractive. However, with the advance of quantum mechanics this has changed: for according to the dominant interpretation of quantum mechanics, physical laws are indeterministic (for an introduction to the various interpretations, see Loewer 1998, the paper from which Chapter 53 was taken). We should not underestimate the significance of this. Some critics claim (as we shall presently see) that indeterministic physics is no solution to the problem of free will. Nonetheless, however that may be, with the development of quantum mechanics libertarians are at least in the position of offering a view which is compatible with generally accepted scientific opinion.

6. Free will in an indeterministic world

Believers in libertarian free will are convinced by the incompatibility of freedom and determinism, and therefore they claim that the world is indeterministic. A problem with their position is that there is an argument, as old and as influential as the first incompatibility argument, which is supposed to show that freedom cannot be accommodated by *indeterminism*. We can illustrate this with an early version of the libertarian view, held by Epicurus. Epicurus was an atomist, and he maintained that the two primary causes of an atom's movement are its weight and its collision with other atoms. In addition, according to various sources, he thought that atoms are capable of entirely undetermined 'swerves'; changing their trajectory spontaneously without a cause. One important function of the swerves is to make the world indeterministic, and hence provide space for freedom and moral responsibility. What is difficult to see, however, is how a random jump of atoms in our bodies should make us free and responsible. True, our actions would not be determined, but here the alternative seems to be that they come about by mere chance. If it is mere chance whether we do something right or wrong, why should we be responsible for it?

This is also the upshot of Hume's argument in Chapter 50. He starts with rehearsing his views about causation with respect to bodies: that we draw our idea of cause and effect only from the 'uniform and regular conjunction' of events. Necessity enters into the idea of cause through the mind's determination to pass from one event to another. 'Necessity' here means 'necessary connection', or 'determination'; that is, causes being invariably followed by their effects. Hume uses the word 'liberty' in a somewhat specific sense: liberty is simply the denial of necessity, that is, of necessary connection. So since necessary connection (in the way Hume understands it) is indispensable for causation, liberty is the denial of causes, 'and is the very same thing with chance'. So when Hume investigates whether liberty or necessity operates in the mind, his question is really this: do *causes* operate in the mind? The first part of his argument draws from observation: he thinks that constant conjunction—that is, causation—is as prevalent in human affairs as it is among bodies; there is a constant connection between the situation, temper, motives, and character of an agent on the one hand, and her actions on the other. 'There is a general course of nature in human actions, as well as in the operations of the sun and the climate.' The second part of Hume's argument aims to show that the observed determination of our actions, instead of being detrimental to their value for us, is in fact indispensable to moral responsibility. For he thinks, plausibly, that the true case of responsibility is when an action is caused by the agent's decisions, character, motives, and so on; if, as the doctrine of 'liberty' would have it, the action has no such cause, we cannot hold the person responsible. If actions 'proceed not from some cause in the characters and disposition of the person, who perform'd them, they infix not themselves upon him, and can neither redound to his honour, if good, nor infamy, if evil'.

7. Agent causation, probabilistic causation

Hume's argument assumes that the only alternative to determinism is admitting events with no cause. But this assumption can be questioned. Let us now look at two ways of doing this.

We saw that according to one line of thought, determinism is the consequence of two principles:

(1) Every event has a cause.
(2) Causes are invariably followed by their effects.

In formulating the first of these, we did not lay a special emphasis on whether we mention 'event' or 'fact' or simply 'thing'. We have already seen, in Part VI: Causation, that the question of what sort of entities are the relata of causal relations is a substantial one. So it seems that we have overlooked the fact that the validity of the argument requires a more precise formulation of the first premiss:

(1*) Every event is caused by *another event*.

What happens if we deny (1*) and accept only (1)? In that case, if an event is caused by something which is *itself not an event*, the principle of universal causation does not apply to the cause. And this is precisely the proposal Roderick Chisholm presents in Chapter 54. According to Chisholm, when causes are inanimate, causation holds between events or states of affairs. But in the case of responsible human actions the situation is different. Let's return to our earlier example: Franz Jozef signing the declaration of war. The event of signing was caused by the event of a movement of muscles in the arm, this was caused by an event of decision, this was caused by another event of deliberation . . . If we describe what led to the signing as a series of events in this way, something crucial will be left out: that it was *Franz Jozef*, he himself, not some event in his mind or brain, who did the signing. In order to do justice to this intuition, Chisholm suggests that we should recognize a special kind of causation, called *agent causation*; when an agent does something, she or he, and not an event, is the ultimate cause of the action. Since agents are not events, they are not caused; and in this way we can stop following back the causal chain to where it originated: in the agent.

One problem with agent causation is addressed by Chisholm. The theory states that an agent *directly* causes some event—presumably an event in the brain, which then causes some movement of the body. The event in the brain is not caused by another event, like making a decision, or an act of the will. This means that the agent causes the event without herself undergoing any change. For if the agent changes in some way when causing A to happen—for example, by forming a decision—then the respect in which she changed might plausibly be regarded as the cause, and this would be just another event. The question is this: what is the difference between the agent existing, and A simply occurring, on the one hand, and the agent's *causing* A to occur on the other? Chisholm thinks that the difference is just this—that is, the presence or absence of causal connection—and there is no more puzzle in this than in the case of ordinary event causation. For we could ask, in the same way: what is the difference between *B* happening and then *A* happening on the one hand, and *B*'s causing *A* on the other? But the reply may not satisfy us for the following reason: with event causation, once *B* has occurred, we expect *A* to occur. In the case of agent causation, however, the matter is less straightforward: it is not true that once the agent comes into existence, the occurrence of *A* is expected. Further elaboration is needed to defend agent causation.

Agent causation is one way of arguing that the admission of uncaused events is not the only alternative to determinism, but it is not the only one. Let's return to our two principles again:

(1) Every event has a cause.
(2) Causes are invariably followed by their effects.

What about the second principle? In Part VI: Causation, we saw that on Hume's definition of causation, causation indeed has to be deterministic—but also that there are alternative analyses of causation which can accommodate indeterministic causes. Indeterministic causation has also the advantage that it fits well into the indeterministic understanding of quantum mechanics. So, as we saw above, here is some hope for the libertarian. Denying determinism, we do not deny that all events are caused; we state simply that some—our free choices being among them—are caused by probabilistic causes. Maybe we are still tempted to say that these events are 'random' or 'happen by chance', but only if we mean by this that they are not determined. But as we saw with the example of the atomic explosion in Part VI: Causation, it is easy to see how to understand probabilistic causation as a case of causation.

One philosopher who is sceptical about this way to develop libertarianism is Barry Loewer (Chapter 53). He considers a certain interpretation of quantum mechanics, according to which the world is indeterministic. A further assumption is that physics is causally complete; that is, every physical event is governed or fixed by previous physical events in accordance with physical laws. (On the completeness of physics, see also Part IX: Mind and Body.) Loewer maintains that an argument very similar to the consequence argument can be constructed to show that a physically closed indeterministic world is incompatible with freedom. If someone accepts the first incompatibility, she should accept the second incompatibility too. The only way out for the libertarian, according to Loewer, is to deny the completeness of physics.

8. Compatibilism

Loewer calls the notion of freedom he discusses 'libertarian' freedom: it is essential to libertarian freedom that it should be causally undetermined by events that lie outside the agent's control; that the free choices should *originate* in the agent. It is freedom understood in this way which is incompatible with determinism, and, if Loewer is right, also with complete physical indeterminism. But as we already indicated in section 2, this is not the only understanding of freedom. There is a long tradition in philosophy holding that freedom, appropriately understood, is in fact compatible with determinism. This is known as *compatibilism*. The motivation for compatibilism is the belief in determinism—on either metaphysical or scientific grounds—coupled with the reluctance to renounce freedom. Another weighty motivation can be a conviction that something like Hume's argument is right: indeterminism cannot accommodate freedom and responsibility. However, compatibilists need not believe in determinism: they are simply committed to the claim that *if* determinism is true, it is compatible with freedom.

Initially, we characterized freedom in terms of two ideas: that it is *up to us* what we do, and, in the case of free actions, *we could have done otherwise*. Compatibilists think that this characterization can be interpreted in a way which allows the world to be deterministic. One possibility is to say that it is 'up to us' what we do when there is no external force or constraint on our actions, but, rather, when what we do is caused by our beliefs, desires, etc. We have already encountered a similar suggestion by Locke. Second, a number of compatibilists have argued that the requirement '*X* could have done otherwise' should be understood as '*X* would have done otherwise, if *X* had chosen to do otherwise.' This is compatible with determinism, since *X* could have chosen to do otherwise, if the world in the primeval state had been appropriately different. Both van Inwagen and Chisholm critically discuss this compatibilist suggestion.

A more sophisticated compatibilist account is presented by Harry Frankfurt in Chapter 51. Frankfurt's account goes beyond that of Locke: for Frankfurt does think that we can raise the question about the freedom of the will, rather than simply about freedom of actions. He would not agree with Locke and Hobbes that 'we cannot will the will'; in fact, something like the ability to 'want the will' to be a certain way is the key to freedom. Freedom of the will is analogous to freedom of action: the second is freedom to do what we want to do; the first is freedom to want what we want to want. As Frankfurt points out, this account is compatible with determinism; for it is possible that it is causally determined that we are free to want what we want to want. However, Frankfurt would agree with Locke and Hobbes that the will should ultimately be understood in terms of a (sophisticated kind of) want or desire. And it could be objected that desires are simply too passive (not sufficiently 'up to us') to account for what we really understand by freedom (see Pink 2004).

Chapter 50

Selection from *Treatise of Human Nature*

David Hume

Of liberty and necessity

WE come now to explain the *direct* passions, or the impressions, which arise immediately from good or evil, from pain or pleasure. Of this kind are, *desire and aversion, grief and joy, hope and fear.*

Of all the immediate effects of pain and pleasure, there is none more remarkable than the WILL; and tho' properly speaking, it be not comprehended among the passions, yet as the full understanding of its nature and properties, is necessary to the explanation of them, we shall here make it the subject of our enquiry. I desire it may be observ'd, that by the *will*, I mean nothing but *the internal impression we feel and are conscious of, when we knowingly give rise to any new motion of our body, or new perception of our mind.* This impression, like the preceding ones of pride and humility, love and hatred, 'tis impossible to define, and needless to describe any farther; for which reason we shall cut off all those definitions and distinctions, with which philosophers are wont to perplex rather than clear up this question; and entering at first upon the subject, shall examine that long disputed question concerning *liberty and necessity*; which occurs so naturally in treating of the will.

'Tis universally acknowledg'd, that the operations of external bodies are necessary, and that in the communication of their motion, in their attraction, and mutual cohesion, there are not the least traces of indifference or liberty. Every object is determin'd by an absolute fate to a certain degree and direction of its motion, and can no more depart from that precise line, in which it moves, than it can convert itself into an angel, or spirit, or any superior substance. The actions, therefore, of matter are to be regarded as instances of necessary actions; and whatever is in this respect on the same footing with matter, must be acknowledg'd to be necessary. That we may know whether this be the case with the actions of the mind, we shall begin with examining matter, and considering on what the idea of a necessity in its operations are founded, and why we conclude one body or action to be the infallible cause of another.

David Hume, selection from *Treatise of Human Nature*, book II, part iii, § 1 and 2, edited by E. C. Mossner (Penguin Books, 1969).

It has been observ'd already, that in no single instance the ultimate connexion of any objects is discoverable, either by our senses or reason, and that we can never penetrate so far into the essence and construction of bodies, as to perceive the principle, on which their mutual influence depends. 'Tis their constant union alone, with which we are acquainted; and 'tis from the constant union the necessity arises. If objects had not an uniform and regular conjunction with each other, we shou'd never arrive at any idea of cause and effect; and even after all, the necessity, which enters into that idea, is nothing but a determination of the mind to pass from one object to its usual attendant, and infer the existence of one from that of the other. Here then are two particulars, which we are to consider as essential to necessity, *viz.* the constant *union* and the *inference* of the mind; and wherever we discover these we must acknowledge a necessity. As the actions of matter have no necessity, but what is deriv'd from these circumstances, and it is not by any insight into the essence of bodies we discover their connexion, the absence of this insight, while the union and inference remain, will never, in any case, remove the necessity. 'Tis the observation of the union, which produces the inference; for which reason it might be thought sufficient, if we prove a constant union in the actions of the mind, in order to establish the inference, along with the necessity of these actions. But that I may bestow a greater force on my reasoning, I shall examine these particulars apart, and shall first prove from experience that our actions have a constant union with our motives, tempers, and circumstances, before I consider the inferences we draw from it.

To this end a very slight and general view of the common course of human affairs will be sufficient. There is no light, in which we can take them, that does not confirm this principle. Whether we consider mankind according to the difference of sexes, ages, governments, conditions, or methods of education; the same uniformity and regular operation of natural principles are discernible. Like causes still produce like effects; in the same manner as in the mutual action of the elements and powers of nature.

There are different trees, which regularly produce fruit, whose relish is different from each other; and this regularity will be admitted as an instance of necessity and causes in external bodies. But are the products of *Guienne* and of *Champagne* more regularly different than the sentiments, actions, and passions of the two sexes, of which the one are distinguish'd by their force and maturity, the other by their delicacy and softness?

Are the changes of our body from infancy to old age more regular and certain than those of our mind and conduct? And wou'd a man be more ridiculous, who wou'd expect that an infant of four years old will raise a weight of three hundred pound, than one, who from a person of the same age, wou'd look for a philosophical reasoning, or a prudent and well-concerted action?

We must certainly allow, that the cohesion of the parts of matter arises from natural and necessary principles, whatever difficulty we may find in explaining them: And for a reason we must allow, that human society is founded on like principles; and our reason in the latter case, is better than even that in the former; because we not only observe, that men *always* seek society, but can also explain the principles, on which this universal propensity is founded. For is it more certain, that two flat pieces of marble will unite together, than that two young savages of different sexes will copulate? Do the children arise from this copulation more uniformly, than does the parents care for their safety and preservation? And after they have arriv'd at years of discretion by the care of their parents, are the inconveniencies attending their separation more certain than their foresight of these inconveniencies and their care of avoiding them by a close union and confederacy?

The skin, pores, muscles, and nerves of a day-labourer are different from those of a man of quality: So are his sentiments, actions and manners. The different stations of life influence the whole fabric, external and internal; and different stations arise necessarily, because uniformly, from the necessary and uniform principles of human nature. Men cannot live without society, and cannot be associated without government. Government makes a distinction of property, and establishes the different ranks of men. This produces industry, traffic, manufactures, law-suits, war, leagues, alliances, voyages, travels, cities, fleets, ports, and all those other actions and objects, which cause such a diversity, and at the same time maintain such an uniformity in human life.

Shou'd a traveller, returning from a far country, tell us, that he had seen a climate in the fiftieth degree of northern latitude, where all the fruits ripen and come to perfection in the winter, and decay in the summer, after the same manner as in *England* they are produc'd and decay in the contrary seasons, he wou'd find few so credulous as to believe him. I am apt to think a travellar wou'd meet with as little credit, who shou'd inform us of people exactly of the same character with those in *Plato's* republic on the one hand, or those in *Hobbes's Leviathan* on the other. There is a general course of nature in human actions, as well as in the operations of the sun and the climate. There are also characters peculiar to different nations and particular persons, as well as common to mankind. The knowledge of these characters is founded on the observation of an uniformity in the actions, that flow from them; and this uniformity forms the very essence of necessity.

I can imagine only one way of eluding this argument, which is by denying that uniformity of human actions, on which it is founded. As long as actions have a constant union and connexion with the situation and temper of the agent, however we may in words refuse to acknowledge the necessity, we really allow the thing. Now some may, perhaps, find a pretext to deny this regular union and connexion. For what is more capricious than human actions? What more inconstant than the desires of man? And what creature departs more widely, not only from right reason, but from his own character and disposition? An hour, a moment is sufficient to make him change from one extreme to another, and overturn what cost the greatest pain and labour to establish. Necessity is regular and certain. Human conduct is irregular and uncertain. The one, therefore, proceeds not from the other.

To this I reply, that in judging of the actions of men we must proceed upon the same maxims, as when we reason concerning external objects. When any phaenomena are constantly and invariably conjoin'd together, they acquire such a connexion in the imagination, that it passes from one to the other, without any doubt or hesitation. But below this there are many inferior degrees of evidence and probability, nor does one single contrariety of experiment entirely destroy all our reasoning. The mind balances the contrary experiments, and deducting the inferior from the superior, proceeds with that degree of assurance or evidence, which remains. Even when these contrary experiments are entirely equal, we remove not the notion of causes and necessity; but supposing that the usual contrariety proceeds from the operation of contrary and conceal'd causes, we conclude, that the chance or indifference lies only in our judgment on account of our imperfect knowledge, not in the things themselves, which are in every case equally necessary, tho' to appearance not equally constant or certain. No union can be more constant and certain, than that of some actions with some motives and characters; and if in other cases the union is uncertain, 'tis no more than what happens in the operations of body, nor can we conclude any thing from the one irregularity, which will not follow equally from the other.

'Tis commonly allow'd that mad-men have no liberty. But were we to judge by their actions, these have less regularity and constancy than the actions of wise-men, and consequently are farther remov'd from necessity. Our way of thinking in this particular is, therefore, absolutely inconsistent; but is a natural consequence of these confus'd ideas and undefin'd terms, which we so commonly make use of in our reasonings, especially on the present subject.

We must now shew, that as the *union* betwixt motives and actions has the same constancy, as that in any natural operations, so its influence on the understanding is also the same, in *determining* us to infer the existence of one from that of another. If this shall appear, there is no known circumstance, that enters into the connexion and production of the actions of matter, that is not to be found in all the operations of the mind; and consequently we cannot, without a manifest absurdity, attribute necessity to the one, and refuse it to the other.

There is no philosopher, whose judgment is so riveted to this fantastical system of liberty, as not to acknowledge the force of *moral evidence*, and both in speculation and practice proceed upon it, as upon a reasonable foundation. Now moral evidence is nothing but a conclusion concerning the actions of men, deriv'd from the consideration of their motives, temper and situation. Thus when we see certain characters or figures describ'd upon paper, we infer that the person, who produc'd them, wou'd affirm such facts, the death of *Caesar*, the success of *Augustus*, the cruelty of *Nero*; and remembering many other concurrent testimonies we conclude, that those facts were once really existant, and that so many men, without any interest, wou'd never conspire to deceive us; especially since they must, in the attempt, expose themselves to the derision of all their contemporaries, when these facts were asserted to be recent and universally known. The same kind of reasoning runs thro' politics, war, commerce, economy, and indeed mixes itself so entirely in human life, that 'tis impossible to act or subsist a moment without having recourse to it. A prince, who imposes a tax upon his subjects, expects their compliance. A general, who conducts an army, makes account of a certain degree of courage. A merchant looks for fidelity and skill in his factor or super-cargo. A man, who gives orders for his dinner, doubts not of the obedience of his servants. In short, as nothing more nearly interests us than our own actions and those of others, the greatest part of our reasonings is employ'd in judgments concerning them. Now I assert, that whoever reasons after this manner, does *ipso facto* believe the actions of the will to arise from necessity, and that he knows not what he means, when he denies it.

All those objects, of which we call the one *cause* and the other *effect*, consider'd in themselves, are as distinct and separate from each other, as any two things in nature, nor can we ever, by the most accurate survey of them, infer the existence of the one from that of the other. 'Tis only from experience and the observation of their constant union, that we are able to form this inference; and even after all, the inference is nothing but the effects of custom on the imagination. We must not here be content with saying, that the idea of cause and effect arises from objects constantly united; but must affirm, that 'tis the very same with the idea of those objects, and that the *necessary connexion* is not discover'd by a conclusion of the understanding, but is merely a perception of the mind. Wherever, therefore, we observe the same union, and wherever the union operates in the same manner upon the belief and opinion, we have the idea of causes and necessity, tho' perhaps we may avoid those expressions. Motion in one body in all past instances, that have fallen under our observation, is follow'd upon impulse by motion in another. 'Tis impossible for the mind to penetrate farther. From this constant union it *forms* the idea of cause and effect, and by its influence *feels* the necessity. As there is the same constancy, and the same influence in what we call moral evidence, I ask no more. What remains can only be a dispute of words.

And indeed, when we consider how aptly *natural* and *moral* evidence cement together, and form only one chain of argument betwixt them, we shall make no scruple to allow, that they are of the same nature, and deriv'd from the same principles. A prisoner, who has neither money nor interest, discovers the impossibility of his escape, as well from the obstinacy of the gaoler, as from the walls and bars with which he is surrounded; and in all attempts for his freedom chuses rather to work upon the stone and iron of the one, than upon the inflexible nature of the other. The same prisoner, when conducted to the scaffold, foresees his death as certainly from the constancy and fidelity of his guards as from the operation of the ax or wheel. His mind runs along a certain train of ideas: The refusal of the soldiers to consent to his escape, the action of the executioner; the separation of the head and body; bleeding, convulsive motions, and death. Here is a connected chain of natural causes and voluntary actions; but the mind feels no difference betwixt them in passing from one link to another; nor is less certain of the future event than if it were connected with the present impressions of the memory and senses by a train of causes cemented together by what we are pleas'd to call a *physical necessity*. The same experienc'd union has the same effect on the mind, whether the united objects be motives, volitions and actions; or figure and motion. We may change the names of things; but their nature and their operation on the understanding never change.

I dare be positive no one will ever endeavour to refute these reasonings otherwise than by altering my definitions, and assigning a different meaning to the terms of *cause, and effect, and necessity, and liberty, and chance.* According to my definitions, necessity makes an essential part of causation; and consequently liberty, by removing necessity, removes also causes, and is the very same thing with chance. As chance is commonly thought to imply a contradiction, and is at least directly contrary to experience, there are always the same arguments against liberty or free-will. If any one alters the definitions, I cannot pretend to argue with him, 'till I know the meaning he assigns to these terms.

The same subject continu'd

I BELIEVE we may assign the three following reasons for the prevalance of the doctrine of liberty, however absurd it may be in one sense, and unintelligible in any other. First, After we have perform'd any action; tho' we confess we were influenc'd by particular views and motives; 'tis difficult for us to persuade ourselves we were govern'd by necessity, and that 'twas utterly impossible for us to have acted otherwise; the idea of necessity seeming to imply something of force, and violence, and constraint, of which we are not sensible. Few are capable of distinguishing betwixt the liberty of *spontaniety*, as it is call'd in the schools, and the liberty of *indifference*; betwixt that which is oppos'd to violence, and that which means a negation of necessity and causes. The first is even the most common sense of the word; and as 'tis only that species of liberty, which it concerns us to preserve, our thoughts have been principally turn'd towards it, and have almost universally confounded it with the other.

Secondly, There is a *false sensation or experience* even of the liberty of indifference; which is regarded as an argument for its real existence. The necessity of any action, whether of matter or of the mind, is not properly a quality in the agent, but in any thinking or intelligent being, who may consider the action, and consists in the determination of his thought to infer its existence from some preceding objects: As liberty or chance, on the other hand, is nothing but the want of that determination, and a certain looseness, which we feel in passing or not passing from the idea of one to that of the other. Now we may observe, that tho' in reflecting on human actions we seldom feel such a looseness or indifference, yet it very commonly happens, that in performing the actions themselves we are sensible of something like it: And as all related or resembling objects are readily taken for each other, this has been employ'd as a demonstrative or even an intuitive proof of human liberty. We feel that our actions are subject to our will on most occasions, and imagine we feel that the will itself is subject to nothing; because when by a denial of it we are provok'd to try, we feel that it moves easily every way, and produces an image of itself even on that side, on which it did not settle. This image or faint motion, we persuade ourselves, cou'd have been compleated into the thing itself; because, shou'd that be deny'd, we find, upon a second trial, that it can. But these efforts are all in vain; and whatever capricious and irregular actions we may perform; as the desire of showing our liberty is the sole motive of our actions; we can never free ourselves from the bonds of necessity. We may imagine we feel a liberty within ourselves; but a spectator can commonly infer our actions from our motives and character; and even where he cannot, he concludes in general, that he might, were he perfectly acquainted with every circumstance of our situation and temper, and the most secret springs of our complexion and disposition. Now this is the very essence of necessity, according to the foregoing doctrine.

A third reason why the doctrine of liberty has generally been better receiv'd in the world, than its antagonist, proceeds from *religion*, which has been very unnecessarily interested in this question. There is no method of reasoning more common, and yet none more blameable, than in philosophical debates to endeavour to refute any hypothesis by a pretext of its dangerous consequences to religion and morality. When any opinion leads us into absurdities, 'tis certainly false; but 'tis not certain an opinion is false, because 'tis of dangerous consequence. Such topics, therefore, ought entirely to be foreborn, as serving nothing to the discovery of truth, but only to make the person of an antagonist odious. This I observe in general, without pretending to draw any advantage from it. I submit myself frankly to an examination of this kind, and dare venture to affirm, that the doctrine of necessity, according to my explication of it, is not only innocent, but even advantageous to religion and morality.

I define necessity two ways, conformable to the two definitions of cause, of which it makes an essential part. I place it either in the constant union and conjunction of like objects, or in the inference of the mind from the one to the other. Now necessity, in both these senses, has universally, tho' tacitly, in the schools, in the pulpit, and in common life, been allow'd to belong to the will of man, and no one has ever pretended to deny, that we can draw inferences concerning human actions, and that those inferences are founded on the experienc'd union of like actions with like motives and circumstances. The only particular in which any one can differ from me, is either, that perhaps he will refuse to call this necessity. But as long as the meaning is understood, I hope the word can do no harm. Or that he will maintain there is something else in the operations of matter. Now whether it be so or not is of no consequence to religion, whatever it may be to natural philosophy. I may be mistaken in asserting, that we have no idea of any other connexion in the actions of body, and shall be glad to be farther instructed on that head: But sure I am, I ascribe nothing to the actions of the mind, but what must readily be allow'd of. Let no one, therefore, put an invidious construction on my words, by saying simply, that I assert the necessity of human actions, and place them on the same footing with the operations of senseless matter. I do not ascribe to the will that unintelligible necessity, which is suppos'd to lie in matter. But I ascribe to matter, that intelligible quality, call it necessity or not, which the most rigorous orthodoxy does or must allow to belong to the will. I change, therefore, nothing in the receiv'd systems, with regard to the will, but only with regard to material objects.

Nay I shall go farther, and assert, that this kind of necessity is so essential to religion and morality, that without it there must ensue an absolute subversion of both, and that every other supposition is entirely destructive to all laws both *divine* and *human*.

'Tis indeed certain, that as all human laws are founded on rewards and punishments, 'tis suppos'd as a fundamental principle, that these motives have an influence on the mind, and both produce the good and prevent the evil actions. We may give to this influence what name we please; but as 'tis usually conjoin'd with the action, common sense requires it shou'd be esteem'd a cause, and be look'd upon as an instance of that necessity, which I wou'd establish.

This reasoning is equally solid, when apply'd to *divine* laws, so far as the deity is consider'd as a legislator, and is suppos'd to inflict punishment and bestow rewards with a design to produce obedience. But I also maintain, that even where he acts not in his magisterial capacity, but is regarded as the avenger of crimes merely on account of their odiousness and deformity, not only 'tis impossible, without the necessary connexion of cause and effect in human actions, that punishments cou'd be inflicted compatible with justice and moral equity; but also that it cou'd ever enter into the thoughts of any reasonable being to inflict them. The constant and universal object of hatred or anger is a person or creature endow'd with thought and consciousness; and when any criminal or injurious actions excite that passion, 'tis only by their relation to the person or connexion with him. But according to the doctrine of liberty or chance, this connexion is reduc'd to nothing, nor are men more accountable for those actions, which are design'd and premeditated, than for such as are the most casual and accidental. Actions are by their very nature temporary and perishing; and where they proceed not from some cause in the characters and disposition of the person, who perform'd them, they infix not themselves upon him, and can neither redound to his honour, if good, nor infamy, if evil. The action itself may be blameable; it may be contrary to all the rules of morality and religion: But the person is not responsible for it; and as it proceeded from nothing in him, that is durable or constant, and leaves nothing of that nature behind it, 'tis impossible he can, upon its account, become the object of punishment or vengeance. According to the hypothesis of liberty, therefore, a man is as pure and untainted, after having committed the most horrid crimes, as at the first moment of his birth, nor is his character any way concern'd in his actions; since they are not deriv'd from it, and the wickedness of the one can never be us'd as a proof of the depravity of the other. 'Tis only upon the principles of necessity, that a person acquires any merit or demerit from his actions, however the common opinion may incline to the contrary.

But so inconsistent are men with themselves, that tho' they often assert, that necessity utterly destroys all merit and demerit either towards mankind or superior powers, yet they continue still to reason upon these very principles of necessity in all their judgments concerning this matter. Men are not blam'd for such evil actions as they perform ignorantly and casually, whatever may be their consequences. Why? but because the causes of these actions are only momentary, and terminate in them alone. Men are less blam'd for such evil actions, as they perform hastily and unpremeditately, than for such as proceed from thought and deliberation. For what reason? but because a hasty temper, tho' a constant cause in the mind, operates only by intervals, and infects not the whole character. Again, repentance wipes off every crime, especially if attended with an evident reformation of life and manners. How is this to be accounted for? But by asserting that actions render a person criminal, merely as they are proofs of criminal passions or principles in the mind; and when by any alteration of these principles they cease to be just proofs, they likewise cease to be criminal. But according to the doctrine of *liberty* or *chance* they never were just proofs, and consequently never were criminal.

Here then I turn to my adversary, and desire him to free his own system from these odious consequences before he charge them upon others. Or if he rather chuses, that this question shou'd be decided by fair arguments before philosophers, than by declamations before the people, let him return to what I have advanc'd to prove that liberty and chance are synonimous; and concerning the nature of moral evidence and the regularity of human actions. Upon a review of these reasonings, I cannot doubt of an entire victory; and therefore having prov'd, that all actions of the will have particular causes, I proceed to explain what these causes are, and how they operate.

Chapter 51

Freedom of the will and the concept of a person

Harry Frankfurt

WHAT philosophers have lately come to accept as analysis of the concept of a person is not actually analysis of *that* concept at all. Strawson, whose usage represents the current standard, identifies the concept of a person as 'the concept of a type of entity such that *both* predicates ascribing states of consciousness *and* predicates ascribing corporeal characteristics . . . are equally applicable to a single individual of that single type'.[1] But there are many entities besides persons that have both mental and physical properties. As it happens—though it seems extraordinary that this should be so—there is no common English word for the type of entity Strawson has in mind, a type that includes not only human beings but animals of various lesser species as well. Still, this hardly justifies the misappropriation of a valuable philosophical term.

Whether the members of some animal species are persons is surely not to be settled merely by determining whether it is correct to apply to them, in addition to predicates ascribing corporeal characteristics, predicates that ascribe states of consciousness. It does violence to our language to endorse the application of the term 'person' to those numerous creatures which do have both psychological and material properties but which are manifestly not persons in any normal sense of the word. This misuse of language is doubtless innocent of any theoretical error. But although the offence is 'merely verbal', it does significant harm. For it gratuitously diminishes our philosophical vocabulary, and it increases the likelihood that we will overlook the important area of inquiry with which the term 'person' is most naturally associated. It might have been expected that no problem would be of more central and persistent concern to philosophers than that of understanding what we ourselves essentially are. Yet this problem is so generally neglected that it has been

---

1. P. F. Strawson, *Individuals* (London: Methuen, 1959), 101–2. Ayer's usage of 'person' is similar: 'it is characteristic of persons in this sense that besides having various physical properties . . . they are also credited with various forms of consciousness' (A. J. Ayer, *The Concept of a Person* (New York: St. Martin's, 1963), 82). What concerns Strawson and Ayer is the problem of understanding the relation between mind and body, rather than the quite different problem of understanding what it is to be a creature that not only has a mind and a body but is also a person.

Harry Frankfurt, 'Freedom of the Will and the Concept of a Person', from the *Journal of Philosophy*, 68/1 (Jan. 1971), copyright © *Journal of Philosophyhy*, 1971.

possible to make off with its very name almost without being noticed and, evidently, without evoking any widespread feeling of loss.

There is a sense in which the word 'person' is merely the singular form of 'people' and in which both terms connote no more than membership in a certain biological species. In those senses of the word which are of greater philosophical interest, however, the criteria for being a person do not serve primarily to distinguish the members of our own species from the members of other species. Rather, they are designed to capture those attributes which are the subject of our most humane concern with ourselves and the source of what we regard as most important and most problematical in our lives. Now these attributes would be of equal significance to us even if they were not in fact peculiar and common to the members of our own species. What interests us most in the human condition would not interest us less if it were also a feature of the condition of other creatures as well.

Our concept of ourselves as persons is not to be understood, therefore, as a concept of attributes that are necessarily species-specific. It is conceptually possible that members of novel or even of familiar non-human species should be persons; and it is also conceptually possible that some members of the human species are not persons. We do in fact assume, on the other hand, that no member of another species is a person. Accordingly, there is a presumption that what is essential to persons is a set of characteristics that we generally suppose—whether rightly or wrongly—to be uniquely human.

It is my view that one essential difference between persons and other creatures is to be found in the structure of a person's will. Human beings are not alone in having desires and motives, or in making choices. They share these things with the members of certain other species, some of whom even appear to engage in deliberation and to make decisions based upon prior thought. It seems to be peculiarly characteristic of humans, however, that they are able to form what I shall call 'second-order desires' or 'desires of the second order'.

Besides wanting and choosing and being moved *to do* this or that, men may also want to have (or not to have) certain desires and motives. They are capable of wanting to be different, in their preferences and purposes, from what they are. Many animals appear to have the capacity for what I shall call 'first-order desires' or 'desires of the first order', which are simply desires to do or not to do one thing or another. No animal other than man, however, appears to have the capacity for reflective self-evaluation that is manifested in the formation of second-order desires.[2]

---

2. For the sake of simplicity, I shall deal only with what someone wants or desires, neglecting related phenomena such as choices and decisions. I propose to use the verbs 'to want' and 'to desire' interchangeably, although they are by no means perfect synonyms. My motive in forsaking the established nuances of these words arises from the fact that the verb 'to want', which suits my purposes better so far as its meaning is concerned, does not lend itself so readily to the formation of nouns as does the verb 'to desire'. It is perhaps acceptable, albeit graceless, to speak in the plural of someone's 'wants'. But to speak in the singular of someone's 'want' would be an abomination.

The concept designated by the verb 'to want' is extraordinarily elusive. A statement of the form 'A wants to X'—taken by itself, apart from a context that serves to amplify or to specify its meaning—conveys remarkably little information. Such a statement may be consistent, for example, with each of the following statements: (a) the prospect of doing X elicits no sensation or introspectible emotional response in A; (b) A is unaware that he wants to X; (c) A believes that he does not want to X; (d) A wants to refrain from X-ing; (e) A wants to Y and believes that it is impossible for him both to Y and to X; (f) A does not 'really' want to X; (g) A *would rather die than X*; and so on. It is therefore hardly sufficient to formulate the distinction between first-order and second-order desires, as I have done, by suggesting merely that someone has a first-order desire when he wants to do or not to do such-and-such, and that he has a second-order desire when he wants to have or not to have a certain desire of the first order.

As I shall understand them, statements of the form 'A wants to X' cover a rather broad range of possibilities.[3] They may be true even when statements like (a) through (g) are true: when A is unaware of any feelings concerning X-ing, when he is unaware that he wants to X, when he deceives himself about what he wants and believes falsely that he does not want to X, when he also has other desires that conflict with his desire to X, or when he is ambivalent. The desires in question may be conscious or unconscious, they need not be univocal, and A may be mistaken about them. There is a further source of uncertainty with regard to statements that identify someone's desires, however, and here it is important for my purposes to be less permissive.

Consider first those statements of the form 'A wants to X' which identify first-order desires—that is, statements in which the term 'to X' refers to an action. A statement of this kind does not, by itself, indicate the relative strength of A's desire to X. It does not make it clear whether this desire is at all likely to play a decisive role in what A actually does or tries to do. For it may correctly be said that A wants to X even when his desire to X is only one among his desires and when it is far from being paramount among them. Thus, it may be true that A wants to X when he strongly prefers to do something else instead; and it may be true that he wants to X despite the fact that, when he acts, it is not the desire to X that motivates him to do what he does. On the other hand, someone who states that A wants to X may mean to convey that it is this desire that is motivating or moving A to do what he is actually doing or that A will in fact be moved by this desire (unless he changes his mind) when he acts.

It is only when it is used in the second of these ways that, given the special usage of 'will' that I propose to adopt, the statement identifies A's will. To identify an agent's will is either to identify the desire (or desires) by which he is motivated in some action he

---

3. What I say in this paragraph applies not only to cases in which 'to X' refers to a possible action or inaction. It also applies to cases in which 'to X' refers to a first-order desire and in which the statement that 'A wants to X' is therefore a shortened version of a statement—'A wants to want X'—that identifies a desire of the second order.

performs or to identify the desire (or desires) by which he will or would be motivated when or if he acts. An agent's will, then, is identical with one or more of his first-order desires. But the notion of the will, as I am employing it, is not coextensive with the notion of first-order desires. It is not the notion of something that merely inclines an agent in some degree to act in a certain way. Rather, it is the notion of an *effective* desire—one that moves (or will or would move) a person all the way to action. Thus the notion of the will is not coextensive with the notion of what an agent intends to do. For even though someone may have a settled intention to do X, he may none the less do something else instead of doing X because, despite his intention, his desire to do X proves to be weaker or less effective than some conflicting desire.

Now consider those statements of the form 'A wants to X' which identify second-order desires—that is, statements in which the term 'to X' refers to a desire of the first order. There are also two kinds of situation in which it may be true that A wants to want to X. In the first place, it might be true of A that he wants to have a desire to X despite the fact that he has a univocal desire, altogether free of conflict and ambivalence, to refrain from X-ing. Someone might want to have a certain desire, in other words, but univocally want that desire to be unsatisfied.

Suppose that a physician engaged in psychotherapy with narcotics addicts believes that his ability to help his patients would be enhanced if he understood better what it is like for them to desire the drug to which they are addicted. Suppose that he is led in this way to want to have a desire for the drug. If it is a genuine desire that he wants, then what he wants is not merely to feel the sensations that addicts characteristically feel when they are gripped by their desires for the drug. What the physician wants, in so far as he wants to have a desire, is to be inclined or moved to some extent to take the drug.

It is entirely possible, however, that, although he wants to be moved by a desire to take the drug, he does not want this desire to be effective. He may not want it to move him all the way to action. He need not be interested in finding out what it is like to take the drug. And in so far as he now wants only to *want* to take it, and not to *take* it, there is nothing in what he now wants that would be satisfied by the drug itself. He may now have, in fact, an altogether univocal desire *not* to take the drug; and he may prudently arrange to make it impossible for him to satisfy the desire he would have if his desire to want the drug should in time be satisfied.

It would thus be incorrect to infer, from the fact that the physician now wants to desire to take the drug, that he already does desire to take it. His second-order desire to be moved to take the drug does not entail that he has a first-order desire to take it. If the drug were now to be administered to him, this might satisfy no desire that is implicit in his desire to want to take it. While he wants to want to take the drug, he may have *no* desire to take it; it may be that *all* he wants is to taste the desire for it. That is, his desire to have a certain desire that he does not have may not be a desire that his will should be at all different than it is.

Someone who wants only in this truncated way to want to X stands at the margin of preciosity, and the fact that he wants to want to X is not pertinent to the identification of his will. There is, however, a second kind of situation that may be described by 'A wants to X'; and when the statement is used to describe a situation of this second kind, then it does pertain to what A wants his will to be. In such cases the statement means that A wants the desire to X to be the desire that moves him effectively to act. It is not merely that he wants the desire to X to be among the desires by which, to one degree or another, he is moved or inclined to act. He wants this desire to be effective— that is, to provide the motive in what he actually does. Now when the statement that A wants to want to X is used in this way, it does entail that A already has a desire to X. It could not be true both that A wants the desire to X to move him into action and that he does not want to X. It is only if he does want to X that he can coherently want the desire to X not merely to be one of his desires but, more decisively, to be his will.[4]

Suppose a man wants to be motivated in what he does by the desire to concentrate on his work. It is necessarily true, if this supposition is correct, that he already wants to concentrate on his work. This desire is now among his desires. But the question of whether or not his second-order desire is fulfilled does not turn merely on whether the desire he wants is one of his desires. It turns on whether this desire is, as he wants it to be, his effective desire or will. If, when the chips are down, it is his desire to concentrate on his work that moves him to do what he does, then what he wants at that time is indeed (in the relevant sense) what he wants to want. If it is some other desire that actually moves him when he acts, on the other hand, then what he wants at that time is not (in the relevant sense) what he wants to want. This will be so despite the fact that the desire to concentrate on his work continues to be among his desires.

II

Someone has a desire of the second order either when he wants simply to have a certain desire or when he wants a certain desire to be his will. In situations of the latter kind, I shall call his second-order desires 'second-order volitions' or 'volitions of the second order'. Now it is having second-order volitions, and not having second-order desires generally, that I regard as essential to being a person. It is logically possible, however unlikely, that there should be an agent with second-order desires but with no volitions of the second order. Such a creature, in my view, would not be a person. I shall use the term 'wanton' to refer to agents who have first-order

---

4. It is not so clear that the entailment relation described here holds in certain kinds of cases, which I think may fairly be regarded as non-standard, where the essential difference between the standard and the non-standard cases lies in the kind of description by which the first-order desire in question is identified. Thus, suppose that A admires B so fulsomely that, even though he does not know what B wants to do, he wants to be effectively moved by whatever desire effectively moves B; without knowing what B's will is, in other words, A wants his own will to be the same. It certainly does not follow that A already has, among his desires, a desire like the one that constitutes B's will. I shall not pursue here the questions of whether there are genuine counter-examples to the claim made in the text or of how, if there are, that claim should be altered.

desires but who are not persons because, whether or not they have desires of the second order, they have no second-order volitions.[5]

The essential characteristic of a wanton is that he does not care about his will. His desires move him to do certain things, without its being true of him either that he wants to be moved by those desires or that he prefers to be moved by other desires. The class of wantons includes all non-human animals that have desires and all very young children. Perhaps it also includes some adult human beings as well. In any case, adult humans may be more or less wanton; they may act wantonly, in response to first-order desires concerning which they have no volitions of the second order, more or less frequently.

The fact that a wanton has no second-order volitions does not mean that each of his first-order desires is translated heedlessly and at once into action. He may have no opportunity to act in accordance with some of his desires. Moreover, the translation of his desires into action may be delayed or precluded either by conflicting desires of the first order or by the intervention of deliberation. For a wanton may possess and employ rational faculties of a high order. Nothing in the concept of a wanton implies that he cannot reason or that he cannot deliberate concerning how to do what he wants to do. What distinguishes the rational wanton from other rational agents is that he is not concerned with the desirability of his desires themselves. He ignores the question of what his will is to be. Not only does he pursue whatever course of action he is most strongly inclined to pursue, but he does not care which of his inclinations is the strongest.

Thus a rational creature, who reflects upon the suitability to his desires of one course of action or another, may none the less be a wanton. In maintaining that the essence of being a person lies not in reason but in will, I am far from suggesting that a creature without reason may be a person. For it is only in virtue of his rational capacities that a person is capable of becoming critically aware of his own will and of forming volitions of the second order. The structure of a person's will presupposes, accordingly, that he is a rational being.

The distinction between a person and a wanton may be illustrated by the difference between two narcotics addicts. Let us suppose that the physiological condition accounting for the addiction is the same in both men, and that both succumb inevitably to their periodic desires for the drug to which they are addicted. One of the addicts hates his addiction and always struggles desperately, although to no avail, against its thrust. He tries everything that he thinks might enable him to overcome his desires for the drug. But these desires are too powerful for him to withstand, and

5. Creatures with second-order desires but no second-order volitions differ significantly from brute animals, and, for some purposes, it would be desirable to regard them as persons. My usage, which withholds the designation 'person' from them, is thus somewhat arbitrary. I adopt it largely because it facilitates the formulation of some of the points I wish to make. Hereafter, whenever I consider statements of the form 'A wants to want to X', I shall have in mind statements identifying second-order volitions and not statements identifying second-order desires that are not second-order volitions.

invariably, in the end, they conquer him. He is an unwilling addict, helplessly violated by his own desires.

The unwilling addict has conflicting first-order desires: he wants to take the drug, and he also wants to refrain from taking it. In addition to these first-order desires, however, he has a volition of the second order. He is not a neutral with regard to the conflict between his desire to take the drug and his desire to refrain from taking it. It is the latter desire, and not the former, that he wants to constitute his will; it is the latter desire, rather than the former, that he wants to be effective and to provide the purpose that he will seek to realize in what he actually does.

The other addict is a wanton. His actions reflect the economy of his first-order desires, without his being concerned whether the desires that move him to act are desires by which he wants to be moved to act. If he encounters problems in obtaining the drug or in administering it to himself, his reponses to his urges to take it may involve deliberation. But it never occurs to him to consider whether he wants the relation among his desires to result in his having the will he has. The wanton addict may be an animal, and thus incapable of being concerned about his will. In any event he is, in respect of his wanton lack of concern, no different from an animal.

The second of these addicts may suffer a first-order conflict similar to the first-order conflict suffered by the first. Whether he is human or not, the wanton may (perhaps due to conditioning) both want to take the drug and want to refrain from taking it. Unlike the unwilling addict, however, he does not prefer that one of his conflicting desires should be paramount over the other; he does not prefer that one first-order desire rather than the other should constitute his will. It would be misleading to say that he is neutral as to the conflict between his desires, since this would suggest that he regards them as equally acceptable. Since he has no identity apart from his first-order desires, it is true neither that he prefers one to the other nor that he prefers not to take sides.

It makes a difference to the unwilling addict, who is a person, which of his conflicting first-order desires wins out. Both desires are his, to be sure; and whether he finally takes the drug or finally succeeds in refraining from taking it, he acts to satisfy what is in a literal sense his own desire. In either case he does something he himself wants to do, and he does it not because of some external influence whose aim happens to coincide with his own but because of his desire to do it. The unwilling addict identifies himself, however, through the formation of a second-order volition, with one rather than with the other of his conflicting first-order desires. He makes one of them more truly his own and, in so doing, he withdraws himself from the other. It is in virtue of this identification and withdrawal, accomplished through the formation of a second-order volition, that the unwilling addict may meaningfully make the analytically puzzling statements that the force moving him to take the drug is a force other than his own, and that it is not of his own free will but rather against his will that this force moves him to take it.

The wanton addict cannot or does not care which of his conflicting first-order desires wins out. His lack of concern is not due to his inability to find a convincing basis for preference. It is due either to his lack of the capacity for reflection or to his mindless indifference to the enterprise of evaluating his own desires and motives.[6] There is only one issue in the struggle to which his first-order conflict may lead: whether the one or the other of his conflicting desires is the stronger. Since he is moved by both desires, he will not be altogether satisfied by what he does no matter which of them is effective. But it makes no difference *to him* whether his craving or his aversion gets the upper hand. He has no stake in the conflict between them and so, unlike the unwilling addict, he can neither win nor lose the struggle in which he is engaged. When a *person* acts, the desire by which he is moved is either the will he wants or a will he wants to be without. When a *wanton* acts, it is neither.

III

There is a very close relationship between the capacity for forming second-order volitions and another capacity that is essential to persons—one that has often been considered a distinguishing mark of the human condition. It is only because a person has volitions of the second order that he is capable both of enjoying and of lacking freedom of the will. The concept of a person is not only, then, the concept of a type of entity that has both first-order desires and volitions of the second order. It can also be construed as the concept of a type of entity for whom the freedom of its will may be a problem. This concept excludes all wantons, both infrahuman and human, since they fail to satisfy an essential condition for the enjoyment of freedom of the will. And it excludes those suprahuman beings, if any, whose wills are necessarily free.

Just what kind of freedom is the freedom of the will? This question calls for an identification of the special area of human experience to which the concept of freedom of the will, as distinct from the concepts of other sorts of freedom, is particularly germane. In dealing with it, my aim will be primarily to locate the problem with which a person is most immediately concerned when he is concerned with the freedom of his will.

According to one familiar philosophical tradition, being free is fundamentally a matter of doing what one wants to do. Now the notion of an agent who does what he wants to do is by no means an altogether clear one: both the doing and the wanting, and the appropriate relation between them as well, require elucidation. But although its focus needs to be sharpened and its formulation refined, I believe that this notion does capture at least part of what is implicit in the idea of an agent who

---

6. In speaking of the evaluation of his own desires and motives as being characteristic of a person, I do not mean to suggest that a person's second-order volitions necessarily manifest a *moral* stance on his part toward his first-order desires. It may not be from the point of view of morality that the person evaluates his first-order desires. Moreover, a person may be capricious and irresponsible in forming his second-order volitions and give no serious consideration to what is at stake. Second-order volitions express evaluations only in the sense that they are preferences. There is no essential restrictions on the kind of basis, if any, upon which they are formed.

acts freely. It misses entirely, however, the peculiar content of the quite different idea of an agent whose *will* is free.

We do not suppose that animals enjoy freedom of the will, although we recognize that an animal may be free to run in whatever direction it wants. Thus, having the freedom to do what one wants to do is not a sufficient condition of having a free will. It is not a necessary condition either. For to deprive someone of his freedom of action is not necessarily to undermine the freedom of his will. When an agent is aware that there are certain things he is not free to do, this doubtless affects his desires and limits the range of choices he can make. But suppose that someone, without being aware of it, has in fact lost or been deprived of his freedom of action. Even though he is no longer free to do what he wants to do, his will may remain as free as it was before. Despite the fact that he is not free to translate his desires into actions or to act according to the determinations of his will, he may still form those desires and make those determinations as freely as if his freedom of action had not been impaired.

When we ask whether a person's will is free we are not asking whether he is in a position to translate his first-order desires into actions. That is the question of whether he is free to do as he pleases. The question of the freedom of his will does not concern the relation between what he does and what he wants to do. Rather, it concerns his desires themselves. But what question about them is it?

It seems to me both natural and useful to construe the question of whether a person's will is free in close analogy to the question of whether an agent enjoys freedom of action. Now freedom of action is (roughly, at least) the freedom to do what one wants to do. Analogously, then, the statement that a person enjoys freedom of the will means (also roughly) that he is free to want what he wants to want. More precisely, it means that he is free to will what he wants to will, or to have the will he wants. Just as the question about the freedom of an agent's action has to do with whether it is the action he wants to perform, so the question about the freedom of his will has to do with whether it is the will he wants to have.

It is in securing the conformity of his will to his second-order volitions, then, that a person exercises freedom of the will. And it is in the discrepancy between his will and his second-order volitions, or in his awareness that their coincidence is not his own doing but only a happy chance, that a person who does not have this freedom feels its lack. The unwilling addict's will is not free. This is shown by the fact that it is not the will he wants. It is also true, though in a different way, that the will of the wanton addict is not free. The wanton addict neither has the will he wants nor has a will that differs from the will he wants. Since he has no volitions of the second order, the freedom of his will cannot be a problem for him. He lacks it, so to speak, by default.

People are generally far more complicated than my sketchy account of the structure of a person's will may suggest. There is as much opportunity for ambivalence, conflict, and self-deception with regard to desires of the second order, for example, as there is with regard to first-order desires. If there is an unresolved conflict among someone's second-order desires, then he is in danger of having no second-order volition; for unless this conflict is resolved, he has no preference concerning which of his first-order desires is to be his will. This condition, if it is so severe that it prevents him from identifying himself in a sufficiently decisive way with *any* of his conflicting first-order desires, destroys him as a person. For it either tends to paralyse his will and to keep him from acting at all, or it tends to remove him from his will so that his will operates without his participation. In both cases he becomes, like the unwilling addict though in a different way, a helpless bystander to the forces that move him.

Another complexity is that a person may have, especially if his second-order desires are in conflict, desires and volitions of a higher order than the second. There is no theoretical limit to the length of the series of desires of higher and higher orders; nothing except common sense and, perhaps, a saving fatigue prevents an individual from obsessively refusing to identify himself with any of his desires until he forms a desire of the next higher order. The tendency to generate such a series of acts of forming desires, which would be a case of humanization run wild, also leads toward the destruction of a person.

It is possible, however, to terminate such a series of acts without cutting it off arbitrarily. When a person identifies himself *decisively* with one of his first-order desires, this commitment 'resounds' throughout the potentially endless array of higher orders. Consider a person who, without reservation or conflict, wants to be motivated by the desire to concentrate on his work. The fact that his second-order volition to be moved by this desire is a decisive one means that there is no room for questions concerning the pertinence of desires or volitions of higher orders. Suppose the person is asked whether he wants to want to concentrate on his work. He can properly insist that this question concerning a third-order desire does not arise. It would be a mistake to claim that, because he has not considered whether he wants the second-order volition he has formed, he is indifferent to the question of whether it is with this volition or with some other that he wants his will to accord. The decisiveness of the commitment he has made means that he has decided that no further question about his second-order volition, at any higher order, remains to be asked. It is relatively unimportant whether we explain this by saying that this commitment implicitly generates an endless series of confirming desires of higher orders, or by saying that the commitment is tantamount to a dissolution of the pointedness of all questions concerning higher orders of desire.

Examples such as the one concerning the unwilling addict may suggest that volitions of the second order, or of higher orders, must be formed deliberately and that a person characteristically struggles to ensure that they are satisfied. But the conformity of a person's will to his higher-order volitions may be far more thoughtless and spontaneous than this. Some people are naturally moved by kindness when they want to be kind, and by nastiness when they want to be nasty, without any explicit forethought and without any need for energetic self-control. Others are moved by nastiness when they want to be kind and by kindness when they intend to be nasty, equally without forethought and without active resistance to these violations of their higher-order desires. The enjoyment of freedom comes easily to some. Others must struggle to achieve it.

IV

My theory concerning the freedom of the will accounts easily for our disinclination to allow that this freedom is enjoyed by the members of any species inferior to our own. It also satisfies another condition that must be met by any such theory, by making it apparent why the freedom of the will should be regarded as desirable. The enjoyment of a free will means the satisfaction of certain desires—desires of the second or of higher orders—whereas its absence means their frustration. The satisfactions at stake are those which accrue to a person of whom it may be said that his will is his own. The corresponding frustrations are those suffered by a person of whom it may be said that he is estranged from himself, or that he finds himself a helpless or a passive bystander to the forces that move him.

A person who is free to do what he wants to do may yet not be in a position to have the will he wants. Suppose, however, that he enjoys both freedom of action and freedom of the will. Then he is not only free to do what he wants to do; he is also free to want what he wants to want. It seems to me that he has, in that case, all the freedom it is possible to desire or to conceive. There are other good things in life, and he may not possess some of them. But there is nothing in the way of freedom that he lacks.

It is far from clear that certain other theories of the freedom of the will meet these elementary but essential conditions: that it be understandable why we desire this freedom and why we refuse to ascribe it to animals. Consider, for example, Roderick Chisholm's quaint version of the doctrine that human freedom entails an absence of causal determination.[7] Whenever a person performs a free action, according to Chisholm, it's a miracle. The motion of a person's hand, when the person moves it, is the outcome of a series of physical causes; but some event in this series, 'and presumably one of those that took place within the brain, was caused by the agent and not by any other events' (18). A free agent has, therefore, 'a prerogative which some would attribute only to God: each of us, when we act, is a prime mover unmoved' (23).

This account fails to provide any basis for doubting that animals of subhuman species enjoy the freedom it defines. Chisholm says nothing that makes it seem less likely that a rabbit performs a miracle when it moves its leg than that a man does so when he moves his hand. But why, in any case, should anyone *care* whether he can interrupt the natural order of causes in the way Chisholm describes? Chisholm offers no reason for believing that there is a discernible difference between the experience of a man who miraculously initiates a series of causes when he moves his hand

---

7. 'Freedom and Action', in *Freedom and Determinism*, ed. Keith Lehrer, (New York: Random House, 1966), 11–44.

and a man who moves his hand without any such breach of the normal causal sequence. There appears to be no concrete basis for preferring to be involved in the one state of affairs rather than in the other.[8]

It is generally supposed that, in addition to satisfying the two conditions I have mentioned, a satisfactory theory of the freedom of the will necessarily provides an analysis of one of the conditions of moral responsibility. The most common recent approach to the problem of understanding the freedom of the will has been, indeed, to inquire what is entailed by the assumption that someone is morally responsible for what he has done. In my view, however, the relation between moral responsibility and the freedom of the will has been very widely misunderstood. It is not true that a person is morally responsible for what he has done only if his will was free when he did it. He may be morally responsible for having done it even though his will was not free at all.

A person's will is free only if he is free to have the will he wants. This means that, with regard to any of his first-order desires, he is free either to make that desire his will or to make some other first-order desire his will instead. Whatever his will, then, the will of the person whose will is free could have been otherwise; he could have done otherwise than to constitute his will as he did. It is a vexed question just how 'he could have done otherwise' is to be understood in contexts such as this one. But although this question is important to the theory of freedom, it has no bearing on the theory of moral responsibility. For the assumption that a person is morally responsible for what he has done does not entail that the person was in a position to have whatever will he wanted.

This assumption *does* entail that the person did what he did freely, or that he did it of his own free will. It is a mistake, however, to believe that someone acts freely only when he is free to do whatever he wants or that he acts of his own free will only if his will is free. Suppose that a person has done what he wanted to do, that he did it because he wanted to do it, and that the will by which he was moved when he did it was his will because it was the will he wanted. Then he did it freely and of his own free will. Even supposing that he could have done otherwise, he would not have done otherwise; and even supposing that he could have had a different will, he would not have wanted his will to differ from what it was. Moreover, since the will that moved him when he acted was his will because he wanted it to be, he cannot claim that his will was forced upon him or that he was a passive bystander to its constitution. Under these conditions, it is quite irrelevant to the evaluation of his moral responsibility to inquire whether the alternatives that he opted against were actually available to him.[9]

---

8. I am not suggesting that the alleged difference between these two states of affairs is unverifiable. On the contrary, physiologists might well be able to show that Chisholm's conditions for a free action are not satisfied, by establishing that there is no relevant brain event for which a sufficient physical cause cannot be found.

9. For another discussion of the considerations that cast doubt on the principle that a person is morally responsible for what he has done only if he could have done otherwise, see my 'Alternate Possibilities and Moral Responsibility', *Journal of Philosophy*, 1969, 829–39.

In illustration, consider a third kind of addict. Suppose that his addiction has the same physiological basis and the same irresistible thrust as the addictions of the unwilling and wanton addicts, but that he is altogether delighted with his condition. He is a willing addict, who would not have things any other way. If the grip of his addiction should somehow weaken, he would do whatever he could to reinstate it; if his desire for the drug should begin to fade, he would take steps to renew its intensity.

The willing addict's will is not free, for his desire to take the drug will be effective regardless of whether or not he wants this desire to constitute this will. But when he takes the drug, he takes it freely and of his own free will. I am inclined to understand his situation as involving the overdetermination of his first-order desire to take the drug. This desire is his effective desire because he is physiologically addicted. But it is his effective desire also because he wants it to be. His will is outside his control, but, by his second-order desire that his desire for the drug should be effective, he has made this will his own. Given that it is therefore not only because of his addiction that his desire for the drug is effective, he may be morally responsible for taking the drug.

My conception of the freedom of the will appears to be neutral with regard to the problem of determinism. It seems conceivable that it should be causally determined that a person is free to want what he wants to want. If this is conceivable, then it might be causally determined that a person enjoys a free will. There is no more than an innocuous appearance of paradox in the proposition that it is determined, ineluctably and by forces beyond their control, that certain people have free wills and that others do not. There is no incoherence in the proposition that some agency other than a person's own is responsible (even *morally* responsible) for the fact that he enjoys or fails to enjoy freedom of the will. It is possible that a person should be morally responsible for what he does of his own free will and that some other person should also be morally responsible for his having done it.[10]

On the other hand, it seems conceivable that it should come about by chance that a person is free to have the will he wants. If this is conceivable, then it might be a matter of chance that certain people enjoy freedom of the will and that certain others do not. Perhaps it is also conceivable, as a number of philosophers believe, for states of affairs to come about in a way other than by chance or as the outcome of a sequence of natural causes. If it is indeed conceivable for the relevant states of affairs to come about in some third way, then it is also possible that a person should in that third way come to enjoy the freedom of the will.

10. There is a difference between being *fully* responsible and being *solely* responsible. Suppose that the willing addict has been made an addict by the deliberate and calculated work of another. Then it may be that both the addict and this other person are fully responsible for the addict's taking the drug, while neither of them is solely responsible for it. That there is a distinction between full moral responsibility and sole moral responsibility is apparent in the following example. A certain light can be turned on or off by flicking either of two switches, and each of these switches is simultaneously flicked to the 'on' position by a different person, neither of whom is aware of the other. Neither person is solely responsible for the light's going on, nor do they share the responsibility in the sense that each is partially responsible; rather, each of them is fully responsible.

Chapter 52

The incompatibility of free will and determinism*

Peter van Inwagen

IN this paper I shall define a thesis I shall call 'determinism', and argue that it is incompatible with the thesis that we are able to act otherwise than we do (i.e. is incompatible with 'free will'). Other theses, some of them very different from what *I* shall call 'determinism', have at least an equal right to this name, and, therefore, I do not claim to show that *every* thesis that could be called 'determinism' without historical impropriety is incompatible with free will. I shall, however, assume without argument that what I call 'determinism' is legitimately so called.

In Part I, I shall explain what I mean by 'determinism'. In Part II, I shall make some remarks about 'can'. In Part III, I shall argue that free will and determinism are incompatible. In Part IV, I shall examine some possible objections to the argument of Part III. I shall not attempt to establish the truth or falsity of determinism, or the existence or non-existence of free will.

I

In defining 'determinism', I shall take for granted the notion of a proposition (that is, of a non-linguistic bearer of truth-value), together with certain allied notions such as denial, conjunction, and entailment. Nothing in this paper will depend on the special features of any particular account of propositions. The reader may think of them as functions from possible worlds to truth-values or in any other way he likes, provided they have their usual features (e.g. they are either true or false; the conjunction of a true and a false proposition is a false proposition; they obey the law of contraposition with respect to entailment).

* The writing of this paper was supported by a stipend from the National Endowment for the Humanities for the summer of 1973. The paper was read at a colloquium at the University of Maryland at College Park. Earlier versions were read at the University of Rochester and Syracuse University. The audiences at these colloquia are thanked for useful comments and criticism. Special thanks are due to Rolf Eberle, Keith Lehrer, Raymond Martin, and Richard Taylor. I wish to thank Carl Ginet for his acute comments on an earlier draft, and the referee [of *Philosophical Studies*] for several helpful suggestions. Of course, none of these people is responsible for any mistakes that remain.

Peter van Inwagen, 'The incompatibility of Freewill and Determinism', from *Philosophical Studies*, 27 (1975).

Our definition of 'determinism' will also involve the notion of 'the state of the entire physical world' (hereinafter, 'the state of the world') at an instant. I shall leave this notion largely unexplained, since the argument of this paper is very nearly independent of its content. Provided the following two conditions are met, the reader may flesh out 'the state of the world' in any way he likes:

(i) Our concept of 'state' must be such that, given that the world is in a certain state at a certain time, nothing follows *logically* about its states at other times. For example, we must not choose a concept of 'state' that would allow as part of a description of the momentary state of the world, the clause, ' . . . and, at *t*, the world is such that Jones's left hand will be raised 10 seconds later than *t*.'

(ii) If there is some observable change in the way things are (e.g. if a white cloth becomes blue, a warm liquid cold, or if a man raises his hand), this change must entail some change in the state of the world. That is, our concept of 'state' must not be so theoretical, so divorced from what is observably true, that it be possible for the world to be in the *same* state at t_1 and t_2, although (for example) Jones's hand is raised at t_1 and not at t_2.

We may now define 'determinism'. We shall apply this term to the conjunction of these two theses:

(a) For every instant of time, there is a proposition that expresses the state of the world at that instant.
(b) If *A* and *B* are any propositions that express the state of the world at some instants, then the conjunction of *A* with the laws of physics entails *B*.

By a proposition that expresses the state of the world at time *t*, I mean a true proposition that asserts of some state that, at *t*, the world is in that state. The reason for our first restriction on the content of 'state' should now be evident: if it were not for this restriction, 'the state of the world' could be defined in such a way that determinism was trivially true. We could, without this restriction, build sufficient information about the past and future into each proposition that expresses the state of the world at an instant, that, for every pair of such propositions, each *by itself* entails the other. And in that case, determinism would be a mere tautology, a thesis applicable to every conceivable state of affairs.

This amounts to saying that the 'laws of physics' clause on our definition does some work: whether determinism is true depends on the character of the laws of physics. For example, if all physical laws were vague propositions like 'In every nuclear reaction, momentum is *pretty nearly* conserved', or 'Force is *approximately* equal to mass times acceleration', then determinism would be false.

This raises the question, What is a law of physics? First, a terminological point. I do not mean the application of this term to be restricted to those laws that belong to physics in the narrowest sense of the word. I am using 'law of physics' in the way some philosophers use 'law of nature'. Thus, a law about chemical valences is a law of physics in my sense, even if chemistry is not ultimately 'reducible' to physics. I will not use the term 'law of nature', because, conceivably, *psychological* laws, including laws (if such there be) about the voluntary behaviour of rational agents, might be included under this term.[1] Rational agents are, after all, in some sense part of 'Nature'. Since I do not think that everything I shall say about laws of physics is true of such 'voluntaristic laws', I should not want to use, instead of 'laws of physics', some term like 'laws of nature' that might legitimately be applied to voluntaristic laws. Thus, for all that is said in this paper, it may be that some version of determinism based on voluntaristic laws is compatible with free will.[2] Let us, then, understand by 'law of physics' a law of nature that is not about the voluntary behaviour of rational agents.

But this does not tell us what 'laws of nature' are. There would probably be fairly general agreement that a proposition cannot be a law of nature unless it is true and contingent, and that no proposition is a law of nature if it entails the existence of some concrete individual, such as Caesar or the earth. But the proposition that there is no solid gold sphere 20 feet in diameter (probably) satisfies these conditions, though it is certainly not a law of nature.

It is also claimed sometimes that a law of nature must 'support its counter-factuals'. There is no doubt something to this. Consider, however, the proposition, 'Dogs die if exposed to virus V'. The claim that this proposition supports its counter-factuals is, I think, equivalent to the claim that 'Every dog is such that if it were exposed to virus V, it would die' is *true*. Let us suppose that this latter proposition *is* true, the quantification being understood as being over all dogs, past, present, and future. Its truth, it seems to me, is quite consistent with its being the case that dog-breeders *could* (but will not) institute a programme of selective breeding that *would* produce a sort of dog that is immune to virus V. But if dog-breeders *could* do this, then clearly 'Dogs die if exposed to virus V' is not a law of nature, since in that case the truth of the corresponding universally quantified counter-factual depends upon an accidental circumstance: if dog-breeders were to institute a certain programme of selective breeding they are quite capable of instituting, then 'Every dog is such that if it were exposed to virus V, it would die' would be false. Thus a proposition may 'support its counter-factuals' and yet not be a law of nature.

I do not think that any philosopher has succeeded in giving a (non-trivial) set of individually necessary and jointly sufficient conditions for a proposition's being a law of nature or of physics. *I* certainly do not know of any such set. Fortunately, for the purposes of this paper we need not know how to analyse the concept 'law of physics'. I shall, in Part III, argue that certain statements containing 'law of physics' are analytic. But this can be done in the absence of a satisfactory analysis of 'law of physics'. In fact, it would hardly be possible for one to *provide* an analysis of some concept if one had no pre-analytic convictions about what statements involving that concept are analytic.

1. For example, 'If a human being is not made to feel ashamed of lying before his twelfth birthday, then he will lie whenever he believes it to be to his advantage.'
2. In 'The Compatibility of Free Will and Determinism', *Philosophical Review*, 1962, J. V. Canfield argues convincingly for a position that we might represent in this terminology as the thesis that a determinism based on voluntaristic laws could be compatible with free will.

For example, we do not have to have a satisfactory analysis of memory to know that 'No one can remember future events' is analytic. And if someone devised an analysis of memory according to which it was possible to remember future events, then, however attractive the analysis was in other respects, it would have to be rejected. The analyticity of 'No one can remember future events' is one of the *data* that anyone who investigates the concept of memory must take account of. Similarly, the claims I shall make on behalf of the concept of physical law seem to me to be basic and evident enough to be data that an analysis of this concept must take account of: any analysis on which these claims did not 'come out true' would be for that very reason defective.

II

It seems to be generally agreed that the concept of free will should be understood in terms of the *power* or *ability* of agents to act otherwise than they in fact do. To deny that men have free will is to assert that what a man *does* do and what he *can* do coincide. And almost all philosophers[3] agree that a necessary condition for holding an agent responsible for an act is believing that that agent *could have* refrained from performing that act.[4]

There is, however, considerably less agreement as to how 'can' (in the relevant sense) should be analysed. This is one of the most difficult questions in philosophy. It is certainly a question to which I do not know any non-trivial answer. But, as I said I should do in the case of 'law of physics', I shall make certain conceptual claims about 'can' (in the 'power' or 'ability' sense) in the absence of any analysis. Any suggested analysis of 'can' that does not support these claims will either be neutral with respect to them, in which case it will be incomplete, since it will not settle *all* conceptual questions about 'can', or it will be inconsistent with them, in which case the arguments I shall present in support of these claims will, in effect, be arguments that the analysis fails. In Part IV, I shall expand on this point as it applies to one particular analysis of 'can', the well-known 'conditional' analysis.

I shall say no more than this about the meaning of 'can'. I shall, however, introduce an idiom that will be useful in talking about ability and inability in complicated cases. Without this idiom, the statement of our argument would be rather unwieldy. We shall sometimes make claims about an agent's abilities by using sentences of the form:

S can render [could have rendered] . . . false.

---

3. See, however, Harry Frankfurt, 'Alternate Possibilities and Moral Responsibility', *Journal of Philosophy*, 1969.

4. Actually, the matter is rather more complicated than this, since we may hold a man responsible for an act we believe he could not have refrained from, provided we are prepared to hold him responsible for his being unable to refrain.

where ' . . . ' may be replaced by names of propositions.[5] Our ordinary claims about ability can easily be translated into this idiom. For example, we translate:

He could have reached Chicago by midnight.

as

He could have rendered the proposition that he did not reach Chicago by midnight false.

and, of course, the translation from the special idiom to the ordinary idiom is easy enough in such simple cases. If we were interested only in everyday ascriptions of ability, the new idiom would be useless. Using it, however, we may make ascriptions of ability that it would be very difficult to make in the ordinary idiom. Consider, for example, the last true proposition asserted by Plato. (Let us assume that this description is, as logicians say, 'proper'.) One claim that we might make about Aristotle is that he could have rendered this proposition false. Now, presumably, we have no way of discovering *what* proposition the last true proposition asserted by Plato was. Still, the claim about Aristotle would seem to be either true or false. To discover its truth-value, we should have to discover under what conditions the last true proposition asserted by Plato (i.e. that proposition having as one of its accidental properties, the property of being the last true proposition asserted by Plato) would be false, and then discover whether it was within Aristotle's power to produce these conditions. For example, suppose that if Aristotle had lived in Athens from the time of Plato's death till the time of his own death, then the last true proposition asserted by Plato (whatever it was) would be false. Then, if Aristotle could have lived (i.e. if he had it within his power to live) in Athens throughout this period, he could have rendered the last true proposition asserted by Plato false. On the other hand, if the last true proposition asserted by Plato is the proposition that the planets do not move in perfect circles, then Aristotle could not have rendered the last true proposition asserted by Plato false, since it was not within his power to produce any set of conditions sufficient for the falsity of this proposition.[6]

It is obvious that the proposition expressed by 'Aristotle could have rendered the last true proposition asserted by Plato false', is a proposition that we should be hard put to express without using the idiom of rendering propositions false, or, at least, without using some very similar idiom. We shall find this new idiom very useful in

---

5. In all the cases we shall consider, ' . . . ' will be replaced by names of *true* propositions. For the sake of logical completeness, we may stipulate that any sentence formed by replacing ' . . . ' with the name of a *false* proposition is trivially true. Thus, 'Kant could have rendered the proposition that $7 + 5 = 13$ false' is trivially true.

6. Richard Taylor has argued (most explicitly in 'Time, Truth and Ability' by 'Diodorus Cronus', *Analysis*, 1965) that every true proposition is such that, necessarily, no one is able to render it false. On my view, this thesis is mistaken, and Taylor's arguments for it can be shown to be unsound. I shall not, however, argue for this here. I shall argue in Part III that we are unable to render *certain sorts of* true proposition false, but my arguments will depend on special features of these sorts of proposition. I shall, for example, argue that no one can render false a law of physics; but I shall not argue that this is the case because laws of physics are *true*, but because of other features that they possess.

discussing the relation between free will (a thesis about abilities) and determinism (a thesis about certain propositions).

III

I shall now imagine a case in which a certain man, after due deliberation, refrained from performing a certain contemplated act. I shall then argue that, if determinism is true, then that man *could not have* performed that act. Because this argument will not depend on any features peculiar to our imagined case, the incompatibility of free will and determinism *in general* will be established, since, as will be evident, a parallel argument could easily be constructed for the case of any agent and any unperformed act.

Here is the case. Let us suppose there was once a judge who had only to raise his right hand at a certain time, T, to prevent the execution of a sentence of death upon a certain criminal, such a hand-raising being the sign, according to the conventions of the judge's country, of a granting of special clemency. Let us further suppose that the judge—call him 'J'—refrained from raising his hand at that time, and that this inaction resulted in the criminal's being put to death. We may also suppose that the judge was unbound, uninjured, and free from paralysis; that he decided not to raise his hand at T only after a period of calm, rational, and relevant deliberation; that he had not been subjected to any 'pressure' to decide one way or the other about the criminal's death; that he was not under the influence of drugs, hypnosis, or anything of that sort; and finally, that there was no element in his deliberations that would have been of any special interest to a student of abnormal psychology.

Now the argument. In this argument, which I shall refer to as the 'main argument', I shall use 'T_0' to denote some instant of time earlier than J's birth, 'P_0' to denote the proposition that expresses the state of the world at T_0, 'P' to denote the proposition that expresses the state of the world at T, and 'L' to denote the conjunction into a single proposition of all laws of physics. (I shall regard L itself as a law of physics, on the reasonable assumption that if A and B are laws of physics, then the conjunction of A and B is a law of physics.) The argument consists of seven statements, the seventh of which follows from the first six:

(1) If determinism is true, then the conjunction of P_0 and L entails P.

(2) If J had raised his hand at T, then P would be false.

(3) If (2) is true, then if J could have raised his hand at T, J could have rendered P false.[7]

(4) If J could have rendered P false, and if the conjunction of P_0 and L entails P, then J could have rendered the conjunction of P_0 and L false.

---

7. 'J could have raised his hand at T' is ambiguous. It might mean either (roughly) 'J possessed, at T, the ability to raise his hand', or 'J possessed the ability to bring it about that his hand rose at T'. If J was unparalysed at T but paralysed at all earlier instants, then the latter of these would be false, though the former might be true. I mean 'J could have raised his hand at T' in the latter sense.

    (5) If J could have rendered the conjunction of P_0 and L false, then J could have rendered L false.

    (6) J could not have rendered L false.

∴ (7) If determinism is true, J could not have raised his hand at T.

That (7) follows from (1) through (6) can easily be established by truthfunctional logic. Note that all conditionals in the argument except for (2) are truth-functional. For purposes of establishing the *validity* of this argument, (2) may be regarded as a simple sentence. Let us examine the premises individually.

    (1) This premiss follows from the definition of determinism.

    (2) If J had raised his hand at T, then the world would have been in a different state at T from the state it was in fact in. (See our second condition on the content of 'the state of the world'.) And, therefore, if J had raised his hand at T, some contrary of P would express the state of the world at T. It should be emphasized that 'P' does not *mean* 'the proposition that expresses the state of the world at T'. Rather, 'P' *denotes* the proposition that expresses the state of the world at T. In Kripke's terminology, 'P' is being used as a *rigid designator*, while 'the proposition that expresses the state of the world at T' is perforce non-rigid.[8]

    (3) Since J's hand being raised at T would have been sufficient for the falsity of P, there is, if J could have raised his hand, at least one condition sufficient for the falsity of P that J could have produced.

    (4) This premiss may be defended as an instance of the following general principle:

    If S can render R false, and if Q entails R, then S can render Q false.

This principle seems to be analytic. For if Q entails R, then the denial of R entails the denial of Q. Thus, any condition sufficient for the falsity of R is also sufficient for the falsity of Q. Therefore, if there is some condition that S can produce that is sufficient for the falsity of R, there is some condition (that same condition) that S can produce that is sufficient for the falsity of Q.

    (5) This premiss may be defended as an instance of the following general principle, which I take to be analytic:

    If Q is a true proposition that concerns only states of affairs that obtained before S's birth, and if S can render the conjunction of Q and R false, then S can render R false.

Consider, for example, the propositions expressed by

    The Spanish Armada was defeated in 1588.

and

    Peter van Inwagen never visits Alaska.

---

8. See Saul Kripke, 'Identity and Necessity', in *Identity and Individuation*, ed. Milton K. Munitz (New York, 1971).

The conjunction of these two propositions is quite possibly true. At any rate, let us assume it is true. Given that it is true, it seems quite clear that I can render it false if and only if I can visit Alaska. If, for some reason, it is not within my power ever to visit Alaska, then I *cannot* render it false. This is a quite trivial assertion, and the general principle (above) of which it is an instance is hardly less trivial. And it seems incontestable that premiss (5) is also an instance of this principle.

(6) I shall argue that if anyone *can* (i.e. has it within his power to) render some proposition false, then that proposition is not a law of physics. This I regard as a conceptual truth, one of the data that must be taken account of by anyone who wishes to give an analysis of 'can' or 'law'. It is this connection between these two concepts, I think, that is at the root of the incompatibility of free will and determinism.

In order to see this connection, let us suppose that both of the following are true:

(A) Nothing ever travels faster than light.
(B) Jones, a physicist, can construct a particle accelerator that would cause protons to travel at twice the speed of light.

It follows from (A) that Jones will never exercise the power that (B) ascribes to him. But whatever the reason for Jones's failure to act on his ability to render (A) false, it is clear that (A) and (B) are consistent, and that (B) entails that (A) is not a law of physics. For given that (B) is true, then Jones is able to conduct an experiment that would falsify (A); and surely it is a feature of any proposition that is a physical law that no one *can* conduct an experiment that would show it to be false.

Of course, most propositions that look initially as if they might be physical laws, but which are later decided to be non-laws, are rejected because of experiments that are actually performed. But this is not essential. In order to see this, let us elaborate the example we have been considering. Let us suppose that Jones's ability to render (A) false derives from the fact that he has discovered a mathematically rigorous proof that under certain conditions *C*, realizable in the laboratory, protons would travel faster than light. And let us suppose that this proof proceeds from premises so obviously true that all competent physicists accept his conclusion without reservation. But suppose that conditions *C* never obtain in nature, and that actually to produce them in the laboratory would require such an expenditure of resources that Jones and his colleagues decide not to carry out the experiment. And suppose that, as a result, conditions *C* are never realized and nothing ever travels faster than light. It is evident that if all this were true, we should have to say that (A), while *true*, is not a law of physics. (Though, of course, 'Nothing ever travels faster than light except under conditions *C*' might be a law.)

The laboratories and resources that figure in this example are not essential to its point. If Jones *could* render some proposition false by performing *any* act he does not in fact perform, even such a simple act as raising his hand at a certain time, this would be sufficient to show that that proposition is not a law of physics.

This completes my defence of the premises of the main argument. In the final part of this paper, I shall examine objections to this argument suggested by the attempts of various philosophers to establish the compatibility of free will and determinism.

IV

The most useful thing a philosopher who thinks that the main argument does not prove its point could do would be to try to show that some premiss of the argument is false or incoherent, or that the argument begs some important question, or contains a term that is used equivocally, or something of that sort. In short, he should get down to cases. Some philosophers, however, might continue to hold that free will and determinism, in the sense of Part I, are compatible, but decline to try to point out a mistake in the argument. For (such a philosopher might argue) we have, in everyday life, *criteria* for determining whether an agent could have acted otherwise than he did, and these criteria determine the *meaning* of 'could have acted otherwise'; to know the meaning of this phrase is simply to know how to apply these criteria. And since these criteria make no mention of determinism, anyone who thinks that free will and determinism are incompatible is simply confused.[9]

As regards the argument of Part III (this philosopher might continue), this argument is very complex, and this complexity must simply serve to hide some error, since its conclusion is absurd. We must treat this argument like the infamous 'proof' that zero equals one: It may be amusing and even instructive to find the hidden error (if one has nothing better to do), but it would be a waste of time to take seriously any suggestion that it is sound.

Now I suppose we do have 'criteria', in some sense of this over-used word, for the application of 'could have done otherwise', and I will grant that knowing the criteria for the application of a term can plausibly be identified with knowing its meaning. Whether the criteria for applying 'could have done otherwise' can (as at least one philosopher has supposed[10]) be taught by simple ostension is another question. However this may be, the 'criteria' argument is simply invalid. To see this, let us examine a simpler argument that makes the same mistake.

Consider the doctrine of 'predestinarianism'. Predestinarians hold (i) that if an act is foreseen it is not free, and (ii) that all acts are foreseen by God. (I do not claim that anyone has ever held this doctrine in precisely this form.) Now suppose we were to argue that predestinarianism must be compatible with free will, since our criteria for applying 'could have done otherwise' make no reference to predestinarianism. Obviously this argument would be invalid, since predestinarianism is incompatible with free will. And the only difference I can see between this argument and the 'criteria' argument

---

9. Cf. Antony Flew, 'Divine Omniscience and Human Freedom', *New Essays in Philosophical Theology*, ed. Antony Flew and Alasdair MacIntyre (London: SCM Press, 1955), 149–51 in particular.
10. Flew, loc cit.

for the compatibility of free will and determinism is that predestinarianism, unlike determinism, is *obviously* incompatible with free will. But, of course, theses may be incompatible with one another even if this incompatibility is not obvious. Even if determinism cannot, like predestinarianism, be seen to be incompatible with free will on the basis of a simple formal inference, there is, nonetheless, a conceptual connection between the two theses (as we showed in our defence of premiss (6)). The argument of Part III is intended to draw out the implications of this connection. There may well be a mistake in the argument, but I do not see why anyone should think that the very idea of such an argument is misconceived.

It has also been argued that free will *entails* determinism, and, being itself a consistent thesis, is *a fortiori* compatible with determinism. The argument, put briefly, is this. To say of some person on some particular occasion that he acted freely is obviously to say at least that *he* acted on that occasion. Suppose, however, that we see someone's arm rise and it later turns out that there was *no cause whatsoever* for his arm's rising. Surely we should have to say that *he* did not really raise his arm at all. Rather, his arm's rising was a mere chance happening, that, like a muscular twitch, had nothing to do with *him*, beyond the fact that it happened to involve a part of his body. A necessary condition for this person's really having raised his hand is that *he* caused his hand to rise. And surely '*he* caused' means '*his* character, desires, and beliefs caused'.[11]

I think that there is a great deal of confusion in this argument, but to expose this confusion would require a lengthy discussion of many fine points in the theory of agency. I shall only point out that if this argument is supposed to refute the conclusion of Part III, it is an *ignoratio elenchi*. For I did not conclude that free will is incompatible with the thesis that every event has a cause, but rather with determinism as defined in Part I. And the denial of this thesis does not entail that there are uncaused events.

Of course, one might try to construct a similar but relevant argument for the falsity of the conclusion of Part III. But, so far as I can see, the plausibility of such an argument would depend on the plausibility of supposing that if the present movements of one's body are not completely determined by physical law and the state of the world before one's birth, then these present movements are not one's own doing, but, rather, mere random happenings. And I do not see the least shred of plausibility in this supposition.

I shall finally consider the popular 'conditional analysis' argument for the compatibility of free will and determinism. According to the advocates of this argument—let us call them 'conditionalists'—what statements of the form:

(8) *S* could have done *X*

11. Cf. R. E. Hobart, 'Free Will as Involving Determination and Inconceivable Without It', *Mind*, 1934; A. J. Ayer, 'Freedom and Necessity', in his collected *Philosophical Essays* (New York, 1954); P. H. Nowell-Smith, 'Freewill and Moral Responsibility', *Mind*, 1948; J. J. C. Smart, 'Free Will, Praise, and Blame', *Mind*, 1961.

mean is:

   (9) If *S* had chosen to do *X*, *S* would have done *X*.[12]

For example, 'Smith could have saved the drowning child' means, 'If Smith had chosen to save the drowning child, Smith would have saved the drowning child.' Thus, even if determinism is true (the conditionalists argue), it is possible that Smith did not save but *could have* saved the drowning child, since the conjunction of determinism with 'Smith did not save the child' does not entail the falsity of 'If Smith had chosen to save the child, Smith would have saved the child'.

   Most of the controversy about this argument centres around the question whether (9) is a correct analysis of (8). I shall not enter into the debate about whether this analysis is correct. I shall instead question the relevance of this debate to the argument of Part III. For it is not clear that the main argument would be unsound if the conditional analysis *were* correct. Clearly the argument is *valid* whether or not (8) and (9) mean the same. But suppose the premises of the main argument were rewritten so that every clause they contain that is of form (8) is replaced by the corresponding clause of form (9)—should we then see that any of these premises is false? Let us try this with premiss (6), which seems, prima facie, to be the crucial premiss of the argument. We have:

   (6a) It is not the case that if *J* had chosen to render *L* false, *J* would have rendered
         L false.

Now (6a) certainly seems true: If someone chooses to render false some proposition *R*, and if *R* is a law of physics, then surely he will fail. This little argument for (6a) *seems* obviously sound. But we cannot overlook the possibility that someone might discover a mistake in it and, perhaps, even construct a convincing argument that (6a) is false. Let us, therefore, assume for the sake of argument that (6a) is demonstrably false. What would this show? I submit that it would show that (6a) does not mean the same as (6), since (6) is, as I have argued, *true*.

   The same dilemma confronts the conditionalist if he attempts to show, on the basis of the conditional analysis, that any of the other premises of the argument is false. Consider the argument got by replacing every clause of form (8) in the main argument with the corresponding clause of form (9). If all the premises of this new argument are true, the main argument is, according to the conditionalist's own theory, sound. If, on the other hand, any of the premises of the new argument is false, then (*I* would maintain) this premiss is a counter-example to the conditional analysis. I should not be begging the question against the conditionalist in maintaining this, since I have given arguments for the truth of each of the premisses

12. Many other verbs besides 'choose' figure in various philosophers' conditional analyses of ability: e.g. 'wish', 'want', 'will', 'try', 'set oneself'. Much of the important contemporary work on this analysis, by G. E. Moore, P. H. Nowell-Smith, J. L. Austin, Keith Lehrer, Roderick Chisholm, and others, is collected in *The Nature of Human Action*, ed. Myles Brand (Glenview Ill., 1970). See also 'Fatalism and Determinism', by Wilfrid Sellars, in *Freedom and Determinism*, ed. Keith Lehrer (New York, 1966), 141–74.

of the main argument, and nowhere in these arguments do I assume that the conditional analysis is wrong.

Of course, any or all of my arguments in defence of the premises of the main argument may contain some mistake. But unless the conditionalist could point to some such mistake, he would not accomplish much by showing that some statement he *claimed* was equivalent to one of its premises was false.[13]

---

13. For an argument in some respects similar to what I have called the 'main argument', see Carl Ginet's admirable article, 'Might We Have No Choice?' in Lehrer, 87–104. Another argument similar to the main argument, which is (formally) much simpler than the main argument, but which is stated in language very different from that of traditional statements of the free-will problem, can be found in my 'A Formal Approach to the Problem of Free Will and Determinism', *Theoria*, 1974.

Chapter 53

Selection from *Freedom from Physics: Quantum Mechanics and Free Will*

Barry Loewer

> If . . . the atoms of our bodies follow physical laws as immutable as the motion of the planets, why try? What difference can it make how great the effort if our actions are already predetermined by mechanical laws. . . .
>
> —Arthur Holly Compton,
> *The Freedom of Man*

Introduction

Robert Nozick describes the experience of making a free choice thus:

Making choices feels like this. There are various reasons for and against doing each of the alternative actions or courses of actions one is considering, and it seems and feels as if one could do any one of them. In considering the reasons, mulling them over, one arrives at a view of which reasons are more important, which ones have more weight. . . . What picture emerges if we take seriously the feeling that the (precise) weights to be assigned to reasons is "up to us"? It is causally undetermined (by prior factors) which of the acts we will decide to do.[1]

I will call a choice that *is*, not merely *feels*, as Nozick describes 'libertarian free' and philosophers who believe that our choices are sometimes libertarian free 'libertarians.'

We have cut section 2 of this paper, which gives a summary of two indeterministic interpretations of quantum mechanics: the orthodox or Copenhagen interpretation, and the non-orthodox GRWP interpretation (named after its founders Ghiradhi, Rimini, Weber, and Pearle). The third interpretation summarized is Bohm's deterministic 'hidden variable' interpretation. Loewer argues in this section that 'since Bohmian mechanics is as well supported by empirical evidence as indeterministic quantum theories we currently have as much reason, at least as far as physics is concerned, to believe that our world is one at which determinism is true'; and that 'if quantum theory is to provide any support at all for libertarian freedom it will be some indeterministic version like the orthodox account or GRWP'. It is not essential to understand the details of these interpretations in order to grasp the philosophical points made in the rest of Loewer's paper.

1. Robert Nozick, *Philosophical Explanations* (Cambridge, Mass.: Harvard University Press, 1981), 294.

Barry Loewer, 'Freedom from Physics: Quantum Mechanics and Free Will', from *Philosophical Topics*, 24 (1998), reprinted with permission of Philosophical Topics and the author.

On the libertarian conception of freedom, a choice is free only if, as Nozick says, the agent's choice or the weight she assigns to her reasons is *up to her*. The phrase 'up to the agent' is frequently invoked by libertarians to express the idea that the choice *originates* in the will of the agent.[2] While factors prior to making the choice (including the agent's prior mental states) may limit possibilities or incline the agent one way or another, they don't causally determine which option she chooses. The choice originates in her. But exactly what does it mean for a decision to *originate* in the will of the agent? Robert Kane explains what it is for a decision to originate in an agent's will in terms of her being *ultimately responsible* for her decision and explains this notion thus:

(UR) An agent is ultimately responsible for E's occurring only if (R) the agent is personally responsible for E's occurring in a sense which entails that something the agent voluntarily did or omitted, and for which the agent could have done otherwise, either was, or causally contributed to, E's occurrence and made a difference to whether or not E occurred; and (U) for every X and Y if the agent is personally responsible for X and if Y is an *arche* (or sufficient ground or cause or explanation) for X then the agent must be personally responsible for Y.[3]

If a decision satisfies (UR), then there is some part of the causal history of the decision that involves the agent's making a choice when she could have chosen otherwise and there is no sufficient cause of that choice. (UR) doesn't require the agent to be responsible for every part of the cause of her choice. It is enough if there is some part of the cause that cannot be accounted for by factors external to the agent. I think that (UR) goes some distance toward clarifying libertarian freedom. Whether it provides a sufficient condition is a matter I will return to later.

Are there any choices (decisions or actions) that satisfy (UR)? Libertarians all agree that if there are libertarian free choices, then *determinism* is false. Determinism is the doctrine that the laws of nature are such that two possible worlds that agree on their states at time *t* and on the laws of nature agree on their states at all times. It is obvious that the existence of choices satisfying (UR) is incompatible with determinism. The reason is that if determinism is true, then for any choice *X* by an agent *A* there is a *Y* such that *Y* is a sufficient cause of *X* but *A* is not responsible for *Y*. For example, *Y* can be the conjunction of the deterministic laws and the state of the universe at a time prior to *A*'s birth.

Libertarian conceptions of freedom contrast with *compatibilist* conceptions. Compatibilists agree with libertarians that for a choice to be free it must be up to the agent, but they understand this notion quite differently. According to compatibilists,

2. According to Nozick, libertarian free choices possess 'originative value.' He says:

A being with originative value, one whose acts have originative value, can make a difference. Due to his actions, different value consequences occur in the world than otherwise would; these were not in the cards already. . . . Puppets and marionettes lack originative value (except in fairy stories), and the way we resemble them, if causal determinism is true, is that we lack originative value too (Nozick, op. cit., 312).

3. Robert Kane, *The Significance of Free Will* (New York: Oxford University Press, 1996), p. 35.

a choice is up to an agent if it is causally and counterfactually sensitive to the agent's reasons—her beliefs, preferences, plans, etc.—in an appropriate fashion. Sophisticated compatibilist accounts further require that these reasons are themselves causally and counterfactually sensitive in an appropriate way to prior and higher-order reasons and so forth.[4] A precise characterization of 'appropriate' is elusive, but it involves the implementation of rational relations among the agent's beliefs, preferences, choices, etc. However 'appropriate' is spelled out, compatibilists think that the existence of free choice is compatible with those choices and the reasons for them being covered by deterministic laws; that is, it is compatible with there not being more than one choice that is genuinely possible prior to making the choice. Obviously, a decision that is *merely* compatibilist free may fail to satisfy Kane's (UR) condition, since it may have a sufficient cause that is entirely outside of the agent.

As long as it was thought that the fundamental physical laws of nature supported determinism—as Newtonian theory was generally thought to—it appeared that physics excluded libertarian freedom.[5] For philosophers who, like Kant, thought that morality and even rationality require libertarian freedom, this consequence is absurd and paradoxical. On the one hand, scientific rationality seemed to lead to determinism and, on the other hand, the exercise of that rationality apparently requires libertarian freedom. But with the overthrow of Newtonian physics and its replacement with quantum theory, some physicists and philosophers have thought that the physics of our world may be compatible with libertarian freedom after all.[6] Among the claims that have been made about quantum theory are that its laws are ineliminably indeterministic, that properties sometimes fail to possess determinate values, that physical laws are ineliminably incomplete, and that physics cannot be formulated without reference to consciousness. All this has given hope to proponents of libertarian freedom. If physical laws require reference to consciousness for their formulation, it has been thought, they cannot exclude the possibility of freedom.

The primary aim of this paper is to investigate the claim that quantum theory is hospitable to libertarian freedom. . . .

4. A classic development of a compatibilist account of freedom is Harry Frankfurt, 'Freedom of the Will and the Concept of a Person,' *The Journal of Philosophy* 18 (1971): 5–20. Frankfurt emphasizes the importance of second-order preferences directing first-order preferences. For accounts of libertarian and compatibilist conceptions of control, see also John Martin Fischer, *The Metaphysics of Free Will* (Cambridge, Mass.: Blackwell, 1994).

5. Dualism might be thought to allow for libertarian freedom even if determinism holds, say, in the physical world. But although it might allow for freedom in the realm of the mental, it seems like a freedom hardly worth having, since the mental would be epiphenomenal with respect to the physical.

6. This hope is expressed in Arthur H. Compton, *The Freedom of Man* (New Haven, Conn.: Yale University Press, 1935); Karl Popper, *Objective Knowledge* (Oxford: Clarendon Press, 1972); Peter van Inwagen, *An Essay on Free Will* (Oxford: Clarendon Press, 1983); Robert Kane, *Free Will and Values* (Albany, N.Y.: SUNY Press, 1985); and 'Two Kinds of Incompatibilism,' in Timothy O'Connor, ed., *Agents, Causes, and Events* (Oxford: Oxford University Press, 1995); and Nozick, op. cit.

Indeterminism and freedom

It has often been claimed (especially by compatibilists) that it is actually indeterminism (and not determinism) that is incompatible with freedom. For example, Ayer says:

Either it is an accident that I chose to act as I do or it is not. If it is an accident, then it is merely a matter of chance that I did not choose otherwise; and if it is merely a matter of chance that I did not choose otherwise, it is surely irrational to hold me morally responsible for choosing as I did. But if it is not an accident that I choose to do one thing rather than another, then presumably there is some causal explanation of my choice; and in that case we are led back to determinism.[7]

Ayer seems to identify choices that are not determined by prior conditions and laws with 'accidental' choices and these latter choices with ones that are 'merely a matter of chance.' He claims that choices that are merely a matter of chance are not free, at least not in the sense relevant to moral responsibility. If Ayer were right, then libertarian freedom would require free choices both to be determined and not determined (given the laws) by prior events. Quantum mechanics could not rescue it. But Ayer's argument is too quick. First of all, an event's being nonaccidental and its being determined by prior events are quite different things. Otherwise, were the laws to be deterministic, there would be no accidents, and were the fundamental laws to be probabilistic, then every event with an objective chance less than 1 would be an accident. Second, Ayer seems to assume that every event must either be determined by prior events or have some chance different from 1 of occurring. But this is not obviously so. Recent philosophical accounts of laws and probabilities allow for the possibility of events that are not covered by any laws and that don't have probabilities.[8] Third, and most importantly, it is not obvious that if a choice is the outcome of a probabilistic process, it is irrational to hold a person morally responsible for it. As we will see, libertarians have developed models on which deliberation is an indeterministic quantum mechanical process. They claim that on these models choices may be caused by an agent's reasons in a way that underwrites their being up to the agent. If they are correct, then it is rational to hold a person morally responsible for such choices. So we need to examine indeterministic quantum mechanical models of libertarian freedom within quantum theory to see whether they provide adequate accounts of libertarian freedom.

7. A. J. Ayer, 'Freedom and Necessity,' in his *Philosophical Essays* (New York: St Martin's Press, 1954), p. 275.
8. The two most important recent accounts are to be found in David Lewis, *Philosophical Papers* (New York: Oxford University Press, 1983) and David M. Armstrong, *What Is a Law of Nature?* (Cambridge: Cambridge University Press, 1983). Lewis advocates a *Humean* account of laws and probabilities according to which the laws are the contingent generalizations, including probabilistic generalizations, entailed by the theory that best combines informativeness, fit, and simplicity. Armstrong's account is *non-Humean*, specifying that laws, including probabilistic laws, are facts composed of relations of contingent necessity and probilification between universals. Both these accounts allow for the possibility of events that are not covered by any laws and that fail to have objective probabilities.

The idea that quantum theory makes room for or supports libertarian freedom goes back to the origins of the theory.[9] Before discussing suggestions about how that might be accomplished, I want to address the frequently made claim that quantum mechanics is irrelevant to discussions of free will, since quantum indeterminacy only involves microevents, while human choices and actions are a macroscopic phenomena.[10] This claim is almost certainly mistaken. If an indeterministic version of quantum theory like GRWP is true, then it is very likely that many macroevents—including mental events and actions—evolve indeterministically. Quantum theory assigns probabilities to macroscopic events (assuming that these are constituted by or supervene on microscopic events) in all sorts of usual situations. For example, if a measurement of the x-spin of a y-spin particle is recorded in the position of a macroscopic pointer, then the post-measurement position of that pointer is assigned an objective probability by quantum theory. If GRWP is true, then all sorts of typical measurement-like interactions between macroscopic and microscopic systems (i.e., interactions in which macroscopic properties become correlated with microscopic properties) evolve indeterministically. Since ordinary chemical reactions involve the breaking and forming of chemical bonds and such interactions are indeterministic according to quantum theory, those interactions involving small numbers of molecules will also be indeterministic. These indeterminacies may with high probability cancel out at the macroscopic level if the relevant macroscopic property is an average of microscopic qualities. But that need not be the case. The microscopic indeterminacy may be amplified at the macroscopic level as it is in measurements. Of course, the quantum mechanical probabilities of choices and actions (and other mental events) are an empirical matter and are not known. But if GRWP is true, then it is very plausible that these probabilities are never exactly 1 or 0 and sometimes deviate appreciably from these extremes.

I now want to discuss some quantum mechanical models of libertarian freedom. Nozick makes the following suggestion:

According to the currently orthodox quantum mechanical theory of measurement, as specified by John von Neumann, a quantum mechanical system is in a superposition

---

9. Compton, op. cit., was an early and enthusiastic advocate of the idea that quantum theory permitted the existence of freedom of the will.
10. Ted Honderich seems to follow this line of reasoning. He says that:

if . . . micro-indeterminism does produce chance events in the ordinary world, what about the evidence for that? Why have we not noticed one of these chance events? Why has a spoon not levitated before now, when the random lurches of little events within it all happened to combine in the right way? The common answer made to this is that any levitations, for several reasons, are so totally improbable as in some sense or other to be out of the question. It does not quite satisfy me. If it *is* true that there is indeterminism in the real world, and finding it would get someone a Nobel Prize, I would have expected a little unquestioned progress by now. *Some* kind of unquestioned progress. (Ted Honderich, *How Free Are You?* [Oxford: Oxford University Press, 1993], 66).

Honderich is looking in the wrong place (e.g., for spoons to levitate) for indeterministic macroscopic events. Every macroscopic measurement of a quantum mechanical observable on a system that is not in an eigenstate of that observable is indeterministic; e.g., the noise made by a Geiger counter detecting alpha particles.

of states, a probability mixture of states, which changes continuously in accordance with the quantum mechanical equations of motion, and which changes discontinuously via a measurement or observation. Such a measurement "collapses the wave packet," reducing the superposition to a particular state; which state the superposition will reduce to is not predictable. Analogously, a person before decision . . . is in a superposition of (precise) weights, perhaps within certain limits, or a mixed state (which need not be a superposition with fixed probabilities). The process of decision reduces the superposition to one state . . . but it is not predictable or determined to which state of the weights the decision (analogous to a measurement) will reduce the superposition.[11]

Nozick says that he is not literally proposing that the process of making a decision is a quantum mechanical measurement but that he intends the analogy to show that a certain model of choosing an action is coherent.[12] Despite his disclaimer it is worthwhile to examine the model, since if quantum theory is to provide space for libertarian freedom, there must be some quantum mechanical account of acting freely. On Nozick's model, prior to making the decision the agent is in a superposition of states corresponding to different evaluations of reasons that favor different actions. Making the decision involves measuring this observable. The measurement collapses this state into one of its components, i.e., a state in which the weight of reasons favors a particular action over its alternatives.[13]

There is a problem about the particular way Nozick employs quantum theory in his account that arises from the nature of quantum mechanical superpositions. Prior to coming to a decision we expect that a person will report that she has not yet made up her mind, that is, that she hasn't yet decided what action her reasons favor. But if an agent is in a superposition of states, each corresponding to having made up her mind but in different ways, it follows from the linearity of the Schrödinger equation that in this state she has definitely made up her mind.[14] If she sincerely reports the state of her mind, then in the state Nozick describes, she will report that she has made up her mind. But of course prior to deciding on a particular action a person has not

---

11. Nozick, op. cit., 298.
12. Popper, op. cit.; David Wiggins, 'Toward a Reasonable Libertarianism,' in Ted Honderich, ed., *Essays on Freedom of Action* (London: Routledge and Kegan Paul, 1973); Kane, *Free Will and Values,* 'Two Kinds of Incompatibilism,' and *The Significance of Free Will*; J. R. Lucas, *The Freedom of the Will* (Oxford: Clarendon Press, 1970); and practically every other contemporary supporter of libertarian freedom appeal to quantum mechanics to argue that libertarian freedom is possible.
13. On the GRWP theory, the superposition will be stable only if it involves an isolated system with very few degrees of freedom or is close to an eigenstate of position. The latter is more plausible since weighing reasons likely corresponds to a physical process involving many degrees of freedom. If so, then the observable being measured (the observable corresponding to the superposition of reasons) must involve some property other than position; e.g., the spins of many particles.
14. The state c|decided to do A> $+ c^*$|decided to do B> is an eigenstate of the operator corresponding to the property of having made up one's mind. For a discussion of this elementary but still, to some, surprising result, see David Albert, *Quantum Mechanics and Experience* (Cambridge, Mass.: Harvard University Press 1992) and David Albert and Barry Loewer, 'Tails of Schrödinger's Cat' in J. S. Bell (ed.), *The Speakable and the Unspeakable in Quantum Mechanics* (Cambridge: Cambridge University Press 1987).

made up her mind and, if she is sincere, won't report that she has. This is a bit surprising since one might think that a superposition of mental states would be experienced as a feeling of uncertainty. But that is not so.

This particular defect in the proposal is not difficult to repair. Robert Kane has suggested a slightly different account of how quantum mechanics might ground libertarian free will that avoids the problem.[15] Kane's picture of the process of making a free choice is similar to Nozick's. But he adds that the process of deliberation involves making an *effort of will*. This is where Kane locates quantum indeterminateness. He says:

Let us suppose that the effort of will (to resist temptation) in the moral and prudential choice situations . . . is (an) *indeterminate* (event or process), thereby making the choice that terminates it *undetermined*.[16]

On this account, at the outset of deliberation the agent is in a superposition of states corresponding to initiating various degrees of efforts of will. The deliberation process is the evolution of this state, which at a certain point collapses into a state corresponding to exerting a specific effort of will. And that state leads to making a particular choice. Presumably, the greater effort of will is required for the action that is supported by moral or prudential reasons than the action that is supported by current whims. In any case, Kane's account doesn't suffer from the defect in Nozick's, since prior to the collapse the agent hasn't made a decision and will so report and after the collapse the agent has made a decision and will so report.

Kane's model of free will appears to satisfy some of the features that libertarians think free will possesses. Prior to making a choice there are various alternative choices open to the agent and making the choice involves mental processes internal to the agent. Conditions outside of or external to the agent do not *determine* which choice she makes. Further, the choice she makes will be rational by her own lights, since she will have reasons for it.

On Kane's account, do free choices satisfy his condition (UR)? Recall that (UR) requires that an agent's choice X is libertarian free only if each Y that is a *sufficient* cause of X is such that the agent is responsible for Y. Since the choices that are free on Kane's model are ones that don't have *any* causally sufficient conditions it is clear that they satisfy (UR). And if the fundamental laws are indeterministic, choices may very well not have any causally sufficient conditions. In spite of this

---

15. See Kane, *Free Will and Values*; 'Two Kinds of Incompatibilism'; and *The Significance of Free Will*. As far as I know, Kane was unaware of this problem with Nozick's account. His own account has a similar, although not as troubling, consequence. Even though prior to the collapse the agent does not exert a particular degree of effort—the state is a superposition of various degrees—she will report that she is exerting a specific degree of effort. But this doesn't seem to be a defect.

16. Kane, *The Significance of Free Will*, 128. Kane makes a distinction between what he calls 'Epicurean worlds' in which the laws are indeterministic but properties are never indeterminate (that is, in which there are no superpositions) and quantum mechanical worlds in which properties can be indeterminate. He thinks that the latter is required for libertarian free will, but it is not clear to me exactly why this should be so.

and the other appealing features of Kane's account, I don't think that a libertarian should be satisfied with it. It will be tricky to argue for this claim, since it is open to a libertarian to claim that choices that fit Kane's model are exactly what he *means* by a choice being free. However, given a widely accepted principle concerning chancy causation, it will follow by reasoning parallel to the reasoning that the libertarian uses to show that determinism is incompatible with freedom that a complete indeterministic theory (like GRWP) is incompatible with freedom.

To set the stage for my argument we will need to discuss a few points concerning objective physical probabilities and causation. I will suppose that the laws of physics are complete and that they assign objective probabilities to every event. For example, in GRWP, the quantum state $|\$_t>$ of the universe at time t and the dynamical law both determine objective probabilities for every possible evolution of $|\$_t>$. I'll call the claim that the laws are like this 'objective indeterminism.' On objective indeterminism, the objective probability of an event is indexed to two times: the time at which the event occurs and a second time at which the objective probability is evaluated given the history up to that time.[17] How this works will be clearer with an example.[18] Suppose A enters a labyrinth at time t_0 planning to choose whether to turn left or right when she comes to a branch point by flipping a coin (the outcome of which I assume to be genuinely chancy). Suppose also that the possible outcomes of each flip—heads or tails—each have objective chances of 1/2. Call the event of A's reaching the center of the labyrinth at t_n $C(t_n)$. Suppose that at t_0 the chance of A's reaching the center at t_n is .7, i.e., $Pt_0(C(t_n)) = .7$. At the first branch point, A turns left, away from the most direct path to the center. Then at t_1 (the time she turns left) the chance of $C(t_n)$ drops to .4. At t_2, A turns right and thus raises her chances of reaching the center by t_n to .6. Had A turned left at that point, the chance of $C(t_n)$ would have dropped to .2. As A advances through the labyrinth, the chance of her reaching the center by t_n will generally vary until finally at t_n it is either 1 or 0.

Suppose that A does reach the center of the labyrinth by t_n. It is reasonable to say that among the causes of $C(t_n)$ is A's turning right at t_2, i.e., $R(t_2)$. This is a case of *probabilistic causation*. It is probabilistic in that at t_2 the state of the world doesn't determine whether or not A reaches the center by t_n. It is causation in that it raises the chance of A's reaching the center by t_n. That event would have been less likely had A turned to the left. There are various accounts of probabilistic causation that have been proposed. According to Lewis, c probabilistically causes e if c and e are distinct events that occur and c's occurrence raises the chance of e's occurrence.[19] Lewis's account and all other accounts I know of conform to the following principle:

(P) If e is a chancy event (i.e., at times prior to its occurrence there are objective chances of its occurring or not occurring), then if c causes e, it does so by altering the chance of e (at the

---

17. By the chance at t of an event occurring at t^* I mean the chance of a particular type of event occurring at that time. If the event does occur, then it can be named and we can talk about the chance at various times of that very event.

18. This example is adapted from Lewis, *op. cit.*

19. Lewis explains c's occurrence raising the chance of e's occurrence as follows: If t is the time immediately after c's occurrence, then (i) $P_t(Oe) = x$, (ii) $-O(c) > P_t((Oe)) = y$, and x is greater than y.

time immediately after *c*) or by altering the chance of some event in a causal chain leading from *c* to *e*.

(P) expresses the idea that the only way to causally influence the occurrence of a chancy event is by influencing its chance. It seems to me to be obviously true. I will use (P) to argue that if every event (including choices) possesses an objective chance at all times (as on GRWP), then no choice is genuinely libertarian free. Put slightly differently, my argument is that anyone who thinks that determinism is incompatible with free will should also think that objective indeterminism is also incompatible with free will. If this is correct, then accounts of free choice, like Nozick's and Kane's, that attempt to characterize free choice in terms of objective probabilities are not *genuine* libertarian accounts and indeterministic quantum theories like GRWP are not compatible with libertarian freedom.

Kane's condition (UR) is intended to capture the idea that a genuinely free choice originates in the will of the agent in such a way that it is *the agent* and not anything else that is ultimately responsible for the choice. Clearly, it does express the idea that nothing external to the agent is completely responsible (i.e., is a sufficient cause) for the choice. But libertarians also think that the agent must be responsible for her choice. Now whatever this amounts to, it is clear that the agent thinks that such responsibility is incompatible with determinism. What I propose to do is to show that the very considerations that persuade the libertarian that free choice is incompatible with determinism are equally effective in showing that free choice is incompatible with objective indeterminism.

The incompatibility argument is this:[20]

1. No agent is free to influence the past.
2. No agent is free to influence the laws of nature.
3. The past and the laws logically imply the future.
4. If an agent is not free to influence Q and Q logically implies R, then that agent is not free to influence R.
5. No agent is free to influence the future.

The usual compatibilist response to this argument is to reject (4). While the libertarian notion of freedom may not be entirely clear, it is clear that libertarians think that it satisfies (4). I don't want to enter into the discussion of whether our ordinary notion of a 'free choice' does or doesn't support (4), but I do want to examine a parallel argument that apparently establishes the incompatibility of objective indeterminism and freedom.

The argument for the incompatibility of libertarian free will and objective indeterminism is straightforward. Given (P) the only way that A can influence what choices she makes at time t is to influence the chances of those choices at prior times. But the only way that A can influence *those* chances is by influencing prior

---

20. There are various versions of this argument, some of which employ conditions that are thought to be necessary for acting freely. See van Inwagen, *op. cit.*, and Fischer, *op. cit.*

states that determine (together with the laws) those chances. And the only way A can influence those further states is by influencing *their* chances; and so forth. Clearly, this will take us back to a time at which A cannot influence events because she hasn't yet been born. It will follow then that A cannot influence her choices; i.e., they are not *up to her* in the way that libertarianism requires. Here is another version of the same argument. For perspicuity's sake I will assume that time is discrete. Let t_0 be a time at which A has no control (in the libertarian sense) over anything occurring at that time (say, before A's birth). At t_0, A has no control over the chances indexed to t_0. Since A has libertarian control over an event only if A can influence that event, it follows from (P) that A has no control over an event that occurs at t_1. The events that occur at t_1 determine the probabilities indexed to t_1 of events at t_2. But then it follows from (P) that A has no control over events at t_2, and so on. It follows that at no time does A have control over subsequent events, including her choices.

It is not surprising that objective indeterminism is incompatible with libertarian freedom, since determinism is the limit of objective indeterminism in which all the chances are 1 or 0.[21] A libertarian who, like Kane, thinks that objective indeterminism makes all the difference to whether freedom is possible would seem to be committed to the view that as soon as the chances depart from 1 and 0, however slightly, freedom becomes possible. It is difficult to see why such a slight difference in the physics should make such a vast difference in our wills (i.e., whether they are free or not). If the above argument is correct, then satisfaction of Kane's condition (UR), although it may be necessary, is not sufficient for a choice to be free. It captures the idea that nothing other than the agent is ultimately responsible for her choice. But it doesn't guarantee that *the agent* is responsible. Specifically, it allows that nothing is ultimately responsible for the choice, since it is a matter of chance.

Some libertarians have argued that freedom involves a sui generis relation of *agent causation.*[22] Agent causation is supposed to relate the agent directly to her choices and is not explainable in terms of causal relations—deterministic or probabilistic— between an agent's mental states and her choices. O'Connor characterizes agent causation this way:

The decision I make is no mere vector sum of internal and external forces acting upon me during the process of deliberation. . . . Rather, *I* bring it about—directly, you might say—in response to the various considerations: I am the source of my own activity, not merely in

---

21. One might object that a chance of 0 doesn't mean impossibility, since, for example, it is usual to say that the chance of a spinner landing on any particular point is 0 although, of course, it is possible for the pointer to land at each point. The answer is, as Lewis points out (op. cit.), that the objection confuses infinitesimal chance with 0 chance.

22. See Roderick Chisholm, 'Freedom and Action,' in Keith Lehrer, ed., *Freedom and Determinism* (New York: Random House, 1966); O'Connor, 'Agent Causation,' in *Agents, Causes, and Events*, and 'Indeterminism and Free Agency: Three Recent Views,' *Philosophy and Phenomenological Research* 53 (1993): 499–526; and Randolph Clarke, 'Toward a Credible Agent-Causal Account of Free Will,' in *Agents, Causes, and Events.*

a relative sense as the most proximate and salient locus of an unbroken chain of causal transactions leading up to the event, but fundamentally, in a way not prefigured by what has gone before.[23]

It is often complained that agent causation is mysterious and merely labels the puzzle of freedom rather than helps to solve it. However that may be, it is clear that agent causation is also incompatible with objective indeterminism, since advocates of agent causation accept the view that the agent has libertarian control over her choices.

Neither deterministic versions of quantum mechanics like Bohm's theory nor objective indeterministic theories like GRWP make room for libertarian freedom. It appears that if libertarian freedom is coherent at all, it must be that free choices (or events leading up to free choices) are outside of the nomological order. In fact, there is a way of thinking about quantum mechanical measurements—one that has been around for some time—according to which quantum mechanical measurements are initiated by 'anomalous' events of conscious observation. This view is sufficiently intriguing to see whether it can be used to ground libertarian freedom. Eugene Wigner proposed that a quantum mechanical measurement occurs when a sentient being makes a conscious 'observation.'[24] So, for example, when a person observes a pointer in the quantum mechanical state $|M>$ that act of observation causes the state to 'collapse' into a state in which the pointer has a determinate position. Wigner doesn't say anything about how this process takes place, but he does seem to assume that acts of consciousness are themselves not physical events at all and so exempt from quantum theoretical laws.[25] I will call this version of quantum theory 'Wignerian mechanics.' Wignerian mechanics seems best understood within a dualist framework. It claims that the laws of physics are not causally closed, since certain changes of physical states would have nonphysical causes (e.g., acts of consciously making measurements) and could not be accounted for in terms of prior physical states. Notice that the world described in this account has two sources of physical indeterminism. First, there is quantum mechanical indeterminism. Once a measurement is made on a system, the system evolves according to the collapse postulate. Second, there is the indeterminism that results from the fact that exactly how a system evolves depends on whether or not conscious acts occur.

If *agent causation* is coherent at all, then it seems that Wignerian mechanics describes the sort of possible world in which it can be implemented. I won't discuss whether *agent causation* is coherent, but I do want to explore a suggestion for how Wignerian quantum mechanics might accommodate it.[26] Suppose that when

23. O'Connor, 'Agent Causation,' 173.
24. See Eugene Wigner, *Symmetries and Reflections* (Bloomington: Indiana University Press 1967).
25. I am assuming that not only are acts of consciousness nonphysical but they don't supervene on physical states. So a complete characterization of the physical state of a system may leave it open whether an act of consciousness associated with that system occurs.
26. I haven't seen this proposal explicitly made in print but Wigner, *op. cit.*, suggests it and I have heard it made in conversation.

a person consciously deliberates about whether to do d or d^* that act of consciousness involves measuring a quantum mechanical observable. *Agent causation* consists in the agent's making this measurement (although, of course, that is not how the agent thinks of what she is doing). The measurement initiates a collapse of state in conformity with the collapse postulate, with the quantum mechanical chances either in a state corresponding to her deciding to do d or in a state corresponding to her deciding to do d^*. The process of conscious deliberation (i.e., the quantum mechanical measurement) is itself not subject to law. That is, there is no law connecting prior conditions (mental or physical) to making a choice (or to the chance of making a choice).

Notice that the indeterminism that is peculiar to quantum mechanical laws is not essential to this account of libertarian freedom.[27] The indeterminism that is supposed to make room for libertarian freedom is not the quantum mechanical indeterminism (i.e., the probabilities associated with the collapse of the quantum state) but rather the indeterminism that results from its not being determined by prior conditions whether or not a conscious measurement (an act of deliberation) will take place. This is what leaves room for the libertarian to say that it is *up to the agent* whether or not the measurement occurs.

Wignerian quantum mechanics is the only interpretation of quantum mechanics that is at all favorable to libertarian freedom. But it is a very implausible interpretation. All the evidence that has ever been obtained in laboratories and by observation supports the view that every physical event is governed by quantum mechanical laws; i.e., that the quantum mechanical laws are complete. And there is absolutely no evidence that acts of measurement fall outside these laws and of course no evidence that mental acts bring about collapses of states or that they are not covered by the laws of quantum theory. It might be replied to this that although there is no 'scientific' evidence that contravenes the completeness of quantum mechanics, still, it is just a conjecture that all events, including acts of decision, are covered by quantum mechanical—or any—laws. And if libertarian freedom requires there to be events outside of the nomological order, then since we have reason to think that we are libertarian free, we have reason to think that the laws of nature are incomplete.[28] But this is a very frail line of thought. Libertarians may be correct that it *feels* to us that our choices are up to us in a way that exempts them from natural law. But it is preposterous to think that we can draw reliable conclusions about physics on the

---

27. Neither the indeterminateness of some observables nor the indeterminism of the evolution of state that is characteristic of quantum mechanics are essential to this approach to making room for libertarian freedom. Suppose that the fundamental laws are Newtonian but *ceteris paribus*—the ceteris paribus condition being that no events of libertarian freedom associated with a system occur. Suppose that an event of libertarian freedom can alter the momentum (or some other classical quantity) of some particles in the brain in ways that violate the Newtonian laws and that these alterations result in various intentions and that events of libertarian freedom are not covered by deterministic or probabilistic laws.

28. O'Connor, 'Agent Causation,' and Clarke, op. cit., argue in this way.

basis of such feelings. It is more plausible to suppose that this feeling—to the extent we have it—is an illusion.[29]

Conclusion

The results of this paper can be summarized thus: Libertarian freedom requires that an agent's free choices originate in her will. Whatever that means, the libertarian is clear that freedom is incompatible with determinism. It is widely thought that quantum theory is incompatible with determinism. This has suggested that there may be no incompatibility between what physics tells us our world is like and our possessing libertarian freedom. But we have seen that quantum theory provides scant support to the libertarian. We considered three interpretations of quantum theory—Bohm's theory, GRWP, and Wignerian mechanics. The first is deterministic and the latter two are indeterministic. The first two are complete (i.e., cover all events), while the latter allows for events not covered by its laws. Since libertarian freedom is incompatible with determinism, it is incompatible with Bohm's theory. GRWP assigns objective probabilities to every physically possible event at every time. I argued that since events that have objective probabilities can be influenced only by influencing their probabilities, reasons for holding that freedom is incompatible with determinism are also reasons for holding that it is incompatible with objective indeterministic theories like GRWP. Wignerian mechanics posits the existence of events that neither are determined by prior events nor have objective probabilities. Perhaps, then, it allows for libertarian freedom. But there is little reason to believe Wignerian mechanics. I conclude that there is little prospect for gaining (libertarian) freedom from physics.[30]

29. Colin McGinn suggests that this illusion may arise because we in fact generally don't know the complete cause of our choices. (See Colin McGinn, *Problems in Philosophy: The Limits of Inquiry* [Oxford: Basil Blackwell, 1993].) One can speculate that the belief that it is 'up to the agent' which action is actualized—so that prior to making a choice various possibilities are open—although false, plays an important role in the causal history of the action. Perhaps we are such that if we didn't have this belief, rational action would be more difficult.

30. Thanks to David Albert, Michael Bradie, Noa Latham, Brian Loar, and Timothy O'Connor for comments on earlier versions of this paper.

Chapter 54

Human freedom and the self

Roderick M. Chisholm

'A staff moves a stone, and is moved by a hand, which is moved by a man.

Aristotle, *Physics*, 256a.

1. The metaphysical problem of human freedom might be summarized in the following way: Human beings are responsible agents; but this fact appears to conflict with a deterministic view of human action (the view that every event that is involved in an act is caused by some other event); and it *also* appears to conflict with an indeterministic view of human action (the view that the act, or some event that is essential to the act, is not caused at all.) To solve the problem, I believe, we must make somewhat far-reaching assumptions about the self or the agent—about the man who performs the act.

Perhaps it is needless to remark that, in all likelihood, it is impossible to say anything significant about this ancient problem that has not been said before.[1]

2. Let us consider some deed, or misdeed, that may be attributed to a responsible agent: one man, say, shot another. If the man *was* responsible for what he did, then, I would urge, what was to happen at the time of the shooting was something that was entirely up to the man himself. There was a moment at which it was true, both that he could have fired the shot and also that he could have refrained from firing it. And if this is so, then, even though he did fire it, he could have done something else instead. (He didn't find himself firing the shot 'against his will', as we say.) I think we can say, more generally, then, that if a man is responsible for a certain event or a certain state of affairs (in our example, the shooting of another man), then that event or state of affairs was brought about by some act of his, and the act was something that was in his power either to perform or not to perform.

But now if the act which he *did* perform was an act that was also in his power *not* to perform, then it could not have been caused or determined by any event that was not itself within his power either to bring about or not to bring about. For example,

---

1. The general position to be presented here is suggested in the following writings, among others: Aristotle, *Eudemian Ethics*, bk. ii ch. 6: *Nicomachean Ethics*, bk. iii, ch. 1–5; Thomas Reid, *Essays on the Active Powers of Man*; C. A. Campbell, 'Is "Free Will" a Pseudo Problem?' *Mind*, 1951, 441–65; Roderick M. Chisholm, 'Responsibility and Avoidability', and Richard Taylor, 'Determination and the Theory of Agency', in *Determinism and Freedom in the Age of Modern Science*, ed. Sidney Hook (New York, 1958).

if what we say he did was really something that was brought about by a second man, one who forced his hand upon the trigger, say, or who, by means of hypnosis, compelled him to perform the act, then since the act was caused by the *second* man it was nothing that was within the power of the *first* man to prevent. And precisely the same thing is true, I think, if instead of referring to a second man who compelled the first one, we speak instead of the *desires* and *beliefs* which the first man happens to have had. For if what we say he did was really something that was brought about by his own beliefs and desires, if these beliefs and desires in the particular situation in which he happened to have found himself caused him to do just what it was that we say he did do, then, since *they* caused it, *he* was unable to do anything other than just what it was that he did do. It makes no difference whether the cause of the deed was internal or external; if the cause was some state or event for which the man himself was not responsible, then he was not responsible for what we have been mistakenly calling his act. If a flood caused the poorly constructed dam to break, then, given the flood and the constitution of the dam, the break, we may say, *had* to occur and nothing could have happened in its place. And if the flood of desire caused the weak-willed man to give in, then he, too, had to do just what it was that he did do and he was no more responsible than was the dam for the results that followed. (It is true, of course, that if the man is responsible for the beliefs and desires that he happens to have, then he may also be responsible for the things they lead him to do. But the question now becomes: *is* he responsible for the beliefs and desires he happens to have? If he is, then there was a time when they were within his power either to acquire or not to acquire, and we are left, therefore, with our general point.)

One may object: But surely if there were such a thing as a man who is really *good*, then he would be responsible for things that he would do; yet, he would be unable to do anything other than just what it is that he does do, since, being good, he will always choose to do what is best. The answer, I think, is suggested by a comment that Thomas Reid makes upon an ancient author. The author had said of Cato, 'He was good because he could not be otherwise', and Reid observes: 'This saying, if understood literally and strictly, is not the praise of Cato, but of his constitution, which was no more the work of Cato than his existence'.[2] If Cato was himself responsible for the good things that he did, then Cato, as Reid suggests, was such that, although he had the power to do what was not good, he exercised his power only for that which was good.

All of this, if it is true, may give a certain amount of comfort to those who are tender-minded. But we should remind them that it also conflicts with a familiar view about the nature of God—with the view that St. Thomas Aquinas expresses by saying that 'every movement both of the will and of nature proceeds from God as the Prime Mover'.[3] If the act of the sinner *did* proceed from God as the Prime

---

2. Thomas Reid, *Essays on the Active Powers of Man*, essay iv, ch. 4 (*Works*, 600).
3. *Summa Theologica*, First Part of the Second Part, qu. vi ('On the Voluntary and Involuntary').

Mover, then God was in the position of the second agent we just discussed—the man who forced the trigger finger, or the hypnotist—and the sinner, so-called, was *not* responsible for what he did. (This may be a bold assertion, in view of the history of western theology, but I must say that I have never encountered a single good reason for denying it.)

There is one standard objection to all of this and we should consider it briefly.

3. The objection takes the form of a stratagem—one designed to show that determinism (and divine providence) is consistent with human responsibility. The stratagem is one that was used by Jonathan Edwards and by many philosophers in the present century, most notably, G. E. Moore.[4]

One proceeds as follows: The expression

(a) He could have done otherwise,

it is argued, means no more nor less than

(b) If he had chosen to do otherwise, then he would have done otherwise.

(In place of 'chosen', one might say 'tried', 'set out', 'decided', 'undertaken', or 'willed'.) The truth of statement (b), it is then pointed out, is consistent with determinism (and with divine providence); for even if all of the man's actions were causally determined, the man could still be such that, *if* he had chosen otherwise, then he would have done otherwise. What the murderer saw, let us suppose, along with his beliefs and desires, *caused* him to fire the shot; yet he was such that *if*, just then, he had chosen or decided *not* to fire the shot, then he would not have fired it. All of this is certainly possible. Similarly, we could say, of the dam, that the flood caused it to break and also that the dam was such that, *if* there had been no flood or any similar pressure, then the dam would have remained intact. And therefore, the argument proceeds, if (b) is consistent with determinism, and if (a) and (b) say the same thing, then (a) is also consistent with determinism; hence we can say that the agent *could* have done otherwise even though he was caused to do what he did do; and therefore determinism and moral responsibility are compatible.

Is the argument sound? The conclusion follows from the premises, but the catch, I think, lies in the first premiss—the one saying that statement (a) tells us no more nor less than what statement (b) tells us. For (b), it would seem, could be true while (a) is false. That is to say, our man might be such that, if he had chosen to do otherwise, then he would have done otherwise, and yet *also* such that he could not have done otherwise. Suppose, after all, that our murderer could not have *chosen*, or could not have *decided*, to do otherwise. Then the fact that he happens also to be a man such that, if he had chosen not to shoot he would not have shot, would make no difference. For if he could *not* have chosen *not* to shoot, then he could not have done anything other than just what it was that he did do. In a word: from our statement (b) above ('If he

4. Jonathan Edwards, *Freedom of the Will* (New Haven, 1957); G. E. Moore, *Ethics* (Home University Library, 1912), ch. 6.

had chosen to do otherwise, then he would have done otherwise'), we cannot make an inference to (a) above ('He could have done otherwise') unless we can *also* assert:

(c) He could have chosen to do otherwise.

And therefore, if we must reject this third statement (c), then, even though we may be justified in asserting (b), we are not justified in asserting (a). If the man could not have chosen to do otherwise, then he would not have done otherwise—*even if* he was such that, if he *had* chosen to do otherwise, then he would have done otherwise.

The stratagem in question, then, seems to me not to work, and I would say, therefore, that the ascription of responsibility conflicts with a deterministic view of action.

4. Perhaps there is less need to argue that the ascription of responsibility also conflicts with an indeterministic view of action—with the view that the act, or some event that is essential to the act, is not caused at all. If the act—the firing of the shot—was not caused at all, if it was fortuitous or capricious, happening so to speak out of the blue, then, presumably, no one—and nothing—was responsible for the act. Our conception of action, therefore, should be neither deterministic nor indeterministic. Is there any other possibility?

5. We must not say that every event involved in the act is caused by some other event; and we must not say that the act is something that is not caused at all. The possibility that remains, therefore, is this: We should say that at least one of the events that are involved in the act is caused, not by any other events, but by something else instead. And this something else can only be the agent—the man. If there is an event that is caused, not by other events, but by the man, then there are some events involved in the act that are not caused by other events. But if the event in question is caused by the man then it *is* caused and we are not committed to saying that there is something involved in the act that is not caused at all.

But this, of course, is a large consequence, implying something of considerable importance about the nature of the agent or the man.

6. If we consider only inanimate natural objects, we may say that causation, if it occurs, is a relation between *events* or *states of affairs*. The dam's breaking was an event that was caused by a set of other events—the dam being weak, the flood being strong, and so on. But if a man is responsible for a particular deed, then, if what I have said is true, there is some event, or set of events, that is caused, *not* by other events or states of affairs, but by the agent, whatever he may be.

I shall borrow a pair of medieval terms, using them, perhaps, in a way that is slightly different from that for which they were originally intended. I shall say that when one event or state of affairs (or set of events or states of affairs) causes some other event or state of affairs, then we have an instance of *transeunt* causation. And I shall say that when an *agent*, as distinguished from an event, causes an event or state of affairs, then we have an instance of *immanent* causation.

The nature of what is intended by the expression 'immanent causation' may be illustrated by this sentence from Aristotle's *Physics*: 'Thus, a staff moves a stone, and is moved by a hand, which is moved by a man' (VII, 5, 256a, 6–8). If the man was responsible, then we have in this illustration a number of instances of causation—most of them transeunt but at least one of them immanent. What the staff did to the stone was an instance of transeunt causation, and thus we may describe it as a relation between events: 'the motion of the staff caused the motion of the stone.' And similarly for what the hand did to the staff: 'the motion of the hand caused the motion of the staff'. And, as we know from physiology, there are still other events which caused the motion of the hand. Hence we need not introduce the agent at this particular point, as Aristotle does—we *need* not, though we *may*. We *may* say that the hand was moved by the man, but we may *also* say that the motion of the hand was caused by the motion of certain muscles; and we may say that the motion of the muscles was caused by certain events that took place within the brain. But some event, and presumably one of those that took place within the brain, was caused by the agent and not by any other events.

There are, of course, objections to this way of putting the matter; I shall consider the two that seem to me to be most important.

7. One may object, firstly: 'If the *man* does anything, then, as Aristotle's remark suggests, what he does is to move the *hand*. But he certainly does not *do* anything to his brain—he may not even know that he *has* a brain. And if he doesn't do anything to the brain, and if the motion of the hand was caused by something that happened within the brain, then there is no point in appealing to "immanent causation" as being something incompatible with "transeunt causation"—for the whole thing, after all, is a matter of causal relations among events or states of affairs.'

The answer to this objection, I think, is this: It is true that the agent does not *do* anything with his brain, or to his brain, in the sense in which he *does* something with his hand and does something to the staff. But from this it does not follow that the agent was not the immanent cause of something that happened within his brain.

We should note a useful distinction that has been proposed by Professor A. I. Melden—namely, the distinction between 'making something A happen' and 'doing A'.[5] If I reach for the staff and pick it up, then one of the things that I *do* is just that—reach for the staff and pick it up. And if it is something that I do, then there is a very clear sense in which it may be said to be something that I know that I do. If you ask me, 'Are you doing something, or trying to do something, with the staff?', I will have no difficulty in finding an answer. But in doing something with the staff, I also make various things happen which are not in this same sense things that I do: I will make various air-particles move; I will free a number of blades of grass from the pressure that had been upon them; and I may cause a shadow to move from one place to another. If these are merely things that I make happen, as distinguished from things that I do, then I may know nothing whatever about them; I may not have the slightest idea that, in moving the staff, I am bringing about any such thing as the motion of air-particles, shadows, and blades of grass.

5. A. I. Melden, *Free Action* (London, 1961), especially ch. 3. Mr. Melden's own views, however, are quite the contrary of those that are proposed here.

We may say, in answer to the first objection, therefore, that it is true that our agent does nothing to his brain or with his brain; but from this it does not follow that the agent is not the immanent cause of some event within his brain; for the brain event may be something which, like the motion of the air-particles, he made happen in picking up the staff. The only difference between the two cases is this: in each case, he made something happen when he picked up the staff; but in the one case—the motion of the airparticles or of the shadows—it was the motion of the staff that caused the event to happen; and in the other case—the event that took place in the brain—it was this event that caused the motion of the staff.

The point is, in a word, that whenever a man does something A, then (by 'immanent causation') he makes a certain cerebral event happen, and this cerebral event (by 'transeunt causation') makes A happen.

8. The second objection is more difficult and concerns the very concept of 'immanent causation', or causation by an agent, as this concept is to be interpreted here. The concept is subject to a difficulty which has long been associated with that of the prime mover unmoved. We have said that there must be some event A, presumably some cerebral event, which is caused not by any other event, but by the agent. Since A was not caused by any other event, then the agent himself cannot be said to have undergone any change or produced any other event (such as 'an act of will' or the like) which brought A about. But if, when the agent made A happen, there was no event involved other than A itself, no event which could be described as *making* A happen, what did the agent's causation consist of? What, for example, is the difference between A's just happening, and the agents' *causing* A to happen? We cannot attribute the difference to any event that took place within the agent. And so far as the event A itself is concerned, there would seem to be no discernible difference. Thus Aristotle said that the activity of the prime mover is nothing in addition to the motion that it produces, and Suarez said that 'the action is in reality nothing but the effect as it flows from the agent'.[6] Must we conclude, then, that there is no more to the man's action in causing event A than there is to the event A's happening by itself? Here we would seem to have a distinction without a difference— in which case we have failed to find a *via media* between a deterministic and an indeterministic view of action.

The only answer, I think, can be this: that the difference between the man's causing A, on the one hand, and the event A just happening, on the other, lies in the fact that, in the first case but not the second, the event A *was* caused and was caused by the man. There was a brain event A; the agent did, in fact, cause the brain event; but there was nothing that he did to cause it.

This answer may not entirely satisfy and it will be likely to provoke the following question: 'But what are you really *adding* to the assertion that A happened when you utter the words "The agent *caused* A to happen"?' As soon as we have put the question this way, we see, I think, that whatever difficulty we may have encountered is

6. Aristotle, *Physics*, bk. iii, ch. 3; Suarez, *Disputations Metaphysicae*, Disputation 18, s. 10.

one that may be traced to the concept of causation generally—whether 'immanent' or 'transeunt'. The problem, in other words, is not a problem that is peculiar to our conception of human action. It is a problem that must be faced by anyone who makes use of the concept of causation at all; and therefore, I would say, it is a problem for everyone but the complete indeterminist.

For the problem, as we put it, referring just to 'immanent causation', or causation by an agent, was this: 'What is the difference between saying, of an event A, that A just happened and saying that someone caused A to happen?' The analogous problem, which holds for 'transeunt causation', or causation by an event, is this: 'What is the difference between saying, of two events A and B, that B happened and then A happened, and saying that B's happening was the *cause* of A's happening?' And the only answer that one can give is this—that in the one case the agent was the cause of A's happening and in the other case event B was the cause of A's happening. The nature of transeunt causation is no more clear than is that of immanent causation.

9. But we may plausibly say—and there is a respectable philosophical tradition to which we may appeal—that the notion of immanent causation, or causation by an agent, is in fact more clear than that of transeunt causation, or causation by an event, and that it is only by understanding our own causal efficacy, as agents, that we can grasp the concept of *cause* at all. Hume may be said to have shown that we do not derive the concept of *cause* from what we perceive of external things. How, then, do we derive it? The most plausible suggestion, it seems to me, is that of Reid, once again: namely that 'the conception of an efficient cause may very probably be derived from the experience we have had . . . of our own power to produce certain effects'.[7] If we did not understand the concept of immanent causation, we would not understand that of transeunt causation.

10. It may have been noted that I have avoided the term 'free will' in all of this. For even if there is such a faculty as 'the will', which somehow sets our acts agoing, the question of freedom, as John Locke said, is not the question '*whether the will be free*'; it is the question '*whether a man be free*'.[8] For if there is a 'will', as a moving faculty, the question is whether the man is free to will to do these things that he does will to do— and also whether he is free *not* to will any of those things that he does will to do, and, again, whether he is free to will any of those things that he does not will to do. Jonathan Edwards tried to restrict himself to the question—'Is the man free to do what it is that he wills?'—but the answer to this question will not tell us whether the man is responsible for what it is that he *does* will to do. Using still another pair of medieval terms, we may say that the metaphysical problem of freedom does not concern the *actus imperatus*; it does not concern the question whether we are free to accomplish whatever it is that we will or set out to do; it concerns the *actus elicitus*, the question whether we are free to will or to set out to do those things that we do will or set out to do.

---

7. Reid, *Works*. 524.
8. *Essay concerning Human Understanding*, bk. ii, ch. 21.

11. If we are responsible, and if what I have been trying to say is true, then we have a prerogative which some would attribute only to God: each of us, when we act, is a prime mover unmoved. In doing what we do, we cause certain events to happen, and nothing—or no one—causes us to cause those events to happen.

12. If we are thus prime movers unmoved and if our actions, or those for which we are responsible, are not causally determined, then they are not causally determined by our *desires*. And this means that the relation between what we want or what we desire, on the one hand, and what it is that we do, on the other, is not as simple as most philosophers would have it.

We may distinguish between what we might call the 'Hobbist approach' and what we might call the 'Kantian approach' to this question. The Hobbist approach is the one that is generally accepted at the present time, but the Kantian approach, I believe, is the one that is true. According to Hobbism, if we *know*, of some man, what his beliefs and desires happen to be and how strong they are, if we know what he feels certain of, what he desires more than anything else, and if we know the state of his body and what stimuli he is being subjected to, then we may *deduce*, logically, just what it is that he will do—or, more accurately, just what it is that he will try, set out, or undertake to do. Thus Professor Melden has said that 'the connection between wanting and doing is logical'.[9] But according to the Kantian approach to our problem, and this is the one that I would take, there is no such logical connection between wanting and doing, nor need there even be a causal connection. No set of statements about a man's desires, beliefs, and stimulus situation at any time implies any statement telling us what the man will try, set out, or undertake to do at that time. As Reid put it, though we may 'reason from men's motives to their actions and, in many cases, with great probability', we can never do so 'with absolute certainty'.[10]

This means that, in one very strict sense of the terms, there can be no science of man. If we think of science as a matter of finding out what laws happen to hold, and if the statement of a law tells us what kinds of events are caused by what other kinds of events, then there will be human actions which we cannot explain by subsuming them under any laws. We cannot say, 'It is causally necessary that, given such and such desires and beliefs, and being subject to such and such stimuli, the agent will do so and so'. For at times the agent, if he chooses, may rise above his desires and do something else instead.

But all of this is consistent with saying that, perhaps more often than not, our desires do exist under conditions such that those conditions necessitate us to act. And we may also say, with Leibniz, that at other times our desires may 'incline without necessitating'.

13. Leibniz's phrase presents us with our final philosophical problem. What does it mean to say that a desire, or a motive, might 'incline without necessitating'? There

9. Melden, 166.
10. Reid, *Works*, 608, 612.

is a temptation, certainly, to say that 'to incline' means to cause and that 'not to necessitate' means not to cause, but obviously we cannot have it both ways.

Nor will Leibniz's own solution do. In his letter to Coste, he puts the problem as follows: 'When a choice is proposed, for example to go out or not to go out, it is a question whether, with all the circumstances, internal and external, motives, perceptions, dispositions, impressions, passions, inclinations taken together, I am still in a contingent state, or whether I am necessitated to make the choice, for example, to go out; that is to say, whether this proposition true and determined in fact, *In all these circumstances taken together I shall choose to go out*, is contingent or necessary.'[11] Leibniz's answer might be put as follows: in one sense of the terms 'necessary' and 'contingent', the proposition 'In all these circumstances taken together I shall choose to go out', may be said to be contingent and not necessary, and in another sense of these terms, it may be said to be necessary and not contingent. But the sense in which the proposition may be said to be contingent, according to Leibniz, is only this: there is no logical contradiction involved in denying the proposition. And the sense in which it may be said to be necessary is this: since 'nothing ever occurs without cause or determining reason', the proposition is causally necessary. 'Whenever all the circumstances taken together are such that the balance of deliberation is heavier on one side than on the other, it is certain and infallible that that is the side that is going to win out'. But if what we have been saying is true, the proposition 'In all these circumstances taken together I shall choose to go out', may be causally as well as logically contingent. Hence we must find another interpretation for Leibniz's statement that our motives and desires may incline us, or influence us, to choose without thereby necessitating us to choose.

Let us consider a public official who has some moral scruples but who also, as one says, could be had. Because of the scruples that he does have, he would never take any positive steps to receive a bribe—he would not actively solicit one. But his morality has its limits and he is also such that, if we were to confront him with a *fait accompli* or to let him see what is about to happen ($10,000 in cash is being deposited behind the garage), then he would succumb and be unable to resist. The general situation is a familiar one and this is one reason that people pray to be delivered from temptation. (It also justifies Kant's remark: 'And how many there are who may have led a long blameless life, who are only *fortunate* in having escaped so many temptations'.[12] Our relation to the misdeed that we contemplate may not be a matter simply of being able to bring it about or not to bring it about. As St. Anselm noted, there are at least four possibilities. We may illustrate them by reference to our public official and the event which is his receiving the bribe, in the following way: (i) he may be able to bring the event about himself (*facere esse*), in which case he would actively cause himself to receive the bribe; (ii) he may be able to refrain from

---

11. 'Lettre à Mr. Coste de la Nécessité et de la Contingence' (1707), in *Opera Philosophica*, ed. Erdmann, 447–9.

12. In the Preface to the *Metaphysical Elements of Ethics*, in *Kant's Critique of Practical Reason and Other Works on the Theory of Ethics*, ed. T. K. Abbott (London, 1959), p. 303.

bringing it about himself (*non facere esse*), in which case he would not himself do anything to insure that he receive the bribe; (iii) he may be able to do something to prevent the event from occurring (*facere non esse*), in which case he would make sure that the $10,000 was *not* left behind the garage; or (iv) he may be unable to do anything to prevent the event from occurring (*non facere non esse*), in which case, though he may not solicit the bribe, he would allow himself to keep it.[13] We have envisaged our official as a man who can resist the temptation to (i) but cannot resist the temptation to (iv): he can refrain from bringing the event about himself, but he cannot bring himself to do anything to prevent it.

Let us think of 'inclination without necessitation', then, in such terms as these. First we may contrast the two propositions:

(1) He can resist the temptation to do something in order to make A happen;
(2) He can resist the temptation to allow A to happen (i.e. to do nothing to prevent A from happening).

We may suppose that the man has some desire to have A happen and thus has a motive for making A happen. His motive for making A happen, I suggest, is one that *necessitates* provided that, because of the motive, (1) is false; he cannot resist the temptation to do something in order to make A happen. His motive for making A happen is one that *inclines* provided that, because of the motive, (2) is false; like our public official, he cannot bring himself to do anything to prevent A from happening. And therefore we can say that this motive for making A happen is one that *inclines but does not necessitate* provided that, because of the motive, (1) is true and (2) is false; he can resist the temptation to make it happen but he cannot resist the temptation to allow it to happen.

---

13. Cf. D. P. Henry, 'Saint Anselm's *De "Grammatico"* ', *Philosophical Quarterly*, x (1960), 115–26. St. Anselm noted that (i) and (iii), respectively, may be thought of as forming the upper left and the upper right corners of a square of opposition, and (ii) and (iv) the lower left and the lower right.

Study questions

1. What is the connection between the issue of compatibilism versus incompatibilism, and the issue of whether we define freedom in terms of freedom to act or freedom to will?
2. List the different ways in which someone could deny that the world is deterministic.
3. Can you avoid the problem of the incompatibility of free will and determinism, if you are a Cartesian dualist?
4. Do you think that Frankfurt's account of free will can answer the worries raised by the case of a thoroughly manipulated person, like Winston Smith at the end of *1984*?

Further reading

There are a number of good collections on free will: Honderich (1973), Watson (1982), O'Connor (1995). An excellent recent collection is Kane (2002), with helpful editorial introduction. A good—and short—general introduction is Pink (2004). An enlightening study of the question of free will in Stoic philosophy is Bobzien (1998).

In a famous paper, Harry Frankfurt argues that moral responsibility does not require alternative possibilities; see Frankfurt (1969). On the question of determinism in physics, see Earman (1986). A more detailed discussion of van Inwagen's consequence argument is in his (1983). For criticism, see Lewis (1981) and Dennett (1984). Ayer (1954)—reprinted in Watson (1982)—gives another clear version of the Humean argument that freedom requires determinism. Agent causation is developed by a number of authors (O'Connor, Clarke, and Rowe) in O'Connor (1995). One of the most influential contemporary libertarians is Robert Kane; see his contribution in Kane (2002) and, for a detailed discussion, Kane (1996). Watson (1982: part II) contains an exchange on the understanding of 'could have done otherwise'. An easily accessible defence of compatibilism is Dennett (1984).

References

ADAMS, MARILYN MCCORD, and ADAMS, ROBERT MERRIHEW (1990). *The Problem of Evil.* Oxford: Oxford University Press.

ADAMS, ROBERT (1994). *Leibniz: Determinist, Theist, Idealist.* Oxford: Oxford University Press.

ANSCOMBE, G. E. M. (1971). 'Causality and Determination'. Inaugural Lecture at Cambridge University. Reprinted in G. E. M. Anscombe, *Metaphysics and the Philosophy of Mind.* Oxford: Blackwell, 1981.

—— (1981). 'Substance', in *Collected Philosophical Papers,* ii: *Metaphysics and the Philosophy of Mind.* Oxford: Blackwell.

—— and GEACH, P. T. (1961). *Three Philosophers.* Oxford: Blackwell.

Anselm of Canterbury (1965). Selection from *Proslogon,* translated by M. Charlesworth, Oxford: Oxford University Press.

AQUINAS, ST THOMAS (1967). *Summa Theologiae,* ed. Thomas Gilby. London: Eyre and Spottiswoode.

ARMSTRONG, D. M. (1968). *A Materialist Theory of the Mind.* London: Routledge and Kegan Paul.

—— (1978). *Universals and Scientific Realism.* 2 vols. Cambridge: Cambridge University Press.

—— (1980). 'Identity through Time', in Peter van Inwagen (ed.), *Time and Cause.* Dordrecht: Reidel.

—— (1989a). *A Combinatorial Theory of Possibility.* Cambridge: Cambridge University Press.

—— (1989b). *Universals: An Opinionated Introduction.* Boulder, Colo.: Westview Press.

—— (1997). *A World of States of Affairs.* Cambridge: Cambridge University Press.

AYER, A. J. (1936). *Language, Truth and Logic.* 2nd edn. Harmondsworth: Penguin Books, 1971.

—— (1954). 'The Identity of Indiscernibles', in *Philosophical Essays.* London: Macmillan.

AYERS, MICHAEL (1991). *Locke.* 2 vols. London: Routledge.

BACON, JOHN, CAMPBELL, KEITH, and REINHARDT, LLOYD (eds.) (1993). *Ontology, Causality and Mind.* Cambridge: Cambridge University Press.

BARCAN MARCUS, RUTH (1947). 'The Identity of Individuals in a Strict Functional Calculus of First Order', *Journal of Symbolic Logic,* 12: 12–15.

BARNES, JONATHAN (1972). *The Ontological Argument.* London: Macmillan.

—— (1995). 'Metaphysics', in Jonathan Barnes (ed.), *The Cambridge Companion to Aristotle.* Cambridge: Cambridge University Press.

BEALER, GEORGE (1998). 'Universals and Properties', in Laurence and Macdonald (1998).

BENNETT, JONATHAN (1988). *Events and their Names.* Cambridge: Cambridge University Press.

BERKELEY, GEORGE (1710). *Principles of Human Knowledge,* in Berkeley (1996).

—— (1713). *Three Dialogues between Hylas and Philonous,* in Berkeley (1996).

—— (1996). *Principles of Human Knowledge and Three Dialogues between Hylas and Philonous,* ed. Howard Robinson. Oxford: Oxford University Press.

BLACK, M. (1952). 'The Identity of Indiscernibles', *Mind,* 61: 153–64.

BLACKBURN, SIMON (1990). 'Filling in Space', *Analysis,* 50: 62–5.

BOBZIEN, SUSANNE (1998). *Determinism and Freedom in Stoic Philosophy.* Oxford: Clarendon Press.

BOGHOSSIAN, PAUL A. (1996). 'Analyticity Reconsidered', *Noûs*, 30/3: 360–91.

BOSTOCK, DAVID (1988). 'Time and the Continuum', *Oxford Studies in Ancient Philosophy*, 6: 148–69.

BROAD, C. D. (1938). *An Examination of McTaggart's Philosophy*. Cambridge: Cambridge University Press.

BROACKES, JUSTIN (1993). 'Did Hume hold a Regularity Theory of Causation?', *British Journal for the History of Philosophy*, 99–114.

BURGESS, JOHN P. (2001). 'Set Theory', in Lou Goble (ed.), *The Blackwell Guide to Philosophical Logic*. Oxford: Blackwell.

BURKE, MICHAEL (1992). 'Copper Statues and Pieces of Copper', *Analysis*, 52: 12–17.

—— (1994). 'Preserving the Principle of One Object to a Place', *Philosophy and Phenomenological Research*, 54: 591–624. Reprinted in Rea (1997).

BURNYEAT, MYLES (1982). 'Idealism and Greek Philosophy: What Descartes Saw and Berkeley Missed', *Philosophical Review*, 91: 3–40.

CAMPBELL, KEITH (1970). *Body and Mind*. South Bend, Ind.: Notre Dame University Press.

—— (1990). *Abstract Particulars*. Oxford: Blackwell.

CARNAP, RUDOLF (1947). *Meaning and Necessity*. Chicago: University of Chicago Press.

—— (1955). *Logical Syntax of Language*. Berkeley and Los Angeles: University of California Press.

CASULLO, ALBERT (1977). 'Kripke on the A Priori and the Necessary', *Analysis*, 37: 152–9.

CHALMERS, DAVID (1996). *The Conscious Mind*. Oxford: Oxford University Press.

CHISHOLM, R. M. (1969). 'The Observability of the Self', *Philosophy and Phenomenological Research*, 30: 7–21. Reprinted in Q. Cassam (ed.), *Self-Knowledge*. Oxford: Oxford University Press, 1994.

—— (1976). *Person and Object*. LaSalle, Ill.: Open Court.

CHURCHLAND, P. M. (1981). 'Eliminative Materialism and the Propositional Attitudes', *Journal of Philosophy*, 78: 67–90.

COFFA, ALBERTO (1991). *The Semantic Tradition from Kant to Carnap*. Cambridge: Cambridge University Press.

COLLINS, J., HALL, NED, and PAUL, LAURIE (eds.) (forthcoming). *Causation and Counterfactuals*. Cambridge, Mass.: MIT Press.

CRAIG, WILLIAM LANE (1980). *The Cosmological Argument from Plato to Leibniz*. London: Macmillan.

CRANE, TIM (1995a). 'The Mental Causation Debate', *Proceedings of the Aristotelian Society, Supplementary Volume*, 69: 211–36.

—— (ed.) (1995b). *Dispositions: A Debate*. With contributions by D. M. Armstrong, C. B. Martin, and U. T. Place. London: Routledge.

—— (2003). *The Mechanical Mind*. 2nd edn. London: Routledge.

DAINTON, BARRY (2001). *Space and Time*. Chesham: Acumen.

DAVIDSON, DONALD (1970). 'Mental Events', in L. Foster and J. Swanson (eds.), *Experience and Theory*. London: Duckworth. Reprinted in Donald Davidson, *Essays on Actions and Events*. Oxford: Oxford University Press, 1982.

DAVIES, BRIAN (1993). *An Introduction to the Philosophy of Religion*. Oxford: Oxford University Press.

—— (2000). *Philosophy of Religion: A Guide and Anthology*. Oxford: Oxford University Press.

DAWKINS, RICHARD (1986). *The Blind Watchmaker.* Harmondsworth: Penguin.

DENNETT, DANIEL C. (1984). *Elbow Room: The Varieties of Free Will Worth Wanting.* Cambridge, Mass.: MIT Press.

DESCARTES, RENÉ (1641). *Meditations on First Philosophy,* in Descartes (1984: vol. ii).

—— (1644). *Principles of Philosophy,* in Descartes (1984: vol. i).

—— (1984). *Philosophical Writings of René Descartes,* 3 vols., ed. trans. J. Cottingham, R. Stoothof, D. Murdoch, and A. Kenny. Cambridge: Cambridge University Press.

DIVERS, JOHN (2002). *Possible Worlds.* London: Routledge.

DOWE, PHIL (2000). *Physical Causation.* Cambridge: Cambridge University Press.

DRETSKE, FRED I. (1977). 'Laws of Nature', *Philosophy of Science,* 39: 69–71.

DUMMETT, MICHAEL (1960). 'A Defence of McTaggart's Proof of the Unreality of Time', *Philosophical Review,* 69: 497–504. Reprinted in Dummett (1978).

—— (1978). *Truth and Other Enigmas.* London: Duckworth.

EARMAN, JOHN (1986). *Primer on Determinism.* Dordrecht: Reidel.

EHRING, DOUGLAS (1997). *Causation and Persistence.* Oxford: Oxford University Press.

EVANS, GARETH (1982). *The Varieties of Reference.* Oxford: Clarendon Press.

EVNINE, SIMON (1991). *Donald Davidson.* Oxford: Polity Press.

FEIGL, HERBERT (1958). 'The "Mental" and the "Physical" ', in H. Feigl, M. Scriven, and G. Maxwell (eds.), *Minnesota Studies in the Philosophy of Science,* vol. ii. Minneapolis: University of Minnesota Press. Reprinted as a monograph by the same publisher, 1967.

FOGELIN, ROBERT (2001). *Berkeley and the Principles of Human Knowledge.* London: Routledge.

FOSTER, JOHN (1982). *The Case for Idealism.* London: Routledge and Kegan Paul.

—— (1985). *A. J. Ayer.* London: Routledge.

—— and ROBINSON, HOWARD (eds.) (1985). *Essays on Berkeley.* Oxford: Clarendon Press.

FRANKFURT, HARRY (1964). 'On the Logic of Omnipotence', *Philosophical Review,* 73: 262–3.

—— (1969). 'Alternate Possibilities and Moral Responsibility', *Journal of Philosophy,* 66: 829–39.

FREGE, GOTTLOB (1884). *Foundations of Arithmetic,* trans. J. L. Austin. Oxford: Blackwell, 1953.

GALE, RICHARD M. (1968). *The Philosophy of Time: A Collection of Essays.* London: Macmillan.

GALLOIS, ANDRÉ (2003). *Occasions of Identity.* Oxford: Clarendon Press.

GARDNER, SEBASTIAN (1999). *Kant and the Critique of Pure Reason.* London: Routledge.

GARRETT, BRIAN (1998). *Personal Identity and Self-Consciousness.* London: Routledge.

GEACH, P. T. (1962). *Reference and Generality.* Ithaca, NY: Cornell University Press.

—— (1969). *God and the Soul.* Cambridge: Cambridge University Press.

—— (1977). *Providence and Evil.* Cambridge: Cambridge University Press.

GENDLER, TAMAR SZABÓ, and HAWTHORNE, JOHN (eds.) (2001). *Conceivability and Possibility.* Oxford: Oxford University Press.

GIBBARD, ALAN (1975). 'Contingent Identity', *Journal of Philosophical Logic,* 4: 187–221. Reprinted in Rea (1997).

HANKINSON, R. J. (1995). 'Philosophy of Science', in Jonathan Barnes (ed.), *The Cambridge Companion to Aristotle.* Cambridge: Cambridge University Press.

HASLANGER, SALLY (1989). 'Endurance and Temporary Intrinsics', *Analysis,* 49: 119–25.

—— (2003). 'Persistence through Time', in Michael Loux and Dean Zimmerman (eds.), *Oxford Handbook of Metaphysics*. Oxford: Oxford University Press.

HEIL, JOHN (2003). *From an Ontological Point of View*. Oxford: Oxford University Press.

HELLER, MARK (1990). *The Ontology of Physical Objects: Four Dimensional Hunks of Matter*. Cambridge: Cambridge University Press.

HELM, PAUL (1999). *Faith and Reason*. Oxford: Oxford University Press.

HEMPEL, C. G. (1965). *Philosophy of Natural Science*. Englewood Cliffs, NJ: Prentice Hall.

HICK, JOHN (1975). *Evil and the God of Love*. London: Fontana.

HOBBES, THOMAS (1651). *Leviathan*, ed. Richard Tuck. Cambridge: Cambridge University Press, 1991.

—— (1655). *Elementorum Philosophiae Sectio Prima, De Corpore*, in *The English Works of Thomas Hobbes of Malmesbury*, ed. Sir W. Molesworth, 11 vols. London, 1839–45. Reprinted Darmstadt: Scientia, 1962.

HONDERICH, TED (ed.) (1973). *Essays on Freedom of Action*. London: Routledge and Kegan Paul.

HORWICH, PAUL (1990). *Asymmetries in Time*. Cambridge, Mass.: MIT Press.

HUGHES, CHRISTOPHER (1997). 'Same-Kind Coincidence and the Ship of Theseus', *Mind*, 106: 53–67.

HUME, DAVID (1739–40). *Treatise of Human Nature*, 2nd edn., ed. L. A. Selby-Bigge, rev. P. H. Nidditch. Oxford: Clarendon Press, 1978.

—— (1748). *An Enquiry Concerning Human Understanding*, 3rd edn., ed. L. A. Selby-Bigge, rev. P. H. Nidditch. Oxford: Clarendon Press, 1975.

—— (1778). *Dialogues Concerning Natural Religion*, ed. Norman Kemp Smith. Oxford: Clarendon Press, 1935.

IRWIN, T. H. (1999). 'The Theory of Forms', in Gail Fine (ed.), *Plato 1: Metaphysics and Epistemology*. Oxford: Oxford University Press.

JACKSON, FRANK (1977). 'Statements about Universals', *Mind*, 86: 427–9.

—— (1998). *From Metaphysics to Ethics*. Oxford: Oxford University Press.

JACQUETTE, DALE (2002). *Ontology*. Chesham: Acumen.

JAMES, SUSAN (2000). 'The Emergence of the Cartesian Mind', in Tim Crane and Sarah Patterson (eds.), *History of the Mind–Body Problem*. London: Routledge.

JOHNSTON, MARK (1987a). 'Human Beings', *Journal of Philosophy*, 84: 59–83.

—— (1987b). 'Is there a Problem about Persistence?', *Proceedings of the Aristotelian Society Supplementary Volume*, 61: 107–35.

JOHNSTON, W. E. (1921). *Logic*. Part 1. Cambridge: Cambridge University Press.

KANE, ROBERT (1996). *The Significance of Free Will*. Oxford: Oxford University Press.

—— (ed.) (2002). *Free Will*. Oxford: Blackwell.

KANT, IMMANUEL (1787). *Critique of Pure Reason*, 2nd edn., trans. Norman Kemp Smith. London: Macmillan, 1929.

KEEFE, ROSANNA, and SMITH, PETER (eds.) (1997). *Vagueness: A Reader*. Cambridge, Mass.: MIT Press.

KENNY, ANTHONY (1969). *The Five Ways*. London: Macmillan.

KIM, JAEGWON (1989). 'Mechanism, Purpose and Explanatory Exclusion', in James E. Tomberlin (ed.), *Philosophical Perspectives 3: Philosophy of Mind and Action Theory*. Atascadero, Calif.: Ridgeview. Reprinted in Jaegwon Kim, *Supervenience and Mind*. Cambridge: Cambridge University Press, 1993.

KIM, JAEGWON (1996). *Philosophy of Mind*. Boulder, Colo.: Westview.

—— (1998). *Mind in a Physical World*. Cambridge, Mass.: MIT Press.

—— and SOSA, ERNEST (eds.) (1999). *Metaphysics: An Anthology*. Oxford: Blackwell.

KIRK, ROBERT (1974). 'Zombies versus Materialists', *Proceedings of the Aristotelian Society Supplementary Volume*, 48: 135–52.

KITCHER, PHILIP (1980). 'Apriority and Necessity', *Australasian Journal of Philosophy*, 58: 89–101. Reprinted in Moser (1987).

KNEALE, WILLIAM, and KNEALE, MARTHA (1962). *The Development of Logic*. Oxford: Oxford University Press.

KRIPKE, SAUL A. (1971). 'Identity and Necessity', in Milton K. Munitz (ed.), *Identity and Individuation*. New York: New York University Press. Reprinted in A. W. Moore (ed.), *Meaning and Reference*. Oxford: Oxford University Press, 1993.

—— (1972). 'Naming and Necessity', in Donald Davidson and Gilbert Harman (eds.), *Semantics for Natural Language*. Dordrecht: Reidel. Reprinted in book form Oxford: Blackwell, 1980.

LAURENCE, STEPHEN, and MACDONALD, CYNTHIA (eds.) (1998). *Contemporary Readings in the Foundations of Metaphysics*. Oxford: Blackwell.

LEIBNIZ, G. W. (1686). *Discourse on Metaphysics*, in Leibniz (1998).

—— (1714). *Monadology*, in Leibniz (1998).

—— (1765). *New Essays on Human Understanding*, trans. and ed. Peter Remnant and Jonathan Bennett. Cambridge: Cambridge University Press, 1996.

—— (1956). *The Leibniz–Clarke Correspondence*, ed. H. G. Alexander. Manchester: Manchester University Press.

—— (1998). *Philosophical Texts*, trans. and ed. R. S. Woolhouse and Richard Francks. Oxford: Oxford University Press.

LE POIDEVIN, ROBIN (2003). *Travels in Four Dimensions: The Enigmas of Space and Time*. Oxford: Oxford University Press.

—— and MACBEATH, MURRAY (eds.) (1993). *The Philosophy of Time*. Oxford: Oxford University Press.

LESLIE, JOHN (1989). *Universes*. London: Routledge.

LEVINE, JOSEPH (2000). *Purple Haze*. Oxford: Oxford University Press.

LEWIS, DAVID (1966). 'An Argument for the Identity Theory', *Journal of Philosophy*, 63: 17–25. Reprinted in *Philosophical Papers*, vol. i. Oxford: Oxford University Press, 1983.

—— (1968). 'Review of Putnam', in Ned Block (ed.), *Readings in the Philosophy of Psychology*, vol. i. London: Methuen, 1980.

—— (1973). *Counterfactuals*. Oxford: Blackwell.

—— (1981). 'Are We Free to Break the Laws?', reprinted in Lewis (1986a).

—— (1986a). *Philosophical Papers*. Vol. ii. Oxford: Oxford University Press.

—— (1986b). *On the Plurality of Worlds*. Oxford: Blackwell.

—— (1994). 'Reduction of Mind', in Samuel Guttenplan (ed.), *A Companion to the Philosophy of Mind*. Oxford: Blackwell. Reprinted in David Lewis, *Papers in Metaphysics and Epistemology*. Cambridge: Cambridge University Press, 1999.

—— (2000). 'Causation as Influence', *Journal of Philosophy*, 97: 182–97.

LOCKE, JOHN (1690). *Essay Concerning Human Understanding*, ed. P. H. Nidditch. Oxford: Oxford University Press, 1975.

LOEWER, BARRY (1998). 'Freedom from Physics: Quantum Mechanics and Free Will', *Philosophical Topics*, 24: 91–112.

—— (2001). 'From Physics to Physicalism', in Carl Gillett and Barry Loewer (eds.), *Physicalism and its Discontents*. Cambridge: Cambridge University Press.

LONG, A., and SEDLEY, DAVID (eds.) (1987). *The Hellenistic Philosophers*. Vol. i. Cambridge: Cambridge University Press.

LOUX, MICHAEL J. (ed.) (1979). *The Possible and the Actual*. Ithaca, NY: Cornell University Press.

—— (ed.) (2001). *Metaphysics: Contemporary Readings*. London: Routledge.

LOWE, E. J. (1989). *Kinds of Being*. Oxford: Blackwell.

—— (1998). *The Possibility of Metaphysics: Substance, Identity and Time*. Oxford: Oxford University Press.

—— (2002). *A Survey of Metaphysics*. Oxford: Oxford University Press.

MACBEATH, MURRAY (1993). 'Time's Square', in Le Poidevin and MacBeath (1993).

MACBRIDE, FRASER (1998). 'Where are Particulars and Universals?', *Dialectica*, 52: 203–37.

MCCULLOCH, GREGORY (1989). *The Game of the Name*. Oxford: Oxford University Press.

—— (2003). *The Life of the Mind*. London: Routledge.

MACDONALD ROSS, GEORGE (1984). *Leibniz*. Oxford: Oxford University Press.

MCDOWELL, JOHN (1994). *Mind and World*. Cambridge, Mass.: Harvard University Press.

—— (1998). 'Anti-realism and the Epistemology of Understanding', in *Meaning, Knowledge and Reality*. Cambridge, Mass.: Harvard University Press.

MACKIE, J. L. (1965). 'Causes and Conditions', *American Philosophical Quarterly*, 2: 245–64.

—— (1982). *The Miracle of Theism*. Oxford: Oxford University Press.

MARTIN, C. B. (1980). 'Substance Substantiated', *Australasian Journal of Philosophy*, 58: 3–10.

—— (1993). 'Power for Realists', in Bacon, Campbell, and Reinhardt (1993).

—— (1994). 'Dispositions and Conditionals', *Philosophical Quarterly*, 44: 1–8.

MELLOR, D. H. (1981). *Real Time*. Cambridge: Cambridge University Press.

—— (1993). 'Properties and Predicates', in Bacon, Campbell, and Reinhardt (1993). Reprinted in Mellor and Oliver (1997).

—— (1995). *The Facts of Causation*. London: Routledge.

—— (1998). *Real Time II*. London: Routledge.

—— (2002). 'Time Travel', in K. Ridderbos (ed.), *Time*. Cambridge: Cambridge University Press.

—— and OLIVER, ALEX (eds.) (1997). *Properties*. Oxford: Oxford University Press.

MENZIES, PETER (1989). 'Probabilistic Causation and Causal Processes: A Critique of Lewis', *Philosophy of Science*, 56: 642–63.

—— (1996). 'Probabilistic Causation and the Pre-emption Problem', *Mind*, 105: 85–117.

—— (2003). 'Is Causation a Relation?', in H. Lillehammer and G. Rodriguez-Pereyra (eds.), *Real Metaphysics*. London: Routledge.

MERRICKS, TRENTON (1994). 'Endurance and Indiscernibility', *Journal of Philosophy*, 91: 165–84. Reprinted in Loux (2001).

—— (2001). *Objects and Persons*. Oxford: Oxford University Press.

MOLNAR, GEORGE (2003). *Powers*, ed. Stephen Mumford. Oxford: Oxford University Press.

MOSER, PAUL K. (ed.) (1987). *A Priori Knowledge*. Oxford: Oxford University Press.

MUMFORD, STEPHEN (1998). *Dispositions*. Oxford: Oxford University Press.

NEALE, STEPHEN (1995). 'The Philosophical Significance of Gödel's Slingshot', *Mind*, 104: 761–825.

NEWTON, SIR ISAAC (1729). *Mathematical Principles of Natural Philosophy*, trans. A. Motte and F. Cajori. Berkeley and Los Angeles: University of California Press, 1962.

NOLAN, DANIEL (1997). 'Three Problems for "Strong" Modal Fictionalism', *Philosophical Studies*, 87/3: 259–75.

O'CONNOR, TIMOTHY (ed.) (1995). *Agents, Causes, and Events: Essays on Indeterminism and Free Will*. Oxford: Oxford University Press.

OAKLANDER, L. NATHAN, and SMITH, QUENTIN (eds.) (1994). *The New Theory of Time*. New Haven: Yale University Press.

OLSON, ERIC (1997). *The Human Animal*. Oxford: Oxford University Press.

OPPY, GRAHAM (1995). *Ontological Arguments and Belief in God*. Cambridge: Cambridge University Press.

ORWELL, GEORGE (1949). *1984*. London: Secker and Warburg.

OWEN, G. E. L. (1979). 'Aristotle on Time', in J. Barnes, M. Schofield, and R. Sorabji (eds.), *Articles on Aristotle*, iii: *Metaphysics*. London: Duckworth.

PAPINEAU, DAVID (2001). 'The Rise of Physicalism', in Carl Gillett and Barry Loewer (eds.), *Physicalism and its Discontents*. Cambridge: Cambridge University Press.

PATTERSON, SARAH (2000). 'How Cartesian was Descartes?', in Tim Crane and Sarah Patterson (eds.), *History of the Mind–Body Problem*. London: Routledge.

PERCIVAL, PHILIP (2002). 'A Presentist's Refutation of Mellor's McTaggart', in Craig Callendar (ed.), *Time, Reality and Experience*. Cambridge: Cambridge University Press.

PINK, THOMAS (2004). *Free Will: A Very Short Introduction*. Oxford: Oxford University Press.

PLANTINGA, ALVIN (1974). *The Nature of Necessity*. Oxford: Clarendon Press.

—— (1975). *God, Freedom and Evil*. New York: Harper and Row.

PRICE, HUW (1996). *Time's Arrow and Archimedes' Point*. New York: Oxford University Press.

PUTNAM, HILARY (1975). 'The Nature of Mental States', in *Mind, Language and Reality: Philosophical Papers*, vol. ii. Cambridge: Cambridge University Press.

—— (1999). *The Threefold Cord: Mind, Body and World*. New York: Columbia University Press.

QUINE, W. V. (1951). 'Two Dogmas of Empiricism', *Philosophical Review*, 60: 20–43. Reprinted in Quine (1961*a*).

—— (1953). 'Reference and Modality', in Quine (1961*a*).

—— (1958*a*). *The Ways of Paradox*. Cambridge, Mass.: Harvard University Press.

—— (1958*b*). 'On Mental Entities', in Quine (1958*a*).

—— (1958*c*). 'A Logistical Approach to the Ontological Problem', in Quine (1958*a*).

—— (1958*d*). 'Quantifiers and Propositional Attitudes', in Quine (1958*a*).

—— (1958*e*). 'Truth by Convention', in Quine (1958*a*).

—— (1958*f*). 'Carnap and Logical Truth', in Quine (1958*a*).

—— (1960). *Word and Object*. Cambridge, Mass.: MIT Press.

—— (1961*a*). *From a Logical Point of View*. 2nd edn. Cambridge, Mass.: Harvard University Press.

—— (1961*b*). 'Identity, Ostension and Hypostasis', in Quine (1961*a*).

—— (1981). 'On the Individuation of Attributes', in *Theories and Things*. Cambridge, Mass.: Harvard University Press.

QUINN, PHILIP, and TALIAFERRO, CHARLES (1997). *A Companion to the Philosophy of Religion.* Oxford: Blackwell.

RAMSEY, F. P. (1925). 'Universals', in *F. P. Ramsey: Philosophical Papers*, ed. D. H. Mellor. Cambridge: Cambridge University Press, 1990.

—— (1927). 'Facts and Propositions', in *F. P. Ramsey: Philosophical Papers*, ed. D. H. Mellor. Cambridge: Cambridge University Press, 1990.

REA, MICHAEL C. (ed.) (1997). *Material Constitution: A Reader.* Lanham, Md.: Rowman and Littlefield.

REICHENBACH, HANS (1956). *The Direction of Time.* Berkeley and Los Angeles: University of California Press.

RODRIGUEZ-PEREYRA, GONZALO (2002). *Resemblance Nominalism: A Solution to the Problem of Universals.* Oxford: Oxford University Press.

ROSEN, GIDEON (1990). 'Modal Fictionalism', *Mind*, 99: 327–54.

ROSENTHAL, DAVID (ed.) (1991). *The Nature of Mind.* Oxford: Oxford University Press.

RUSSELL, BERTRAND (1905). 'On Denoting', *Mind*, 14: 479–93.

—— (1912). *The Problems of Philosophy.* Oxford: Oxford University Press.

—— (1918). 'On the Notion of Cause', in *Mysticism and Logic and Other Essays*. Reprinted London: Routledge, 1994.

RYLE, GILBERT (1948). *The Concept of Mind.* London: Hutchinson.

SAINSBURY, MARK (1995). *Paradoxes.* 2nd edn. Cambridge: Cambridge University Press.

SALMON, NATHAN (1986). *Frege's Puzzle.* Cambridge, Mass.: MIT Press.

SCHAFFER, JONATHAN (2000). 'Trumping Pre-emption', *Journal of Philosophy*, 97: 165–86.

SHOEMAKER, SYDNEY (1969). 'Time without Change', in Le Poidevin and MacBeath (1993).

—— and SWINBURNE, RICHARD (1984). *Personal Identity.* Oxford: Blackwell.

SIDER, THEODORE (2001). *Four-Dimensionalism.* Oxford: Oxford University Press.

SIMONS, PETER (1998*a*). 'Farewell to Substance: A Differentiated Leave-Taking', *Ratio*, NS 11: 235–52. Also in D. S. Oderberg (ed.), *Form and Matter: Themes in Contemporary Metaphysics.* Oxford: Blackwell, 1998.

—— (1998*b*). 'Particulars in Particular Clothing: Three Trope Theories of Substance', in Laurence and Macdonald (1998).

SMART, J. J. C. (1953). 'Sensations and Brain Processes', *Philosophical Review*, 68: 141–56.

SMITH, A. D. (1990). 'Of Primary and Secondary Qualities', *Philosophical Review*, 99/2: 221–54.

SORABJI, RICHARD (1988). *Time, Creation and the Continuum.* London: Duckworth.

SOSA, ERNEST, and TOOLEY, MICHAEL (eds.) (1993). *Causation.* Oxford: Oxford University Press.

SPINOZA, BENEDICT (BARUCH) DE (1985). *Ethics*, in *Spinoza: Collected Works*, ed. E. Curley, vol. i. Princeton: Princeton University Press.

STALNAKER, ROBERT (1984). *Inquiry.* Cambridge, Mass.: MIT Press.

STONEHAM, TOM (2002). *Berkeley's World.* Oxford: Clarendon Press.

STRAWSON, GALEN (1989). *The Secret Connexion: Causation, Realism and David Hume.* Oxford: Clarendon Press.

STRAWSON, P. F. (1974). 'Freedom and Resentment', in *Freedom and Resentment and Other Essays.* London: Methuen.

STRAWSON, P. F. (1976). 'Entity and Identity', in H. D. Lewis (ed.), *Contemporary British Philosophy*, 4th series. Reprinted in P. F. Strawson, *Entity and Identity and Other Essays*. Oxford: Oxford University Press, 1997.

STROUD, BARRY (1981). *Hume*. London: Routledge.

STUMP, ELEONORE, and MURAY, MICHAEL J. (1999). *Philosophy of Religion: The Big Questions*. Oxford: Blackwell.

STURGEON, SCOTT (2000). *Matters of Mind: Consciousness, Reason and Nature*. London: Routledge.

SWINBURNE, RICHARD (1968). 'The Argument of Design', *Philosophy*, 43. Reprinted in Davies (2000).

—— (1984). 'Personal Identity: The Dualist Theory', in Shoemaker and Swinburne (1984).

—— (1986). *Is There a God?* Oxford: Oxford University Press.

—— (1996). *Does God Exist?* Oxford: Clarendon Press.

THOMSON, JUDITH JARVIS (1983). 'Parthood and Identity across Time', *Journal of Philosophy*, 80: 201–20. Reprinted in Kim and Sosa (1998), and in Rea (1997).

VAN CLEVE, JAMES (1985). 'Three Versions of the Bundle Theory', *Philosophical Studies*, 47: 95–107. Reprinted in Loux (2001) and in Laurence and Macdonald (1998).

VAN INWAGEN, PETER (1981). 'The Doctrine of Arbitrary Undetached Parts', *Pacific Philosophical Quarterly*, 62: 123–37.

—— (1983). *An Essay on Free Will*. Oxford: Clarendon Press.

—— (1990). *Material Beings*. Ithaca, NY: Cornell University Press.

—— (1993). *Metaphysics*. Boulder, Colo.: Westview Press.

VESEY, G. (ed.) (1980). *Idealism: Past and Present*. Cambridge: Cambridge University Press.

WATSON, GARY (ed.) (1982). *Free Will*. Oxford: Oxford University Press.

WIGGINS, DAVID (1968). 'On Being in the Same Place at the Same Time', *Philosophical Review*, 77: 90–5.

—— (1976). 'Frege's Problem of the Morning Star and the Evening Star', in M. Schirn (ed.), *Studies on Frege II: Logic and Philosophy of Language*. Stuttgart-Bad Cannstatt: Frommann-Holzboog.

—— (1980). *Sameness and Substance*. Oxford: Blackwell.

—— (2001). *Sameness and Substance Renewed*. Cambridge: Cambridge University Press.

WILLIAMS, BERNARD (1973). *Problems of the Self*. Cambridge: Cambridge University Press.

—— (1981). *Moral Luck*. Cambridge: Cambridge University Press.

WILLIAMSON, TIMOTHY (1994). *Vagueness*. London: Routledge.

WITTGENSTEIN, LUDWIG (1922). *Tractatus Logico-Philosophicus*, trans. D. Pears and B. McGuinness. London: Routledge, 1961.

WOOLHOUSE, R. S. (1993). *Descartes, Spinoza, Leibniz: The Concept of Substance in Seventeenth-Century Metaphysics*. London: Routledge and Kegan Paul.

WRIGHT, CRISPIN (1992). *Truth and Objectivity*. Cambridge, Mass.: Harvard University Press.

YABLO, STEPHEN (1992). 'Mental Causation', *Philosophical Review*, 101: 245–80.

Index